A CASEBOOK ON THE IRISH

Also by the authors:
THE IRISH LAW OF TORTS (1981)

To Mary and Alice

A CASEBOOK ON THE IRISH LAW OF TORTS

by

BRYAN M. E. McMAHON
B.C.L., LL.B., LL.M. (HARVARD), Ph.D.
Solicitor, Professor of Law,
University College, Cork

and

WILLIAM BINCHY
B.A., B.C.L., LL.M.
Barrister-at-Law, Research Counsellor,
The Law Reform Commission

with a

FOREWORD

by

The Honourable Mr. Justice **BRIAN WALSH**
M.A. (N.U.I.), LL.D. (h.c.) (Dublin)
Senior Ordinary Judge of the Supreme Court of Ireland,
Judge of the European Court of Human Rights,
President, The Law Reform Commission

PROFESSIONAL BOOKS
ABINGDON, OXON.
1983

Published in 1983 by
Professional Books Limited
Milton Trading Estate, Abingdon, Oxon.
Typeset by Inforum Ltd, Portsmouth
and printed in Great Britain by
Billing and Sons Ltd, Worcester

ISBN: Hardback: 0 86205 0502
Paperback: 0 86205 0561

FOREWORD

The law of tort is a growth area. While it is not primarily the function of the courts to endeavour to remedy all the ills of society the combined function of judges and juries is to do justice according to law between plaintiff and defendant. This is achieved by working out a system of checks and balances between judge and jury. The aims of the law of tort combine punitive and deterrent objectives as positive objectives. It has, of course, other objectives such as that of offering reasonable compensation to those who suffer injuries, and the negative objective of judging according to reasonable standards so as not to unduly inhibit ordinary human activity. Courts are not ordinarily expected to assume the burden of legislating to the extent of radically changing the underlying policy of the law nor are judges expected to abdicate completely to juries the function of applying that policy in the actual cases. Nevertheless, it has to be recognised that only the most compelling needs are likely to attract the attention of the legislators. Legislative inaction cannot be regarded as an indication of approval of the law as it stands. The many demands upon parliamentary time, and the fact that in particular areas where reform of the law would be highly desirable the majority of legislators have no individual views, leads to a situation where reform of tort law increasingly depends upon court decisions, particularly at the appellate level. The study of judicial decisions enables the reader to evaluate to what extent the objectives of the law of tort have in reality been served by the courts and judicial decisions.

In the area of the Irish law of tort this casebook will enable both student and practitioner alike to discover for themselves the application of the law in this area by the courts in Ireland in addition to discovering the principles of the Irish law of tort. A casebook such as the present one which reproduces so extensively the full text, or almost the full text, of judgments is of great value in bringing home to student and practitioner alike the practical application of the relevant legal principles which have already been learned from the systematic textbook. This particular work has a special value in that it reproduces many unreported Irish cases, regrettably very numerous, and thus for the first time reproduces these decisions in published form. It is scarcely two years since the learned authors produced their excellent textbook. So by publishing the present casebook they cannot be said to commit themselves to the casebook method of teaching law. The casebook method of teaching, much more commonly used in American law schools than elsewhere, first came into prominence just over one hundred years ago and revolutionised the study of law in the universities and law schools of the United States. In Europe the systematic textbook has remained the basis for the teaching of law because there was not the same faith in the belief that a student could discover the law inductively by an examination of decided cases.

Contemporary Irish law students and practitioners have had the benefit of a much wider course of studies and have been more intensively taught than their predecessors. This gives them a much wider knowledge of the whole basis of law together with some knowledge of other subjects which are highly relevant to the modern study and practice of law.

Every reader of judicial opinions should bear in mind that the primary function of the judge is to decide the case. He should state plainly the legal basis of his decision because it is the court's function to declare the law and because the litigants understand that one or other of them usually loses. Therefore judicial opinions should be neither timid nor apologetic. Neither should they be founded on concessions wrung from reluctant counsel. The student should beware of judicial opinions which are a mere collection of precedents or a litany of well stated platitudes from earlier decisions. Such decisions tend to stifle rather than assist the progressive development of law by analysis and construction. Dean Wigmore in his great treatise on evidence critically analysed a great mass of judicial opinions and came to the conclusion that the greatest defects disclosed in them were a lack of acquaintance with legal history, a lack of discrimination in the use of expository authorities, and a lack of knowledge of both the philosophy and the jurisprudence of the law. In so far as these faults exist in any common law system they can be attributed not only to defects in the judges themselves but also to defects in the counsel who appear in court. A high standard at the Bar is necessary to force the judges to the highest standard just as a commonplace standard at the Bar will tend to limit judicial achievement. In appellate courts, and particularly in the court of final appeal, our system permits any member of the Bar, no matter how inexperienced or how lacking in knowledge, to conduct a case. Thus the judges will never know from day to day whether the case will be presented by specialists who themselves know all of the subject and can skillfully present the essence of the actual controversy or by one who cannot offer such necessary assistance to the court.

Therefore the intelligent law student in studying judgments should also study the arguments of counsel and the submissions made in so far as they can be detected in law reports. In recent years the Supreme Court of Ireland has developed the practice of inviting counsel to make written submissions and this has had the double effect of concentrating counsel's mind in advance on the points to be made in court and of giving the members of the court itself an opportunity to ascertain, before the hearing, the exact perameters of the case and to suggest, if necessary, that some particular points might be developed in some greater detail. However, total reliance on law reports can itself constitute a trap because some reports leave the impression that counsel had not made particular submissions or had made none at all or had omitted to refer to certain relevant judicial decisions when in fact counsel had presented a fuller and a better assembled case than appears from the reports. Indeed this is a trap into which judges themselves have fallen on more than one occasion when they have been led to either overruling or adversely commenting on some earlier decision by thinking that the judge or the court, as the case may be, had not been referred to such-and-such a case because the law report in question did not attribute such a reference to counsel and was not referred to in the judgements. In more than one case a perusal of the court book kept by the Registrar would have indicated that the point in question had in fact been brought to the court's attention and had been discussed. It is not the function of a judicial opinion to refer expressly to everything said in court. Therefore the absence of any reference to a particular case or matter is not to be taken as conclusive evidence that the matter was never raised in or considered by the court. More particularly the function of a court of final appeal must be to state plainly the rule upon which its decision proceeds, not merely for the information of the litigants but also so that practitioners will know exactly what rule they can follow in advising clients. With that aim in mind the judgment should be clear and unambiguous. When, after careful study of all the relevant authorities, the judge feels that he can pronounce a clear decision it is unnecessary to encumber it by having every step of the reasoning laden with citations of other authorities. There is nothing more irritating to the reader than the rambling judicial opinion which pieces together great numbers of semi-irrelevant propositions of law, wanders through numerous cited cases and ends up by giving the impression that somewhere or other the judgment has said what the law is but leaves unclear what detail of the rule is newly decided. Worse still is undue deference to or uncritical acceptance of the decisions of courts of foreign jurisdictions, particularly when preceded by such expressions as "I respectfully agree." In the appropriate instance there is nothing wrong in following or not following, as the case may be, the reasoning of a court of another jurisdiction but it is not appropriate to give utterance to expressions of agreement or disagreement with the judges of other jurisdictions. Moreover, as has been sadly demonstrated more than once, to base a decision wholly or even substantially on the acceptance of a decision in another jurisdiction wihtout more can lead to somewhat embarrassing results when the court of that other jurisdiction subsequently abandons the decision relied upon or substantially alters the basis of it. Fortunately our Supreme Court released itself almost twenty years ago from undue servitude to the bondage of precedent. That now permits new and special elements to have effect. If the materials at the disposal of the judge are permitted to remain fluid then he will be enabled to find the answer which will satisfy and establish one more point as a basis for future growth. The test should be, will the reader, whether he be a layman or a lawyer, as soon as he reads the decision, recognise the result as the right result and therefore the inevitable result.

There is much more to reading judicial decisions than simply endeavouring to track down the *ratio decidendi* and endeavouring to find in the case a set of facts indistinguishable in any material particular from those of the precedent case to which the decision might be thought to be applicable. One should always bear in mind Lord Dunedin's warning of "the fallacy of the similarity of facts." Every student is taught to distinguish between *ratio decidendi* and *obiter dictum* but in reality the distinction is not as clear or as readily ascertainable as students are taught. The discovery of *ratio decidendi* may itself be a matter of considerable difficulty, particularly in cases where several principles are stated in justification of the decision (and indeed each of them may be as distinct and binding as the other) and particularly in a multi-judge court where the judges, or a majority, may concur in the result but may enunciate different reasons for the result. Many *dicta* are carefully considered statements which have been made after hearing the point argued in court and acquire substantial authority which in subsequent cases may be of great persuasive value. Even those *dicta* which may strictly speaking be irrelevant to the case may be highly relevant to collateral matters. The practice of interpreting decisions so as to downgrade certain parts of what had hitherto been thought to be *ratio* to mere *dicta* is not one to be commended.

The student should not be too critical of the apparent lack of logic in some decisions. As Mr. Justice Oliver Wendell Holmes said: "Other tools are needed besides logic." The law's barren logic must yield to the conception of justice as an element in every case. Lastly, the contemporary, socially orientated and thoroughly educated law student should be cautious in searching judgments for clues to whatever preconceived notions, economic or otherwise, which the judge may be thought to harbour and to the extent, if any, by which his opinion may have been thus affected. William James in his "Lectures on Pragmatism" said:

> "There is in each of us a stream or tendency, whether you choose to call it philosophy or not, which gives coherence and direction to thoughts and actions. Judges cannot escape that current any more than other mortals."

He said that inherited instincts, traditional beliefs and acquired convictions, even if not recognised, are tugging at judges all of their lives. Mr. Justice Cardozo in his famous statement on the point directed this idea to the decisional process in judging. However, to attempt to explain judicial behaviour in terms of the background of judges is simply to be confronted with the problem which confronts historians – the problem of never knowing precisely how the past has influenced the present. One should never underestimate the influence of the institution upon the individual. Perhaps the decision-making process of collegial courts should be studied under the rubric of small group sociology.

This excellent casebook will provide student and practitioner alike with ample material to enable him or her further pursue any of these varied elements of judicial decision making. More importantly, it will complement the authors' excellent text-book and will enable readers to discover and understand the foundations of Irish tort law. Professor McMahon and Mr. Binchy have once again rendered a great service to Irish legal studies.

BRIAN WALSH
The Supreme Court
September 1983

PREFACE

This volume is intended to be a companion to the authors' earlier publication, *The Irish Law of Torts*. The title of the present work indicates both the book's content and the policy that underlies the selections. It concentrates on court cases, reported and unreported, and does not reproduce other materials relevant to the study of tort law. Occasional exceptions have been made and important Irish statutory material is reproduced to inform the foreign reader and to provide the essential background without which the significance of some of the cases could not fully be appreciated.

The object of the present publication is further restricted by the policy that it should contain Irish cases only. We have firmly held to this approach throughout, even to the extent that important common law precedents which occupy a central place in Irish jurisprudence, such as *Donoghue* v. *Stevenson* and *Rylands* v. *Fletcher*, have not been reproduced. We could find no merit in presenting those well known cases once more to the legal public. Undoubtedly of more interest for the local and foreign reader are the Irish cases on the *Donoghue* v. *Stevenson* and *Rylands* v. *Fletcher* problems. Further, this restrictive policy in relation to common law precedent has enabled us to present more Irish cases than would otherwise have been possible. As we have mentioned, we have not confined ourselves to reported cases only: the book also includes a substantial number of unreported judgments of the Supreme Court on important issues of principle.

With regard to these unreported judgments, it is only fair to say that they have been reproduced faithfully, although on a very few occasions, to avoid pedantry, we have made minor grammatical or spelling alterations. In some cases these judgments were available in handwritten form only and this editorial intervention is made without apology. One other matter should be mentioned in this connection. In some of the recently reported Irish judgments, case references are given at the foot of the page. In this book these references have been lifted and appear in the body of the text. Moreover, to avoid multiple references to the same case on the same page, references have occasionally been omitted where such omission would cause no inconvenience to the reader. Lastly, it should be mentioned that we have in the main tried to present cases which represent the law as it is in Ireland. Some casebooks reproduce, for didactic and discursive reasons, decisions that are clearly wrong or non-representative. We have refrained from this practice for the most part and the cases that have been selected, by and large, stand as authoritive propositions for what the law is in Ireland at present. Where this is not so, the notes and questions clearly signal the departure.

The book includes decisions available to us up to the end of March 1983. In a few cases we have managed to add brief references to later decisions in the "Notes and Questions" section at the end of the extracts of decisions.

A significant case which appeared too late for inclusion in the appropriate chapter is *Morgan* v. *Park Developments Ltd*. [1983] I.L.R.M. 156, (High Court, Miss Justice Carroll, 2 Feb. 1983). In this case Miss Justice Carroll refused to follow the recent House of Lords decision in *Pirelli General Cable Works Ltd.* v. *Oscar Faber & Partners* [1983] 2 W.L.R. 6, which held that in the case of defective buildings the period of limitations runs from the date the damage came into existence and not the date of discoverability. While there are differences in the statutory provisions between the two jurisdictions, Miss Justice Carroll's refusal to follow the House of Lords is more broadly based and relies *inter alia* on the Constitution. The central portion of her judgment merits quotation:

"It was acknowledged by Lord Reid in *Cartledge* v. *E. Joplin and Sons Ltd*. [1963]

A.C. 758 (which was the decision applied in the *Pirelli case*) that it was unreason-able and unjustifiable in principle that a cause of action should be held to accrue before it is possible to discover any injury. But he felt constrained by the Statute to reach a decision which was wholly unreasonable.

It was acknowledged by Lord Scarman in the *Pirelli case* that he agreed with Lord Reid's comments and also with Lord Pierce's comment in the *Cartledge case* that a law which produced such a result was harsh and absurd. But nevertheless he felt constrained to come to the same decision.

The [Statute of Limitations] 1957 . . . is a post-1937 Statute and has the benefit of the presumption of constitutionality. If there are two interpretations, one of which is unconstitutional and one of which is constitutional, it must be presumed that the Oireachtas intended the interpretation which was constitutional.

The English Parliament do not operate within the confines of a written constitution whereas in this country the Oireachtas can only pass laws which are compatible with the Constitution. It seems to me that no law which could be described as 'harsh and absurd' or which the courts could say was unreasonable and unjustifiable in principle (as did the English Courts) could also be constitutional.

Mr. Fitzsimons [counsel for the defendant] took issue with the word 'absurd'. He said that harshness is not the test. The result may be harsh but it is necessary. He said there is nothing unconstitutional *per se* in a harsh interpretation.

If I interpret accrual as denoting the date of the negligent act, it may have the effect of depriving an injured party of a right of action before he knows he had one. If I interpret accrual as denoting the date of discoverability, it may operate with hardship as a defendant in that action may not be brought for many years after-wards.

This was a consideration which was an important factor in the Supreme Court decision of *Moynihan* v. *Greensmyth* [1977] IR 55 [*infra*, p. 640 – *eds*.]. In the *Sparham-Souter case* [1976] Q.B. 858, one of the principles applied was that the Statute of Limitations cannot begin to run unless two things are present, a party capable of suing and a party liable to be sued.

There cannot be a party capable of suing unless he knows or should know that he has suffered damage.

The original House of Lords decision in *Cartledge* v. *E Joplin & Sons Ltd*. is based on the reasoning that because the Limitation Act 1939 made special provision for fraud or mistake, this necessarily implied that if fraud or mistake were not involved, time must begin to run whether or not the damage could be discovered.

However, it seems to me that the provisions regarding fraud or mistake do not preclude the interpretation which takes the date of discoverability as the date of accrual. In my opinion the provisions of s.71 can co-exist with that interpretation. Therefore of the two possible interpretations I prefer the one adopted in the *Sparham-Souter case* which has the date of discoverability as the date of accrual. Whatever hardship there may be to a defendant in dealing with a claim years afterwards, it must be less than the hardship to a plaintiff whose action is barred before he knows he has one. The latter interpretation appears to me indefensible in the light of the Constitution.

Accordingly I hold that the date of accrual in an action for negligence in the building of a house is the date of discoverability, meaning the date the defect either was discovered or should reasonably have been discovered."

The decision is analysed by Mr. Tony Kerr in 5 Dublin U.L.J. 133 (1983).

Another case worthy of note is *Dempsey* v. *Eastern Health Board*, High Court, Finlay P. with jury, 8 July 1983. In this case a nine-year-old plaintiff who contracted meningitis was awarded £387,000 in a medical malpractice action against the Eastern Health Board. The jury held that the defendant's servants or agents failed to carry out timely tests which would have given an early diagnosis.

The report of the case in the *Irish Times* (9 July 1983, pp. 1,7) states that Finlay P. stressed to the jury that in assessing the conduct of the defendants, 'the golden word was "reasonable".' The report adds that:

"Mr. Justice Finlay read to the jury extracts from Supreme Court judgments on the question of care in medical matters which stated, *inter alia*, (which Mr. Justice Finlay said was of crucial importance) it must be established that the course a doctor adopted was one which no professional man of ordinary skill would have taken if he had been acting with reasonable care."

The Supreme Court decision of *Reddy* v. *Bates*, 29 July 1983 (199–82), suggests a slight retrenchment on the question of assessment of damages. Griffin J. noted that in a case where damages are to be assessed under several headings:

"When the jury has added the various sums awarded and arrived at a total for damages, they should then consider this total sum, as should this Court on any appeal, for the purpose of ascertaining whether the total sum awarded is, in the circumstances of the case, fair compensation for the plaintiff for the injury suffered, or whether it is out of all proportion to such circumstances."

McCarthy J. considered it "appropriate that this Court, in reviewing awards under the heading of general damages, should look both to the items separately and as a whole."

It should also be noted that section 1 of the *Trade Disputes (Amendment) Act, 1982*, substitutes a new subsection (3) in section 5 of the *Trade Disputes Act, 1906*, the effect being to extend the protection to "workmen" afforded by section 5 of the 1906 Act to all persons employed, whether or not in the employment of the employer with whom a trade dispute arises. The only exceptions are members of the Defence Forces and the Garda Síochána. See Daly, 77 Inc. L. Soc. of Ireland Gaz., No. 6, p. 149 (1983).

Our thanks are due to many people who helped in the preparation of this book. We are most grateful to Mr. Justice Brian Walsh for agreeing to provide a foreword. We also wish to thank Professor L. Wrigley, Department of Management, University College, Cork, who, through the Management Fund, University College, Cork, generously supported this publication, and we must acknowledge the generosity of the Law Society in agreeing to launch the book at Blackhall Place.

We would like to record our sincere thanks to Miss Peggy McQuinn of the Supreme Court Office for her great help to us in tracking down the unreported decisions of the Supreme Court. Our thanks are also due to Miss Mary Neylon, B.L., Librarian, King's Inns Library, Dublin and Ms. Margaret Byrne, Librarian, The Law Society, for their assistance. Mr. Gary Lynch gave us considerable help and advice, for which we are most grateful.

BRYAN M.E. McMAHON
WILLIAM BINCHY
15 August 1983

ACKNOWLEDGMENTS

The publishers and the authors gratefully acknowledge permission from the following to reproduce materials from the sources indicated:

The Incorporated Council of Law Reporting for Ireland: *The Irish Reports*.
The Jurist Publishing Company: *The Irish Jurist Reports*.
Round Hall Press, Irish Academic Press: *The Irish Law Times Reports, The Irish Law Reports Monthly*.
Several members of the Irish Judiciary: the Unreported Judgments handed down in their names.
The Irish Times Limited: *The Irish Times*.
The Stationery Office and the Department of Justice: excerpts from statutory material and unreported judgments.

TABLE OF CONTENTS

TABLE OF STATUTES

STATUTES IN OTHER JURISDICTIONS

THE 1922 CONSTITUTION OF THE IRISH FREE STATE

THE 1937 CONSTITUTION

TABLE OF CASES

Chapter 1

CAUSATION AND REMOTENESS OF DAMAGE

1. *CAUSATION*

Before the defendant can be held liable in tort it must be shown that he *caused* the complained of injury to the plaintiff. By this is meant that there must be an appreciable connection between the plaintiff's injury and the defendant's conduct. The problem of causation, therefore, while most frequently manifesting itself in the context of the tort of negligence, is a general one for the law of torts and indeed is a problem also encountered in locating liability in other areas of the law.

For our purposes it is most fruitful to concentrate on cases where the plaintiff has failed to prove the defendant's causal connection, or at least where the defendant has argued (even if unsuccessfully) that there was no causal link.

The criterion most favoured by the courts in determining whether the defendant caused the injury is the 'but for' test: would the injury suffered by the plaintiff have been avoided but for the defendant's tortious conduct? Although satisfactory in many cases this test provides an inadequate explanation where multiple causes exist. This situation can arise, for example, where concurrent wrongdoers inflict an injury on the plaintiff (*cf. infra*, pp. 47–59), or indeed where the plaintiff's injuries are caused both by the defendant's conduct and the plaintiff's own negligence. (This latter situation gives rise to the problem of contributory negligence; *cf. infra*, pp. 204–208.)

The selection from the cases given in this section of the chapter is intended to illustrate the above points and the reader's attention is also drawn to the following points:

(i) Exceptionally in the case of vicarious liability, the law may impose liability on the master/employer even where there is no causal connection between the defendant's conduct and the plaintiff's injuries.

(ii) In some cases although it may be true to say that the defendant's act was the cause, the law will exonerate the defendant because some new intervening act comes between the defendant's act and the plaintiff's injuries. This new intervening act the becomes, for legal purposes, the sole operative cause. The exact circumstances where such a *novus actus interveniens* will break the chain of causation between the plaintiff and the defendant has preoccupied the courts for many years.

(iii) Intervening human acts may not break the chain of causation between the plaintiff and the defendant's act where such intervening acts are foreseeable and are reflex actions or are almost 'programmed' by the initial act of the defendant as, for example, where a person tries to rescue another who has been placed in imminent danger by the defendant's negligence.

The defendant's act must cause the plaintiff's injury. It is for the plaintiff to prove this.

MARTIN V. MILLAR & CO. LTD.
Unreptd. Sup. Ct. 12 May 1972

Walsh J.:

In this case the plaintiff, who was a wood working machinist, sued his employers, the defendants, for injuries he sustained in the working of a revolving cutter spindle which he was operating in the course of his employment. This was a wood working machine which was electrically driven and was stopped and started by a switch which turned on or off the electric power.

The plaintiff alleged that the defendants had been in breach of statutory duty (1) in failing to have the machine securely fenced, (2) in failing to warn the plaintiff of the danger of cleaning the machine while the cutters were in motion, and (3) in failing to provide sufficient and suitable lighting conditions during the operation of the machine. The case was tried before Mr. Justice Henchy and a jury on the 3rd and 4th December, 1968, and the jury found against the plaintiff on each of three matters referred to. Judgment was entered for the defendants and against this judgment the plaintiff has appealed. In my view, this appeal should be dismissed.

The accident in question occurred after the plaintiff had switched off the machine and when he was attempting to remove some wood shavings from it. I choose this version as the one most favourable to the plaintiff's case because he has given other versions which at times indicated that he was not sure whether he had or he had not switched it off or that he was not removing wood shavings but was wiping a piece of oil from the platform of the machine near the cutting blades while it was in motion. On the version which I accept as being the most favourable to the plaintiff for the purpose of this appeal the plaintiff was of opinion that possibly the blades continued to revolve after the current had been switched off and he put his hand close to them too soon. It was alleged during the hearing on behalf of the plaintiff that the dangerous part of the machine was not fenced. This is not correct as the evidence indicates that there was a form of guard which performed a double function, namely, by being spring-loaded it pressed the board which was to be grooved against the back plate, holding it over the cutting edge and when the board was not there the effect of the springs in these rollers was to thrust the rollers forward so that they overhung the cutting edges. While there might be some question as to the adequacy of this fencing while the machine was actually operating, that is to say, grooving timber, there can be little doubt that when there was no timber in the machine, as there was not on this occasion, a person could not bring his hand in contact with the revolving blades unless he put his hand in there for some purpose. That is what happened in the present case and it seems clear on the evidence that the plaintiff came in contact with the blades by inserting his hand in a position where a board would normally go to be grooved. In the circumstances, in my view, the jury was perfectly justified on the evidence in holding that the defendants had not been in breach of statutory duty in failing to have the machine securely fenced. In the first place it was fenced to the degree I have described but, secondly, the defect or deficiency in the fencing, if any, was not a causative factor in this accident. The immediate causative factor was the insertion by the plaintiff of his hand into the position of danger for a purpose other than that of the normal working of the machine.

On the second point, as to the question of the warning which the plaintiff ought to have received as to the danger of cleaning the machine while the cutters were in motion, the jury also answered in the negative. In my view, this was also justified on the evidence. The plaintiff had been employed on this machine for something over four years, was thoroughly familiar with the machine and before he ever started working on it had received instruction about the dangers of it. The object of such warning is, of course, to bring home to the operator the dangers which may arise and that knowledge, if it does not completely remove the danger, would certainly reduce it considerably by bringing home to the plaintiff what he has to avoid. In the present case there is ample evidence to indicate that the plaintiff was fully aware of all the dangers of this machine and that what he did was apparently an act of forgetfulness, which, although it might not amount to negligence on his part, does not mean that because it occurred it must necessarily reflect negligence on the part of the defendants. The plaintiff very likely on the evidence overlooked the fact that the machine does not come to a stop instantly upon the disconnection of the current.

On the question of the adequacy or otherwise of the lighting there was really no evidence upon what was the condition of the lighting on the date of the accident. There was evidence upon which the jury could hold from the tests made by Mr. Doherty, an expert called on behalf of the plaintiff, that the natural lighting on that occasion was probably bad. On the other hand the same expert stated that he had no difficulty in observing whether the machine was on or off. Furthermore he could not recollect whether there was artificial light on at the time of his test and there is no evidence whatever as to whether there was or there was not artificial light at the time of the accident. The plaintiff in the course of his evidence made no reference to the question of lighting. As the jury heard all the evidence on this point, in my view there was ample evidence to uphold their finding on the question of lighting either on the basis that it was not inadequate or alternatively that the adequacy or otherwise of it was not a causative factor in this accident. In either event the plaintiff obviously failed.

For these reasons I am of opinion that the verdict of the jury cannot be disturbed and the appeal must be dismissed.

Budd J. concurred with **Walsh J.**'s judgment and **McLoughlin J.** delivered a separate judgment also dismissing the appeal.

More than one person may cause the plaintiff's injury, and several persons may be liable at the same time to the plaintiff. The rules relating to the liability of concurrent wrongdoers and contribution between concurrent wrongdoers are now to be found in Part III of the Civil Liability Act 1961 (*infra* pp. 48–59).

What is the quality of a human novus actus *if it is to completely dislodge a previous factual cause and become the sole legal cause of the accident?*

CONOLE V. REDBANK OYSTER CO.
[1976] I.R. 191 (Sup. Ct.)

Henchy J.:

The plaintiff's daughter was one of nine young people who were drowned when the defendants' boat capsized in the sea off New Quay, County Clare, on Sunday the 29th June, 1969. It was a new boat which had been specially constructed by the third party (Fairway) for the defendants. The defendants were going to use the boat for dredging oysters. The fourth party were involved in the contract for the building of the boat because, as they were giving a grant to the defendants, they required the boat to be built to their satisfaction.

The plaintiff's claim against the defendants for damages resulting from the death of his daughter through the defendants' negligence was settled for £1,000 and £666 costs. A separate issue then came before Pringle J. on third-party procedure to determine whether the defendants were entitled to an indemnity or contribution against Fairway and, if so, whether they were entitled to an indemnity or contribution against the fourth party. Mr. Justice Pringle held that the circumstances did not warrant any contribution or indemnity. The fourth party is not involved in this appeal which is confined to the question whether Pringle J. was correct in holding that Fairway were not bound to make any indemnity or contribution on the ground that they were not a 'concurrent wrongdoer' for the purposes of s. 21 of the Civil Liability Act, 1961.

Let us first proceed on the hypothesis that Fairway, through want of reasonable care, sent forth a boat with a propensity to ship water and sink which the defendants could not have been reasonably expected to discover in time to avoid the consequences. Of course, Fairway would be liable if the accident had happened in those circumstances. Those drowned in the accident would have come within the range of people whom Fairway should have foreseen as likely to suffer injury because of their carelessness in putting into circulation a boat with such a defect. They might not be solely and totally liable – if, for example, the defendants were also wanting in reasonable care through allowing too many people to travel on the boat – but, on the authority of cases such as *Donoghue v. Stevenson* [1932] A.C. 562, they could not escape liability in one degree or another.

Consider, however, what actually happened in this case after the boat had been delivered to the defendants. They took her to sea on a few trial runs and, while it was observed that she took water in through the freeing ports, she did not ship water to an extent that could not be cleared by the use of a pump. On the day of the fatal accident, when the ceremony of naming and blessing the vessel took place, she was taken out on six trips – the sixth being the fatal one. On the fifth trip, Mr. Hugman (the manager of the defendant company) was at the controls and he had on board with him five people, including the second defendant and some members of his family. This was a speed and manoeuvrability trial. Mr. Hugman manoeuvred the vessel at half speed and then at full speed; the result was nearly a disaster. Water poured on to the deck in such quantities through the freeing ports, particularly when the vessel did a sharp turn, that the pumps could not clear the water from the deck – no matter how hard they were worked. The second defendant was frightened and he ordered Mr. Hugman to slow down and return to harbour. When they landed, the second defendant told Mr. Hugman to tie up the boat and to come into the company's office to take part in the festivities that were going on there in connection with the naming and blessing ceremony.

The fact of the vessel's unseaworthiness had been brought fully home to the second defendant by his frightening experience. In telling Mr. Hugman to tie up the boat the second defendant, in effect, was announcing that the boat was now out of commission because she had proved to be unseaworthy and dangerous. He said in evidence that, if he had known that she was going to be used again, he would have forbidden it. His response to his alarming experience of the boat's propensity to become waterlogged, with only six people aboard, is summed up in the answer he gave to one question put to him in cross-examination:–

'Q. – If you knew the boat was going to go out again after your trip, you would have forbidden it?
A. – I told Mr. Hugman to tie up the boat for the night. I knew that boat was very dangerous. I believe, my lord, that boat was absolutely unseaworthy.'

Mr. Hugman's knowledge that the boat was dangerous must be deemed to have been no less than that of the second defendant. In the circumstances it was clearly the duty of the defendants to see that the boat did not put to sea again with passengers. But, mark what did happen. Within an hour of the earlier harrowing experience, and despite the second defendant's order to tie up the boat for the night, Mr. Hugman unaccountably agreed to take some local boys and girls out for a pleasure trip on her. That was not all; he allowed some fifty of them to come aboard. The boat was thus dangerously overloaded with a moving cargo of unsupervised young people. Inevitably, as the experience on the previous trip should have foretold, the deck was soon deeply awash. The pumps were not properly manned. The children panicked and the boat capsized. A number of the children, including the plaintiff's daughter, were drowned. It was a tragic and avoidable accident.

It goes without question that the defendants were negligent. They should not have taken the boat out once they knew it was unseaworthy, and they made matters worse by allowing too many people aboard. However, the sole issue now is whether the defendants are entitled to an indemnity or contribution from Fairway on the ground that the accident was caused or contributed to by Fairway.

Assuming that Fairway were negligent in sending forth an unseaworthy boat, reliance on this negligence must, on the authorities, be confined to those whom Fairway ought reasonably to have foreseen as likely to be injured by it. Furthermore, the negligence must be such as to have caused a defect which was unknown to such persons. If the defect becomes patent to the person ultimately injured and he chooses to ignore it, or to an intermediate handler who ignores it and subjects the person ultimately injured to that known risk, the person who originally put forth the article is not liable to the person injured. In such circumstances the nexus of cause and effect, in terms of the law of tort, has been sundered as far as the injured person is concerned.

When the defendants discovered that the boat was unseaworthy and, nevertheless, proceeded to put to sea with passengers aboard, the defendants in effect decided to supplant Fairway as tortfeasor in the event of an accident. Leaving aside the added factor of taking too many passengers on board, the mere circumstances that the defendants put to sea at all with passengers when they knew the boat to be dangerously unseaworthy meant that the defendants were consciously undertaking the primary responsibility if an accident happened, and that Fairway were being relegated to an area of remoteness within which responsibility in negligence does not operate. Of course, the defendants are entitled to say that there would have been no accident if Fairway had not been in default in supplying an unseaworthy boat. If the defendants are correct in that assertion, it is merely something they can put forward to support a complaint by them that Fairway were in breach of the contract between the defendants and Fairway. However, as far as the negligence that resulted in the drownings is concerned, any such default by Fairway would have been merely a *causa sine qua non* and not a *causa causans*.

In terms of legal causation, there was only one act of negligence in this case: it was the defendants' act of putting to sea in a boat which they knew to be unseaworthy and which was overloaded with unsupervised young people. Once the defendants are shown to have been aware of the danger involved in that act, they are no more entitled to shed any part of their responsibility on to Fairway, on the ground that Fairway supplied an unseaworthy boat, than they would be entitled to saddle another person with part of the liability if the unseaworthiness of which they had knowledge had been caused by an earlier act done by that other person, *e.g.*, a negligent collision or a malicious injury caused by him.

The direct and proximate cause of this accident was the decision of the defendants, acting through Mr. Hugman, to put to sea with passengers when they had a clear warning that the boat was unfit for the task. The defendants were the sole initiators of the causative negligence. Because that negligence derives from the defendants' knowledge of the risk to which the passengers were being subjected, the plaintiff could not have joined Fairway as defendants successfully. It follows for the same reason, since Fairway cannot rank as a concurrent wrongdoer, that the defendants are not entitled to transfer to Fairway any part of their liability in negligence to the plaintiff. I would dismiss the appeal.

Walsh J. and **Budd J.** agreed with **Henchy J.**

If the act of the third party (novus actus) *was the very thing which the defendant was under a duty to take precautions against the defendant cannot claim that the chain of causation between himself and the plaintiff has been broken.*

CUNNINGHAM V. MacGRATH BROS.
[1964] I.R. 209 (Sup. Ct.)

Kingsmill Moore J. delivered the unanimous judgment of the Court.

Kingsmill Moore J.:

The plaintiff, a chief buyer in Brown Thomas Ltd., left the premises for her luncheon by the side door which leads into Duke Lane and was walking up Duke Lane towards Duke Street when she was hit by a falling ladder very shortly before she reached the end of the lane. Neither she nor any other witness saw the ladder fall and the reason for its fall is conjectural. There was a very strong gusty wind which might have caused a ladder if propped insecurely against the wall to topple over, or it may have been jolted by some passer-by who disappeared rapidly to avoid complications. No other reason for its fall was suggested, nor, in the view that I take, is the exact reason material.

The ladder belonged to MacGrath Brothers, the defendants, who have been sued in negligence and nuisance. The jury made no finding on the issue of negligence, but found the defendants guilty of creating a public nuisance causing injury to the plaintiff and assessed damages. The defendants now appeal, alleging that the findings of the jury were inconsistent, that there was no evidence to support the finding of nuisance, that any such finding was against the weight of evidence, and that the trial Judge should have withdrawn the case from the jury. A further ground of appeal was that the damages were excessive, but this ground was not argued.

Substantially, the defence was that the fall of the ladder was not due to the act or default of the defendants but was due to the action of some person or persons unknown, who removed the ladder from a safe position in Duke Street and put it in an unsafe position in Duke Lane, an action which could not reasonably have been foreseen by the defendants.

The accident took place on the 1st January, 1959. Some six months before Brown Thomas Ltd. had employed the defendants to install two electrically controlled awning blinds over their display windows in Duke Street. One of these blinds was not working properly and the defendants were asked to come and put it right. Shortly before 10 a.m. on the day of the accident the defendants' workmen arrived, bringing with them two double ladders about eight feet long. These double ladders are a familiar type, each consisting of two single ladders joined together at their tops by a metal fitting which allows the bases of the single ladders to be separated so that the combined ladder, when viewed from the side, is like the capital letter 'A' without the cross stroke. The fitting holds the combination in this position. The distance between the feet of the side members of each single ladder is over two feet, the distance between the bases of the respective single ladders, when open, is some four feet. Thus, when opened and set up, the double ladder has a high degree of stability, lateral and longitudinal, which would preclude it being overturned by even a violent wind or by any light jostle from a passer-by. If placed on a busy side-walk a person not expecting such an obstacle might, in the throng, inadvertently bump into it or catch his toe on one of its legs but the danger of it being knocked over, if it was properly set up, would be very slight.

The workmen set up the two double ladders along the wall of the premises of Brown Thomas Ltd., which abuts on Duke Street, in such a way that the 'A's were parallel to the wall and the inside foot of each of the single ladders was touching the wall. The ladders were then fully open and secure. Between the corner formed by the intersection of Duke Lane and Duke Street and the entrance into the premises of Brown Thomas Ltd. there are four small display windows. One ladder was opposite the window nearest the corner, the other opposite a window further down. So placed, the ladders were an obstruction and inconvenience to passers-by on the footpath and prevented proper inspection of the articles on display in the windows. The workmen then mounted the ladders and examined the blind. They discovered that one reason why it was not working properly was that portion of the edge of the plaster recess, into which the blind fitted when drawn up, was somewhat proud and needed to be chipped back. In addition some adjustments to the mechanism of the blind were required which necessitated the removal of the blind to the workshop. Mr. Mac-Grath, the proprietor of the defendant firm, came on the scene some time after 10 a.m. and was shown the difficulty. He got into touch with a Mr. Murphy, a foreman carpenter in the employment of Brown Thomas Ltd. The accounts of what happened next vary widely. I will give first the account as told by Mr. MacGrath and corroborated by his workman, McLoughlin. Mr. MacGrath, Mr. McLoughlin and Mr. Murphy went across to the opposite side of the street to get a general view. Then they came back to the Brown Thomas side and Mr. McLoughlin went up the ladder to point out in detail the work which was necessary to be done. Mr. Murphy said he would have it done immediately and Mr. MacGrath said that if it were done straight away he would leave the ladders for the use of whoever would do it. McLoughlin says that another employee of Brown Thomas Ltd. was present at the time and was shown by Mr. Murphy the work to be done. It was now about 11 a.m. and this man said he would get on to the job as soon as he had finished his tea. Apparently there is a short break for tea at 11 o'clock.

Mr. MacGrath then telephoned for a vehicle to take the blind away, and left. His workmen dismantled the blind and loaded it on the vehicle. They moved the ladders slightly so that the feet of the two double ladders were touching each other and left at about 11.30. When they left the work of chipping had not yet started. They did not return until 4 p.m. when they brought the repaired blind. On arrival they found the two ladders lying on their sides in Duke Lane and the work of chipping the plaster completed. They refitted the blind and took away the ladders.

Mr. Murphy's evidence was confused and contradictory. He admitted that he was told by someone that a small job of chipping was required and that it had been done under his instructions by a man named Hollingsworth, who had died since. He denied that there was any conversation about the ladder and said he did not know what ladder was used by Hollingsworth. There were, he said, plenty of suitable ladders available in the stores of Brown Thomas Ltd. What is without doubt is that the ladders were left by Mr. MacGrath's men at about 11.30 in a position where they were a very considerable obstruction to persons using the footpath and that the men did not return for them till about 4 p.m. In the meantime somebody had moved at least one of the ladders and had left it in a dangerous position near the corner of Duke Lane. Who moved it we do not know. It may have been Hollingsworth when he had finished his job of chipping which, it was agreed, should not take more than an hour. It may have been a neighbouring frontager who objected to the pavement of Duke Street being obstructed. It may have been any of the staff of Brown Thomas Ltd. who wished to allow easy inspection of the goods in their display windows. It might even have been a well-meaning passer-by.

Mr. MacGrath, whose evidence impresses me as being fair and candid to an unusual degree, agreed that in the ordinary way he would never leave ladders unattended, that it would be unsafe to leave ladders unattended in a public place, and that he would not do it. His explanation for his action on the day in question was that he left the ladders to facilitate Mr. Murphy and that they were in his charge. That he tacitly assumed Mr. Murphy would take over control of the ladders and see that they were in a safe position need not be questioned. It seems to me extremely probable. But he does not say that he made any express arrangement with Mr. Murphy to look after the ladders and Mr. Murphy, if he is to be believed, certainly did not accept any responsibility. A jury would be entitled to take the view that there was no express arrangement with Mr. Murphy to look after the ladders and that if there was any implied arrangement it was limited to the period when the ladders were being used to enable the work of chipping to be carried out.

Now, speaking generally, any obstruction of the public highway is a public nuisance, prosecutable on indictment and a tort sounding in damages if any member of the public should suffer particular injury thereby. But the owner of property abutting on the highway may, for proper purposes connected with his property, cause such an obstruction, provided that neither in quantum nor duration does it extend beyond what is necessary; and this exception would extend to cover those doing the necessary work. Thus, although the ladders when in position obstructed the footpath, so long as their presence was necessary for chipping the plaster or fixing the blind they did not constitute a public nuisance: but as soon as the chipping was done and there was no need for the ladders to remain in position they did become a public nuisance and if anyone had been injured by them in the position in which they had been left by the defendants' workmen and defendants would clearly have been liable. But it is contended for the defendants that there was no direct causal connection between the leaving of the ladders in a safe position and the injury to the plaintiff. The accident was due to the intervention of an unknown person who removed at least one of the ladders from a position of relative safety to a position of danger. There was a '*novus actus interveniens*.'

It is not every '*novus actus*' which breaks the chain of causation. 'If what is relied upon as *novus actus interveniens* is the very kind of thing which is likely to happen if the want of care which is alleged takes place, the principle embodied in the maxim is no defence. The whole question is whether or not, to use the words of the leading case, *Hadley v. Baxendale*, 9 Ex. 341 (1854) the accident can be said to be "the natural and probable result" of the breach of duty. If it is the very thing which ought to be anticipated . . . or one of the things likely to arise as a consequence of his wrongful act, it is no defence, it is only a step in the way of proving that the damage is the result of the wrongful act . . .

'It is not necessary to show that this particular accident and this particular damage were probable; it is sufficient if the accident is of a class that might well be anticipated as one of the reasonable and probable results of the wrongful act': *Haynes v. Harwood* [1935] 1 K.B. 146, per Greer L.J., at p. 156.

A case which bears some resemblance to the present was *Clark v. Chambers*, 3 Q.B.D. 327. The defendant had unlawfully placed a spiked barrier so as to partially to obstruct a private road. Someone removed the barrier and put it on the neighbouring footpath. A lawful user of the road, coming along it in the dark, felt his way to that portion of the road which he knew to be unobstructed and then, going on to the footpath, ran into the spikes on the portion of the barrier which had been removed. Cockburn C.J., giving the judgment of the Divisional Court, held the plaintiff entitled to recover. After a detailed review of authorities dealing with the defence of *novus actus interveniens*, he said, at p. 338:–'. . . a man who unlawfully places an obstruction across either a public or private way may anticipate the removal of the obstruction, by someone entitled to use the way, as a thing likely to happen; and if this should be done, the probability is that the obstruction so removed will, instead of being carried away altogether, be placed somewhere near: thus, if the obstruction be to the carriageway, it will very likely be placed, as was the case here, on the footpath. If the obstruction be a dangerous one, wheresoever placed, it may, as was the case here, become a source of damage, from which, should injury to an innocent party occur, the original author of the mischief should be held responsible.'

I am of opinion that the test to be applied is whether the person responsible for creating the nuisance should anticipate as a reasonable and probable consequence that some person in pursuance of his rights would attempt to abate the nuisance and in so doing would create a danger. Applying this test it seems to me that Mr. MacGrath should have anticipated as reasonable and probable that someone – a passer-by, a frontager, or an employee of Brown Thomas Ltd. – would remove the ladder and put it somewhere near in a position where it would be less of an obstruction but might constitute more of a danger. This is what happened. The ladder was moved round the corner to Duke Lane, a relatively unimportant side street which is not a thoroughfare. It was probably folded up and put leaning against the wall. In this position, though more dangerous, it would be less of an obstruction to pedestrians and would not obscure the window display of Brown Thomas Ltd. That an unattended ladder, even if spread out, involves some element of danger is recognised by the admitted practice of the men to take down the ladders during the luncheon interval and put them on a hand cart, and by Mr. MacGrath's acquiescence in the suggestions that 'it would be unsafe to leave a ladder unattended in a public place' and that 'it was a thing you would not do.' Indeed, the whole tenor of his evidence was that he only left the ladders because he thought they would be taken care of by Mr. Murphy. A jury were entitled to consider that he should have made an express stipulation to that effect and that, as he did not do so, the accident was a reasonable and probable result of his action in leaving the ladders without making some provision for their removal to a safe place when no longer needed. I would dismiss the appeal.

Notes and Questions

1. See also *Stansbie* v. *Troman* [1948] 2 K.B. 48, *McKenna* v. *Stephens* [1923] 2 I.R. 112, *Sullivan* v. *Creed, infra*, p. 153. Consider the liability of the defendant where the act of the third party is:
   (a)   unforeseeable;
   (b)   foreseeable;
   (c)   very likely.
2. Consider the liability of the defendant when the action taken by the third party is:
   (a)   reasonable;
   (b)   negligent;
   (c)   objectively reckless;
   (d)   subjectively reckless;
   (e)   intentionally malicious.
3. Is the result of the Irish cases that for the defendant to be relieved of liability the intervening acts of the third party must be:
   (a)   unforeseeable; *or*
   (b)   if foreseeable in a general way, subjectively reckless or intentionally malicious?
   Put another way, is it true to say that the defendant will continue to be liable even where there is an intervening human act if:
   (a)   the intervening act is foreseeable (or very likely?); and
           the third party has not been subjectively reckless or intentionally malicious?

4. If the defendant's act merely *accelerates* an event which would have happened anyway, can it be said to have *caused* the event? *Cf. Smith* v. *Leavy,* unreported, Supreme Court, 7 November 1960.

2. *REMOTENESS*

The law does not always make a person who causes an injury liable for *all* the consequences of his acts. The courts have spent much time debating the criterion which should be used to cut off those consequences for which the defendant ought to be accountable from those consequences for which he should not have to answer. The 'direct consequence' rule established in *Re Polemis* ([1921] 3 K.B. 560) was routed, at least in negligence and nuisance, by the reasonable foreseeability rule established in the *Wagon Mound* litigation ([1961] A.C. 388). *Wagon Mound* was followed in Ireland in several cases and the 'direct consequence' rule has clearly been ousted now in negligence and nuisance cases. The 'egg-shell skull' principle has survived, however, and in some strict torts at least the direct consequence rule still persists.

In recent years, at least in some English cases, there has been a more open acknowledgement that the causation, duty and remoteness concepts tend to run into each other and that each of these can be seen as judicial devices to limit the circumstances when the plaintiff will be allowed to recover. This intermingling is accompanied by a frank acknowledgement that the courts' decisions in these circumstances are essentially policy decisions. In considering these cases therefore it is worth asking what factors influence the courts when they are coming to conclusions on these matters. Attention is drawn in particular to two recent English cases: *Lamb* v. *London Borough of Camden* ([1981] 2 All E.R. 408) and *McKay* v. *Essex Area Health Authority* ([1982] 2 All E.R. 771).

RING V. POWER
[1961] Ir. Jur. Rep. 51 (Sup. Ct., 1958)

Lavery J.:
The plaintiff, on the night of the 13th September, 1956, was a passenger in a motor vehicle driven by the defendant. The vehicle was a Volkswagen van and in the bench seat three persons were seated. The defendant, the driver, was on the right. Next to him was the plaintiff's sister, Mrs O'Riordan, and the plaintiff was on the extreme left next to the door.

As the van took a right hand turn the plaintiff, it is alleged, was thrown against the door which was opened and she fell out on the roadway and suffered injury. She claimed damages alleging negligence against the defendant in the driving of the van.

The handle of the door was so constructed and fitted that it lay above the position where the passenger sat; it opened the door by a downward pressure and the hand, arm, elbow, or body of the passenger seated on the left pressing against it could easily release the catch and cause the door to swing open.

It was accepted that this is what happened.

It was not alleged that the construction of the van or of the door or of the fitting of the handle made the defendant responsible unless it was established that he should have anticipated what happened.

The claim was rested on the ground that the defendant drove the car so fast at the turn that the plaintiff was thrown against the door and, in the event, probably by reason of the nature of the door handle fitting, the door opened and she fell out and was injured. It is claimed that the speed at which the van was driven was unreasonable in the circumstances and was therefore negligent and that the damage and loss suffered by the plaintiff is the consequence of such negligence and the defendant is therefore liable therefor.

There is no fact in controversy except whether the speed at which the van was driven was or was not excessive in the circumstances.

The action was tried before Mr. Justice Murnaghan and a jury in the City of Cork in July, 1957.

The learned judge left two questions to the jury, apart from damages:– 1. Was the defendant guilty of negligence? 2. If so, was the plaintiff guilty of contributory negligence?

The jury answered that the defendant was not negligent. The second question did not, therefore, arise.

On this finding the learned judge entered judgment for the defendant.

This appeal is brought against this verdict and judgment. The appeal is based on an alleged misdirection by the learned judge in his charge to the jury.

It is necessary to set out in full the passage from the charge which, it is submitted, was a misdirection:– 'If you decide that he was going too fast for the particular place it may follow that act of his threw the plaintiff on the handle and opened the door. So far we have got. But even if that happened it would be a long way to fix the defendant with liability because we now come to the part of the case which will probably cause most difficulty. Even if you felt that the defendant drove too fast and the speed threw the plaintiff on the door handle which opened and she fell out that would not be sufficient unless you would have happened [*sic* – eds.]. I want you to be quite clear on that. Supposing that happened and in his wildest dreams the defendant could not have anticipated that it would happen you could not make a mark of him. You can even go much further. You must be satisfied that he could reasonably have anticipated that this might have happened. I think a test, not necessarily conclusive, which you might apply is, say to yourselves this: This defendant, from what we know of the case and from what we know he knew of the car, would it be reasonable that he should have told anybody "Mind that door and keep away from it"? Would you think he should be obliged to say that to every passenger on that side. If you do not think he should have said that I do not think he is liable in this case. If on the other hand you think he should have it helps in coming to the conclusion that he might have anticipated what happened and should have driven more carefully. That seems to be the real hub of this case and on that part of things the evidence is, as the car was a standard model at the time and for a considerable time afterwards, in his favour.' (*sic*).

The learned judge has reported that objection to his charge was taken by counsel for the plaintiff 'in the sense of the first ground of appeal'. That ground of appeal reads:– '1. That the learned High Court judge misdirected the jury by telling them that they would have to be satisfied that the defendant should have anticipated that the plaintiff would be thrown against the door of his said motor vehicle, that the door would open and that she would be thrown on to the public road'.

This submission is based on the decision of the Court of Appeal in England in the case of *Polemis and Furness Withy & Co.* [1921] 3 K.B. 560.

The Court is informed and it is accepted that the learned trial Judge was referred to this decision and was asked to direct the jury to consider the issues on the basis of this decision, which it was submitted applied, and that he declined to recall the jury. This decision is not binding on this Court. It has been the subject of discussion both by courts and by jurists in Great Britain. It has not met with universal acceptance and though it was followed by the Court of Appeal in *Thurogood v. Van den Berghs & Jurgens Ltd.* [1951] 2 K.B. 537, which considered it was bound by it, the principle which it is said it states has not yet been examined, been accepted or rejected by the House of Lords.

The case has been cited on several occasions in this Court but, so far as counsel have submitted or as I have been able to discover, no judicial pronouncement has been made upon it. Mr. McKenna referred the Court to an article by Dr. Goodhart in 68 Law Quarterly Review (1952) which makes interesting reading. I would not hesitate to give my opinion, for what it is worth, on the decision if the evidence requires the application of the so-called principle.

If not, then it would be inappropriate to discuss the decision further and the matter must be left for consideration until the occasion arises.

What is the principle stated?

I quote first from the headnote and then from the judgments of the three judges what appear to be the grounds of their decision. The claim was for damages for negligence. The headnote sets out:– 'The question whether the damage could reasonably have been anticipated is relevant only on the question whether the act is or not negligent.'

Banks L.J. said at p. 572:– 'Given the breach of duty which constitutes the negligence, and given the damage as a direct result of that negligence, the anticipations of the person whose negligent act has produced the damage appear to me to be irrelevant'.

Warrington L.J. said at page 574:– 'The result may be summarised as follows: The presence or absence of reasonable anticipation of damage determines the legal quality of the act as negligent or innocent. If it is thus determined to be negligent, then the question whether particular damages are recoverable depends only on the answer to the question whether they are the direct consequences of the act'; and Scrutton L.J. said at p. 577:– 'To determine whether an act is negligent, it is relevant to determine whether any reasonable person would foresee that the act would cause damage; if he would not, the act is not negligent. But if the act would or might probably cause damage, the fact that the damage it in fact causes is not the exact kind of damage one would expect is immaterial, so long as the damage is in fact directly traceable to the negligent act, and not due to the operation of independent causes having no connection with the negligent act, except that they could not avoid its results. Once the act is negligent, the fact that its exact operation was not foreseen is immaterial.'

If these statements are to be treated as general propositions and not limited to the circumstances of the particular case they raise questions fundamental in the law of negligence. This has been recognised.

It certainly would be right that this Court, as the final Court of Appeal, should pronounce on such a question but it can only do so if, in its opinion, it arises for decision in a case before it.

Moreover, I doubt whether in any particular case the law of negligence well established and generally understood will not be found adequate to determine liability or non liability.

So far as this case is concerned I think it is so.

I have stated the principle alleged to have been established by the case of *Polemis and Furness Withy & Co.* at length in order to show that I have fully considered it.

In my opinion any difficulties which it may raise do not arise for decision in this case.

Under the direction of the learned trial judge the jury has found, interpreting their verdict in the manner most favourable to the plaintiff, that the defendant was not negligent in the manner in which he drove the van in the sense that he could not reasonably have anticipated that his conduct would cause the door to open and the plaintiff to fall out and suffer injury.

The learned judge's charge clearly asked them to consider the case on this basis and their verdict thereon is clear.

It is argued that apart from occasioning the opening of the door, the manner in which the van was driven might, in the opinion of the jury if they had been required to consider it, have caused some injury to the plaintiff by bruising of her shoulder or some other physical injury by impact with the door or side of the car, and that the defendant should reasonably have anticipated this and that therefore his culpability would be established and any damage directly following, though not anticipated, would be his responsibility.

This contention is, on the evidence, in my opinion, entirely fanciful and unsupported.

Therefore, while accepting, but most certainly not deciding, that the appellant would be entitled to recover damages for the injuries which she in fact suffered but which were not, as the jury have found, reasonably to have been foreseen as a consequence of anything the defendant did there is, in my opinion, no evidence which would support a finding – if such had been asked for and made – that the defendant was guilty of negligence in the sense of conduct – which would have caused and been foreseen as likely to cause – injury to the plaintiff apart from the unexpected opening of the door.

Mr. Gleeson, for the plaintiff, appellant, speaking in reply, stated the ground of appeal thus:– The jury have been asked to consider whether the defendant's conduct in the manner of his driving might have caused some injury to the plaintiff which he should, acting reasonably, have anticipated.

This submission is made on the basis that the jury has found against the plaintiff's contention that the opening of the door should reasonably have been contemplated by the defendant as a probable consequence of his conduct.

The defendant's counsel, accepting for the moment the principle of *Polemis and Furness Withy & Co.*, says that it is not sufficient that there should be a mere possibility of injury, there must be a likelihood of injury to the plaintiff from being thrown against the door.

It was emphasized that the onus of establishing this was on the plaintiff and this of course is true.

It is to be accepted that the learned trial judge was asked to direct the jury on the proposition put forward on behalf of the plaintiff and that he declined to do so.

In my opinion there is nothing in the evidence to suggest – much less to establish – that any witness, the plaintiff included, considered that the manner in which the car was driven would have caused any injury to the plaintiff if the door had not opened.

The Court was referred to the evidence in detail. Naturally I have examined it but I do not consider it necessary in this judgment to set forth the questions or answers in full but I quote the crucial answers later. It was not suggested in evidence, though it may have been in argument, that there was or could have been any injury from a blow or any violence involved in the impact of the plaintiff's body with the door or side of the car caused by the turning of the van.

I refer to questions 30 to 34, 151, 156 *et seq.* in the plaintiff's evidence and questions 340 and 342 in the evidence of Mrs. O'Riordan, the plaintiff's sister, the other passenger in the van. The plaintiff in reply to question 30 said: 'When we came to the bend I felt I was being thrown out, before I knew . . . I felt a swerve and I was thrown out . . .'

'I would say he was driving fast' (151). Asked was she worried about the speed she said: 'No, but when we came to the bend I felt swerved over' (*sic* 156). 'I went with the car like when we came to the turn' (162). Mrs. O'Riordan said:– 'I cannot say at what speed it (the car) was travelling but it was going considerably fast I thought' (340).

Asked what happened at St. Luke's Cross she said: 'The car I thought tilted slightly to the left . . . at the turn' (342 and 343).

Neither lady said or suggested that there would have been a violent impact with the door which could have caused injury. It should be mentioned that the width of the seat on which three adults were seated was no more than fifty-eight inches and that the two passengers were seated to the left of a central gear lever which afforded them only $30\frac{1}{2}$ inches or $15\frac{1}{4}$ inches each.

The plaintiff must have been seated right up against the door.

If the trial judge had asked the jury to find a special verdict and had put to them the question:– Was the defendant negligent in the driving of the van in that he should have anticipated injury to the plaintiff by being thrown against the door of the van? and the jury had answered in the affirmative, in my opinion, their finding would have been unsustainable.

It follows that the learned judge would have been wrong if he had directed the jury to consider this.

In my opinion, on the evidence, the directions of the learned trial judge to the jury were proper and correct. The finding of the jury must be accepted and this appeal should be dismissed.

Maguire C.J. and **Ó'Dálaigh J.** agreed.

Questions

1. What did the Court decide in *Ring v. Power*?
2. If you were counsel for the plaintiff in a similar case today how would you plead and argue the case?
3. What did the Court have to say about *Re Polemis*?

BURKE V. JOHN PAUL & CO. LTD.
[1967] I.R. 277 (Sup. Ct.)

The plaintiff, an employee of the defendant, was injured while cutting steel bars by means of the hand-operated cutting machine with which he had been furnished by the defendant. The blades of the cutter were blunt and caused the plaintiff to exert a greater physical effort during his work than would have been necessary had the blades of the cutter been maintained properly. The plaintiff's abdominal muscles were torn and he developed a hernia. At the trial on the 17th and 18th June, 1963, of the plaintiff's action against the defendant in the High Court before McLoughlin J. and a jury, in which the plaintiff claimed damages for the negligence of the defendant, the trial judge withdrew the plaintiff's case from the jury and entered judgment for the defendant on the ground that, as there was evidence that a hernia usually develops where there is an area of congenital weakness of the abdomen, there was not sufficient evidence to justify a finding that the defendant could have reasonably foreseen that the plaintiff would have developed a hernia as a result of operating the cutting machine. The plaintiff appealed to the Supreme Court.

Budd J.:

At the conclusion of the plaintiff's case, counsel for the defendants asked the trial judge to non-suit the plaintiff on the ground that the defendants could not reasonably be expected to anticipate and foresee that the plaintiff might develop a hernia from having to exert such extra pressure as might be involved in the use of a blunt instrument. The learned trial judge acceded to this request. I quote two paragraphs from his decision on that application which I think fairly represent his views on the matter:– 'I do not think I can permit the jury to say that an employer should reasonably have anticipated because a labourer is asked to do labouring work, the kind that was done in this case, that he should anticipate that the labourer might suffer a hernia as a result of overstrain of the muscles of the abdomen . . . There is only one aspect of the evidence that can be taken in this regard and that is that the exertion that he was able to make, his body was not able to take. That is a thing that the employers could not possibly have anticipated.'

The plaintiff appealed to this Court from the order of the High Court on the following grounds:– '(a) That the trial judge was wrong in law and in fact in holding that the jury could not reasonably find for the plaintiff. (b) That the trial judge's said ruling was contrary to the evidence and completely unsupported thereby. (c) That the question of the defendants' negligence was one for the jury and should have been left for the jury.' On the pleadings, the run of the case and the evidence given, the questions which the jury would have to answer in the affirmative to enable the plaintiff to succeed would be, first, were the defendants negligent in failing to provide the plaintiff with a proper appliance with which to do the work he was required to do, or in failing to maintain it in a proper condition; secondly, if the answer to the first question is in the affirmative, was the hernia caused by the negligent breach of duty; thirdly, if so, was the type of injury suffered one which an employer could and should reasonably have foreseen. The point to be decided is whether a reasonable jury could have answered these questions in the affirmative on the evidence adduced.

With regard to the first matter at issue, the contention of the defendants was that there was not sufficient evidence to show that the plaintiff was supplied with defective equipment. It was submitted that the furthest that the evidence went was that the blades were blunt and that a greater effort was therefore required to cut but that, nevertheless, the instrument was efficient to cut and had not in fact failed to cut. The duty of an employer to his servants is to take reasonable care for their safety in all the circumstances of the case; the contract between them, as Lord Herschell observed in *Smith* v. *Baker & Sons* [1891] A.C. 325, 362, 'involves on the part of the former the duty of taking reasonable care to provide proper appliances, and to maintain them in a proper condition, and so to carry on his operations as not to subject those employed by him to unnecessary risk.' There is the evidence of the plaintiff that the blades of the guillotine were badly worn, that he had difficulty in cutting the steel bars, that it required more pressure and extra force to cut the steel bars (meaning presumably more pressure than if they were sharp), and that he complained to the foreman on the first day about the condition of the instrument. There was thus some evidence upon which a jury could find, if they saw fit, that the defendants had failed to supply the plaintiff with a proper appliance to cut the steel bars or, alternatively, had failed to maintain the appliance in a proper condition so that the plaintiff was caused to exert a greater pressure on the instrument than would have been necessary if the blades were sharp and in proper condition, thus exposing him to the added risk of injury that the additional pressure might impose on him – such risk being unnecessary as it was easily avoidable. . . .

There then remains the question of foreseeability. The test of foreseeability as adopted in *Overseas Tankship (U.K.) Ltd.* v. *Morts Dock & Engineering Co. Ltd. (The Wagon Mound)* [1961] A.C. 388, has been accepted in this Court (and indeed was accepted in the argument in this case) and I proceed on the basis that, in determining liability for the consequences of a tortious act of negligence, the test is whether the damage is of such a kind as a reasonable man should have foreseen. What is said by the defendants is that there was no evidence given in this case to show that the type of injuries sustained might reasonably have been anticipated by the defendants. The argument, as it was developed, was that the medical evidence showed that before a person can develop a hernia there must be some congenital weakness – some predisposition to getting a hernia, and that, since this could not be discovered on any ordinary examination, it was impossible for the defendants to know of any predisposition of the plaintiff to develop a hernia, and that consequently they could not foresee that the use of extra exertion and pressure by the plaintiff in cutting the bars would result in a hernia developing. It was clearly implicit in the medical evidence that unwonted bodily exertion may cause straining or tearing of the muscles. It cannot, I think, be suggested that it is necessary to have the statement of a medical expert that an employer should know that if one of his employees is forced to use great exertion in the course of his work that may cause a straining, or even a tearing, of muscles, as that is a matter of common knowledge; but the point taken is that it could not be reasonably anticipated that a hernia would result without knowledge that the plaintiff had a predisposition to hernia. The answer to this, I think, is what is generally referred to as 'the egg-shell skull rule' and I do not think that that rule has been impugned in any way by the *Wagon Mound* decision.

A somewhat similar point arose in the case of *Smith* v. *Leech Brain & Co. Ltd* [1962] 2 Q.B. 405. The case was a claim by the widow of a workman under the Fatal Accidents Acts, 1846 to 1908, and the Law Reform (Misc. Provs.) Act, 1934. The workman suffered an injury by reason of a piece of molten metal striking him on the lower lip and causing a burn. The burn was the promoting cause of cancer from which the workman died. The cancer developed in tissues which already had a premalignant condition. It was alleged that the employers were negligent in not providing adequate protection for the workman, the risk of his being burned being one which was readily foreseeable. Lord Parker C.J. took the view that, but for the decision in the *Wagon Mound* case, it seemed perfectly clear to him that, assuming negligence was proved and the burn caused in whole or in part of the cancer and death, the widow would be entitled to recover.

With regard to the effect of the *Wagon Mound* decision on the case he was dealing with, Lord Parker said at pp. 414 and 415 of the report:– 'For my part, I am quite satisfied that the Judicial Committee in the *Wagon Mound* case did not have what I may call, loosely, the thin skull cases in mind. It has always been the law of this country that a tortfeasor takes his victim as he finds him. It is unnecessary to do more than refer to the short passage in the decision of Kennedy J. in *Dulieu* v. *White & Sons* [1901] 2 K.B. 669, where he said: "If a man is negligently run over or otherwise negligently injured in his body, it is no answer to the sufferer's claim for damages that he would have suffered less injury, or no injury at all, if he had not had an unusually thin skull or an unusually weak heart." To the same effect is a passage in the judgment of Scrutton L.J. in *The Arpad* [1934] P. 189, 202, 203. But quite apart from those two references, as is well known, the work of the courts for years and years has gone on on that basis. There is not a day that goes by where some trial judge does not adopt that principle, that the tortfeasor takes his victim as he finds him. If the Judicial Committee had any intention of making an inroad into that doctrine, I am quite satisfied that they would have said so. It is true that if the wording in the advice given by Lord Simonds in the *Wagon Mound* case is applied strictly to such a case as this, it could be said that they were dealing with this point. But, as I have said, it is to my mind quite impossible to conceive that they were and, indeed, it has been pointed out that they disclose the distinction between such a case as this and the one they were considering when they comment on *Smith* v. *London & South Western Railway Company*, L.R. 6 C.P. 14. Lord Simonds in dealing with that case said: "Three things may be noted about this case: the first, that for the sweeping propositions laid down no authority was cited: the second, that the point to which the court directed its mind was not unforseeable damage of a different kind from that which was forseen, but more extensive damage of the same kind." In other words, Lord Simonds is clearly there drawing a distinction between the question whether a man could reasonably anticipate a type of injury, and the question whether a man could reasonably anticipate the extent of injury of the type which could be foreseen. The Judicial Committee were, I think, disagreeing with the decision in the *Polemis* case that a man is no longer liable for the type of damage which he could not reasonably anticipate. The Judicial Committee were not, I think, saying that a man is only liable for the extent of damage which he could anticipate, always assuming the type of injury could have been anticipated. I think that view is really supported by the way in which cases of this sort have been dealt with in Scotland. Scotland has never, so far as I know, adopted the principle laid down in *Polemis* [1921] 3 K.B. 560, and yet I am quite satisfied that they have throughout proceeded on the basis that the tortfeasor takes the victim as he finds him. In those circumstances, it seems to me that this is plainly a case which comes within the old principle. The test is not whether these employers could reasonably have foreseen that a burn would cause cancer and that he would die. The question is whether these employers could reasonably foresee the type of injury he suffered, namely, the burn. What, in the particular case, is the amount of damage which he suffers as a result of that burn, depends upon the characteristics and constitution of the victim.'

With respect, I entirely adopt the reasoning of Lord Parker. Applying his reasoning to this case, the test is not whether the defendants could reasonably have foreseen that a straining or tearing of the muscles would cause a hernia in this particular man, but the question is rather whether they could have reasonably foreseen the type of injury that he did suffer, namely, the tearing or straining of the muscles which resulted in the hernia. A reasonable jury could, in my view, certainly find on all the facts and circumstances of the case that the defendants ought to have anticipated that a man in the plaintiff's position, being given a blunt instrument with which to cut steel bars, might, by reason of the unusual exertion he would be called upon to exercise, strain or injure his muscles; it is immaterial that the defendants could not anticipate the full extent of the damage. It follows that a reasonable jury could properly have answered the third question that I have posed in the affirmative, as well as the other two. The case, therefore, should not have been withdrawn from the jury and in the circumstances a new trial becomes necessary.

Ó Dálaigh C.J. and **Haugh J.** agreed with **Budd J.'s** judgment

REEVES V. CARTHY AND O'KELLY
Unreported Sup. Ct. 28 April 1982

O'Higgins C.J.:

These proceedings have been brought by the plaintiff against the two defendants who are general medical practitioners, because of a serious and incapacitating stroke which he suffered on the 9th June 1977. The two defendants are members of a medical service known as 'Doctor on Call' and each, on separate occasions on that date, answered a sick call made by the plaintiff's wife to a designated doctor who was unable to attend. The plaintiff alleges that each defendant, in his attendance upon and treatment of him, was guilty of negligence and breach of duty and that as a result he, later that day, suffered a stroke which was serious and permanently incapacitated him. The plaintiff's claim was tried over several days in the High Court before Mr. Justice Gannon and a jury. At the conclusion of all the evidence in the case the learned trial Judge acceded to an application made on behalf of both defendants that the case should be withdrawn from the jury. He did so on the grounds advanced on behalf of the defendants that even if there was evidence of negligence or breach of duty against the defendants or either of them, the occurrence of a stroke was not reasonably foreseeable and accordingly liability could not be established. Against this decision this appeal has been brought by the plaintiff.

[Having reviewed much of the evidence **O'Higgins C.J.** continued:]

On this evidence which I have outlined it seems to me that a jury could arrive at the following conclusions.

(1) On the 8th June 1977 the plaintiff, who was suffering from an undiagnosed condition of Crohn's Disease, perforated from the small intestine into the abdominal cavity.

(2) Over the ensuing hours this perforation continued to progress, and, at 3 a.m. on the 9th June, when seen by Dr. Carthy, he was suffering from peritonitis.

(3) This fact would have been apparent to any doctor who examined the plaintiff's abdomen.

(4) Dr. Carthy failed to carry out such an examination and as a result failed to recognise the plaintiff as an acutely ill person in need of immediate hospitalisation.

(5) The administration of the drug cyclomorph was, in the circumstances, contrary to accepted medical practice and dangerous because it could mask the plaintiff's symptoms.

(6) Peritonitis affects and lowers the blood supply and, as it persists, weakens the circulatory system. A period of circulatory weakness or hypotension lasting a number of hours involves the risk of a stroke occurring. The existence of such a risk should be known to any doctor attending a patient exhibiting symptoms of circulatory disorder.

(7) When Dr. O'Kelly examined the plaintiff the plaintiff was suffering from peritonitis, with a fast, weak pulse or tachycardia, he was exhibiting signs of circulatory weakness and was developing shock. In these circumstances Dr. O'Kelly should have recognised his patient as being acutely ill and in danger of death and should have insisted on his immediate removal to hospital.

(8) The administration by Dr. O'Kelly of the drug largactil was, in the circumstances, contrary to proper medical practice and was dangerous because it added to the process of circulatory collapse.

(9) The plaintiff's stroke was caused by circulatory weakness or hypotension lasting over a prolonged period.

On the basis that a jury could reach these conclusions the question now to be considered is whether a case in negligence has been made out against the defendants or either of them. To succeed in an action based on negligence it is necessary to establish a breach of that duty to take care which the law requires in the circumstances. It is also necessary to show that such breach of duty has resulted in damage. Carelessness without damage is not actionable nor is a person in breach of duty liable for consequences which he could not reasonably have foreseen.

[Having examined the nature of the duty of care owed by the doctors and having concluded that a jury could have found the doctors in breach **O'Higgins C.J.** turned to the question of whether the plaintiff's stroke was a reasonably foreseeable consequence.]

Being satisfied as I am that there was evidence of negligence to go to the jury against both defendents, I have now to consider the ground upon which this case was withdrawn from the jury by the learned trial Judge. He formed the view that even if some want of care or negligence could be established on the part of both defendants, or either one of them, the occurrence of a stroke as a consequence could not reasonably have been foreseen. In making the application for a direction, both Mr. Liston and Mr. Sutton on behalf of the respective defendants relied on the fact that the plaintiff had Crohn's Disease. This meant, they submitted, that he had a disposition to a stroke. While the defendants might have foreseen an abdominal perforation, they could not have foreseen the occurrence of a stroke as such was not a consequence of the perforation but of a perforation with Crohn's Disease. The learned trial Judge seems to have accepted and adopted his submission. In my view, in doing so he was incorrect. While undoubtedly Crohn's Disease was a factor, there was a considerable amount of evidence to the effect that, apart altogether from Crohn's Disease, the subjecting of a patient even of the Plaintiff's age to a prolonged period of hypotension carried with it the risk of a stroke. There was further evidence that the existence of such a risk would have been known to any doctor. In addition, there was clear evidence that untreated peritonitis leads to circulatory weakness and hypotension. From this it seems to me to follow that any doctor who fails, culpably, to diagnose a perforation must be taken as foreseeing that his failure to do so could lead to hypotension which if prolonged could in turn lead to a stroke. The fact that the patient had an additional predisposing medical condition is, in my view, irrelevant. I appreciate that the administration of largactil by Dr. O'Kelly was, so far as Dr. Carthy is concerned, a complicating factor. However, in my view, a jury could well take the view on the evidence that the administration of this drug was merely an accelerating factor in the circulatory collapse which was inevitable as long as the plaintiff's condition was not properly diagnosed and treated in hospital, and for this both defendants could be held responsible.

I have come to the conclusion, therefore, on the evidence, that because the result of the defendants' negligence was an untreated abdominal perforation, the inherent danger therein of a circulatory collapse and prolonged hypotension made the risk of a stroke foreseeable.

Even if the view which I have taken of the effect of the medical evidence be incorrect and if the most that can be said is that foreseeability was limited to the perforation which the plaintiff suffered, I do not see that this can assist the defendants. The stroke was directly caused by the fact that this plaintiff suffered an abdominal perforation which was not diagnosed or treated in time. The fact that another person would not have suffered a stroke or that a doctor being told of abdominal pains would not think of the danger of the stroke or that the plaintiff had Crohn's Disease are to my mind irrelevant considerations. The failure to diagnose or treat a perforated abdominal cavity was capable of causing great harm to the person concerned, leading eventually to an abdominal catastrophe. The fact that in this plaintiff with Crohn's Disease and predisposition to a stroke the harm done was more extensive and severe than might have been anticipated does not excuse the defendants. In my view, the case viewed in this light is very similar to *Burke* v. *John Paul* [1967] I.R. 277.

New trial ordered. (**Hederman J.** concurred).

Griffin J.:
On behalf of the plaintiff, Mr. McGrath submitted that once damage of a *type*

which is foreseeable occurs, the full extent of that damage is the liability of the defendants, although the *extent* of the damage might not be foreseeable. That submission is in my opinion well-founded.

In *Overseas Tankship (U.K.) Ltd.* v. *Morts Dock and Engineering Co. Ltd.* (*The Wagon Mound*) [1961] 2 W.L.R. 126, Viscount Simonds, in the course of giving the advice of the Privy Council, said at p. 142 that the essential factor in determining liability is whether the damage is of such a kind as the reasonable man should have foreseen and that thus foreseeability becomes the effective test. In *Overseas Tankship (U.K.) Ltd.* v. *The Miller Steamship Company Pty.*, [1966] 3 W.L.R. 498 (*The Wagon Mound No. 2*) Lord Reid said at p. 506:

> 'It has now been established by the *Wagon Mound (No. 1)* and by *Hughes* v. *Lord Advocate*, [1963] A.C. 837 that in such cases damages can only be recovered if the injury complained of was not only caused by the alleged negligence but was also injury of a class or character foreseeable as a possible result of it.'

The test of foreseeability as adopted in the *Wagon Mound* has been accepted in this Court in *Burke* v. *John Paul,* [1967] I.R. 277. The relevant passage from the judgement of Budd J. in that case has been cited by the Chief Justice in his judgment. I agree with the Chief Justice that the reasoning of Budd J. in that passage can properly be said to be applicable to this case.

Since the *Wagon Mound* and *Burke* v. *John Paul* the law does not therefore require that the precise nature of the injury must be reasonably foreseeable before liability for its consequences follows. Professor Heuston in *Salmond on the Law of Torts*, 16th edn., para. 202 at p. 564 has, with his customary clarity, concisely and conveniently summarised this branch of the law as follows:

> '*Type of damage must be foreseen*. It has been made plain that the precise details of the accident, or the exact concatenation of circumstances, need not be foreseen. It is sufficient if the type, kind, degree, category or order of harm could have been foreseen in a general way. The question is, was the accident a variant of the perils originally brought about by the defendant's negligence? The law of negligence has not been fragmented into a number of distinct torts'.

In this case, the damage which occurred was of a type that was foreseeable (i.e. circulatory damage and shock), so that even if the stroke was not, as such, foreseeable by the defendants, if they or either of them was held to be negligent then they or he would be answerable for the stroke, because that was the extent of the damage suffered.

One final matter arises. On behalf of Doctor Carthy Mr. Sutton submitted that, even assuming negligence on the part of Doctor Carthy, this did not lead to the stroke because Doctor O'Kelly did fully examine the plaintiff later and his intervention broke the chain of causation. In my view, the intervention of Doctor O'Kelly was not a *novus actus interveniens*. He, if at all, merely contributed an additional act of negligence. Doctor Carthy's original negligence continued to operate until the stroke occurred around midday. The refusal of the plaintiff to accept Doctor O'Kelly's advice to go to hospital may be a good ground for contributory negligence, but it was not a *novus actus*.

I would allow the appeal and direct a new trial against each of the defendants on the ground, in Doctor Carthy's case, that there was evidence to go to the jury in relation to whether or not he carried out an abdominal examination, and, in Doctor O'Kelly's case, in relation to the administration of largactil.

Notes

1. Reasonable foreseeability is the criterion in public nuisance (*Wall* v. *Morrissey* [1969] I.R. 10 (Sup. Ct.)), but the direct consequence rule still survives in actions for deceit: *Northern Bank Finance Corporation Ltd.* v. *Charlton* [1979] I.R. 149 (Sup. Ct.). As to cattle trespass see *McCabe* v. *Delaney* [1951] Ir. Jur. Rep. 10, *infra*, pp. 572–577. Would this decision still command support if the issue came before the Court today?

2. If the plaintiff has to borrow to mitigate the loss caused by the wrong of the defendant, is the plaintiff entitled to the interest on such borrowings as part of his loss? *Cf. Riordans Travel Ltd.* v. *Acres & Co. Ltd. (No. 2)*, unreported, High Ct., McWilliam, J., 17 January 1979. See also Kerr, 74 Inc. L.S. Ir. Gazette 51 (1980).

Chapter 2

MINORS AND MENTALLY ILL PERSONS

O'BRIEN V. McNAMEE
[1953] I.R. 86 (High Ct., Davitt, P., 1952).

1. *MINORS*

The defendant, aged seven years and one month, obtained matches and brought a lighted paper into the plaintiff's barn. He put the paper down in the middle of the floor, but the flame spread to the hay in the barn and the barn was burnt down.

Davitt P.:

Strange as it may seem, the defendant is liable. A child over seven years of age is liable for the torts he commits, provided there is no question of intention involved in the tort and provided that it does not arise out of contract. When the act may or may not be a malicious act, intent may be material. It is then a question whether he wills the consequences.

. . .[A]ll that is necessary to establish the tort of trespass is that the act should be voluntary. If a man is sitting on a wall and is pushed so that he falls into someone's land and thereby commits trespass his act is involuntary and he is not liable in tort; but if he is out shooting and thinks he has a right to be on the particular land, when in fact he has no such right, his act is voluntary and he is liable for trespass even though he has no intention of trespassing. It seems to me that if intention is out of the matter, the only question is whether the defendant's act was voluntary; if it was voluntary, he is liable.

In *Stanley* v. *Powell* [1891] 1 Q.B. 86, the defendant, when out shooting, fired, and a beater was hit by a ricochet; negligence was negatived on the ground of the act being involuntary. In *Clissold* v. *Cratchley* [1910] 2 K.B. 244, the plaintiff had recovered judgment against the defendant. The solicitor for the plaintiff had two offices. The account was paid at the country office, but not to the knowledge of the plaintiff or his solicitor who issued execution. Though there was no intention to do a wrong act, there was a trespass, for the judgment had been satisfied. Accordingly, if the only essential of trespass is that it be voluntary and no question arises as to whether there is intention or malice, the defendant is liable. There is very little authority, but the textbooks support the liability of an infant in such a matter.

Judgment for plaintiff.

Notes and Questions

1. Davitt P.'s reference to the liability of a 'child over seven years of age' may mislead in that it suggests that a child under that age would be exempt from responsibility in tort. The textbooks writers all agree that there is no arbitrary minimum age below which a child may not be held liable; see also *Cotton* v. *Comm'r. for Road Transport & Tramways*, 43 S.R. (N.S.W.) 66, at 69 (Sup. Ct., *per* Jordan, C.J., 1942). But see *Kingston* v. *Kingston*, 102 I.L.T.R. 65, at 67 (Sup. Ct., *per* Walsh, J., 1965).
2. Is it sound legal policy to hold a young child liable in trespass, when he may lack full appreciation of the seriousness of his acts or of their consequences?

FLEMING V. KERRY COUNTY COUNCIL
[1955–56] Ir. Jur. Rep. 71 (Sup. Ct., 1953).

The plaintiff, aged nine and a half years, was returning from school with a group of other children along the public road, when they were attracted by a road repairing unit belonging to the defendants, which included a steam roller and a tar boiler. The children swarmed around the vehicles, and in spite of being warned repeatedly by the driver and his helper to keep away, they returned to them. The plaintiff was injured, apparently by the wheel of the tar boiler passing over her foot.

The trial judge, having ruled that the plaintiff was capable of contributory negligence, left it to the jury to determine if she had been guilty of contributory negligence, notwithstanding application for a direction made on behalf of the defendants that the plaintiff had been so clearly guilty of contributory negligence that she could not succeed in the action. The jury found in favour of the plaintiff and awarded her £3,000 damages. The defendants appealed to the Supreme Court.

Maguire C.J.:

. . . The trial Judge held that [the plaintiff] was capable of contributory negligence but despite objection he asked the jury to say whether in fact she was negligent.

Unquestionably this combination of vehicles being drawn along the public road at a walking pace was tempting to children. In my opinion it is a question for the jury whether the plaintiff in going to play around, catch on to or clamber upon the tar boiler, showed prudence to as great a degree as she could be expected to show it.

For this reason I consider that the learned Judge acted properly in leaving the question of contributory negligence to the jury.

In my opinion the appeal fails and ought to be dismissed.

O'Byrne J.:

I agree. In the case of a person of full age and capacity contributory negligence means a failure to take such precautions for his own safety as might reasonably be expected from a reasonable person placed in the position in which the plaintiff was called upon to act. In such a case no question arises as to whether the plaintiff is capable of being guilty of contributory negligence.

In the case of a child of tender years there must be some age up to which the child cannot be guilty of contributory negligence. In other words, there is some age up to which a child cannot be expected to take any precautions for his own safety. In cases where contributory negligence is alleged against a child, it is the duty of the trial Judge to rule, in each particular case, whether the plaintiff, having regard to his age and mental development, may properly be expected to take some precautions for his own safety and consequently be capable of being guilty of contributory negligence. Having ruled in the affirmative, it becomes a question of fact for the jury, on the evidence, to determine whether he has fallen short of the standard which might reasonably be expected from him having regard to his age and development. In the case of an ordinary adult person the standard is what should be expected from a reasonable person. In the case of a child, the standard is what may reasonably be expected, having regard to the age and mental development of the child and other circumstances of the case. There may be cases in which, even in the case of a child, the want of care is so gross that he could not reasonably be acquitted of negligence and in such a case it is a matter for the Judge to direct the jury on this question. That is not the position in this case, in which, in my view, it was entirely a question for the jury to determine whether the plaintiff fell short of the standard of care which might properly be expected from her and was, therefore, guilty of contributory negligence.

Lavery, Kingsmill Moore and **Ó'Dálaigh JJ.** concurred.

Notes and Questions

1. What is the minimum age below which a child cannot be guilty of contributory negligence? Is it three? Cf. *Macken* v. *Devine*, 80 I.L.T.R. 121 (Circuit Ct., Gleeson, J., 1946). Four? *Cf. Lipschitz* v. *Caulfields Ltd*, unreported, Sup. Ct., 20 December 1960 (32–1960). Five? *Cf. Curran* v. *Lapedus*, 73 I.L.T.R. 89 (High Ct., O'Byrne, J., 1939). Or even older? *Cf. Menton* v. *C.I.E.*, unreported, Sup. Ct., 27 July 1966 (149–1965), *Brennan* v. *Savage Smyth & Co. Ltd.*, unreported, Sup. Ct., 2 February 1982. Is this the question the courts should ask? *Cf. McMahon & Binchy*, pp. 68–69.
2. In *Duffy* v. *Fahy*, 102 I.L.T.R. 65 (Sup. Ct., 1965), Lavery J. expressed uncertainty as to the meaning of O'Bryne J.'s statement in *Fleming's* case that the standard to be applied in determining whether a child was guilty of contributory negligence was 'what may reasonably be expected, having regard to the age and mental development of the child and the other circumstances of the case.' Lavery, J. considered this to be –

    'susceptible of meaning either the mental development of the individual concerned or the mental development of the normal or average child of that age.'

    The balance of authority clearly favours the former interpretation: *cf. McMahon & Binchy*, pp. 69–71, *Brennan* v. *Savage Smyth & Co. Ltd.* [1982] I.L.R.M. 223 (Sup. Ct.), *McNamara* v. *E.S.B.* [1975] I.R.I., *infra*, pp. 250–264.

    In the recent Canadian decision of *Wessell* v. *Kinsmen Club of Sault Ste. Marie Ontario Incorporated*, 21 C.C.L.T. 10 (Ont. H.C. 1982), Walsh, J. stated:

    'The test is a subjective one. The total child must be assessed. All of the individual qualities and defects of the child, as well as all of the opportunities or lack of them, which he might have had to become aware of the particular danger or duty of care thus imposed, must be considered.'

    Does this go further than Irish law? If a child is particularly impulsive, should this be taken into account? *Cf.* Gray, 'The Standard of Care for Children Revisited' 45 Missouri L. Rev. 597, at 602–603 (1980).
3. There appears to be no Irish decision on the question of negligence (as opposed to contributory negligence) of a child. There is a dearth of judicial authority in most other common law jurisdictions. The commentators tend to the view that the same standard should be applied to both negligence and contributory negligence. See, however, *Kingston* v. *Kingston*, 102 I.L.T.R. 65, at 67 (Sup. Ct., *per* Walsh J. 1965).

2. *MENTALLY ILL PERSONS*

The liability of mentally ill persons in tort is a matter of considerable uncertainty. Some aspects of the problem are, however, reasonably clear. Where a person's mental condition prevents him from having a specific mental ingredient – malice for example – then he will not be liable for a tort requiring proof of his ingredient. The position relating to negligence and contributory negligence has not yet been resolved in Ireland. In *Kingston* v. *Kingston*, 102 I.L.T.R. 65, at 67 (Sup. Ct., 1965) Walsh, J. stated:

'It is sufficient to say that the question of the standard of care required of a plaintiff who is . . . mentally infirm is still open.'

On trespass, the leading English decision is *Morriss* v. *Marsden* 1952] 1 All E.R. 925 (Q.B.D., 1952). Stable J. accepted (at 928) that a condition of complete automatism would relieve a defendant of liability, but that –

'where there is the capacity to know the nature and quality of the act, that is sufficient although the mind directing the hand that did the wrong was diseased.'

In the Circuit Court decision of *Donohue* v. *Coyle*, [1953–1954] Ir. Jur. Rep. 30, Judge Sheehy imposed liability for battery, stating (at 31) that –

'In the circumstances I feel that I must follow the recent English decision of *Morriss* v. *Marsden*.'

Questions

What policies should tort law seek to serve in relation to mentally ill persons? Is its function to punish wrongdoing or to compensate the injured? Is it possible to reconcile these competing policies? Should the law of negligence be treated differently from that of trespass in this context? If so, why? Some of these questions are considered by Fridman, 'Mental Incompetency' Part II, 80 L. Q. R. 84, at 84–96 (1964); Todd, 'The Liability of Lunatics in the Law of Tort' 26 Austr. L. J. 299 (1952); Bohlen, 'Liability in Tort of Infants and Insane Persons' 23 Mich. L. Rev. 9 (1924); Picher, 'The Tortious Liability of the Insane in Canada' 13 O.H.L.J. 193 (1975).

Chapter 3

PARTIES

1. *CORPORATIONS*

A corporation has the same capacity as an individual to sue for torts committed against it. Certain torts (assault and battery, for instance) cannot by their nature be committed against a corporation; but it seems that, in actions for defamation, a corporation can sue in respect of statements tending to cause actual damage to its property or business where it is a trading corporation (*Irish People's Assurance Society* v. *Dublin City Assurance Co.* [1929] I.R. 25) and the better opinion nowadays appears to be that any corporation can sue in respect of any defamatory statement about the conduct of its affairs.

A corporation may be sued as being vicariously liable for the acts of its servants and agents; moreover, where an act is that of the central governing authority, liability may attach to the corporation, not because of *respondeat superior*, but because the wrong may be properly said to be that of the corporation itself: *Salmond & Heuston*, pp. 404–406. As to cases where the tort committed by a servant is *ultra vires*, see *McMahon & Binchy*, pp. 75–76.

2. *UNINCORPORATED ASSOCIATION AS DEFENDANT*

CREAN V. NOLAN & OTHERS
97 I.L.T.R. 125 (C. Ct., 1963)

Judge O'Briain:

It is pleaded in the Civil Bill that the plaintiff is a farmer and is the occupier of certain lands at Tonevane, Blennerville, Tralee in the County of Kerry. The defendants are members of the Festival of Kerry Committee, and were, at the time of the matters complained of, the President, Secretary and joint Treasurers respectively of the said Committee. On or about the 3rd day of September, 1961, the defendants organised and managed a drag-hunt in the vicinity of the said lands in the occupation of the plaintiff and, prior to the commencement of the said drag hunt, the defendants their servants and agents brought together a large number of beagle dogs on premises occupied by the defendants.

It is alleged that, in the course of said hunt, the defendants led and brought the dogs into the lands in the occupation of the plaintiff and trespassed thereon, and that one or more of the dogs made an attack upon the plaintiff's sheep and as a direct result, eleven of the sheep died or were lost.

I am satisfied that trespass has not been proved, and there is no evidence that the drag hunt was laid on the lands of the plaintiff.

I am also satisfied, however, as a matter of probability that one or more of the dogs that had been participating in the hunt did attack the plaintiff's sheep as alleged. A large loss of this kind is serious for a small farmer but I have to decide the case on the evidence alone. Had it not been for the hunt the damage to the sheep would not have taken place, but the plaintiff must show that the cause of the damage was the wrongful act of the defendants.

It is pleaded in paragraph 8 of the Civil Bill that the dogs were of a fierce and ferocious nature and accustomed to so attack sheep, and that the defendants well knew that the said dogs were of such a fierce and ferocious nature and were so accustomed. *Prima facie* there is no liability for trespass of cats and dogs in the absence of proof of *scienter*, or the incitement by the owner of the dogs to trespass and commit damage. The proof of *scienter* must, however, relate to the particular dogs which killed the sheep, and known to the defendants or the owners. There is no evidence that either of them knew that the dogs were fierce and ferocious, and so this plea also must fail.

A claim may suceed under the Dog's Act, 1906, in which it is not necessary to prove either *scienter* or negligence, but this applies only against the owner or owners of the dogs and has no relevance in relation to the defendants in this case.

In paragraph 9 of the Civil Bill it is pleaded that the defendants their servants and agents were neglegent in the care, management and control of the said dogs at the time of the matters complained of. This plea raises the question as to whether the owners of the dogs were the agents of the defendants. The whole Festival of Kerry is described as the greatest free show on earth, and the committee decided to put on a drag hunt and they did it by inviting a number of dog owners to come and enter their dogs for the drag-hunt. But they did so, not *per se*, but through others, and the owners were agents for the Festival Committee.

The mere organising of a hunt is not *per se* a negligent act and the assembling of the dogs is not evidence of negligence. Nobody saw the dogs breaking away but they got away from the pack and dispersed. While I hold that the owners were agents for the defendants, there must be a time limit to the continuance of the agency. I hold that they were agents from the time of assembly to the dispersal of the owners and the giving of the prizes, but, at what exact time this was, the evidence is flimsy.

At 8.30 p.m. a single dog was seen crossing the mountain, and, two days later, two other dogs were caught by a local farmer. Accordingly three of the beagles which had taken part in the hunt had not been re-assembled with the others, but there is no evidence that these beagles escaped from the pack during the hunt, and, on the evidence, it is open to me to hold that they may have escaped after the hunt but, at that time the agency had terminated. While I hold that there was agency, I am not satisfied that the onus of proving that the damage was done by beagles who had strayed away after the hunt has shifted on to the defendants, and, while there is some moral obligation on the committee of the Festival of Kerry to make good the loss to the plaintiff, in law I hold that the plaintiff has not proved his case and I must dismiss his claim with costs. I will make a similar order in the case of *O'Connor* v. *Nolan and Others*.

3. *PARTNERSHIPS*
Persons who have entered into a partnership with each other may sue and be sued in the firm's name by virtue of Order 14 of the Rules of the Superior Courts. Partners are jointly and severally liable for the tortious actions of any one of their members committed against outsiders during the ordinary course of the firm's business or with the authority of the other partners: *Partnership Act 1890*, sections 10 and 12.

4. *TRADE UNIONS*
It has long been established that a trade union may sue and be sued in its own name. Generally speaking, however, since 1906, trade unions are not liable in tort. The scope and limitations of this exemption from liability will be considered *infra*, pp. 472–506.

5. *THE STATE*

BYRNE V. IRELAND AND THE A.G.
[1972] I.R. 241

Walsh J.:

The plaintiff claims that when she was lawfully walking along the public highway at Bray in the County of Wicklow the footpath upon which she was walking subsided, and that this was due to the negligence and breach of duty of persons employed in the Department of Posts and Telegraphs when they had been laying installations under the footpath. The plaintiff has claimed that these persons were employees of the State and that the State is vicariously liable for their negligence. The portions of the defence relevant to this appeal are those which claim that the Court cannot exercise jurisdiction over the State as the judicial power granted by the Constitution does not of common right extend to actions against the sovereign authority. It claims further that the action, being one based on an alleged tortious act or omission, was not maintainable in law by reason of the immunity of the State against such actions as sovereign authority. It is also claimed that the action could not be maintained against the Attorney General as a representative of the State and that the representative order, which the plaintiff seeks, could not be made. By order of the President of the High Court dated the 6th November, 1967, it was directed that special issues be tried by a judge without a jury.

By the Constitution which was adopted and enacted by the People and came into force on the 29th December, 1937, the People created a State which is described in Article 5 of the Constitution as 'a sovereign, independent, democratic state' and under Article 4 the name of the State in the English language is 'Ireland'. If the State can be sued, then in my opinion it can be sued by its official name which is 'Ireland' in the English language.

Article 6 of the Constitution provides that all powers of government – legislative, executive and judicial – 'derive, under God, from the people, whose right it is to designate the rulers of the State and, in final appeal, to decide all questions of national policy, according to the requirements of the common good.' Article 46 of the Constitution provides that every proposal for an amendment of the Constitution shall, upon having been passed or deemed to have been passed by both Houses of the Oireachtas, be submitted by referendum to the decision of the People, and Article 47 provides that every such proposal for an amendment shall be held to have been approved by the People if, upon having been so submitted, a majority of the votes cast at such referendum shall have been cast in favour of its enactment into law. The preamble to the Constitution is a preamble by the People formally adopting, enacting and giving themselves a Constitution.

It appears to me abundantly clear from those provisions that the State is the creation of the People and is to be governed in accordance with the provisions of the Constitution which was enacted by the People and which can be amended by the People only, and that in the last analysis the sovereign authority is the People. This is in contrast to the position in the United States of America where Chief Justice John Marshall initially established the basic premise that the United States was created by the States and the people of the States, and not by the people separated from the States. It is also in contrast to the position which prevailed in England and now in Great Britain that the King was the personification of the State and that, even with the development of constitutional monarchy where the distinction between the King in his public and private capacities could be perceived, no legal acknowledgment of this distinction was made with the consequence that the King, or the Crown, was and remains the personification of the State in Great Britain.

Article 6 of our Constitution, having designated the powers of government as being legislative, executive and judicial and having declared them to have been derived from the People, provided that these powers of government are exercisable only by or on the authority of the organs of State established by the Constitution. The question which now arises for decision is whether the judicial power of government which is exercised by the judiciary through the Courts is exercisable so as to bind the State itself, one of whose organs is the judiciary.

It has already been established that the State is a juristic person capable of holding property: see *Comyn v. The Attorney General* [1950] I.R. 142 and *Commissioners of Public Works v. Kavanagh* [1962] I.R. 216. It was implicit in the judgments in those cases that the State could have been sued as such. Drummond's famous dictum that property has its duties as well as its rights is no less true in this context. Even in mediaeval England the petition of right was available for all proprietary actions in the wide sense of the term in that it lay not merely for the recovery of land but for claims for damages for interference with proprietary rights, and also for the recovery of chattels. Not only in England but in many other countries in Europe the inviolability of property was acknowledged in law as a right superior even to that of sovereignty itself. The petition of right fell into disuse from the fifteenth century onwards until the nineteenth century during which time it was superseded by the real actions. In a very full investigation of the history of the petition of right, Lord Sommers in the *Bankers' Case* (1700) 14 St. Tr. 1 was able to treat as precedents (for the competence of the petition of right in contract) cases in which the facts corresponded to those in modern suits in contract but which had been decided as proprietary actions. Therefore, the concept of proprietary actions lying against the State, even when the King was the personification of the State, is not a new one.

The point which arises in the present case is whether a right of action lies against the State for a wrong and, in particular, whether the State is vicariously liable for the wrongs committed by its servants. The learned High Court judge, Mr. Justice Murnaghan, who tried these issues came to the conclusion that the State is not so liable and he based his rejection of the submission on the statement in Article 5 of the Constitution that Ireland is 'a sovereign . . . state.' He says that 'the simple statement that "Ireland is a sovereign . . . state" is completely inconsistent with the propositions that the State is subject to one of the organs of State, the judicial organ, and can be sued as such in its own courts.' This appears to me to assume that, even if the State is the sovereign authority and not simply the creation of the acknowledged sovereign authority, the People, the concept of being sued in court is necessarily inconsistent with the theory of sovereignty. In the first place I think that the learned trial judge misconstrued the intent of Article 5 if he construed it as a constitutional declaration that the State is above the law. Article 1 of the Constitution affirms that the Irish nation has the 'sovereign right to choose its own form of Government.' Our constitutional history, and in particular the events leading up to the enactment of the Constitution, indicate beyond doubt, to my mind, that the declaration as to sovereignty in Article 5 means that the State is not subject to any power of government save those designated by the People in the Constitution itself, and that the State is not amenable to any external authority for its conduct. To hold that the State is immune from suit for wrong because it is a sovereign state is to beg the question.

In several parts in the Constitution duties to make certain provisions for the benefit of the citizens are imposed on the State in terms which bestow rights upon the citizens and, unless some contrary provision appears in the Constitution, the Constitution must be deemed to have created a remedy for the enforcement of these rights. It follows that, where the right is one guaranteed by the State, it is against the State that the remedy must be sought if there has been a failure to discharge the constitutional obligation imposed. The Oireachtas cannot prevent or restrict the citizen from pursuing his remedy against the State in order to obtain or defend the very rights guaranteed by the Constitution in the form of obligations imposed upon the State; nor can the Oireachtas delegate to any organ of state the implementation of these rights so as to exonerate the State itself from its obligations under the Constitution. The State must act through its organs but it remains vicariously liable for the failures of these organs in the discharge of the obligations, save where expressly excluded by the Constitution. In support of this it is to be noted that an express immunity from suit is conferred on the President by Article 13, s. 8, sub-s. 1, and that a limited immunity from suit for members of the Oireachtas is contained in Article 15, s. 13, and that restrictions upon suit in certain cases are necessarily inferred from the provisions of Article 28, s. 3, of the Constitution.

It is also to be noted that Article 45 of the Constitution, which sets forth certain principles of social policy intended for the general guidance of the Oireachtas, contains an express provision that the application of those principles 'shall not be cognisable by any Court under any of the provisions of this Constitution.' This express exclusion from cognisance by the Courts of these particular provisions reinforces the view that the provisions of the Constitution obliging the State to act in a particular manner may be enforced in the Courts against the State as such. If, in particular cases, the State has already by law imposed on some organ of State or some servant of the State the duty to implement the right or protection guaranteed by the Constitution then, in cases of default, it may be sufficient and adequate in particular instances to bring proceedings against the person upon whom the duty has been so imposed; but that does not absolve the State, upon which the primary obligation has been imposed, from responsibility to carry out the duty imposed upon it. If under the Constitution the State cannot do any act or be guilty of any omission save through one or more of its organs or servants, it is nonetheless answerable because of the identification declared by the provisions of Article 6 of the Constitution.

The suggestion advanced in this case that the State cannot be made amenable for civil wrong stems from the English feudal concept that 'the King can do no wrong.' There is some authority for believing that this phrase originally meant precisely the contrary to what it now means, and that its original meaning was that the King must not, was not allowed to, and was not entitled to, do wrong. However, while for many centuries past there has been no doubt as to the meaning of the phrase 'the King can do no wrong', that is a concept which differs from the concept that he was immune from suit. A great variety of devices emerged for obtaining relief against the Crown; some of these took the form of suits against the officers or agents of the King personally where no consent was necessary, and some of them took the form or suits against the King himself where it was permitted by the grant of the petition of right rather than by suing by writ. The grant of a petition of right in such a case was based precisely on the proposition that the King had acted contrary to law. In the sphere of tort the petition of right did not normally lie outside real actions. Tortious immunity was a judge-made rule. It would appear to have been based on the view that it would be a logical anomaly for the King to issue or enforce a writ against himself. The theory was that the King, as the source of all justice, was incapable of committing a wrong. But the theory was reserved for torts which lay outside the sphere of interference with proprietary rights. There does not appear to be any record of how this doctrine fared in England during the years of the republic under the Cromwellian régime. The theory at least included the safeguard, frequently of little practical worth, that the servant of the Crown was personally liable for the wrongs committed by him in the performance of his service; this was based on the presumption that the officer who committed the wrongful act did so of his own accord and was thus liable for it because the King, who was incapable of committing a wrong, could not have authorised it.

By contrast, when the doctrine of sovereign immunity was imported into the United States, the doctrine was extended to cover the officers and agents of the State and over the course of years it could be availed of even by municipal authorities. The doctrine appears to have been imported into the common law in the United State as basic to the common law without, perhaps, a proper recognition of the nature of its origin, namely, that it rested upon the King being the personification of the State and, therefore, was applied only to a person. The fact that this English theory of sovereign immunity, originally personal to the King and with its roots deep in feudalism, came to be applied in the United States where fuedalism had never been known has been described as one of the mysteries of legal evolution. It appears to have been taken for granted by the American courts in the early years of the United States – though not without some question, since Chief Justice Jay in *Chrisholm* v. *Georgia* (1893) 2 Dall. 419 said:– 'I wish the state of society was so far improved and the science of government advanced to such degree of perfection that the whole nation could in the peaceable course of law be compelled to do justice and be sued by individual citizens.' In later cases the United States courts defended the doctrine of immunity on the grounds that it was vital for the efficient working of government. Mr. Justice Holmes sought to justify it in *Kawananakoa* v. *Polyblank* (1907) 205 U.S. 349, 353 by saying that 'a sovereign is exempt from suit, not because of any formal conception or absolute theory, but on the logical and practical ground that there can be no legal right as against the authority that makes the law on which the right depends.' It had also been suggested that the immunity rested on a policy imposed by necessity. In *United States* v. *Lee* (1882) 106 U.S. 196 after full historical investigations the Supreme Court of the United States reached the conclusion at p. 206 of the report 'that it has been adopted in our courts as a part of the general doctrine of publicists, that the supreme power in every State, wherever it may reside, shall not be compelled, by process of courts of its own creation, to defend itself from assaults in those courts.' Other decisions based it on public policy. In England the enactment and operation of the Crown Proceedings Act, 1947, and in the United States the Federal Torts Act, 1945, would appear to have invalidated these rationalisations.

Under our own constitutional provisions it is the Oireachtas which makes the laws and it is the judiciary which administers them; there is no apparent reason why the activities of either of these organs of state should compel the State itself to be above the law.

That the concept of state liability is not a juristic problem is also evident from the laws of several other countries. In France prior to the revolution the principle of *le Roi ne peut mal faire* prevailed as in the English legal theory upon the same basis of the King being the personification of the state. Since the revolutionary period the liability of the state gradually grew until finally, in the Blanco case of 1873, it was clearly established that the state was liable for the tortious act of its servant if it amounts to a *faute de service*, though the public servant involved may be personally liable for actions which are clearly outside the scope of his employment. In France these actions against the state for the tortious actions of its servants are heard in the administrative courts. In Germany the law developed in a somewhat similar way.

Article 839 of the German Civil Code of 1896 and Article 34 of the Constitution of the Federal Republic of Germany make the state liable to a third party for the tortious activities of the state's servants in the exercise of their public functions, and these actions may be brought before the ordinary civil courts.

Many other countries in the world have imposed, to a greater or lesser extent, liability on the state for the tortious acts of public servants, and included in these are common-law countries, in the British Commonwealth. Section 78 of the Constitution of the Commonwealth of Australia (appearing in s. 9 of the Commonwealth of Australia Constitution Act, 1900) provided that the legislature of Australia might make laws for conferring rights to proceed against the Commonwealth or a State in respect of matters within the limits of the judicial power. Part 9 of the Judiciary Act of 1903 permitted suits by and against the Commonwealth and the States; it gave a right to sue the Commonwealth both in contract and tort without a petition of right and laid down that 'in any suit in which the Commonwealth or a State is party the rights of parties shall as nearly as possible be the same and judgment may be given the costs awarded on either side as in a suit between subject and subject.' Under the Canadian Petition of Right Act the Crown can be sued in the Court of Exchequer and Separate Court on petition of right in contract and tort. Although a previous limitation in tort to 'public work' was abolished by the Exchequer Act, 1938, a petition of right is still required. In New Zealand the Crown can now be sued in contract and tort under the Crown Proceedings Act, 1950. Under the Crown Liability Act, 1910, the former Union of South Africa could be sued without petition of right in contract and for torts arising 'out of any wrong committed by any servant of the Crown acting in his capacity within the scope of his authority as such servant.' In India a distinction has been drawn between acts of State and ordinary acts done under cover of municipal law. The latter case would include the negligence of the driver of a military vehicle in the ordinary use of that vehicle, as distinct from acts arising out of the exercise of a sovereign power like that of making war for which the State would not be liable: see *Union of India* v. *Jasso* A.I.R. 1962 Punj. 315. (F.B.).

In our own context it is to be noted that the Factories Act, 1955, applies to factories belonging to or in the occupation of the State: see s 3, sub-s. 9, and s. 118 of the Act of 1955. Section 59 of the Civil Liability Act, 1961, makes the Minister for Finance liable for the negligent use of a motor vehicle belonging to the State; that section replaced virtually identical provisions in s. 116 of the Road Traffic Act, 1961, which had replaced s. 170 of the Road Traffic Act, 1933. For an example of a similar statutory provision enacted by the Oireachtas of Saorstát Éireann, see s. 6 of the Conditions of Employment Act, 1936.

I have referred to these several different matters for the purpose of indicating that there is ample support for my view that immunity from suit for wrong is not a necessary ingredient of State sovereignty.

For many years in this country, like the American experience, the notion of sovereign immunity of the State seems to have been accepted as part of the common law, without full regard to its true origin in the common law. The confusion was increased by the fact that the King enjoyed some place under the Constitution of the Irish Free State, 1922, and by the fact that in these years the law was practised and interpreted by persons who, quite naturally, had been mostly orientated by education and practice towards a system in which this concept of sovereign immunity of the Crown held sway.

However, I have not found any Irish case decided since 1922 which deals with the point at issue here. There were cases which dealt with the question of whether or not the Crown, or the State, enjoyed prerogative rights of exemption from statutory provisions. In *In re Maloney* [1926] I.R. 202 a question arose under s. 4 of the Preferential Payments in Bankruptcy (Ireland) Act, 1889, whether the Land Commission could rely on the prerogatives of the Crown to give their claim priority. In that case the Land Commission were acting for and on behalf of the Minister for Finance and counsel in the course of his argument conceded that the prerogative of the Crown, on which the Land Commission relied, could not be disputed. In his judgment Johnston J., in referring to the concession made by counsel, omitted to refer to the point of whether or not the Constitution of the Irish Free State, 1922, had impaired or extinguished the prerogative. In that case it was also conceded by counsel that the royal prerogative of not being bound by a statutory provision, unless it was expressly or by necessary implication referred to, remained in full force and effect in the Irish Free State because Article 12 of the Constitution of the Irish Free State, 1922, provided that the Oireachtas should consist of the King, the Dáil and the Senate, and because Article 51 of that Constitution provided that the executive authority of the Irish Free State was to be vested in the King and would be exercisable in accordance with the law and constitutional usage governing the exercise of the executive authority in the case of the Dominion of Canada by the representative of the Crown. In my view, the reference to the constitutional usage of Canada, in addition to being the basis of a concession, was used too generally in the context because it did not follow that, because in the law of Canada the Crown had the prerogative right to claim priority in the payment of debt, the right necessarily existed also in the Irish Free State. Five years later in *Galway County Council* v. *Minister for Finance* [1931] I.R. 215 Johnston J. at p. 232 of the report rejected the plea of the Galway County Council, that sums claimed by the Minister were statute barred, by saying:– 'There can be no doubt, and it has not been argued in the present case to the contrary, that the prerogative and prerogative right can be relied upon by the Irish Free State, and is part of the law of the land . . . I can see nothing in sect. 51, sub-sect. 7, that suggests that it was intended to have any applicability to the Crown or the State, and I think, therefore, that the defendant is entitled to rely on this set-off.' In this context it is to be noted that by virtue of s. 3 of the Statute of Limitations, 1957, a State authority is now put on the same footing as a private citizen where limitations of many kinds of actions are concerned. A State authority means a Minister of State, or the Commissioners of Public Works in Ireland, or the Irish Land Commission, or the Revenue Commissioners or the Attorney General. There are certain exceptions which prevent the statute being pleaded in actions for the recovery of tax or duty under the care and management of the Revenue Commissioners, or certain other fines, taxes or duties. It is to be noted that in the *Galway C.C. Case* [1931] I.R. 215 a further reference is made to the position in Canada and that reliance was placed on *Maritime Bank of Canada (Liquidators)* v. *Receiver General of New Brunswick* [1892] A.C. 437 where it was decided that the prerogative right could be relied upon not only by the Dominion Government but also by the Provincial Governments in Canada.

In *Cork County Council* v. *Commissioners of Public Works* [1945] I.R. 561 the question before the former Supreme Court was whether the Commissioners of Public Works were liable for the rates on houses which had formerly belonged to the Crown. That case, like the *Galway C.C. Case*, is unsatisfactory as an examination of the question on principle because the Cork County Council admitted that, in so far as the houses in question were concerned, the State enjoyed the same right of prerogative immunity as that which had been enjoyed by the Crown. The constitutional question propounded was whether the defendants, the Minister for Finance and the Commissioners of Public Works, were 'entitled to enjoy the like immunity from liability for rates as was formerly claimed and enjoyed by the Crown prior to the Constitution of the Irish Free State.' Murnaghan J. stated at p. 571 of the report that it was unnecessary to give any answer to that question because of the admission made by the plaintiffs, and that the case then was concerned only with the extent of the prerogative. Formerly, the Crown was not liable for rates unless it was engaged in private trading. At p. 578 of the report O'Byrne J. referred to Article 73 of the Constitution of the Irish Free State in this context. Article 73 was the one which carried forward all the laws in force at the date of the coming into operation of that Constitution – save to the extent to which such laws were inconsistent with that Constitution. He treated Article 12 and Article 51 of that Constitution as saying that the prerogative rights of the Crown, being part of the common law of England and of Ireland up to the date of that Constitution, continued to apply as part of the common law in the Irish Free State by virtue of Article 73. The implication being, though not expressly stated, that there was nothing in that Constitution inconsistent with such continuance.

In my view, that was an erroneous over-simplification of the issues. He appears to have overlooked the fact that the basis of the Crown prerogatives in English law was that the King was the personification of the state. Article 2 of the Constitution of the Irish Free State declared that all the powers of government and all authority, legislative, executive and judicial, in Ireland were derived from the people of Ireland and that the same should be exercised in the Irish Free State through the organisations established by or under and in accord with that Constitution. The basis of the prerogative of the English Crown was quite inconsistent with the declaration contained in that Article. The King enjoyed a personal pre-eminence; perfection was ascribed to him. These were the prerogatives pertaining to the royal dignity. It was under this heading that he was personally immune from civil or criminal proceedings. So far as the royal authority was concerned, the prerogative relating to this was a general one by virtue of which the King was the supreme head of the executive; he had the prerogative right to make treaties and alliances with foreign states and the power to declare war and to make peace, and he was regarded as the fountain-head of justice and the general conservator of the peace of the kingdom. In the early days the King sat in person to administer justice and all jurisdictions in the civil courts were derived from him, either mediately or immediately. To this very day in England every civil suit in the High Court commences in the form of a command by the Sovereign to the defendant to enter an appearance. In criminal proceedings the Sovereign acts as prosecutor, and judges derive their appointments from the Sovereign. In Ireland it is to be noted that by Article 30, s. 3, of the Constitution of Ireland, 1937, all crimes and offences in any court, other than a court of summary jurisdiction, shall be prosecuted in the name of the People, who are the sovereign authority.

The provisions of Article 2 of the Constitution of the Irish Free State expressly rejected the concept that any of the powers of government, legislative, executive or judicial, derived from the Crown. The position of the King in the Constitution of the Irish Free State was confined to the express provisions in that regard which were contained in that Constitution; and that position was owed not to any right on the part of the King but rather to the election of those who enacted the Constitution to give him a place in it. Article 12 of that Constitution made him a part of the Oireachtas and Article 51 vested the executive authority of the Irish Free State in him to be exercisable 'in accordance with the law, practice and constitutional usage governing the exercise of the Executive Authority in the case of the Dominion of Canada, by the Representative of the Crown.' The reference to 'the law, practice and constitutional usage . . . of Canada' had its origin in Article 2 of the Agreement for a Treaty between Great Britain and Ireland of the 6th December, 1921, and has been examined by Kingsmill Moore J. (when he was in the High Court) in *In re Irish Employers Mutual Insurance Association Ltd.* [1955] I.R. 176 at p. 218 of the report. It is unnecessary to investigate what was the law, practice and constitutional usage of Canada governing the exercise of the executive authority by the King; Article 51 of that Constitution by its very terms circumscribed the exercise by the King of the executive authority vested in him by the Article. It covered such matters as the declaration of war (although active participation in war, save in the case of invasion, required the assent of the Oireachtas under Article 49 of that Constitution), the making of treaties, the accrediting of diplomats and the dissolution of parliament. These were powers expressly granted to the King and could not be enforced in so far as they conflicted with the rights of any private individual, whether existing by virtue of the provisions of the constitution of the day or the law of the day. As supreme head of the executive the King, through the officers and departments of the executive, was primarily concerned with carrying into execution all the Acts passed by the Oireachtas of Saorstát Éireann. Even assuming that in such capacity he enjoyed the royal prerogative of being personally immune from any civil or criminal proceedings, it did not mean that everything transacted by the then executive council was just and legal; nor was any personal immunity thereby afforded to individual officers or servants of Saorstát Éireann. He was but the executive organ of Saorstát Éireann, and if he had a personal immunity that did not relieve the principal, Saorstát Éireann, from making good the damage caused by the executive organ in carrying out the executive powers of government of the principal, Saorstát Éireann, which itself was the creation of the sovereign People.

So far as the judicial sphere was concerned, Article 68 of that Constitution provided that judges of the Supreme Court, the High Court and other courts established under that Constitution should be appointed by the representative of the Crown on the advice of the executive council; and Article 66 of that Constitution, which dealt with the finality of the decisions of the Supreme Court, added a proviso to the effect that a person should retain the right to petition the King for special leave to appeal from the Supreme Court to 'His Majesty in Council' or, in other words, to the Privy Council. The position and power granted to the King in that Constitution owed everything to the express provisions to that effect in that Constitution. In Saorstát Éireann he was not the personification of the State and, therefore, the common-law immunities or prerogatives of the King which were personal to him did not exist in Saorstát Éireann because any such claim postulated, of necessity, the acceptance in the Constitution of Saorstát Éireann of the King as the personification of the State. All royal prerogatives to be found in the common law of England and in the common law of Ireland prior to the enactment of the Constitution of Saorstát Éireann 1922, ceased to be part of the law of Saorstát Éireann because they were based on concepts expressly repudiated by Article 2 of that Constitution and, therefore, were inconsistent with the provisions of that Constitution and were not carried over by Article 73 thereof. I am fortified in this view by the opinion expressed by Murnaghan J., and concurred in by all the members of the former Supreme Court, in *In re Irish Employers Mutual Insurance Association Ltd.* at p. 240 of the report. In my view, the assumptions and the concessions in the cases which I have mentioned, tha the former royal prerogatives were carried over by common law into the law of Saorstát Éireann, were incorrect. While those cases dealt with statutory provisions and the question whether or not the State was bound by the statutory provisions, the observations which I have made as to the question of the prerogatives apply with even greater force to causes of action which are not based upon statutory provision.

So far as statutory provisions are concerned, it is to be noted that in the *Cork C.C. Case* [1945] I.R. 561, both O'Byrne J. and Black J. referred to *United States* v. *Hoar* (1821) 26 Fed. Cas. 329 which was decided by Mr. Justice Story, a justice of the United States Supreme Court, while he was acting as a Circuit Justice. The case involved the question of whether the United States could be barred from recovering in assumpsit in the Federal Court in Massachusetts by the Massachusetts statutes of limitations. Section 34 of the Judiciary Act of 1789 provided that 'the laws of the several states, except where the constitution, treaties, or statutes of the United States shall otherwise require or provide, shall be regarded as rules of decision in trials at common law in the courts of the United States, in cases where they apply.' Mr. Justice Story framed the issue as to whether that was the case where the statutes of limitations of Massachusetts applied. He held that the federal sovereign was privileged not to be bound by the statutes of limitations of a state and that, in the absence of a federal statute waiving the privilege, the state statute did not apply to the United States. Mr. Justice O'Byrne cited a passage from p. 330 of the report of *United States* v. *Hoar*; I now propose to cite that passage with a sentence from the passage which was omitted by O'Byrne J.:– 'We find accordingly in our own state, the doctrine is well settled, that no laches can be imputed to the government, and against it no time runs, so as to bar its rights (*Inhabitants of Stoughton* v. *Baker* 4 Mass. 528); so, that it is clear, that the statutes of limitations pleaded in this case would be no bar to a suit brought to enforce any right of the state in its own courts. *But, independently of any doctrine founded on the notion of prerogative, the same construction of statutes of this sort ought to prevail, founded upon the legislative intention.* Where the government is not expressly or by necessary implication included, it ought to be clear from the nature of the mischiefs to be redressed, or the language used, that the government itself was in contemplation of the legislature, before a court of law would be authorized to put such an interpretation upon any statute. In general, acts of the legislature are meant to regulate and direct the acts and rights of citizens; and in most cases the reasoning applicable to them applies with very different, and often contrary force to the government itself. It appears to me, therefore, to be a safe rule founded in the principles of the common law, that the general words of a statute ought not to include the government, or affect its rights, unless that construction be clear and indisputable upon the text of the act.' The text that I have quoted appears in the American report which I have already cited; the sentence which I have placed in italics does not appear in the passage as quoted by O'Byrne J. In my view it is a most vital sentence because it rationalises the principle expressed by Story J. Mr. Justice O'Byrne went on to say that he would be prepared, apart from any special reason arising out of the Constitution, to follow the reasoning of Story J. and to hold that the same rule was applicable in this State. It is to be noted that the state referred to by Story J. in the passage quoted is the State of Massachusetts and not the United States. Mr. Justice Black in his judgment also referred to the American decision. I think Professor Kelly in his book 'Fundamental Rights in Irish Law and Constitution' (2nd ed, at p. 326) is correct in his observation that these two judges, of the three who decided that case, relied not only upon their view of the constitutional provisions but also upon the rationalisation of the principle underlying the prerogative right in question.

So far as the constitutional provision in question is concerned, I have already dealt with the observations of O'Byrne J. in his reliance upon the provisions of Articles 12, 51 and 73 of the Constitution of the Irish Free State. He also relied upon the provisions of Article 49 of the Constitution of Ireland, 1937, as carrying over the Crown prerogatives which, for the reasons he stated, he felt had been part of our common law after the year 1922. If, however, I am correct in the view I have expressed that this was an erroneous construction of the Constitution of Saorstát Éireann, then such privileges, prerogatives, and other rights which are carried over by Article 49 of the Constitution of Ireland are only those which were exercisable in or in respect of Saorstát Éireann immediately before the 11th December, 1936, whether by virtue of the Constitution of Saorstát Éireann or otherwise by the authority in which the executive power of Saorstát Éireann was then vested. Exemption from the provisions of a statute by virtue only of a royal prerogative existing at common law is not one of them.

At this point it is also relevant to note *In re The Irish Aero Club; Gillic* v. *Minister for Industry and Commerce* [1939] I.R. 204. In the winding up of the company the Minister for Defence claimed priority against other general creditors. His claim was grounded on s. 38, sub-s. 2, of the Finance Act, 1924, and he also submitted that the State was entitled to enjoy the prerogative which had accorded to the British Crown a right to a payment in full in priority to its subjects. At p. 209 of the report Gavan Duffy J. said:– '. . . in the course of the hearing, Mr. Dixon, on behalf of the two Ministers, has expressly abandoned this second claim, very properly, if I may say so, for such a claim would be hard to reconcile with the Constitution.' Gavan Duffy J. emphatically rejected the claim of the Minister for Posts and Telegraphs in *In re P.C.* [1939] I.R. 306 to be entitled to the common-law royal prerogative of payment in priority to other debtors: see pp. 314–16 of the report. He observed at p. 314 of the report that it was well established that whenever the King's claims and those of his subjects 'came into competition, the King's claims must be preferred, not because he was the executive authority, but by reason of the pre-eminence which he enjoyed at common law over all persons, on the principle expressed in the phrase *detur digniori*.' He pointed out, as had Kennedy C.J. in *In re K.* [1927] I.R. 260, 273, that in Saorstát Éireann the Central Fund was a State fund and was in no sense a royal exchequer, and that the latter concept would have been in violation of Article 61 of the Constitution of Saorstát Éireann.

In so far as the State may be exempted from the provisions of a statute, it may possibly be capable of being rationalised on the basis on which it was done in *United States* v. *Hoar* (1821) 26 Fed. Cas. 329 and which was adopted by O'Byrne J. as one of his reasons; but it is not necessary to decide that matter in this case as we are not concerned with the construction of a statute or with the question of whether or not the State is bound by the restrictive provisions of some statute. With reference to the quotation from *United States* v. *Hoar* (1821) 26 Fed. Cas. 329, it is well to bear in mind that the vital words are:– 'Where the government is not expressly *or by necessary implication* included, it ought to be clear from the nature of the mischiefs to be redressed, or the language used, that the government itself was in contemplation of the legislature, before a court of law would be authorized to put such an interpretation upon any statute.' Immediately before the passage cited from the judgment of Story J., there appears the sentence:– 'And though this is sometimes called a prerogative right, it is in fact nothing more than a reservation, or exception, introduced for the public benefit, and equally applicable to all governments.' It is already apparent from the provisions of s. 3 of the Statute of Limitations, 1957, which I have mentioned earlier in this judgment, that in areas outside the collection of the public revenues and taxes and kindred subjects the public benefit no longer appears to the Oireachtas to require that the State, in its several departments therein mentioned, should have exemption from the provisions of the limitation periods laid down in that statute.

I wish to make it clear that nothing I have said is to be taken as expressing any view, one way or the other, upon the competence of the Oireachtas to exempt the State in respect of general statutory duties from liability for breaches of those duties committed by its officers, servants or employees within the scope of their service or employment. This case is concerned with the ability of the plaintiff to maintain a common-law action against the State for the tortious acts of its employees.

I have already stated the reasons for my opinion that the King had no place in the Irish legal system after 1922, save that which was expressly provided by the terms of the Saorstát of Saorstát Éireann. The power and position granted to him by Article 51 of that Constitution did not purport to grant immunity from suit in exercise of the executive authority of the Irish Free State thereby declared to be vested in him. In my view, for the reasons I have already stated, no such immunity was available in Saorstát Éireann by virtue of any inherent quality in the royal person. If immunity from suit could have been claimed for the State, it could only have been on the basis of a rationalisation such as that enunciated in *United States* v. *Hoar* (1821) 26 Fed. Cas. 329 and adopted by O'Byrne J. in *Cork County Council* v. *Commissioners of Public Works* [1945] I.R. 561; that immunity, if it existed, would have been enjoyed by Saorstát Éireann and not by the King.

There is no basis, theoretical or otherwise, for a claim that the State can do no wrong or, in the particular context, that Saorstát Éireann could do no wrong; and there is no basis, in theory or otherwise, for a submission that the State cannot be made vicariously liable for a wrong committed by its officers, employees and servants in the course of the service of the State. Earlier in this judgment I have given my reasons for holding that immunity from suit is not a necessary ingredient of State sovereignty.

Several provisions of the Constitution of the Irish Free State imposed obligations upon the State and conferred rights on the citizens as against the State and a breach of these, or a failure to honour them, on the part of the State would clearly have been a wrong or a breach of obligation; it is of no consequence that the wrong or breach might not be within the recognised field of wrongs in the law of tort. In principle, a wrong which arises from the failure to honour an obligation must be capable of remedy, and a contest between the citizen and the State in the pursuit of such a remedy is a justiciable controversy cognisable by the Courts save where expressly excluded by a provision of the Constitution if it is in respect of obligations and rights created by the Saorstát, or save where expressly excluded by law if it is simply in respect of rights or obligations created by law. To take one example, Article 10 of the Saorstát of Saorstát Éireann provided that all citizens of the Irish Free State 'have the right to free elementary education.' In my view, that was clearly enforceable against Saorstát Éireann if no provision had been made to implement that Article of its Constitution. There are several instances in the Constitution of Ireland also where the State undertakes obligations towards the citizens. It is not the case that these are justiciable only when some law is being passed which directly infringes these rights or when some law is passed to implement them. They are justiciable when there has been a failure on the part of the State to discharge the obligations or to perform the duties laid upon the State by the Constitution. It may well be that in particular cases it can be shown that some organ of the State already has adequate powers and in fact may have had imposed upon it the particular duty to carry out the obligation undertaken by the State, but that would not mean that the State was not vicariously liable for the non-performance by its various organs of their duties.

Even if one were to adopt the concept that the State can do no wrong because, as it acts by its organs, agents or employees, any wrong arising must be attributed to them rather than to the State itself, the doctrine of *respondeat superior* would still apply. That doctrine is not invalidated by showing that the principal cannot commit the particular tort. It rests not on the notion of the principal's wrong but on the duty of the principal to make good the damage done by his servants or agents in carrying on the principal's affairs. It may well be that in many cases the appropriate organ of State, or the officer or person, charged with the particular duty could be compelled by mandamus proceedings to carry out the duty imposed including, if necessary, an order to apply to the Oireachtas for the necessary finance: see *Conroy* v. *Minister for Defence* [1934] I.R. 342, 679. However, that does not exonerate the State as the principal from the damage accruing from the failure to do so or from the damage accruing from the wrongful manner in which it was done.

Where the People by the Constitution create rights against the State or impose duties upon the State, a remedy to enforce these must be deemed to be also available. It is as much the duty of the State to render justice against itself in favour of citizens as it is to administer the same between private individuals. The investigation and the adjudication of such claims by their nature belong to the judicial power of government in the State, designated in Article 6 of the Constitution of Ireland, which is vested in the judges and the courts appointed and established under the Constitution in accordance with the provisions of the Constitution.

In my view, the whole tenor of our Constitution is to the effect that there is no power, institution, or person in the land free of the law save where such immunity is expressed, or provided for, in the Constitution itself. Article 13, s. 8, sub-s. 1 (relating to the President) and Article 15, ss. 12 and 13 (relating to the Oireachtas) are examples of express immunities. For an example of provision for the granting of immunity, see Article 29, s. 3, by which diplomatic immunities may be granted. There is nothing in the Constitution envisaging the writing into it of a theory of immunity from suit of the State (a state set up by the People to be governed in accordance with the provisions of the Constitution) stemming from or based upon the immunity of a personal sovereign who was the keystone of a feudal edifice. English common-law practices, doctrines, or immunities cannot qualify or dilute the provisions of the Constitution: see *The State (Browne)* v. *Feran* [1967] I.R. 147. I think it is apposite to quote here the words of Murnaghan J. in *In re Tilson* [1951] I.R. 1 where he said at p. 32 of the report:– 'The archaic law of England rapidly disintegrating under modern conditions need not be a guide for the fundamental principles of a modern state. It is not a proper method of construing a new constitution of a modern state to make an approach in the light of legal survivals of an earlier law.'

While the King had a limited place in the Constitution of Saorstát Éireann, he had no place in the present new republican form of constitution which was enacted in 1937 and came into force on the 29th December, 1937. The present Constitution provides at Article 28, s. 2, that the executive power of the State shall, subject to the provisions of the Constitution, be exercised by or on the authority of the Government. Section 3 of that Article provides that war shall not be declared and that the State shall not participate in any war save with the assent of Dáil Éireann, except that in the case of actual invasion the section provides that the Government may take whatever steps it may consider necessary for the protection of the State and that the Dáil, if not sitting, shall be summoned to meet at the earliest practicable date. Article 29, s. 4, reserves exclusively to the authority of the Government the exercise of the executive power of the State in connection with its external relations. By Article 15 the national parliament (to be known as the Oireachtas) consists of the President of Ireland, Dáil Éireann and Seanad Éireann. Article 34 expressly reserves the administration of justice to the judges and the courts to be appointed and established under the Constitution, subject to the provision in Article 37 for the exercise of limited functions and powers of a judicial nature by other persons or bodies duly authorised by law to exercise such functions in matters other than criminal matters. The defendants have placed reliance upon the provisions of Article 49 of the Constitution. Section 1 of that Article provides as follows:–

'All powers, functions, rights and prerogatives whatsoever exercisable in or in respect of Saorstát Éireann immediately before the 11th day of December, 1936, whether in virtue of the Constitution then in force or otherwise, by the authority in which the executive power of Saorstát Éireann was then vested are hereby declared to belong to the people.'

This is a reference to the Constitution (Amendment No. 27) Act, 1936, which provided in s. 1 that several Articles of the Constitution of Saorstát Éireann set out in the schedule to that Act were amended, or otherwise dealt with, in the manner set out in the schedule. The Act came into force on the 11th December, 1936, and the effect of it was to remove from the Constitution of Saorstát Éireann all references to the King, the representative of the Crown, and the Governor General. In particular the effect of the changes, in so far as Article 51 of that Constitution was concerned, was to divest the King of the executive authority of Saorstát Éireann and to vest it in the Executive Council. At that date the King was Edward VIII who had abdicated from the throne of England on the 10th December. On the 12th December, 1936, the Executive Authority (External Relations) Act, 1936, came into force and it provided that the diplomatic representatives of Saorstát Éireann should be appointed on the authority of the Executive Council, and that every international agreement concluded on behalf of Saorstát Éireann should be concluded by or on the authority of the Executive Council. Section 3 of that Act provided that so long as the King recognised by Australia, Canada, Great Britain, New Zealand and South Africa as the symbol of their co-operation continued to act on behalf of those nations on the advice of their several governments for the purpose of the appointment of diplomatic and consular representatives and the conclusion of international agreements, and so long as Saorstát Éireann was associated with those nations, the King so recognised was thereby authorised to act on behalf of Saorstát Éireann for the like purposes as and when advised by the Executive Council to do so. The same section provided that, immediately upon the passing of that Act (12th December, 1936), King Edward VIII should cease to be King for the purpose of those activities and for all other, if any purposes and that his successor for the time being would be his successor under the law of Saorstát Éireann. The joint effect of those two Acts was to remove the King entirely from the Constitution of Saorstát Éireann, to remove from him all powers and functions in relation to the executive or other authority of Saorstát Éireann or the exercise of any of the powers of government of Saorstát Éireann, and to authorise him to act on behalf of Saorstát Éireann only when so advised by the Executive Council to do so in respect of certain matters concerned only with external relations. It is to be noted that neither of these Acts made any reference whatever to the immunities or prerogatives of the King, if any, which existed in Saorstát Éireann on the 10th December, 1936; these Acts made no reference whatsoever to any question of succession to or transmission of these prerogatives or immunities, if any.

It is unnecessary to enquire what powers, functions, rights or prerogatives were exercisable by the King on the 10th December, 1936, in or in respect of Saorstát Éireann as, for the reasons I have already given, they did not include a right of immunity from suit in the courts of Saorstát Éireann. Therefore, the provisions of Article 49, s. 1, of the Constitution of Ireland which vested in and declared to belong to the People all the powers, functions, rights and prerogatives whatsoever exercisable in or in respect of Saorstát Éireann immediately before the 11th December, 1936, whether in virtue of the Constitution of Saorstát Éireann or otherwise, did not carry over or set up an immunity from suit. It was quite within the competence of the People in enacting the Constitution of 1937 to provide for an immunity from suit which did not exist prior to the coming into operation of the Constitution, but no such provision was made. Section 2 of Article 49 provides that save to the extent to which provision is made by the Constitution or might thereafter be made by law for the exercise of any such power, function, right or prerogative by any of the organs established by the Constitution, the powers, functions, rights and prerogatives mentioned in s. 1 shall not be exercised or be capable of being exercised in or in respect of the State, save only by or on the authority of the Government. Even assuming that such a common-law immunity from suit did exist so as to be capable of being carried over by Article 49 of the Constitution in accordance with the terms of that Article, it would become thereby the immunity of the People as distinct from the State. While the present action in its original form was an action brought against the People, the parties were changed so that it is now an action against the State and the Attorney General, and the original plea in the defence claiming the immunity of the People as the sovereign authority from such action must be read as a plea claiming such immunity on behalf of the State. In either its original form or in its present form the plea would, in my view, fail even if such immunity were vested in and belonged to the People, because there is no evidence of any authority from the Government for the assertion of any such claim and, by virtue of s. 2 of Article 49 of the Constitution, no such claim could be set up in respect of the State save only by or on the authority of the Government. It is to be noted that the same situation arose in *In re P.C.* [1939] I.R. 306, 311 where Gavan Duffy J. expressed the same view on the necessity for evidence of authority from the Government for the assertion of the claim of immunity.

As the pleadings and the evidence already taken in the present case indicate, the claim of the plaintiff arises out of an allegation of negligence in the carrying out of certain works on the public road in County Wicklow, which works consisted in the laying of telephone or telegraph cables for the Department of Posts and Telegraphs by persons employed in that Department. Section 1 (ix) of the Ministers and Secretaries Act, 1924, sets out the functions of that Department and provides that the head of the Department shall be the Minister for Posts and Telegraphs. The Minister is a corporation sole with perpetual succession and, as such, may be sued under his style or name: see s. 2, sub-s. 1, of the Act of 1924. The officials and other employees in that Department are not the employees of the Minister for Posts and Telegraphs, and he cannot be made liable in damages for the tortious acts committed by these employees even though they may have been appointed by him to their particular employment. Both they and the Minister are persons employed by or under the State and in my view it makes no difference if, being civil servants, they are civil servants in the service of the Government or are civil servants in the service of the State – a distinction which was adverted to in *McLoughlin* v. *Minister for Social Welfare* [1958] I.R. 1. All such persons employed in the various Departments of the Government and the other Departments of State, whether they be in the Civil Service or not, are in the service of the State and, for the reasons I have already given, the State is liable for damage done by such persons in carrying out the affairs of the State so long as that person is acting within the scope of his employment. The decision of this Court in *The Attorney General* v. *Ryan's Car Hire Ltd* [1965] I.R. 612 provides no support for a contrary view. That case simply decided that the State employee who was involved in the case was not a servant of the menial status in respect of the loss of whose services the State could seek to avail of the action *per quod servitium amisit*, which action was based on a feudal concept having its origins in the rules of law applicable to villein status.

The concept of a Minister or a member of the Government being a fellow servant or fellow employee of the other persons employed in his Department was fully discussed in *Carolan* v. *Minister for Defence* [1927] I.R. 62 and, while the constitutional position has altered since that decision, I think the concept is still valid. In that particular case it was held by the High Court that members of the Defence Forces and the Minister for Defence were fellow servants in the employment of the Government. The real point of the case, however, was whether the Minister for Defence was the employer of such members or their fellow employee. The court's view that they were both in the employment of the Government is not, I think, of any great materiality because no point was raised as to whether they were in the employment of the Government as distinct from the State. In *McLoughlin* v. *Minister for Social Welfare* [1958] I.R. 1 it was indicated that persons in the Civil Service may be in the Civil Service of the State rather than the Civil Service of the Government, but I think that the correct view is that they are all in the service of the State. In *Carolan* v. *Minister for Defence* [1927] I.R. 62 Sullivan P. referred at p. 66 of the report to the Minister for Defence and his subordinates as 'both being servants of the public' and at p. 68 he referred to the subordinates as 'servants of the public in the employment of the Government, and, as such, fellow-servants of the Minister for Defence . . .' As the Minister is not a servant of or in the employment of the Government, it seems quite clear that the court in that case was not deciding that the subordinate was in the service of the Government as distinct from the State. It is in the latter instance only tha he is a fellow servant with the Minister. This latter concept is one which was recognised by s. 64 of the Workmen's Compensation Act, 1934, just as it is recognised by s. 59 of the Civil Liability Act, 1961, in relation to motor vehicles used by the different Departments of Government or of the State. The Government is the organ of State established by the Constitution to exercise the executive power of the State subject to the provisions of the Constitution, and by the Constitution it is bound to act as a collective authority and to be collectively responsible for the Departments of State administered by the members of the Government. It is responsible to Dáil Éireann. It was not claimed in the present case that the plaintiff's action should have been more properly brought against the Government than against the State, and I do not think that such claim would have been sustainable; but it is ironic to note that, if such were the case, the very provisions of Article 49, s. 2, of the Constitution which were relied upon by the defendants to enforce their claim for immunity from suit would not be applicable to a suit against the Government itself.

I come now to deal with the joining of the Attorney General as a defendant in these proceedings. Article 30 of the Constitution constitutes the office of Attorney General. It provides that the Attorney General shall be the adviser of the Government in matters of law and legal opinion, and that he shall exercise and perform all such powers, functions and duties as are conferred or imposed on him by the Constitution or by law. By virtue of the Constitution he is an independent constitutional officer of State with powers and duties some of which are of a quasi-judicial nature and some of an executive nature. However, he is not in any sense the servant of the executive, and any exercise by him of executive powers is not the exercise of the executive powers of the Government but rather those of the Attorney General himself: see Ó Dálaigh J. (as he then was) in *McLoughlin* v. *Minister for Social Welfare* [1958] I.R. 1 at pp. 24 and 25 of the report. The Attorney General is not answerable for the acts of the Government or of its members, or for the acts of those in the service of the State. Section 6, sub-s. 1, of the Ministers and Secretaries Act, 1924, specifies particular powers, functions and duties which are vested in the Attorney General, including the administration and business generally of public services in connection with the representation of the Government and of the public in all legal proceedings for the enforcement of law and the assertion or protection of public rights and all powers, duties and functions connected with the same. In the case of *O'Doherty* v. *The Attorney General* [1941] I.R. 569 a somewhat similar point was raised with regard to the propriety of joining the Attorney General in an action in which, ultimately, an order for mandamus was made to compel the referee under the Military Service Pensions Act, 1934, to carry out his functions in accordance with law. It would appear from the report that the mandamus was directed only to the referee. At p. 585 of the report Gavan Duffy J. said:– 'My view is that the plaintiff was right in joining the Attorney General. The Referee is a statutory delegate, reporting upon some 60,000 cases for the Minister for Defence; he is doing very difficult work of an administrative character, but so extensive that the normal machinery of the Department of Defence could not cope with it; the Minister is necessarily interested in an attack of this kind upon the proceedings of the Referee, an attack which in some cases might have far-reaching effects, if successful; and the State is interested, because the work of the Referee in the case of every successful applicant leads directly to a demand on public funds. The Minister for Defence was not sued and the Minister for Finance was not sued; the public interest was represented by the Attorney-General instead. I think that was right.' He went on to note that no additional costs would be incurred by joining the Attorney General as the referee and the Ministers or the Attorney General, when sued, should have the same solicitor and counsel, except in a case where the referee was defending his own conduct which was not supported by the Government and where he had decided to fight the case though the Government disapproved.

In the present case I think the same general reasoning applies. There can be no doubt that when the State is sued it is entitled to defend itself; this power or right to defend itself is one which can be exercised in respect of the State only by or on the authority of the Government by virtue of the provisions of Article 49, s. 2, of the Constitution. If in such a case it is the Attorney General's opinion that the Government should authorise the defence by the State of the claim brought against it, the defence is a matter of public interest and is properly financed out of public moneys. If the Government does not wish to authorise the defence by the State, then the Attorney General would not defend the case either. In all such cases it is my view that the correct procedure would be to sue the State and to join the Attorney General in order to effect service upon the Attorney General for both parties. In effect the Attorney General would be joined in a representative capacity as the law officer of State designated by the Constitution. If the claim should succeed, judgment would be against the State and not against the Attorney General.

It is unnecessary at this juncture to consider how such a decree would be executed or enforced but it is sufficient to say that an order for mandamus to compel compliance with the judgment would be an appropriate step and not without precedent.

For the reasons I have given, the order of the High Court should be reversed and in lieu thereof an order should be made answering in the affirmative the question raised in each of the four issues directed to be tried by the Order of the 6th November, 1967. I have had the privilege of reading the judgment about to be delivered by Mr. Justice Budd and I agree with it.

Budd J. delivered a judgment supporting **Walsh J.'s** position and **Ó Dálaigh C.J.**, agreed with both **Walsh J.** and **Budd J.**

FitzGerald J. *(dissenting)*:

In my opinion this appeal should be dismissed. The facts relating to the plaintiff's accident have been stated in the judgments already delivered and it is unnecessary for me to repeat them. As the majority of the Court are of the opinion that the appeal should be allowed, I also consider it unnecessary to discuss the details of the cases mentioned in the judgments already delivered, other than to summarise my view of their effect.

This country by Article 5 of its Constitution is declared to be a 'sovereign' state. A State to be sovereign does not have to have a king. The immunity which exists in England and which existed in this country prior to 1922 (based, as it was, on the royal prerogative) no longer exists in this country. In my opinion, it does not follow that the State is not entitled to immunity, it being declared to be 'sovereign.' If the State is sovereign internationally, as appears to be accepted, I see no reason why the word 'sovereign' should be differently construed in relation to the State's relationship with a citizen.

Since the year 1922 the position of the State in relation to one of its citizens has been the subject of the judicial decisions in the cases already mentioned. They appear to establish that the State is a 'juristic person' in the context of the particular issue with which the court in each case was then concerned, but limited to that extent. No case has gone the length of holding that the State is a juristic person which is liable in tort for the action or neglect of a public servant. It appears to me to have been accepted since 1922 that a liability of the State for tort did not exist, unless created by statute – like the liability for negligence imposed on the Minister for Finance under the Road Traffic Act and liability under the Workmen's Compensation Act, 1934.

In my view, the extension of the liability of the State as a 'juristic person' to the law of tort involves such a radical change in the accepted view both of the Courts and of the Legislature that this Court should decline to undertake such a step. Such an extension of the meaning of juristic person would appear to leave the State liable to the same control and sanctions which are applicable to a private individual, including the criminal and bankruptcy jurisdictions.

If the liability of the State for the tort of a public servant is to be established, in my view it should be imposed by the Legislature as has already been done in this country under the Road Traffic Act and the Workmen's Compensation Act. It is significant that in the United States, Canada, Australia and in England, as late as 1947, such liability on those states was imposed by statute. In my opinion, the judgment of Mr. Justice Murnaghan was correct and this appeal should be dismissed.

Notes and Questions

1. *Byrne's* case is comprehensively analysed by Professor Osborough in 'The State's Immunity in Tort' 8 Ir. Jur. (n.s.) 275 (1973), and 'The State's Tortious Liability: Further Reflections on Byrne v Ireland' 11 Ir. Jur. (n.s.) 11, 279 (1976). See also J.M. Kelly, *The Irish Constitution*, 560 ff. (1980).
2. *After Byrne's case*, may the State be sued as an occupier or employer, rather than merely on the basis of vicarious liability? *Cf.* Osborough, 11 Ir. Jur. (n.s.), at 13–14 (1976).
3. Who are servants of the State, for the purpose of rendering the State vicariously liable for their wrongs? *Cf.* Osborough, 11 Ir. Jur. (n.s.), at 14–17 (1976).
4. In what circumstances may the State be sued in respect of torts committed by the Gardái? *Cf.* Osborough, 11 Ir. Jur. (n.s.), at 17–22.
5. Does *Byrne's* case repeal, modify or supplement section 59 of the *Civil Liability Act 1961? Cf.* Osborough, 11 Ir. Jur. (n.s.), at 297–301.

6. *DIPLOMATIC IMMUNITY*
Diplomatic Privilege does not confer immunity from legal responsibility, but merely

immunity from local jurisdiction. It lapses when a diplomatic agent ceases to be accredited.

NORTON V. GENERAL ACCIDENT, FIRE AND LIFE ASSURANCE COMPANY
74 I.L.T.R. 123 (1939)

This was an application under s. 78 s.-s. 1 (d), of the Road Traffic Act, 1933 for leave to issue proceedings against the General Accident Assurance Co., Ltd., in lieu of John Cudahy, quondam Minister to Éire for the United States of America. The plaintiff was an infant suing by John Norton, his father and next friend.

John Norton stated in his affidavit that on the 11th day of June, 1938, the bus in which his son was travelling came into collision with a motor car the property of John Cudahy, the then American Ambassador, and as a result the plaintiff sustained severe injuries. In May, 1939, a plenary summons was issued against John Cudahy, but no appearance was entered until January, 1940, by which time the defendant had left the country. Mr. Cudahy stated, as appeared from the affidavit of the Insurance Company's inspector, that he did not propose to waive his diplomatic privilege. This original action was then discontinued, and on February 10, 1940, notice was served on the General Accident Assurance Company as required by s. 78 of the Road Traffic Act. This application then came before Maguire, J., for leave to institute proceedings against the company under the 78th section.

The application was made *ex parte* in the first instance by Mr. Hamill and Mrs. Justice Hanna gave leave to the applicant to serve notice upon the Insurance Company of the application.

C. Campbell, S.C. (with him *Wm. Hamill*) in support of the motion: When Mr. Cudahy left the country his diplomatic privilege ceased and his Insurance company are liable. The policy of the Road Traffic Act, as appears from ss. 56 and 78, is to give monetary damages to anyone injured. If Mrs. Cudahy is to be sued leave must be given by the Court to serve out of the jurisdiction. Diplomatic privilege does not confer immunity from legal responsibility: *Dickinson* v. *Del Solar; Mobile and General Insurance Company Limited (Third Parties)* [1930] 1 K.B. 376.

Cecil Lavery, S.C. (with him *W. O'Brien Fitzgerald*) for the defendant company: Mr. Cudahy never waived his diplomatic privilege. The original summons was served while he was still accredited to Éire. When service was accepted there was an action in existence. The plaintiff cannot now abandon procedure against the proper defendant and make the company liable. A plaintiff cannot delay his claim indefinitely until the diplomat leaves the country and then proceed against the Insurance Company.

Maguire, J.:

In the course of his judgment, said that his only difficulty lay because of the previous action brought against Mr. Cudahy after he had left the country. His Lordship could not understand why that action had been voluntarily discontinued before any application had been brought to set aside the proceedings and without waiting for any such application. If that had been the only factor in the case he would have no hesitation, but there were further matters to be considered.

The facts were simple and clear. An accident took place at a time when Mr. Cudahy was insured against third party claims. As a result the infant plaintiff was injured; there was no dispute about the injuries. The case was taken in hand at that time but it was not until the May of 1939 that the present firm of solicitors took charge of it. A plenary summons was issued in that month when Mr. Cudahy was still resident in Ireland. Mr. Cudahy did not leave Ireland until January 1940, subsequent to which date a conditional appearance was entered on his behalf without prejudice to his right to raise his diplomatic privilege. Although no application was made to have the proceedings set aside they were voluntarily discontinued. As a result this application was now made.

The Road Traffic Act, 1933, was intended to protect the public and to ensure as far as possible that if they were injured they would have a remedy against the person responsible for the accident, or in certain circumstances against the Insurance Company. It was quite clear that that was the intention of the Act which compelled all motor owners to insure. In so far it might be said the Road Traffic Act threw a burden upon insurers. The question here turned on the construction to be placed upon section 78, s.-s. 1 (d), of the Road Traffic Act, which gives injured parties the right to apply to the Court for liberty to proceed against insurers or guarantors. The words were 'and such Court is satisfied that such owner or driver is not in Saorstát Éireann, or cannot be found, or cannot be served with the process of such Court, or that it is for any other reason just and equitable that such application should be granted, may grant such application.' He was not prepared to hold that the defendants could not be found or could not be served, but he would hold that it was for other reasons just and equitable, because the plaintiff would be greatly impeded and delayed in obtaining relief if the application was not granted.

The reason for the delay was that the proper defendant had raised his diplomatic privilege. His Lordship accepted the reasoning of Lord Hewart in *Dickinson* v. *Del Solar (supra)* with regard to diplomatic privilege, reasoning which was founded upon the cases referred to by Lord Hewart.

He accepted the proposition that the exemption was from local jurisdiction only and not from legal responsibility. Although a Minister of a foriegn power could not be sued while he was here he became a mark when he left the country. This had meant delay and he thought it just and equitable that the application should be granted. The original action should not have been discontinued. Accordingly he granted the application but made no order for costs.

Note

On diplomatic immunity, generally see the *Diplomatic Relations and Immunities Act 1967*. Immunities and privileges of employees of the European Communities are contained in the *Protocol on Privileges and Immunities of the European Communities*.

Chapter 4

CONCURRENT WRONGDOERS

In tort, as in other branches of law, responsibility for the plaintiff's injuries may rest on more than one person. The plaintiff may be entitled to sue multiple defendants in respects of the injuries he has suffered. If the injury complained of is tortious then the defendants may be spoken of as concurrent tortfeasors; if the injury is contractual or a breach of trust the more general term, concurrent wrongdoers, is now more appropriate in Ireland. Traditionally, concurrent tortfeasors were classified into two categories: joint tortfeasors and several tortfeasors. Generally speaking, the law considered persons to be joint tortfeasors whenever it felt that in addition to being liable individually they should also be liable to the plaintiff *as a group*. When no group activity was involved, however, (e.g. where there was no conspiracy or concerted action) liability to the plaintiff was said to be several only, i.e. each defendant might be liable to the plaintiff individually, but there was no liability as a group.

Until 1961 the law relating to joint tortfeasors and several concurrent tortfeasors in Ireland was contained in common law principles as amended and supplemented by the *Joint Tortfeasors Act 1951*. The *Civil Liability Act 1961* now contains the principal rules on this subject. Part III of the 1961 Act, however, is not confined to joint tortfeasors or several concurrent tortfeasors: it also covers wrongdoers other than tortfeasors, such as persons in breach of contract or in breach of trust. Consequently, Part III of the Act deals with the liability of concurrent wrongdoers, which term, it may be noted for our purposes, embraces joint tortfeasors and several concurrent tortfeasors.

1. *CONTRIBUTION AND CONCURRENT WRONGDOERS*

Part III of the Civil Liability Act 1961 contains the principal rules on this topic and is reproduced hereunder. Three principles underline these provisions:
  '(i) Subject to the rule that the plaintiff cannot recover more than the total amount of the damages he has suffered, the injured plaintiff must be allowed full opportunity to recover the full compensation for his injuries from as many sources as possible;
  (ii) Concurrent wrongdoers should be entitled to recover fair contributions from each other in respect of damages paid to the plaintiff;
  (iii) All matters relating to the plaintiff's injuries should as far as possible be litigated in one action.' (*McMahon & Binchy*, pp. 86–87)

THE CIVIL LIABILITY ACT 1961 (Extracts)

11. – (1) For the purpose of this Part, two or more persons are concurrent wrongdoers when both or all are wrongdoers and are responsible to a third person (in this Part called the injured person or the plaintiff) for the same damage, whether or not judgment has been recovered against some or all of them.
  (2) Without prejudice to the generality of subsection (1) of this section –
  (a) persons may become concurrent wrongdoers as a result of vicarious liability of one for another, breach of joint duty, conspiracy, concerted action to a common end or independent acts causing the same damage;
  (b) the wrong on the part of one or both may be a tort, breach of contract or breach of trust, or any combination of them;

(c) it is immaterial whether the acts constituting concurrent wrongs are contemporaneous or successive.

(3) Where two or more persons are at fault and one or more of them is or are responsible for damage while the other or others is or are free from causal responsibility, but it is not possible to establish which is the case, such two or more persons shall be deemed to be concurrent wrongdoers in respect of the damage.

(4) Where there is a joint libel in circumstances normally protected by the defences of qualified privilege or fair comment upon a matter of public interest, the malice of one person shall not defeat the defence for the other, unless that other is vicariously liable for the malice of the first.

(5) Where the same or substantially the same libel or slander or injurious falsehood is published by different persons, the court shall take into consideration the extent to which it is probable that the statement in question was published directly or indirectly to the same persons, and to that extent may find the wrongdoers to be concurrent wrongdoers.

(6) For the purpose of any enactment referring to a specific tort, an action for a conspiracy to commit that tort shall be deemed to be an action for that tort.

12. – (1) Subject to the provisions of sections 14, 38 and 46 concurrent wrongdoers are each liable for the whole of the damage in respect of which they are concurrent wrongdoers.

(2) Where the acts of two or more persons who are not concurrent wrongdoers cause independent items of damage of the same kind to a third person or to one of their number, the court may apportion liability between such persons in such manner as may be justified by the probabilities of the case, or where the plaintiff is at fault may similarly reduce his damages; and if the proper proportions cannot be determined the damages may be apportioned or divided equally.

(3) Subsection (2) of this section shall apply to two or more persons whose acts taken together constitute a nuisance, even though the act of any one of them taken alone would not constitute a nuisance, not being unreasonable in degree.

13. – An action may be brought against all of concurrent wrongdoers or against any of them without joining the other or others, but the court shall have power –

(a) in an action for the execution of trusts, to require the trust estate to be properly represented;

(b) in an action where the title to property is in question, to require the joinder of all those interested or claiming to be interested in the property.

14. – (1) Where judgment is given against concurrent wrongdoers who are sued together, the court may give judgment against the defendants together or against the defendants separately and, if the judgment is given against the defendants together, it shall take effect as if it were given against them separately.

(2) Subject to subsections (3) and (6) of this section and to sections 38 and 46, each of the said judgments shall be for the full amount of the plaintiff's damages in respect of which the defendants are concurrent wrongdoers, together with any further damages in respect of which the particular defendant against whom judgment is given is individually liable and, if the same jury has in its verdict apportioned damages between the defendants on the basis that the total of the damages awarded is meant to be equivalent to the plaintiff's loss resulting from the concurrent wrongs, the plaintiff shall be entitled to judgment against the defendants for the aggregate of such damages.

(3) The plaintiff may agree to accept an apportionment of his damages among the defendants according to their degrees of fault and, in this event, the following provisions shall take effect –

(a) satisfaction of one judgment shall not operate as satisfaction of the others;

(b) the defendants shall have no right of contribution among themselves;

(c) the plaintiff, at any time within the period limited by law for the enforcement of judgments and upon proof that, after taking reasonable steps, he has failed to obtain satisfaction of any judgment in whole or in part, shall have liberty to apply for secondary judgments having the effect of distributing the deficiency among the other defendants in such proportions as may be just and equitable.

(4) Where the court would be prepared to award punitive damages against one of concurrent tortfeasors, punitive damages shall not be awarded against another of such tortfeasors merely because he is a concurrent tortfeasor, but a judgment for an additional sum by way of punitive damages may be given against the first-mentioned tortfeasor.

(5) The judgment mentioned in subsection (4) of this section may specify that such additional sum is awarded by way of punitive damages, and no contribution shall be payable in respect thereof by a tortfeasor against whom such judgment could not properly have been given.

(6) Where, in an action for libel or slander, one of concurrent tortfeasors would have been entitled to a mitigation of the damages payable by him had he been a single tortfeasor, but another of the said tortfeasors would not have been so entitled, the first-mentioned tortfeasor shall be entitled to the said mitigation of damages and shall not be compellable to make contribution except in respect of the amount of damages payable by him; and the judgment against him may be given accordingly.

15. – (1) Where one of concurrent wrongdoers who are sued together makes default of appearance or defence, the plaintiff may obtain an interlocutory judgment against him and damages shall be assessed against him –

(a) at the same time as damages are assessed at the trial against the other defendants who appear;

(b) if the plaintiff fails against such other defendants or discontinues his action against them, separately under the interlocutory judgment.

(2) If the plaintiff fails against the defendants who appear for a reason that goes to the liability of all, the interlocutory judgment shall be discharged.

(3) If the plaintiff's damages against the defendants who appear are reduced under subsection (1) of section 34 on account of the plaintiff's contributory negligence, damages shall be assessed under the interlocutory judgment as if the defendant had appeared.

(4) This section shall not apply to any head of damage in respect of which the defendant who makes default and the defendants who appear are not concurrent wrongdoers.

16. – (1) Where damage is suffered by any person as a result of concurrent wrongs, satisfaction by any wrongdoer shall discharge the others whether such others have been sued to judgment or not.

(2) Satisfaction means payment of damages, whether after judgment or by way of accord and satisfaction, or the rendering of any agreed substitution therefor.

(3) If the payment is of damages, it must be of the full damages agreed by the injured person or adjudged by the court as the damages due to him in respect of the wrong; otherwise it shall operate only as partial satisfaction.

(4) An injured person who has accepted satisfaction from one alleged to be a wrongdoer, whether under a judgment or otherwise, shall, in any subsequent proceeding against another wrongdoer in respect of the same damage, be estopped from denying that the person who made the satisfaction was liable to him; and the liability

of such person shall be conclusively assumed for the purpose of the said proceeding: but the injured person may litigate in the said proceeding any question of law or fact relative to the liability of the defendant to such proceeding, other than the question whether or not the said satisfaction was made by one liable to the injured person.

17. – (1) The release of, or accord with, one concurrent wrongdoer shall discharge the others if such release or accord indicates an intention that the others are to be discharged.

(2) If no such intention is indicated by such release or accord, the other wrongdoers shall not be discharged but the injured person shall be identified with the person with whom the release or accord is made in any action against the other wrongdoers in accordance with paragraph (h) of subsection (1) of section 35; and in any such action the claim against the other wrongdoers shall be reduced in the amount of the consideration paid for the release or accord, or in any amount by which the release or accord provides that the total claim shall be reduced, or to the extent that the wrongdoer with whom the release or accord was made would have been liable to contribute if the plaintiff's total claim had been paid by the other wrongdoers, whichever of those three amounts is the greatest.

(3) For the purpose of this Part, the taking of money out of court that has been paid in by a defendant shall be deemed to be an accord and satisfaction with him.

18. – (1) Where damage is suffered by any person as a result of concurrent wrongs –

    (a) judgment recovered against any wrongdoer liable in respect of that damage shall not be a bar to an action against any other person who would, if sued, have been liable as concurrent wrongdoer in respect of the same damage;

    (b) if more than one action is brought in respect of that damage by or on behalf of the person by whom it was suffered, or for the benefit of his estate, or for the benefit of his dependents, against wrongdoers liable in respect of the damage, the sums recoverable under the judgments given in those actions by way of damages shall not in the aggregate exceed the amount of the damages awarded by the judgment first given; and in any of those actions, other than that in which judgment is first given, the plaintiff shall not be entitled to costs unless the court is of opinion that there was reasonable ground for bringing the action: but this paragraph shall not apply where the judgment first given was an apportioned judgment given in pursuance of section 14, section 38 or section 46.

(2) The reference in this section to 'the judgment first given' shall, in a case where the judgment is reversed on appeal, be construed as a reference to the judgment first given which is not so reversed and, in a case where a judgment is varied on appeal, be construed as a reference to that judgment as so varied.

19. – (1) Where the injured person sues one or more of alleged concurrent wrongdoers and judgment is given for one defendant, the injured person shall be bound by the findings of fact in favour of such defendant in the injured person's present or subsequent action against another or others of the alleged concurrent wrongdoers.

    (2) (a) For the purpose of subsection (1) of this section, where judgment is given for the said defendant on the ground of the injured person's discontinuence, the injured person shall be bound by the allegations and denials in the said defendant's defence as if they had been found in favour of the said defendant, so far as they are relevant to the defence of that defendant.

        (b) Paragraph (a) of this subsection shall not apply unless, on the facts, the injured person is barred by his discontinuance from bringing a second action against the said defendant.

(3) Where an action is brought against concurrent wrongdoers and judgment is given against one and for another for a reason that goes to the liability of all, the first-mentioned judgment shall be discharged.

(4) Where an action is brought against concurrent wrongdoers and judgment is given against one without reduction of damages and against another subject to a reduction of damages under subsection (1) of section 34 on account of the plaintiff's contributory negligence, the damages under the first-mentioned judgment shall be assessed subject to the same proportionate reduction, and the provisions of section 38 shall apply.

20. – For the purpose of the Statute of Limitations or any other limitation enactment concealed fraud by one of concurrent wrongdoers shall not suspend time for another or others.

Chapter II

Contribution between concurrent wrongdoers

21. – (1) Subject to the provisions of this Part, a concurrent wrongdoer (for this purpose called the claimant) may recover contribution from any other wrongdoer who is, or would if sued at the time of the wrong have been, liable in respect of the same damage (for this purpose called the contributor), so, however, that no person shall be entitled to recover contribution under this Part from any person entitled to be indemnified by him in respect of the liability in respect of which the contribution is sought.

(2) In any proceedings for contribution under this Part, the amount of the contribution recoverable from any contributor shall be such as may be found by the court to be just and equitable having regard to the degree of that contributor's fault, and the court shall have power to exempt any person from liability to make contribution or to direct that the contribution to be recovered from any contributor shall amount to a complete indemnity.

22. – (1) Where the claimant has settled with the injured person in such a way as to bar the injured person's claim against the other concurrent wrongdoers, the claimant may recover contribution in the same way as if he had suffered judgment for damages, if he satisfies the court that the amount of the settlement was reasonable; and, if the court finds that the amount of the settlement was excessive, it may fix the amount at which the claim should have been settled.

(2) Where the claimant has settled with the injured person without barring the injured person's claim against the other concurrent wrongdoers or has paid to the injured person a sum on account of his damages, the claimant shall have the same right of contribution as aforesaid, and for this purpose the payment of a reasonable consideration for a release or accord shall be regarded as a payment of damages for which the claimant is liable to the injured person: but the contributor shall have the right to claim repayment of the whole or part of the sum so paid if the said contributor is subsequently compelled to pay a sum in settlement of his own liability to the injured person and if the circumstances render repayment just and equitable.

23. – (1) Where, in accordance with the provisions of this Part, judgment is given for contribution in respect of damages for which the claimant is or has been liable to the injured person, execution shall not be issued on such judgment until after satisfaction by the claimant in whose favour it is given before or after the said judgment of the whole or part of the damages for which he is liable to the injured

person, and execution shall then issue only in respect of the amount by which the sum paid by him exceeds his just proportion of that particular amount, as such proportion is determined by the court in accordance with this Part.

(2) Notwithstanding anything in subsection (1) of this section, execution may be issued on such judgment as aforesaid after satisfaction by the claimaint in whose favour it is given of his just proportion of the damages for which he is liable to the injured person, provided that in this case the court makes provision, by obtaining the personal undertaking of the claimant's solicitor or otherwise, for applying the sum received under the said judgment towards satisfaction of the damages due to the injured person.

(3) In this section 'damages for which he is liable to the injured person' means damages for which the claimant is liable at the time when satisfaction is made to the injured person or his representatives or lawful assignees.

(4) A payment of damages by the claimant at a time when the injured person's cause of action against the claimant is barred by the Statute of Limitations or any other limitation enactment shall not found a claim to levy execution under a judgment for contribution: but such a payment shall found such a claim if, at the time when it was made, the injured person's cause of action against the contributor was not barred.

24. – A judgment for contribution may be given in respect of costs payable to the injured person or incurred by the claimant: but, where the injured person has sued the claimant and the contributor together and has recovered judgment for costs against both of them, the provisions of section 23 shall apply, with the substitution of the word 'costs' for the word 'damages' wherever it there appears.

25. – Where, of three or more concurrent wrongdoers, one is omitted from the claim for contribution, contribution shall be awarded to the claimant on the basis that responsibility for the damage is to be borne by the claimant and the contributor or contributors without regard to the responsibility of the omitted wrongdoer, and, in such a case, a claimant whose net remaining liability is increased or a contributor whose contribution is increased by reason of the fact that judgment has not been given against the omitted wrongdoer may claim contribution from such omitted wrongdoer in accordance with the provisions of this Part: but, where such last-mentioned claim for contribution is made by a contributor in respect of his own liability to make contribution and judgment is given in such contributor's favour, execution shall not be issued on that judgment –

    (a) except in accordance with the provisions of section 28, with the substitution of 'contribution' for 'damages' and of 'original claimant for contribution' for 'injured person' wherever they there appear, and 'just proportion' in the said section being understood to mean for this purpose just proportion as between the contributor in whose favour judgment for contribution is now given and the wrongdoer against whom the said judgment is given, and in any case

    (b) to an amount greater than the sum that, when added to the amount (if any) still due to the injured person, will equal the just proportion of the damages payable by the wrongdoer against whom the said judgment is given.

26. – For the purpose of a claim for contribution –

    (a) a person who restores property to its true owner shall be deemed to be a concurrent wrongdoer with one through whom he originally claimed the property and who was a wrongdoer in respect of it towards the true owner, and

    (b) such restoration of property shall, as against such wrongdoer, be deemed to be a payment of damages to the extent of the value of the property.

27. – (1) A concurrent wrongdoer who is sued for damages or for contribution and who wishes to make a claim for contribution under this Part –

(a) shall not, if the person from whom he proposes to claim contribution is already a party to the action, be entitled to claim contribution except by a claim made in the said action, whether before or after judgment in the action; and

(b) shall, if the said person is not already a party to the action, serve a third-party notice upon such person as soon as is reasonably possible and, having served such notice, he shall not be entitled to claim contribution except under the third-party procedure. If such third-party notice is not served as aforesaid, the court may in its discretion refuse to make an order for contribution against the person from whom contribution is claimed.

(2) The provisions of subsection (1) of this section shall not apply to any contribution claim where the parties to the claim are precluded by agreement or otherwise from disputing any earlier determination by a court of the amount of the injured person's damages and the proportion in which contribution should be made.

(3) Where it is sought to serve a third-party notice making a claim for contribution, or making a claim for damages in respect of a wrong committed to the third-party plaintiff, such claim for damages having arisen in whole or in part out of the same facts as the facts giving rise to the principal plaintiff's claim, leave to serve a third-party notice shall not be refused merely because the issue between the third-party plaintiff and the third party will involve a difficult question of law.

(4) Where a concurrent wrongdoer makes a payment to the injured person without action in settlement of the injured person's claim against himself and subsequently claims contribution in accordance with section 22, the contributor shall have the right to have the injured person joined as co-defendant for the purpose of binding him by the determination of the proportions of contribution, unless the injured person is co-plaintiff in the action or the injured person has effectively agreed to be bound by such determination or the injured person has no claim against the contributor or the injured person has already sued the contributor to judgment.

(5) A claim may be made or a notice may be served pursuant to subsection (1) of this section notwithstanding that the person making the claim or serving the notice denies or does not admit that he is a wrongdoer, and the making of the claim or serving of the notice shall not be taken as implying an admission of liability by him. [inserted by *Civil Liability (Amendment) Act 1964*, section 3 – *eds.*]

28. – Where, of three or more concurrent wrongdoers, judgment for contribution is given in favour of one against two or more, the claimant, at any time within the period limited by law for the enforcement of judgments and upon proof that, after taking reasonable steps, he has failed to obtain satisfaction of any judgment in whole or in part, shall have liberty to apply for secondary judgments having the effect of distributing the deficiency among the other defendants in such proportions as may be just and equitable.

29. – (1) In any proceeding for contribution, the contributor shall not be entitled to resist the claim on the ground that the claimant who has paid the injured person was not liable to such person; but, subject to this section and to the general law of estoppel, he may resist the claim on the ground that he himself is not liable to such person and, for this purpose, may dispute any question of law or fact even though that question arises also on the liability of the claimant to the injured person; and the contributor may in the same way dispute the amount of the damage suffered by the injured person.

(2) Where a claim for contribution is made by third-party notice in the injured person's action and the third party is given leave to defend the main action, he shall

be bound by the finding of the court upon the questions that he is given leave to defend.

(3) Where the contributor had knowledge of an action brought by the injured person against the claimant, and unreasonably failed to make a proposal for assisting the claimant in the defence of the action, and the injured person obtained judgment against the claimant, the contributor shall, in any proceedings brought against him by the claimant, be estopped from disputing the property or amount of the judgment obtained by the injured person or any question of law or fact common to the claimant's liability to the injured person and the contributor's liability to the injured person: but the contributor shall not be so estopped where the claimant submitted to judgment in fraud of the contributor.

(4) In any proceeding for contribution the claimant shall be bound by any finding of law or fact in the injured person's action against him that was necessary to establish his liability to the injured person.

(5) Where the injured person has sued the claimant and contributor together and failed against the contributor, the claimant shall, in any proceeding for contribution, be bound by any finding of law or fact that was necessary to negative the contributor's liability to the injured person: provided that –
   (a) the claimant shall not be so bound where the injured person submitted to judgement in fraud of the claimant;
   (b) his subsection shall not apply where the injured person's action was brought in a court outside the State, unless by the law of the court the claimant had an opportunity of presenting evidence against the contributor, of appealing against a judgment in his favour and of contesting an appeal by him.

(6) (a) A decision on the proportion of fault between claimant and contributor on a claim for contribution shall be binding upon the same persons in a subsequent claim in respect of damage suffered by one or both of them arising out of the same facts, and conversely, such a decision in a claim in respect of such damage shall be binding upon the same persons in a subsequent claim for contribution.

(6) (b) Paragraph (a) of this subsection shall apply between two parties notwithstanding that one of them is party to the two actions in different capacities.

(7) A concurrent wrongdoer who makes a payment to the injured person without action in settlement of the injured person's claim against himself and who subsequently claims contribution under section 22 shall, where the injured person has sued the contributor, be bound by the apportionment made by the court in the injured person's action in accordance with paragraph (h) of subsection (1) of section 35.

(8) It shall not be a defence to a claim for contribution merely to show that the injured person has failed in an action against the contributor to which the claimant was not a party.

30. – The right to ask the court for an award of contribution shall be deemed to be in the nature of a quasi-contractual right which shall pass to the personal representatives of the claimant for the benefit of his estate, and shall avail against the personal representatives of the contributor; and the right to contribution shall be deemed to be a cause of action within section 9.

31. – An action may be brought for contribution within the same period as the injured person is allowed by law for bringing an action against the contributor, or within the period of two years after the liability of the claimant is ascertained or the injured person's damages are paid, whichever is the greater.

32. – (1) Where an action is brought against two or more persons as concurrent wrongdoers, each defendant shall have the right to present evidence against the other or others.

(2) Where an action is brought against two or more persons as concurrent wrong-doers and the plaintiff obtains judgment and the judgment is satisfied by one of such wrongdoers, another of such wrongdoers may appeal against the judgment notwith-standing that it has been satisfied.

(3) Where an action is brought against two or more persons as concurrent wrongdoers and the plaintiff obtains judgment and one defendant appeals against the judgment, another defendant may, upon giving such notice as may be required by rules of court, contest the appeal as respondent.

(4) Where an action is brought against two or more persons as concurrent wrong-doers and the plaintiff succeeds against one and fails against another, the unsuccess-ful defendant may appeal against the judgment in favour of the successful defendant .

33. – (1) For the purpose of a contract insuring against liability for a wrong or against a liability to pay damages, the liability of a wrongdoer to make contribution under this Part to a concurrent wrongdoer shall be deemed to be a liability to pay damages for a wrong, unless the contrary intention appears from the contract.

(2) Where a claim for contribution between wrongdoers is made under a contract for contribution between them, the provisions of subsection (1) of this section shall apply to the extent that the claim could have been made under the provisions of this Part instead of under the contract for contribution.

38. – (1) Where an action is brought against one or more of concurrent wrongdoers by an injured person who is found in such action to have been guilty of contributory negligence and it is held to be just and equitable that the plaintiff's damages should be reduced under subsection (1) of section 34 having regard to his contributory negligence, the judgment against one wrongdoer shall not be for the whole of the plaintiff's recoverable damages but the court shall determine the respective degrees of fault of the plaintiff and of all the defendants to the plaintiff's claim at the time of judgment, leaving out of account the degrees of fault of persons who are not such defendants, and shall give the plaintiff a several judgment against each defendant for such apportioned part of his total damages as the court thinks just and equitable having regard to that defendant's degree of fault determined as aforesaid.

(2) The plaintiff, at any time within the period limited by law for the enforcement of judgments and upon proof that, after taking reasonable steps, he has failed to obtain satisfaction of any judgment in whole or in part, shall have liberty to apply for secondary judgments having the effect of distributing the deficiency among the other defendants in such proportions as may be just and equitable.

(3) This section shall not apply where one of the defendant wrongdoers is respons-ible for the acts of another; such wrongdoers shall, subject to subsection (1) of section 34, be liable to the plaintiff for a single portion of his damages.

(4) After judgment has been given in accordance with subsection (1) of this section, the plaintiff shall not be entitled to bring a second or subsequent action against a concurrent wrongdoer against whom judgment has not been given, unless he satisfies the court in such action that it was not reasonably possible for him to join such wrongdoer as co-defendant in the first action.

(5) The plaintiff, when commencing such second or subsequent action, shall be under a duty to the wrongdoers already successfully sued who have a right of contribution against the wrongdoer now sued or proposed to be sued to take reasonable steps to notify them of such second or subsequent action at least fourteen days before the institution of proceedings in such action or as soon as is reasonably possible after the commencement of such period.

(6) A wrongdoer receiving such notice shall have the right to become co-plaintiff in the action if the proceedings have not been instituted and otherwise to apply to the

court for leave to be joined as co-plaintiff or for consolidation of actions; and a wrongdoer who unreasonably fails to take any of those steps as aforesaid shall be barred from his right of contribution.

(7) If the plaintiff is successful in such second or subsequent action, he shall be entitled to the difference between the total of the damages awarded to him in the previous judgment or judgments and the total of damages that in the view of the court would have been awarded if the said wrongdoer had been joined with the previous defendant or defendants as co-defendant in the earlier action or actions; and he shall be entitled in addition to the provision mentioned in subsection (2) of this section: provided that –

(a) nothing in this subsection shall entitle a plaintiff to recover from such wrong-doer more than he could have recovered had he not brought such previous action or actions;

(b) nothing in this subsection shall preclude such wrongdoer from disputing any issue that he is otherwise entitled to dispute and, if the plaintiff's damages are found to be less than they were held to be by the court in the earlier action or actions, such wrongdoer shall not be liable for more than his due proportion as between himself, the plaintiff and the previous defendant or defendants of the damages so found;

(c) such wrongdoer may at his option avail himself of any matter decided against the plaintiff in such previous action or actions as though such matter were *res judicata* between them.

(8) Where damages are awarded against a wrongdoer in accordance with the provisions of this section, such wrongdoer may recover contribution from any other wrongdoer not sued at the same time where such recovery is just and equitable subject to the provisions of Chapter II of this Part.

(9) A wrongdoer, when commencing such action for contribution, shall be under a duty to the injured person who has a right of action against the contributor and to the other wrongdoers already successfully sued by the injured person who have a right of contribution against the contributor to take reasonable steps to notify them of such action for contribution at least fourteen days before the institution of proceedings in such action or as soon as is reasonably possible after the commencement of such period.

(10) The injured person or a wrongdoer receiving such notice shall have the rights specified in subsection (6) of this section, and if he unreasonably fails to take advantage of his rights he shall be barred from his right of action for damages or for contribution as the case may be.

(11) Where the injured person brings a second or subsequent action in accordance with the provisions of this section, and where a wrongdoer brings an action for contribution as provided in subsection (8) of this section, the parties to the action shall be bound by the apportionment of fault made in the earlier action or actions: but the defendant shall not be bound by such apportionment if provision comes to be made for distributing any deficiency caused by the failure to obtain satisfaction of any judgment in whole or in part from one of the wrongdoers already sued.

(12) Where –

(a) the plaintiff sues one wrongdoer and either because he obtains judgment by default or because the court negatives contributory negligence the plaintiff recovers judgment in respect of the whole of his damages against such wrongdoer, and

(b) the plaintiff subsequently sues another wrongdoer who is held to have been a concurrent wrongdoer with the first, the plaintiff also being held to have been guilty of contributory negligence as regards both wrongdoers, the defendant secondly sued shall be entitled to credit for the same proportion of the sum received from the defendant first sued as the proportion of the damage adjudged to be borne by the plaintiff as between himself and the defendant secondly sued, and in the event of overpayment shall be entitled to repayment.

39. – Where it is made to appear to the court that –

(*a*) one wrongdoer in whose favour judgment is given is or may become a bankrupt, or

(*b*) the estate of one wrongdoer for the benefit of which judgment is given is or may be insolvent,

provision shall be made to ensure that such first-mentioned wrongdoer or such estate, as the case may be, shall be deprived of recovery to the extent that the wrongdoer or estate is liable to another party or in the aggregate to other parties as a result of the same accident, occurrence or transaction; and for that purpose judgment in favour of the wrongdoer or for the benefit of the estate shall, where necessary, be attached in whole or in part for the benefit of another party in whose favour judgment is given.

40. – (1) Where damages are awarded to any person by virtue of subsection (1) of section 34, the jury or if there is no jury then the judge or arbitrator shall find and record –

(*a*) the total damages that would have been awarded if there had not been contributory negligence;

(*b*) where the plaintiff's damages are reduced under the said subsection, the proportion of such damages that shall not be awarded to the plaintiff and the proportion that shall be payable by the defendant, or the respective proportions that shall be payable by each of the defendants if more than one, expressed in each case in percentage of the total fault of the plaintiff and defendant or defendants;

(c) [Para. *(c)* was repealed by section 6 of the *Civil Liability (Amendment) Act 1964 – eds.*]

(2) It shall be the duty of the judge or arbitrator to make the requisite calculations following upon such findings.

LYNCH V. LYNCH & ALLIANCE & DUBLIN CONSUMERS GAS CO.
Unreported H. Ct. 24 Nov. 1976. Murnaghan J. (1974–3554)

Apportionment between concurrent wrongdoers and between the plaintiff who has contributed to the accident.

Murnaghan J. (at conclusion of legal argument in the absence of the Jury):

This question arose because Mr. Sutton in opening the case stated that the jury – having told them that he would ask them to find that each of the defendants were negligent – may have to work out the proportions of blame as between the two defendants. He went on from that to discuss with the jury the injuries which he alleged his client had sustained, and, as an apparent afterthought, producing a new sheet of paper, he reminded the jury that contributory negligence had been pleaded by both defendants, and there the matter was left.

I then asked Counsel for the defendants what their attitude to Mr. Sutton's opening statement was. Mr. Liston shortly submitted that the apportionment of fault should be between three parties, namely, each of the two defendants and the plaintiff. In other words, a three-cornered division of the 100. I will come back to that in a moment. Mr. O'Connor, on the other hand, thought that the apportionment should be as between the plaintiff on the one hand and the two defendants looked at collectively on the other hand with a further question, as suggested by Mr. Sutton to the Jury, of assessment of blame or fault in percentages as between the two defendants. Mr. Sutton in his submission seemed to agree with the submission of Mr. Liston, namely, that there should be an assessment of fault in percentages looking at the plaintiff and each of the two defendants all at the same time.

In my view the view propounded by Mr. Liston is the more correct one and the one that I think is the correct one to adopt.

The next question I then have to consider is how and when this matter of apportionment has got to be determined? I have said many times before that the Civil Liability Act is a very difficult and sometimes an impossible Act to construe, and the Courts have made valiant efforts for the last fifteen years to try to make the Act work, and I have been a party to that effort, sometimes perhaps not altogether successfully. The section that I have to construe is section 38(1) and it deals in its opening words with the case where the action is brought against 'one or more concurrent wrongdoers by an injured person who is then found guilty of contributory negligence.' Well, if an injured person brings it against one wrongdoer and if the plaintiff is found negligent there is no difficulty, that situation is dealt with earlier in the Act. Consequently, this section can only be read as referring to the case of two or more negligent defendants. In a case where the plaintiff has been found negligent and two or more defendants have been found negligent, the section applies. It then goes on to provide as follows: 'and it is held to be just and equitable that the plaintiff's damages should be reduced under sub-section 1 of section 38, having regard to his contributory negligence.' I stop at that point to give it as my opinion that that is something that can only be done by a judge, it is a matter of law, it is not a function of a jury.

The section further goes on to provide as follows: 'the judgment against one wrongdoer shall not be for the whole of the plaintiff's recoverable damages, but the Court shall determine the respective degrees of fault of the plaintiff and of all the defendants to the plaintiff's claim at the time of judgment'.

As a matter of practicality it is impossible to deal with the situation where a jury finds that a number of wrongdoers are negligent and that the plaintiff is negligent, if the judge should then have to make the decision that it is just and equitable that the plaintiff's damages should be reduced and that following such a decision the matter should go back to the Jury to determine the degrees of fault of both the plaintiff and all the defendants.

In my view the proper construction of this section is that where the word 'Court' is used before the words 'shall determine in respect of degrees of fault' that that must mean a judge. That has, I am bound to say, always been my view, but, while it is a matter for the judge to determine, it is always open to a judge in his discretion in any case – and I emphasise 'in any case' – to ask for the assistance of a jury to determine a question or questions of fact. Consequently, it is open to me if I think fit to ask for the jury's assistance in determining the degrees of fault, which are issues of fact, and I agree with Counsel that it has been the practice where the issue of negligence is before the jury to ask the jury further to consider the question of degrees of fault.

In my experience it has rarely been the practice – where the issue of the plaintiff's negligence was not in issue – to have the matter of the defendant's degrees of fault decided by a jury. That is normally in my experience determined by a judge without a jury. In my view, a party does not have the right, and I emphasise the word 'right' to have the question of degrees of fault determined by a jury. I repeat again that a judge, in his discretion, may ask the jury to assist him in determining these matters. If he does he should formally say that he adopts what the jury had decided. . . .

Now, having said that, I come to the present case. In the present case I propose to leave questions to the jury to elicit from them their view as to whether either or both of the defendants were negligent, and then a question as to whether the plaintiff was negligent. I will ask them these three questions. I will also ask them for their view if they should consider that the answers to all of these questions should be in the affirmative, to assess what, in their opinion, would be the degrees of fault attributable to each of the three, looked at as individuals, in percentages, and that is the only question I propose to leave on this issue of fault. I will then determine the matter myself depending on the various answers to the various questions I will leave them. These are the only questions I propose to leave on liability.

Note

Section 21 of the Civil Liability Act 1961 provides that a concurrent wrongdoer may recover contribution from another wrongdoer who would have been liable to the plaintiff if he had been sued in respect of the same damage. Actions for contribution are common and are frequently defended on the grounds that the defendant in the contribution action would not have been liable to the plaintiff in the original action. See, *e.g.*, *Conole* v. *Redbank Oyster Co. Ltd. et al.*, *supra*, pp. 3–6, *Keenan* v. *Bergin, infra*, pp. 344–348, *Patterson* v. *Murphy, infra*, pp. 512–524.

Chapter 5

VICARIOUS LIABILITY

Sometimes the law will make a person liable for the torts of another person even when the first person is in the ordinary sense not at fault at all, and in some cases even when he may not be causally linked to the wrongdoer's act or the plaintiff's injury. Guilt by attribution is understandable when a legal person such as a company is involved, but it can be equally justified on policy grounds even when human persons are the targets of the legal action.

The primary example of such liability, called vicarious liability, in law, occurs in the case of a master's liability for the torts of his servant. We say that liability is justified in this case because the act is done for the master and in the interest of the enterprise, and in such cases it is only right that the master or enterprise should carry the loss. The rule is extended to principals, in respect of the acts of their agents, and in respect of the acts of 'de facto' servants and, in appropriate cases, in respect of acts of gratuitous volunteers.

In contrast to the rule that a master is liable for the torts of his servants is the negative proposition that the employer is not normally liable for the wrongs of independent contractors hired by him. Exceptions exist, however, and both statutory rules (e.g. *Factories Act, 1955*) and common law exceptions (e.g. in respect of inherently dangerous activities) impose liability on the employer with regard to wrongs committed by independent contractors in such circumstances.

The master is not liable for all the torts of his servants, however. Liability attaches only for those torts which are committed 'within the scope of the servant's employ-ment.' There has been much litigation as to the meaning of this phrase. Similarly, there has been much litigation as to who is a servant for the purpose of the rule.

It should also be mentioned that, while the rule of vicarious liability imposes liability on the master for the torts of his servants, it does not exonerate the servant from liability. In other words, the injured person may sue both the servant and the master, in appropriate circumstances, and indeed the master and servant are concur-rent wrongdoers for the purposes of the *Civil Liability Act 1961*. Moreover, it should not be thought that vicarious liability represents the only possible basis of the employer's liability. The employer may also become liable to the injured person because of a breach of his *personal* duty to take care. Although vicarious liability represents for the plaintiff an attractive basis for liability when it applies, it should not be allowed to blind the plaintiff to other possible grounds of liability.

A master is liable for the torts of his servant committed in the course and scope of his employment.
Who is a servant?

MOYNIHAN V. MOYNIHAN
[1975] I.R. 192 (Sup. Ct.)

Walsh J.:

The infant plaintiff was born on the 11th October, 1968, and her accident occurred on the 10th November, 1970. The defendant is the paternal grandmother of the infant plaintiff. The defendant was the owner and occupier of the house where the accident occurred and in which the defendant resided at Victoria Road in the City of

Cork. The defendant's adult daughter, Marie, resided with her in the house on the relevant date and no domestic servant was employed by the defendant. The only other person residing in the house was another daughter, Anne, and both she and Marie were in employment in Cork and resided with their mother, the defendant. These two daughters shared the domestic work in the house with their mother.

The father of the plaintiff, a son of the defendant, had lived abroad with his wife and the plaintiff and had returned to Ireland only about two weeks before the date of the accident out of which this action arises; they then resided in Cork with the parents of the plaintiff's mother. Prior to the date of the accident the plaintiff's parents had visited the mother of the defendant but had not been there for a meal. On the date of the accident the plaintiff's father and mother and the plaintiff were invited by the defendant for an evening meal which was served in the breakfast-room which opened off the kitchen of the house. The evening meal, which consisted of dinner, was at about 6.30 or 7.00 p.m. and those present were the defendant, who sat at the head of the table, her two daughters (Marie and Anne), the plaintiff's father and mother, and the plaintiff. It was proposed to have tea after the meal, but before that the dishes used at the dinner were cleared off the table and brought to the kitchen. The tea was to be served at the table in the breakfast-room where the meal had been served. Before the tea was served Anne went upstairs, the plaintiff's father left the house, the plaintiff's mother went into the kitchen to wash the dishes and the defendant went in to dry them; Marie went to make the tea. During the dinner the plaintiff was present in the breakfast-room and was seated at the table.

When Marie had made the tea, she brought it into the breakfast-room and put the teapot [In a brightly-coloured tea cosy. Eds. (See Henchy J., at 199)] upon the table there; all that time the plaintiff was in the breakfast-room. The telephone rang and that caused Marie to leave the breakfast-room to go into the hall to answer the telephone and, at that stage, the only person in the breakfast-room was the plaintiff. This is the account given in evidence by Marie. The evidence of the plaintiff's mother is also to the effect that the plaintiff was in the breakfast-room immediately before the accident. The plaintiff's mother said that the plaintiff was over in a corner of the breakfast-room playing quietly. The defendant did not give evidence.

Therefore, there is evidence from which the jury could have held that the plaintiff was in the breakfast-room at the time the teapot was placed on the table. The teapot was placed in what Marie described as 'the usual position' but, whatever position it was placed in, it was placed in one which was within the reach of the plaintiff, because it appears from the evidence that the plaintiff went over to the table when Marie had left the room (and when nobody else was in the room) and succeeded in pulling down the teapot on top of herself and caused most serious burns to her body. There was evidence from which a jury might hold that, although the plaintiff's mother was in the kitchen washing the dishes which the defendant was drying, the communicating door between the kitchen and the breakfast-room was such that the plaintiff's mother, if she had looked, would have had a view of the plaintiff in the room and would have observed that she was alone in the room with the teapot on the table. It was suggested that this is what the plaintiff's mother ought to have done when the telephone rang, that it would have alerted her attention to the fact that somebody had to answer it and that it was Marie who left the room to answer it and thereby left the plaintiff alone.

These were all matters which the jury would have had to consider if the case had been left to the jury, but the learned trial judge withdrew the case from the jury on the application of counsel for the defendant. The case was withdrawn from the jury on the grounds that there was no evidence upon which a jury could reasonably hold that the defendant was liable. The action against the defendant was brought for negligence on her part and on the basis of vicarious liability for the alleged negligence of her daughter, Marie. It is the latter aspect of the case which falls to be considered in this judgment.

Therefore, the first question to be considered is whether on the evidence a jury could hold that Marie was negligent. If the jury had found, as in my view they could have found, that Marie put a teapot with freshly-made tea in a position on a table which was within reach of a two-year-old child and then left the room, leaving the child alone in the room, it would be open to a jury to hold that Marie was negligent. It is not the law that, in the circumstances of the case, the mother of the plaintiff was the only person who had to watch out for the plaintiff's safety or who owed her a duty to take care.

The next question is whether the defendant is vicariously liable for the negligence of her daughter Marie, if she was negligent. If the person who left the teapot on the table, in the circumstances already outlined, had been a domestic servant or other employee of the defendant, there could be no doubt about the defendant's vicarious liability for the negligence, if established, of that person. The question to be decided is whether, in the circumstances of the case, the relationship between the defendant and her daughter Marie was sufficient to make the defendant vicariously liable for the negligence alleged against Marie.

If the defendant had put the teapot there herself, she could have been found guilty of negligence and the case would not depend on whether or not she was the occupier of the premises in question or whether the child was or was not an invitee: see *Purtill* v. *Athlone U.D.C.* [1968] I.R. 205. In my view the present case turns upon the position of the defendant as the person extending hospitality to the child.

The defendant invited to her house for dinner the plaintiff and her parents. As the evidence shows, the defendant was the owner and occupier of the house and was the head of the household. She had two daughters employed outside the household but who resided with her and assisted her in the domestic chores. One of the domestic duties on the day in question was the giving of this dinner; in the service of this meal the daughter Marie, apart from whatever other duties may have been assigned to her, was given or permitted the task of making the tea and putting the teapot upon the table. The negligence attributed to Marie was not the casual negligence of a fellow guest but may be regarded as the negligence of a person engaged in one of the duties of the household of her mother, the defendant, which duties were being carried out in the course of the hospitality being extended by the defendant. The nature and limits of this hospitality were completely under the control of the defendant, and to that extent it may be said that her daughter Marie in her actions on this occasion was standing in the shoes of the defendant and was carrying out for the defendant a task which would primarily have been that of the defendant, but which was in this case assigned to Marie. As the defendant was the person providing the hospitality, the delegation of some of that task to her daughter Marie may be regarded as a casual delegation. Marie's performance of it was a gratuitous service for her mother. It was within the control of the defendant to decide when the tea would be served and where it would be served and, indeed, if it was to be served at all. It was also within the control of the defendant to decide how it would be served.

This power of control was not in any way dependent upon the relationship of mother and daughter but upon the relationship of the head of a household with a person to whom some of the duties of the head of the household had been delegated by that head. The position would be no different, therefore, from that of a case where the head of a household had requested a neighbour to come in and assist in the giving of a dinner-party because she had not any, or not sufficient, hired domestic help. It would produce a strange situation if in such a case the 'inviter' should be vicariously liable for the hired domestic help who negligently poured hot sauce over the head of a guest but should not be equally liable for similar negligence on the part of the co-helper who was a neighbour and who had not been hired. In my view, in the latter case the person requested to assist in the service, but who was not hired for that purpose, is in the *de facto* service of the person who makes the request and for whom the duty is being performed.

Most, if not all, of the cases of gratuitous service in respect of which a vicarious liability has been imposed upon the person for whom the service is performed relate to motor cars, but these cases confirm the view that, even if the doctrine of vicarious liability depends upon the existence of service, the service does not have to be one in respect of which wages or salary is paid but may be a gratuitous service or may simply be a *de facto* service. For example, in the present case if the defendant had requested or permitted her daughter Marie to drive the plaintiff home in the defendant's motor car and the plaintiff, had been injured through Marie's negligence, there would have been no doubt about the vicarious liability of the defendant. It may well be, as has been suggested by one noted writer, that the fact that this imposition of vicarious liability has apparently been confined to motor-car cases is because it was developed as a means of reaching the insurance company of the owner of the car. Whatever may be the reasons for the development of the doctrine in a particular area, the reasons cannot mask the basic principle of law involved.

In my view, on the evidence so far adduced in the present case, the necessary element of control was vested in the defendant and her daughter Marie was in the *de facto* service of the defendant for the purpose of the act in which Marie was alleged to be negligent. If further or other evidence should indicate that the household was a joint one and the defendant and her two daughters were engaged in a joint enterprise and were offering joint hospitality, then different considerations might arise; but it is not at this stage necessary to express any view whether in such a case persons engaged in such a joint enterprise would be vicariously responsible for each other.

In my view, the learned trial judge was wrong in withdrawing the case from the jury on the ground that in law the defendant could not be held vicariously liable for the act of negligence alleged against her daughter Marie. I would allow the appeal and direct a new trial.

O'Higgins C.J. agreed with **Walsh J.**, but **Henchy J.** dissented. The relevant portion of **Henchy J.'s** dissent is given next.

The plaintiff's advisers have chosen to sue the plaintiff's grandmother rather than the plaintiff's aunt Marie; the claim is founded on an allegation that the defendant was negligent, through her agent Marie, in leaving the plaintiff unattended in the breakfast-room when it ought to have been anticipated that she would be allured to and injured by the teapot of hot tea. When the action came on for hearing in the High Court before Mr. Justice Murnaghan and a jury, counsel for the defendant applied at the close of the plaintiff's case to have the case withdrawn from the jury on the ground that it would not be open to the jury, on the then state of the evidence, to find that the defendant was negligent. Having heard legal argument, the judge was persuaded that the submission of counsel for the defendant was correct; and thereupon the judge directed the jury to find for the defendant. This appeal is taken from that decision.

The first question to be considered is whether, even if Marie was negligent, the defendant could be held liable for that negligence. For the purpose of dealing with this question I assume that, in making and serving the tea, Marie was acting for her mother, the defendant, and that the jury would have so found if that point had been put to them as a question. On that assumption, counsel for the plaintiff submits that what Marie did in connection with making and serving the tea was done as the defendant's agent; that there fell within the scope of that agency the negligent sequence of leaving the teapot on the table within reach of the child and then leaving the child unattended in the room when Marie went out to answer the telephone; and that for that negligence the defendant could have been held liable by the jury.

Behind this submission is the large implication that when a person chooses to do an act for another at his request or with his consent, that other becomes liable for any negligence committed in doing that act. In the present case it would seem that, if the defendant had received and accepted an offer from the plaintiff's mother to make and serve the tea on the defendant's behalf, and if the plaintiff's mother in doing so had acted as Marie did, the defendant would be liable for the negligence of the plaintiff's mother. One's first reaction to the sweep of this submission, which implies a vicarious liability for negligence in the countless acts of that kind that are done in the course of the daily round, is that one would expect to find many cases illustrating the operation of such a rule. Yet, counsel for the plaintiff is unable to put forward any case in support of his proposition. He relies instead on the maxim *qui facit per alium facit per se*, and he says that the defendant is liable on the simple basis that the act of negligence was committed by her through her agent, Marie.

I am satisfied that the maxim *qui facit per alium facit per se* has no application in this case, for in the law of tort it is referable only to circumstances where a person has authorised or procured the commission of a specific tortious act by another, in which case the principal is just as liable as if he had committed the act himself. The maxim does not apply in a case such as this where the tortious act complained of has not been specifically authorised, but arose incidentally in carrying out an authorised act.

Therefore, since it was conceded both in the High Court and in this Court that Marie was not the servant of the defendant, the plaintiff's case falls back on the proposition that the defendant is liable on the ground of agency. If, as I am prepared to assume, Marie was bringing in the tea at the tacit request of the defendant and on her behalf, it must be agreed that Marie was acting as the defendant's agent when the act of negligence took place. But Marie was the defendant's agent only in a very general sense, and Marie would have to be fitted into the more specific category of agency that is required for vicarious liability in the law of torts before the defendant could be held liable for Marie's negligence.

While Marie may be said to have been acting for the defendant when the act of alleged negligence was committed, she was not acting under any contract of service so as to be the defendant's servant, nor under any contract for services so as to be an independent contractor. She was simply a gratuitous obligor or undertaker who was carrying out an ordinary household chore on behalf of the defendant. As such, liability for Marie's negligence could not fall on the defendant any more than if Marie had been an independent contractor, such as a caterer employed for the occasion. If Marie had been an independent contractor, responsibility for her negligence could have passed to the defendant as her employer only if the act of negligence arose in circumstances in which it could be said that the defendant herself was in breach of a duty owed by her to the plaintiff, e.g., a duty imposed by statute or a duty, because of the inherently dangerous nature of what was to be done, to see that care was taken. This was not such a case. If a permissible inference from the facts is that the defendant allowed Marie to make a pot of tea and to bring it into the breakfast-room, there were no special circumstances capable of taking the commonplace delegation of a normally harmless household chore out of the general rule that the negligence of an independent contractor or a gratuitous obligor does not fall on the employer or the person benefited.

The general rule was stated by Dixon J. (as Sir Owen Dixon then was) in *Colonial Mutual Life Assurance Society Ltd* v. *Producers and Citizens Co-operative Assurance Co. of Australia Ltd*. (1931) 46 C.L.R. 41, 48 as follows:-

> 'In most cases in which a tort is committed in the course of the performance of work for the benefit of another person, he cannot be vicariously responsible if the actual tortfeasor is not his servant and he has not directly authorized the doing of the act which amounts to a tort. The work, although done at his request and for his benefit, is considered as the independent function of the person who undertakes it, and not as something which the person obtaining the benefit does by his representative standing in his place and, therefore, identified with him for the purpose of liability arising in the course of its performance. The independent contractor carries out his work, not as a representative but as a principal.'

The exceptions to the general rule are to be found in cases where a primary duty – arising either under statute or at common law – rests on the defendant to take a particular precaution and there has been a breach of the primary duty. In *Cassidy* v. *Ministry of Health* [1951] 2 K.B. 343, Denning L.J. said at p. 363 of the report:- 'I take it to be clear law, as well as good sense, that, where a person is himself under a duty to use care, he cannot get rid of his responsibility by delegating the performance of it to someone else, no matter whether the delegation be to a servant under a contract of service or to an independent contractor under a contract for services.' Denning L.J. was there referring to cases of personal or non-delegable duty of care.

Here the act of negligence, if negligence it was, cannot be viewed as the breach of a primary duty resting on the defendant. It was a collateral or incidental act of negligence on the part of a person who was a gratuitous helper (and not a servant or an independent contractor) and whose services were accepted for the purpose of carrying out a simple and normally harmless domestic task. What caused the accident was the fact that the carrying out of that task became enmeshed in an unforeseeable sequence of fortuities – the teapot being left near the edge of the table; the sudden ringing of the telephone; the unconsidered rush from the room by Marie to answer it, thus leaving the child alone in the room; and the failure of the plaintiff's mother to see the plaintiff approach the teapot. Undoubtedly, what Marie undertook to do for the defendant was capable of causing injury if done negligently, but it was essentially a task of a routinely harmless nature which the defendant had no reason to think would not be carried out safely by Marie. It is conceded that Marie was not the defendant's servant, and the circumstances of the accident do not fit into any of the exceptions to the rule that a principal is not liable for the negligence of an independent contractor or a gratuitous helper or a delegate who is not a servant.

Much as one might wish that the law would allow this plaintiff to recover damages from some quarter for the consequences of the unfortunate accident that befell her, the inescapable fact is that there is a complete absence of authority for the proposition that liability should fall on the defendant (who was innocent of any causative fault) rather than on Marie whose conduct is alleged to have been primarily responsible for the accident. I see no justification for stretching the law so as to make it cover the present claim when, by doing so, the effect would be that liability in negligence would attach to persons for casual and gratuitous acts of others, as to the performance of which they would be personally blameless and against the risks of which they could not reasonably have been expected to be insured. To transfer or extend liability in those circumstances from the blameworthy person to a blameless person would involve the redress of one wrong by the creation of another. It would be unfair and oppressive to exact compensatory damages from a person for an act done on his behalf, especially in the case of an intrinsically harmless act, if it was done in a negligent manner which he could not reasonably have foreseen and if – unlike an employer, or a person with a primarily personal duty of care, or a motor-car owner, or the like – he could not reasonably have been expected to be insured against the risk of that negligence.

Since in my view it would not have been open to the jury to hold that the defendant was liable for Marie's negligence, it is not necessary to come to any firm conclusion as to how the jury might permissibly have dealt with the question of Marie's negligence, having regard to the dicta of Devlin J. in *Phipps* v. *Rochester Corporation* [1955] 1 Q.B. 450 as to the degree of care that is owed to a child of tender years who comes accompanied by a parent or other custodian. I am prepared to hold, for the purpose of this judgment, that it would have been open to the jury to find that Marie was negligent. However, even if the jury were to make such a finding, they could not have gone on (for the reasons I have given) to hold the defendant liable for that negligence. I would therefore dismiss this appeal.

Questions

1. Was the result in this case a *fair* one? Would your answer be different if you knew that the defendant householder (a) was (b) was not, covered by insurance? Do you think that such a fact should be disclosed to the Court?
2. Did Walsh J.'s decision involve the creation of new law? If so, in what way? Would you consider it to be an acceptable judicial extension?
3. Consider the concept of 'de facto service' as used in Walsh J.'s judgment.
4. From the judgments in *Moynihan*, can you state the law in relation to liability for the acts of:
    (a) independent contractors;
    (b) servants;
    (c) 'de facto servants';
    (d) agents;
    (e) gratuitous helpers;
    (f) persons engaged in a joint enterprise?

Servant or Independent Contractor?

WALSHE V. BAILIEBOROUGH CO-OPERATIVE AGRICULTURAL & DAIRY SOCIETY, LTD. AND GARGAN
[1939] Ir. Jur. Rep. 77 (H. Ct.)

Johnston J. [Sitting at Cavan, as an additional judge of the High Court, for the hearing of Circuit Appeals (Northern Circuit: No. 4)]:

This is an appeal from a decree granted by Judge Sheehy and dated May 9, 1939, in an action in which Miss Margaret Walshe, Kingscourt, sued the Bailieborough Co-operative Agricultural and Dairy Society Ltd., and a second defendant named Owen Gargan for damages for negligence. Gargan is the person who collects and delivers milk on a specified round for the Society from the farmers who on that round send their milk for treatment to the creamery. Miss Walshe is an oldish lady of feeble appearance whose sight and hearing are not too good. On September 1, 1938, she proceeded from her house to walk to Bailieborough. Gargan had called at the house of one of the customers of the Society, a man named Fisher, to collect the daily can of milk. He left his horse and cart unattended on the road while he went to Fisher's house for the can. The horse, frightened apparently by a passing lorry, bolted, overtook Miss Walshe, and knocked her into the gully at the roadside. Her arm was broken and she was detained in hospital for treatment for some little time, and Judge Sheehy, holding that there had been negligence upon Gargan's part in leaving his horse unattended on the road, and that Gargan was the servant or agent of the Society, granted a decree for £50 against both defendants. From this decree both the defendants have appealed – Gargan on the ground that he was not guilty of any negligence, and the Society on that ground and on the further ground that Gargan was an independent contractor, and that they had no responsibility for his conduct.

I am satisfied beyond doubt that Gargan was negligent, and that he, at any rate, is responsible for the damage which the plaintiff suffered. Mr. FitzSimon contends on his behalf that the leaving of horses and vehicles unattended upon the public streets and roads is an everyday occurrence – in fact, that it is a universal practice – and that the affairs of the community could not be carried on if such a practice were to be held in every case to be an act of negligence. I doubt very much the correctness of that statement as a general proposition, but in this particular case there was something more. Gargan tied up his horse by the reins to an 'outshoot' on the cart. In that way he showed that some control was necessary, even though his horse was an ancient animal of some twenty-two summers. Further, shortly after the horse bolted the shafts of the cart slipped from the harness by reason, no doubt, of some faulty construction in the harness, or of something wrong with the mechanism of the cart. I am sure that the horse was further startled by this mishap, and I have no doubt that the injury which the plaintiff suffered arose through the negligence of Gargan.

The only real difficulty in the case is the point which is relied upon by the other defendants. They allege that whatever liability Gargan may have incurred, they have incurred none, seeing that (as they allege) Gargan was altogether an independent contractor, and not their servant or agent in any sense. Now there are certain situations under which an independent contractor and a contracting owner may be jointly liable for negligence which arose through the mistake or default of the former. Two well-known cases illustrative of that principle are *Penny* v. *Wimbledon Urban District Council* [1899] 2 Q.B. 72, and *Holiday* v. *National Telephone Co* [1899] 2 Q.B. 392, in which it was decided that a public body which carries out statutory works – works from which danger is likely to arise to the public in connection with the doing of it unless sufficient precautions are taken – may be liable in damages to injured persons jointly with the contractor, the negligence of the contractor not being casual or collateral to his employment. Lord Blackburn in a classic statement in *Dalton* v. *Angus* (6 App. Cas. 740, at p. 829) put the matter thus: 'Ever since *Quarman* v. *Burnett* 6 M. & W. 499 it has been considered settled law that one employing another is not liable for his collateral negligence unless the relation of master and servant existed between them. So that a person employing a contractor to do work is not liable for the negligence of that contractor or his servants. On the other cannot escape from the responsibility attaching on him of seeing that duty performed by delegating it to a contractor.' Now in the present case there was no such duty, and I agree with Mr. McGonigal to this extent that this is not one of those cases in which an independent contractor, and the person employing him, can be jointly liable for the negligence of the former.

That brings me to the last question in the case, the question as to the nature of Gargan's employment. Was he employed by the company as an independent contractor or as a servant doing 'piece-work' for his employer and paid for it as such? The learned Circuit Judge took the latter view. There was no written contract in the case, and the minutes of the company contain no reference to the engagement of this man or to any regulation in respect of the work. The question depends upon the circumstances of the case, and must be decided, in this common law action, totally irrespective of the analogous questions which arise under the Workmen's Compensation Acts, the National Health Insurance Acts, and the Unemployment Insurance Acts.

It is true that Gargan used his own horse and cart to enable him to carry out his contract expeditiously and satisfactorily, and that, no doubt, is a point in favour of the company; but the work that he was called upon to do was largely of a manual character – carrying the cans of milk, placing them on the cart, removing them at the creamery, and carrying out the reverse process with the empty cans. For this work he was paid at the 'piece-work' rate of one penny per gallon for the quantity of milk carried. This work was done regularly and daily by Gargan personally (although occasionally his son did the work for him) during the summer months, and less often during the remaining part of the year. He was under the control of the company as to the doing of this work on a fixed round, and at an hour each day to suit the work of the creamery undertaking. It was the daily toil of a labouring man, and in no sense could he be said to be his own master. It seems to me that the only factor in the case which favours the company's point of view is the use of the horse and cart, and, in my opinion, that fact cannot be allowed to outweigh all the other circumstances in the case. I should like to refer to two cases, by way of analogy, in which a similar question arose in past years. The case of *Clarke* v. *Bailieborough Co-operative Dairy Society* 47 I.L.T.R. 113 is a very remarkable case because it was concerned with the very same point that arises in this case, namely, the question as to the status of a man who carted milk to a creamery company's premises using his own horse and cart – and the order was made against the very same company as are defendants in this case. It was held by the Court of Appeal (O'Brien, L.C., and Holmes and Cherry, L.JJ.) that the use by the carter of his own horse and cart could not be regarded by the Court as outweighing the other circumstances in the case (which was an application by the carter for compensation under the Workmen's Compensation Act, 1906). So clear was the Court in regard to this question that it did not consider it to be necessary to call upon counsel for the employee. The case of *Bray* v. *Kirkpatrick & Sons* 53 I.L.T.R. 81 is also one of a useful character. That application was also under the Workmen's Compensation Act, 1906, in which a man who had been injured whilst carting timber for a saw-mill owner claimed compensation. It was held by the Court of Appeal (Sir James Campbell, Bart., L.C., Ronan and O'Connor, L.JJ.) that the applicant was an independent contractor and not an employee, and the application was dismissed; but that was done for the following reasons as set out in the Lord Chancellor's judgment, and the reasoning shows clearly where the dividing line between the two classes of cases is to be found. He said 'The applicant in this case was nothing more nor less than a casual carter. He had his own horse and cart and supplied his own tackle, and he undertook to remove fallen timber. He might work for two, three or four days as he pleased, and the respondents had no right to call on him to work on any particular day. He was his own master . . . It is true he was under the control of respondents' foreman to the extent that he was told where the timber was, what class of timber to take, whether to leave the timber on the ground, or to put it in the railway waggons; but there was no control such as is involved in a contract of service. We cannot find any of the elements necessary to constitute the relationship of master and servant in this case, in fact they are all absent.'

These two decisions show clearly the distinction in principle between the two classes of cases. There will, therefore, be a dismissal of the appeal in this case and the defendants will pay to the plaintiff the taxed costs of the appeal. The appeal will, of course, be remitted to the County Registrar of Cavan. I may add that I received great assistance from the counsel who appeared for the various parties, and particularly from Mr. McWilliam who fought the case on behalf of the plaintiff.

Appeal dismissed

Note

The concept of servant may also have significance for other branches of the law – employment law, tax law, social security law, etc. To what extent is it legitimate to borrow precedents from those areas to guide the Courts in determining who are servants for the purpose of vicarious liability in tort?

One cannot serve two masters. Whose servant?

LYNCH V. PALGRAVE MURPHY LTD
[1964] I.R. 150

Kingsmill Moore J.:

'The defendants, Palgrave Murphy Ltd., are well-known stevedores who were unloading a ship in the port of Dublin on the day of the accident. The plaintiff, a casual dock labourer, was employed by them in the work. Mr. Henry Crosbie is a carrier and haulier who owns a number of vehicles of different types which he is accustomed to hire out, with their operators, to anyone who may need them and the defendants hired from him a machine known as a fork-lift at a price of £1 an hour which included the services of its driver, a man named Byrne, to assist them in unloading the ship.

No photograph or diagram of the fork-lift was supplied to the Court but the general nature of the machine was agreed by counsel. It consists of a mobile truck with two long bars projecting in front like the prongs of a fork, and it is used for lifting, transporting and depositing loads which are too heavy for a man to carry. The prongs are power-operated and the general method of use is to insert the prongs under the load, raise the prongs to take the weight of the load, transport it to the warehouse and deposit the load in the desired place by lowering the prongs. The prongs are then withdrawn from under the load and the truck returns to take the next load in the same manner.

On the day in question – there is some doubt as to the exact date, but it was some time in the month of October, 1957 – Byrne had been sent by Mr. Crosbie with his fork lift to assist the defendants in unloading a ship and Byrne was directed by the defendants' foreman to lift heavy bales of paper from the quayside, bring them to a shed and stack them in tiers where indicated. The plaintiff was assigned to assist in the work. The withdrawal of the forks after the load had been deposited had to be done in rather a complicated way owing to the weight of the bales, nearly half a ton each, and to the fact that they were being stacked in tiers one on top of the other. If the top bale had been deposited flat on the one below it and an attempt had then been made to withdraw the forks, the friction between the forks and the bales above and below might have upset the tier. In order to avoid this, a short batten of wood, about three inches thick, was placed upon the lower bale so that, when the next bale came to be deposited and the forks were lowered, the upper bale came to rest supported by the batten, with a space left for the withdrawal of the forks. The batten itself, known to the workmen as 'the podger,' had now to be removed and to facilitate this the forks were not withdrawn entirely but left projecting a few inches under the near edge of the bale. They were then lifted so that the bale was tilted, the far edge resting on the bale below and the near edge raised and supported on the forks. This enabled another man to put in his hand and remove the podger. When he had removed it, he called out to the man in charge of the fork lift, 'O.K.' or 'Lower,' to indicate that it was safe to let down the forks and pull them away. The last few inches of the forks could be pulled out, apparently, from between the bales without disturbing them.

No evidence was given as to who devised this method originally but it appears to have been standard and the plaintiff described it as if it was day-to-day practice. The familiarity of the practice is further indicated by the existence of the special technical word for the batten.

The plaintiff was the man engaged in placing and removing the podger. At some time in the day, when the forks had been partially withdrawn and the nearside of the bale lifted, Byrne called out to the plaintiff to remove the podger and the plaintiff started to do so but, before his hand was clear, Byrne lowered the forks and caught the plaintiff's thumb between the lower bale and the edge of one of the forks, thereby injuring the thumb severely. That Byrne was guilty of negligence in so doing was not disputed before us.

The plaintiff sued Palgrave Murphy Ltd., alleging that Byrne was their servant and that they were vicariously responsible for his negligence. The defendants answered that Byrne was not their servant but the servant of Crosbie. At the trial the defendants applied to the Judge for a direction at the conclusion of the evidence for the plaintiff and, when this was refused, did not tender any evidence. The Judge then left to the jury two questions – whether James Byrne was at the time of the accident the servant or agent of the defendants and whether the defendants their servants or agents had been guilty of negligence – to both of which questions the jury answered, 'Yes.' They assessed damages at £1,200. From this verdict and the judgment consequent thereon the defendants' appeal on the ground (amongst others) that there was no evidence to warrant the submission to the jury of the question whether Byrne was a servant of the defendants and that the trial Judge should have withdrawn the case from the jury.

This appeal raises once again the question as to when and in what circumstances a workman, whose services have been lent temporarily by his permanent employer to another employer, can be considered to have become the servant of the second employer so as to make the second employer liable vicariously for his negligence. Various terms have been used in the decided cases to describe the second employer, such as '*dominus pro tempore*' and '*dominus pro hac vice*.' I will use the terms, 'permanent master' and 'temporary master,' as being the simplest, though I realise that the use of the word 'master' begs the question to a certain degree.

It was accepted by counsel on both sides that it was a question of fact whether in all the circumstances the control and direction of the workman could be said to have passed so completely from the permanent master to the temporary master as to make the workman a servant of the temporary master to the extent that the temporary master became responsible for his negligence; and it was conceded by counsel for the defendants that in certain circumstances such a result could be brought about. But counsel for the defendants contended that the presumption always was that the workman remained in the service of the permanent master and that the onus of disproving this rested on anyone who wished to challenge it; moreover, he said that the onus was very heavy and that the burden could only be shifted in exceptional circumstances, none of which had been proved in the present case.

The evidence at the trial did not establish all the circumstances quite as clearly as might be desired, but they may, I think, be summarised as follows. Byrne was employed, paid and subject to dismissal by Crosbie. He was a skilled manipulator of the truck and the fork-lift and his services were included in the price paid for the hire of the fork-lift by whoever hired it. He alone had control of the levers and mechanical devices which operated the fork-lift. The temporary master – in this case the defendants, Palgrave Murphy Ltd. – had no right to give him orders in regard to his actual method of working the controls. On the other hand, Palgrave Murphy Ltd., through their foreman stevedore, could assign the task to be performed, the end to be procured and, to a certain extent, the manner of performance and procurement. The foreman could say what loads were to be lifted, and from where and to what place they were to be transported, and how they were to be stacked. I will assume that, if the nature of the load required special precautions in its transport, the foreman could insist on those precautions being observed: Mr. Crosbie said that the stevedore might check the operator if he were not handling the cargo in the proper manner. The actual manipulation of the controls was admittedly a matter for the operator. Mr. Crosbie was asked:– 'Would you have any right or power to direct him (the operator) how he was to operate the controls of his truck?' and his answer was:– 'No, I don't think so, because the operator becomes quite an expert after a few months of that, so I don't think anyone could advise him how to handle it.' I think that this answer must be interpreted as a disclaimer by Mr. Crosbie of the technical knowledge which would induce or warrant his interference, and not as a denial of the legal right to give instructions if, in any event, instructions appeared to him to be necessary.

There is no evidence that the foreman ever attempted to interfere with the manner of driving the truck or the operation of the controls and it is clear that the accident was due to a negligent operation of the controls, namely, lowering the forks before the plaintiff had his hand clear.

A great number of cases, ranging over a century, were cited but it is unnecessary to review them in detail. Though the question whether the permanent master or the temporary master is responsible for the negligence of the workman is a conclusion of fact based on the establishment or non-establishment of various other facts, it seems to be established by authority that the mere power to assign the task to be done – and even to direct in a general way how the desired object is to be accomplished – does not, by itself, make the temporary master responsible for the workman's negligence, unless there is also the power to control the way in which the act involving negligence was done. In the present case Crosbie engaged, paid and could dismiss Byrne. He directed him each day where to go to work. He left the driving of the truck and the operation of the controls to the discretion of Byrne, but he, Crosbie, would have had the power, by himself or by an engineer if he had chosen to employ one, to direct Byrne in his method of handling the controls. The defendants could only indicate to Byrne the load to be taken, the place from which it was to be taken, the place where it was to be deposited and the arrangements made to facilitate the depositing. The lifting of the forks, the driving of the truck and the management of the forks to deposit the load were not under the control of the defendants. This being so, there was no fact which would warrant a jury in finding that Byrne had become a servant of the defendants so as to involve them in vicarious liability. Nor is the position altered by the fact that, in order to achieve the desired end of stacking the bales in tiers, Byrne had so to operate his forks as to co-operate with a servant or servants of the defendants.

Mr. Micks, for the plaintiff, relied chiefly on *Donovan* v. *Laing, Wharton, and Down Construction Syndicate, Limited* [1893] 1 Q. B. 629. There the defendants lent one of their cranes and a driver to wharfingers, Jones & Co., who were discharging a ship at their wharf. The crane driver, according to the statement of facts, worked the crane in conformity with instructions received from the wharfingers. The plaintiff, one of the wharfingers' servants, gave instructions to the crane driver for the raising and lowering of the chain attached to the load. The statement of facts does not indicate that he did more. He was injured, as the jury found, by the negligent operation of the crane. The trial judge entered judgment for the defendants on the ground that the crane driver had become, for the purpose of his operations, the servant of the wharfingers. The Court of Appeal upheld this finding, but passages in the judgments suggest that the control exercised by the wharfingers went much further than appears in the statement of facts. Thus Lord Esher M. R. says, at p. 631:– '. . . every act in connection with the working of the crane must be done according to the orders of those who are directing the loading,' and at p. 632:– 'The man was bound to work the crane according to the orders and under the entire and absolute control of Jones & Co.'; and the Master of the Rolls also said that the man was '. . . bound to work under the orders of Jones & Co., and, if they saw the man misconducting himself in working the crane or disobeying their orders, they would have a right to discharge him from that employment.' Bowen L.J. says, at p. 634:– 'It is clear here that the defendants placed their man at the disposal of Jones & Co., and did not have any control over the work he was to do,' and 'in the present case the defendants parted for a time with control over the work of the man in charge of the crane, and their responsibility for his acts ceased for a time.'

   M'Cartan v. *Belfast Harbour Commissioners* [1910] 2 I. R. 470; [1911] 2 I. R. 143 was a case where the facts closely resembled *Donovan* v. *Laing, Wharton and Down Construction Syndicate* [1893] 1 Q.B. 629. The Commissioners hired out one of their cranes with its driver to the master of a ship which was discharging at their wharves. The craneman raised and lowered the buckets containing the cargo, and swung the jib, in the direction of a servant of the shipmaster. Owing to the negligence of the craneman in lowering a bucket at a high speed, the plaintiff was injured and he sued the Commissioners. The jury found that the plaintiff was injured as a result of the negligence of the craneman who let the bucket get out of control; but in answer to the special question, 'Had the hirer authority to control Duffy otherwise than in respect of the time and place of movement of the crane, and the time of raising and lowering the buckets?' they replied, 'No.' On those findings the trial judge entered judgment for the plaintiff. Upon motion by the defendants, the King's Bench Division set aside the judgment for the plaintiff and entered a verdict and judgment for the defendants with costs. The judgment of the King's Bench Division was reversed by the Court of Appeal who were affirmed by the House of Lords. In the Court of Appeal Holmes L.J., who gave the judgment of the Court, said that the work of unloading the vessel was a joint operation, but in that part of it which consisted of the manipulation of the crane the shipmaster had no control over the craneman. For this reason he held that he had not become the servant of the ship-master so as to make the ship-master liable for the craneman's negligence in conducting that operation.

   In the House of Lords the decision again rested on the limited amount of control exercised by the ship owner. *Donovan's Case* was distinguished because in that case all control over the craneman had passed to the wharfinger while in *M'Cartan's Case* the control was limited as found by the jury. Lord Dunedin cited with approval the words of Bowen L.J. in *Moore* v. *Palmer* 2 T.L.R. 781 (a case almost identical in the relevant facts):– 'The great test was this, whether the servant was transferred or only the use and benefit of his work.' *M'Cartan's Case*, as a judgment of our Court of Appeal and of the House of Lords before 1922, would normally be regarded as a precedent which, even if not absolutely binding on us, should be followed in the absence of very special reasons, and if there is any discrepancy between *Donovan's Case* and *M'Cartan's Case* then the latter should be followed.

   Mersey Docks and Harbour Board v. *Coggins and Griffith (Liverpool), Ltd.*

[1947] A. C. 1 in its facts again echoes *M'Cartan's Case* [1910] 2 I. R. 470; [1911] 2 I.R. 143. The plaintiff, McFarlane, was employed by forwarding agents who had engaged the respondent company as stevedores to load cargo on a ship. While so employed the plaintiff was injured by the negligence of a craneman in the management of his crane. The crane and its driver had been hired by the appellant Board to the respondent company. Lord Simon, at p. 10 of the report, compendiously states the facts which seemed to him relevant, and his conclusion:– 'The appellant board had engaged Newall, and it paid his wages: it alone had power to dismiss him. On the other hand, the respondent company had the immediate direction and control of the operations to be executed by the crane driver with his crane, e.g., to pick up and move a piece of cargo from shed to ship. The respondent company, however, had no power to direct how the crane driver should work the crane. The manipulation of the controls was a matter for the driver himself. In the present case the accident happened because of the negligent way in which the crane driver worked his crane, and since the respondent company had no control over how he worked it, as distinguished from telling him what he was to do with the crane, it seems to me to follow that Newall's general employers must be liable for the negligence and not the hirers of the apparatus . . . It is not disputed that the burden of proof rests on the general or permanent employer – in this case the appellant board – to shift the *prima facie* responsibility for the negligence of servants engaged and paid by such employer so that this burden in a particular case may come to rest on the hirer who for the time being has the advantage of the service rendered. And, in my opinion, this burden is a heavy one and can only be discharged in quite exceptional circumstances.'

Lord Simon refers to the test laid down by Bowen L.J. in *Donovan's Case* [1893] 1 Q. B. 629 when the latter said:– '. . . by the employer is meant the person who has a right at the moment to control the doing of the act,' and Lord Simon accepts such test only if the words are construed as meaning 'to control the way in which the act involving negligence was done.' At page 12 of the report he presents the test as being 'where the authority lies to direct, or to delegate to, the workman, the manner in which the vehicle is driven,' and he goes on to say:– 'It is this authority which determines who is the workman's "superior." In the ordinary case, the general employers exercise this authority by delegating to their workmen discretion in method of driving, and so the Court of Appeal correctly points out . . . that in this case the driver Newall, "in the doing of the negligent act, was exercising his own discretion as driver – a discretion which had been vested in him by his regular employers when he was sent out with the vehicle – and he made a mistake with which the hirers had nothing to do".'

Lord Macmillan, Lord Porter, Lord Simonds and Lord Uthwatt, in slightly varying language, agreed with Lord Simon. Thus Lord Macmillan states, at p. 13: 'The stevedores were entitled to tell him where to go, what parcels to lift and where to take them, that is to say, they could direct him as to what they wanted him to do; but they had no authority to tell him how to handle the crane in doing his work,' and at p. 14:– 'Here the driver became the servant of the stevedores only to the extent and effect of his taking directions from them as to the utilization of the crane in assisting their work, not as to how he should drive it.' Lord Porter says that a change of employer must always be proved in some way and not presumed: and that the test is to ask who is entitled to tell the employee the way in which he is to do the work on which he is engaged. He says, at p. 17:– 'But it is not enough that the task to be performed should be under his control, he must also control the method of performing it. It is true that in most cases no orders as to how a job should be done are given or required: the man is left to do his own work in his own way. But the ultimate question is not what specific orders, or whether any specific orders, were given but who is entitled to give the orders as to how the work should be done. Where a man driving a mechanical device, such as a crane, is sent to perform a task, it is easier to infer that the general employer continues to control the method of performance since it is his crane and the driver remains responsible to him for its safe keeping.'

Finally, I would quote Lord Uthwatt, who says, at p. 21:– 'The principles established by the authorities are clear enough. The workman may remain the employee of his general employer, but at the same time the result of the arrangements may be that there is vested in the hirer a power of control over the workman's activities sufficient to attach to the hirer responsibility for the workman's acts and defaults and to exempt the general employer from that responsibility. The burden of proving the existence of that power of control in the hirer rests on the general employer. The circumstance that it is the hirer who alone is entitled to direct the particular work from time to time to be done by the workman in the course of the hiring is clearly not sufficient for that purpose. The hirer's powers in this regard are directed merely to control of the job and the part the workman is to play in it, not to control of the workman, and the workman in carrying out the behests of the hirer as to what is to be done is not doing more than implementing the general employer's bargain with the hirer and his own obligations as a servant of his general employer. To establish the power of control requisite to fasten responsibility on him, the hirer must in some reasonable sense have authority to control the manner in which the workman does his work, the reason being that it is the manner in which a particular operation (assumed for this purpose to be in itself a proper operation) is carried out that determines its lawful or wrongful character. Unless there be that authority the workman is not serving the hirer, but merely serving the interests of the hirer, and service under the hirer in the sense I have stated is essential.'

Donovan's Case [1893] 1 Q. B. 629 was considered by Lord Simon, Lord Macmillan, Lord Porter and Lord Simonds and was explained by the special finding of fact that 'entire and absolute control' over the workman had passed to the wharfingers – though some of their lordships question whether such a finding could be justified.

The *Mersey Docks Case* [1947] A. C. 1 is not binding on us but must command the full weight of so distinguished a Court. I am in agreement with the opinions expressed in that case and, applying the tests laid down, I can find no evidence in the present case to suggest that the defendants had been granted or had assumed any power to control the driver in his actual operation of the machinery of the fork-lift. In my opinion the case should have been withdrawn from the jury. The appeal must be allowed and judgment entered for the defendants.

It is claimed on behalf of the respondent that the appellants are liable by reason of the application of the doctrine of *respondeat superior* because, it is said, James Byrne was the servant of the appellants at the time of the accident.

It was not suggested that the contract of service existing between Crosbie and Byrne was at any time terminated or suspended. It follows, therefore, that Crosbie remained at all material times the person who paid Byrne and was the only person who could dismiss him. It also raised the presumption that at all material times Crosbie had the right to determine not only what work Byrne should do, but the manner of doing it. There is abundant authority for stating that, while such matters as payment and power of dismissal may be taken into consideration, the decisive factor in deciding whether a person doing work for another is or is not the servant of that other is whether the latter has complete control as to how the particular work shall be done.

Thus, as the relation of master and servant is in each case a question of fact, the respondent at the trial of this action undertook to discharge the burden of proving that at the time of the accident Byrne was the servant of the appellants, though not in the sense that there was any contract of service between them, thereby rebutting the presumption that Byrne remained the servant of Crosbie. In my view the respondent was in law thereby obliged to prove as a fact that at the time of the accident Crosbie had completely relinquished his right to control Byrne in his operation of the truck and its fork-lift and that the appellants at that time had complete and exclusive authority over Byrne in that matter. That is the effect, in my view, of the line of authorities which includes, amongst others, *Rourke* v. *White Moss Colliery Co.* 2 C. P. D. 205; *M'Cartan* v. *Belfast Harbour Commissioners* [1911] 2 I. R. 143: *Bain* v. *Central Vermont Railway Co.* [1921] 2 A. C. 412: *Century Insurance Co.* v. *Northern Ireland Road Transport Board* [1942] A. C. 509; *Mersey Docks and Harbour Board* v. *Coggins and Griffith (Liverpool) Ltd.* [1947] A. C. 1; and *O'Reilly* v. *Imperial Chemical Industries, Ltd.* [1955] 3 All E. R. 382. It is also the basis of the decision in *Donovan* v. *Laing, Wharton, and Down Construction Syndicate, Limited* [1893] 1 Q. B. 629 upon which the respondent in this case sought to rely. That decision turned upon the finding that, to quote Lord Esher M. R., at p. 632, 'the man was bound to work the crane according to the orders and under the entire and absolute control of Jones and Co.' This also appears from the judgment of Bowen L.J. when he says, at p. 634:– 'It is clear here that the defendants placed their man at the disposal of Jones and Co., and did not have any control over the work he was to do.' That such a finding of fact is necessary in any case where it is sought to establish that a loaned workman becomes the servant of the person temporarily in receipt of his services was repeated in the decision of the House of Lords in *M'Cartan* v. *Belfast Harbour Commissioners* [1911] 2 I. R. 143. In that case the learned Law Lords thought *Donovan's Case* [1893] 1 Q. B. 629 had been correctly decided having regard to the particular finding of fact upon which it was based. Lord Dunedin, dealing with the facts of *M'Cartan's Case* [1911] 2 I. R. 143, stated, at page 150:– '. . . that the general authority and control of the defendants over Duffy had not, *pro hac vice*, been surrendered by them, and transferred to Chambers, but that the control given to Chambers was limited to the right to give directions to move the crane alongside the hold, and to lower or raise the bucket. Any control, however limited, is not, *per se*, enough to transfer the service, and the jury has not held this control to be sufficient so to transfer it.' Indeed, when one bears in mind that *Donovan's Case* [1893] 1 Q. B. 629 was so clearly decided upon the finding that the defendants there did not retain any control over the work which their man was to do when they put him at the disposal of Jones and Company, one may venture to suggest that the criticism, levelled at Bowen L.J. for his reference to the 'carriage cases,' by Lord Dunedin in *M'Cartan's Case* [1911] 2 I.R. 143, at p. 151, and by Lord Simon in the *Mersey Docks Case* [1947] A.C. 4 at page 11, were undeserved. Bowen L.J. did not suggest that the principle of law applicable in the 'carriage cases' was different from that applicable in the 'crane case,' but rather that the facts of the 'carriage cases' where, as he says, the owner of the carriage 'in no sense places the coachman under the control of the hirer,' were so fundamentally dissimilar from the facts upon which *Donovan's Case* [1893] 1 Q. B. 629 was being decided that the 'carriage cases' clearly could not be used for the purpose of ruling *Donovan's Case* [1893] 1 Q. B. 629 by what Lord Dunedin himself described in *M'Cartan's Case* [1911] 2 I. R. 143 as the fallacious test of similarity of facts. There is no necessity to attempt to distinguish *Donovan's Case* [1893] 1 Q. B. 629 from *M'Cartan's Case* [1911] 2 I. R. 143 or from the *Mersey Docks Case* [1947] A. C. 4 so far as the legal principle involved is concerned, unless it is sought to suggest that the finding of fact upon which the decision was expressed to be based was not justified by the evidence in the case. In my view that is a field of enquiry which is not open for the purpose of endeavouring to show that the legal principle enunciated in *Donovan's Case* [1893] 1 Q. B. 629 is other than that which it is expressed to be.

The burden of proving that the hirer is answerable for the negligence of the loaned servant has been described by Lord Simon in the *Mersey Docks Case* [1947] A.C. 4, at p. 10, as a heavy one and one that can only be discharged in quite exceptional circumstances. He stated:– 'It is not easy to find a precise formula by which to determine what these circumstances must be.' If by 'precise formula' is meant a precise statement of legal principle, I venture to suggest that it is the one which is found in the cases I have referred to, namely, that the act involving the negligence must be one in respect of which the general employer has completely relinquished his right to control the way in which it should be performed and has completely transferred that right to the hirer at the time of the accident. The difficulty which arises is one of fact in that it may be only in exceptional circumstances that such an arrangement is the case. In *Denham* v. *Midland Employers Mutual Assurance Ltd.* [1955] 2 Q. B. 437 Denning L.J., dealing with this topic, says, at p. 444:– 'Such a transfer rarely takes place, if ever, when a man is lent with a machine, such as a crane or a lorry: nor when a skilled man is lent so as to exercise his skill for the temporary employer. In such case the parties do not contemplate that the temporary employer shall tell the man how to manipulate his machine or to exercise his skill. But a transfer does sometimes take place in the case when an unskilled man is lent to help with labouring work: see *Garrard* v. *A. E. Southey & Co.* [1952] 2 Q. B. 174. The temporary employer can then no doubt tell the labourer how he is to do the job. The labourer becomes so much part of the organisation to which he is seconded that the temporary employer is responsible for him and to him.' That describes the circumstances usually encountered but it does not of course raise the standard of proof required in a civil action when the facts are that such a complete transfer did take place, even in the case of a skilled person, as was the situation in *Rourke* v. *White Moss Colliery Co.* 2 C. P. D. 205. In this context it may be relevant to note the dictum of Murnaghan J. in *Graham* v. *Minister for Industry and Commerce and Molloy* [1933] I. R. 156, where he said, at p. 165:– 'Again, when a person engages a skilled artisan or tradesman, the presumption is that the person engaged is his own master over the work to be done and it is not under the control of the other so as to be his servant.' That was a case which turned upon the question of whether the individual concerned was an independent contractor or a servant, but I think it is permissible to equate a machine and its operator with a skilled artisan or tradesman.

Turning to the facts of the present case, the question is whether the evidence adduced on behalf of the respondent is sufficient in law to establish *prima facie* that Crosbie had surrendered and transferred to the appellants the right to completely control Byrne in the operation and manipulation of the fork-lift truck. In this Court Mr. Micks, on behalf of the respondent, relied upon the answers to questions 413, 451, 452 and 464 as showing that no control remained in Crosbie. Question 413 and its answer must, in my opinion, be read with question 412 and its answer. They are as follows:–

'412. Q.: Mr. Guiden would tell you and the fork driver where to go and what to do?

'A.: He would tell us where to put the fork lifter to put the stuff. He would tell us and we would have to tell him.

'413. Q.: And then you would go over as a team with the fork driver and you would do the unloading that Guiden had told you to do in the way Guiden told you?

'A.: Yes.'

The witness was a dock labourer and a fellow-employee of the respondent with the appellants and was working with the respondent at the tiering of the bales. Guiden was the appellant's foreman. Even assuming that 'team' in question 413 included Byrne as well as the witness and the respondent, the answers only deal with the appellants' foreman indicating the place where the bales were to be deposited by the fork-lift truck.

The witness who answered questions 451, 452 and 464 was Crosbie and the questions and answers are as follows:–

'451. Q.: When the driver and truck were on hire in that way, who would have the power of checking if something was done wrong?

'A.: I would solely depend on my operator.

'452. Q.: Suppose he did something wrong, was there someone who would have the right to check him, to correct him?

'A.: Yes, the stevedore might check him if he was not handling the cargo in the proper manner.

'464. Q.: Would you have any right or power to direct him how he was to operate the controls of his truck?

'A.: No, I don't think so because the operator becomes quite an expert after a few months of that, so I don't think anyone could advise him how to handle it.'

This evidence reveals only that the foreman might remonstrate with Byrne if he was mishandling the cargo but falls very far short of showing that Crosbie had transferred to the appellants the right of controlling the operation of the fork-lift truck. Crosbie's answer at question 464 is clearly directed to the necessity for his exercising the power rather than the right to exercise it. The matter was not pursued further with him. This evidence and the other evidence in the case did not go further than to establish that the appellants could indicate where and when the truck was to be operated by Byrne; and even those directions were, in my view, given to Crosbie as the owner of the truck and the employer of Byrne, although they were received not by him personally but by Byrne whom the had sent to do the work. The position was no different than if Crosbie had been present on the quayside during the whole of the operation of the truck and had received the orders in person and then passed them on to Byrne. The transaction between the appellants and Crosbie was essentially one for the conveyance of goods, already unloaded, from the quayside to the transit shed and there to be deposited in accordance with the direction of the appellants: see the observations of Lord Wright in *Century Insurance Co. Ltd.* v. *Northern Ireland Road Transport Board* [1947] A. C. 509, at pp. 517 and 518.

In my view therefore the learned trial Judge should have acceded to the application of the appellants to withdraw the case from the jury. Accordingly this appeal should be allowed.

Note and Question

1. See also *Davey* v. *C.I.E.* 103 I.L.T. & Sol. J. 164 (High Ct., 1968).
2. Do you think that employers generally are conscious of the requirements of law articulated in *Lynch* v. *Palgrave Murphy Ltd.*?

Arising out of or within the scope of servant's employment

KIELY V. McCREA & SONS, LTD.
[1940] Ir. Jur. Rep.1

Appeal by the defendants. Messrs. McCrea & Sons, Ltd., from the judgment and order of the Circuit Court at Cork awarding a sum of £63 11s. 6d. to the plaintiffs on foot of a claim for damages for negligence arising out of a collision between two motor-cars, the property of the plaintiffs and the defendants respectively.

At the time of the accident the defendants' car was being driven by one, Thomas Murphy, a commercial traveller employed by them and the terms of whose employment were governed by a written agreement. At the trial of the action in the Circuit Court Murphy was called as a witness by the plaintiffs for the purpose of establishing that at the time of the accident he was acting within the scope of his authority as an employee of the defendant company. The further facts appear sufficiently from the judgement of the Circuit Judge, the material portion of which was as follows:–

'In this case I shall first deal with paragraph 9 in the Agreement dated 3rd October 1934, and made between Messrs. Edward McCrea & Sons, Ltd., of the one part, and Mr. Thomas Murphy, of the other part. Mr. Binchy has quoted to me that paragraph which I have read very carefully. Paragraph 9 says:- "The Company undertakes to provide a motor car to enable the said Thomas Murphy to carry out his duties as traveller in the Counties before mentioned, and will also pay for all petrol, oil, and repairs necessary for the carrying on of these duties; and also the hotel expenses incurred, except in the City of Cork, and the said Thomas Murphy undertakes to supply receipted bills for all such petrol, oils, repairs and renewals to the motor car and all hotel expenses incurred while on the Company's business, and the said Thomas Murphy undertakes not to use the motor car for his private purposes and it is clearly understood that the motor car shall be used only for the legitimate purposes of the Company's business."

'Now, I have to distinguish the use by Mr. Murphy of this car for his own personal private business. Mr. Murphy himself tells me that he is the representative in the South of Ireland of the defendant company, as traveller for the sale of the company's shirts, collars, and overalls. He is provided with a motor car on that business, and, according to the agreement (paragraph 2), he, the said Thomas Murphy, "agrees to use his utmost endeavours to effect the sale of the goods of the company in the districts agreed upon." Mr. Murphy tells me that he is connected with the Gaelic Athletic Association here in the City of Cork, and that for the purposes of business he finds that connection is very valuable to him. He further says, that in order to carry on that business, to make new customers, and to encourage old customers, he had to do certain things as we know all travellers, at least in Ireland, have to in order to keep old customers or to acquire new ones. The use of the motor car in such work and with that object is clearly, in my view, not for the traveller's own private use but "for the legitimate purposes of the company's business," and complies with paragraph 2 of the agreement to "use his best endeavours to affect the sale of the goods of the company." On the night of the accident there was a football dance, somewhere outside or in the City, and Mr. Murphy being connected with football in the City went there in the interests of his principals, and, for their benefit as he interpreted it, he did use this motor car. He carried in that car parties who were working in houses with which he did business, and, in his interpretation of the interests of his principals, he invited those people to go with him in this car to the dance. In doing this I feel he, a trusted traveller, was acting in the interests and for the benefit of the legitimate purposes of the business of the company. The company who employed him say by their amended Defence and by their Counsel to-day that that is private business and not their (the company's) business. I cannot so interpret it. I could understand that the Company would say to Mr. Murphy: 'you cannot take your wife and children down to the seaside for your own personal business.' That would be undoubtedly personal and private business, and could have no connection whatever with the furthering or advancing or the popularising of the company's business which he represented. On the other hand, I feel that if a trusted traveller, who is working for a company that has other serious competitors in his district is anxious to extend and popularise his business and to gain new friends and supporters, in his discretion thinks that taking out to a popular dance, a number of employees of a firm with which he does business, is of advantage to his company, and will help him in getting orders, then I think he is acting in the company's interest and for the legitimate purposes of the company's business.

'If a dance is organised and held by a body that has great public influence throughout Munster and throughout the Irish Free State, if Mr. Murphy thought it would be in the interest of his Company to associate himself with it and take people to a dance to make the dance a success, then, equally I hold he was acting in the company's interest and in their legitimate business. Therefore, for all these reasons I hold that the defence based on the agreement fails. I hold that the car in question was driven by Mr. Murphy, the agent and servant of the defendants at the time of the accident, and that he was driving it in the course of his employment.'

The defendants appealed on the ground that Murphy was not at the material time acting within the scope of his authority as their servant or agent, the appeal being heard upon the report of the official stenographer.

Hanna, J.:

I think the decree in this case should be reversed. The Circuit Judge held that the driver of the defendants' car was acting within the scope of his employment at the time of the accident. Now, we start with the agreement between the driver and his employers. [His Lordship read paragraph 9 of the agreement]. The evidence is that the car was at the time being used for the driver's private purposes and his firm had no knowledge of the journey. When he used the car for purposes of the firm they paid for the petrol; when he used it for his own purposes he paid for the petrol himself. The evidence is that he paid for the petrol himself on this occasion.

I could not possibly accept the submission that he was on his firm's business, on the evidence given by Murphy himself. In essence it was a private journey of Murphy upon which he took his friends.

O'Byrne, J.:

I agree.

Note   *Appeal allowed.*
Contrast this case with *Boyle* v. *Ferguson* [1911] 2 I.R. 489.

SECTION 59 OF THE CIVIL LIABILITY ACT, 1961

59 – (1) Where a wrong is committed by the use of a mechanically propelled vehicle belonging to the State, the Minister for Finance shall be liable to an action for damages

in respect of damage resulting from the wrong in like manner as if the Minister for Finance were the owner of the vehicle, and the person using the vehicle shall, for the purposes of such liability, be deemed to be the servant of the Minister for Finance in so far as such person was acting in the course of his duty or employment.

(2) Proceedings may be brought against the Minister for Finance by virtue of this section without obtaining the fiat of the Attorney General.

(3) Nothing in this section shall operate to relieve any person from liability in respect of damage resulting from his own wrong.

(4) For the purposes of this section, a mechanically propelled vehicle not belonging to the State shall –

(a)   while being used when it is under seizure by a person in the service of the State in the course of his duty or employment, or

(b)   while being used by a member of the Garda Siochána or an officer of any Minister for the purpose of a test, removal or disposition of the vehicle pursuant to the Road Traffic Act, 1961, or any regulation thereunder,

be deemed to belong to the State.

(5) In this section –

'mechanically propelled vehicle' means a vehicle intended or adapted for propulsion by mechanical means, including –

(a)   a bicycle or tricycle, with an attachment for propelling it by mechanical power, whether or not the attachment is being used,

(b)   a vehicle the means of propulsion of which is electrical or partly electrical and partly mechanical;

'use' includes keeping or leaving stationary.

MURRAY V. MINISTER FOR FINANCE, IRELAND AND THE A.G.
(Unreported. H. Ct. Irish Times 27 May 1981 p. 13 (Doyle, J.); Sup. Ct. Irish Times 22 April 1982 p. 11)

[In this case the plaintiffs were injured when they were in collision with a Garda patrol car. In the High Court Mr. T. Murray, the driver of the other car, was awarded £9,101. The Supreme Court reversed. The Irish Times report of the Supreme Court decision is given hereunder. (There was no written judgment by the Supreme Court).]

The Supreme Court yesterday decided that a garda was acting outside the period of his duty when the patrol car he was driving near Cork was in collision with another car injuring its driver and his wife.

The court upheld an appeal by the State against a jury verdict in the High Court in which Timothy Murray, a lorry driver, of Oliver Bond House, Dublin, and Kilmichael, Macroom, Co. Cork, was awarded £9,101 damages for injuries received in the collision at Carrigrohane Road, on December 27th 1974.

In the High Court it had been stated that Garda David Brosnan and another garda had been on duty with a squad car at a coursing meeting at Blarney and that Garda Brosnan, who had been seen drinking in the marquee, had taken the squad car and had later been seen drinking with a man named Cahill from Cahirciveen who had been at the coursing meeting.

Garda Brosnan was due to have gone off duty at 6 p.m. and when the collision occurred about 20 minutes after that time, the patrol car was being driven in the direction of Cork, away from Blarney where Garda Brosnan was stationed. In the collision, Garda Brosnan and Mr Cahill were killed outright.

The defendants had denied liability, claiming that at the time of the accident,

Garda Brosnan was not acting in the course of his authority, or duty. They denied that they knew, or ought to have known, that Gards Brosnan was in dereliction of duty, as alleged, or unfit to drive at the time. The jury had found that Garda Brosnan was driving the patrol car in the course of his duty and assessed damages.

In a subsequent action, Mr Murray's wife was also awarded damages in the High Court on the basis of the jury's finding of negligence in her husband's case.

The Chief Justice, Mr O'Higgins, said that he would concede the general principle that a garda was always on duty, but Section 59 of the Civil Liability Act related to a particular duty and he felt that the trial judge should have refused to allow any question under that Section to go to the jury.

It was clear that the other gardai had no idea that Garda Brosnan was off on a skite. A direction should have been granted, and a verdict for the defendant given.

However, the court strongly recommended in view of the fact that a garda car was involved that the authorities might consider compensating the innocent victims of the accident. Mr Justice Henchy and Mr Justice Hederman agreed. The question of costs was adjourned.

Questions

Consider the liability of the State or the Minister for Finance in the following circumstances: A Garda who is on duty at a coursing meeting until 6 p.m. –
(a) gets drunk at 4 p.m. and causes an accident at the coursing meeting at 5.00 p.m.;
(b) gets drunk at 4 p.m. and causes an accident at the coursing meeting at 6.30 p.m.;
(c) gets drunk at 4 p.m. and causes an accident on his way back to his barracks at 6.30 p.m.;
(d) gets drunk at 4 p.m. and causes an accident at 6.30 p.m. on his way to Cork city, *i.e.* in a totally different direction from his barracks.

DOWLING V. MOORE
31 I.L.T. 367 (Co. Ct. 1897)

A pony and van, the property of defendant, was driven to the Cork terminus of the Gt. S. W. R. When there, the servant in charge went into the railway station, and left the pony unattended. The pony got frightened at some paper which blew upon a telegraph wire, and ran into a cart-horse near by, injuring the horse a good deal. The defendant's servant was at that time some seven or eight yards from the pony, and the carman some few yards from his horse. *Held*, the defendant was liable owing to the twofold duty cast upon his servant of driving the van to the station and taking parcels into it, which would prevent the most attentive man from minding the pony.

Question

From this meagre report can you say whether the liability imposed on the defendant was personal or vicarious?

Normally the employer is not liable for the negligence of independent contractors. But the employer will be liable even for the negligence of his indpendent contractors where the work involved is 'inherently dangerous'

BOYLAN V. NORTHERN BANK LTD. & JAMES CORCORAN LTD.
Unreported. H. Ct. 21 July 1977 (Costello J)

In demolishing a building, contractors employed by the Northern Bank caused damage to the plaintiff's house. The plaintiff sued both the contractors and the Bank.

Costello J.:
The liability of the Defendants

The manner in which the contractors demolished the bank's premises caused injury to the plaintiff's premises as a result of which she has suffered loss and damage. Later in this judgment I will examine the extent of the injury and assess her damages. I will now deal with the question of the liability of each of the defendants arising from the facts which I have found to have been established.

No difficulty arises in relation to the contractor's liability. Every witness in the case expressed the opinion that the proper way to demolish the Bank's gable wall was by hand. I have found that it was not done in this way. The submissions made by Mr. Landy in closing on behalf of the contractors relating to the liability for damage caused by acts which, though properly performed by an occupier nonetheless cause injury to a neighbour's land, might have been of relevance if I had accepted the contractor's evidence. But in the light of my findings it follows that the contractors were guilty of negligence in the demolition of the bank's premises entitling the plaintiff to damages against them.

But is the bank liable to the plaintiff? The plaintiff's case against the bank has been put in the course of the proceedings in three different and alternative ways. Firstly, it was said that this is a case which falls within one of the exceptions to the general rule that an employer is not liable for the negligence of his independent contractor: the operations undertaken by the Bank were, it is said, extra-hazardous ones and the bank is accordingly liable. Secondly, it was alleged that Mr. Ellison, the bank's architect, was negligent and that the bank is liable because of this. Thirdly, it was claimed that a liability arises because of the undertaking given by the bank's architect to the plaintiff's architect at the meeting of the 7th November that care would be taken in the demolition of the gable wall and that it would be taken down by hand. As to the third submission, I have already indicated that I do not consider that any legal obligation arose from the discussions between the architects, and in my opinion no cause of action can arise from them. The bank's duty to the plaintiff was not a contractual one. As to the allegation relating to the architect's negligence, it should be pointed out that he was a consultant and not an employee of the bank and accordingly if he was negligent the bank would only be liable if the case fell within the exception to the general rule relating to liability for the acts of an independent contractor to which I have referred. But in my opinion he was not negligent. Whilst it is true that he was of the opinion that the gable wall should have been taken down by hand and that he did not so specifically provide in the contract documents he prepared prior to the commencement of the work, nonetheless he had secured an agreement from the contractor that the wall would be demolished in the way he thought proper. Nor do I think that his supervision was inadequate. He carried out regular on-site inspections and I do not consider that he could have done more than he did to secure the safe demolition of the bank's premises.

I come, then, to what I consider to be the plaintiff's main submission. There are a number of well-established exceptions to the rule that an employer is not liable for the negligence of his independent contractor. One of the principal exceptions has been formulated as follows:

> 'When a person through a contractor does work which from its nature is likely to cause danger to others, there is a duty on his part to take all reasonable precautions against such danger, and he does not escape from liability for the discharge of that duty by employing the contractor if the latter does not take these precautions'

(see: *Belvedere Fish Guano Co. Ltd.* v. *Rainham Chemical Works Ltd.* [1920] 2 I. B. 487, 504)

This formulation of the principle was quoted with approval in one of the judgments in the Court of Appeal in England in the case of *Salsbury* v. *Woodland* [1970] 1 Q.B.

324. This was a case in which the plaintiff suffered injury due, it was claimed, to the negligence of a number of persons who were joined as Defendants. The first defendant was the occupier of a house and he employed the second defendant to remove a large hawthorn tree from his front garden. It was established that the second defendant was negligent in the way he felled the tree and, as it was also established that he was an independent contractor, a question arose as to whether or not the occupier (the first defendant) was liable for the contractor's negligence. It was held that he was not. As pointed out by Harman, L.J. the act of felling the tree *did* involve danger to others because it was negligently done, but it was a perfectly simple job to remove the tree without causing any danger to anybody and it was not work which was inherently dangerous so as to come within the exception to which I have referred (p. 345).

It was suggested by Counsel for the Bank in the present case that the exception to which I have referred (the existence of which is not contested) relating to the liability of an employer for work which is inherently dangerous is limited to cases where operations dangerous from the use of explosives or inflammable materials arise. It is clear, however, from the authorities that this is not so. For example in *Salsbury* v. *Woodland* Sachs, L.J. (at p. 348) stated the legal principle in the following passage:

'. . . there is, to my mind, a sharp distinction between cases in which the work done is inherently dangerous and cases where there is no such danger, although there may be risks entailed if the work is done incompetently. The dividing line between the two classes of cases may sometimes be difficult and may involve questions of degree; but generally speaking this is a matter of common sense as to what, in plain English is "inherently dangerous" having regard, inter alia, to the distance from the highway of the place where the work is being done. In the present case it seems clear to me that there was nothing "inherently dangerous" in the operation of removing this particular hawthorn tree . . . The whole position as regards "inherent danger" might be very different if the case was concerned with the removal of a sixty foot tree'.

The issue, therefore, of the Bank's liability to the plaintiff depends on whether the demolition of the gable wall was an inherently dangerous operation. I think it was. It was a masonry wall, about two feet thick measuring 22 feet by 55 feet. It was standing within two inches of the plaintiff's premises. Even if it was not connected to the plaintiff's gable wall by the concrete beam the operation of demolishing such a mass of masonry in such close proximity to the plaintiff's premises carried inherent dangers in it. The danger was increased by the fact that the two walls were connected by the concrete connecting beam (a factor of which the Bank was aware by reason of the knowledge of the manager of its Skerries premises). The expert evidence in the case (which I accept) was to the effect that extreme care would be required in demolishing the wall and that it should be taken down by hand in small pieces. The need to take special care arose in my view from the dangers inherent in the operation being undertaken. Those dangers, not only related to the possibility of local damage from falling masonry or damage resulting from the removal of the connecting beam or the flashing but also from the vibrations which could be caused by the wall if it was allowed to fall in large segments.

It follows therefore that the bank is liable because of the negligent way the wall was demolished and that the plaintiff is entitled to judgment against both defendants.

KELLY V. LOMBARD MOTOR CO. LTD
[1974] I.R. 142 (High Ct., Kenny, J., 1973)

Kenny J.:

In this action the plaintiff claims damages for injuries which she suffered on the 24th December, 1967, when she was a passenger in a motor car owned by the defendants and driven by Patrick O'Donnell. The defendants admit that they owned the motor car and that O'Donnell was careless but say that they are not liable to compensate the plaintiff because O'Donnell had obtained possession of the car from them by fraud and so was not using it with their consent.

In December, 1967, Patrick O'Donnell was working in England and had decided to return to Galway for the Christmas holidays. He had not a driving licence issued in Ireland or in Britain and he wanted to hire a car for the holidays. He knew that the companies in Dublin which hire cars required the production of a driving licence by a person who wished to hire a car from them, and so he got possession of one which had been issued in the Republic of Ireland to Michael Kelly who was then in England and was a friend of his. Some time afterwards, Matthew O'Donnell, who was also in England and who wanted to hire a car from the defendants, telephoned them and, when his conversation had finished, Patrick O'Donnell told the defendants that he was Michael Kelly and asked them to keep a car for him. On the 16th December Patrick O'Donnell called to the offices of the defendants in Dublin and said that he was Michael Kelly and produced Kelly's licence.

The defendants had an arrangement with the Irish National Insurance Company Ltd. by which the defendants are insured against their liability in connection with the negligent driving of any cars on hire from them and under which they can allow the person seeking to hire a car to drive it at once without reference to the insurance company, provided that such person produces a valid driving licence. Patrick O'Donnell answered questions put to him and the information was entered on a form headed 'Irish National Insurance Company Limited.' He gave the hirer's name as Michael Kelly and his address in London and stated that he had a private car insurance certificate. He also stated that he had a driving licence and its number is on the form. Patrick O'Donnell then signed the form with the name of Michael Kelly, he was given the car and drove it away. Each of these statements was fraudulent. Patrick O'Donnell had never had a driving licence in any country.

Counsel for the defendants said that O'Donnell's fraud vitiated the consent to drive which they gave; while counsel for the plaintiff argued that the defendants had given their consent to the car being driven by the person whom they saw on the 16th December. No authorities were cited by either side.

At common law the owner of a motor car is liable for the negligence of the person driving it if that person is his servant acting in the course of his employment, or if that person is his agent. The driver is regarded as the owner's agent when the driver, with the owner's consent, is driving the car on the owner's business or for the owner's purposes. Mere consent by the owner of a car to another person driving does not make the driver the servant or agent of the owner: *Hewitt* v. *Bonvin* [1940] 1 K.B. 188; *Ormrod* v. *Crosville Motor Services Ltd.* [1953] 1 W.L.R. 1120; and *Rambarran* v. *Gurrucharran* [1970] 1 W.L.R. 556.

When insurance against negligence in the driving of a motor vehicle was made compulsory by the Road Traffic Act, 1933, the law was changed by s. 172 of that Act. It provided that whenever a person drove a mechanically propelled vehicle with the consent (whether expressed or to be implied from the circumstances) of the owner, the person driving should, for the purposes of determining the liability of the owner for injuries caused by the negligent driving by such person, be deemed to drive the vehicle as the servant of the owner, but only in so far as the person driving acted in accordance with the terms of the consent. This section was repealed by the Road Traffic Act, 1961, which provides in s. 118 that:– 'Where a person (in this section referred to as the user) uses a mechanically propelled vehicle with the consent of the owner of the vehicle, the user shall, for the purposes of determining the liability or non-liability of the owner for injury caused by the negligent use of the vehicle by the user, and for the purposes of determining the liability or non-liability of any other person for injury to the vehicle or persons or property therein caused by negligence occurring while the vehicle is being used by the user, be deemed to use the vehicle as the servant of the owner, but only in so far as the user acts in accordance with the terms of such consent.'

The defendants consented to the person whom they thought was Michael Kelly driving the car because they believed that he had a valid driving licence. The defendants would not have been insured against their liability in connection with the driving of the car if the person to whom they hired it had not a driving licence. On principle it seems to me that a fraudulent mis-statement made at the time of the hiring would prevent the apparent consent which was given being effective only if it procured the consent and if it related to the matter of identity in such a way that, if the defendants had known the true facts, they would not have given their consent. The identity of the person hiring the car mattered nothing to the defendants but his possession of a driving licence did matter because they were insured against their liability only if the person hiring the car had a driving licence.

This approach gets support from the law in relation to the type of fraud which invalidates the apparent consent which is the foundation of the marriage ceremony. Fraud is a ground for annulling a marriage, but only when it procures the appearance without the reality of consent. A marriage cannot be annulled on the ground that the consent was included by fraud unless it relates to the identity of the person getting married. *Swift* v. *Kelly* (1835) 3 Knapp 257 is a decision of a Privy Council which included Lord Brougham and Baron Parke and so is of the highest authority. It was a suit brought by a husband for the restitution of conjugal rights. The husband and wife were Irish and, when they were in Rome both abjured the Protestant religion and became Roman Catholics. They obtained a licence to marry from the Vicar General of Rome and were then married by a Roman Catholic priest. The wife alleged that she never intended to abjure the religion to which she belonged and that her marriage was therefore invalid because the person who gave the licence and the priest who celebrated the marriage believed that she had become a Roman Catholic. The Court of Arches decided that there was not a valid marriage but this decision was reversed by the Privy Council. In the course of the advice given by Lord Brougham this passage appears at p. 293 of the report:– 'It should seem, indeed, to be the general law of all countries, as it certainly is of England, that unless there be some positive provision of statute law, requiring certain things to be done in a specified manner, no marriage shall be held void merely upon proof that it had been con-tracted upon false representations, and that but for such contrivances, consent never would have been obtained. Unless the party imposed upon has been deceived as to the person, and thus has given no consent at all, there is no degree of deception which can avail to set aside a contract of marriage knowingly made. If such be the law touching consent to the marriage itself, and the fraud whereby that consent was obtained, it would be extraordinary indeed if another rule were allowed to govern the case where fraud has been practised upon a third party, acting immaterially in granting the licence to celebrate it.'

The apophthegm 'fraud vitiates consent' has also been applied in the criminal law. When the criminal act charged consists of trespass to the person or to property, the consent of the person injured is a complete defence; but the consent must be by a person who knows the nature of the act to which he is consenting and fraud as to that or as to the identity of the person doing it vitiates the consent: *R. v. Case* (1850) 4 Cox C.C. 220.

It seems to me that the consent in this case by the defendants to the driving of the car was given to a person who held a driving licence. There was never a consent to a person driving the car who did not have a licence and, therefore, the defendants did not consent to Patrick O'Donnell driving the car. They gave their consent to a Michael Kelly, the holder of a driving licence, driving the car. The result is that the defendants did not consent to Patrick O'Donnell (or to Patrick O'Donnell masquerading as Michael Kelly) driving the car and so the defendants are not liable to the plaintiff.

Notes and Questions

1. Does this case raise the same problem as that arising in the law of contract where mistake as to identify is alleged? *Cf.* Clarke, *Contract* pp. 94–96 (Irish Law Texts, 1982). What relevance had the law of nullity of marriage or the criminal law to the issue before the Court?
2. The whole subject of vicarious liability of motor vehicle owners has been comprehensively analysed by Professor Osborough in a number of important articles: see 'The Vicarious Liability of the Vehicle Owner' 6 Ir. Jur. (n.s.) 77 (1971), 'The Regime of Protection for Road Accident Victims' 5 Ir. Jur. (n.s.) 217 (1970); 'Consensual User in the Vicarious Liability of the Vehicle Owner' 65 Gazette of the Incorp. L. Soc. of Ir. 7 (1971).

Chapter 6

SURVIVAL OF ACTIONS AND FATAL INJURIES

1. *SURVIVAL OF ACTIONS*

CIVIL LIABILITY ACT, 1961

PART II

Survival of Certain Causes of Action on Death

Preliminary

6. – In this Part 'excepted cause of action' means–

(*a*) a cause of action for breach of promise to marry or for defamation or for seduction or for inducing one spouse to leave or remain apart from the other or for criminal conversation, or

(*b*) any claim for compensation under the Workmen's Compensation Act, 1934.

Causes of action vested in deceased person

7.–(1) On the death of a person on or after the date of the passing of this Act all causes of action (other than excepted causes of action) vested in him shall survive for the benefit of his estate.

(2) Where, by virtue of subsection (1) of this section, a cause of action survives for the benefit of the estate of a deceased person, the damages recoverable for the benefit of the estate of that person shall not include exemplary damages, or damages for any pain or suffering or personal injury or for loss or diminution of expectation of life or happiness.

(3) Where–

(*a*) a cause of action survives by virtue of subsection (1) of this section for the benefit of the estate of a deceased person, and

(*b*) the death of such person has been caused by the circumstances which gave rise to such cause of action,

the damages recoverable for the benefit of his estate shall be calculated without reference to any loss or gain to his estate consequent on his death, except that a sum in respect of funeral expenses may be included.

(4) The rights conferred by this section for the benefit of the estate of a deceased person are in addition to the rights conferred on the dependants of deceased persons by Part III of the Air Navigation and Transport Act of 1936 and Part IV of this Act.

Causes of action subsisting against deceased person

8.–(1) On the death of a person on or after the date of the passing of this Act all causes of action (other than excepted causes of action) subsisting against him shall survive against his estate.

(2) Where damage has been suffered by reason of any act in respect of which a cause of action would have subsisted against any person if he had not died before or at the same time as the damage was suffered, there shall be deemed, for the purposes of subsection (1) of this section, to have been subsisting against him before his death such cause of action in respect of that act as would have subsisted if he had died after the damage was suffered.

9.–(1) In this section 'the relevant period' means the period of limitation pre-scribed by the Statute of Limitations or any other limitation enactment.

(2) No proceedings shall be maintainable in respect of any cause of action what-soever which has survived against the estate of a deceased person unless either–

> (a) proceedings against him in respect of that cause of action were commenced within the relevant period and were pending at the date of his death, or
>
> (b) proceedings are commenced in respect of that cause of action within the relevant period or within the period of two years after his death, whichever period first expires.

10.–In the event of the insolvency of an estate against which proceedings are maintainable, any liability in respect of the cause of action in respect of which the proceedings are maintainable shall be deemed to be a debt provable in the administ-ration of the estate, notwithstanding that it is a demand in the nature of unliquidated damages arising otherwise than by a contract or promise.

Notes and Questions

1. Recently in England the House of Lords has held that where a person is wrongfully killed and his working-life cut short, his estate may recover in respect of the earnings (less the cost of maintaining himself) which he would have made during the working years lost as a result of the accident: *cf. Gammell* v. *Wilson*, [1981] 1 All E.R. 578 (H.L.); *Pickett* v. *British Rail Engineering Ltd.*, [1980] A.C. 136 (H.L.).
   Should the same approach be followed here? *cf.* White, 'Insurers at Bay – Repercussions of Gammell v. Wilson' 75 Inc. L. Soc. of Ir. Gazette 77 (1981); Pigot, 'Gammel v. Wilson and Ors. – A Further Commentary' 76 Inc. L. Soc. of Ir. Gazette 65 (1982).
2. See also *Moynihan* v. *Greensmyth, infra*, pp. 640–645 (unsuccessful challenge to constitu-tionality of two-year limitation period).
3. In relation to s. 6, note that actions for enticement of spouses, for criminal conversation and under the *Workmen's Compensation Act 1934* have been abolished.

2. *FATAL INJURIES*

Since 1846 (Lord Campbell's Act) a person who wrongfully caused the death of another was liable to be sued by the dependants of the deceased for the pecuniary loss suffered by the dependants. The statutory provisions allowing this action, originally contained in the *Fatal Accidents Acts 1846–1908*, and later in the *Fatal Injuries Act 1956*, are now re-enacted with amendments in sections 47 to 51 (Part IV) of the *Civil Liability Act 1961*.

The essential features of this action, apart from its statutory basis, are twofold: first, it is available only to *dependants* of the deceased – a group which is defined to include only the immediate family of the deceased; second, the action is primarily designed to cover only the *pecuniary loss* which the dependants suffer as a result of the wrongful death. In addition, in Ireland since 1961 the plaintiffs in such an action may also claim as an additional head of damages compensation for the *mental distress* resulting to each of the dependants (i.e. for what is known in Scots law as *solatium*). The original maximum compensation payable under this heading (£1,000) was recently increased to £7,500 by the *Courts Act 1981*.

Many of the cases on this topic are concerned with the method of calculating what exactly was the dependants' economic loss as a result of the wrongful death.

CIVIL LIABILITY ACT 1961

PART IV

47.–(1) In this Part–

'dependant', in relation to a person whose death is caused by a wrongful act, means any member of the family of the deceased who suffers injury or mental distress;

'member of the family' means wife, husband, father, mother, grandfather, grandmother, stepfather, stepmother, son, daughter, grandson, granddaughter, stepson, stepdaughter, brother, sister, half-brother, half-sister;

'wrongful act' includes a crime.

(2) In deducing any relationship for the purposes of this Part–

(*a*) a person adopted under the Adoption Act, 1952, shall be considered the legitimate offspring of the adopter or adopters;

(*b*) subject to paragraph (*a*) of this subsection, an illegitimate person shall be considered the legitimate offspring of his mother and reputed father;

(*c*) a person *in loco parentis* to another shall be considered the parent of that other.

48.–(1) Where the death of a person is caused by the wrongful act of another such as would have entitled the party injured, but for his death, to maintain an action and recover damages in respect thereof, the person who would have been so liable shall be liable to an action for damages for the benefit of the dependants of the deceased.

(2) Only one action for damages may be brought against the same person in respect of the death.

(3) The action may be brought by the personal representative of the deceased or, if at the expiration of six months from the death there is no personal representative or no action has been brought by the personal representative, by all or any of the dependants.

(4) The action, by whomsoever brought, shall be for the benefit of all the defendants.

(5) The plaintiff shall furnish the defendant with particulars of the person or persons for whom and on whose behalf the action is brought and of the nature of the claim in respect of which damages are sought to be recovered.

(6) The action shall be commenced within three years after the death.

49.–(1) (*a*) The damages under section 48 shall be–

(i) the total of such amounts (if any) as the jury or the judge, as the case may be, shall consider proportioned to the injury resulting from the death to each of the dependants, respectively, for whom or on whose behalf the action is brought, and

(ii) subject to paragraph (*b*) of this subsection, the total of such amounts (if any) as the judge shall consider reasonable compensation for mental distress resulting from the death to each of such dependants.

    (*b*) The total of any amounts awarded by virtue of subparagraph (ii) of paragraph (*a*) of this subsection shall not exceed one thousand pounds. [Now £7,500 – *eds*.]

    (*c*) Each amount awarded by virtue of paragraph (*a*) of this subsection shall be indicated separately in the award.

    (*d*) [Para. (*d*) was repealed by s. 6 of the *Civil Liability (Amendment) Act 1964 – eds*.]

(2) In addition, damages may be awarded in respect of funeral and other expenses

actually incurred by the deceased, the dependants or the personal representative by reason of the wrongful act.

(3) It shall be sufficient for a defendant, in paying money into court in the action, to pay it in one sum as damages for all the dependants without apportioning it between them.

(4) The amount recovered in the action shall, after deducting the costs not recovered from the defendant, be divided among the persons entitled in such shares as may have been determined.

50. – In assessing damages under this Part account shall not be taken of–

(*a*) any sum payable on the death of the deceased under any contract of insurance,

(*b*) any pension, gratuity or other like benefit payable under statute or otherwise in consequence of the death of the deceased.

51. – A reference in any enactment to the Fatal Accidents Acts, 1846 to 1908, or to any of them shall be construed as a reference to this Part.

Difficulty of assessing what future loss to dependants would have been.
DOWLING V. JEDOS
Unreported Sup. Ct. 30 March 1977

Walsh J. (for the Court):

On the 23rd May, 1973, Jeremiah Dowling was killed in the course of his employment at the defendants' factory at Monkstown in the County of Cork. The death was caused by the negligence of the defendant company. The plaintiff in these proceedings is the mother of the late Jeremiah Dowling and is a dependant within the meaning of the Civil Liability Act, 1961. She brought the action for the benefit of herself and of the dependants of the deceased.

The action was heard at Cork by Mr. Justice Murnaghan sitting without a jury. The learned trial judge found that in addition to the plaintiff nine other persons qualified as dependants of the deceased. He assessed damages in respect of the injury resulting from the death of the deceased in the sum of £3,060, which included £135.75 for funeral and other expenses. For mental distress resulting from the death of the deceased to the ten dependants the judge assessed compensation in the sum of £940. The total sum for damages and compensation for mental distress was £4,000.

The plaintiff has appealed against this award and has asked this Court to set it aside. She claims in the notice of appeal that the trial judge failed to have regard to the evidence of the actuary in assessing the amounts of damages proportioned to the injury resulting from the death to each of the dependants and that the total sum awarded was perverse, inadequate and against the weight of the evidence. It was also claimed that the trial judge had regard to matters not raised in the evidence and not forming part of the evidence.

According to the evidence the deceased was born on the 7th July, 1955. His death therefore occurred approximately six weeks before his eighteenth birthday. He had been employed by the defendants for five or six months prior to his death. He was employed as a helper in industrial cleaning and was employed at an hourly rate, apparently payable according to the number of hours he worked. His wages for the last six weeks of his life were £18.75, £14.50, £38.75, £14.88, £19 and £19.25 per week respectively. The differences in the sums reflect the difference in the number of hours worked. According to the evidence he would in all probability have continued in employment, if not in the direct employment of the defendants then in the direct employment of main contractors for whom the defendants worked. He was one of nine children born to his parents. The eldest child was born in 1949. Further children were later born, including the deceased and his twin brother. The deceased had no girl friend and there was no evidence to suggest that he was contemplating marriage in the near future. His elder brother was married at the age of twenty-one. One of his sisters was married at the age of twenty-two and none of the other brothers or sisters was married. The plaintiff was married at the age of nineteen and her husband at the age of twenty-two.

The deceased paid about £12 a week to his mother and the net value to the family of his contribution was £8. An actuary who gave evidence on behalf of the plaintiff, and who gave the only actuarial evidence offered in the case, made certain calculations which were based on the assumption that the net weekly contribution of the deceased to the family at the date of death was £8 a week. The calculation allowed for the fact that the deceased's parents were alive and were based on a rate of interest of 5% and allowed for the probability of the deceased marrying in due course in accordance with the statistics derived from the 1971 Irish Census Returns which apparently were the last available census returns. On that basis the multiplier offered by the actuary was the sum of £516 capital value for each pound per week. It was clear from his evidence that the figure was based on an assumption of the probability of the marriage of the deceased in accordance with the pattern afforded by the statistics. From a purely mathematical point of view, however, the calculations were based on the probability of his not being married each year in the future and therefore the average age of marriage would not come into a calculation based on the probability of marriage in accordance with statistics.

On the assumption that the deceased would have married at the age of twenty-two then the multiplier upon the actuarial evidence would be £280 for each pound loss and if the marriage took place at the age of twenty-three it would be approximately £320. At the age of twenty-four it would be approximately £370. Referring to his figure based on the probability of marriage in accordance with the statistics of the Census Returns the actuary gave the following answer:

> 'In that in my other calculations, in considering loss, I allowed for the probability of marriage over the three years up to now, but if we are talking of marriage at 22, 23 or 24, I do not have to allow for that in the tots.'

All the figures given by the actuary were based on an assumption that upon marriage the contribution of the deceased to his family would cease.

In the course of his judgment giving the reasons for his decision the learned trial judge expressed himself as being 'quite satisfied that the reasonable probability in this case is that certainly – and I emphasise the word "certainly" – by the time he reached the age of twenty-three the deceased would have left home and probably would have got married, by the time he would have reached the age of twenty-three, the picture of the family as they existed on the date of his death would have changed quite considerably in the interval between his death and his attaining the age of twenty-three if he lived.' He therefore took the figure of £320 as being the multiplier for marriage or departure from home at the age of twenty-three and added 10% to it in accordance with the suggestion of the actuary by adding 10% for adjustment. That gave the judge a multiplier of approximately £350 which he multiplied by eight to give him the figure of £2,800. He awarded £940 for the mental distress and the total with the funeral and other testamentary expenses standing at £135.75 made a total of £3,875.75 which the judge rounded off to the sum of £4,000.

If there was evidence on which the judge could reasonably hold that the probability was that the boy wold have married or left home at the age of twenty-three then no fault could be found with the judge's reasoning or his figures. In view of the fact that the deceased was not quite eighteen years old at the date of his death and that there was no direct evidence of any kind touching upon his intentions in so far as marriage was concerned the only evidence available to the judge was what might be called the family pattern of marriage, namely, the early age of marriage of each of the parents of the deceased and of his brother and sister. In my opinion that is insufficient evidence upon which to base a finding of the reasonable probability in the case being that the deceased would have married or would have left home at the age of twenty-three. There was no evidence whatever of the boy's views on matrimony or of the family's views on matrimony or of any discussion between the deceased and the members of his family with regard to the probability or even possibility of marriage. The only evidence was that of the example of early marriage offered in the cases of his parents and of his brother and sister. Such evidence is not sufficient to take the matter outside the realm of conjecture or speculation, although such conjecture or speculation would not be without foundation. However, such conjecture is not sufficient to warrant the finding made by the learned trial judge on this matter. One has every sympathy with the position in which the trial judge found himself called upon to deal with a matter in respect of which there was such a paucity of evidence. But the lack of such evidence may not be the fault of anyone because if evidence does not exist it cannot be produced. In a fatal case the deceased is not there to be questioned as to his future intentions as would be the position in a case where a person had been so grievously injured that all future prospects of marriage had been ruled out by the injury. This type of problem is peculiar to fatal cases or cases in which the injuries have been so great that the plaintiff in a non-fatal case has been rendered unfit or unable to give any evidence and no other evidence exists. What then is a court to do in such a situation? In my view a court then can only have resort to such probable pattern as may reasonably be deduced from available statistics and indeed the court must have resort to such evidence in the absence of more direct evidence.

In the present case the actuary was not asked any detailed questions either in direct examination or cross-examination about the quality of the statistics or the particular patterns which might be deduced from them such as for example the difference in the marriage patterns of rural dwellers and urban dwellers. The deceased was one of the latter. In the present case it may well be that neither the plaintiff's side nor the defendants' side really expected anything more to happen than a figure being awarded more or less in accordance with the figure the actuary gave. That, however, does not absolve the plaintiff from the primary duty of discharging the necessary burden of proof which in this case would, in my view, require not merely the evidence given by the actuary but a more detailed analysis of that evidence than was in fact given. The learned trial judge stated that he specifically rejected the statistical basis 'as realistically providing a reasonable probability of the age at which the deceased would have married.' While I think the learned judge was wrong in principle in taking this view of the statistical evidence, I can appreciate the degree of exasperation he may have felt at the remarkable paucity of evidence in the case. It appears to me, however, that he misunderstood the nature of the actuarial evidence and that is indicated by his reference to the evidence as being unable to realistically provide a reasonable probability of the age at which the deceased would have married. It had already been explained in evidence by the actuary that the figure in question was based on a calculation which related particularly to a case of a person who was unmarried but who would probably get married in accordance with the statistics and was not based upon a calculation of an average of marriage.

For the reasons I have given I am of opinion that a new trial should be ordered in respect of the damages resulting from the loss of dependancy. If the non-statistical actuarial evidence is in no better condition than it was at the trial before the learned trial judge in the present case then in my view the statistical evidence must be analysed by the necessary witness in far greater detail so as to isolate, as nearly as possible, the picture which would be most referable to the position of the deceased, his environment, his station in life, his prospects and, so far as is possible, be based on the most up-to-date figures available. It is now approximately six years since the census of 1971. While no census has been taken since then, if other figures are available which can be reasonably relied upon they should also be adduced or alternatively evidence should be given to indicate that no reliable figures which could be safely used are available.

So far as the figure awarded for mental distress is concerned it is not possible to detect upon what evidence or basis the judge arrived at the particular figure which he awarded. The total which he awarded was £940 and the maximum permitted under the statute is £1,000. It has, however, already been pointed out in this Court in *McCarthy* v. *Walsh* [1965] I. R. 246 that this figure of £1,000 is not to be regarded as being available only for the worst possible case and accordingly it would be incorrect to approach all cases less serious than the worst possible case on the assumption that £1,000 could never be awarded. In my view, the correct approach is for the judge to make a notional award in the sum which he would on the evidence be justified in giving to each of the persons who suffered mental distress without taking into account at that stage that the maximum possible total is £1,000. When the notional figures have been arrived [at,] if their total exceeds £1,000 then as the ratio between them is already known they should be scaled down proportionately so that the total is reduced to £1,000. It does not appear to me that this was the method followed in the present case and for that reason I would direct that the compensation for mental distress should be re-assessed.

In the result I would allow the appeal and make the order sought, namely, to set aside the award and direct a new trial on the issue of damages and compensation for mental distress.

Questions

What kind of evidence should be given as regards future marriage prospects of the deceased? Who should give the evidence? Statisticians? Sociologists? Psychologists? Family friends and relations?

Difficulties in assessing future loss in certain cases e.g. where deceased was a self-employed farmer.

O'SULLIVAN V. C.I.E.
[1978] I.R. 409

The plaintiff's husband was killed when a tractor which he was driving was in collision with a C.I.E. lorry.

Murnaghan J. (High Court):

. . .

Having considered the submissions made by counsel for the plaintiff and by counsel for the defendants on this question, I am clear that the proper approach is to ascertain as accurately as is possible:–

1. The income of the deceased. In the case of a wage earner this is relatively simple; the question becomes difficult, and at times very difficult, in the case of self-employed persons such as farmers, shopkeepers, or professional people, particularly where no adequate accounts are kept.

2. In the majority of cases, it is necessary to discover how much of the deceased's income was brought into the household for the benefit of the household.

3. In other cases, one must discover how much of the deceased's income, apart from what was contributed to the household, was contributed to the upkeep of any other 'member of the family' within the meaning of that expression in s. 47 sub-s. 1, of the Act of 1961.

4. The part of the sum contributed by the deceased to his or her household which must be attributed to the maintenance and upkeep of the deceased in the household.

5. The manner in which the amount contributed by the deceased to the household, less the amount attributed to his or her own maintenance and upkeep, should be allocated among the surviving members of the household and, where appropriate, any other 'member of the family' of the deceased.

6. The actual loss sustained by the 'dependants,' as defined by s. 47 sub-s. 1, between the date of death of the deceased and the hearing of the action.

7. The interest on the amount found in para. 6 to the date of the hearing.

8. The future financial loss, calculated on an actuarial basis on the findings under paras. 1–5, taking into account an estimation of the reasonable probabilities of a future increase (if any) on such findings.

9. The saving which the deceased was able to make.

10. The material benefits (if any) which came to the 'dependants' by reason of the death of the deceased.

I have said many times before, and I now repeat that it should be made obvious that assessments and calculations on the general basis indicated by Kingsmill Moore J. and, in addition, on the further bases which I have indicated are not suitable matters to be determined by a jury. In my experience, no matter what instructions are given by the trial judge, a jury is generally incapable of approaching a consideration of all the questions involved in coming to a proper decision in cases such as the present. This case is itself an excellent example of how difficult it is, even for a judge, to make a correct estimation of the actual financial loss. If a jury has a function at all in this type of case, in my opinion that function should be restricted to the assessment of the amount of damages for 'mental distress' which, by virtue of s. 49, sub-s. 1(*a*) (ii), of the Act of 1961 is reserved to the judge. The amount found by a jury for 'mental distress', if it exceeded the maximum, could be scaled down by the judge so that the total would not exceed the total amount of £1,000 fixed by s. 49, sub-s. 1(*b*), of the Act of 1961.

The appeal to the Supreme Court from this judgment was dismissed.

Griffin J.:

On the 2nd April, 1974, a collision occurred at Farranfore in the county of Kerry between a tractor driven by Timothy O'Sullivan (the husband of the plaintiff) and a motor lorry which was the property of the defendants. As a result of the collision, the plaintiff's husband received injuries from which he died on the same day. This action is brought by the plaintiff to recover the loss which has been suffered by her and her four young children (one of whom was born posthumously) as a result of the death of her husband. The action was tried at Cork by Mr. Justice Murnaghan sitting without a jury on the 29th and 30th July, 1976. Liability was not contended by the defendants.

In his reserved judgment the trial judge assessed the damages, in respect of the injury resulting to the dependants from the death of the deceased, as the sum of £21,139.50p. The plaintiff has appealed to this Court from that judgment. The relevant facts are sufficiently set out in the judgment of the trial judge and it is not necessary for me to repeat them.

By virtue of the provisions of s. 49, sub-s. 1 (*a*), of the Civil Liability Act, 1961, the damages to be recovered by the dependants of the deceased (apart from compensation for mental distress and funeral and other expenses actually incurred by the deceased or the personal representative by reason of the wrongful act of the defendants, in respect of which there is no dispute in this case) are 'the total of such amounts (if any) as the jury or the judge, as the case may be, shall consider proportioned to the injury resulting from the death to each of the dependants, respectively, for whom or on whose behalf the action is brought.' Accordingly, the damages are to be based on the reasonable expectation of pecuniary benefit or other benefit which can be reduced to a monetary value. It is to be noted that the action is given to the dependants as individuals, so that each of them is entitled to be compensated for the loss resulting to him personally. How this loss should have been ascertained by the trial judge is the question that arises in this appeal. The plaintiff alleges that the trial judge erred in principle in adopting the method which he applied and in not adopting one or other of two alternative methods which were proposed by the plaintiff.

At the trial the plaintiff's case was presented on three alternative bases, *i.e.*, what were called the conventional method of assessing the loss, the differential basis and the capitalised value of the service of the deceased. In respect of each basis, it was assumed by the plaintiff's actuary that each of the four children would have been dependant on the deceased until it was twenty years old and that, upon each child reaching that age, one half of what had been expended on that child would have reverted to the wife and one half to the husband. The defendants' actuary acted on the same assumption. Further, Dr. Bielenberg, an agricultural economist, called on behalf of the plaintiff, gave it as his opinion that profits from dairy farming increased by some 50% between the years 1974 and 1976, and both actuaries took this into account in their calculations.

In assessing the damages under s. 49, sub-s. 1 (*a*) (i), of the Act of 1961 (i.e., those excluding the undisputed amounts), the trial judge adopted the conventional method of assessing the loss to the dependants. He ascertained, as best he could, the contributions of the deceased in money, services and kind to his wife and children for their support and maintenance; and he capitalised these by applying appropriate actuarial multipliers. This was the manner in which the plaintiff's case was made in the pleadings. Very detailed particulars had been sought by the defendants and were furnished by the plaintiff. This information was to the effect that at the time of his death the deceased was contributing on average the sum of £30 per week towards the expenses of the family household (which included the deceased) and that, in addition, he was providing vegetables and turf which were valued at £3 per week. He had purchased a car in 1971 for approximately £1,000, and this car was used in the main by the deceased. In relation to the £33 per week which the deceased contributed to the household, the defendants' actuary proposed an apportionment of £10 per week towards the support of the plaintiff, an apportionment of £4 per week towards that of each child (including the posthumous child), and £7 per week towards the support of the deceased. In addition, he proposed a sum of £5 per week in respect of the plaintiff's loss of the use of the family car, thus bringing her weekly loss up to £15. Having regard to Dr. Bielenberg's evidence in relation to the increase of 50% in dairying profits between 1974 and 1976, this actuary considered that it was reasonable to assume that the contributions of the deceased to the household would have increased in the same proportion, if he had lived. Accordingly, this actuary added 50% to his figures to bring them up to 1976 values and arrived at a sum of £22.50 per week towards the plaintiff's support and £6 per week towards that of each of the four children, which made a total of £46.50 per week. These amounts were then capitalised by the application of the multipliers set out in the judgment of the trial judge, and this produced a gross loss of £38,660.

In applying the conventional method, the plaintiff's actuary approached the problem in a somewhat different way. Dr. Bielenberg had given evidence that a profit of £4,383 p.a. (or £84 per week) might reasonably be expected from a well-run dairy farm of 56 acres in 1976. The sum of £84 per week was distributed by him as to £60 for the support of the plaintiff and as to £6 for the support of each child, and he capitalised these sums to produce a gross loss of £77,000.

Faced with this evidence from the two actuaries, the trial judge had to make a choice; he accepted the approach and the calculations made by the defendant's actuary. He was entitled to do so and, in my view, he was quite justified in doing so. The notional sum of £84 per week represented gross *profit*, which is not to be equated with gross *loss*. Assuming that the deceased, if he had lived, would have made that profit, he himself would require to be supported and maintained out of it. No deduction was made for his own support and maintenance, although approximately £60 per week had been allowed for the support of his wife. Again, as the trial judge accepted, there was an unrealistic division amongst the members of the household of the notional amount coming into the household each week. In addition, the multipliers used by the plaintiff's actuary were significantly higher than those of the defendants' actuary. They had been calculated on the basis of the full amount of the future loss, discounted back to the date of death, with the addition of interest from the date of death to the date of trial; the future loss was calculated on the notional losses in 1976, which were almost double the notional losses in 1974. The defendants' multipliers were obtained by discounting all future losses back to the date of trial, and by accumulating past losses, with interest added, from the date of death to the date of trial – past losses are capable of reasonably accurate assertainment taking into account all the events that have occurred between the date of the death of the deceased and the date of trial. The trial judge accepted the method of calculating the multipliers adapted by the defendants' actuary and in my opinion, he was quite correct in doing so. When an appropriate allowance is made for the support and maintenance of the deceased, and a more realistic distribution amongst the members of the family is made of the notional amount coming into the household, and when the correct multipliers are used, the figure of £77,000 is reduced to a figure somewhat less than the £38,660 calculated by the defendant's actuary.

As the deceased died intestate, the plaintiff became entitled to two thirds of the estate and the four children became entitled to one twelfth each, pursuant to s. 67, sub-s. 2, of the Succession Act, 1965. The deceased owned 44 acres of land at the date of his death. He had applied to the Land Commission for additional land and the application was successful so that he was in the process of getting 12 acres which adjoined his own lands; but this 12 acres was not allotted until a few months after his death. The agreed value of the assets on the basis of a 44 acre farm (but excluding the value of the family dwelling-house and the curtilage of approximately 2 acres) was £29,458. From the sum of £38,660, which he accepted as the gross loss, the trial judge deducted the sum of £23,566 in respect of the assets left by the deceased and inherited by the plaintiff and the four children.

The plaintiff submitted that no deduction should have been made in respect of the value of the assets inherited by the plaintiff and the children. In computing the loss suffered by the dependants, the actual pecuniary loss of each individual entitled to sue can only be ascertained, as stated (p. 612) by Lord Wright in *Davies* v. *Powell Duffryn Associated Collieries* [1942] A.C. 601, by balancing, on the one hand, the loss to him of the future pecuniary benefit and, on the other, any pecuniary advantage which comes to him by reason of the death. It is well settled that the assets of the deceased which pass to the dependants must be taken into account. Section 50 of the Act of 1961 provides that, in assessing damages, account should not be taken of any sum payable on the death of the deceased under any contract of insurance or of any pension, gratuity or any other like benefit payable under statute or otherwise in consequence of the death of the deceased. This section is identical in terms with, and replaced, s. 5 of the Fatal Injuries Act, 1956. In *Byrne* v. *Houlihan* [1966] I.R. 274 at p. 278 of the report, Kingsmill Moore J. said:– 'That in computing the "injury resulting from the death" gains are in general to be set off against losses is shown by s. 5 [*of the Fatal Injuries Act, 1956*] which, by specifically excluding from such computation certain benefits by way of insurance monies and pensions, implies that benefits not so expressly excluded must be taken into account.' His observations apply equally to s. 50 of the Act of 1961.

However, in the case of a farm or a family business, the value to be put on deductible assets can present some difficulty. In the instant case, if the deceased had lived out his normal span and had been survived by the plaintiff, it is reasonably certain that the farm would have gone to the plaintiff or to the plaintiff and some, at least, of the children. In any event, by surviving the deceased the plaintiff would have been entitled to one third of his estate pursuant to s. 111, sub-s. 2 of the Succession Act, 1965. Therefore there was acceleration in the timing of the receipt of the inheritance and it is only that acceleration which should be taken into account in valuing deductible assets. According to the valuation of the acceleration made by the plaintiff's actuary, almost the entire of the £29,458 should be deducted from the gross loss to obtain the net loss. The evidence of the defendants' actuary was to the effect that he would normally deduct only 80% of the value of the assets but that in this case, as the loss of support was being valued in 1976 values, the value of the assets (which were valued as of 1974) should likewise be increased to 1976 values and that, as that increase and the reduction due to the fact that only the acceleration should be taken into account almost exactly balanced each other out, the entire of the 1974 value of the assets should be deducted. The value of the assets on the basis of a 56 acre farm was agreed to be £35,458. As the *loss* to the dependants was calculated on the basis of a 56 acre farm, it is reasonable that the *asset value* should also be based on 56 acres and not 44 acres. It is to be noted that the value of the house and the curtilage of 2 acres was very properly excluded from the deductible assets. The house was the family home; if it were sold, the plaintiff would have to find another house so there is no element of 'gain' to the family in inheriting the house: see *Heatly* v. *Steel Company of Wales* [1953] 1 W.L.R. 405.

In arriving at his valuation of the acceleration, the trial judge did not accept the opinion of either actuary. He measured the acceleration by taking 80% of £29,458 which gives a figure of £23,566 to be deducted. This he stated to be a somewhat arbitrary percentage. For myself I would be inclined to deduct only two thirds of the value of the assets but, as this also is an arbitrary figure, it could not be said that the trial judge's figure of 80% was wrong in principle. However, the trial judge did in fact deduct approximately two thirds of the value of the estate since, in making his calculations, he apparently overlooked the fact that the value of the additional 12 acres was omitted from the value of the assets. This is understandable because the particulars on which the value was based were taken from the schedule of assets, which had not included the 12 acres. The correct value of the assets was £35,458 and not £29,458 so that the trial judge deducted only £23,566 from the total value of £35,458. In doing so, he did not err in principle in my view.

The amount of the deduction made in respect of assets was also criticised in that it was alleged that it failed to take into account the probable future savings of the deceased; alternatively, it was said that if a deduction is made for acceleration then an addition to the award should be made for the loss of future savings. In my view, this criticism was not warranted on the facts proved. Undoubtedly, the value of the dependancy can include not only that part of the earnings of a deceased which he would have expended in maintaining his dependants, but also that part of his earnings which he would have saved and which would most likely have come to his dependants on his death in any event. But appropriate evidence should be led on behalf of the plaintiff if a claim is to be made in respect of future savings. In this case, the evidence of the plaintiff on the question of savings was given at questions 71 to 73. The effect of this evidence was that she and her husband first saved for a car, then for a tractor, and that some machinery had been purchased; but no effort whatever was made to quantify any savings, other than to say that the car cost £1,000. The savings were stated to have been kept in a bank account and used when necessary, but no effort was made to produce the account or to give any evidence in relation to it. There was no material upon which evaluation of any savings might be calculated. The defendants' actuary, in his calculations, did build into his figures an element of saving in respect of the car as his figures allowed for the capitalisation of £7.50 per week in respect of the loss by the plaintiff of the use of the car. If an effort had been made to quantify any savings, it would have been possible for the actuaries to calculate the value of probable future savings. Indeed, the defendants' actuary, when asked about savings by counsel for the plaintiff at question 579, stated that he was unable to put a value on any savings as he was given no figures. As no figures were available, the trial judge cannot be blamed for having failed to include a capital sum in respect of future savings.

In the result, the sum of £23,566 was deducted from the gross loss of £38,660, which left a net loss of £15,094; as that figure was based on a farm of 44 acres, the loss on 56 acres was calculated to be £19,210. The trial judge then distributed that sum amongst the wife and children and arrived at the figures set forth in his judgment.

The two alternative methods of calculation which were proposed by the plaintiff i.e., the differential basis and the capitalised value of the services of the deceased (either of which, they allege, should have been used) can be dealt with briefly.

The differential basis. As a result of the death of her husband, the plaintiff, as trial judge found, is unable to carry on the farm as a dairy farm and, by the time of the trial, she had changed over to dry stock. According to Dr. Bielenberg, the differential between running this farm as a dairy farm by the deceased had he been alive to run it, and as a dry stock farm by the plaintiff, for the years 1974, 1975 and 1976 was £24 per week, £31 per week, and £46 per week respectively. The plaintiff's actuary capitalised this difference at £42,618. This calculation, however, made no allowance for the support of the deceased, who would have had to be supported and maintained out of the profits of the dairy farm. When the cost of his support and maintenance is taken into account, and the correct multipliers used, this figure is reduced to £18,158 and if it is assumed that as little as £1.50 per week out of the profits of the additional 12 acres would have gone to the deceased, the loss would be £16,324 – both sums being less than the plaintiff was awarded in damages.

The loss of services of the deceased. If the plaintiff decided to carry on the more profitable business of dairy farming, it would have been necessary for her to employ labour to do so. Dr. Bielenberg estimated the cost of replacing the labour of the deceased on a farm of 56 acres would be the sum of £49.75 per week in 1976. For the purpose of estimating the net loss and of capitalisation thereof, it would be necessary to deduct from the £49.75 the cost of the support and maintenance of the deceased. The plaintiff's actuary, who proposed this basis of calculation, estimated the cost of maintaining the deceased at £4.75 per week, leaving a net balance of £45 per week. In respect of the £45 per week, he allocated £25 to the wife, and £5 per week to each of the four children. He capitalised these sums at £41,640, again using the higher (and incorrect) multipliers. Under cross-examination, the actuary was invited to justify the sum of £4.75 to support the husband when £25 was allowed for the wife and £5 was allowed for each of the four childen. The £4.75 was explained as 'a notional accounting figure which the farm accounts will show when they come to be made for income tax purposes.' Allocating £4.75 per week for the husband, who would have to be fully clothed, fed, and maintained out of it, and who was a moderate drinker, bore no relation whatever to reality and this view was apparently taken by the trial judge who was, in my opinion, fully justified in rejecting it. If a realistic sum were allocated to the support and maintenance of the deceased, the capitalization of the remainder, using the correct multipliers, would produce a figure considerably less than that awarded by the trial judge. Therefore, there would have been no advantage to the plaintiff in adopting this method or the differential basis.

Before the Court can interfere with the award of damages by the trial judge, it must be satisfied that he has acted on a wrong principle of law, or that he has misunderstood the facts, or that he has made a wholly erroneous assessment (whether inadequately or excessively) of the loss suffered by the dependants. There is no one method of arriving at the appropriate damages which is suitable to all circumstances as each case must depend on its own facts. In any given case, the jury or trial judge must apply the method which appears most suitable to that case. In this case, the method adopted by the trial judge in arriving at his figures was a reasonable one: it led him to a reasonable conclusion and the damages awarded by him were within the reasonable range of awards which might be made in respect of the loss to the dependants. Accordingly, I would dismiss this appeal.

There is one matter mentioned by the trial judge on which I should like to comment. The trial judge expressed the opinion that this type of case is one which is inappropriate for trial by jury; I am in entire agreement with his observations. With rare exceptions, cases of this type require reasonable familiarity with, and an appreciation of, actuarial calculations. When they are tried by a judge sitting without a jury it is usual, by consent, to have copies of the actuaries' reports made available to the judge: in this case there were six reports, all of which were made available for the use of the judge. The trial judge found it necessary to reserve judgment in this case although he had the assistance of the reports, which a jury probably would not have had. Had the case been tried by a jury, the jury, after a comparatively short retirement, would have been expected to bring in a verdict assessing the loss to each of the dependants, without having the benefit of the actuaries' reports and with little or no appreciation of the methods whereby the actuaries arrived at their conclusions under the different approaches to the problem of the loss. Trial by jury of matters such as this are not conducive to the due administration of justice.

Henchy and **Parke JJ.** concurred.

Should the expectation which the children had in benefiting from their father, the plaintiff, be taken into account in assessing the extent of their dependency?
Meaning of 'funeral and other expenses'

BYRNE V. HOULIHAN & DE COURCY
[1966] I.R. 274

Kingsmill Moore J.:

This action was brought by the plaintiff, as personal representative of his dead wife, claiming damages under the provisions of the Fatal Injuries Act, 1956, on behalf of himself and the other dependants of his wife who was killed as a result of the negligence of the defendants. That the death was caused by the 'wrongful act, neglect, or default' of the defendants was not, and is not, challenged. The grounds of the appeal are that the damages awarded to the several dependents were grossly excessive and that the learned Judge misdirected the jury as to matters which should be taken into account in arriving at the amount of their award.

The action was brought on behalf of ten alleged dependants. It is only necessary to mention those in respect of whom the jury made awards, namely, the five sons of the deceased, aged, respectively, at the date of their mother's death, 21, 19½, 16, 13½ and 8.

To them the jury awarded damages as follows: to the first and second sons, £500, each; to the third son, £1,800; to the fourth son, £3,500; and to the fifth son, £700.

The deceased woman was aged 50 when she died and her husband, the plaintiff, was then aged 55. He was a bank manager, earning, at that date, between his salary, a rank allowance and insurance commissions, about £1,250 per year, a sum which has since increased to about £1,375. In addition, he had a free house, fuel and light. His wife owned 1,376 shares in a private company and their value at the date is agreed to have been about £9,000. They paid a very handsome dividend of £550 per year, free of tax, and continue to pay this amount. As his wife died intestate, these valuable shares passed in their entirety to her husband, the plaintiff, and the children got nothing.

The contention put forward on behalf of the children is that, having regard to the normal social conventions, traditions and mores which prevail in an Irish family in the upper middle class range, the children had a reasonable expectation of sharing in the income of their mother's property during her life and of succeeding eventually to the capital under her will, an expectation of which they have been deprived by her sudden death intestate. The probability of sharing in such benefits was to some degree enhanced by evidence that the deceased had talked of her intention of transferring property to her children before her death so as to avoid death duties, but, as her husband was due to retire within ten years on a very modest pension, it would seem likely that the wife's money would have been needed to keep up the family establishment.

An examination of the aptitudes and prospects of the children suggests that they were likely to receive, or have applied for their benefit, some portion of the income of the fund. The two elder children are now earning for themselves but their remuneration is not large and they could expect some occasional small subventions. The youngest is a bright boy who has still to be educated. Of the remaining two, one is slightly retarded and does not show any avidity for work. It was planned to send him to a relative in Australia in the hope that the more energising climate – natural and social of that continent might help to activate him. This plan would involve at least the provision of an outfit and journey expenses. The remaining boy is definitely retarded and might easily become a permanent charge on the family exchequer. The primary obligation to meet such expenditure, as I have indicated, would be on the father, but it would be reasonable to expect that a mother with an independent income would assist and she had already shown a willingness so to do, having incurred an overdraft of £1,100 for monies which she had applied to family purposes, in particular the education of the children.

It seems to me that a jury could properly come to the conclusion that the children, but for their mother's untimely death, would eventually have inherited the bulk of their mother's capital, though probably not till after the death of the father and meantime would have received some assistance out of the income of the shares.

The defendants do not seriously contest these assumptions but say that the sums awarded are grossly excessive. In the first place, they say that there is not sufficient discount for the present payment of a benefit which was likely to be postponed to a distant future. The deceased was aged 50, the husband 55. Though no actuarial evidence was offered the probability would be that the death of the survivor would not have occurred for at least 15 or 20 years and it was not likely that the capital would become available till after the death of the survivor. The necessary discount would, it was suggested, reduce the present value to something like half of the £9,000. Secondly, they say that, as the whole of the property of the deceased passed by reason of her death to the husband, the children would have a reasonable expectation that they would receive from their father, whose obligation to look after his children was as great if not greater than that of the mother, as substantial benefits out of her fortune as if she had not been killed. This expectation has been diminished by the second marriage of the father, but a jury might well think that it is still very considerable. The learned trial Judge ruled and instructed the jury that expectations from the father were to be left out of account. This ruling and direction are said to be erroneous, and they form a principal ground of appeal. The authorities on the subject are not conclusive.

The relevant Irish statute is the Fatal Injuries Act, 1956, entitled 'An Act to make better provision for compensating members of the family of any person killed by the wrongful act or default of another.' The action is one 'for damages for the benefit of the dependants of the deceased' (s.3 sub-s. 1) and the damages 'shall be the total of such amounts as the jury or the judge, as the case may be, may think proportioned to the injury resulting from the death to each of the dependants, respectively, for whom or on whose behalf the action is brought, and each such amount shall be separately indicated in the award' (s. 4, sub-s.1). In addition, it is provided that damages may be awarded in respect of funeral and other expenses actually incurred by the deceased, the dependants or the personal representative by reason of the wrongful act, neglect or default (s.4, sub-s. 2); and that in assessing damages account shall not be taken of any sum payable on the death of the deceased under any contract of insurance or 'any pension, gratuity or other like benefit payable under statute or otherwise in consequence of the death of the deceased' (sect. 5).

From the wording of the Act itself certain deductions may be made. There is to be no punitive element in the damages – they are by way of 'compensation'. As they are given not to all members of a family but only to dependants, and as they are to be proportioned to the injury resulting from the death to each of the dependants, there is a clear indication that the compensation is to be based on monetary loss of prospective benefits and does not include a '*solatium.*' [Remedied in the 1961 Act, *Eds*.] That in computing the 'injury resulting from the death' gains are in general to be set off against losses is shown by s. 5 which, by specifically excluding from such computation certain benefits by way of insurance monies and pensions implies that benefits not so expressly excluded must be taken into account.

The Act, apart from the provisions of s. 5 and the inclusion of funeral and other expenses in the compensation, follows in general the model of the Fatal Accidents Act, 1846, commonly known as Lord Campbell's Act, and the Fatal Accidents Act, 1864. The wording 'damages . . . proportioned to the injury resulting from such death to the parties respectively for whom and for whose benefits such action shall be brought,' occurs in s. 2 of Lord Campbell's Act, and it was agreed by counsel that our Act must have been drafted with the knowledge of decisions given under the earlier Act and must be construed in the light of such decisions.

Before Lord Campbell's Act, the law was that 'in a civil Court, the death of a human being could not be complained of as an injury . . .': *Baker v. Bolton* 1 Camp. 493; and the cause of action introduced by the Act was accepted as being ' . . . new in its species, new in its quality, new in its principle, in every way new . . .' *Seward* v. *Vera Cruz*, 16 App. Cas, 59, per Lord Blackburn, at p. 70. Six years after the passing of Lord Campbell's Act it was decided by the Court of Queen's Bench, with Lord Campbell himself presiding, that damages could only be given under the Act for loss admitting of a pecuniary estimate and that nothing could be given by way of *solatium*: *Blake* v. *Midland Railway Company* 18 Q.B. 93. Four years later, in *Dalton* v. *South Eastern Railway Company* 4 C.B. (N.S.) 296, Willes J. held that in computing damages, not merely pecuniary loss which could be proved to have occurred but the reasonable expectation of pecuniary advantage if the deceased had not been killed must be taken into account, and damages could be given for loss of such expectation. This view was upheld in the Exchequer Chamber in *Pym* v. *Great Northern Railway Company* 4 B & S.396 where Erle C.J., with whom the other members of the Court concurred said (at p. 406) that the jury must consider if there was ' . . . evidence of a reasonable probability of pecuniary benefit to the parties if the death of the deceased had not occurred: and was it lost by reason of that death . . .' The same case established that any pecuniary benefits arising by reason of the death must be set off against the loss of financial benefit or the deprivation of a reasonable expectation of such benefit. On this principle deductions were regularly made where an insurance or a pension became payable by reason of the death, until subsequent legislation provided that these items were to be disregarded. All these principles were recognised in this court by Kennedy C.J. and FitzGibbon J. in *Gallagher* v. *Electricity Supply Board* [1933] I. R. 55S.

If pecuniary benefits arising by reason of the death are to be set off against pecuniary loss incurred thereby, and if not merely actual and demonstrable loss but the loss of reasonable expectation of benefit is to form the ground of damages, I can see no logical reason why the gain of a reasonable expectation of benefit by reason of the death should not also form a subject of set-off. As I have pointed out the Act is designed to give compensation to dependants and damages are to be proportionate to the injury resulting to the dependants from the death. If by reason of the death, a dependant loses a reasonable expectation of benefit from the deceased and at the same time gains a reasonable expectation of benefit from another person, the injury resulting from the death must be the loss on balancing of the two expectations. This seems to have been the view of all the members of the Court in *Baker* v. *Dalgleish Shipping Company* [1922] I. K. B. 361. In that case the question was whether there should be a deduction from the damages to be given to a widow because, on the death of the deceased husband under circumstances giving rise to a claim under the Fatal Accidents Act, 1846, a pension became payable to the widow from the Crown. The pension was voluntary, could be (but was unlikely to be) withdrawn, and might be reduced if there was a substantial award of damages in the action. Bankes L.J. says at p.368: 'I cannot myself see why, when assessing compensation under Lord Campbell's Act, any distinction should be drawn between an assessment of what is a reasonable expectation of benefit had the deceased person lived, and what is reasonable expectation of benefit in consequence of the deceased person's death. Both must be taken into consideration in arriving at the real loss. Both may legitimately, in my opinion, be arrived at by the same process.' Scrutton L.J. says at p.372:– 'Just as in assessing the loss by the death the probability of voluntary contribution destroyed by the death of the contributor may be included to swell the claim, so the probability of voluntary contribution bestowed in consequence of the death may be used to reduce the claim by showing what loss the claimant has in fact sustained by the death.' Younger L.J. held that the probability of future payments of a pension arising from the death, even though such payments were voluntary and could be discontinued (an unlikely contingency), must be taken into account in reduction of the amount to be awarded.

Counsel for the plaintiff relied on *Peacock* v. *Amusement Equipment Co. Ltd.* [1954] 2 Q. B. 347. In that case a husband had been living with his wife in a house where she carried on a small business out of which she maintained him and herself, though he was earning substantial wages from an outside employment. She was killed in an accident which gave rise to a claim under the Fatal Accidents Acts, 1846–1908. By her will she had left the house to her two children by a former marriage. They sold the house and out of the proceeds made a voluntary gift to the plaintiff of £575. The defendant in the action sought to have this sum deducted from the amount which would otherwise have been payable as damages to the plaintiff. It was held that the sum should not be deducted as it was attributable to the spontaneous generosity of the children and was not a sum which he could have had any reasonable expectation of receiving as a result of his wife's death. Somervell L.J. in *Baker v. Dalgleish Steam Shipping Company* [1922] 1 K.B. 361 goes on to say, at p. 353: '. . . in considering whether claims other than claims of legal right are to be brought in, whether payments have been made or not, it is important to consider the position as at the time of the death: Was there at that time any probability or reasonable expectation of a benefit? Applying that test to the present case, I think that it is plain on the evidence that there was none. These stepchildren were evidently fond of their father and they realised that he had benefited from their mother's business and they determined out of the assets realised to make a present, but there was no expectation by him of a present when the deceased died.' Birkett L.J. says, at p. 355:– 'When it turned out that he (the husband) was not even mentioned in the wife's will he certainly had no expectations that he would receive any part of what his wife left.' In his view the payment, being a mere expression of generosity was not such a payment as should be taken into account. In the circumstances it was not money paid 'by reason of the death.' I can understand the criterion being whether at the time of the death, and by reason of the death and the circumstances brought about by it, a reasonable expectation of pecuniary benefit in the future arose. If that is the ground of the decision in *Peacock's Case* [1954] 2 Q.B. 347 – and I think it is – then *Peacock's Case* is of little avail to the plaintiff. In the present case I think there arose at the time of the wife's death and because, by reason of that death, her property passed to her husband, a reasonable expectation that the husband would apply part of the income for the benefit of the children and would eventually bequeath to them a considerable portion and perhaps all of the capital. The husband has now married again and may have further children. This would go to reducing the expectation of the children of the first marriage and may be taken into account by the jury in their estimation of damages. But that a reasonable expectation still exists I cannot doubt, and I think the learned Judge was in error in directing the jury to leave such expectation out of account.

I find, however, considerable difficulty in reconciling *Peacock's Case* [1954] 2 Q.B. 347 with the subsequent case of *Mead* v. *Clarke Chapman & Co. Ltd.*[1956] 1

All E. R. 44, also a decision of the English Court of Appeal. The deceased was killed in the course of employment with the defendants, who admitted liability for negligence, leaving a widow and a daughter aged 4 months. Eight months after the death the widow re-married, her new husband being financially in the same position as her former one. The step-father was fond of the child and supported it. The trial judge allowed sums in respect of the period between the death of the first husband and the re-marriage, but held that the effect of the re-marriage was to put the wife and child in as good a position as before the death. On appeal it was held that the prospects of benefit from the step-father must be taken into account, but that something more than had been awarded by the trial judge must be allowed to the child because the obligations of the natural father to look after the child were legal and those of the step-father, being only moral, were of less value. A very moderate sum, £200 in all, was allowed by way of compensation to the child. This case seems to me to conflict with *Peacock's Case* [1954] 2 Q.B. 347 in as much as, if the matter is to be looked at as of the date of death, there was no real expectation of benefit to the child accruing from the death by reason of the possibility of a future marriage to a kind step-father. Such a possibility seems to me too remote and speculative to form a basis for computation. Had the case been heard promptly before any question of re-marriage arose, damages must have been awarded on the assumption that the death had deprived the child of a means of support to which he had a legal claim and that there was no reasonable expectation of a compensating benefit. The case is an authority to show that the actual state of affairs at the date of the trial must be considered.

However, even assuming that *Peacock's Case* [1954] 2 Q.B. 347 is in all respects correctly decided, it does not, in my view and for the reasons I have stated, affect the present case. In my opinion there must be a retrial.

One further matter calls for decision. The jury awarded the sum of £200 for funeral and other expenses. The funeral expenses came to £121 and the remainder of the £200 must have been awarded in the light of the evidence given by the plaintiff that in consequence of losing the assistance of his wife he had to incur greater expense for domestic help and for some private tuition for his children. It was argued for the defendants that there must be set off against this sum of £200 the financial gain which had accrued to the plaintiff by reason of his wife's death. This was contested by the plaintiff. The £200 was awarded under s. 4, sub-s, 2, which provides as follows:– 'In addition, damages may be awarded in respect of funeral and other expenses actually incurred by the deceased, the dependants or the personal representative by reason of the wrongful act, neglect, or default.' The first question which presents itself is whether the £79 awarded in recompense of payments made for services which the deceased might have been expected to perform falls within the category of 'other expenses actually incurred by the . . . dependants or the personal representative by reason of the wrongful act, neglect, or default.' Under the Fatal Accidents Act, 1846, and under s.4, sub s. 1, of our Fatal Injuries Act, services rendered to the dependants and which were likely to continue could be estimated in money, capitalised, and added to the damages: *Berry* v. *Humm & Co.* [1915] I K. B. 627. To allow the amounts paid in respect of the loss of such services to form a separate heading of award would be to recompense twice over for the same item of loss. I cannot believe that such was the intention of the Act. Sect. 4, sub-s 2, in my view provides only for items of loss which could not, on the authorities, be compensated under s. 4, sub-s, 1. Funeral expenses, which are specifically mentioned, could not have been taken into account under the Fatal Accidents Act, 1846: *Clarke* v. *London General Omnibus Co. Ltd.* [1906] 2 K. B. 648. and do not come under s. 4 sub-s, 1, of our Act Expenses under s. 4, sub-s, 2. are distinguished from loss arising by reason of the death; they are expressed to be such as arise 'by reason of the wrongful act, neglect, or default.' Expenses for medical treatment of the deceased, to give but one example, could be awarded under s. 4, sub-s, 2, and would not come under s. 4, sub-s, 1. If, as I think s, 4, sub-s, 2, is meant to cover only items which could not be compensated by damages under s. 4, sub-s. 1, then the £79 cannot be awarded under this head.

If I am right in my view as to the intention of s. 4, sub-s. 2, there should be no deduction from damages properly awarded under this head by reason of any advantage which may incidentally have accrued to dependants by reason of the death. The Fatal Accidents Act, 1846, and s. 4, sub-s, 1, of our Act are conceived in terms of dependency. The real monetary loss to the dependents which arises by reason of the death can only be arrived at by taking into account such benefits as may accrue by reason of the death. There does not seem to me any scope for such accountancy under s. 4, sub-s, 2. This sub-section deals with concrete expenditure incurred by reason of the wrongful act, neglect or default. I can see no reason in the wording of the Act, or in common sense, why the wrongdoer should not have to pay these expenses which are analogous to the items of special expenses in an ordinary negligence action. The £200 should be reduced to £121, but no further.

Ó Dálaigh C.J. and **Haugh J.** agreed.

Calculating deceased's likely income. 'Gratuity and like benefit' within meaning of Sec. 50 of Civil Liability Act, 1961.

MURPHY V. CRONIN
[1966] I.R. 699

Having emerged from a side road on a bicycle the plaintiff's husband was killed when he was struck by defendant's motor car.

Kingsmill Moore J.:
The jury assessed the total figure for damages for injury to the dependents resulting from the death at £10,118.5s.0d., a figure which may be taken as £10,000, for £118.8s.0d. was awarded in respect of funeral expenses. It is submitted that this sum is excessive. The estate of the deceased, which passed to his dependants was approximately £5,000. The figure of loss to dependants, as calculated and submitted by an actuary, was £7,663. The defendent says that from the actuary's figure of £7,663 must be deducted the £5,000 which accrued to the dependants by reason of the death, leaving a sum of £2,663 as the total pecuniary loss to the dependants arising from the death, and that therefore the sum of £10,000 awarded by the jury is out of all proportion to the loss sustained. To this the plaintiff answers that the sum calculated by the actuary is inadequate, because he has left out of account the probability that the earnings of the deceased would have substantially increased: and that the full sum of £5,000 should not be deducted because in all probability the assets of the deceased would have come to the dependants on his death, whenever it occurred. The only advantage accruing to them was, it is submitted, an acceleration of the time when they received such assets.

Under s.49, sub-s 1 (a), of the Civil Liability Act, 1961, the damages (apart from compensation for mental distress) are to be 'the total of such amounts (if any) as the jury or the judge, as the case may be, shall consider proportioned to the injury resulting from the death to each of the dependants, respectively, for whom or on whose behalf the action is brought . . .' This section reproduces s. 4, sub-s, 1, of the Fatal Injuries Act, 1956, and a similar phrasing 'damages . . . proportioned to the injury resulting from such death to the parties respectively for whom and for whose benefit such action shall be brought' was used in the Fatal Accidents Act, 1846, commonly known as Lord Campbell's Act. The general principles governing the award of damages under these words have been laid down in numerous decisions and were recently considered by this Court in *Byrne* v. *Houlihan* [1966] I.R. 274. What has to be ascertained as accurately as possible is the net pecuniary loss incurred by the dependants in consequence of the death of the deceased. In arriving at the sum the loss of a 'reasonable expectation of pecuniary benefit . . . from the continuance of the life' must be taken into account as well as the pecuniary benefit which can be demonstrated to have been lost: *Franklin* v. *South Eastern Railway Co*. 3 H & N. 211, 214; *Dalton* v. *South Eastern Railway* 4 C.B.(N.S.) 296, *Pym* v. *Great Northern Railway Company* 4 B. & S. 396. But 'the damages . . . must take into account any pecuniary benefit accruing to that dependant in consequence of the death of the deceased. It is the net loss on balance which constitutes the measure of damages' – *Davies* v. *Powell Duffryn Associated Colleries Ltd*. [1942] A.C. 601, 609. A reasonable possibility of benefit accruing from the death must also be taken into account in reduction of damages. Byrne v. *Houlihan* [1966] I.R. 274.

Evidence was given for the plaintiff by Mr. Rowe, an actuary, who based his calculations on the following facts and assumptions. At the time of his death the deceased was aged 50, his wife 39, and the eight children range from 8 months to 10 years. The deceased was earning, as a collecting agent for the Royal Liver, approximately £23 a week in the last year of his life. He gave £13 a week to his wife which she expended for the benefit of the family as a whole, and Mr Rowe assumed that of this £13 she would expend £2 for the benefit of her husband. In addition the deceased paid sums for rent, rates, repairs, heating and lighting which amounted to £2 a week. Mr. Rowe further assumed that the annual earnings would remain the same till the deceased was 70 when he would have to retire on a pension of nearly two thirds of his current salary, that each child would cease to be dependent at the age of 16, and that when each child became independent the money so released would be divided equally between husband and wife. On these assumptions, using actuarial bases which were not challenged, he worked out the value of the sums which would have been expended on the wife and children as having a present value of £7,109 at the date of death, and, adding interest on that notional sum to the day of the hearing arrived at a total figure of £7,630.

It is clear that a jury might regard some of Mr. Rowe's assumptions as being somewhat conservative. It does not seem likely that the income of the deceased would have remained static. He was dedicated to his work and though the collection, when he took it over nineteen years before his death, was small, he had by his efforts increased it to 2½ times its original amount. The figures of his earnings for the three years before his death show increases of £50, £25 and (approximately) £33 10s. 0d. Mr Brady, senior inspector in Ireland for the Royal Liver, thought that in time he could easily have doubled his earnings. If we take into account the principle of diminishing returns and the decreasing activity which comes with the advance of years, this may sound optimistic, but a jury might accept Mr. Brady's view that he could have doubled his income with the result that by the date of his retirement, which would come in 20 years, he might have added to his yearly income a sum of nearly £1,200, this figure based on the fact that he earned £1,143 for the 353 days before his death; his financial year would not have been completed till another twelve days had elapsed. If we assume the increase in earnings to have come about in regular increments of £60 a year over the 20 years, reaching £1,200 in the last year, the total addition to his earnings would have been £12,600. This would seem to be a generous view, as the average yearly increment for the three years before his death was only £36 as against the £60 average yearly increment which I have assumed, but it is one which on the evidence a jury might take.

The deceased was a frugal man who had already accumulated some £3,135 in savings and spent little on himself. Again I think a jury could make the assumption that of the £12,600 he would only expend about £2,600 on himself and that of the remaining £10,000 he would have expended £5,000 on his family and saved £5,000. Leaving aside the question of the savings, the notional £5,000 which he would have expended on his family must be discounted for present payment. If we were to assume the total extra payments to dependants to have been spread equally over 20 years we can regard the £5,000 as if it were one sum payable in ten years. This may seem too favourable to the dependants as the sums paid for their benefit in the earlier years, when the income was only gradually increasing, would be smaller and the sums paid in later years, when discount would be greater, would be larger. But it would be natural for the deceased to call temporarily on his savings in the earlier years and to replace his withdrawals in later years. The present value of £5,000 payable in 10 years, on a 5% basis, is £3,070. Adding this sum to Mr. Rowe's figure of £7,663 we reach a figure of £10,733 as against £10,000 awarded by the jury.

We have still to estimate the pecuniary benefits which accrued to the dependants in consequence of the death. Leaving out of account repayment by the Royal Liver of sums paid by the deceased during his lifetime as contributions towards a pension, and also leaving out of account the value of the house and furniture on the ground that these would have continued to be used as family property had deceased lived, we find that the dependants became entitled to a sum of approximately £5,000 from the assets of the deceased. In many cases it may be proper to deduct the whole amount of the assets so received. But, it is submitted, such a deduction would not be warranted in this case. The deceased was a model family man and it can be assumed that he would have left all his assets to his dependants when he died. The only benefit his dependants got is an acceleration of payment. It is also submitted that the deceased would have continued to save and that his savings would have been left to his dependants. I think a jury could reasonably assume both these submissions to be probable and I will further assume that the deceased by the age of 70 would have been able to save a further sum of £5,000 so that the total assets available for distribution among his dependants at his death would have been £10,000. Mr. Rowe did not give a figure for the expectation of life of the deceased, a healthy male of 50, but he assumed that he would live to receive a pension which was not payable till the age of 70; and the actuarial tables which I have been able to consult justify the view that he had over 20 years' expectation of life. The actual expectation according to the latest tables would appear to be not less than 22 years. The sum of £10,000 would not then have been payable for at least 20 years. Taking interest at 5% the present value of £10,000 payable in 20 years would, at the date of the death, have been £3,769 (on the revised Innwood's Tables). This means that the sum of £5,000 received is £1,231 more than the present value of what the dependants might have expected to receive had the deceased lived to the age of 70 and left assets of £10,000. I have assumed that there should be added to Mr. Rowe's figure a sum of £3,070 making it £10,733. From this has to be taken the sum of £1,231 as representing the immediate financial benefit accruing as a result of the early death, leaving the sum of £9,502. The jury awarded £10,000. On these figures they awarded only £500 too much.

I think that in arriving at these figures I have made every possible assumption in favour of the dependants. At the time of his death, on Mr. Rowe's figures, based on the evidence of the plaintiff, just under half of the income of the deceased was spent on his dependants. The remainder must have been spent on the expenses of the deceased or put into savings. Of the increase in income, which I have assumed, I have allotted notionally only about 1/5th to the deceased and about 4/5ths between the dependants and savings. Mr. Rowe assumed that the children would become independent at the age of 16 – an age which would be reached in 6 years in the case of the eldest child and in $14\frac{1}{2}$ years in the case of the youngest. It seems to me that at least some of the children would not cease to be dependent till they were much older than 16. An effort might have been made to give some of them a university or other advanced education. For this reason I have assumed that some of the children as well as the wife would have been dependent in greater or less degree for the full remaining period of the probable life of the deceased and that the money released, when one or more became independent, would be applied for the benefit of the wife and those still dependent. Mr. Rowe assumed that money released as each child became independent would be applied equally between husband and wife. I have made no allowance for the application of any portion of the money so released to the use of the husband as I have already allotted to him £2,600 out of the increased earnings. Many of these assumptions may be unduly favourable to the dependants but I could not say that a jury might not make them reasonably. On these assumptions it would appear that the verdict of the jury in their favour was £500 too much. I do not think this excess is so disproportionate as to warrant setting this sum aside.

I should mention that I have not deducted from the damages two sums which the defendant says should be deducted. By the rules governing the Royal Liver Superannuation Fund, if a member of the fund dies before being superannuated, there is payable to his legal personal representative the member's own accumulated contributions to the fund with compound interest, and there is payable to his widow a sum equal to 25% of such accumulated contributions. Those sums, in the events which have happened, accrue to the dependants (the widow and children) in consequence of the death of the deceased. Sect. 50 of the Civil Liability Act, 1961, provides as follows:– 'In assessing damages under this Part account shall not be taken of – (a) any sum payable on the death of the deceased under any contract of insurance, (b) any pension, gratuity or other like benefit payable under statute or otherwise in consequence of the death of the deceased.' The sum payable to the widow seems clearly a gratuity which falls within the wording of Sec. 50 (b). The return of contributions with interest seems to me to be a 'like benefit' within the same paragraph. It is a lump sum payable instead of a pension where the deceased has not reached pensionable age. A lump sum payable in lieu of a pension is often loosely referred to as a gratuity even where it is paid under a contractual arrangement. It can, I think, fairly be regarded as a 'like benefit.' To my view it is not deductible.

Ó Dálaigh C.J., Haugh J. and **Walsh J.** agreed with **Kingsmill Moore J. Lavery J.** dissented.

Who is entitled to be compensated for mental distress? Must one be a 'dependant' or may a member of the deceased's family who is not a dependant also be compensated for mental distress? Damages under this heading must be reasonable.

McCARTHY V. WALSH
[1965] I.R. 246

Ó Dálaigh C.J.:

This appeal arises in proceedings under Part IV of the Civil Liability Act, 1961, which replaces, with amendment the provisions of the Fatal Injuries Act, 1956: see s. 5 and Schedule, Part V, item 2.

The plaintiff as personal representative and father of Mary Margaret Patricia McCarthy, deceased, brought the action as such personal representative on his own behalf and for and on behalf of his wife, the deceased's mother, and the deceased's seven infant brothers and sisters, all of whom, it was alleged, were dependants of the deceased at the date of her death.

The deceased, who was aged 16 years, was a shop assistant earning £2 10s. 0d. per week out of which she contributed £2 5s. 0d. to her mother for the household budget. Her death was caused by her being knocked from her bicycle by the defendant's motor car. The jury found both the defendant and deceased negligent, the former 90 per cent and the latter 10 per cent. The plaintiff and his wife were found to be the only dependants and the damages were assessed at £1,027 15s. 10d. of which £367 15s. 10d. was allocated to the plaintiff and £660 to his wife. Subsequently the trial Judge, pursuant to the statute fixed damages for mental distress for the plaintiff and his wife in the sum of £150 each, making a total verdict of £1,327 15s. 10d., but an actual verdict of £1,195. There was a sum of £1,251 lodged in Court with the defendant's defence and accordingly judgment was entered for the defendant as from the date of lodgment.

In considering the question of mental distress the trial Judge ruled that the infant plaintiffs were not entitled to damages for mental distress as they had not recovered damages for 'injury'.

Sect. 47 sub-s. (1) defines the terms, 'dependant' and 'member of the family,' 'Dependant' means any member of the family of the deceased who suffers injury or mental distress. 'Member of the family' means wife, husband, father, mother, grandfather, grandmother, stepfather, stepmother, son, daughter, grandson, granddaughter, stepson, stepdaughter, brother, sister, half-brother, half-sister. Sect. 48. sub-s. 1, creates the cause of action in these words: 'Where the death of a person is caused by the wrongful act of another such as would have entitled the party injured, but for his death to maintain an action and recover damages in respect thereof the person who would have been so liable shall be liable to an action for damages for the benefit of the dependants of the deceased.' Sect. 49 then provides what the damages under s. 48 are to be. It will be enough to cite the first three paragraphs, (*a*), (*b*), (*c*), of sub-s. 1 of s. 49:–

'(1) (*a*)   The damages under section 48 shall be–

        (i) the total of such amounts (if any) as the jury or the judge, as the case may be shall consider proportioned to the injury resulting from the death to each of the dependants respectively, for whom or on whose behalf the action is brought, and

        (ii) subject to paragraph (*b*) of this subsection, the total of such amounts (if any) as the judge shall consider reasonable compensation for mental distress resulting from the death to each of such dependants.

(*b*)   The total of any amounts awarded by virtue of sub-paragraph (ii) of paragraph (*a*) of this sub-section shall not exceed one thousand pounds.

(*c*)   Each amount awarded by virtue of paragraph (*a*) of this subsection shall be indicated separately in the award.'

The trial Judge began his judgment by observing that he thought it was fair to say that it is probable that each member of the family would suffer mental distress to a greater or less extent, and that if the Legislature took this view and intended that each member of the family should get damages for mental distress resulting from the death it would have been simple to have provided that damages for mental distress should be awarded to each member of the family. That course, he said, was not adopted and that in itself suggested to him that it was not intended that each member of the family who suffered mental distress should benefit. He pointed out that the words, 'such dependants,' in sub-paragraph (ii) were intended to indicate the dependant referred to in sub para (i). These dependants are the 'dependants . . . for whom or on whose behalf the action is brought.' The Judge considered that the words following the word, 'dependants,' did not add anything to the meaning of the word, 'dependants', and that as a matter of construction it must be assumed some purpose lay behind their use and that they were not tautological. He concluded that the words effected a limitation and referred to the class of persons who were alleged to have suffered and did in fact suffer 'injury resulting from the death'.

On that basis he held that damages for mental distress were intended to be additional to the damages which a Court could award under earlier legislation, that is to say, damages for 'injury'. Moreover, he was of opinion that the conjunction 'and' linking sub-paras (i) and (ii), supported this view. Finally, he observed that the only support for the construction contended for by plaintiff's counsel was the word 'or' in the definition of 'dependants' in s. 47, but only, as he said, if the word 'or' was to be read disjunctively. He held that it was also possible to read the word conjunctively and he concluded that for the harmonious interpretation of Part IV it should be so read.

The appellant has submitted that the Judge has misconstrued the Act, and that the clear effect of the definition of 'dependant' in s. 47, read with ss. 48 and 49, is to confer a right to damages on a member of the family who has suffered mental distress even though no 'injury' has been suffered. The respondent has not sought to support the Judge's view that the word, 'or,' in the definition section (s. 47) is to be construed as 'and,' but he has submitted that the words 'such dependants,' in sub-para, (ii) of s. 49, sub-s. (1) (a) do limit the right to compensation for mental distress to dependants who have had an award of compensation for 'injury' under sub-para (i).

As has been pointed out, Part IV of the Act of 1961 is a re-enactment of the provisions of ss. 2, 3, and 4 of the Fatal Injuries Act, 1956, with amendments. It is these amendments which have caused the difficulty. The words, 'or mental distress' in the definition of 'dependant' in s. 47, sub-s. (1) of the Act of 1961 are new. (The substitution of 'injury' for 'loss' is of no importance). Paragraph (i) of s. 49, sub-s. (1) (a) of the Act of 1961 is in effect a re-enactment of s. 4 sub-s. (1) of the indicated separately contained in s.4 sub-s. 1, of the Act of 1956 appears in s. 49 sub-s. 1 as sub-para. (c) of the Act of 1961.] a re-enactment of s. 4 sub.-s. (1) of the Act of 1956 with the not insignificant addition of the words, 'if any,' after the word, 'amounts.' Sub-paragraph (ii) is, of course, new. It will be noted that s. 4, sub-s. (1) of the Act of 1956 had after the word, 'dependants' the clause 'for whom or on whose behalf the action is brought.' The clause served no particular purpose in s. 1, sub-s. (1)

of the Act of 1956; a dependant was a member of the family who had suffered 'loss' and, as in the Act of 1961, s. 48, sub-s. (1) (a), the action was required to be brought for the benefit of all the dependants (s. 3, sub-s. 4 of the Act of 1956). What was the need to add this clause? The answer is, the clause is unnecessary. If we are to seek a reason for its existence, the probable explanation is that originally the draftsman transcribed it, with modification, from s. 2 of the Fatal Accidents Act 1846. The clause was there needed and served a purpose. The Act of 1846 did not use the term 'dependant'. Sect. 2 of that Act reads:– 'Every such action shall be for the benefit of the wife, husband, parent and child of the person whose death shall have been so caused and shall be brought by and in the name of the executor or administrator of the person deceased and in every such action the jury may give such damages as they may think proportional to the injury resulting from such death to the *parties* respectively *for whom and for whose benefit* such action shall be brought.'

The amending Act of 1864 (27 & 28 Vict., c. 95) allowed the action to be brought by all or any one of the persons for whose benefit the action would formerly have been brought by the personal representative where no representation was raised within six months of the death.

In any event, whatever its origin, the clause, 'for whom or on whose behalf the action is brought,' following 'dependants' does not operate to cut down in any way the definition of the term, 'dependant.' The action must be brought for the benefit of all the dependants: s. 48, sub-s. 4. The clause could be done without, but its insertion does nothing to alter the meaning of the term, 'dependants.' The 'such dependants' in sub-para. (ii) does no more than to hark back to sub-para. (i); again, one can say the word, 'such,' adds nothing and alters nothing.

Sub-paragraph (i), far from purporting to say that dependants must recover under it, that is to say, in respect of 'injury,' acknowledges with the words, 'if any,' following the words, 'the total of such amounts,' the possibility of there being a nil award under the sub-paragraph. The words 'if any,' are new: and they are appropriate, looking to the terms of the definition in s. 47; although I may say that I cannot see that their absence would make any difference to the construction. It has been pointed out that damages for mental distress is a new head of damage in actions arising out of fatal injuries. If it were merely a head of damage to be added only in the case of those dependants who suffered 'injury' (or 'loss'), as the respondent contended, no alteration was needed in the definition of 'dependant.' It would have sufficed to have added sub-para, (ii) without more. Further, the view accepted in the High Court that 'or' may be read as 'and,' while surprising, has also the effect that an action by a person who would have been entitled to recover under the Act of 1956 and the original Act in respect of loss of financial benefit would now fail if he or she were unable to establish 'mental distress.' The judgment in the High Court having begun (as has been noted) by observing that it was *probable* that every member of the family of the deceased would suffer mental distress to a greater or less extent, proceeds later to the basis that mental distress could be established by every member of the family. This is not necessarily so. Grand-children may be wholly unknown to grand-parents; step-children may not know their step-father; half-sisters may be wholly unacquainted. Even close relatives may quarrel bitterly and their affections turn to hate. All this is regrettable but true. Its only relevance here is to point out that a member of the family is far from being necessarily synonymous with a member of a family who suffers mental distress; and it is by making this equation, as it seems to me, the judgment of the High Court is in error.

It is unnecessary in this case to examine the unusual circumstances in which Courts have considered themselves justified in reading 'or' as being used conjunctively.

Whenever such a construction is adopted it involves violence being done to the language which only compelling context can justify. It is enough that in the case under consideration, there is no such justification; but, on the contrary, the context here fully accords with 'or' being given its ordinary disjunctive meaning.

For the reasons I have given, at too great length as I now feel, I am of opinion that the infant brothers and sisters of the deceased are entitled to recover compensation for mental distress resulting from the deceased's death.

The picture of the deceased's family as presented in the evidence, though not very detailed, is nevertheless sufficient to allow this Court to assess compensation.

The deceased's father is a station foreman in the employment of Córas Iompair Éireann, earning £9 15s. 0d. per week.

The eldest child Eileen, was aged 18 at the date of the deceased's death; she worked in a bacon factory. The deceased (aged 16) came next in the family. The other children in descending order of age were Elizabeth (14), John (12½), Denis (11½), Michael (10), Anne (5) and Anthony (4). The family, in the words of the deceased's mother, was very united and very happy: and her brothers and sisters 'missed the deceased.' In my opinion it would be a modest assessment to allow a sum of £200 for mental distress among the 7 children. The two eldest surviving children were closest in age to the deceased and I think they should be allocated half of the sum of £200, to be shared equally, £50 each. The balance of £100 I would allocate as to £75 equally between John, Denis and Michael £25 each, and as to the balance £25 equally between the two youngest, £12 10s. 0d. each.

The plaintiff has also contended that the allocation by the trial judge of £150 each to himself and his wife for damages for mental distress is inadequate. The figure requires considerable adjustment in the light of what I consider reasonable in the case of the children. I would allow the parents a total of £500 dividing the compensation equally, as the trial Judge did, and awarding £250 each.

The test to be applied in assessing damages for mental distress is that they shall be reasonable. This test does not differ from the test to be applied in the other branch of the case – that of reasonableness. The term, 'reasonable,' is not to be equated with moderate or small. 'Reasonable' is what is fair in the circumstances of the case. This precludes the damages being measured by reference to an imagined worse case, fixing damages for such case at the statutory limit of £1,000 and then measuring all other cases by reference to that case. The statutory limit of £1,000 is a limit on what may be recovered. It is not a limit on what is reasonable. If reasonable damages for mental distress exceed £1,000 then the figure must be reduced to the statutory maximum and if there are two or more dependants their damages will abate proportionately. Here, as the award of £700 does not reach the maximum there is no adjustment to be effected.

It will be apparent that the new allowances must suffer a diminution of 10 per cent in view of the jury's finding of 10 per cent fault on the part on the part of the deceased in contributing to the accident.

In the result this appeal will be allowed and judgment will be entered for the plaintiff.

Lavery J.:

I agree with the judgment of the Chief Justice.

I wish to add a few words on the measure of damages. Sect 49, sub-s. 1 (*a*) (ii), provides that the judge shall 'consider reasonable compensation for mental distress resulting from the death.'

Obviously it is difficult to translate mental distress into money values. But this is not a new problem in principle.

The same difficulty arises where damages for pain and suffering have to be assessed and in innumerable other cases damages are equally difficult to assess.

All damages are to be assessed on a reasonable basis. The word, 'moderate,' has been used in argument but this does not help. The word is not used in the statute and all damages are to be assessed moderately and not immoderately.

In my opinion the judge uses his discretion in fixing reasonable damages. He is fairly at large.

Sect. 49, sub-s. 1 (*b*), provides that the total amounts awarded shall not exceed £1,000. This is arbitrary, but it may perhaps be regarded as an indication by the Legislature of what it considered reasonable.

There will however, be cases where such a sum could not be regarded as reasonable. I instance the case of a wife, widowed by the tragic death of her husband, who suffers a mental breakdown in consequence. Such a case is not far-fetched.

Perhaps a judge might consider £5,000 reasonable compensation in such a case. He assesses this sum and then faces the application of the overriding maximum. The statute here involves a contradiction which the judge must resolve as best he can.

If there is only the widow concerned he awards her £1,000. If there are others to be considered he might take the course of setting down all his assessments in proportion so that the total shall not exceed £1,000. The Chief Justice has indicated that this in his view is the course the judge should take. I agree this would normally be the proper course but I can visualise exceptional cases where a different course might be appropriate.

In the present case this problem does not arise.

I have only ventured these observations because we were told that the judges of the High Court felt difficulties in the application of the section which is certainly understandable.

Whether what the Chief Justice and I have said will be of any help to them. I cannot say. It does not bind them.

Haugh, Walsh and O'Keeffe JJ. agreed with the Chief Justice.

Note . . .

See also Walsh J.'s judgment in *Dowling* v. *Jedos Ltd.* (*supra* pp. 90–93) on the effect which the statutory limit (then £1,000) has when one is assessing the award for mental distress where several dependants are involved.

Chapter 7

TRESPASS TO THE PERSON

Trespass to the person embraces a variety of specific torts, including battery, assault, false imprisonment and (it seems) intentional infliction of emotional suffering. Each of these specific torts will be considered in turn.

1. *BATTERY*

The direct application of physical contact upon the person of another without his consent may constitute a battery. (The tort is frequently referred to as 'assault', following criminal terminology, but this should not cause any difficulty once the practice is known.) Mere passive obstruction does not constitute a battery. Whether or not the victim of the battery appreciated that the act was about to take place is irrelevant: thus, if I approach somebody from the rear and hit him on the back of the head I will be liable to him, even though he knew nothing about what was to happen to him. Conversely, if the victim of the injury does not appreciate that he has been injured (as, for example, where a sleeping person is injured or killed) liability will nonetheless attach. Contrast the position in relation to the tort of assault, discussed, *infra*, pp. 116–120.

CORCORAN V. W. & R. JACOB & CO. LTD.
[1945] I.R. 446 (Supreme Court, 1944)

Murnaghan J.:

This is an appeal brought by the defendant company against a verdict and judgment for £500, damages, in an action tried before the President of the High Court, in which the causes of action which went to the jury were: 1, slander, and 2, assault.

The respondent, Corcoran, was for many years employed by Messrs. W. & R. Jacob & Co., Ltd., and, as a result of the incidents which led up to the trial, he lost his position there, and brought this action. The action also included a claim for damages for wrongful dismissal, but it was admitted at the trial that the plaintiff could not sustain any claim founded on wrongful dismissal.

Now, in Messrs. Jacob's factory it is the custom to employ commissionaires. We do not live in an ideal world, and hence the firm employ men whose duty it is to examine employees with a view to ascertaining whether they have taken property of the firm. It is admitted by both sides that the commissionaires carry out their duty for that purpose.

On the 17th September, 1943, the respondent, a storekeeper in the appellants' employment, went into the city on messages on behalf of the company. He had to make two calls. On his discovery that he had forgotten a parcel he returned to the factory after the first call. While he was at or near the gate he was accosted by a commissionaire, Noonan. As a result of his conversation with Noonan he went into an office adjoining the entry, where the events occurred which gave rise to his claim for assault.

[**Murnaghan J.** went on to consider the plaintiff's action for slander based on words spoken by Noonan shortly afterwards; he held that the jury could not have found that they were spoken with malice on an occasion of qualified privilege. He continued:]

As regards the respondent's claim in respect of an alleged assault, booklets have been produced here, and evidence was given at the trial of notices exhibited in the factory, showing the firm's regulations as to their employees' liability to be searched. As I understand it, the case proceeded on the basis that Corcoran agreed that he was liable to search, as that word is ordinarily understood. There was no limitation of the right of the searcher to put his hands upon the person searched.

The only question which arises, then, is whether there was any unnecessary violence used in Noonan's search of Corcoran. The respondent spoke of a 'power drive.' That is ambiguous, but might lead a jury to believe that excessive strength was used which might be unreasonable in the circumstances. The appellants' servant said he only used such force as was necessary, and desisted when objection was made, and it is agreed that he did at once desist. My view is that this is a question of fact, in one sense, for a jury. I do not think the mere pulling about of his clothes was such as in any way injuriously to affect the respondent. He was not injured, but merely lost a button. Counsel for the appellant practically admit that it was a question for the jury whether any unnecessary violence was used, and in these circumstances, I do not think that the Court should interfere with the jury's findings on this issue.

At the trial the jury awarded the sum of £500 damages for both claims, and there was no segregation of amounts. It is impossible for this Court to segregate the amounts assessable to the respective claims, and, accordingly, the jury's finding as to the amount of damages will be set aside, and the case must be remitted to the High Court on the assault issue for the assessment of damages by a jury.

In the result, the appeal, in my opinion, should be allowed with costs, and judgment entered for the applicants in the issue of slander, and the case must be remitted to the High Court to assess damages on the claim for assault.

Geoghegan J. concurred.

O'Byrne J.:

I concur with the judgment just delivered by Mr. Justice Murnaghan concerning the slander issue for the reasons he has given.

As regards the assault issue I understood counsel for the appellants to concede that the jury's finding of liability for assault might stand. Accordingly, I concur with the jury's verdict on that issue.

Black J.:

Under our system of law a jury's verdict is looked upon as sacrosanct for several reasons: they hear the direct evidence in the first instance, they can observe the witnesses and they must form and act upon their own view of what the evidence in their judgment proves. We, therefore, have only to consider whether the jury's finding of malice in this case is reasonable, and not perverse.

What is the meaning of the word 'perverse'? FitzGibbon L.J., in *Quinlane* v. *Murnane* 18 L.R.Ir. 53, says, at p. 59:– 'The meaning of the word "perverse" is that the jury misconducted themselves in coming to the conclusion they did.' Accepting that definition, in my opinion this appeal cannot succeed on the ground of the perversity of the verdict.

Is the jury's finding of malice here unreasonable? There was evidence of the assault, and the jury may have come to the conclusion that excessive zeal was used. In my view the respondent's story of the assault was credible, and, therefore cannot be disturbed by this Court.

[**Black J.** went on to state that in his opinion the Court should not disturb the jury's finding of malice in respect of the slander action.]

Notes and Questions

1. Does touching the clothes a person is wearing constitute a battery? *Cf. Humphries* v. *Connor*, 17 Ir.C.L.1 (1864). Is it a battery if I strike the horse a person is riding? *Cf. Dodwell* v. *Burford*, 1 Mod. 24, 86 E.R. 703 (1670). Is it a battery or trespass to chattels (or both) if I beat on the roof of a car which a person is driving? Am I liable for battery of all the passengers as well? What about a bus?
3. Is physical injury an ingredient of the tort of battery? Does *Corcoran* v. *W. & R. Jacob & Co.* hold that it is?

2. ASSAULT

An assault consists of an act that places another person in reasonable apprehension of an immediate battery being committed upon him. Mere passive obstruction does not suffice, although taking active steps to block or obstruct another may do so. This distinction may, of course, be difficult to draw in specific cases.

Where a person has no apprehension of a battery before it takes place – as where he is asleep or is stabbed in the back – he may not sue for assault, for the tort consists of 'a touching of the mind, not the body': *Kline* v. *Kline*, 64 N.E. 9 (Ind. S.C., 1902).

The apprehension must be of an immediate battery, a limitation which the courts have interpreted narrowly.

DULLAGHAN V. HILLEN AND KING
[1957] Ir. Jur. Rep. 10 (Circuit Court, Judge Fawsitt, 1956)

Judge Fawsitt.:

In his civil bill (claiming damages) the plaintiff alleges *inter alia* that (1) he was assaulted and beaten; (2) held prisoner and arrested; and (3) maliciously prosecuted by the defendants.

In their joint defence the defendants deny *inter alia* that (1) they assaulted and beat the plaintiff; (2) they held the plaintiff prisoner or had him arrested; and (3) they subsequently maliciously prosecuted him.

In further defence the defendants aver that (4) if the defendant Hileen assaulted or beat the plaintiff he did so in necessary self-defence; (5) if the defendants held the plaintiff prisoner or procured his arrest or detention they did so in discharge of their duty as officers of customs and by virtue of the powers and duties conferred on them by the Customs Acts.

What are the facts and circumstances which gave rise to his claim?

County Louth (in which the Court sits) is a border county. It is notorious as the scene of much cross-border smuggling. To prevent this unlawful activity the State has stationed a number of preventative officers of customs, including the present defendants, at Dundalk, whose duty it is to prevent smuggling of certain classes of merchandise and livestock into and out of the State in their area of jurisdiction. These officers are supplied with a distinctive uniform not customarily worn by them when on patrol duty. For the purposes of transport to and from the land frontier or border certain main roads are classified as 'approved' roads, whilst other roads also leading to and from the border are classified as 'unapproved' roads. Merchandise and livestock lawfully leaving or entering the County Louth by or from the border are transported over 'approved' roads only; it is notorious that the 'unapproved' roads are those used by persons engaged in the unlawful cross-border smuggling racket. Among other duties and powers imposed by statute and statutory regulations upon officers of customs, in the County Louth area, is one authorising such officers to stop and examine vehicles travelling upon a route within twenty miles of the land frontier (popularly called 'the border'). For the more efficient discharge of their onerous duties the State provides motor cars for preventative officers of customs, thereby enabling them to patrol both 'approved' and 'unapproved' roads leading to and from the border. These cars carry no distinctive marks or badges to distinguish them from privately owned motor vehicles.

On the 24th September, 1954, the plaintiff was driving a hired motor van along an unapproved road in the direction of Kilkerly in this County; that is to say the van was being driven at the time by him from the direction of the border. It was a van which had previously been seized by customs officers when it was found to be transporting into County Louth smuggled fish allegedly landed at a County Louth port. The van was known to certain officers of customs, including the defendant, Francis Hillen. At the same time on the same day a customs officer's motor car driven by the defendant John King, the senior officer of the party, and carrying the defendant Hillen and two other assistant preventative officers, Messrs. Gallagher and Farren, was proceeding along the same 'unapproved' road towards the border. Both vehicles passed each other and, it appears, that the van was recognised by one of the customs officers in the car, whereupon the driver, King, stopped it, turned it round on the road, and drove it after the receding van. On its journey the van's progress was hindered by a flock of sheep then being driven from the Kilkerly direction, and it stopped to allow the sheep to pass by in safety. Whilst so stopped, the following customs car overtook the van, and it stopped immediately behind the van. There was evidence that all four customs officers immediately left the car and proceeded towards the van, one officer proceeding to the left of the van, another, the defendant Hillen, to the right of the van. A third officer went to the back door of the van. This case has arisen out of what occurred immediately afterwards. What had occurred prior to this point on both vehicles' journeys was made the subject of a separate summons against the plaintiff for an alleged offence under s. 13 of the Adaptation of Enactments Act, 1922, for a breach of article 11 (2) of the Customs (Land Frontier) Regulations, 1923. The said summons was brought by order dated 28th September, 1954, made by the Revenue Commissioners. It was heard by the Justice of the District Court sitting at Dundalk on the 20th October, 1954. The summons charged the defendant (the plaintiff in this action) that at Newtownbalryan, County Louth, he, on the 24th September, 1954, 'being the person in charge of a vehicle travelling upon a route within 20 miles of the land frontier did fail, upon request by a customs officer, to stop such vehicle and allow such officer to examine the said vehicle and any goods therein and to take an account of such goods.' The complainant in the summons was the Attorney General. After hearing evidence on behalf of the complainant, the learned District Justice dismissed the summons. From that order no appeal was taken to the Circuit Court. At the same sitting of the District Court two further summons, each brought by the Attorney General as complainant, were heard by the same District Justice against the present plaintiff. The District Justice convicted him on both charges, viz.: (1) on a charge that he did on the 24th September, 1954 . . . obstruct officers in discharge of their duty contrary to section 12 (5) of the Customs and Inland Revenue Act, 1881, and (2) on a charge that he did on the 24th September, 1954 . . . assault Francis Hillen, Officer of Customs and Excise, a person employed for the prevention of smuggling and in the discharge of his duties, contrary to section 12 (5) of the Customs and Inland Revenue Act, 1881. Each such conviction carried with it a penalty of £5. 0s. 0d., and in default two months' imprisonment.

From each of these two convictions and orders the present plaintiff appealed to this Court on its criminal side. Both appeals were listed before and heard together by me in this Courthouse, on 21st March, 1955. At the close of the evidence for the complainant in each summons, counsel for the present plaintiff applied to me for a direction in each case, and after hearing him and counsel for the complainant in reply, on the facts and the relevant law, I granted the direction asked for and in each case I allowed the appeal of the plaintiff and reversed the order of the learned District Justice and dismissed the summons.

The matters at issue between the respective parties then stood as follows: The complainant had failed to prove to the satisfaction of the District Court that the plaintiff: (1) had failed upon request by a customs officer to stop the van which he drove at Newtownbalryan, County Louth, on 24th September, 1954, and allow such officer to examine the said van and any goods therein, and to take an account of such goods; (2) on the same date and place, obstructed officers in discharge of their duty, contrary to section 12 (5) of the Customs and Inland Revenue Act, 1881, and; (3) on the same date and place, assaulted Francis Hillen an officer of customs and excise in the discharge of his duties, contrary to s. 12 (5) of the Customs and Inland Revenue Act, 1881. In effect, all that this means, is that, since in criminal issues, charges as laid must be strictly proved, the strict proofs required had not been produced in the District Court or in the criminal side of this Court, and the three charges as laid had therefore to be dismissed, one by order of the District Justice and two by order of this Court. The same strictness of proof is not required or called for on the civil side of our Court of law, where probabilities as well as facts are taken into consideration when weighing up the evidence on one side and the other tendered before the Court. I am, here, dealing, not with a criminal or quasi-criminal charge or matter, but with a civil action for damages.

I propose to deal in this judgment, firstly, with the claim based on the alleged assault and battery. . . .

(1) Assault and battery: Security for the person is among the first conditions of civilised life. The law, therefore, protects us, not only against actual hurt and violence, but against every kind of bodily interference and restraint not justified or excused by allowed cause, and against the present (immediate) apprehension of any of these things. Blackstone said: 'the least touching of another's person wilfully, or in anger, is a battery; for the law cannot draw the line between different degrees of violence and, therefore, totally prohibits the first and lowest stage of it; every man's person being sacred and no other having a right to meddle with it in any the slightest manner.' Battery indicates assault, and the word 'assault' is to-day commonly made to include battery. Hostile or unlawful intention is necessary to constitute an indictable assault, and such touching, pushing or the little as belongs to the ordinary conduct of life and is free from the use of unnecessary force, is neither an offence nor a wrong. Words cannot of themselves amount to an assault, under any circumstances. When one is wrongfully assaulted, it is lawful to repel force by force, provided that no unnecessary violence is used. How much force and of what kind it is reasonable and proper to use, in the circumstances, is a question of fact. Resistance must 'not exceed the bounds of mere defence and prevention,' or that the force used in defence must be not more than commensurate with that which provoked it.

The plaintiff alleged in his civil bill, and testified in Court, that the defendant, Hillen, both assaulted and beat him. It is implicit in the joint defence that the defendant, Hillen, did assault and beat the plaintiff. The first question which I have to determine is: did Hillen beat the plaintiff in self-defence? In addition to hearing the evidence on the issues of assault and self-defence, I saw both protagonists on the witness stand in this Court, and so had opportunity to note their respective physiques as well as their dimensions, intelligence, alertness, et cetera. In a ring-match or a fracas, my money (if I had any to spare and were a betting man) would be placed on Francis Hillen. On the date and at the place in which this action is laid, the defendant Hillen, clearly and convincingly demonstrated his superior skill, strength and fisticuff agility in his short one-round encounter with the plaintiff. The scandalous scene in that public highway is one to be regretted and, above all, one to be avoided by a state servant, acting, as it is claimed for Hillen he was acting on that morning and place, in the discharge of his duty as customs officer.

[After reviewing the evidence concerned with the commencement of the altercation between the parties, the judge continuing, said]:

I have to find that the defendant, Hillen's approach and address, on the occasion was not a polite approach or address, nor was it an approach or address in keeping with his status of public servant and officer of customs. He was engaged in an unpopular and risky task, and ought to have exercised a wise, a scrupulously careful and a forbearing discretion towards the plaintiff. Mr. Hillen forgot one of the chief golden rules of public conduct, namely, to speak to others as you would be spoken to by them. Passions were not confined to one side only, as became manifest when in reply, the plaintiff uttered a filthy and insulting remark towards Hillen, which still further inflamed Hillen's temper. But for his agitated state of mind Hillen would, no doubt, have recollected the commonplace but trite couplet which runs: 'Sticks and stones may break your bones but words will never hurt you,' and in which there is a definition of the law of assault, namely that mere words, no matter how harsh, lying insulting and provocative they may be, can never amount in law to an assault. When the plaintiff refused to withdraw and apologise to Hillen for the insulting words which the plaintiff used towards and of Hillen, the assault on, and beating up of, the plaintiff, by Hillen, immediately followed. The plaintiff, his passion, too, now aroused, then made a kick at Hillen which, if it struck Hillen, did him no injury, and could properly in the circumstances, be described as having been made by the plaintiff in his self-defence. Hillen's rejoinder was the series of brutal blows which he delivered on the nose of the plaintiff, resulting in the breaking of that organ, and a copious and continuing outflow of blood from it. This series of blows by Hillen on the plaintiff's nose was not delivered by him in his (Hillen's) self-defence; nor was the beating up of the plaintiff justified by the filthy language employed by the plaintiff towards Hillen; nor was it justified or merited by the refusal of the plaintiff to give his name and address to the customs officers; nor was it done by Hillen in discharge of his duty as customs officer. It was committed by Hillen in excess of the limits of the powers which he possessed as customs officer. The plaintiff must succeed on his part of his claim. . . .

Notes and Questions

1. The statement that '[w]ords cannot of themselves amount to an assault, under any circumstances' is too broad. When spoken in particular contexts suggesting the imminent use of force, words may well do so. *Cf.* Handford, 'Tort Liability for Threatening or Insulting Words.' '54 Can. Bar. Rev. 563, at 566–571 (1976). See also *Grealy* v. *Casey*, 1 N.I.J.R. 121, at 122 (C.A., *per* Porter, M.R., 1901); *Walsh* v. *Pender*, 62 I.L.T.R. 8 (High Court, 1927). *Cf.* Williams, 'Assault and Words' (1957) Crim. L. Rev. 219.

2. In some circumstances words may have the effect of rendering legally harmless conduct that would otherwise constitute an assault. Thus, in *Turberville* v. *Savage* 1 Mod. 3, 86 E.R. 684 (1669), the Court held that no liability would attach to a man who laid his hand menacingly

on his sword but remarked: 'If it were not assize-time, I would not take such language from you.'

3. As to provocation and joint participation in a fight, English and Canadian courts have evinced an increasing disposition to deny the claim or reduce damages where the victim actively brought the injury on himself. *Cf. Murphy* v. *Culhane* [1977] Q.B. 94 (C.A.), *Holt* v. *Verbruggen*, 20 C.C.L.T. 29 (B.C. Sup. Ct., Berger, J., 1981). For an excellent comparative analysis, see Osborne, 'Annotation,' 20 C.C.L.T. 29 (1982).

4. It is not necessary that the victim of an assault be frightened by the prospect of imminent physical contact: awareness is all that is required. *Cf. Brady* v. *Schatzel* [1911] Q.S.R. 206.

5. How imminent must the apprehended contact be? If I threaten to beat you up tomorrow and you have every good reason to believe me, have I assaulted you? If not, have I committed some other tort? *Cf. State Rubbish Collectors Association* v. *Siliznoff* 38 Cal. 2d 330, 240 P.2d 282 (1952).

6. What is the position in relation to conditional threats? If I seek payment of a bill, saying that if it is not paid immediately, I will strike you, is this an assault?

3. *INFLICTION OF EMOTIONAL SUFFERING*

Where a person intentionally or recklessly inflicts emotional suffering on another he may be guilty of a tort. The precise scope of the tort is somewhat uncertain.

The leading decision is *Wilkinson* v. *Downton* [1897] 2 Q.B. 57; 66 L.J.Q.B. 493 (Wright J.). The defendant, as a practical joke, told the plaintiff that her husband had been injured in a road accident, that he was lying on the ground with both legs broken and that she was to go at once to fetch him. The entire tale was false. It gave the plaintiff a violent shock resulting in severe injuries. The action did not fit easily into any established categories, but the Court 'obviously had no love for the defendant; and as in many another hard case, the enormity of the outrage overthrew the settled rule of law.' *Prosser*, p. 55. Liability was imposed on the basis that the defendant had 'wilfully done an act calculated to cause physical harm to the plaintiff, that is to say, to infringe her legal right to personal safety, and has in fact thereby caused physical harm to her. That proposition without more appears to me to state a good cause of action, there being no justification alleged for the act. The wilful *injuria* is in law malicious, although no malicious purpose to cause the harm which was caused nor any motive of spite is imputed to the defendant.'

Of particular interest to Irish readers is the treatment of *Victorian Railways Comrs.* v. *Coultas* (1888) 13 App. Cas. 222, the decision in which the Privy Council had held that illness which was the effect of shock caused by fright was too remote a consequence of a negligent act which caused the fright, no physical harm having been caused immediately to the plaintiff. Wright, J. stated that *Coultas* was –

'inconsistent with an earlier decision of the Court of Appeal in Ireland (*Bell* v. *Great Northern Rly. Co. of Ireland* 26 L.R.Ir. 428 (1890)) where the Irish Exchequer Division declined to follow *Victorian Railways Comrs.* v. *Coultas*, and it has been disapproved in the Supreme Court of New York . . . Nor is it altogether in point, for there was not in that case any element of wilful wrong, nor was perhaps the illness so direct and natural a consequence of the defendant's conduct, as in this case.

On these grounds it seems to me that *Victorian Railways Comrs.* v. *Coultas* is not an authority on which this case ought to be decided.'

The whole question of negligently inflicted nervous shock is considered *infra*, pp. 170–177.

There has been a surprising dearth of reported decisions in this country and in England on this subject, but in the United States an avalanche of cases has given some shape to the tort.

The precise scope of liability in this country is thus a matter of speculation. It would appear that an intention to produce the harm is essential, at all events in the sense that intention includes cases of presumed intent in respect of the natural consequences of conduct. In this context, it might be asked whether the basis of the tort is (a) that the defendant told a lie; (b) that what he said was untrue; (c) that what he said was harmful. *Cf. Weir*, pp. 270–271.

Although the reported cases deal only with the imposition of shock, fear or other psychological harm, is there any reason in principle why liability should not extend to all intentionally caused physical harm which the plaintiff suffers other than that falling within the scope of actions for trespass to the person? *Cf. McMahon & Binchy*, p. 134.

4. *FALSE IMPRISONMENT*

DULLAGHAN V. HILLEN

[1957] Ir. Jur. Rep. 10 (Circuit Court, Judge Fawsitt, 1956)

[The facts of the case have been set out on pp. 116–119, *supra*., Judge Fawsitt continued his judgment as follows:]

. . . (2) False imprisonment: The second ground of the plaintiff's claim is that he was held prisoner and arrested: that is, he was unlawfully detained and arrested by the defendants. This is an allegation of false imprisonment. It has been judicially stated that 'interference with the liberty of the subject by a private person has ever been jealously guarded by the common law of the land. At common law a police constable may arrest a person if he has reasonable cause to suspect that a felony has been committed, although it afterwards appears that no felony had been committed, but that is not so when a private person makes or causes the arrest, for to justify his action, he must prove among other things that a felony has actually been committed.' (See per Lord Tenterden, C.J., in *Beckwith* v. *Philby* 6 B. & C. 635). Suspicion only, without a felony committed, is no cause for the arrest of another by a private person. The Constitution of the State deals among other matters with Fundamental Rights. Sub-article 3 (1) of article 40 declares that 'the State guarantees in its laws to respect, and, as far as possible, by its laws, to defend and vindicate the personal rights of the citizen,' and sub-article 4 (1) of the said article 40 lays down that 'no citizen shall be deprived of his personal liberty save in accordance with the law.' Freedom of the person includes immunity, not only from the actual application of force, but from every kind of detention and restraint not authorised by law. The infliction of such restraint is the worry [sic] of false imprisonment, which though generally coupled with assault, is nevertheless a distinct wrong. False imprisonment is the unlawful and total restraint of the personal liberty of another whereby by constraining him or compelling him to go to a particular place or continuing him in a prison or police station or private place or by detaining him against his will in a public place. The essential element in the offence is the unlawful detention of the person, or the unlawful restraint on his liberty. The fact that a person is not actually aware that he is being imprisoned does not amount to evidence that he is not imprisoned, it being possible for a person to be imprisoned in law, without his being conscious of the fact and appreciating the position in which he is placed, laying hands upon the person of the party imprisoned not being essential. There may be an effectual imprisonment without walls of any kind. The detainer must be such as to limit the party's freedom of motion in all directions. In effect, imprisonment is a total restraint of the liberty of the person. The offence is committed by mere detention without violence.

When an action of false imprisonment is brought and defended, the real question in issue is: was the imprisonment justified? All the plaintiff has to prove is the detention: it is then for the defendant to show that he was justified in what he did, and that the imprisonment was lawful. The present defendants are persons with limited authority, under the customs, statutes and regulations, to arrest persons in certain circumstances. 'The general rule of law as to actions of trespass against persons having a limited authority is plain and clear. If they do any act beyond the limit of their authority . . . they thereby subject themselves to an action of trespass: but if the act be within the limit of their authority, although it may be done through an erroneous or mistaken judgment, they are not liable to such action.' (*Doswell* v. *Impey* 1 B. & C. 163). Has the plaintiff in this action, proved that he was detained and imprisoned? His evidence (and on this aspect of the case against the defendants his evidence was not controverted) was to the effect that he was forced to leave his van twice, and was ordered to enter the customs officers' car in which he was brought to Dundalk town, his van, too, being driven to Dundalk by a customs officer. After being detained in the car outside the customs office in Dundalk for from 15 to 30 minutes he was brought in the car to the garda station at Dundalk, where he was given in charge to the station orderly for the time being. He was detained in the garda station until a peace commissioner was obtained and a special court was held at which certain charges were formulated against the plaintiff, and on those charges he was remanded on bail for trial before the District Court at its next sitting in Dundalk. On these facts I must find that there was a detaining and imprisonment of the person of the plaintiff by and at the instance of the defendant, King, although the defendant had not himself actually applied the restraint, but he had directed and authorised the detention of the plaintiff and had caused him to be brought to the garda station to be charged with certain customs offences. Was that arrest and detention of the plaintiff within or in excess of the limited powers possessed by the defendant King as customs officer?

[After referring to the evidence given before this Court on this part of the plaintiff's claim his Lordship continued:] On this evidence I must find that the plaintiff's van when it was just observed that morning by the customs officers was being driven over an 'unapproved road' from the direction of the border; it was a vehicle which had previously to the knowledge of one of the customs officers – the defendant, Hillen – been employed in contravening certain customs regulations relating to the importation of fish into the State; its driver (i.e. the present plaintiff) had seemingly disregarded the repeated blowing of the horn of the following and overtaking customs car; he stopped the van only to allow a flock of sheep to pass it by in safety. It was at this moment that the customs car overtook the van and stopped behind it, the four customs officers alighting from it, with the intention of searching the van for unaccustomed or prohibited goods. Any such search, if carried out, would be, in the circumstances, fully within the powers of the defendants as customs officers. After the fracas with the defendant, Hillen, the plaintiff, on being asked by the defendant, King, refused to give his name and address, basing his refusal on the assault and beating he had suffered at the hands of the defendant, Hillen. When he so refused, the plaintiff knew that his questioner and the companions of his questioner were customs officers. Since obstruction need not be physical obstruction only, the plaintiff by refusing to give the defendant, King, his name and address was in law technically guilty of the offence of obstructing a customs officer in the discharge of his statutory duty as such officer. It was this refusal which caused the defendant, King, to order his brother officers to take possession not only of the van, but also of the plaintiff's person, thus causing him to leave his van and to be seated instead in the car outside the customs office. In Dundalk the plaintiff was again asked by the defendant,

King, for his name and address, and was told there, that on giving same to Mr. King, he (plaintiff), would be released. The plaintiff's reply to this request was to refuse to give his name and address to Mr. King, whereupon he was brought in the custom's car to the garda station at Dundalk, at which place he was given in charge to the garda then on duty there. On these facts and findings I must hold that the plaintiff's detention and imprisonment was within the limited powers of the defendant, King, as customs officer, and done in the discharge of his duty as such officer; accordingly, as the detention and arrest of the plaintiff in the special circumstances was justified by the defence, I must disallow this part of the plaintiff's claim in this action.

Before I leave this part of the present case I take leave to say, for the information and reflection of officers with limited authority, that a resort to arrest should be the last resort when all ordinary peaceful and less provocative means have failed. Officers confronted with a situation, of the kind outlined in this action, should exercise a discretion as to the necessity for arrest and should apply to the circumstances principles which are just and humane, for the arrest and detention of an innocent person is undertaken at the peril of the officer responsible for the arrest. . . .

Notes and Questions

Why should it be a tort to imprison someone without his knowledge? What harm has he suffered? Is liberty of movement so important a value that it must be protected even in such cases? In England the law on this point is uncertain: cf. *Herring* v. *Boyle*, 1 Cr. M. & R. 377, 149 E.R. 1125 (1834), *Meering* v. *Grahame-White Aviation*, 122 L.T. 44 (C.A.). For an excellent analysis of the issue, see Prosser, *False Imprisonment: Consciousness of Confinement*, 55 Colum. L. Rev. 847 (1975). As to the defence of lawful authority, see further pp. 143–152, *infra*.

PHILLIPS V. GREAT NORTHERN RAILWAY CO. LTD.
4 N.I.J.R. 154 (K.B.D., 1903)

Motion on behalf of the defendants for judgment, on the grounds that there was no evidence of false arrest to go to the jury, and also that by virtue of section 5 of the Railway Regulation Act, 1889, the defendants were, on the evidence, entitled to judgment. The action was to recover damages for assault and false imprisonment. The alleged wrongful act took place on August 1st, 1902. It appeared from the notes of the Lord Chief Baron, who tried the action on December 16th, 1902, that the plaintiff on August 1st, with her two daughters, travelled on the defendants' railway from Skerries to Dublin. The plaintiff had a second-class villa ticket, one of the daughters had a second-class ticket, and the other had a return third, on which second-class excess fare had been paid. Before the train arrived at Dublin the guard examined the tickets, and there was some confusion about them, so two halves of the second-class ticket being shown as the tickets on which the plaintiff's two daughters were travelling, instead of one half of that ticket and the third-class ticket. The plaintiff alleged that at Amiens-street Station the ticket-collector said, 'You are travelling on a false ticket,' which the plaintiff denied. The mistake about the two halves of the second-class ticket was then discovered by the plaintiff and rectified. The ticket-collector then asked for the villa ticket on which the plaintiff herself was travelling. When it was handed to him he said, 'This is dated July 31st.' The plaintiff then went to the secretary's office, where some conversation took place. When she got back to the arrival platform of the station where her two daughters were waiting for her, the incident took place which formed the cause of action. That incident is stated fully in the judgment of Lord O'Brien. The plaintiff admitted, on cross-examination, that she had a dog with her, for which she had a ticket from Dublin to Skerries, but not one from Skerries to Dublin. However, she paid the cost of the return dog ticket at Amiens-street. The plaintiff's two daughters and a cabman (whose evidence also is stated in Lord O'Brien's judgment) were examined also on behalf of the plaintiff. At the close of the plaintiff's case, counsel for the defendants asked the judge to direct a verdict for the defendants, on the ground that there was no evidence of either arrest or false imprisonment. The Lord Chief Baron thought that there was some evidence of false imprisonment, and refused to direct. Richard Maxwell, the guard of the train, was the first witness for the defendants, and he stated that when he saw that the two halves of the second-class ticket were off one ticket, he thought that they were trying to defraud the company. Richard Buckley, the ticket-collector, stated in his evidence that on the arrival platform, after the interview in the secretary's office, as the plaintiff was walking towards her cab, he told the plaintiff that he would have to draw the station-master's attention to her, and to wait a moment till he got him. The station-master then went with the ticket-collector to the cab. Buckley had not previously told the cabman to stop. The station-master raised his hat politely, and said, 'There is some misunderstanding between you and the collector as regards the tickets.' Buckley was in the act of handing the two halves to the station-master, to show that they corresponded, when the lady snapped the outward portion of it out of his hand, and tore it up, saying, 'That is how I treat you people.' He picked it up. The station-master said her conduct was not ladylike, and said, 'Will you kindly give me your name and address?' She said she would report both of them, walked to the cab, got in, and told the cabman to drive on. The station-master closed the door of the cab. Buckley did not touch or assault her, and did not detain her, save by asking her to stop. The Lord Chief Baron left the following questions to the jury:– (1) Did the company imprison the plaintiff? (Yes.) 2. Did Buckley know the plaintiff's name and address? (No.) 3. Did the company through their officers in fact know her name and address? (No.) 4. Was the plaintiff asked to pay her fare? (No.) 5. Did the proper officers of the company give the plaintiff the ticket as an authority to travel up to the 1st August inclusive? (No.) 6. Assess the damages contingently upon the judge or the court above being of opinion, on your findings, that the plaintiff is entitled to succeed (£5.) Judgment was entered for the plaintiff for £5.

Lord O'Brien, L.C.J.:

The jury found that the plaintiff was imprisoned by one of the servants of the company, and awarded £5 damages, and the question that we have to determine now is whether there was any evidence to justify that finding. The facts of the case are comprised within a very narrow ambit. It appears that Mrs. Phillips, the plaintiff, was travelling to Dublin from Skerries on the 1st August last, and a series of mistakes was made about their tickets. There was no ticket for the dog which was with the plaintiff, and both the guard and the collector thought the plaintiff intended to defraud the company. It is right, at this stage, to point out that there is nothing in the case but a pure mistake. There is no imputation whatsoever against Mrs. Phillips, whose integrity is unimpeachable. This should be clearly understood, and the only point to be decided is the dry legal question – whether there is any evidence to warrant the finding. It is better, at this stage, to read from the notes of the plaintiff's evidence what exactly occurred. When they arrived at Amiens-street Station the collector asserted that the plaintiff and her daughters had been travelling on a false ticket. While the altercation was going on, the daughter had the luggage placed in the cab. This is the critical period in the case, and I now turn to the plaintiff's evidence. She says, 'When I got round, one of my daughters said to me, "I have a cab, and the luggage is all right; come along." As I was stepping into the cab, and giving the cabman the address where to drive to, the ticket-collector told me not to move. I asked the cabman whom he was to obey – was it I or the ticket-collector? The cabman said, "You; but we dare not move." The ticket-collector went away, and brought back the station-master. The station-master refused to hear my explanation, and said I was travelling on a false ticket. The ticket-collector kept waving the wrong half of the ticket in my face. I was annoyed at this, and took it out of his fingers, and tore it up. The station-master said that I was a dishonest woman, that I was acting most dishonestly, and that I was no lady. I gave him the bits of the torn ticket, and said I would report him. He laughed at that and said, "Oh, do, ma'am, and I will take the law on you." I got into the cab. The station-master shouted, "We have the number of that cab." We drove away.' Now, that is what the lady says. Turn now to what the cabman, John Keegan, says:– 'On the 1st August I had a cab at Amiens-street. Was engaged by the young lady. The passengers were nearly all gone when the lady and her mother came to the cab. The ticket-collector told me to stay there till the station-master came. The station-master, after a few minutes, told me I might go. I did not mind what they were saying when I was driving away. There was some altercation.' These were the facts as set out in the evidence on the plaintiff's side. On the defendants' side there is a denial that there was any arrest or false imprisonment. It is plain from the evidence that the plaintiff experienced a certain delay. She would have left sooner but for the conduct of the station-master. On consideration, however, I think that there was no evidence of imprisonment within the meaning of the authorities. There is no evidence that the plaintiff was so dominated by the action of the ticket-collector that, succumbing to that domination, she lost her liberty. Her intended means of egress were interfered with, but she plainly could have left the station, and in the words of Mr. Justice Patteson in *Bird* v. *Jones*, 7 Q.B. 742, there was not 'a total restraint of the liberty of the person.' In that case Mr. Justice Coleridge said, 'And I am of opinion that there was no imprisonment; to call it so appears to me to confound partial obstruction and disturbance with total obstruction and detention.' In the same case, Mr. Justice Williams says, 'If a partial restraint of the will be sufficient to constitute an imprisonment, such undoubtedly took place.' But then he goes on to say that there was no total restraint by force – 'I think that, in this case, there was no total restraint by force.' Mr. Justice Patteson said, 'I have no doubt that in general if one man compels another to stay in any given place against his will, he imprisons that other just as much as if he locked him up in a room, and I agree that it is not necessary, in order to constitute imprisonment, that a man's person should be touched; but I cannot bring my mind that if one man merely obstructs the passage of another in a particular direction, whether by threat of personal violence or otherwise, leaving him at liberty to stay where he is, or to go in any other direction if he pleases, he can be said thereby to imprison him.' Lord Denman, in that case, dissented. He thought that there was evidence of false imprisonment, and said, 'The plaintiff, wishing to exercise his right of way, is stopped by force, and ordered to move in a direction which he wished not to take'; but I do not think that there is anything in this case like that. I think there is no evidence of total restraint of the person, and the verdict therefore must be set aside, and judgment entered for the defendants, with costs. It is not necessary to refer to the other point arising under the Act of 1889.

Notes and Questions

1. Do you agree that there was not 'a total restraint of the liberty of the person' in this case? *Cf. Dillon* v. *Dunnes' Stores Ltd., infra.* pp. 123–130.

2. Why should it be false imprisonment only where there is a *total* restraint of liberty? In *Bird* v. *Jones* (1845) 7 Q.B. 742, at 755, 115 E.R. 668, at 673, Lord Denman, C.J., dissenting, considered that where there was a total deprivation of liberty 'with reference to the purpose for which [the plaintiff] lawfully wished to employ his liberty,' this amounted to a tortious restraint of the person. Had he a point?

3. Where the means of egress involve the risk of danger or some embarrassment to the plaintiff, an action may still lie: *cf. McMahon & Binchy*, p. 135.

4. Obstructions on the highway may in certain cases constitute a public nuisance where they force those using the highway to take the long way round: *cf. Boyd* v. *Great Northern Ry., infra*, pp. 510–511. The possibility of an action for negligence should also not be dismissed: *cf. Star Village Tavern* v. *Nield* [1976] 6 W.W.R. 80 (Man. Q.B.). What are the prospects of a successful action in negligence where the obstruction takes place on private property rather than on the highway?

5. For a variety of psychological reasons, people who are kidnapped may become closely attached to their captors and may, on occasion, be reluctant to escape when opportunities present themselves to do so without risk of injury. Has their imprisonment ended after the first of these opportunities has arisen?

DILLON V. DUNNE'S STORES (GEORGE'S STREET) LTD.
Unreported, Supreme Court, 20 December 1968, (139/5/6–1966)

Ó Dálaigh C.J. (for the Court):

This appeal is taken by the defendants against a judgment of £5,000 for plaintiff against the defendants, entered up by Mr Justice McLoughlin on 17th November, 1966, after a jury trial lasting fifteen days.

The plaintiff was a shop assistant in the employment of the first-named defendant, a limited company, Dunne's Stores (George's Street) Ltd., and the second and third named defendants, who are father and daughter, the directors of the company. The fourth- and fifth-named defendants are Sergeant and Garda respectively in the Garda Síochána, and at the time of the matters complained of by the plaintiff were also store detectives in the employment of the company. The plaintiff was then aged 17 years.

On Friday, 24th January, 1964 the plaintiff was at her work in the defendant company's shop at Sth. Great George's Street, Dublin. At 4.45 p.m. on that date she was instructed by a Miss Elizabeth Dunne, who is also a director of the company, to go to an upstairs office. The office to which she was taken was Miss Margaret Dunne's office. She was not long in this office until she was told to come into another office immediately adjoining it. While in this office she was questioned by Garda Molloy and Sergeant Culloty, apparently working in relay; and, eventually, she signed a statement in the course of which she purported to confess to having stolen goods and moneys belonging to the company, crimes of which she now says she is innocent. This questioning, on the plaintiff's account, would appear to have lasted for approximately two hours.

Some time after 7 p.m. the plaintiff, again on her account, was told that Mr. Ben Dunne would like to see her and she went into Mr. Ben Dunne's office, which was across the corridor. There she was questioned by Mr. Ben Dunne, and the interview ended when she was told by Mr. Dunne that she was suspended from her employment. She then left the company's premises which had been closed since 6 p.m.; it was then about 8 p.m.

The plaintiff in her statement of claim claimed damages for (i) false imprisonment, (ii) wrongful dismissal, (iii) defamation of character, (iv) injurious falsehood and (v) conspiracy (a) to injure, (b) defame, (c) falsely imprison and (d) maliciously prosecute. The plaintiff, however, in the body of her statement of claim (para. 14) alleged only a single conspiracy, to wit, conspiracy to furnish the alleged confession to the police authorities. At the trial the plaintiff was granted leave to amend her statement of claim by adding an allegation of conspiracy (a) to injure and (b) falsely to imprison (para. 4a). The questions eventually left to the jury deal with two only of the alleged causes of action: (i) conspiracy to imprison unlawfully and (ii) unlawful (or, false) imprisonment.

The jury found that the 2nd, 3rd, 4th and 5th named defendants conspired to imprison the plaintiff and that both 4th and 5th named defendants unlawfully imprisoned the plaintiff and that there was agreement between them and the 2nd and 3rd named defendants that they should unlawfully imprison the plaintiff. Damages arising out of the conduct of 4th named defendant, Sergeant Culloty, were assessed at £2,500 and arising out of the conduct of the 5th named defendant, Garda Molloy, at a like sum. The trial Judge gave judgment for the total of these sums £5,000, against each of the five defendants. All five defendants have appealed.

Certain other employees of the company were also interviewed by Garda Molloy and Sergeant Culloty and also by the Dunnes, the subject of inquiry in each case being the same as in the case of the plaintiff i.e. alleged pilfering; and as alleged, these girls were also unlawfully imprisoned. Some of these interviews took place on Thursday, 23rd January 1964 and others on the following day, Friday, 24th January, 1964, the day on which the plaintiff was interviewed. Counsel for the plaintiff in opening the case informed the jury that he proposed to call a number of these girls as witnesses, and he summarised for the jury what their evidence would be. At the close of counsel's address objection was taken by counsel for the company and the Dunnes to the introduction of this evidence as prejudicial to the defence; he applied for the jury's discharge. Counsel for Sergeant Culloty, and Garda Molloy, who was appearing in person, supported the objection. In reply Counsel for the plaintiff submitted the evidence was admissible on three grounds – (i) as part of the *res gestae* – that there was one continuing transaction which commenced on Thursday, 23rd January and ended on Friday evening, 24th January; (ii) to establish proof of the employment of the 4th and 5th named defendants by the company and that they were acting as agents for the company; and (iii) as evidence of the conspiracy alleged, which if established would, it was submitted, let in all this evidence against all the defendants.

The trial Judge was of opinion that the evidence of the other girls might be relevant; and, on that ground he said, that being so, it would be quite wrong for him to discharge the jury at that stage. The evidence of these girls was admitted, and a great part of the trial was taken up with it.

Sergeant Culloty was engaged by Dunne's Stores as a store detective in the month of July, 1963. He was to work in his spare time on Thursdays, Fridays and Saturdays and to be paid 7/6d. per hour. It was agreed he could find a deputy when he could not attend; the deputy he chose was Garda Molloy. Sergeant Culloty kept a tally of the hours worked by both; he was paid by Miss Margaret Dunne, and in turn, he paid Garda Molloy.

Garda Molloy's evidence was that some days prior to Saturday, 18th January, 1964 he had obtained confidential information that there was pilfering going on in Dunne's Stores. This he communicated to Sergeant Culloty on 18th, and Sergeant Culloty, in response, told him he already had similar information. On the following Wednesday, 22nd January, on the instructions of Sergeant Culloty Garda Molloy went to Dunne's Stores to interview an employee named Miss Christina Conroy, which he did, having first obtained the permission of Miss Margaret Dunne. As a result of what Miss Conroy told him he took possession of her overcoat. He communicated the result of this interview to Sergeant Culloty. Later, the same evening,

Garda Molloy went to Jury's Hotel where he saw Mr. Ben Dunne and the Dunne family. He asked Mr. Dunne if he might interview members of his staff at the stores the next day. Mr. Dunne said it was a matter for the Garda's authorities; Garda Molloy said he was making these enquiries with his authorities' knowledge. Mr. Dunne then said that as far as he was concerned that was quite all right.

On Thursday morning, 23rd January, Garda Molloy received instructions from Chief Superintendent Culhane, through Sergeant Culloty, to go to Dunne's Stores. He arrived some time after 9 a.m. and had a conversation with Mr. Ben Dunne and Miss Margaret Dunne. Then he began interviewing shop assistants, and the interviewing continued throughout the day. Assistants were interviewed singly, and Sergeant Culloty and Ban-Ghárda O'Reilly took part in this operation. The interviewing was continued on Friday, 24th January; and the plaintiff was the last person interviewed that day. The plaintiff, in her statement of claim, alleges that she was falsely imprisoned on three separate occasions on the evening of Friday 24th; but the only occasion relied upon at the trial is that which is alleged to have occurred in the course of the interview or interrogation of the plaintiff conducted by Garda Molloy and Sergeant Culloty. Garda Molloy began the interview and left the room. Next, Sergeant Culloty entered and continued the interview and then left. The interviewers alternated in this way, the Garda being replaced by the Sergeant. Eventually the plaintiff signed a document in the course of which she purports to confess to having stolen shop goods and money, both the property of her employers. During one of these several interviewing sessions, when she was questioned about taking money and had denied it she asked Garda Molloy if she could go. Her evidence is that he said 'yes'. She says she then got up and walked to the door. At that point, according to the plaintiff, Garda Molloy interposed with the words – 'When you admit taking the money'. The plaintiff also says that the Garda said that 'he was going to telephone for a squad car to take her to Mountjoy for six months'; that he picked up the telephone, as if to do so, and at that point she commenced to cry. Garda Molloy then left the room, and after an interval he was, she says, replaced by Sergeant Culloty. The Sergeant, she says, inquired why she was crying, and she says she told him it was because Molloy had said she had taken money. She says that the Sergeant had a long sheet of paper in his hand, that he wrote for a few minutes and then said to the plaintiff she could go home if she signed the paper: she signed the paper. Garda Molloy then entered the room, and he and Sergeant Culloty left together. As Garda Molloy left the room he said, again according to the plaintiff, 'I will be back'. He did not in fact return. The plaintiff remained on in the room until after an interval, she was brought into Mr. Ben Dunne's room.

It was the plaintiff's case that what occurred during this interview constituted false imprisonment.

The defendants' first ground of appeal is that there was no evidence that the plaintiff was falsely imprisoned; that what the plaintiff alleges occurred did not constitute false imprisonment. This, in my opinion, is a submission which does not bear examination. One can fix in the plaintiff's evidence a point at which Garda Molloy in effect told the plaintiff that she was not free to leave until she signed a confession of theft. However it may be argued that prior thereto the plaintiff was under no constraint and might have broken off the interview at any moment and left the room, it is quite impossible to say that after Garda Molloy uttered the words sworn to by the plaintiff the jury, accepting the plaintiff's evidence, had not the clearest evidence of false imprisonment.

Next, it was argued by Sergeant Culloty that there was no evidence that he had falsely imprisoned the plaintiff. It is true that there is no evidence that he personally falsely imprisoned the plaintiff. The plaintiff's case is that the act of Garda Molloy in falsely imprisoning the plaintiff was also the act of Sergeant Culloty; that they were acting in concert. The plaintiff's account of how the interview was conducted, with Garda and Sergeant alternating, affords ample evidence from which a jury could infer that the several steps taken in the course of obtaining the plaintiff's confession were agreed upon by both officers and that the Garda in declining to let the plaintiff go until she signed a confession was acting on the directions and on behalf of his superior. The interview was, on the terms of the plaintiff's evidence, a conjoint operation by the Garda and the Sergeant. One took up where the other left off, and they had, after each 'session', an opportunity of consulting outside the room as to the progress the other had made and agreeing how matters should go forward. The jury had more than enough material from which they could infer that the Garda in detaining the plaintiff was acting on the Sergeant's authority and as his agent.

The next ground of appeal for consideration raises the question whether the Dunnes agreed with the Gardaı to falsely imprison the plaintiff. The jury found they did. The submission on behalf of the Dunnes is that there is no evidence to sustain this finding.

The evidence pointed to on behalf of the plaintiff in support of the jury's finding is as follows: (i) the Gardaı were also the company's store detectives; (ii) there is evidence that statements obtained from other assistants, under not dissimilar conditions, were proved to be in the possession of the Dunnes immediately after each of such Garda interviews terminated; (iii) that Garda Molloy had said to Miss Whelan during the course of her interview that he didn't like doing this any more than she did and on account of knowing all the girls, but that Ben Dunne had asked specially at the station for him and Sergeant Culloty (2261); (iv) that Garda Molloy had said to Miss Nolan (later Mrs. FitzGerald) that he did not want to do it but Mr. Ben Dunne had asked him to; (2077) that, according to Miss Brady, Miss Margaret Dunne on the previous evening had first refused a request of a Miss Purcell to go to the toilet and then allowed it, but under surveillance (2791).

None of these matters amounts to evidence that the false imprisonment of the plaintiff was effected by the Gardaı in agreement with the Dunnes. The inference is open that the Dunnes wanted the Gardaı to obtain for them confessions in writing from the assistants who were suspected of pilfering. But this falls short of authorising or agreeing to falsely imprison. The fact that the Gardaı also were in the employment of the company as store detectives, a jury might reasonably think, may have made them excessively zealous in their pursuit of evidence of pilfering by members of the shop staff; but this is not enough. Nor does what Garda Molloy is alleged to have said either to Miss Whelan or Miss Nolan put the matter any further. In the one instance what the Garda was doing when he is alleged to have said he didn't like doing *this* was merely questioning Miss Nolan not detaining her against her will; and in the other instance what the Garda said he 'didn't want to do' was somewhat similar: he was moving from one counter to another counter asking Miss Nolan if she had taken goods from any of these counters. Further, Miss Margaret Dunne's surveillance of Miss Purcell was something which occurred not before but after the Garda interview.

Nowhere in the cross-examination was a suggestion put to Mr. Ben Dunne or any of his co-directors that they agreed with the Gardaı that they should detain the plaintiff until she confessed to theft. The submission made on behalf of the Dunnes (Ben and Margaret) is, in our opinion, correct. There is, as has been said, evidence to support an inference of an agreement to obtain statements; but we do not find any evidence that would warrant the jury holding that the Dunnes agreed with the Gardaí falsely to imprison the plaintiff, and the Court must, therefore, set aside the jury's findings that Ben and Margaret Dunne had so agreed.

In the result the plaintiff's action against the Dunne's and against the Company for false imprisonment fails, and judgment must be entered up in their favour in respect of that cause of action.

[Ó Dálaigh C.J. proceeded to consider the question whether the defendants were guilty of conspiracy to falsely imprison the plaintiff. This passage from the judgment is extracted *infra* pp. 460–461. He continued:]

... The appellants, Garda Molloy and Sergeant Culloty, have also appealed against the judgment on two other grounds. The first of these grounds is a challenge to the admissibility of the evidence of the other assistants who alleged they were treated in much the same way as the plaintiff viz. falsely imprisoned, compelled to make confessions, threatened with imprisonment etc.

This evidence is not relevant to the issue whether or not the defendants falsely imprisoned the plaintiff. The resolution of that issue depends on what the jury find occurred in the course of the interview of Garda Molloy and Sergeant Culloty with the plaintiff: what happened to other girls is irrelevant to that issue. It was submitted on the plaintiff's behalf that the evidence of the other girls was admissible on three grounds: conspiracy, agency, pattern.

On none of these grounds, in our opinion, was this evidence admissible. First, the evidence did not establish a conspiracy. Secondly, while there were observations made by Garda Molloy to two girls (Miss Whelan and Miss Murray) which bore on the question whether the Gardaí were acting as private store detectives as well as Gardaí in carrying out this inquiry, the rest of the evidence of the girls had no relevance to agency. Thirdly, the principle that evidence of other like transactions is admissible to prove pattern had no relevance whatever to the issue which the jury had to try. What occurred in Mr. Ryan's room either amounted to false imprisonment or it didn't. Nothing that occurred before or after to other girls could effect the answer to that question.

The admission of evidence of these other girls was highly prejudicial to the defence of Garda Molloy and Sergeant Culloty; and there is no room for doubt that it rendered [their] trial unsatisfactory – indeed, rendered the trial not a trial but a commission of inquiry into the alleged misdeeds of the defendants.

The judgment for false imprisonment against Garda Molloy and Sergeant Culloty cannot, in the circumstances, be allowed to stand; but as there is evidence to go to a jury in support of this cause of action a new trial should be ordered.

We should not conclude without adverting briefly to certain matters raised with regard to the question of damages. It is, in our opinion, not open to question that in an action for false imprisonment a jury may award punitive damages. The existence of the category of damages known as punitive damages has received statutory recognition: see Civil Liability Act, 1961, s. 14(4).

We should also add that it is proper that the attention of juries should be called to the provisions of section 14 (4) wherever it is open to distinguish between the roles of several defendants. A jury which held that Garda Molloy and Sergeant Culloty had jointly falsely imprisoned the plaintiff could not, however, on the evidence, here distinguish between their several roles.

In the result, this appeal will be allowed.

In the case of the 1st, 2nd and 3rd named defendants judgment will be entered up in their favour; and in the case of the 4th and 5th named defendants the Court will direct a new trial but confined to the action for false imprisonment. . . .

Notes and Questions

1. Does this case hold that authorisation to falsely imprison must be express? If not, must it involve some communication between the parties? (*Cf.* the interpretation of section 34 (1),

(b) of the *Civil Liability Act 1961, infra*. pp. 217–219. Does this have any light to throw on the present problem or can no analogy be drawn?)
2. If a Garda says to a suspect: 'You may leave if you tell the truth', does this constitute imprisonment? What is the position if instead he says: 'You may leave when you have told me what happened'?

BURNS V. JOHNSTON

[1916] 2 I.R. 445 (King's Bench Division) (affirmed by Court of Appeal, [1917] 2 I.R. 137)

Cherry L.C.J.:

This is a test action brought by the plaintiff, who is a workman in the employment of the defendant's firm, to recover damages for alleged false imprisonment by the defendant, under the circumstances fully set out in the case stated. A number of their actions, about 130 in all, depend upon the result of the present action; so that, apart from the question of law involved, the case is of some importance.

The plaintiff has been a weaver in the defendant's factory for about eighteen years; the hours of employment in the factory are regulated by the Factory Acts. Normally these hours are from 6 a.m. till 6 p.m., but at various times the hours of employment have been changed. It is customary to put up a notice of intended change of hours for one fortnight prior to a change coming into operation.

In the month of August, 1915, the defendant applied to the Home Secretary, under sect. 150 of the Factory Act, 1901, for permission to extend the hours of work in the factory beyond those sanctioned by the Factory Acts, and received an order on the 25th August sanctioning that course. The working hours were then extended for half an hour, to 6.30 p.m. A notice to that effect was on the 30th August posted up in the factory, and was seen on that date by the workers, including the plaintiff. The change was to begin on the 14th September, 1915. The defendant stated that some workers gave notice to leave his employment in consequence of the change of hours, but that none of the 130 plaintiffs gave any such notice.

During working hours the yard gate of the factory was always kept locked; and if a worker had to leave the factory during working hours, he or she had to obtain a pass, which had to be given to the gate-keeper before leaving. Without such a pass a worker could not leave the factory during working hours.

The defendant's counsel contended that this custom of keeping the yard gate locked during working hours, and preventing the workers from leaving without sufficient cause during those hours, formed part of the contract by which the work-people were bound. The learned judge has not stated that he arrived at any such conclusion, and it may be necessary, inasmuch as the case is stated on a question of law only, for us to draw inferences of fact from the evidence, and both sides agree that we should be allowed to do so. Acting on this permission, I arrive at the conclusion that the defendant's contention is right on this point, and that the work-people are bound, as a term of their contract, by the rule as to the closing of the gates.

On the 14th September, 1915, the defendant gave instructions that the yard gate was to be kept locked until 6.30 p.m. On this evening, at six o'clock, 130 of the workers, including the plaintiff, came out of the factory, and demanded to be let out. The defendant refused to allow the gate to be opened until 6.30 p.m., and the plaintiff was, with the other workers, detained until that hour. None of the workers on the occasion had a pass.

The question now arises: Were the plaintiff and the other workers bound by the rule as to the closing of the gates during the last half hour of work in the same way as, in my opinion, they were bound during the ordinary hours, 6 a.m. to 6 p.m.? In my opinion they were. Having had notice of the intended change for a fortnight, and not having served any notice of intention to leave the defendant's employment, they must, I think, be taken to have agreed to the change in the hours. Otherwise they should not have gone to work on the 14th September.

The case, in my opinion, comes within the principles laid down by the House of Lords in the recent case of *Herd* v. *Weardale Steel, Coal, and Coke Co., Ltd.* [1913] A. C. 67, and the facts in the present case strongly resemble those proved in that case. There, a coal miner descended a coal mine for the purpose of working therein for his employers at 9.30 a.m. On arriving at the bottom of the mine he was ordered to do certain work which he wrongfully refused to do, and at 11 a.m. he requested to be taken to the surface in a lift, which was the only means of egress from the mine. In the ordinary course he would have been entitled to be raised to the surface at 4 p.m. The employers refused to permit him to use the lift until 1.30 p.m., although it had been available for the carriage of men to the surface from 1.10 p.m., and in consequence he was detained in the mine against his will. It was held by the House of Lords that an action for false imprisonment could not be maintained, because the contract was to remain in the mine until 4 p.m.; and the principle of *volenti non fit injuria* therefore applied. 'The man,' Lord Haldane says, at page 73 of the report, 'chose to go to the bottom of the mine under these conditions – conditions which he accepted. He had no right to call upon the employers to make use of special machinery put there at their cost, and involving cost in its working, to bring him to the surface just when he pleased.'

In my opinion, these remarks of Lord Haldane apply to the present case. It was part of the conditions of his employment that the plaintiff should remain at work until 6.30 p.m.; and although the defendant might not be entitled to interfere actively to prevent his leaving before that time, he was not bound to afford facilities to him for doing so. He was, in my opinion, not bound to open the gates contrary to the ordinary rule for the working of the factory. Had the plaintiff applied for and been refused a pass out, different considerations might arise, but this he did not do.

Mr. Maguire contended in his able argument that even assuming that the plaintiff was not entitled to leave his work, the action of the defendant in refusing to allow the gates to be opened was punitive in character, and such action having been taken with the intention of imprisoning the plaintiff, an action for false imprisonment would consequently lie, even though the plaintiff was leaving in violation of his contract of service. But Lord Haldane, in his judgment in *Herd's Case* [1915] A. C. 67, deals with this very point, and assumes that an action would not lie under the circumstances, even though the intention was to punish. 'There was,' he says (p. 72), 'no refusal to bring him up at the ordinary time which was in his bargain; but there was a refusal – and I am quite ready to assume that the motive of it was to punish him, I will assume it for the sake of argument, for having refused to go on with his work – by refusing to bring him up at the moment when he claimed to come. Did that amount to false imprisonment? In my opinion it did not.' Even though, therefore, we were to draw the inference which plaintiff's counsel suggests, it would not materially assist him.

For all these reasons I am of opinion that the facts proved in this case do not constitute false imprisonment, and that the question put by the learned judge should be answered in the negative.

Gibson J.:

This case primarily depends on inferences of fact which the Court has no proper jurisdiction to draw, its function being confined to questions of law arising on ascertained facts. Counsel, however, have agreed that the Court should be at liberty to draw inferences, and I shall dispose of the controversy on that footing.

There are the following questions of fact to be determined:– 1. Did the plaintiff accept the defendant's term that the day should be prolonged for the extra half-hour? 2. Did he accept as a term of his employment the defendant's right to keep the gate locked? 3. On what terms was the gate to be unlocked?

1. Prima facie, on the course of dealing stated in the case, the plaintiff would have been bound to serve for the extended period. What is relied on is the letter of O'Neill (who is assumed to have been the plaintiff's representative) asking for a war bonus. This was refused on August 31st, 1915, by letter. The plaintiff, on August 30th, knew of the change of hours, and the terms on which he would be employed. He did not give the usual fortnight's notice, or any notice determining his employment, and on September 14th went to work as usual. Unless he accepted his employer's terms he had no right to be there. Had he objected, he might not have been employed at all. It would be in complete violation of the principles of the law of contract, where a proposal is acted on by the other party without objection, to allow such party to evade the prima facie contract by alleging that he did not intend to be found. The work was piece-work, and the plaintiff ought to have repudiated the time extension in express terms. He knew that the defendant was only employing him on the new basis, and that the war bonus application was to stand over. I find, therefore, as a fact, that there was a tacit contract (whether the plaintiff in his own mind intended it or not) that the hours were to be extended to 6.30 p.m. Contract, when not evidenced by express language, depends on acts and conduct, and not on secret ideas in the mind of either of the parties. When the plaintiff entered the premises and began to work with an employer who had postponed the increase of pay, but was insisting on the additional time, the defendant was justified in concluding that the plaintiff was assenting to the master's terms. He, by his conduct, held himself out as so assenting, and his employer was entitled so to assume.

2. On the same reasoning, I think it must be taken that the gate was to be kept locked when the shorter working day was in force, and that this was a term of employment accepted by the plaintiff. The same term must be applied to the longer day. It would be absurd that the defendant should be at liberty to have the gate locked up to 6 o'clock, but not from 6 to 6.30 o'clock. The old terms applied to the new arrangement, which only affected duration of work. The plaintiff must have known on September 14th that the gate was locked as previously.

3. The gate was not to be opened without a pass. The case does not inform us on what terms such pass was to be issued. The gate was kept locked in the employer's interest, and plainly the pass was intended to be for his protection. It was not for the purpose of getting a time-sheet filled, for the work was piece-work. It was, in accordance with familiar factory discipline, to control the workers, avoid irregularity of work, and prevent absence without knowledge of the employer. It would presumably be asked for and given on a special occasion on reasonable personal grounds. I do not think that anyone who wished could at any time demand a pass when he had no reason for going out. On that view, the locking of the gate and the pass would be a meaningless form; the employee could leave when he liked; the pass would be a piece of worthless paper without any effect. The case does not state that the employee was entitled to the pass as of right. If it was unreasonably refused, a different question would have arisen. What was done by the plaintiff and his comrades was a complete

repudiation of the pass system. At the lowest, the pass was to enable a note or record to be kept in the foreman's list, book, or memory, of the individual quitting work. Where 130 persons required at once to get out, the issue of passes to each individually would take a considerable time, possibly half an hour. It was necessary to distinguish those quitting from those remaining behind. The plaintiff and his fellow-workers asked for no pass, and their demand was founded on no pass being necessary, as the day's work was done.

It is admitted that if the plaintiff was minded to leave, though in breach of contract, the defendant could not have detained him by locking him in, whether with the object of forcing him to work or by way of punishment. Such detention would be false imprisonment. The defendant's contention is, that this gate was locked in pursuance of contract, and that he was under no contractual duty to issue a pass in the circumstances proved, or to open the gate. He *abstained* from acting, as Lord Justice Buckley puts it in *Herd's Case* [1913] 2 K. B. 771. He was under no obligation to facilitate or assist the plaintiff in going away before his time in violation of his bargain.

Herd's Case [1915] A. C. 67, with the judgments in the Court below, was relied on by both sides. Lord Haldane, at page 72, treats the motive of the defendants' act – whether to punish or otherwise – as immaterial. There were two grounds of decision: (1) that the principle *volenti non fit injuria* applied, and that there was no breach of contract by the defendants; (2) that there was no duty on the defendants to supply the plaintiff with facilities for leaving the mine before the regular hour. The circumstances were, no doubt, different from those before us here; but the question is, does the principle of the decision apply? I think the case falls within Lord Haldane's reasoning. What the plaintiff wanted was to get out before his duty had expired, and for that purpose to require the defendant to do an act interrupting the existing physical situation in his own favour. This brings in the second ground of the decision in *Herd's Case*. Whether the means of egress is by a cage from a mine, or by laying a gangway, or by using a key in a lock, though the cost may be different, all agree in this, that assistance is required from an affirmative act. Suppose a cook in the middle of the night – the outer door being locked, and her employer in bed – wished on a sudden nocturnal caprice to get away, could she sue for false imprisonment if her master declined to get up and open the door to enable her to carry out her breach of contract? The opening of a locked door involves voluntary action which may cause trouble and delay, especially if the staff controlling the key was away at any distance, or where (as here) a number were going and many remaining. If all the dissatisfied workers did not go at the same time, was the gate-keeper to keep unlocking and locking the gate for the thirty minutes? All that the defendant did was that he abstained from an act which the plaintiff was not, by his contract or otherwise, entitled to demand. The defendant did nothing not warranted by his contract. His locking was legitimate, and he was not bound to unlock. If (as I think clear) the workman during working hours could not leave without a pass, he could not complain because he was kept in from not having got or asked for such pass. No pass was asked for, the attitude of the workers being that all their day was finished, and no pass was therefore necessary. The legal position is the same as if the exodus had been attempted before 6 o'clock. The pass, whatever the terms regulating its issue, was a material provision of factory discipline which the employees were not at liberty to repudiate. Probably, had passes been demanded (a step which would have admitted that the factory hours were in force), they would have been refused on the ground that passes were not applicable to simultaneous concerted action of a body seeking to violate their contract. Supposing that passes would have been refused, that would not help the plaintiff. A wrongful refusal would be necessary; and his case is that after six o'clock he was free from all factory restrictions and regulations, and thus needed no pass. In my opinion he was bound by his contract to accept the locking of the gate as legitimate, and *Herd's Case* is directly in point. The plaintiff by wrongfully refusing to work cannot get rid of the employer's right to maintain the existing physical condition of the factory premises, or impose in him a duty of doing an act which he never undertook to do, and which would be contrary to the terms of his bargain with the plaintiff.

My conclusion is based on the nature and effect of the contract as inferred by me from the facts stated in the case. The action fails. There was no false imprisonment.

On appeal, the Court of Appeal summarily affirmed the judgment of the King's Bench Division: [1917] 2 I.R. 137.

Notes and Questions

1. What limits, if any, are there to the concept of contractually-imposed self restraints on freedom of movement? *Cf.* Keng Feng Tan, 'A Misconceived Issue in the Tort of False Imprisonment' 44 Modern L. Rev. 166 (1981), Williams, 'Two Cases on False Imprisonment' ch. 5 of *Law, Justice and Equity*. Would *Burns* v. *Johnston* be decided the same way today, in your opinion? If not, why not? Would it be because of a change in relevant legal principles or for some other reason?
2. What would the Court's decision have been if the plaintiff had suddenly needed to go to hospital because (a) he had a heart attack? (b) he became unconscious from having drunk too much when on the job? (c) his wife had just been brought to the hospital after a serious accident?
3. If I agree to work as a domestic servant in your house from 2 to 5 p.m. every weekday, and one day, after a row with you at 3 p.m., I make for the door, may you lawfully lock the door before I reach it?

5. *DEFENCES TO TRESPASS TO THE PERSON*
A variety of defences may be available to actions for trespass to the person: they will be considered in turn.
(a) *Consent*
Where an individual consents to physical contact that would otherwise constitute a trespass to his or her person this will render the contact lawful. As Palles, C.B. said in *Hegarty* v. *Shine* 4 L. R. Ir. 288, at 296 (C.A., 1878):

> 'It is indisputable that an act cannot be an assault unless it be against the will of the person assaulted.'

Consent may be expressed or implied. An area of implied consent which has come under increasing discussion in recent years is that relating to physical contact sports. See *McMahon & Binchy*, p. 140. We are still awaiting a definitive modern statement of the law on this subject by an Irish court; the general trend in other countries is to construe the defence of implied consent more narrowly than was generally understood in previous years.

When a defendant pleads consent he must show that he did not exceed the terms of the consent. If, as part of the terms of my employment in a factory, I agree to be liable to be searched by security personnel when I am leaving the factory, this will not justify a security officer making a 'power drive' at me when attempting to search me: *cf. Corcoran* v. *W. & R. Jacob, supra*, pp. 114–118.

It is clear that consent may be vitiated by fraud or duress. The courts have, however, tended to interpret the scope of these concepts narrowly.

HEGARTY V. SHINE
4 L.R. Ir. 289 (Court of Appeal, 1878)

Ball L.C.:

This action is brought by a female Plaintiff against a male Defendant for breach of promise of marriage, and for assault of the Plaintiff, and infecting her with venereal disease; and the second, that the Defendant assaulted and beat the Plaintiff, and infected her with venereal disease. Of the first cause of action (for breach of promise of marriage) there was upon the trial no evidence. The rest of the complaint was founded upon the following facts:– Between the Plaintiff and the Defendant there had for about two years subsisted an illicit intercourse, and during its continuance the Plaintiff contracted from the Defendant disease. As the questions to be decided by us arise upon the charge of the learned Judge before whom the trial took place, and in respect of the view taken by him of the legal considerations applicable to a case of this character, I think it unnecessary to enter into the details of the evidence. There was a verdict for the Plaintiff, but, if the jury were misdirected, of course it cannot be upheld. The charge is reported by the learned Judge in the terms which I shall now state:–

'I charged the jury, carefully reviewing the evidence. Without expressing any opinion on my own part, I adopted as law, and, as applicable to a civil action, the cases of *Reg.* v. *Bennett* 4 F. & F. 1105 and *Reg.* v. *Sinclair* 13 Cox, C.C. 28, and I in substance directed the jury, as matter of law, that an assault implied an act of violence committed upon a person against his or her will, and that, as a general rule, when the person consented to the act there was no assault; but that if the consent was obtained by the fraud of the party committing the act, the fraud vitiated the consent, and the act became in view of the law an assault; and that therefore, if the Defendant, knowing that he had venereal disease, and that the probable and natural effect of his having connexion with the Plaintiff would be to communicate to her venereal disease, fraudulently concealed from her his condition, in order to induce, and did thereby induce, her to have connexion with him, and if but for that fraud she would not have consented to have had such connexion, and if he had with her the connexion so procured, and thereby communicated to her such venereal disease, he had committed an assault, and one for which they might on the evidence award substantial damages.'

This charge and the objections to it were brought before the Queen's Bench Division, when a majority of the Judges held that the views presented by the learned Judge to the jury (not, indeed, according to his own opinion, but in deference to the authority of the two cases in the Criminal Courts cited by him) were a misdirection, and they consequently awarded a new trial upon this ground. The propriety of this ruling we have now to examine.

The charge of the learned Judge assumes that, in order to constitute an assault upon a person, the act done should be against his or her will, without his or her consent. With that proposition I entirely agree. To strike a person minaciously or in anger is a matter very different in character from a blow in sport or play. Sexual intercourse with the consent of the female (supposing no grounds for invalidating that consent) cannot be an assault on the part of the male. The charge then proceeds to assert, that although consent be given, yet if that consent was obtained by the fraud of the party committing the act, the fraud vitiated the consent, and the act became in view of the law an assault. From this proposition, when laid down in reference to the particular facts of the present case, I dissent. We are not dealing with deceit as to the nature of the act to be done, such as occurred in the instance cited in argument, of the innocent girl who was induced to believe that a surgical operation was being per-formed. There was here a lengthened cohabitation; deliberate consent to the act or acts, out of which the cause of action has arisen. If deceit by one of the parties to such a cohabitation as to the condition of his health suffices to alter the whole relation between them, so as to transform their intercourse into an assault on his part, why should not any other deceit have the same effect? Suppose a woman to live with her paramour, under and with a distinct and reiterated promise of marriage, not fulfilled, nor, it may be, ever intended to be fulfilled – is every separate act of sexual intercourse an assault? Let the same happen in conjunction with a violated engage-ment to provide for her maintenance and protection against poverty – does a similar consequence here also follow? No one, I think, would be prepared to answer these questions in the affirmative. In the present case, the fraud relied upon to annul the Plaintiff's consent is the concealment of a fact which if known would have induced her to withhold it; but before this effect is attributed to such concealment, it seems to me reasonable to demand – what is required in contract – that from the relation between the parties there should have arisen a duty to disclose, capable of being legally enforced. And how can this be, when the relation is itself immoral and for the indulgence of immorality; the supposed duty with the object of aiding its con-tinuance? To support obligation founded upon relation, it appears to me the relation must be one that we can recognise and sanction. I do not think these opinions conflict with the cases in Criminal Courts referred to by the learned Judge in his charge. Considerations affect prosecutions not applicable to civil actions. In the former we are concerned with public interests and consequent public policy; in the latter, with the reciprocal rights and liabilities of individuals. Mutual consent to a prize-fight might prevent the pugilists having a remedy *inter se*; but would not make it less a breach of the peace, or exonerate those engaged from punishment.

These reasons, in my opinion, justify the order of the Queen's Bench Division directing a new trial upon the ground of misdirection by the learned Judge. I think it right to add that I also concur with the majority of that Court in holding an action of this character cannot be maintained. The consequence of an immoral act – the direct consequence – is the subject of complaint. Courts of Justice no more exist to provide a remedy for the consequences of immoral or illegal acts and contracts, than to aid or enforce those acts or contracts themselves. Some striking illustrations of this are afforded by authorities cited in the argument of this appeal. Thus Judges have refused to partition the plunder obtained by robbery, to acknowledge or protect property in an indecent book or picture, to compel payment of the wages of unchas-tity. Are the same tribunals to regulate the relative rights and duties of the parties to an illicit intercourse? No precedent has been cited, no authority suggested, for an action like the present; and I am not disposed to make, in the interest of immorality, either precedent or authority for it.

Palles C.B.:

. . . [T]wo propositions have been advanced on the part of the Plaintiff – first, that there was evidence that she did not consent in fact to the act constituting the cause of action; and second, that if she did consent, there was evidence that that consent was procured by fraud. Unless she can establish either of these propositions, the present appeal must fail.

I cannot entertain any doubt that the Plaintiff must, in law, be taken to have consented in fact to the act constituting the alleged trespass. In reference to this, which I deem a cardinal question to the right decision of the case, I abstain from referring to any matter of form. I assume the alleged infecting to be pointedly laid as a substantive trespass. I also assume that which I much doubt, that the contention is open upon the direction at the trial which the Plaintiff is here to support. Apart from matters of form, the case is, that the Plaintiff consented to have sexual intercourse with an individual who then, but without her knowledge, was affected with this foul disorder, and that the physical contact thus consented to communicated the disease to the Plaintiff.

Without entering into any refinements – without considering whether one act is the consequence of the other, or whether each is a separate act, which, but for the Plaintiff's consent, would have been a separate assault – I hold that the consent proved must, in law, be taken to extend to both. That which the Plaintiff consented to involved the communication of the infection, and in consenting to the former she consented to the latter. Such a case is wholly distinguished from *Reg.* v. *Lock* 2 Cr. Cas. R. 10 and *Reg* v. *Flattery* 2 Q. B. Div. 410. In the first there was not a consent to anything; there was not an exercise of a positive will – there was submission, but nothing more. In the second, the prosecutrix consented to a surgical operation: in no sense did she consent to the prisoner having connexion with her.

I have the satisfaction of believing that, upon this part of the case, my view is not in conflict with that of the Lord Chief Justice. No doubt, after putting the case of a surgeon using a poisoned instrument, the learned Chief Justice says: 'Could he not establish that to such an operation, involving such consequences, he did not consent, though he did permit an operation of a different character?' The Chief Justice had, however, immediately previously, stated his view of the law, of which he gave that as an example. 'It appears to me,' he says, 'that the doctrine laid down by Mr. Justice Willes and other Judges in England, that consent procured by fraudulent conceal-ment is void in point of law, is applicable to an action like the present before a civil tribunal.' And again, at the end of his judgment, he bases his conclusion, that the wrong was done without the plaintiff's consent, upon the authority of the cases which he had previously referred to, viz., *Reg.* v. *Bennett* 4 F. & F. 1005, *Reg.* v. *Saunders* 8 C. & P. 263, and *Reg.* v. *Williams* 8 C. & P. 286, each of which was a case of consent in fact, held to have been avoided by fraud.

Being then of opinion that the alleged trespass was an act done with the consent, in fact, of the Plaintiff, the next inquiry is, was that consent avoided by fraud?

Now, I may at once say that I am not prepared to overrule the long line of cases which establish that consent may be avoided by fraud. It is familiar to us all that a contract procured through fraud may be avoided by the innocent party, unless such a change of circumstances has supervened as renders it impossible to reinstate the parties in the condition in which they were before the contract. I see no good reason why the same principle should not be applicable to a bare consent, although it lack the other incidents of a binding contract. Nor do I see why the principle should not be pushed to the extent of converting into an assault that which was in fact the subject of a contract procured through fraud. *Reg.* v. *Saunders* 8 C. & P. 263, and *Reg.* v. *Williams* 8 C. & P. 286, decided upwards of forty years ago, depend for their validity upon this application of the principle; and in relation to the question now in hand, these cases have been since not only uniformly followed in Courts of first instance, but in *Reg.* v. *Case* 1 Den. C. C. 580 have been recognised in the Court for Crown Cases Reserved.

It is not necessary for the purposes of this case to consider whether the fraud which is sufficient to avoid such a consent must not amount (as it did in the three cases to which I have referred) to a false representation that the thing to be consented to is materially different from that which it really was. The logical result of such a limitation might, and indeed I think would, be that the true *ratio decidendi* in such cases should be an absence of consent, not its avoidance for fraud. This, however, could not be held without overruling the many authorities which establish that the obtaining possession of the person of a married woman by fraudulently pretending to be her husband does not amount to rape. If these cases are to be reconsidered (which I am far from saying is not desirable), it certainly must be in the Court of Criminal Appeal. Fully adopting, however, the law as laid down in these several cases, and assuming that there can be fraud of such a description as will be capable of avoiding a consent to commit an immoral act, I think it clear that such fraud must consist of active misrepresentation, as distinguished from suppression or concealment. Concealment, although wilful, and resorted to for the purpose of deception, cannot amount to fraud unless a duty be shown to communicate the fact concealed to the party deceived. In the case of an agreement to commit an immoral act, the sole relation between the parties from which it can be said that a duty to communicate arises is that they have entered into such agreement. From such a relation – illegal and immoral in itself – no duty can arise; and in the absence of such duty, the concealment is neither fraud nor evidence of fraud. This applies as well to a criminal prosecution as to a civil action.

Applying these principles to the facts of the present case, I am of opinion that there has not been any evidence of fraud, and that for that reason the verdict ought to have been directed for the Defendant. In this view the question of necessity of pleading the illegality does not arise.

Assuming, however, for argument's sake, that there was evidence of fraud; assuming also that *Reg.* v. *Bennett* 4 F. & F. 1105 and *Reg.* v. *Sinclair* 13 Cox, C. C. 28 were rightly decided; and even assuming, lastly (which appears to be pushing admissions to nearly an unreasonable extent), that upon the facts proved at the trial of the present case an indictment would have lain against the Defendant for the alleged assault, I am still of opinion that this action is not maintainable.

I am of opinion that the cause of action here is a *turpis causa*, incapable of being made the foundation of an action. The cause of action is the very act of illicit sexual intercourse. The fraud relied upon is not the representation of the existence of a state of facts under which the act of intercourse would have been a moral act on the Plaintiff's part. This is not the case of an innocent party to a bigamous marriage, or of a false representation by the man that he was the husband of the woman. The act was admittedly immoral, irrespective of the belief alleged to have been produced by the fraud. The cause of action is, therefore, an immoral act to which the Plaintiff was knowingly a party. This appears to me to be a typical illustration of the maxim *ex turpi causa non oritur actio*. The answer which has been given to this is one certainly entitled to consideration, as it carries with it all the weight of the authority of the Lord Chief Justice. It is that this maxim applies to cases of contract only. To that proposition I feel unable to assent. 'A promise' – as the Lord Chief Justice truly says – 'cannot be supported – on the contrary, is vitiated – by an immoral consideration . . . nor can a contract be enforced if its object be to promote and encourage immorality.' But why? Because the immorality, which is the consideration in the one case and the object in the other, pervades the contract and renders it immoral. Is it either logical, or consistent with our jurisprudence, to hold that an act of such a character as to vitiate as immoral a contract in reference to it, can itself be capable of sustaining an action? That incapacity to obtain support or audience in a Court of Justice which it communicates to every contract of which it is the subject-matter or the purpose, is necessarily inherent in itself. Every contract relating to this act of illicit intercourse is *turpis*, because the act itself is *turpis*: and as the contract cannot support an action because it is *turpis*, neither, *a fortiori*, can the *turpis* act itself.

It remains but to refer to the argument founded upon the absence of the plea of illegality. No doubt illegality must be pleaded. If, for instance, the plaint had been so framed as to have driven the Defendant to plead the Plaintiff's consent, and there had been a replication that such consent had been procured by fraud, I should have thought a rejoinder of the illegality would have been necessary; but to the plaint as framed here the Defendant had no opportunity of so pleading. The only allegation is of an assault. The denial of the assault puts in issue the Plaintiff's consent. Consent in fact is admitted, and the attempt to avoid it by fraud is made, not by pleading, but in evidence. Under such circumstances the Defendant is, in my opinion, entitled to give in evidence the same answer to such an attempt as, were the fraud alleged in pleading, ought to have been made upon the record. If, to a replication that the consent was procured by fraud, a rejoinder relying upon the immorality would have been an answer, so evidence of the fraud is answered by evidence of the immorality. When consent in fact is, as it was, admitted in evidence by the Plaintiff, the Judge was, in my opinion, bound, in consequence of the immorality of the thing consented to, to have declined to allow inquiry into the circumstances under which such consent was given, and to have directed a verdict for the Defendant.

Deasy L.J.:

I quite concur in the judgments pronounced by the Lord Chancellor and the Lord Chief Baron. This is an action of the first impression. Since the time the disease in question was imported into Europe – as it is said to have been – we have never heard of such an action before. If we were to yield to the compassion which everyone must entertain for the serious injuries which this poor woman has incurred – if we were to make a precedent now, it would be one of very dangerous and wide application. The Plaintiff led an immoral life for two years; and if at the end of that period she can maintain an action against her comrade in sin for a common consequence of that sort of intercourse, we should have many such actions, and also, perhaps, verdicts obtained from motives of compassion. I think such actions are contrary to public policy and public decency, and that no Court should lend its aid to make a precedent for their institution. There is no such precedent. The two cases before Judge Willes and Judge Shee were peculiar; I do not wish to add to or detract from their authority; I leave them where they are, and I say they are no authority for the doctrine that consent to such an act as the present Plaintiff complains of can support such an action as this. The Lord Chancellor put a stronger example – the case of a woman seduced under promise of marriage. Has it ever been suggested that an action for assault could be maintained by her? Let me put an even stronger illustration – the case of a bigamous marriage, where a woman is induced, by the greatest fraud that can be practised, to submit to the embraces of a man. Has it ever been suggested that she could bring an action against him for assault, though the woman in that instance would stand in a very different moral position from the Plaintiff here? Here she has led an immoral life for two years, and one of the not uncommon consequences of that is the disease which she has contracted. Therefore she has no right to complain. The case affords an instance of the mischiefs which would arise from the Court's establishing the doctrine for which the Plaintiff contends. We have had here a very eminent Judge and a jury for two days investigating the time at which, and the circumstances under which, this unfortunate but immoral woman contracted a disease which is incident to the life she led. In my opinion the subject is not a fit one for the consideration of Judges or juries. The action is contrary to public policy and decency, and the decision below must be affirmed.

Notes and Questions

1. Do you agree with the holding in the decision on the question of consent? If considerations

of sexual morality were to be ignored, would the decision have been the same? If a man with an infectious fatal disease were to give a woman the disease by shaking hands with her at a party, should the woman lose her action for battery because unquestionably she intended to shake hands with the man? Is this analogy a sound one?

2. Deasy L.J.'s rhetorical question regarding a woman defrauded into contracting a bigamous marriage has received an emphatic answer in *Graham* v. *Saville* [1945] O.R. 301 (C.A.) and *Smythe* v. *Reardon* [1948] Q.S.R. 74. See also *Shaw* v. *Shaw* [1954] 2 K.B. 429 (proceedings for breach of promise of marriage).

3. The criminal law raises different policy questions: cf. *R.* v. *Clarence* 22 Q.B.D. 23 (1888).

4. Would the plaintiff in *Hegarty* v. *Shine*, if she sued today, succeed on the basis of (a) battery; (b) deceit; (c) negligence; (d) intentional infliction of emotional suffering; (e) a constitutional tort of invasion of bodily integrity? Or would she still be denied any remedy?

(i) *Consent to Medical Procedures*

Medical procedures raise particular problems relating to consent. Clearly, where the medical practitioner fully explains to the patient the nature of the proposed treatment and the patient consents, there is no problem: the difficulties arise where no such explanation is given or no attempt is made to obtain the patient's consent at all, whether on account of the patient's unconscious condition or his young age.

The question of 'informed consent' is discussed *infra*, pp. 177–181. At present consideration will be given to the cases of failure to obtain any consent for the treatment carried out.

It is quite possible, of course, that consent may be implied in the circumstances of the case. The patient may well have authorised the practitioner to behave in the way he did by a general permission, such as telling him to 'do what you consider best', or some similar injunction. The failure by the patient to prohibit ordinary and foreseeable modes of treatment may also be considered to amount to implied consent in certain cases.

Where, however, something out of the ordinary is done by the practitioner, it is less easy to establish implied consent. The decisions hold that it will not be sufficient for the practitioner to show that what he did was for the benefit of the patient: he must show that it was urgently necessary for him to do so without letting the patient first decide on whether he wishes the treatment to be carried out: 'The law prefers

entitlement of the doctor to act in cases of emergency should properly be regarded as being based on the implied consent of the patient or on the broader concept of necessity has been debated in decisions.
self-determination of paternalism': *Salmond & Heuston*, p. 467. Whether the

(ii) *Minors*

The capacity of minors to consent to medical treatment – and, more broadly, any other types of physical contact – is a matter of some uncertainty. The better view, according to Skegg, 36 M.L.R. 370, at 373, appears to be that

> '[i]t all depends on whether the minor can understand what is involved in the procedure in question. At least in theory, this is a factual test, the application of which cannot be determined in the abstract.'

Where a minor is incapable of providing consent, and, indeed, even in some cases where he is, the practice in this country and abroad is for medical practitioners to obtain the consent of his parents or guardian for the proposed treatment. How such consent, given by a third party, can logically provide a defence is difficult to understand but it clearly has the support of decisions in this country and in other jurisdictions. It may perhaps be justified on the ground of necessity, implied consent or agency.

HOLMES V. HEATLEY

[1937] Ir. Jur. Rep. 74 (High Court, Maguire, J., with jury, 1936)

Witness Action before a judge and jury.

The plaintiffs, the parents of a deceased minor, claimed damages under the Fatal Accidents Act, 1846 (9 & 10 Vict c. 93) (Lord Campbell's Act), from the defendant, a medical surgeon, for the death of the minor during a surgical operation which took place in a hospital in Dublin.

The statement of claim set out (*inter alia*):– 'The plaintiffs have suffered damage from an assault and battery committed upon the 23rd day of November, 1934, by the defendant upon one Richard Holmes, a minor, at Mercer's Hospital. Dublin, by causing to be administered to the said Richard Holmes a drug or anaesthetic and by performing upon the said Richard Holmes a surgical incision or operation whereby the said Richard Holmes died upon the said day.'

The defence set out (*inter alia*):– 'The defendant never assaulted or beat the said Richard Holmes as alleged or at all. The acts which are alleged to have constituted an assault and battery were done with the leave and by the consent of the said Richard Holmes and/or the plaintiffs.'

From the evidence at the trial it appeared that advice had been obtained from a general medical practitioner to the effect that the minor, who was sixteen years of age, should undergo an operation for a toxic exophthalmic goitre. The deceased and his parents (the plaintiffs) consented to the necessary operation, the plaintiff Annie Holmes having been informed that only a local anaesthetic would be required and that the proposed operation would not be serious. The minor spent several weeks in hospital during which *inter alia* a cardiograph and an X-ray photograph were prepared and revealed that the left auricle of the minor's heart was slightly enlarged.

The anaesthetist and members of the nursing staff attended under sub-poena and gave evidence that at the actual operation the minor, who was of a nervous disposition, became restless and hysterical, was shouting and kicking, and had to be held down. He also put his hand to the incised part of his back. In order to stitch up the wound it became necessary to administer a general anaesthetic, but on chloroform being administered the patient became weak and died upon the operation table.

An extract from the register of operations of the hospital which was put in evidence stated: 'Operation was started under local anaesthesia; patient became very restless and excitable. Chloroform about two drachms was administered in usual manner. Breathing became shallow and eventually ceased altogether. Usual stimulants were given and artificial respiration performed.'

At the close of the evidence adduced on behalf of the plaintiffs, counsel for the defendant asked for a direction.

Mr. Kingsmill Moore, S.C. (with him, Mr. Ernest Wood), for the defendant: In the case of an adult there is no relevant reported authority for the proposition that consent under such circumstances is necessary. 'A reasonable patient should be told what is about to be done to him that he may take courage and put himself in such a situation as to enable him to undergo the operation': *Slater* v. *Baker and Stapleton* 2 Wils. 359, 95 E.R. 860 (1767). Apparently a tacit consent may be implied even against the instructions of the patient where the operation is necessary: *Beatty* v. *Cullingsworth* (1896), unreported, noted in Halsbury: Laws of England, vol. 20, p. 333. *Pollock on Torts* (at p. 160) expresses the view that consent is unnecessary. It appears that the necessity for preserving health and life justifies an assault even though the plaintiff has not consented, *e.g.* forcible feeding: *Leigh* v. *Gladstone* 26 T.L.R. 139 (K.B., 1909). It is not necessary formally to plead consent as a defence to trespass to the person since it is implied in the denial of assault: *Christopherson* v. *Bare* 11 Q.B. 473, 116 E.R. 554 (1848). *Pollock on Torts*, p. 216, note (q).

In the case of an infant there is no reported authority as to the necessity for a parent's consent. By analogy the consent of the infant should be sufficient. An infant could take part in boxing or football without the consent of a parent being obtained in respect of anything that might happen to him, and the absence of the parent's consent would not give the infant a right of action against opponents who might injure him in the course of the sport. At common law the consent of an infant is a defence even in cases of indecent assault unless a breach of the peace is caused: *Reg.* v. *Banks* 8 C.P. 574 (1838); *Reg.* v. *Meredith* 8 C. & P. 589 (1838); *Reg.* v. *Martin* 9 C. & P. 213 (1839).

Where a person is of such an age of discretion as to understand the nature of and necessity for an operation his consent is sufficient to prevent the operation being *wrongful*, and the Fatal Accidents Act, 1846, applies only where death is caused by a *wrongful* act, neglect, or default. As to the meaning of 'age of discretion' see the *Oxford Dictionary*, vol. 3, p. 436. In the emergency which arose, if consent were necessary, the antecedent consent given in respect of the local anaesthetic tacitly implied consent to the general anaesthetic. A relevant test is whether the boy, had he recovered, could have maintained an action.

Mr. Lennon, for the plaintiffs: It was improper to perform such an operation without the consent of the parents: *Slater* v. *Baker and Stapleton* 2 Wils. 359, 95 E.R. 860 (1967); *Mitchell* v. *(Magistrates of) Aberdeen* 20 S.C. (Rettie) 253 (Ct. of Session, 1893); *Sutherland* v. *(Magistrates of) Aberdeen* 22 S.C. (Rettie) 95 (Ct. of Session, 1894); *Halsbury: Laws of England*, vol. 27, pp. 877–8 (including notes). The nature of the case and the possible dangers should have been previously communicated to the plaintiffs and their consent to the administration of the general anaesthetic obtained.

Maguire J.: I am of the opinion that the direction asked for should be granted. There is no evidence here which would entitle a jury to hold that there was an assault. I am not deciding the question as to whether there is any necessity for the consent of the parents for an operation or whether the consent of the boy of the age of the deceased is sufficient. In my view the surgeon was bound to act as he did in the emergency with which he was faced. On the uncontradicted evidence in this case the giving of the general anaesthetic was the only course open to him. I accordingly withdraw the case from the jury and direct a verdict for the defendant.

Questions

May a parent give a valid proxy consent to medical research being carried out on a minor where the research may confer a benefit on mankind but is neither intended nor expected to confer any particular benefit on the minor? If the answer is no, how may medical research be effectively carried out on children?

(b) *Lawful Authority*

KAVANAGH V. HAMROGUE
Unreported, Supreme Court, 12 March 1965 (33–1964)

Kingsmill Moore J.:

The defendant, Gregory Allen, a Sergeant in the Civil Guards then stationed at Wicklow, was cycling towards Wicklow at about 11.45 p.m. on Sunday, September 25th 1960, when he met a group of cyclists returning from a cinema at Wicklow. All the cyclists, save one, had lights on their bicycles. The exception was the plaintiff, a boy just over sixteen, whose bicycle lamp had been stolen while he was in the cinema. The sergeant switched on a torch which he had in his hand, turned it towards the plaintiff and called out to him to stop, but the plaintiff instead of stopping swerved, put on speed past the sergeant, who had now halted, and made off as fast as he could down the road to Rathnew.

In the past year there had been about 30 bicycles stolen or taken away without the owner's permission from places in Wicklow town, such thefts usually taking place on Saturdays or Sundays. The behaviour of the plaintiff made the sergeant suspicious that he was riding a bicycle which he had just stolen and so the sergeant turned his bicycle and set off in pursuit. After going about a mile the sergeant caught up with the plaintiff and again called out to him to halt but the plaintiff put on a spurt and outdistanced the sergeant. The sergeant, feeling doubtful whether he could overtake so nimble a fugitive, and with his earlier suspicions now confirmed, stopped a passing car driven by a Mr. Hamrogue, got in, and took up the chase in the car. At Dowling's public house in the village of Rathnew the car came up with the plaintiff, who was riding as fast as he possibly could. On the sergeant's instigation, Mr. Hamrogue passed the plaintiff and, when some distance ahead, pulled in to the left of the road near a petrol filling-station owned by Mr. Doolin, where there was some illumination from lights over the petrol pumps. The sergeant jumped out of the rear left door, ran round the back of the car, and put himself in the centre of the plaintiff's half of the road about 6 feet out from the road edge, with his hands up and his torch alight. His intention was to stop the plaintiff, who was then at a distance of 5 or 6 bicycle lengths according to the sergeant and a distance of 5 or 6 yards according to the plaintiff. The plaintiff however, made no attempt to slow or brake but continued to cycle at full speed swerving at the same time to his right in order to round the sergeant. The sergeant thereupon jumped further to his left, intending to catch some portion of the bicycle or of the plaintiff as he passed, and at the same time turned sideways with his right shoulder to the oncoming plaintiff so as to take the shock of any collision. As the plaintiff came level with him the sergeant made a grab. The sergeant thinks he caught the handlebars, the plaintiff says that the grab caught some portion of his person. It does not matter which story is correct for the momentum of the cyclist was sufficient to break the hold; but the grab had been sufficient to throw the rider out of equilibrium and losing control he careered across to the far side of the road and collided with a motor which was coming the opposite way from Dublin and which had not been noticed by either the sergeant or the plaintiff. As a result of the collision his right leg had to be amputated.

The plaintiff admits that he became aware that he was being chased by a guard, that he was trying to escape, that he saw the sergeant get out of the car and take up his position waving his hands, that he knew the sergeant was signalling to stop him and was going to try to stop him and that he did not slacken speed or try to put on brakes but 'kept going' and swerved to his right. Though he does not actually say so it is clearly implicit in his account that he swerved to try and get round the sergeant and escape. It is undisputed that the plaintiff had no idea that the sergeant suspected him of having stolen the bicycle, but thought that he was being stopped for the venial offence of having no light on his bicycle, and that his attempts to escape were the product of youthful exuberance and bravado. It is also clear that the sergeant had no intention of injuring the boy but was merely doing what appeared to him his plain duty, namely to stop a suspected felon, question him, and if unsatisfied, take him to the Guard station. The tragic outcome was anticipated by no one. A little over a hundred yards from where Mr. Hamrogue's car pulled up there is a turn on the road which would conceal a car coming from Dublin. Whether the car which did the injury was in sight when the sergeant started to come out from the rear of Mr Hamrogue's car is doubtful but from the time he came out of Mr Hamrogue's car the sergeant had his back to the oncoming car and would not have seen it. The plaintiff on the other hand was facing the oncoming car and should have seen it, but did not. It would appear that both the sergeant and the plaintiff were so intent, the one in making, the other in avoiding, an arrest that they had eyes only for each other.

The President rules that the sergeant had reasonable grounds for suspecting that the plaintiff had committed a felony. The jury, in answer to a question left to them by the President, have found that the sergeant honestly suspected that the plaintiff was riding a bicycle which he had stolen. There is no appeal against either ruling or finding, and on his ruling and finding the sergeant was justified in endeavouring to arrest the plaintiff and it was his duty to do so. If the plaintiff resisted or tried to escape from arrest the sergeant would be entitled to use such force as was reasonably necessary to attain his purpose – Russell on Crimes 11th Ed. Vol. 1. 730, *Small's Case*, Select Coroners Rolls 79. – the reasonableness of the force and its proportion to the exigencies of the case being judged in the light of all the circumstances. It does not appear to me that the amount of force which the sergeant intended to use to stop the boy, though it was calculated to cause a fairly vigorous collision of their bodies and very possibly a fall, was in itself unreasonable or greater than was necessary to stop a person who had already on two occasions shown his determination to escape, and no question was left to the jury on assault. What was left to the jury was a question whether the sergeant was negligent, and in leaving this question I understand the President to have accepted that the amount of force intended to be used and used by the sergeant was not in itself excessive nor were such results as the sergeant must be deemed to have intended of a nature calculated to make the force unlawful. What was left to the jury to decide was whether the sergeant was negligent in failing to foresee that results which he did not intend and did not anticipate might reasonably and probably eventuate from his action.

We have not been referred to any case, nor have I been able to find any case, where an action was taken based on negligence in the course of a lawful arrest.

But negligence, certainly extreme negligence, may be an element to be considered when judging of the reasonableness of the force employed, if a guard were to take action similar to that taken by the sergeant against a boy riding a bicycle at full speed in a Dublin street crowded with traffic it could well be said that his failure to appreciate the probability of severe injury arising from his action was negligence of such a character as to make the force unreasonable. In such a case a judge might leave to a jury a question as to whether in endeavouring to effect the arrest the guard used such force as was not reasonably necessary, explaining to them that in considering the reasonableness of the force they should take into consideration whether the guard was negligent in failing to foresee what actually happened as a reasonably probable course, but if a judge considered that there was no ground on which the force could be considered unreasonable, other than a failure to foresee as reasonably probable the actual result, he might simplify the matter by leaving the question as one of negligence alone, explaining, as did the President, the way in which the question was to be approached.

The circumstances in this case were very different from those which I have supposed in my hypothetical case. Although the Dublin-Wicklow road is a main artery, traffic in the Wicklow area is not dense at midnight and in the excitement of the moment, the sergeant might well be excused for not anticipating such an event as happened. But if a question as to negligence may properly be left in a case where it is the main ingredient in the larger question whether or not the force used was reasonable I think that in this case there was enough evidence to justify submitting the question on negligence to a jury and that the finding of the jury on this issue was sustainable on the run of the case and the way it was presented to them.

If the question left to the jury had been one as to the reasonableness of the force used it would have had to be considered in the light of the action of the boy for it could be said that the final grab of the sergeant was a natural and automatic response to the final snipe-like swerve of the boy.

If on the other hand the question was left as one of negligence it seems to me that the conduct of the boy should have been considered under the heading of contributory negligence.

The President did not leave any question on contributory negligence as, in his view, the plaintiff could and would have got safely by if the guard had not jumped to the left and tried to grab his handlebars. But this action or something very like it, must have been anticipated by the plaintiff. He knew the man in front of him was a guard in uniform, and on his own statement he knew that he was signalling to him to stop and was going to try to stop him. He must, or ought, to have anticipated that the sergeant would throw himself in his way and try to seize him and he deliberately elected not to brake, not to cease pedalling, not to move to his left between the sergeant and the car or to the left of the car, but to keep on speed and try to beat the sergeant by a swerve outside him. He ought, I think, to have anticipated the probability that in the course of the sergeant's attempt to stop him he would be forced off balance and might even have a fall. While the sergeant had his back to the oncoming vehicle the plaintiff was facing it and ought to have seen the lights which were on full. A jury might very reasonably have come to the conclusion that the real cause of the accident was his attempt to escape being apprehended and that he was negligent in so doing. It was his duty, when challenged by an officer of the law, to stop. 'The law does not encourage the subject to resist the authority of one whom he knows to be the officer of the law.' 'The right to resist is always limited by the duty to submit to arrest by an officer of the law, even though the reason for arrest is not at once stated'. *Christie* v. *Leachinsky* [1947] A.C. 573, Lord du Parcq at 599, 601. Taking a broad view it might be argued that it was the action of the plaintiff that brought his calamity upon him. His conduct justified the sergeant in using force and he apparently anticipated that the sergeant would try to do so. It seems to me that a jury could hold that he was at least as negligent as the sergeant in not realising that his attempt to escape at high speed combined with the probable and legitimate efforts of the sergeant to prevent him might result in injury which neither of them desired to happen. I find it difficult to divorce, either in time or place, the final action of the sergeant from the final action of the boy. They seem to me intimately interconnected and it appears to me almost impossible to say that the lamentable result was due solely to the negligent action of the sergeant, uncontributed to by the negligent action of the boy.

In my view there should be a new trial on all issues and the trial judge must be at liberty to leave to the jury such questions as he thinks fit, not necessarily the questions left by the President.

Ó Dálaigh C.J.:

The infant plaintiff was injured when the defendant, a sergeant of the Garda Siochána, attempted to stop him to ascertain if the unlighted bicycle which he was riding along the public highway was a stolen bicycle. The precise circumstances of the encounter are narrated in the judgments my two colleagues have prepared and it is unnecessary to repeat them.

The defendant made the defence that he suspected the plaintiff was riding a stolen bicycle. On this basis he claimed that he was entitled to arrest the plaintiff using such reasonable force as was necessary for the purpose. The issue of the defendant's right to arrest the plaintiff was determined in the High Court in the defendant's favour; it has not been reopened here. As the case will, in my opinion go for retrial this issue, with the other issues, will require fresh consideration.

As to the rest of the trial, its course was that it was treated as an action for negligence. The jury were asked to say if the Sergeant was negligent. The learned President ruled that in all the circumstances there was no room for a finding of contributory negligence on the part of the plaintiff.

The question as to negligence of the defendant (as I follow the course of the trial) is to be understood as raising the issue whether the force, in manner and quantum, used by the defendant, in attempting to effect the arrest, was, in all the circumstances, in excess of what was reasonable necessary. I think it would have been more satisfactory if the trial had proceeded on that basis. The parties, however agreed to this course, and they have made no complaint of it in this Court.

What has been urged here on behalf of the defendant is that there was no evidence that he was negligent, that is to say, no evidence that he used excessive force; or alternatively (another aspect of the same submission) that there was coercive evidence of contributory negligence, again, meaning that the force used was not excessive; and, in the further alternative, that in any event there was evidence of contributory negligence which should have been left to the jury to consider, meaning, once more, that if plaintiff's own conduct at the ultimate stage of the encounter be taken into account the jury could well say that the force used was not excessive.

The need for this exegesis seems to me to indicate that it could have been more satisfactory if the trial had proceeded as to its second branch on the simple issue of the reasonableness in all the circumstances of the force used – e.g. the conduct of both parties, the degree of seriousness of the suspected offence, the suddenness or otherwise of the Sergeant's confrontation of the plaintiff, the traffic and other perils to be anticipated.

My view is that there was evidence to be considered by the jury as to whether the force employed by the Sergeant was, in all the circumstances, in excess of what was reasonably necessary. Among these circumstances were the plaintiff's knowledge and conduct – his knowledge: that a member of the Garda Síochána wished to stop and interview him, and his conduct: that, not withstanding this, he determined to persist in his attempt to flee.

I do not think that the plaintiff must necessarily be found guilty of contributory negligence; but I do think that it is not possible to say, as the President ruled, that the last moments of this encounter are so clearly severable from what went before that the plaintiff must be acquitted of contributory negligence.

I confess embarrassment at having to use terms which seem to me not wholly appropriate to raise clearly the only issue arising on the second branch of the case – the reasonableness, or otherwise, of the force used by the Sergeant in his attempt to effect the arrest.

The case should therefore in my opinion go for retrial.

I feel I should, however, repeat what I said in the course of the argument – that this is a case in which, it seems to me, the parties, looking to the tragic consequences of what was not a great deal more than a boyish escapade, should consider whether they cannot adjust their differences without further litigation.

Lavery J. (dissenting):

' . . . The only question, in my opinion, requiring serious consideration is whether the judge should have left the question of contributory negligence to the jury.

The first ground does not arise for consideration on this appeal. The President ruled that the defendant had reasonable grounds for suspecting the plaintiff of having committed a felony – to wit, the larceny of a bicycle: and left to the jury the question whether he honestly believed this.

The jury answered this in the defendant's favour. They could hardly have done otherwise in view of the President's ruling that there were reasonable grounds unless they convicted the defendant of a gross and unprovoked assault.

This they certainly would not have been justified in doing.

I confess, however, that I consider the President's ruling that there were reasonable grounds for suspecting the plaintiff of a felony as exceedingly lenient.

The defendant said that in the district many bicycles were being stolen or taken unlawfully by young persons in order to get home – particularly on Sunday nights. He said thirty bicycles had been taken in the preceding year of which seven had not been recovered.

There was no evidence that any bicycle had been taken that night and the defendant's reasonable and honest belief that the plaintiff had stolen a bicycle was based solely on his endeavour to escape capture which in fact was because he had no light.

I do not think I would have taken the same view as the learned President but the defendant has the benefit of it and it is not now an issue. Nevertheless it has a bearing on the issues.

The conduct of the defendant must be reasonable in the circumstances of the case and the action of a police officer in stopping for the purpose of arrest a fugitive must be related to those circumstances. If a crime of violence has been committed and the criminal is trying to escape – that is one extreme case.

The present case is surely at the other extreme. Accepting that the defendant was acting within the scope of his authority in attempting to stop the plaintiff – though I entertain doubts about it – the defendant was bound to use that authority in a reasonable way and the jury were clearly justified in finding that he had not done so.

The defendant jumped out of the car which had overtaken the plaintiff and ran round to the back of the car and surprised the plaintiff who did not anticipate that his path would be barred as it was by the defendant with hands up and moving out as he, the plaintiff, swerved to pass.

At midnight on Sunday on the main road from Dublin such a manoeuvre without giving any attention to traffic was plainly negligent and the disastrous result of his action was reasonably to be expected.

The unexpected and reckless conduct of the defendant has a direct bearing on the only real issue on this appeal – the alleged contributory negligence of the plaintiff.

The ground upon which the President refused to leave the question of contributory negligence on the part of the plaintiff to the jury is thus stated by him in the course of his charge to the jury:

'I am not leaving you any question as to whether Mr. Kavanagh was careless as regards his own safety. You are probably of the opinion that he was. He saw the position with Mr. Hamrogue's car parked on his side of the road and the sergeant on the middle of his half and he knew the Sergeant was trying to stop him.

Notwithstanding that he elected to pedal on as hard as he could and try and avoid the sergeant. That is a risky thing to decide to do but notwithstanding that risky performance it is common case, it is his case and it is the Sergeant's case, both said the same thing, that he could safely have got by the Sergeant and Mr. Hamrogue's car if the Sergeant hadn't done what he did, that is jump to the left, right in front of him and tried to grab his handlebars. Accordingly I am not leaving any question as to the plaintiff's negligence. Assuming he was negligent it had nothing to do with what happened.'

In my opinion the ruling was correct.

I hesitate to state my reasons as I consider the President has done so adequately.

The picture of the accident is clear. The plaintiff cycling fast suddenly is confronted by his pursuer, he swerves and could have passed safely around the car and the police officer. But the defendant makes a lunge to his left to grab the plaintiff or his bicycle and the plaintiff, thrown out of balance goes to his right out of control and into the path of the oncoming car.

The plaintiff said – 'I was going too fast to stop so I went to pass the car. I could have passed inside the white line.'

To me it seems clear that the sole and effective cause of the accident was the action of the defendant.

If that action was negligent and the jury have so found the defendant is liable.

The defendant has had a full and careful trial. There is no blame to be imputed to him save an excess of zeal.

In my opinion this appeal should be dismissed.

Notes and Questions

1. The present relationship between actions for trespass to the person and actions for negligence is not clear. *Cf. McMahon & Binchy*, pp. 127–129. Do you see any reason why the plaintiff should not have proceeded in negligence? Would the position have been different if the defendant had intentionally pushed the plaintiff in the path of oncoming traffic? See also *Marshall* v. *Osmond* [1982] 2 Q.B. 857.

2. As to police powers of arrest and related questions, see Charleton, 'The Powers of the Police: A Critical Overview' 76 Incorp. L. Society of Ireland Gazette 77, 101 (1982).

DUNNE V. CLINTON
Unreported, Supreme Court, 12 December 1931 (42/4–1930), aff'g [1930] I.R. 366
(High Court, 1930)

A felony having been committed, a Civic Guard requested the two plaintiffs, whom he suspected of complicity in the crime, to go to the Civic Guards' Barracks, which the plaintiffs voluntarily did. When they reached the barracks they were questioned by the defendant, the Chief Superintendent of the Civic Guards for the county, and were then detained in the barracks while the Guards were endeavouring to procure evidence. They were not charged with any crime, nor were they formally arrested. They were detained in the barracks from an early hour of the morning of one day until the evening of the following day, when, in consequence of a letter of complaint from their solicitor, they were formally arrested and charged with the crime and brought before a Peace Commissioner, who remanded them on bail to the next District Court. At that Court the charge was dismissed. It was admitted that the plaintiffs could have been brought before a Peace Commissioner on either of the two days during which they were detained. Each of the plaintiffs then brought a civil bill against the defendant for damages for false imprisonment. The Circuit Court Judge gave a decree in favour of one of the plaintiffs, and dismissed the other civil bill. On appeal to the High Court, the High Court held first, that the detention of the plaintiffs amounted in law to imprisonment, as it was a total restraint of their liberty imposed on them by the action of the Guards; and, secondly, that it was the duty of the defendant, as the officer responsible for such detention, to have brought the plaintiffs before a Peace Commissioner as soon as he reasonably could. Accordingly, as he did not do so, he was liable to the plaintiffs in damages in respect of the period that elapsed between the time when the defendant could reasonably have brought the plaintiffs before a Peace Commissioner and the time when he in fact did so.

The Defendant appealed to the Supreme Court.

Kennedy C.J.:

It is hardly necessary to reserve judgment in this case. We are all perfectly clear on the position. If it called for any elaborate consideration – we don't think it does – we would reserve it, but I think as the Court of Criminal Appeal laid down in *Cox's case* 9 April 1929, there is no difference between detention and imprisonment. Taking a classical definition of imprisonment from the *Terme de la ley*:

'Imprisonment is the restraint of a man's liberty, whether it be in the open field, or in the street or cage in the streets, or in a man's own house as well as in the common goal. And in all these places the party so restrained is said to be a prisoner for so long as he hath not his liberty freely to go at all times to all places whether he will without bail or mainprize.'

Now, this thing for which this new term of 'detention' has been invented and is sought to be introduced is imprisonment within the recognised definition of the law. Taking that old definition as a standard, on the evidence here there is no question, because with all the astuteness and ability of Mr. Lynch, he has not been able to show that those men were voluntary boarders for two days in the police barracks. On the evidence they were not free men from the hour when their prolonged interrogation terminated. There is no question of the proper grounds of their arrest or of their interrogation. The only question is whether they were illegally detained, so as to have a cause of action for false imprisonment from the end of that interrogation until they were subsequently brought before a Peace Commissioner. Mr. Binchy puts his theory of the commencement of the detention at 10 o'clock of the morning of the next day after their arrest, because he does not attempt to make the case that a Peace Commissioner should have been summoned from his bed at four o'clock in the morning when the interrogation had ended to determine whether those men should have been remanded on bail or in custody. They were, however, brought into contact with a Solicitor who intervened on their behalf, and were brought before a Peace Commissioner. No justification is brought for the imprisonment, beyond this, that the guards were entitled to detain those suspected of crime. But the question is, whether it is a justification for a prolonged detention or imprisonment to say that the crime was being investigated. I am of opinion that that is not a sufficient answer, because that may run to any length of time, and the time test is not whether the police had a reasonable time to formulate a charge which they propose to bring, but when they could conveniently bring them before a Peace Commissioner in order to have their fate determined validly in law so as to be an answer, if a *habeas corpus* had been applied for under the article of the Constitution which declares that that most important principle laid down there cannot be waived aside for the sake of some indefinite investigation within the will and determination of the police officers themselves.

Now, in my opinion they may be detained only until they can be brought before – and this is to be done as soon as can conveniently be done – a Peace Commissioner and a charge preferred and an order made, either that they be remanded in custody or bail, and the only alternative is to discharge them from custody. The Defendant has taken the responsibility of detaining in both of these cases and detention is nothing different from imprisonment and having gone beyond a period at which the services of a Peace Commissioner could have been conveniently obtained, the imprisonment is not justified and the appeal must be dismissed.

FitzGibbon J.:

I agree. I have very little to add. I think that the proposition that the plaintiffs were not under restraint up to the moment at which they were finally arrested and brought before a Peace Commissioner is not only not open on the evidence, but I don't think that Mr. Clinton himself really desired to put it forward at all. He considered he was acting within his rights and performing no more than his duty in seeing that those men were not allowed to depart from the barracks and go away while he was investigating the alleged burglary. The result of this case will be to save other energetic and diligent Superintendents from exceeding their powers in what they honestly believe to be the performance of their duties, for it has now been decided definitely, not only by the Central Criminal Court, but by this Court, that there is no such thing as detention which is not arrest. A man is not at liberty if under detention. Mr. Clinton fully understood the action of his subordinates and accepted responsibility for it. So far as the rest of the case is concerned, I agree that the reasonableness of the duration of the detention is to be measured by the facilities for requisitioning the services of a District Justice or Peace Commissioner and not by the exigencies of preparing a good or plausible case against a suspected person. The Peace Commissioner before whom a person charged has been brought on the mere suspicion of the Garda has no option to discharge the prisoner. He must if any evidence is offered remand either in custody or on bail and remit the case for hearing to the District Court and in a proper case the prisoner will be brought up on a formal charge before the District Court and the case must go on and be ended by the discharge of the prisoner or by his return for trial. The provisions of Sec. 88(4) of the Courts of Justice Act (No. 10 of 1924) as to the bringing of a person charged with an offence before a Peace Commissioner have been amended in the Courts of Justice Act 1928 s.10 by the omission of the word 'forthwith' but this omission does not exempt the Garda from the duty of exercising all reasonable promptitude and in each case the Peace Commissioner's jurisdiction attaches only if a District Justice is not *immediately* available. The effect of the Constitution is that a person may not be kept under restraint at the will of a Police Officer or civilian except upon the order of some judicial officer such as a District Justice, or, where a District Justice is not immediately available, of a Peace Commissioner.

Murnaghan J.:

I also agree. The authorities cited in argument show that when a person is apprehended by a police officer on a reasonable suspicion of having been implicated in a felony within a reasonable time previously – this form of apprehension is imprisonment – it would be justifiable if the police had gone either before a Peace Commissioner or District Justice within a reasonable time. 'Reasonable time' is ascertained by considering when a Peace Commissioner is available and not the time when the police authorities thought they would have a good case formulated against the accused. The Peace Commissioner or District Justice is the person to determine whether he should be allowed to be detained in a case like the present.

Notes and Questions

1. See generally J.M. Kelly, *The Irish Constitution*, pp. 384–385 (1980); *The People (at the suit of the D.P.P.)* v. *Walsh,* [1980] I.R. 294 (Sup. Ct.).
2. Where a mentally ill person is received and detained in a mental hospital without the prior making of a valid chargeable patient reception order, for what tort, if any, is the health board liable? Negligence? False imprisonment? *Cf. O'Dowd* v. *North Western Health Board*, unreported, Supreme Court, 16 July 1982 (4–1981) (no liability on facts of case). Henchy, J. dissenting, stated:

    'Even as a mentally ill person [the plaintiff] could not have been lawfully incarcerated in the mental hospital without the making of a valid chargeable patient reception order. . . . Such involuntary detention, with its accompanying stigma of dangerous lunacy in the eyes of the neighbours, must be accounted a false imprisonment no less than when a person is arrested without a warrant in a case where the law requires a warrant. If it should transpire that this applicant's mental condition would have warranted the making of a chargeable patient reception order, that fact could be put forward on the issue of damages. But it would not excuse the false imprisonment.'

    Do you agree?
3. Other defences to actions for trespass to the person are self-defence; defence of others or of property; necessity and discipline. See *McMahon & Binchy*, pp. 143–146, 147–148.

Chapter 8

NEGLIGENCE

1. *GENERAL*

Until relatively recently, negligence was not regarded as a separate tort. The word was used in a number of senses, generally suggesting culpable inadvertence or inattention on the part of the defendant. In the nineteenth century negligence began to emerge as a separate basis of liability but it was not until the present century that the conceptual elements of the tort were fully developed.

Negligence has been defined as 'the omission to do something which a reasonable man, guided upon those considerations which ordinarily regulate the conduct of human affairs, would do or doing something which a prudent and reasonable man would not do': *Blyth* v. *Birmingham Waterworks Co.* 11 Exch. 781, at 784, 156 E.R. 1047, at 1049 (*per* Alderson, B., 1856). The standard of 'the reasonable man' imposes an objective norm: the jury are required to decide not how *they would have acted*, but rather how *a reasonable person ought to have acted*.

The law allows some deference to individual factors, such as minority (see pp. 23–24, *supra*), and physical disability, but its approach to mental disability seems somewhat inconsistent and confused: *cf. McMahon & Binchy*, p. 154.

While the standard of the reasonable man gives some substance to the concept of negligence, a number of more specific indicators have been mentioned in the cases in an effort to elaborate more particularly what is or is not reasonable in the circumstances. Four factors in particular have been mentioned. These are:

(*a*) the *probability* of an accident;
(*b*) the *gravity* of the threatened injury;
(*c*) the *social utility* of the defendant's conduct; and
(*d*) the *cost* of eliminating the risk.

(*a*) *The Probability of an Accident*
Children are likely to meddle with certain dangerous objects

SULLIVAN V. CREED
[1904] 2 I.R. 317 (Court of Appeal, affirming King's Bench Division, 1903)

This was an application on behalf of the plaintiff to set aside a verdict and judgment entered for the defendant, and to enter judgment for the plaintiff for £50 damages, or for a new trial.

The action was brought by the plaintiff, a boy of sixteen years of age, by his next friend, for the recovery of damages against the defendant for negligence.

The action was tried before Kenny, J., and a common jury of the city of Cork, at the Spring Assizes, 1903, when the following facts were proved:– On the 10th August, 1902, the plaintiff was returning home from Mass by a public road which passed the defendant's lands. On his way he met Daniel Creed, a son of the defendant, aged between fifteen and sixteen, and two other boys. Daniel Creed left them at a gap leading to the defendant's house. This gap consisted of two pieces of deal, with a narrow passage between, level with the road, and from the gap a private path led to defendant's house, forming a short cut to it. The plaintiff and the two other boys continued along the high road, and had gone about 25 yards when the plaintiff heard Daniel Creed, who had come back to the high road, cry 'Hi, lads.' The plaintiff looked round, and saw a gun in Daniel Creed's hands pointed towards him. The gun went off, and the plaintiff was hit in the eye, and in consequence lost the eye. The plaintiff stated in his evidence that he heard the defendant say that in the morning he went out to shoot rabbits, but got none, and that he met a couple of neighbours and walked along the road with them, and then went to a cottage and read a paper, and before going left his gun. The plaintiff's mother stated she heard the defendant say that he went and took his gun; that he loaded it, and that it was near the road; that he put the gun inside the stile out of his hand, and that it was on full cock; that he went along with two men to show them a field of 'spuds,' and then went to a cottage and remained there reading newspapers till the people were coming back from Mass, and that after coming out he heard the shot of a gun. Daniel Creed, the defendant's son, was called as a witness for the plaintiff, and stated: 'I saw the gun. It was up against the ditch near the gap. I saw it the moment I went in through the gap. I was fiddling with the gun; I did not know it was loaded; I was playing with it.'

The defendant called no evidence, and asked for a direction on the following grounds:– 1. That the injuries arose from the wilful act of a third party of upwards of fourteen years of age, and that there was no legal liability on the defendant for the act of such a party. 2. That there was no legal duty on the party of the defendant towards the general public to guard against the boy obtaining possession of the gun. 3. That the injuries were not the reasonable and natural result of any failure of duty by the defendant.

It was admitted on both sides at the trial that the question was one of law, and that it was desirable to take the opinion of the jury on the question of damages. The only question left to the jury was, to what damages was the plaintiff entitled, assuming that he was entitled in point of law to succeed. They found £50, and then by direction of Kenny, J., the jury found a verdict for the defendant, and the learned Judge gave judgment for the defendant. It was agreed that the Court should be at liberty to draw all proper inferences of fact, and that if the verdict was changed the damages were to be £50.

The King's Bench Division held by a majority that verdict should be entered for the plaintiff for the £50 damages assessed at the trial. The defendant appealed to the Court of Appeal.

FitzGibbon L.J.:

This is in any view a deplorable case. The plaintiff has lost an eye, for which the sum awarded by the jury cannot adequately compensate him. If the defendant is legally responsible for the act of his son, who did the mischief, the litigation may ruin him, and in any event he must feel that but for what was at best his thoughtlessness, the misfortune would not have happened.

The question for us is one of legal liability; it depends upon principles illustrated by many cases. The Judges in the Court below thought this case near the border line, that is, almost admitting a decision either way, as often happens where the result depends upon a balance of considerations.

It is clear to us from what occurred at the trial that the only question now open is whether there was sufficient evidence to sustain a verdict for the plaintiff upon whatever issues properly arose upon the evidence given. . . .

The principle to be derived from the numerous authorities seems to be this:– Where an injury has been suffered which would not have happened but for the action of more than one person, no one of the several persons whose action led up to the injury will be answerable in damages for it unless his action *caused* it; and it should be held to have caused it, if a man of ordinary prudence, having regard to all the circumstances, ought to have anticipated the injury as a not improbable – *'likely'* is too strong – consequence of his action. If so, he is responsible, notwithstanding that the injury would not have happened but for the independent act of a third party. All third party cases are difficult, because in tracing the chain of cause and effect, circumstances often make it almost impossible to distinguish between a flaw and a break, or to say whether the intervention of the third party has not so far predominated in bringing about the injury as to make it right to say that the act of the original party was not an effective cause of the ultimate result.

What are the facts? The defendant on a Sunday morning was going to shoot rabbits, carrying a loaded gun on full cock; being called away, he laid the gun in that state out of his hand, leaning against a fence of his own field, inside a gap or stile on a pathway from a high road to his house, where anyone using the pathway would see it. I must express my surprise that Boyd, J., should have thought that the defendant was not guilty of actionable negligence in thus leaving the gun. Would not anyone finding it in such a position be justified in assuming that it was not loaded and on full cock? If the son, in picking it up to take it home, had shot himself, would not the father have been morally and legally responsible? If it had fallen, or had been accidentally knocked down, and had gone off and done mischief, would the result not have been caused by its having been left in an improper place, and in a dangerous condition? Books and newspapers are full of accidents happening from the incautious handling of loaded guns, especially often by persons most familiar with their use, *e.g.* soldiers and sportsmen; the victims are usually relatives or friends, and the intention to do harm is wholly absent. To suggest that a man who lays a loaded gun on full cock against the fence of the pathway to his house, in full view of every passer-by, is not guilty of negligence, is contrary to my estimate of the judgment of ordinary men. How often have we heard young people warned, even about unloaded guns – 'Charged, or not charged, she's dangerous.' 'Don't point that gun: the devil might load it unbeknownst' – are proverbial Irish cautions, but they are none the less prudent counsel.

We should not unreasonably extend the duty. But the duty is to use reasonable care to prevent any mischief of which there ought to be a reasonable apprehension. The measure of reasonable care is to be gauged by the measure of risk. In the case of a gun loaded and on full cock, the measure of care is at its *maximum*. The scope of duty is the scope of danger, and it extends to every person into whose hands a prudent man might reasonably expect the gun to come, having regard to the place where he left it. The ground of liability here is not that the boy was the defendant's son, but the fact that the gun was left without warning, in a dangerous condition, within reach of persons using the pathway, and the boy was one of the very class of persons whom the defendant knew to be not only likely but certain to pass by, viz. his own household. If they were at Mass, the very time at which they were to pass coincides with the moment when he interrupted the reading of his newspaper on remembering the gun, unfortunately just too late.

So far, I hold that the defendant must be responsible for every direct consequence of the gun being taken up by his son under circumstances which reasonably entitled anyone who found it to assume that it was not both loaded and cocked. There was a breach of duty towards the son himself if he had been injured by its going off as he lifted it. Initial negligence of the father being thus shown, the question is reduced to this – whether the son's act, when he got the gun, was so independent of the father's negligence, and so far outside the range of reasonable anticipation, as to make it the sole cause of the injury, and to absolve the father.

Numerous cases have established that leaving a dangerous thing within the reach of others, without warning, creates a responsibility, by way of cause and effect, for the result of an unauthorised and negligent, reckless, or even criminal act of a third person into whose hands the dangerous thing has fallen. The negligence, recklessness, or criminality of the act of the third person is treated as mitigated by his right to assume that the thing was not so dangerous, or was not in a condition so dangerous, that leaving it where or as he found it exposed him or others to any special and undisclosed risk of injury. Injury directly and not unnaturally arising from the third party's acting on that assumption is treated as the effect of the negligence which originated the danger.

What the boy did is thus stated in the Judge's note:–

'I saw the gun. It was up against the ditch near the gap. I saw it the moment I went in through the gap. I was fiddling with the gun. I did not know it was loaded. I was playing with it.'

The anticipation of any misfortune which was not improbable as a consequence of his act was the defendant's duty, and every person who might not improbably be injured was within the scope of that duty. Several cases have already gone further than is necessary to fix liability on the present defendant. . . .

[After a review of these authorities, FitzGibbon L.J. continued]:

No one can say that the jury here would have been wrong in finding that the gun, as and when it was left by the defendant, was dangerous. He took no precaution whatever. The thoughtless boy here turned a grossly negligent act into an injurious one. The handling of the dangerous gun by the defendant's son as he was coming home ought to have been anticipated, and so ought his 'fiddling with it,' in ignorance of its dangerous condition.

I must read a passage of great interest on the law of Homicide from 'Foster's Crown Law' (Dublin Edition, 1767, p. 263). The learned author on the subject of 'due caution' says:–

'I cannot pass over a case reported by Keiling (Keil. 41), because I think it an extreme hard case and of very extensive influence. A man found a pistol in the street, which he had reason to believe was not loaded, *having tried it with a rammer*. He carried it home and showed it to his wife, and she standing before it, he pulled up the cock and touched the trigger. The pistol went off and killed the woman. This was ruled manslaughter. It appeareth that the learned editor was not satisfied with the judgment. It is one of the cases he, in the preface to the report, recommendeth to further consideration. Admitting that the judgment was strictly legal, it was, to say no better of it, *Summum Jus*. I cannot help saying that the rule of law I have been considering in this place touching the consequences of taking or not taking due precaution doth not seem to be sufficiently tempered with mercy. . . . This I have said upon a supposition that the judgment reported by Keiling was strictly legal. I think it was not. For the law in these cases doth not require the *utmost* caution that *can* be used; it is sufficient that a reasonable precaution, what is *usual and ordinary* in the like cases, be taken. . . . The man in the case under consideration examined the pistol in the ordinary way. Perhaps the rammer, which he had not tried before was too short, and deceived him. But having used the ordinary caution, found to have been effectual in like cases, he ought to have been excused.

I have been the longer upon this case because accidents of this lamentable kind may be the lot of the wisest and best of mankind, and most commonly fall amongst the nearest friends and relations. And in such a case the forfeiture of goods rigorously exacted would be heaping affliction on the head of the afflicted, and galling an heart already wounded past cure. It would even aggravate the loss of a brother, a parent, a child, or wife, if such a loss under such circumstances is capable of aggravation.

I once upon the circuit tried a man for the death of his wife by the like accident. Upon a Sunday morning the man and his wife went a mile or two from home with some neighbours, to take dinner at the house of their common friend. He carried his gun with him, hoping to meet with some diversion by the way. But before he went to dinner he discharged it, and set it up in a private place in his friend's house. After dinner he went to church, and in the evening returned home with his wife and neighbours, bringing his gun with him, which was carried into the room where his wife was, she having brought it part of the way. He, taking it up, touched the trigger, and the gun went off and killed his wife, whom he dearly loved. It came out in evidence that while the man was at church a person belonging to the family privately took up the gun, charged it, and went after some game; but before the service at church was ended, returned it loaded to the place whence he took it, and where the defendant, who was ignorant of all that had passed, found it, to all appearance as he left it. I did not inquire whether the poor man had examined the gun before he carried it home; but being of opinion, upon the whole evidence, that he had *reasonable grounds to believe that it was not loaded*, I directed the jury that if they were of the same opinion they should acquit him, and he was acquitted.'

Does not this passage furnish a conclusive argument to show that to leave a gun as this defendant left it was even criminally negligent, and that he would have been answerable upon an indictment for the misfortune which followed?

I am clearly of opinion that the defendant's thoughtless, reckless conduct gave occasion to the plaintiff's injury, and so far *caused* that injury as to make the defendant liable in damages. Accordingly, I hold that the appeal must be dismissed, with costs.

Walker and **Holmes L.JJ.** concurred.

Notes and Questions

1. If the defendant's son had used the gun in anger, would the defendant have been liable? Cf. *Cunningham* v. *Blake* [1937] Ir. Jur. Rep. 20 (High Ct.)
2. To what extent was the fact that the defendant was the parent of the person who caused the injury relevant to the outcome of the case? *Cf.* Binchy, 'Liability in Tort of Parents for Damage Caused by their Children' 74 Incorp. L. Soc. Gazette of Ireland 35 (1980).
3. Do you consider that *Foster's Crown Law* was of relevance to the case? Why?

O'GORMAN V. RITZ (CLONMEL) LTD

[1947] Ir. Jur. Rep. 35 (High Court, Geoghegan, J.)

The plaintiff claimed damages for personal injuries suffered by her and caused, as alleged, by the negligence of the defendants, their servants and agents in that certain rows of seats in the Ritz Cinema, Clonmel, the property of the defendants, were placed too closely together and were consequently dangerous to persons seated therein and had caused injuries and damage to the plaintiff.

The facts as proved or admitted were as follows: The plaintiff paid for admission to and occupied a parterre seat in the Ritz Cinema, the property of the defendant company, for the purpose of attending a cinematograph performance. During the course of the performance she allowed her ankles or legs to project under the seat immediately in front of her, which was occupied by another person. While she was sitting in that position the occupant of that seat, in rising to his feet to allow other patrons to pass, tilted the front of his seat upwards, thereby causing the back of the movable portion to come closer to the floor and to catch the plaintiff's legs, cutting her left shin, which became septic and required medical treatment for two months.

The backs of the row of seats in which the plaintiff was sitting were 2 feet 4½ inches from the backs of those immediately in front, and there was uncontradicted evidence that in practice this was regarded as a minimum safe distance and was generally adopted for the cheaper seats in cinemas. It was also proved that in the more expensive seats in such theatres a greater distance was allowed between the rows of seats, sometimes as much as 3 feet 4 inches; that it was impracticable to provide seating which did not allow a member of the audience to place his feet under the seat in front; that seating similar to that in question existed in another cinema in Clonmel; that in the previous seven years, notwithstanding that approximately one million people had used the parterre seats in the Ritz Cinema, no complaints regarding the same had been received by the management.

The civil bill alleged that the defendants knew or should have known of the danger but neglected to give the plaintiff any or sufficient warning thereof, or to take any or any adequate steps to protect her or reasonable care to make the said cinema and the seating thereof reasonably safe for patrons. She further pleaded the doctrine of *res ipsa loquitur*, and that the defendants impliedly warranted to her that the cinema and the seating accommodation therein were as safe for her use and accommodation, as a patron of the said cinema, as reasonable skill and care could make them.

The Circuit Judge of the South-Eastern Circuit granted a decree for £20. The defendants appealed.

Geoghegan J.:

I have to deal with this action on the basis that the defendants warranted their premises to be reasonably safe for patrons who paid to see the pictures. The defendants are not insurers and it seems to me that the plaintiff seeks a degree of diligence, foresight, and precaution to which an ordinary theatre-goer is not entitled. I am satisfied on the particular facts, that to guard against a remote contingency such as that which led to the injuries here would need precautions of a well-nigh fantastic nature, which could not reasonably be expected in the construction or management of a theatre. The defendants could not foresee that Mrs. O'Gorman would get her feet into the position that led to the injuries from which she suffered. Accordingly, the appeal should be allowed and the action dismissed.

Notes and Questions

1. Do you agree that cinema proprietors could not foresee that a patron would extend her feet under the seat in front of her? Have you ever done such an 'unforeseeable' act?
2. In *Tullgren* v. *Amoskeag Mfg. Co.* 82 N.H. 268, 133 A. 4 (1926), the court stated:
   'For a person to be careless it is not necessary that damage as a more rather than a less probable result should be anticipated . . . Danger consists in the risk of harm, as well as the likelihood of it, and a danger calling for anticipation need not be of more probable occurrence than less. If there is some probability of harm sufficiently serious that ordinary men would take precautions to avoid it, then failure to do so is negligence. That the danger will more probably than otherwise not be encountered on a particular occasion does not dispense with the exercise of care.'
   Is the holding in *Ritz* in any way inconsistent with this statement?
3. See also *Donaldson* v. *Irish Motor Racing Club, infra*, pp. 220–228.
4. *Cf. Lamb* v. *London Borough of Camden* [1981] 2 All E.R. 408 (C.A.).

(*b*) *The Gravity of the Threatened Injury*

Where the potential injury is great, the creation of even a slight risk may constitute negligence. See, *e.g. Hughes* v. *Ballynahinch Gas Co.* 33 I.L.T.R. 74 (Palles, C.B., 1898). The gravity of the threatened injury is a matter depending on the circumstances of the defendant but also of the plaintiff. Although the risk of an accident happening may be exactly the same for two people, the results may be more serious for one than the other, and accordingly greater care may be owed to the former. An obvious example is where a one-eyed employee is required to do work that involves the risk of his losing the sight in his other eye: *Paris* v. *Stepney Borough Council* [1951] A.C. 367.

(*c*) *The Social Utility of the Defendant's Conduct*

WHOOLEY V. DUBLIN CORPORATION
[1961] I.R. 60 (High Court, McLoughlin, J., 1960)

McLoughlin J.:

The plaintiff claims damages from the defendant Corporation for injuries received by her by reason of the alleged negligence of the servants of the Corporation in the maintenance of a fire hydrant box in the public footway at Oxford Road, Ranelagh. On the night of the 11th November, 1958, the plaintiff was walking along the footway when her foot went into the uncovered box of a fire hydrant causing her to fall to the ground whereby she was injured. The fire hydrant box is normally covered by a flush-fitting cast iron lid measuring superficially 11 inches by 14 inches by $\frac{1}{4}$-inch in depth and weighing about 3 lbs. On this night the lid had been removed and was lying some distance away and the box was full of water; the latter circumstance may have been due to the fact that it was a wet night, which I think was unlikely, or to escape of water from the hydrant caused by a defect in the valve or to unwarranted interference with the valve by some person, which last cause I consider most likely.

It is not contended that the Corporation are not under a duty to maintain these hydrants on the footway and that they must be readily accessible for use by the Corporation fire brigade in case of fire, but reliance is placed by the plaintiff on the evidence of an engineer called on her behalf who stated that the type of hydrant and box in this case was thirty to forty years old, that the lid could be removed by a child inserting a stick or some instrument into a slot provided along one side of the lid for that purpose, and that a more modern type has a heavier, though smaller, lid without a slot but with a hole in the centre for the insertion of a simple type of key. He did not, however, suggest that this more modern type of lid was designed to make, or would make, interference by mischievous persons more difficult.

There was evidence also by a lady that some days previous to the accident water was spurting from a hydrant without a lid in Oxford Road which, I am inclined to believe, was this same hydrant.

For the defendant Corporation there was evidence that for paving purposes the hydrants in Oxford Road, including this particular one, were in use during that period, 21st October to 4th November, after which they were inspected and were left in proper and safe condition. There was also evidence of a turncock who was notified of the accident on the same night, shortly after its happening, and inspected this hydrant box and found nothing wrong with it. How the lid came to be replaced is not known.

Having carefully considered all the circumstances and the authorities quoted to me by counsel I cannot find that the Corporation through its officials maintained this hydrant box in a negligent way so as to cause the plaintiff's injuries. There is, in my view, no reason for holding that this type of hydrant box is of the kind that is likely to be interfered with by young irresponsible children to the knowledge of the Corporation's officials or that any such knowledge should be imputed to them. It is my opinion that this hydrant was interfered with by some mischievous person and that no other type of hydrant which could be devised, consistent with its necessary purpose, would be safe from such malicious interference.

Accordingly, this action must be dismissed and the order of the Circuit Judge reversed.

Notes and Questions

1. Are ambulance drivers to be judged by the same standard of care as ordinary motorists? *Cf. Daborn* v. *Bath Tramways Motor Co. Ltd.* [1946] 2 All E.R. 333 (C.A.).
2. If I brake suddenly to avoid hitting a dog and a car runs into the back of my car, can I argue that I was not negligent? *Cf. Molson* v. *Squamish Transfer Ltd.* 7 D.L.R. (3d) 553 (1969). Would your answer be different if the animal was a horse? Or a rat?
3. Contrast this case with *Cunningham* v. *MacGrath*, *supra*, p. 6.

(d) The Cost of Eliminating the Risk

Regard may be had to the cost of eliminating the risk of injury. 'A slight risk may be run if the cost of remedying it is unreasonably high': *Kirwan* v. *Bray U.D.C.*, unreported, Supreme Court, 30 July 1969 (30–1969), *per* Ó'Dálaigh, C.J. In some cases relating to employers' liability, the courts have on occasion made statements that appear to afford considerable deference to cost factors. In *Christie* v. *Odeon (Ireland) Ltd.* 91 I.L.T.R. 25, at 29 (Sup. Ct., 1956), Kingsmill Moore, J. observed that 'to make accidents impossible would often be to make work impossible'; and, in *Bradley* v. *C.I.E.* [1976] I.R. 217, at 223 (Sup. Ct.), Henchy, J. went so far as to assert that 'even where a certain precaution is obviously wanted in the interests of the safety of this workman, there may be counteracting factors which would justify the employer in not taking that precaution.'

In other cases, the courts have shown far less sympathy to the defence that cost considerations should prevail over those of safety. See, *e.g., McGovern* v. *Clones Urban District Council* [1944] I.R. 282 (High Ct., Black, J., 1943).

2. DUTY

In *Donoghue* v. *Stevenson* [1932] A.C. 562, at 580 (H.L. (Sc.)), in a passage which has been cited with approval many times in our courts, Lord Atkin outlined what he described as 'a general conception of relations giving rise to a duty of care, of which the particular cases found in the books are but instances.' He said:

> 'The rule that you are to love your neighbour becomes in law you must not injure your neighbour; and the lawyer's question, who is my neighbour? receives a restricted reply. You must take reasonable care to avoid acts or omissions which you can reasonably foresee would be liable to injure your neighbour. Who then, in law, is my neighbour? The answer seems to be – persons who are so closely and directly affected by my act that I ought reasonably to have them in contemplation as being so affected when I am directing my mind to the acts or omissions which are called in question.'

In *Anns* v. *Merton London Borough Council*, [1978] A.C. 728, in a passage extracted *infra*, pp. 280–284. Lord Wilberforce posited a two-step approach. First one asks whether there is a sufficient relationship of proximity or neighbourhood that, in the reasonable contemplation of the defendant, carelessness on his part may be likely to cause damage, in which case a *prima facie* duty of care arises. Secondly, assuming that this hurdle has been crossed, one must consider whether there are any considerations which ought to negative or to reduce or to limit the scope of the duty or the class of person to whom it is owed or the damages to which a breach of it may give rise.

English courts in recent years have increasingly been willing to articulate these policy considerations in determining the 'duty' question. So far Irish courts have shown less desire to abandon 'legal' concepts in favour of a more open discussion of policy. (See further p. 196, *infra*.) Whatever language is used, of course, the question remains the same and the task of the legal adviser, especially in areas where the duty issue has not recently come before the courts, is an unenviable one.

To what extent is the Duty Concept Determined by Objective Criteria?

McCOMISKEY V. McDERMOTT
[1974] I.R. 75 (Supreme Court, 1973)

Henchy J.:

In October, 1968, the plaintiff and the defendant were students in University College, Dublin. The plaintiff was studying medicine and the defendant engineering. Their common interest was motor cars and, more particularly, the sport of motor rallying. In a motor rally the competing cars start one after the other at fixed intervals from the same point, and they are expected to arrive at a series of checkpoints at predetermined times. If they are late at any checkpoint, they incur penalty marks; if they are early, they are penalised even more. Each car is manned by a team consisting of a driver and a navigator. The navigator's task is to guide the driver by reference to a map and to act as time-keeper.

The plaintiff and the defendant decided to enter as a team in a rally for novices that was being held on the night of the 25th October, 1968, by the Dublin University Motor Club. The plaintiff had been rallying for three years, but this was only the defendant's second rally. They were to compete in the defendant's car, and the defendant was to be the driver. The plaintiff, with the help of a special lamp, a half-inch road map and a compass, was to be the navigator. They started off from Kilmacanogue, County Wicklow, on what was a dark, wet night. The cars moved off at one-minute intervals and were expected to pass 35 checkpoints. To cover the route (of which the teams were informed only shortly before starting) without incurring penalties, the drivers would have to maintain an average speed of 35 m.p.h.

The plaintiff and the defendant had negotiated four checkpoints without incurring penalties when they found themselves on a narrow secondary road in the Wicklow hills. The plaintiff advised the defendant that in a matter of seconds they would arrive at the fifth checkpoint. Just then they came to a sharp left-hand bend. The defendant says that when he came around the bend he saw, about 45 yards ahead and downhill, two cars blocking the road. It later transpired that this was the next checkpoint and that one of the cars, which was not blocking the road, was that of an official who was checking the competitors' cars as they arrived there, and that the other car, which was causing the obstruction, was that of a competitor. The defendant braked as soon as he saw the obstruction but, because of the muddy downhill road, the braking was not effective and the defendant, believing that he could not pull up before he reached the two parked cars, released the brake and directed his car into the ditch at the right-hand side of the road. The car overturned and the plaintiff was injured.

The plaintiff instituted proceedings in the High Court in which he claimed damages for negligence against the defendant, but judgment was given against him for the jury held (*a*) that his claim was defeated because he had impliedly agreed to waive his legal right in respect of any negligence of the defendant causing injury to him, and (*b*) that the defendant was not negligent. From those findings the plaintiff now appeals to this Court.

[Henchy, J. went on to consider the first of these grounds; see *infra*, pp. 218–219. He continued:]

. . . There remains the finding by the jury, in answer to the second question, that the defendant was not negligent. Counsel for the plaintiff suggest, in the first place, that this finding may be vitiated because it was made after the jury had wrongly held, in answer to the first question, that the plaintiff had waived his right to sue in respect of the negligence of the defendant. Having regard to the sequence of the directions given by the judge to the jury, I do not think it can be assumed that the jury necessarily answered the first question before they answered the second. However, even if they did, the fact that they unnecessarily and incorrectly answered the first question does not invalidate their answer to the second question. They had been fully and correctly instructed by the trial judge as to the legal approach to each of those questions and there was nothing in the judge's charge to suggest that the answer to the first question should, or could, govern the answer to the second. Therefore, if the answer to the second question is otherwise sustainable, I do not think that it should be set aside because of the answer to the first question.

However, counsel for the plaintiff contend that the answer cannot stand in the light of the evidence. It is conceded that the relevant evidence for the purpose of this submission is the version given by the defendant. Briefly, that evidence is that the defendant rounded a sharp bend on this narrow, muddy, second-class, mountain road on a dark night with heavy rain. When he came round the bend he saw, about 45 yards ahead of him on a 1:10 downhill slope, the car of the preceding competitor blocking the road. He braked ineffectively because of the muddy surface and, believing that he would not be able to stop before reaching the car ahead, he drove into the ditch at the side of the road thus causing his car to overturn and the plaintiff to be injured.

Was that conduct negligence on his part? Counsel for the plaintiff say that it was; they say that he should have been driving at a speed which would have enabled him to cope with an emergency such as this, and that the duty he owed to the plaintiff was no more nor less than the duty to show care that a motorist owes to other users of the road. I think it is important to bear in mind that, while the general duty owed by a motorist to other users of the road is the objective one of showing due and reasonable care, the duty becomes particularised and personalised by the circumstances of the case. For example, it might be negligence to drive at 50 m.p.h. past a group of boisterous children coming from school, and yet it may not be negligence to drive at that speed past a group of adults. Therefore, it is necessary in each case to consider who is the person claiming to be owed the duty of care, who is the person it is claimed against, and what are the circumstances.

The essential feature of the relationship between the plaintiff and the defendant in this case is that they were bound together as a team engaged in a joint competitive venture. Each undertook to use his skills towards the common end of scoring as well as possible in the competition. To achieve this the plaintiff, as navigator, had to act as a map-reader and the time-keeper and to convey the necessary information to the defendant, as driver; and then it was for the defendant to use his driving skill to the best advantage in the light of that information. All this had to be done in the context of the prevailing climatic and other conditions, the fact that to keep up with the time schedule laid down for the event an average speed of 35 m.p.h. had to be maintained, and the fact that a team had started out one minute before them and another one minute after them.

The law of negligence lays down that the standard of care is that which is to be expected from a reasonably careful man *in the circumstances*. Because the particular circumstances dictate the degree of care required, decisions in other cases are frequently of little guidance. In the present case we have been referred to cases such as *Insurance Commissioner* v. *Joyce* (1948) 77 C.L.R. 39 and *Nettleship* v. *Weston* [1971] 2 Q.B. 691 which raise the vexed question as to the standard or degree of care required to be shown by a driver towards a passenger who knows that the driver lacks the capacity to drive with reasonable care. In my view, such cases are not to the point in the present case where the passenger, far from committing himself to the care of a driver whom he knew to be incompetent, allied himself to the driver as navigator in the hope that by the assiduous application of their respective skills they would win a prize in the competition.

I consider that the duty of care owed by the defendant to the plaintiff was to drive as carefully as a reasonably careful, competitive rally-driver would be expected to drive in the prevailing circumstances. The jury were fully and carefully instructed by the trial judge to apply that standard to the facts as they found them. The jury were entitled to find that the accident happened because on a wet, dark night on a muddy, narrow road in the Wicklow hills, in the course of a motor rally, the defendant drove around a bend in the road only to find an unexpected motor car 45 yards ahead on a pronounced downhill slope, blocking the road and that, not being able to brake effectively because of the muddy downhill surface, he had to drive his car against a bank at the side of the road thus causing it to overturn.

The question whether the defendant was negligent on that version of the circumstances of the accident was pre-eminently one for the jury, and their answer in the negative cannot be disturbed unless it could be said to be unreasonable. I am unable to say that it was. For those reasons, I would uphold the jury's verdict of no negligence and dismiss this appeal.

Griffin J. concurred with **Henchy J.**

Walsh J. (dissenting):

. . . In the main, the submissions made on behalf of the defendant in the course of this appeal were to the effect that since a negligence action is an action for breach of duty, the duty is to be measured in the light of the circumstances governing the situation in which the act complained of happened. Reduced to simpler terms, the defendant has submitted that the only duty the defendant owed to the plaintiff was to act in accordance with the standards of the ordinary, reasonable and prudent rally driver. In my view this submission is an over-simplification. The most important and the governing circumstance of this episode was that it occurred on the public highway at a time when the highway was open to use and was being used by other members of the public. If this particular competition had taken place in a private place or on the highway at a time when it was closed to ordinary use by members of the public, the circumstances would be different even for such members of the public as attended as spectators. There have been a number of cases dealing with episodes leading to injury to either participants or spectators at horse shows, motor races, motor-cycle races or competitions held in places which were not open to ordinary public traffic. One of these cases (*Wilks* v. *Cheltenham Cycle Club* [1971] 1 W.L.R. 668) was cited and relied upon in the present case. In my view, there is no parallel between the circumstances of that case and the present one. *Nettleship* v. *Weston* [1971] 2 Q.B. 691 is closer to the present case; in that case the act of a learner driver caused injury to a passenger instructor, who was seated beside the learner, while the car was being driven on the public highway and it was held by the English Court of Appeal that the duty owed by the learner driver to the passenger instructor was the same objective standard as was owed by every driver on the public highway to other persons using the highway. The fact that the driver in question was so inexperienced or so unskilled as not to have the ability or skill of the ordinary reasonable and prudent driver was irrelevant.

In my view, in the present case the governing circumstance is that the motor car was being driven on the public highway at a time when the highway was being used as such. The duty which the defendant owed to all persons using that highway, including the passenger in his own car, was the same. To hold otherwise would lead to rather absurd results. For example, if during the course of the rally the defendant had picked up a passenger who knew that he was in a participating motor car (but who was not himself in any sense a participant) and if the car had been involved in an accident, due to the negligent driving of the defendant, which injured not merely the navigator but also the casual passenger and a pedestrian who happened to be walking along the road at the same time, it could not be seriously contemplated that the liability of the driver of the motor car to each of the injured parties would be governed by different standards of duty. Apart from facts which would warrant the application of the statutory defence given by s.34, sub-s. 1, of the Act of 1961, the conduct of the plaintiff during the course of the exercise or the fact that he partici- pated in this competitive venture with the driver may be relevant in terms of contributory negligence but they are not relevant in determining the standard of care which is to be observed by the defendant. It was the duty of the defendant to use proper care not to cause injury to persons using the highway, including his own passengers, and that involved not merely avoiding excessive speed but also keeping a proper look out. This duty was owed to the plaintiff as he was a person who might reasonably expect to be injured by the omission to take such care. If a pedestrian had been hit by the defendant's motor car and the facts of the case warranted a finding of negligence against the defendant, then the plaintiff would have been equally entitled to a verdict on this issue against the defendant.

The immediate cause of the accident in question was the fact that the defendant approached and rounded a bend without knowing what a bad bend it was and without making provision for the possibility of something being on the roadway around the bend, which in fact was the case. While it is true that he relied upon the plaintiff, or passenger-navigator, to inform him of the nature of the bend, I do not think that that exonerates him from taking care. Furthermore, the navigator could not have told him that there was something, which was invisible to both of them, on the road around the bend. Persons rounding a bend, particularly one which is unknown to them, should always anticipate at least the possibility of there being something on the roadway around the bend and should take precautions as the circumstances would dictate to enable them reasonably to cope with such a situation. This the defendant did not do and when the situation revealed itself he found he was unable to control the situation because of the bad road surface and the downward gradient, so he chose to go into the ditch. In his evidence he agreed that he knew there would be such a risk because of the nature of the roads used. According to his evidence he was also aware that every time he came to a bend he had to have due regard to the fact that he might encounter a pedestrian or an animal or another vehicle around the bend. In my view, the defendant's evidence was such as to make a finding of negligence against him coercive.

Apart from that conclusion, it should be noted that the learned trial judge in his directions to the jury correctly pointed out to them that the defendant had to take care by looking out for the ordinary things one might expect to meet on a road. The learned trial judge also informed the jury that a person driving a motor car had a duty to take such care 'as the circumstances demand not to cause injury to anybody else.' The learned trial judge did not, however, explain to the jury that the duty which the defendant owed to the plaintiff was no less than that which he owed to other users of the road. In fact his address to the jury tended to give a somewhat opposite impression by the amount of attention and time he devoted to the allegations of negligence on the part of the plaintiff, and by indicating that part ot the case against the plaintiff was that he had failed to give proper instructions to the defendant as to the location and severity of the bend and the position of the checkpoint. Speaking of the defendant's duties, he said:– 'But at the same time he has to remember the other things to do. This is to try to drive so as to be at a certain point at a certain time and, as I say, at all times influenced by this element of competition. These are the matters that have to be borne in mind, as I say, to keep this case in proper perspective.' In my view, this, taken in conjunction with his observations about the possibility of the failure of the plaintiff at his task as navigator, were calculated to give the jury the impression that the duty owed by the defendant was something other than the ordinary duty of care and was something special and peculiar to the plaintiff. . . .

Notes and Questions

1. Do you prefer the approach favoured by Henchy and Griffin JJ., or that proposed by Walsh J.? Why? Is the answer to the question a legal one at all? Has it more to do with what is the desirable range of the compensation rather than that of liability? See Symmons, 'The Impact of the Third Party Insurance Legislation on the Development of the Common Law' 4 Anglo-Amer. L. Rev. 426 (1975), especially at 436–437.
2. Of what relevance (if any) is section 34(1)(b) of the *Civil Liability Act 1961*? Cf. *Deskau* v. *Dziama* 36 D.L.R. (3d) 36 (Ont. High Ct., Keith, J., 1973).
3. A passenger takes a lift from a driver whom the passenger knows to be drunk? Does the driver owe a different duty of care to the passenger from that he owes to other drivers and road-users? Does not *McComiskey* v. *McDermott* require us to say that he does? See further pp. 217–219, *infra*.
4. What duty (if any) does a burglar driver owe his passenger, a fellow burglar, when fleeing from the police? Cf. *Aston* v. *Turner* [1981] Q.B. 137. What duty do the police owe persons fleeing from them in a stolen car? Cf. *Marshall* v. *Osmond* [1982] 2 Q.B. 857. What duty do the police owe the general public when chasing suspects? Cf. *Priestman* v. *Colangelo* [1959] S.C.R. 615.

Failure to Act

Tort law has traditionally set its face against imposing a *general* duty to assist others or to protect them from harm. In *specific* instances, however, it does impose a duty, having regard to the particular relationship between plaintiff and defendant.

Where a railway company accepts a drunken passenger it falls under a duty to take care that his presence does not result in injury to other passengers.

ADDERLEY V. GREAT NORTHERN RAILWAY CO.
[1905] 2 I.R. 378 (Court of Appeal, 1905)

FitzGibbon L.J.:

The plaintiff sues, as a passenger of the defendant Company, for damages for an injury sustained while he was sitting in a carriage of the Company at the Omagh platform. He was sitting next to the window, on the platform side. The injury was done by the violence of a drunken fellow-passenger, who, standing on the platform within reach of the window, struck out suddenly, broke the window, and seriously injured the plaintiff's eye. The case has so far resulted in a trial at the Derry Assizes, at which a common jury returned a verdict for the Plaintiff with £850 damages. In the King's Bench Division the Court was divided.

As I hold that there must be a new trial, I cannot discuss the evidence in detail, but I must refer to it sufficiently to explain my view of the duty of the defendants, and the application of the facts to the law, as I understand it. The amount of the damages, and the extent of the injury, were both serious; but the importance of the legal principles which are at stake, as to the duties and liabilities of Railway Companies in respect of passengers more or less under the influence of drink, appears to me to transcend anything concerning the present plaintiff.

I must distinctly say, at the outset, that in my opinion it is impossible to withdraw from the jury the evidence of breach of duty which the facts supply against the defendants, and if I was satisfied that the jury had found their verdict, and had assessed the damages, on due consideration of the measure of the defendants' duty, I should hold that we had no jurisdiction to interfere.

The circumstances of the case may be shortly described. The train in which the plaintiff was seated was at rest. But it was just about to start, and it is not immaterial to determine how near it was to the point of starting when the injury occurred. The plaintiff was on his journey, sitting in a nearly empty compartment, at an intermediate station. He was where he had a right to be, and where he had a right to be protected by a due exercise of reasonable care on the part of the Company, so that he might attain the object for which he had paid his fare, that of completing his journey with ordinary comfort and in personal safety.

The story of the man who did the injury is not an uncommon one. He was seen approaching the station manifestly under the influence of drink, and exhibiting signs of excitement. He had a season ticket, and therefore, if not otherwise disqualified, he was entitled to enter the station and the train. At the outer door of the station it was the duty of an officer of the Company to check the tickets of all intending passengers. He checked the ticket of this particular man, and he passed him into the station. After he got into the station and on to the platform, perhaps in consequence of his condition – he was attempting to enter a first-class carriage, having only a third-class ticket. A porter seeing what he was at, and doing his duty, stopped him. Almost at the same moment, the station master, the most responsible representative of the Company, and answerable for maintaining order, saw what was going on, and called out to the porter, 'Keep that man back.' Whether he did this merely because the train was on the point of starting, or whether he did so because he saw that the man was not in a proper condition to travel, may be doubtful; but, whatever the reason was, this direction was not obeyed. The porter, who had stopped the man from entering the first-class carriage, really took personal charge of him. He took him under the arm, and proceeded to walk with him parallel to the train, in the direction away from the engine, alongside and within arm's length of the carriages. He passed at least one first-class carriage; and though the evidence may not be quite clear, I think that down to the moment when the injury happened, the train had not begun to move. The time that elapsed between the injury and the starting of the train was certainly very short, but the injury was done while the porter, arm-in-arm, was conducting the drunken man along-side the train. The immediate motive or occasion of the act of violence that did the mischief is doubtful. It may have been a sudden perception that he was going to be left behind, or a sudden spasm of intoxication, or an angry gesture; but whatever was the motive or occasion, the drunken man struck out and, whether with his fist or hand, and whether with or without any definite intention, he broke the window, close to which the plaintiff was lawfully and quietly sitting, the glass flew into the plaintiff's eye, and the injury was sustained.

The evidence of the ticket-checker at the gate, and the porter on the platform, has been subjected here, and at the trial, to observation. The jury are the ultimate judges of the truth. We have no right to discuss what is within the exclusive jurisdiction of the jury. The main questions submitted by the Judge to the jury, and to which no substantial objection was made at the trial except that there was no sufficient evidence to sustain them, were divided into two classes: the first concerned the conduct and responsibility of the ticket-checker in admitting this drunken man to the defendants' premises; and the second question related to the conduct of the porter who took charge of him on the platform. To these were added the question about cause and effect, and the question of damages.

The wording of the principal question about the ticket-checker was taken from the judgments in *Murgatroyd's Case* 2 T.L.R. 180, 451, and I must observe that it is, in my opinion, almost impossible to apply words relating to the particular facts of one case to the facts of another, without creating difficulty. In *Murgatroyd's Case*, a man 'obviously drunk' was permitted to mount a London omnibus which was at the time greatly overcrowded. When he got on to the top of the bus, there being no seat for him he propped himself against the side rail. Lurching forward from that unstable position, he precipitated a woman and her child down the steps. The child was killed, the woman was severely injured, and an action for damages was brought. The questions in that case were in every respect apposite to its facts; but they cannot be applied, as if they were mathematical definitions, to every case where a drunken passenger does mischief, without altering and extending their effect. On the Omagh platform the state of facts was wholly different from what it was on the top of the London omnibus. Before I can apply the unqualified terms defining the responsibility of the London Company with respect to the conduct of a person who, when obviously drunk, was allowed to mount the omnibus and balance himself against the side rail, while in motion, to the case of an intoxicated passenger on a railway platofrm, I must compare the circumstances, because, in my opinion, the measure of reasonable care depends on them, and the duty and responsibility are not unqualified or absolute. To permit a man obviously drunk to stand – or try to stand – on the top of a moving omnibus, where there was no seat for him, appears to me to warrant the statement of the law in the terms applied to that case. But the questions put to the jury, and the arguments addressed to us, in this case, appear to me to rest on the assumption that once a man visibly under the influence of drink has been permitted by a ticket-checker to enter a railway station, the Company becomes absolutely responsible for everything he does. This assumption appears to me to be incompatible with common sense, and unsupported by law, at least in a country where total abstinence is far from universal. The same observation seems to me to apply to the conduct of the porter. At the trial, the question whether the man was 'obviously drunk' when he was allowed to pass the door was treated as decisive, and it was assumed that once he was permitted to enter the premises, if the checker ought to have seen that he was not sober, this was in itself evidence of negligence sufficient to maintain the action. Similarly, as regards the porter, the question really debated was whether at the moment of the mischief the porter was engaged in trying to place him in a third-class carriage, and to let him go on his journey. It is a mere detail whether he was trying to find an empty compartment for him, or to put him into the charge of a friend, or to put him into the compartment where he broke the window; the real question that was tried, and treated as decisive, was whether the porter was conniving at a drunken man's being allowed to travel at all?

Counsel for the plaintiff have relied on a by-law as a legal foundation for the extreme measure of liability adopted at the trial. The by-law is in terms a positive enactment that if any person under the influence of drink is found on the premises, he *shall* be forthwith removed; and I read this as an equally positive enactment that he shall not be admitted. What is the scope of that by-law?

Does it make the admission, or non-removal, of a person under the influence of drink illegal, and so illegal that the violation of it, or any delay or neglect in acting on it, entails the absolute responsibility consequent on the commission of a crime? I cannot think so, especially as I find an equally Draconic law as to any person who plays any game of chance on the Company's premises.

But I do not think that the by-law is to be overlooked in measuring the duty of the Company, and furthermore I do not think that its scope is limited to clearing railway premises of objectionable people. It indicates to my mind the duty to protect sober passengers from annoyance or injury by drunken men, and it empowers the Company to remove them. But when the Company chooses to accept a drunken passenger, the measure of responsibility is to be governed by the same principle which regulates the responsibility of carriers of dangerous things. A carrier who accepts a dog, or a carboy of vitriol, does not become absolutely answerable for everything that may happen, but he accepts a responsibility, and he undertakes a duty, regulated by the nature and the circumstances of the case. It was the duty of the man who checked the tickets to use reasonable care to admit no one who was dangerous, and if he did allow a man to come in who was, in the words of the jury, and of *Murgatroyd's Case* 2 T. L. R. 180, 451, 'obviously drunk,' it became the duty of the Company to take due and reasonable care, having regard to his condition, to prevent any inconvenient or injurious consequences to other passengers arising from his condition. The duty was undertaken by the porter, when he prevented him from entering a wrong carriage.

The duty of the porter then was to use all reasonable care to see that the man of whom he took charge should not get the opportunity of doing any mischief reasonably likely to be done by a drunken man. But I am not satisfied that it was his absolute duty to prevent him from travelling in the train. He walked with him down the train. It is for the jury to say whether it was not his duty to keep him sufficiently away from the train to prevent him from doing mischief to himself or to anyone else by staggering against it, or in struggling to get into it, and the direction of the station master to 'keep that man back' could not be withdrawn from the jury as material to the reasonableness of what the porter did in leaving him within reach of the train as it was starting.

As to the question of cause and effect which seems to have led Mr. Justice Wright to his conclusion, it appears to me that if the duty to use reasonable care to prevent injury from any particular cause is established, and if injury occurs, but happens in some most improbable way, or causes some most unlikely mischief, neither the particular manner of the injury, not the particular extent of the mischief, can affect the question of the relation of cause and effect. But if the injury could not have reasonably been expected, or if the mischief was of a kind that could not reasonably be regarded as the consequence of what was done, if would be open to the jury to find that the relation of cause and effect does not exist. All this, and the cases and the law upon it, were discussed in *Sullivan* v. *Creed* [1904] 2 I. R. 317, where though the defendant's act did not directly cause the accident, and notwithstanding that the chances against its happening as it did were almost incalculable, the defendant's negligence was held to be the cause of the injury, because it was a result which reasonably might or ought to have been anticipated as a consequence of his act.

This matter which caused the difficulty with Wright, J., did not receive any attention at the trial. It was not considered by the jury, because the risk which the Company undertook by accepting this man as a potential passenger was treated as in itself evidence of their liability, on the act of the ticket-checker alone, even without considering the action of the porter.

The measure of duty might, and in fact does, affect the assessment of damages. The measure of duty laid down at the trial was, in my opinion, too strict; and although I am of opinion that the case must go to the jury again, I cannot hold the defendants bound by a verdict based on an exaggerated standard of duty, and therefore possibly resulting in an exaggerated measure of damages. The case is complicated by other circumstances. The injury occurred in March; the trial took place in July. It was opened here as a case in which the plaintiff had lost his eye. As a matter of fact the vision of both eyes remains, although the sight of one has been seriously affected. It was stated at the time that he suffered no pain, and that the sight of the injured eye was then improving. The amount of the damages – £850 – is *prima facie* very large. The danger of sympathetic injury to the remaining eye has been much pressed as justifying the damages, but one of the medical witnesses qualified this risk by the chance that some glass might have remained in the eye. The amount given challenges careful consideration; and with respect to the grounds which I have mentioned, the experience of twelve months instead of four is now available to test the risk on which the damages were assessed at £850. If we judge by our own experience, it is remarkable what a number of people have shared the misfortune of Hannibal, Nelson, and Gambetta; how many have but one eye, and how many more have only one useful eye? In how many cases has injury to one eye afterwards caused the loss of the other? But if the defendants are allowed the second trial which they ask, the additional expense must not diminish the plaintiff's compensation if he ultimately succeeds; and the costs of both trials, and of the new trial motion, must abide the result of the action. It has been said here that the damages were increased by the unpopularity of the Great Northern Railway Company in Derry. I do not believe that the jury acted from such a motive, and if the allegation was true, how do the defendants explain their entrusting the case to a common jury?

In my opinion the verdict ought not to stand, not on the amount of damages alone, but because the measure of duty and responsibility laid down as against the defendants, and the standard of duty applied to the conduct of their servants, the ticket-checker and porter, were incorrect, and may have affected the amount of damages. Accordingly, I am of opinion that the appeal should be allowed and a new trial directed. The appellant should have his costs of this appeal against the defendants; and the costs of the previous trial and of the motion in the King's Bench Division should be costs in the action.

Holmes L.J. delivered a concurring judgment. **Walker L.J.** delivered a dissenting judgment.

Notes

Cf. Cannon v. *Midland Great Western Railway Co.* 6 L. R. Ir. 199 (C.A., 1880) (unruly crowd on station platform, rushing forward, caused passenger to be killed by train).

CAHILL V. KENNEALLY
[1955–1956] Ir. Jur. Rep. 15 (Circuit Court, Judge Roe, 1955)

The plaintiff brought an action against the defendant in the following circumstances. The defendant's bus was hired to bring a party to a darts competition in a licensed premises in Clonmel. The driver of the bus having dropped his passengers at their destination, parked the bus some distance away and locked it. Later, by arrangement, he returned to collect the party. Outside the premises he met two of the passengers, and, at their request, he admitted them to the main portion of the bus, while he went in search of the rest of the party, leaving the bus unlocked and unattended. Access could be had from the main portion of the bus to the driver's cabin, and the ignition switch in use at this time was not operated by a key but merely by turning a knob. In the driver's absence one of the two passengers in the bus entered the driver's cabin, succeeded in starting the bus, and drove it into the plaintiff's car which was parked on the street.

Judge Roe:
I must hold the defendant is liable in the circumstances of this case. When the driver parked the bus, having dropped his party, he locked it so that it would be safe while unattended. Later he came back to collect the party again and allowed two men into the bus to rest. He opens the bus to let them in and leaves it open and unattended while he goes in search of the rest of the party. The construction of the bus is such that the two men have access from the passenger portion of the bus to the driver's cabin, and the ignition can be switched on merely by turning a knob. It was negligence on the part of the driver, when he obviously knows that the bus, if unattended, should be locked, so that it may be safe, and it was clearly dangerous to allow these men into the bus. One of the men succeeded in starting the bus and drove it against the plaintiff's car. I hold that the plaintiff is entitled to recover damages from the defendant.

Notes

See also *Davoren* v. *FitzPatrick*, [1935] Ir. Jur. Rep. 23 (Circuit Court, Judge Shannon) (car started by children). For a stimulating analysis of the scope of liability in negligence for ommissions, see Smith and Burns, 'Donoghue v. Stevenson – The Not So Golden Anniversary' 46 Modern L. Rev. 147 (1983).

Negligent Infliction of Nervous Shock

BELL V. THE GREAT NORTHERN RAILWAY CO. OF IRELAND
26 L.R. (Ir.) 428 (Ex. Div., 1890)

The action was brought by the plaintiffs, who were husband and wife, to recover £600 damages for personal injuries alleged to have been sustained by the plaintiff Mary Bell through the negligence of the defendants; and the plaintiff George Bell claimed a further sum of £200 for loss of the society and services of his wife, and for medical expenses.

The statement of claim alleged that the plaintiff Mary Bell became a passenger on the defendants' railway upon a journey from Armagh to Warrenpoint, and that the defendants so negligently and unskilfully conducted themselves in carrying the said plaintiff upon said railway on the said journey, in managing the said railway and the carriage in which the said plaintiff was a passenger, that the said plaintiff was wounded and injured; and further alleged that, by reason of the premises, the plaintiff George Bell had lost the society and services of the said Mary Bell, and had been put to expense.

The defendants by their defence traversed – 1, the alleged negligence; 2, that Mary Bell sustained any injuries; 3, that it was by reason of any negligence on their part that she had sustained the injuries; and, 4, that George Bell had been deprived of the society or services of his wife, or that he had been put to any loss or expense.

The plaintiffs joined issue.

The action was tried before Mr. Justice Andrews and a jury of the city of Dublin, in the Michaelmas Sittings, 1889. The plaintiff Mary Bell was examined, and deposed that she was forty-nine years old, and up to June, 1889, was in good health. She was a passenger in the excursion train which left Armagh about 10 o'clock a.m. on the 12th June, 1889. The carriage she was in was the last carriage of that part of the train which remained connected with the engine after the train was divided. The train was not able to go up the incline of Dobbin's Bridge. She heard the unhooking. The train stopped, and was then unhooked. Before the carriage started, after the stop, a man sitting on the seat behind her dropped on her shoulder from the jerk at starting. The portion of the train she was in went on, and then it gave a jerk, and reversed towards Armagh, and went back very fast. She heard rattling of chains, and heard cries of 'Jump out; jump out: you'll all be killed.' The carriage doors were locked; and she saw people jumping out through the windows. There was a steep embankment at one side; and the train was going back very fast. Witness and all the people in the carriage were frightened. The train came to a curve, and pulled up suddenly. Witness was then standing up, and was thrown down; and the people in the carriage were all thrown about. She remembered nothing more of how she got out of the carriage; and she was in Armagh till the Monday week after the accident, and then went home to Carrickfergus. [Witness then deposed to the injuries she received.] Her general employment was house-keeping for her husband, who was a land-steward; and she was unable since the accident to do anything owing to the injuries she received. She had four children, one of whom was living with her.

On cross-examination the witness deposed that the carriage she was in did not collide with any other train or carriage, and she was not in the runaway part of the train. She felt a jerk when the train was put back to be loosed before it was unhooked: that was the first jerk; but it did not cause her injuries. The last jerk was the only one. She did not know anyone in the carriage but her daughter and grandchild. At the last jerk of the carriage she was thrown down; but she did not know if anyone else in the carriage was thrown down.

Other witnesses were examined, and proved the uncoupling of the carriages, and the shock sustained by the passengers when the train jerked.

The plaintiffs' daughter was examined, and proved that in June, 1889, the plaintiff went on a visit to a lady in Armagh, and was up to that time in good health. The plaintiff came back about the Monday week after the accident, and witness hardly knew her; she looked as white as death, and trembled. She could not sleep at night; and if she fell asleep she awoke screaming. The plaintiff got gradually worse, and continually complained of her head and side. On the morning of the 7th July, 1889, at 3 o'clock, plaintiff had been in bed; and witness, who was sleeping in the next room, found her on the floor, screaming. The doctor was then called in. The plaintiff's mind was entirely deranged; and she began throwing things out of the bed. Ever since the accident plaintiff had been in bad health; previously she was the strongest woman in the house.

On cross-examination the witness deposed that the plaintiff was very nervous, and seemed as if she had got a great fright, and been shocked. She was always talking about the train, and people jumping out, and, before the last shock, about a soldier lying dead. After the 7th July she got slightly better.

The plaintiff's son-in-law deposed that he resided in Armagh; and hearing of the accident, drove out to the scene of its occurrence. He found the plaintiff lying on her side on the embankment, and she did not know him. He carried her to the car, and put her into it, and brought her to Armagh, where, on her arrival, she was put to bed. Witness did not believe she would live till the next morning. When the plaintiff recovered consciousness she talked very queer. She remained in Armagh till the Monday week following. Witness knew her for twenty years; and she was, up to the time of the accident, a strong, healthy woman.

Three medical witnesses were then examined, and deposed that the plaintiff was suffering from fright and nervous shock; and one of these witnesses deposed that her condition might result in paralysis.

The plaintiffs' case then closed.

Counsel for the defendants then submitted – 1, that there was no evidence of negligence *quoad* the female plaintiff and the carriage she was in; and, 2, if there were such evidence, the damages were too remote.

His Lordship declined to direct a verdict for the defendants.

On behalf of the defendants three persons who were in the front portion of the train which remained attached to the engine were examined, and deposed that there was no sudden or violent jerk felt, and that the only jerk felt was like that usually felt on the ordinary stoppage of a train.

Medical evidence was also given, to show that the symptoms from which the plaintiff was alleged to be suffering were not serious, and that they were not likely to develop into brain-disease or paralysis. The plaintiff suffered from shock from fright.

The defendants' case then closed; and their counsel repeated his requisition to direct a verdict for them. His Lordship declined, and left the following questions to the jury, the answers to which respectively are annexed:–

1. Was there negligence on the part of the defendants in relation to the excursion train before it was divided? – Yes.

2. After it was divided, was there negligence on the part of the defendants in relation to the front part thereof, in which the plaintiff Mary Bell was? – Yes.

3. Were injuries to Mary Bell's health occasioned while she was in the excursion train? – Yes.

4. Were those injuries occasioned by negligence on the part of the defendants? – Yes.

5. Did those injuries reasonably and naturally result from negligence on the part of the defendants in relation to the front part of the train in which Mary Bell was? – Yes.

6. If not, did they reasonably and naturally result from negligence on the part of the defendants before and after the train was divided? – (No answer.)

7. Assess the plaintiffs' damages for Mary Bell's injuries. – £300.

8. Assess the plaintiff George Bell's damages for loss of society and services of his wife, and for expenses incurred for medical attendance upon her. – £50.

His Lordship reported as follows:–

'In charging the jury, I told them that if great fright was in their opinion, a reasonable and natural consequence of the circumstances in which the defendants had placed Mary Bell, and she was actually put in great fright by these circumstances, and if injury to her health was, in their opinion, a reasonable and natural consequence of such great fright, and was actually occasioned thereby, damages for such injury would not be too remote, and might be given for them if they found for the plaintiff.

After the jury retired, Mr. Walker, on behalf of the defendants, handed me in the following requisition in writing:–

"*Bell* v. *Great Northern Railway Co*. – His Lordship left to the jury the question of negligence. On the part of the defendants, we ask his Lordship to tell the jury – 1, that there was no evidence of negligence naturally and reasonably tending to the injury of which the plaintiff complains; 2, that the injury was not the natural and reasonable result of any negligence of the defendants; 3, if damages or injury were the result of, or arose from, mere fright, and not accompanied by any actual physical injury, even though there might be a nervous or mental shock occasioned by the fright, such damages would be too remote."

I declined to direct the jury.

The MacDermot, on behalf of the plaintiffs, handed me in the following requisition in writing as what he wished me to tell the jury:–

"That even although there was, under the special circumstances, namely, first, the running away of the unhooked part of the train, and secondly, its collision with the ordinary train, causing the block on the road, no negligence in following with the engine division of train, or in the pulling up of that portion, yet, if the pursuit of the runaway train, and the pulling it up at place of collision, exposed the plaintiff to peril, and she, as a reasonable consequence of it, sustained the injuries complained of, the defendants would be liable by reason of their antecedent negligence."

The MacDermot said he did not present this by way of objection to my charge, but as a request to put it to the jury in the way he had put it in his requisition. I said that I had not told the jury anything to the contrary of his requisition; and I declined to recall the jury, and alter the manner in which I had left the case to them, which I thought was the proper one; and I said that in receiving the requisition I was not to be taken as indicating that I had not left what I regard as the substance of his requisition to the jury.'

His Lordship gave judgment for the plaintiffs, in accordance with the findings of the jury.

The defendants having obtained a conditional order, the plaintiffs now showed cause.

Palles C.B.:

Two of the questions argued – viz. (1) that there was no evidence of negligence in the management of the portion of the train in which the plaintiff was travelling; and (2) that there was no evidence of injury to the plaintiffs sufficient to sustain the action – were disposed of during the argument, and indeed were substantially abandoned by the defendants' counsel. There remains, then, only the third question, that the jury were misdirected as to the elements which they were entitled to take into consideration in measuring the damages.

In summing up, my brother Andrews told the jury that, if great fright was, in their opinion, the reasonable and natural consequence of the circumstances in which the defendants, by their negligence, had placed the female plaintiff, and that she was actually put in great fright by those circumstances; and if the injury to her health was, in their opinion, the reasonable and natural consequence of such great fright, and was actually occasioned thereby, damages for such injury would not be too remote. The defendant's counsel objected to this direction, and required the Judge to tell the jury that if the injury was the result of, or arose from, mere fright, and was not accompanied by any physical injury, even though there might be a *nervous* or mental shock occasioned by the fright, such damages would be too remote.

This objection presupposes that the plaintiff sustained, by reason of the defendants' negligence, 'injury' of the class left to the consideration of the jury by summing-up, *i.e.* injury to health, which is bodily or physical injury; and the proposition presented is that damages for such injury are not recoverable, if two circumstances occur: (1) if the only connexion between the negligence and this bodily injury is that the former caused fright, which caused nervous or mental shock, which shock caused the bodily injury complained of; and (2) that this so-called bodily injury did not accompany the fright, which I suppose means that the injury, although in fact occasioned by the fright, assumed the character of bodily injury subsequently to, and not at, the time of the negligence or fright. To sustain this contention, it must be true whether the shock which it assumed to have been caused was either mental or nervous; and as the introduction of the word 'mental' may cause obscurity, by involving matter of a wholly different nature, unnecessary to be taken into consideration here, I eliminate it from the question. If there be a distinction between mental shock and nervous shock, and if the proposition be not true in the case of nervous shock, then the objection cannot be sustained.

It is, then, to be observed: (1) that the negligence is *a* cause of the injury, at least in the sense of a *causa sine quâ non*; (2) that no intervening independent cause of the injury is suggested; (3) that jurors, having regard to their experience of life, may hold fright to be a natural and reasonable consequence of such negligence as occurred in the present case.

If, then, such bodily injury as we have here, may be a natural consequence of fright, the chain of reasoning is complete. But the medical evidence here is such that the jury might from it reasonably arrive at the conclusion that the injury, similar to that which actually resulted to the plaintiff from the fright, might reasonably have resulted to any person who had been placed in a similar position. It has not been suggested that there was anything special in the nervous organization of the plaintiff which might render the effect of the negligence or fright upon her different in character from that which it would have produced in any other individual I do not myself think that proof that the plaintiff was of an unusually nervous disposition would have been material to the question; for persons, whether nervous or strong-minded, are entitled to be carried by railway companies without unreasonable risk of danger; and my only reason for referring to the circumstance is to show that, in this particular case, the jury might have arrived at the conclusion that the injury which did, in fact, ensue was a natural and reasonable consequence of the negligence which actually caused it.

Again, it is admitted that, as the negligence caused fright, if the fright contemporaneously caused physical injury, the damage would not be too remote. The distinction insisted upon is one of time only. The proposition is that, although, if an act of negligence produces such an effect upon particular structures of the body as at the moment to afford palpable evidence of physical injury, the relation of proximate cause and effect exists between such negligence and the injury, yet such relation *cannot* in law exist in the case of a similar act producing upon the same structures an effect which, at a subsequent time – say a week, a fortnight, or a month – must result, without any intervening cause, in the same physical injury. As well might it be said that a death caused by poison is not to be attributed to the person who administered it because the mortal effect is not produced contemporaneously with its administration. This train of reasoning might be pursued much farther; but in consequence of the decision to which I shall hereafter refer, I deem it unnecessary to do so.

In support of their contention, the defendants relied upon the *Victorian Railway Commissioners* v. *Coultas* 13 App. Cas. 222. That was a remarkable case. The statement of claim alleged that through the negligence of the servants of the defendants, in charge of a railway gate at a level crossing, the plaintiffs, while driving over it, were placed in imminent peril of being killed by a train, and by reason thereof the plaintiff, Mary, received a shock, and suffered personal injuries. It appeared that the female plaintiff, whilst returning with her husband and brother in the evening, from Melbourne to Hawthorn, in a buggy, had to cross the defendants' line of railway at a level crossing. When they came to it the gates were closed; the gatekeeper opened the gates nearest to the plaintiffs, and then went across the line to those on the opposite side. The plaintiffs followed him, and were partly on to the up-line (the further one), when the train was seen approaching on it. The gatekeeper directed them to go back, but James Coultas, who was driving, shouted to him to open the opposite gate, and went on. He succeeded in getting the buggy across the line, so that the train, which was going at a rapid speed, did not touch it, although it passed close at the back of it. As the train approached, the plaintiff, Mary, fainted. The medical evidence showed that she received a severe *nervous* shock from the fright, and that the illness from which she afterwards suffered (and which is stated in Mr. Beven's book on Negligence to have included a miscarriage) was the consequence of the fright. One of the plaintiffs' witnesses said she was suffering from profound impression on the nervous system – *nervous shock*; and that the shock from which she suffered would be a natural consequence of the fright. Another said he was unable to detect any physical damage; he put down her symptoms to *nervous shock*.

It is to be observed that from this evidence the jury might have inferred that physical injury was sustained by the female plaintiff at the time of the occurrence in question. Although one witness spoke of nervous shock, as contradistinguished from physical damage, the question would still have been open for the jury whether the nervous shock was not – as in the generality of, if not indeed in all, cases it necessarily must be – physical injury. The jury found for the plaintiffs. Upon an appeal, the Privy Council without deciding that impact was necessary to sustain the action not only set aside the verdict, but entered judgment for the defendants. In delivering judgment, Sir R. Couch says, 'Her fright was caused by seeing the train approaching, and thinking they were going to be killed. Damages arising from mere sudden terror, unaccompanied by any actual physical injury, but occasioning a nervous or mental shock, cannot, *under such circumstances* (their Lordships think), be considered *a consequence* which, in the ordinary course of things, would flow from the negligence of the gatekeeper.'

Amongst the reasons stated in the judgment in support of this conclusion are: 1, that a contrary doctrine would involve damage on account of *mental* injury being given in every case where the accident caused by the negligence had given the person a severe *nervous* shock; 2, that no decision of an English court had been produced in which, upon such facts, damages were recovered; 3, that a decision of the Supreme Court of New York (*Vandenbury* v. *Truax* 4 Denio. Sup. Ct. N.Y. Rep. 464), which was relied upon, was distinguishable, as being a case of *palpable* injury.

Of these reasons, the first seems to involve that injuries, other than mental, cannot result from nervous shock; and the third implies that injuries resulting from such a shock cannot be 'palpable.' I am unable (I say it with deference) to follow the reasoning; and further, it seems to me that even were the proposition of law upon which the judgment is based sustainable, the Privy Council were not warranted in assuming as a fact, against the verdict of the jury, and without any special finding with regard to it, that the fright was, in that particular case, unaccompanied by any actual physical injury. Further, the judgment assumes, as a matter of law, that nervous shock is something which affects merely the mental functions, and is not in itself a peculiar physical state of the body. This error pervades the entire judgment. Mr. Beven states, in his recent work on Negligence (p. 67), and I entirely concur with him, that 'the starting-point of the reasoning there is that nervous shock and mental shock are identical; and that they are opposed to actual physical injury.'

Possibly, were there no decision the other way, I should, from courtesy, defer my opinion to that of the Privy Council, and leave it to the plaintiff to question our decision upon appeal. The very point, however, had been, four years before the decision of the Privy Council in the *Victorian Railway Commissioners* v. *Coultas* 13 App. Cas. 322, decided in this country, first in the Common Pleas Division, then presided over by the present Lord Morris, and afterwards in the Court of Appeal, in a judgment delivered by the late Sir Edward Sullivan; and it is a sad commentary upon our system of reporting that a decision so important and so novel has never found its way into our Law Reports. The case I refer to is *Byrne* v. *Great Southern and Western Railway Company*, unreported. It was tried before me on the 5th and 6th December, 1882; and a motion to enter a verdict for the defendants was heard in 1883 by the Common Pleas Division; and by the Court of Appeal in February, 1884. It was an action by the Superintendent of the Telegraph Office at the Limerick Junction station of the defendants' railway. His office consisted of a small building at the end of one of the defendants' sidings, between which and the office there was a permanent buffer strongly fixed. On the 7th December, 1881, through some railway points having being negligently left open, a train entered this siding, broke down the permanent buffer, and the wall of the telegraph office. The plaintiff's case was that by hearing the noise, and seeing the wall falling, he sustained a nervous shock, which resulted in certain injuries to his health. On cross-examination he said, 'A hair of my head was not touched; I swear I received no physical injury; I got a great fright and shock; I do not mean a physical shock; it was the crash and falling in of the office, and shouts of the clerks saying they were killed; I saw part of the office falling in; I believed it was all falling in.' A verdict having being found for the plaintiff with £325 damages, a motion to set it aside, and enter a verdict for the defendants, on the ground that there was no evidence of injury sufficient to sustain the action, was refused by the Common Pleas Division; and this refusal was affirmed by the Court of Appeal.

That case goes much further than is necessary to sustain the direction here, as in it there was nothing in the nature of impact. As between it, by which we are bound, and the decision of the Privy Council, by which we are not, I must prefer the former. I desire, however, to add that I entirely concur in the decision in *Byrne* v. *Great Southern and Western Railway Co.*, and that I should have been prepared to have arrived at the same conclusion, even without its high authority. Its importance in the present case is that it renders unnecessary for me to yield my own opinion to the decision in the *Victorian Railway Commissioners* v. *Coultas* 13 App. Cas. 322.

In conclusion, then, I am of opinion that, as the relation between fright and injury to the nerve and brain structures of the body is a matter which depends entirely upon scientific and medical testimony, it is impossible for any Court to lay down, as a matter of law, that if negligence cause fright, and such fright, in its turn, so affects such structures as to cause injury to health, such injury cannot be 'a consequence which, in the ordinary course of things would flow from the' negligence, unless such injury 'accompany such negligence in point of time.'

In my opinion the verdict should stand.

Andrews and **Murphy JJ.** concurred.

Notes and Questions

1. What limits (if any) to recovery for injury from nervous shock does this decision lay down? *Cf. Hogg* v. *Keane* [1956] I.R. 155, (Supreme Court, 1955). What light does it throw on the question?
2. If reasonable foreseeability is the only test, will liability be too extensive, from a policy standpoint?
3. In England a greater willingness to articulate policy considerations is now apparent: see *McLoughlin* v. *O'Brian* [1982] 2 All E.R. 298 (H.L.), analysed by Hutchinson & Morgan, 45 Modern L. Rev. 693 (1982); Teff, 'Liability for Negligently Inflicted Nervous Shock' 99 L.Q. Rev. 100 (1983).
4. In determining which plaintiffs are within the range of reasonable foreseeability should the social utility of their conduct be taken into consideration? Is a rescuer who suffers shock more deserving of compensation than a mere bystander? *Cf. Chadwick* v. *British Railways Board* [1967] 1 W.L.R. 912; *Weir*, pp. 54, 71. Could it on the other hand be argued that bystanders are, in practice, more foreseeable than rescuers? *Cf. Hay (or Bourhill)* v. *Young* [1943] A.C. 92, and *McLoughlin* v. *O'Brian, supra.*

3. *MEDICAL NEGLIGENCE*

DANIELS V. HESKIN

[1954] I.R. 73 (Supreme Court, 1953)

Kingsmill Moore J.:

The plaintiffs are a labourer and his wife, living some five miles from Waterford, and the defendant is the dispensary doctor of the district in which the plaintiffs reside. The plaintiffs claim damages for negligence, or alternatively for breach of contract, alleging that the defendant was employed to treat the female plaintiff and that in so doing he was negligent in three ways, in as much as he allowed a surgical needle to break while stitching her perineum, failed to remove the broken portion of the needle from the perineum or to take early steps to have it removed, and failed to inform the plaintiffs that the broken portion had been left in the perineum.

At 11 o'clock p.m. on the 17th June, 1951, the wife gave birth to her first baby, and in the course of the delivery the perineum became torn to an extent which required stitching. Accordingly, Nurse Power, a midwife of over thirty years' experience, who was in attendance at the birth, sent next day for the defendant. He arrived at 11 o'clock a.m., selected from his bag the needles he required, and gave them to the nurse who sterilised them, and threaded in the sutures. The first stitch was inserted without mishap, but in the course of inserting the second stitch the needle broke and about $1\frac{1}{2}$ inches remained buried, fairly deeply, in the perineum. Another needle and suture were got ready, and with them the second stitch was put in place. Both doctor and nurse searched for, but could not find, the broken portion of the needle and the doctor told the nurse that 'it must be in there,' meaning that it was in the perineum, and said 'we will have to have an X-ray,' and subsequently 'you will have to have an X-ray.' Before leaving he told the nurse to look after the patient, to watch her pulse and temperature and to report to him if anything went wrong, or if she was worried about anything, or if the patient was suffering any discomfort. He does not seem to have given specific directions about the needle, but Nurse Power understood that these directions were given with reference to the needle, and she also understood that if the needle was not found in six weeks the patient was to be X-rayed.

The patient remained under the care of Nurse Power and had a normal convalescence. After nine days the stitches were removed, and the patient got up, and began to take up her ordinary life. She did suffer from what she called 'ire,' a word which apparently means 'chafing' and which, according to Nurse Power, is a normal feature after delivery, and when she bent down, according to her testimony in the box, she felt as if there was a piece of wire in her flesh which pricked her. Nurse Power attended her daily for nine days after the birth and saw her out walking, or on a social call, about twice a week after that. No complaint was made to Nurse Power about the sensation of wire, but the patient did complain of the 'ire.' Nurse Power in the course of the six weeks after the birth saw and reported to the defendant about three or four times, and told him that she had not been able to find the needle. When the six weeks had expired Nurse Power, without any additional instructions from the defendant, but in pursuance of what she thought had been agreed on the day of the stitching, took her patient into Waterford to a Dr. O'Keeffe, who is a surgeon and gynaecologist, and he made arrangements for an X-ray. The X-ray showed the broken needle lying fairly deep in the perineum. After a delay of about a fortnight, till a bed should be vacant, the patient was operated on, and the broken needle removed, not without some little difficulty, on the 13th August. On the 26th August she was discharged from hospital with the operation scar healed and her health has progressed normally. At the trial she said that she was due to have another child on the 24th June – just over twelve months after her first baby was born.

Nurse Power kept the defendant informed of the steps which were being taken by her and believed herself to be carrying out his instructions. She says that when she told Dr. Heskin that she had taken the patient to Dr. O'Keeffe he appeared pleased.

For the plaintiffs, Dr. O'Keeffe and Dr. Davidson, ex-Master of the Rotunda Hospital, gave expert evidence. For the defendant, Dr. Arthur Chance, a very eminent surgeon, was called, and his evidence was for convenience interposed after the plaintiffs' doctors had given their evidence. The defendant himself was too ill to attend the trial. At the conclusion of the case for the plaintiffs the trial Judge withdrew the case from the jury on the ground that there was no evidence of negligence, and entered judgment for the defendant, and against this ruling and order the plaintiffs appeal.

There was very little controversy as to facts and the case turns on whether, on the admitted facts, there was any evidence that the defendant was negligent in the treatment of his patient in any of the three ways suggested, and the answer depends chiefly on the expert evidence of the doctors.

The first negligence alleged was permitting the needle to break in the tissues of the patient. All the doctors agreed that needles may, and do, break owing to flaws in the steel, without the slightest error being imputable to the user. As I understand the evidence, all the doctors also agreed that a sound needle may be broken by a doctor in the course of an operation if the doctor asks too much of it, either by taking up rather too big a fold of tissue, or by forcing the needle slightly, or subjecting it to some other strain. This Dr. Chance termed an 'imperfection of technique,' but he made it quite clear that it was such an imperfection as was inherent in the limitations of human nature, and did not amount to negligence: 'there is no living surgeon that has not broken a needle many times,' 'all the most skilful people in the world have done it,' 'the most competent surgeons in the world have broken needles. The masters have broken them.' Dr. Davidson said:– 'I have broken needles often myself – trying to get too much into the needle, or putting too big a strain on it,' and in cross-examination he reaffirmed that needles had frequently broken with him, but disclaimed any negligence on his part. Dr. O'Keeffe appeared to have been more fortunate than his colleagues, having only broken needles on two occasions.

If a needle may be broken through a flaw in the steel, or through some failure to reach perfection in handling, which does not amount to negligence, there can be no question of the application of the maxim, *res ipsa loquitur*, and there must be evidence of some definite act of negligence by the doctor. It was suggested that the doctor used a wrong type of needle. The usual needle used for such stitching is the semi-circular, or fully-curved perineal needle, and the X-ray showed that the doctor had used a less fully-curved needle. But on this, Dr. Davidson said:– 'I should say that not all people use a fully-curved needle. Some use the semi-curved needle. Some may use the less fully-curved.' Dr. O'Keeffe agreed that different kinds of needles were used, depending on individual choice.

It was also suggested that the needle was too thin, but it was admitted that a fine needle had the advantage of minimising pain, and no doctor said that the needle used was improperly fine.

I am unable to find any evidence such as would warrant a jury in finding that the fracture of the needle was due to any negligence of the defendant, rather than to an unforeseen weakness in the steel, or to a mishap such as may happen to the most skilful operator, especially when he is working in difficult conditions. To fall short of perfection is not the same thing as to be negligent.

If the doctor was not negligent in breaking the needle, was he negligent in leaving the broken piece in the tissues, to be removed subsequently? There was a divergence of opinion between the doctors as to what was the most suitable course. Dr. Davidson said that if he was a country practitioner, stitching the patient in her own home, and found it difficult to get at the broken needle at once, he thought that he would stitch up the patient and leave her to see if the needle would show up at a later date; but if the needle had not worked itself out by three or four months time, he would operate, and he would operate at an earlier period if pain or temperature suggested any harm was being done. Dr. O'Keeffe said:– 'I think I would take the patient into hospital straight away . . . giving an anaesthetic and attempt to remove the needle.' He made it clear that, unless he could be certain of operating within twenty-four hours of the time when the needle was fractured, he would prefer to have the needle *in situ* for some weeks or months before operating. Dr. Chance was of opinion that if the needle were broken in the course of an operation in a hospital theatre, the best course would be to locate and remove the broken portion at once, but if the damage occurred in a private house, and the broken portion could not be at once located and removed, then the better course was to sew up the patient and remove the needle after six weeks or so had elapsed.

None of these eminent medical men purported to be dogmatic; none of them suggested that a course, other than the course he preferred, would have been necessarily erroneous: certainly no one of them suggested that the adoption of the alternative course was negligence. I should like to say with emphasis that an honest difference of opinion between eminent doctors, as to which is the better of two ways of treating a patient, does not provide any ground for leaving a question to the jury as to whether a person who had followed one course rather than the other has been guilty of negligence. It would be different if a doctor had expressed the opinion that the course adopted was definitely erroneous. The defendant in this case adopted the course which Dr. Davidson, a Master of the Rotunda, who for many years was responsible for teaching the best practice of midwifery, considers to have been correct, and the one which ought to have been adopted in the circumstances. Neither the honesty nor the competency of this opinion has been challenged – indeed Dr. Davidson was called as the expert witness for the plaintiffs. I do not understand Dr. O'Keeffe to have suggested that there was anything negligent in leaving the needle *in situ* to be removed subsequently, though he himself would probably have attempted an early removal if he could be sure of doing the operation within twenty-four hours. There was no evidence that the defendant, faced with an emergency, could have been sure of making suitable arrangements for an operation to take place within the period assigned, and in Dr. O'Keeffe's own opinion, if this could not be ensured, the most proper course was that taken by the defendant.

There seems to me to be no evidence fit to be considered by a jury to suggest that the defendant was negligent in leaving the needle in the tissues for removal at a subsequent period when the tissues should have healed and risk of infection would have diminished.

The third head of negligence alleged against the defendant was his failure to give immediate information to the patient or her husband that a portion of the needle was buried in the tissues.

Counsel for the plaintiffs suggested that there was a rule of law that such information should be given. He relied first on the words of Mr. Justice du Parcq in a case of *Gerber* v. *Pines*, very shortly reported in 79 Sol. J. 13. The learned Judge is there alleged to have said that 'it seemed to him that a patient in whose body a doctor found he had left some foreign substance was entitled to be told at once. That was a general rule, but there were exceptions.' Counsel next referred to an American case, noted in Taylor's Medical Jurisprudence, 9th ed., vol. 1, at p. 83, *Eislein* v. *Palmer* Amer. Law Dig. 1899, at p. 1870, in which it was apparently decided that there was no duty on a physician to tell a patient or her husband that a broken needle had been left in the patient's body so long as she remained a patient, but that there was a duty to tell her when discharging her from his care.

I doubt very much whether the judges in either of these cases intended to enunciate a rule of law. If they did I must respectfully disagree. A doctor owes certain well recognised duties to his patient. He must possess such knowledge and skill as conforms to the recognised contemporary standards of his profession and, if he is a specialist, such further and particularised skill and knowledge as he holds himself out to possess. He must use such skill and knowledge to form an honest and considered judgment as to what course, what action, what treatment, is in the best interests of his patient. He must display proper care and attention in treating, or in arranging suitable treatment for, his patient. Any attempt to substitute a rule of law, or even a rule of thumb practice, for the individual judgment of a qualified doctor, doing what he considers best for the particular patient, would be disastrous. There may be cases where the judgment of the physician is proved by subsequent events to have been wrong, but if it is honest and considered and if, in the circumstances known to him at the time, it can fairly be justified, he is not guilty of negligence. There may indeed be cases where the nature of the judgment formed or the advice given is such as to afford positive evidence that the physician has fallen short of the required standard of knowledge and skill, or that this judgment could not have been honest and considered, but it lies on the plaintiff to adduce evidence from which such a failure of duty can reasonably be inferred.

I cannot admit any abstract duty to tell patients what is the matter with them or, in particular, to say that a needle has been left in their tissues. All depends on the circumstances – the character of the patient, her health, her social position, her intelligence, the nature of the tissue in which the needle is embedded, the possibility of subsequent infection, the arrangements made for future observation and care, and innumerable other considerations. In the present case the patient was passing through a *post-partum* period in which the possibility of nervous or mental disturbance is notorious; the needle was not situated in a place where any immediate damage was to be anticipated; husband and wife were of a class and standard of education which would incline them to exaggerate the seriousness of the occurrence and to suffer needless alarm; and arrangements were made to keep the patient under observation during the period when sepsis might occur, and to have the patient X-rayed at a period when the bruising and injuries caused by the birth should have subsided. If it were open to me to speak as a juror I would say that the defendant's action was correct. That question is not directly before this Court. What we have to consider is whether it was so incorrect as to provide evidence on which a jury could reasonably conclude that the defendant had failed in any of the duties toward his patient which I have already enumerated. In my opinion there is no such evidence.

All the doctors who were examined were of opinion that it would be wise for a doctor to tell a patient or some member of her family of such a mishap – but wise in a self-regarding way, so as to protect the doctor from the possibility of future vexatious actions. Thus Dr. Davidson said he would inform the patient as otherwise he might 'find himself in an awful mess.' 'From my own point of view I would inform her, looking after my own interest.' In cross-examination he admitted that there was a choice between 'either keeping yourself right by informing the patient, or taking a chance and saving her anxiety.' Dr. O'Keeffe said he would have told one of the family; but agreed that there were patients who should not be informed immediately after a confinement, that in every case a doctor must make up his own mind, and that as Dr. Heskin and Mrs. Power knew the patient and the circumstances of the case they were in the best position to form a correct judgment. Mr. Chance thought the patient should not have been informed; that there was no reason to inform her except the doctor's self-protection; that in his own interest a doctor should tell somebody.

Here the defendant told Mrs. Power. No doubt he would have been wise in his generation to tell the husband and so avoid future trouble for himself. But his policy, though justifiable from motives of narrow self-interest, may seem to some less laudable than the other alternative of 'taking a chance' to save the patient anxiety.

Nor can I see how the patient's interests in this case would have been secured by informing her husband, thus causing anxiety to him and, if he revealed his knowledge, to her. It has been suggested that if her husband had been informed he might have got into touch with Dr. O'Keeffe, who in turn might have been able to get a bed and remove the needle within the period of twelve to twenty-four hours in which he considered operation would be desirable. The husband, though examined, never suggested that he would have taken this course, and, if we are to pay attention to the evidence given by Dr. Davidson for the plaintiffs, it is a matter of doubt whether such an operation at this time was the best treatment. Even if there was a duty to inform, which in this case I do not think there was, I cannot find that any damages have been incurred by failure in such duty.

To avoid any misconstruction I may add that I do not wish to suggest that a doctor would always be justified in keeping such knowledge to himself. In every case there is a clear duty to take precautions against injury to the patient from the presence of the needle. The nature of those precautions must vary with each case. In the present case the arrangements made with Mrs. Power, to keep a close watch on the patient and have an X-ray at the appropriate time, were such that it would be impossible to find that the doctor had not exercised his judgment honestly, responsibly and with a due regard to his patient's interest.

Lavery J. delivered a judgment to similar effect (with which **Murnaghan** and **O'Byrne JJ.** concurred). **Maguire C.J.** also delivered a concurring judgment.

Notes and Questions

1. The issues of principle raised in this decision have come under increasing international scrutiny in recent years. See Robertson, 'Informed Consent to Medical Treatment' 97 L.Q. Rev. 102 (1981). Do you think that doctors should set the disclosure standard or are broader issues involved? *Cf.* Seidelson, 'Medical Malpractice: Informed Consent Cases in "Full Disclosure" Jurisdictions' 14 Duquesne L. Rev. 309 (1976). Where does *Daniels* v. *Heskin* stand on this question? *Cf. McMahon & Binchy*, p. 178.
2. Would an Irish court in 1983 consider the social class of the plaintiff to be relevant to the outcome of the decision in the way that Kingsmill Moore J. did?
3. A sick patient says to his doctor: 'Tell me truthfully: am I dying?' Is the doctor under any legal responsibility to tell the truth?
4. Who may be treated as an expert witness in actions for medical malpractice? *Cf. Reynolds* v. *Dublin Skin & Cancer Hospital*, unreported, Supreme Court, 18 December 1958 (68–1957).
5. See also *Reeves* v. *Carthy, supra*, pp. 17–20 (allegation of negligent diagnosis).
6. A person represents to others that he is possessed of special skill and knowledge in the diagnosis, treatment and cure of tuberculosis, but does not hold himself as having any professional or academic qualifications in medicine. By what standard of care is he to be judged? *Cf. Brogan* v. *Bennett* [1955] I.R. 119 (Sup. Ct.). Contrast *Philips* v. *Whiteley Ltd.* [1938] 1 All E.R. 566.
7. Is it lawful for a medical researcher to pay a substantial sum of money to a human 'guinea-pig' to induce him to undergo a trial of a drug whose side-effects are not known? Assuming that all the risks have, so far as possible, been brought to the attention of the subject of the trial, is his consent a legally valid one? *Cf.* M. Somerville, *Consent to Care*, pp. 49–52 (L. R. Com. of Canada, 1979).

4. *LIABILITY OF SCHOOLS*

LENNON V. McCARTHY
Unreported, Supreme Court, 13 July 1966 (5–1965)

The plaintiff, a pupil at a rural two-teacher school in Co. Roscommon, was injured at play during the mid-day lunch-break. He was then within a few weeks of his tenth birthday.

He and four or five other companions, one of whom was a boy called James Dunne climbed from the school playground over a wall more than three feet high into the 'hollow' of an adjoining field and there began playing the game of 'tig'. Dunne was older than the plaintiff, being two classes ahead of him. The plaintiff was chasing Dunne to touch him, or give him 'tig'. Dunne was running along by a flat fence in the 'hollow' on which a number of trees were growing. Some of these trees were limes and others were hawthorn bushes. A branch projected out horizontally for 7 feet from one of the hawthorn bushes at a height of 3 feet above ground level. Dunne as he ran along by the fence pushed this branch out of his way and then let it back. The plaintiff in close pursuit was struck in the eye by the rebounding branch.

The plaintiff sued the manager and principal teacher of the school for negligence. In his evidence, he stated that the principal teacher and his assistant remained in the school during the playtime and that the principal teacher only came into the yard to ring the bell for re-assembly. The trial judge withdrew the case from the jury and the plaintiff appealed to the Supreme Court.

Ó Dálaigh C.J. (for the Court):

. . . The duty of a schoolmaster is to take such care of his pupils as a careful father would of his children (per Lord Esher, M.R. in *Williams* v. *Eady* (1893) 10 T.L.R. 41). But when normally healthy children are in the playground it is not necessary that they should be under constant supervision: *Rawsthorne* v. *Ottley* [1937] 3 All E.R. 902.

The accident here complained of occurred outside the school playground and, in my opinion, a jury could find that there was an absence of adequate supervision.

Starting from that point [Counsel for the plaintiff] submits that it might reasonably have been foreseen by the principal teacher that the plaintiff, playing in the 'hollow' without supervision, would be injured, though not necessarily in the manner in which he was injured. This field was not safe, it is said. [Counsel for the plaintiff] points to the evidence about the slope down to the 'hollow' and he adds that boys of 9/10 years of age at school are likely to be more vigorous at play than when at home.

In my opinion it is not shown that the slope constituted any kind of peril for boys. The plaintiff's engineer did not say it was; nor would measurements indicate this. He appears to have been concerned to show no more than that boys playing in the 'hollow' could not be easily seen from the school playground.

It was also suggested that the projecting branch was a feature of danger because of its height from the ground. The plaintiff's engineer described it as a typical whitethorn branch.

In effect the Court is being invited to say that a careful father looking into this field would consider it an unsuitable – a dangerous – field for boys of 9 to 10 years of age to play in; that he would, or rather should, foresee that children would be likely to be injured there.

I am wholly unable to accept this view. It is unreal. Its effect would be to proscribe the playing of ordinary simple games like 'tig' in the ordinary surroundings of rural Ireland. What happened here was an accident such as is inseparable from life and action and no circumstances exist which would warrant placing responsibility for it on the plaintiff's school teacher.

Absence of supervision had nothing whatever to do with this accident.

The appeal should be dismissed.

Notes and Questions

1. *Cf. O'Gorman* v. *Crotty* [1946] Ir. Jur. Rep. 34 (High Court, O'Byrne, J., (1945). Can *Lennon* v. *McCarthy* and *O'Gorman* v. *Crotty* be reconciled?
2. See generally, V.T.H. D[elany], 'Injuries to Schoolchildren: The Principles of Liability'

28–29 Ir. Jur. 15 (1962–1963), Linehan, 'The School Teacher and the Law of Negligence' 31 Ir. Jur. 38 (1965).
3. Where, as a result of the negligence of the school, a child is placed in danger and a third party is injured when trying to save the child, will the school be liable? *Cf. Carmarthenshire Co. Co.* v. *Lewis,* [1955] A.C. 549 (H.L. (Eng.)).

5. *SOLICITOR'S NEGLIGENCE*

Formerly, the duty of a solicitor was regarded as resting exclusively on contract, and no right of action in tort for negligence was recognised. With the development and extension of the 'neighbour' principle, this limitation came to be questioned.

FINLAY V. MURTAGH
[1979] I.R. 249 (Supreme Court, 1978)

Henchy J.:

When a client complains that he has suffered loss because his solicitor has failed to show due care in the performance of his duty as solicitor, does the client's cause of action lie in contract or in the tort of negligence? Or has he a choice? That is the problem presented in this appeal. The plaintiff client has founded his claim against the defendant solicitor in negligence, his case being (and it has not been denied) that the defendant did not, within the period fixed by the statute of limitations, bring an action for damages for personal injuries sustained by the plaintiff as a result of the alleged negligence of a third party. The plaintiff has served notice of trial against the defendant before a judge sitting with a jury, which he would be entitled to do if his cause of action lies, as has been pleaded, in tort. But the defendant contends that the cause of action is breach of contract, that is to say that it is founded on a breach of the implied term in the contract that he would carry out his duties as solicitor with due professional care and skill. If the defendant is correct in that contention, the notice of trial should have been for a judge sitting without a jury. So the defendant has moved in the High Court for an order setting aside the notice of trial which was served. Mr. Justice D'Arcy refused to make that order as he held that the plaintiff's action lies in the tort of negligence. It is from that refusal that the present appeal has been brought by the defendant.

There has been no decision of this Court on the point at issue but we have been referred to three decisions of the High Court. In *McGrath* v. *Kiely* [1965] I.R. 497 the client sued his solicitor for negligence and, alternatively, for breach of contract in failing to show due professional care in the preparation of an action for damages for personal injuries. The claim was pursued in Court as one for breach of contract and no effort was made to pursue the claim in negligence. The parties agreed to treat the solicitor's default as a breach of contract. Therefore, that case throws no light on the present problem.

The second case, *Liston* v. *Munster and Leinster Bank* [1940] I.R. 77, was an action by the personal representative of a customer of the bank against the bank for damages for negligence, for conversion, and for money had and received. The issue being whether the entire cause of action arose out of a contract, in which case notice of trial by a judge without a jury would be appropriate, or whether it lay partly in tort, in which case the notice of trial that had been served specifying trial by a judge with a jury would have been correct. In holding that the claim was partly for breach of contract and partly for conversion, O'Byrne J. applied the following test which had been laid down by Greer L.J. in *Jarvis* v. *Moy, Davies, Smith, Vandervell & Co.* [1936] 1 K.B. 399 at p. 405 of the report:–

'The distinction in the modern view, for this purpose, between contract and tort may be put thus: where the breach of duty alleged arises out of a liability independently of the personal obligation undertaken by contract, it is tort, and it may be tort even though there may happen to be a contract between the parties, if the duty in fact arises independently of that contract. Breach of contract occurs where that which is complained of is a breach of duty arising out of the obligations undertaken by the contract.'

The third High Court case to which we were referred is *Somers* v. *Erskine* [1943] I.R. 348. There the question was whether an action commenced by a client against a solicitor for negligence, and sought to be continued against the solicitor's personal representative, had abated with the solicitor's death as an action in tort, or whether it survived his death as an action in contract. In an unreserved judgment Maguire P. applied the same test as was applied by O'Byrne J. in *Liston* v. *Munster and Leinster Bank* [1940] I.R. 77, and held that the client's claim was essentially one in contract rather than in tort and that, therefore, the claim had survived the solicitor's death. In my opinion, the conclusion that an action by a client against a solicitor for damages for breach of his professional duty of care is necessarily and exclusively one in contract is incompatible with modern developments in the law of torts and should be overruled. In my view, the conclusion there reached does not follow from a correct application of the test laid down by Greer L.J. in the *Jarvis Case* [1936] 1 K.B. 399.

The claim made by the plaintiff in the *Jarvis Case* [1936] 1 K.B. 399 was one by a client against stockbrokers 'for damages for breach of contract arising out of the defendants' relationship with the plaintiff as stockbrokers and client.' Therefore, it is clear that the action was one for breach of contract, at least in form. But the particulars given in the writ show that the substance of the complaint was that the stockbrokers had departed from the specific instructions given by the client. Therefore, the cause of action arose from the breach of a particular binding provision created by the parties, and not from any general obligation of care arising from the relationship of stockbroker and client. The nub of the matter was that the stockbrokers had defaulted on a special personal obligation which was imposed by the contract. They could not have been made liable otherwise than in contract and the court held correctly that the claim was 'founded on contract' in the words of the statute which was being applied.

The test adumbrated by Greer L.J., which commended itself to O'Byrne J. in *Liston* v. *Munster and Leinster Bank* [1940] I.R. 77 and to Maguire P. in *Somers* v. *Erskine* [1943] I.R. 348, correctly draws a distinction between a claim arising out of an obligation deriving from, and owing its existence to, a personal obligation undertaken pursuant to a contract (in which case it is an action in contract) and a claim arising out of a liability created independently of a contract and not deriving from any special obligation imposed by a contract (in which case an action lies in tort). The action in tort derives from an obligation which is imposed by the general law and is applicable to all persons in a certain relationship to each other. The action in contract is founded on the special law which was created by a contract and which was designed to fit the particular relationship of that contract. As I understand it, therefore, the test propounded by Greer L.J. does not support the conclusion reached by Maguire P. that, because the contract of retainer implies a duty of professional care and skill and because a default in that duty has occurred, the cause of action lies exclusively in contract.

It has to be conceded that for over a hundred years there has been a divergence of judicial opinion as to whether a client who has engaged a solicitor to act for him, and who claims that the solicitor failed to show due professional care and skill, may sue in tort or whether he is confined to an action in contract. In *Somers* v. *Erskine* [1943] I.R. 348 (and in some English cases) it was held that the sole cause of action was the solicitor's failure to observe the implied term in the contract of retainer that he would show due professional skill and care. It is undeniable that the client is entitled to sue in contract for breach of that implied term. But it does not follow that the client, because there is privity of contract between him and the solicitor and because he may sue the solicitor for breach of the contract, is debarred from suing also for the tort of negligence. Since the decision of the House of Lords in *Hedley Byrne & Co. Ltd.* v. *Heller & Partners Ltd* [1964] A.C. 465 and the cases following in its wake, it is clear that, whether a contractual relationship exists or not, once the circumstances are such that a defendant undertakes to show professional care and skill towards a person who may be expected to rely on such care and skill and who does so rely, then if he has been damnified by such default that person may sue the defendant in the tort of negligence for failure to show such care and skill. For the purpose of such an action, the existence of a contract is merely an incident of the relationship. If, on the one side, there is a proximity of relationship creating a general duty and, on the other, a reliance on that duty, it matters not whether the parties are bound together in contract. For instance, if the defendant in the present case had not been retained for reward but had merely volunteered his services to the plaintiff, his liability in negligence would be the same as if he was to be paid for his services. The coincidence that the defendant's conduct amounts to a breach of contract cannot affect either the duty of care on the common-law liability for its breach, for it is the general relationship, and not any particular manifestation such as a contract, that gives rise to the tortious liability in such a case: see *per* Lord Devlin in the *Hedley Byrne Case* [1964] A.C. 465 at p. 530 of the report.

A comprehensive survey of the law governing the liability of a solicitor to his client in negligence is to be found in the judgment of Oliver J. in *Midland Bank* v. *Hett, Stubbs & Kemp* [1979] Ch. 384, in which it was held that the solicitor's liability in tort exists independently of any liability in contract. That conclusion, which was reached at first instance and with which I agree, may be said to be reinforced by dicta in the judgments of the Court of Appeal in *Batty* v. *Metropolitan Realisations Ltd.* [1978] Q.B. 554 and *Photo Production Ltd* v. *Securicor Ltd.* [1978] 1 W.L.R. 856.

On a consideration of those cases and the authorities mentioned in them, I am satisfied that the general duty of care created by the relationship of solicitor and client entitles the client to sue in negligence if he has suffered damage because of the solicitor's failure to show due professional care and skill, notwithstanding that the client could sue alternatively in contract for breach of the implied term in the contract of retainer that the solicitor will deal with the matter in hand with due professional care and skill. The solicitor's liability in tort under the general duty of care extends not only to a client for reward, but to any person for whom the solicitor undertakes to act professionally without reward, and also to those (such as beneficiaries under a will, persons entitled under an intestacy, or those entitled to benefits in circumstances such as a claim in respect of a fatal injury) with whom he has made no arrangement to act but who, as he knows or ought to know, will be relying on his professional care and skill. For the same default there should be the same cause of action. If others are entitled to sue in tort for the solicitor's want of care, so also should the client; that is so unless the solicitor's default arises not from a breach of the general duty of care arising from the relationship but from a breach of a particular and special term of the contract in respect of which the solicitor would not be liable if the contract had not contained such a term. Thus, if the client's instructions were that the solicitor was to issue proceedings within a specified time, or to close a sale by a particular date or, generally, to do or not to do some act, and the solicitor defaulted in that respect, any resulting right of action which the client might have would be in contract only unless the act or default complained of falls within the general duty of care owed by the solicitor.

The modern law of tort shows that the existence of a contractual relationship which impliedly deals with a particular act or omission is not, in itself, sufficient to rule out an action in tort in respect of that act or omission. For instance, in *Northern Bank Finance Corporation Ltd.* v. *Charlton* [1979] I.R. 149 it was unanimously held by this Court that a customer of a bank can sue the bank for the tort of deceit where the deceit arises from fraudulent misrepresentations made by the bank in the course of carrying out the contract between the bank and the customer. The existence of a contract, for the breach of which he could have sued, did not oust the customer's cause of action in tort.

Therefore, I conclude that where, as in the instant case, the client's complaint is that he has been damnified by the solicitor's default in his general duty of care, the client is entitled to sue in negligence as well as for breach of contract. In the plaintiff's statement of claim, after reciting his accident and his retainer of the defendant as the solicitor to prosecute his claim for damages in respect of it, the plaintiff pleads that the defendant 'negligently failed to issue proceedings on behalf of the plaintiff in respect of the accident aforesaid within the time limited by the Statute of Limitations, 1957.' That was intended to be, and is, a claim in negligence. Such being the case, by virtue of the provisions of s. 94 of the Courts of Justice Act, 1924, as amended, the plaintiff was entitled to serve notice of a trial by a judge and jury. Mr. Justice D'Arcy was correct in refusing to set aside the notice of trial so served. I would dismiss this appeal.

Griffin. J.:

... A solicitor holds himself out to the client who has retained him as being possessed of adequate skill, knowledge and learning for the purpose of carrying out all business that he undertakes on behalf of his client. Once he has been retained to pursue a claim for damages for personal injuries, it is the duty of the solicitor to prepare and prosecute the claim with due professional skill and care. Therefore, he is liable to the client in damages if loss and damage are caused to the client owing to the want of such skill and care on the part of the solicitor as he ought to have exercised.

Mr. Kinlen, for the defendant, contends that the duty owed by a solicitor to his client under his retainer is a duty which arises *solely* from the contract and excludes any general duty in tort; he submits that this action is one founded upon contract, in which event the plaintiff would not be entitled to have the action tried by a jury. Mr. Walsh, for the plaintiff, submits that, apart from the duty which arises from contract, there is a general duty to exercise skill and care on the part of the solicitor, for breach of which he would be liable in tort if damage is suffered by the client as a result of the want of such skill and care. He submits that, as one claiming damages for negligence, his action is properly a claim in tort, in which case the plaintiff is entitled as of right to have the action tried before a judge and jury pursuant to s. 94 of the Courts of Justice Act, 1924, as amended.

There is abundant, if somewhat conflicting, authority on the question in England, and in argument we were referred also to two Irish cases in which the question arose.

In *Groom* v. *Crocker* [1939] 1 K.B. 194 the Court of Appeal in England had to consider whether the mutual rights and duties of a solicitor and his client were regulated by the contract of employment alone, and whether the solicitor was liable in tort. It was there held that the contract of employment regulated the relationship and that the solicitor was not liable in tort. In the course of his judgment, Sir Wilfred Greene M.R. said at p. 205 of the report:–

'In my opinion, the cause of action is in contract and not in tort. The duty of the appellants was to conduct the case properly on behalf of the respondent as their client . . . The relationship of solicitor and client is a contractual one: *Davies* v. *Lock* (1844) 3 L.T. (O.S.) 125; *Bean* v. *Wade* (1885) 2 T.L.R. 157. It was by virtue of that relationship that the duty arose, and it had no existence apart from that relationship.'

Scott L.J. at p. 222, having set out the duty of a solicitor, said that the tie between the solicitor and the client is contractual and that no action lies in tort for the breach of such duties. MacKinnon L.J. put the position succinctly at p. 229 where he said:– 'I am clear that this is a claim for damages for breach of contract . . .'

After that unanimous decision of the Court of Appeal, it was generally accepted in England, at least until very recently, that the liability of a solicitor to his client was contractual only and that he could not be sued in tort either in the alternative or cumulatively. The case has been almost universally followed and applied there since it was decided; see, for example, *Bailey* v. *Bullock* [1950] 2 All E.R. 1167; and Hodson and Parker L.JJ. at pp. 477 and 481 respectively of the report of *Hall* v. *Meyrick* [1957] 2 Q.B. 455; *Cook* v. *Swinfen* [1967] 1 W.L.R. 457. At p. 510 of the report of *Clark* v. *Kirby-Smith* [1964] Ch. 506 Plowman J. said:– 'A line of cases going back for nearly 150 years shows, I think, that the client's cause of action is in contract and not in tort: see, for example, *Howell* v. *Young* (1826) 5 B. & C. 259 and *Groom* v. *Crocker* [1939] 1 K.B. 194. In *Heywood* v. *Wellers* [1976] Q.B. 446 James L.J. said at p. 461 of the report:– 'It is well known and settled law that an action by a client against a solicitor alleging negligence in the conduct of the client's affairs is an action for breach of contract: *Groom* v. *Crocker* [1939] 1 K.B. 194.' However, in that case Lord Denning did say at p. 459 that *Groom* v. *Crocker* might have to be reconsidered, and in *Esso Petroleum* v. *Mardon* [1976] Q.B. 801 at p. 819 of the report he 'ventured to suggest' that that case, and cases which relied on it, are in conflict with other decisions of high authority which were not cited in them – decisions which show that, in the case of a professional man, the duty to use reasonable care arises not only in contract but is also imposed by the law apart from contract and is, therefore, actionable in tort; it is comparable to the duty of reasonable care which is owed by a master to his servant or vice versa; it can be put either in contract or in tort. In *Midland Bank* v. *Hett, Stubbs & Kemp* [1979] Ch. 384, on which the plaintiff relied strongly, Oliver J., in a judgment in which he examined exhaustively all the leading cases on the subject of a solicitor's liability, held that a solicitor was liable in tort quite independently of any contractual liability.

In *Somers* v. *Erskine* [1943] I.R. 348 the client sued his solicitor for damages for negligence in the discharge of his professional duty to the client. The solicitor died after the action was commenced and one of the issues which then arose was whether or not the cause of action had survived against his executrix. It was held by Maguire P. that the action was in substance founded in contract and that, in considering whether an action is founded on contract or on tort, the court must look not merely at the form of the pleadings but at the substance of the action and decide whether it is founded on contract or tort. He adopted and applied the following passage from the judgment of Greer L.J. in *Jarvis* v. *Moy, Davies, Smith, Vander-well and Co.* [1936] 1 K.B. 399 (a claim against a stockbroker) at p. 405 of the report:– 'The distinction in the modern view, for this purpose, between contract and tort may be put thus: where the breach of duty alleged arises out of a liability independently of the personal obligation undertaken by contract, it is tort, and it may be tort even though there may happen to be a contract between the parties, if the duty in fact arises independently of that contract. Breach of contract occurs where that which is complained of is a breach of duty arising out of the obligations undertaken by the contract.' That passage had been accepted and approved by O'Byrne J. in *Liston* v. *Munster and Leinster Bank* [1940] I.R. 77. Applying that test, the learned President held that the substance of the client's claim was the breach of a duty arising out of an obligation created by contract, and said that he found it difficult to dissociate that duty from the contract. Counsel for the defendant in that case had urged that the duty which was alleged to have been broken was merely the ordinary common-law duty, the breach of which constituted negligence, *i.e.*, the duty to take reasonable care in the particular circumstances; but the President held that the duty arose out of a contractual obligation only.

I have had the advantage of reading in advance the judgment of Mr. Justice Henchy and I agree with him that Maguire P. did not correctly apply the test laid down by Greer L.J. in the *Jarvis Case* [1936] 1 K.B. 399. I agree with the analysis made by Mr. Justice Henchy of the passage quoted from the judgment of Lord Justice Greer.

The only other Irish case cited in argument was *McGrath* v. *Kiely* [1965] I.R. 497 in which the client sued a surgeon and a solicitor, founding her claim for damages on both negligence and breach of contract. In the course of the hearing before Mr. Justice Henchy it was conceded on behalf of the client that the liability sought to be imposed on each of the defendants arose *ex contractu*, so that the question of the liability of the defendants in tort was not argued and did not fall to be decided.

In *Somers* v. *Erskine* [1943] I.R. 348, the learned President was not prepared to accept that, in the case of a solicitor, there was a general duty to use reasonable care imposed by the law quite apart from contract. He took the view that because there was a contractual relationship between the solicitor and the client, and a liability in contract for breach of the duty owed to the client, there was no duty in tort. Counsel for the defendant had cited the passage in Beven on Negligence (4th ed. at p. 1384) that states:– 'A solicitor is liable for negligence both in contract and in tort. He is liable in contract where he fails to do some specific act to which he has bound himself. He is liable in tort where, having accepted a retainer, he fails in the performance of any duty which the relation of solicitor and client as defined by the retainer imposes on him.' Authorities to support that proposition were not cited; if they had been cited, it is likely that the President would have come to a different conclusion. The law is concisely and clearly summed up in a few sentences in the well-known passage in the speech of Viscount Haldane L.C. in *Nocton* v. *Ashburton* [1914] A.C. 932 at p. 956 of the report:– 'My Lords, the solicitor contracts with his client to be skilful and careful. For failure to perform his obligation he may be made liable at law in contract or even in tort, for negligence in breach of a duty imposed on him.' See also what was said by Tindal C.J. in *Boorman* v. *Brown* (1842) 3 Q.B. 511, (1844) 11 Cl. & Fin. 1 in the Court of Exchequer Chamber at p. 525 of the report and by Lord Campbell in the House of Lords at p. 44 of the report of the appeal. It is to be noted that these cases also were not cited in *Groom* v. *Crocker* [1939] 1 K.B. 194, or in the cases which followed it, and that the failure to do so led to the criticism of these cases by Lord Denning in *Esso Petroleum* v.

Mardon [1976] Q.B. 801. In my opinion, the President was wrong in holding that the liability of the solicitor to the client was solely in contract. *Somers* v. *Erskine* [1943] I.R. 348 should not be followed.

Quite apart from the fact that *Somers* v. *Erskine* [1943] I.R. 348 was decided without the citation of relevant authorities and on an incorrect application of the test laid down by Greer L.J. in the *Jarvis Case* [1936] A.C. 465, the decision is inconsistent with developments in the law of tort since the case was decided. It is now settled law that whenever a person possessed of a special knowledge or skill undertakes, quite irrespective of contract, to apply that skill for the assistance of another person who relies on such skill, a duty of care will arise: see the speech of Lord Morris of Borth-y-Gest at p. 502 of the report of *Hedley Byrne and Co. Ltd.* v. *Heller & Partners Ltd*. [1964] A.C. 465. At p. 538 of the report of Lord Pearce said:– 'In terms of proximity one might say that they are in particularly close proximity to those who, as they know, are relying on their skill and care although the proximity is not contractual.' See also Lord Hodson at p. 510 and Lord Devlin at p. 530 of the report. Where damage has been suffered as a result of want of such skill and care, an action in tort lies against such person, and this applies whether a contractual relationship exists or not. This doctrine applies to such professional persons as solicitors, doctors, dentists, architects and accountants. Although in the *Hedley Byrne Case* [1964] A.C. 465 the claim was in respect of a non-contractual relationship, the statements of the Law Lords were general statements of principle, and it is clear from their speeches that they did not in any way mean to limit the general principle and that their statements were not to be confined to voluntary or non-contractual situations.

Therefore, where a solicitor is retained by a client to carry out legal business (such as litigation) on his behalf, a general relationship is established, and 'Where there is a general relationship of this sort, it is unnecessary to do more than prove its existence and the duty follows' – *per* Lord Devlin at p. 530 of the report of the *Hedley Byrne Case* [1964] A.C. 465. If, therefore, loss and damage is caused to a client owing to the want of such care and skill on the part of a solicitor as he ought to have exercised, there is liability in tort even though there would also be a liability in contract. Even if the relationship between the solicitor and the client was a non-contractual or voluntary one, the same liability in tort would follow.

In my opinion it is both reasonable and fair that, if the issues of fact are such that he would be entitled to succeed either in contract or in tort, the plaintiff should be entitled to pursue either or both remedies; there can be nothing wrong in permitting the plaintiff, who is the injured party, to elect or choose the remedy which to him appears to be that which will be most suitable and likely to attract the more favourable result.

In my judgment, the plaintiff in the instant case has a good cause of action in tort as well as in contract and is entitled to sue in respect of either or both remedies since he has suffered loss and damage as a result of the negligence of the defendant, as the plaintiff's solicitor, in failing to institute proceedings within the time limited by the Statute of Limitations, 1957. Accordingly, the plaintiff is entitled as of right to have his action tried before a judge and jury, and Mr. Justice D'Arcy was correct in so deciding. Accordingly, I would dismiss this appeal.

Kenny J.:

I have had the advantage of reading the judgment prepared by Mr. Justice Henchy and I agree with the conclusion he has reached that this motion seeking a trial of this action by a judge sitting without a jury should be dismissed.

When a client retains a professional person (*e.g.* a solicitor, an architect, an accountant or a doctor) to do work for reward, there is implied from the retainer a contract between them, one of the terms of which is that the professional person has the competence to do the work and that he will act with that degree of care and skill which is reasonably expected from a member of that profession. If he is negligent in the performance of the work, an action for damages for breach of contract may be successfully brought against him.

The professional person, however, owes the client a general duty, which does not arise from contract but from the 'proximity' principle (*Donoghue* v. *Stevenson* [1932] A.C. 562 and *Hedley Byrne & Co. Ltd.* v. *Heller & Partners Ltd* [1964] A.C. 465), to exercise reasonable care and skill in the performance of the work entrusted to him. This duty arises from the obligation which springs from the situation that he knew or ought to have known that his failure to exercise care and skill would probably cause loss and damage. This failure to have or to exercise reasonable skill and care is tortious or delictual in origin.

So a plaintiff in such an action may successfully sue in contract or in tort or in both. In the instant case, the plaintiff has sued in tort and so is entitled to have his case tried by a jury: see s. 94 of the Courts of Justice Act, 1924. I would dismiss the appeal.

O'Higgins C.J. and **Parke J.** concurred with the judgments of **Henchy** and **Griffin JJ.**

Notes and Question

1. See also the very important decision of *Wall* v. *Hegarty, infra,* pp. 415–420.
2. A solicitor is retained by a pedestrian who was struck by a car. The solicitor fails to issue proceedings against the driver within the required time and the claim becomes statute barred. Assuming that the solicitor is liable in negligence to the pedestrian, how are damages to be assessed? *Cf. Hayes* v. *Kenefick*, unreported, High Ct., Finlay, P., with jury, 24 February 1982, *Irish Times*, 25 February 1982.

6. BARRISTERS' NEGLIGENCE

Historically barristers have been immune from liability in negligence in respect of their work, at all events so far as it relates to litigation. Various policy reasons have been advanced in support of this position. It has been said that the administration of justice requires that a barrister should be allowed to perform his or her duty independently and discharge fully the higher duty to the court. Moreover, actions against barristers for negligence in the performance of courtroom work would prolong litigation, against the public interest. A barrister is perhaps unique among professionals in being obliged to accept any client. Finally, it has been argued that a barrister must be permitted, in the interests of the efficient administration of justice, to prepare the case and make decisions as to what is relevant and what is not: if he or she were constantly to have regard to a prospective action for negligence by the client, the Court could be burdened with much unnecessary evidence and argument as an insurance against having his or her discretionary judgment questioned subsequently.

The policy issues are analysed in the Committee on Court Practice and Procedure's Fourteenth Interim Report, *Liability of Barristers and Solicitors for Professional Negligence* (Prl. 238, 1971). See also Keane, 'Note: Negligence of Barristers' 2 Ir. Jur. (n.s.) 102 (1967); *Rondel* v. *Worsley*, [1969] A.C. 991; *Saif Ali* v. *Sydney Mitchell & Co. (a firm)*, [1980] A.C. 198; Smith, 'Liability for the Negligent Conduct of Litigation: The Legacy of *Rondel* v. *Worsley*' 47 Sask. L. Rev. 211 (1983).

7. NEGLIGENCE ON THE HIGHWAY

Road accidents have given rise to a large volume of negligence litigation. The guiding principles tend to be little more than generalities, with not much substance to them. When the courts have erected 'rules of law' in this area, they have frequently not worked out satisfactorily in practice and the courts have been obliged to think again.

Driving when vision is occluded

O'REILLY V. EVANS
[1956] I.R. 269 (Supreme Court)

Kingsmill Moore J.:

The facts are hardly in dispute. The defendant's motor car, a black saloon Ford Prefect, was drawn up, unlighted, on the road leading from Midleton to Cork. It was facing towards Cork and its left side was about 2 feet out from the left-hand edge of the road, which is here some 26 feet wide.

The plaintiff's husband was riding a motor-assisted bicycle along the road from Midleton towards Cork. According to an eye-witness he was moving at a moderate speed of about 10 miles per hour. His lamp was lighted but, if we can trust the estimate of the same witness, it was only illuminating the road for 7 to 10 feet in front of it. The rider failed to see the motor car in time and, although he attempted to pull clear, some part of his bicycle touched the right rear corner of the motor car, and he fell on the road fracturing his skull so badly that he died.

The night was dark, and there are hedges on both sides of the road which would tend to increase the darkness, so that the driver of any vehicle would have to depend on his own lights to give him adequate warning of an obstruction. The road is nearly straight with a very slight trend to the left as one comes from Midleton, but at one point the hedge on the left-hand side projects somewhat, so that a cyclist keeping well in to his own side would not get a full view of the motor car till he had come within 22 yards of it.

The jury found the defendant negligent and absolved the deceased man of contributory negligence. The defendant now appeals on the ground that the contributory negligence of the deceased is so manifest that the trial Judge should have withdrawn the case from the jury and entered judgment for the defendant, and that the refusal of the jury to find contributory negligence was perverse.

Prima facie, a man riding or driving along a public road at night must so control his bicycle or vehicle as to be able to avoid any obstacle which he is reasonably likely to encounter. His pace must be regulated by the distance which his lamp or lamps illuminate, the stopping power of his brakes, and the nature of his own vision. It was for some time accepted in England that if a man collided with a stationary and unlit obstacle at night it was an inescapable conclusion that he was guilty of negligence: *Baker v. E. Longhurst and Sons Ltd* [1933] 2 K. B. 461: *Tart v. G. W. Chitty and Co.* [1933] 2 K.B. 453: *Evans v. Downer and Co. Ltd*. [1933] 2 K. B. 465 (*note*). This is no longer the law either in England or in Ireland. *Tidy v. Battman* [1934] 1 K. B. 319: *Stewart v. Hancock* [1940] 2 All E. R. 427: *Hayes v. Finnegan and Others* [1952] I. R. 98. It is a question of fact in each case. There may be circumstances of an embarrassing nature, or such as are not reasonably to be anticipated, which are sufficient to account for a collision without necessarily involving negligence on the part of the plaintiff. I may instance deceptive lighting, a sudden drift of fog, interference or confusion caused by other road users, the small size and partial concealment of the obstacle, and so on. Nevertheless, in the absence of some such unusual circumstances, the conclusion that there was negligence may be so cogent that a judge should withdraw the case from the jury.

Are there any circumstances in this case to displace the *prima facie* presumption of negligence? The vision of the driver of a motor car with strong headlights might have been somewhat curtailed by the bulge in the hedge, but as the bulge was some 22 yards from the motor car it could not adversely affect a man riding a bicycle whose lamp only illuminated for a distance of 7 to 10 feet. The estimate of the extent of the illumination may well be inaccurate, but even multiplying it by six the bulge cannot have affected the cyclist's power to pick up the stationary car. It is argued that the car was black and so more difficult to see; but even so it was a large object and one of a type which every road user must expect to encounter: nor could it have been devoid of some reflecting portions. Lastly, it was pressed that the darkness of the night and the hedges on each side of the road might provide an excuse: but drivers on the highway at night must depend on the illumination which they carry themselves unless there is adequate street lighting.

I am of opinion that there is no way of escaping the conclusion that this unfortunate man was guilty of negligence and that the appeal must be allowed.

Lavery, Maguire and **Ó Dálaigh JJ.** concurred with **Kingsmill Moore J. Maguire, C.J.** dissented.

8. *DUTY OF DRIVER IN RELATION TO CAR DOORS*

CURLEY V. MANNION
[1965] I.R. 543

Walsh J.:
This is an appeal by the plaintiff against a ruling by the trial Judge in her action for personal injuries against the defendant that on the evidence adduced the jury could not reasonably find for her and consequent on which the learned trial Judge entered judgment for the defendant with costs.

Briefly the facts of the case are that on the 29th May, 1961, the plaintiff was cycling along Connaught Street in the town of Athlone and as she overtook the stationary motor car of the defendant, a four-door Ford Prefect motor car parked on the left hand side of the street, she was struck and knocked from her bicycle by the opening of one of the doors on the off-side of the defendant's motor car. The door had been opened without any prior warning being given to the plaintiff. The defendant was sitting in the driving seat of the motor car. He lived some miles outside the town of Athlone and on that day he had driven into town with his wife and his two daughters. The latter were then aged about thirteen years and twelve years respectively. When they reached Athlone, the wife left the car to do some shopping and the defendant remained seated in the stationary motor car which was parked with the near side next to the footpath. The two daughters remained with him but were in the rear seat of the car. At one stage the younger daughter got out of the motor car by the rear off side door to purchase an ice-cream at a nearby shop. After a few minutes she returned and entered the car again by the same door, closed it, and then, apparently in an attempt to fasten it more securely, re-opened it with a view to closing it again. It was at or about the moment of the re-opening of the door that the accident occurred. The defendant was aware of his daughter's exit and entrance by the off-side door and he took no steps to ensure that it was safe for her to do so or to warn her of the danger of so doing. The defendant gave evidence to the effect that at the moment the girl re-entered the car a lorry was passing along the street coming towards the motor car. The defendant says that he did not recollect any other traffic. In the course of her evidence the girl stated that it was while she was pulling in the door to close it for the second time after her re-entry into the car that the door hit the plaintiff and that the point of impact was the edge of the door and, she thought, the front wheel of the bicycle. The result of the impact was that the plaintiff was knocked from her bicycle and sustained personal injuries.

In her statement of claim, the plaintiff claimed that the accident was due to the negligence of the defendant, his servants or agents, in or about the care, management, driving, control and supervision of the motor car. The case made at the hearing was that it was either the defendant's own door that was opened and hit the plaintiff or that it was the rear door on the same side, that is, the off-side, which caused the accident by striking her. Until the defendant and his daughter gave evidence after the close of the plaintiff's case there was no direct affirmative evidence that the accident had been occasioned or caused by the opening of the rear door by the daughter. A witness called for the plaintiff who had a view of the scene of the accident from some distance away, had heard the noise of the collision, and had seen the plaintiff on the ground immediately after falling, gave evidence to the effect that she saw the defendant's door open at about the same time though she could not say that she actually saw the defendant's door strike the plaintiff. The plaintiff could not say which door struck her. The defendant, in his defence, pleaded that it was not his door which had opened but that a door had been opened by a passenger in the car and disclaimed liability for the action of that passenger.

At the end of the plaintiff's case, the trial Judge refused an application on behalf of the defendant to have the case withdrawn from the jury. The trial Judge ruled that upon the evidence of the onlooker there was a case from which the jury could infer that the opening of the defendant's door had caused the accident. At the close of the defendant's case the learned trial Judge acceded to the defendant's application to have the case withdrawn from the jury. This he did on two grounds. The first was that no jury could reasonably hold that the defendant had himself opened the door which struck the plaintiff. The second ground was that the defendant was not responsible for the action of the passenger, in this case the action of his own child, which it was admitted was the cause of the accident. In dealing with this matter he said:– '. . . as to the responsibility of the driver for passengers who act in the way in which this passenger did, got in on the traffic side and having got in, opened the door, I could not hold as a matter of law that there could be some responsibility on the driver of the car in the circumstances. If a jury were so to hold, I am afraid that any such finding would be upset in the Supreme Court if an appeal were taken. I must consider whether I could allow a proposition of that sort to pass me. I don't see how I could. The parent is not responsible for the negligent acts of his children. He may be responsible for any such want of care in regard to them under certain circumstances but not under circumstances such as this. There is no authority for any such proposition. I could not allow it to stand.'

With regard to the first ground I am of opinion that the learned trial Judge was correct in his ruling. At the close of the plaintiff's case it could have been inferred by a jury in the absence of any direct evidence that the fact that an onlooker saw the defendant's door open at the time she saw the plaintiff on the ground immediately after the collision even though she did not see the door striking the plaintiff would warrant the inference that the opening of the door was the cause of the accident. It did transpire subsequently on the evidence in the defendant's case that the defendant had opened the door, but according to him he had done it when he saw the plaintiff fall. This explanation coupled with the direct and affirmative evidence and admission that the plaintiff was in fact struck by the rear door of the car in my view invalidates the inference which was available in the absence of such evidence and in the circumstances therefore the only evidence upon which the jury could act in relation to the question of which door was opened was that which affirmed that the rear door was the offending one.

With regard to the second ground upon which the case was withdrawn from the jury, it appears to me that the learned trial Judge in this matter had in mind only the question of vicarious liability and in fact the submission made to him on behalf of the defendant on this part of the case also proceeded on the same basis. Both the Judge and defendant's counsel assumed that the plaintiff's case was based either upon the allegation that the defendant himself opened the door which struck the plaintiff or that the defendant was vicariously liable for the action of the passenger. A perusal of the discussion which took place on this aspect of the case reveals quite clearly that the latter was not the only alternative relied upon by the plaintiff's counsel, but that he also relied upon the submission that if the defendant was not personally liable by reason of himself opening the door he was still personally liable for negligently permitting the door to have been opened by his passenger in the circumstances. It does not appear to me that this aspect of the case was ruled upon at all by the learned trial Judge. But if I am not correct in this, it does not affect the view I am about to express. The learned trial Judge was quite correct in holding that the relationship of parent and child could not of itself impose upon the defendant any vicarious liability for the act of the girl. That, however, did not dispose of the matter.

In my view the defendant, as the owner and driver of the motor car in question, owed a duty to other persons using the highway not merely not to use or drive the car negligently but to make reasonable precautions to ensure that the car, while under his control and supervision, was not used in a negligent fashion. It would indeed be a startling proposition that a person in charge of a motor vehicle on a public highway should not owe any duty to third parties save in respect of his own negligent act in the use of the vehicle, or in respect of omissions relating to his own use of the vehicle, and that he should not be liable in negligence for failing to take reasonable steps to prevent the negligent use of a motor car by a passenger therein while it is under his control and supervision when such negligent use is actually known to or ought to be foreseen by him. In the streets of a town the opening and closing of doors on the traffic side of a stationary motor car is so notoriously fraught with danger that a person in control of a motor car who permits this to be done in his motor car without first ascertaining that it is safe to do so or without taking reasonable steps to ensure that it is done without danger, is in my view failing in the duty which he, as the person in control and supervision of the motor car, owes to other users of the highway.

The steps which such a person should take must, of course, be determined in the light of the exact circumstances of each case. In this case the defendant by reason of the fact that he was the parent of the tortious child could be held to have had an authority over the child. By reason of his proximity to the child he could be held to have been in a position to exercise that authority. By reason of his knowledge of the child's previous actions of leaving the car by the off-side door and of re-entering by the same door, it could be held to be foreseeable that it was not improbable that the same child, or even the other child, would again open the off-side door. Was it foreseeable that the child might do so without taking proper care to do so without danger to the other users of the street? In my view a jury might reasonably answer that question in the affirmative and find the defendant personally negligent for not taking the opportunity open to him to obviate that danger. It was certainly reasonably foreseeable that if the door was opened without first seeing that it was safe to do so some other person upon the street might be injured. What might be sufficient warning to an adult may not be sufficient warning to a child of twelve. These would be matters for the jury. But in this case there was no warning given to the child and no steps taken to prevent the child using the off-side door.

There is no lack of authority, if authority be needed, for the proposition that a parent may be liable for his own personal negligence in allowing his child the opportunity to commit a tort. For examples, see *Sullivan* v. *Creed* [1904] 2 I.R. 317; *Newton* v. *Edgerley* [1959] 1 W.L.R. 103; *Bebee* v. *Sales* 32 T.L.R. 413.

In my view, the plaintiff was entitled to have the case considered by the jury on the question of the defendant's personal negligence in not seeking to prevent the child using the off-side door or at least in not endeavouring to ensure that it would be used without danger. I would allow the appeal.

[**O'Keeffe J.** agreed with **Walsh J.** and on this issue **Ó Dálaigh C.J.** said:]

As to the second ground: in my judgment a person in charge of a motor car must take reasonable precautions for the safety of others, and this will include the duty to take reasonable care to prevent conduct on the part of passengers which is negligent. In the present case that duty is, it seems to me, reinforced by the relationship of parent and child; and a parent, while not liable for the torts of his child, may be liable if negligent in failing to exercise his control to prevent his child injuring others.

The evidence here is that the defendant took no interest in the exit and re-entry of his young daughter through the off-side rear door in a busy street. It is a matter for a jury to consider whether this conduct on his part fell short of reasonable care for the safety of other road users.

On this ground I am of opinion that the plaintiff's case should have been allowed to go to the jury. I would direct a new trial.

Questions

1. Precisely how is the driver of a car to prevent a passenger from opening a door dangerously? To what extent does your answer depend on who is driver and who is passenger? Is a chauffeur in a different position to a taxi-driver? If the passenger is an adult, fully *compos mentis* and experienced in urban life, what must the driver do?
2. When (if ever) must the driver of a car ensure that all the doors are securely locked or fastened? *Cf. Ryan* v. *Walsh*, 73 I.L.T.R. 98.

9. ECONOMIC LOSS

IRISH PAPER SACKS LTD. V. JOHN SISK & SON (DUBLIN) LTD.
Unreported, High Court, O'Keeffe, P., 18 May 1972 (1971 No. 115P)

O'Keeffe P.:

The plaintiffs in this action claim damages for the negligence of the defendants who are building and civil engineering contractors. The plaintiffs have their factory at Ballymount Road, Walkinstown, Dublin. They manufacture paper sacks. Their machines are powered by electric current, which is brought to the factory by underground cable. On 23 November, 1970, there was a failure of the electric power, due to a break in the underground cable. The cable was not restored until the morning of 25 November, and in the meantime the plaintiffs had to cease production. They claim that their loss amounts to £270 for labour, £650 for overheads, and £263 for loss of profit, giving a total of £1183. These figures were not questioned.

The plaintiffs gave evidence that about the end of 1969 or early 1970 a factory for O'Dea & Co. Ltd. was nearing completion, and it became necessary to re-arrange the supply of electricity of the factories at Ballymount Road, where there are a number of factories on an industrial estate. It was agreed that the Defendants should excavate a trench in which the cable would be run. The trench was excavated to a depth of about 2 feet, which should afford adequate cover for the cable. The cable was laid about March of 1970. It was a very strong cable, and well protected. At the point where the cable ran under the line of an intended access road to the site the cable was carried in concrete ducts, as an additional protection.

When the power failure occurred the approximate point of breakage was established. It was about one-third way across the access road, and in a place where the cable ran through the ducts. An attempt was made to pull away the damaged cable, but the duct had been so damaged that the cable could not be withdrawn. A second duct was also blocked. Mr. Fanning, the E.S.B. Engineer in charge of the area, who was responsible for the laying of the cable, expressed the view that the damage must have been caused by a bulldozer used to excavate the area for the laying of a concrete access road over the site of the cable. He thought it likely that the bulldozer gripped the cable and pulled it and damaged the insulation. This was, in his view, done when the excavation was being carried out, with the result that, the insulation being damaged, the cable ultimately failed as a result of a percolation of water. He agreed that the bulldozer driver would be aware of it, if his machine caught the cable as suggested.

The defendants called their general foreman on the site, Mr. Albert Kavanagh, who said that after the cable was laid, the E.S.B. covered it over for a depth of about six inches, and the defendants then backfilled by machine, which merely pushed the soil into the trench. This machine worked along the trench, travelling astride the trench, and would not have damaged the cable or the ducts. The road was concreted in June, but no machine worked in the area after the month of March, when the trench was filled in.

The defendants argued that the plaintiffs' claim must be dismissed on two grounds: first, the claim was for economic loss indirectly caused only, and not for damage to the plaintiffs' property, and secondly, the plaintiffs had not established any negligence on the part of the defendants.

In support of the first ground reference was made to: *Weller & Co.* v. *Foot and Mouth Disease Research Institute* [1965] 3 All E.R. 560; *Electrochrome Ltd.* v. *Welsh Plastics Ltd.* [1968] 2 All E.R. 205; *Elliot* v. *Sir Robert McAlpine & Sons Ltd.* [1966] 2 Ll. L. R. 482, and *S.C.M. Ltd.* v. *Whittall & Son Ltd.* [1970] 2 All E.R. 417, [1970] 3 All E.R. 245. Reference was also made to *Hedley Byrne & Co. Ltd.* v. *Heller & Partners Ltd.* [1964] A.C. 465. The principle to be derived from these cases is that a plaintiff suing for damages suffered as a result of an act or omission of the defendant cannot recover if the act or omission did not directly injure the plaintiff's person or property, but merely caused consequential loss.

After a full consideration of the matter I think that I must apply the principle of the cases above cited. For this reason I must hold that the plaintiffs in this action are not entitled to succeed. I consider, further, that the plaintiffs have failed to establish that the injury to the cable was caused by any act of the defendants, and on this ground, also, the defendants are entitled to succeed.

1. The question of recovery for pure economic loss raises important questions of policy which have not yet been satisfactorialy resolved. Increasingly the courts in several countries, notably England, Canada and the United States, are setting aside the legal concepts of duty, remoteness and causation in favour of more general policy guidelines. Whether this approach will prove more useful is a matter of debate. See generally, *McMahon & Binchy* pp. 191–195.
2. In Ireland, the courts still tend to adopt the conventional legal concepts. An important decision in respect of recovery for pure economic loss is *Wall* v. *Hergarty, infra*, pp. 415–420. It may be argued that that decision renders obsolete the general principle that pure economic loss, as such, is not compensable: henceforth the issue is to be resolved on the straightforward negligence principles endorsed in *Donoghue* v. *Stevenson*. Perhaps this is reading too much into *Wall* v. *Hegarty*: only time will tell.

10. *PROOF OF NEGLIGENCE AND* RES IPSA LOQUITUR

(a) *Proof of Negligence: The General Principle*

As a general rule a plaintiff in an action for negligence must plead and prove negligence on the part of the defendant in order to succeed. In proceedings in the High Court he must convince the jury on the balance of probabilities that the defendant was negligent. In this regard the judge and jury have different functions. It is the judge's function to say whether any facts have been established by evidence from which negligence *may reasonably be inferred*: the jurors have to say whether, from these facts, negligence *ought to be inferred*. If the judge considers that sufficient evidence has not been adduced from which negligence may reasonably be inferred, he must withdraw the case from the jury. Moreover, an appeal may be taken to the Supreme Court on the basis that the judge ought (or, as the case may be, ought not) to have withdrawn the case from the jury.

Of the nature of things, evidence may sometimes be indirect or circumstantial. This can give rise to particular difficulties in deciding whether there is sufficient evidence to go to the jury.

MAHON V. DUBLIN & LUCAN ELECTRIC RY. CO.

39 I.L.T.R. 126 (K.B. Div., 1905)

Motion that a nonsuit directed at the trial be set aside, and for a new trial. The action was tried before Wright, J., and a common jury, on Jan. 16th, 1905. The action was brought by Ellen Mahon, widow of James Mahon, on behalf of herself and her three children, under Lord Campbell's Act, for damages, sustained by the death of her husband by reason of the negligence of the defendant company or their servants. The plaintiff stated – 'My husband was a labourer, at 12s. a week, in the employment of Mr. Dease. I last saw my husband alive at 6.45 p.m. on Aug. 17th in our house, he was then starting for Dublin; next day was cattle market day. He had been three months with Mr. Dease, and four years in service before that He was about twenty-seven. I saw his dead body next day.' Sergeant Cullen, R. I. C., stated – 'I heard of the accident at about three quarters of an hour after midnight. I went at once to the scene, three quarters of a mile off. I arrived there at 1.15 a.m. and saw the dead body of James Mahon; it was in front of the engine; the intestines were protruding; the front wheel of the engine was derailed. I saw a lamp lighted – it was in the front and centre of the engine; it was an oil lamp; it did not give as brilliant a light as an electric light. The body was removed at 4 a.m. The engine had to be raised to extricate the body. The ground was roughened for about nine feet;

there was blood for three or four feet from where the body was found. The dead body was lying across the outer rail; all the trunk of the body was inside the rail. The rails are raised nine inches above the level of the road. There is a footpath on the opposite side of the road. The width of the road is thirty-two feet. The body was in front of the wheel; there is a fire-box in front, and the body was under it.' Michael Bird stated – 'I was at the scene of the accident at 3 a.m. on the 18th. I saw the corpse lying alongside the engine. I saw no light on the engine, but one of the company's servants had a lamp in his hand. There may have been a lamp there, but it was not lighting when I got there.' Denis Dowd stated – 'I saw the deceased at 10 p.m. that night; he was then perfectly sober. The place where I saw him was about one mile to one and a quarter miles from where his dead body was found.' A man named Quigley, who was also in charge of cattle for the Dublin market, was stated to have been in company with the deceased from the time they left Celbridge up to the time of the accident, and when the policeman arrived, and was subpœnaed by the plaintiff, but did not appear.

Shaughnessy, K.C. on behalf of the company, asked for a direction, and cited *Wakelin* v. *London & S. W. Ry. Co.*, 12 A.C. 44, and *Redmond* v. *Clontarf & Hill of Howth Tramway Co.* (Ct. of App. Ireland, unreported).

Wright J.: directed a verdict for the defendants with costs.

O'Shaughnessy, K.C., *Chambers*, K.C., and *T.J. Smyth*, appeared for the defendants on the new trial motion.

No appearance for the plaintiff.

Lord O'Brien, L.C.J.:

Mr. O'Shaughnessy has placed the facts clearly before us, and we are of opinion that there is no evidence of actionable negligence, and we therefore discharge the notice of motion and confirm the direction of the judge at the trial.

Notes and Questions

1. Do you agree with this decision? Contrast the case with *Kielthy* v. *Ascon* [1970] I.R. 122 (Sup. Ct.).
2. Does this decision mean that the plaintiff must always have to 'have a story'? *Cf. O'Rourke* v. *McGuinness* [1942] I.R. 554 (Sup. Ct.)

(b) *Res Ipsa Loquitur*

The doctrine of *res ipsa loquitur* has given rise to much controversy but little clarity. The doctrine traces its origin to a comment made by Chief Baron Pollock during the course of argument in *Byrne* v. *Boadle* 2 H. & C. 722, at 726, 159 E.R. 299, at 300 (1863). The plaintiff had been injured by a barrel of flour which fell from a window above the defendant's shop. The defendant did not explain how the accident occurred. The assessor granted a non-suit. On appeal to the Court of Exchequer, counsel for the defendant contended that the plaintiff 'was bound to give affirmative proof of negligence. But there was not a scintilla of evidence, unless the occurrence is of itself evidence of negligence.' Pollock, C.B. responded that: 'There are certain cases of which it may be said *res ipsa loquitur* and this seems one of them . . .'

In his judgment Pollock C.B. stated that

'The learned counsel was quite right in saying that there are many accidents from which no presumption of negligence can arise, but I think it would be wrong to lay down as a rule that in no case can presumption of negligence arise from the fact of an accident.'

It is fairly clear that Pollock C.B. 'was totally unaware that he was creating a new doctrine' in *Byrne* v. *Boadle*. He was speaking at a time when litigation regarding railway accidents was beginning to fashion a rule of law that a presumption of negligence should arise in certain cases – as, for example, where there was a collision between trains run by the same company. Whilst there was nothing amiss in Pollock C.B. making the Latin remark in *Byrne* v. *Boadle*, it was very shortly afterwards elevated to the status of a principle, in respect of which some courts have been guilty of very loose language and lack of conceptual clarity.

Two fundamental questions arise in relation to the principle: when will it apply and what is its procedural effect?

When Will the Principle Apply?

In *Scott* v. *London & St. Katherine Docks Co*. 3 H. & C. 596 at 601 (1865), Erle, C.J., in a passage that has been very influential in subsequent decisions, stated:

'There must be reasonable evidence of negligence. But where the thing is shown to be under the management of the defendant or his servants, and the accident is such as in the ordinary circumstances does not happen if those who have the management use proper care, it affords reasonable evidence, in the absence of explanation by the defendants, that the accident arose from want of care.'

These elements require specific elucidation.

(i) *Management of the Defendant*

TREACY V. HAGEN
Unreported, Supreme Court, 6 March 1973 (153–1970)

FitzGerald C.J.:

In this case the plaintiff, a maintenance fitter employed by Industrial Mouldings Limited, sustained an injury to the middle finger of his left hand on the 10th December, 1965, when engaged in trying to trace and remedy a fault in a machine in his employers' factory. The employers manufacture, amongst other things, plastic bottles which are produced by a machine which they purchased from the defendants who are the manufacturers of such machines. The particular machine on which the plaintiff was working had been in the factory for some six months before the accident happened, and it was part of the plaintiff's duty to service it.

The source of power to the machine is by compressed air. After six months in use, the machine developed a fault as a result of a break in a welded joint which resulted in a leak of the compressed air into the machine. Subsequent to the accident, the fault was located and repaired by a member of the defendants' staff who replaced the defective part. He did the work which the plaintiff was endeavouring to do at the time of the accident.

The basis of the claim by a person injured against the manufacturer of an article which injures him, is laid down in *Donoghue* v. *Stevenson* [1932] A.C. 562, and is limited to cases where a defective article when manufactured, is not likely to be examined and the defect discovered before it reaches the injured person.

In the present case the employers undertook the servicing of the machine which they purchased from the defendants. Their workman, the plaintiff, was actually in the course of doing this work when injured and another workman, Millar, actually remedied the defect after the accident. In my opinion, the facts do not come within the principle of *Donoghue* v. *Stevenson* at all. The defendants were no longer in control of the machine once they sold and delivered it to the plaintiff's employers and the defect which developed was one which the employers could have, and did ultimately locate and repair.

It was submitted on behalf of the appellants that the case came within the principle of *res ipsa loquitur* on the ground that negligence of the defendants in the manufacture of the machine on the proved facts, were more consistent with negligence on their behalf than with any other cause. [*sic*.] This does not appear to me to be so on the facts. The accident may have been due to faulty manufacture; it may have been due to the negligence of the plaintiff in failing to locate and remedy the defect as his co-worker, Millar, subsequently did, and particularly due to his failure to keep a recessed button depressed as he said he did, the effect of which would have been to prevent the nozzle in the machine rising and striking his finger.

For these reasons I am of the opinion that there was no evidence which could properly be submitted to the jury on a question as to the defendant's negligence, and Mr. Justice Pringle was correct in his decision to non-suit the plaintiff. I would dismiss this appeal.

Walsh J.:

. . . As the plaintiff elected to sue the defendant the case against the defendant is one in which the defendant is sought to be made primarily liable although at the time in question the machine was the property of the plaintiff's employers.

In my view, the appeal should fail. The plaintiff has alleged that the malfunctioning of the machine was the cause of his injury and that malfunctioning was due to a defect in the manufacture or design of the machine. I do not think this is a case where the plaintiff can rely upon the maxim *res ipsa loquitur*. The fact that the accident happened does not of itself constitute prima facie proof that the machine must have been at fault in its design or construction. As I pointed out in my judgment in *Millington* v. *C.I.E.*, 23 March, 1972, the effect of the application of the maxim is that the res proved is itself evidence establishing a prima facie case of negligence. The burden of proof, however, remains at all times upon the plaintiff, although in the appropriate case the very fact of the incident or accident may itself be sufficient to establish a prima facie case of negligence.

As I have already indicated, at the time of the accident the machine in question was the property of and was being used by the plaintiff's employers. There was no evidence that it was at any material time under the control or the management of the defendant or that at the time of the accident it was in the condition in which it had been provided by the defendant. On that ground alone it is my view that the allegation of a malfunction, even if it were proved, would not in itself be sufficient to constitute a prima facie case of negligence against the defendant, even on the assumption that the alleged malfunction could not have occurred save as a result of negligence on someone's part.

The plaintiff also set out to establish that the malfunctioning alleged was due to a particular specified defect, namely, a flange which broke due to bad welding in manufacture. The evidence seems to clearly establish that there was such a defect in the machine. However, the evidence did not establish a prima facie case that this particular defect was the cause of the sudden emergence of the pressure valve which caused the injury to the plaintiff. In as much as the plaintiff undertook to establish this chain of causation, in my view he failed to establish a sufficient case to go to the jury. It was put to him in cross-examination that in fact the accident was due to his own action, knowingly or unknowingly in taking his thumb off a button which prevented the emergence of the nozzle. He, however, testified that he did not do so and at the point at which the non-suit was given the judge had to proceed upon the basis that the accident was not caused by the plaintiff. The state of the evidence at that stage was therefore that the machine was shown to have had a defect in construction but there was no evidence of a causal connection between the defect and the emergence of the part of the machine which caused the injury.

For these reasons I am satisfied that the learned trial judge was correct in giving a non-suit in this case as the evidence stood. Firstly that the maxim *res ipsa loquitur* was not applicable on the ground that the machine, not being under the control or the management of the defendant, had not been proved to have been in the condition in which he provided it; and secondly on the ground that in so far as the plaintiff attempted to indicate the precise cause of the accident there was not sufficient evidence to go to the jury to enable them to find a causal connection between the broken flange and the actual incident which caused the injury.

Henchy J.:

I agree that, because the circumstances of the accident did not raise a prima facie case that defective construction or design of the machine was the reason why the plaintiff was injured, the maxim *res ipsa loquitur* did not apply. Consequently, before the plaintiff could succeed he had to prove some specific negligence on the part of the defendants as manufacturers of the machine. He sought to do that by adducing evidence to show that the accident happened because of a defectively welded flange in the machine. However, at the end of the evidence given at the trial, it was not possible for the trial judge to hold that the jury could reasonably conclude that the allegation of negligence had been sustained by the evidence. Accordingly, in my opinion, he was correct in withdrawing the case from the jury.

I concur in the order dismissing the appeal.

(ii) *The accident must be such as in the Ordinary Course of Things does not Happen with Use of Care by those in Control of the Thing*

NEILL V. MINISTER FOR FINANCE
[1948] I.R. 88 (Supreme Court, 1946)

Maguire C.J.:

This is an appeal by the plaintiff from a judgment of Davitt J. in an action tried with a jury in which the plaintiff claimed damages for personal injuries arising out of alleged negligence on the part of the defendant's servants. The appellant asks that the direction given by the learned trial Judge in favour of the respondent should be set aside and a new trial ordered.

The main evidence as to the accident in respect of which the claim arose was given by one witness, Mrs. Hannah Hazell, who described how a postal van, the property of the respondent, drove up to the block in which the appellant lived with his father and mother at Arbour Hill Barracks. The driver got out of the driving seat or the front of the van, went to the rere of the van, opened the door, and took out a parcel which he delivered at the appellant's home. After a few minutes he returned to the van, one of the rere doors of which appears still to have been open.

The appellant, a child of two and one-half years, followed him from the house. In close proximity there were other children, but it seems that the appellant was the only one near the rere of the van. Mrs. Hazell said that he was near one of the rere mud-guards when she last observed him before the accident. The next thing described is the screaming of the child and the postman ejaculating: 'My goodness.' The child was found to have sustained serious injuries to a finger and thumb. Subsequently he lost two pads of the thumb and index finger of the right hand. The driver is said, at one stage, to have called upon the children to go away from near the van. At the close of the appellant's case, the trial Judge withdrew the case from the jury. In his Report to this Court the learned Judge says that he gave the direction on the grounds:– (*a*) that there was no evidence of any negligence on the part of any servant or agent of the Minister for Posts and Telegraphs; and (*b*) that, assuming that there was negligence on the part of any servant or agent of the Minister for Posts and Telegraphs, such did not constitute 'negligent driving' within the meaning of s. 170, sub-s. 1, of the Road Traffic Act, 1933. . . .

[**Maguire C.J.** held that the trial judge was correct in holding that the injury did not arise from negligent driving on the part of the Minister's servant or agent. He continued:]

Holding that view, it is unnecessary for me to deal with the other point raised by the appellant, but, as the point has been fully argued and as I have formed a clear view on it I shall deal with it. As I have already indicated, there was nothing in the evidence to show exactly how the accident occurred. The evidence was that the door of the van was open, the driver was at the back of the van, near the door. The child was near the mudguard. The door was closed. The next incident of which there is evidence was that the child screamed and was discovered to have suffered an injury. As to how, precisely, the injury was caused there is a blank in the evidence. Mr. McBride, however, contends that the case is of the same type as *Scott v. London Dock Co.* 3 H. & C. 596 and that the doctrine of *res ipsa loquitur* applies. The principle there laid down is that where an accident occurs where the instrument or machinery causing the injury is shown to be under the management of the defendant or his servants, and the accident is such that it does not happen in the ordinary course of things if those who have the management use proper care, it affords reasonable evidence, in the absence of explanation by the defendant, that the accident arose from want of care. I cannot see how that principle can be applied in the present case. The gap which exists between the evidence as to the movements of the driver and the injury to the child could reasonably be filled in a number of ways. Granted that it is reasonable to conclude that the child's fingers were caught in some way in the door of the van when it was being closed, the actions of the child may have been such as could not reasonably have been anticipated by the driver. On that ground also, therefore, I hold that the learned trial Judge was right in withdrawing the case from the jury.

. . . Accordingly in my view this appeal should be dismissed.

Black J.:

The first ground upon which Davitt J. granted a direction in this case was that there was no evidence of any negligence on the part of any servant or agent of the Minister for Posts and Telegraphs, and Mr. McBride and Mr. Hartnett seek to get over the lack of evidence showing negligence by arguing that the accident would not have happened without it. There are cases where the *res ipsa loquitur* principle applies, but I do not think that this is one of them. In my view Mr. Murnaghan is correct in suggesting that a reasonable alternative to negligence could be that the child manipulated the door himself. Accordingly, I agree that the learned trial Judge was entitled to give a direction upon the ground which I have mentioned, namely, that there was not sufficient evidence as to how the accident was caused to eliminate all reasonable possibility that the driver was not to blame, or to justify a verdict for the appellant. . . .

Murnaghan J. concurred with **Maguire C.J.**

(iii) *The Procedural Effect of* Res Ipsa Loquitur

One of the most difficult and unsatisfactory aspects of the operation of the *res ipsa loquitur* principle arises in relation to the procedural effect of the principle. If the plaintiff has established that *res ipsa loquitur* applies, this could have one of three consequences. *First*, it could mean no more than that he has established a case sufficient to go to the jury. *Secondly*, it could mean that the defendant is obliged to establish either that he was not negligent or to provide a reasonable explanation, equally consistent with negligence and no negligence on his part. *Thirdly*, it could shift the onus onto the defendant to establish affirmatively that the accident was not caused by his negligence.

The courts have been somewhat remiss in the language they have used to describe the law on this question. One even finds decisions in which inconsistencies are apparent within the same judgment.

There is much to be said in favour of the *first* interpretation, which has won favour in courts in the United States, Canada, Australia, and, it seems, New Zealand. Why should one species of circumstantial evidence (which is referred to as *res ipsa loquitur*) have greater evidential weight than direct evidence? To regard *res ipsa loquitur* as merely having the effect of ensuring that the plaintiff gets his case before the jury means, however, that it ceases to be a distinctive doctrine and such concepts as 'control' of the object that causes the danger lose their significance.

The tendency in the Irish courts is not to favour the first interpretation (although a few decisions seem to give some support to it). The second, and more particularly the third, interpretations are generally adopted. See *McMahon & Binchy*, pp. 209–211.

11. *CONTRIBUTORY NEGLIGENCE*

Contributory negligence means a lack of reasonable care, by the plaintiff for his own safety. Formerly, proof of contributory negligence was an absolute defence, qualified only by the counter-charge by the plaintiff that the defendant had had the 'last opportunity' – or even 'constructive last opportunity' – to avoid the accident. If the jury found that the defendant had had the last opportunity to avoid the accident, then the plaintiff, in spite of being guilty of contributory negligence, would recover his damages in full.

Since 1961 this all-or-nothing approach has been replaced by a system of apportionment. Section 34 of the *Civil Liability Act 1961* provides as follows:

'(1) Where, in any action brought by one person in respect of a wrong committed by any other person, it is proved that the damage suffered by the plaintiff was caused partly by the negligence or want of care of the plaintiff or of one for whose acts he is responsible (in this Part called contributory negligence) and partly by the wrong of the defendant, the damages recoverable in respect of the said wrong shall be reduced by such amount as the court thinks just and equitable having regard to the degrees of fault of the plaintiff and defendant: provided that –

(*a*) if, having regard to all the circumstances of the case, it is not possible to establish different degrees of fault, the liability shall be apportioned equally;

(*b*) this subsection shall not operate to defeat any defence arising under a contract or the defence that the plaintiff before the act complained of agreed to waive his legal rights in respect of it, whether or not for value; but, subject as aforesaid, the provisions of this subsection shall apply notwithstanding that the defendant might, apart from this subsection, have the defence of voluntary assumption of risk;

(*c*) where any contract or enactment providing for the limitation of liability is applicable to the claim, the amount of damages awarded to the plaintiff by virtue of this subsection shall not exceed the maximum limit so applicable.

(2) For the purpose of subsection (1) of this section –

(*a*) damage suffered by the plaintiff may include damages paid by the plaintiff to a third person who has suffered damage owing to the concurrent wrongs of the plaintiff and the defendant, and the period of limitation for claiming such damages shall be the same as is provided by section 31 for actions for contribution;

(*b*) a negligent or careless failure to mitigate damage shall be deemed to be contributory negligence in respect of the amount by which such damage exceeds the damage that would otherwise have occurred;

(*c*) the plaintiff's failure to exercise reasonable care for his own protection shall not amount to contributory negligence in respect of damage unless that damage results from the particular risk to which his conduct has exposed him, and the plaintiff's breach of statutory duty shall not amount to contributory negligence unless the damage of which he complains is damage that the statute was designed to prevent;

(*d*) the plaintiff's failure to exercise reasonable care in the protection of his own property shall, except to the extent that the defendant has been unjustly enriched, be deemed to be contributory negligence in an action for conversion of the property;

(*e*) damage may be held to be caused by the wrong of the defendant notwithstanding any rule of law by which the scope of the defendant's duty is limited to cases where the plaintiff has not been guilty of contributory negligence: but this paragraph shall not render the defendant liable for any damage in respect of which he or a person for whose acts he is responsible has not been careless in fact;

(*f*) where an action is brought for negligence in respect of a thing that has caused damage, the fact that there was a reasonable possibility or probability of examination after the thing had left the hands of the defendant shall not, by itself, exclude the defendant's duty, but may be taken as evidence that he was not in the circumstances negligent in parting with the thing in its dangerous state.

(3) Article 21 of the Warsaw Convention (which empowers a court to exonerate wholly or partly a carrier who proves that the damage was caused by or contributed to by the negligence of the injured person) shall have effect subject to the provisions of this Part.'

(a) *Contributory Negligence and the Particular Risk*

MOORE V. NOLAN
94 I.L.T.R. 153 (Supreme Court, 1956)

The plaintiff pedestrian, when crossing a road, was injured by a car driven by the defendant. There was evidence from which a jury might find that the defendant had violated a red light. The jury found in favour of the plaintiff and acquitted him of contributory negligence. The defendant appealed to the Supreme Court, alleging that, if the plaintiff had been paying proper attention in respect of the possible danger of a car approaching through the green light, he would have seen the defendant's car.

Kingsmill Moore J. (For the Court):
. . . The verdict of the jury must mean that the plaintiff was not bound to foresee that traffic might come across Annesley Bridge and so was under no obligation to take steps to look out for and avoid such traffic. On analysis therefore the argument for the defendant must run something like this. I admit I was negligent in creating a danger whereby the plaintiff was injured, and I admit the plaintiff was not negligent in failing to anticipate this danger. But he was negligent in failing to anticipate another possible danger. I cannot say that if this danger had existed his failure to anticipate it would have caused him injury, but I do say that if he had taken proper precautions against this possible and to be anticipated danger those precautions would have been adequate to safeguard him from the danger he was not bound to anticipate. Therefore, I am not liable.

I find two difficulties in accepting this argument. The law does not, in general, require of any man that he be careful of his safety. I may indulge in rock climbing and other dangerous pursuits if I like. What it does say is that a man who has negligently created a danger whereby another person is injured may plead as a way of avoiding liability that the injured person by his negligence contributed to create the danger. But it seems to me that the injured person must be shown to have been negligent in respect of the particular danger which actually eventuated, in failing to foresee it and failing to take steps to avoid it. Otherwise the way of a transgressor with an ingenious imagination would be made easy, for he could call in his aid a series of possible and potential dangers which in theory a careful man should anticipate and take steps to guard against. As against his own proved and effective negligence he could set a hypothetical negligence of the injured man. I am unaware of any authority which goes this length and, in the absence of such authority, I am not prepared to yield to an argument which seems to me to favour unduly a negligent defendant.

Secondly, there is the practical difficulty. It is often a difficult task for a jury to say whether a plaintiff has been guilty of negligence contributing to the actual danger created by the defendant, so that the accident and his injuries can fairly be regarded as resulting from his combination of the two negligences. To ask them to consider whether the Plaintiff's conduct was negligent in regard to a hypothetical danger, and whether such negligence in regard to hypothetical danger would have resulted or have been likely to result in a hypothetical accident and the accident to cause hypothetical injuries would be to impose on them a fantastic task. Yet if his negligence in regard to the hypothetical danger would not have produced an accident and injuries (as might well be the case) how can such negligence debar him from recovering from the injuries caused to him by the actual proved negligence of the Defendant?

I have said that to establish contributory negligence the Plaintiff must be shown to have been guilty of a failure to take proper precautions for his own safety against the particular danger which eventuated. This statement perhaps requires elaboration. It does not mean that the particular form in which the danger manifested itself should actually have occurred to his mind. It is sufficient if it is a danger of a particular class whose occurrence he should anticipate and take reasonable precautions to guard against. Persons crossing a street must anticipate that the street may be used by any form of traffic which is legitimately entitled to be traversing it and danger from such traffic, whatever its nature, is to be guarded against. No doubt a pedestrian ordinarily thinks in terms of motor cars, horse traffic, bicycles and other pedestrians. But if he were to run under the legs of an elephant belonging to a travelling circus which was being taken along the road he could not justify his failure to look out on the ground that a pedestrian is not expected to think in terms of elephants. An elephant is in the class of legitimate road users. On the other hand he would not be expected to look out for a helicopter making a forced descent. Whether he is bound to anticipate and take steps against the danger which eventuates on the ground that, though unusual, it is a danger of that particular class which he is bound to anticipate and guard against must usually be a question for the jury. It seems to me that the jury were entitled to say, and have said, that the danger of being hit by traffic disregarding the lights was not a danger of this class. . . .

Notes and Questions

1. See now section 34 (2) (c), *supra*, p. 205, reaffirming Kingsmill Moore J.'s approach.
2. Is the concept of 'particular risk' sufficiently definite? Is it not open to very elastic interpretation? If I travel with an obviously drunk driver, to what risk or risks am I exposing myself? *Cf. Judge* v. *Reape* [1968] I.R. 226 (Supreme Court); *Lauritzen* v. *Barstead* 53 D.L.R. (2d) 267 (Alba. Sup. Ct., Kirby, J., 1965).

(b) *Apportionment of Fault*

CARROLL V. CLARE COUNTY COUNCIL
[1975] I.R. 211 (Supreme Court)

Kenny J.:

The principal grounds of appeal in this case are (1) that the trial judge erred in the way in which he advised the jury to apportion the fault for the accident if they held that both parties were negligent; (2) that the apportionment which the jury made was grossly disproportionate to the admitted facts; and (3) that the general damages were excessive. The case raises important questions about the construction of s. 34 of the Civil Liability Act, 1961, and as to the form of questions to be submitted to the jury in regard to general damages, when these are claimed for disability and pain suffered before the trial and to be suffered after it.

A motorist who wishes to drive from the city of Limerick to Shannon airport takes the main trunk road from Limerick to Ennis until he comes to the Ballycasey cross. There the trunk road to Ennis turns sharply to the right while the secondary road to Shannon, which was 20 feet wide before it was altered in 1966, continues in a straight line. Drivers coming from Shannon who wanted to go to Limerick tended to go from the secondary road from Shannon into the trunk road without stopping, and this caused many accidents.

In 1966 the defendants decided that they would carry out extensive road works at the junction so that drivers travelling from Shannon to Limerick would know that they had to stop. As the defendants could not get immediate possession of all the lands which they required for the work, they decided to carry out an interim scheme. They erected a large sign 6' wide and 6' high which was put on top of a pole 180 yards back from the junction and on the left-hand side of a driver coming from Shannon. On the upper half of this sign there was an illustration which showed the road to Limerick going straight on and that to Ennis going left. On the lower half the words 'Major Road Ahead' were written in large letters. The secondary road at the junction where it entered the trunk road was widened by 7' 6". There were three lines of traffic to be catered for, the traffic going to the left to Ennis, that going from Shannon to Limerick and that coming from Limerick to Shannon. The defendants erected two traffic islands at the point where the road from Shannon entered the trunk road. That on the left of the driver coming from Shannon was a small triangular traffic island with a large stop sign facing towards Shannon. The stop sign was on a pole and was 2' 6" wide; it was octagonal in shape and had the word 'Stop' in large white capital letters on a red reflectorised surface so that the lights from a car showed it up very clearly. The second traffic island was 12' on the right of the triangular one for a driver coming from Shannon, and was intended to separate the traffic coming from Shannon from that coming from Limerick; it was 29' 3" long, 2' wide and 6" high and was painted in black and yellow colours. It ran parallel with the side of the road but at the time of the accident did not have any bollards or fixed lights on it. Arrangements for lighting these two islands had been made with a man who lived five-miles away and who was to place the usual red bull's eye lamps on the two islands.

Before this work was carried out, there had been a broken white line in the middle of the road. The effect of the widening of the road was to change the centre-line of the road and so the defendants blacked out the old broken white line in the centre with paint for some distance back from the long traffic island; in its place, and to the left of it as a driver from Shannon approached the island, there was a continuous and clearly visible white line, which, as it advanced to the long traffic island, became a cross-hatched white section where the lines were a maximum width of 2 ft. This continuous white line and the cross-hatched section were 116' long and led to a double-dashed white line where the lines were 2' from each other. This double-dashed line was 42' long and pointed to the narrow traffic island which I have described. The total length of the continuous white line, the cross-hatched portion of the double white line and the double-dashed line was thus 158 feet. This new centre line continued back for more than 158' and merged with the broken white line which had not been blacked out. A driver from Shannon who kept to the left of the hatched line and the two double lines could not collide with the long traffic island in the middle of the road. The black paint, which had been used to obliterate the broken white line, became slightly worn so that a faint sign of the old line could be seen but it was not as bright as the new one. A driver who had his right-hand wheels on the old line would collide with the long island if he continued in that direction.

The plaintiff, who was 32 years of age at the time of the accident, left Dublin at 8.30 a.m. to drive to Limerick on business. He arrived in Limerick at midday and spent the entire day at conferences which lasted until 7 p.m. At 9 p.m. he went to visit some friends living at Shannon and he had 'four or six beers' there. He left Shannon at 3 a.m. on the 27th May and was driving at 40–50 m.p.h. as he approached the 'major road ahead' sign. He was driving on his headlights but he was not sure whether they were dipped or not. He saw the 'major road ahead' sign but did not slow down. He had his right front wheel on the broken line. He did not see the stop sign at all or any light on either of the islands. He continued with his right wheel on the faint old line which was to the right of the new line and finished up on the right-hand side of the long island. He did not see anything until he was on top of the junction when he saw the traffic island which, in his evidence, he called 'the blobs.' He then swerved violently to the left. His right front wheel struck the long narrow traffic island. He had no recollection of coming to the unbroken line or of seeing the hatched part of the double line or the double line which led to the traffic island. When the plaintiff swerved to the left, he struck the traffic island on which the stop sign was and his car went across the road and struck a wall. There was evidence that there were two bull's-eye lamps on the islands but the jury were entitled to conclude that these had either not been lit or that the light had gone out when the accident happened.

Proceedings for damages were commenced by the plaintiff against the defendants on the 26th April, 1968. There was lengthy skirmishing about interrogatories and the action did not come to trial until March 1974, when it was heard by Mr. Justice Butler sitting with a jury. The plaintiff's case was that the defendants were negligent in failing to light the islands and in allowing the broken white line which he followed to become visible so that he collided with the island.

The first question submitted to the jury was whether the junction as it existed at the time of the accident was a danger to the public. The answer was 'yes.' The second question was, if the answer to the first question was 'yes', whether the defendants were negligent in relation to the junction in (a) its design and construction, (b) its maintenance and (c) its lighting. To each of these questions the jury answered 'yes.' They found that the plaintiff was negligent in failing to keep a proper look out and in driving too fast and that he was not negligent in driving on his incorrect side of the road. They apportioned 70% of the degrees of fault to the defendants and 30% to the plaintiff. They awarded £50 for damage to property, £9,650 for special damages (these were two agreed figures) and £36,000 for general damages. This amounted to an award of £45,700 and the judge gave judgment for the plaintiff for £31,990.

In my opinion the first question should not have been submitted to the jury as it served no purpose and tended to mislead them. The question whether the junction, as it existed at the time of the accident, was a danger to the public had no relevance to the questions which had to be tried; it involved the risk that the jury were asked to make a decision on a general matter which was not related to any specific issue relied on by the plaintiff. Moreover, the jury were asked to consider the issue of the defendants' negligence only if they answered 'yes' to the first question; they were thereby led to believe that what they had to try was whether the junction was a danger to the public generally, and not the real question which was whether the defendants were negligent in relation to the plaintiff.

There was, in my opinion, no evidence upon which the jury could conclude that the defendants were negligent in relation to the junction in its design and construction. There was nothing negligent in the design or construction of the traffic islands; the work was done to make the road safer and the defendants had made adequate arrangements for the lighting of the junction until bollards were erected. There was, however, evidence to support the finding that the defendants were negligent in the maintenance of the junction because they allowed the old broken line to become visible and there was evidence to support the finding that neither of the islands was lit. There was abundant evidence that the plaintiff was negligent in failing to keep a proper look out and in driving too fast.

Section 34, sub-s. 1, of the Civil Liability Act, 1961, in so far as it is relevant to this action, reads:–

'(1) Where, in any action brought by one person in respect of a wrong committed by any other person, it is proved that the damage suffered by the plaintiff was caused partly by the negligence or want of care of the plaintiff or of one for whose acts he is responsible (in this Part called contributory negligence) and partly by the wrong of the defendant, the damages recoverable in respect of the said wrong shall be reduced by such amount as the court thinks just and equitable having regard to the degrees of fault of the plaintiff and defendant. . . .'

The section does not say that the damages are to be reduced by such amount as the court thinks just and equitable having regard to the degrees of negligence, but the section refers to fault of the plaintiff and the defendant.

In *O'Sullivan* v. *Dwyer* [1971] I.R. 275, Mr. Justice Walsh (with whose judgment Ó Dálaigh C.J. and FitzGerald J. agreed) said at p. 286 of the report:–

'It appears to me then that Mr. Liston is correct in his general submission that a judge, in directing a jury, must direct their minds to the distinction between causation and fault and that they should be instructed that degrees of fault between the parties are not to be apportioned on the basis of the relative causative potency of their respective causative contributions to the damage, but rather on the basis of the moral blameworthiness of their respective causative contributions. However, there are limits to this since fault is not to be measured by purely subjective standards but by objective standards. The degree of incapacity or ignorance peculiar to a particular person is not to be the basis of measuring the blameworthiness of that person. Blameworthiness is to be measured against the degree of capacity or knowledge which such a person ought to have had if he were an ordinary reasonable person: see the judgment of this Court in *Kingston* v. *Kingston* (1968) 102 I.L.T.R. 65.'

I think that 'fault' in s. 34 of the Act of 1961 means a departure from a norm by a person who, as a result of such departure, has been found to have been negligent and that 'degrees of fault' expresses the extent of his departure from the standard of behaviour to be expected from a reasonable man or woman in the circumstances. The extent of that departure is not to be measured by moral considerations, for to do so would introduce a subjective element while the true view is that the test is objective only. It is the blameworthiness, by reference to what a reasonable man or woman would have done in the circumstances, of the contributions of the plaintiff and defendant to the happening of the accident which is to be the basis of the apportionment. I think that the use of the word 'moral', when addressing a jury in connection with blameworthiness, is likely to mislead them. Two examples may illustrate this: if an elderly lady is driving a motor car towards a traffic light which is showing red to her and if she, intending to put her foot on the brake, puts her foot on the accelerator and causes a serious accident, she is morally blameless but seriously blameworthy. If the plaintiff admits that some hours before the accident he had a glass of beer and if a member of the jury is of opinion that one should not drive when one has any alcoholic drink taken, the juryman may apply his particular standard of morality to apportioning blameworthiness and may decide to attribute blameworthiness to the plaintiff on moral grounds although no suggestion is made by either party that the plaintiff was unfit to drive or that his driving was affected by the alcoholic drink which he had consumed. Therefore, I think that judges, when addressing juries, should not under any circumstances use the word 'moral' when speaking of blameworthiness, but that they should emphasise that the jury are to apportion the fault according to their view of the blameworthiness of the causative contributions to the accident and that it is to be measured and judged by the standards of conduct and care to be expected from a reasonable person in the circumstances.

I wish to emphasise that I agree with the principle in the passage which I have quoted from the judgment of Mr. Justice Walsh and I make these remarks only because 'moral blameworthiness' (which he was so careful to define in exact language) when used to a jury introduces a subjective element which is not consistent with the objective standard laid down in the passage and which will probably be misunderstood by juries and so will produce verdicts of apportionment on a wrong legal basis.

The trial judge put before the jury for their consideration the view that somebody who maintains a danger must be the more blameworthy when compared with a driver who is guilty of one act of negligence. When the jury had retired, Mr. Liston (for the defendants) objected to this passage in the charge and the judge said that the view that a person who maintains a danger is more blameworthy than a person guilty of a casual act of negligence approaching that danger was supported by the decision of this Court in *Walsh* v. *The Galway Harbour Commissioners* (18th December, 1972). The trial judge in this case said that his statement of this had been approved by Ó Dálaigh C.J. in his judgment in the Supreme Court in *Walsh's Case, supra*. That case was heard at first instance by Mr. Justice Butler sitting without a jury; in the course of his judgment in that case he said that in normal circumstances he would be inclined to apply the principle that, when there has been an accident, a person who maintains or permits an unusual danger must be more at fault than one who is guilty of what might be described as a casual act of negligence which contributes to the accident. In his judgment in the Supreme Court, Ó Dálaigh C.J. did not either approve or disapprove of this statement – though he did say that the trial judge's apportionment of 50% to the defendants was the least which he could have allocated.

However, it is not a principle of law that a person who maintains or permits an unusual danger must bear a higher share of fault than that attributed to a person guilty of a casual act of negligence. Pressed to its logical conclusion, this leads to the result that a motorist is entitled to recover more than half the damages resulting from a collision at night between his vehicle and a traffic island which was insufficiently lighted, even though he had passed warning signs and had consumed far too much alcoholic drink and had been driving at an excessive speed. This is not the law.

In each case it is a question of fact whether a person who creates or maintains a danger is more blameworthy than a person who collides with it. As Lord Wright said in *Tidy* v. *Battman* [1934] 1 K.B. 319, it is unfortunate that questions which are questions of fact alone should be confused by importing into them, as principles of law, a course of reasoning which has properly been applied in deciding other cases on other sets of facts. The dangers of stating general principles in relation to what are essentially questions of fact is well illustrated in our law reports. In *O'Beirne* v. *Hannigan* [1937] I.R. 237, 246, FitzGibbon J. said that a motorist who plunged into a 'black shadow' without being able to see in front of him, and who collided with a stationary vehicle, must be held to have been guilty of contributory negligence. This statement was made at a time when contributory negligence was a complete defence to an action. Mr. Justice FitzGibbon's remarks were frequently distinguished and explained (though much of the explaining was explained away) until they were finally overruled in *Hayes* v. *Finnegan* [1952] I.R. 98.

As it is not a principle of law that a driver who drives on when he cannot see ahead of him and collides with an unlighted object is necessarily guilty of contributory negligence (because this is essentially a question of fact which should not be judged by general principles), so in the same way someone who erects or maintains what is a danger in a public place need not, in the particular circumstances, necessarily have attributed to him the greater share of fault for an accident.

This Court will not generally interfere with the apportionment of fault made by a jury if it is not substantially different from the way in which the Court would have apportioned it. However, if there is gross disproportion between the apportionment by the jury and that which this Court would have made having regard to the undisputed facts, or if there has been a gross error on the part of the jury on the undisputed facts, this Court will reverse or review the verdict of the jury on this issue: *Donoghue* v. *Burke* [1960] I.R. 314; *Murphy* v. *Cronin* [1966] I.R. 699; and *O'Leary* v. *O'Connell* [1968] I.R. 149.

In this case the jury found that the defendants were negligent in failing to light the traffic islands and in failing to ensure that the old traffic lines did not become visible in any way: for this the jury held that the defendants were 70% at fault. They also found that the plaintiff was negligent in failing to take reasonable care because he did not keep a proper look out and because he drove too fast: for that they attributed 30% of the fault to him. In my opinion this apportionment bore no relation to the undisputed facts and to a proper and rational assessment of the degrees of fault of the plaintiff and the defendants for this unfortunate accident.

The plaintiff must have known that he was tired and should have known that his reaction was bound to be slow because his day had started at 8 a.m. in Dublin. He saw the 'major road ahead' sign and continued to drive at 40/50 m.p.h. He failed to see the vivid cross-hatched marks on the road, which he drove over, and the double line on the road. These together measured 158 feet and the plaintiff could have stopped his car so that there would have been no accident if he had slowed down when he had seen the 'major road ahead' sign, and if he had seen the stop sign which he could not have failed to see for a considerable distance if he had kept any reasonable look out. Drinking four or six beers at his friends' house certainly did not help his concentration. If he had been paying any attention to the road in front of him, the plaintiff would have seen the vivid cross-hatched part of the road and the stop sign and he would have realised that he had to keep to the left of the cross-hatched part and of the white double line which led to the island. The defendants were negligent in failing to light the islands and in failing to ensure that the marks of the old line did not become visible again. In my opinion the proper apportionment of fault in this case is 30% to the defendants and 70% to the plaintiff.
. . .

Henchy and **Griffin JJ.** concurred.

(c) *The 'Agony of the Moment'*

KEARNEY V. GREAT SOUTHERN & WESTERN RAILWAY CO.
18 L.R. Ir. 303 (Queen's Bench Division, 1886)

May C.J.:

This was a motion of the plaintiff in the action to set aside a verdict and judgment, directed by the Judge at the trial to be entered for the defendant.

The action was one against the defendants, the Railway Company, to recover damages for injuries caused to the plaintiff by their negligence.

The facts, which appeared at the trial, which took place before Mr. Justice O'Brien, at the last Spring Assizes for the county of Cork, are as follows:–

The plaintiff, on the 30th June, 1885, was a third-class passenger on the railway, from Lismore. At six o'clock when the train was approaching Castletownroche station, the plaintiff felt a shock, and some pebbles struck the windows of the carriage, and the carriage, as the plaintiff thought, became filled with smoke. A man in the same compartment as the plaintiff looked out of the window, and cried out that the train was on fire. The train was moving very slowly at the time; the plaintiff was greatly frightened, and jumped out of the carriage, and was, in consequence, injured.

It appeared that some portion of the machinery had broken, which caused water and steam to issue from the engine, which, it would seem, the plaintiff mistook for smoke. In fact, the carriage was not on fire, nor was the plaintiff, in fact, in any danger, when the accident happened. A brake was put on, and the train had nearly stopped when the plaintiff jumped out.

The Judge was of opinion that there was no evidence that the injury to the plaintiff was caused by any negligence or default of the defendants, and directed a verdict and judgment to be entered for the defendants. The plaintiff has moved to set aside this verdict and judgment, and the question is, whether the Judge was right in the direction he gave.

In my opinion, no evidence had been given showing that the injury to the plaintiff was occasioned by any negligence or default of the defendants, and the Judge properly directed the verdict and judgment. Had the carriage, in which the plaintiff was, been overturned by the defect in the machinery, or the plaintiff been injured by the direct consequences of that defect, the case would have assumed a different aspect. But the law must regard the proximate, not remote and imaginary, causes. No immediate injury was caused to the plaintiff by the accident; but she heard some man call out 'Fire,' and immediately, without inquiry, she rashly jumped out of the carriage, and was injured by the fall. The injury was caused by the plaintiff's own act, not by any act of the defendants.

The case of *Jones* v. *Boyce* 1 Stark, 493 was relied upon by the plaintiff's counsel. In that case the plaintiff was on the top of a coach, the horses became unruly and unmanageable, and, there being a real danger that the coach might be upset, the plaintiff jumped down from the coach, and was injured. The Judge (Lord Ellenborough) stated: 'If, through the default of a stage-coach owner neglecting to provide proper means of conveyance, a passenger is placed in so perilous a situation as to render it prudent for him to leap from the coach, whereby his leg is broken, the proprietor will be responsible, though the coach was not actually overturned.' That ruling of the Judge was, no doubt, perfectly sound.

O'Brien J. concurred.

Johnson J.:

The questions are – Was there evidence proper to be submitted to the jury (*a*) of negligence on the part of the defendants in the condition of the engine attached to the train of carriages? and, if so (*b*) was it by reason of that negligence the plaintiff sustained the injuries of which she complained?

I agree in the judgment of the Court, on the ground that, even assuming negligence on the defendants' part, it was not by reason of that negligence plaintiff was injured. It is therefore unnecessary for me to decide whether there was evidence of negligence for the jury. A carrier of passengers is, however, bound to provide a road-worthy conveyance, not in all events, but as far as human care and foresight can go; and if the conveyance is defective, it is for him to excuse his default. In this case the engine was defective – the coupling-rod broke – and therefore it was, in my opinion, a question of fact for a jury, whether the defendants were as careful and foreseeing as they were bound to be in reference to it. But, even so, on the second question, I think there was not evidence for the jury of a peril justifying the plaintiff's dangerous act of jumping out of the carriage. The rule laid down by Lord Ellenborough in *Jones* v. *Boyce* 1 Stark. 495 is:– 'It is sufficient if the person is placed, by the misconduct of the defendant, in such a situation as obliged him to adopt the alternative of a dangerous leap, or to remain at certain peril.' As stated by Field, J., in *Robson* v. *The North-Eastern Railway Company* L. R. 10 Q. B. 271:– 'If a person, by a negligent breach of duty, expose the person towards whom the duty is contracted to obvious peril, the act of the latter, in endeavouring to escape from the peril, although it may be the immediate cause of the injury, is not the less to be regarded as the wrongful act of the wrongdoer: *Jones* v. *Boyce* 1 Stark. 495; and this doctrine has, we think, been rightly extended in more recent times to "a grave inconvenience" when the danger to which the passenger is exposed is not in itself obvious.' In the present case there was not, in my opinion, evidence of peril or grave inconvenience within these authorities which ought to have gone to the jury. The coupling-rod of the engine broke; one end pierced the boiler; steam escaped thence, and smoke from the furnace; the train yielded at once to the action of the vacuum brake – was slowing, and shortly came to a standstill. It does not appear how the engine-driver and stoker came by the serious injuries they sustained; but no passenger in the train was injured, or (except the plaintiff and the girl O'Connor) even alarmed. These two seem to have been terrified by the cry – a statement of some men being passengers in the same compartment – that the train was on fire. The defendants are not responsible for this cry or statement: it was unfounded, in fact; but the plaintiff, in panic, jumped through the carriage door, which the girl O'Connor had opened, and she was injured. The injuries, however, were, in my opinion, the result of her unfortunate rashness, and not of the defendants' negligence. On this ground, therefore, I think the case was rightly withdrawn from the jury.

Note and Questions

1. Do you agree with the holding in this decision? How do you think the case would have been decided if section 34 of the *Civil Liability Act 1961* had then been part of the law?
2. For another harsh decision, see *Kelly* v. *McElligott*, 85 I.L.T.R. 4 (1949).

(d) *The Seat Belt Defence*

HAMILL V. OLIVER

[1977] I.R. 73 (Supreme Court)

Griffin J.:

On the 2nd September, 1973, the plaintiff was a passenger in her husband's car when it was involved in a collision with a car the property of the defendant on the main Dublin-Derry road near Slane in the county of Meath. She claimed damages against the defendant and her action came on for trial in the High Court on the 26th February, 1976. At the trial the defendant admitted negligence, but his counsel sought to have a question on contributory negligence left to the jury on the ground that at the time of the accident the plaintiff was not wearing a seat belt, although one was fitted in the car for use by the front-seat passenger. The learned trial judge refused to allow this question to go to the jury in the absence of evidence on behalf of the defendant that the accident would not have happened, or that the plaintiff would not have suffered the type of injury sustained by her, if the plaintiff had been wearing a seat belt. The only question left to the jury was that of damages, and the plaintiff was awarded £6,000 for general damages in addition to agreed special damages.

The two questions which arise for consideration in this appeal are (1) whether the judge was correct in deciding that the question of contributory negligence did not arise, and (2) whether the jury's award of £6,000 for general damages was excessive.

The final question is whether the trial judge should have ruled out contributory negligence although the plaintiff was not wearing the seat belt provided in her husband's car. Neither the plaintiff nor her husband was wearing a seat belt at the time. This was a new car, being only a few months old, but she said in evidence that they had never worn the seat belts provided.

The Road Traffic (Construction, Equipment and Use of Vehicles) (Amendment) Regulations, 1971 – S.I. No. 96 of 1971 – made it obligatory to fit safety belts and anchorage points in motor cars for use by the driver and the front-seat passenger farthest from him. The regulations apply to all cars first registered on or after the 1st June, 1971, and the car in which the plaintiff was travelling was so fitted. Since March, 1973, all main roads in the country display large road-safety posters with the slogan 'Live with a safety belt' painted in very large letters thereon. Advertisements appear regularly on television advocating the wearing of seat belts and drawing attention to the risks involved to those who travel in the front seat of a motor car without wearing such belts. When the Oireachtas made it compulsory to fit seat belts to a motor car, it must have been intended that they should be worn although the *wearing* of seat belts was not made compulsory. The plaintiff cannot but have been aware of the advisability of wearing a seat belt and of the risks incurred if she failed to do so.

In the accident, the plaintiff, as she herself described it, was 'thrown on to the gear handle' of the car, and received injuries to her chest and ribs. She fractured the fifth, sixth and seventh ribs on the right side, and she suffered a right pneumothorax with collapse of the lung on that side. The nature of the accident, coupled with these injuries, shows that the primary cause of her injuries was an impact with the gear lever, which would have been situated to her right. She was obviously thrown forward and to the right. This was a type of accident which could not have happened if she had been wearing a seat belt.

Prima facie, therefore, there was contributory negligence on her part. As was held in *Froom* v. *Butcher* [1976] Q.B. 286, any person who travels in the front seat of a motor car, be he passenger or driver, without wearing an available seat belt must normally be held guilty of contributory negligence if the injuries in respect of which he sues were caused wholly or in part as a result of his failure to wear a seat belt. There may be excusing circumstances for not wearing the seat belt, such as obesity, pregnancy, post-operative convalescence, and the like, where the wearing of a seat belt may be thought to do more harm than good; but it is for the plaintiff who has not worn it to raise and prove such excusing circumstances.

In this case, the trial judge ruled out contributory negligence on the ground that there was no evidence that the wearing of a seat belt would have prevented the accident. However, as was decided in *Froom* v. *Butcher* [1976] Q.B. 286, that is not the correct test. The question is whether the wearing of a safety belt would have prevented or reduced the injuries. Here, as in most cases, no special evidence was required on the point. The jury could not but have come to the conclusion that the impact injuries the plaintiff received when her right chest and ribs struck the gear lever would not have happened if she had been wearing a seat belt. Therefore, the issue of contributory negligence was incorrectly ruled out.

As to the question of damages, the plaintiff was detained in hospital for three weeks during which time it was necessary to insert a tube into the right side of her chest to relieve her extreme difficulty in breathing and to allow the air which had accumulated between the chest wall and lung to escape. She suffered very considerable distress while in hospital. Subsequently, she had pain in her chest, right shoulder, and right arm and this subsisted to a greater or lesser degree up to the date of the trial, which was almost $2\frac{1}{2}$ years after the accident. In addition, she suffered acute gastritis, and developed an anxiety condition; the medical evidence at the trial was to the effect that it would probably be a further six to twelve months before her anxiety, gastritis and pain cleared up. Having regard to the total extent of her pain, discomfort and worry, I do not think that the award of £6,000 is in any way excessive. It is not, at any rate, so excessive as to justify interfering with it. Therefore, I would reject this ground of appeal.

I would order a new trial confined to the question of contributory negligence and the question of apportionment of fault. If, at that trial, the plaintiff does not adduce special circumstances capable of excusing her failure to wear a seat belt, the trial judge should direct the jury that she should be found guilty of contributory negligence because of such failure. At the same time, as the *accident* was caused by the negligent driving of the defendant, and as the injuries resulted only to a minor extent by reason of the failure to wear a seat belt, the jury should be directed that, in the apportionment of degrees of fault between the plaintiff and the negligent defendant, much the greater attribution of fault should be held to fall on the defendant as the person primarily responsible for the plaintiff's injuries.

O'Higgins C.J. and **Henchy J.** concurred.

Questions

1. Do you think it wise that 'in most cases' no special evidence should be required to prove that the wearing of the seat belt would have prevented or reduced the injuries?
2. In determining the proportion by which damages should be reduced for failure to wear a seat belt, is the extent to which the injuries were enhanced by this failure relevant to the calculation? If, for example, the injuries were enhanced by only £5,000 from £95,000 to £100,000, would it be possible for a jury to find the plaintiff 10% responsible?

12 *VOLUNTARY ASSUMPTION OF RISK*

Formerly it was a complete defence to show that the plaintiff had 'voluntarily assumed the risk', that is to say, had absolved the defendant in advance for his negligence. The precise scope of the defence was not very clear: frequently, it merged with other defences, notably that of contributory negligence, then also an absolute defence. Moreover, if the plaintiff was the author of his own misfortune, his case would be rejected, the courts sometimes inaccurately couching their rejection in the language of voluntary assumption of risk.

Section 34(1)(b) of the *Civil Liability Act 1961*, set out *supra*, p. 205, now expresses the defence in statutory form. Some aspects of this provision have given rise to judicial analysis.

M'COMISKEY V. McDERMOTT
[1974] I.R. 75 (Supreme Court, 1973)

[The facts of this case have already been set out *supra*, pp. 161–162. The extracts from the judgments set out below deal with the defence under section 34(1)(*b*) of the *Civil Liability Act 1961*.]

Henchy J.:

. . . The question whether the plaintiff had agreed to waive his legal rights in respect of the defendant's negligence so as to enable the defendant to rely on the statutory defence given by s. 34, sub-s. 1, of the Civil Liability Act, 1961, arose in this way. When the defendant purchased this car in England it had attached to the instrument fascia a notice to the effect that passengers travelled in the car at their own risk. The defendant had not bothered to remove the notice. The plaintiff was present when the car was bought by the defendant and consequently knew of the notice. The only reference made to it before the accident was on one occasion when the plaintiff jokingly said to the defendant that unless he removed the notice no one would sit in the car. The plaintiff denied in evidence that he took the notice seriously when he travelled as a passenger in the car; and the defendant, although his defence formally pleaded that the plaintiff had waived his right to sue, failed to state in evidence that he was relying on the notice when he carried the plaintiff as a passenger. Because the plaintiff was present when the defendant bought his car, he knew that it was the former owner who put the warning notice in the car, so the mere continuance of the notice in the car would not be sufficient to absolve the defendant unless it was proved, or could be inferred, that the defendant adopted the notice as one coming from him and intended to bind the plaintiff and that the plaintiff so accepted it: see *O'Hanlon* v. *Electricity Supply Board* [1969] I.R. 75. The evidence fell short of that. In fact, the plaintiff said in evidence that he disregarded the notice, and the defendant failed to assert that he intended or expected the plaintiff to treat the notice as a binding or effective one. In these circumstances, I consider the jury's verdict that the plaintiff had waived his right to sue to be unsupported by evidence and to be therefore invalid. . . .

Griffin J.:

. . . The first question is based on what used to be called the defence of *volenti non fit injuria* which, since the Civil Liability Act, 1961, is 'the defence that the plaintiff before the act complained of agreed to waive his legal rights in respect of it. The law on this topic was settled by this Court in *O'Hanlon* v. *Electricity Supply*

Board [1969] I.R. 75. The majority decision of the Court was delivered by Mr. Justice Walsh and, having set out the terms of s. 34 of the Act of 1961, he stated at pp. 91–2 of the report:– 'Under the terms of the Act of 1961 the defendants must establish that the plaintiff agreed to waive his legal rights in respect of the act complained of and that such agreement was made before that act. As no question of statutory duty arises in this appeal it is unnecessary to consider whether any such agreement, if it did exist, would be contrary to statute or to public policy. In my opinion, the use of the word 'agreed' in the Act of 1961 necessarily contemplates some sort of intercourse or communication between the plaintiff and the defendants from which it could be reasonably inferred that the plaintiff had assured the defendants that he waived any right of action that he might have in respect of the negligence of the defendants. A one-sided secret determination on the part of the plaintiff to give up his right of action for negligence would not amount to an agreement to do so. Such a determination or consent may be regarded as "voluntary assumption of risk" in terms of the Act but, by virtue of the provisions of the Act and for the purposes of the Act, this would be contributory negligence and not the absolute defence mentioned in the first part of sub-s. 1(*b*) of section 34.' Later, at p. 95, Mr. Justice Walsh stated:– 'The real question, and it was not put to the jury, was whether the plaintiff undertook the operation in question in circumstances from which it could be inferred, if it was not actually expressed, that he had agreed with the defendants before the dangerous operation was undertaken that he was exonerating them from liability for their negligence in not furnishing him with the means of disconnecting the current. The judge's charge erroneously permitted the jury to infer agreement from knowledge only and erroneously permitted them to equate a unilateral private determination with an agreement between two parties.'

Counsel for the plaintiff submitted that there was no evidence of any 'communication' between the plaintiff and the defendant from which the inference could be drawn that the plaintiff waived his right of action against the defendant, and that the existence of the notice on the dash-board of the car did not convey a message from the defendant to the plaintiff nor did it represent the state of mind of the defendant. Counsel for the defendant cited *Bennett* v. *Tugwell* [1971] 2 Q.B. 267 in which the defendant successfully relied on the defence of *volenti non fit injuria* where the plaintiff was injured whilst travelling in the defendant's car to which had been affixed a notice stating:– 'Passengers travelling in this vehicle do so at their own risk.' On the facts of that case Ackner J. held that the consent of the plaintiff was clearly to be inferred from the facts. The trial judge in that case did not, of course have to consider the provisions of s. 34 of the Act of 1961. In an appropriate case the affixing of a notice to the dashboard might lead to the inference that there was agreement between the passenger and the owner sufficient to set up the statutory defence under the Act of 1961, but such an inference could not, in my view, be drawn from the facts in the present case. In view of the fact that the defendant himself in evidence at no time relied on the notice, Mr. Ellis was driven to concede that there was no evidence to indicate that the notice in the car on this occasion did in fact represent a communication to the plaintiff by the defendant or the state of mind of the defendant and, in my opinion, there was no evidence which warranted leaving the first question to the jury and, accordingly, the question should not have been left for their consideration. . . .

Walsh J. (dissenting) (but dissent not affecting this issue):

. . . The circumstances which caused the judge to leave the first question to the jury were that there was attached to the instrument board of the defendant's motor car a notice to the effect that passengers travelled in the car at their own risk. In fact this notice was on the car when the defendant purchased it second-hand in England and he had not bothered to remove the notice. The plaintiff was aware that this notice was on the car when the defendant bought it and it is abundantly clear from the evidence in this case that neither the plaintiff nor the defendant regarded the notice as affecting their relationship. It was not intended by the defendant to be an intimation to the plaintiff of the terms or conditions under which he travelled in the car, nor was it accepted by the plaintiff as such. For the reasons given in *O'Hanlon* v. *Electricity Supply Board* [1969] I.R. 75, the statutory defence afforded by s. 34, sub-s. 1, of the Civil Liability Act, 1961, did not arise in this case. In so far as the plaintiff's appeal is being taken against the fact that the judge left this question the jury, it should succeed. There was no evidence in this case which warranted leaving the question to the jury. . . .

Questions

Should section 34 (1) (*b*) be interpreted as involving the requirement that there be 'some sort of intercourse or communication' between the plaintiff and the defendant, in your view? Do cases in the law of contract on the question of implied agreement support this requirement?

Chapter 9

OCCUPIERS' LIABILITY

On this subject generally, see McMahon, *Reform of Law of Occupiers' Liability in Ireland: Survey and Proposals for Reform* (Prl. 4403, 1975).

The law relating to occupiers' liability is in a state of transition and the process of judicial reform is in an unfinished and rather untidy state at present. The courts are beginning to set aside the approach which categorised different entrants onto property and which ascribed different levels of duty on the part of the occupiers towards each of these categories. But in order to understand the present law it is necessary to look at its earlier development.

Categories of Entrant

Contractual entrants are those who enter premises in pursuance of a contract between themselves and (normally) the occupier. Subject to any particular terms in a contract, there is an implied term that reasonable care has been taken to make the premises safe for the purposes contemplated by the contract. Apart from contractual entrants, those who come on to the premises are classified into three categories: invitees, licensees and trespassers. Trespassers have no right to be on the premises; licensees are permitted to be on the premises, but are there only for their own benefit; invitees come on to the premises on business in which the occupier has an interest. There are no other sub-divisions; these categories are exhaustive.

Until the recent Supreme Court decision of *McNamara* v. *E.S.B.* ([1975] I.R. 1) the law on this topic could be stated in the following way. (The effect of *McNamara's* decision on this is a matter of uncertainty.) The occupier's duty on such entrants varies, and depends largely on the category into which the entrants are classified. Briefly, with regard *to the state of the premises*, he owes little or no duty to the trespasser: to the licensee he owes a duty to warn of concealed dangers of which he knows; to the invitee he owes a duty to take reasonable care to prevent damage from unusual dangers of which he knows or ought to know. With regard *to his own acts* while those people are on his premises he owes the same duty to invitees and licensees and trespassers: the duty to take reasonable care. Until *McNamara's* case the duty to trespassers were merely not to injure them by intentional or reckless conduct.

DONALDSON V. IRISH MOTOR RACING CLUB AND THOMPSON
Unreported Sup. Ct. 1st Feb. 1957 (66–1956)

Kingsmill Moore J.:

On August 28th, 1954, motor races were held on the Curragh road racing circuit, organised by and under the auspices of the Irish Motor Racing Club Ltd., one of the defendants. Among the competing motor cars was one owned by John Thompson, the second defendant, which was driven by a driver named Quinn. This car, for reasons which are not clear, swerved off the track and continued, apparently still under full power, over the grass plain of the Curragh, along a course diverging from the track, till it came into contact with a line of posts connected with rope behind which a number of spectators were standing. It broke two or three of the posts and the rope, and then, swerving sharply to its left, regained and crossed the track, and finished on the far side of the road facing back in the direction from which it had come, having travelled a course of nearly 1 mile from the point where it left the track. The car was still on all four wheels and the driver was in his seat dead, or on the point of death, apparently from injuries received when the car struck the posts. Two of the spectators were also killed and one seriously injured.

This action was taken by the parents of one of the dead spectators, against the Club and Mr. Thompson, claiming damages under the Fatal Accidents Act. The claim was laid both in negligence and nuisance, but, as the roads over which the race was held had been closed to the public by order of the Minister for Local Government acting under statutory authority, the allegation of nuisance was not pursued in this Court.

At the trial the learned Judge withdrew the case from the jury at the conclusion of the evidence for the plaintiff, and directed the jury to find for the defendants, holding that there was no evidence on which a jury could properly find negligence against either defendant. From this verdict and the judgment consequent thereon the plaintiffs appeal. Counsel for the plaintiffs maintained, as against the Club, that it had chosen an unsuitable course for a race, that it had failed to take proper precautions to make the course suitable, and that it had neglected to provide proper protection for the spectators; as against Mr. Thompson he maintained that his driver had chosen an unsuitable place to pass another car and that, when passing, he tried to shave the other car too closely with the result that his wheels touched it and he was deflected onto the grass margin, or, alternatively, that he went onto the grass margin in the course of giving an unnecessarily wide berth.

The track used for the races was about five miles long and roughly triangular. Save for a short distance, where it ran through the Curragh Camp, the road was unfenced and stretched across the open grass plain, sometimes a little higher and sometimes a little lower than the surrounding levels. From time to time road sweepings had been deposited on the grass margins and had themselves become grass grown so that in a number of places low mounds, rising to a height of a little over a foot, lay along the grass margins parallel to the road. Through those mounds water channels had been cut for the purpose of draining surface water from the road and these channels varied in depth according to the height of the mound, being a foot or more deep at the places where the mound was highest. A car travelling at high speed if for any reason it was driven onto this alternation of mounds and water channels, would be liable to be damaged and might for a time get out of control; but the danger was clearly visible and could not be overlooked by any driver who had examined the track or even made a preliminary practise circuit.

The point where the car left the road is towards the end of a long straight. About 250 yards further on the track begins to curve very gradually to the left, and in another 100 yards it comes to Ballymany crossroads, one of the critical parts of the course where cars have to take a sharp corner. The road is 18 feet wide, slightly cambered, and of an excellent surface. Though important races had been held over this track on four or five previous occasions there was no evidence that a car had ever left the road surface on a straight section of the road. At a corner, however, it was not unusual for a car to skid off the road onto the surrounding grass.

At Ballymany corner a stand had been erected, for the use of which a charge was made, and it was protected from skidding cars by a heavy barrier. On other parts of the circuit the public were free to watch the racing without payment. They were kept from encroaching too closely on the track by stewards and by the line of posts, joined by a rope, to which I have referred. This was sited roughly parallel to the road and about 20 yards from its edge. The barrier made by the posts and rope was not intended in any way to protect spectators from a car which had got out of control but was to facilitate the stewards in keeping spectators at a distance which was considered to be safe. At a bend or a corner a car which had got out of control in any way would tend to go off at a tangent to the curve, but if the accident occurred on a straight portion the tendency would be to continue along the track without diverging from it.

How the accident originated was left somewhat obscure. The car driven by Quinn was following another car which one witness thought, somewhat hesitantly, was on the crown of the road. Other witnesses put it further to its left. Quinn attempted to pass and, just as his front wheels were level with the car in front, his car appeared to swerve suddenly onto the grass margin and to continue over the series of bumps and water channels which are present at this point. The irregularities buffetted the car and caused it to bounce into the air, but it remained on its wheels and passed over the bumps onto the slope which leads down to the plain, and over the plain at high speed, diverging from the line of the road, until at a distance of 220 yards from where it left the road it touched one of the posts. This it broke, and the rope seems to have become entangled in some way with the car for although the car swerved away immediately from the line of posts (as was shown by the tracks left on the grass) three more posts were found broken after the car had passed. Somehow in the collision the driver sustained the injuries from which he died, and the Plaintiff's son who was standing behind the rope was also fatally injured.

No evidence was given of any defect in the car and no expert evidence was offered as to the nature of the risks which were normally undertaken by racing drivers. There was however some evidence that the place chosen for passing by Quinn was a normal place for passing and that cars had passed each other safely at this place during the course of the race, and there was also evidence that there was room for Quinn to pass the car in front of him. While all the witnesses agreed that the overtaking car had made a sharp swerve as it was coming up on the car in front, one witness thought there had been a glancing contact between the two cars. On this somewhat meagre evidence the case was presented.

There was considerable argument as to the legal category into which a spectator, who had paid nothing for his right to look on, should properly be placed. Was he merely a 'neighbour', in the sense ascribed to that term by Lord Atkin in *Donoghue* v. *Stevenson*? Or was he a licensee? or an invitee? or entitled to require the same standard of care for his safety as a person who had paid money for admission and who could base his claim on contract? I find great difficulty in holding that a spectator who has not paid anything should be entitled to the higher standard of care which is required toward those who have paid for their right to be on premises, nor do I see how the relationship of invitor and invitee can be established unless there is a common interest between the occupier of the premises and the person who comes upon them, and no such common interest was suggested, (though I am not sure that one could not be discovered). The true relationship seems to me probably to be that of licensor and licensee. It is not, however, necessary to give a concluded opinion for two reasons. First the case is capable of being decided on considerations which are equally applicable to a 'neighbour', a licensee, an invitee, or a person who has paid for admission: and secondly Mr. McGonigal [counsel for the Club], accepting for the purpose of argument that the spectator who had not paid might have the same rights as one who had, maintained – successfully in my opinion – that even applying this standard the Club was not liable.

Whatever be the category the Club are not insurers against any injury however improbable. 'You must take reasonable care to avoid acts or omissions which you can reasonably foresee would be likely to injure your neighbour' said Lord Atkin in *Donoghue* v. *Stevenson* [1932] A.C. 562 at 580. 'To determine whether an act is negligent it is relevant to determine whether any reasonable person would foresee that the act would cause damage.' *Polemis and Furness Withy* [1921] 3 K.B. 560, 577 (*per* Scrutton L.J.).

'The mere possibility of accident is not enough to establish liability' *Searle* v. *Wallbank* [1947] A.C. 341. Lord Maugham at 351. 'Two elements appear to be necessary to create liability, foreseeability of the risk and the possibility by reasonable care and skill of guarding against it.' *Coleman* v. *Kelly* 85 I.L.T.R. 48. Maguire C.J. at 51. See also *Glasgow Corporation* v. *Muir* [1943] A.C. 448. *Bolton* v. *Stone* [1954] A.C. Lord Normand at 861, Lord Porter at 858 and Lord Reid at 867.

Just as there is no absolute liability to protect against every danger however improbable, so there is no absolute standard of care to be taken even against those risks which come within the realm of probability. In none of the categories suggested is there a duty to take such care as would effectuate complete insurance. The care taken need only be reasonable care, and what is reasonable care depends on all the circumstances, including the probability of an occurrence causing danger, the probability of injury ensuing if such an occurrence takes place, the practicability of precautions, the legal categories involved, and other matters too diverse and numerous to be catalogued.

Of the categories suggested the greatest care is demanded 'where for reward persons are invited to use premises.' This view was expressed by Slesser L.J. in *Hall* v. *Brooklands Auto Racing Club* [1933] 1 K.B. 205 at 227 and approved by Maguire C.J. in *Coleman* v. *Kelly* 85 I.L.T.R. 48 at 50 and Lavery J. in the same case at 56. The standard of care required in this category was expressed by McCardie J. in *Maclenan* v. *Seager* [1917] 2 K.B. 325 as 'an implied warranty that the premises are as safe (for the purpose mutually contemplated by the occupier and the injured person) as reasonable care and skill on the part of anyone can make them.' In *Hall* v. *Meath Hospital* (unreported) Sullivan C.J. expressed the obligation as being one 'to take reasonable care that the premises are safe', a test adopted by Lavery J. in *Coleman's* case at 56. In the same case Maguire C.J. uses the words 'to ensure that the premises were reasonably safe' and speaks of risks 'which it is possible by reasonable skill and care to guard against.' In *Gilmore* v. *L.C.C.* [1947] 4 All E.R. 331 du Parcq J. speaks of 'an implied warranty of reasonable care that the premises are reasonably safe for the contemplated purpose.' I do not think that it matters whether the adjective 'reasonable' is attached to the word 'care' or to the word 'safety' or to both. What does matter is that, even in this category, the standard of care is not absolute but relative to the circumstances.

The circumstances which prevail when persons are allowed by organisers of sports or games, either in consideration of payment or otherwise, to be spectators of the performances on property of which they are occupiers, have been considered in a number of decisions, both Irish and English. Such performances usually involve violence in the form of high speed or vigorous muscular exertion or both, and it is impossible to confine the results of such violence entirely to the arena in which the performance is taking place. To remove spectators to such a distance, or to guard them with such protective screens, as would ensure complete safety, would in most cases so diminish the view as to render watching unattractive and put an end to the entertainment. Where the arena of the sport extends linearly over a great distance, as in horse or motor racing, the provision of an unbreakable barrier alongside the whole course would be impracticable on the ground of expense. Yet it is in the public interest, alike from the point of view of players, competitors, and spectators that games and sports should be carried on. Moreover it corresponds to common sense and reality to suppose that the spectators appreciate and take the risk of certain accidents inherent in the nature of the game or sport. If it were pointed out to the ordinary spectator at a point to point or a motor race that horse or car might get out of control and run into him, causing him serious injuries, he would probably reply 'I know that, but the chances are so small that I am willing to risk it'; and if a spectator on the touch line at a hockey match or round the green at a golf championship was reminded that it was by no means an improbability that he would be hit by a ball he would say 'Yes, but the chances of any serious injury resulting are so remote that I am prepared to disregard them.' Where the liability of the promoter rests on contract (as where the spectator pays) effect can be given to these considerations by implying a term to accept such risks; and, where it lies in tort, the same result can be arrived at by applying the doctrine of *volenti non fit injuria*. The decisions appear to me to have arrived at a practical compromise. The promoters of the sport or game are bound to take normal, reasonable and practicable precautions to protect spectators from the risk of injuries the occurrence of which is not improbable and the result of which would be likely to be serious, but the spectator accepts the risks of occurrences, which, though inherent in the nature of the activity, are either unlikely to happen or, though not unlikely to happen are unlikely to cause injuries of any seriousness. The leading case is *Hall* v. *Brooklands Auto Racing Club* [1933] 1 K.B. 205, where the facts were not dissimilar to those in the present case. The finishing straight at Brooklands was bounded by a 6″ kerb and, at 4′5″ from its edge, by a railing behind which spectators were allowed to stand. The fence was of moderately strong construction, sufficient to stop a skidding car but not sufficient to stop a car which charged it under power. Owing to a driver's mistake two cars, racing down the straight, collided, and one of the cars half crashed through, half leaped over, the railing and injured a spectator behind it.

The Court of Appeal reversed a jury finding in favour of the plaintiff. Scrutton L.J. pointed out that the case raised questions of general application to any cases where landowners admit for payment to their land persons who desire to witness sports or competitions carried on thereon, if those sports may involve risk of danger to persons witnessing them, and asks himself 'What is the duty of the defendant Company who take money from the spectator for their permission to him to view the racing on their premises?' (at 212) and 'What then is the term to be implied on payment to see a spectacle, the nature of which is known to all people of ordinary intelligence who go to see it?' (at 214.) He concludes that there 'is not an absolute warranty of safety, but a promise to use reasonable care to ensure safety. What is reasonable care would depend on the perils which might be reasonably expected to occur, and the extent to which the ordinary spectator might be expected to appreciate and take the risk of such perils. Illustrations are the risk of being hit by a cricket ball at Lords or the Oval where any ordinary spectator in my view expects and takes the risk of a ball being hit with considerable force among the spectators, and does not expect any structure which would prevent any ball from reaching spectators. An even more common case is one which may be seen all over the country every Saturday afternoon, spectators admitted for payment to a field to witness a football or hockey match, and standing along a line near the touch line. No one expects the persons receiving payment to erect such structures or nets that no spectator can be hit by a ball kicked or hit violently from the field of play towards the spectators. The field is safe to stand on and spectators take the risk of the game.' After examining a number of other cases and dicta he says. 'I think to all those statements there must be added a term that there is no obligation to protect against a danger incident to the entertainment which any reasonable spectator foresees and of which he takes the risk.' He finally based his judgment on the view that 'I cannot think it is a failure to use reasonable care or negligence not to inform spectators of a motor race that with cars running at a rate of 100 m.p.h. there is a risk of cars skidding or leaving the track, especially when for 23 years no such car had reached a spectator.'

Greer L.J. regarded the occurrence as 'an extraordinary and unlikely event, which no one would have anticipated.' He accepted that the relationship between the parties was contractual, and that McCardie J.'s pronouncement in *Maclenan* v. *Seager* as to the liability created by this relationship was correct. He continues – 'It is clear law that there is no absolute warranty that the premises are safe but only that reasonable skill and care have been used to make them safe. But the question arises whether the term I have mentioned is the only term to be implied as between a spectator who takes a ticket to see a cricket match, a race, or other spectacle, which in certain events may be attended by a risk of danger.

In my judgment both parties must have intended that this person paying for his licence to see a cricket match, or a race, takes upon himself the risk of unlikely and improbable accidents provided that there has not been on the part of the occupier a failure to take usual precautions.' He instances as an example of a possible but improbable accident the risk of a horse getting out of hand and running loose among spectators at the Derby and continues. 'In the same way a man taking a ticket to see motor races would know quite well that no barrier would be provided which would be sufficient to protect him in the possible but highly improbable event of a car charging the barrier and getting through to the spectators. The risk of such an event would be so remote that he would quite understand that no provision would be made to prevent it happening and that he would take the risk of any such accident. In my judgment there was an implied term in the contract between the plaintiff and the defendants under which the plaintiff agreed to take the risk of the kind of accident that happened in the present case, but if I should be wrong about this I am prepared to hold that there was no evidence that the defendants failed to take reasonable care to make their premises reasonably safe for spectators. I do not think the defendants are under any obligation to provide safety in all circumstances, but only to provide against damage to spectators which any reasonable occupier in their position would have anticipated as likely to happen.'

Slesser L.J. did not rest himself on an implied term whereby the spectator took the risk. In his view there were two considerations, first whether the misadventure was of so unusual a kind that it could not reasonably have been expected, and secondly whether, if it could have been expected, the defendants had used reasonable care to avoid the danger. He came to the conclusion, on the facts, that there was no evidence that the unusual danger was one which the defendants ought to have known. 'The obligation is to guard against dangers which might reasonably be anticipated, not against all and every danger.'

The *Brooklands* case was applied in England in *Murray* v. *Harringey Arena Ltd.* [1951] 2 K.B. 529. An infant spectator at an ice hockey match was injured by a blow from the puck which was driven out of the rink and among the onlookers. There was evidence that it was a fairly common event for a puck to be driven out in this way. Injury could be avoided by the erection of netting, and this was done at the ends of the rink behind the goals (where missed shots at goal would be frequent and would travel with great velocity), but netting at the sides would impede the view and it was not usual to provide such netting. The Court of Appeal upheld the trial judge in absolving the defendants from liability. Singleton L.J., with whose judgment Cohen L.J. and Morris L.J. agreed, said at 536: 'I regret it as clear from the authorities that the implied term is not that the occupiers shall guard against every known risk. There are some which every reasonable spectator foresees and of which he takes the risk. ... The implied term is to take reasonable care, and in measuring that one must have regard to the reasonable man or spectator, and the duty arising under it does not involve an obligation to protect against a danger incident to the entertainment which any reasonable spectator foresees and of which he takes the risk.' He held that the injury resulted from a danger incidental to the game of which spectators took the risk.

In two cases the questions involved in this case have come before our Supreme Court – *Coleman* v. *Kelly* 85 I.L.T.R. 66 and *Callaghan* v. *Killarney Race Course Ltd.* somewhat perfunctorily reported in 90 I.L.T.R. 134. [Subsequently reported in [1958] I.R. 366 – *eds.*] In *Coleman's* case a horse, engaged in a jumping competition, threw its rider and, alarmed by a loose saddle, galloped back through the unfenced opening to the saddling enclosure. The plaintiff who was standing in the gap with the consent, and perhaps under the direction of, one of the stewards, was knocked down. The majority of the court, Maguire C.J., O'Byrne J., Black J. and Lavery J., took the view that on the evidence given a jury might consider that the occurrence was not improbable and that reasonable care had not been taken by proper stewarding or otherwise to protect the spectator. Murnaghan J. dissented. I have already referred to the views of the different members of the Court on the liability of occupiers of premises to persons whom they admit to those premises for payment. The question as to whether the plaintiff had accepted a risk inherent in the sport was not fully considered because of the evidence that the spectator had taken up his position on the suggestion of a steward. O'Byrne J. considered that there was no evidence that the Plaintiff voluntarily accepted or realised the risk. Black J., however, considered that there were many potential dangers incident to such an entertainment which the reasonable man expected to encounter and did not expect to be guarded against, and this he attributed to two factors, the remoteness of such dangers and the magnitude of the trouble and expense necessary to provide efficient protection. Lavery J. said: 'Spectators undertook to accept, subject to the discharge by the defendants of their responsibilities, the dangers inherent in the entertainment.'

In the *Killarney* case a racehorse, instead of jumping a hurdle in the ordinary way, jumped sideways over the wing and over or through the rails marking the course, injuring a spectator who was standing behind the rails. The court set aside a jury finding in favour of the plaintiff. Ó Dálaigh J. was of the opinion that the accident was so unusual and unexpected that the defendants were not bound to anticipate it. 'It was not the duty of the defendants to provide against improbable and unlikely happenings.' The Chief Justice, with whom Lavery J. agreed, also took this view, but he accepted that the risk of a horse swerving off the course was an obvious possibility which both the plaintiff and the defendants should know. The defendants had not failed in taking reasonable precautions and the plaintiff took the risk of such an occurrence which was inherent in the sport of racing. It also took the view that there was no evidence of a want of reasonable care on the part of the defendants and that the plaintiff took the risk of a possible but unlikely occurrence inherent in the nature of the sport.

In the present case I will assume that the defendant Club is to be regarded as being the occupier of the roads over which the race was run and of the ground on each side of those roads, and will assume further (though this seems to me doubtful) that it was under the same liability to a spectator, who had not paid for his right to be where he was, as it would have been to a paying spectator. I also assume, and if necessary am prepared to hold, that a spectator, who does not pay, accepts at least the same risks as, on the decisions, are accepted by a spectator who pays. Three questions appear to me to be raised:

(1) Was the occurrence of such an unusual and unexpected nature that there was no duty on the Club to take precautions against it?

(2) If it was not of such an unusual and expected nature, and if the Club were bound to take some precautions, did they take reasonable precautions?

(3) Was the risk one inherent in the sport of which the ordinary spectator must be deemed to be aware and of which he takes the risk?

That the occurrence was unusual and unexpected is not in issue. There was no evidence that in any previous race a car had left the course on a straight, nor was there evidence that this had happened on straight portions of other road racing courses. The possibility of such an occurrence however was one which, to my mind, must have been known to the Club and the ordinary spectator alike. Burst tyres, mechanical failures, minor errors of judgment, all these are inherent in the nature of the performance. It may well be that the occurrence was so rare and unusual that there was no obligation on the Club to safeguard spectators against it, and that the remote possibility of such a happening was inherent in the nature of the sport and was accepted as a risk by the ordinary spectator. But even if the Club were bound to anticipate as a reasonable probability that something might occur which would temporarily interfere with a driver's control of his vehicle, I consider that the Club took reasonable precautions against injury to spectators by such an occurrence, in as much as they took steps to keep spectators at a distance of 20 yards from the edge of the track. A burst tyre, or a collision, would ordinarily result in a car overturning or skidding down the road more or less in a straight line. If a car remained on its wheels the driver should be able by releasing the accelerator, applying the brakes, and using the steering wheel to prevent the car from diverging to the extent of 20 yards from the straight track. The circumstances of this accident are almost incomprehensible. The car remained on its wheels, apparently running under power, slanting gradually away from the line of the road and travelled for a distance of 220 yards before it reached the spectators. There was no evidence of any attempt to steer or brake the car. Such a combination of circumstances could not have been anticipated. I consider that the Club took reasonable precautions to keep the spectators out of the zone of any danger which could be anticipated, and that a jury could not properly hold otherwise, and I consider that, when such precautions had been taken, the risk of injury to a spectator was so excessively improbable that there was no obligation to guard against it.

Accordingly, even on the assumption that nonpaying spectators were entitled to the same rights as if they had paid, the Club is not liable to compensate the plaintiffs.

There remains the more difficult question of the liability of the owner of the car. The original swerve of the car and its subsequent behaviour when it safely reached the grass plain are completely unexplained. There is no evidence of any defect in steering or other mechanical defect. Undoubtedly the behaviour of the car is consistent with negligence on the part of the driver. It is also consistent with an error of judgment falling short of negligence, followed by an injury to the driver, when the car hit the mounds, which temporarily deprived that driver of consciousness and prevented him from controlling the car. Could a jury reasonably arrive at an inference, as opposed to a conjecture, that the facts were more consistent with negligence than with the absence of negligence? With great hesitation I have come to the conclusion that, failing any evidence or explanation on the part of the defendant, they might not unreasonably take this view. (I do not suggest that it is my own view.) Very little evidence on the part of the defendants would be sufficient to displace any such conclusion, but I think there must be a new trial as against Mr. Thompson at which, of course, the defendant will have the opportunity of giving such evidence, if available.

[**Maguire C.J.** in a separate judgment agreed with **Kingsmill Moore J. Lavery J.** agreed with **Maguire C.J.**'s judgment in so far as the case against the Irish Motor Racing Club was concerned, but felt that a jury could not convict, on the evidence, the deceased driver.]

Notes and Questions

1. To which category of entrant did the deceased spectator belong, in your opinion? Why?
2. What arguments would you make to show that the Club was under the same liability to a non-paying spectator as to a paying spectator?
3. Why should a non-paying spectator accept 'at least the same risks as . . . are accepted by a spectator who pays'? If a farmer tending his sheep on the Curragh on the day of the accident had taken a few minutes off to look at the race, what risks (if any) would he have assumed and why?
4. What is the effect of the enactment of section 34 (1) (*b*) of the *Civil Liability Act 1961? Cf. supra*, p. 205.
5. See also *White* v. *Blackmore* [1972] 3 All E.R. 158.
6. Is the duty of the Club to the spectators the same as the duty of the driver?
7. Is the duty of the Club the same to (a) a paying spectator and (b) the child of such a paying spectator whose ticket was paid for by his parent?

Invitee or Trespasser?

O'KEEFFE V. IRISH MOTOR INNS
[1978] I.R. 85

The plaintiff sustained serious injuries when he fell over a collection of beer barrels at the rere of the defendants' hotel. The jury awarded substantial damages. The defendants appealed.

O'Higgins C.J.:
. . . [I]n the first instance one must look at the evidence to see if it establishes the capacity in which the plaintiff was on the premises at the time. The critical time is the time of the accident and this cannot be established exactly by the evidence – but some approximation can be obtained. It appears that between 3.45 a.m. and 4 a.m. the plaintiff was found lying face downwards, unconscious, outside the kitchen door in the enclosed yard furthest from the front of the hotel. He had, of course, by then fallen. At a time stated to be between 3.15 a.m. and 3.30 a.m. the plaintiff had been let out of the front door of the hotel by Mr. Dorgan. It follows, therefore, that some time in the ensuing half-hour or so the plaintiff received his injuries somewhere on the hotel premises.

The permitted drinking period in the hotel had ended at midnight and the residential part of the hotel had been closed to non-residents from that time on. The dance had concluded in the function-room at 2 a.m. The plaintiff was shown out of the main hotel door by the manager long after the dance was over and after all the guests had departed. The circumstances of the plaintiff's departure from the hotel and the exchange of good-nights clearly indicated that the plaintiff was leaving, not remaining on, the hotel premises. So clear is the evidence in this respect that, in my view, it is incapable of any other construction.

Apparently, instead of leaving the hotel premises as he was expected to do, the plaintiff went to the function-room and later around by the side of the building towards the rere of the hotel. He did so, according to his own evidence, in the mistaken belief that the dance was still on and that he might get a lift home from one of the guests. Accepting that this was his reason in not proceeding to leave the defendants' premises, what effect, if any, did it have on his continued presence on these premises? It was clearly the defendants' intention (and they were certainly entitled to believe and expect) that the plaintiff, having been shown out of the front door and having been wished a good-night, would proceed to leave the hotel premises. The fact was that at this stage (at 3.15 or 3.30 a.m.) all the hotel activities had ceased and all visitors had long since gone home. In such circumstances could an independent decision of the plaintiff not to leave, based on an erroneous belief that the dance was still on, clothe his continued presence on the defendants' premises with authority from them, or put him in the position of having been invited by them so to remain? In my view, this could not be so. An objective test must be applied.

If the plaintiff was on the defendants' premises earlier that night as an invitee, this does not mean that he continued to be such so long as he remained on the premises. He would have to comply with the terms of the invitation as to where he went and as to how long he could remain. When his legitimate visit as a hotel guest or customer came to an end, as it most certainly did when he was conducted out of the front door by the manager, so did his invitation apart from the time required to permit him to leave the hotel grounds. The fact that he had been an invitee up to that point did not authorise or permit him to wander at his will, without the knowledge and contrary to the expectation of the defendants, over the hotel grounds long after all hotel activities had ceased.

In my view, the evidence clearly established, without any question, that not only was the plaintiff at the time of his accident not an invitee of the defendants but that in law he was a trespasser on their premises at that time since he was there without their knowledge or permission. The term trespasser is a word which has an unfortunate connotation, but in law it simply means a person who is on another's land without permission. This can be quite an innocent presence which carries no sinister, disrespectful or ugly implication. However, the fact that the plaintiff was a trespasser does not mean the end of the case.

It is now necessary to consider what duty was owed by the defendants to the plaintiff in the circumstances. The injuries were sustained on the defendants' premises by a person who at the time was a trespasser in law. It used to be said that in such circumstances the only duty owed by the occupier of property was not to act with reckless disregard of the trespasser's presence or of his safety, but this is not a correct statement of the law; see *McNamara* v. *Electricity Supply Board* [1975] I.R. 1. Irrespective of the capacity in which a person is on another's land, regard must be had to the actual circumstances and to what in those circumstances is known by or can reasonably be expected from the occupier as to such person's presence or actions. If the presence of persons on one's property without permission is habitual and well known, it may well be negligence if one acts in disregard of that fact. It is a question of foreseeability and regard must be had to all the circumstances including, of course, the time and the actual place where the person is at the time of the accident or injury. Indeed the test of reasonable foreseeability is, in my view, sufficiently flexible to cover all such cases where a person is injured on another's land.

Accordingly, in my view, in the circumstances of this case regard must be had to what the defendants could expect or could have reasonably foreseen in relation to the presence and conduct of the plaintiff at the time and place of the accident. As hoteliers the defendants were entitled to, and did, have their hours of business and their closed periods. In addition, they had areas of their premises open to their guests and areas not so open. If the plaintiff's fall and injuries were caused by his coming in contact with a collection of beer barrels, it must have occurred at the corner of the short wall marking the boundary of the outer yard. The evidence clearly established that the only collection of barrels at the time of the plaintiff's accident was at this point. Again, if the plaintiff's accident was so caused it must have been caused when the plaintiff, if on foot, was travelling at a high speed. This is clearly established by the medical evidence.

The accident, wherever and however it occurred, must have happened between about 3.30 a.m. and 4 a.m. when the hotel was, and had been for some time, closed for the night. Could it be said that the defendants ought to have anticipated such an occurrence? I find it absolutely impossible to say that they could. It seems to me to be bordering on the absurd to say that Mr. Dorgan, or any of the defendants' staff, could or ought to have expected that a man who had left the hotel in order to go home long after all the hotel activities had ceased would still be on the outside of the hotel premises at about 4 a.m. and, further, that he would at that time be running in darkness towards the rere kitchen quarters of the hotel in such a manner as to crash into a collection of barrels collected at the corner of this yard wall. In these circumstances to suggest placing some blame on the defendants is virtually to suggest that the defendants must be to blame because the plaintiff had his accident. I am driven to the conclusion that in the circumstances of this case there was no evidence to suggest that the defendants could be in any way to blame for the plaintiff's unfortunate and tragic accident.

Kenny J.:

. . . On principle it would seem that the occupier's invitation extends to those places into which he, as a prudent man, may anticipate that the invitee will be likely to go *and* where the invitee may reasonably believe that he is entitled or invited to go. If the invitee goes outside this area, he becomes a trespasser. It would also seem that the invitation may be limited by time. An invitation to enter during working hours may not continue after working hours have ended; and an invitation to enter during the day time may not survive into the night. This statement is, I think, in accordance with the authorities and with the best text-books on the subject.

In *Walker* v. *Midland Railway Co.* 55 L.T. 489 (1886) the Earl of Selborne, when delivering the judgment of the majority of the House of Lords on the ambit of the invitation to a guest in a hotel, said at p. 490 of the report:– 'I think it impossible to hold that the general duty of an innkeeper to take proper care for the safety of his guests extends to every room in his house, at all hours of night or day, irrespective of the question whether any such guests may have a right, or some reasonable cause, to be there. The duty must, I think, be limited to those places into which guests may reasonably be supposed to be likely to go, in the belief, reasonably entertained, that they are entitled or invited to do so.' This passage in the Earl of Selborne's judgment was cited by Kingsmill Moore J. when sitting as a judge of the High Court on Circuit in *Reaney* v. *Thomas Lydon & Sons Ltd* [1957] Ir. Jur. Rep. 1. He went on to formulate the test in these words at p. 3 of the report:– 'The ambit of invitation extends to those places and is limited to those places into which guests may reasonably be supposed to be likely to go, in the belief, reasonably entertained, that they are entitled or invited to do so.' The judge then considered the question of the liability to a guest who had bona fide strayed from the apparent area of invitation and said:– '. . . if a person has entered on an area to which he was clearly invited and if he has strayed from that area, the question is not so much whether or not he has been invited to stray, as whether or not there was anything to delimit the apparent area of invitation.'

Mr. Justice Kingsmill Moore's statement of the law as to straying invitees deals with invitees who reasonably believe that they are entitled to go into the area which is not within the ambit of the invitation. It is a good general rule but not a universal one. The surroundings, the place entered or the appearances may be such that without an express delimitation, the area is outside the ambit of the invitation. In Lord Justice Scrutton's famous illustration of the man sliding down the bannisters, it surely is not necessary to put a delimitation notice on them before inviting a guest into one's house for dinner.

In *Hillen* v. *I.C.I. (Alkali) Ltd*. [1936] A.C. 65 Lord Atkin, when speaking of the duty of the invitor to an invitee, said at p. 69 of the report:– . . . this duty to an invitee only extends so long as and so far as the invitee is making what can reasonably be contemplated as an ordinary and reasonable use of the premises by the invitee for the purposes for which he has been invited'.

In Professor Prosser's text-book [Handbook of the Law of Torts, 4th ed., 1971], the area of the invitation is discussed in detail at pp. 391 and 392. He wrote:– 'The special obligation towards invitees exists only while the visitor is upon the part of the premises which the occupier has thrown open to him for the purpose which makes him an invitee. The "area of invitation" will of course vary with the circumstances of the case. It extends to the entrance to the property, and to a safe exit after the purpose is concluded; and extends to all those parts of the premises to which the purpose may reasonably be expected to take him, and to those which are so arranged as to lead him reasonably to think that they are open to him . . . If the customer is invited or encouraged to go to an unusual part of the premises, such as behind the counter or into a storeroom, for the purpose which has brought him, he remains an invitee: but if he goes without such encouragement and solely on his own initiative, he is only a licensee if there is consent, or a trespasser if there is not . . . *There are similar limitations of time*; and if the invitee remains on the land beyond the time reasonably necessary to accomplish the purpose for which he came, and to withdraw from the premises, he becomes at most a licensee thereafter.' I have added the emphasis.

Stone v. *Taffe* [1974] 1 W. L.R. 1575 is the latest case on the matter which I have been able to find. I do not think that it states any new principle: it is an application of existing ones only. It illustrates the view that a limitation as to time on an invitation to enter and remain on premises must be communicated to the invitee before it binds him.

I come now to apply the general principle I have stated and those enunciated by the Earl of Selborne, by Kingsmill Moore J. and by Professor Prosser. The first aspect of the matter relates to the defendants, the invitors: could they have foreseen that it was likely that at a time between 3 a.m. and 3.30 a.m. the plaintiff, instead of leaving the premises, would go along the front of the hotel and then walk along the footpath at the side for a distance of 69 feet? They knew that the tarmacadam surface extended back for 69 feet from an imaginary line created by extending the line of the front of the building across the strip, and they knew that cars were sometimes parked there. They also knew that the bars for the sale of intoxicating liquor had closed at midnight, that the dance had ended at 2 a.m. and that the plaintiff was the last non-resident guest to leave. They were aware that the car-park in the front was brightly illuminated, that there were no cars on it and that the strip was in complete darkness. In my opinion they as prudent men, could not have foreseen that the plaintiff, who was not a resident guest, would go into the dark strip which led only to the doors (long since closed) of the kitchen and stores, instead of leaving the grounds by crossing the illuminated car-park and going down the avenue. No prudent person could have anticipated this.

The second aspect relates to the plaintiff, the invitee: could he have reasonably had the belief that he was entitled or invited to walk along the footpath at the side of the strip for a distance of 69 feet or, indeed, for any length? The best answer is provided by his own words when giving evidence:– 'I was going from light into darkness. I was in a dangerous position. I was actually blind at that time.' He could not have believed that he was entitled or invited by the defendants to put himself in a dangerous position. Walking along the footpath in complete darkness was very foolish, particularly as he knew that it had a considerable risk attached to it. When he turned the corner he did not see any cars with lights on the tarmacadam and he must have realised that there was no chance of getting a lift from any car which might be parked on the strip. There was a car parked there which belonged to a member of the staff and one of the mysteries of the case is how he got past it without seeing it. When he turned the corner, he was leaving a brightly lit area and going into a dark one. The defendants did not delimit this area so as to exclude it from the area to which he was invited but it is difficult to see how they could have done so at night because the area was not outside the ambit of the invitation in daytime. As I have already said, the circumstances and appearance may amount to a delimitation. The lighting of the front and the complete absence of light in the side amounted, in my opinion, to a sufficient delimitation. On this aspect of the case, the time element is critical. He could not have believed that he, a non-resident invitee, was entitled or invited to go into the area at the side at 3 a.m. or 3.30 a.m. In my opinion, the plaintiff became a trespasser when he started to walk along the footpath at the strip side of the building.

If the plaintiff was a trespasser when he turned the corner and continued to walk, the question arises what duty the defendants owed him and whether they committed a breach of it. I have had the advantage of reading the judgment of the Chief Justice and I agree with what he has written on this branch of the case. I think that this case should have been withdrawn from the jury's consideration at the end of the evidence, and this appeal succeeds and that the action should be dismissed.

Henchy, Griffin and Parke J.J. concurred with **O'Higgins C.J.**

Notes and Questions

Canadian courts have considered the question of the 'area of invitation' in several cases over the past twenty years: see, *e.g. Stephens* v. *Corcoran* 65 D.L.R. (2d) 407 (Ont., 1965); *Jones* v. *Triton Centres Ltd.* 4 D.L.R. (3d) 327 (n.s., 1969); *Sanders* v. *Frawley Lake Lumber Co. Ltd.* 19 D.L.R. (3d) 378 (Ont., 1971); *Jesmer* v. *Bert Katz Real Estate Ltd.* 33 D.L.R. (3d) 662 (Ont., 1972); *Lichty* v. *K.E. Holidays Ltd.* 35 D.L.R. (3d) 561 (B.C., 1973). See also the English cases, *Pearson* v. *Coleman Bros.* [1948] 2 K.B. 359; *Stone* v. *Taffe* [1974] 1 W.L.R. 1575 (mentioned in Kenny J.'s judgment).

Effect of a warning to the invitee.

MAGUIRE V. PACIFIC STEAM NAVIGATION CO. LTD. & NEWMAN & SONS LTD.

Unreported Sup. Ct. 26 May 1955

Maguire C.J.:

The plaintiff, a docker, was employed by the second named defendants who are stevedores, in the unloading of a part cargo of nitrate of soda on the Steamship

'Santander' the property of the first named defendants, when bags of sugar, part of the cargo, fell upon him and injured him.

His action for damages for negligence was tried before McLoughlin J. and a jury.

At the conclusion of the plaintiff's case the learned Trial Judge on the application of Counsel for the second-named defendants dismissed the action as against them with costs. The jury found that the cargo of sugar constituted an unusual danger that the defendants knew or ought to have known of such danger, that they failed to take reasonable care to prevent injury being caused to the plaintiff by such danger and that the injuries were caused by such danger. They found also that the plaintiff did not know of such danger; that he was not negligent and that he did not voluntarily accept the risk. They assessed damages at £3,500 for which sum Judgment was entered. The Trial Judge ordered that the plaintiff be recouped against the appellants the cost which he is liable to pay and does pay to the defendants.

The appellants appeal against the Order and Judgment in favour of the plaintiff and also against the part of the Order which makes them responsible for the costs which the plaintiff is ordered to pay to the other defendants.

The plaintiff appeals against the Order and Judgment dismissing the action against the second named defendants.

In the argument before this Court these appellants confined their argument to their contention that the jury's findings that the plaintiff did not know of the danger and that he did not voluntarily accept the risk should be set aside as not being supported by the évidence and that they should not be ordered to recoup the plaintiff the costs which he was ordered to pay the second named defendants. No difficulty arises if it be held that the evidence supports the finding of the jury that the plaintiff was unaware of the existence of the dangerous state of the premises and that he was not negligent. If this stands the finding brings the case exactly within the principle laid down in the well-known passage in the Judgment of Willes J. in the Court of Common Plea in *Indermaur* v. *Dames*, L.R.1 C.P. 274: L.R.2 C.P. 311, which runs:– 'With respect to such a visitor at least, we consider it settled law, that he, using reasonable care on his part for his own safety, is entitled to expect that the occupier shall on his part use reasonable care to prevent damage from unusual danger, which he knows or ought to know; and that, where there is evidence of neglect, the question whether such reasonable care has been taken, by notice, lighting, guarding, or otherwise, and whether there was contributory negligence in the sufferer, must be determined by a jury as matter of fact.'

If, however, the finding that the plaintiff did not know of the danger which threatened him is set aside the question which arose in: *The London Graving Dock Co.* v. *Horton*, [1951] A.C. p. 737, and in *Long* v. *The Saorstat & Continental Shipping Co.* (unreported [when judgment issued, but reported now 93 I.L.T.R. 137 (1953) – *eds.*[ ) in this country, has to be considered.

I have come to the conclusion that the finding that the plaintiff did not know of the danger cannot stand. I am however of opinion that the finding of the jury that he did not voluntarily accept the risk cannot be interfered with.

This being the position the question to be considered is whether an invitor can be held liable in tort for injury caused by the dangerous state of his premises of which he knew or ought to have known to an invitee who though sciens was neither volens nor careless of his own safety. This is how Lord MacDermott stated the problem in: *Horton's Case*, [1951] A.C. 737 at 760. This question was argued before this Court in: *Long* v. *Saorstát & Continental Steamship Co.* 93 I.L.T.R. 137 (1953). In that case the plaintiff had been over-balanced and thrown into the hold by the tipping upwards of a gangway where it rested upon the deck of a ship which, as a docker, he was helping to unload. The Court were unanimously of opinion that if the gangway was tethered in such a way that it could only swing or tip upwards without swaying to either side that it could not be held to be an unusual danger. A majority of the Court however considered that there was evidence from which the jury might find that the injury was caused by the end of the gangway 'splaying' or swinging laterally. As it was considered that his question was not fully or properly investigated and that the trial in that respect was unsatisfactory the case was sent back for a new trial.

In the course of his Judgment however, Kingsmill Moore J. deemed it necessary to deal with the question raised in *Horton's Case*. He said – 'The dispute has centred round the effect which knowledge of the danger to the invitee had upon the liability of the occupier. Does such knowledge whether conveyed to the invitee by the occupier or independently acquired by the invitee absolve the occupier from the need to take further precautions? Does it affect the classification of a danger as usual or unusual and can it turn an unusual danger into a usual? On these questions Judges and writers of text books alike have been divided.'

The conflicting views are succinctly stated in the speech of Lord MacDermott at page 761 and by other Law Lords in varying terms but all to the same effect. The majority of the Law Lords held that the invitee's knowledge of the usual risk exonerated the occupiers from liability for the damage sustained by the invitee. Kingsmill Moore J. finds himself unable to accept this view. He stated his opinion as follows:– 'It is for a jury to determine under proper direction whether in all the circumstances the occupier has failed to discharge his duty by taking reasonable care to prevent injury to the invitee from unusual danger. There are many such dangers which an invitee exercising reasonable care for his own safety can avoid if he had knowledge of their nature and extent while at the same time carrying out the purpose for which he has come. The matter may be so clear that a Judge can decide that there is no evidence of any neglect on the part of the occupier and no question to be left to a jury. When the matter is doubtful a jury should be directed to find for the occupier if in their opinion an invitee exercising reasonable care for his own safety and with such knowledge of the danger as he has been proved to possess could adequately carry out the purpose for which he has come without running risk of injury.' At a later stage in his Judgment he sums up his view as follows:– 'An occupier of premises is liable for injury caused to his invitees by a danger on his premises which he knows or ought to know is unusual, in the sense above explained, unless he has taken reasonable precautions to safeguard the invitee, or unless the invitee has knowledge of the danger. The duty to take reasonable precautions may be discharged by taking measures which should give the invitee knowledge of the danger. But even knowledge on the part of the invitee, whether imparted to him by the occupier or independently possessed by the invitee, will not excuse the occupier unless the invitee by virtue of such knowledge can efficiently carry out the task for which he has come without exposing himself to such danger.' O'Byrne J. and Lavery J., agreed with this view.

Is this opinion to be regarded as a decision binding upon this Court? Counsel for the appellant contended that it is not and re-argued the question as if it was still open. As the case went back to be re-tried on the ground above-mentioned it was open to the jury on the re-trial to find that the plaintiff was aware of the unusual danger from a gangway so fastened that it might swing laterally in its upward tilt when someone proceeded along it to leave the ship. It was therefore necessary that the extent of the duty of an invitor in such circumstances should be explained, as the Trial Judge would require to have an authoritative exposition of the law on this point. The opinion of the Court on this point cannot be regarded as merely obiter and is therefore binding on this Court. I may add that if it were still open my view would be the same as that of Kingsmill Moore J.

The only difficulty which then arises is whether the jury have found and whether the evidence supports a finding that the defendants failed to take adequate precautions for the safety of the plaintiff. An effort had been made by placing a net in position to prevent the danger to the plaintiff. This proved ineffective. It would seem clear that something more could have been done and that in the last resort danger could have been avoided by removing the portion of the cargo from which danger threatened.

I am accordingly of opinion that this appeal fails.

The question as to whether these defendants should have been ordered to recoup the plaintiff the costs against him in favour of the other defendants must await the determination of the appeal of the plaintiff against the Order dismissing the action against them.

Kingsmill Moore J. agreed with **Maguire C.J.'s** judgment and adhered to the view already expressed in *Long's* case. No other judgment is recorded.

'Unusual danger'. Workman also viewed as invitee.
KENNY V. IRISH SHIPPING LIMITED
Unreported Sup. Ct. 4 Nov. 1968

Budd J.:

The plaintiff in these proceedings was employed as a donkey-man by the defendant company. Part of his duties consisted of greasing and oiling the ship's engines and he also assisted in cleaning the decks around the engines. He was at the time of the matters complained of a member of the crew of the Irish Plane, one of the ships constituting the defendant company's fleet of vessels. The proceedings arise out of an accident which the plaintiff alleges occurred to him when the vessel was approaching the port of Ilo Ilo, which is situate in the Philippine Islands, on the 5th October, 1965.

On the occasion in question the plaintiff had reported for duty on the lower deck of the engine-room at about 9 a.m. At sometime shortly after this he was instructed to squeeze some water pumps situate on the lowest deck in the engine-room. It was necessary to get some hot water for this purpose which was to be found in the crew's quarters. He, therefore, went to the crew's quarters, collected the water in a bucket and returned by way of a short staircase leading to the middle deck of the engine-room. This middle deck of the engine-room is made of steel plates which have diamond grooves on the surface. He says that when he stepped on the plates 'his feet went from underneath him and he fell.' Broadly speaking his allegation was that he had fallen by reason of the plates of the deck being greasy or oily.

The plaintiff claims that his injuries were caused by the negligence of the defendants as owners of the ship in failing to provide a safe place of work and a safe system of working by reason of their allowing grease or oil to be on the deck and because of their failure to remove such oil or grease.

The action came on for hearing before Mr. Justice Butler and a jury on the 23rd January, 1968. Counsel for the defendants applied at the end of the plaintiff's case for a direction on the basis that there was no evidence of any actionable negligence. This application was refused and the defendants went into evidence. The jury failed to answer any of the questions left to them and were discharged, the trial being adjourned.

This appeal is taken by the defendants from the learned trial judge's refusal to grant a direction and the defendants also seek judgment in their favour.

The defendants submitted in the first place that there was no evidence from which a jury could reasonably infer that the plaintiff had slipped on oil or grease or indeed as to what caused him to slip. The plaintiff was, however, cross-examined in detail about the fall and he gave the following evidence: 'I slipped on grease, a greasy surface.' On being asked if he looked to see what it was he said: 'Yes. The surface was greasy.' On again being asked if he saw any grease he answered: 'I seen a dirty oily surface beneath where I fell. I could not be sure whether it was grease or oil.' The plaintiff's evidence was, admittedly, somewhat contradictory in that when first asked about what made him slip he had said: 'It is obvious I slipped on something, a greasy surface or oil or something.' It might well be suggested that the plaintiff had improved his evidence as he went along but it was a matter for the jury to assess the weight which they would give to the evidence taken as a whole and in my view it would have been quite within the province of the jury to find that the plaintiff had fallen on a greasy or oily surface.

The fact that there was evidence from which a jury might infer, if so minded, that the plaintiff slipped on grease or oil does not mean that the plaintiff is entitled to succeed in the action. The defendants are not in law insurers of the plaintiff's safety. It is their duty to him as an invitee not to expose him to any unusual danger or risk, that is to say, one which is not usually found in carrying out the task which he had in hand (*London Graving Dock Company Limited* v. *Horton* [1951] A.C. 739).

The defendants submitted that there was no evidence from which the jury could reasonably infer that the plaintiff was exposed to any unusual risk in his service and that the learned trial judge was, therefore, in error in leaving the case to the jury on such a ground. The trial judge in fact left the matter to the jury on the basis that it was for them to decide whether or not an unusual danger existed by reason of there being an undue accumulation of oil or grease at the place where the plaintiff slipped, that is to say an accumulation greater than was normally to be found on the surface of the plates in the engine-room.

The evidence indicates that there were several persons employed to grease and oil the engines and to keep the decks of the engine-room clean. It is an inescapable inference from this and other evidence that there must inevitably be a certain amount of oil or grease on the decks surrounding the engine. Some oil must be spilled or grease dropped in the course of going round the engines. A great heat must be generated by the engines of a ship, causing the dripping or splashing of oil and grease. It must, therefore, have been a normal feature of this engine-room that there should be a certain amount of oil or grease on the plates from time to time. In addition to the evidence of the plaintiff to which I have already referred touching on the condition of the plates on which he fell there was some important evidence bearing on the very point as to the quantum of oil or grease on the plate on which he slipped. The plaintiff was asked: 'As a matter of fact is there not always a certain amount of grease or oil around the engine room?' and his answer was: 'Not a thick layer of grease.' Incidentally the clear implication from that answer is that a certain amount of grease and oil is always to be expected. The judge then observed: 'This is the first time I have heard about a thick layer.' Mr. Micks then asked the plaintiff: 'Are you now saying there was a thick layer of grease?' and the plaintiff's answer was a simple 'No'.

Taking the evidence as a whole and the last-mentioned answer of the plaintiff in particular it is to my mind clear that there was no evidence on which the jury could properly have found that the plaintiff was exposed to any unusual danger and the case, therefore, should not have been left to the jury on that issue.

The plaintiff's case was also put on the basis that it was the duty of his employers to have in operation a safe system of work in particular by way of inspection to see that the plates of the engine-room decks were not left in a slippery and dangerous condition. The defendants submit that there was no evidence of any failure on the part of the defendants to have a proper system of inspection and cleaning of the engine-room decks.

The evidence with regard to the system of inspection and cleaning of the engine-room was as follows. Mr. Byrne, the second engineer, was responsible for seeing that the engine-room was kept clean. His evidence was to the effect that there were four men whose duty it was to keep the engine-room clean and that there were three of them engaged on his particular task on the morning when the accident occurred. There was no evidence that I have been able to discover suggesting that an inadequate team of cleaners was provided. The evidence does not, moreover, indicate that there was any failure in the operation of the system of work by those whose duty it was to carry out the cleaning of the engine-room.

There was in particular no evidence from which it would be reasonable to draw the inference that there had been a failure to inspect the plates of the engine-room as for example by showing that the plate in question had been in an oily or greasy condition for some considerable time. The evidence in fact was all the other way because it would appear that the plaintiff himself had passed over this particular plate to mount the ladder to the crew's quarters where he collected the water to wash the pumps a short while before the accident and he did not notice anything the matter with the plate on that occasion. The reasonable inference is that the presence of oil or grease on the plate was of recent origin. There was in fact no evidence of such oil or grease as may have been on the plate being left there for any unreasonable time or that the defendants knew or ought to have known of its presence nor was there any evidence of failure of inspection.

In the circumstances which I have just detailed there was no evidence of any failure on the part of the defendants to perform their duty of providing a safe system of work by way of inspection or otherwise. The plaintiff's case, therefore, fails on this ground also.

In the foregoing circumstances the case should have been withdrawn from the jury and I would allow this appeal.

[**Ó Dálaigh C.J.** (with whom **Haugh J.** concurred) delivered a judgment to the same effect.]

Notes and Questions

1. Cases where infants have been injured when motor vehicles have been put in motion are now normally dealt with on straight negligence principles. A former tendency to deal with these cases in occupiers' liability language seems now to have been abandoned in favour of the negligence approach.

   Contrast, for example, the Court's approach in *Donovan* v. *Landy's Ltd,* ([1963] I.R. 441) with the approach taken in *Brennan* v. *Savage Smyth & Co. Ltd.* [1982] I.L.M.R. See also *Breslin* v. *Brennan* [1937] I.R. 350 and *Griffin* v. *Daniels* 223 (Sup. Ct.). 86 I.L.T.R. 38.

2. Why do not injured workmen more frequently base their claims on the grounds of their status as invitees?

Children injured by dangerous objects taken without authority from occupier's premises.

BYRNE V. MacDONALD
Unreptd. Sup. Ct. 7 Feb. 1957

Kingsmill Moore J.:

In these two actions, which have been consolidated, Michael Byrne, an infant, now aged fourteen, sues the Wexford County Council and Alan MacDonald, one of their assistant engineers, claiming damages for negligence. As against MacDonald the allegation is that, having detonators in his custody, he failed to keep them safely and allowed them to fall into the hands of young children with the result that the Plaintiff was injured. As against the Wexford County Council it is alleged that they for their own purposes store and use detonators, that MacDonald was acting as their servant when in control of the detonators and that accordingly they are liable for his negligence. At the trial, when the plaintiff's case was concluded the learned judge withdrew from the jury the case against the County Council on the ground that there was not sufficient evidence to justify a jury in finding that MacDonald, if he left the detonators in the shed, was acting as a servant of the County Council within the scope of his employment in so doing.

The case proceeded against MacDonald and the jury found that the detonators were taken by his son Alan from a box in his shed and given to Jimmy Byrne, a brother of the plaintiff, that MacDonald senior was negligent, but that the Plaintiff was guilty of contributory negligence. The plaintiff now appeals to this court on the ground that the learned judge was wrong in withdrawing from the jury the case against the County Council, and that there was no evidence to justify him in leaving to the jury an issue of contributory negligence in the case against MacDonald. He also complains that the charge of the learned judge did not correctly lay down the law in regard to contributory negligence by young children.

The story as to the procurement of the detonator and the circumstances which led up to the accident depends on the evidence of young boys and there are minor discrepancies between their accounts, but the jury by their finding have accepted the essential part of the story that the detonators were in a shed belonging to the Defendant MacDonald and were given by his son Alan to the plaintiff's brother. In more detail the evidence given by the plaintiff's witnesses was as follows:

On Sunday January 24th 1954 after lunch the plaintiff, then aged 10½ went with his brother Jim aged 8 to the premises of the defendant MacDonald to play with his two sons Donald aged 11 and Alan aged 6 and two other boys Robert O'Leary aged 14 and Patsy O'Leary aged 11. After a short while the plaintiff and Donald MacDonald went to the plaintiff's house to exchange some 'comics'. While they were away Alan MacDonald, the plaintiff's brother Jim, and Patsy O'Leary went into a tool shed opening off the garage of the Defendant MacDonald. The shed was locked but there was a key in the lock and Alan turned the key and went in. When they had got in Alan took down a round paint tin which was full, or partly full, of metal objects, which were in fact detonators. He poured some into his hand and gave six or seven to Jim, and one to Patsy. According to Patsy, Alan said that 'If you put oil in it and hit it with a hammer it would blow up and make a bang'. Jim says that the words were 'If you hit them with a hammer or put oil in them they would blow you up'. The tin was then replaced, the boys pocketed the detonators they had been given, went out and resumed their play. The detonators were harmless looking things being as far as the eye could see: tubes of thin bright metal closed at one end about $1\frac{1}{2}$ inches long and the diameter of a pencil. Specimens were produced at the trial and also to us. The detonating chemicals were packed at the closed end and there was a considerable empty space at the open and left for the insertion of a fuse. The general appearance was that of the top of the case of a clinical thermometer. Patsy says he thought they were pencil tops. It is clear from the way in which Patsy and Jim subsequently handled them that they had not the slightest conception of the concealed danger. Patsy took his detonator home with him and next day threw it in the fire where it exploded, fortunately without doing any injury to anyone. Jim also took back his six or seven detonators to his home and that night openly played with them in the kitchen before his parents, rolling them round the floor. At one time he gave them to his father to hold and his father saw nothing in them to make him think they had any harmful potentialities.

That night, or perhaps next morning, Jim gave the detonators to his brother, the Plaintiff, and in the morning he started to play with them before the fire in the kitchen, where his mother and a baby sister were also present. He rolled them about in his handkerchief and put some on a chair. Then he did a thing which at first seems inexplicable. He cut the red phosphorus heads off three matches and put the heads into the hollow end of the detonator. Having done this, holding the detonator in his left hand, with another match he lighted the match heads. As a result he blew away a considerable portion of his left hand and inflicted a wound on his thigh.

The explanation of his action lies in a boy's trick which the Plaintiff knew and had tried before. The hollow end of a key is stuffed with one or more match heads. A nail is then inserted and driven in by hitting it against something. The result is that the match heads produce a tiny and harmless explosion and a most satisfying bang. It was not suggested that this procedure when carried out with a key was in any way dangerous. To the plaintiff the hollow detonator casing carried no more promise of danger than a key. He said that he hoped the result of his action would be to make a bang – a loud bang – and that no one had told him it would explode.

He was cross-examined as to whether the detonators were 'like bullets' and he assented. He said he had seen bullets before and that they were wider but not so long. He was asked if he knew what would happen if he put a match to a bullet and he said 'I never put a match to it before'. Counsel then suggested to him 'I suppose it would explode' and he said, 'Yes, sir'. He then reverted to his statement that he wanted to make a bang, and was just trying it for pleasure.

I confess that I do not understand this cross-examination.

In any correct usage 'bullet' means a metal projectile which has not in itself any explosive properties. It was alleged, however, that in popular speech 'bullet' is used as being equivalent to a loaded and unfired rifle or revolver cartridge, and that this word was used by counsel and understood by the witness in this sense. Whichever meaning was in counsel's mind I find great difficulty in assuming that the witness understood the word in the sense suggested for the detonator produced bears not the slightest resemblance to a loaded and unfired rifle or revolver cartridge. It does bear a resemblance to a small calibre empty cartridge case from which the bullet has already been fired, but such an empty case would, of course, have been harmless. Whatever counsel meant or whatever the boy understood, I cannot find any justification for attributing to the plaintiff any knowledge or even suspicion that the result of his action would produce any harmful or dangerous results or indeed anything different in character from his experiments with match heads and a key, nor can I find any reason why he should have anticipated any danger. The making of bangs has a fascination for children and the practice is tolerated, though without much enthusiasm, by their elders. What child has not with its parents' permission owned a pistol firing percussion caps (which cause small explosions), or let off a 'slap-bang', or squib?

I am unable to find any evidence of contributory negligence on the part of the plaintiff. Contributory negligence consists in failing to take reasonable care for one's own safety. The act or omission must be judged in the light of the knowledge, actual or imputed, which the plaintiff has, for if there is, or should be, no knowledge that the act or omission involves danger then the Plaintiff cannot be convicted of failing to take reasonable care. To every adult is imputed the knowledge of risks which the normal reasonable man may be assumed to have, and to children the knowledge which children of the age of the actor may be assumed to have. Even the normal and reasonable adult could not, in my opinion, be assumed to know that these apparently harmless metal tubes contained a dangerous explosive, and still less could such knowledge be imputed to a child. If the tubes had not contained an explosive the experiment with the match heads would not have been calculated to cause any injury and the action of the boy could not, in my opinion, have been regarded as negligent. The presence of a dangerous explosive could not have been known to the boy unless he had been expressly warned, and there is no evidence that anyone had ever given him any warning. The cryptic remark about oil and a hammer was made to his brother Jim who did not repeat it.

The issue of contributory negligence should not, in my opinion, have been left to the jury, for there was no evidence to support an affirmative finding.

The next question is whether the learned judge was correct in directing that there was no evidence fit to be submitted to the jury as against the County Council. The main store of gelignite and detonators owned by the County Council is a magazine at Wexford, and when considerable quantities are needed for any work the explosives are brought in a special van from the magazine to the scene of operations. Any large quantity unused is brought back by the same van, but small quantities left over, both of gelignite and detonators, may be kept in locked huts at the various quarries. The defendant MacDonald as assistant county engineer was entitled to draw from the magazine detonators for use in the quarries under his charge and usually drew them in boxes of 100 at a time. He might draw more than one box. On April 23rd 1953 he drew 300 and he says that from that date up to the date of the accident (January 24th 1954) he was 'making use of those detonators which had been issued to me.' It was part of his duty to carry these detonators to the places where they were required for use. He would bring detonators from the magazine to the quarries and from quarry to quarry and would allow some to be kept in the quarry huts. Sometimes he kept detonators in his office in Enniscorthy but, although he said it would not be a breach of duty for him to take them to his house, he denied that he had ever brought any to his house or to his shed. He said that he did no private work as engineer, did not have any detonators in the house in his private capacity or for his personal use, and did not have any detonators in his possession that were not the property of the County Council. He could not remember having had any detonators under his control at the relevant period that were not the property of the County Council. The jury, in the action against MacDonald, found that the detonators were in his shed and that he was negligent. There was ample evidence to justify both these findings. To make the County Council liable a jury would also have to find that the detonators in question were part of a stock which he had obtained as engineer to the County Council and which it was his duty to keep from getting into the hands of unauthorised persons. It was admitted that as such engineer he drew large quantities of detonators up to 300 at a time, and he said that he had no detonators from any other source. From where did the detonators in the shed (according to one witness there were about 30) come? I am of opinion that a jury might reasonably come to the conclusion that on a balance of probabilities those detonators were part of a stock drawn by him as engineer to the County Council and which he had brought home and put in the shed, with the intention of keeping them there till they were requested and which, he may, perhaps, have forgotten about. If this were the fact he would have been negligent in carrying out his duty as their servant to keep the detonators safely and see that they did not come into unauthorised, inexperienced, or ignorant hands, and the County Council would be liable for his negligence. In my view the case should not have been withdrawn from the jury.

These issues as far as they affect the County Council have not been determined. There should be a new trial as against the County Council and a verdict should be entered against MacDonald in the action against him. As the jury did not consider the question of damages there must be an enquiry as to damages.

[**Maguire J.** agreed that the direction should not have been given in favour of the defendants, the Wexford County Council and that a re-trial of all issues should be granted. No other written judgment was delivered.]

Liability to Trespassers.

PURTILL V. ATHLONE URBAN DISTRICT COUNCIL
[1968] I.R. 205 (Sup. Ct.)

Walsh J.:

On the relevant dates the defendants owned and operated an abattoir in the town of Athlone. The method of slaughter of the animals, carried out by the defendants' employees, was by the use of a humane killer which is a pistol-like instrument in which the power is supplied by the explosion of a detonator. A separate detonator is employed for each use of the instrument and the defendants kept a stock of these detonators on the premises for the purpose of carrying on the work of the abattoir. The premises were situated about a half a mile from the residence of the plaintiff and he passed the abattoir every day going to, and coming from, school. The doors of the abattoir were open from 9 a.m. until about 6 p.m. and apparently it was customary for boys to go into the premises without objection from the caretaker of the premises or the employees working at the slaughter of the animals. At the time of the accident in respect of which he has sued, the plaintiff was fourteen years old and he had visited the abattoir premises on about ten occasions in the previous five years, always with other boys. The visits were during the periods when the doors were open and apparently the gate leading into the premises was never shut during those hours. In the course of his visits he had seen the method used for killing the animals and had observed that the detonators were kept on a shelf in the office and also in the actual place of killing, where they were left on a stool.

On Thursday, the 14th November, 1963, he went to the premises with another boy, named John O'Brien, at about 3 or 4 p.m. when they saw some men killing sheep. The boys spent about half an hour there and afterwards lent a hand in cleaning up the premises. The plaintiff said in the course of his evidence that this was the first time he had ever assisted in any work in the premises. While the boys were there, the plaintiff observed fifteen detonators on the stool in the slaughter-house and he took seven or eight of these without the knowledge of the employees and without their consent. This, according to the evidence, was the first time he had ever taken detonators but he had seen other boys in possession of some on earlier occasions, though he did not actually see them take any from the premises. It is, however, an inference, which is open on the evidence, that the boys had obtained these detonators in the premises. The plaintiff and his friend then went home and exploded the detonators in the back garden of the plaintiff's house by wrapping them in paper and setting fire to the paper. On the same afternoon, at about 5 p.m., he went back to the abattoir and went into the slaughter house and took another five detonators from the stool. None of the employees of the defendants were in the slaughter house at that time. The plaintiff then left and went to another boy's house and exploded the detonators in a similar fashion to the earlier ones.

On the following day, which was the day of the accident, he deliberately played truant from school and went down to the abattoir at about 10 a.m. While he was there, three employees of the defendants were also there. When they were not observing him, he went into the office and took about twelve detonators from the shelf in the office. This shelf was within easy reach as it was no higher than the boy's chest or shoulders. Later he went back to the office and took some more of the detonators, making in all about forty which he had taken without the consent or knowledge of the defendants or their employees. The plaintiff brought these detonators home to his own house and proceeded to explode them in the back garden of his house. Later on the same day, at about 1.30 p.m., he returned to the abattoir and went into the office, which was open, and saw some more detonators scattered on the shelf in the office. He took about nine of these. On this occasion he was accompanied by another boy. The boys then went off to another place, which was not the plaintiff's home, and proceeded to explode the detonators. The plaintiff did not explode them all and when he went home to his own house he still had about seven. Four or five of these he exploded in a shed at the end of his own garden. After igniting the paper, holding one of the detonators, he threw it on the ground but it failed to explode. Thinking that the rain had affected it, he picked it up and it then exploded causing the severe injuries which resulted in the subsequent removal of his right eye. There is no doubt whatever that on this day his sole purpose in visiting the abattoir was neither to watch the men at work nor to assist in the cleaning up, but simply to steal the detonators. The employees were aware of his presence but they were not aware, apparently, of his purpose in being there. There was no evidence that the defendants or their employees were actually aware that the plaintiff, or any other boys who frequented their premises, had taken detonators from the defendants' premises at any time.

The plaintiff sued the defendants for negligence. The negligence alleged was that the defendants knew or ought to have known that young boys, including the plaintiff, had access to their premises and in fact resorted there from time to time during the hours of work and without objection from the defendants or their servants, and that the defendants took no steps to keep the humane killer and the detonators in a place where they would not be accessible to the boys, including the plaintiff, frequenting the premises. Furthermore, it was alleged that in the circumstances the defendants were negligent in leaving the detonators readily available on the premises, either on the stool in the slaughter house or on the shelf in the office, and that the detonators should have been kept in a safe place under lock and key, and that the defendants should have foreseen that the boys, including the plaintiff, would be tempted to interfere with these detonators and that they would constitute an allurement for boys. It was further alleged that the defendants took no steps to warn the boys of the danger which could result from the handling or misuse of these detonators, or generally of the danger of interfering or tampering with them.

The defendants contended that they were not guilty of any of the alleged acts of negligence and further contended that the plaintiff was at all material times a trespasser on their premises and that, in effect, they owed him no duty. They also pleaded that the plaintiff himself had been guilty of negligence and that the injuries and loss suffered by him were too remote.

The defendants did not go into evidence but, at the close of the case for the plaintiff, the defendants submitted to the learned trial judge that they had no case to meet and that the plaintiff's claim should be withdrawn from the jury. It was submitted on behalf of the defendants that the plaintiff was a trespasser and that there was no evidence that the defendants had consciously or wilfully caused him any injury, and that the full extent of their duty to a trespasser did not amount to any more than that.

The learned trial judge ruled that on the day in question the plaintiff, while he was on the defendants' premises, was a trespasser and that the only duty owed by the defendants to the plaintiff as a trespasser was not to set a trap. He ruled, however, that there was a case to go to the jury on the question of the defendants' negligence on the basis that, in the circumstances, it was for the jury to decide whether or not the defendants had failed to observe the degree of care in the control of the detonators that one would expect from a reasonably prudent person and whether such want of care resulted in the plaintiff's injury. The circumstances that the judge was dealing with were the circumstances of an abattoir to which these boys had resort, without objection from the defendants or their employees, at times when these detonators were being used and were accessible to such boys.

The jury found that the defendants were guilty of negligence and they also found that the plaintiff was guilty of contributory negligence and they assessed damages at the sum of £4,242. They apportioned the degrees of fault between the parties on the basis of 85% of the fault being the defendants' and 15% being the plaintiff's. Against these findings and the verdict the defendants have appealed. They seek an order directing judgment to be entered for the defendants on this appeal or, alternatively, an order for a new trial. The grounds upon which the appeal is based are that the trial judge misdirected himself and was wrong in law in not acceding to the application of counsel for the defendants at the close of the plaintiff's case to have the action completely withdrawn from the jury, and that the apportionment of the degrees of fault between the parties was perverse and not in accordance with the evidence. It was also submitted in the notice of appeal that the damages awarded by the jury were excessive and unreasonable and were not in accordance with the evidence offered at the trial.

The defendants base their appeal primarily upon the submission that the plaintiff was a trespasser on the day in question and that he cannot, therefore, be heard now to say that any greater duty was owed to him than that of not laying a trap for him. The learned trial judge ruled that the plaintiff in this case was a trespasser. The defendants, in their submission to the learned trial judge, had submitted that the plaintiff was a trespasser because his real object in coming into the premises of the defendants was to steal the detonators even though his actual entry was not sought to be prevented or indeed objected to, by the defendants through their employees at the time. On the evidence the defendants, through their servants, could be said to have acquiesced in his presence on the premises. The acquiescence was, of course, based on the assumption that the plaintiff was coming upon the premises for the purpose of watching the defendants' employees at work or of participating, in some minor degree, in that work. If in fact the plaintiff had gone to the premises for the purpose of assisting at the work or even merely as a spectator without the intention of stealing, it could not be maintained that he was a trespasser in the circumstances of the present case. Whether he be an invitee rather than a licensee, or vice versa, is not, in my view, decisive in this case. If he were there in either category and, having entered without any intention of stealing, he then formed the intent to steal, does he become a trespasser as from the moment he forms the intent on the grounds that once he exceeds the terms of his invitation or his licence he becomes a trespasser *ab initio*? If the answer to that question is in the affirmative then *a fortiori* he is a trespasser if he forms the intention before he enters at all.

For the purposes of the present decision I do not think it is necessary to answer this question because it would only be relevant if the plaintiff had sustained injuries as a consequence of some defect or danger in the static condition of those premises, or if the defendants' liability is attributable only to their duty as occupiers. The plaintiff's claim against the defendants is not wholly, or even primarily, based upon the neglect of the defendants as occupiers of the premises so much as upon the neglect by the defendants of a duty which, it is claimed, they owed to the plaintiff and which did not depend upon the defendants being the occupiers of any premises but rather upon the defendants being the custodians of chattels which, if not properly controlled by them, might foreseeably cause injury to the plaintiff.

The liability, if established, is therefore one which arose by virtue of the proximity of the parties and it would be the same wherever the parties might find themselves, provided their proximity to each other was the same. In other words the liability is not based upon any special relationship such as occupier and invitee, or licensee or even trespasser, but simply upon proximity.

The first question, therefore, is whether the parties were sufficiently proximate so that the defendants might owe a duty to the plaintiff. In my view the answer to this question is in the affirmative. The plaintiff was one of a class (namely, a class of local boys), who frequented the premises in question for the purpose of watching the men at work and the plaintiff himself had on a number of occasions been on the premises for that purpose. The defendants' employees were therefore accustomed to having these young boys around them while performing their work. The degree of physical proximity was quite close on such occasions. It was sufficiently close to make the employees conscious of the possibility of injury to any of these boys, as well as to themselves, by any untoward incident during the operation. The detonators were admittedly of a nature calling for care and ones which were known, or ought to have been known, to be capable of causing injury if wrongly used. If the employees, or one of them, were to give some of these detonators to any of these boys as playthings, or to use as they wished, with or without a warning of the nature of the detonators, and injury befell the recipient due to that nature, there would be little doubt but that the employee who gave it would be personally liable in negligence. The very nature of the detonators and their function were, in my view, sufficient to enable a jury to hold that the detonators would constitute a source of attraction or an allurement for boys. That would be a matter which a jury would be entitled to hold as something which ought to be foreseen by the defendants' employees. If, without any question of stealing arising, the boys were allowed to handle the detonators while on the premises, or to play with them, and injury resulted, it would be difficult to hold that such an event was not foreseeable by the defendants or their employees.

In the present case it is submitted that the defendants could not be held to have been able to foresee that some of these materials would be stolen and removed from their premises by these boys. When the objects in question are sufficiently small to be removed without attracting attention and are very easily concealed and are of such a nature that they constitute an allurement to boys frequenting the place where the objects are to be found, it is a matter for the jury to say whether, in all circumstances, the owners of these objects ought reasonably to have foreseen that the attraction of these objects for the boys might be sufficient to tempt them to steal some of them. In my view the evidence in the present case was sufficient to justify the learned trial judge leaving the matter to the jury upon this basis and was sufficient to warrant the jury taking the view that the defendants owed a duty to the plaintiff and that they failed in that duty.

In what way would the liability have been different if the accident had occurred on the defendants' premises? The plaintiff was on the premises, at the time when he took the detonators, with the tacit permission of the defendants' employees. Unknown to the defendants' employees the plaintiff was in law a trespasser, because the ostensible purpose for his being on the premises was not his real purpose which was unlawful. Nonetheless the defendants' employees were in charge and control of the detonators, which could be held to be an allurement to a boy of the plaintiff's age because of the knowledge he had gained of them during his lawful visits to the premises. When the proximity of the parties is voluntary on both sides and when, because of that proximity, the lack of control over the detonators may be a danger, is the duty to keep these detonators safe from interference by the boy any the less because one of the parties has achieved that proximity by concealing the real purpose of his presence? I do not think so. When the danger is reasonably foreseeable, the duty to take care to avoid injury to those who are proximate, when their proximity is known, is not abrogated because the other party is a trespasser. The duty to those in proximity is not based on any implied term of an invitation or a licence, or upon any warranty for safety which might be thought to be inherent in any such invitation or licence. Rather is it based upon the duty that one man has to those in proximity to him to take reasonable care that they are not injured by his acts. What amounts to sufficient care must vary necessarily with the circumstances, the nature of the danger, and the age and knowledge of the person likely to be injured.

The next matter to be considered is the question of the apportionment of the fault. The plaintiff undoubtedly knew, and was old enough to appreciate, that these objects had an explosive effect and were therefore likely to be dangerous. He knew from experience that they could be detonated by wrapping them in lighted paper. If, therefore, on this occasion he had kept one in his hand while the paper was igniting and the explosion had occurred then, it might rightly be regarded as a very dangerous activity consciously engaged in, and a high proportion of the fault might well be attributed to him. In the present case, however, what happened was that the detonator failed to explode and the plaintiff then retrieved it from the ground and it then exploded. The plaintiff's knowledge of the dangers of these objects and his experience of them may not have been sufficient, and there is nothing to indicate that it was, to warn him of the danger of a delayed explosion. In those circumstances, therefore, his negligence in retrieving the object which had apparently failed to explode might well be held by the jury to have been far less culpable than the doing of an act of whose danger he had full knowledge and appreciation. While the jury's apportionment may appear to be generous in some degree to the plaintiff, it is not one which, in the circumstances and on the evidence, must necessarily be held to be unreasonable and perverse.

The last matter to be considered is the question of the amount of damages. The damages awarded in this case, £4,242, are claimed by the defendants to be excessive and unreasonable and not in accordance with the evidence offered at the trial. The most serious consequence of the accident to the plaintiff was the loss of one eye. There are a number of cases in which it has been held by this Court that a sum of £3,000 is not an unreasonable award for the loss of an eye, as such, of a person under middle age, apart from any question of economic loss which may result from it. Applying that standard to the present case it would leave a sum of approximately £1,200 to cover all the other matters which fell under the heading of pecuniary loss and economic loss in the future. The evidence on the question of the boy's future as an earning unit is not very satisfactory. At the time of the trial he was working as an apprentice jockey but he complained that having only one eye was something of a disadvantage in that occupation. After the accident he worked for about nine months in a bakery where it does not appear that his disability was anything of a handicap. His future employment would seem to lie in the category of semi-skilled or unskilled employment, probably of a manual nature. Experience in the Courts shows that, although, the loss of an eye may not be such a great handicap to a man in such an occupation as it would to one doing precision work, it can nevertheless be an inhibiting factor in obtaining employment mainly because every prospective employer knows that his workman has but to lose one eye to achieve total blindness. In my view, a sum of £1,200 as compensation for a boy of sixteen (the plaintiff's age at the date of the trial) is not to be regarded as unreasonably large for the purpose of covering, for the rest of his life, all the contingencies of the labour market which may arise because of his one eyed condition. I would not disturb the damages. For the reasons I have already stated, in my view the appeal should be dismissed.

Ó Dálaigh C.J. and **Budd J.** agreed with **Walsh J's** judgment.

Notes and Questions

1. *Byrne* v. *McDonald, supra*, pp. 238–241 was not cited in *Purtill* v. *Athlone U.D.C.*, why do you think this was so?
2. Are *Purtill* and *Byrne* true cases of occupiers' liability?
3. Contrast Walsh J.'s approach in *Purill* where he cites no authorities, but relies on principle, with the House of Lords approach to the trespasser problem in *British Railways Board* v. *Herrington* [1972] A.C. 877; [1972] 1 All E.R. 749.

M'NAMARA V. E.S.B.
[1975] I.R.1 (Sup. Ct.)

Walsh J.:

This appeal concerns an accident which occurred on the 9th July, 1965, when the plaintiff was 11 years old. The action for personal injuries arising out of the accident brought by the plaintiff against the defendants was heard before Mr. Justice Butler and a jury in February, 1972. The jury held that the defendants had been negligent and that the plaintiff had not been negligent. Damages amounting to £74,772 were awarded by the jury to the plaintiff for the very serious injuries which he sustained, and judgment was entered for the plaintiff in that sum. The defendants have appealed to this Court against the whole of the judgment and the findings of the jury and have asked for judgment to be entered for the defendants or that a new trial should be ordered.

The plaintiff's injuries were suffered when he came into contact with high-voltage electricity conductors at a sub-station of the defendants situated at Garryowen in the City of Limerick. The conductor in question carried a voltage of 10,000 volts. The sub-station was built in 1929 and, when originally built, was a concrete structure enclosed by chain-link fencing and one entrance gate. The fencing was a 2″ mesh and as originally erected was 5′ high, the entrance gate being 5′ 6″ high. At that time the nearest point of the fence to the building was about 20 feet. There were transformers outside the building but inside the fence. The electric current entered the concrete building at a voltage of 38,000 and emerged from it stepped down to 10,000 volts. The 10,000-volt conductors, as they emerged from the side wall of the building, were uninsulated and they then entered a box known as a cable-end box to carry the current away in an insulated cable running down the side wall of the building. The distance between the ground and the nearest point of the uninsulated conductor was 10½ feet. The transformers outside the building, with which this case is not directly concerned, also had conductors which were a minimum of 8½ feet above ground level and were also uninsulated.

About the year 1956, a flat-roofed addition to the building was erected which was 9′4″ over ground level. Where the flat-roofed structure is attached to the main structure, there is a drain-pipe coming from the patched roof of the main structure and running down to the ground. This drain-pipe is only a matter of inches from where the flat roof joins the main building. Three of the uninsulated conductors running down the wall of the main building were close to this drain-pipe; the nearest one was within easy reach, being only one foot from the drain-pipe.

When the sub-station was originally erected there was a small number of houses about 50 or 60 yards away from the sub-station, and the area was not a built-up area. In the 1960s a new housing estate was built which was completed about 1964. In the result this sub-station was flanked by a large housing estate, and only a small portion of waste ground separated the two.

About the time of the completion of the housing estate, discussions had taken place between Limerick Corporation and the defendants' representatives on the question of surrounding the whole sub-station by a wall 8′9″ high – the wall of the internal transformer compound was to be 12′ high. The 8′9″ wall was to be built in such a way that no abutments or embellishments or any other matter in the design of the wall would facilitate climbing. Some of the wall around the area had been completed prior to the accident, and some five or six weeks before the accident a portion of the wire-fencing was moved to facilitate the building of the wall. The portion of fencing which was moved was the one nearest to the conjunction of the flat roof and the drain-pipe which I have already described; it was moved to a point where the distance from the top of the wire to the flat roof was 3′1″ before any pressure was put upon it.

Over the years certain changes in the fencing itself had occurred. The gate had been replaced and, due to the deposit of soil, the level of the ground had been changed so that the original wire-mesh fence was only 5′ high at the point of the fence with which this case is concerned, and was supplemented by the addition of barbed wire which raised the total height to about 6′8″. The barbed wire was arranged in the form of a large mesh fence. The original fencing post was extended by the addition of another angle-iron piece to a total height of 7′9″ which is about 1 foot higher than the highest point of the wire.

For some time before the date of the accident, the local officials of the defendants were aware that the sub-station was an object of attention for the local children. The station had suffered damage caused by children throwing stones;

glass was broken and children were known to play around the area immediately outside the boundaries of the sub-station. The defendants' officials were also conscious of the danger of persons crossing the fence into the sub-station and it was this appreciation which led them to raise the height of the fence by the addition of the barbed wire. The instructions issued to the defendants' charge-linesman who carried out the work were 'to make it like a concentration camp' and they illustrate the defendants' appreciation of the gravity of the danger.

The fence, as it existed at the date of the accident, was the subject of very adverse criticism in evidence given by an architect and an engineer called on behalf of the plaintiff. There was no engineer or architect called on behalf of the defendants. The evidence by the plaintiff's experts, one of whom described the fence as 'laughable,' was to the effect that the fence was quite unsuitable for the purpose of keeping persons out; that it constituted 'a man-made ladder to give access to the flat roof'; and that in general it could be described as a rather 'rickety arrangement' – to use the words of the architect. This general description was certainly borne out by the photographs of the portion of the fence in question. The main criticisms were that the fence posts were loose and that the wire was slack. Both of these factors made it easier to climb the fence in the sense that the loose posts would cause the fence to lean inwards and the slackness of the wire would make it easier to climb. In particular, the barbed-wire addition was in such a wide mesh that it would offer a foothold; and the extension of the fence post offered a handhold to persons who were going to reach the top of the fence and pass from it to the flat roof which, at best, was 3'1" away – and that distance would be shortened by the weight of a person leaning in towards the fence. The view was offered that a boy of 10 or 11 years would have no trouble in climbing the fence.

The plaintiff and his brother in their evidence stated that they had often played around the area outside the sub-station over a period of years and for two years prior to the accident had frequently played inside the wire and had no difficulty in getting over it; on at least one occasion they had gone over the wire fence on to the flat roof. They had been shown this by other children. When they got on to the flat roof they descended by sliding down the drain-pipe which I have described. A number of children, including themselves, played games of cowboys and Indians around the station, and it was in the course of this game that entry was made. On previous occasions when they and other children had been playing around the station, they had been told to go away by passers-by; they had also been told to go away by their father. The plaintiff in his evidence said that he would not enter the station if any employee of the defendants was present; but he also said that he did not know the station was for electricity, or that it would be dangerous to go there. He agreed that he could read and that he had seen the warning notices which were posted around the fence of the station.

On the day in question the plaintiff and his brother, David, who was one year younger than himself, climbed up the fence on to the flat roof of the station. The first person over was the younger brother and the plaintiff followed him. They stayed some time on the flat roof and observed that there were many stones there. In their evidence the defendants' employees stated that they had on many occasions found stones on the roof which had been thrown up there by the children who played around the place. The plaintiff, in his description of the climbing, mentioned that as they climbed the fence the wire leaned forward sufficient to enable them to put one hand on to the roof to steady themselves and then, when they were steady, they jumped from the top strand of wire on which they were standing with the support of the upright pole. After the short time they spent on the roof the younger brother, David, said he was going down. The plaintiff observed David going down and observed him putting his hand around the corner of the wall and he followed his example also for the purpose of coming down. The object of putting their hands out was apparently to catch the drain-pipe and slide down. The plaintiff remembers no more than putting his hand around the corner of the wall. His brother David saw him putting his hand around and apparently grasp the electric conductor. While the plaintiff thought he had used his right hand, it is quite obvious that this would have been impossible and it is much more likely that it was his left hand which came in contact with the conductor. A burn mark, which is clearly visible on the conductor in the photographs and which was mentioned in evidence by the architect, probably indicates the point of contact. What is not clear is whether the first hand which the plaintiff put out was his left hand and that that reached out far enough to grasp the conductor, or whether he had first used one of his hands, if not both, to grasp the drain-pipe and then put out one hand to give himself a greater hold in reaching for the conductor. It does not really matter in this case what was the sequence of events because the facts have clearly demonstrated that the live conductor was within the reach of the boy's hand. As a result of this contact he suffered very severe injuries which it is unnecessary to refer to in this portion of the judgment and I will pass from them.

The first three questions on the issue paper referred to the allegation of negligence on the part of the defendants, and by them the jury were asked (1) whether the defendants were aware, or should they have known, that children were liable to cross the wire and trespass on the sub-station; (2) if so, whether the defendants should have foreseen the risk of injury to such children by coming into contact with electric wire; and (3) if so, whether the defendants were negligent in failing to provide and maintain proper fencing at the sub-station. The jury answered each of these questions in the affirmative.

In their appeal against the jury's findings on the question of the defendants' negligence, the defendants have relied strongly upon the claim that the plaintiff was a trespasser, as they did at the trial, and have submitted that the defendants owed no duty of care to the plaintiff when he was a trespasser or that the only duty they owed him was a duty not to act with reckless regard for his safety and that there was no evidence of any such reckless disregard on their part. This particular plea is an echo of the decision in *Robert Addie and Sons (Collieries) Ltd.* v. *Dumbreck* [1929] A.C. 358.

A great deal of the hearing of this appeal was taken up with a discussion of the decision in *Addie's Case*, and of the decisions in *Videan* v. *British Transport Commission* [1963] 2 Q.B. 650 and *Herrington* v. *British Railways Board* [1972] A.C. 877. It was submitted that this Court should follow the decision in *Addie's Case* [1929] A.C. 358 on the ground that this Court followed it in *Donovan* v. *Landy's Ltd.* [1963] I.R. 441 (which was itself followed in *O'Leary* v. *Wood Ltd.* [1964] I.R. 269) and should not follow the views expressed in *Videan's Case* [1963] 2 Q.B. 650 or in *Herrington's Case* [1972] A.C. 877. It is to be noted that in *O'Leary* v. *Wood Ltd.* [1964] I.R. 269 the Court held that it was bound by the decision of the majority in *Donovan* v. *Landy's Ltd.* [1963] I.R. 441. This was before the Court, in *The Attorney General* v. *Ryan's Car Hire Ltd.* [1965] I.R. 642, finally rejected the practice or doctrine of *stare decisis*.

This Court laid down in *Purtill* v. *Athlone U.D.C.* [1968] I.R. 205 that the occupier of premises could not claim exemption from liability on the grounds that the person injured by the occupier's acts or omissions was a trespasser, and that that was the position even when the occupier's act was not done with the deliberate intention of doing harm to the trespasser or done with reckless disregard for the presence of the trespasser. In my view, the learned trial judge was quite correct in holding that the defendants' claim to be exempt from any duty to the plaintiff, on the ground that he was a trespasser, was unfounded in law. As was pointed out in that case, when a danger has been created by a person and it was reasonably foreseeable that the danger might cause injury to those who were proximate to him, it is that person's duty to take care to avoid that injury, and that duty is not abrogated because the danger was created on his land and resulted in injury to a trespasser. It is of interest to note the opinion of the Privy Council in *Southern Portland Cement Ltd.* v. *Cooper* [1974] A.C. 623 which was given since the present appeal was argued. There the duty of an occupier to a trespasser at common law is stated in the following terms at p. 644 of the report:– 'The rights and interests of the occupier must have full consideration. No unreasonable burden must be put on him. With regard to dangers which have arisen on his land without his knowledge he can have no obligation to make inquiries or inspection. With regard to dangers of which he has knowledge but which he did not create he cannot be required to incur what for him would be large expense. If the occupier creates the danger when he knows that there is a chance that trespassers will come that way and will not see or realise the danger he may have to do more. There may be difficult cases where the occupier will be hampered in the conduct of his own affairs if he has to take elaborate precautions. But in the present case it would have been easy to prevent the development of the dangerous situation which caused the plaintiff's injuries. The more serious the danger the greater is the obligation to avoid it. And if the dangerous thing or something near it is an allurement to children that may greatly increase the chance that children will come there.'

In *Purtill's Case* [1968] I.R. 205 this duty was stated in relation to a situation where the proximity was known, and that is also the fact in the present case. In erecting the sub-station with the exposed conductors carrying high voltages, the defendants created a foreseeable danger to parties coming in close contact with them. That is one of the reasons why they erected a fence around the sub-station in the first instance, in addition, of course, to the reason of protecting the property itself. The duty was a continuing one and the degree of care which was cast upon them must necessarily depend upon the surrounding circumstances.

One of the outstanding features of the present case is that the circumstances altered radically between the date of the erection of the sub-station and the date of the accident. The most radical change was the presence of a large new housing estate in the immediate vicinity of the sub-station and the known presence of children playing around the immediate area of the sub-station itself. The second important change was the addition of the flat-roofed structure built as an extension to the original sub-station. The third important change was the re-positioning of approximately 30 yards of fencing a few weeks before the accident so that the fence was brought to within 3 feet or so of the corner of the flat roof.

Was it reasonably foreseeable to the defendants that children might enter their premises unless reasonable steps were taken to keep them out? On the evidence placed before the jury, I think they were quite entitled to answer the question in the affirmative. The question must then arise of whether the steps taken by the defendants to keep out children were reasonable in all the circumstances. Again, on the evidence before the jury, I think the jury were quite entitled to answer that question in the negative. The fence in question, because of its slackness and its very close proximity to the flat-roofed building, was one which could reasonably be held to have been at the time easily within the climbing capacity of a child of the plaintiff's age, and that was a matter which could be held to have been reasonably foreseeable to the defendants. If so, the steps taken by the defendants were not reasonably sufficient to discharge the duty they owed to children who would be in danger of severe injury if they secured access to the building. It has been said that it is not the duty of the occupier of property to make any fence child-proof. I think that particular phrase does not have any precise meaning. However, if it means that there is no duty on the person creating the danger to take more steps than are reasonably necessary to prevent injury, then it is correct, but not otherwise. The known physical facts were the condition of the fence, its proximity to the building, and the habit of the local children to play around the immediate area of the fence. In those circumstances it was the duty of the defendants to take reasonable steps to ensure that the children, or any of them, would not be able to enter the danger area. In a case such as the present, that means taking reasonable steps to prevent the children trespassing. On the facts of the present case, having regard to the nature of the fence in question and notwithstanding the notices giving warning of danger, I think the jury had ample evidence upon which to find that the defendants had been guilty of negligence and to answer in the affirmative the first three questions.

In so far as *Donovan* v. *Landy's Ltd.* [1963] I.R. 441 decided that the only duty owed to a person who was in law a trespasser was a duty not to act with reckless disregard of his presence or his safety, I am of opinion that it was wrongly decided. In that case Lavery J., who did not subscribe to that view, stated at p. 445 of the report that the obligation of a defendant in any claim against him for negligence has to be measured by all the circumstances of the case. On the same page he said: 'These need not be enumerated but they include such circumstances as the time and place and the persons who may be expected to be exposed to danger.' He goes on then to quote with approval the words of Lord Macmillan in *Read* v. *J. Lyons & Co. Ltd.* [1947] A.C. 156, 173:– 'The sound view, in my opinion, is that the law in all cases exacts a degree of care commensurate with the risk created.' That appears to have been the basis of the assent of Lavery J. to the decision in that case. Earlier in his judgment he stated that in his opinion the appeal did not call for the consideration of any special, peculiar or novel principle and that the well-understood principles of the common law of negligence considered as a tort were sufficient to enable it to be determined. He did not use the words 'trespass' or 'trespasser' anywhere in the course of his judgment. It is true that he stated that he agreed with the conclusions and, in the main, with the reasons given by Kingsmill Moore J.: but he went on to state immediately afterwards that he was 'in some doubt as to whether the distinction between negligence and reckless disregard is necessary to be drawn . . .' However, Kingsmill Moore J. did appear to reject the view that any greater duty than the duty not to act with reckless disregard was owed to a trespasser. I do not think that that is a correct statement of the law. While it is true that the appellant in *Donovan* v. *Landy's Ltd.* [1963] I.R. 441 relied mainly on the decision in *Breslin* v. *Brennan* [1937] I.R. 350 and while a great number of authorities are cited in the case, both in the arguments as reported and in the judgment of Kingsmill Moore J., a notable exception is *Donoghue* v. *Stevenson* [1932] A.C. 562. It does not appear that the case was argued or decided upon any consideration of the 'neighbour' principle enunciated in *Donoghue* v. *Stevenson* [1932] A.C. 562 or the application of that principle to the facts in *Donovan* v. *Landy's Ltd.* [1963] I.R. 441. The appellant's counsel in that case also sought to distinguish between cases involving the occupancy of land and cases where the liability arises from the ownership of a vehicle on the public highway; it was in the latter context that they relied upon *Breslin* v. *Brennan* [1937] I.R. 350. Mr. Justice Kingsmill Moore confessed that the decision in *Breslin* v. *Brennan* [1937] I.R. 350 left him in considerable doubt, to say the least of it, about the then state of the law of this country on the subject.

In *Breslin* v. *Brennan* [1937] I.R. 350 the standard of reasonable care appears to have been applied and Sullivan C.J. records in his judgment at p. 355 of the report that counsel for the defendants admitted that if the driver knew that the boy was on the running board 'even as a trespasser' the driver would be guilty of negligence if he started the car, as the act would be 'a wilful act involving something more than absence of reasonable care' and an act 'done with reckless disregard of the presence of the trespasser.' On the other hand, FitzGibbon J. appears to have decided the case on the basis of the standard to exercise reasonable care which would constitute ordinary negligence. Finally, Murnaghan J. and Meredith J. accepted the view that, if the jury came to the conclusion that it would have been reasonable for the driver to have anticipated that the child would climb upon the car, the driver would have been negligent if he started the car without seeing whether the child was on it. That case appears to have been decided on the basis that the driver should have reasonably anticipated the presence of the boy and that the jury were entitled to say that his failure to see the boy amounted to negligence.

I turn now to the question of whether or not the evidence was such that the plaintiff must be found guilty of negligence. I think the trial judge was correct in leaving to the jury the question of negligence on the part of the plaintiff. He was of an age when he could be found guilty of negligence in failing to take ordinary care for his own safety, so the question is whether it was open to the jury to acquit him on the evidence. The judge left two questions to the jury on this point; they were asked whether the plaintiff was negligent (a) in crossing the wire when he knew or ought to have known that the sub-station might be a dangerous place, and/or (b) in descending from the flat roof without paying due regard to the risk of injury if he came into contact with electric wires. The jury answered each of these questions in the negative, and both of them are based upon the jury having to be satisfied about whether the plaintiff knew, or ought to have known, that entry over the fence into the area of the sub-station would be an act fraught with grave danger of serious injury if not death.

There was uncontradicted evidence that the plaintiff knew that the sub-station was a place where he ought not to be, and he admitted as much. But the reason why he ought not to be there is the vital point in so far as this aspect of the case is concerned. In his own evidence he stated that he did not know that it would be dangerous, and his brother also said that he was not aware of danger. Each of them said that he did not know that the sub-station had anything to do with electricity The plaintiff's father appreciated the danger from the sub-station and had often warned the plaintiff to keep away from it. It does not appear, however, from the evidence that, beyond telling his son he had no business to be there, he ever explained to him, or even mentioned to him, the nature of the danger or the fact that there was a danger. While there was also evidence that other persons from time to time chased the boys away, there is no evidence that any of them ever conveyed to the boys, or to the plaintiff in particular, that there was danger involved in playing around the sub-station. On the other hand there were around the fence a number of notices on which was written: 'Danger, Keep Away. It is dangerous to touch the electric wires.' In small writing underneath there was written:– 'Beware of fallen wires.' These were yellow enamelled metal notices with a red lightning symbol above the writing. There were about a dozen of these notices displayed around the perimeter and each one measured about 8 inches by 8 inches. Although the engineer gave evidence for the plaintiff describing the two notices on the gates as being in one case legible but damaged and in the other case half obliterated, the plaintiff in his evidence said he had seen the notices but that he had never read them although he was able to read. He said that he did not know they were warnings of danger.

Therefore, the test to be applied is that stated by O'Byrne J. in *Fleming* v. *Kerry County Council* [1955–56] Ir. Jur. Rep. 71, which is that it is for the jury to determine whether the boy fell short of the standard which might be reasonably expected from him having regard to his age and his development. If the jury believed that he did not read the notices and that he did not understand that there was a danger and a serious danger must they hold that, at his age and having regard to the other matters which occupied his mind while playing his games around the area, he fell short of the standard expected of a boy of his age in not reading and appreciating the effect of the notices or in not appreciating, from the construction or the appearance of the sub-station, that it was a place which could seriously injure him by the discharge of electricity if he entered it? I think that on the evidence the jury were entitled to accept that the plaintiff did not actually know the danger, and I do not think the evidence is such that the jury must find that he ought to have known of it even applying the fully objective standard of measuring him by what is to be expected of the ordinary eleven-year-old boy whose experience of the sub-station always appears to have been that of a boy playing cowboys and Indians or other similar games around the immediate area of the sub-station. The evidence was such that the jury were quite entitled to hold that the defendants had not discharged the burden of proving as a probability that the plaintiff was negligent. I have put the matter in this way because of the phraseology of paragraph 7 of the notice of appeal which states one of the grounds of appeal as being that 'there was no evidence to support the jury's finding that the plaintiff was not negligent and accordingly the jury's answer to question No. 4 was contrary to the evidence and perverse.' The form of that ground of appeal appears to have overlooked the burden of proof which was on the defendants. The plaintiff could not possibly be found guilty of negligence unless the evidence adduced in the case was such that the plaintiff could be found to have been negligent, and the burden of proof was on the defendants to satisfy the jury on that point.

[**Walsh J.** went on to examine the question of damages and came to the conclusion that the jury award was grossly excessive and that a new trial should be ordered on this issue alone.]

Budd J. concurred with **Walsh J.**'s judgment.

Henchy J.:

It is common ground that the plaintiff was a trespasser on the defendant's property when he was injured. What has been primarily in dispute, both at the trial and in this appeal, is the test by which the defendants' liability for negligence at common law should be determined. Is it, as counsel for the defendants contends, the test laid down by the House of Lords in *Robert Addie & Sons (Collieries) Ltd.* v. *Dumbreck* [1929] A.C. 358, as restated by this Court in *O'Leary* v. *Wood Ltd.* [1964] I.R. 269? Or should it be founded, as the plaintiff's counsel submit, on the more general duty owed to a 'neighbour' in the sense in which that word was used by Lord Atkin in *Donoghue* v. *Stevenson* [1932] A.C. 562.

It was laid down in *O'Leary* v. *Wood Ltd.* [1964] I.R. 269 at p. 272 of the report (following a line of cases running from *Addie's Case* [1929] A.C. 358 to the decision of this Court in *Donovan* v. *Landy's Ltd.* [1963] I.R. 441) that an occupier of property owes no duty to trespassers unless he is aware of their presence or of the high probability of their presence and, even then, that the duty is merely not to do 'any act of positive misfeasance which is intended to do harm to those within the ambit of the operation of the act, nor to any act which involves a reckless disregard of their safety.' This duty is less than that owed to a licensee, and much less than that owed to an invitee. Considering that in law the word 'trespasser' covers every person who enters on another's property in circumstances in which he is neither a licensee nor an invitee, it is difficult to see why the same inferior duty should be owed by the occupier to every person who comes within that category. Why, for example, should no higher duty be owed to a child openly but innocently trespassing in pursuit of a lost ball than to a burglar furtively and knowingly trespassing for the purpose of committing a crime? For the fact is that the wide and heterogeneous selection of people who fall into the category of 'trespasser' are compressed into a simplistic stereotype when the law says that the occupier owes a common unvarying duty to each of them.

In founding this important aspect of the law governing the social obligations of occupiers of property on the artificial uniformity of the concept of a trespasser, the law has produced palpable injustices from which the courts have been constrained in some cases by what must be accounted strained and not very convincing reasoning – to rescue plaintiffs from defeat by treating them as licensees: see *Cooke* v. *Midland Great Western Railway of Ireland* [1909] A.C. 229. In other cases, such as *Videan* v. *British Transport Commission* [1963] 2 Q.B. 650, efforts have been made to distinguish the application of *Addie's case* [1929] A.C. 358 and to found liability on the broader base of the 'neighbour' principle as enunciated in *Donoghue* v. *Stevenson* [1932] A.C. 562. In certain jurisdictions the legislature has intervened to abolish or modify the rule that an occupier's duty to a trespasser is that laid down in *Addie's Case* [1929] A.C. 358 and cases derived from it: see the Occupiers' Liability (Scotland) Act, 1960.

Since in this State there has been no legislative intervention, this Court has to choose between a test of the defendants' liability based on the mere fact that the plaintiff was a trespasser and those decisions which say that liability should be decided by applying the 'neighbour' principle of *Donoghue* v. *Stevenson* [1932] A.C. 562. The degree of certainty, continuity and predictability that judicial decisions should have, to enable people to arrange their conduct so as to avoid legal liability, would normally dictate that this Court should follow its own decisions in *Donovan* v. *Landy's Ltd.* [1963] I.R. 441 and *O'Leary* v. *Wood Ltd.* [1964] I.R. 269 which restated the law as laid down in *Addie's Case* [1929] A.C. 358. But there are exceptional and compelling reasons for not doing so.

Modern judicial decisions in jurisdictions in different parts of the common-law world show a widespread desire to escape from *Addie's Case* [1929] A.C. 358 on the ground of its unsuitability to modern social conditions and, perhaps more so, because a test of liability based on that case, whatever its original validity, runs counter to the principle that pervades the law of negligence since *Donoghue* v. *Stevenson* [1932] A.C. 562 which is that a man is liable to damages if he has failed to take all reasonable steps to avoid injuring those whom he ought reasonably to have foreseen as likely to be injured by his conduct. In particular, the House of Lords (where the *Addie* test was originally laid down) has now ruled that *Addie's Case* [1929] A.C. 358 was wrongly decided and that an occupier is liable to a trespasser if, by the standards of common sense and common humanity, he could be said to be culpable in failing to take reasonable steps to avoid a danger to which the trespasser was likely to be exposed: see *Herrington* v. *British Railways Board*

[1972] A.C. 877. In summing up the different ways in which the Law Lords in that case stated the occupier's duty, Lord Denning M.R. has said:– 'The long and short of it is that you have to take into account all the circumstances of the case and see then whether the occupier ought to have done more than he did' – see *Pannett* v. *McGuinness & Co.* [1972] 2 Q.B. 599, 606. The application of such a test does not mean that a trespasser would necessarily succeed if the injury was foreseeable by the occupier but that it would be for the judge or jury (as the case may be) to say, in the light of all relevant circumstances, whether liability should fall on the occupier. The most recent statement of the test is to be found in *Southern Portland Cement Ltd.* v. *Cooper* [1974] A.C. 623 which is a decision of the Privy Council given since the present appeal was argued.

In my opinion, such a test correctly represents the law. Whether on the ground of juridical consistency, the social obligations of occupiers of property, or plain justice, I think it should be preferred to the principle of liability enunciated by *Addie's Case* [1929] A.C. 358 and last restated by this Court in *O'Leary* v. *Wood Ltd.* [1964] I.R. 269. If, instead of encountering and being injured by a dangerous object while trespassing on the premises, the plaintiff had found a dangerous object there which he had taken away and which later injured him, the plaintiff would be entitled to succeed against the occupier regardless of the fact that the plaintiff had been a trespasser, provided that he passed the test of proximity and foreseeability: this Court so held in *Purtill* v. *Athlone U.D.C.* [1968] I.R. 205. I can think of no good reason why the law should be different when the injury happened on the premises.

The limits of the range of trespassers to whom an occupier owes a duty of care are set by the words of Lord Atkin in *Donoghue* v. *Stevenson* [1932] A.C. 562 at p. 580 of the report:

'You must take reasonable care to avoid acts or omissions which you can reasonably foresee would be likely to injure your neighbour. Who, then, in law is my neighbour? The answer seems to be persons who are so closely and directly affected by my act that I ought reasonably to have them in contemplation as being so affected when I am directing my mind to the acts or omissions which are called in question.'

As a general rule, trespassers do not come within that category since they are unpermitted and, usually, unexpected entrants on the property. Thus, a burglar who falls down an unlit stairs will normally have no cause of action against the occupier because the presence and conduct of the burglar put him beyond the scope of what a reasonable occupier should have guarded against in the circumstances. Apart from cases of injury caused intentionally or through recklessness (with which we are not concerned here), a trespasser injured on property while trespassing is not entitled to recover damages from the occupier unless he can satisfy the court of trial of all of the following matters: (i) that the injury was caused by a hidden or unexpected danger to which he was exposed; (ii) that the danger was one created, maintained, or at least tolerated by the occupier; (iii) that the circumstances were such as would not entitle a reasonable occupier to disregard the risk of injury to trespassers, or a particular class of trespassers such as children; (iv) that, having regard to such risk, the element of danger involved, the expense, difficulty or impracticability of eliminating or reducing the danger, and all other relevant factors, the occupier should have done more than he did in the interests of safety; (v) that the occupier's failure to take due precaution caused or contributed to the accident. It needs to be stressed that the existence of, or failure to observe, a duty of care should not be determined with the hindsight derived from the accident but in the light of the circumstances, actual and potential, that ought to have been present to the mind of a reasonably conscientious occupier of property before the trespass took place.

I would hold that the defendants, having created and maintained the danger, are liable if the plaintiff was one of a class of persons whom they ought reasonably to have foreseen as being likely to be injured by the danger, and if they failed to take reasonable steps to avert the injury. In substance, that is the test by which Mr. Justice Butler directed the jury to decide the question of the defendants' negligence. I would uphold the direction as being correct.

The next point that arises is whether there was evidence to support the jury's findings that the defendants were negligent.

[On an examination of the evidence **Henchy J.** found that the defendants were negligent. On the issue of contributory negligence he went on to say –]

I find it impossible to hold that in those circumstances the jury were justified in finding that the plaintiff in no way contributed to the accident by way of reasonable care for his own safety. The jury were, of course, entitled to accept the plaintiff's evidence that he was ignorant of the danger from electricity if he climbed over the fence. But they were not entitled to excuse that ignorance when it resulted from his culpable failure to read the warning notices, and when that failure contributed substantially to the happening of the accident. Judged by the standard of care for his own safety to be expected from a boy aged 11 years of the plaintiff's education and general background, he cannot be excused for his failure to read the notices, particularly when he had such ample opportunity to read them and when they were so prominently displayed on a fence clearly designed to separate him from what he well knew to be a forbidden area. I would set aside the finding of the jury that the plaintiff was not guilty of negligence, for the reason that it was perversely indulgent of them to excuse his unaccountable failure to read notices which he admitted having seen and which, if he had read them, would have brought home to him the fact that danger awaited him if he climbed over the fence.

[**Henchy J.** went on to order a new trial on the ground that the damages awarded were excessive. His treatment of the breach of statutory duty argument is omitted.]

Griffin J.:

The facts have been fully set out in the judgment of Mr. Justice Walsh and it is not necessary for me to repeat them. The plaintiff was clearly and admittedly a trespasser, and the question which arises in this appeal is the duty owed by the defendants to him. Counsel for the defendants submitted that the law is well settled that a trespasser trespasses at his peril and that the occupier owes no duty to him other than that of not inflicting damage intentionally or recklessly to him. They relied on *Robert Addie and Sons (Collieries) Ltd.* v. *Dumbreck* [1929] A.C. 358; *Donovan* v. *Landy's Ltd.* [1963] I.R. 441 and *O'Leary* v. *Wood Ltd.* [1964] I.R. 269 as authorities for this proposition. It is therefore necessary to consider what was said in these cases.

In *Addie's Case* [1929] A.C. 358, Lord Hailsham L.C. said at p. 365 of the report:– 'Towards the trespasser the occupier has no duty to take reasonable care for his protection or even to protect him from concealed danger. The trespasser comes on to the premises at his own risk. An occupier is in such a case liable only where the injury is due to some wilful act involving something more than the absence of reasonable care. There must be some act done with the deliberate intention of doing harm to the trespasser, or at least some act done with reckless disregard of the presence of the trespasser.' Viscount Dunedin, at p. 370 of the report, cited the following passage from the judgment of Hamilton L.J. in *Latham* v. *R. Johnson Ltd.* [1913] 1 K.B. 398, 411, with every word of which he stated he agreed:– 'The owner of the property is under a duty not to injure the trespasser wilfully; "not to do a wilful act in reckless disregard of ordinary humanity towards him"; but otherwise a man "trespasses at his own risk." On this point Scotch law is the same. In English and Scotch law alike, when people come on the lands of others for their own purposes without right or invitation, they must take the lands as they find them, and cannot throw any responsibility upon the person on whose lands they have trespassed . . .' The rather harsh principles laid down in *Addie's Case* [1929] A.C. 358 were accepted as correct and followed in England for many years: see *Edwards* v. *Railway Executive* [1952] A.C. 737; *Commissioner for Railways* v. *Quinlan* [1964] A.C. 1054.

In *Donovan* v. *Landy's Ltd.* [1963] I.R. 441, a decision of this Court, Kingsmill Moore J. approved of *Addie's Case* [1929] A.C. 358 and adopted the reckless-disregard test; the test of recklessness being an objective test in his view. He said at p. 462 of the report:– 'In regard to a trespasser I am liable only if my failure to exercise care is such that in the eyes of the ordinary man it would appear so gross as to be reckless.' In *O'Leary* v. *Wood Ltd.* [1964] I.R. 269 Kingsmill Moore J., delivering the judgment of the Court, said at p. 272 of the report:– 'To a trespasser of whose presence he is unaware and has no reason to be aware an owner or occupier owes no duty. If, however, he is aware of the presence of trespassers, or is aware of the high probability of the presence of trespassers, the owner or occupier must not do any act of positive misfeasance which is intended to do harm to those within the ambit of the operation of the act, nor do any act which involves a reckless disregard of their safety. Recklessness is more than a mere failure to exercise reasonable care. It involves a lack of care so extreme that in the eyes and parlance of the ordinary man it would be properly described as "gross carelessness" or "recklessness," though it need not comprise a full appreciation of the risk involved coupled with a deliberate election to take that risk: *Donovan* v. *Landy's Ltd.* [1963] I.R. 441.' If the rather rigid rule in *Addie's Case* [1929] A.C. 358 is to be applied, the plaintiff could not succeed in this action.

By reason of the harshness of the rule, the courts found means to circumvent it. With comparative ease and frequently without sufficient justification, child trespassers were converted into licensees. This practice was criticised by Lord Goddard and by Lord Reid in *Edwards* v. *Railway Executive* [1952] A.C. 737; by Lord Denning M.R. in *Videan* v. *British Transport Commission* [1963] 2 Q.B. 650 and by the High Court of Australia in *Commissioner for Railways (N.S.W.)* v. *Cardy* (1960) 104 C.L.R. 274. Again, the distinction was drawn between the permanent or static condition of the premises and the activities occurring on the land: Pearson L.J. in *Videan's Case* [1963] 2 Q.B. 650 could see no sound basis for this distinction. The rule was held to apply when it was sought to make the occupier liable *as occupier* for the condition of the premises but not in the case of a contractor carrying on activities on the land: Lord Denning M.R. in *Videan's Case* [1963] 2 Q.B. 650 too the view that there was no distinction in principle between the duty owed by an occupier and a contractor; and finally, though the occupier was not liable as occupier, he may be liable *as neighbour* for negligence.

If, by reason of its rigidity or harshness, a rule is found to be unsatisfactory, it is undesirable that efforts to circumvent it should be made rather than that it should be reconsidered. This has been done in recent years with regard to the rule in

Addie's Case [1929] A.C. 358. In *Commissioner for Railways (N.S.W.)* v. *Cardy* (1960) 104 C.L.R. 274, the plaintiff was a boy aged 14 years. Notwithstanding the fact that the boy was a trespasser, Dixon C.J. said at p. 286 of the report:– 'In principle a duty of care should rest on a man to safeguard others from a grave danger of serious harm if knowingly he has created the danger or is responsible for its continued existence and is aware of the likelihood of others coming into proximity of the danger and has the means of preventing it or of averting the danger or of bringing it to their knowledge.' This passage has frequently been cited with approval in dealing with trespass cases within the past ten years.

The plaintiff relied on *Videan's Case* [1963] 2 Q.B. 650, which was described by Lord Reid in *Herrington* v. *British Railways Board* [1972] A.C. 877 as 'opening a new chapter.' In *Videan's Case* [1963] 2 Q.B. 650 the Court of Appeal decided that the duty of the occupier of land towards a trespasser was the duty to take care not to injure a trespasser whose presence was foreseeable or reasonably to be anticipated. Lord Denning M.R. stated the true principle in the following terms at pp. 665–6 of the report:– 'In the ordinary way the duty to use reasonable care extends to all persons lawfully on the land, but it does not extend to trespassers, for the simple reason that he cannot ordinarily be expected to foresee the presence of a trespasser. But the circumstances may be such that he ought to foresee even the presence of a trespasser: and then the duty of care extends to the trespasser also.' And in relation to children he said:– 'Once he foresees their presence, he owes them the common duty of care, no more and no less. I would not restrict it to a duty "to treat them with common humanity," for I do not know quite what that means. I prefer to say that he is to take reasonable care. This simple test (which is based on foreseeability) is sufficient to explain all the cases, though not all the statements contained in them. You must remember that, in applying the test of foreseeability, you have to consider all the circumstances of the particular case . . .'

The test of reasonable foresight adopted in *Videan's Case* [1963] 2 Q.B. 650 was expressly disapproved by the Judicial Committee of the Privy Council in *Commissioner for Railways* v. *Quinlan* [1964] A.C. 1054 in which the *Addie* principle was adopted. The judgments in *Videan's Case* [1963] 2 Q.B. 650 did not thereafter have the authority which, in my view, was their due.

The duty owed to a trespasser was reconsidered by the House of Lords in *Herrington* v. *British Railways Board* [1972] A.C. 877 and a considerable portion of the argument in the court below and in this Court was devoted to that decision. In *Herrington's Case* [1972] A.C. 877, *Addie's Case* [1929] A.C. 358 was not followed and, indeed, it was stated that the case had been wrongly decided. At p. 929 of the report Lord Pearson said:– 'It seems to me that the rule in *Addie's Case* [1929] A.C. 358 has been rendered obsolete by changes in physical and social conditions and has become an incumbrance impeding the proper development of the law. With the increase of the population and the larger proportion living in cities and towns and the extensive substitution of blocks of flats for rows of houses with gardens or back yards and quiet streets, there is less playing space for children and so a greater temptation to trespass. There is less supervision of children, so that they are more likely to trespass. Also with the progress of technology there are more and greater dangers for them to encounter by reason of the increased use of, for instance, electricity, gas, fast-moving vehicles, heavy machinery and poisonous chemicals. There is considerably more need than there used to be for occupiers to take reasonable steps with a view to deterring persons, especially children, from trespassing in places that are dangerous for them. In my opinion the *Addie* v. *Dumbreck* [1929] A.C. 358 formulation of the duty of occupier to trespasser is plainly inadequate for modern conditions, and its rigid and restrictive character has impeded the proper development of the common law in this field. It has become an anomaly and should be discarded.' In relation to the duty owed by the occupier of land to a trespasser, Lord Reid said at p. 899 of the report:– 'So it appears to me that an occupier's duty to trespassers must vary according to his knowledge, ability and resources. It has often been said that trespassers must take the land as they find it. I would rather say that they must take the occupier as they find him. So the question whether an occupier is liable in respect of an accident to a trespasser on his land would depend on whether a conscientious humane man with his knowledge, skill and resources would reasonably have been expected to have done or refrained from doing before the accident something which would have avoided it.' In applying a subjective test, Lord Reid introduced a new approach to this branch of the law. Lord Morris of Borth-y-Gest, at p. 909 of the report, expressed the duty as 'a duty to take such steps as common sense or common humanity would dictate'; at p. 940 of the report Lord Diplock said of the occupier that 'Where he does know of physical facts which a reasonable man would appreciate involved danger of serious injury to the trespasser his duty is to take reasonable steps to enable the trespasser to avoid the danger.'

Since *Herrington's Case* [1972] A.C. 877, therefore, the law in relation to the duty owed to a trespasser has been settled in England. Lord Denning M.R. in *Pannett* v. *M'Guinness & Co.* [1972] 2 Q.B. 599 has summarised the present state of the law in the following terms at pp. 606–7 of the report:– 'The long and short of it is that you have to take into account all the circumstances of the case and see then whether the occupier ought to have done more than he did. (1) You must apply your common sense. You must take into account the gravity and likelihood of the probable injury . . . The more dangerous the activity, the more he should take steps to see that no one is injured by it. (2) You must take into account also the character of the intrusion by the trespasser . . . You may expect a child when you may not expect a burglar. (3) You must also have regard to the nature of the place where the trespass occurs . . . (4) You must also take into account the knowledge which the defendant has, or ought to have, of the likelihood of trespassers being present. The more likely they are, the more precautions may have to be taken.' I find no difficulty in agreeing with that statement.

Counsel for the defendants urge strenuously that this Court should not follow *Herrington's Case* [1972] A.C. 877 but I can see no valid reason why the rule in *Addie's Case* [1929] A.C. 358, which has been considered obsolete in England and which in my view is equally obsolete here, should be applied any longer.

The decision of this Court in *Purtill* v. *Athlone U.D.C.* [1968] I.R. 205 is also of considerable importance. In that case the plaintiff, a boy aged 14 years, was held to be a trespasser; he had taken some detonators from the defendants' abattoir and was injured at his home when one of the detonators exploded. The defendants alleged that they owed the plaintiff no duty because he had been a trespasser. The test of reasonable foresight was applied and, in delivering the judgment of the Court, Mr. Justice Walsh said at p. 212 of the report:–

'When the danger is reasonably foreseeable, the duty to take care to avoid injury to those who are proximate, when their proximity is known, is not abrogated because the other party is a trespasser. The duty to those in proximity is not based on any implied term of an invitation or a licence, or upon any warranty for safety which might be thought to be inherent in any such invitation or licence. Rather is it based upon the duty that one man has to those in proximity to him to take reasonable care that they are not injured by his acts. What amounts to sufficient care must vary necessarily with the circumstances, the nature of the danger, and the age and knowledge of the person likely to be injured.'

Purtill's Case [1968] I.R. 205 was criticised by counsel for the defendants on the basis that it was breaking new ground and that the notion of proximity was being introduced for the first time in that case. However, this is not so as it is to be found in *Heaven* v. *Pender* [1883] 11 Q.B.D. 503, in *Le Lievre* v. *Gould* [1893]1 Q.B. 491 and in Lord Atkin's well-known judgment in *Donoghue* v. *Stevenson* [1932] A.C. 562; so that, like *Donoghue* v. *Stevenson* [1932] A.C. 562, *Purtill's Case* [1968] I.R. 205 could be said to be restorative rather than revolutionary.

In my view, the test to be applied in the present case is to ask whether the defendants could reasonably have foreseen that child trespassers were likely to climb the fence at their sub-station, gain access to the roof, and sustain injury there; and whether, in all the circumstances of the case, the defendants took reasonable care to see that child trespassers were not injured. The sub-station was in the centre of a large housing estate and, to the knowledge of the defendants' employees, children tended to congregate very much in the locality. The danger to be guarded against could hardly have been more serious; it was the risk of someone coming into contact with high-voltage electricity. The employees of the defendants were alive to the danger of children coming on to the defendants' premises, and it was for this very reason that the fence was heightened. The instructions given to the employee who raised the height of the fence were 'to make the fence like a concentration camp.' In view of the fact that the live portion of the copper conductor was not less than 10'7" from the ground, there was no real danger unless and until a child got on to the flat roof. Once there, however, he was in close proximity to the conductor which carried 10,000 volts. The engineer who gave evidence on behalf of the plaintiff described the fence as being a man-made ladder giving easy access to the roof, and the jury were entitled to accept this evidence. In my opinion there was evidence on which the jury were entitled to reach a finding that there was negligence on the part of the defendants and to answer the questions in favour of the plaintiff.

[**Griffin J.** held, however, that the jury should have found that the plaintiff contributed to the accident and that the damages awarded were excessive. He declared that a new trial should be ordered on all issues. **Fitzgerald C.J.** dissented: *cf. McMahon* v. *Binchy*, p. 259, fn. 171.]

KEANE V. E.S.B.
[1981] I.R. 44

Henchy J.:

This case seems to have its origin in the decision, in July, 1974, of this Court in *McNamara* v. *Electricity Supply Board*.

That important decision represented a departure from earlier authorities as to the principle on which the liability of an occupier of premises to a trespasser, especially a child trespasser, should be determined. As the headnote correctly summarizes the effect of the judgments, in order to succeed in an action against the occupier for negligence such a plaintiff must be able (inter alia) to get an affirmative answer from the jury to the dual test:– 1. Could the occupier have *reasonably* foreseen that the child trespasser would try to make an entry into the area of danger. 2. Did the occupier fail to take *reasonable* steps to prevent the entry and the consequent injury?

Were it not for the new turn that the law had taken in *McNamara* v. *Electricity*

Supply Board [1975] I.R. 1, the present action would scarcely have seen the light of day. This plaintiff, being 23 years old, instituted these proceedings in June, 1977 (three years after the decision of this Court in *McNamara* v. *Electricity Supply Board* [1975] I.R. 1) in respect of an injury which he had suffered 12 years earlier when he was almost 11 years old. By any standards of the reasonably expeditious prosecution of a claim for damages for negligence, this was a stale action. It did not come on for hearing until January, 1979, which was nearly 14 years after the accident. Such delay, for which no explanation has been vouchsafed, could hardly be described as providing the ideal route to a just and fair trial. For one thing, the attendant at the electricity sub-station where the accident took place had died by the time of the trial. In the event, the plaintiff lost his case in the High Court for, at the end of the evidence for the defence, the trial judge withdrew the case from the jury on the ground that the evidence would not warrant a finding in the plaintiff's favour on the issue of negligence. It is from that ruling that the present appeal has been taken by the plaintiff.

This case shares certain features with *McNamara* v. *Electricity Supply Board* [1974] I.R. 1. Each boy was about 11 years old at the time of his accident; they each managed to climb over a wire-mesh fence which was topped with barbed wire, they each disregarded boldly-displayed warning notices; each of them, as a trespasser, got into a danger area where there was an uninsulated high-tension cable or conductor; and each of them, by coming into contact with the cable or conductor, suffered severe arm injuries. In almost every other respect, I find crucial differencies between the two cases.

I have already indicated the salient feature in *McNamara* v. *Electricity Supply Board* [1975] I.R. 1 that made a finding of negligence sustainable against the defendants in that case. By way of distinction and contrast, let me point to certain factors that put the present case in a different category. The sub-station where the accident happened was not situate in a city, let alone in the middle of a densely populated urban housing estate; it was in the middle of a field in the country at about half a mile from the small town of Cloyne in the county of Cork. There was no history of the field having been frequented previously by children to the knowledge of the defendants. To get into the field from the road the plaintiff had to climb over a locked gate. The occasion of his visit – to look for fluffy-topped bulrushes as playthings – was not to be expected by the defendants; it was out of season for bulrushes in that state of bloom. In the field there were two fences surrounding the transformer where the plaintiff was injured. He got over the first or outer fence by climbing over a six-bar iron gate. He then was faced with the inner or security fence which was 5' 9" high and was made of 2½ inch square chain links. On the security fence were mounted three strands of barbed wire which made the total height 6' 9" at the point where he climbed over. The inner gate at this point, up which the plaintiff clambered, carried a large notice which read 'Electricity Supply Board H.T. Sub-Station. No Unauthorised Persons Admitted.' Having disregarded or not observed this notice, the plaintiff managed to get over the 6' 9" fence in his unlikely search for bulrushes. Diverting himself from that search, he proceeded to do something no less unlikely and no less outside the reasonable foresight of the defendants: he climbed on to the transformer and then clutched one of the high-tension cables. The serious injury to his left hand was the inevitable consequence.

Bearing in mind that the legal test was whether it was reasonably foreseeable that a youth such as the plantiff would attempt to get inside the security fence and, if so, whether the defendants had, in the light of all the prevailing relevant circumstances, taken reasonable steps to keep him out, and assuming for the purpose of this appeal that the plaintiff satisfied the first part of that test, let us see how the evidence went at the trial as to the second part. In this context I repeat what I said in my judgment in *McNamara's Case* (at pp. 24–5):–

'It needs to be stressed that the existence of, or failure to observe, a duty of care should not be determined with the hindsight derived from the accident but in the light of the circumstances, actual and potential, that ought to have been present to the mind of a reasonably conscientious occupier of property before the trespass took place.'

The plaintiff's advisers relied on the evidence of two engineers to prove that the defendants had failed to take reasonable steps to prevent the plaintiff's entry into the area of danger. The evidence of the first of these witnesses (Mr. Tennyson) as to the defendants' alleged default might be summed up in the following replies he gave to questions put to him about the adequacy of the security fence:– 'This fence wouldn't be regarded as being sufficiently child-proof to protect a high-tension station to make a fence child-proof . . . It is climbable by children . . . As I said, the criterion you should use is one of preventing access so that people cannot get in without tools [*to cut their way in*].' The evidence of the other engineer (Mr. Brennan) was to the effect that the fence would not be adequate or effective unless the posts, on which the barbed wire at the top was strung, were cranked outwards, thus debarring ingress to everybody, child or adult, who did not use a wire-cutting implement or a ladder. In other words, he postulated a fence that would be proof against access by young or old, or, at least, a child-proof fence.

In my judgment, that evidence pitched the test for negligence higher than that laid down by *McNamara's Case* and by the relevant modern decisions which are mentioned in that case. An occupier of dangerous premises, even when he has reason to foresee the possibility of an attempted trespass, is bound to do no more than to take all reasonable steps to prevent the trespass or the injury likely to result from it; he is not bound to render the premises so safe that they will be immune from intrusion by the trespasser: see *Videan* v. *British Transport Commission* [1963] 2 Q.B. 650; *Pannett* v. *McGuinness & Co.* [1972] 2 Q.B. 599 and *Herrington* v. *British Railways Board* [1972] A.C. 877. To impose such a duty on the occupier would be akin to making him an insurer of the trespasser's safety.

By way of rebuttal of the plaintiff's case, the defendants adduced expert evidence that the security fence was of a standard design and construction; that it was supervised and maintained adequately; that there are about 180 similar stations in the State; that from the time of the construction of this sub-station in 1961 until the trial of the action in 1979 there was (apart from this case) no known trespass or attempted trespass there; that it is only in the case of sub-stations in urban areas where attempted trespass or vandalism is to be expected that, in recent times, the extra precautions suggested by the plaintiff's engineers are considered advisable (*i.e.* the outward overhanging barbed wire on top), but that even that precaution has not succeeded in preventing trespass; that at the relevant time security fences of this kind were to be found in use by electricity boards in England, Wales, Northern Ireland and elsewhere; and that experience had shown that this security fence was an adequate precaution because, up to the time of this accident and later, the design of such a fence in 180 sub-stations had led to no such accident: in short, that at the time of this accident there was nothing to suggest that it would be reasonable to take any precautions against trespass other than those taken.

In those circumstances, I am of the opinion that the judge was correct in holding, in effect, that a jury which was properly directed as to the law would be bound to find for the defendants on the basis of the uncontroverted evidence that was given on their behalf, and to which I have referred. Of course, as the two engineers who gave evidence for the plaintiff said, the security fence could have been made higher and more complex and, therefore, more likely to repel trespassers. But that is not the test. The test is whether the occupier did all that he could reasonably be expected in the circumstances to have done to avert the trespass and injury that followed on it. The defendants adopted what was then considered (justifiably, on the basis of standard design and widespread experience) the mode of deterrence (*i.e.*, by warning notices and attempted physical exclusion) which could reasonably have been expected to avert this kind of accident.

Counsel for the plaintiff, in suggesting that the defendants' duty was to go further and to take all such precautions as would have made this kind of accident, as he put it, 'almost impossible,' places the duty of an occupier vis-à-vis a trespasser on too high a plane. Where the default complained of is not obviously risky or imprudent, and is no more than an adherence to a widely observed practice which has hitherto proved safe, to hold the occupier liable for injury to a trespasser would impose a higher duty of care on an occupier towards a trespasser than the law imposes on an employer towards an employee. That would be both illogical and unfair, having regard to the respective social relations and obligations of such parties in the eyes of the law. As Lord Reid said in his speech in the House of Lords in *M'Glone* v. *British Railways Board* 1966 S.C. 1 at p. 13 of the report:– 'It would put occupiers in an impossible position if, having provided adequate protection, they then had to weigh possible further reduction of risk of accidents against the trouble and expense of taking further precautions. An occupier must do what he is bound to do, but he is not in fault in failing to do more, however easy it might have been to do that.'

I would uphold the ruling of the trial judge and dismiss this appeal.

[**Griffin J.** in a separate judgment agreed with **Henchy J. O'Higgins C.J.** however, dissented, holding that the case should have been left go to the jury at the trial, on the issue of whether the defendant had taken reasonable care.]

Note

In Northern Ireland and in England lawful visitors are now, by legislation, entitled to 'the common duty of care'. (See the *Occupiers' Liability Act (Northern Ireland), 1957* and the *Occupiers' Liability Act 1957*). The duty to trespassers, however, was not dealt with in those Acts and is still a matter for the common law. In *Herrington* v. *British Railways Board* [1972] A.C. 877 the House of Lords reviewed the law relating to trespassers and held that the occupier owes foreseeable trespassers a duty to act in a conscientious and humane manner. In *Lowry* v. *Buchanan* N.I.L.R. Bull. 1980 No. 3 in Northern Ireland McDermott J., quoted Henchy J. in *McNamara* with approval, adding 'As a gloss to that quotation and having regard to the observations in *Herrington* I would simply add that in deciding what is reasonable care to exercise towards a trespasser, the Judge, or Jury, must apply the standards of Lord Reid's [in *Herrington*] conscientious and humane man.'

Chapter 10

LIABILITY OF BUILDERS, VENDORS AND OTHERS

Vendors and lessors of real property had certain immunities at common law. Builders did not enjoy any such immunity and contract builders are liable in both contract and tort in the appropriate circumstances. A difficulty arises, however, in respect of a vendor/builder (or a lessor/builder). Is such a person, who may build a house and then sell it to a stranger, liable to the stranger for defects in the premises or for damage which the defects cause? In other words is the vendor/builder to be classified as a vendor when he will be entitled to the common law immunities (including the benefit of the maxim *caveat emptor*) or will he be classified as a builder who will be liable for damage caused to his neighbour? And what of the liability of public authorites in relation to powers, duties and discretions imposed by statute on them in respect of buildings? Are they to be liable for failure to exercise those functions properly? These, and related matters are discussed in the cases that follow.

The traditional rule, in the case of real property, was that there was no implied conditions as to fitness for habitation, etc. Caveat emptor *applied.*

McGOWAN V. HARRISON
[1941] I.R. 331

Sullivan C.J.:

This is an appeal by the plaintiff from the judgment in favour of the defendant pronounced by the President of the High Court on the trial of the action without a jury.

The action was brought to recover damages for breach of contract on the sale to the plaintiff of the house, 48 Orwell Road, Dublin. The house in question is one of several houses that the respondent erected on a plot of ground, which he held under a sub-lease, dated the 8th July, 1931, for a term of 500 years from the 29th September, 1925 (save the last day thereof) at a rent of £55 14s. Od.

The appellant was anxious to purchase the house, and after some negotiations he entered into an agreement with the respondent, dated the 27th January, 1933, to take from him a sub-lease of the premises for the term of 450 years at a yearly rent of £8 and to pay therefor the sum of £775. To enable him to carry out that agreement the appellant obtained from the Dublin Corporation under the provisions of the Small Dwellings Acquisition Act, 1899, the Housing (Ireland) Act, 1919, and the Housing (Miscellaneous Provisions) Act, 1931, an advance of £600: and by indenture of lease and charge, dated the 16th May, 1933, and made between the respondent, the appellant and the Corporation, the respondent, in consideration of the payment of the sum of £775, demised the house to the appellant for the term of 500 years from the 29th September, 1925 (save the last day thereof) subject to the yearly rent of £8, and the appellant charged in favour of the Corporation the premises with the sum of £600 and interest.

The appellant and his family occupied the house from the date of the lease until the end of the year 1937 when, owing to the subsidence of the foundations and the cracking of the walls, the house was, as found by the learned President, 'in a deplorable condition and not fit for human habitation.' He then left the house and shortly afterwards instituted this action.

At the trial it was contended on behalf of the appellant (1) that, as the house was, to the knowledge of the respondent, required by the appellant for his immediate habitation, there was an implied warranty that it was reasonably fit for that purpose; and, in the alternative, (2), that by virtue of s. 31 sub-s. 1, of the Housing (Miscellaneous Provisions) Act, 1931 there was an implied condition in the contract that the house was, at the commencement of the tenancy, and would be kept by the respondent during the tenancy, reasonably fit for human habitation. That argument was rejected by the learned President, and the action was dismissed.

The only question argued on this appeal was whether s. 31, sub-s. 1, of the Housing (Miscellaneous Provisions) Act, 1931, applied in this case. If the indenture of lease and charge, dated the 16th May, 1933, is a 'contract for letting for habitation a dwelling-house' within the meaning of that sub-section, then there must be read into it the condition mentioned in the sub-section. In form that indenture is a letting of the premises, but the transaction between the parties was in substance a sale to the appellant of the entire interest of the respondent in the premises – a term of 500 years from the 29th September, 1925 – in consideration of the payment of a sum of £775.

The fact that the sale to the appellant was carried out by means of an underlease does not, in my opinion, suffice to establish that he is a tenant holding under a 'contract for letting for habitation a dwelling-house' within the meaning of the sub-section. I do not think that he is.

I am therefore of opinion that this appeal should be dismissed.

[**Murnaghan, Meredith and Johnson JJ.** all agreed in separate judgments with the Chief Justice. **Maguire P.'s** holding in the High Court that there was no implied warranty on the part of the defendant that the house was fit for habitation, was not appealed. In the High Court **Maguire P.** had said:]

At one stage it was contended that the house when purchased was an incomplete house, but that is not persisted in now. The position is, and I so hold, that in 1933 the house was a complete house. Mr. Binchy has suggested that, even if it were a complete house, the plaintiff having intimated that he wanted a dwelling-house, the purpose for which it was required was well known to the defendant, and that, consequently, there was an implied warranty that it was reasonably fit for habitation. He referred to the case of *The Moorcock* 14 P.D. 64 as authority for this proposition. I am afraid that I cannot accept that contention. I am of opinion that the law as stated by Atkinson J. in *Otto v. Bolton and Norris* [1936] 2 K.B. 46 is the law in this country. Atkinson J., in the case referred to, at p. 52 says:– 'It is settled law that the vendor of a house, even if also the builder of it, gives no implied warranty as to its safety. A purchaser can make any examination he likes, either by himself or by somebody better qualified so to do. He can take it or leave it, but if he takes it, he takes it as he finds it. It is, perhaps, the strongest example of the application of the maxim *caveat emptor*. I can find in no case any suggestion that a builder, selling a house after completion is, in his capacity of builder, under any obligation to take care towards a future purchaser, let alone other persons who may come to live in it.'

I hold that there was no implied warranty on the part of the defendant that the house was fit for habitation, or as regards the quality of the material used.

Certain conditions are implied when the purchaser is buying a dwelling-house in the course of erection.

BROWN V. NORTON
[1954] I.R. 34

Davitt P.:

These three cases are concerned with three dwelling houses which were built by a Mr. Joseph Fennell for the defendants, James Norton and Bridget Norton, and by them sold to the plaintiffs. Each plaintiff alleges that at the time he contracted to purchase his house it was in course of erection and not completed, and that in the circumstances there is to be implied an agreement by the defendants that they would complete the erection of his house, and would do so in a proper and work-manlike manner with sound and suitable materials; and that his house when completed would be fit for human habitation. The only issue in these cases are whether in the circumstances of each case a warranty should be implied, and if so, of what nature, and whether there has been any breach thereof.

[Having examined the facts and the nature of the defects complained of, **Davitt P.** continued:]

These are the material facts in these three cases. As I have already said each plaintiff pleads that his purchase agreement was an agreement for the purchase of a house in the course of erection: that the defendants impliedly agreed that they would complete the erection of his house and that it would be completed of sound and suitable materials and in a proper and workmanlike manner, and when complete would be fit for human habitation. Each alleges a breach of the implied agreement as subsequently described in his evidence. In each case the defendants plead that the agreement was for the sale of a completed house; they deny that there was any such implied agreement: and deny that there are any defects which would constitute a breach of such an agreement. In the cases of Brown and Burgess they plead that if there was any such implied agreement it became merged and extinguished in the sub-leases which were granted. In O'Connor's case they plead that the sub-lease was granted to Mr. and Mrs. O'Connor as joint tenants and that Mr. O'Connor has no cause of action. In hearing the only deferences relied on were that in O'Connor's case the agreement was for the sale of a completed house, that in Burgess's case the purchase agreement in its terms negatived any implied agreement, and that in all the cases there were no defects which constituted any breach of the alleged agreements. Counsel for the defendants also relied upon my interpretation in the unreported cases of *Fitzpatrick* v. *Brady* and *Fitzpatrick* v. *Brennan* of the decision in the *Cannon Hill Estates Case* [1931] 2 K.B. 113 as to the nature of the agreements, if any, to be implied.

The plaintiffs rested their cases almost entirely upon the authority of the decision in *Miller* v. *Cannon Hill Estates Ltd.* [1931] 2 K.B. 113 as accepted and applied in this country. It is sufficient at this stage to say that I consider that that case is an authority for the proposition that where a building contractor agrees to sell to a purchaser a dwelling-house which is in the course of erection, and both parties understand that the purchaser is buying for the purpose of occupying it as a residence as soon as it is completed, a Court may, in the absence of any circumstances negativing such an implication, hold that the vendor impliedly agrees that he will complete the house, and will do so in such a way that when complete it will be reasonably fit for immediate occupation as a residence. In this sense I believe that the decision has been readily accepted and applied during the last twenty years by the High Court and the Circuit Court in this country. In no case, however, that I am aware of has the basis on which that decision rests been examined; and it can do no harm now to attempt an examination of that decision and the other relevant authorities.

Before the decision in the *Cannon Hill Estates Case* [1931] 2 K.B. 113 the following principles of law appear to me to have been regarded as established. The mere sale of land, and *a fortiori* a mere agreement to sell, carried no implication of any agreement that the land was fit for any particular purpose: *Loundes* v. *Lane* (1789) 2 Cox. Eq. Cases 363, per Lord Thurlow; *Spoor* v. *Green* L. R. 9 Ex. 99, per Cleasby B. at p. 109; Halsbury's Laws of England (2nd ed.), vol. 29, at p. 248, paras. 330 *et seq.*: Williams on Vendor and Purchaser (4th ed., 1936), at p. 759. The mere letting of land, with or without an unfurnished dwelling-house upon it likewise carried no such implication: *Sutton* v. *Temple* 12 M. & W. 52; *Hart* v. *Windsor* 12 M. & W. 68. In the case of a written agreement for the letting of a dwelling-house unfurnished, which contained no such provision, there could be a collateral *express* warranty as to the fitness of the house for habitation: *De Lassalle* v. *Guildford* [1901] 2 K.B. 215. In the case of a written agreement for the letting of a furnished house which was silent upon the matter there could be implied a collateral agreement that the house would be at the commencement of the term in a good and tenantable condition and reasonably fit for human occupation: *Smith* v. *Marrable* 11 M. & W. 5; *Wilson* v. *Finch Hatton* 2 Ex. D. 336; *Collins* v. *Hopkins* [1923] 2 K.B. 617. Where a builder contracted with an employer to build a dwelling house for him, in the absence of any circumstances negativing such an implication, he impliedly agreed that he had the necessary skill and would execute the work in a good and workmanlike manner and with sound and suitable materials and that the house would be fit for the purpose for which it was built: *Norris* v. *Staps* Hobart 210; 80 E.R. 357; *Farnsworth* v. *Garrard* [1807] 1 Camp. 38; *Harmer* v. *Cornelius* (1858) 5 C.B. (N.S.) 236; *Pearce* v. *Tucker* 3 F. & F. 136; *Duncan* v. *Blundell* 3 Stark. (N.P.) 6; *G. H. Myers and Co.* v. *Brent Cross Service Co.* [1934] 1 K. B. 46; *Hall* v. *Burke* 3 T. L. R. 165. Where two parties contracted and it was clearly to be inferred from the circumstances that some provision which it was their common will and intention should be part of their agreement was taken for granted and left unexpressed, such a provision would be implied: *The Moorcock* (1889) 14 P. D. 64; *In re Comptoir Ancorsois* v. *Power, Son & Co.* [1920] 1 K. B. 868 (per Scrutton L.J., at p. 899); *Lamb* v. *Evans* [1893] 1 Ch. 218 (per Bowen L.J., at p. 229); *Shirlane* v. *Southern Foundries* (1926) *Ltd* [1939] 2 K. B. 206 (per MacKinnon L.J., at p. 227).

It is not easy to appreciate exactly the grounds for the distinction between the letting of an unfurnished house and the letting of a furnished house. In *Wilson* v. *Finch Hatton* 2 Ex. D. 336 Keely C.B. thought it quite clear that both parties contemplated that the house should be ready for occupation on the day on which the tenancy began; that they both intended that it should be then fit for occupation in the sense that it should be reasonably healthy; and that accordingly effect should be given to their common intention. Pollock B. (at p. 344) put the matter in a nut shell when he said:– 'Apart, however, from authority, it is, I think, clear, that the plaintiffs have not supplied to the tenant that which both parties intended they should supply.' In *Smith* v. *Marrable* 11 M. & W. 5 Parke B. apparently considered that there was no distinction between furnished and unfurnished lettings; but in *Hart* v. *Windsor* 12 M. & W. 68 he had to abandon this position. In that case, in which he delivered the judgment of the Court, he appears to have approached the matter by considering whether on the old authorities there was any general rule of law which attached to the word, 'demise,' in a lease, or to the mere fact of a letting, the implication of an agreement that the subject of the letting was fit for the purpose for which it was intended. He does not appear to have considered the question as to what was the actual and common, though unexpressed, intention of the parties. He appears to be mainly concerned with the effects and consequences of deciding what terms should be deemed to be incorporated in every contract for the letting of lands or houses, and not specifically with determining what in the particular case was the unexpressed will of the contracting parties. So far as the reported cases go nobody appears ever to have succeeded in convincing a Court that in the case of the sale of a completed house, or of the letting of an unfurnished house, that the real question was, as Pollock B. considered in *Wilson* v. *Finch Hatton* 2 Ex. D. 336, whether the vendor or the landlord, as the case might be, had supplied to the purchaser or tenant what both parties intended that he should supply. In *Bunn* v. *Harrison* 3 T. L. R. 146 in respect of an unfurnished letting the plaintiff sought to rely upon an implied warranty as an alternative to an express one. He succeeded on the express warranty. The Court of Appeal (Esher, Lindley and Lopes L.JJ.) expressly left open the question whether the principles of *Smith* v. *Marrable* 11 M. & W. 5 and *Wilson* v. *Finch Hatton* 2 Ex. D. 336 applied to the case where both parties understood that the unfurnished house was intended for immediate habitation. In *Collins* v. *Hopkins* [1923] 2 K. B. 617 McCardie J. (at p. 618) observed:– 'In the case of an unfurnished house there is ordinarily no warranty of fitness for occupation. Special circumstances may create such a warranty. . . . Normally, however, no warranty exists.' In *Bottomley* v. *Bannister* [1932] 1 K. B. 458, however, Scrutton L.J. (at p. 468) said:– 'Now it is at present well established English law that, in the absence of express contract, a landlord of an unfurnished house is not liable to his tenant, or a vendor of real estate to his purchaser, for defects in the house or land rendering it dangerous or unfit for occupation even if he has constructed the defects himself or is aware of their existence.' This was followed by Atkinson J. in *Otto* v. *Bolton and Norris* [1936] 2 K. B. 46 who said (at p. 52):– 'It is settled law that the vendor of a house, even if also the builder of it, gives no implied warranty as to its safety. A purchaser can make any examination he likes, either by himself or by somebody better qualified so to do. He can take it or leave it, but if he takes it, he takes it as he find it. It is, perhaps, the strongest example of the application of the maxim *caveat emptor*. I can find in no case any suggestion that a builder selling a house after completion is, in his capacity of builder, under any obligation to take care towards a future purchaser, let alone other persons who may come to live in it.' In *Hoskins* v. *Woodham* [1938] 1 All E.R. 692 Macnaghten J. (at p. 695), says:– 'It is quite certain that, in the sale of a completed house, where a sale is duly executed, and possession taken of the house after conveyance, there is no implied warranty that the house is reasonably fit for habitation.' In that case it would appear that the only circumstances from which the Court was asked to imply such a warranty were that the house was a new house, part of a building estate, and was purchased from the builder. The latest case I have found upon the matter is *Edler* v. *Auerbach* [1950] 1 K. B. 359 in which Devlin J. (at pp. 373–4), applies the principle as enumerated in *Hart* v. *Windsor* 12 M. & W. 68 and *Bottomley* v. *Bannister* [1932] 1 K. B. 458.

In *Lawrence* v. *Cassell* [1930] 2 K. B. 83 the defendant agreed in writing to sell to the plaintiff a plot of land, part of a building estate, with a dwelling-house thereon in course of erection, and to complete the house in accordance with plans of other houses, with fittings similar in all material particulars to those in other houses, erected on the estate. The contract was duly completed and a deed of conveyance executed which was silent as regards the building of the house. The house proved not to be weatherproof and the plaintiff sued for damages for breach of the written contract to complete the house, alleging that by that contract the defendant had undertaken to carry out the work in a proper, efficient and workmanlike manner and that the materials used should be fit and proper for the purpose. The defendant pleaded that there were no terms in the contract except what was expressed; that before the contract was made the house was fully completed except that no plastering or decoration had been done and the fireplaces had not been fitted nor the fittings supplied; that in any event the contract had merged in the conveyance. Swift J. gave judgment for the plaintiff for £150 damages but the grounds upon which he did so do not appear. On appeal two points were argued on behalf of the defendant: that the contract had merged; and that if not the contract to complete the house related only to the work which still remained to be done at the date of the contract and had no reference to the work already done at that date. The Court of Appeal (Scrutton, Greer and Slesser L.JJ.), held that the contract to complete the house was collateral to the contract of sale and did not merge in the conveyance; and expressly refrained from deciding anything else. They did not deal with the second point argued on behalf of the defendants as this had not been raised at the trial. Scrutton L.J. (at p. 89), said:– 'I agree that it might require very careful consideration whether the agreement to complete the house referred exclusively to work to be done subsequently; accepting what had already been done as executed according to the contract, or whether it included the whole of the work to be done on the house – that which purported to be completed as well as that which was plainly unfinished. There is a good deal to be said for the view that a contract to complete a house is not performed by making a house full of defects some of which subsequently appear in consequence of work badly done before the contract and some of which are due to bad work done after the contract. But on this question I say nothing. . . .'

In the *Cannon Hill Estates Case* [1931] 2 K. B. 113 the plaintiff, having been assured by the defendants' secretary and sales manager that the material and workmanship used and employed in the construction of the houses on the estate were 'of the best,' signed an agreement to purchase one for £915 0s. 0d. Clause 7 of the agreement provided that the interior of the house was to be finished off similar to a show house and that the defendants undertook to furnish and complete the same to the purchaser's reasonable satisfaction. The same was duly completed by conveyance and the plaintiff went into occupation. The weather proved to be abnormally wet and serious damp penetrated the house. The plaintiff sued for damages for breach of the express warranty, and alternatively of an implied warranty by the defendants that they would complete the house in a good and workmanlike manner with materials of good quality and description so as to be fit for habitation. The case was tried in the County Court, with a jury who found in favour of the express warranty and the judge gave judgment for £91 0s. 0d. On appeal counsel for the defendants argued that there was not sufficient evidence of an express warranty; that if the contract was only a contract for the sale of a house the maxim *caveat emptor* applied; but admitted that, if the contract was a double one – to build a house and to sell a completed house – the question of an implied warranty did arise. The Court of King's Bench held that the jury were justified in finding in favour of the express warranty relied on; but went on to consider the question of implied warranty. Swift J. thought that it was plain from all the facts of the case that the law would imply a warranty that the house *which was to be built* by the defendants for the plaintiff should be a house which was habitable and fit for human beings to live in. He distinguished the case from the case of a purchaser buying an unfurnished house, in regard to which he said (at p. 120):– 'I think it is quite clear law that if one buys an unfurnished house, there is no implication of law, and there is no implied contract that the house is necessarily fit for human habitation.' He said that where there is a contract to build a house, or to purchase a house in the course of erection, the whole object, as both parties know, is that there shall be erected a house in which the intended purchaser shall come to live; that it was the very essence and nature of the transaction that he will have a house erected which is fit for him to come into as a dwelling-house; and that it was plain that in those circumstances there was an implied warranty that the house would be reasonably fit for the purpose for which it was required, namely, for human dwelling. He said that if the plaintiff had no such implied warranty the consideration for which he bought the house wholly failed. He considered *Lawrence* v. *Cassell* [1930] 2 K. B. 83 an authority in favour of an implied warranty; and concluded by saying that there was in this case an implied agreement by the defendants to complete the house and to do so in an efficient and workmanlike manner and with proper materials. Macnaghten J. said that it was an implied term between the parties that the defendants should complete the house in a good and workmanlike manner, with materials of good quality and description, so as to be fit for habitation.

With all respect I cannot agree with some of the grounds upon which Swift J. based his opinion. There would have been, for instance, no total failure of consideration in the absence of the implied warranty. The plaintiff paid £915 0s. 0d. for the house. He was awarded £91 0s. 0d., damages, which presumably was the cost of remedying the defects, or the amount by which the value of the house was diminished by reason of them. Instead of 100 per cent. failure of consideration it seems to me that there was at most a 10 per cent. failure. Moreover, *Lawrence* v. *Cassell* [1930] 2 K.B. 83 seems to me to be an authority merely for the proposition that the purchase agreement did not wholly merge in the conveyance. I hold that the judgments in the *Cannon Hill Estates Case* [1931] 2 K. B. 113 if they did not make new law did break new ground in the sense that it is the first reported case, so far as I am aware, in which in a contract for the acquisition of an unfurnished house a term was implied as to its fitness for a particular purpose. *Hart* v. *Windsor* 12 M. & W. 68 was decided upon the basis that the letting was for the purpose of the tenant dwelling in the house; and it seems to be that most, if not all, the stock arguments against implying a term as to fitness in such a contract, or in a contract for the sale of an unfurnished house for the same purpose, applied to the sale of a house in the course of erection. Such a term had never before been implied in any reported case; the tenant or purchaser had as compared with the purchaser of a completed house at least an equal opportunity of inspecting the work already done; he had an equal chance of getting an express warranty if he was prepared to pay an enhanced price, and he could have taken it without an express warranty or have left it. However that may be, the main basis for the decision to imply the term in question in the *Cannon Hill Estates Case* [1931] 2 K.B. 113 was that the circumstances of the case justified the inference that it was the common intention of the parties, and the object of their contract, that the defendants should supply the plaintiff with a house to live in and therefore reasonably fit for that purpose. In other words the real basis for the decision is the same as that in *Wilson* v. *Finch Hatton* 2 Ex. D. 336. In *Wilson* v. *Finch Hatton* reliance was placed upon *Smith* v. *Marrable* 11 M. & W. 5 as an authority. The basis of the judgment of Abinger C.B. in the later case appears to have been much the same as the basis of the judgments in the former. In attempting, however, to distinguish the latter case in *Sutton* v. *Temple* 12 M. & W. 52 Abinger C.B. appears to have been anxious to shift the basis somewhat. He explained that the letting of a furnished house was a mixed contract which involved a hiring of chattels as well as a demise of a house and land; that from the point of view of value the hiring was much the more important element; and that in the hiring of a chattel there was to be implied an agreement that it was fit for the purpose for which it was hired; if then, he reasoned, the tenant is entitled to expect that a house will be supplied with furniture suitable for its use and occupation, common sense and justice required the lessor to let the house itself in a habitable state. In the *Cannon Hill Estates Case* [1931] 2 K.B. 113 similarly Swift J. appears to have regarded the contract as a mixed contract – to build and sell when built. It seems clear that the circumstance that a contract to build involved the usual warranty as to workmanship, materials and fitness substantially influenced his decision. In either of these cases the parties, had they so desired, could have expressly kept separate the obligations arising from the different parts of their mixed contract and could have provided in the one case that while there was to be a warranty in regard to the furniture there was to be none with regard to the house; and in the other that while there was to be a warranty with regard to future work there was to be none as regards what had already been done. In determining what was implied in the agreement of the parties I see no difficulty in observing the same distinction; and I see no compelling reason why an obligation which applies to one part of a contract must necessarily apply to the whole. However that may be, the real basis of the decision in the *Cannon Hill Estates Case* [1931] 2 K.B. 113 was, I think, as far as principle is concerned the same as that in *Wilson* v. *Finch Hatton*, 2 Ex. D. 336, considered from that angle the basis if I may say so with all respect seems firm and solid enough.

In the *Cannon Hill Estates Case* [1931] 2 K. B. 113 there appears to have been no necessity to draw any distinction between the defendants' obligation to the plaintiff with regard to the work already done at the date of the purchase agreement and the work which was done thereafter. It seems to me however that, having considered the case of *Lawrence* v. *Cassell* [1930] 2 K. B. 83, the Court had the distinction in mind. When the judgments deal with the contract as a whole they speak of implying a term that the house should be reasonably fit for habitation; when they deal with the particular obligation to complete the house they speak of implying a term that this should be done in an efficient and workmanlike manner and that proper materials should be used. Many years ago in the Circuit Court in a judgment dealing with two cases of this kind, *Fitzpatrick* v. *Brady* and *Fitzpatrick* v. *Brennan* (unreported) I held, following the decision in the *Cannon Hill Estates Case* [1931] 2 K. B. 113, that there should be implied a warranty that the house in each case would be completed and when completed would be reasonably fit for immediate occupation; that this warranty covered the work already done on the houses at the dates respectively of the agreements to sell and the work to be done thereafter; that as regards what was already done it was a warranty that the work and the material used was such that the house when complete would be reasonably fit for immediate occupation; that as regards what was to be done it was a warranty that the work and material was of that same quality; that as regards what was to be done there was the further warranty implied that the work would be done in a good and workmanlike manner and with materials of good quality and description. It seems to me that upon a careful reading of the judgments in the *Cannon Hill Estates Case* [1931] 2 K. B. 113 and upon consideration of the other relevant authorities to which I have referred, this is the true effect of that decision.

The following consideration gives further support to this view. In my opinion no term should be implied in the contract in a case of this kind unless the Court which is asked to do so is prepared to say of it:– 'That is what both parties wanted at the time they were making their contract.' If that cannot truthfully be said then the Court, if it were to hold that the term was implied, would not be determining what the contract was; it would be itself making the agreement between the parties. The parties are legally free to make whatever lawful contract they wish; and, questions of estoppel aside, it cannot be a contract at all unless it represents their common will in the matter. A fair test would seem to be:– imagine the parties about to close their bargain on certain expressed terms, and that then the term which it is sought to imply is mentioned; if the probability is that one or other party would say:– 'I will not agree to that,' can the term ever fairly be said to be implied in their agreement? It is easy to envisage the sale of a house which is incomplete and where certain work, say, plastering and woodwork, which does not affect its habitability has been crudely or badly done. If the purchaser were to say:– 'Of course, it is understood that when the house is complete it will be fit to live in,' I can well imagine the vendor saying:– 'Yes, that is understood.' If the purchaser, however, were to add:– 'And you will tear down that woodwork and hack off that plastering and do it again in a workmanlike manner?' I should think that the reply would probably be:– 'Yes, if you pay me extra for doing it, but not otherwise.' For these reasons I think that the view which I took as to the warranties to be implied in the cases of *Fitzpatrick* v. *Brady* and *Fitzpatrick* v. *Brennan* (unreported) was correct and I propose to adhere to it.

The *Cannon Hill Estates Case* [1931] 2 K. B. 113 was considered by the Court of Appeal in England in *Perry* v. *Sharon Development Co.* [1937 4 All E.R. 390. The agreement in that case was for the sale of a house which was stated to be erected or in the course of erection. At the date of the agreement the house, in addition to decoration, lacked such things as water-taps, baths and grates, and the plastering of the walls in the dining-room and drawing-room was incomplete. The agreement provided that the contract was to be completed on a certain date 'or so soon thereafter as the premises shall be completely finished and ready for occupation.' The house being defective the purchaser sued for damages, relying upon an implied warranty as to fitness. The vendor contended that the transaction was the sale of a completed house; and that the maxim *caveat emptor* applied. The principle of the *Cannon Hill Estates Case* [1931] 2 K. B. 113 was approved though the judgments appear to rest upon the construction of the written contract rather than upon the implication of a warranty as in the *Cannon Hill Estates Case* [1931] 2 K. B. 113. The Court reiterated the opinion that there was no such warranty to be implied in the case of the sale of a completed house; but took the view that the transaction was not such a sale.

So much for the English authorities; the Irish authorities of which I am aware are few. In *Murray* v. *Mace* I. R. 8 C. L. 396 the Irish Court of Exchequer followed and applied *Hart* v. *Windsor* 12 M. & W. 68 and *Sutton* v. *Temple* 12 M. & W. 52. In *Doyle* v. *Youell* 72 I. L. T. R. 253 Mr. Justice Hanna apparently followed the decision in the *Cannon Hill Estates Case* [1931] 2 K.B. 113. In *McGowan* v. *Harrison* [1941] I. R. 331 the Chief Justice, then President of the High Court, was of opinion that the law as stated by Atkinson J. in *Otto* v. *Bolton and Norris* [1936] 2 K. B. 46 in the passage already quoted was the law in this country. That was a case of a sale of a completed house in which it must have been clear to the vendor that the purchaser wanted the house as a residence for himself and his family, and that he was anxious to leave the flat he was in and move into the house as soon as he could.

I confess that I am unable to appreciate any difference in principle between cases on the one hand of a sale of a dwelling-house in the course of erection and the letting of a furnished dwelling-house, and on the other hand cases of the sale of a newly completed dwelling-house or the letting of a dwelling-house unfurnished, if in all cases it is clearly the common though unexpressed will of the parties that what the purchaser or lessee is contracting to acquire and the vendor or lessor is contracting to supply is a dwelling-house for the purchaser or lessee to live in at the earliest opportunity. The same considerations seem to me to apply to all cases and the arguments to be adduced in favour of implying a warranty in cases in the first category appear to me to apply to cases in the second; and all the stock arguments against implying it in cases in the second category seem also to apply to cases in the first. I doubt if a general rule against implying a warranty in cases within the second category can be supported in principle and suspect that if it exists it must rest solely upon authority.

The only authorities cited by Scrutton L.J. in *Bottomley* v. *Bannister* [1932] 1 K. B. 458 (at pp. 468–9) are *Hart* v. *Windsor* 12 M. & W. 68; *Robbins* v. *Jones* 15 C. B. (N.S.) 221; *Lane* v. *Cox* [1897] 1 Q. B. 415 and *Sutton* v. *Temple* 12 M. & W. 52; and the only authority mentioned in *Otto* v. *Bolton and Norris* [1936] 2 K. B. 46 by Atkinson J. in support of the rule is *Bottomley* v. *Bannister* [1932] 1 K. B. 458. When these cases are closely examined they appear to me not to afford a very solid support for a rule of such a general nature. *Hart* v. *Windsor* 12 M. & W. 68 and *Sutton* v. *Temple* 12 M. & W. 52 were actions for rent brought by the landlords. Many matters were discussed in the arguments but to me the judgments appear to show that the question which was being mainly considered was whether there was to be derived from the authorities any general rule of law which attached to the word, 'demise,' in a lease, or to the mere fact of a letting, the implication of a condition or warranty as to fitness. (In *Sutton* v. *Temple* 12 M. & W. 52 see Abinger C.B. at p. 62, Parke B. at p. 64, and Rolf B. at p. 66; and in *Hart* v. *Windsor* 12 M. & W. 68 see Parke B. at p. 85 and the concluding paragraph on pp. 87–8). In neither case did the Court consider what must have been the *common* intention of the parties in each particular case. *Robbins* v. *Jones* 15 C. B. (N.S.) 221 was an action under Lord Campbell's Act brought by the widow of a man who had been killed as the result of the collapse of a flagged footpath constructed over what had been the area of a house adjoining the highway which belonged to the defendant. The report is a very lengthy one in which many matters are discussed. In the judgment, at p. 240, several propositions of law are set out *seriatim*. The only one of these which appears to have any relevance is the first one, which Scrutton L. J. refers to. This is as follows:– 'If the passage over the area be considered as a private way to the houses, then the reversioner is not liable, but the occupier. A landlord who lets a house in a dangerous state, is not liable to the tenant's customers or guests for accidents happening during the term: for, fraud apart, there is no law against letting a tumbledown house; and the tenant's remedy is upon his contract, if any.' This passage seems clearly to deal with the landlord's freedom from liability in tort, and his liability, if any, in contract is not dealt with. It is hard to see how the passage can afford any support for the rule in question. *Lane* v. *Cox* [1897] 1 Q. B. 415 was an action for damages for personal injuries by a workman employed by the tenant of a house leased from the defendant. At the time the house was let the staircase, which had caused the injuries, was in an unsafe condition. It was held that the landlord was under no liability to the workman. Lopes L.J. (at p. 417) said:– 'There is no liability either on the landlord or the tenant to put or to keep the demised premises in repair, unless such liability is created between them by contract. No contractual relation in this respect is implied on the letting of an unfurnished house.' This appears to be the only passage in the judgments which deals with the question of the landlord's liability to the tenant in contract. As regards the Irish cases

Murray v. *Mace* I. R. 8 C. L. 396 was decided expressly on the authority of *Sutton* v. *Temple* 12 M. & W. 52 and *Hart* v. *Windsor* 12 M. & W. 68, *Smith* v. *Marrable* 11 M. & W. 5 being regarded as of questionable authority; while in *McGowan* v. *Harrison* [1941] I. R. 331 Maguire P. accepted the rule as stated by Atkinson J. in *Otto* v. *Bolton and Norris* [1936] 2 K. B. 46. I am strongly inclined to the opinion that the only general proposition which can be safely derived from the earlier authorities is that there is no rule of law which provides that, on the mere sale or letting of an unfurnished but completely built house, there shall be implied a warranty that it is reasonably fit for habitation. To say that in no case of such a sale or letting, no matter how compelling the circumstances, can a Court hold that such a warranty is implied seems to me to be a wholly different and very much wider proposition. The Legislature may be competent to lay down such a sweeping provision but I take leave to doubt whether it is within the competence of a Court to do so. In some of the later cases, however, this appears to be the sense in which the earlier authorities have been understood and applied. The complete absence from the reports of any case in which a plaintiff has succeeded on the basis of any such implied warranty indicates that this is the sense in which the authorities have been generally understood; and affords strong, but perhaps not conclusive support for the wider and more drastic proposition.

I think that the law which I have to apply in these cases may be stated thus: where there is an agreement to purchase a house in the course of erection, and it is clearly understood by the parties that what the purchaser is contracting to buy and the vendor is contracting to sell is a dwelling-house in which the purchaser can live as soon as it is completed by the vendor, the Court may hold, in the absence of any circumstances negativing such an implication, that the vendor impliedly agrees (1) that he will complete the building of the house; (2) that as regards what has already been done at the date of the agreement the quality of the work and materials *is* such, and as regards what then remains to be done the quality *will be* such, that the house when completed will be reasonably fit for immediate occupation as a residence; and (3) that as regards what then remains to be done the work will be carried out in a good and workmanlike manner and with sound and suitable materials. The expressions, 'completed house' and 'house in course of erection,' so frequently used in cases of this kind are not, of course, to be treated as if they were expressions used in an enactment of the Legislature. In no case has it been sought to define them nor would it be advisable to make an attempt at definition. All that now remains to be done to conclude this already too lengthy judgment is to apply the law as I see it to the facts as I have found them.

In Brown's case I am satisfied to hold that agreements and warranties of the nature I have stated above were implied in the contract between the parties and to interpret them as follows: the vendors impliedly agreed (1) that they would have the building of the house completed; (2) that the walls had been soundly and properly constructed; (3) that the ground floors had been or would be properly constructed so as to be damp-proof; and (4) that the woodwork of the doors, having due regard to the difficulties of supply at the time, would be constructed in a good and workmanlike manner and of sound and suitable materials. I am satisfied that there were breaches of the agreements mentioned as (2), (3) and (4), and assess damages at £35 0s. 0d., £140 11s. 6d., and £25 0s. 0d. respectively. There will be judgment in this case for £200 11s. 6d.

In Burgess's case I am likewise satisfied to hold that the vendors impliedly agreed (1) that they would have the building of the house completed; (2) that the ground floors would be damp-proof; and (3) that the woodwork of the doors on the ground-floor and of the door of the linen-press having due regard to supply difficulties, would be constructed in a good and workmanlike manner and of sound and suitable materials; and (4) that the fireplace flue, and boiler-grate in the dining-room had been constructed and fitted in such a manner that the room would be habitable. I am satisfied that there were breaches of agreements (2), (3) and (4), and assess damages at £91 6s. 9d., £17 0s. 0d., and £32 12s. 6d., respectively. As regards the walls which were already built at the time of the purchase agreement I take the view that the clause which I have quoted from the agreement negatives the implication of any warranty in respect of them. There will be judgment for £140 19s. 3d. in this case.

As I have said, it is inadvisable to attempt any definition of the expressions 'a completed house' or 'a house in course of erection.' With regard to O'Connor's case I can only express the opinion that the evidence does not justify me in considering the house as a house which at the time of the purchase agreement was still in course of erection. Mr. O'Connor very frankly and fairly said in evidence that it was then to all intents and purposes almost complete. I am very doubtful as to what exactly, if it was anything substantial, remained to be done with respect to the boiler-grate in the dining-room; but assuming that it still had to be fitted I am not prepared to hold that this prevented the transaction from being a contract from the sale of a completed house and placed it in the other category. The other trivial matters mentioned by Mr. O'Connor do not in my view affect this conclusion in any way. I am unable to distinguish this case from *McGowan* v. *Harrison* [1941] I.R. 331 and must come to the conclusion that Mr. O'Connor has failed to establish his claim. There will accordingly be judgment in favour of the defendants.

Questions

1. What justification is there for imposing less onerous obligations in respect of the sale of 'a completed house' than in respect of a house 'in the course of erection'?
2. When is a house completed? Is a house that still requires the fininshing plaster still 'in the course of erection'?
3. Does the rule in *Brown* v. *Norton* benefit the house owner's child who is injured when a ceiling in the house collapses?
4. What effect would the adoption of a rule like that favoured in *Junior Books* v. *Veitchi* [1982] 2 All E.R. 201, have on *Brown* v. *Norton*?

No duty owed by landlord to wife of tenant.

CHAMBERS V. LORD MAYOR OF CORK
93. I.L.T.R. 45 (High Ct., 1958)

On the 15th of December, 1955, the plaintiff's husband became the weekly tenant, under a written agreement, of No. 28 Nun's Walk, Ballyphehane, Cork, a house owned by the defendants and recently built by them under a direct labour scheme. The rent, which was on a differential basis, was £2 10s. a week, there being nothing in the agreement about repairs. The tenant, with his wife, the plaintiff, went to live in the house on the 17th December, 1955. The yard of the house measured approximately fifteen feet by sixteen feet, the fuel-house being situated therein some eleven feet away from the kitchen door. A gully trap to take waste water and surface water was situated some eight feet from the kitchen door and in a direct line to the fuel-house door, some three feet further on. The gully trap, ten and a quarter inches in diameter, had an iron grating cover which was set two and a half inches below the level of the surrounding surface of the yard, which was of fairly rough concrete.

The plaintiff's husband, the tenant of the house, stated in evidence that as he thought the gully trap would be a danger to his wife and himself, he reported its condition to the foreman in charge of defendants' housing scheme, who promised to convey the complaint to defendants' general foreman. As nothing was done he reported the matter himself to the general foreman, and later, in January, 1956, as nothing still had been done, he reported it direct to defendants' engineer, who promised to detail a man to deal with the gully traps in all the Corporation's houses in the neighbourhood, as well as that in 28 Nun's Walk. Towards the end of January, 1956, a Corporation official came to 28 Nun's Walk and inspected the gully trap and agreed it needed resetting; as no action followed his visit, witness covered the iron grating with a piece of wood, but as this did not fit into the trap it was constantly being displaced by the wind or otherwise. The plaintiff's husband saw the plaintiff leave the kitchen on the 1st of May, 1957, and go out into the yard to get coal from the fuel-house; he did not see her fall but heard her groan and ran out and picked her up.

After the accident the plaintiff's husband brought the level of the cover of the trap up to the level of the surrounding surface of the yard but the defendants' workmen later cut away the concrete he had used and restored the trap to its original condition. Later still, when written to by witness's solicitor, the defendants had the trap and cover raised to the proper level but they denied that the trap as originally installed was dangerous.

The plaintiff in evidence stated that, on the 1st of May, 1957, as she was walking across the yard from the kitchen door to the fuel-house, she caught her foot in the trap and fell injuring her back, with the result that she now has to wear a steel brace and can only walk with the aid of two sticks. In cross examination the plaintiff agreed she knew the grating covering the trap was not flush with the surface of the yard and that it was dangerous and for that reason they had put a wooden cover over it. Before crossing the yard on the day of the accident she had looked to see if the wooden cover was in place and saw that it was not. She took great care in crossing the yard but her foot got caught.

An engineering witness called on behalf of the plaintiff testified that the normal position for the iron grating cover of a gully trap would be flush with the surrounding surface of the yard but that the grating at 28 Nun's Walk was two and a half inches below the level of the yard. He could see no reason for this.

The general foreman employed by the defendants at the time of the accident gave evidence on behalf of the plaintiff and agreed that the plaintiff's husband had reported to him 'once or twice' the condition of the gully trap in the yard of 28 Nun's Walk. He had inspected the trap and thought it dangerous and had made a report to the Corporation Engineer, who said he would inspect the trap himself and let witness know what he should do about it. There were, stated this witness, some 900 of these traps (known as D. A. D. or Dublin Artisan Dwellings gully traps) in use in Ballyphehane and they were all installed close to the wall in the various yards, the depth of the iron grating cover below the level of the surrounding surface varying in different houses from a half-inch to two inches depending on the slope of the yard in each case. He agreed that the present complaint was the only one that had come to his notice about these traps.

Dixon J.:

I do not see how this claim can succeed. No evidence whatsoever was produced to show that the gully trap constituted a nuisance; and, even if there had been such evidence, the plaintiff might have had difficulty in showing that she had a

As to the issue of negligence, it is well settled law that in circumstances such as those present here a landlord owes no duty to the wife of a tenant. Even if it were found that the gully trap was defective, the law is that a tenant takes a house as he finds it with all its defects. And, except by special agreement, the landlord is not liable to the tenant for defects in the house rendering it dangerous and unfit for occupation, even if he has brought about the defects himself or is aware of their existence. That, of course, is all the more so where, as here, the defects are obvious to the tenant, and if the landlord owes no duty to the tenant in this respect then the wife of the tenant could be in no better position and could have no greater claim.

Although, therefore, I have great sympathy for the plaintiff. I must decide that no legal liability attaches to the defendants in respect of this claim. Accordingly I must withdraw the case from the jury and dismiss the action.

Note and Questions

1. Even if it were found that there had been an implied warranty on the part of the defendant could the plaintiff have relied on it?
2. Would you feel that the same attitude would now be taken on the negligence issue?
3. See also *McGeary* v. *Campbell,* [1975] N.I. 7.

Liability of builder to owner of a dwelling house who is not in contractual relationship. Effect of intermediate examination. What damages are recoverable?

COLGAN V. CONNOLLY CONSTRUCTION CO. (IRELAND) LTD.
Unreptd. H. Ct. 29 Feb. 1980

McMahon J.:

This is an action brought by the owner and occupier of a dwellinghouse against a builder claiming damages for the financial loss which the plaintiff will incur in making good defects in the dwellinghouse alleged to be due to the negligent manner in which it was constructed by the builder. The plaintiff is not the first owner of the house and has no contractual relationship with the builder but he claims to be entitled to recover damages in tort on the principle of *Donoghue* v. *Stevenson*.

The house No. 54 Lucan Lodge Estate, Lucan, was built by the defendants in the year 1973 under a written contract with the first owner, Mr. Eunan Murray. The site belonged to a development company named Whitewater Limited and when the house was completed the defendants procured that company to grant a lease of it to Mr. Murray for a term of 250 years. The lease was executed in December 1973 and the house was occupied by Mr. Murray and his family from that time until it was sold to the plaintiff in 1976. The plaintiff and his family have occupied it since then. The house was not professionally surveyed before the plaintiff bought it but the plaintiff and his wife inspected it several times. The only defect they observed was a crack in the plaster on the lintel over a window in the main bedroom. It is admitted that the defects now complained of would not have been apparent on examination by a lay-man in 1976 and I am satisfied that all would have been discovered had the house been professionally surveyed at that time.

Early in 1979 the plaintiff employed a decorator to renew the wallpaper in the house and it was then discovered that large areas of the walls had plaster which was not adhering to the blockwork. The plaintiff called in an architect who discovered other defects.

The duty of care owed by the maker of an article under the principle of *Donoghue* v. *Stevenson* relates to defects which the maker can foresee are not likely to be discovered by the kind of examination he can reasonably expect to be made before the article is put into use. I have no evidence to show the kind of examination which could reasonably be anticipated by the builder of a house in this class which cost approximately £20,000 when Mr. Colgan bought it in 1976. If I were entitled to use my own knowledge I would think that it is not usual for the buyer of a house in this price class to have it professionally surveyed. Under the *Donoghue* v. *Stevenson* principle in order to establish negligence I think the onus was on the plaintiff to establish that the manufacturer should have anticipated that his product would be put into use without such an examination as would have discovered the dangerous defect. Section 34(2) (f) of the Civil Liability Act 1961 seems to me to have shifted the onus of proof to the defendants in product liability cases. That section provides that the fact that there has been a reasonable possibility or probability of examination after the thing had left the hands of the defendants shall not, by itself, exclude the defendant's duty but may be taken as evidence that he was not in the circumstances negligent in parting with the thing in its dangerous state. I hold that the builder's liability is not excluded by the fact that the defects could have been discovered by the plaintiff if he had the house professionally surveyed before he bought it.

Having considered the evidence on both sides I find that the builder of this house was careless in regard to certain matters in its construction and that in consequence the roof is defective, the internal plastering is defective, the porch roof is leaking and the cavity in the external walls is not of the proper width which is a minimum of two inches. I am not satisfied that the plaintiff has established that the sitting room window lintel is inadequate for the span or that the flashing of the chimney is defective.

I am satisfied that the defect in the cavity has not caused any problems to date with damp penetration and is unlikely to do so in the future. The effect of the cavity not being of adequate width is that the house is not as well insulated as it ought to be but this does not threaten the health or safety of the occupiers. In my view the width of the cavity can be regarded only as a defect in the quality of the house.

The trouble with the porch roof is due to an inadequate flashing which did not cause trouble until after the plaintiff had bought the house. It is now causing dampness in the sitting room and this will spread in the course of time if not remedied and will cause physical deterioration in the fabric of the house. It is not, in my view, a defect which can be a cause of danger to health or safety.

There is no evidence that the internal plastering is dangerous to health or safety except in one place, that is, on the lintel over the arch between the dining room and the sitting room. If the loose plaster at that point were to fall it could possibly cause injury to someone but apart from that the loose plaster in my view amounts to a defect of quality only.

The roof defects consist of the absence of diagonal bracing for the roof trusses and inadequate support for the roof sprockets and the fact that the blockwork walls are not carried up to meet the underfelt of the roof. These are defects which threaten the stability of the roof and in storm conditions could result in personal injury as the result of falling tiles or other possibly more serious roof damage.

In the case of *Siney* v. *The Mayor etc. of Dublin* ([1980] I. R. 400) the Supreme Court held the Corporation liable in negligence to the plaintiff in providing him with a flat which was not fit for habitation because of the defective design of the ventilation system. The ventilation system in the flat was found to amount to a serious concealed defect which the plaintiff could not have been expected to discover. The flat was provided by the Corporation in the exercise of statutory powers conferred by the Housing Act 1966 and the Supreme Court held that the condition of the flat was a breach of an implied warranty in the contract of letting that the flat would be habitable. The Court also considered a claim against the Corporation in negligence and held that the Corporation in their capacity as Housing Authority owed a duty to the plaintiff to see that the flat he was provided with was fit for habitation and that they were negligent in failing to perform that duty. The Chief Justice and Mr. Justice Henchy who delivered the judgments in the appeal expressly confined their decision on negligence to the duty which they held the Corporation owed to the plaintiff under the Housing Act 1966. They held that the question whether the Corporation would have been liable to the plaintiff apart from the Housing Act 1966 under the principle of *Donoghue* v. *Stevenson* did not arise. Mr. Justice Henchy said:

'Following on *Donoghue* v. *Stevenson* [1932] A.C. 562 it has been established by a line of decisions (examples of which are *Dutton* v. *Bognor Regis U.D.C.* [1972] 1 Q.B. 373, *Anns* v. *London Borough of Merton* [1977] 2 All E.R. 492 and *Batty* v. *Metropolitan Property Realisations* [1978] Q.B. 554) that where a person including a builder or a local authority carelessly provides a dwelling in which there is a concealed defect which the occupier could not have discovered by inspection the person who provided the dwelling may be liable in negligence for personal injury or economic loss suffered as a result of the defect. The precise conditions for or limitations of that liability need not now be considered for I have no doubt that the principle of liability involved in those cases is applicable to the circumstances of this case.'

I am satisfied by the reasoning of Lord McDermott L.C.J. in *Gallagher* v. *McDowell Ltd.* [1961] N.I. 26 and the decisions referred to by Mr. Justice Henchy that the principle of *Donoghue* v. *Stevenson* applies to the relationship between the builder of a house and a subsequent occupier so as to entitle the occupier to recover damages against the builder for personal injuries caused by defects in the house which are attributable to the negligence of the builder and which are not discoverable by the kind of examination which the builder could reasonably expect the occupier to make before occupying the house. The facts of the present case make it necessary to consider some of the conditions and limitations on that liability referred to by Mr. Justice Henchy.

I think it is clear in the case of defects in the dwelling which threaten the health or safety of the occupier that he is entitled to recover expense incurred in removing such defects where he discovers them before they have caused injury. The right to recover damages of that kind was considered to be beyond question by Lord Justice Denning in *Dutton* v. *Bognor Regis Building Company* ([1972] All E.R. 464 at p. 474) and by Lord Justice Sachs in his judgment in the same case at p. 490. It was also the view of Lord Wilberforce in *Anns* v. *Merton L.B.C.* ([1977] 2 All E.R. 492) because at p. 505 Lord Wilberforce dealing with the application of the Statute of Limitations held that a cause of action arose,

'when the state of a building is such that there is a present or imminent danger to the health or safety of persons occupying it.'

I therefore hold that the plaintiff is entitled to the cost of making the roof safe and making good the small portion of defective plaster which I have mentioned as a possible danger. I assess the damages under this head at £300.

The defect in the porch roof is due to an inadequate flashing and this is admitting moisture which is causing a damp patch on the sitting room wall. It is a defect which did not appear until the last year or so but unless it is remedied there will be a gradual deterioration of the fabric of adjoining parts of the dwellinghouse. It is not, in my view, a defect which threatens the health or safety of the occupiers. The defect in the internal plasterwork consists of the absence of a proper bond between the plaster and the blockwork walls over large areas. This defect has existed since the house was built and is probably due to the fact that the plaster was applied before the blockwork was properly dried out. I do not consider it a threat to the health or safety of the occupiers and it is in the nature of a defect of quality in the house. The existence of an inadequate cavity in the external walls is also a defect of quality. The house is not as well insulated as if the walls had a cavity of proper width. The defect does not affect the health or safety of the occupiers or the durability of the dwelling.

I have therefore to consider whether these defects which reduce the value of the dwellinghouse and, in the case of the leak from the porch roof, damaged the fabric of it are matters for which damages can be recovered by the occupier under the principle of *Donoghue* v. *Stevenson*.

I do not think that the English decisions already referred to recognise any right to recover damages for defects of these kinds. In *Anns* v. *Merton* L.B.C. ([1977] 2 All E.R. 492) damages were to be recoverable in respect of damage to the dwellinghouse itself from defective foundations. That case was an action brought not against the builder but against the local authority for breach of their duty to take reasonable care to secure compliance with the building bye-laws. The defect was a danger to the health and safety of the occupiers of the dwelling. Lord Wilberforce said (p. 505).

'In my opinion they (the damages) may also include damage to the dwellinghouse itself; for the whole purpose of the bye-laws in requiring foundations to be of a certain standard was to prevent damage arising from weakness of the foundation which is certain to endanger the health or safety of the occupants.'

In my opinion it does not follow from this that damages for damage to the dwellinghouse itself which does not threaten health or safety is recoverable against the builder. The builder's breach of duty is not a duty arising under a bye-law designed to ensure that the foundations are adequate to bear the house and thereby protect health and safety but is the common law duty of care recognised by the principle of *Donoghue* v. *Stevenson*. I think that it is a duty to take care to avoid defects in the product which may cause personal injury or damage to property but the product itself has not been regarded as falling within the scope of the duty. The obligation of the builder or manufacturer in regard to the quality of his product is, in my view, something which ought to rest in contract only. It is not of the same nature as his common law duty under the principle of *Donoghue* v. *Stevenson* because that duty is founded upon the concern of the law to see that the product is not a cause of injury or damage to persons or property subsequently affected by it. Where a defect is such that no question of such injury or damage arises I see no good reason for extending the principle of *Donoghue* v. *Stevenson* to defects in the quality of the product itself. I would therefore hold that the plaintiff is not entitled to recover damages for the defects in the internal plaster (other than that mentioned), for the defect in the porch roof and for the builder's failure to provide an adequate cavity in the external walls.

Notes

1. *Colgan's* case is analysed by Kerr, 'Tort-Builder's Liability' [9181] D.U.L.J. 118.
2. See also the important decision of the House of Lords in *Junior Books* v. *Veitchi,* mentioned *infra*, p. 328; in this context note the Canadian decisions cited by Kerr, *supra*, n. 1, at 121, fn. 20.
3. The Northern Ireland decision of *Gallagher* v. *N. McDowell Ltd.*, [1961] N.I. 26 should be read for the comprehensive analysis of the relevant authorities by Lord McDermott L.C.J. in his judgment.
4. In *Anns* v. *Merton London Borough Council* [1978] A.C. 728, the House of Lords was required to decide on two important points of principle as to the liability of local authorities for defects in dwellings constructed by builders in their area namely: (1) whether a local authority is under any duty of care towards owners or occupiers of any such houses as

regards inspection during the building process; (2) what period of limitation applies to claims by such owners or occupiers against the local authorities.

Lord Wilberforce's speech merits extensive quotation:

'. . . *The duty of care*

Through the trilogy of cases in this House, *Donoghue* v. *Stevenson*, [1932] A.C. 502, [1932] All ER Rep. 1, *Hedley Byrne & Co. Ltd.* v. *Heller & Partners Ltd.* [1963] 2 All ER 575, [1964] AC 405, and *Home Office* v. *Dorset Yacht Co. Ltd,* [1970] 2 All ER 294, [1970] AC 1004, the position has now been reached that in order to establish that a duty of care arises in a particular situation, it is not necessary to bring the facts of that situation within those of previous situations in which a duty of care has been held to exist. Rather the question has to be approached in two stages. First one has to ask whether, as between the alleged wrongdoer and the person who has suffered damages, there is a sufficient relationship of proximity or neighbourhood such that, in the reasonable contemplation of the former, carelessness on his part may be likely to cause damage to the latter, in which case a prima facie duty of care arises. Secondly, if the first question is answered affirmatively, it is necessary to consider whether there are any considerations which ought to negative, or to reduce or to limit the scope of the duty or the class of person to whom it is owed or the damages to which a breach of it may give rise (see the *Dorset Yacht case,* [1970] 2 All ER 294 at 297, 298 [1970] AC 1004 at 1027, per Lord Reid). Examples of this are *Hedley Byrne & Co. Ltd.* v. *Heller & Partners Ltd,* [1903] 2 All ER 575, [1904] AC 405, where the class of potential plaintiffs was reduced to those shown to have relied on the correctness of statements made, and *Weller & Co.* v. *Foot and Mouth Disease Research Institute* [1965] 3 All ER 560, [1966] 1 QB 569, and (I cite these merely as illustrations, without discussion) cases about "economic loss" where, a duty having been held to exist, the nature of the recoverable damages was limited (see *SCM (United Kingdom) Ltd.* v. *W. J. Whittal & Son Ltd,* [1970] 3 All ER 245, [1971] 1 QB 337, *Spartan Steel and Alloys Ltd.* v. *Martin & Co (Contractors) Ltd,* [1972] 3 All ER 557, [1973] QB 27.

The factual relationship between the council and owners and occupiers of new dwellings constructed in their area must be considered in the relevant statutory setting, under which the council acts. That was the Public Health Act 1936. I must refer to the relevant provisions. [Having examined the statutory position Lord Wilberforce continued]

To summarise the statutory position. The Public Health Act 1936, in particular Part III, was enacted in order to provide for the health and safety of owners and occupiers of buildings, including dwelling houses, by inter alia, setting standards to be coplied with in construction and by enabling local authorities, through building byelaws, to supervise and control the operations of builders. One of the particular matters within the area of local authority supervision is the foundations of buildings, clearly a matter of vital importance, particularly because this part of the building comes to be covered up as building proceeds. Thus any weakness or inadequacy will create a hidden defect which whoever acquires the building has no means of discovering: in legal parlance there is no opportunity for intermediate inspection. So, by the byelaws, a definite standard is set for foundation work (see byelaw 18(1) (b) referred to above); the builder is under a statutory (*sc.* byelaw) duty to notify the local authority before covering up the foundations; the local authority has at this stage the right to inspect and to insist on any correction necessary to bring the work into conformity with the byelaws. It must be in the reasonable contemplation not only of the builder but also of the local authority that failure to comply with the byelaws' requirement as to foundations may give rise to a hidden defect which in the future may cause damage to the building affecting the safety and health of owners and occupiers. And as the building is intended to last, the class of owners and occupiers likely to be affected cannot be limited to those who go in immediately after construction.

What then is the extent of the local authority's duty towards these persons? Although, as I have suggested, a situation of proximity existed between the council and owners and occupiers of the houses, I do not think that a description of the council's duty can be based on the "neighbourhood" principle alone or on merely any such factual relationship as "control" as suggested by the Court of Appeal. So to base it would be to neglect an essential factor which is that the local authority is a public body, discharging functions under statute: its powers and duties are definable in terms of public not private law. The problem which this type of action creates, is to define the circumstances in which the law should impose, over and above, or perhaps alongside, these public law powers and duties, a duty in private law towards individuals such that they may sue for damages in a civil court. It is in this context that the distinction sought to be drawn between duties and mere powers has to be examined.

Most, indeed probably all, statutes relating to public authorities or public bodies, contain in them a large area of policy. The courts call this "discretion", meaning that the decision is one for the authority or body to make, and not for the courts. Many statutes, also, prescribe or at least presuppose the practical execution of policy decisions: a convenient description of this is to say that in addition to the area of policy or discretion, there is an operational area. Although this distinction between the policy area and the operational area is convenient, and illuminating, it is probably a distinction of degree; many "operational" powers or duties have in them some element of "discretion". It can safely be said that the more "operational" a power or duty may be, the easier it is to superimpose on it a common law duty of care.

I do not think that it is right to limit this to a duty to avoid causing extra or additional damage beyond what must be expected to arise from the exercise of the power or duty. That may be correct when the act done under the statute *inherently* must adversely *affect* the interest of individuals. But many other acts can be done without causing any harm to anyone – indeed may be directed to preventing harm from occurring. In these cases the duty is the normal one of taking care to avoid harm to those likely to be affected.

To say that councils are under no duty to inspect is not a sufficient statement of the position. They are under a duty to give proper consideration to the question whether they should inspect or not. Their immunity from attack, in the event of failure to inspect, in other words, though great is not absolute. And because it is not absolute, the necessary premise for the proposition "if no duty to inspect, then no duty to take care in inspection" vanishes.

Passing then to the duty as regards inspection, if made. On principle there must surely be a duty to exercise reasonable care. The standard of care must be related to the duty to be performed, namely to ensure compliance with the byelaws. It must be related to the fact that the person responsible for construction in accordance with the byelaws is the builder, and that the inspector's function is supervisory. It must be related to the fact that once the inspector has passed the foundations they will be covered up, with no subsequent opportunity for inspection. But this duty, heavily operational though it may be, is still a duty arising under the statute. There may be a discretionary element in its exercise, discretionary as to the time and manner of inspection, and the techniques to be used. A plaintiff complaining of negligence must prove, the burden being on him, that action taken was not within the limits of a discretion bona fide exercised, before he can begin to rely on a common law duty of care. But if he can do this, he should, in principle, be able to sue.

Is there, then, authority against the existence of any such duty or any reason to restrict it? It is said that there is an absolute distinction in the law between statutory duty and statutory power – the former giving rise to possible liability, the latter not; or at least not doing so unless the exercise of the power involves some positive act creating some fresh or additional damage.

My Lords, I do not believe that any such absolute rule exists: or perhaps, more accurately, that such rules as exist in relation to powers and duties existing under particular statutes, provide sufficient definition of the rights of individuals affected by their exercise, or indeed their non-exercise, unless they take account of the possibility that, parallel with public law duties there may coexist those duties which persons, private or public, are under at common law to avoid causing damage to others in sufficient proximity to them. This is, I think, the key to understanding of the main authority relied on by the council, *East Suffolk Rivers Catchment Board* v. *Kent,* [1940] 4 All ER 527, [1941] AC 74. [After an examination of that case Lord Wilberforce continued].

* * *

My Lords, I believe that the conception of a general duty of care, not limited to particular accepted situations, but extending generally over all relations of sufficient proximity, and even pervading the sphere of statutory functions of public bodies, had not at th[e] time [of the *East Suffolk* case] become fully recognised. Indeed it may well be that full recognition of the impact of *Donoghue* v. *Stevenson,* [1932] AC 562, [1932] All ER Rep 1, in the latter sphere only came with the decision of this House in *Home Office* v. *Dorset Yacht Co. Ltd,* [1970] 2 All ER 294, [1970] AC 1004.

* * *

So in the present case, the allegations made are consistent with the council or its inspector having acted outside any delegated discretion either as to the making of an inspection, or as to the manner in which an inspection was made. Whether they did so must be determined at the trial. In the event of a positive determination, and only so, can a duty of care arise. I respectfully think that Lord Denning MR in *Dutton's* case, [1972] 1 All ER 402 [1972] 1 QB 373 at 392, puts the duty too high.

To whom the duty is owed. There is, in my opinion, no difficulty about this. A reasonable man in the position of the inspector must realise that if the foundations are covered in without adequate depth or strength as required by the byelaws, injury to safety or health may be suffered by owners or occupiers of the house. The duty is owed to them, not of course to a negligent building owner, the source of his own loss. I would leave open the case of users, who might themselves have a remedy against the occupier under the Occupiers' Liability Act 1957. A right of action can only be conferred on an owner or occupier, who is such when the damage occurs (see below). This disposes of the possible objection that an endless, indeterminate class of potential plaintiffs may be called into existence.

The nature of the duty. This must be related closely to the purpose for which powers of inspection are granted, namely to secure compliance with the byelaws. The duty is to take reasonable care, no more, no less, to secure that the builder does not cover in foundations which do not comply with byelaw requirements. The allegations in the statements of claim, insofar as they are based on non-compliance with the plans, are misconceived.

The position of the builder. I agree with the majority in the Court of Appeal in thinking that it would be unreasonable to impose liability in respect of defective foundations on the council, if the builder, whose primary fault it was, should be immune from liability. So it is necessary to consider this point, although it does not directly arise in the present appeal. If there was at one time a supposed rule that the doctrine of *Donoghue* v. *Stevenson,* [1932] AC 502, [1932] All ER Rep 1, did not apply to realty, there is no doubt under modern authority that a builder of defective premises may be liable in negligence to persons who thereby suffer injury: see *Gallagher* v. *N McDowell Ltd,* [1961] NI 26, per Lord MacDermott CJ, a case of personal injury. Similar decisions have been given in regard to architects (*Clayton* v. *Woodman & Son (Builders) Ltd,* [1962] 2 All ER 33, [1962] 1 WLR 585, *Clay* v. *A.J. Crump & Sons Ltd,* [1963] 3 All ER 687, [1964] QB 533). *Gallagher's* case [1961] NI 26, expressly leaves open the question whether the immunity against action of builder-owners, established by older authorities (e.g. *Bottomley* v. *Bannister,* [1932] 1 KB 458, [1931] All ER Rep 99) still survives.

That immunity, as I understand it, rests partly on a distinction being made between chattels and real property, partly on the principle of "caveat emptor" or, in the case where the owner leases the property, on the proposition that (fraud apart) there is no law against letting a "tumbledown house" (*Robbins* v. *Jones,* (1863) 15 CBNS 221, [1861–73] All ER Rep 544, per Erle C.J. But leaving aside such cases as arise between contracting parties, when the terms of the contract have to be considered (see *Voli* v. *Inglewood Shire Council,* (1963) 110 CLR 74 at 85, per Windeyer J), I am unable to understand why this principle or proposition should prevent recovery in a suitable case by a person, who has subsequently acquired the house, on the principle of *Donoghue* v. *Stevenson,* [1932] AC 562, [1932] All ER Rep 1: the same rules should apply to all careless acts of a builder: whether he happens also to own the land or not. I agree generally with the conclusions of Lord Denning MR on this point (*Dutton's* case [1972] 1 All ER 462 at 471, 472, [1972] 1 QB 373 at 392–394). In the alternative, since it is the duty of the builder (owner or not) to comply with the byelaws, I would be of opinion that an action could be brought against him, in effect, for breach of statutory duty by any person for whose benefit or protection the byelaw was made. So I do not think that there is any basis here for arguing from a supposed immunity of the builder or immunity of the council.

Nature of the damages recoverable and arising out of the cause of action. There are many questions here which do not directly arise at this stage and which may never arise if the actions are tried. But some conclusions are necessary if we are to deal with the issue as to limitation. The damages recoverable include all those which foreseeably arise from the breach of the duty of care which, as regards the council, I have held to be a duty to take reasonable care to secure compliance with the byelaws. Subject always to adequate proof of causation, these damages may include damages for personal injury and damage to property. In my opinion they may also include damage to the dwellinghouse itself; for the whole purpose of the byelaws in requiring foundations to be of certain standard is to prevent damage arising from weakness of the foundations which is certain to endanger the health or safety of occupants.

To allow recovery for such damage to the house follows, in my opinion, from normal principle. If classification is required, the relevant damage is in my opinion material, physical damage, and what is recoverable is the amount of expenditure necessary to restore the dwelling to a condition in which it is no longer a danger to the health or safety of persons occupying and possibly (depending on the circumstances) expenses arising from necessary displacement. On the question of damages generally I have derived much assistance from the judgment (dissenting on this point, but of strong persuasive force) of Laskin CJ in the Canadian Supreme Court case of *Rivtow Marine Ltd.* v. *Washington Iron Works,* [1973] 6 W.W.R. 692 at 715, and from judgments of the New Zealand Court of Appeal (furnished by courtesy of that court) in *Bowen* v. *Paramount Builders (Hamilton) Ltd and McKay,* (22nd December 1976) unreported [1977] 1 N.Z.L.R. 394—*Eds.*].

When does the cause of action arise? We can leave aside cases of personal injury or damage to other property as presenting no difficulty. It is only the damage for the house which required consideration. In my respectful opinion the Court of Appeal was right when, in *Sparham-Souter* v. *Town and Country Developments (Essex) Ltd,* [1976] 2 All ER 65, [1976] 1 QB 858, it abjured the view that the cause of action arose immediately on delivery, i.e. conveyance of the defective house. It can only arise when the state of the building is such that there is present an imminent danger to the health or safety of persons occupying it. We are not concerned at this stage with any issue relating to remedial action nor are we called on to decide on what the measure of the damages should be, such questions, possibly very difficult in some cases, will be for the court to decide. It is sufficient to say that a cause of action arises at the point I have indicated.

The Limitation Act 1939. If the fact is that defects to the maisonettes first appeared in 1970, then, since the writs were issued in 1972, the consequence must be that none of the present actions are barred by the Act.

Conclusion. I would hold: (1) that *Dutton* v. *Bognor Regis United Building Co. Ltd,* [1972] 1 All ER 462, [1972] 1 QB 373, was in the result rightly decided; the correct legal basis for the decision must be taken to be that established by your Lordships in this appeal; (2) that the question whether the council by itself or its officers came under a duty of care toward the plaintiffs must be considered in relation to the powers, duties and discretions arising under the Public Health Act 1936; (3) that the council would not be guilty of a breach of duty in not carrying out inspection of the foundations of the block unless it were shown (a) not properly to have exercised its discretion as to the making of inspections, and (b) to have failed to exercise reasonable care in its acts or omissions to secure that the byelaws applicable to the foundations of the block were complied with; (4) that the council would be liable to the plaintiffs for breach of duty if it were proved that its inspector having assumed the duty of inspecting the foundations and acting otherwise than in the bona fide exercise of any discretion under the Act, did not exercise reasonable care to ensure that the byelaws applicable to the foundations were complied with; (5) that on the facts as pleaded none of the actions is barred by the Limitation Act 1939. And consequently that the appeal should be dismissed with costs.'

Lord Diplock, Lord Simon of Glaisdale and Lord Russell of Killowen agreed with Lord Wilberforce. Lord Salmon delivered a separate concurring speech.

5. Commenting on *Anns, Weir,* p. 29 states: 'So far as the decision relates to the local authority it restricts rather than enlarges the ambit of *Dutton* v. *Bognor Regis,* [1972] 1 Q.B. 373. After all, governments are elected in order to decide how to waste the citizens' money. It would be wrong to make them liable just for that. Accordingly, they are liable only if they waste the citizen's money *inadvertently*, by the incompetent execution of their constitutional decisions. This will still cost local authorities (that is the ratepayers) a pretty penny.'

6. See generally Craig, 'Negligence in the Exercise of a Statutory Power' 94 L. Q. Rev. 418 (1978).

7. Recent English decisions on the liability of local authorities include *Dennis* v. *Charawood Borough Council* [1982] 3 W.L.R. 1064 (C.A.) and *Acrecrest Ltd.* v. *W.S. Hattrell & Partners,* [1982] 3 W.L.R. 1076 (C.A.). See also the New Zealand decision of *R.A. & T. J. Carll Ltd.* v. *Berry,* [1981] N.Z.L.R. 76 (High Ct., Hamilton, J.).

8. See generally Fennelly, *Defective Buildings: Liability of Builders, Supervisory Authorities and Others in Contract and Tort,* Society of Young Solicitors Lecture No. 109, 21 October 1978.

9. For analysis of the Law Reform Commission's proposals for reform of the law, contained in its *Report on Defective Premises* (LRC 3–1982), see Kerr, 5 Dublin U. L. Rev. 133 (1983).

Warranty implied on the part of Dublin Corporation as a housing authority, in the case of an unfurnished letting under the Housing Act 1966, that the premises were reasonably fit for human habitation.

SINEY V. CORPORATION OF DUBLIN

[1980] I.R. 400 (Sup. Ct.)

O'Higgins C.J.:

This is a Case which was stated pursuant to the provisions of s. 16 of the Courts of Justice Act, 1947, by His Honour Judge G. A. Clarke of the Circuit Court; he seeks the opinion of the Supreme Court on certain questions of law which arise on the facts as he has found them. It is necessary at the outset to set out these facts very generally.

The plaintiff, being in need of housing accommodation, applied to the defendant corporation for a house. On the 23rd August, 1973, he was allotted by the defendants a flat at No. 56 Avonbeg Gardens, Tallaght. This flat was intended for the accommodation of the plaintiff, his wife and two children. On the same day he signed a form which was stamped 'First Letting.' This form contained the standard letting conditions of the defendants and a description of the flat as 'a dwelling provided by the Corporation under the Housing Act, 1966.' The undertaking in the form which was signed by the plaintiff was an undertaking by him to observe these standard letting conditions. The flat in question was one of a number at Avonbeg, Tallaght, which were built and provided for the defendants through the National Building Agency. The designs for these flats were prepared by the principal architect for the National Building Agency in consultation with the defendants' engineering and administrative staff. The work of building was carried out by a private contractor under the supervision of the architect of the National Building Agency. Upon completion and handing over to the defendants, the flats were inspected by their officials.

The plaintiff and his family were the first family to live in the flat in question. When they moved in, water appeared under the floor covering in the bedroom. Later, a putty-like fungus appeared on the bedroom wall under the window. This then spread to other walls and to the skirting in the bedroom and later to the sittingroom and kitchen. This fungus was accompanied with a heavy damp smell and a cold feeling to anyone entering the rooms. Efforts to eliminate this problem were made but did not prove successful.

On the evidence he heard, the learned Circuit Court judge found the cause of the problem to be insufficient ventilation. He found this defect to be such that, despite a reasonable and proper use of the heating and ventilation systems by the plaintiff and his family, dampness and humidity in the flat could not be overcome. This defect in the ventilation system could have been discovered prior to the letting to the plaintiff if a relative humidity test had been carried out. Such test was neither carried out by the architect for the National Building Agency nor by anybody else. By reason of the inadequacy of the ventilation system, the learned Circuit Court judge found that the flat was unsuitable to the plaintiff and his family. The judge also found that, as a consequence, the plaintiff had suffered certain damage. On the facts as found by the judge, he has submitted the following questions for determination by this Court.

'(*a*) Do the facts, as found, constitute a breach by the defendants of their contract with the plaintiff herein? If the answer is Yes, is the plaintiff entitled to damages?

(*b*) Do the facts as found by me constitute a breach by the defendants of their statutory duty under the Housing Act, 1966, and the regulations made there-under? If the answer to (*b*) is Yes, is the plaintiff entitled to damages?

(*c*) Do the facts as found constitute negligence on the part of the defendants, their servants or agents? If the answer to (*c*) is Yes, is the plaintiff entitled to damages?

(*d*) Do the facts as found by me constitute a nuisance created by or maintained by the defendants, their servants or agents? If the answer to (*d*) is Yes, is the plaintiff entitled to damages?'

Breach of contract

The first question involves a consideration as to whether, in the particular letting of this flat to the plaintiff, a warranty can be implied as to its fitness or suitability for habitation by the plaintiff and his family. This is so because the document which was signed on the 23rd August, 1973, contains 32 conditions which either define the rights of the defendants or specify the obligations of the plaintiff tenant. There is no express warranty on the part of the defendants as to the suitability of the flat for any particular purpose, nor is such a warranty expressly excluded. Therefore, it becomes a question as to whether such a warranty can be implied in this particular letting in the circumstances. The law as to the circumstances under which a warranty may be implied in a contract was stated many years ago by Bowen L.J. in this well-known passage from p. 68 of his judgment in *The Moorcock* 14 P. D. 64 (1889):–

'Now, an implied warranty, or, as it is called, a covenant in law, as distinguished from an express contract or express warranty, really is in all cases founded on the presumed intention of the parties, and upon reason. The implication which the law draws from what must obviously have been the intention of the parties, the law draws with the object of giving efficacy to the transaction and preventing such a failure of consideration as cannot have been within the contemplation of either side; and I believe if one were to take all the cases, and they are many, of implied warranties or covenants in law, it will be found that in all of them the law is raising an implication from the presumed intention of the parties with the object of giving to the transaction such efficacy as both parties must have intended that at all events it should have.'

At once the question arises as to whether this principle of law has any application or relevance in a case such as the present. Counsel for the defendants submit very strongly that it has not. As this was a letting of an unfurnished flat or dwelling, they assert that no such warranty can be implied. In this respect they rely on a long line of authorities as illustrated by *Sutton* v. *Temple* 12 M. & W. 52 (1843); *Hart* v. *Windsor* 12 M. & W. 68 (1843); *Brown* v. *Norton* [1954] I.R. 34 and *Chambers* v. *Cork Corporation*, 93 I.L.T.R. 45 (1958). Those authorities established the proposition that the mere letting of land, with or without an unfurnished dwellinghouse upon it, carried no such implication of a warranty with regard to fitness for any particular purpose. Those cases applied the rule of *caveat emptor* to all lettings of land, with or without a house thereon, in the same way as it was applied to contracts for the sale of land.

An exception, which is not relevant to this case, was recognised where a furnished house was let for occupation; in such a case a covenant on the part of the landlord that the premises could be fit for such occupation at the commencement of the tenancy is implied: *Smith* v. *Marrable* 11 M. & W. 5 (1843); *Wilson* v. *Finch Hatton* 2 Ex. Div. 336 (1877); *Collins* v. *Hopkins* [1923] 2 K.B. 617 and *Brown* v. *Norton* [1954] I.R. 34. A further exception was recognised where a lessor sold by way of lease a house under construction; in such circumstances terms could implied with regard to the completion of the house, and suitability of the materials used, the quality of the workmanship and its fitness for habitation: *Norris* v. *Staps* Hob. 210 (1616); *Pearce* v. *Tucker* 3 F. & F. 136 (1862); *G. H. Myers & Co.* v. *Brent Cross Service Co.* [1934] 1 K.B. 46; *Hall* v. *Burke* (1886) 3 T.L.R. 165 and *Brown* v. *Norton* [1954] I.R. 34.

There can be no doubt that the authorities mentioned (and others which are too numerous to cite) do establish the proposition that a mere letting of land, with or without an unfurnished house thereon, carried with it no implication that either the land or the house would be fit for any particular purpose. This rule probably developed when the main subject of conveyances and leases was land, and when buildings and houses were often of secondary importance in a society that was thinly urbanised. To-day the application of such a rule in a society which is becoming more and more urbanised, and in which the building and sale of houses has become a major industry, may appear somewhat harsh and inappropriate. However, whether the rule has or has not survived changes in society is not in issue in this case. The issue is whether it can be applied, or ought to be applied, in the particular circumstances of this letting by the defendants to the plaintiff.

To answer this question, regard must be had to the Housing Act, 1966, under which this letting was made, and to the position, powers and obligations of the defendants under that Act. The Act of 1966 is a major piece of social legislation which is aiming at dealing with the distressing problem of families that are unable to provide for themselves and being either homeless or living in overcrowded, unhealthy and unfit houses. The Act sought to establish administrative machinery under which such conditions could be eliminated gradually throughout the country, and by means of which new and suitable dwellings could be provided for those in need. Under its provisions the defendant corporation became a housing authority. As such the defendants were given the statutory duty of inspecting and assessing the adequacy of the supply and the condition of houses in their functional area, having regard to unfitness or unsuitability for human habitation and overcrowding: see section 53. The defendants were also obliged to prepare and to adopt a building programme which would have many objectives, but amongst which were 'the repair, closure or demolition of houses which are unfit or unsuitable for human habitation' and 'the elimination of overcrowding' and 'the provision of adequate and suitable housing accommodation for persons (including elderly or disabled persons) who . . . are in need of and are unable to provide such accommodation from their own resources' – see section 55.

The defendants were also obliged to draw up a scheme of priorities for the letting of available housing accommodation, having regard to the primary objectives of 'the repair, closure or demolition of houses which are unfit in any respect for human habitation' and 'the elimination of overcrowding' and 'the provision of adequate and suitable housing accommodation for persons . . . who, in the opinion of the housing authority are in need of and are unable to provide such accommodation from their own resources' and 'the provision of adequate and suitable housing accommodation for persons suffering from pulmonary tuberculosis' – see section 60. To deal with the problem of overcrowding and unfit houses, the defendant corporation was given specific statutory powers to enforce the repair of such or their closure or demolition: see ss. 63, 65, 66, of the Act of 1966 as extended by s. 5 of the Housing Act, 1969. These various duties and powers were amplified in detail in various other provisions of the Act.

The Act also empowers the Minister for the Environment to provide grants for persons endeavouring to provide their own houses, either by building, or by repairing or reconstructing existing accommodation: see sections 13–23. The Minister was also empowered to give grants to housing authorities in order to promote and finance schemes for the assistance of people seeking to build or otherwise provide their own housing accommodation: see sections 24–43. In considering whether a house was or was not fit for human habitation, the defendant corporation (and every other housing authority) was obliged to have regard to the extent to which the house was deficient as respects each of the matters set out in the second schedule to the Act of 1966: see sub-s. 2 of section 66. Among the matters mentioned in that second schedule are 'resistance to moisture' and 'air space and ventilation.'

Generally, it may be said that under the Act of 1966 the defendant corporation, as a housing authority, was charged with the task, in respect of its own functional area, of ending overcrowding and of eliminating substandard and unsuitable housing for poor people. The defendants were also empowered, and obliged, to let such housing accommodation as they were able to provide, on a priority basis, to people released from these conditions. In short, the aim of the Act of 1966 was to bring into existence decent housing which, in each functional area, would be introduced by the housing authority and the standards of which would be maintained by that authority. It is now necessary to consider the particular letting made to the plaintiff.

This letting was expressed to be a letting of a 'dwelling provided by the Corporation under the Housing Act, 1966.' Moreover, it was a letting of one of a number of newly-built flats. Therefore, it was a letting made by the defendant corporation of a dwelling provided under its building programme and let by it in accordance with its scheme of priority for, inter alia, the ending of overcrowding and the elimination of houses unfit in any respect for human habitation. Under these circumstances, can it be said that such a letting carried no implication that the accommodation thereby provided for a necessitous family would be fit for habitation by them? It seems to me that to not imply such a condition or warranty would be to assume that the defendant corporation was entitled to disregard, and was disregarding, the responsibilities cast upon it by the very Act which authorised the building and letting of the accommodation in question.

However, counsel for the defendants relied on the provisions of s. 114 of the Act of 1966 and, accordingly, that section requires to be noted. Sub-sections 1, 2 and 5, of s. 114 provide:–

'(1) Subject to subsection (2) of this section, in any contract entered into after the commencement of this section for letting for habitation a house at a rent not exceeding one hundred and thirty pounds per annum there shall, notwithstanding any stipulation to the contrary, be implied a condition that the house is at the commencement of the tenancy and an undertaking that the house will be kept by the landlord during the tenancy, in all respects reasonably fit for human habitation but nothing in this section shall affect the liability of the tenant or occupier of any such house for any wilful act or default of such tenant or occupier whereby the house is rendered other than reasonably fit for human habitation.

(2) The condition and undertaking mentioned in subsection (1) of this section shall not be implied in any case in which–

(a) a house is let for a term of not less than three years on the terms that it be put by the lessee into a condition reasonably fit for habitation, and

(b) the tenancy agreement is not determinable at the option of either the landlord or the tenant before the expiration of three years . . .

(5) In this section, "landlord" means any person who lets for habitation to a tenant any house under a contract to which this section applies, and includes his successor in title.'

Because of s. 114, counsel for the defendants contended that, as a special condition as to fitness for human habitation was implied by the section in respect of houses let at a rent not exceeding £130 p.a., no such condition ought to be implied in respect of houses let at a higher rent. Since the letting to the plaintiff was at a higher rent it was said that, on this account, the implication of such a condition in the plaintiff's letting was not possible. This argument rests on the assumption that the section applies to the defendant corporation, as a housing authority. In my view, this assumption is not well founded. The section refers both to a condition that the house is at the commencement of the tenancy and to an undertaking that it will be kept by the landlord during the tenancy in all respects reasonably fit for human habitation. As the condition and the undertaking are to the same effect and relate to the same tenancy, it seems clear that they are both intended to be binding on the landlord as defined in the section. It would seem improbable that the condition was intended to be binding on a wider category of landlords than the undertaking. Sub-section 2, in excluding the implication of both the condition *and* the undertaking in the circumstances mentioned at (*a*) *and* at (*b*) where 'the tenancy agreement is not determinable at the option of either the landlord or the tenant before the expiration of three years,' again envisages the same type or category of landlord as being bound by, or excluded from, both the condition and the undertaking. By sub-s. 5 of s. 114 the word 'landlord' is given the meaning of 'any *person* who lets for habitation to a tenant any house . . .' However, by s. 2, sub-s. 1, of the Act the word 'person', when used in the Act, is given a special meaning. The word is there defined as follows:–

' "person", except in this section and in sections 15 and 34 of this Act, does not include a housing authority.'

It seems to follow that the 'landlord' in s. 114 cannot include a housing authority and that, therefore, the section does not apply to the defendant corporation. If I am right in this view, then this entire argument is without substance. Indeed, it probably follows that the reason why housing authorities were not included in and covered by s. 114 is that they were already burdened with a clear statutory responsibility to provide and to let only dwellings which complied with the terms of the condition and undertaking imposed by the section.

Accordingly, I have come to the conclusion that the letting made to the plaintiff by the defendants did include an implied warranty that the premises let would be reasonably fit for human habitation and, therefore, I would answer affirmatively the first question in the Case Stated. In my view the plaintiff is entitled to damages on this account.

Statutory duty

In my view the second question in the Case Stated should be answered in the negative. I will merely say that the statutory duties imposed by the Housing Act, 1966, are so imposed for the benefit of the public. Under the Act they are enforceable under s. 111 by the Minister. In these circumstances no right of action is given to a private citizen if the complaint is *merely* that the duties so imposed, or any one of them, have or has not been carried out. The mere fact that a housing authority has failed to discharge a duty imposed upon it does not give to a complaining or aggrieved citizen a right of action for damages.

Negligence

On behalf of the defendants it was submitted that, as the lessors of the flat, they could be under no liability at common law in respect of injury or damage caused by a defect existing in the premises at the time of the letting. If correct, this submission means that what is known as the principle in *Donoghue* v. *Stevenson* [1932] A.C. 562 has no application in the circumstances of this case and that, as landlords, the defendants cannot be made liable in negligence in respect of defects existing in the premises which they have let. This submission is supported by an impressive series of decisions commencing before *Donoghue* v. *Stevenson* [1932] A.C. 562 but continuing after the date of that decision: see *Robbins* v. *Jones* 15 C.B.N.S. 221 (1863); *Cavalier* v. *Pope* [1906] A.C. 428; *Bottomley* v. *Bannister* [1932] 1 K.B. 458; *Otto* v. *Bolton and Norris* [1936] 2 K.B. 46; *Davis* v. *Foots* [1940] 1 K. B. 116; *McGowan* v. *Harrison* [1941] I.R. 331 and *Chambers* v. *Cork Corporation* 93 I.L.T.R. 45 (1958). The immunity originated as an immunity enjoyed by vendors or lessors of land but seems to have been extended to vendors and lessors of buildings erected upon land and to defects in such buildings. It is not easy to see the basis in logic for the existence of such an immunity, particularly where the defect which causes the damage was known or could have been known to the lessor, were it not for his carelessness, and was not known and could not have been known to the tenant or to those whom he brought into the building or house pursuant to the letting. Because of this difficulty of finding a logical basis to justify a general immunity accorded to all vendors and all lessors in relation to defects in premises sold or let, it is not surprising to find in recent decisions certain clear exceptions being established.

In *Gallagher* v. *N. McDowell Ltd.* [1961] N.I. 26 the Court of Appeal in Northern Ireland refused to regard the immunity as being one which attached to reality. In that case the court held that the builders were liable for injury to the wife of the tenant of a house let by the Northern Ireland Housing Trust; the wife's injury had been caused by a defect in the house. Lord MacDermott L.C.J. said at p. 38 of the report:–

'In my opinion, the cases since *Donoghue* v. *Stevenson* [1932] A.C. 562 show that the land-owner's immunities, which I have described as settled before that decision, have not been disturbed by it. But the fact that these immunities arise in relation to defects and dangers on land does not mean that the law imposes no neighbourly duty of reasonable care as respects defects and dangers of that kind. The immunities attach to land-owners as such, and I do not think one is at liberty to jump from that to saying that the law of negligence in relation to what is dangerous draws a clear distinction between what are chattels and what, by attachment or otherwise, form part of the realty. Why should it? Such a distinction does not justify itself, and it is not required by the immunities I have mentioned when one is not dealing with land-owners as such.'

In that passage from his judgment, Lord MacDermott seems to assume a continuing immunity for land-owners, as such, from the rule in *Donoghue* v. *Stevenson* [1932] A.C. 562 in respect of defects or dangers on their land. Such a view of the law is not consistent with the decisions of this Court in *Purtill* v. *Athlone U.D.C.* [1968] I.R. 205 and *McNamara* v. *Electricity Supply Board* [1975] I.R. 1. In relation to their particular facts, those cases regarded the liability of the occupier of land (whether as owner or otherwise) in respect of defects or dangers found on the land as proper to be treated under the principles of *Donoghue* v. *Stevenson* [1932] A.C. 562.

In *Dutton* v. *Bognor Regis U.D.C.* [1972] 1 Q.B. 373 it was held that a local authority could be liable in respect of its building inspector's negligence in certifying that a building, which was defective, complied with local bye-laws. In *Sparham-Souter* v. *Town Developments* [1976] Q.B. 858 the English Court of Appeal confirmed both the developer's and the local authority's liability in similar circumstances. In the recent decision of the House of Lords in *Anns* v. *Merton London Borough* [1978] A.C. 728 it was held that a local authority, which was negligent in the exercise of its powers or functions with the result that a defective building was constructed and the occupiers were thereby injured, could be held liable at common law. Whether these decisions, some of which suggest a liability on the part of the builder although he was a vendor or lessor, indicate a trend towards applying the principles of *Donoghue* v. *Stevenson* [1932] A.C. 562 irrespective of whether the defective premises were sold or let, if the circumstances justify the application, is a question which does not arise in this case.

In this case it is sufficient to say that many of these recent decisions recognise a possible liability where the exercise of statutory powers in a negligent manner results in injury to persons occupying houses for whose protection or benefit these powers were intended. Here the defendants were given by the Housing Act, 1966, the power to provide dwellings for persons, such as the plaintiff, who were unable to provide houses for themselves. In this instance, the defendants chose to exercise this power through the medium of the National Building Agency Ltd. Having decided to do so, the defendants remained privy to the design of the dwellings to be erected and exercised a supervision over what was being done.

Before accepting the completed flat, which was intended for allotment or letting to a family such as the plaintiff's, the defendants carried out an inspection. Obviously, that inspection should have been carried out to ensure that what had been built or provided accorded with the statutory requirements as to fitness for human habitation. Had the inspection by the defendants been so carried out, it would have disclosed that the ventilation system in this particular flat was defective and inadequate and that the defect was likely to lead to excessive humidity and to the kind of conditions of which the plaintiff and his family subsequently complained. In the circumstances the undetected defect in the ventilation was a serious concealed danger of which the incoming tenant, the plaintiff, could not have been aware and which he could not reasonably have been expected to discover. In these circumstances I can see no basis for suggesting that the principle of *Donoghue* v. *Stevenson* [1932] A.C. 562 should not apply. The inspection should have been carried out on the basis that the flat was to be handed over for occupation as a dwelling to a family entitled to expect that it would be one which was fit for human habitation. Because the inspection was defective, the flat was handed over in a condition in which it was not so fit. The result was that damage and injury was caused to the incoming family. In my view, on the facts found by the Circuit Court judge the defendants ought to be held liable in negligence.

As to the suggestion that liability in negligence should not be held to attach to the defendants because of the contractual relationship existing between them and the plaintiff, I agree with what will be said by Mr. Justice Henchy in this regard in the judgment he is about to read.

Accordingly, I would answer the third question affirmatively and say that, as a result, the plaintiff is entitled to damages in respect of such injury or damage as was caused to him as a result of the defendants' negligence.

Nuisance

The fourth question has not been argued in this Court. On the facts as found by the learned Circuit Court judge, it does not seem to me that any question of liability for nuisance could arise. Therefore, it follows that this question should be answered in the negative.

Damages

I should like to add something with regard to damages. These were found by the Circuit Court judge to be £325, of which £175 was for damage to furniture and clothing. With regard to what was termed 'interference with the ordinary comfort and convenience' of the plaintiff and his family, the Circuit Court judge measured damages at £150. It was objected on behalf of the defendants that this sum in respect of inconvenience was not recoverable and that the damages should be confined to what was described as physical or material damage. I think that this is too sweeping a submission. It is true that damages arising from a breach of contract may not be recovered for annoyance, or loss of temper or vexation or disappointment. However, damages may be recovered for physical inconvenience and discomfort: see McGregor on Damages, (14th ed. p. 61). It seems to me that it is this kind of discomfort and inconvenience which the Circuit Court judge had in mind in his findings as to damages at paragraph 5 of the Case Stated. On the facts of this case I cannot see that any different consideration applies in relation to damages for negligence.

Henchy J.:

Breach of contract

While there is no express finding on the matter, I take it to be inherent in the judge's findings of fact that the flat was not fit for habitation when the plaintiff began living in it. Within two months of going into occupation in 1973, he found water oozing through the bedroom floor. After another three weeks the fungus began to appear. From then until he left the flat in 1975 the damp and the fungus, with their accompanying chilly atmosphere and pervasive smell, made life so intolerable for the plaintiff and his family that he was compelled to leave as soon as he was able to get another flat from the defendants. Therefore, it would be in the teeth of the evidence to say that the flat was fit for habitation when the plaintiff moved in. As far as appearances went, everything was then in order but, as events were shortly to prove, the hidden defects made the flat far from habitable when the tenancy commenced.

As the judge has found, the reason for the unfitness of the flat for habitation was a flaw in the design. Specifically, the ventilation was inadequate so that there was excessive condensation. There was a failure by the experts to make the necessary calculations so as to eliminate the danger of excessive relative humidity. The condensation, which was the immediate cause of the trouble, was found by the judge to have been preventable and foreseeable.

The facts found by the judge further show that the defendants were privy to all decisions made as to design. The architect's plans, drawings and decisions were made in consultation with the defendants' experts. The design of the heating system was carried out on the advice of a consultant in heating engineering who was highly qualified. He was employed by the National Building Agency but he advised in consultation with the defendants' experts and those of the Electricity Supply Board. It has been urged on behalf of the defendants that the fault for the defective ventilation design should not be attributed to them. I cannot agree. Whether secondary or partial fault lies with others need not now be considered. The principals in the operation of building the flats were the defendants. On them fell the duty under statute of providing flats which would fulfil their housing obligations under the Act of 1966. If, as was the case, the ventilation design was so defective that some 10–15% of the flats had condensation problems, and this particular flat was so badly affected that the plaintiff and his family had to flee from it, the defendants cannot shed responsibility by saying that they relied on expert advice which proved to be faulty. As the housing authority, the defendants were expected by the legislature to ensure that dwellings provided by them under the Act would not have defects which would make them uninhabitable. While the defendants may possibly have rights against third parties, the primary responsibility for the defective design falls on them. They cannot rid themselves of that responsibility by pleading that they delegated the observance of their statutory obligations to others.

It is against that background that an answer must be given to the question whether there is to be read into the plaintiff's tenancy agreement an implied term that the flat was fit for habitation.

The Act of 1966 is markedly different from previous Housing Acts in the extent to which it makes it the duty of a housing authority to plan, control, oversee and provide for the supply of adequate housing in its area. Section 53, sub-s. 1, imposes a duty on a housing authority, at intervals of not more than five years, to inspect the houses in its functional area and to ascertain (inter alia) to what extent there exist in the area houses which are in any respect unfit or unsuitable for human habitation. Section 55, sub-s. 1, makes it the duty of a housing authority, at least once in every five years, to prepare and adopt a building programme. Section 55, sub-s. 3, requires that, in preparing such building programme, the housing authority shall have regard to seven objectives, the first of which is 'the repair, closure or demolition of houses which are unfit or unsuitable for human habitation.' The second schedule to the Act of 1966 numbers 'resistance to moisture' and 'resistance to transmission of heat' among the tests of habitability.

When the defendants, as the housing authority, prepared and adopted a building programme and then exercised their powers under s. 56, sub-s. 1, to provide these flats for letting, it was a necessary postulate of the statutory scheme of things that the flats would not add to the stock of houses unfit or unsuitable for human habitation. Indeed, it would be positively inconsistent with the powers and duties of the defendants, as a housing authority under the Act, to provide a flat that was not fit for habitation. The defendants' powers (set out in ss. 66–69) of getting uninhabitable houses repaired, or closed and demolished if not repairable, are so specific and drastic that it must be deemed a necessary element of the statutory intent that the defendants are to use their powers under the Act in such a way that a dwelling built and let by them is fit for habitation, and that the tenant of the dwelling may act on an unarticulated assurance by them that it is fit for habitation. In other words, the letting agreement in this case should be read as if it contained an express term warranting the flat to be habitable.

The tenancy agreement entered into by the plaintiff fully bears out that deduction. The flat was provided under s. 56, sub-s. 1, as a 'dwelling,' and that fact alone would have made it incumbent on the defendants to give the plaintiff at least an implied warranty that it was a flat which was fit to dwell in. But apart from that, many of the 32 terms of the written tenancy agreement are directed to specifying what the plaintiff tenant shall do or may not do when dwelling in the flat; there is even a specific term requiring him to dwell in the flat. The tenancy agreement, which was executed by the plaintiff but not by the defendants, begins with the words 'in consideration of being allotted a dwelling provided by the Corporation under the Housing Act, 1966, I hereby agree to observe, perform and comply with' the conditions of the letting. Such being the basis of the letting, the defendants must be deemed to have attached to the written words a tacit assurance that the flat was being duly provided under the Act of 1966, *i.e.*, in a habitable condition.

It has been argued on behalf of the defendants that such an implied term is not reconcilable with s. 114, sub-s. 1, of the Act. Subject to specified exceptions, s. 114, sub-s. 1, stipulates that in any contract entered into after the commencement of the section for the letting for habitation of a house at a rent not exceeding £130 p.a. there shall, *notwithstanding any stipulation to the contrary*, be implied a condition that at the commencement of the tenancy the house is reasonably fit for human habitation and an undertaking that during the tenancy the landlord (a term which, by the definition in the Act, does not include a housing authority) will keep it so. That provision does not apply directly to this case, because the rent payable by the plaintiff was over £130 p.a. It is urged, however, that the exclusion from the range of s. 114, sub-s. 1, of lettings for a rent above the prescribed limit necessarily excludes an intention that a condition as to habitability should be inferred in such lettings. I do not agree. This provision replaces a corresponding provision in the Housing (Miscellaneous Provisions) Act, 1931, which replaced a like provision in the Housing of the Working Classes Act, 1890, and is merely the re-enactment of a protection given to the tenants of low-rented houses of the kind specified, regardless even of an express covenant to the contrary. As the Chief Justice has pointed out in his judgment, this provision does not appear to apply at all to houses let by a housing authority. Even if it did apply to them, the existence of such a provision could not be treated as a guide to what is to be implied in the letting of a dwelling provided under the Act. To determine what is implied in such a letting, it is the powers and duties of the housing authority under the Act that must be examined and, as I hope I have shown, these necessarily require the housing authority to ensure that the dwelling, when let, is fit for human habitation.

I do not find it necessary or desirable to express an opinion as to the wider question whether there should be held to be implied a condition as to habitability in the letting of every kind of dwellinghouse.

As I construe the law, the plaintiff is entitled to succeed in contract for the particular reason that this flat was provided under the Act of 1966. Therefore, it is academic to consider whether he would be entitled to succeed if the flat had not been provided under the Act. Whether in such circumstances he would be entitled to sue on an implied condition as to habitability is a point on which this Court has never pronounced. Were it necessary to decide the point, it is not unlikely that the Chief Justice would consider it necessary to convene a full Court for that purpose, for there are long-standing judicial authorities which hold that a condition as to habitability is not to be implied in the letting of an unfurnished dwellinghouse. If those authorities are to be set aside, it would probably be better to do so by statute, with prospective effect, rather than by judicial decision with its necessarily retrospective effect. If statutory effect in relation to tenancies is given to the legislative proposals in this respect set out in the Law Reform Commission's Working Paper No. 1 (The Law Relating to the Liability of Builders, Vendors and Lessors for the Quality and Fitness of Premises), the decision of this Court on the point is not likely to be called for.

In all the circumstances, therefore, I find it appropriate to rule on the plaintiff's claim in contract by holding that he is entitled to rely on a breach of an implied condition as to habitability arising from the fact that the flat was provided under the Act of 1966.

Negligence

Just as the question of the liability of the defendants in contract may be decided on the basis that the flat was provided under the Act of 1966, so also the question of liability in negligence lends itself to resolution on the same footing. It would be beyond the true scope of the essential circumstances of this case to decide whether there would be liability in negligence if the flat had not been provided under the Act. That broader question will be given a legislative solution if the proposals in the Law Reform Commission's Working Paper No. 1 are given effect by Parliament.

Following on *Donoghue* v. *Stevenson* [1932] A.C. 562 it has been established by a line of decisions (such as *Dutton* v. *Bognor Regis U.D.C.* [1972] 1 Q.B. 373; *Anns* v. *Merton London Borough* [1978] A.C. 728 and *Batty* v. *Metropolitan Realisations Ltd.* [1978] Q.B. 554) that where a person, including a builder or a local authority, carelessly provides a dwelling in which there is a concealed defect which the occupier could not have discovered by inspection, the person who provided the dwelling may be liable in negligence for personal injury or economic loss suffered as a result of the defect. The precise conditions or limitations of that liability need not now be considered, for I have no doubt that the principle of liability evolved in those cases is applicable to the circumstances of this case.

Despite ample opportunity of vetting the design of the ventilation system, the defendants were wanting in due care and skill in passing and accepting it. They should have made the necessary calculation as to relative humidity, or ensured that it was made. If they had done so, they would have discovered that the ventilation system was likely to produce the excessive condensation which made this flat unfit for habitation. As the ventilation system in the flat amounted to a serious concealed defect which the plaintiff could not have been expected to discover, and as the defendants (in their capacity as a housing authority providing a dwelling under the Act) owed a duty to the plaintiff to see that the flat he was getting was fit for habitation, the defendants were negligent in failing to observe the duty. The plaintiff was entitled, apart from any contractual obligation, to rely on the defendants to ensure that the flat would be habitable. The duty placed on the defendants by the Act of 1966 justified the plaintiff in so thinking. It is the defendants' failure, *vis-à-vis* the plaintiff as tenant under the Act, to observe that duty that was the particular source of negligence.

It has been suggested in argument that liability in negligence should not be held to attach to the defendants because of the contractual link between them and the plaintiff. I do not think that the existence of a contract of tenancy, or of liability under that contract, excludes liability in negligence. Liability under both heads may exist simultaneously: this Court so held in *Finlay* v. *Murtagh* [1979] I.R. 249. Where, as in the present case, there was a proximity of relationship creating a general duty on one side and a justifiable reliance by the other side on the observance of that duty, it is immaterial that the parties were bound together in contract.

I would dispose of the matters argued by holding that the plaintiff is entitled, both in contract and in negligence, to recover from the defendants the damages found by the Circuit Court judge.

Kenny J.:

I have had the advantage of reading the judgments of the Chief Justice and of Mr. Justice Henchy, and I agree with both judgments.

Note and question

For a comprehensive analysis of the decision, see Kerr and Clark, 'Council Housing, Implied Terms and Negligence – A critique of *Siney* v. *Dublin Corporation*' Irish Jurist (n.s.) 32 (1980). Has *Weir* v. *Dun Laoghaire Corporation*, Sup. Ct., 20 December 1982 (15–1982) any implications in relation to the liability of housing authorities, in your view?

Chapter 11

BREACH OF STATUTORY DUTY

The question whether a breach of statute gives rise to civil liability is a difficult one in tort law. In general, the orthodox approach at common law suggests that whether a statute gives a remedy to an injured person is a matter of interpretation in each case. The courts in this country have been quick to express 'principles of interpretation' but slower to attempt to articulate the policy on which this interpretation should be based. This formalism contrasts with the position in North America, where much discussion of policy is apparent.

In certain cases no problem arises. A statute sometimes provides explicitly that a civil action may or may not be taken in relation to a breach of certain of its provisions. Where, however, the statute is silent as regards any civil remedy, the courts may be called on to determine whether it was the intent of the legislature that such a remedy should exist. In truth, the legislature probably had no 'intent', one way or the other, on the matter; indeed, its failure to provide explicitly for a remedy might reasonably be considered to imply that it did not intend that any remedy should be available to persons injured by breach of any of the statute's provisions.

A number of guidelines have been developed by the courts in determining the legislative 'intent' of such statutory provisions. These will be considered in turn.

1. *BENEFIT OF THE PUBLIC OR A CLASS OF PERSONS*

The courts have frequently held that where a legislative provision was enacted for the benefit of a particular class of persons rather than for the benefit of the general public, members of that class ought to be able to obtain damages for breach of the provision. On other occasions, they have found that only a public benefit was intended.

WALSH V. KILKENNY COUNTY COUNCIL
Unreported, High Court, Gannon, J., 23 January 1978 (1976–No.2535P)

Gannon J.:

This is a claim for £2,480, the agreed value of the loss sustained by the plaintiff upon the occasion of the death by poisoning of eight milch cows, his property, on the 11th November 1975. These animals were from a herd of 130 cows that had free-run grazing upon a substantial area of pasture which was bounded as a short stretch by a cemetery in which two yew trees were growing. The cattle had gained access to the yew trees by passing through a gap in the boundary wall between the cemetery and the plaintiff's pasture and by going across some 70 to 77 yards of the cemetery.

The plaintiff said in evidence that he had this farm at Danesfort County Kilkenny, which adjoins the old graveyard or burial ground, for 27 years. He said he never knew that there were yew trees in the cemetery. The maintenance of the wall which separated the cemetery from his land was always understood by him to be the responsibility of the County Council. At one portion there was a small gap in the wall for some years, but the wall at this point was sufficient to prevent cattle from going through. About twelve months prior to the occasion giving rise to the claim he had observed that in a storm a portion of the wall had split along its length. The effect was to cause a portion of the split wall to spill in on his land while the corresponding portion innermost to the cemetery remained standing. He expressed the opinion that ivy growing along the wall kept the damaged portion standing. It was this portion which collapsed and left the gap through which his cows had gone into the cemetery on the morning of the 11th November 1975. There was no evidence of any particular incident which might have caused this damaged portion of wall to collapse. The plaintiff said that during the twelve month period prior to that morning he did not think his cows would go into the cemetery or that it was necessary to tell the County Council of the condition of the wall or that it would be necessary to take any steps to prevent his cows going into the cemetery. He said he knew that yew was poisonous to cattle and that the cattle were fond of eating ivy. He thought that if there was ivy near the yew the cattle while eating the ivy might also eat yew. The cows at that time were left out for grazing day and night but were fed at the yard when milked morning and evening, and the plaintiff considered that they had plentiful grazing pasture at that time.

On behalf of the defendants, the County Council of Kilkenny, evidence was given by Peter Doran who stated that the cemetery was maintained by the County Council and the damaged wall has since been repaired by the County Council. He produced a plan of the location. He stated that the cemetery was inspected and cleaned up annually, the grass was usually cut in the summer months, probably in July, and any repairs required were done. He said that if the County Council had known of the split in the wall they would have repaired it, and if it had appeared to be in danger of collapse they would have repaired it immediately. It was his evidence that the portion of wall of which the plaintiff complains on inspection had appeared to be all right on the defendants' side.

The following facts which appear to me to be material were proved to my satisfaction in evidence. The defendants accepted the obligation to, and did, maintain the wall between the cemetery and the plaintiff's pasture in a state of repair sufficient to prevent entry by cattle from the pasture into the cemetery. For a period of about twelve months prior to the 10th November 1975 a portion of this wall was in a damaged state to the knowledge of the plaintiff but unknown to the defendants. During this period the plaintiff did not think it necessary to inform the defendants of the condition of the wall, nor did he think his cows would break into the cemetery, nor did he think it necessary to take steps to prevent his cows getting into the cemetery. During this period the damaged portion of wall was effective to prevent the plaintiff's cattle getting into the cemetery. Between the 10th and 11th November 1975 the plaintiff's cows did get into the cemetery through a gap in the wall corresponding to the damaged portion which was then found to be collapsed. The plaintiff's cattle were poisoned by eating yew in the cemetery. How or why the damaged portion of the wall ceased on the night of the 10th November 1975 to continue to be effective to prevent the plaintiff's cattle getting into the cemetery has not been proved. Other than to suggest that that portion of wall collapsed without some force or activating agency the plaintiff, on whom the burden of proof lies, gives no answer to this query. On the evidence I have heard I think the inference most consistent with probabilities is that some of the plaintiff's cattle commenced eating ivy growing along the damaged portion of the wall and in the course thereof caused that portion of the wall to collapse. No evidence was given to establish whether or not the cemetery is a burial ground attached to or contiguous to a church, chapel or place of worship. The plan and photographs admitted in evidence seem to indicate that the cemetery was a burial ground which had been attached to and contiguous to a church, chapel or place of worship.

On these facts the plaintiff seeks to establish liability in the defendants for the amount of his loss on the basis either of breach of the statutory duty imposed on the County Council as the Health Authority by section 185 of the *Public Health (Ireland) Act 1878*, or alternatively under the Statutory Rules made pursuant to section 181 of that Act on the 6th July 1888, or in the further alternative on the basis of negligence at common law.

In relation to the statutory duty the plaintiff contends that under Rule 1 of the regulations for burial grounds dated 6th July 1888 made pursuant to section 181 of the *Public Health (Ireland) Act 1878* the defendants were obliged to maintain the cemetery 'sufficiently fenced'. Rule 1 of the 1888 regulations is as follows: 'Every burial ground shall be kept sufficiently fenced, and, if necessary, shall be under-drained to such a depth as will prevent water remaining in any grave or vault.' The plaintiff contends that the defendants failed to maintain the cemetery 'sufficiently fenced' and that the plaintiff is a person for whose benefit the duty was created by Statute and who has suffered damage from the failure of the defendants to perform this duty. It was submitted that, in the absence of any statutory penalty prescribed for failure to perform the duty, the remedy in damages lies for any person damnified by the breach of statutory duty. The defendants in answer, on this aspect, submit that the injury alleged to have been sustained by the plaintiff is not attributable to any breach of this statutory duty, and further that the plaintiff is not a person within the ambit of the purposes of the statutory duty imposed upon the County Council by the *Public Health (Ireland) Act 1878*.

Not every failure to comply with a statutory duty from which damage ensues entitles a person damnified to recover compensation from the party in breach of the Statute in a claim for damages founded on that ground alone. As stated by Maughan L.J. in *Monk* v. *Warbey* [1935] 1 K.B. 75 at page 85:

'The Court has to make up its mind whether the harm sought to be remedied by the Statute is one of the kind the Statute is intended to prevent; in other words it is not sufficient to say that harm has been caused to a person and to assert that the harm is due to a breach of the Statute which has resulted in the injury.'

Furthermore the fact that the Statute does not exact a penalty from the defaulting party is not the only factor which signifies that damages may be recovered in a civil action founded on the breach of the statutory duty. In *Philips* v. *Britannia Hygienic Laundry Company Limited* [1923] 2 K. B. 832 at page 840 Atkin L.J. says:

'When a Statute imposes a duty of commission or omission upon an individual, the question whether a person aggrieved by a breach of the duty has a right of action depends on the intention of the Statute. Was it intended that a duty should be owed to the individual aggrieved as well as to the State, or is it a public duty only? That depends upon the construction of the Statute as a whole, and the circumstances in which it was made, and to which it relates. One of the matters to be taken into consideration is this: does the Statute on the face of it contain a reference to a remedy for the breach of it? If so, it would, prima facie, be the only remedy, but that is not conclusive. One must still look to the intention of the Legislature to be derived from the words used, and one may come to the conclusion that, although the Statute creates a duty and imposes a penalty for the breach of that duty, it may still intend that the duty should be owed to individuals.'

Romer L.J. in *Solomons* v. *Gertzenstein Limited* [1954] 2 Q.B. 243 at 266 observed:

'No universal rule can be formulated which will answer the question whether in any given case an individual can sue in respect of a breach of statutory duty. "The only rule" said Lord Simonds in *Cutler*'s case (*Cutler* v. *Wandsworth Stadium* [1941] All E.R. 544 at 547) "which in all circumstances is valid is that the answer must depend on a consideration of the whole Act, and the circumstances, including the pre-existing law in which it was enacted." '

The Statute under consideration in the present case is the *Public Health (Ireland) Act 1878* and in particular Part III thereof which is a re-enactment with amendments of most of the *Burial Grounds (Ireland) Act 1856* and its amending Act of 1860 both of which were repealed. Sections 58 and 59 of the *Cemeteries Clauses Act 1847*, which relate to the protection of cemeteries, were expressly incorporated by Section 193 of the *Public Health (Ireland) Act 1878*. By Section 234 of the Act it is provided, inter alia, that the expenses incurred by a Burial Board established by the Act shall be charged on and paid out of the poor rates in cases of rural districts, and in cases of urban districts a rate to be levied specially for the purpose. Taking the provisions of this Act as a whole and in particular the provisions of Part III and the other Sections related to that Part I am in no doubt that this is an enactment for the benefit only of the public at large, and that the duties and obligations therein are imposed for the benefit only of the public at large, and not for the benefit of any class of persons nor of any individuals. The several Sections within Parts VI and VII of the Act make provision for claims by the Public Authority upon whom the statutory duties are imposed and by persons who may be aggrieved by the performance or the breach of any of the duties imposed by the Act. None of these Sections is capable of being construed as constituting the plaintiff in this case as a person for whose benefit the statutory obligations alleged w[ere] imposed on the defendants. Having regard to Sections 161 to 181 inclusive of Part III of the Act it would appear that the declared and primary purposes of the duties imposed on the defendants are the protection of public health, the maintenance of public decency, and the prevention of the violation of the respect due to the remains of deceased persons. The provisions of Section 171 and of Section 58 of the *Cemeteries Clauses Act 1847* incorporated by Section 193, which confer powers on the defendants to punish trespassers are inconsistent with the imposition of any duty on the defendants to trespassers. The duty to fence imposed by the Regulations of the 6th July 1888 made pursuant to Section 181 seems to be a duty to protect the property vested in the Burial Board from desecration or other interference by trespassers. The plaintiff, who is admittedly a trespasser, cannot claim that he is a person for whose benefit this duty is laid upon the defendants. Section 185 must be read in conjunction with Sections 186 and 187, and on the facts of this case these Sections have no application and do not assist the plaintiff. . . .

Note

See also *Siney* v. *Dublin Corporation, supra*. pp. 285–289.

2. *NATURE OF PENALTY OR REMEDY PROVIDED BY THE STATUTORY PROVISION*

In attempting to define whether a civil remedy ought to be made available under a statute the courts also look to the penalty provisions of the Act in question for inspiration in their deliberations. Here, however, the courts have attempted the impossible in trying to draw a conclusion, one way or the other, from the nature of the penalty or remedy provided by the statutory provision. If the penalty is low or if no penalty at all or some other remedy not involving a specific right to damages is provided, does this mean that the legislature regarded it as improper for there also to be a civil action (as some courts have concluded) or does it indicate, on the contrary that the legislature must have intended that the criminal sanction should be supplemented and reinforced by a civil remedy (as other courts have said)? Conversely, if the penalty is high, does this suggest that the legislature regarded it as sufficient punishment, or can one conclude that a breach which the legislature so clearly considered to be serious must be supplemented by a civil remedy? Even a cursory glance at the authorities shows that the courts have not been consistent in their approach to this general question. See *McMahon & Binchy*, p. 281.

3. OTHER TECHNIQUES OF STATUTORY INTERPRETATION

The courts have used other techniques of statutory interpretation. They may, for example, examine the preamble or other sections of the statute in order to determine whether an intention to create civil liability for breaches of specific sections may be inferred. The previous statutory background to the Act under consideration or a contrast of the language of the Act under consideration with that of other Acts may also throw light on its interpretation. The courts may also apply the principle of construction, *expressio unius est exclusio alterius*, so as to deny a civil remedy where civil liability is expressly stated in certain sections of the Act but not in the particular section under consideration.

Limitations on Recovery

LONG V. SAORSTÁT & CONTINENTAL STEAMSHIP CO.
93 I.L.T.R. 137 (Supreme Court, 1953)

Maguire C.J.:
The defendants in this action move the Court to set aside the verdict of the jury and the order and judgment of the President of the High Court in favour of the plaintiff for the sum of £5,261 and costs and to enter judgment for them with costs or for such order as to the Court may seem meet.

On April 18th, 1951, the plaintiff was employed as a stevedore in the unloading of a cargo from the S.S. City of Cork, the property of the defendants, then berthed at the North Wall Extension in the Port of Dublin. A gangway connecting the ship with the shore was free at the shore end, but was held in position by ropes which were lashed to rings on the coaming surrounding a hatch on board the ship which was open. At the time of the accident out of which this action arises the fall of the tide brought the deck below the level of the quay. As a result, the gangway was at an angle with its free end in the air. The plaintiff was standing near the end which rested upon the deck. He was engaged in superintending the unloading of long iron. Two men who were talking to the plaintiff turned and proceeded up the gangway. As they approached the shore the gangway tipped upwards from the deck. The lashing was so arranged that this could happen. The plaintiff had turned to face the open hold. In this position he was struck by the upward-swinging gangway. He was thrown into the hold, suffering serious injuries.

He brought this action claiming damages for negligence and breach of statutory duty. In their defence, the defendants deny this and plead contributory negligence on the part of the plaintiff. . . .

The jury . . . found that the defendants were guilty of a breach of statutory duty in failing to comply with Statutory Rules and Orders, 1928, No. 69. The relevant part of that order is art. 9, which provide:–

'If a ship is lying at a wharf or quay for the purpose of loading or unloading or coaling, there shall be safe means of access for the use of *persons employed* at such times as they have to pass from the ship to the shore or from the shore to the ship as follows:–

(a) where a gangway is reasonably practicable, a gangway not less than twenty-two inches wide, properly secured, and fenced throughout on each side to a clear height of two feet nine inches by means of upper and lower rails, taut ropes or chains or by other equally safe means.'

It is clear that this regulation is intended to provide that there shall be a safe means of access from ship to shore and *vice versa*. The accident out of which this action arose was not in any way connected with the use of the gangway as such. Even if the gangway had not complied with the terms of the regulation, I am of opinion that the plaintiff would have no cause of action arising out of a breach of the duty imposed by the order. In *Gorris* v. *Scott* L. R. 9 Exch. 125 it was held that the plaintiff could not recover for sheep which were washed overboard from a ship by reason of the defendant's neglect to take a precaution required by a Statutory Order on the ground that the object of the statute was to prevent the spread of disease among animals and not to protect them from perils of the sea. The evidence here is that the gangway was properly constructed. No evidence was given that in its structure it failed to comply with the regulations. The manner in which it was secured prevented any danger to persons using it as a means of going to or from the ship. It accordingly complied with the statutory regulation.

In my opinion, the answers to the questions whether the danger was unusual and whether there was a breach of statutory duty had no evidence to support them. The verdict should, accordingly, be set aside and judgment entered for the defendants.

O'Byrne J.:

I concur in the view expressed by the Chief Justice that the statutory regulation, on which the plaintiff sought to rely, was made for the benefit of persons passing and re-passing from the ship to the shore and that the plaintiff, who was not using it as means of access between the ship and the shore, cannot rely upon it. . . .

Kingsmill Moore, J.:

. . . The relevant portions of Article 9 are as follows:

'If a ship is lying at a wharf or quay for the purpose of loading or unloading, there shall be safe means of access for the use of persons employed at such times as they have to pass from the ship to the shore or from the shore to the ship. . . .'

It appears to me plain that this article is for the purpose of securing a means of access which is safe for persons passing from the ship to the shore and the shore to the ship, and only persons who come within that category can complain of a breach. The plaintiff is outside the ambit of this regulation, which imposes to duty on the shipowner or his servants towards persons not using the gangway as a means of access . . .

Murnaghan and **Lavery JJ.** concurred.

Notes

1. *Cf. McNamara* v. *E.S.B.* [1975] I.R. 1 (Sup. Ct., 1974) (regulations under *Factories Act 1955* for safety of 'persons employed' did not extend to person who was trespassing on an electricity sub-station), *Daly* v. *Greybridge Co-Operative Creamery Ltd.* [1964] I.R. 497 (Sup. Ct., 1963); *Roche* v. *P. Kelly & Co. Ltd.* [1969] I.R. 100 (Sup. Ct.)
2. See also *Córas Iompair Éireann* v. *Carroll and Wexford Co. Ltd.*, unreported, High Court, Gannon, J., 14 June 1982 (1976 No. 4925P).

Nature of Obligation Imposed by Statute

It is a matter of statutory construction to determine the nature of the obligation imposed by a statutory provision on the defendant. Generally it will not be sufficient for him to show that he behaved with due care, although occasionally a statutory provision may prescribe an obligation expressed in such specific terms: *cf.*, e.g., the *Safety in Industry Act 1980*, section 9(1) (no.9). More frequently, the courts impose 'absolute' or 'strict' liability for breaches of statutory provisions.

GALLAGHER V. MOGUL OF IRELAND LTD.
[1975] I.R. 204 (Supreme Court)

Walsh J.:

On the relevant date the defendants were the owners and managers of a mine known as the Silvermines mine at Nenagh in County Tipperary; the plaintiff, who is a miner, was employed by them in the mine. On the 16th January, 1971, when the plaintiff was engaged in drilling operations in a tunnel in the mine, there was a fall of rock from the roof of the tunnel causing injury to the plaintiff.

The plaintiff brought an action for damages in the High Court against the defendants and claimed that his injuries were caused by breach of statutory duty and by negligence on the part of the defendants. The defendants, who denied they were guilty of either breach of statutory duty or of negligence, claimed in turn that the plaintiff was guilty of negligence. The matter was heard before the then President of the High Court, Mr. Justice O'Keeffe, and a jury in January, 1974, and resulted in a net award being made to the plaintiff in the sum of £10,370 damages. The total sum awarded by the jury was £13,700, but the jury had apportioned the fault between the defendants and the plaintiff as to 80% to the defendants and 20% to the plaintiff. Allowing for this apportionment and deducting a sum of £590 paid under the Social Welfare (Occupational Injuries) Act, 1966, the trial judge gave judgment for the net sum already mentioned.

The defendants have brought their appeal against the award of damages on the ground that it was excessive, perverse, and unsupported by the evidence; they have also appealed against the apportionment of fault on the grounds that this was also a perverse and unsupportable apportionment. The defendants have also appealed against the learned trial judge's ruling in directing the jury to find them guilty of a breach of statutory duty to keep the working-place safe and secure.

The statute in question is the Mines and Quarries Act, 1965. Section 49 of the Act, which deals with the question of support, is as follows:–

'(1) It shall be the duty of the manager of every mine to take such steps by way of controlling movement of the strata in the mine and supporting the roof and sides of every road or working place as may be necessary for keeping the road or working place secure.

(2) It shall be the duty of the manager of every mine to secure that he has at all material times all information relevant for determining the steps necessary to discharge efficiently the duty imposed on him by subsection (1).'

Section 138 of the Act provides that the owner of a mine or a quarry is not absolved from liability to pay damages in respect of a contravention in relation to the mine or quarry, by a person employed by him, of a provision of the Act or an order made thereunder (or regulations or a prohibition, restriction or requirement imposed by a notice served under or by virtue of the Act by an inspector) 'by reason only that the provision contravened was one which expressly imposed on that person or on persons of a class to which, at the time of the contravention, he belonged, a duty or requirement or expressly prohibited that person, or persons or such a class or all persons from doing a specified act or, as the case may be, that the prohibition, restriction or requirement was expressly imposed on that person or that that person was, in pursuance of this Act or regulations, appointed by a person other than the owner.'

Section 137 of the Act provides:–

'It shall be a defence in any legal proceedings to recover damages . . . in so far as the proceedings . . . are or is based on an allegation of a contravention, in relation to a mine or quarry, of (a) a provision of this Act . . . to prove that it was impracticable to avoid or prevent the contravention.'

Section 49 of the Act imposes duties on the manager of a mine and the effect of s. 138 is that, if there is a contravention by the manager of the duties imposed by s. 49, the employers will not be absolved from liability by reason only of the fact that the obligation was expressly imposed upon the manager. In such a case in proceedings against either the manager or against his employers s. 137 provides that it shall be a defence to prove that it was impracticable to avoid or prevent the contravention. That section makes it quite clear that the burden of such proof is upon the defence and it would be no defence under this section simply to show that it would not have been reasonable to take the steps necessary to avoid such contravention.

The learned trial judge ruled that the duty imposed by s. 49 of the Act was an absolute duty; if he was correct in that ruling, it would mean that the only defence available would be the one provided in section 137. In the present case the defendants did not seek to set up a defence under s. 137, so the first matter to be considered in this appeal is whether or not s. 49 imposes an absolute obligation.

Section 49 of the Coal Mines Act, 1911, provided that 'The roof and sides of every travelling road and working place shall be made secure . . .' This section, as indeed was the whole Act of 1911, was repealed by the Act of 1965, and it may be said that s. 49 of the Act of 1965 replaced s. 49 of the Act of 1911. So far as I have been able to discover, there is no reported Irish case which deals with the construction of this section or which examines the nature of the obligation which it imposed. A number of English cases did hold that the duty imposed by s. 49 of the Act of 1911 was an absolute duty.

In my view, the obligation imposed by s. 49 of the Act of 1911 was an absolute duty and this view is confirmed by the decision of this Court in *Doherty* v. *Bowaters Irish Wallboard Mills Ltd.* [1968] I.R. 277 in which it was held that the provisions of s. 34, sub-s. 1(a), of the Factories Act, 1955, imposed an absolute duty when it enacted that 'a chain, rope or lifting tackle shall not be used unless it is of good construction, sound material, adequate strength and free from patent defect.' It had been submitted in that case that the provision in question did not impose an absolute obligation because the provisions of s. 33, sub-s. 1, of the same Act, in imposing an absolute obligation in the case of hoists or lifts, did so in the terms of providing that the hoist or lift should 'be properly maintained' whereas s. 34, sub-s. 1(a), made no reference whatever to the maintenance of the chain, rope or lifting tackle. The Court, while being of opinion that s. 33 of the Act of 1955 did create an absolute obligation, was also of opinion that s. 34, sub-s. 1(a), did so by the use of the expression 'shall not be used unless it is of good construction, sound material, adequate strength and free from patent defect.'

In the present case the learned trial judge ruled that s. 49 of the Act of 1965 imposed an absolute duty; his ruling was based upon his view that the effect of the decision of this Court in *Doherty's Case* [1968] I.R. 277 was to compel such a construction of s. 49 of the Act of 1965.

It has been submitted on behalf of the defendants that the wording of s. 49 of the Act of 1965 is so different from the wording of s. 49 of the Act of 1911 that it must be assumed that the intention of the Oireachtas was to make a different provision. It is submitted that the duty imposed by s. 49 of the Act of 1965 is not an absolute duty. If that be so, it would appear that it was the intention of the Oireachtas to diminish the force of the obligation created by the Act of 1911. It is true that there are differences in the section of the Act of 1965. The first important difference is that it imposes an obligation or a duty upon the manager personally, for breach of which his employers may also be answerable. The Act of 1911 speaks of making secure the roof and sides of every travelling road and working place. The Act of 1965 is also directed towards keeping the road and working place secure. Both sections refer to the roof and sides, but the Act of 1965 refers in addition to the movement of the strata in the mine. It is clear that the Act of 1965 makes the duty more extensive than did the Act of 1911, so the question is whether it altered the nature of the duty in the manner suggested by the defendants.

If s. 49 of the Act of 1911 had read that it was 'the duty of the manager to make secure the roof and sides of every travelling road and working place,' I do not think that the nature of the duty would be any different than it was under the wording which was in fact used in the section. The Act of 1965 says that it shall be the duty of the manager to take such steps by way of controlling movement of the strata in the mine and supporting the roof and sides of every road or working place as may be necessary for keeping the road or working place secure. By referring expressly to controlling the movement of strata and to supporting the roof and sides, it appears to me that the duty imposed (whatever may be its nature) does not relate to matters which might affect the safety or security of the road or working place which do not come within the ambit of movement of strata or support for the roof and sides. Therefore, if the road or working place become unsafe by reason of a fall or collapse of the roof and sides, it does not appear to me that there would be any contravention unless it were shown that the fall or collapse was of a type which was preventable by the provision of support. Similarly, a movement of strata, which results in making the road or working place unsafe, must be a movement of the type which is controllable before there is a contravention of the section.

However, if the insecurity is brought about by an insufficiency of support or inadequate control of movement of the strata, it appears to me that it would be no defence to show that the support which was provided (if any) or the control which was exercised (if any) was as much as reasonable foresight would have required. In other words, the duty imposed by the statute, within the limits which I have indicated, is certainly greater than the ordinary common-law duty to take care. I am fortified in this view by the fact that s. 137 of the Act of 1965, *supra*, contains an escape clause, but an escape clause which is not conditioned by considerations of either reasonable-ness or foresight.

Counsel for the defendants have submitted that the learned trial judge was incorrect in holding that the section imposed strict liability. Their submission was based principally upon the decision and the reasoning of the House of Lords in *Brown* v. *The National Coal Board* [1962] A.C. 574. Under a similar statutory provision in the (English) Mines and Quarries Act, 1954, it was held by the House of Lords that strict liability was not imposed upon the manager, and that the manager of a mine is not in breach of his duty under the relevant English statutory provision if he has obtained all the information that sub-s. 2 of the English provision requires him to obtain, and if he has acted in the light of that information with all the care and skill which a manager ought to bring to bear.

Before considering this decision it is desirable to refer to the provisions of the relevant English section which is s. 48 of the Mines and Quarries Act, 1954, and it reads as follows:–

'(1) It shall be the duty of the manager of every mine to take, with respect to every road and working place in the mine, such steps by way of controlling movement of the strata in the mine and supporting the roof and sides of the road or working place as may be necessary for keeping the road or working place secure: Provided that nothing in this subsection shall require the taking of such steps as aforesaid with respect to a road or part of a road which is, or is comprised in, a part of the mine every entrance to which is for the time being provided, in pursuance of section thirty-three of this Act, with such an enclosure or barrier as is therein mentioned.

(2) It shall be the duty of the manager of every mine to take such steps as may be necessary for securing that he is at all material times in possession of all information relevant for determining the nature and extent of any steps which it is requisite for him to take in order to discharge efficiently the duty imposed on him by the foregoing subsection.'

It will be seen from this that, while the section in general terms appears to be similar, there are differences. In *Brown* v. *The National Coal Board* [1962] A.C. 574 the view of Lord Reid appears as follows, beginning at the bottom of p. 587 of the report:–

'Logically subsection (2) comes first: it requires the manager to obtain all the information necessary to enable him to discharge his duties under subsection (1). It is hardly possible to suppose that subsection (2) imposes an absolute duty. The manager is to take "such steps as may be necessary" for securing that he has all relevant information. Investigation after an accident may disclose information which it was physically impossible for him to obtain earlier, but which, if it could have been known earlier, would have enabled him to prevent the accident. I cannot read subsection (2) as laying on him the impossible duty of obtaining that information before the accident: "such steps as may be necessary" must at least be limited to such steps as it is possible to take."

At p. 588 he refers to the fact that sub-s. 1 of s. 48 contains the same phrase ('such steps . . . as may be necessary') and he continues by saying:–

'Then I think that further light on the meaning of subsection (1) can be got from subsection (2). It assumes that if he carries out his duties under it the manager will be in possession of *all* information relevant for determining the nature and extent of the steps which subsection (1) requires him to take. If that is right, then the manager cannot be in breach of his duty under subsection (1) if he has obtained all the information which subsection (2) requires him to obtain and has acted in light of that information with all the care and skill which a manager ought to bring to bear. So again the conclusion is that the manager is not under any absolute duty.'

The main judgment was delivered by Lord Radcliffe, with whom Lord Reid and Viscount Simonds agreed; all of these members accepted the view that an obligation in strict liability was created by s. 49 of the Coal Mines Act, 1911. On the other hand, Lord Denning, who arrived at the same conclusion as his colleagues that the duty created by s. 48 of the Act of 1954 was not an absolute one, expressed the view at p. 599 of the report that the duty under the Act of 1954 was in no way less than the duty under the Act of 1911; but he took the view that the Act of 1911 did not impose an absolute duty. The Court of Appeal in England, against whose decision ([1961] 1

Q.B. 303) the appeal was taken to the House of Lords, had agreed that the appellant's action must fail; but were not unanimous in their analysis of the import of s. 48 of the Act of 1954. According to Lord Radcliffe their division occurred in describing the meaning of the words 'such steps as may be necessary.' One member of the Court of Appeal, Lord Morris of Borth-y-Gest, took the view that the obligation to take the necessary steps was an entirely objective one and independent of what was or could be known, or provided for, before a fault took place. The other two members of the Court, Holroyd Pearce L.J. and Pilcher J., did not consider that the failure to take a step, the necessity for which could only have been ascertained after the event, would constitute a breach of the manager's duty. They took the view that whether steps are necessary or not had to be decided in the light of all the facts which were known or ought to have been known at the time when the decision to take those steps fell to be made and when it was still possible for those steps to be taken. Lord Radcliffe took the same view, and at p. 590 of the report he said:–

> 'The natural meaning of these words seems to me to be plain. A duty is imposed upon the manager from time to time to do certain things described as "taking steps" and it is so far absolute that, once the obligation falls, the only excuse permitted is that to be found in section 157 of the Act, which provides generally that it is to be a defence in any legal proceedings or prosecution based on an alleged contravention of requirements imposed by the Act to prove that it was impracticable to avoid or prevent the contravention. But "steps" to achieve what? One must first, I think, be clear what is meant by the word "secure" in this section. It does not mean in my view that the roof is to be impregnable, in the sense that it is to be kept in such a state that there can never be a fall of or from it.'

The conclusion of Lord Radcliffe is that the duty imposed is an absolute one once the obligation falls. In his view the absolute duty imposed by the statute was that of taking such steps as are necessary in the light of all the facts which were known, or ought to have been known, at the time when the decision to take those steps fell to be made and when it was still possible for them to be taken. Lord Denning took the view that the duty imported was that the manager must take not only such steps as may be reasonable or desirable but also those which may be necessary to keep the road secure. Both Lord Radcliffe and Lord Denning took the view that the use of the words 'as may be necessary' imported the element of foreseeability. Lord Denning expressed it as being the duty of the manager to take steps to guard the workmen against those foreseeable dangers which are a possible cause of injury in circumstances which may reasonably be expected to occur.

The outstanding difference between the relevant section of the Act of 1911 and the corresponding section of the Act of 1965 is that in the latter provision a duty is cast upon the manager. It cannot be assumed that in so doing the legislature intended to diminish the nature of the liability imposed by the Act of 1911. Far more likely is the explanation that to designate a particular person as having a particular responsibility was to ensure the probability of greater safety, because the absence of a statutory designation would leave the precautions which should be taken open to the criticism that what was everybody's business was nobody's business; so that it appeared more logical to make it the business of a particular person. A reading of the Irish sections and of the corresponding British sections certainly demonstrates a difference in wording apart altogether from the proviso which appears in the first sub-section of the British section. However, in my view the difference in wording does not reflect much more, if anything, than a difference in drafting style.

It has been submitted, as was submitted and held in *Brown's Case* [1962] A.C. 574, that sub-s. 2 of s. 49 of the Act of 1965 would logically come before sub-s. 1 of that section and that one should construe the intention of the Oireachtas as being one of reducing what was an absolute liability to a less than absolute liability. In my view, to say that sub-s. 2 logically comes before sub-s. 1 is to beg the question. If the duty imposed by sub-s. 1 is less than absolute, then it might well be said that sub-s. 2 should logically come first; but if the duty imposed by sub-s. 1 is an absolute duty, then that imposed by sub-s. 2 is a separate duty although ancillary to, or connected with, the first duty. It may be very desirable, if not indeed necessary, to impose upon persons a duty to take such steps as may be open to them to take to assist in, if not succeeding in, the fulfilment of an absolute duty. It is, however, well known that there can be a breach of an absolute duty without fault on anybody's part; the law fully recognises this. See [*O'Sullivan* v. *Dwyer*] [1971] I.R. at p. 285. Therefore, if the duty imposed by sub-s. 1 is an absolute duty, a breach of it does not in any way depend upon proving a breach of the duty imposed by sub-s. 2; indeed it may be clearly established that in such a case there was no breach of sub-section 2. On the other hand, there can be a situation where there is a clearly-established breach of sub-s. 2 without there having been any breach of sub-s. 1, as where the road and working place in a mine are secure even though that happy position has come about, or is being maintained, notwithstanding the failure of the manager of the mine to furnish himself with all the information required by sub-section 2.

For the reasons I have already given earlier in this judgment, I do not think the duty imposed upon the manager is a general one to keep the road and working place secure but rather it is one to keep the road and working place secure in so far as the same can be made secure by the control of movement of the strata and the support to the roof and sides of the road or working place.

However, the important phrase is 'as may be necessary.' It is submitted that the use of this phrase imports a connotation of a duty less than absolute duty. In my view, that is not a correct construction of the statutory provision. If a road or working place can be made secure or kept secure by the provision of a sufficient amount of support by way of the provision of a sufficient control of movement, then the failure to provide the safeguards in the sufficiency actually required is a failure to provide the necessary amount. In my view, the trial judge was quite correct in his application of the decision of this Court in *Doherty* v. *Bowaters Irish Wallboard Mills Ltd.* [1968] I.R. 277. In that case the Court held that an absolute duty was imposed by a statutory provision which contained a requirement that a chain or rope or lifting tackle should not be used unless it was of '. . . adequate strength . . .' in the context of the provision of the Factories Act in issue in that case and the present statutory provision, I do not see any distinction which can be drawn between the use of the word 'adequate' and the use of the word 'necessary.' If anything 'necessary' imports a greater sense of obligation than the word 'adequate.' If the road or working place becomes insecure by reason of a deficiency in the support to the roof or sides of the road or working place, or a deficiency in the degree of control of movement of the strata in the mine, then it is clear beyond doubt that the support and control which was provided was less than was necessary. The test is not 'less than was reasonably foreseen to have been necessary.'

Therefore, I am of opinion that, where the working place or the road is not secure and where it could have been made secure by a sufficient degree of control or support, there has been a failure to provide the necessary degree of control or support. The statutory obligation is absolute in the sense that it is independent of what could reasonably have been foreseen or of what was capable of being ascertained only after the event. But even in respect of this stringent statutory obligation the Oireachtas has provided the statutory defence contained in para. (*a*) of s. 137 of the Act of 1965. In other words, in legal proceedings to recover damages based on the contravention of sub-s. 1 of s. 49 it is still a defence for the defendant to prove that it was impracticable to avoid or prevent the contravention, even in a case where the precautions which the statute required to be taken could only have been ascertained after the event. In my view, therefore, the appeal against the ruling or finding that the defendants were guilty of breach of statutory duty in failing to keep the working place secure should be dismissed. . . .

Budd and **Griffin JJ.** concurred.

Contributory Negligence

O'SULLIVAN V. DWYER
[1971] I.R. 275 (Supreme Court)

Walsh J.:

This is an appeal taken against the judgment and order of the President of the High Court in this action which was tried before the learned President and a jury at Cork from the 17th–22nd July, 1969. It was an action for negligence and breach of statutory duty which the plaintiff alleged had resulted in him sustaining very serious personal injuries. The jury awarded a total sum of £64,024 as damages but judgment was entered for the plaintiff in the sum of £38,414. 8. 0d. because the jury apportioned the degrees of fault between the parties by attributing 60% to the defendant and 40% to the plaintiff. Part of the gross sum of £64,024 consisted of an award of £35,000 for general damages. While this appeal is taken on questions of liability as well as on damages, the appeal as to damages is limited to this particular sum of £35,000 which was awarded for general damages. Therefore, it will be unnecessary to consider the other heads under which damages were awarded. The jury in fact found damages under four headings of which the fourth was general damages.

The accident in this case arose out of building operations which are sufficiently described in the judgment of this Court given on the 27th March, 1969, in an earlier appeal in this action and it is unnecessary to repeat them here. At the retrial the case was conducted on behalf of the plaintiff on the basis that he was the servant of the defendant or, alternatively, that he was an independent contractor employed by the defendant. The learned trial judge at the conclusion of the evidence ruled that the plaintiff was not a servant and, as the defendant was not contesting the fact that the plaintiff was an independent contractor, the case went to the jury on that basis though no finding to that effect was either necessary or made.

In the light of the decision of this Court in *Roche* v. *Kelly & Co. Ltd.* [1969] I.R. 100 and the previous decision of this Court in this case, the matter went to the jury on the basis of an alleged breach of the Building (Safety, Health and Welfare) Regulations, 1959, and substantially on the basis that contrary to the Regulations the defendant had failed to provide a hand-rail or a toe-board or other effective means to prevent the plaintiff falling from the flat roof upon which he was working.

The learned trial judge, following the earlier judgment of this Court in this case, allowed the case to go to the jury on the basis that the provisions of Regulation 6, para. 1, of the Regulations of 1959 were applicable and the jury were asked whether the flat roof in question was a working platform and they answered that question in the affirmative. At the hearing of this appeal the defendant has submitted that the learned trial judge should have ruled as a matter of law that the flat roof was not a working platform within the meaning of para. 1 of Regulation 6. In my view, this submission is quite unsustainable as this Court in this case has already decided that it was a working platform.

It has been suggested in this Court in the present appeal that, if any regulation applies, the appropriate regulation is para. 4 of Regulation 8. That paragraph refers to flat roofs and to persons working on flat roofs, and the submission was made to the learned trial judge on behalf of the defendant that that paragraph did not apply because, as the roof had not been completely constructed but was simply a roof in the course of construction, it could not be regarded as a roof terminating in an unprotected edge for the purpose of that paragraph. The plaintiff had fallen off the edge of a flat roof which had been completed to the extent that only a piece of board of three or four feet long remained to be placed upon it to complete it. The evidence clearly discloses that the surface in question was the surface upon which the plaintiff worked and was obliged to work. It terminated in an unprotected edge. The clear object of the Regulations of 1959 in this respect is to compel employers to take precautions against workmen (or independent contractors in the cases in which they are protected – *Roche* v. *P. Kelly & Co. Ltd.* [1969] I.R. 100) falling off such unprotected surfaces where they are working upon them. In my opinion, no jury could find that this was not a flat roof within the meaning of para. 4 of Clause 8 of the Regulations of 1959. At what point a flat roof in the course of construction may be regarded as a roof rather than as a platform from which the roof is being constructed may be a question of degree but in this particular case, where only a small piece of wood remained to be inserted, it would be quite absurd to regard this as anything but a flat roof. If the roof had been completed and then it had been found to be necessary to remove the same small piece of wood to make some further adjustment, could it be seriously suggested that the roof had ceased to be a roof because the piece of wood was taken out of it? In my view the learned trial judge could have left the question to the jury under the provisions of para. 4 of Regulation 8 also, but he was persuaded from so doing by the submissions made on behalf of the defendant.

However, the trial judge was correct in holding that para. 1 of Regulation 6 was applicable. As I mentioned, that particular point has already been decided by this Court. If a flat roof is used as a platform upon which work is to be carried out, it is a working platform. If work is being done upon a flat roof or if it is used as a platform for the purpose of carrying out work upon some other structure or part of the building for which it can be used as a platform, in my view it would be wholly unrealistic to suggest that the flat roof is not a working platform because it is a platform which is permanent in the sense that it is a roof rather than a temporary platform erected for a particular job. If a temporary structure were laid upon a flat roof so as to be supported by it, it is not contested that the structure would qualify as a working platform within the meaning of the Regulations. If that is so, then it would be a complete negation of the purposes of the Regulations to withdraw the statutory protection because the workman stands upon the flat roof itself instead of standing upon a few boards placed upon it. Not every flat roof would qualify as a working platform within the meaning of the Regulations; it would depend on the width of the roof. For example, a flat roof over a passage might not have the minimum width required by the Regulations, which prescribe platforms of not less than 42 to 51 inches in width for certain types of work: see para. 3 (*c*) and (*d*) of Regulation 6. In such a case, if the roof was to be used, it would have to be temporarily extended in width and provided with the necessary guards to qualify as a working platform. However, when it is the necessary width and is being used as a working platform then it is a working platform. In view of the previous decision of this Court in the matter, it is not now open to the defendant to contend otherwise. In my view, this ground of appeal fails.

It had already been ruled in the previous decision of this Court that para. 1 of Regulation 29 of the Regulations of 1959 did govern this case, and the ground of appeal which claims that the learned trial judge was wrong in ruling in accordance with the decision of this Court is not sustainable.

The jury also found that the absence of a hand-rail or a toe-board, or other effective means to prevent the fall of the plaintiff, was a cause of the accident and against this finding there is no appeal. The finding is amply justified by the evidence.

The plaintiff cross-appealed in respect of the judge's failure to leave the matter to the jury under para. 4 of Regulation 8. I think the plaintiff is correct in this but it does not now arise in view of the fact that I am of opinion that the judge's ruling with reference to the applicability of Regulation 6 was correct.

It was also submitted on behalf of the defendant that the apportionment of fault in this case was such that no reasonable jury could have attributed 60% of the fault to the defendant and only 40% to the plaintiff and that, therefore, the apportionment ought to be set aside. In support of this it was submitted, as set out in the notice of appeal, that the learned trial judge should have directed the jury that the apportionment of degrees of fault should be on the basis of culpability and that he did not fully or correctly direct the jury on this topic in accordance with the provisions of the Civil Liability Act, 1961.

In the course of his directions to the jury the learned trial judge said at p. 332 of the transcript:– 'now, if you answer these two questions "Yes" the result is that the defendant must pay damages to the plaintiff because the defendant would have been guilty of a breach of duty under statute and that would have contributed to the accident, but you would then have to consider the extent to which the plaintiff himself may have been responsible for his injuries.' Later at p. 333 he said:– 'On the other hand, if you think he [*the plaintiff*] was guilty of something, neglecting to take the care a reasonable man would for his own safety, you answer the question "Yes" and if you do, you now have to come along and attribute, not the blame, for blame in the sense of criticism does not really arise in this case at all, but the responsibility or the legal fault in terms of percentages as between the plaintiff and the defendant . . .' At p. 334 he said:– 'But, anyway, I cannot – if you come to the conclusion that both were to blame, in the sense of responsibility for this accident – I cannot do any more than say to you that you must view this on the basis of a legal fault on the part of the defendant and a lack of care on the part of the plaintiff for his own safety and try and say among yourselves what way in terms of percentages do we attribute the responsibility for this accident, the actual causation, was it due to the absence of the rail . . .' The learned trial judge then went on to deal at some length with the question of damages but at the end of that part of his directions he said at p. 342 of the transcript:– 'I have this to say to you and it is just as well to renew it now for I would have to bring you back to tell you – if you find the plaintiff guilty of contributory negligence, of course, you take off a proportion of the damages because of that but you don't take it off, you give him exactly the same as if you found him guilty of no negligence and I will then deal with negligence, so that, if you thought he was 50% to blame, you would not take 50% off the damages, you would give him the whole damages and I will take the 50% off, so don't take anything off if you think that the plaintiff was guilty of contributory negligence.'

When the jury had retired, Mr. Liston, on behalf of the defendant submitted to the learned trial judge that he had used the word 'responsibility' and that he had intended to convey to the jury that they should apportion according to causation. He submitted that the proper basis for apportionment, particularly having regard to the words used in the Act, is not degrees of negligence but degrees of fault. He said:– 'In this case it could be of great importance for the jury might well take the view that my client was at fault because he did not treat this as a working platform and say, at the same time, every other man building a flat roof did the same thing and the amount of fault was small and they might say that nobody cuts timber over the edge of a roof and on the basis of culpability, a man who did that was very much at fault, but on the question of causation you might say that each might equally well cause it, so I would ask you to suggest that it should be on the basis of culpability. That is the true meaning of the word "fault" where it is not degrees of negligence. There is little guidance in the Act beyond the fact it uses the word "fault".' To that the learned trial judge remarked that he assumed that in the Act it meant legal fault with which Mr. Liston agreed but he added that it must be fault in the sense that there was a breach of legal obligation but on the other hand it would be simple to put it as simply apportioning degrees of negligence.

Mr. McCarthy, for the plaintiff, did not agree with Mr. Liston's interpretation of the law and submitted that there was no difference between fault and responsibility. The learned trial judge pointed out that the provisions of s. 11, sub-s. 3, of the Act of 1961 appeared to indicate that fault and causal responsibility were not the same thing. The learned trial judge interpreted Mr. Liston's submissions in the following words at p. 345 of the transcript:– 'No, he wants us to approach this on the basis of both being at fault legally, both being in some way responsible for causation of injuries, one is the more blameworthy.' To that Mr. McCarthy said:– 'Which, I presume, is some sort of subjective test. Is Mr. Dwyer less to blame because he did not know he was responsible under the building regulations?' Judge:– 'The jury is going to say which.' Mr. McCarthy:– 'I trust not. I trust they are not going to be permitted to say that a man is less at fault because he did not know of the existence of the building regulations.' Judge:– 'I don't think it is necessary to recall the jury on this.'

It is quite clear that no question of the apportionment of fault arises at all unless both the plaintiff and the defendant have contributed causatively. If the defendant has not contributed causatively there can be no verdict against him, and if the defendant has contributed causatively but the plaintiff has not then there is no question of apportionment of fault. In the English Law Reform (Contributory Negligence) Act, 1945, 'fault' is defined in terms which are virtually identical with the definition of 'wrong' in our Civil Liability Act, 1961.

Under the provisions of s. 34 of the Act of 1961 the question of apportionment of fault only arises when the plaintiff has been found guilty of contributory negligence and not in the case of any other wrong on the part of the plaintiff, although the defendant's wrong may not necessarily be negligence at all. The provisions of the Act of 1961 indicate clearly that fault is not equated to causation but that it does flow from causation in the sense that if there is no causation there can be no fault.

Section 1 of the English Act of 1945 says:– 'Where any person suffers damages as the result partly of his own fault and partly the fault of any other person or persons, a claim in respect of that damage shall not be defeated by reason of the fault of the person suffering the damage, but the damages recoverable in respect thereof shall be reduced to such extent as the Court thinks just and equitable having regard to the claimant's share in the responsibility for the damage.' That Act appears to distinguish between fault and responsibility as our Act distinguishes between wrong and fault.

Under our statutory provision one party may be guilty of several wrongs and the other be guilty of one only, or vice versa, but it appears to me that fault, in the sense in which it is used in the Act of 1961, is not apportioned by comparing the sum of the wrongs on one side with the sum of the wrongs on the other side. A single wrong on one side may have done far more to bring about the damage than the sum of the wrongs on the other side. This seems to me to indicate that blameworthiness is involved in the sense of a party being more to blame or less to blame, as the case may be, in the normal sense – as if one were to say, in respect of somebody's action, that he ought to have known better or that he could hardly have been expected to know that. That this is so appears to be recognised by the provisions of s. 43 of the Act of 1961 which provide that where the defendant's wrong is the breach of strict statutory or common-law duty without fault there shall be no apportionment of fault as against him.

However, it appears to me that in the apportionment of fault this indicates that, where a defendant's causative contribution to damage has been his breach of such strict duty, there must also be negligence on his part before any apportionment of the fault can be attributed to him. In my view, this indicates that under our law an action for breach of strict duty is not an action for negligence although some breaches of statutory duty may give rise to an action for negligence: see the definition of 'negligence' in s. 2 of the Act of 1961. Breach of strict duty is in itself actionable and appears to me to be a cause of action in which foreseeability is not a necessary ingredient. On the other hand the torts of negligence and of public nuisance, as distinct from the tort of breach of strict duty, are based upon personal culpability arising from the failure to avoid the foreseeable. It appears to me that this conclusion necessarily follows from the statutory distinction which the Act of 1961 makes between the wrong of breach of strict duty and the wrongs importing fault. Of course, it is possible to show that in many (if not most) cases of breach of strict duty there has also been culpable wrong or fault on the part of the defendant, but that is a different situation.

The result, however, appears to be somewhat anomalous. Under the terms of the Act of 1961 a person who has caused damage by the commission of a wrong which amounts to a breach of strict duty is liable in damages to the person injured thereby, even though the wrongdoer was not guilty of any fault, provided that the person injured was not guilty of contributory negligence. The position appears to be that, once he has been found guilty of contributory negligence, the person injured will fail to recover anything if the defendant wrongdoer cannot be shown to have been at fault. For example, the occupier of a factory may be under a strict duty not to use a certain piece of equipment unless it is of adequate strength, which is a continuing obligation; if the equipment proves not to be of adequate strength because of a defect which was not patent and which could not have been discovered by reasonable care or inspection (as in *Doherty* v. *Bowaters Irish Wallboard Mills Ltd.* [1968] I.R. 277) and this causes injury, the defendant would be liable in full to the injured party if the latter is not shown to have been guilty of any contributory negligence. On the other hand, if the injured party is shown in such case to have been guilty of any degree of contributory negligence amounting to causation, no part of the fault would be attributed to the defendant unless it could be shown that he was at fault in addition to being guilty of breach of strict duty. In such a case, therefore, it would be necessary to prove that the defendant was guilty not merely of breach of strict duty but also of some other causative factor from which fault could be deduced. It is right, however, to add that in a case of breach of strict duty only, a plaintiff could scarcely be found guilty of contributory negligence unless he had knowledge of the breach of strict duty found against the defendant.

It appears to me then that Mr. Liston is correct in this general submission that a judge, in directing a jury, must direct their minds to the distinction between causation and fault and that they should be instructed that degrees of fault between the parties are not to be apportioned on the basis of the relative causative potency of their respective causative contributions to the damage, but rather on the basis of the moral blameworthiness of their respective causative contributions. However, there are limits to this since fault is not to be measured by purely subjective standards but by objective standards. The degree of incapacity or ignorance peculiar to a particular person is not to be the basis of measuring the blameworthiness of that person. Blameworthiness is to be measured against the degree of capacity or knowledge which such a person ought to have had if he were an ordinary reasonable person: see the judgment of this Court in *Kingston* v. *Kingston* (1968) 102 I.L.T.R. 65. To that extent the act can be divorced from the actor. In many cases greater knowledge may attract a greater share of the blame or fault, but so also may greater ignorance. Fault or blame is to be measured against the standard of conduct required of the ordinary reasonable man in the class or category to which the party whose fault is to be measured belongs; but both common sense and public policy require that ignorance of the law is not a factor to be taken into account in the diminution of fault.

In the present case the jury could not have been told that they might take into account in favour of the defendant the fact, if it were the fact, that he was unaware of the provisions of the building regulations or that he was no worse in ignoring them than was every other person engaged in the building of a flat roof. Persons engaged in the building trade are expected to know the safety regulations which govern their activities in the employment of others; ignorance of the regulations, or a failure to follow them because nobody else follows them, is not a factor which may be taken into consideration in diminution of the fault attributable to a person who is bound to observe the regulations. In the present case there was not merely a breach of the statutory duty to provide the necessary safeguards but there was ample evidence from which the jury could find that the defendant was at fault.

It is true that the learned judge, in addressing the jury, used the term 'legal fault' on a number of occasions without explaining the difference between it and causation, but on the other hand there is no point at which he did equate it to causation, at least to the jury, and in his closing remarks to the jury he used the term 'blame.' Having regard to the fact that the defendant's requisition to the judge was based solely upon the defendant's apparent ignorance of the building regulations and the fact that he was only doing what others did, I am of opinion that the learned trial judge's failure to explain more fully than he did the question of fault did not result in any injustice because these were factors which could not have been taken into account in the diminution of the defendant's fault.

So far as the amount of fault attributed to the plaintiff is concerned, the jury might very well in this case have divided the fault equally but, in my view, the evidence is not coercive to the point where a reasonable jury could not attribute more of the fault to the defendant than to the plaintiff. There was ample evidence upon which the jury could have held that the plaintiff was, or ought to have been, as fully alive to the necessity for safeguards as the defendant but, in apportioning blame between the parties, the jury would be quite entitled to take into account that the plaintiff, by reason of his preoccupation with the particular work he was doing, might well overlook the immediate danger when it arose and that the defendant ought to have foreseen such an event. Therefore, in apportioning blame between the parties, a jury might reasonably come to the conclusion that the defendant was really more to blame than the plaintiff; on such a view the apportionment of 60% of the fault to the defendant and 40% to the plaintiff would be quite sustainable. In my view, therefore, the apportionment is not one which no reasonable jury could arrive at and there are no grounds for disturbing it.

I have already dealt with one ground of the plaintiff's cross-appeal. The other more substantial ground of cross-appeal by the plaintiff was the ruling of the trial judge that on the evidence the jury could not find that the plaintiff was a servant rather than an independent contractor which was the reason why the judge refused to leave that question to the jury. I find it unnecessary to deal with this point because, in my view, it would not affect the outcome of this appeal. Upon the grounds I have already given, the plaintiff is entitled to hold the verdict on the liability and the apportionment of liability. Even if the jury had held that the plaintiff was a servant, he would have been a servant of such a skilled character as to put him, so far as the question of fault was concerned, in no different position from that of an independent contractor. I do not think that there was anything to suggest that the jury's attribution of 40% of the fault to the plaintiff would in any way have been diminished by their finding that he was a servant rather than an independent contractor. . . .

FitzGerald J.:

I agree, but I want to add that I was a member of the Court which decided that the roof was a working platform. I now have considerable doubt as to whether this was a good decision. . . .

Ó'Dálaigh C.J. concurred with **Walsh J.**

Notes and Questions

1. Does section 43 require the interpretation given to it by Walsh J.? In using the word 'may', does it foreclose the possibility of a court being entitled either to apportion the damages or to hold the defendant fully liable in a case involving liability without fault on the part of the defendant and contributory negligence on the part of the plaintiff? See generally *Williams*, para. 79.
2. Why, in a case of breach of strict duty only, should a plaintiff 'scarcely be found guilty of contributory negligence unless he had knowledge of the breach of strict duty found against the defendant'? What necessary relevance does such knowledge have to the question of the contributory negligence of the plaintiff?
3. As to the meaning of 'fault', see further *Carroll* v. *Clare County Council* [1975] I.R. 221 (Sup. Ct.) extracted *supra*, pp. 207–212.

Infringement of a statutory right

COSGRAVE V. IRELAND
[1982] I.L.R.M. 48 (High Court, McWilliam, J., 1981)

McWilliam J.:

In December of last year, in an action brought by the plaintiff in which he claimed that his constitutional rights and his rights under the Guardianship of Infants Act, 1964, had been infringed. I held that the plaintiff's rights as joint guardian of his children under the Act of 1964 had been infringed by the issue of passports for them to his wife after the Department of Foreign Affairs had been notified by him that he was objecting to the issue of the passports. I was of opinion that, after such notice as aforesaid, the passports should not have been issued without an application to the court.

The children have been in Holland with the plaintiff's wife since March, 1975 and are still there, and the plaintiff's wife has stated that she will not agree to the children coming to Ireland. She has obtained a divorce from the plaintiff in Holland. The parties were married in 1970. The plaintiff was a small farmer and his wife was a qualified nurse. They were not compatible and by the end of 1974, the marriage had hopelessly broken down. It is always difficult to apportion blame when a marriage breaks down but there is no doubt but that the plaintiff was, at least, eccentric, and after his wife's departure from the matrimonial home, he spent a short period in a psychiatric hospital. One of the psychiatrists at the hospital formed the opinion that he suffered from paranoia. After she left the matrimonial home the wife and her children were accommodated in a home for battered wives in Harcourt St., Dublin. It is not unreasonable to suppose that she went to such an institution as a last resort, whether her apprehensions were justified or not. It was while she was there that the passports for her children were issued to her.

Having given my decision that the plaintiff's rights had been infringed, the matter now comes before me to determine what relief, if any, the plaintiff is entitled to obtain. Orders are sought directing the defendant to make representations to the authorities in Holland regarding the custody of the children and access to them by the plaintiff but no argument ha[s] been addressed to me which persuades me that I have jurisdiction to make any such orders even if they had been sought in the Statement of Claim. The main arguments have centred round the plaintiff's claim for damages.

On behalf of the plaintiff I have been referred to an old case in the reign of Queen Anne, *Ashby* v. *White* (1703) 2 Ld. Raym. 938. The substantial effect of this decision was that, if there is a right, there is a remedy and, if there is no other remedy, the remedy will be in damages. It is significant that, in this case, there was no pecuniary loss of any sort, merely the deprivation of a right to vote for a member of parliament. I was also referred to the judgment of Walsh J., giving the judgment of the Supreme Court in the case of *Meskell* v. *Coras Iompair Eireann* [1973] IR 121, in which he said, at page 136, that, for the breach of a constitutional right, a person is entitled to such damages as may, upon inquiry, be proved to have been sustained by him; and, at page 138, he said that a person may sue for damages suffered by reason of the infringement of his constitutional rights. I was further referred, on behalf of the plaintiff, to the case of *Heywood* v. *Wellers* [1976] QB 446. This was a case in which solicitors had been grossly negligent in their conduct of, or failure to conduct at all, proceedings on behalf of their client to restrain an objectionable form of molestation. It was there held that it was foreseeable by the solicitors at the time of their retainer that failure to take the appropriate steps on behalf of their client would result in a continuance of the molestation or, at least, in a risk of its continuance. The solicitors having failed to take the appropriate steps, the client was further molested and it was held that she was entitled to recover damages for the distress resulting from the negligent failure of the solicitors to obtain the relief which they were employed to obtain.

I have also read the judgment of Birkett, J., in the case of *Constantine* v. *Imperial Hotels Ltd* [1944] KB 693. This was a case brought by a traveller against an innkeeper who had wrongfully refused to receive and lodge him. The issue related to the right to sue for a breach of a common law right without proof of special damage. It was held that there was such a right and that the plaintiff was entitled to succeed in the action. This issue does not arise in the present case but, in his judgment, Birkett, J having reviewed a great many decisions, including that in *Ashby* v. *White*, held that he was not entitled to award substantial or exemplary damages although he found that the plaintiff had suffered much unjustifiable humiliation and distress, and awarded only nominal damages.

The position as to damages for mental distress was considered by all the judges in *Heywood* v. *Wellers*. Lord Denning, MR said (at 459)

> It was suggested that even if the solicitors had done their duty and taken the man to court he might still have molested her. But I do not think they can excuse themselves on that ground. After all, it was not put to the test: and it was their fault that it was not put to the test. If they had taken him to court as she wished – and as they ought to have done – it might well have been effective to stop him from molesting her any more. We should assume it would have been effective to protect her unless they prove it would not.

James, LJ (at 461–2) referred to an earlier judgment of Lord Denning in *Cook* v. *Swinfen* [1967] 1 WLR 457. Lord Denning said in that case, at 461, 'So both in tort and in contract the measure of damages depends on what may reasonably be foreseen. In these circumstances I think that, just as in the law of tort, so also in the law of contract, damages can be recovered by nervous shock or anxiety state if it is a reasonably foreseeable consequence.' Bridge, LJ said (at 463–4)

> There is, I think a clear distinction to be drawn between mental distress which is an incidental consequence to the client of the misconduct of litigation by his solicitor, on the one hand, and mental distress on the other hand which is the direct and inevitable consequence of the solicitor's negligent failure to obtain the very relief which it was the sole purpose of the litigation to secure. The first does not sound in damages: the second does.

Although I was not referred in argument to the case of *Constantine* v. *Imperial Hotels Ltd*, it was submitted that I am not entitled to award any damages for mental distress. However I prefer to adopt the views expressed in the later cases, as I can see no reason why the principles there applied in cases of contract and tort should not also be applied in the case of the infringement of a statutory right. Accordingly, I am of opinion that the plaintiff is entitled to recover such damages as have been proved to have been sustained by him and also general damages for foreseeable mental distress, anxiety and inconvenience.

The plaintiff visited Holland in the autumn in each of the years 1976, 1977, 1978 and 1979. His evidence in that he spent sums, not very satisfactorily estimated, in travelling to Holland and staying there on these four occasions. He has also claimed sums in respect of defending divorce proceedings brought against him by his wife in Holland. I have also had evidence from a travel agent as to the costs of travelling to Holland and from an actuary as to the capital value now of the sums required to meet such costs until the children reach ages varying from 16 to 18 years. This amounts to a substantial sum and is claimed on behalf of the plaintiff.

Although the Department adopted an incorrect procedure and thereby infringed the rights of the plaintiff, I think I am bound to consider, in relation to any special damage, what was the difference between the damage actually sustained and the probable damage had the correct procedure been adopted. It appears to me, from the evidence I have heard, that the result would probably have been the same had an application been made to the court except that the court might have tried to impose some condition on the wife that the issue of the passports would be made subject to suitable arrangements for access by the plaintiff to his children. How such a condition could have been implemented I do not know but, had it been made, it is possible that some condition would also have been made requiring the plaintiff to contribute to the support of his children. He has not contributed anything towards the support of his wife or children since they left Ireland. The behaviour of the plaintiff while the parties were in Ireland was such that his access to the children would probably have been very greatly restricted had his wife and children remained in Ireland. It is quite inconceivable that he would have been given custody of the children when the parties separated.

The plaintiff's visits to Holland were unsatisfactory from the point of view both of the plaintiff and of his wife. I am not satisfied that meetings would have been any more satisfactory had they taken place in Ireland except that the children would have been able to speak in English to the plaintiff. One unsatisfactory aspect of the visits was that the plaintiff made no prior arrangements with his wife regarding them and did not adopt any normal procedures for arranging the visits. In addition he refused to furnish the addresses at which he stayed in Holland and made no attempt to co-operate with his wife or her family while he was there.

Having regard to all the circumstances of the case, I cannot accept the figures put forward on the plaintiff's behalf as justified. I am satisfied that he did sustain some expense as a result of the issue of the passports in the way in which they were issued but, in my opinion, this was very small and I will award a sum of £250 on this account. I am also satisfied that the claim for substantial general damages is not justified either, but the plaintiff must have suffered considerable distress when his request, in effect, that the proper procedures should be observed was ignored. Accordingly, he is entitled to more than mere nominal damages and I will award a sum of £1,000 on this account, making a total of £1,250.

Notes and Questions

1. How significant is the decision? Does it open up an entirely new area of liability in tort? See generally Cooney & Kerr, 'Constitutional Aspects of Irish Tort Law' [1981] D.U.L.J.I.
2. What limits, if any, are there to the concept of 'infringement' of a statutory right? Must the infringement be (*a*) malicious; (*b*) intentional; (*c*) reckless; (*d*) negligent; (*e*) 'wrongful'? Must it result directly or foreseeably from the defendant's conduct? Can there be infringement through omission? (If there can, ponder for a moment on the repercussions in such areas as health, employment, educational and housing policy, for example.) Should the Court, before granting a remedy in damages for infringement of a statutory right, ask itself questions similar to those it asks in relation to actions for breach of statutory *duty*? For example, is the intention of the legislature to grant a remedy a relevant factor? Can there be a 'public' statutory right in the sense that infringement by an individual should not imply a duty to compensate?
3. What defences, if any, are available in an action for infringement of a statutory right?
4. In actions for common law negligence, courts are increasingly willing to articulate policy considerations. Should they do the same in relation to the action for infringement of a statutory right?

Chapter 12

PRODUCTS LIABILITY

Liability in negligence for dangerous or defective products is in the course of radical transformation. In the nineteenth century, the courts imposed liability only in cases where injury was caused by the negligent control, management or supply of a dangerous product. They evinced little desire to hold manufacturers of products responsible for injuries suffered by consumers: to do so would, according to the thinking of former times, contradict the basic privity rule of contract law, whereby a person who is not a party to a contract may not derive rights of action under it. In recent years the position has been transformed. The changes in marketing of products, the increase in consumerism and the internationalisation of commerce have all led to a changed approach. The concept of negligence has been applied and expanded. The trend is to go further, in line with the thinking in many other European and North American jurisdictions, and impose strict liability for defective products.

A manufacturer is bound to take reasonable care to protect consumers of his products from injury.

KIRBY V. BURKE AND HOLLOWAY
[1944] I.R. 207 (High Ct., Gavan Duffy, J.)

Gavan Duffy J.:

This appeal from the Circuit Court turns on a point of law of exceptional public inportance, unquestionably fit for the decision of the final tribunal, but neither party has asked me to state a case for the Supreme Court and there is no other right of appeal.

In the Circuit Court the plaintiffs, a father and three little children, recovered damages in tort against the defendant for his negligence in manufacturing and issuing for sale a pot of jam unfit for human food, bought by the housewife for the family, and eaten by the plaintiffs to the sad mischief of their internal economy.

On 6th May, 1942, Mrs. Josephine Kirby, finding butter to be unobtainable, bought for her family from a grocer a pot of rhubarb and ginger jam; the pot was wrapped in cellophane of amber hue, and the jam had a cardboard cover and under the cover, immediately over the jam, a piece of waxed paper. This was the sort of jam known to the trade as 'slip' jam, from a slip of paper affixed to the pot, designating the fruit; the main attraction of slip jam seems to have been that it passed with an innocent public as homemade; and it bore no tell-tale label with the maker's names.

Mrs. Kirby brought the pot home, opened it forthwith and spread the jam on slices of bread for her husband's lunch; shortly afterwards she gave a similar luncheon to three of her young children, who had the like meal again for their supper. Mr. Gerald Kirby, the husband, suffered that afternoon and subsequently from an attack of gastroenteritis, and that night the children had very severe attacks of the same malady with its unpleasant symptoms, which persisted; the eldest boy, Gabriel, aged 9 years, recovered very slowly. Mrs. Kirby herself had a toothache and took no jam, and she gave none to her baby daughter; neither she nor the baby fell ill.

I am satisfied that the members of the family who suffered did so as the direct result of eating that jam, and that 'war bread,' though laxative, would not have induced the same symptoms. I am satisfied that the jam was unwholesome, when seen by Dr. Masterson next day. I am satisfied that the evidence points strongly to the conclusion that the jam was in the same condition when Mrs. Kirby brought it from the grocer. But she had no reason whatever to treat the product as suspect.

I find that the pot of jam came from the defendant, Holloway, through two intermediate grocers, one of whom had kept it for six months; and, though neither of these reluctant gentlemen was an impressive witness, I do not on the evidence see any reason to believe that there had been any tampering with the jam pot after it left the defendant's factory.

Professor Bayley Butler, with whose views generally Dr. John Magrath, the pathologist, agreed, gave learned evidence for the plaintiffs. He knew Mrs. Kirby's story and he examined the jam; while he could not, as a scientist, be certain of the genesis of the contamination whereof he saw symptoms in the jam, he reached the conclusion that some species of fly, carrying bacteria, must have made its way into the jam pot at the factory, probably while the jam was cooling or before its cardboard cap was affixed; that seemed to me a probable theory, unless it should be rebutted or countered by evidence for the defendant. The plaintiffs could not be expected in the circumstances to do more than put forward a probable case through witnesses of authority, and it was not to be expected that any expert witness would find himself in a position to trace the infection to its origin beyond doubt. (*Cp.* the judgment of Lord Greene M.R. in *Dawson* v. *Murex Ltd.* [1942] 1 All E. R. 483, at p. 487.) In my opinion, the initial burden of proof was discharged by the plaintiffs, and it remained for the defendant, with his own special knowledge of the conditions under which his jam was made, to displace that *prima facie* case, and to call any expert evidence which might undo it.

The two distinguished men of science called for the defendant gave their opinions in detail on the probabilities against the plaintiffs, but they were not able to exclude the possibility that the theory for the plaintiffs corresponded with the actual facts; the suggestion that the jam may have become infected after Mrs. Kirby opened the pot is practically excluded by the size of the larvae found in the jam by the plaintiffs' doctor on the 7th of May. On the scientific aspect of the case, I think that the honours are clearly with the plaintiffs' witnesses; no adequate counter-theory was opposed to them.

It still remained to be seen whether the defendant could prove that his jam-making process was unexceptionable and thus put the plaintiffs' theory out of Court; and, as in *Daniels* v. *White & Sons, Ltd.* [1938] 4 All E. R. 258 a fool-proof process, established by the defendant lemonade-makers, carried the day, the defendant here could reasonably expect to win this action on establishing a fly-proof procedure after his jam is made; but the actual evidence fell decidedly short of proving any effort to attain so high a standard.

Two, and only two, witnesses were called from the factory, the sole owner, Mr. James J. Holloway, and a Miss Brady. The evidence was that Mr. Holloway himself supervised the whole process of jam-making, while Miss Brady was in immediate control of the more important operations; these consisted, where rhubarb was concerned, of slicing, sieving and steaming first, and then of boiling and cooling, and of affixing the waxed paper to the jam; there followed the stacking of the pots; the subsequent packing was under its own charge-hand. There is no State control of jam-making as such, but a factory inspector calls once or twice a year. Mr. Holloway has had thirty years' experience as a jam-maker in Dublin; I do not known if he has other qualifications. Miss Brady seems to be a very busy lady and she holds a highly responsible post; but she is called a charge-hand; she has had fourteen years' experience and her pay, apart from overtime, amounts to £2 17s. 6d. a week.

Mr. Holloway says that three boiling pans are kept going together in one room, a room with good light from a glass roof and an electric fan to clear away steam. In October, 1941, when the jam in question was made, Mr. Holloway was, he states, making 7,000 lbs. of jam *per diem* and the factory was working overtime. After the jam is boiled, it is emptied with buckets into a copper cooling pan and then, almost immediately, while still quite hot, filled into jam pots. The boiling and cooling is done in one room, and next to that room is the stacking room, where the pots are stacked in layers, with ply-wood between them, for two or three days, (three or four days, he said later), with the wax paper on top; there is no special supervisor here. Then the jam pots go to the packing room, where the cardboard top is affixed and the cellophane placed round the pots. The packing girl has to see that the caps are properly adjusted and that the pots going out are clean. The rooms and utensils are washed and kept clean. Mr. Holloway says that he had some thirty-five employees at the material time.

I have omitted from this summary acount of the process the evidence as to the covering of the jam with waxed paper, because that evidence calls for separate examination. Here Mr. Holloway and Miss Brady differed in material particulars. Mr. Holloway, the general supervisor, says that, when the jam pots have been filled, they are then run to the stacking room and the wax caps are put on immediately and the pots are then stacked. He states that two girls are employed on the wax paper and one on stacking. There are in the stacking room two windows, kept open in summer and closed in winter; they would be closed in October.

Miss Brady says that experienced hands are necessary and that all her girls have been employed for many years; she has thirteen girls under her. Two girls are employed all day on the capping and stacking; here possibly she was speaking of some different period from her employer. 'The wax capping,' she goes on, 'is generally done as soon as the jam is filled; *it's part of my work.*' Then, in cross-examination, she says that she was told of Mrs. Kirby's complaint, the first of its kind; she does not think she would be responsible, if there were such a complaint; Mr. Holloway always supervises after her, to see that everything is right; he himself boils when she is on holiday. 'The pots are nearly always capped when filled out; sometimes they are not, a matter of a few minutes; sometimes they would be moved into the stacking room; it's nearly always done in the room where the cooling is done; the cooling is a matter of a minute or two; very rarely the exposed trays are taken into the stacking room; the girl nearly always does it at the cooling table; the jam is capped immediately; a tray might be missed and taken into the stacking room uncapped, but it does not often happen, a few times during the day; it very seldom happens.' And then:– '*I've no need to go into the capping room.*' It was, of course, not suggested that the proprietor himself checks the wax capping of every tray-load of pots done in the stacking room; the universal supervisor would not, if he could.

Thus there is no supervision at all, on any occasion when the wax cap is put on in the stacking room. A tired girl in a rush period may put on the cap badly; then a fly will have plenty of time to get in, after the jam has cooled. I do not know what precautions the packing girl takes afterwards, if any, on finding a wax cap loose. Though complaints be very rare, this was no fly-proof process, and I find that reasonable diligence was not used to ensure the continued purity of the jam, a most important matter, after the boiling was complete. Too much was taken on trust. Mr. Holloway received the impugned jam pot from one of the intermediary grocers on 8th May, 1942, and was told by telephone of the complaint; he admits that the jam had not the normal glitter and appeared to have fermented; Mrs. Kirby and her doctor said that they saw maggots in it, but he could discern none. He says he just put the jam on a shelf; he did not show the pot to Miss Brady; he did not probe it; he did not cause any portion of the jam to be analysed. A day or two later Mrs. Kirby called to recover her pot; he offered her another, which she refused; she says that he then kept her waiting for some time and that, when eventually he returned her pot, some of the jam seemed to have been replaced with fresh jam and that she told him so, but he said the jam was exactly the same. He denies this account of her protest and his reply, and says that he gave her back the pot as he received it and without any delay. Professor Bayley Butler, to whom the jam was then submitted for analysis, found the top layer brighter in colour than the rest, which had numerous bubbles, suggesting fermentation; the top layer was free from bubbles. I accept Mrs. Kirby's evidence on this matter. I pass over other discrepancies between her evidence and Mr. Holloway's. His failure to have a serious analysis made was a bad error of judgment.

I have now to consider whether the law sustains the claim of the plaintiffs to make the manufacturer liable for the unpleasant consequences to them of eating his jam. The defendant manufactures a common article of food, jam, made from fruit of the particular season; he then distributes it for sale by retail grocers to members of the public; he intends it to be sold as food for human consumption and bought as food for human consumption. Before sending it out he pots the jam and places waxed paper over it, closes the pot with a cover and packs it in a coloured cellophane wrapper, with the result that the jam, when sold over the counter, will be taken to be (as it is meant to be) in the condition in which it left the factory, and that the purchaser will have no reasonable opportunity to examine the contents for any visible defects; and a manufacturer must know, as a matter of ordinary experience, that a housewife, the probable purchaser, does not usually, on opening the pot at home, begin by scrutinising the contents for signs of corruption; why should she?

A particular pot of jam turns out to be unwholesome, when bought, and injurious to the consumers, and the question at once arises on what principle is the alleged liability of the maker, who intended no injury and made no contract with the consumers, to be determined? The inquiry involves the ascertainment of the foundation, upon the authorities, of liability for tort at common law.

In 1869, an Irish Court, following English decisions, held on demurrer that, in the absence of fraudulent misrepresentation, the law could give no redress against the manufacturers to a man (the purchaser's servant) injured by the explosion of a boiler in a steam engine, upon an allegation that the boiler was unsafe by reason of negligence in its construction: *Corry* v. *Lucas* I. R. 3 C. L. 208. The confusion and conflict in later cases in England left the basis of liability in tort at common law so uncertain that at the time of the Treaty nobody could find in case law any sure guide to the actual legal position, and I have no Irish decision to guide me.

I am thus thrown back upon first principles in the endeavour to ascertain where the line is drawn at common law between conduct resulting in unintended hurt which entails liability for damage, and conduct resulting in unintended hurt which entails no liability.

In the quandary produced by the baffling inconsistencies among the pre-Treaty judicial pronouncements, I turn from the Courts to one of the outstanding juristic studies of the nineteenth century, 'The Common Law' by Oliver Wendell Holmes, afterwards Mr. Justice Holmes of the Supreme Court of the United States. The work was published in London in 1887. The law which I apply to this case is taken from his penetrating Lectures III and IV on torts and the theory of torts.

That master of the common law shows that the foundation of liability at common law for tort is blameworthiness as determined by the existing average standards of the community; a man fails at his peril to conform to those standards. Therefore, while loss from accident generally lies where it falls, a defendant cannot plead accident if, treated as a man of ordinary intelligence and foresight, he ought to have foreseen the danger which caused injury to his plaintiff.

Applying that norm to the facts, I have to inquire whether a man in the position of the defendant, making jam for the public to eat, is bound, according to the standards of conduct prevailing among us, to take specific precautions against the danger, to the hurt of consumers, of infection to his jam from external causes before it finally leaves his factory; or, more exactly, though he may not have anticipated the precise injury that ensued to the plaintiffs from infection, was he bound, in conformity with those standards, to safeguard his jam from access by flies, as notoriously ubiquitous as they are notoriously dirty, during the interval between the moment when jam is poured into a jam pot after boiling and the moment, three or four days later, when the jam pot is finally enveloped for sale and sent out? I answer this question, as I believe a jury of practical citizens would answer it, in the affirmative, because our public opinion undoubtedly requires of a jam manufacturer that he shall take care to keep flies out of his jam. Any novice would foresee that a fly might get in, given the chance, and I have already found as facts that the defendant failed to take adequate precautions and that the buyer was in no way at fault.

On the facts of the case now before me, there is no question of remoteness of damage. The test, as Holmes J. puts it, is whether the result actually contemplated was near enough to the remoter result complained of to throw the peril of that result upon the actor. The plaintiffs are therefore entitled to succeed.

The much controverted 'Case of the Snail in the Bottle,' while leaving subsidiary questions open, has settled the principle of liability on a similar issue finally against the manufacturer in Great Britain. But the House of Lords established that memorable conclusion only twelve years ago in *Donoghue* v. *Stevenson* [1932] A.C. 562, by a majority of three Law Lords to two, 'a Celtic majority,' as an unconvinced critic ruefully observed, against an English minority. Where lawyers so learned disagreed, an Irish Judge could not assume, as I was invited to assume, as a matter of course, that the view which prevailed must of necessity be the true view of the common law in Ireland. One voice in the House of Lords would have turned the scale; and it is not arguable that blameworthiness according to the actual standards of our people depends upon the casting vote in a tribunal exercising no jurisdiction over them. Hence my recourse to the late Mr. Justice Holmes. His classic analysis supports the principle of Lord Atkin and the majority. And to that principle I humbly subscribe.

As to damages, this appeal is a re-hearing; so that I must exercise my own judgment on the *quantum* to award. I shall affirm the decree of the Circuit Court with variations award to Mr. Gerald Kirby, the father of the family, the sum of £27 7s. 0d., to include the fees of £7 7s. 0d. payable to the doctor; Mr Kirby was the breadwinner for the family. I award to Gabriel Kirby, an infant, the sum of £20; I award to Winifred Kirby, an infant, the sum of £12; I award to Noel Kirby, an infant, the sum of £12. I shall follow the order of the learned Circuit Court Judge in every respect as to the payment into Court and investment of the moneys payable to the three infants.
. . .

Notes and Questions

1. Do you think that Gavan Duffy, J. was wise to have recourse to Holmes rather than the 'Celtic majority'? Why?
2. Does *Kirby* v. *Burke and Holloway* distinguish clearly between the 'duty' question and that

of the standard of care in negligence? In being guided by Holmes, does it apply a standard of reasonable care, without the limitations of *Donoghue* v. *Stevenson*? Or does Gavan Duffy, in 'humbly subscrib[ing]' to 'the principle of Lord Atkin', limit the scope of the holding? Lord Atkin articulated *two* principles. The first was the broad 'neighbour' principle, set out *supra* p. 160. The second, more restrictive, principle related to the duty of manufacturers. Lord Atkin stated (at 599) that:

'A manufacturer of products, which he sells in such a form as to show that he intends them to reach the ultimate consumer in the form in which they left him with no reasonable possibility of intermediate examination, and with the knowledge that the absence of reasonable care in the putting up of the products will result in an injury to the consumer's life or property, owes a duty to the consumer to take that reasonable care.'

3. If a *guest* at the Kirby's had been injured by the jam, do you think that Gavan Duffy, J. would have imposed liability? How about a case where a burglar at the Kirby residence took a spoonful and became ill?

4. In *Power* v. *Bedford Motor Co.* [1959] I.R. 391 (Sup. Ct.), Lavery J. referred to Lord Atkin's 'neighbour' principle and said:

'Lord Atkin's opinion commanded the support of the majority of the House – three against two – a division of opinion which demonstrates that the law was then difficult and unsettled. However, it must now be taken as settled.

It is clear in principle that the obligation is not confined to manufacturers of goods but extends to persons undertaking repairs to articles which will be dangerous to users who should be in contemplation if there is a want of reasonable care in the work. It must also apply to persons doing work on an article which they foresee would be used by others without examination.

This view has been taken in many cases in Great Britain, e.g., *Haseldine* v. *C.A. Daw & Son, Ltd.* [1941] 2 K.B. 343 (defective lift), *Andrews* v. *Hopkinson* [1957] 1 K.B. 229 (motor car), *Herschtal* v. *Stewart and Arden, Ltd.* [1940] 1 K.B. 155 (reconditioned motor car), *Stennett* v. *Hancock* [1939] 2 All E.R. 579 (motor lorry defectively repaired).

This Court was not referred to any such case in this country, but if my memory serves me the liability of a repairer to persons injured, for defective work, the other conditions being satisfied, has been maintained in actions in the High Court.'

Lavery J. expressed the opinion that this was the law in Ireland.

O'SULLIVAN V. NOONAN AND TRANSIT LTD.
Unreported, Supreme Court, 28 July 1972 (89/103/109 – 1970)

The plaintiff was injured when a defective tyre burst in the car in which she was a passenger. The car had been bought secondhand from a dealer by the driver who, having previously driven a lorry and having owned five different cars at different times, was a person with 'a little more knowledge of cars than perhaps the average purchaser or driver.' (Page 20 of Walsh J.'s judgment.) The evidence indicated that the tyre was defective at the time the car was sold by the dealer, but that the owner had not discovered the defect before the accident. The plaintiff sued the driver and the dealer. The jury found that the tyre had burst before the collision, that the driver had been negligent and that the dealer had supplied a car to the driver with a dangerous and defective tyre of which condition he knew or ought to have known, but added to their latter finding the words 'not knowingly'. They apportioned the degrees of fault between the defendants by attributing 30% of the fault to the driver and 70% to the dealer. Both defendants appealed to the Supreme Court on the question of damages.

Walsh J.:

. . . [T]he important question of law in the case [concerns] the liability of Transit Limited, as the vendors of this car, for the injury occasioned to persons resulting from the bursting of the tyre due to a defect in the tyre existing at the date of the sale. There was ample evidence to go before the jury, mainly produced by Transit Limited, to the effect that there had been a pre-sale examination of the tyres of the car and that in fact two new remoulds had been fitted to the car. That coupled with the evidence of [the previous owner] and Mr. Noonan leaves uncontradicted the fact that the tyres had been handled and examined to some degree at least by Transit Limited before they sold the motor car.

According to [an expert]'s evidence the defect in the tyre was one which was visible on examination even of the outer surface of the tyre as from the time it was caused. If it was in existence at the time the car was sold, which the jury found it was, then it should have been discovered on a reasonable examination by the staff or the employees of Transit Limited who were concerned with the handling and the fitting of these tyres and whatever examination of them was made which resulted in some of the tyres being changed. On the evidence the jury was entitled to hold, as it did, that at the time of the sale the motor car in question was in a dangerous condition because of the defective tyre. While the plaintiff in this case had no contractual relationship with Transit Limited, nevertheless under the doctrine of *Donoghue* v. *Stevenson* [1932] A.C. 562 Transit Limited could be liable in negligence to the plaintiff. There can be little doubt on the evidence that when the car was sold it was intended to be used by Mr. Noonan in the condition in which it was delivered to him and it could not be contested that it was foreseeable that any person using the highway or any passenger in the car could be injured if the car was in fact in a defective condition at the time it was supplied. A motor car is not in itself a dangerous thing but if it suffers from such a defect as renders it a dangerous thing then it is a dangerous chattel. If the motor car is sold with the actual knowledge of its dangerous condition then there is a peculiar duty on the vendor to take precaution against danger to the party to whom the car is supplied. The most obvious one is to give the person actual notice of the defect so that he is fully aware of the dangerous nature of the object which he is purchasing. As a motor car is an object which may become a dangerous one by reason of the existence of a defect the person who sells in conditions or circumstances which indicate that he intends it to be used in the form in which it leaves him is under a duty to take reasonable care to see that it is safe or alternatively to warn the purchaser that he, the vendor, has made no reasonable examination of the vehicle before selling it so as to put the purchaser on notice that the motor is not being sold and delivered to him in a form which the vendor intends it to be used without prior examination. A dealer in motor cars, whether they be new motor cars or second-hand cars, who sells a vehicle to the ordinary purchaser must be presumed to intend the car to be used in the condition in which he has sold it unless he has given express notice to the contrary. If the car in fact contains a defect which would have been discoverable on a reasonable examination by the vendor then he would be liable for the damage which may be caused to persons injured by that defect if they be passengers in the motor car or other users of the highway or other parties who would foreseeably come into proximity with the motor vehicle. The fact that the purchaser may have an opportunity for examination would be no defence to the vendor unless the vendor could show that he should reasonably have expected that the purchaser would have used the opportunity for inspection in such a way as to give him warning of the danger. Again, in such a situation it is a question of what could have been contemplated by the vendor as being a reasonable examination on the part of the purchaser because if the purchaser is the ordinary motorist he could not in the ordinary way be reasonably contemplated to have carried out the type of examination which would be open to a dealer in motor cars even if it were in the contemplation of the vendor that the purchaser would make an examination. The jury was quite entitled to accept the evidence of [the expert] that the defect in this tyre was apparent and would have been discoverable on any reasonable examination of the tyre. The fact that there had been some form of examination of the tyre is beyond doubt and the only conclusion is, which the jury was quite entitled to arrive at, that the examination was negligently carried out in either being of a very cursory character or being perhaps carried out by either being confined to one side of the tyre or perhaps an examination of the tread of the tyres only. It is true that before Mr. Noonan bought the motor car he heard the engine running, had a look at the tread in the tyres and generally speaking had a brief superficial examination of the motor car. He did not look on the inner surface of the tyre in question or indeed of any other tyre. Mr. Noonan in his evidence said that when he bought the car he was not informed that there were two remoulds fitted to the car but that he was informed that the two front tyres had been replaced. He said that they conveyed to him that the two which had been on the car previously had been replaced by the two which he saw on the car when he bought it. He said he looked at the tyres and he described them as 'good looking tyres' but he was not sure whether they were new or used. He said these tyres had been cleaned up and polished. It was put to him that when he purchased the car he was furnished with an invoice or docket which referred to the car, quoted the price and registration number and had written on the bottom of if the phrase 'bought as is.' Mr. Noonan stated he did not get any such document and perhaps that is not surprising even if such document were furnished because the actual purchaser of the car in law was a hire purchase company through which Mr. Noonan did state, however, and it was accepted that when he purchased the car he was told by Transit that the car was being guaranteed for six months but he understood that to be a reference to the mechanical condition of the car and he did not allege that it included a guarantee or warranty as to the tyres. The original of the alleged invoice containing the words 'bought as is' was not produced but the General Manager of Transit Limited produced a carbon copy and he said the ordinary practice was to deliver the original to the purchaser either immediately or subsequently by post but that in this case that would probably have been delivered, if it was delivered, to the hire purchase company. He stated that in the trade the words 'bought as is' meant that you bought the car as inspected or, as he agreed when put to him by his counsel, quoting Oliver Cromwell, 'warts and all.' It was suggested on cross-examination that if the words 'bought as is' had the meaning he put on them it would appear to be in conflict with the guarantee as to the mechanical condition of the car which was given at the same time, if the mechanical condition was not what it was warranted to be. The witness's own view was that a customer who was not in the trade himself should get somebody to inspect a car before he purchased it and that in fact that occurs sometimes. He seemed to be surprised to think that any person would buy a car without a trial, although the evidence in the present case was that Mr. Noonan had bought it without a trial.

In my view, the words 'bought as is', even if they had been brought to the attention of Mr. Noonan before he purchased the car, would be quite inadequate as notice to a purchaser of a motor car from a dealer if it was intended to convey to the purchaser that the vendors had carried out no reasonable examination of the car before the sale to ascertain whether or not it was safe to be used in the condition in which it was being sold. A motor car may very well be in a condition in which as to appearance, mechanical performance and various other matters which a person would like to see improved before he bought it but which would not affect the safety of the car. 'Bought as is' may cover that aspect of the transaction, namely that the vendor will not carry out any improvements on the car but that is a very far cry from indicating to the purchaser that it is up to him to discover whether or not car is in a dangerous condition. Even if the jury had come to the conclusion that Mr. Noonan had bought the car with notice of this phrase 'bought as is' they would still have been justified in finding against Transit Limited. However, on the evidence they would also have been justified in finding that the qualification, such as it was, was not brought to his notice at all.

In my view, there was ample evidence on which the jury could hold, as they did hold, that the motor car was in a dangerous condition in so far as the tyre was concerned at the time it was sold and that the defect was one which could have been discovered upon a reasonable examination and that Transit Limited were negligent in allowing the car out in the condition either because the examination they made was less than reasonable or that they had made no examination for defects at all and that the accident was the result of this negligence. In my view, the finding of the jury on this matter cannot be disturbed.

In so far as the apportionment of fault was concerned I think the jury was amply justified on the evidence in attributing 70% of the fault to Transit Limited.

The appeal on behalf of the defendant, Noonan, is against the jury's finding of negligence against him and against the attribution of 30% of the fault to him. The negligence which was suggested against Noonan was that he ought to have discovered the defect in the tyre himself sometime before the accident occurred. [Counsel] has argued very cogently on behalf of Mr. Noonan to the effect that Mr. Noonan was informed at the time he bought the car that the two front tyres had been replaced and that that amounted to a representation to him that they would require little, if any, attention for some time to come and that in view of the fact that he had the car for a comparitively short time and had only used it for 600 miles it would be unreasonable to expect him to have discovered the defect particularly as the defect in the tyre was on the surface furthest from the outside of the car. The learned trial judge in the course of his directions to the jury expressed the view that he thought the evidence against Mr. Noonan was not very strong but that there was some evidence on which the jury could hold that Mr. Noonan could have discovered the defect if he had taken reasonable care. The jury may well have regarded Mr. Noonan as being a little out of the ordinary run of motor car drivers and owners. He had previously driven a lorry for about twelve years and had owned about five different motor cars during the course of his driving career. He generally bought second-hand cars but he sometimes bought a new car. He said he always checked the pressure of the tyres himself and would know when a tyre should be replaced. As part of his business he ran a petrol pump though did not provide any other garage service to customers. Generally speaking it might be said that he had a little more knowledge of cars than perhaps the average purchaser or driver and the jury could reasonably come to the conclusion that in his case, even in the relatively short period he had this car, he might have taken the precaution of having a look over the car and the tyres in particular while he had it and that in not doing so he was guilty of some degree of negligence. I personally think that their attribution of 30% of the fault to him was in the circumstances somewhat higher than I would have been prepared to attribute but I cannot say that the difference is so great that I must necessarily regard the jury's apportionment as being so excessive as to warrant being set aside. I would not, therefore, disturb the verdict against the defendant, Noonan. . . .

Ó Dálaigh C.J., **Budd** and **McLoughlin JJ.** concurred.

Fitzgerald J. (dissenting):

. . . Having regard to the fact that Noonan had possession of the car for two months and drove it some 600 miles before the accident, coupled with the fact that he is the owner of what could be described as a 'petrol station', where he had a petrol pump for the sale of petrol and a power-driven air line for the inflation of tyres, the jury would have been entitled to hold either that he had caused the initial damage to the tyre by negligent driving or alternatively that having bought the car with a defective tyre and having regard to the evidence of . . . the expert called on behalf of the plaintiff, that the defect would have become progressively worse and hence, presumably, more apparent, he should, having regard to his mechanical knowledge and experience, have observed the defect while he had the car. In view of the jury's answer to the third question it is obvious that they decided against him on the ground that he was negligent in failing to observe an existing defect.

In my opinion, this finding was open to the jury and should not be upset.

In my opinion, the jury's answer to the third question was, if not ambiguous, certainly unsatisfactory and insufficient to justify a judgment against Transit. It appears to me that while the supplying of a car, which to their knowledge had a defective tyre, would justify a verdict against them in the plaintiff's favour, the supplying of a car with a defective tyre without their knowing of the defect would not leave them liable to the plaintiff. Since the decision in *Donoghue* v. *Stevenson* in 1932 when it was decided that a manufacturer of defective goods owed a duty to the ultimate consumer, and the extension of that doctrine to make the repairer of an article, liable to a person ultimately damaged it appears to me that that falls far short of imposing liability on the seller of a second-hand article which is without an express warranty. In my view, to impose such a liability on a motor dealer would involve not only an implied warranty to the purchaser in respect of unknown defects but a corresponding liability in tort to the world at large. This involves an extension of the *Donoghue* v. *Stevenson* doctrine to which I decline to subscribe. In any event there was ample opportunity for intermediate examination by Noonan and the jury have in fact found him negligent in failing to discover the defect. In these circumstances I consider that Transit were entitled on the jury's answer to question 3 to have the action against them dismissed. . . .

Notes and Questions

1. Section 13 of the *Sale of Goods and Supply of Services Act 1980* provides as follows:
   '(1) In this section "motor vehicle" means a vehicle intended or adapted for propulsion by mechanical means, including –
       (a)   a bicycle or tricycle with an attachment for propelling it by mechanical power, and
       (b)   a vehicle the means of propulsion of which is electrical or partly electrical and partly mechanical.
   (2) Without prejudice to any other condition or warranty, in every contract for the sale of a motor vehicle (except a contract in which the buyer is a person whose business it is to deal in motor vehicles) there is an implied condition that at the time of delivery of the vehicle under the contract it is free from any defect which would render it a danger to the public, including persons travelling in the vehicle.
   (3) Subsection (2) of this section shall not apply where –
       (a)   it is agreed between the seller and the buyer that the vehicle is not intended for use in the condition in which it is to be delivered to the buyer under the contract, and
       (b)   a document consisting of a statement to that effect is signed by or on behalf of the seller and the buyer and given to the buyer prior to or at the time of such delivery, and
       (c)   it is shown that the agreement referred to in paragraph (a) is fair and reasonable.
   (4) Save in a case in which the implied condition as to freedom from defects referred to in subsection (2) is either not incorporated in the contract or has been effectively excluded from the contract pursuant to that subsection, in the case of every sale of a motor vehicle by a

person whose business it is to deal in motor vehicles a certificate in writing in such form as the Minister may by regulations prescribe shall be given to the buyer by or on behalf of the seller to the effect that the vehicle is, at the time of delivery, free from any defect which would render it a danger to the public, including persons travelling in the vehicle.

(5) Where an action is brought for breach of the implied condition referred to in subsection (2) by reason of a specific defect in a motor vehicle and a certificate complying with the requirements of this section is not proved to have been given, it shall be presumed unless the contrary is proved that the proven defect existed at the time of delivery.

(6) Regulations under subsection (4) may apply to motor vehicles generally or to motor vehicles of a particular class or description (defined in such manner and by reference to such things as the Minister thinks proper) and different forms of certificate may be prescribed for different classes or descriptions of vehicles.

(7) A person using a motor vehicle with the consent of the buyer of the vehicle who suffers loss as the result of a breach of the condition implied by subsection (2) in the contract of sale may maintain an action for damages against the seller in respect of the breach as if he were the buyer.

(8) The Statute of Limitations, 1957, is hereby amended –
   (I) by the insertion in section 11 (2) of the following paragraph –
      '(d) An action for damages under section 13 (7) of the Sale of Goods and Supply of Services Act, 1980, shall not be brought after the expiration of two years from the date on which the cause of action accrued';
  (II) by the insertion in section 49 of the following subsection –
      '(5) In the case of an action claiming damages under section 13 (7) of the Sale of Goods and Supply of Services Act, 1980, subsection (1) of this section shall have effect as if for the words "six years" there were substituted the words "two years".'

(9) Notwithstanding section 55 (1) of the Act of 1893 (inserted by section 22 of this Act) any term of a contract exempting from all or any of the provisions of this section shall be void.'

Do you consider it advisable to base liability, as the section does, on a contractual rather than a tortious basis? Can you see any difficulties or advantages resulting for an injured person? Of course, the principle established in *O'Sullivan* v. *Noonan* has been merely supplemented, and not overruled, by the enactment of section 13. Do you regard the principle as capable of easy extension to other products? A complicated do-it-yourself tool, for example?

2. What do you think of Fitzgerald, J's dissenting judgment? Section 34(2)(*f*) of the *Civil Liability Act 1961* provides that:
    'where an action is brought for negligence in respect of a thing that has caused damage, the fact that there was a reasonable possibility or probability of examination after the thing had left the hands of the defendant shall not, by itself, exclude the defendant's duty, but may be taken as evidence that he was not in the circumstances negligent in parting with the thing in its dangerous state.'

Does this provision have any relevance to the case, in your view? Note that in *Colgan* v. *Connolly Construction Company (Ireland) Ltd.*, *supra*, pp. 277–280, McMahon, J. interpreted the provision as having 'shifted the onus of proof to the defendants in product liability cases.' Does it go that far?

Colgan's case holds that contract rather than tort is the proper avenue for recovery where an article is simply defective rather than dangerous. But the House of Lords has recently taken a radically different view: see *Junior Books Ltd.* v. *Veitchi Co. Ltd.*, [1982] 2 All E.R. 201 (H.L. (Sc.)).

FLEMING V. HENRY DENNY & SONS

Unreported, Supreme Court, 29 July 1955 (8–1954)

The plaintiff, while eating a slice of black pudding which had been manufactured by the defendant company, purchased from a retailer by her husband, and cooked by herself, bit upon a small irregular lump of steel and injured her jaw. She sued the company, and at the trial the jury found that the piece of metal was in the black pudding when delivered by the company to the retailer; that the plaintiff was injured by eating the black pudding; that the company did not have a reasonably safe system for the production of the black pudding; but, that if the system was reasonably safe, the company was negligent in the operation of the system. The company appealed to the Supreme Court against the finding of the jury that the system was not reasonably safe, on the ground that this finding was without evidence, contrary to the evidence, and perverse.

Kingsmill Moore J. (for the Court):

The plaintiff's case was rested on the well known words of Lord Atkin in *Donoghue* v. *Stevenson* [1932] A.C. 562, at 599. 'A manufacturer of products, which he sells in such a form as to show that he intends them to reach the ultimate consumer in the form in which they left him, with no reasonable possibility of intermediate examination, and with the knowledge that the absence of reasonable care in the preparation or putting up of the products will result in an injury to the consumer's life or property, owes a duty to the consumer to take that reasonable care.'

It is not disputed that the black pudding, which was enclosed in a casing at the time of manufacture, was intended to reach the consumer in that form and that there was no reasonable possibility of intermediate examination, but it is alleged that, on the evidence adduced, no jury could properly find that the company was lacking in reasonable care.

The plaintiff did not attempt to give evidence of any specific negligent acts or omissions, but rested her case on the principle of *res ipsa loquitur*, alleging that pieces of steel were not normal or desirable components of black puddings, and that the presence of such a piece of steel was in itself eloquent of some negligence on the part of the company. Lord Macmillan in *Donoghue* v. *Stevenson* at 662 said 'there is no presumption of negligence in such a case as the present, nor is there any justification for applying the maxim "*res ipsa loquitur*" . . .' but this remark appears to be *obiter* for the point had not been raised in argument. Moreover it appears inconsistent with the views of the Court of Appeal in *Chaproniere* v. *Mason* 21 T.L.R. 633 (where a stone was found in a Bath Bun and the court accepted the view that the maxim applied) and also with the decision of the Privy Council in *Grant* v. *Australian Knitting Mills Limited* [1936] A.C. 95, where the case for the Plaintiff rested on the maxim, and Lord Wright in giving judgment said 'The appellant is not required to lay his finger on the exact person in all the chain who was responsible, or to specify what he did wrong. Negligence is found as a matter of inference from the existence of the defects, taken in conjunction with all the known circumstances.' It appears to me that the maxim is applicable. But its application only shifts the onus of proof. The Defendant can give evidence to negative negligence on his part by demonstrating that his system of production is one which is reasonably safe (or, as I would prefer to phrase it, that he has taken all reasonable care to provide a safe system) and that there has been no negligence on the part of his servants in the operation of the system provided.' Such a defence was successful in *Daniels* v. *R. White & Sons* [1938] 4 All E.R. 258 where a bottle of lemonade contained 38 grains of carbolic acid but the manufacturer convinced the trial judge that he had a 'fool proof' system of cleaning, washing, and filling bottles. Evidence of a fool proof system will not in itself usually be sufficient . . . In *Grant's* case there was evidence that the system was the most up to date possible and that over four million garments had been sold without complaint, yet the Privy Council supported a verdict for the Plaintiff on the ground that 'the coincidences of time and place and the absence of any other explanation told in favour of the Plaintiff.' Lord Duneden in *Ballard* v. *North British Ry.* 1913 S.C. 43 and Langton, J. in *The Kite* 1933 P. 154 held that the defendants in such cases should give a reasonable explanation which is equally consistent with the accident happening without their negligence as with their negligence. In the present case however the jury seem to have negatived negligence in the operation of the system. It is true that the jury had already answered 'No' to the question 'Had the Defendants a system which was reasonably safe for the production of black pudding[?]' and so it was unnecessary for them to answer the succeeding question 'If the Defendants had a system which was reasonably safe were they negligent in the operation of that system at the time the black pudding was made[?]' – which they also answered 'No'. But it seems that they meant to find that there was no negligence in the actual operations of the system, be it safe or unsafe. At an earlier stage in their deliberation they had submitted to the judge the question. 'Can the jury answer Question No. 2 (the question as to system) in the affirmative, and Question No. 3 (the question as to the operation of the system) in the negative, and still award the Plaintiff damages?' The learned judge had directed them that if they answered Question 2 'Yes' they must answer Question 3 'Yes' in order to find for the Plaintiff. When subsequently the jury answered Question 3 'No' I think they must have intended to negative any negligence on the part of those operating the system.

Could a jury, having regard to the evidence given for the Defendant company, properly find that the company had been negligent in failing to provide a reasonably safe system? The obligation to take care in the preparation of articles intended to be eaten is high and it is incumbent on those who put up the food to take great care that it is not injurious in any way – whether through the presence of deleterious substances or foreign bodies – to the prospective consumer. The company gave very detailed evidence by the mouths of responsible witnesses, the veracity of whose testimony was not challenged as to the way in which the puddings were made and the precautions taken. Five substances go to the manufacture of black puddings – blood, meat cured in brine, oatmeal, rusk, and spices. The blood and meat are provided by the company and the evidence established that the blood was carefully strained, the meat scraps collected with due care, pickled, cooked, and conveyed to a mincer in proper utensils, which were properly cleaned. In the mincer they were forced through holes of a quarter inch diameter, this being the smallest diameter which would provide puddings of the consistency which was demanded by the local connoisseurs of black pudding. It was admitted that the piece of steel which did the damage could have passed through a hole of this diameter, but it was alleged that in so doing it would almost certainly make a noise which would attract the attention of the operator and cause the machine to be spotted and examined. The rusk meal, the oatmeal, and the spices were brought from firms of high repute, long established, and with whom the company have been dealing for many years. Rusk meal and oatmeal come in the manufacturers' bags and are used direct from those bags. The spices come in boxes, and the requisite amounts of each spice for the puddings is measured out by a girl operator from the various boxes. When the meat has been minced all the ingredients are agitated and mixed together in a special machine mixer, and are then filled by another machine into casings which are tied, cooked, packeted and sent to the retailers.

Evidence was given that all the apparatus used had been inspected within a fortnight of the accident, and that there was no sign of any chipping or damage. . . . Evidence was also given of the precautions taken to prevent anything falling from the clothes or persons of the operators into the mixture, and of the periodical cleaning and inspection of all utensils. If the evidence of the witnesses for the company was accepted as being informed and veracious – and it does seem to have been challenged – I am of opinion that a jury could not properly find a lack of reasonable care in the system of preparing, utilising and incorporating in the finished puddings those ingredients which were prepared, from their origin, by the company. But it is urged by the Plaintiff that no proper care was taken to make reasonably sure that the materials purchased from other manufacturers, namely, the spices, rusk meal, and oatmeal, were free from foreign bodies. It is suggested that a simple operation, such as sieving, would have removed the piece of steel and that the failure to sieve showed a lack of reasonable care.

It was admitted that these materials, coming from outside manufacturers, were only inspected with a view to seeing that they had not got musty or in any way out of condition, and it was admitted that the piece of steel might have been contained in those materials [but it is argued on behalf of the defendant that since the materials came] from a reputable firm, it was not bound to duplicate the precautions which they knew were to be used for human consumption. Indeed the Defendant company can go further and suggest that the true explanation of the presence of the steel lay in the default of one of the manufacturers of the outside materials, a default which in all the circumstances it was not bound to anticipate or guard against.

It is, I think, impossible to lay down a universal rule. The nature of the material purchased, the reputation of the dealer from whom it is purchased, the obligations imposed by law on a vendor, the processes through which the materials have already passed in the hands of the manufacturer dealer, the past experience of the purchaser and the general experience of mankind, all these have their bearing upon the remoteness or otherwise of this contingency. The manufacturer is not bound to take precautions against any contingency however remote, and the nature of the precautions which he is often obliged to take must bear a relation to the probability or improbability of the risk. A manufacturer of cakes may well be bound to take great care that stones are not incorporated in the currants which he uses, for the occasional presence of such items is notorious, but it does not follow that if he purchases flour from millers of unblemished reputation he is bound to test it for the presence of ergot, and still less would he be bound to examine the sugar which he purchases from reliable sources to see that it is not contaminated with strychnine or other poisonous crystals.

In the present case the outside materials – rusk, oatmeal, and spices – were all bought from firms of high repute with whom the Defendant company had been dealing for many years. All the materials had been subjected to some form of grinding or disintegration which would be calculated to discover such things as pieces of steel. There was a clear duty as the suppliers – a duty in contract and I think also in tort – to supply articles free from contamination or foreign bodies, and to take all necessary precautions for that purpose. Was it part of the duty of the Defendant Company to duplicate tests and examinations which they might reasonably assume already to have been made in order to guard against a contingency which they had no reason to suppose was in any way likely to occur. Its duty was to take reasonable care not to incorporate dangerous matter in its sausages. Was that duty exercised by purchasing high grade materials from highly reputable firms and using them in the form in which they were bought without any examination other than one designed to discover such deterioration as might normally be expected to occur?

Some assistance may be got from the decisions in *Phillips* v. *Britannia Hygienic Company* [1973] 1 K.B. 539 and *Stennett* v. *Hancock* [1939] 2 All E.R. 578. It is the duty of the owner of a vehicle to take reasonable care that it is fit for the road. In each of those cases the owner of the vehicle had put it into the hands of a competent repairer who in fact had been negligent in doing the repairs with the result that when the vehicle was taken on the road a wheel came off with resultant injury to the Plaintiff. The owner of the vehicle was held not to be liable: 'if the duty is, as I hold it is, to take reasonable care to have his vehicle fit, then that duty is discharged by the owner of the vehicle who puts it in the hands of a competent repairer with instructions to do what is necesary to put it in a fit state to use the road.' Bailhache, J. at p. 556 of *Phillips'* case. 'It seems to me that it would be quite wrong to limit the protection given by *Phillips* v. *Britannia Hygienic Laundry Company* to a man who has entrusted his repairs to a competent repairer by superimposing upon it the duty of himself seeing that the repairs have been properly executed. There might be cases in which it would be plain to anybody's knowledge that the vehicle was in an unfit state and I am not saying, of course, that there might not be cases in which the defect was so obvious that an uninstructed owner would observe it. What I do say, however, is that it seems to me, in view of the decision in *Phillips'* case that it would be wrong for me to impose upon a person who has submitted his car to be repaired by a competent repairer a duty to look himself and see whether those repairs have been properly carried out,': [*Stennett* v. *Handcock*, at p. 581 (*per* Branson J.)] Those cases are authority that a duty to take reasonable care may be satisfied by employing a person who is competent and whose duty it is to take similar care in respect of a similar responsibility. It seems to me that a manufacturer whose duty is to take reasonable care not to send out food containing any harmful substance may, insofar as the ingredients of that food are concerned, discharge his duty by obtaining the ingredients from firms of high repute who have a like responsibility to see that the ingredients are free from any harmful substance. It may not be so in every case: the defect may be so obvious that it is a failure of reasonable care not to observe it. There may be special facts which require special precautions. But, viewing the whole facts and circumstances of this case, I have come to the conclusion that failure to detect this small fragment of steel does not warrant a finding of lack of reasonable care and that a jury could not reasonably hold that this presumption of failure to use reasonable care created by this doctrine of *res ipsa loquitur* had not been rebutted by the evidence given, and not substantially challenged, as to the nature of the system employed and the manner in which it was operated.

Notes and Questions

1. Do you agree with the approach favoured by the Court? Why?
2. *Cf. Taylor* v. *Rover Co. Ltd.,* [1966] 1 W.L.R. 1491; *Sullivan* v. *Manhattan Market Co.*, 146 N.E. 673 (Mass. 1925).

Chapter 13

EMPLOYERS' LIABILITY

The law was slow to impose liability in negligence on employers in relation to injuries sustained by their employees. The *laissez-faire* philosophy regarded industrial enterprise as socially beneficial in the long run; the employee should look after his own interests, and if he chose to accept dangerous employment for an appropriate payment he should not look to his employer for compensation when things went wrong.

This philosophy has all but become redundant today (although echoes could be perceived as recently as twenty years ago: *cf. Depuis* v. *Hawlbowline Industries Ltd.*, unreported, Supreme Court, 14 February 1962 (1–1961)). The cases that follow indicate that courts are now generally concerned to ensure that the workplace is subject to close scrutiny so as to ensure that employers take reasonable care for the safety of their employees.

Nevertheless, the courts have consistently stressed that an employer is not an insurer of the safety of his employee: he will not be liable if he has taken reasonable care for the safety of the employee.

BRADLEY V. CORAS IOMPAIR ÉIREANN
[1976] I.R. 217 (Sup. Ct.)

The plaintiff was a railway signalman employed by the defendant company. Part of his duties was the servicing of the lamps of certain signals at the top of vertical signal posts. He reached each lamp by climbing the half-inch round steel rungs of an almost vertical steel ladder attached to each signal post. When the plaintiff was descending one of these ladders while carrying a lamp, his right foot slipped on a rung and he fell to the ground and was injured. In the plaintiff's action for negligence against the defendant, a witness for the plaintiff stated that the plaintiff's fall would have been prevented if an elliptical steel cage had been attached to the ladder so that a climber could ascend and descend the ladder within the cage. There was no evidence that such cages were a feature of similar ladders used in other railway systems. The defendant's evidence established that its 1,000 signal post ladders of the type in question were of a normal design and that, within the period of ten years before the accident there had been no accident arising from the use of these ladders within the defendant's railway system. The jury found that the defendant had been negligent in failing to provide a safe place of work for the plaintiff. The defendants appealed to the Supreme Court.

Henchy J.:

. . . In th[e] circumstances, was it open to the jury on the evidence to hold that the defendants were negligent in not having the suggested cage fitted to this ladder? Although an argument was addressed to the trial judge in support of the submission that the case should be withdrawn from the jury because the evidence could not support a finding against the defendants on the issue of negligence, unfortunately no authorities were cited to the judge as to what the applicable law is in such circumstances.

Where a workman founds a claim for damages for negligence against his employer on an allegation that something was left undone that should have been done in the interests of his safety, the most commonly cited statement of the necessary degree of proof is that formulated by Lord Dunedin at p. 809 of the report of *Morton* v. *William Dixon Ltd* 1909 S.C. 807:–

> '. . . I think it is absolutely necessary that the proof of that fault of omission should be one of two kinds, either – to shew that the thing which he did not do was a thing which was commonly done by other persons in like circumstances, or – to show that it was a thing which was so obviously wanted that it would be folly in anyone to neglect to provide it.'

This rule has been applied in numerous cases including the decision of the Supreme Court in *Christie* v. *Odeon (Ir.) Ltd* (1956) 91 I.L.T.R. 25 usually with the gloss given to it by Lord Normand in *Paris* v. *Stepney Borough Council* [1951] A.C. 367, 382:–

> 'The rule is stated with all the Lord President's trenchant lucidity. It contains an emphatic warning against a facile finding that a precaution is necessary when there is no proof that it is one taken by other persons in like circumstances. But it does not detract from the test of the conduct and judgment of the reasonable and prudent man. If there is proof that a precaution is usually observed by other persons, a reasonable and prudent man will follow the usual practice in the like circumstances. Failing such proof the test is whether the precaution is one which the reasonable and prudent man would think so obvious that it was folly to omit it.'

The Lord Dunedin formulation, as thus glossed, continues to be the generally accepted statement of the standard and mode of proof in such cases, with the qualification that when it refers to 'folly' it means no more than 'important' or 'unreasonable': see *per* Lord Tucker in *Cavanagh* v. *Ulster Weaving Co. Ltd.* [1960] A.C. 145, 162. In fact, it does no more than provide a mode of testing whether in the class of cases to which it refers the employer has taken reasonable care for the safety of his employee or, as it is sometimes put, whether he has subjected him to unnecessary risk.

In the present case, the first part of the test laid down by Lord Dunedin in *Morton's Case* 1909 S.C. 807 was answered by uncontroverted evidence that the safety cage suggested by the plaintiff's engineer was unknown in railway practice. The defendants' engineer (who was the only expert in railway engineering called in evidence) said that although he was familiar with the systems of railway signals in Ireland, the United Kingdom and some continental countries, he had never seen a signal-post ladder with such a cage. His evidence to the effect that such a cage was unheard-of passed without cross-examination or any other attempt to controvert it. That being so, it would have been impossible for counsel for the plaintiff to argue that the provision of a safety cage was 'a thing which was commonly done by other persons in like circumstances.'

To succeed, therefore, the plaintiff had to satisfy the second or alternative part of the test: although the defendants were following general practice in not having fitted the ladder with a safety cage, was such a cage so obviously wanted for the protection of the plaintiff from injury by falling that the defendants could be said to have been imprudent or unreasonable in not providing it? In applying this test it is important to bear in mind what was pointed out by Lord Reid in *General Cleaning Contractors* v. *Christmas* [1953] A.C. 180, 192:–

> 'A plaintiff who seeks to have condemned as unsafe a system of work which has been generally used for a long time in an important trade undertakes a heavy onus:

if he is right it means that all, or practically all, the numerous employers in the trade have been habitually neglecting their duty to their men.'

As far as the evidence in this case goes, it shows that no railway company in Ireland, the United Kingdom or Holland (and possibly other European countries) fits a safety cage to this kind of ladder. Was it open on the evidence for the jury to say, as in effect they did say, that they are all wanting in reasonable care for the safety of their workmen? The answer lies in whether, notwithstanding the general practice, the provision of a safety cage was an obvious safety precaution which could reasonably have been provided.

First, as to whether the defendants ought to have noticed that a safety cage was obviously wanted. There was no suggestion in the evidence that the experience from a century and a half of railway operations had thrown up any need for a safety cage on these ladders. A specific search of the records of the defendants for the ten years prior to this accident showed that, despite the fact that over 1,000 of these uncaged ladders were being operated in the defendants' railway system, not one accident related to their use was reported. Looking outside railways, the plaintiff's engineer could produce from his experience only two instances of a ladder with a safety cage, one being in the Ford factory in Cork city and the other in an Aer Rianta installation in West Cork. But cross-examination elicited that in each of those two cases the ladder in question was used as a stairway for regular access to a higher level of building. So, in fact, no instance was given of a safety cage on an external vertical or near-vertical fixed ladder of this kind, although such ladders are to be seen on quaysides, ships, silos, gasometers, building sites and other buildings and installations. It is impossible, therefore, to say that it was, or should have been, obvious to the defendants that a safety cage was wanted on this ladder. The combination of long-established operation, the widespread use elsewhere of similar ladders, and the unbroken experience of absence of a likelihood that these ladders would cause accidents must be held to rule out the conclusion that a safety cage was obviously wanted. Of course, a ladder such as this carries a risk of injury to a person working on it, particularly if he is carrying an object such as a lamp in one hand, but no more than does any other fixed ladder of this kind on which a person is required to work. In all such cases it might be said, at the most, that a safety cage would be desirable, but certainly as far as this case is concerned, it could not be said that it was obviously wanted.

However, even if the evidence enabled the jury to say that a safety cage was obviously wanted, it would not necessarily follow that the plaintiff had established negligence by proving that the defendants had not fitted one. It would be further necessary in such a case as this for the plaintiff to show that the obviously wanted precaution is one that a reasonably careful employer would have taken. The law does not require an employer to ensure in all circumstances the safety of his workmen. He will have discharged his duty of care if he does what a reasonable and prudent employer would have done in the circumstances. Thus, even where a certain precaution is obviously wanted in the interests of the safety of the workman, there may be countervailing factors which would justify the employer in not taking that precaution. As Lord Reid said in *Morris* v. *West Hartlepool Steam Navigation Co. Ltd.* [1956] A.C. 552, 574.

> '. . . It is the duty of an employer, in considering whether some precaution should be taken against a foreseeable risk, to weigh, on the one hand, the magnitude of the risk, the likelihood of an accident happening and the possible seriousness of the consequences if an accident does happen, and, on the other hand, the difficulty and expense and any other disadvantage of taking the precaution.'

The defendants were entitled to measure against the desirability of installing a safety cage on this ladder the fact that they would also have to install a safety cage on each of the thousand or more similar ladders scattered throughout their railroad system, thus incurring heavy installation and maintenance expenses, notwithstanding that such installations are not deemed necessary in neighbouring countries and notwithstanding the absence over a period of at least ten years of a single accident to suggest the necessity of taking such a precaution. Of even greater weight is the fact that, if they installed a safety cage on this particular ladder, they would reduce the clearance between the steel fixture thus created and each of the two adjoining railway lines from $4'6\frac{1}{2}''$ to $3'9\frac{1}{2}''$ – thus breaching the rule of a minimum clearance of $4'6''$ which the defendants observe. That rule apparently derives from Board of Trade regulations which are not binding in this State. Therefore, it would have been open to the plaintiff to show that the margin of clearance observed by the defendants is unnecessarily wide and that they could reduce it to $3' 9\frac{1}{2}''$ without undue risk. However, no evidence on the matter was given on behalf of the plaintiff. The only witness who dealt with it was the defendants' expert, and he left the witness box without a single question having been put to him in cross-examination to suggest that the observance of a $4'6''$ clearance was unnecessary. Therefore, at the end of the case there was no evidence to support a finding that a $4'6\frac{1}{2}''$ clearance could responsibly be reduced to $3'9\frac{1}{2}''$ clearance. It may be that a minimum clearance of $4'6''$ is pitched unnecessarily high, but it would be unjustifiable to say so without evidence to that effect. It is implicit in the jury's verdict that they reached that conclusion. In doing so without evidence, they took a leap in the dark. For all they knew, a reduction of the clearance to $3'9\frac{1}{2}''$ might have produced a hazard or injury to others that would outweigh the risk of injury to the plaintiff through not fitting the ladder with a safety cage.

For the foregoing reasons, I am of opinion that there was not evidence to support the jury's verdict, and that the application to have the case withdrawn from the jury should have been allowed. I would therefore allow the appeal and in lieu of the order of the High Court, enter judgment for the defendants. I would allow the appeal without costs because counsel for the defendants, when applying to have the case withdrawn from the jury, did not direct the trial judge's attention to any of the authorities relied on in this Court or to any authority.'

Griffin and **Kenny JJ.** concurred.

Notes and Questions

1. Does this case, in its result, hold that safety considerations come second to those of cost? If not, what does it hold regarding the relationship between safety and cost? Is the court the appropriate forum to determine this question?
2. Are there any echoes of Lord Dunedin's 'folly' test still remaining in Irish law? Rather than glossing the Dunedin formulation, would it not be better to exorcise it from our law?
3. Does the passage quoted from Lord Reid's judgment in *Morris* v. *West Hartlepool Steam Navigation Co.* support the proposition for which it is invoked in Henchy J.'s judgment? See also Denning L.J.'s remarks in *General Cleaning Contractors* v. *Christmas* [1952] 1 K.B. 141, at 149.
4. What do you think of the 'clearance' argument?

Scope of the Duty Owed by an Employer to an Employee
Whilst the scope of the duty of care is a matter for individual determination in each case, the courts have tended to analyse the duty under four general headings:
   (a) the provision of *competent staff*;
   (b) the provision of a *safe place of work*;

(c)   the provision of *proper equipment*; and

(d)   the provision of a *safe system of work*.

(Sometimes a fifth, miscellaneous, heading is added.)

Clearly these headings can be difficult to separate in some cases but in practice this does not appear to cause difficulties.

Let us first consider a decision that proceeds on a somewhat general basis and then examine each of these four headings more specifically.

O'DONNELL V. HANNIGAN

Unreported, Supreme Court 19 July 1960 (63–1959)

Ó Dálaigh C.J. (delivering judgment of the Court):

This is an appeal by way of notice of motion for a new trial from the judgment entered for the defendant following the withdrawal of the case from the jury.

The action was one of negligence. The plaintiff was a farm labourer in the employment of the defendant who is a farmer residing some twenty-one miles from the City of Limerick.

In the month of March, 1956, the defendant directed the plaintiff to take a yearling bull to Limerick to be sold at an auction mart there. The defendant told him that he was going to a neighbouring farmer named Power who had also a bull for sale to find out if he, Power, would take the two bulls together. Later the defendant informed him that another farmer named Sheehy, who had a 'pick-up' truck, would take both bulls to Limerick. On the following morning the 'pick-up' truck arrived. It was a Ford 10 cwt. truck. Both Power and Sheehy came with it. Power's bull was in the truck when it arrived. The defendant was not present when the truck arrived. With the help of the others the plaintiff loaded the bull on to the truck and all three took their places on the truck. Power and Sheehy were seated in the cab while the plaintiff sat in the body of the truck with the two bulls. They set out for Limerick. On the journey the truck overturned. The plaintiff was thrown out and injured. He claims damages from the defendant alleging that he was negligent in employing a motor truck which was unsafe and unsuitable for the purpose for which it was used.

At the close of the case for the plaintiff Haugh J. was asked to withdraw the case from the jury on the ground that there was no evidence of negligence on the part of the defendant. It was conceded that there was evidence from which the jury might find that the motor truck was unsuitable for the purpose of transporting a bull. Mr. McMahon submitted however that as there was no evidence that the defendant saw the truck or had anything to do with it, that he had made an arrangement with Power and had no knowledge of what sort of truck it was and that even if the defendant had seen the bulls loaded the plaintiff would have to show that the defendant could judge that the vehicle was unsafe. Mr. McKenna in reply to this submission agreed that, if the defendant had employed well-known hauliers of established reputation such as C.I.E., it would be difficult to convict him of negligence, but that in the circumstances of this case the jury would be allowed to decide whether in the arrangement which he made he had so 'conducted his operations as not to expose his servant to unnecessary risk.' This is the test suggested by Lord Herschell in *Smith* v. *Baker* [1891] A.C. 325, 362. The learned Judge withdrawing the case from the jury said to the jury: 'This is a case where the plaintiff was injured in another man's lorry. That is the type of case which you ordinarily have. That is Mr. Sheehy in this case. He has not been sued. . . . Mr. McMahon asks to have the plaintiff non-suited on the basis that there was no duty on the employer to do more than he did.'

Lord Wright in *Wilsons & Clyde Coal Co.* v. *English* [1938] A.C. 37, 84 succinctly stated the duty of an employer towards his servant to be that he is 'to take reasonable care for the servant's safety in all the circumstances of the case.'

Charlesworth on Negligence, 3rd ed. p. 395 points out that it is usual to consider this duty under certain heads which he sets out as follows:–(1) to provide a safe place of work; (2) to employ competent servants; (3) to provide and maintain adequate appliances; (4) to provide a safe system of work; (5) other cases. While it may be difficult for the plaintiff to fit his claim in this case exactly within any of the first four heads mentioned above, I am of opinion in the circumstances disclosed by the evidence as it stood that a jury might justifiably hold that the defendant had not fulfilled his duty towards the plaintiff.

In my opinion therefore the learned Judge was wrong in withdrawing the case from the jury. This appeal should accordingly be allowed, the judgment set aside, and a new trial ordered.

Question

Do you consider that this decision should be categorised under head (5) ('other cases') or under some combination of the first four heads?

(a) *The Provision of Competent Staff*

HOUGH V. IRISH BASE METALS LTD.
Supreme Court, 8 December 1967 (40–1967)

Ó Dálaigh C.J. (**Walsh** and **Haugh JJ.** concurring):

The appellant is a foreman mechanic. His place of work was the defendant mining company's repair shop and store. This consisted of a large shed. The shed was originally heated by means of a convector gas fire. A fortnight before the date of the appellant's injury this heater was removed by the mine foreman to his offices and an open gas ring was substituted. This ring was about 2 feet in circumference and the gas was fed in from a drum or cylinder through a long flexible hose. The ring had 40 to 50 jets, and until one of the workers made a cover for it from a 10 gallon metal barrel which he perforated, usually burned with a naked flame.

This ring was moveable; and from time to time it was moved about the repair shed. This was done sometimes to clear the floor for a vehicle which was being driven in or out or, again, when a worker decided to pull the ring closer to the particular position in the shed where he was working.

On the 19th February, 1965 the appellant was engaged in cleaning the engine of a Land Rover jeep which had toppled over into a muddy ditch. He was furnished with a basin of paraffin and a cloth and he was lying on his stomach on the flat mudguard of the vehicle with the bonnet of the engine raised up. His legs were projecting out over the edge of the mudguard. Suddenly he felt his left leg on fire. He jumped up, his head struck the bonnet, the paraffin spilled and in an instant his entire clothing was ablaze.

What happened was this, in the language of an eye witness named Horrigan who was standing near the entrance to the repair shop: 'I seen a chap called Reilly – which was done to myself several times – give the gas ring a kick under Paddy (i.e. the appellant) and tipped out the side door laughing.' Horrigan added later: 'He didn't mean to harm the man . . . I often done the thing myself for a bit of fun. It was the general procedure there . . . A bit of devilment . . . As a lark . . . We often shoved it over near each other to give him (i.e. the fellow worker) that extra bit of heat.' And to the judge's question 'Do you mean more heat than he wanted?' the witness replied 'Yes'. Before Reilly kicked the ring over towards the appellant it was about 3 yards distant.

The appellant's evidence amplified Horrigan's evidence about 'larking' in the repair shop. He said: 'There was a lot of tricking with it . . . Fellows would be stooping down working . . . it was a trick to shove it under him.' The judge asked: 'To shove it under him without him noticing it?' to which the appellant answered: 'Yes. Well there is usually a lot of tricking that way on construction jobs. There is not much you can do about it.'

Reilly is identified as an employee of the respondent mining company, but there is no evidence as to his particular employment.

The appellant sued the respondents for failure to provide a safe system of work; and the case made at the trial, which took place before McLoughlin J. and jury, was that the system of work was unsafe because the employers had failed to exercise supervision over the repair shop. It was not said that there was evidence that the employers had actual knowledge of this dangerous larking, but it was submitted that the employers ought to have known of it and prevented it and could have known of it by [a] proper system of supervision.

Mr. Justice McLoughlin ruled that there was no evidence of a consistent practice which was known, or should be known, or could be known, to the employer and withdrew the case from the jury. He pointed out that Reilly's act was an act which was done for his own purposes and not for his employers' and therefore was not an act for which his employers could be vicariously liable.

Appellant's counsel accepted that there was no evidence that the employers had actual knowledge of the 'larking' complained of, but his submission here has been that the larking was so general that it ought to have been known to the employers if they had a proper system of supervision. And it is said that an employer who ought to know should be in no better position than an employer who does know.

Counsel for the respondents submitted that actual knowledge is necessary; then he added a number of alternative submissions. He said there was evidence that the plaintiff was a person in authority, in charge not only of the fitters but also of general maintenance; in effect that the plaintiff was himself the supervisor and that as he was in default in not reporting the larking he cannot be heard to complain of his injuries. Further it was submitted that the plaintiff had given no evidence of absence of supervision; further still that the conduct complained of occurred momentarily and was of a kind that would most probably be concealed in the presence of a supervisor.

The supervision which is in question here is supervision which is referable to the ordinary work of the repair shop. The evidence affords no assistance as to what amount of supervision would be required in a repair shop and store of this type; and moreover the evidence was not directed to what, if any, supervision took place. If by supervision of a kind and frequency normally required in a repair shop such as this the existence of dangerous larking would probably have been discovered then there is much to be said for the view that an employer who neglected such supervision should be in no better position than an employer who fulfilled his obligation to supervise and had become aware of it. But we have no material which would require a close examination of the validity of this proposition. The evidence is silent both as to the degree of supervision that would ordinarily be required in a repair shop-cum-store and as to the supervision that in fact took place. It is therefore not possible to accept the submission that there was evidence from which the jury could infer that the employers ought to have known of this dangerous larking. It may be added that the ultimate sanction against dangerous larking is dismissal. Before dismissal it would be reasonable to admonish.

It is to be noted that there is no evidence that either the plaintiff or any of his fellow-workers made any complaint to anyone in authority in respect of this larking. It seems rather to have been looked upon by all as a 'bit of fun' or 'devilment'. The whole thing would be over in an instant. The subject of the fun would immediately become aware that the fire had been pushed close to him and he would presumably either move away or push the fire away. The nature of the larking was therefore such as to make it not easily detectable; and in any event it could not reasonably be said that an employer who did not detect it had failed in his duty to provide a safe system of supervision as the larking in question was of such recent origin and was not of such frequency as must necessarily have been detected in any system of reasonable supervision.

In all the circumstances I am satisfied that Mr. Justice McLoughlin was right in withdrawing the case from the jury, and this appeal should therefore be dismissed.

Note and Questions

1. In what circumstances would vicarious liability be more likely to succeed than *personal* liability on the part of the employer?
2. See also *Walker* v. *McCormack*, unreported, Supreme Court, 4 March 1968 (130–1965).

(b) *The Provision of a Safe Place of Work*

As *O'Donnell* v. *Hannigan, supra*, indicates, it is well settled that an employer must ensure that a reasonably safe place of work is provided and maintained for the benefit of the employee. Some courts have expressed this duty in terms of occupiers' liability, generally according the employee the status of invitee (*cf. McMahon & Binchy*, p. 314); but the general tendency has been to regard the duty owed to the employee as being that of reasonable foresight unencumbered by the distinctive rules attaching to the different categories of entrant.

KIELTHY V. ASCON LTD.
[1970] I.R. 122 (Supreme Court)

The plaintiff's husband, an employee of the defendants, was killed when he fell from an unfinished wall on his way to the defendants' office. The jury awarded damages, answering in the affirmative the second question submitted to them, as to whether the fall had been "caused or contributed to by the failure of the defendants to provide and maintain proper and safe means of passage on the building site." The jury also absolved the deceased of contributory negligence. The defendants appealed.

Ó Dálaigh C.J.:
. . .[I]t was submitted that the deceased's employers could not be held to be negligent if, in addition to the wall passage (assuming the wall passage to be unsafe), they provided other means of access which were safe. At the trial the defendants' counsel said he accepted that the wall passage was what he called a 'recognised' route to the office. In my opinion if an employer offers without distinction a number of modes of access to the company's office of which all, except one, are safe, he cannot be relieved of his liability because a workman happens to choose to use the one which turns out to be unsafe. His duty is not to see that *some* modes of access which he offers are safe but to see that all of them are safe.

Next, it was submitted that the jury's answer to the second question submitted to them should not be allowed to stand because the deceased's employers had provided several safe modes of access to the company's office but the deceased had chosen one which was dangerous. Much of what I have said in dealing with the defendants' main ground of appeal is again in point here. The employer does not escape liability merely by providing safe means of access; if he also provides or 'recognises' other modes of access which are not safe, he is answerable if a workman is injured while using one of such other modes of access. It should also be added that the point taken in this ground of appeal had in fact vanished from the case before the questions came to be settled; the defendants accepted that they provided or recognised the wall route and made the case that it was a safe route.

Finally, the defendants have complained that there should have been a finding of contributory negligence against the deceased as the wall was held not to have been a safe means of passage. At the trial the defendants made the case that their allegation of contributory negligence was as to the manner of the deceased's user of the wall route. Understandably they chose this course in order that they might present a consistent case to the jury. They were unwilling to present the alternative case that the wall route was unsafe. Having chosen to allege negligence only as to the *manner* of using the wall route, the difficulty presented itself that the onus rested on them to offer evidence of negligence in the manner of user. This they were unable to do and the jury, in my opinion, therefore properly made a finding of no contributory negligence on the part of the deceased. . . .

Walsh and **McLoughlin JJ.** concurred.

(c) *The Provision of Proper Equipment*

An employer has the duty to take 'reasonable care to provide proper applicances, and to maintain them in a proper condition, and so to carry on his operations as not to subject those employed by him to unnecessary risk.' (*Burke* v. *John Paul & Co. Ltd.* [1967] I.R. 277, at 281 (Sup. Ct.,*per* Budd, J.), quoting from *Smith* v. *Baker & Sons,* [1891] A.C. 325, at 362 (H.L. (Eng.),*per* Lord Herschell.)) Frequently the employee will be as well aware of the defect in the appliance as his employer; the employer may seek to argue that on this account the employee should not be entitled to succeed in his action, either on the basis of failure to establish the breach of a duty of care, contributory negligence or what was formerly referred to as voluntary assumption of risk.

DEEGAN V. LANGAN
[1966] I.R. 373 (Supreme Court)

Walsh J.:

This is an appeal against an award of £10,500 damages recovered by the respondent who was a carpenter from his employer, the appellant. The appellant was found guilty of negligence in providing for use by the respondent, in the course of a building operation being carried on by the appellant, a particular type of steel masonry nail which was dangerous in that it was apt to disintegrate when struck by a hammer. Such a disintegration occurred when the respondent was using the nail in the course of his employment for the appellant with the result that the respondent lost the sight of one eye.

There was evidence that the appellant was aware of the dangerous quality of the nail in question when he provided the same for use by the respondent and permitted him to use it with a hammer. There was also evidence that the respondent himself was aware of this dangerous quality in the nail and that the appellant's knowledge of this dangerous quality was also known to the respondent. The position was therefore that at the time of the accident the respondent was hammering a nail which to his own knowledge and to his employer's knowledge was dangerous because of its propensity to disintegrate and the respondent was using the nail, which was provided by the appellant, for the purpose of the appellant's work upon which the respondent was engaged.

The appellant complains that the learned trial Judge misdirected himself in law in refusing to allow counsel for the appellant to cross-examine the respondent to the effect that the respondent was himself guilty of negligence in using the nail when he knew it to have this particular dangerous quality. The allegation of negligence against the respondent which the Judge refused to permit to be pursued was that the respondent decided to run the risk of using this dangerous type of nail. There was no question of any negligence on his part after making his decision to use the nail.

It appears to me that the law governing such a situation is that the decision to run the risk does not amount to negligence on the part of the plaintiff provided that his conduct under all the circumstances was that of a reasonable man; that is, whether in this particular case, having regard to all the circumstances, his decision to use the nail was a reasonable one. It has been contended on behalf of the appellant that it should have been left to the jury to decide whether or not the respondent was unreasonable in not making representations to his employer about using this nail and in not having his instructions to use it further confirmed and, it is contended, that for not having done so the jury could find that he had acted unreasonably.

In my view a jury could not so find on the facts in this case. The relevant facts are that the parties were in the position of master and servant; the defective article was consciously and with full knowledge of the deficiency provided by the master for use by his servant; the latter was aware not merely of the defect in the article but also of his master's knowledge of that defect. His instructions were clear and unambiguous and bearing in mind their respective positions it is my view that it would be unreasonable to hold that there still remained an obligation upon the servant to make further representations about the matter to his master. In reality the alternatives open to him were either to do the job as he had been instructed to do it or to refuse to do it. He could not be held guilty of negligence because he chose to do the job he was directed to do.

A further factor emerged later in the case. There was evidence from the master's side to the effect that the master had no other nails available for doing this particular job, so it is quite clear that even if representations had been made by the servant, which as I have already held he was not obliged to make in the circumstances of the case, they would in any event have been fruitless because the only means available for doing the job was the use of this particular type of nail.

In my view the learned trial Judge was correct in refusing to allow this particular cross-examination to be pursued because for the reasons I have stated it was directed only towards sustaining an issue which could not have been decided against the respondent. In my view this ground of appeal fails.

The appellant has also appealed against the award of damages on the grounds that the sum awarded was wholly unreasonable and excessive.

The total of the amount of special damages, that is to say, loss of wages, hospital expenses and other out-of-pocket expenses incurred before the trial, was £1,200. That leaves a sum of £9,300 to cover pain and suffering and the loss which the respondent will suffer in his pleasure in life and his loss in respect of the other amenities of life because of the fact that he now has sight in only one eye, and to cover the effect it will have upon his earning capacity for the remainder of his life.

The respondent, who at the time of the trial was twenty-eight years old, was a skilled carpenter. At the date of the trial his earnings would have been almost £14 a week. The injury to the eye has caused complete blindness in the eye but did not result in the removal of the eye. He suffered very severe pain in the eye at the time of the accident and this persisted for a few days. Taken all in all, a sum of £3,000 might not be regarded as unreasonable for the loss of sight with its consequent loss of enjoyment of life and for the pain and suffering involved. That leaves approximately £6,000 to be considered as appropriate to future loss of earnings resulting from the effect of blindness in one eye on his future earning capacity. On an approximate actuarial calculation based upon the normal expectation of life for a person of his age and assuming that all would go well for him in the labour market, a sum of £6,000 would represent a loss of approximately 50 per cent of his present and future earning capacity.

The respondent in his own evidence was of the opinion that he could not go back to carpentry work because a carpenter's normal work involved going up on ladders and working at heights and standing on scaffolding and that for such work two eyes were essential. He felt quite fit for it so far as his limbs and the rest of his body were concerned. In the view of his doctor it would be extremely dangerous for him to work upon scaffolding or walls or to climb along parapets and that because of his loss of binocular vision he would be unable to accurately measure the relative positions of objects.

Giving this evidence its full value it is at least established that there are certain types of carpentry work which may not be open to the respondent in the future. It is not disputed, however, that there are other types of carpentry work which would not involve climbing up ladders or working upon scaffoldings or upon parapets. In my view the evidence adduced in this trial did not adequately, if at all, explore the possibility of the types of carpentry work that would be open in the future to the respondent, even assuming that all the ones already referred to would not be open to him or what loss of earning capacity, if any, would result from any such restriction upon him in the field of carpentry. On the evidence the figure arrived at by the jury can at best be an estimate unsupported by the necessary evidence, a result for which the jury are not to be blamed. As has been done in other cases, and I mention as one example, the case of *Ebbs* v. *Forkin* 1960, No. 1344 P. (unreported), evidence can be adduced to provide some picture of the probable future diminution in earning capacity. For example, in the case I have just referred to, the diminution in earnings capacity was estimated at between 25 and 30 per cent. This may require the calling of specialist type evidence in respect of conditions in the labour market, the types of carpentry work which are available, the earnings available in such branches of carpentry, and other such relevant material. Even if such evidence is available to indicate a likely percentage of loss of earnings capacity it is highly unsatisfactory that a jury should be expected to assess the value of this loss as a present lump sum without the expert advice of an actuary which could provide them with the present value of £1 per week loss on the assumption that the respondent's working life would continue for a certain number of years and on various other assumptions which would necessarily be involved and which can be founded only upon evidence. Once the jury, as the judges of fact in the case, have made the necessary findings of fact as to the probable duration of working life, the probable changes in the normal wage rate, employment prospects, etc., the figure provided by the actuary would enable them to arrive at an almost exact computation of the correct sum for present compensation. On previous occasions it has been stated by this Court that in cases where the damages claimed contain a substantial element of loss of future earnings it is most desirable that expert evidence of the type referred to should be available for the assistance of the jury. In this type of case there can be no justification for allowing it to go to the jury to be decided on inspiration, uninformed guesses or crude rule of thumb methods. It is regrettable that it should still be necessary for this Court to repeat this. The present case is but another of the many cases in which the jury was not provided with this evidence. It may well be that evidence can be secured and adduced which would justify the award in this case but no such evidence was in fact adduced. On the evidence adduced the most the jury could say is that there would be probably some diminution in the earnings capacity of the plaintiff in the future but there is no evidence upon which they could make any reasonable finding of the degree of such diminution, if any, and on the evidence adduced in this case there is no alternative but to hold that the figure of about £6,000, which one may properly assume was awarded for loss of future earnings, is such that no reasonable jury could award it and the verdict must be set aside and a new trial directed on the issue of damages.

Lavery and **O'Keeffe JJ.** concurred.

It should be noted that an employer is not an insurer of the safety of the equipment supplied to his employees; reasonable care on his part is all that is required.

KEENAN V. BERGIN
[1971] I.R. 192 (Supreme Court)

Walsh J.:

The first defendant was a haulage contractor and he was the owner of a trailer of the type which is used for carrying goods containers and it is drawn by a motor vehicle which is detachable from the trailer but which, when attached to the trailer, bears the weight of one end of the trailer. At the other, or rear, end of the trailer are ordinary double wheels on each side which are of the type seen on heavy trucks. The connection between the tractor and the trailer is an articulated one and the whole assembly is more usually known by the proprietary name of one manufacturer, namely, Scammell truck and trailer.

When the tractor is detached from the trailer the front end of the trailer is supported by what are known as jockey wheels. This is an assembly which is retracted under the floor of the trailer while it is attached to the tractor but, upon detachment of the tractor, descends into a vertical position, enabling the front end of the trailer to rest upon the wheels at the foot of that assembly. This enables the tractor to be used for other purposes while the trailer is being loaded or unloaded or is being used otherwise when not needed for immediate haulage. The jockey-wheel assembly contains as one of its components a locking mechanism or device the purpose of which is to prevent the jockey-wheel assembly from retracting while the trailer is resting upon the jockey-wheels. The trailer is also designed in such a way that, in addition to its facility to be pushed directly forwards or backwards when resting on its road wheels and jockey wheels, a special pulling bar can be attached to the front of it so that the jockey-wheel assembly can be pivoted, thus enabling the person or persons manhandling the trailer to steer it. If the locking mechanism is not in position or is inadequate or for any reason fails in its primary purpose, there is the danger that upon the trailer being drawn forward by manhandling the assembly may collapse into the retracted position thereby causing the whole front end of the trailer to fall to ground level. As this trailer can weigh several tons when laden, it is obviously capable of causing very serious injury to anybody who may be struck by it if it should collapse in the manner described. Trailers of this type are in very common use and people in the business of carriage of goods by road, and people who are engaged in loading or unloading such trailers, are quite familiar with them and they are also familiar with the mechanism of the jockey-wheel support.

On Friday, the 23rd January, 1970, the first defendant in the course of his business carried goods on the said trailer in a container from the premises of the British and Irish Steam Packet Company to the premises of the second defendants. The second defendants carry on business in the City of Dublin manufacturing sacks. When the first defendant arrived in the yard premises of the second defendants on the day in question his intention was to leave the trailer on the premises to be unloaded and he was directed by the servants and agents of the second defendants where to leave the trailer. He left it in the place indicated and uncoupled the tractor from the trailer and the jockey wheels then fell into position and the trailer was left supported by its ordinary rear wheels and by the jockey wheels in front. The first defendant thereupon departed with his tractor.

The jockey-wheel assembly was in fact defective on that date by reason of some violent injury it had suffered previously, the effect of which was to prevent the locking mechanism being operative. It was a defect of a type which would be easily observable to anybody looking at the assembly either from underneath the front end of the trailer or even from a side view. As the front end of the trailer was at least four feet above ground level, there would be no appreciable difficulty in inspecting or looking at the assembly in question for the purpose of ascertaining whether or not it was apparently in working order. The defect in the locking mechanism did not affect the ability of the jockey-wheel assembly to support the trailer in the position in which it had been left, and the work of unloading the trailer proceeded without incident. No inspection or examination of any kind was made of the trailer assembly by the second defendants, or their servants or agents, prior to the commencement of the unloading on the date in question and there was no direct evidence that the defect was known to the first defendant.

On Monday, the 26th January, when the unloading had been completed, it was decided by the employees of the second defendants that the trailer should be moved to another portion of the yard to get it out of the way. There was not available, nor had there been furnished by the first defendant, any bar or other standard instrument for attaching to the front of the trailer for steering it. An effort was made by a number of the employees (including the assistant manager of the second defendants and, eventually, the plaintiff as foreman) to move the trailer by manual exertion. The assistant manager's effort consisted in using a wooden pole in an effort to move one of the jockey wheels and possibly to affect the direction of the movement of the trailer. The trailer had already been moved some distance before the plaintiff joined in the operation. The surface of the yard was uneven in places and after moving some distance in the manner indicated the jockey-wheel assembly collapsed, possibly due to coming in contact with and meeting the resistance of an unevenness in the yard. In the collapse of the trailer which followed, the plaintiff sustained serious personal injuries in respect of which he has brought this action. As nothing in this appeal turns upon the nature or extent of his injuries it is unnecessary to make any further reference to them.

The second defendants, and their servants and agents, were quite familiar with the use and the loading and unloading of trailers of this type and they were also accustomed to manhandling them in the way indicated, including using a piece of wood of the type mentioned for assisting them in this operation when a handling device was not available. The necessity to move trailers of the type indicated to other places in the yard was due, as on this occasion, to the necessity of clearing away an empty trailer from the unloading chute or bay so as to enable another trailer to be brought to that point for unloading. On this occasion the arrangement with the first defendant had apparently been that the trailer would be removed by him the first thing on Monday morning but as that did not happen the plaintiff, who was the foreman, decided that it ought to be moved to another portion of the yard pending its removal from the premises by the first defendant. For that purpose he rang up the assistant manager of the second defendants, informed the manager of what he proposed to do and asked the manager for the necessary additional workmen to enable him to do so. The assistant manager went along with the additional men and the pushing of the trailer commenced upon his arrival with the additional men, even though the plaintiff himself was not there at the time. The assistant manager was the person who used the stick in the manner indicated on this particular morning. After some movement, the plaintiff came along and was furnished with the stick by the assistant manager who then left the scene. There was a suggestion made during the trial that the use of a stick on this occasion was in fact the cause of the defect in the locking mechanism, and a question to this effect was put to the jury by the learned trial judge on the basis that the plaintiff might be thought to be guilty of contributory negligence in interfering with the locking device with the stick. This was denied in evidence by the plaintiff. The jury answered this question in the negative and it is agreed that the effect of the question and the answer is that the jury found as a fact that the use of the stick by the plaintiff was not a causative factor in the accident. It could scarcely be contested on the evidence that the injury to the mechanism which affected the locking device was of long standing.

The plaintiff sued both defendants for negligence. In answer to the first question put to the jury by the judge, the jury found that the locking device was in a dangerous condition when the trailer was left at the premises of the second defendants on the date in question. The jury found that the first defendant was negligent in failing to anticipate that the trailer would be manhandled and thereby collapse because of its defective condition, and they found that the second defendants were negligent in failing to ascertain that the trailer was in a safe condition before permitting the plaintiff to assist in manhandling it. Although the manhandling did not take place until the 26th January no inspection had been carried out by the defendants, their servants or agents, at any time from the arrival of the trailer on the 23rd to its collapse on the 26th January. The jury apportioned the degrees of fault between the two defendants by attributing 80% of the fault to the first defendant and 20% of the fault to the second defendants. Against this verdict each of the defendants has appealed.

The first defendant has submitted that the trial judge should have acceded to the application made on his behalf at the close of the evidence for the plaintiff that the case should be withdrawn from the jury on the ground that he could not reasonably have foreseen or anticipated that the trailer would be moved while it was in the yard of the second defendants. This defendant has also appealed against the apportionment of fault and has claimed that the attribution of 80% to him was excessive and so unreasonably excessive as to warrant it being set aside. At the close of the submissions in this Court made on behalf of the first defendant, the Court indicated that this ground of appeal was unsustained. There was ample evidence on which the jury could hold, as they did, that not only was the locking device in a dangerous condition when the first defendant left the trailer with the second defendants but that, if the first defendant did not actually know of it, he certainly ought to have known of it and that he ought to have anticipated that the trailer would be manhandled while on the second defendants' premises. That was the normal method of dealing with a trailer when it was desired to move it from one place to another and in fact it was designed for manhandling. The second defendants have no complaint on the question of the apportionment of fault, if they are to be found negligent, but they have strenuously submitted that there were no reasonable grounds upon which a jury could find that they were guilty of negligence. They also submitted that the learned trial judge misdirected himself in failing to accede to their request to withdraw the case against them from the jury.

The second defendants have submitted that they could not reasonably be expected to have foreseen that the trailer would be unsafe to manhandle. In effect, the question is whether a jury should reasonably expect that the second defendants should have satisfied themselves, probably by inspection, that the trailer was in a fit condition to be manhandled before permitting or directing their employees to carry out that operation.

In my opinion, the jury's finding against the second defendants in relation to such a potentially dangerous piece of equipment was one which was open to them on the evidence. It could not be disputed that these defendants would be liable if the trailer had been their property. Whether the employees of these defendants are working on the property of these defendants or upon the property of another person upon the direction or instructions of their employer, the duty of these defendants not to expose their employees to unnecessary risk continues to exist even though the conduct which may amount to a discharge of that duty may vary with the circumstances of the case because the question of what may be reasonable must necessarily depend upon the circumstances. In this particular case the second defendants had taken into their premises a trailer of a type with which they were very familiar – familiar both as to the mechanism and the manhandling of it. On the evidence they must be taken to know that, if the locking device was not in working order, the pulling or the pushing forward of the trailer carried with it a very high degree of danger that the jockey-wheel assembly would collapse, particularly if its progress was impeded by the resistance of unevenness in the surface over which it was being pushed. In the present case the defect may be regarded as a patent defect in that it would be immediately apparent to anybody who, understanding the mechanism, took the trouble to look at it; and in view of the construction and the height of the trailer even a cursory inspection would have revealed the defect in question and such an inspection could have been carried out in a couple of moments without any difficulty. The second defendants had not made any inquiry of the first defendant as to the condition of the trailer or as to the risk, if any, in manhandling it. The second defendants elected to instruct their workmen to carry out this work without any prior inspection or observation of the mechanism when they knew that a defect in the locking mechanism would render the operation a highly dangerous one.

The fact that they had no ground for thinking that an inspection might be necessary in this particular case affords the second defendants no defence as they had taken no steps whatever to satisfy themselves as to the condition of the vehicle. It is not a case of some steps having been taken which proved to be inadequate, the reasonableness of which might be in dispute. There is no comparison between this case and the type of case where an employer discharges his duty by buying from a reputable supplier a standard tool whose latent defect he had no means of discovering and which causes injury. In such a case an employer may be held to have discharged his duty by taking care to buy a standard tool from a reputable supplier. In the present case the second defendants had taken no steps whatever to discharge the duty and in effect their appeal really turns upon submitting that they could not have been reasonably expected to foresee that there could be a danger against which some precaution would have to be taken, even though it might amount to no more than an inspection. The precaution of inspection in this case was one which would have caused no measure of inconvenience or expense. In my view, the jury were amply justified in holding that the second defendants were negligent in not making this prior inspection as the risk was one which was inherent in the very construction and design of the vehicle because the working or non-working of the locking mechanism determined whether the trailer was dangerous or not if manhandled.

On the question of the apportionment of fault I would not disturb the figures at which the jury arrived. On the evidence they are quite justified. In comparing the blameworthiness of each of the defendants the jury could quite reasonably have come to the conclusion that the first defendant was far more blameworthy than the second defendants. He had created the danger initially and had failed to give any warning of it. The second defendants had not created the danger but had failed to observe it before exposing their employees to it. I would dismiss both appeals and affirm the order of the High Court.

Ó Dálaigh C.J. and **Fitzgerald J.** concurred.

Note and Question

1. See also *Simpson* v. *Pollard,* unreported, Supreme Court, 3 June 1963 (129–1963), Osborough, 'Employer's Liability and Defective Tools,' 4 Ir. Jur. (n.s.) 119 (1969).
2. Where the employee himself is charged with the task of ensuring that the equipment is safe, what approach should the law take? *Cf. Tracey* v. *Hayes*, unreported, Supreme Court, 6 March 1973 (153–1970).

(d) *The Provision of a Safe System of Work*

GUCKIAN V. CULLY
Unreported, Supreme Court, 9 March 1972 (162–1970)

Walsh J.:

The plaintiff was a baker who worked in a bakery business owned and conducted by the defendant's late husband. On the 28th November, 1968, in the course of his employment he sustained injuries to his right hand while feeding dough into a dough machine in the bakery premises. In his action for damages for personal injury which was tried in the High Court on the 26th and 27th November, 1970, the jury found that his employer had been negligent and that the plaintiff was negligent. They apportioned the degrees of fault by attributing 60% of the fault to the employer and 40% to the plaintiff. They assessed damages at a total sum of £3,226 made up as follows: £1,126 special damages up to the date of trial; £1,700 special damages for the future; and general damages, £400.

The plaintiff has appealed against these findings, firstly on the ground that there was no evidence upon which the jury could have found the plaintiff guilty of any negligence, secondly, that the apportionment of fault as between the parties was wholly disproportionate in so far as it attributed 40% of the fault to the plaintiff and, thirdly, the appeal was brought on the ground that the damages were so low as could not be arrived at by any reasonable jury.

The machine in question was one into which dough was fed through a hopper. The machine was a free standing machine and the total height of the machine from the ground to the top of the hopper was 5 feet 4 inches. When the dough went into the hopper it passed down through the hopper into a chamber where a moving blade, which was adjustable, cut it into lumps of the desired weight. The principal if not the only motive force which propelled the dough down into the cutting chamber was the action of atmospheric pressure from above forcing the dough down into a chamber in which there was a vacuum created by reason of the air beneath having been extracted by a piston. The custom was for the baker, the plaintiff in this case, to carry in his arms a large lump of dough, weighing about 2 stone, and dropping it into the hopper. Some of the dough used was of such a heavy consistency that it sometimes did not seal itself against the sides of the hopper but left a space down through which air would be drawn between it and the sides of the hopper and thus prevented a vacuum being formed in the chamber underneath. It was also subject to the possibility of air pockets being within the dough itself, caused perhaps on occasions by one lump of dough being placed on top of another and some pockets of air being trapped between the two. It was dough of this type which was being used at the time of the accident. To enable the dough to be put in or to enable it to be tended to while in the hopper it was customary to stand upon a form or stool placed near the machine, which form was itself rather unstable by reason of the nature of its supports. By reason of the consistency of this type of dough which was frequently used the machine required fairly frequent attention for the purpose of pushing the dough by hand or otherwise against the sides of the hopper so as to form an air seal. This procedure was commonplace while this type of dough was used in the machine. On a former occasion the plaintiff had suggested to his employer that he should use a stick for the purpose of pushing the dough when it was necessary to do so, but the employer prohibited this on the grounds that there was a danger that a piece of wood might be cut by the cutter and it would get into the dough which would be baked into loaves. The cutter blade was 1 foot 10 inches from the top of the hopper but when the hopper was fully loaded with dough it came to within 4 inches of the top so that effectively with a full load of dough the distance from the top of the dough to the blade was 1 foot 6 inches. The practice of pressing on the dough by hand apparently continued when it was necessary to do so and this, it may be inferred from the evidence, was quite well known to the employer and in so far as he prohibited the use of a stick may be said to have been authorised by him. As the effort to eliminate air pockets or to complete the seal sometimes involved pushing the hand of the operative into the dough there was always the danger that if the level of the dough was sufficiently low or the hand was pushed too far that the operative's hand might get caught in the machine. That is precisely what happened to the plaintiff and which gave rise to the present action.

On the day of the accident when the plaintiff was engaged in this procedure he apparently leaned over sufficiently in pushing the dough to cause the pressure of his feet or legs to push outwards the stool upon which he was standing, which was in any event a rather unstable one, thereby causing him to lose his balance momentarily. With his left hand he grabbed the side of the hopper and his right hand, already in the dough, went further down into it. Possibly he instinctively sought for a grip in the dough, but the tops of the two middle fingers of his right hand were severed by the blade.

There can be no doubt whatever that the jury was quite correct in finding the employer negligent in this matter. Not merely was he negligent in providing a stool of the type mentioned for support where a proper catwalk or gangway should have been provided, but the whole system of the work carried great dangers for the operative. It was reasonably clear from the design of the machine that it was never intended to have dough pushed into it by hand as was done in the present case and the machine so long as it was used simply by pouring the dough into the hopper had no inherent danger. The danger arose when the dough was pushed round by hand. It is true to say that the employer was not himself a baker in the sense that he was not apparently skilled in the actual making of bread but he did own the business and gave his first attention to the vending of the commodity rather than its making. He did, however, exercise control over the way it was done as was evidenced by the fact that he prohibited the use of a stick.

The plaintiff was also found guilty of negligence and I would not be inclined to disturb this finding although on the evidence it was quite open to the jury to have acquitted him of any negligence. However, on the evidence and having regard to the fact that he was aware of the possible danger in the type of work he was doing which was an unavoidable danger because of the way the work was laid out the jury might well have taken the view that none the less he might have been more careful with the knowledge which he had, not merely of the unstable nature of the stool but of the danger of putting his hand into this opaque mixture.

The next question to be considered is the question of the apportionment of fault. This, as has been explained in other cases, is not to be measured by the causative potency of the negligent acts of each party but is to be judged on the standards of blameworthiness having regard to all the circumstances as was elaborated in *O'Sullivan* v. *O'Dwyer* [1971] I.R. 275 and *Snell* v. *Haughton* [1971] I.R. 305 and more recently in *Kelly* v. *Jameson*, Sup. Ct., 1 March 1972. The Court's approach to deciding whether the jury's apportionment of fault should be disturbed is that laid down in the line of cases beginning with *Donoghue* v. *Burke* [1960] I.R. 314 and the other subsequent cases referred to in *O'Leary* v. *O'Connell* [1968] I.R. 149 and in *Kelly* v. *Jameson*. On the evidence, in my view, it would have been perverse on the part of the jury not to have attributed more of the fault to the defendant than to the plaintiff. This they did but it now becomes necessary to examine the actual percentages attributed. Looking at the behaviour of the plaintiff and his employer in this particular accident, one could only conclude that the blameworthiness of the employer was considerably greater than that of the plaintiff. The plaintiff was guilty of the negligence of which the jury found him negligent but, that being said, there is very little else to be said against the plaintiff. He was working a system which he himself did not devise and which he had made an effort to cure but was not permitted to cure. He was in effect carrying out the dangerous operation exactly as he had been directed to do by his employer. Nothing which he did was unauthorised or without the knowledge of his employer and while he may have had some control over the way the job was carried out in that he carried it out himself he was not responsible either for the machine provided or for the means of access to the machine, both of which were dangerous having regard to the requirements of the handling of the particular type of dough being used. In all the circumstances I am of opinion that the jury's apportionment of 40% of fault to the plaintiff was so disproportionate as to warrant being set aside by this Court. It follows, of course, that a substantially greater degree of fault should be attributed to the employer than the 60% which the jury attributed to him.
. . .

Counsel for each side has intimated to the Court their willingness to have the fault reapportioned by this Court . . .

I am of opinion that the plaintiff was to some extent, but a small extent, blameworthy for the accident which befell him and the injury he suffered. Bearing in mind that he was not under anybody's immediate supervision he could therefore have sought and provided himself with a more stable platform. He could have determined the pace of his own work and knowing the dangers as he did, he could have undertaken the dangerous part of the operation already referred to in a manner which would reduce in so far as possible, though it could not eliminate, the risk to which he was exposed. Giving the matter careful consideration I am of opinion that the highest degree of fault which could be attributed to him is 20%. It is my view that in this case the full amount of the 20% should be attributed to him. I would therefore reapportion the fault so as to attribute 80% to the employer and 20% to the plaintiff. . . .

Ó Dálaigh C.J.:

I concur in the conclusion reached by Mr. Justice Walsh . . . that the jury's apportionment at 40% fault to the plaintiff is so disproportionate as to warrant its being set aside by this Court . . .

I wish to say briefly that in my opinion the jury's apportionment of 40% fault to the plaintiff is explicable only on the basis that the jury misconceived the case they had to try. Perhaps an apportionment of fault of 40% would have been warranted if the facts of this case had been that the plaintiff had permitted his hand to come in contact with the hopper blade while merely engaged in pressing the dough down into the hopper in such a way as to ensure that the measuring mechanism was able to operate correctly. But those were not the facts as proved in evidence and accepted at the trial. The plaintiff was, of course, engaged in pressing the dough down into the hopper to ensure that the edges were properly sealed, but it was not this which brought his hand into contact with the hopper blade but his involuntary lurch when the stool on which he was required to stand in servicing the hopper tilted over. That his hand was in the hopper was a *sine qua non* of the accident, but the *causa causans* was the unsuitable and insecure stool upon which he was required to work.

The two heads upon which it is alleged the plaintiff was guilty of contributory negligence are in my view *nihil ad rem*. The first of these grounds is that the plaintiff should not have pressed down so far. The answer is, the plaintiff did not press down too far; his right hand was involuntarily projected on to the blade because the unstable and unsuitable stool caused him to lurch forward when he was carrying out the pressing down operation with due care. Nor, in my view, is the second ground relied upon, *viz.*, that the plaintiff should have turned off the machine, any more relevant in this case. I repeat, this accident, on the unchallenged evidence of the plaintiff, was due not to any lack of care on the plaintiff's part in bringing his hand, while pressing down the dough into too close proximity to the hopper knife, but because of an involuntary lurch when the stool, which constituted his working platform, tilted over.

Properly evaluated it appears to me that the facts show that the plaintiff was without fault.

[The records state that "Budd J. concurred with both judgments." It is clear, however, from the Court's Order that the plaintiff was held guilty of contributory negligence to the extent of 20% – *eds.*]

Note

See also *Carey* v. *Cork Commission Gas Co.*, unreported, Supreme Court, 5 March 1958 (69–1956).

2. *Contributory Negligence of Employee*

McKEEVER V. DUNDALK LINEN CO. LTD.
Unreported, Supreme Court 26 May 1966 (86–1964)

The plaintiff, aged fifteen years, was employed by the defendant company printing designs on cloth. He was taken one day for the first time to another part of the factory and put to clean the steel rollers on a calendering machine. This machine had large steel rollers at top and bottom and between these was a wooden roller or drum. The machine was driven by an electric motor; the movement of the two steel rollers could be controlled by a clutch, operated by a long handle at one side of the machine. The wooden roller was not driven by the electric motor, but rotated with the steel rollers, either by contact with them or with cloth fed through the machine. The motor was controlled by a switch on the wall some distance from the machine. By means of this switch the motor could be operated to drive the rollers in a clockwise or in an anti-clockwise direction or it could be stopped altogether. When the motor was running the engagement or disengagement of the clutch would also control the movement of the rollers.

The plaintiff was instructed by the foreman to clean rust off the steel rollers with sandpaper. To do this it was necessary to rotate the rollers from time to time to bring forward a fresh part of the face of the roller for cleaning. The plaintiff did this by going to the switch on the wall, and putting the machine in motion, stopping it again with the same switch when a new part of the face was exposed. The plaintiff was left on his own in the room while he was carrying out this work.

When the plaintiff had nearly finished cleaning the top roller, he switched on the motor, causing the rollers to rotate, and moved a small platform on the side of the machine, in order to see if the roller was completely clean. The roller rotated slowly, at about five revolutions per minute, so it would be possible to inspect it readily while it was rotating.

When inspecting the roller the plaintiff had in his hand a piece of cloth which he had used for wiping the roller when cleaning it, and (according to his subsequent evidence), this cloth caught in the roller and his arm was drawn into the space between the top and middle rollers before he realised what was happening. The plaintiff's arm was injured. He sued the defendant company for negligence and breach of statutory duty. The jury found that the defendant was guilty of negligence and the plaintiff guilty of contributory negligence in the proportions of 75% and 25%, respectively. The plaintiff appealed to the Supreme Court.

O'Keeffe J.:
. . . The substantial question argued on this appeal was whether the issue of contributory negligence should have been left to the jury. The Respondents submitted that it was manifest that the accident could not have happened in the manner described by the Plaintiff. They pointed out that there was a space of about 18″ between the 'nip' of the two rollers and the position in which the Plaintiff described himself as having held the cloth, and they submitted that the Plaintiff must have met his injury by attempting to wipe the roller while it was rotating, which, they said, was so obviously dangerous that the Plaintiff was rightly found guilty of contributory negligence.

The hypothesis propounded by the Respondents must be conceded to be open on the evidence, but it does not necessarily follow that the Plaintiff was negligent. The Court has to consider all the facts in order to decide whether a jury could properly convict the Plaintiff of negligence.

It is clear that the Respondents were considered negligent in permitting the Plaintiff to engage in the work of cleaning the machine alone, unsupervised, and without any warning of the danger of approaching near the rollers while they were revolving. On the other hand, the Plaintiff's alleged negligence is in doing that very thing against which the Defendants should have warned him.

An adult engaged in working near machinery of this kind might reasonably be expected to appreciate the risk involved, but the Plaintiff is not, in the opinion of the Court, in quite the same position. He was only just over fifteen years of age, he had no previous experience of this type of machine, he had been directed to start the rollers to bring forward a fresh part for cleaning and no warning had been given to him as to the danger of approaching the machine while it was in motion. The speed at which the roller was rotating (five revolutions a minute) was not such as to convey a sense of danger to a youth of the Plaintiff's age, unused to such machinery, and it cannot be said that in all the circumstances he should have appreciated the risk involved in mounting the platform to inspect the roller while it was moving, or even in attempting to wipe it (if he did so). The negligence found against the Respondents is their failure to warn of this danger and this Court is of opinion that it would be setting too high a standard for this young Plaintiff to expect him to appreciate it without any warning.

For these reasons the Court considers that the question of contributory negligence should not have been left to the jury and that the finding on this question should be set aside, and judgment entered for the Plaintiff (Appellant) for the full amount of the damages assessed by the jury.

Ó Dálaigh C.J. and **Walsh J.** concurred.

Note

See also *Deegan* v. *Langan, supra*, p. 341 and *Guckian* v. *Cully, supra*, p. 348.

Chapter 14

DEFAMATION

Introduction

The law on defamation is an attempt to balance one person's interest in maintaining a fair reputation against another person's right to free speech. Originally the right to reputation was given precedence, but in latter years the right to free speech has been more to the forefront of judicial consciousness.

The tort of defamation is, of course, primarily concerned with language and the meaning of words. If the meaning is clear one faces the problem of whether the words are defamatory in the eyes of the law. They are if they tend to lower the plaintiff in the eyes of right-thinking members of society. Sometimes, however, the meaning, although clear and innocent on its face, may have a hidden meaning because of the context in which words are spoken or because some additional facts give a barb to apparently innocuous statements. Should the defendant be liable then? It may also be asked whether different rules should apply if the statement is in a permanent form (libel) or is in a transient form (slander)?

As well as examining some of these issues, the litigation has also been concerned with the defences available in the defamation action, in particular with the defences of Justification, Privilege and Fair Comment. The statutory provisions relating to these contained in the *Defamation Act, 1961* are noteworthy as are the provisions in the same Act relating to the offer to make amends in the case of unintentional defamation (section 21) and the admissibility of evidence that an apology was offered, to mitigate the damages for which the defendant might be liable (section 17).

What is defamatory? Criterion used by the Courts.

BERRY V. IRISH TIMES
[1973] I.R. 371

Ó Dálaigh C.J.:

In the issue of the 25th September, 1970, the *Irish Times* published a news story concerning the occupation, by 15 members of Sinn Féin, of the British Overseas Aircraft Corporation in Grafton Street, Dublin. The news item was illustrated with a photograph which has given rise to the present proceedings.

The photograph is of the exterior of the B.O.A.C. offices and shows a poster, hung from the office window, referring to the release of political prisoners being held in Britain, together with copies of the periodical *Hibernia*. The photograph also shows a man bearing a placard with the words upon it which are complained of in this action, namely, – 'Peter Berry – 20th Century Felon Setter – Helped Jail Republicans in England.' The associated commentary stated that the demonstration was for the purpose of demanding the release of Irish prisoners being held in Britain and that the issue of *Hibernia* which was hung from the window contained an article on an appeal against their sentences by two Irishmen named Conor Lynch and Patrick O'Sullivan, who had been sentenced to seven years imprisonment in Britain after being convicted of taking part in a raid for arms in Dagenham. The news item also referred to a statement which was handed out by the demonstrating group which, under the heading 'Imperial Group' included the words:– 'All of these prisoners are political hostages held in Jail by the British Empire which for eight hundred years now has hijacked the peace and prosperity of the Irish nation for imperial purposes. The crime of these prisoners is that they are concerned Irish people trying to do what little they could to loosen the imperial grip on Ireland.'

At the time the demonstration outside the B.O.A.C. offices took place, the plaintiff was the Secretary of the Department of Justice and, as is common ground in this action, was well known as such to the public. There could be little doubt to whom the poster referred. The Department of Justice is the Department which by law comprises the administration and business of public services in connection with the police, among other functions: see the Minister and Secretaries Act, 1924. Whether or not persons who saw the actual poster being displayed on the street were aware that the reference on it concerned Lynch and O'Sullivan, there can be no doubt that the readers of the Irish Times were made so aware by the news item which was printed underneath the photograph.

In the statement of claim the words on the poster which appeared in the photograph were cited in full and it was pleaded that the words meant and were understood to mean 'that the plaintiff had helped in the jailing of Irish republicans in England.' It was pleaded that these words were defamatory. The defendants pleaded that the words were not defamatory and pleaded that the matter as published by them was a fair and accurate photographic report which was of general public interest and concern which the defendants had a duty to communicate to the general public, and that the publication was therefore privileged. The words were claimed to be defamatory in their ordinary meaning and no innuendo was pleaded and no attempt was made in the pleadings, or at the trial, to attribute any special meaning to the words other than their ordinary meaning.

The only witness who gave evidence at the trial was the plaintiff. He gave evidence to the effect that the words were untrue. No attempt was made to controvert this. The trial judge refused an application of non-suit made by the defendants who submitted that the words were not capable of being defamatory. The case went to the jury on three questions. The first question was, whether the material complained of conveyed that the plaintiff had helped in the jailing of Irish republicans in England. The trial judge directed the jury to answer this question in the affirmative. The second question was:– 'Was the publication defamatory of the plaintiff?' The jury answered this question in the negative. The third question, which related to damages, did not therefore require to be answered. On these findings judgment was entered for the defendants.

The plaintiff has appealed on the ground that no jury, acting reasonably, could answer that the matter complained of was not defamatory, and also on the ground that the answer and finding of the jury was contrary to the evidence and the weight of the evidence, and, thirdly, on the ground that the finding was perverse. There was a fourth and final ground that the trial was unsatisfactory. The plaintiff asks this Court to hold, as a matter of law, that the words complained of could not be held to be other than defamatory. That is to say that the report in the *Irish Times* of the statement that the plaintiff had assisted in the jailing of Irish Republicans in England, particularly in the publication referred to Lynch and O'Sullivan, are words which must hold the plaintiff up to public odium and contempt in the minds of average right-thinking persons in our community.

The law in the matter is most recently set out in the judgment of this Court in *Quigly* v. *Creation Ltd.* [1971] I.R. 269. In the course of his judgment, Mr. Justice Walsh at p. 272 of the report stated the position in law to be as follows:– 'Basically, the question of libel or no libel is a matter of opinion and opinions may vary reasonably within very wide limits. When a jury has found that there has been a libel, this Court would be more slow to set aside such a verdict than in other types of actions and it would only do so if it was of opinion that the conclusion reached by the jury was one to which reasonable men could not or ought not have come. It is true that if words only tend to lower a person in the minds of a particular class or section of society, particularly if the standard of that particular section of society is one which the Court cannot recognise or approve, the words will not be held to be defamatory. On the other hand, words are defamatory if they impute conduct which would tend to lower that person in the eyes of a considerable and respectable class of the community, though not in the eyes of the community as a whole. The test is whether it will lower him in the eyes of the average right-thinking man. If it will, then it is defamatory if untrue. It follows naturally that in an action in this country the standard would be that of the average right-thinking person in this community. The law recognises the right of the plaintiff to have the estimation in which he stands in the opinion of the right-minded people in this community unaffected by false statements to his dis-credit.' The judgement also goes on to state that in defamation, as in perhaps no other form of civil proceedings, the position of the jury is uniquely important. Mr. Justice Budd and Mr. Justice McLoughlin agreed.

There can be little doubt that the person who published on the placard, which appears in the photograph, the words complained of published a statement which, on the evidence is indisputably false; it is a fair inference that the object of the author of the words (and of those displaying the poster) was to injure the plaintiff in his general reputation. The intent of the author or the publisher of a libel may be very relevant on the question of malice, but it does not determine the question whether the material complained of is or is not defamatory. In appropriate cases an action lies for wilful injurious malicious falsehood, and such an action is not governed by the stringent rules of libel and slander: this matter is dealt with in s. 20 of the Defamation Act, 1961. That is not the action before this Court, even though the material on the placard could be proved to be a malicious falsehood. In this case there is no allegation of express malice against the *Irish Times* in respect of their publication of the placard by its reproduction of the photograph in question.

The words in question, in the context in which they appear in the *Irish Times* photograph and in the news item of which the photograph forms a part, amount to an allegation that the plaintiff, by furnishing evidence or in some other way, had assisted in the prosecution to convicton of Lynch and O'Sullivan who were convicted in an English court of an offence against the laws of England. Is it necessarily defamatory to say of a person that he assisted in the conviction of some of his own fellow countrymen in a foreign country for an offence against the laws of that country, committed in that country, if the act alleged is such that if committed here it would amount to an offence against the laws of this country – or, if it be not such, that it is an offence against a provision in the criminal code of another country which is not in itself repugnant to our concepts of law and justice; or when the procedure followed at the criminal trial in question is not one which by our standards of law and justice could be regarded only as a travesty of justice? No such allegation as this was made in the present case, nor was it any part of the plaintiff's case to suggest that the words accused him of assisting in any such repugnant procedure.

It is perhaps surprising that the Supreme Court should be asked to hold, as a matter of law, that it is necessarily defamatory to say of one of the citizens of this country that he assisted in the bringing to justice in another country of a fellow countryman who broke the laws of that country and who was tried and convicted for that offence in the ordinary course of the administration of criminal justice. This Court is bound to uphold the rule of law and its decisions must be conditioned by this duty. Is the matter to be considered differently because the person or persons so convicted were motivated by a desire to resolve, by force of arms, a dispute existing between their own country and the country in which the offence was committed when there is not a state of war between the two countries? To say, in those circumstances, that such an allegation must be defamatory would be to hold that ordinary right-thinking people in this country could not condemn such militant activities – to the extent that one could not but think that a person who assisted in curbing or putting down such militant activities was guilty of disgraceful conduct. That, in effect, is what was alleged against the plaintiff.

If the allegation was that the plaintiff did it as Secretary of the Department of Justice, then he would do so only on the authority of his Minister or of the Government. Alternatively, the allegation might convey that he did so independently of such authority: but unless it were claimed that in doing so he improperly and in breach of his trust as Secretary of the Department used information which came into his possession as such officer, for example, without the authority of his Minister or of the Government, the allegation must not necessarily be held to be defamatory. No such construction was attempted to be put upon these words. If it had been so, the action would have been of quite a different nature as such an accusation would really have been a reflection on the plaintiff's fitness for his position.

The learned trial judge asked the jury to consider the case on the basis of whether the allegation, if true, was such as would make the plaintiff's ordinary right-thinking neighbours think less of him. To that question the jury answered 'No.' It cannot be held as a matter of law that his right-thinking neighbours, or any other right-thinking people in the community in Ireland, must necessarily think less of him for taking such action if he had done so. The fact that the allegation is false does not make it defamatory. The plaintiff in his own evidence said he understood it to suggest that he was 'an informer.' If for historical reasons it is to be assumed that the word 'informer' has a special and defamatory meaning and is, because of such special meaning, to be distinguished from the word 'informant' which itself certainly is not defamatory in its ordinary meaning, the fact is that the word 'informer' was not used in the publication complained of and no innuendo was pleaded to suggest that the words actuall; published were so understood. This ground of appeal must fail.

Was the trial unsatisfactory? This fourth ground of appeal was not in any way particularised in the notice of appeal. In the hearing of this appeal it has been sought to argue that the trial judge's approach to the jury on the question of damages was such that he tended to diminish damages so much in the jury's mind as perhaps to have caused the jury to think the matter was not defamatory at all. The judge's direction to the jury quite clearly indicates that he rather expected them to find the words were defamatory, and the main theme in his address on the question of damages seems to have been to point out to the jury that no damage had been proved and not to encourage them to give extravagant damages. No objection whatsoever was taken to his direction to the jury at the trial, and there was not the slightest hint at the trial that what he said to the jury was in the least degree unsatisfactory or that his conduct of the case was unsatisfactory. This complaint was made for the first time in this Court. The judge's treatment of the issue of damages, while certainly aimed at keeping the damages within moderate dimensions, could not in any way be construed as such a discouragement to the jury as in effect to encourage them to find that the words were not defamatory. This ground of appeal, as it appeared in the notice of appeal, gave no hint whatever that it related to the second question put to the jury and, in view of the fact that no requisition whatever was made on this subject at the trial, one may conclude that it did not convey that impression to those present. Under the fourth ground of appeal it was also objected that the trial judge's interventions were so frequent and unfair to the plaintiff's case as to render the trial unsatisfactory. There is no substance in this complaint.

In my opinion the appeal must fail. In the event it is not necessary to give any opinion on the special defence of privilege raised by the defendants.

Walsh J.:
I agree.

Budd J.:
I agree.

Fitzgerald J. (dissenting):
... It appears to me, and I think it would appear to any Irishman of normal experience and intelligence, that the words complained of were clearly a libel. 'Felon-setter' and 'Helped jail republicans in England' were not words in respect of which one has to have recourse to a dictionary to know what they meant to an Irishman; they were equivalent to calling him a trator. The words are now admittedly untrue. They were a concoction by the author of the placard.

The defendants have pleaded that there was privilege. They have advanced no evidence of any sort to establish a claim to privilege. The trial judge acted correctly in not leaving any question on it to the jury, and in my view the effort to raise it in the Supreme Court clearly fails.

It is clear that the cross-examination of the plaintiff was mainly directed to the issue of damages. In the judge's charge to the jury, he dealt almost exclusively with the issue of damages – obviously anticipating that the jury would find that the words were defamatory.

Complaint was made on behalf of the plaintiff that the trial judge's interventions had produced an unfair result but it has been suggested by counsel for the defendants that the interventions were in assistance of the plaintiff. Why a judge should presume to assist the plaintiff, who was represented by leading members of the Bar, I do not know. In any event, if that was the purpose of his interventions they were singularly ineffective.

In my view, a gross injustice was done to the plaintiff and the action should be re-tried. The meaning of the words was plainly defamatory and the jury should be so directed and the case re-tried on the issue of damages only.

McLoughlin J. (dissenting):
I propose to deal first in this judgment with the grounds of appeal that the finding of the jury was unreasonable and perverse.

When I got the book of appeal the first document I saw was a photograph of a man carrying a placard with the words:–

'Peter Berry

20th Century
Felon Setter
Helped Jail
Republicans
in
England.'

The impression this conveyed to me was that this publication was so clearly defamatory of the plaintiff that it was beyond all argument. It is important that I should state my first impression because it could well be, in my view, the first impression of others seeing no more than was seen by me in the photograph. To have one's name displayed on a placard in the public street is something which most people would regard as objectionable. It is almost axiomatic that if one's name is placarded one is blackguarded. Followed by the words '20th Century Felon Setter' makes it particularly obnoxious. What do the words mean? Literally, I suppose, designating some person a felon so that he may be proceeded against as such; but more, it means doing it in a malevolent way. As an expression it is clearly vituperative and reviling. The words which follow 'Helped Jail Republicans in England' do not take away from the vituperative nature of the expression '20th Century Felon Setter.' They seem to convey only the reason why he is so vilified. He is called a felon setter because he has designated republicans, by giving information as to names and locations, addresses perhaps in England, and so assisted the British authorities to have such persons jailed. Put in other words, the suggestion is that this Irishman, the plaintiff, has acted as a spy and informer for the British police concerning republicans in England, thus putting the plaintiff into the same category as the spies and informers of earlier centuries who were regarded with loathing and abomination by all decent people.

It is the fact that there is no evidence of the effect of this publication in the minds of persons who saw it. There is evidence of its effect on the plaintiff. Asked why the publication appalled and distressed him, he said:– 'I can think of nothing more ugly, more horrible in this life than to be called an informer. It has a peculiarly nauseating effect in Irish life. It was totally untrue.' Not only was he not cross-examined to suggest that this was not a reasonable reaction on his part to the publication but, on the contrary, it was suggested to him that placards with similar wording on an occasion prior to the publication by the defendants (one bearing the words 'Quisling Berry – helped Britain to gaol Irish political prisoners') were such that he would find them extremely offensive and hurtful.

Reading the charge of the learned trial judge, it is clear that he expected the jury to answer the second question in the affirmative. When charging on the question of damages he said:– 'Prima facie, as a matter of reasonable inference, to suggest of a person of his standing, a reputable public servant, that he is an informer would lower his reputation.' He then goes on to tell the jury in so many words that there was no evidence to indicate that his reputation was in fact lowered. I think the jury may have been misled into thinking that, because there was no evidence that his reputation was in fact lowered by the publication, the publication was not defamatory *of him*; although nowhere in the charge or in the evidence is there any indication that a view could be taken of the publication which was not defamatory.

A publication is defamatory of a person if it injures or tends to injure his good reputation in the minds of right-thinking people. That is a simple definition but the difficulty is to discover what is meant by 'right-thinking people.' It does not mean all such people but only some such people, perhaps even only one, because if a plaintiff loses the respect for his reputation of some or even one right-thinking person he suffers some injury. I put the matter squarely to Mr. Micks and he said that some right-thinking people might regard a publication as defamatory and other right-thinking people might come to a diametrically opposite conclusion.

This plaintiff, and plaintiffs in like cases, are up against a difficulty in this regard and the higher the reputation the greater the difficulty. Friends of the plaintiff, if asked what effect the publication had on their minds, would probably say something like this:– 'Oh, that scurrilous placard; of course I didn't believe a word of it, your reputation is still good with me.' But there must be others whom he may not even know but who know him on account of his exalted position and good repute, who, taking the publication to be true, would toss him from his high pedestal and look on him with disgust and contempt; for what they would believe of him is that, having in his official capacity information about militant Republicans in England, he went out of his way for private reasons, it being no part of his official duty to do so, to supply information to the British police authorities about such persons resulting in their being jailed in England.

An aspect of what the plaintiff was alleged to have done (*viz.*, 'helped jail republicans in England') arose during the argument in this Court but not at the trial; I had not thought of it at the start. It could be put in this way. It is the policy of the Government to regard the actions of militant republicans in England as being injurious to the welfare of this country and, therefore, assistance given to jail them was consistent with this policy. To allow a jury to find that an allegation that the plaintiff had given such assistance was defamatory would amount to approval of the acts of militant republicans in England and to disapproval of the Government's policy.

Logically, this is correct, but I cannot accept it entirely. While I accept that it is Government policy to regard the acts of militant republicans in England as being injurious to the welfare of the State, I am not aware that the Government counsels or encourages or approves either officials or private citizens to supply information to British police authorities with a view to having them jailed. I think it can fairly be inferred from the evidence given at the trial that no such information was ever supplied by the Department of Justice.

In this regard I think it is also relevant to refer to the Extradition Act, 1965. Under that Act if a warrant issued in England is brought here for endorsement and execution, and if the warrant is in respect of a political offence or an offence connected with a political offence, the person concerned shall not be handed over to the English police under the English warrant (See [1972] I.R. 36). In these circumstances the Minister for Justice has the power to direct that such an English warrant shall not be endorsed for execution here. Suppose a person had committed some act of a political nature for which he could be jailed in England. If before his arrest he escaped to and sought sanctuary in this country, he would not be handed over to the British police under an English warrant because of the Act of 1965.

It is my view that there must be many right-thinking persons who, although they do not approve of or positively disapprove of the acts of militant republicans in England, would regard the plaintiff with contempt if they believed that he had gone out of his way to supply information to the British police so as to have such persons jailed in England. It may be that one's views on matters of this sort are conditioned by one's up-bringing and education. The school sneak who, however justified, 'splits to the head' was regarded with contempt by all his fellows.

For the reasons stated, I would not allow the jury's answer to Question 2 to stand, and I would direct a new trial on damages only.

Mr. Micks argued before this Court the defence of qualified privilege, *viz.*, a fair and accurate photographic report of a matter of public interest. I do not see that this Court can do anything about the matter as it does not appear from the transcript that it was made an issue at the trial.

A person's good name deserves the special protection of the law: see Article 40, s. 3, of the Constitution. I do not think that the plaintiff's good name has received that protection.

1. Which judgment do you favour? Why?
2. Is a statement to be considered defamatory because of what right-thinking members of society *in fact* think or because of what they *ought* to think? *Cf. Quigley* v. *Creation Ltd.* [1971] I.R. 269 at 272 (Sup. Ct., *per* Walsh, J.).
3. How does the criterion 'right thinking members of society' differ from 'the reasonable man'?
4. Would it be defamatory now to say of a person that he was (a) 'a Provo' (b) 'a rabid Nationalist' (c) 'a Black Protestant' (d) 'an Orange Billy'? Or to say of a woman that she was raped or that her husband left her?
5. If you were faced now with facts similar to those of the *Berry* case how would you plead the case?
6. Do you think that the plaintiff's grievance in *Quigley's* case fitted easily within the scope of a defamation action? Do you consider that some other action might have been more appropriate?

Whether allegation of intolerance or bigotry capable of being a libel.

TEACY V. McKENNA

I.R. 4 C.L. 374 (1869)

The writ of Summons and Plaint complained that, 'before and at the time of the committing of the grievances hereinafter mentioned, the Plaintiff was a job coach and hotel proprietor, and carried on business as such at Caledon, in the county of Tyrone; and the Defendant falsely and maliciously printed and published of the Plaintiff, in a newspaper called the 'Northern Star,' the words following, that is to say:–

A BAD CASE

TO THE EDITOR OF THE 'NORTHERN STAR'

Sir, – Will you kindly permit me space in the columns of your truly patriotic journal, to make known to the public a case of gross intolerance which occurred in this village on last Sunday. The remains of all that was mortal of a Crimean veteran, who fought for his Queen and country, and received a wound thereby which was the cause of his death, being about to be interred, deceased's brother-in-law applied to Mr. William Teacy (meaning the Plaintiff), a Presbyterian in religion, and proprietor of the Caledon Arms hotel, for a hearse to convey the poor old soldier's lifeless body to interment; but will it be believed that this humane specimen of orthodox Presbyterianism (meaning the Plaintiff) refused to give his hearse, for no other reason than this, that the corpse was to be interred in a Roman Catholic burying ground, saying at the same time that he would give it free if deceased had been buried in Tynan, a Protestant burial ground. It is worthy of note, that before deceased's death, he abjured Protestantism and became a member of the Roman Catholic Church; and hence the only reason for his being so treated at his burial by his former master (meaning the Plaintiff); for deceased was servant to Teacy (meaning the Plaintiff) for a long length of time previous to his illness.

Caledon, 20th April, 1869

The Defendant meaning thereby that the Plaintiff, being a member of the Presbyterian Church, was so actuated by intolerance and bigotry towards the Roman Catholic religion, that he was guilty of the misconduct of refusing in the course of his business to hire a hearse, because it was intended for the conveyance of the remains of the deceased to a Roman Catholic burying ground; and the Plaintiff has, by a reason of the premises, been brought into disfavour and disrepute with his neighbour and customers, and has been greatly injured in his said trade and business; and the Plaintiff claims £500 damages.'

The Defendant pleaded, 'no libel', a denial of the defamatory sense imputed; and a special defence, setting out certain facts; and also demurred.

The Lord Chief Baron intimated that the Court had come to the conclusion, that this case must be tried, and that it occurred to them that it would be right to withhold any discussion of the document itself, as it should be submitted to a jury. It was enough that the Court are not prepared to decide that this document is not capable of a construction, in any reasonable sense, that would make it a libel.

Demurrer overruled

DEFAMATION ACT 1961
Part III Sections 14–28

PART III
Civil proceedings for defamation

14. – (1) In this Part –
'broadcast' has the same meaning as in the Wireless Telegraphy Act, 1926 (in this section referred to as the Act of 1926) and 'broadcasting' shall be construed accordingly;

'broadcasting station' has the same meaning as in the Act of 1926, as amended by the Broadcasting Authority Act, 1960;

'wireless telegraphy' has the same meaning as in the Act of 1926.

(2) Any reference in this Part to words shall be construed as including a reference to visual images, gestures and other methods of signifying meaning.

(3) Where words broadcast by means of wireless telegraphy are simultaneously transmitted by telegraph as defined by the Telegraph Act, 1863, in accordance with a licence granted by the Minister for Posts and Telegraphs, the provisions of this Part shall apply as if the transmission were broadcasting by means of wireless telegraphy.

15. – For the purposes of the law of libel and slander the broadcasting of words by means of wireless telegraphy shall be treated as publication in permanent from.

16. – Words spoken and published which impute unchastity or adultery to any woman or girl shall not require special damage to render them actionable.

17. – In any action for defamation, it shall be lawful for the defendant (after notice in writing of his intention so to do, duly given to the plaintiff at the time of filing or delivering the plea in the action) to give in evidence, in mitigation of damage, that he made or offered an apology to the plaintiff for such defamation before the commencement of the action, or as soon afterwards as he had an opportunity of doing so, in case the action shall have been commenced before there was an opportunity of making or offering such apology.

18. – (1) A fair and accurate report published in any newspaper or broadcast by means of wireless telegraphy as part of any programme or service provided by means of a broadcasting station within the State or in Northern Ireland of proceedings publicly heard before any court established by law and exercising judicial authority within the State or in Northern Ireland shall, if published or broadcast contemporaneously with such proceedings, be privileged.

(2)Nothing in subsection (1) of this section shall authorise the publication or broadcasting of any blasphemous or obscene matter.

19. – In an action for slander in respect of words calculated to disparage the plaintiff in any office, profession, calling, trade or business held or carried on by him at the time of the publication, it shall not be necessary to allege or prove special damage, whether or not the words are spoken of the plaintiff in the way of his office, profession, calling, trade or business.

21. – (1) A person who has published words alleged to be defamatory of another person may, if he claims that the words were published by him innocently in relation to that other person, make an offer of amends under this section, and in any such case –

(*a*) if the offer is accepted by the party aggrieved and is duly performed, no proceedings for libel or slander shall be taken or continued by that party against the person making the offer in respect of the publication in question (but without prejudice to any cause of action against any other person jointly responsible for that publication);

(*b*) if the offer is not accepted by the party aggrieved, then, except as otherwise provided by this section, it shall be a defence, in any proceedings by him for libel or slander against the person making the offer in respect of the publication in question, to prove that the words complained of were published by the defendant innocently in relation to the plaintiff and that the offer was made as soon as practicable after the defendant received notice that they were or might be defamatory of the plaintiff, and has not been withdrawn.

(2) An offer of amends under this section must be expressed to be made for the purposes of this section, and must be accompanied by an affidavit specifying the facts relied upon by the person making it to show that the words in question were published by him innocently in relation to the party aggrieved; and for the purposes of a defence under paragraph (*b*) of subsection (1) of this section no evidence, other than evidence of facts specified in the affidavit, shall be admissible on behalf of that person to prove that the words were so published.

(3) An offer of amends under this section shall be understood to mean an offer –

(*a*) in any case, to publish or join in the publication of a suitable correction of the words complained of, and a sufficient apology to the party aggrieved in respect of those words;

(*b*) where copies of a document or record containing the said words have been distributed by or with the knowledge of the person making the offer, to take such steps as are reasonably practicable on his part for notifying persons to whom copies have been so distributed that the words are alleged to be defamatory of the party aggrieved.

(4) Where an offer of amends under this section is accepted by the party aggrieved –

(*a*) any question as to the steps to be taken in fulfilment of the offer as so accepted shall, in default of agreement between the parties, he referred to and determined by the High Court or, if proceedings in respect of the publication in question have been taken in the Circuit Court, by the Circuit Court, and the decision of such Court thereon shall be final;

(*b*) the power of the court to make orders as to costs in proceedings by the party aggrieved against the person making the offer in respect of the publication in question, or in proceedings in respect of the offer under paragraph (*a*) of this subsection, shall include power to order the payment by the person making the offer to the party aggrieved of costs on an indemnity basis and any expenses reasonably incurred or to be incurred by that party in consequence of the publication in question;

and if no such proceedings as aforesaid are taken, the High Court may, upon application made by the party aggrieved, make any such order for the payment of such costs and expenses as aforesaid as could be made in such proceedings.

(5) For the purposes of this section words shall be treated as published by one person (in this subsection referred to as the publisher) innocently in relation to another person if, and only if, the following conditions are satisfied, that is to say –

    (*a*) that the publisher did not intend to publish them of and concerning that other person, and did not know of circumstances by virtue of which they might be understood to refer to him; or

    (*b*) that the words were not defamatory on the face of them, and the publisher did not know of circumstances by virtue of which they might be understood to be defamatory of that other person,

and in either case that the publisher exercised all reasonable care in relation to the publication; and any reference in this subsection to the publisher shall be construed as including a reference to any servant or agent of the publisher who was concerned with the contents of the publication.

(6) Paragraph (*b*) of subsection (1) of this section shall not apply where the party aggrieved proves that he has suffered special damage.

(7) Paragraph (*b*) of subsection (1) of this section shall not apply in relation to the publication by any person of words of which he is not the author unless he proves that the words were written by the author without malice.

22. – In an action for libel or slander in respect of words containing two or more distinct charges against the plaintiff, a defence of justification shall not fail by reason only that the truth of every charge is not proved, if the words not proved to be true do not materially injure the plaintiff's reputation having regard to the truth of the remaining charges.

23. – In an action for libel or slander in respect of words consisting partly of allegations of fact and partly of expression of opinion, a defence of fair comment shall not fail by reason only that the truth of every allegation of fact is not proved, if the expression of opinion is fair comment having regard to such of the facts alleged or referred to in the words complained of as are proved.

24. – (1) Subject to the provisions of this section, the publication in a newspaper or the broadcasting by means of wireless telegraphy as part of any programme or service provided by means of a broadcasting station within the State or in Northern Ireland of any such report or other matter as is mentioned in the Second Schedule to this Act shall be privileged unless the publication or broadcasting is proved to be made with malice.

(2) In an action for libel in respect of the publication or broadcasting of any such report or matter as is mentioned in Part II of the Second Schedule to this Act, the provisions of this section shall not be a defence if it is proved that the defendant has been requested by the plaintiff to publish in the newspaper in which the original publication was made or to broadcast from the broadcasting station from which the original broadcast was made, whichever is the case, a reasonable statement by way of explanation or contradiction, and has refused or neglected to do so, or has done so in a manner not adequate or not reasonable having regard to all the circumstances.

(3) Nothing in this section shall be construed as protecting the publication or broadcasting of any matter the publication or broadcasting of which is prohibited by law, or of any matter which is not a public concern and the publication or broadcast-

ing of which is not for the public benefit.

(4) Nothing in this section shall be construed as limiting or abridging any privilege subsisting (otherwise than by virtue of section 4 of the Law of Libel Amendment Act, 1888) immediately before the commencement of this Act.

25. – An agreement for indemnifying any person against civil liability for libel in respect of the publication of any matter shall not be unlawful unless at the time of the publication that person knows that the matter is defamatory, and does not reasonably believe there is a good defence to any action brought upon it.

26. – In any action for libel or slander the defendant may give evidence in mitigation of damages that the plaintiff has recovered damages, or has brought actions for damages, for libel or slander in respect of the publication of words to the same effect as the words on which the action is founded, or has received or agreed to receive compensation in respect of any such publication.

27. – (1) The proprietor of every newspaper having a place of business in the State shall, where such proprietor is not a company registered under the Companies Acts, 1908 to 1959, and is not required under the provisions of the Registration of Business Names Act, 1916, to be registered under that Act in respect of the business of carrying on such newspaper, be registered in the manner directed by that Act, and that Act shall apply to such proprietor in like manner as it applies to a firm or individual referred to in section 1 thereof.

(2) Every reference in the Registration of Business Names Act, 1916, to that Act shall be construed as a reference to that Act as extended by subsection (1) of this section.

(3) In this section 'newspaper' means any paper containing public news or observations thereon, or consisting wholly or mainly of advertisements, which is printed for sale and is published in the State either periodically or in parts or numbers at intervals not exceeding twenty-six days.

28. – Nothing in this Part shall affect the law relating to criminal libel.

SECOND SCHEDULE
STATEMENTS HAVING QUALIFIED PRIVILEGE

PART I
Statements privileged without Explanation or Contradiction

1. A fair and accurate report of any proceedings in public of a house of any legislature (including subordinate or federal legislatures) of any foreign sovereign State or any body which is part of such legislature or any body duly appointed by or under the legislature or executive of such State to hold a public inquiry on a matter of public importance.

2. A fair and accurate report of any proceedings in public of an international organization of which the State or the Government is a member or of any international conference to which the Government sends a representative.

3. A fair and accurate report of any proceedings in public of the International Court of Justice and any other judicial or arbitral tribunal deciding matters in dispute between States.

4. A fair and accurate report of any proceedings before a court (including a courtmartial) exercising jurisdiction under the law of any legislature (including subordinate or federal legislatures) of any foreign sovereign State.

5. A fair and accurate copy of or extract from any register kept in pursuance of any

law which is open to inspection by the public or of any other document which is required by law to be open to inspection by the public.

6. Any notice or advertisement published by or on the authority of any court in the State or in Northern Ireland or any Judge or officer of such a court.

PART II
Statements privileged subject to Explanation or Contradiction

1. A fair and accurate report of the findings or decision of any of the following associations, whether formed in the State or Northern Ireland, or of any committee or governing body thereof, that is to say:

(*a*)   an association for the purpose of promoting or encouraging the exercise of or interest in any art, science, religion or learning, and empowered by its constitution to exercise control over or adjudicate upon matters of interest or concern to the association or the actions or conduct of any persons subject to such control or adjudication;

(*b*)   an association for the purpose of promoting or safeguarding the interests of any trade, business, industry or profession or of the persons carrying on or engaged in any trade, business, industry or profession and empowered by its constitution to exercise control over or adjudicate upon matters connected with the trade, business, industry or profession or the actions or conduct of those persons;

(*c*)   an association for the purpose of promoting or safeguarding the interests of any game, sport or pastime, to the playing or exercise of which members of the public are invited or admitted, and empowered by its constitution to exercise control over or adjudicate upon persons connected with or taking part in the game, sport or pastime;

being a finding or decision relating to a person who is a member of or is subject by virtue of any contract to the control of the association.

2. A fair and accurate report of the proceedings at any public meeting held in the State or Northern Ireland, being a meeting *bona fide* and lawfully held for a lawful purpose and for the furtherance or discussion of any matter of public concern whether the admission to the meeting is general or restricted.

3. A fair and accurate report of the proceedings at any meeting or sitting of –

(*a*)   any local authority, or committee of a local authority or local authorities, and any corresponding authority, or committee thereof, in Northern Ireland;

(*b*)   any Judge or Justice acting otherwise than as a court exercising judicial authority and any corresponding person so acting in Northern Ireland;

(*c*)   any commission, tribunal, committee or person appointed, whether in the State or Northern Ireland, for the purposes of any inquiry under statutory authority;

(*d*)   any person appointed by a local authority to hold a local inquiry in pursuance of an Act of the Oireachtas and any person appointed by a corresponding authority in Northern Ireland to hold a local inquiry in pursuance of statutory authority;

(*e*)   any other tribunal, board, committee or body constituted by or under, and exercising functions under, statutory authority, whether in the State or Northern Ireland;

not being a meeting or sitting admission to which is not allowed to representatives of the press and other members of the public.

4. A fair and accurate report of the proceedings at a general meeting, whether in

the State or Northern Ireland, or any company or association constituted, registered or certified by or under statutory authority or incorporated by charter, not being, in the case of a company in the State, a private company within the meaning of the Companies Acts, 1908 to 1959, or, in the case of a company in Northern Ireland, a private company within the meaning of the statutes relating to companies for the time being in force therein.

5. A copy or fair and accurate report or summary of any notice or other matter issued for the information of the public by or on behalf of any Government department, local authority or the Commissioner of the Garda Síochána or by or on behalf of a corresponding department, authority or officer in Northern Ireland.

Notes and questions

Note that the Act does not constitute a code of defamation law. It makes no attempt to define generally what is defamatory, for example, nor does it spell out what constitutes fair comment or 'malice' in qualified privelege.

Note also that section 16 is confined to women and girls. Could a man or boy claim that the section is unconstitutional? What Articles of the Constitution are relevant?

When a plaintiff pleads an innuendo which he fails to prove can libel still be found? Fair comment.

FISHER V. NATION NEWSPAPER CO. AND ROONEY
[1901] 2 I.R. 465 (C.A.)

Holmes L.J.:

There was a period in legal history when the fate of litigation often depended upon questions similar to that discussed in this case. The system under which such questions were possible was for generations the glory of the special pleader and the despair of the law reformer. In the contest between them the former long held his own. Driven by successive statutes passed for the amendment of procedure, from position after position, he was always able to entrench himself in another hardly less formidable. At length a determined frontal attack all along the line proved more successful; and since the Judicature Acts and the Rules thereunder swept away altogether the old methods, and substituted for them a system, at once simple and sensible, an argument such as has been addressed to the Court in this case is rarely heard. Still it occasionally reappears to remind us of an earlier time, 'ere human statute purg'd the gentle weal.' Before referring to the pleadings and the course of the trial, I am led in consequence of the observations made respecting the jury by the leading counsel for the defendants to say a few words about the action in its general aspect. The plaintiff is a shipowner and merchant who has held several important positions both public and private in the town of Newry; and in January, 1899, he was a candidate for the office of Poor Law Guardian for the West Ward of the Newry Urban District. There is nothing in the evidence to show that either in public or private life he had allowed himself to be influenced by a sectarian or intolerant spirit or that by word of act he had shown himself a religious bigot. A short time before the election there was circulated in the constituency a document which in England or Scotland would be considered unique, and for which even in Ireland, where robuster methods of electioneering prevail, it would be difficult to find a precedent. It begins with the words, 'don't vote for Mr. Joseph Fisher, because this gentleman has been as intolerant and exclusive at the Workhouse Board, as Mr. John Quinn Henry.' I pass over some of the following paragraphs which, although very violently worded, might be regarded as more an attack upon the former Board as a whole than upon the plaintiff individually; and I come to this passage, 'Take the treatment recently meted out to Mr. Connolly, Veterinary Surgeon, by the bigotry of the Newry Guardians. Mr. McLoughlin applied with qualification far superior to any other for the last vacant mastership. He was rejected, not because he was disloyal or a politician, but because he was a Catholic. Mr. Fisher – the man who looks for your votes now – those votes he and his party tried to cheat you of – voted against Mr. McLoughlin. Vote against Mr. Fisher, as a protest against his own bigotry as well as that of the old Newry Guardians. Mr. Fisher is enriched by the toil of Catholic working-men. He wishes them to vote for him, that he may use his influence as a public man to keep his feet on the necks of Catholics and crush them down . . . Men and women of Newry, who have votes, are you going to sell your conscientious and religious convictions by voting for a man who, if he had the power, would trample your religion and you who belong to it in the dust? Don't sell your conscience and your honour for any filthy consideration or the hope of any passing little gain.' The plaintiff says that this publication for which the defendants are admitted to be responsible, did him harm; and accordingly he brought the present action. Now it is almost impossible to believe that if the case was to be tried by a jury of fair minded and impartial men, they could have avoided finding for the plaintiff and awarding him at least moderate damages, especially when it appeared that he had nothing to do with the appointment to the vacant mastership, and was not even a member of the Board at the time.

However tolerant juries may be of strong language used in the heat of a political struggle, there is a point beyond which such language ought not to go; and so far from there being any reason to think that the jurors in this case were prejudiced against the defendant, it will be seen, when I refer to their findings, that they did their duty with great caution and moderation. I am, therefore, bound to say that the censure that has been directed against them is entirely without warrant.

The statement of claim, as amended after defence, sets forth the above document broken up into separate portions, to most of which the pleader has attached by way of innuendo a particular meaning. It also contained another cause of action upon which the defendants obtained judgment, and to which it is unnecessary to refer. The defendants severed in their defences, and each of them pleaded that the words complained of are not a libel, that they do not bear or convey the alleged meaning, and that they are a fair comment on a matter of public interest. There are some verbal differences in the way in which each defendant states his defence; but there can be no doubt that if the language is to bear its only possible construction, the first and third defences are applied to the natural meaning of the words, not to the artificial meaning attached to them by the plaintiff's pleading.

The same observation may be made regarding an additional defence of privilege founded on interest and duty relied on by the Rev. Mr. Rooney, alone. Issue having been joined in the usual form, the action went to trial, and at the close of the plaintiff's as also of the defendants' case, Serjeant Dodd asked for a direction on the ground that the occasion was privileged and that the innuendoes were not proved.

The Judge having refused to accede to this requisition, put to the jury the following questions – 1. Were the publications complained of, or some of them, libels? 2. Did they bear the defamatory meanings imputed by the pleadings or some and which of them; 3. Was what was complained of honest fair comment on matters of public interest; and 5. Did the defendants act maliciously? The jury said in answer to the first question, 'Yes, one of the statements in the manifesto, viz. the two paragraphs respecting the candidature of McLoughlin'; and to the second, 'the jury considers the innuendoes all too strongly worded.' They also answered the third question in the

negative, and the fourth in the affirmative, and assessed damages at £50. It is
perfectly clear that the Judge conveyed to the jury, and that the jury thoroughly
understood that the first, third and fourth questions related to the words in the sense
which the jury thought they ought to bear. He says that he at first suggested that the
innuendoes only tended to embarrass the jury, and that the question referring to
them might be struck out; but on Serjeant Dodd objecting, he left it with the others.

Serjeant Dodd's point, urged then and now, is that the plaintiff was bound to prove
the innuendoes, and that having failed to do so, it became immaterial whether the
publication as a whole or any part of it was a libel. The Judge, however, thought
differently, and gave judgment for the plaintiff for £50, with costs as to the portion of
the document specified by the jury, giving at the same time judgment for the
defendants, with costs as to the residue of the action.

The question in this appeal is whether he was right. Now it is to be noted that what
was tried were the issues raised by the defendants themselves, that these issues were
tried fully and exhaustively, and that if the defendants had notice when the statement
of claim was delivered of the course that would be taken by the Judge at the trial, they
could not have made a better or a different case. It has been suggested that they might
have pleaded justification; but if they had, it would not have affected the result, as
they have got judgement on every part of the publication except on that which it is
admitted they could not justify. Besides, in a case of this kind, the defendants have,
under the defence of fair comment, all the advantages both as regards admission of
evidence and consideration by the jury which they would have under a defence of
justification.

It is further to be observed that the course taken by Mr. Justice Gibson would
admittedly have been the proper and legal course in England, and that it is not
unusual in this country. I have it from Mr. Justice Gibson himself, that during his
twelve years of judicial experience he has always acted without objection on the view
that the innuendoes are severable from the libel. I have acted on the same view
during the ten years in which I was engaged in trying jury cases; and I think I could
name other Judges who have done so. Therefore, there has been a trial in which every
possible issue was raised and determined, and which was conducted in a manner that
has received the approbation of all the English and some Irish Judges, with the result
of establishing that the plaintiff had a good cause of action, entitling him to recover
£50 as damages. Is the law regulating legal procedure, after all our reforms still so
imperfect, as to oblige a Court of Justice under such circumstances, not merely to
refuse the plaintiff the damages awarded him, but also to give a judgment against him
for the costs incurred by his adversary in resisting his righteous claim? Mr. Justice
Gibson says in his report that as there was no surprise, an amendment could be made,
but that no amendment was asked for, nor did he think it necessary. This Court also
thinks that it was not necessary, but if it were, I wish to say for myself, that I am of
opinion that we ought now to either make it, or to deal with the case as if it had been
made. An amendment by the terms of the Rule may be allowed at any stage of the
case; and I think it may be reasonably made after trial by either the Divisional Court,
or by the Court of Appeal, for the purpose of bringing the pleadings into conformity
with the issues actually tried by the Judge and jury, when both parties were prepared
for, and neither taken by surprise, at such trial. 'Now, I think, it is a well established
principle,' said Bowen, L. J., in *Cropper* v. *Smith* (24 Ch. D. 305), 'that the object of
Courts is to decide the rights of the parties, and not to punish them for mistakes they
make in the conduct of their cases by deciding otherwise than in accordance with
their rights. Speaking for myself, and in conformity with what I have heard laid down
by the other Division of the Court of Appeal, and by myself as a member of it, I know

of no error or mistake which, if not fraudulent or intended to over-reach, the Court ought not to correct if it can be done without injustice to the other party.'

Although in that case the majority of the Court declined on special grounds to make the amendment needed, I have never heard the soundness of the observations of Lord Justice Bowen doubted. I am glad, however, to say that in this case it is not necessary to amend; and my reasons for this conclusion can be stated with brevity.

I do not propose to discuss the authorities, beginning with Croke, Elizabeth, that have been quoted in the argument. I am satisfied that the English Judges in *Watkin* v. *Hall* (L. R. 3 Q.B. 396), and the Irish Judges in *Hort* v. *Reade* (I. R. 7 C. L. 551), were perfectly familiar with the rules of pleading in their respective countries before the Common Law Procedure Acts of 1852 and 1853, respectively. I assume that these cases show that previous to those enactments the law in both England and Ireland was that the pleader was bound by his innuendo, and that if it was rejected, he could not rely on any other defamatory sense which the words might bear. I also assume that by reason of a difference between the 61st section of the Act of 1852, and the 65th section of the Act of 1853, the former law was not altered in Ireland by the Irish Statute, although the English Act allowed a plaintiff who failed to sustain his innuendo to show that the language complained of bore another defamatory meaning.

In this state of things, the Judicature Acts were passed for England in 1873 and 1875, and for Ireland in 1877. These Statutes provide for the making of Rules for regulating the pleading, practice and procedure in the High Court of Justice and Court of Appeal; and the 65th section of the Irish Statute enacts that, 'in making, altering or annulling Rules of Court in pursuance of this Act, regard shall be had to the Rules of Court for the time being in force under the provisions of the Supreme Court of Judicature Act, 1873 and 1875, so as that the pleading, practice and procedure in the High Court of Justice and Court of Appeal, respectively, constituted by this Act, shall so far as may be practicable and convenient, having regard to the difference of the laws and circumstances of the two countries, be the same as the pleading, practice and procedure in the High Court of Justice and Court of Appeal, respectively, constituted by the said Acts.'

It was evidently the intention that pleading, practice and procedure were to be recast by means of Rules of Court, and that the new point of departure was to be taken advantage of for the purpose of making the systems in the two countries uniform.

Accordingly Rules of Court have been made in England and Ireland which so far as pleading is concerned are identical. That the Legislature believes that the intention of the Judicature Acts had been carried out is shown by the repeal of large portions of the previous statutes regulating pleading and procedure, including the 61st section of the Act of 1852, and the 65th section of the Act of 1853, already referred to. By the rule now in force in both countries, a pleading shall only contain a statement in a summary form of the material facts on which the party pleading relies for his claim or defence. Where, in an action of libel the words complained of are per se innocent, it is no doubt material to set forth by way of innuendo or otherwise some fact or facts showing that as used by the defendant they bear a defamatory meaning; but where the words are in themselves capable of a defamatory sense, an innuendo is immaterial as part of the cause of action, although it may occasionally serve a useful collateral purpose, as, for example, the aggravation of damages. it seems, therefore, to me to be clear that the defendant is at liberty to defend himself by reference to the language he actually used in the sense which it will be determined by the jury it ought to bear, and not in some artificial and fanciful sense invented by the pleader. With all respect for the opinions of an earlier race of lawyers, I think that it might often lead to injustice to oblige a defendant to state his case on whether a jury will accept the pleader's innuendo. It is but fair and reasonable that he should be permitted to show that his publication was not a libel, and to justify or excuse it in its natural sense. But whether fair and reasonable or the contrary, I am of opinion that this is now the law, and I have already shown that the defendants have availed themselves of it in the present action. It follows, that if this is the right of a defendant, a plaintiff may also claim to have the words complained of considered apart from the innuendo. This is the English practice, and if it is not yet definitely settled in this country, it is time that it should be.

It is said that in an unreported case – *Godfrey* v. *Walsh* (1885, unreported) – the Exchequer Division held in 1885 that the old rule was still to be applied in Ireland; and the Queen's Bench Division seems to have considered itself bound thereby. I have no means of knowing the reasons for that decision. It was given, I believe, on an interlocutory motion, and I can understand that it may have rested on grounds that would not apply after judgment. But in any case it cannot relieve this Court from considering the matter for itself.

It would be a subject for regret if the defendants in this action had been placed at a disadvantage by reason of a misapprehension on the part of their counsel as to the mode of pleading. But I have shown that there is no ground for this idea, the defendants having had the benefit of every defence consistent with admitted facts.

For these reasons the Court holds that the appeal be allowed, that the judgment of Mr. Justice Gibson be restored, and that the defendants pay the costs in the Divisional Court and costs of appeal.

Privileged Communications.

HARTERY V. WELLTRADE (MIDDLE EAST) LTD. AND HURLEY
Unreptd. H. Ct. 15 March 1978 (1973/3067 P)

Finlay P.:
This is an action brought by the plaintiff against the first-named defendant for damages for wrongful dismissal and for breach of a contract of employment and against both defendants for defamation in respect of alleged defamatory matter published, in writing, by the second-named defendant as agent of the first-named defendant and orally spoken by the second-named defendant as agent of the first-named defendant.

[Having found against the plaintiff on the matter of wrongful dismissal and breach of the contract of employment, **Finlay P.** went on to examine the case based on defamation.]

Defamation Claim
There remains the second claim by the plaintiff for defamation and it arises on the following facts and events which occurred after those which I have already recited.

The plaintiff's employment was terminated by a letter written by Mr. Sutherland as Managing Director of Welltrade (Middle East) Limited to the plaintiff which was headed 'private and confidential' and dated 2 October 1973. The contents of that letter are of importance in regard to the claim for defamation and I quote it.

'Dear Mr. Hartery

Due to the fact that we have been unable to make contact with you during the past few days, this letter is to serve as notice of the company's intent to instantly dismiss you. This decision is regrettably reached due to your apparent lack of concern over the company affairs in Libya. You were specifically given instructions by both myself and Tony James as to what was required of you in connection with the accounts you were responsible for in Tripoli.

You have blatantly ignored both our requests for your assistance which we are not prepared to tolerate. As far as your affairs in Libya are concerned we are prepared to assist in arranging to dispose of your car and to return any personal effects to England which would of course be at your expense. A final account will be prepared in due course reconciling your account and the return ticket in your possession should be immediately returned to the Shannon office.

Yours faithfully
for Welltrade (Middle East) Limited
M.S. Sutherland
Managing Director'

Upon receipt of that letter the plaintiff brought it to Messrs D.G. O'Donovan, Solicitors, for legal advice and they on the 5th October 1973 wrote the following letter to Mr. Sutherland.

'Dear sir,

Your letter of the 2nd instant addressed to our client Mr. Hartery has been referred to us. The letter purports to instantly dismiss our client from the employment of your firm. The reason that you did not make contact with our client during the past few days was due to the fact that he is on holidays. He is entitled to his holidays by virtue of his contract with the company.

Our client rejects the allegations made about him in your letter. Would you be good enough to supply us with particulars of his apparent lack of concern over the company's "affairs in Libya".

Our client denies that he has blatantly ignored either requests or instructions from persons in authority over him in the firm and we would also be interested to receive particulars of any occasion when he behaved in this fashion.

Our client rejects entirely the allegations made against him which, if true, would entitle the company to dismiss him from service.

'Our client has a contract of employment and he has instructed us to commence proceedings against the company for damages for wrongful dismissal.

Part of these damages will include a claim by him in respect of the trans-shipping of his possessions back to Ireland.

Our client is entitled under the contract to have his personal effects, belongings and possessions shipped to Libya and back at the expense of the company.

In addition as a separate heading of claim our client might be entitled to redundancy.

Furthermore our client is entitled under the circumstances surrounding this matter to cash in lieu of notice.

Our client had given us detailed particulars of certain events which surround the accounts which we can if requested go into which can be substantiated by the Revenue Department of Libya to whom copies of this correspondence may be addressed.'

The contents of that letter received by Mr. Sutherland were immediately communicated to the defendant, Mr. Hurley, Chairman of the defendant company. Upon receipt of that letter he, Mr. Hurley, attempted as a matter of urgency to make contact with his Solicitors, Messrs Arthur Cox and Company, and with Mr. Bergin of that firm who was the partner dealing with his business. Being unable to contact Mr. Bergin by telephone he then contacted Mr. Joseph Dundon, Solicitor, of Limerick. He discussed the letter and its contents with Mr. Dundon and then wrote two letters, one to the Secretary of the Incorporated Law Society of Ireland and the other to Chief Superintendent Lambe of the Garda Síochána Headquarters, William Street, Limerick. The first letter he sent by registered post marked 'private and confidential' and the second letter he delivered by hand interviewing Inspector Creighton in the absence of Chief Superintendent Lambe. In the course of that interview he asked Inspector Creighton to open and read the letter and then, in effect, verbally confirmed its contents and asked Inspector Creighton to investigate the matter. The relevant contents of the two letters are identical and form the basis of the claim for defamation. They are as follows:

'Dear Sir,
Attached is a copy of a letter we have today received from D.G. O'Donovan and Company, 13 William Street, Limerick.

We are most disturbed by the last paragraph of this letter and fear that the activities of D.G. O'Donovan and Company and their client Mr. Hartery will cause irreparable damage to our company unless we pay them the money which they demand. Resulting from his employment with our company Mr. Hartery is in possession of certain secret company information. This information could possibly be extremely damaging to our company if disclosed to an outside source. The last paragraph of the letter sent by D.G. O'Donovan and Company Solicitors is interpreted by us to mean as follows:
(a) A threat has been made to disclose secret company information unless we pay money to Mr. Hartery.
(b) That both Mr. Hartery and D.G. O'Donovan and Company have conspired together to use this threat as a means of obtaining money from our company.
(c) They are demanding money with menaces.
(d) That the letter is an attempt to intimidate our company into paying money under threat of disclosure of certain activities which they deem to be unlawful. In other words we interpret this as blackmail.'

The letter to the Secretary of the Incorporated Law Society then contained an assertion that the company would lose as much as £200,000 sterling if this threat were carried out and asked that the letter be accepted as a formal complaint against Messrs. D.G. O'Donovan and Company. The letter to the Garda Síochána simply asked that the letter be accepted as a formal complaint against Messrs D.G. O'Donovan and Company and Mr. Hartery and a request was made that what was, in the opinion of the writer, a criminal offence should be investigated and that steps should be taken to prevent its continuance.

After the writing of this letter the defendant, Mr. Hurley, apparently again contacted his permanent or usual Solicitors, Messrs Cox and Company, and Mr. Niall McLoughlin of that firm who gave evidence before me, upon seeing the letters which had passed between Messrs O'Donovan and Company and the defendant company and between Mr. Hurley and the Incorporated Law Society and the Garda Síochána, telephoned Mr. O'Donovan. He received an assurance from Mr. O'Donovan that there was no intention to threaten any form of disclosure and, in effect, that the interpretation put upon the letter by Mr. Hurley was incorrect. He accepted that assurance as one colleague to another and advised his client to accept it also. As a result letters were written by Messrs Cox and Company to the Incorporated Law Society and to Messrs O'Donovan and Company in effect withdrawing the complaint and apoligising for it and by the defendant, Mr. Hurley, to the Chief Superintendent Lambe also withdrawing the complaint and apologising for it.

The defendant, Mr. Hurley, who wrote this letter himself had not taken the decision to dismiss Mr. Hartery, he did not know and had no previous dealings with Messrs O'Donovan and Company, Solicitors, and he had met Mr. Hartery shortly on two or three occasions only and had no particular dealings with him. He was, of course, kept informed of the general situation of the defendant company and would have been aware of the tax problems in Libya and their consequences.

In short the plaintiff's submission with regard to the defamation firstly was that the letter written by Messrs O'Donovan and Company was incapable of the interpretation which Mr. Hurley placed upon it and that to have put that interpretation on it was a form of recklessness which destroyed any question of privilege in communication between him, Mr. Hurley, the Incorporated Law Society or the Garda Síochána. Secondly, in relation to the communication to the Incorporated Law Society it was alleged that there was no privilege in respect of any communication between Mr. Hurley and that Society concerning Mr. Hartery over whom the Society had no power or authority. Thirdly, it was contended that the entire concept or project of seeking action in respect of the Solicitors concerned through the Incorporated Law Society and in respect of both the Solicitors and Mr. Hartery through the Garda Síochána to prevent communication to the Libyan Tax Authorities was an irresponsible attempt to misuse the functions of both those bodies which itself constituted evidence of malice. Lastly, it was contended that the terms of both letters and the allegations made in them were so excessive as to indicate malice. Evidence was given before me of the institution of proceedings by Messrs O'Donovan and Company against the defendants for damages for defamation and the settlement of those proceedings by the payment of a sum of money to a charity, the payment of costs and an unreserved apology and withdrawal. The consent however, was explicitly without prejudice to any other proceedings against the defendants or either of them relating to any of the matters arising. I am quite satisfied that the existence of that consent and the settlement by the defendants of that action cannot be a material factor which I am entitled to consider in relation to the present claim for defamation.

I am quite satisfied on the evidence and in particular, having heard Mr. Hurley who impressed me as a witness, that he, bona fide, interpreted the letter from Messrs O'Donovan and Company as a threat on behalf of Mr. Hartery and presumably on his instructions to make disclosures to the Libyan Tax Authorities which would be extremely damaging to his company. Whilst he accepted the advice of Mr. McLoughlin as his Solicitor that this was not the intention of the writer of the letter and whilst, at his instructions, the withdrawals and apologies which I have referred to were subsequently made, one of the more astonishing features of the case in evidence before me was that no explanation was given to me as to what the meaning of the last paragraph of Messrs O'Donovan and Company's letter was. I am satisfied that read as Mr. Hurley must have read this letter against the background of the Libyan tax problems of his company, the phrase 'detailed particulars of certain events which surround the accounts' must have had a sinister meaning so that the statement of the possibility of copies of the correspondence being addressed to the Revenue Department of Libya must have had an extremely threatening aspect. In the absence of the very considerable and undoubted standing and repute of the Solicitors for the plaintiff being personally guaranteed to Mr. Hurley, as it subsequently was by Mr. McLoughlin, I am satisfied that this letter was plainly open to the interpretation which Mr. Hurley put upon it and that he reached a conclusion as to its meaning which was quite bona fide and was not in any sense reckless.

He stated in evidence, and I accept, that he considered in discussion with Mr. Dundon the possibility of taking proceedings for an injunction instead of complaining to the Incorporated Law Society and the Gards Síochána respectively. He rejected that course upon the basis which again I believe he, bona fide, accepted that to institute proceedings for an injunction with the necessary publicity attached to them would be to do as much damage as would be achieved by the carrying out of what he conceived to be the threat contained in the letter.

I am satisfied that the defendant, Mr. Hurley, was not motivated by any anger or ill will against either the plaintiff or the Solicitors who wrote the letter on his behalf but that the letters were written by him in the bona fide belief that he had an interest and a duty on behalf of his company to communicate the matters contained in them to the Law Society and to the Garda Síochána respectively.

Furthermore I am satisfied that once he had interpreted the letter in the way which he did and in which, in my view, was a possible or reasonable interpretation in the particular circumstances then existing the allegations made in his letters to the Society and to the Garda Síochána do not bear any aspect of reckless exaggeration which would constitute evidence of malice.

I have separately considered the point made that in relation to the letter to the Incorporated Law Society the mention of Mr. Hartery went outside any privilege that existed. It does not seem to me possible to make a complaint in the particular circumstances in which the defendant was seeking to make a complaint against a Solicitor without identifying with great particularity precisely what he did. In order to identify that with particularity it was necessary to mention the name of the client on whose behalf he was writing and the relationship between that client and the defendant company. The mention of the name, therefore, of Mr. Hartery in the letter to the Incorporated Law Society was, in my view, covered by the privilege in the communication between the defendant and that body. On these grounds I am satisfied that the plaintiff's claim for defamation must also fail.

Question

Does this case hold that a *bona fide* belief that one has an interest and a duty to make a communication is sufficient to give rise to the defence of qualified privilege?

If the accusation is accidently overheard is the privileged occasion lost?
DEMPSEY V. WALL & CO. LTD. & RYAN
78 I.L.T.R. 73 (Circuit Ct., 1943)

The plaintiff had been the stenographer of the defendant company, and the defendant Ryan was the managing director thereof. The plaintiff was dismissed by the defendant Ryan on the 12th January 1943. The plaintiff alleged that shortly after her dismissal the defendant Ryan said to her: 'Are you taking away the company's property? You are stealing the property of the firm. It is a serious offence to steal the firm's property. If you do not hurry and get out, I will get the police to put you off the premises.' It was alleged that those words were heard by two employees named Hopkins and Murphy; and that the said words were intended by the defendant Ryan and understood by the said Hopkins and Murphy to mean that the plaintiff had been guilty of the criminal offence of stealing or attempting to steal the property of the first named defendants.

The defendants by their defence denied that Ryan spoke the words complained of, or that those words bore the meanings alleged or were capable of any defamatory meaning and contended that if they were spoken they were spoken on a privileged occasion without malice and in the honest belief that they were true.

Judge Shannon:

I find that there is no substantial difference between the words complained of by the plaintiff and admitted to by the defendant: Ryan in the witness-box. But I am coerced into finding that the plaintiff did take this notebook out of her drawer and place it on Miss Hopkin's desk and that Ryan thought that the plaintiff did intend to take this book to her solicitor. The plaintiff had lost her temper and intended to take this notebook which was of no value to either the plaintiff or the defendants. I believe that Ryan thought that the plaintiff was going to take this book. The defendant Ryan in his reference to the police may have used strong language, but that does not necessarily destroy the privilege. It can be construed as an indication of his state of mind. I find that Ryan believed that the plaintiff was about to steal this note-book.

I have a difficulty in reconciling *White* v. *J. & F. Stone Lighting and Radio Limited* 55 T. L. R. 949 with *Toogood* v. *Spyring* (1834) 1 Cr. M. and R. 181. McKinnon, L.J., in *White's Case*, at page 950, applies *Toogood* v. *Spyring*, but the head-note in *White's Case*, in my opinion, is not correct when it states that 'the person to whom it' (the communication complained of) 'is made must be a person other than the plaintiff.' The defendant Ryan in this case had a duty to make the communication to the plaintiff, but not to Hopkins and Murphy. But their presence does not destroy the privilege. Ryan's state of mind helps to establish privilege: he had a duty to make the statement complained of and the plaintiff had an interest in receiving it. I therefore dismiss the action with costs.

Question

Are you clear on the *ratio* of this decision?

Malice will destroy Qualified Privilege. What is malice?

COLEMAN V. KEANES LTD.
[1946] Ir. Jur. Rep. 5

Appeal by the defendants from an award of damages for slander made by the Circuit Court of Justice sitting at Dublin.

The plaintiff called to the defendants' retail shop in Moore Street, Dublin, on the afternoon of 25th September, 1943, for the purpose of purchasing some bacon. There were about fourteen customers in the shop at the time and two assistants. The plaintiff discussed with one of the assistants the price of a piece of bacon which was on the counter, but did not buy it, and the assistant left the plaintiff to serve another customer. When the assistant returned he failed to see the piece of bacon, which, it appeared, had been removed by another assistant to a different part of the counter, and he ran out after the plaintiff, who had just left the shop, and, catching her by the arm in the public street, asked her, in the presence of others, what she had taken and requested her to return to the shop. The plaintiff denied having taken anything, showed the assistant her empty bag, and returned with him to the shop. She subsequently issued a civil bill against the defendants claiming £100 damages for defamation, and the Circuit Court Judge made an award with costs, in her favour. From this order the defendants appealed to the High Court.

E. M. Wood, for the plaintiff.

E. S. FitzSimon, for the defendants: The words complained of were spoken *bona fide* and without malice, upon a privileged occasion, and are not actionable.

E. M. Wood in reply: In order to establish a claim of privilege the defendants must satisfy the Court that their servant acted from a proper motive, since malice, in the sense of an improper motive, destroys privilege. According to his own evidence the servant's only desire was to procure the recovery either of the bacon or of its money value and not to perform his civic duty of apprehending a suspected thief. This was an improper motive and destroys the claim of privilege.

Haugh, J.:

I take the law to be that if a person, who has reasonable grounds to believe that a crime has been committed, uses spoken words in the course of taking steps to apprehend the suspected criminal, the law protects him from actions for slander: *Fowler* v. *Homer*, 3 Camp. 294. It would be a hardship if a shopkeeper, who had good grounds to suspect a person of larceny, felt that his hands were so tied from following up his suspicions that, if he were wrong, he would be a victim of an action for damages.

In this case the words used clearly defamed the character of the plaintiff, and *prima facie*, she is entitled to have her good reputation repaired by an award of damages. The only answer to such a claim is that the occasion was one in which the law attaches privilege, either absolute or qualified, to the publication of the offending words. If the defendants' servant pursued the plaintiff for the purpose of ascertaining whether or not she had stolen the bacon from the shop, in pursuance of the duty imposed on all citizens to combat crime, then privilege would attach. His duty was no greater or less than that which would have been imposed on another customer in the shop who held the same suspicions. If, however, he availed of the circumstances created by what he considered to be her suspicious movements for the sole purpose of recovering the bacon, or its money value, then the position is different. Furthermore, though a person acts *bona fide*, he must have reasonable grounds or evidence before so acting. He must not immediately jump to a rash conclusion. In this case the defendants' servant was rather hasty, but I shall not decide the question on that ground.

On the whole, Mr. Wood is right when he says that if the defendants claim privilege they must satisfy the Court that in fact their servant was acting in pursuance of his duty as a citizen to bring a suspected thief to justice, in which event, the law will allow the defence of privilege to prevail. In this case, however, on his own evidence, the servant acted, not for the purpose of arrest or prosecution, but either to get the bacon back or its money value, that is to say, he was not exercising his civic duty, and hence I hold that the plea of privilege cannot prevail and that the plaintiff is entitled to succeed. I will not disturb the Circuit Judge's award of damages.

Questions

1. Is the decision a fair one, in your opinion?
2. If you were a shopkeeper, how, in the light of this decision, would you advise your employees to act if they thought that a customer had left the shop with a product for which he had not paid?

Qualified Privilege. What constitutes malice?

KIRKWOOD HACKETT V. TIERNEY
[1952] I. R. 185 (Sup. Ct.)

O'Byrne J.:

This is an action for damages for slander. The plaintiff is a student of University College, Dublin, and the defendant is President of the said College. The words complained of are alleged to have been spoken in the President's room in the said College at an interview on the 15th October, 1948, at which there were present the plaintiff, the defendant and Mr. Augustine J. O'Connell, Secretary and Bursar of the said College. The learned trial Judge ruled that the occasion upon which the words were alleged to have been spoken, was a privileged occasion and the jury found that the words were spoken, that they were defamatory in imputing that the plaintiff had committed the criminal offence of obtaining money by false pretences, that the defendant had not an honest belief in the truth of the words, and that the words were spoken and published maliciously and the jury assessed damages at the sum of £750. Judgment was entered for the plaintiff for this amount and for the costs of the action.

Against the judgment so entered, the defendant appeals on the ground that there was no evidence of malice and that the trial Judge, having ruled that the occasion was privileged, should have directed the jury to find for the defendant. The plaintiff has served a cross-notice of appeal in which he alleges that the trial Judge misdirected himself in law in ruling that the occasion was privileged and he asks that the said ruling should be set aside by this Court.

I propose to deal, first, with the question whether the trial Judge was right in ruling that the occasion, upon which the words were spoken, was a privileged occasion. The test for determining whether privilege exists was stated by me in this Court in my judgment in *Reilly* v. *Gill and Others* (85 I. L. T. R. 165) in the following words:–

'It is settled law that an occasion is privileged when the person who makes the communication has an interest or a duty to make it to the person to whom he does, in fact, make it and the person to whom he makes it has a corresponding interest or duty to receive it. The duty referred to need not be a legal duty: it may be a moral or social duty and of perfect or imperfect obligation. The doctrine or privilege is based partly upon matters of presumption and partly upon considerations of the convenience and welfare of society as a whole. Where a communication is made by some person in the discharge of some social or moral duty or on the ground of a common interest between the party making and the party receiving it, it is inexpedient that the person making the communication should be answerable in damages, where he acts in good faith and honestly believes in the truth of the communication. Want of good faith on the part of the person making the communication destroys the privilege and, on this question, the belief or state of mind of such person is of paramount importance. The question, however, as to whether the occasion is privileged depends on the admitted or proved facts in each particular case and does not depend upon the state of mind of the person making the communication.'

In the letter, dated the 4th February, 1947, from the British Ministry of Education to the plaintiff, informing him that an award had been made to him for the purpose of pursuing a full-time course in architecture and obtaining a degree, it is stated that 'the award is tenable subject to satisfactory attendance, conduct and progress, until the end of Autumn Term, 1951, or for such shorter period as may be determined in the light of the reports of your progress.' This clearly contemplated a five-year course and made no allowance for the plaintiff losing a year by failing to pass the annual examination or otherwise. The payment drafts were forwarded, not to the plaintiff, but to the College, and in the letter to the College it is stated that 'In the case of students whose progress and conduct have not been satisfactory, the payment of drafts should not be issued but should be returned to the Ministry together with a statement of the reasons for non-issue.'

Instead of returning the draft in accordance with the foregoing direction the Registrar of the College, at the direction of the defendant, wrote to the Ministry for directions. This letter was written on the 12th October, 1948, and no reply had been received on the 15th October when plaintiff obtained the draft from an official in the office of the College.

As soon as the withdrawal of the draft was reported to him, the defendant directed that the plaintiff should come to his office as soon as possible, and the plaintiff did come to the President's office the same afternoon. He was accompanied by Mr. O'Connell, the Secretary and Bursar of the College, who attended at the request of the defendant. It was at this meeting that the defamatory words were spoken and the publication, relied upon by the plaintiff, was the publication to Mr. O'Connell. It now becomes necessary to consider the position of the defendant and of Mr. O'Connell and their respective rights and duties with reference to the subject-matter of the discussion, viz., the circumstances in which the draft was taken from the College and the steps which should be taken with a view to its recovery.

The defendant is the President of the College and, under the Charter, he is the head and chief officer of the College. The Charter provides that the correspondence of the College is to be conducted under his direction and it is further provided that the President shall exercise a constant supervision over all departments of the College and shall direct his particular attention to the maintenance of order and discipline in the College.

Mr. O'Connell was Secretary and Bursar of the College. It was part of his duty, under the Charter, to take general charge of the buildings and the property of the College, to act as Secretary to the Governing Body and its Committees and to carry out all such directions, in respect of administrative matters, as he might receive from the President. The Charter further provides that he shall observe due secrecy with respect to all official matters and that he shall sign a declaration that he will perform the duties prescribed for him.

In view of the functions so assigned I am of opinion that it was not only the right but that it was the duty, of the President to make full inquiry into the circumstances in which the draft was removed from the College and with reference to the steps which should be taken with a view to having the draft returned to the custody of the College. The words were spoken in the course of this inquiry and were, in my opinion, germane to the inquiry.

Had Mr. O'Connell a corresponding duty, or interest, in receiving the communication? In my opinion he clearly had. The draft had been sent to, and was in the custody of the College and the College, as custodian, had a special property therein. Under the Charter, Mr. O'Connell was bound to take general charge of all the property of the College, including the said draft, and he was bound to carry out the directions of the President in respect of administrative matters. In my view, Mr. O'Connell had a special interest and duty in connection with the draft. As the custodian of the property of the College the draft had been removed from his custody and it was his duty, under the Charter, to take such steps as the President might direct with a view to its recovery. For this purpose it was clearly his right to receive the fullest information as to the circumstances in which the draft had been removed.

It was contended that the communication should have been made, if at all, to the Registrar of the College, who had conducted the correspondence with the Ministry of Education. In my opinion, there is no substance in this contention. Under the Statute, the functions of the Registrar are mainly, if not altogether, academic and he is bound, under the direction of the President, to carry on the correspondence of the College, but only in so far as it relates to academic matters. Correspondence between the College and the Ministry of Education, with reference to the scheme and the position of students thereunder, may well have been regarded as purely academic; but, when the draft was improperly removed from the College, the circumstances in which it was removed and the steps to be taken with a view to its recovery were, in my opinion, strictly administrative matters, in connection with which the President properly called on the services of the Secretary and Bursar.

It is, however, contended that no person is entitled to claim privilege in respect of alleged defamatory words unless he admits that the words were spoken and that, inasmuch as the defendant denied the speaking of the words, he was not entitled to a ruling that the occasion was privileged. There is a strange absence of authority on this matter and this absence of authority is relied upon by both parties in support of their respective contentions.

In my opinion, the plaintiff's contention is not well-founded. The question whether an occasion is privileged depends upon the admitted or proved circumstances surrounding the alleged communication and I see no reason, in principle or on authority, for limiting this to cases in which the defendant admits the speaking of the words.

The plaintiff strongly relied upon a passage in the judgment of Lord Bramwell in the case of *Capital and Counties Bank* v. *Henty* (7 App. Cas. 741). The passage occurs at the end of the judgment (at pp. 793 and 794) and is as follows:– 'If I am wrong in the above, and if the inference, or an inference, to be drawn from the words used is the imputation of insolvency to the plaintiffs, and if the action is otherwise maintainable, I think there is no defence on the ground of privilege. I think that that follows from the defendants' own contention. They say that they did not believe the plaintiffs to be insolvent, and had no intention to say so, and that if that is the inference to be drawn from their language, their language is wrong. But they have no privilege to use wrong language. They have only a right to say what they believe. It may be by mistake that they have said what they do not believe, but for that mistake they are liable.'

It will be seen that in the foregoing passage, the learned Lord is not purporting to consider or deal with the question whether the occasion was privileged. He is dealing with a case where the defendant speaks defamatory words regarding the plaintiff and does not believe in the truth of the charge. He says that 'they have only a right to say what they believe.' I take this to mean, not that the occasion was not privileged, but that the communication was not privileged and that it was not privileged because the making of a false and defamatory charge, without believing in its truth, is clear evidence of malice. The imaginary case with which Lord Bramwell is dealing differs fundamentally from the present case in which it is clear from the evidence of the defendant that he did believe in the truth of the charge and there is no evidence to the contrary.

Various cases were put to counsel in the course of the argument showing the inconvenience, and possible injustice, which would be involved in yielding to the argument of the plaintiff's counsel. Take the following: defamatory words are alleged to have been spoken by a married woman with reference to a former servant and to a prospective employer who has applied to her for a character. It is a classic example of privileged occasion. The lady's husband is sued for his wife's tort. He was not present at the interview and does not know what happened. His wife denies having spoken the words attributed to her. Is the husband, in such circumstances, to be deprived of the plea of privilege so as to throw upon the plaintiff the onus of proving malice? To deprive him of relying on such plea seems to me to be opposed to the whole basis of the law of privilege and would limit the defence, in such a case, in a manner in which, so far, it has not been limited.

So far I have dealt with the case on the basis that there was a categorical denial of the speaking of the words complained of. That is not the present case.

It is true that in portions of his evidence the defendant does emphatically deny having used the words attributed to him; but it would be unreal to concentrate on these portions of his evidence without regard to the remainder.

He prefaces his evidence by saying that he does not pretend to have an accurate verbal recollection of everything that was said. He points out that he had no idea for a month after the interview that any serious consequences were likely to arise and that, therefore, his recollection at best dates from a month after the interview. In his account of the interview he says that he explained to the plaintiff that a rather serious mistake had been made in the College office which might involve the College in some difficulty with the British Ministry of Education and that he went on to point out in a friendly, but serious, way that the defendant's action in taking the draft might easily have a serious construction put upon it. He says he never used the words 'You took that draft under false pretences': but he says that he would not like to swear positively that he did not say that the plaintiff might possibly be accused of having taken the draft under false pretences. Later on, he says that he was not prepared to swear that he did not use the words, 'false pretences,' in warning the plaintiff that a serious view might possibly be taken of his action; but he says that he did not accuse him of having taken the draft under false pretences. Later he is asked (Q. 1164):– 'And you may have used in some context, but not the context alleged, the words, "false pretences"?' Answer:– 'I could not swear that I had not used them.' There are many other answers to the same effect and I am of opinion that on the defendant's evidence alone, it would be fairly open to the jury to find, as a fact, that the defendant did speak the words complained of or words to, substantially, the same effect. That is the reason that I consider the present case far removed from the simple case where a defendant swears that he did not speak the words and yet claims privilege for them.

For all these reasons I am of the opinion that the learned trial Judge was right in his ruling that the occasion was privileged. The question then arises whether there was evidence, proper to be submitted to the jury, that the defendant was actuated by malice – that is, malice in fact.

Malice may be defined as a wrong or improper motive or feeling existing in the mind of the defendant at the time of the publication and actuating that publication. It is not sufficient to show that the defendant acted rashly, improvidently or stupidly so long as he acted in good faith. It must be shown that he acted from an indirect and improper motive. The state of mind of the defendant is the cardinal consideration and the point of time at which that state of mind is to be ascertained, is the moment when the words are spoken and published.

There is no suggestion of any ill-will or enmity existing between the plaintiff and the defendant prior to the 15th October, 1948. The defendant had met the plaintiff on only two occasions prior to the said date and on these occasions the relations between them seem to have been most friendly.

In this case a number of matters, some of them rather trivial, are relied upon as evidence of malice. In such a case I am of opinion that the proper method of considering the evidence is that laid down by Lord Porter in delivering the opinion of the House of Lords in *Turner* v. *Metro-Goldwyn-Mayer Pictures, Ltd.* ([1950] W. N. 83). Lord Porter says (at p. 84):– 'The onus of establishing the existence of malice was on the plaintiff. Each piece of evidence must be regarded separately, and, even if there were several instances where a favourable attitude was shown, one case tending to establish malice would be sufficient evidence on which a jury could find for the plaintiff. If, however, on a careful analysis of each particular instance of alleged malice, the result was to leave the mind in doubt, that piece of evidence was valueless as an instance of malice, whether it stood alone or was combined with a number of similar instances.'

Applying the foregoing principle, which I consider to be sound in law, it is clear that you cannot get evidence of malice from a number of items of evidence, no one of which is, in itself, evidence of malice.

It is alleged that, prior to the interview of the 15th October, at which the defamatory words were spoken, the defendant had not made any, or sufficient, inquiry into the circumstances. There is no substance in this allegation. Prior to the interview, the defendant had received reports from Miss McLoughlin, secretary to the President and Registrar of the College, and from the Secretary, Mr. O'Connell. The defendant was personally aware of the position of the plaintiff in the College and knew that, under the arrangement with the Ministry of Education, he was not entitled to the draft. Indeed, the latter point was scarcely denied by the plaintiff in his evidence. He admits that he had had an interview, on the morning of the 15th October, with Professor Downes, Professor of Architecture, and that the latter told him that he did not think he (the plaintiff) could get another supplemental examination and that the Professor also told him that the regulations precluded the plaintiff from going on to the third year. The plaintiff, according to his own evidence, thereupon said to Professor Downes:– 'This looks like I will lose the grant.' Later on, he says that the Professor told him that he would not get a supplemental, that he knew he could not go on to the third year and that he stood to lose the grant. In view of all this I am of opinion that there is no foundation for the allegation that the defendant did not make sufficient inquiry before the interview. It follows that there is no evidence of malice arising from the failure to make such inquiry.

It is said that the defendant was aggressive and that he exhibited annoyance at the interview. The only reason for the allegation of aggressiveness seems to be that, according to the plaintiff's evidence, the defendant was walking up and down during the interview, though counsel for the plaintiff did not rely on this matter during the argument before us. It may be that the defendant was annoyed and there seems to have been reasonable grounds for such annoyance. I am, however, clearly of opinion that this is not evidence of malice within the meaning of the authorities.

It is also alleged that the plaintiff was given no opportunity to explain his action. It is to be noted that the plaintiff, in his evidence, did not make any complaint on this ground and it also appears from the evidence, and the findings, that most of the words, and all the material words, spoken by the defendant were in the nature of questions to which the plaintiff was called on to reply, if he could do so. Having regard to the plaintiff's own evidence it is difficult to see what explanation he could offer. In my view, there is no substance in this allegation.

It is also contended that the refusal of the defendant to give the plaintiff an interview and to discuss his financial position is evidence of malice. If, as seems to be the fact, the plaintiff was not entitled to remove the draft, it is difficult to see why the demand for its return should be complicated by discussions as to the plaintiff's financial position. This may have been a matter for anxious consideration by the plaintiff; but I cannot see how the refusal of the defendant to embark upon such inquiry is evidence of malice. The plaintiff undoubtedly sought an interview with the defendant on the 19th October; but, according to the plaintiff's evidence (Qq. 243 and 246), this request was in the form of a demand. It is not surprising that such a *demand* from a student to the President of the College was refused.

The plaintiff further contends that the defendant's denial of the speaking of the words complained of shows that the words were spoken from some indirect and improper motive and is evidence of malice. I have already dealt with this matter in considering the question of privilege. There was a denial by the defendant of the precise words attributed to him, but the defendant does not deny speaking words which are substantially to the same effect and which would certainly bear the defamatory meaning of which the plaintiff complains. Having regard to the entire of the defendant's testimony, I am satisfied that it does not contain any evidence of malice on the ground alleged.

In the course of his evidence the plaintiff swore that, at the interview of the 15th October, the defendant stated that, if the draft were not returned, the defendant would have to review the plaintiff's position in the University. It is alleged that this was a threat of expulsion and is evidence of malice. I cannot accept this contention. What could be more proper than a consideration and review of the plaintiff's position in the College in view of what had taken place?

The plaintiff also relies upon the fact that Mr. O'Connell interviewed the manager of the plaintiff's Bank on the morning of the 16th October. Assuming that this interview took place with the concurrence, or on the direction, of the defendant (of which there is considerable doubt) I fail to see how it is any evidence of malice. At the interview of the 15th October, the plaintiff agreed to get the draft back and, in his letter written on the morning of the 16th October to Miss McLoughlin, the plaintiff suggested that the Ministry of Education should be notified so that payment of the draft could be stopped. In approaching the Bank, Mr. O'Connell was trying to assist the plaintiff in his efforts to get the draft back and this course was much less drastic than that suggested by the plaintiff in his letter to Miss McLoughlin. I do not understand how it can be suggested that this is any evidence of malice.

In support of his contention that there was evidence of malice, the plaintiff mainly relied upon certain letters written by or on behalf of the defendant.

The first letter is one of the 18th October, 1948, from the Registrar of the College to the Ministry of Education, informing them about the taking of the draft from the College and that the plaintiff had undertaken to recover the draft and hand it back to the College, but had so far failed to do so. It is alleged that this is not a true statement of the facts. In my view, the letter contains a bald statement of the facts and is true in every particular.

The next letter to which it is necessary to refer is one of the 27th October, from the Ministry of Education to the Registrar of the College, stating that the award to the plaintiff would be continued for the current term and requesting that a special report, with the recommendation of the School, should be forwarded to the Ministry at the end of the term. The plaintiff complains that the contents of this letter were not communicated to him. I know of no reason why this should have been done. The Ministry was seeking a confidential report with reference to the position and progress of the plaintiff and the whole matter was obviously one of confidence between the Ministry and the College.

In reply to the foregoing, the Registrar wrote to the Ministry a letter, dated the

29th October. In this letter the Registrar sets out the position of the plaintiff in the College and does so with strict accuracy. I can see no ground of objection to this letter and know of no reason why its contents should have been communicated to the plaintiff.

The letter upon which most reliance was placed by the plaintiff was a letter, dated the 11th February, 1949, from the defendant to the Ministry of Education. This was written in reply to a letter from the Ministry to the Registrar of the College, dated the 26th January, 1949. That letter is to the following effect:–

'I write with reference to the award under the Further Education and Training Scheme held by Mr. Kirkwood Hackett who has been studying architecture at University College.

'Mr. Hackett's award was suspended following his examination failures in the Summer and Autumn Terms, 1948.

'As you will know, it is not the Ministry's normal policy to continue an award after an examination failure, unless there are extenuating circumstances to account for it or it is felt that the failure does not indicate the student's real ability. I should be glad to know whether, in the light of the work which this student has done during the Autumn Term last and the first part of the present term, you are prepared to make a special recommendation on his behalf for the continuation of his award. If you are prepared to make such a recommendation, would you also say by what date this student is now expected to complete his course for the qualification of A.R.I.B.A.'

Before considering the reply to that letter it is material to state that this action had been instituted by originating summons issued on the 7th January, 1949.

The defendant's letter of the 11th February, 1949, is as follows:–

'Dear Sir,

'Please accept my apologies for the delay in answering your enquiry of the 26th January, addressed to the Registrar.

'The case of Mr. W. B. Kirkwood Hackett has been rendered singularly difficult by his own recent actions. As you are aware he has failed twice in his Second Architecture in the subject of Archaeology. He applied for, and was given, permission to re-attend lectures in this subject, but has not done so. Until he has completed this subject, at his Second Architecture, regulations forbid his proceeding with lectures for his Third Year. Although he should have been aware of this regulation he came to the College office, signed a form, and paid for his Third Architecture Course; and at the same time, withdrew your pay order for £134 6s. 8d. which was intended to cover that Course. As soon as my attention was drawn to his action, I interviewed Mr. Hackett and requested him to arrange for the return of the pay order to the College pending your decision as to whether or not he should be permitted to draw it. This he undertook, but failed to do. Some time later I was informed that he proposed to take a slander action against me, his allegation being that I had stated, in the presence of the Secretary of the College, that he had got his grant from you under false pretences. In due course a summons for alleged slander arrived, and the case is still pending. Beyond a complete and absolute denial of this allegation I do not propose to comment on Mr. Hackett's conduct as the matter is *sub judice*.

'Mr. Hackett's summons was accompanied by another from a student also enjoying a grant from you, Mr. Liam D. Graham. This latter summons was issued against University College for alleged breach of contract. Mr. Graham had failed very badly in his First Agricultural Science Examination and did not present himself for a supplemental, and had been informed that he could no longer be accepted as a student of the College. Both these summonses were served by the same solicitor.'

It is contended that this letter shows pique, bad temper and malice on the part of the defendant. The greater portion of that letter consists of a statement of facts and it has not been suggested that these facts have been stated otherwise than with strict accuracy. I agree that it shows a certain amount of pique and, possibly, bad temper. To what is that due? It seems clear from the history of the case and the contents of the letter, that it is due to the two actions which had been instituted against the defendant.

As I have already stated, in considering the question of the existence or absence of malice, the cardinal consideration is the state of the defendant's mind and the point of time at which that state of mind is to be ascertained, is the moment when the words were spoken. Proceeding on this basis, can it be said that the foregoing letter is evidence of malice that is, evidence from which a jury could be entitled to find, as a fact, that when he spoke the words complained of, the defendant was actuated by some wrong improper or indirect motive? In my opinion, it certainly is not. A period of almost four months had elapsed between the speaking of the words and the writing of the letter and many things had happened in the meantime, including, in particular, the institution of this action. It is not sufficient that the letter should be consistent with the existence of such a motive. To enable the plaintiff to succeed, the letter must be more consistent with the existence of such a motive than with its absence, and, having regard to the lapse of time and the various events that happened in the interval I am of opinion that it is not more consistent with the existence of such a motive, so as to constitute evidence of malice.

Other matters of a trivial nature were mentioned and relied upon; but I do not consider it necessary to deal with them in detail.

In the result, I am of opinion that there was no evidence to justify the jury in holding that the words were spoken and published maliciously and that accordingly the answer to the fifth question should be set aside.

In reply to the fourth question the jury found that the defendant had not an honest belief in the truth of the words spoken by him. The absence of an honest belief in the truth of the words is clear evidence of malice and, if this finding stood, the finding of malice should also stand. In my opinion, it cannot stand. In charging the jury the trial Judge told them that the onus of proof on this matter rested on the defendant. This direction was clearly wrong. The onus of proof rested upon the plaintiff and the plaintiff produced no evidence to discharge that onus. Accordingly the answer by the jury to this question must be set aside.

For all these reasons I am of opinion that the judgment entered for the plaintiff should be set aside and that judgment should be entered for the defendant.

Murnaghan and **Haugh JJ.** agreed with **Byrne J. Maguire C.J.** and **Black J.** dissented. **Black J.** in particular was willing to uphold the jury's finding for the plaintiff on the grounds that there was evidence of malice on the part of the defendants.

Chapter 15

MALICIOUS PROSECUTION, MALICIOUS CIVIL PRO-CEEDINGS AND THE RIGHT TO PRIVACY

Introduction

The law has faced some difficulties in attempting to protect people against being wrongfully exposed to legal proceedings, whether of a criminal or a civil nature, whilst at the same time encouraging persons to bring criminals to justice and to protect their legal rights through recourse to legal proceedings. If, the moment a defendant is acquitted, he may turn around and bring an action against those who prosecuted him, '[t]here would, indeed, be an end of the criminal justice of the country . . .' (*Kelly* v. *Midland Great Western Ry. of Ireland Co.* I.R. 7 C.L. 8, at 16 (Q.B., *per* Whiteside, C.J., 1872)). Similarly, to allow a successful defendant in civil proceedings to pursue the unsuccessful plaintiff might multiply legal proceedings unnecessarily.

The courts have tried to strike a balance between these competing interests in the actions for malicious prosecution and malicious civil proceedings.

1. *MALICIOUS PROSECUTION*

KELLY V. MIDLAND GREAT WESTERN RAILWAY OF IRELAND CO.
I.R. 7 C.L. 8 (Q.B., 1872).

The plaintiff had been employed by the defendant company as a foreman porter, his duty being to charge for extra luggage and to give receipts for the sums received by him on that account. A passenger wrote to the manager of the company, accusing the plaintiff of having charged and received double the amount for which he had given a receipt. The matter was put in the hands of the company's solicitor, who had the passenger brought up from the country and who took down his statement in writing. The solicitor swore (in subsequent proceedings by the plaintiff for malicious prosecu-tion) that he 'sifted [the passenger] closely as to the facts; that he appeared to be very intelligent, and that his answers were satisfactory; that he (the solicitor) believed his statement, and, therefore, directed information to be prepared . . .' The plaintiff was subsequently arrested. In his criminal trial, he was acquitted, although the passenger and his wife swore to the truth of their accusation. In civil proceedings brought by the plaintiff against the company, the company's application for a nonsuit was rejected, and the jury found for the plaintiff, awarding him £200. The defendants sought to have the verdict set aside on the grounds (*inter alia*) that the plaintiff had failed to prove the absence of probable cause and that the defendants had established its existence, and that there was no evidence of malice in the conduct of the defendants.

Whiteside C.J.:

. . . What is the foundation of this form of action, and what is necessary to be established by the Plaintiff? Two things; first, that there was an absence of reason-able or probable cause, and secondly, that the prosecution was malicious. We do not desire to increase the difficulties a Plaintiff may have in establishing his case where he has been acquitted; and on the other hand, we do not intend to deprive Defendants of the protection which the law wisely throws around them when they have instituted a prosecution for which they had reasonable and probable cause. Now, what are the facts of the particular case? [The Chief Justice stated the facts and the evidence given upon the trial.] It was unfortunate that the Plaintiff was arrested on Saturday night, when he could have been summoned on Monday morning; for, when a case of this kind comes before a jury they immediately look to see if there is anything like hardship or oppression in it, and I have upon my notes the following question asked by a juror: 'Why did you get a warrant, instead of summoning him?' However, it is only fair to Mr. Ward to state that he procured the warrant in consequence of a warning he had received from a policeman.

The question now is, whether there was reasonable and probable cause for the prosecution, and whether I was bound at the trial to do what the counsel for the Defendants asked me to do? I am of opinion that I was, and my Brethren on the Bench concur with me in thinking so.

I may here be permitted to refer to two cases that show very clearly the mistake that is sometimes committed by those who entertain the notion that the moment a man is acquitted he may turn round and bring an action against those who prosecuted him. There would, indeed, be an end of the criminal justice of the country if that course of conduct were permitted. In *Perryman* v. *Lister* L.R.3 Ex. 197, it was held by the Courts of Exchequer and Exchequer Chamber that the action lay because the person who made the charge against another of stealing his rifle said that he acted only on hearsay information; and another person being named who had more accurate information, he did not apply to that person, but was satisfied to rely on the earlier statement made to him. It is the rule of law that the jury should find the facts on which the alleged reasonable and probable cause depends, but the Judge must determine whether the facts do constitute such reasonable and probable cause. Upon appeal to the House of Lords it was held that the decision of the Courts below was erroneous, and that there should be a new trial. The principle laid down by Lords Chelmsford and Colonsay as constituting the test in such cases is, whether the circumstances warranted a discreet man in instituting and following up the proceedings – not what impression the circumstances would make on the mind of a lawyer, but what effect they ought to have on the mind of another person, possibly not a lawyer. Taking that rational view of the matter, and applying it to this case, which, undoubtedly, is of great importance to the Plaintiff, it is, upon a review of the facts, impossible to say that a reasonable man would not have acted upon these facts, and that there was not reasonable cause for the prosecution. There is a more recent case of *Walker* v. *South-Eastern Railway Company* L.R. 5 C.P. 640, in which the decision was in favour of the Plaintiff, because there was not proof of any inquiry having been made into the facts, or any report having been made to the Defendants before the proceedings were instituted, so as to show that they undertook the prosecution with a knowledge of the testimony their servants were prepared to give, or after any such careful investigation as the attorney of the Company might have made. But in the case before us the solicitor had all the evidence laid before him, and he carefully examined it. We hold his testimony to be decisive, and, without giving any opinion on the other point in the case, we now decide that no proof was given by the Plaintiff of the absence of reasonable and probable cause, that there was abundant proof given by the Defendants of the existence of such cause, and that therefore we must disallow the cause shown, and order a new trial.

Rule absolute, upon the ground of misdirection.

Notes and Questions

1. Should the Court have taken into consideration the fact that 'the mind of a lawyer' *was* involved in this case, rather than merely that of 'a discreet man'?
2. 'Reasonable and probable cause' was defined by Hawkins J. in *Hicks* v. *Faulkner* 8 Q.B.D. 167, at 171 (1878) as:

   'an honest belief in the guilt of the accused based upon a full conviction, founded upon reasonable grounds, of the existence of a state of circumstances which, assuming them to be true, would lead an ordinary, prudent and cautious man, placed in the position of the accuser, to the conclusion that the person charged was probably guilty of the crime against him.'

   This definition was quoted with approval by Judge Fawsitt in *Dullaghan* v. *Hillen*, [1957] Ir. Jur. Rep. 10, at 17 (Circuit Ct., 1956).

DAVIDSON V. SMYTH
20 L. R. Ir. 326 (C. P. Div., 1887)

A house owned by the defendant's brother was set on fire. Some time afterwards the defendant was told by the plaintiff's sister that the plaintiff had been responsible. The defendant spoke to a police constable and encouraged the plaintiff's sister to make an information before a magistrate, charging the plaintiff with arson. The information was refused and the plaintiff sued the defendant for malicious prosecution. The trial judge refused to grant a direction on the basis that the plaintiff had failed to prove malice, and the absence of reasonable and probable cause. The jury found for the plaintiff £5 damages. The defendant appealed.

Murphy J.:

. . . The law applicable to actions of this character has been for a long time well settled. Still, there has been in many cases a great difficulty in applying the settled principles to the facts that appear in evidence; and in the great number of cases reported on the subject in Ireland and in England, from the time that *Panton* v. *Williams* 2 Q.B. 169 was decided to the present, a diversity of opinion will be found amongst Judges in relation to actions of this nature – as great as appears with respect to actions of any other particular class.

The law was very fully discussed in the case of *Abrath* v. *North-Eastern Railway Co.* 11 Q. B. Div. 440, S.C. on appeal, 11 App. Cas. 247. In addition to what Brett, M.R., says must be proved by plaintiff, it is also, of course, incumbent on him to prove that defendant was, in fact, active in advancing the prosecution.

[Counsel for the defendant] very forcibly contended before us that the evidence did not show that defendant was the prosecutor, and that he could not be held liable in an action because he urged the person who made the information to come before the Justice of the Peace and tell her story. I do not think, on looking at some of the cases cited, that we could yield to what was urged by counsel for defendant as to this part of the case; but I am clearly of opinion that plaintiff did not, by any reasonable evidence, establish what the Court of Appeal, in the case I have referred to, said the plaintiff should establish. It is said by counsel for the plaintiff, this was all for the jury; and they having found, as they did, on questions that should be submitted to them, there is an end of the matter. I entirely dissent from this view of the matter. Before the questions are submitted to the jury, there must be evidence given that, in the opinion of the Court, could reasonably, if believed, discharge the *onus* thrown on the plaintiff. If, on the evidence given in this case, the verdict against defendant could be sustained, the rule should be established that a party who had been prosecuted and acquitted must obtain a verdict in an action of this nature against any person who has taken part in instituting a prosecution against him. Did the sister of plaintiff make an information? Plaintiff's counsel, in the argument, did not, when asked, seem to me prepared to admit or deny that she did. A good deal was said as to her youth, lack of education, and simplicity. I think that, judging from the report, she exhibited no lack of shrewdness on the trial. It is absurd to suppose that a jury could be allowed, if the question were put to them, to say that she did not make the information. Defendant swore that he believed her statements; and where is there evidence to show that this belief was reckless or unreasonable? If he believed she was stating what was true, there was, in my opinion, reasonable and probable cause for instituting a prosecution against the plaintiff. If he were now to believe that she might state or swear, it might be fairly said that, having heard what she swore at the trial, he was indeed very rash in his belief. But it does not appear that he knew anything against her at the time she made the information.

What evidence did the plaintiff give to prove that defendant did not take reasonable care to inform himself of the true state of the case, and did not honestly believe the case placed before the magistrate? Where, or from whom was he to make inquiry to test the truth of the story told by plaintiff's sister? What is there to show that the belief he swears he entertained was not an honest one? The person to whom he gave credence, for which he is to be punished to an extent likely to be ruinous, is the witness to whose testimony plaintiff appeals as truthful, and establishing her case. Defendant knew that the house was destroyed by fire, that the fire was not accidental, that the plaintiff's sister, living in the next house, was a person most likely to know something about the transaction; and when she came forward to swear as she did, I think the course he adopted was reasonable and natural, and that plaintiff's complaint should be against her own sister, whom she could prosecute for perjury, and not against the defendant for having believed her. For these reasons, I am of the opinion that judgment should be entered for the defendant.

Harrison J.:

I have entertained considerable doubts in this case, but they are not sufficiently strong to justify me in differing from the judgment of my brother Murphy.

The *onus* of proving the absence of reasonable and probable cause for instituting the prosecution lay on the plaintiff. I think she failed in proving this, or in adducing evidence from which its absence could reasonably be inferred.

Notes and Questions

1. In an action for malicious prosecution it is essential that the proceedings against the plaintiff were unsuccessful, whether by reason of acquittal, discontinuance, nonsuit or quashing on appeal. Is this requirement justifiable? Is it too blunt a criterion? *Cf. McMahon & Binchy*, p. 377.

2. As well as proving absence of reasonable and probable cause, the plaintiff must prove malice on the part of the defendant. In *Dullaghan* v. *Hillen* [1957] Ir. Jur. Rep. 10, at 16 (Circuit Ct., 1956), Judge Fawsitt stated:

    'The word "maliciously" implies the doing of that which a person has no legal right to do and the doing of it in order to secure some object by means which are improper. An evil motive is required to complete an actionable wrong.'

    Is this test a sufficiently clear one? Note that the issue of malice is one for the jury subject to two provisions: the Court determines whether any particular motive is a proper or improper purpose for the proceedings in question, and it determines whether there is reasonable evidence of malice to go to the jury.

2. *MALICIOUS INSTITUTION OF CIVIL PROCEEDINGS*

Maliciously instituting criminal proceedings against another has long since been recognised as a tort where such proceedings have not been successful and where the person prosecuted has suffered damages. More interesting and perhaps of more relevance nowadays in view of the increasing number of malpractice suits and the damage which the mere threat of such an action can cause, particularly to professional persons, is the little known tort of maliciously maintaining civil proceedings.

DORENE LTD. AND DORENE SEPARATES LTD. V. SUEDES (IRELAND) LTD.
[1982] I.L.R.M. 126 (H. Ct., Costello J.)

Costello J.:

The defendant ('Suedes') owns a factory premises in Clanbrassil Street in Dublin. In the year 1979 the first-named plaintiffs ('Dorene') became interested in leasing it. Negotiations took place between the parties' estate agents and then their solicitors and one of the important issues in the case is whether these negotiations resulted in a concluded enforceable contract. Suedes was of the view that they did not and on 9 October 1979, told Dorene that it was no longer interested in granting a lease. Within a couple of days Dorene had instituted these proceedings for specific performance and registered a *lis pendens* against the property. Suedes immediately riposted by telling Dorene that if it went on with its action Suedes would claim damages as the proceedings were preventing a sale of its property to a third party. Dorene eventually (10 June 1980) abandoned its claim and discontinued the proceedings. But in the meantime pleadings had been filed and Suedes had counterclaimed damages for the wrongful institution and maintenance of the proceedings; its claim, in effect, being one for damages for the malicious abuse of the court's process. This is the claim which I now have to try.

Dorene's counsel have firstly argued that the defendant has no cause of action. He accepts that a claim for maliciously instituting criminal proceedings lies and also for maliciously instituting proceedings in bankruptcy and to wind up a company, but he says that no action lies for instituting a civil action (even one maliciously brought) because the basis of the tort is damage done to the public by the wrongful institution of proceedings and no such injury is suffered by a defendant in an ordinary inter partes action. It is alternatively urged that even if an action for maliciously instituting a claim for specific performance lies, on the facts of this case Suedes' claim is unsustainable. In the light of these submissions I think I should begin this judgment by considering whether the claim which Suedes now is maintaining is one recognised at law, and, if it is, the principles which apply to it.

I have no doubt that at common law an action for maliciously abusing the court's processes lay and that such an action is not limited to claims arising from the institution of a criminal prosecution and to bankruptcy and winding-up proceedings. It is an action which in fact has an ancient lineage. This has been traced in Holdsworth *History of English Law* (Vol. 8 at 385 et seq.), who points out that it was during the 16th and 17th centuries that the development of the action on the case gave rise to both the tort of malicious prosecution and the tort of malicious abuse of the process of the courts. The modern law on the subject is based on a decision of Holt CJ, given at the end of the 17th century in the much cited case of *Saville* v. *Roberts* (1698) I Ld. Raym. 374. It is perfectly clear that at that time an action on the case lay once damage was established, and that the basis of the action was damage to the complainant and not injury to the public. The principles established by *Saville* v. *Roberts* were summarised by Holdsworth as follows (at 391):

> 'It was in substance laid down that to succeed in this action, the plaintiff must show firstly one of three sorts of damage (damage to his 'fair name', damage to his property, damage to his person). Secondly he must show 'express malice and iniquity in prosecution'. Thirdly, the ground of action is not conspiracy but the damage and therefore the action will lie though the indictment be preferred by a single defendant only. Fourthly, no action will as a rule lie for bringing a civil action maliciously. Under the old law the amercement of the plaintiff . . . was, and under the modern law the costs awarded to a successful defendant are, held to be sufficient compensation. But, fifthly, the bringing of the action maliciously or a malicious use of the process of the court may given rise to an action on the case if

special damage be proved. Finally, it was assumed . . . on the action on the case that the proceedings must have terminated in the plaintiff's favour.'

There are many reported cases which show that the view urged on Dorene's behalf is incorrect. For example, a claim for damages for the malicious arrest of a ship is one which the law recognises (see: *In 'The Walter D. Wallet'* (1893) 202). In the course of his judgment the President of the Admiralty Division quoted with approval the words of Lord Campbell in *Churchill* v. *Siggers* 3 E and B 929, at 937: 'To put into force the process of law maliciously and without reasonable or probable cause is wrongful; and, if thereby another is prejudiced in property or person, there is that conjunction of injury and loss which is the foundation of an action on the case', and he held that this principle applied to the process of arrest permitted by the admiralty procedures. On the question of damages he pointed out 'No doubt in an action on the case for commencing or prosecuting an action, civil or criminal, maliciously and without reasonable probable cause, damages must be shown . . . But when a malicious action terminates in an arrest of a person, that wrongful detention must of necessity cause some damage to the person who loses his complete liberty . . . It appears to me that detention of a man's goods stands in this respect on the same footing as detention of his person. It cannot be supposed that no damage results to him from it'. Although no actual damage was established in that case, it was held that the plaintiffs had a good cause of action and nominal damages were awarded.

In more recent times it has been held by the House of Lords in England *Roy* v. *Prior* [1971] AC 470 that an action for damages may lie for maliciously applying for a bench warrant to compel the attendance of the witness at a trial.

The authorities, it seems to me, establish that a claim for damages at common law will lie for the institution or maintenance of a civil action if it can be shown that the action was instituted or maintained (a) without reasonable or probable cause (b) maliciously and (c) that the claimant has suffered special damage or that the impugned action was one which the law presumes will have caused the claimant damage. To support these conclusions I need only refer briefly to some of the authorities.

One of the leading cases on this branch of the law is the *Quartz Hill Gold Mining Company* v. *Eyre* (11 QBD 674), a case which helpfully illustrates the principles I have just mentioned. This was a claim for damages for the malicious presentation of a petition to wind-up a trading company. The trial judge dismissed the claim on the ground that even if an action for maliciously presenting a petition to wind-up a company could be maintained special damage must be shown to support it and none had been established by the plaintiffs. He also held that the plaintiff company had not proved want of reasonable and probable cause in the presentation of the petition. The Court of Appeal held that the trial judge was wrong in ordering a non suit. In the course of his judgment Brett MR said (at 683).

'The first question to which I shall refer is whether an action will lie for falsely and maliciously and without reasonable or probable cause presenting a petition to wind up a company, although the company has suffered no pecuniary damage besides the payment of extra costs. I entirely agree that even although civil proceedings are taken falsely and maliciously and without reasonable and probable cause, nevertheless no action will lie in respect of them, unless they produce some damage of which the law will take notice. The present action is in tort, and in order to support it the plaintiff company must have sustained some damage such as the law takes notice of. I assent to the objection taken by the defendant's counsel that the obligation to pay extra costs is not damage of that kind . . .

When we look back to the decisions of the judges of earlier times . . . we find it laid down by Holt CJ in *Saville* v. *Roberts* 1 Ld. Raym. 374, that there are three heads of damage which will support an action for malicious prosecution. There is damage to a man's person, as when he is taken into custody . . . To take away a man's liberty is damage of which the law will take notice. Secondly, to cause a man to be put to expense is damage of which the law will take notice. But, Holt, CJ, adds a third head of damage, and that is where a man's fair name and credit are injured.

The Master of the Rolls accepted that the obligation to pay 'extra costs' did not amount to special damage but none the less held that the plaintiff had a cause of action. He pointed out that an action for maliciously procuring an adjudication in bankruptcy lay even though no pecuniry loss is suffered because the proceedings injured the plaintiff 'in his fair name'. So, too an action lay for the malicious presentation of a winding-up petition as this would have damaged the company's credit. He then went on to point out that before ruling on a matter of law on the question of reasonable and probable cause the trial judge should have asked the jury to make findings on the disputed question of facts, and that on the question of malice there was evidence to go to the jury that the defendant in presenting the petition was actuated not by a desire to benefit the shareholders but by an indirect motive, namely, a wish to get back the money paid by him for the shares.

In agreeing with the Master of the Rolls Bowen, LJ pointed out that the reason why as a general rule a claim for maliciously instituting an action does not lie is that such an action will not ordinarily cause a defendant damage, but he went on (at 691):

'But although an action does not give rise to an action for malicious prosecution, in as much as it does not necessarily or naturally involve damage, there are legal proceedings which do necessarily and naturally involve damage; and when proceedings of that kind have been taken falsely and maliciously and without reasonable or probable cause, then, in as much as an injury has been done, the law gives a remedy.'

As each of the three essentials of the action for damages for the malicious abuse of civil proceedings, (a) want of reasonable or probable cause, (b) malice and (c) damage, fall to be considered in the present claim so I will say a little bit more about them before turning to the facts of the case.

(a) As to reasonable or probable cause, it is now well established that the test to be applied by the court is an objective test and so when considering a claim for damages based on a civil action the court must itself examine the facts and consider the legal principles applicable to them and decide whether there were reasonable grounds for instituting or maintaining the action which it is claimed was wrongfully instituted or maintained.

The objective nature of the test was adverted to in *Tims* v. *John Lewis and Co* [1951] 2 KB 459 and again referred to in *Tempest* v. *Snowden* [1952] 1 KB 130. The latter case was a case in which the plaintiff claimed damages for malicious prosecution. It was heard in the High Court in England by a judge sitting with a jury. The jury was asked certain questions by the trial judge and having answered them awarded the plaintiff damages. The appeal to the Court of Appeal turned on the correctness of the questions left to the jury. The appeal failed. In the course of their judgments both the Master of the Rolls and Denning, LJ, expressed views on the question of reasonable and probable cause in claims for damages for malicious prosecution. In the course of his judgment Denning LJ, said (at pp. 138–140):

'In my opinion in order to determine the question of reasonable and probable cause, the judge must first find out what were the facts as known to the prosecutor asking the jury to determine any dispute on the matter and then the judge must ask himself whether these facts amounted to reasonable and probable cause. In *Herniman* v. *Smith* [1938] AC 317, Lord Atkin put it quite clearly: "The facts upon which the prosecutor acted should be ascertained; in principle, other facts on which he did not act appear to be irrelevant. When the judge knows the facts operating on the prosecutor's mind, he must then decide whether they afford a reasonable or probable cause for prosecuting the accused". If these facts do afford reasonable and probable cause, then the prosecution is justified and it is not as a rule necessary for an inquiry to be made into the prosecution's belief. The state of his belief goes to malice but not, as a rule, to reasonable and probable cause. This view is supported by the observations of the Lord Chief Justice in the recent case of *Tims* v. *John Lewis and Co* [1951] 2 KB 459, 472; "The question whether there was a reasonable or probable cause is not, I think, to be determined subjectively, as has been suggested. It is a question which objectively the court has to decide on the evidence before it".

It is sometimes said that, in order to have a reasonable and probable cause there must be an honest belief in the guilt of the accused. But I don not think that should be regarded as a universal proposition applicable in all cases. It depends on the particular case . . .

I do not say of course that the prosecutor's belief can never come into the question of reasonable and probable cause. If the prosecutor believed that the man was innocent and preferred the charge simply as a means of inducing him to pay over money to him, there would be no reasonable and probable cause for the prosecution . . . Apart from exceptional cases . . . I think it is right to say that, when once the facts as known to the prosecutor are ascertained, the state of his belief going only to malice, and not to reasonable and probable cause.'

The point was again considered in *Abbott* v. *Refuge Assurance Co Ltd* [1962] 1 QB 432. This is of particular relevance because the defendant in those proceedings, like the plaintiff in the present proceedings, had obtained legal advice prior to the institution of the prosecution on which a claim for damages for malicious prosecution was subsequently based. The Court of Appeal held that even if counsel had advised that a prosecution lay this was not conclusive on the issue of reasonable and probable cause and the the court itself should consider whether counsel's advice was correct. (458).

(b) As to malice, it is to be borne in mind that even if it is shown that the proceedings had been instituted without reasonable or probable cause it is necessary to show in addition that they were instituted maliciously. Malice means the presence of some improper and wrongful motive. And an intent to use the legal process in question for some other than its legally appointed and appropriate purpose can amount to 'malice' in this connection (*Pike* v. *Waldrum* [1952] I Lloyds Report 431, 451 and *Salmond on Torts,* 16th Ed. at 427). Thus as was pointed out in the *Quartz Hill Case* if the motive in presenting a petition to wind-up a company is not a desire to benefit the shareholders but is an indirect one, namely, a wish to get back the money paid for shares (see p. 687), this could be evidence of 'malice'. Obviously where a plaintiff has obtained legal advice before instituting or pending legal proceedings the nature of that advice could be a highly material factor in considering whether he was motivated by an indirect or improper motive, as it may assist in showing whether the plaintiff was using the proceedings for some legally inappropriate purpose.

(c) Finally, as to proof of damage, once a claimant can show that he has suffered some special damages as a result of a civil action which had been brought or maintained without reasonable or probable grounds and maliciously then a cause of action has been established. In the absence of special damages a claimant will have have to show that the impugned action is one which the law regards as causing damage. In the present case Suedes say that the proceedings instituted by Dorene and the registration of a *lis pendens* caused it to lose a sale of its factory to the Industrial Development Authority and that this amounted to special damage. Only if I were to decide on the facts that these proceedings did not cause the loss would it be necessary to consider whether an action would lie in the circumstances of the present case in the absence of proof of special damage.

I now am in a position to consider the facts of this case and to apply to the facts the principles to which I have just referred. I propose to do so in the following way. Firstly, as the test as to reasonable and probable cause is an objective one what I have to consider is whether the negotiations between the parties resulted in a concluded agreement. If I decide they did then Suedes' claim fails as Dorene will have shown that it was entitled to institute proceedings for a specific performance. On the other hand, if there was no concluded agreement then Suedes will have established that the proceedings were instituted without reasonable and probable cause. I will then turn to the question of malice. Here I am concerned with Dorene's motive in (a) instituting and (b) maintaining its proceedings for specific performance. The resolution of the issues which here arises will turn not only on the inferences which can properly be drawn from admitted facts but to a considerable extent on whether I accept certain of the oral evidence tendered on Dorene's behalf. In addition I have had the benefit of a full discovery of all documents (including documents relating to legal advice which Dorene obtained) and these have been by agreement admitted in evidence without the necessity of formal proof. Finally, I must then consider Suedes' claim that Dorene's claim for specific performance and the registration of a *lis pendens* resulted in the loss of a sale to the IDA of the factory premises.

[Having examined the history of the negotiations **Costello J.** concluded that the Dorene offer to lease the premises was a conditional one throughout the negotiations up to the time Suedes called them off.]

Did Dorene (a) institute or (b) maintain the proceedings for specific performance maliciously?

On 11 October 1979 a consultation was held in the offices of Dorene's solicitors. Present at it were Mr Jack Vard, Dorene's managing director, Mr Alan Moore, the financial controller of the Dorene group of companies, Mr Stuart Harrington, Dorene's estate agent, the solicitor who had handled the draft lease on Dorene's behalf and a partner from his firm's litigation department. According to a note kept by Mr Moore of this consultation Dorene was advised that proceedings for specific performance be instituted and that 'on balance' Dorene's solicitor was optimistic of their outcome. The next day the summons was issued, and served a few days later. In the light of this advice it seems to me that there was no evidence to suggest that the proceedings were instituted with an indirect or improper motive. Dorene's wanted to get a lease of the Clanbrassil Street premises, and was advised that on balance it could obtain a court order to that effect. The solicitor who so advised gave evidence and explained his reasons for doing so. I need not detail them here. As I have indicated I think his advice was wrong, but it was quite obviously bona fide given. In fairness to him I think I should point out that I believe his recollection as to what transpired at the consultation is not entirely accurate and that he was far less definite as to Dorene's chances of success than his recollection now suggests. His lack of certainty is evidenced by the fact that in drafting the summons he made no reference to even an approximate date of the agreement which his clients were seeking to enforce. Furthermore, it seems to me that his opinion was based to a considerable extent on his clients' insistence that they had made an agreement with Suedes in the course of the negotiations rather than on his interpretation of the documents which he had perused. He had only had an opportunity to read the file of correspondence on the morning on which the consultation took place and he decided, as the situation was one of some urgency, to issue the proceedings in the absense of a detailed statement of these negotiations. But he requested Mr Harrington to write out a detailed statement and in writing to Suedes' solicitors shortly afterwards in explanation of the delay in filing a statement of claim he said that before counsel could settle the statement of claim 'we are obliged to take full statements from the people involved in negotiating the contract' and added, significantly, 'if we see any reason to reconsider our position when we have obtained the necessary detailed statements of fact then we shall do so'. I think he then believed that the written statements would supply the necessary evidence which was so obviously lacking in the documents which had been furnished to him.

But the finding that Dorene did not institute this action maliciously does not dispose of his case. Suedes' say that the situation was fundamentally altered when counsel's advice was obtained on 13 December. So, I must now turn to the developments which took place after the action was commenced.

[**Costello J.** found that, after proceedings had commenced, Senior Counsel advised on 13 December that Dorene could not succeed in its action. Some of the Dorene directors must have taken the decision to continue the proceedings, knowing that they could not succeed but knowing also that as long as they continued Suedes could not sell its premises. He continued:]

I think they decided to keep the proceedings going because of the pressure the existence of the action and the *lis pendens* would exert on Suedes. They decided at the same time to negotiate with Suedes and the IDA and to use the proceedings to assist their bargaining position. Once they accepted that their claim could not succeed they never intended that the action would go to a hearing. They decided, I believe, to discontinue it when the negotiations terminated one way or the other. They then firstly tried to get the premises from the IDA and obtain Suedes' agreement to waive its option to portion of the premises. When these negotiations failed, they tried to negotiate new terms of lease directly with Suedes. When these, in turn, failed, they dropped their claim for specific performance. And so from shortly after 13 December, Dorene was using these proceedings not for their appropriate purpose, namely to obtain an order for specific performance, but for a different purpose namely, to assist them in the negotiations to which I have referred. The directors' motives in continuing the actions were wrongful; they were actuated by malice in the legal sense of that term. It follows that as the proceedings were in addition maintained without reasonable and probable cause, Suedes' counterclaim will succeed if it can show that it suffered the sort of damage which will support an action for the malicious abuse of the court's procedures.

Proof of Damage

The IDA became interested in buying the freehold of Suedes' Clanbrassil Street factory in the month of September 1979. On 10 October an offer to purchase the premises was made in writing. It is to be noticed that this was made after Suedes' letter of termination of 9 October and it is clear that this letter had been written before Suedes had reached any binding agreement with the IDA. On 11 and again, and finally, on 12 October further letters with amended conditions were sent to Suedes. I am satisfied that but for the institution of these proceedings this offer would have been accepted by Suedes and Suedes would have sold the premises to the IDA, shortly after the receipt of the letter of 12 October. But Suedes as I have pointed out has no cause of action arising from the *institution* of the proceedings; and Suedes must show that the decision taken on or about 13 December to *maintain* the proceedings caused it damage.

Mr Horgan, of the IDA, was telephoned on several occasions on Dorene's behalf and told that Dorene had a good cause of action and that the IDA should withdraw their offer to Suedes. At about the same time Mr Reynolds of Suedes was ringing him and on 20 November he was told that Suedes wished to take up the IDA offer, that it had taken steps to have Dorene's claim struck out and that Mr Reynolds would keep in touch with him. On 11 December he again spoke to Mr Horgan and was told by him that the IDA were still interested in purchasing the property. As a result the letter which the IDA sent on 12 December came as a surprise to Mr Reynolds. But this letter was not a firm refusal to do business with Suedes; it quite clearly kept the door open. Dr Flynn a consultant acting for Suedes then contracted Mr Horgan on 14 December and was told by him that the IDA were still interested and that if there was no impediment the sale could go ahead. It has been urged on me that this conversation did not take place, but I am satisfied that this was the gist of Mr Horgan's comment to Dr Flynn. It is true that Mr Horgan was called as a witness on Suedes' behalf and that he was not questioned about this conversation. But Dr Flynn's testimony satisfies me that it took place and his evidence is consistent with the last sentence in the letter of 12 December in which the IDA suggests that Suedes should contact the IDA should the premises 'be on the market'. Thus the IDA had not irrevocably withdrawn at this time from the sale. This is borne out by the fact that a further letter was written on 17 January. This letter stated that the IDA was not prepared 'at this time' to consider the purchase but that 'if . . . at a future date you succeed in resolving the outstanding problems which affect the premises perhaps you would contact the IDA'. This letter indicates a continuing interest in the premises and would not have been written had the IDA lost interest in the premises at that time. After its receipt Dr Flynn got in touch with the IDA about it and was told 'look at the last paragraph'. A further and final letter was sent to Dr Flynn on 29 February. This time the tone was much more peremptory. The letter stated: 'I have now been instructed by the IDA to inform you that the IDA has had to make alternative arrangements and is no longer interested in purchasing the above premises'.

I have had the benefit of the evidence of Mr Walsh, the manager of the IDA's building division and of Mr Horgan, an industrial adviser in the IDA. Whilst neither witness could positively say what the decision of the board would have been had the proceedings been discontinued I am satisfied that certainly up to the end of December the IDA were still interested in buying the property but that this interest waned as the new year progressed, particularly as a new financial year had started and funds would have to be re-allocated to this purchase. On the balance of probabilities, therefore, I think that had Dorene discontinued the proceedings in the middle of December Suedes would have sold the premises to the IDA on the terms of the IDA's letter of 12 October.

Dorene's counsel have made the point that even if Suedes has shown that it could have sold the premises to the IDA in December, 1979 this loss is not caused by the maintenance by Dorene of the proceedings but by Suedes' failure to apply to have them struck out as vexatious, a course which was open to them according to the Supreme Court decision in *Flynn* v. *Buckley* [1980] I.R. 423, which decided that a *lis pendens* could be vacated in the absence of consent and a recent decision of mine – *Barry* v. *Buckley* [1981] I.R. 306 – in which I held that the court has an inherent jurisdiction to stay a specific performance action when it is clear that the claim cannot succeed. I do not think tha this argument defeats Suedes' claim. In 1979 the law as to the vacation of a *lis pendens* was not as the Supreme Court later said it was. Even if the defendant was minded to apply to have the *lis pendens* vacated it was aware from the affidavit sworn on the motion to dismiss the action for want of prosecution that Dorene's solicitor had sworn that he had advised that his clients had a good cause of action and that he based this advice not only on the correspondence but also on 'his instructions.' In such circumstances the prospect of showing that the proceedings were vexatious was very poor indeed.

I conclude therefore that Suedes has established that by deciding to maintain this action after the middle of December Dorene deprived Suedes of a sale of the premises to the IDA. If it suffered financial loss as a result this damage is sufficient to ground its present claim, and it will be unnecessary for me to consider whether if such loss is not established the law would presume that Suedes must have suffered some damage by being deprived of its ability to deal as it wished with its property.

Suedes is therefore in principle entitled to damages on its counterclaim. By agreement between the parties I deferred hearing evidence on the quantum of Suedes' loss until I had decided the liability issue. I will hear evidence on this outstanding point at a future date.

3. *THE RIGHT TO PRIVACY*

In *McGee* v. *A.G.* [1974] I.R. 284, at 322 (Sup. Ct., 1973), Budd, J. stated that it was 'scarcely to be doubted in our society that the right to privacy is universally recognised and accepted with possibly the rarest of exceptions . . .' This decision was concerned with the constitutional right to privacy, the Supreme Court (by a majority) holding that there is a constitutionally protected right of marital privacy. Interference with this constitutionally protected right may be protected by an action for damages (*Meskell* v. *C.I.E.* [1972] I.R. 330 (Sup. Ct.)) or, in appropriate cases, by an injunction.

The law of tort provides generous protection for privacy interests by means of specific torts, such as trespass to land, to chattels or to the person, intentional infliction of mental suffering, nuisance, defamation and breach of confidence. But in no Irish decision has the issue arisen as to whether there is a substantive general action in tort for invasion of privacy. A statement going some way towards recognising a right of action is that of Powell J. in *Dunlop* v. *Dunlop Rubber Co.* [1920] 1 I.R. 280, at 289 (aff'd. [1921] 1 I.R. 173 (C.A., 1920), aff'd. [1921] 1 A.C. 367 (H.L. (Ir.), 1920):

> 'It may be that if this action comes to trial an additional question may arise on the pleadings as to whether or not, apart from libel, a private person can restrain the publication of a portrait or picture of himself which in the form in which it is published has been designed and published without his authority. The late Lord Collins, when Mr. Justice Collins, in giving judgment in *Monson* v. *Tussands, Ltd.* [1894] 1 Q.B. 671, said that he did not wish to express any opinion on this question. It may be that this point may be decided in the present action, whether it be tried in Ireland or in England; but for the purposes of this motion the case must, I think, be dealt with by the standards applicable to the law of libel.'

In the United States, the action for interference with privacy has been recognised for many years: in other common law jurisdictions, the courts have been slower to take this step but the trend is in this direction: *cf. McMahon & Binchy*, p. 381; *Heath* v. *Weist-Barron School of Television (Canada) Ltd*, 18 C.C.L.T. 129 (Ont. H. Ct., Montgomery, J., 1981); Burns, 'The Law and Privacy: The Canadian Experience' 54 Can. Bar Rev. 1 (1976). There is a discernable trend in Irish decisions on related aspects of the law towards according greater respect to privacy considerations: see, *e.g., Murphy* v. *P.M.P.A.* unreported, High Ct., Doyle, J., 21 February 1978 (analysed by McDonald, 'Some Aspects of the Law on Disclosure of Information' 14 Ir. Jur. (n.s.) 229, at 240 (1979)); *Cook* v. *Carroll* [1945] I.R. 515 (High Ct.); *In re O'Kelly*, 108 I.L.T.R. 97 (Sup. Ct., 1974), *E.R.* v. *J.R.* [1981] I.L.R.M. 125 (High Ct., Miss Justice Carroll). This trend suggests that, should the issue arise, an Irish court could well hold that invasion of privacy constitutes a tort.

Chapter 16

DECEIT AND INJURIOUS FALSEHOOD

1. *DECEIT*

DELANY V. KEOGH
[1905] 2 I.R. 267 (C.A., 1905 rev'g K.B. Div., 1904)

Holmes L.J. (for the court):

The difficulty in this case arises in applying old and well-settled principles of law to an unusual state of facts. There is no doubt that to sustain an action for misrepresentation, there must be proof of fraud on the part of the defendant. It is, I think, equally certain that fraud is proved when it is shown that the defendant made the misrepresentation, knowing it to be false. To use the words of Lord Herschell, in *Derry* v. *Peek* 14 A. C. 337 at 374:– 'To prevent a false statement being fraudulent, there must always be an honest belief in its truth.' To these propositions I add another, suggested by the peculiar facts of the present case. It is not necessary that the misrepresentation which will sustain an action of deceit should be made in actual terms. Words may be used in such circumstances, and in such a connexion, as to convey to the person to whom they are addressed a meaning or inference beyond what is expressed; and if it appears that the person employing them knew this, and also knew that such meaning or inference was false, there is sufficient proof of fraud.

Of course whether the misstatement be express or implied, the plaintiff must show that he has suffered loss by acting on it; but in the foregoing observations, I have only dealt with the mode of proving the defendant's fraud, which is an essential element in the cause of action.

Mr. Keogh, a well-known auctioneer in this city, was employed by Mrs. Martin, a publican, to sell by auction her licensed premises. He was supplied by Mr. Bradley, Mrs. Martin's solicitor, with the necessary particulars; and he published an advertisement, in which the property was described as 'held under lease for a term of sixty-one years, at £25 per annum. A rent of £18 yearly has been accepted by the landlord for several years in lieu of the said rent of £25. The rent, licence duty, and taxes, are less than 11s. weekly' – a calculation made on the basis of the yearly rent being £18. It is, I think, impossible to mistake the meaning of these words. They do not mean that the rent of £25, reserved by the lease, was subsequently legally reduced to £18. They mean that, although the original rent had not been altered, the landlord had, for several years, voluntarily accepted a smaller sum in lieu thereof. The statement was not made for the purpose of informing a would-be purchaser of a past incident with which he was not concerned. It was intended that he should draw the inference that the reduction hitherto made would probably be continued, and, in my opinion, it clearly implied a representation that the vendor had no reason to believe that it would be discontinued. A gentleman of Mr. Keogh's experience knows how usual it has been in Ireland for a landlord to allow, year after year, an abatement in a tenant's rent, and how rarely in such cases it happens that the full rent is insisted on, without a marked change of circumstances, and ample previous notice. I have no doubt that this was in the defendant's mind when he published the advertisement, and that his expectation was that a similar consideration would naturally influence bidders at the auction in their estimate of the value of the premises. Up to this point, there can be no doubt of the defendant's honesty and candour. He not only believed, but he had good grounds for believing, everything that the particulars of sale expressed or implied. Some days before the auction, however, an intending bidder, seeing the importance of the statement as to the rent, determined, if possible, to convert expectation into assurance; and having found out who the landlord was, he inquired from him whether the abatement would be continued. I presume the answer was a decided negative. At all events this enquiry brought the terms of the advertisement to the notice of the landlord, who, for the very purpose of preventing people from being misled by it, wrote at once to the defendant. There is no ambiguity in this letter. Mr. Keogh is told in the clearest terms that thenceforth the full rent would be insisted on. The defendant understood perfectly the significance of this intimation, and brought the letter to Mr. Bradley. That gentleman, who had some previous knowledge of the property, did not hold out any hope that the landlord could be induced to alter his determination to insist on the full rent. On the contrary, this seems to have been assumed; but Mr. Bradley gave an opinion that the landlord was estopped from recovering more than £18. No change was made in the particulars of sale; and the defendant opened the auction, which took place two or three days later, by reading the statement as to rent already quoted without any comment, beyond saying that it was a cheap place. The plaintiff, in ignorance of the landlord's intention, was declared the purchaser at the price of £430; and in the abstract of title, furnished by Mr. Bradley, there was no reference to the amount of rent having been affected by the doctrine of estoppel. The first notice that the plaintiff had of the landlord's intention to insist on the full sum of £25, was some months after the completion of the purchase, when a demand therefor was followed by a writ, to which, of course, there was no defence.

The question is whether, in the foregoing circumstances, the particulars of sale, taken in connexion with the suppression of the contents of the landlord's letter, showed fraud of the kind that entitles the plaintiff to recover in an action of deceit such damages, if any, as he sustained therefrom?

Let me present the case in a way suggested by Mr. Ronan. Let me assume that the defendant, after he received the particulars from Mr. Bradley, but before he made them public, had ascertained from the landlord that he would insist on the full rent for the future, would it not have been manifestly dishonest to frame the advertisement as he did? His doing so would be an example of the trick described by Lord Blackburn in *Smith* v. *Chadwick* 9 A. C. 201; 'If, with intent to lead the plaintiff to act upon it, they' [*i.e.* the defendants] 'put forth a statement which they know may bear two meanings, one of which is false to their knowledge, and thereby the plaintiff, putting that meaning on it, is misled, I do not think they can escape by saying he ought to have put the other. If they palter with him in a double sense, it may be that they lie *like* truth; but I think they lie, and it is a fraud. Indeed, as a question of casuistry, I am inclined to think the fraud is aggravated by a shabby attempt to get the benefit of a fraud without incurring the responsibility.' But the information, which would have made the statement fraudulent if it had been obtained before the advertisement was issued, reached the defendant in time to enable him to prevent persons attending the auction from being misled; and the fact that the landlord communicated with him as auctioneer ought to have impressed, and I am sure did impress, him with the importance of correcting the false inference which his language was calculated and intended to convey. All that was necessary for Mr. Keogh to do was, after reading the particulars at the auction, to have added, that since they had been prepared the landlord had expressed his intention to insist on the rent of £25, but that the vendor's solicitor was of opinion that he was legally estopped from obtaining more than £18.

He did not do this. He allowed the sale to proceed on the basis that the reduced rent might be voluntarily received in the future as in the past, or, at least, that he knew nothing to the contrary.

How does the defendant himself account for this? His evidence on this point is clear:– 'The conditions were Bradley's. I did not get authority to make any change. I was selling under Bradley's orders. I acted on Bradley's directions to me to go on with the sale.' In other words, an intelligent auctioneer, who admits that 'it would have been material to have let those at the auction know of Tench's determination to enforce the higher rent,' kept back this information, because the solicitor under whose orders he was acting did not authorise him to disclose it or make any change in the particulars. In matters of truth and falsehood, of honesty and dishonesty, our law requires a man to judge for himself, and will not allow him to escape responsibility by pleading that he was carrying out the directions of another. Knowing that he could not thus free himself from liability, his counsel relied on his belief in the soundness of Mr. Bradley's legal opinion. I accept Mr. Keogh's statement that he believed what he was told by the solicitor, although this was not his reason for suppressing Tench's letter, and although the solicitor himself had not ventured to state it in the particulars of sale; but the defendant must have understood the difference between a landlord accepting voluntarily an abated rent, and a tenant being forced to fight for the abatement in a doubtful lawsuit. I do not understand either the legal or ethical aspect of Mr. Ronan's argument on this point.

I have observed, not for the first time, in the discussion of this case the prevalence of an idea that *Derry* v. *Peek* 14 A. C. 337 has laid down a new rule in actions of deceit, and has given a latitude to falsehood that did not previously exist. This seems to me to be a great mistake. The directors of a Tramway Co. that had authority to use steam power with the consent of the Board of Trade, believing that this consent would be given as a matter of course, issued a prospectus in which it was stated that they had the right to use steam power without reference to any condition. It was held that this was not actionable, inasmuch as the statement was made in the honest belief that it was true. This is, I think, old law; but if the directors had known, before they issued the prospectus, that the Board of Trade had refused to consent, or had announced its intention to refuse, the case would have been like this, and the directors would have had no defence; nor in such case would their position have been improved if their solicitor had assured them that there would be no difficulty in obtaining from Parliament an amending Act removing the condition.

I am satisfied that when the defendant read in his auction mart to the assembled bidders the particulars of sale, unaccompanied with a statement that there would be no longer a voluntary abatement of the rent, he was knowingly deceiving them, and that the natural effect of the deception was to obtain a higher price for the public-house than it was worth.

I believe that the plaintiff's bid of £430 was considerably higher than what he would have offered if he had the knowledge which the auctioneer possessed; and than the real value of the premises.

The measure of damages is the difference between such real value and £430; and on this point the evidence is not satisfactory. The plaintiff says that if he had known that he would be obliged to pay the full rent, he would not have bid more than £300, but I am of opinion that the premises, subject to £25 a-year, were worth more than £300. There is evidence that the present actuarial value of an increased liability of £7 during the residue of the term would be £110. But £430 was bid on the basis, not that the rent was £18 and no more, but that the landlord might voluntarily accept the same sum in the future as in the past. The extent to which the £110 ought to be reduced by reason of this element of chance, is one of those problems which juries are obliged to answer every day in assessing damages. A jury in this case would probably regard the chances as even, and find a verdict for £55 by the familiar method of splitting the difference. I should be prepared to adopt this amount, especially as it is the figure at which I have arrived by a different mode of calculation; but the other members of the Court consider it to be somewhat excessive; and if there is any subject on which there ought to be 'give and take,' it is that of damages. We have, therefore, fixed the sum for which judgment is to be given at £40.

Notes and Questions

1. What duty of disclosure does this decision require?
2. Do you think that the analogy with *Derry* v. *Peek* which Holmes L. J. presents is a correct one? *Cf. McMahon & Binchy*, p. 390.

GILL V. M'DOWELL
[1903] 2 I.R. 463 (K.B. Div., 1902)

Case stated by the Lord Chief Baron on the hearing of a civil bill appeal.

The following are the material facts as set out in the case:– The case came before the Lord Chief Baron at the Spring Assizes, 1902, for the county of Longford, upon an appeal by the defendant from a decree given by the County Court Judge for £10 damages. The process claimed damages for breach of warranty, and (by amendment made by the County Court Judge) also for false and fraudulent misrepresentation. It was proved in evidence that the defendant had in his possession an animal of the ox tribe which when looked at from the back appeared to be a heifer, but which looked at from certain other directions appeared to be a bullock. The animal was, in fact, and as the defendant knew, a hermaphrodite. It had teats like those of a heifer, but its urinary organs had the outward appearance of those of a bullock. The defendant sent the animal to the April fair of Barry, in the county of Longford, for sale, together with two other animals, a bullock and a heifer. The three animals were purchased in the fair by the plaintiff, a cattle dealer, at the sum of £10 5s. each. A warranty was not asked for or given. Nothing whatever was actually said at the sale as to the sex of the animals, but the plaintiff bought under the belief that he was buying either a bullock and two heifers, or one heifer and two bullocks. The plaintiff to defendant's knowledge would not have purchased had he known of the malformation of the animal the subject of the cause of action. By a careful and skilled examination by the plaintiff the defect could have been discovered, but in point of fact it was not discovered by the plaintiff until the following day, when he sent a notice or message to the defendant to take the animal back, which the defendant refused to do. The animal, which was in bad health from the time of sale, died in the plaintiff's possession in the month of July following from uræmic poisoning occasioned by the retention of urine the result of swellings and abscess caused by the malformation; and the Lord Chief Baron found as a fact that the death was the direct consequence of such malformation.

The question for the Court was, whether the facts stated constituted evidence sufficient to support any cause of action by the plaintiff against the defendant in respect of the animal. If they did the process was, if necessary, to be deemed amended by stating such cause of action.

Lord O'Brien L.C.J.:

This case, which has been stated for our determination by my Lord Chief Baron, is certainly a strange one. It has been said that so many cases have been decided in the course of the administration of the law that it is a cause of wonder that any remain for decision. However, such is the complexity and everchanging nature of human transactions that new facts or new combinations of facts will continue to present themselves, and that new questions, arising on those facts or combinations of facts, will continue to exercise the minds of those engaged in the administration of the law. The facts of this case are few, but what inferences are to be drawn from them is by no means clear. It is all important to consider, not only the facts of the case, but the findings of the Lord Chief Baron and the function imposed upon us by him. Facts and findings and functions are clearly and succinctly set forth. I shall read the special case.

[His Lordship read the case.]

Now, then, this is the special case, and what has the Lord Chief Baron found? That the animal in question was neither a heifer nor a bullock – that it was a hermaphrodite; that it was essentially different in some respects from a heifer and essentially different in some respects from a bullock; that it was an animal, though of the ox tribe, neither a heifer nor a bullock. But what else did my Lord Chief Baron find? This, a very important finding, that the plaintiff bought under the belief that the animals he was buying were a bullock and two heifers, and that the defendant was aware that the plaintiff was buying under the belief that he was buying either a bullock and two heifers or one heifer and two bullocks; he never for a moment believed that any one of the animals was a hermaphrodite, his belief being that the animal in question was either a bullock or a heifer, and the defendant's belief being that the plaintiff believed he (defendant) was contracting to sell things essentially different from a hermaphrodite, that is to say, a heifer or a bullock. The Chief Baron also found that the plaintiff to the defendant's knowledge would not have purchased had he known of the malformation of the animal which was the cause of action. . . . I think . . . there is evidence of misrepresentation sufficient to sustain the action. It is perfectly notorious that a bad animal is often placed among good, so that the defects of the bad animal may, by association with the general lot, escape detection. In the case before us the animal of itself was calculated to give occasion to mistake; from one point of view it might be regarded as a heifer, and from another point of view it might be regarded as a bullock. It would, indeed, be hard to find anything more calculated of itself to deceive, and the defendant, well knowing that it was not a bullock or heifer, drove it into a fair where bullocks and heifers are sold, and deliberately put it into a category to which it did not belong, and to which he knew it did not belong. He associates it with a heifer and a bullock, making it as one of a lot, and thereby the purchaser was, as a matter of fact, deceived, there being, I think, a tacit representation that this animal, standing in this cattle fair with a heifer and bullock, and offered for sale with them, was either a heifer or a bullock. The plaintiff was, as a matter of fact, deceived; the defendant knew he was deceived. In my opinion there is some evidence that he was thrown off his guard by the action of the defendant. I do not think if the case was before a jury that it could be withdrawn from them.

Gibson, J.:

A curious *lusus naturæ* is the subject of this argument. The plaintiff's case is based on one of two grounds: the contract of sale was procured by fraud; or there was no valid contract at all, because the parties were not *ad idem* as to the subject of sale. Three points are relied upon – first, that the plaintiff was sold at an ordinary fair; second, that it was sold with two other beasts – a bullock and a heifer – a circumstance which might have thrown the plaintiff off his guard; and, thirdly, the defendant knew that the plaintiff was buying under the belief that the animal was contracted to be sold as a bullock or a heifer.

The animal was bovine, but from the peculiar nature of its malformation it would be impossible to say that it was male or female. It was not that the organs of generation were deficient or absent; an emasculated boar or a sow subject to spaying remains respectively male or female. This animal was a hermaphrodite of misleading appearance. Looked at from one direction it was a heifer; from another it was a bullock. It possessed no gender.

I now take up the points relied upon by the plaintiff.

First, I cannot say that the fair was appropriated to beasts with a sex. The defendant by selling in the fair cannot be fixed with a tacit affirmation that the animal was male or female. No doubt such animals are usually the subject of a sale, but no implied representation necessarily results from an ordinary fair being the place of sale: *Ward* v. *Hobbs* 4 A. C. 13.

The second point – the sale of the hermaphrodite with two other natural animals at the same price per head – deserves more consideration. The case does not find that the plaintiff had any dishonest intention in so doing, or that the cattle were placed so as to screen the hermaphrodite, or that the sale was calculated to throw the plaintiff off his guard. On the other hand, the fact of the sale of the three animals at the same time, place, and price is expressly stated as a relevant fact; the beast was in its character misleading; defendant knew that plaintiff was buying under a mistake as to the subject of contract; and what is reserved for us is whether there was *any* evidence. It was the duty of the seller to do and say nothing which would disarm the buyer's vigilance. The peculiarity of this animal was so unusual that no ordinary dealer would be on his guard against it as a possible risk. I think the sale of the two beasts, a heifer and bullock, at the same time, place, and price, was calculated to encourage and facilitate the purchaser's oversight, and that the defendant ought to have known this.

There is another point on which an inference of deceit may be possibly based. The animal was misleading – a sort of living lie. Viewed from behind its teats attested its female sex. The plaintiff accepted this silent but false affirmation. The beast told its own lie: it was a machine of fraud which the defendant utilized. Is the case in principle different from that of a book with a forged title-page, or plate with a forged hall-mark which the vendor knows the purchaser buys and pays for in the belief that the vendor is selling it as genuine? If the buyer was in fact deceived, would the result be affected by the circumstance that the forgery was inartistic and that careful examination would have revealed the truth? On the whole, I think there was some evidence of contrivance and deceit. . . .

Boyd J. delivering a concurring judgment.

Madden J. (dissenting on this issue):

The difficulty which I have felt throughout this case has been caused not so much by legal considerations as by the finding of the Lord Chief Baron on a matter of fact as to the mental condition of the contracting parties. It was argued by Mr. Smith that the subject-matter of the contract was three head of cattle, animals of the bovine species, without regard to sex. One of these animals had a malformation which had a relation to sex, and which rendered the animal especially liable to the disease of which it afterwards died. The existence of this malformation was known to the seller. It was unknown to the buyer, but it could have been discovered by a careful and skilled examination, that is to say, such an examination as a cattle dealer would be competent to make. If there were no more than this to be considered, I should be clearly of opinion that the plaintiff had no case. As a general principle a vendor, although bound to employ no artifice for the purpose of concealing a defect of which he is aware, is under no legal obligation to disclose the existence of a defect, even though the non-disclosure is likely to deceive the buyer. In *Ward* v. *Hobbs* it was held by the House of Lords that even when a statute prohibited sending diseased pigs to a market, the conduct of the vendor in exposing pigs for sale in the market did not amount to a representation as between him and the purchaser that they were free from disease.

I asked Mr. Gaussen what the seller ought to have done. I fully accept his statement as to what he himself would have done if he had found himself in the possession of a hermaphrodite in a public fair. But this is a counsel of perfection scarcely applicable to ordinary cattle dealers, who could not be expected to call attention to the peculiarity existing in the present case. Another suggestion is that the animal should have been sold separately, and that the driving of this animal into a fair, and selling it in company with a bullock and a heifer, amounted to fraud. But there is not a special stand provided for hermaphrodites at a fair, and if the seller had treated the animal as one that could not be sold with bullocks or heifers this would practically amount to a representation or admission that the animal suffered from something that rendered it not ordinarily saleable. I do not think that the seller was bound to do this. In my opinion the maxim *caveat emptor* would apply if there were nothing more in the case. . . .

Notes and Questions

1. Do you prefer the approach of the majority or that of Madden J.? Why?
2. Of what exactly did the defendant's misrepresentation consist?
3. On what exactly did the plaintiff rely?
4. On damages in actions for deceit, see *Northern Bank Finance Corporation Ltd.* v. *Charlton* [1979] I.R. 149.

2. INJURIOUS FALSEHOOD

In contrast to deceit where it is the plaintiff himself who is deceived, the essence of the tort of injurious falsehood is that the defendant 'maliciously' deceives *others* about the plaintiff, so as to cause loss to the plaintiff. It is not necessary that what the defendant says should be in any way defamatory of the plaintiff: it is sufficient in this context that the falsity cause the plaintiff loss. The precise scope of 'malice' necessary to commit the tort is not clear. Some judges have equated 'malice' with the absence of a 'just cause or excuse.' Others have gone further and required that some 'indirect, dishonest or improper motive' be established.

It is possible that the tort of negligence may swallow up much of the territory now covered by injurious falsehood. Once the barrier of non-recovery for pure economic loss had been breached it was only a matter of time before this development would be mooted. In *Gallaher (Dublin) Limited, Hergall (1981) Ltd., and Gallaher Ltd.* v. *The Health Education Bureau* [1982] I.L.R.M. (High Ct., Costello, J.), the defendant, in the course of a campaign designed to help members of the public give up smoking cigarettes, made use of the plaintiff cigarette company's trade mark, 'Conquest'. The Bureau acted in good faith and was unaware of the existence of the plaintiff's trade mark, but its campaign irretrievably damaged the trade mark, rendering it impossible to use subsequently in relation to cigarettes.

The court held the defendant liable for infringement of the trade mark under the *Trade Mark Act 1963*. The plaintiff made an alternative claim, based on non-trade mark principles of the common law, contending that the Bureau had breached a duty to care to all persons lawfully engaged in the trade of selling tobacco products not to so conduct its campaign as to damage the legitimate rights of property which such persons were entitled to enjoy. Costello, J. stated (at 248) that since he had held that the plaintiff was entitled to relief under their first claim it was unnecessary for him to express his views on this alternative claim. It is easy to see the attraction such a claim would have for a plaintiff, since it would avoid any difficulties associated with the requirement of proof of malice on the part of the defendant.

Chapter 17

NEGLIGENT MISSTATEMENT

The Old Approach

Tort law was slow to give a remedy for pure economic loss resulting from negligent misstatements unless there was a contractual or fiduciary relationship between the parties or unless the defendant was guilty of fraud. The courts were fearful of imposing 'liability in an indeterminate amount for an indeterminate time to an indeterminate class': *Ultramares* v. *Touche Niven & Co.* 255 N.Y.S. 170, at 179, 174 N.E. 441, at 444 (*per* Cardozo, J., 1931). People notoriously are less careful about what they say than about what they do. Moreover, 'words are more volatile than deeds, they travel fast and far afield, they are used without been expended': *Hedley Byrne & Co. Ltd.* v. *Heller & Partners Ltd.* [1964] A.C. 465, at 534 (H.L. (Eng.), *per* Lord Pearce, 1963).

For many years after the decision of *Donoghue* v. *Stevenson* negligent misstatements continued to be regarded as immune from the application of the 'neighbour' principle of negligence. In time, however, the old law gave way.

The Hedley Byrne Breakthrough

The decision which established definitively in England that liability could arise from negligent misstatement is *Hedley Byrne & Co. Ltd.* v. *Heller & Partners Ltd.* [1964] A.C. 465 (H.L. (Eng.), 1963). The case concerned a reference as to the creditworthiness of its customer given by one bank to another where in giving the reference the bank knew or ought to know that this information would be passed on to the plaintiff company, which was about to do business with the customer.

The reference was negligent and as a result the plaintiff company suffered loss. The reference contained a disclaimer which the House of Lords held was sufficient to relieve the defendant bank of responsibility, but the case is important on account of the fact that the speeches delivered in the House of Lords, despite differences of emphasis, were all to the effect that there can be liability for negligent misstatement in cases where a party seeking information from the defendant relies on his special skill and trusts him to exercise due care.

Lord Reid stated:

> ... A reasonable man, knowing that he was being trusted or that his skill and judgment were being relied on, would, I think have three courses open to him. He could keep silent or decline to give the information or advice sought: or he could give an answer with a clear qualification that he accepted no responsibility for it or that it was given without that reflection or inquiry which a careful answer would require: or he could simply answer without any such qualification. If he chooses to adopt the last course he must, I think, be held to have accepted some responsibility for his answer being given carefully, or to have accepted a relationship with the inquirer which requires him to exercise such care as the circumstances require. ...

Lord Morris of Borth-Y-Gest stated:

> ... it seems to me that if A assumes a responsibility to B to tender him deliberate advice there could be a liability if the advice is negligently given. I say 'could be' because the ordinary courtesies and exchanges of life would become impossible if it were sought to attach legal obligation to every kindly and friendly act. But the principle of the matter would not appear to be in doubt. If A employs B (who might, for example, be a professional man such as an accountant or a solicitor or a doctor) for reward to give advice, and if the advice is negligently given, there could be a liability in B to pay damages. The fact that the advice is given in words

would not, in my view, prevent liability from arising. Quite apart, however, from employment or contract there may be circumstances in which a duty to exercise care will arise if a service is voluntarily undertaken. A medical man may unexpectedly come across an unconscious man, who is a complete stranger to him, and who is in urgent need of skilled attention: if the medical man, following the fine traditions of his profession, proceeds to treat the unconscious man he must exercise reasonable skill and care in doing so. . . .

. . . It is said, however, that where careless (but not fraudulent) misstatements are in question there can be no liability in the maker of them unless there is either some contractual or fiduciary relationship with a person adversely affected by the making of them or unless through the making of them something is created or circulated or some situation is created which is dangerous to life, limb or property. In logic I can see no essential reason for distinguishing injury which is caused by a reliance on words from injury which is caused by a reliance on the safety of the staging to a ship, or by a reliance on the safety for use of the contents of a bottle of hair wash or a bottle of some consumable liquid. It seems to me, therefore, that if A claims that he has suffered injury or loss as a result of acting upon some misstatement made by B who is not in any contractual or fiduciary relationship with him the inquiry that is first raised is whether B owed any duty to A: if he did the further inquiry is raised as to the nature of the duty. There may be circumstances under which the only duty owed by B to A is the duty of being honest: there may be circumstances under which B owes to A the duty not only of being honest but also a duty of taking reasonable care. The issue in the present case is whether the bank owed any duty to Hedleys and if so what the duty was.

Leaving aside cases where there is some contractual or fiduciary relationship there may be many situations in which one person voluntarily or gratuitously undertakes to do something for another person and becomes under a duty to exercise reasonable care. I have given illustrations. Apart from cases where there is some direct dealing, there may be cases where one person issues a document which should be the result of an exercise of the skill and judgment required by him in his calling and where he knows and intends that its accuracy will be relied on by another. . . .

My lords, I consider that . . . it should not be regarded as settled that if someone possessed of a special skill undertakes, quite irrespective of contract, to apply that skill for the assistance of another person who relies on such skill, a duty of care will arise. The fact that the service is to be given by means of, or by the instrumentality of, words can make no difference. Furthermore, if, in a sphere in which a person is so placed that others could reasonably rely on his judgment or his skill or on his ability to make careful inquiry, a person takes it on himself to give information or advice to, or allows his information or advice to be passed on to, another person who, as he knows or should know, will place reliance on it, then a duty of care will arise. . . .

Lord Hodson stated:

. . . I do not think that it is possible to catalogue the special features which might be found to exist before the duty of care will arise in a given case, but since preparing this opinion I have had the opportunity of reading the speech which my noble and learned friend Lord Morris of Borth-y-Gest has now delivered. I agree with him that if in a sphere where a person is so placed that others could reasonably rely on his judgment or his skill or on his ability to make careful inquiry such person takes it on himself to give information or advice to, or allows his information or advice to be passed on to, another person who, as he knows, or should know, will place reliance on it, then a duty of care will arise. . . .

Lord Devlin stated:

. . . In my opinion the appellants in their argument tried to press *M'Alister* (or *Donoghue*) v. *Stevenson* [1932] A.C. 562 too hard. They asked whether the principle of proximity should not apply as well to words as to deeds. I think that it should, but as it is only a general conception it does not yet get them very far. Then they take the specific proposition laid down by *Donoghue* v. *Stevenson* [1932] A.C. 562 and try to apply it literally to a certificate or a banker's reference. That will not do, for a general conception cannot be applied to pieces of paper in the same way as to articles of commerce, or to writers in the same way as to manufacturers. An inquiry into the possibilities of intermediate examination of a certificate will not be fruitful. The real value of *M'Alister* (or *Donoghue*) v. *Stevenson* [1932] A.C, 562 to the argument in this case is that it shows how the law can be developed to solve particular problems. Is the relationship between the parties in this case such that it can be brought within a category giving rise to a special duty? As always in English law the first step in such an inquiry is to see how far the authorities have gone, for new categories in the law do not spring into existence overnight. . . .

I think . . . that there is ample authority to justify your lordships in saying now that the categories of special relationships, which may give rise to a duty to take care in word as well as in deed, are not limited to contractual relationships or to relationships of fiduciary duty, but include also relationships which in the words of Lord Shaw in *Nocton* v. *Lord Ashburton* [1914] A. C. 932, at 972 are 'equivalent to contract' that is, where there is an assumption of responsibility in circumstances in which, but for the absence of consideration, there would be a contract. Where there is an express undertaking an express warranty as distinct from mere representation, there can be little difficulty. The difficulty arises in discerning those cases in whch the undertaking is to be implied. In this respect the absence of consideration is not irrelevant. Payment for information or advice is very good evidence that it is being relied on and that the informer or adviser knows that it is. Where there is no consideration, it will be necessary to exercise greater care in distinguishing between social and professional relationships and between those which are of a contractual character and those which are not. It may often be material to consider whether the adviser is acting purely out of good nature or whether he is getting his reward in some indirect form. The service that a bank performs in giving a reference is not done simply out of a desire to assist commerce. It would discourage the customers of the bank if their deals fell through because the bank had refused to testify to their credit when it was good.

I have had the advantage of reading all the opinions prepared by your lordships and of studying the terms which your lordships have framed by way of definition of the sort of relationship which gives rise to a responsibility towards those who act on information or advice and so creates a duty of care towards them. I do not understand any of your lordships to hold that it is a responsibility imposed by law on certain types of persons or in certain sorts of situations. It is a responsibility that is voluntarily accepted or undertaken either generally where a general relationship, such as that of solicitor and client or banker and customer, is created, or specifically in relation to a particular transaction. In the present case the appellants were not, as in *Woods* v. *Martins Bank, Ltd* [1959] 1 Q.B. 55 the customers or potential customers of the bank. Responsibility can attach only to the single act, i.e., the giving of the reference, and only if the doing of that act implied a voluntary undertaking to assume responsibility. This is a point of great importance because it is, as I understand it, the foundation for the ground on which in the end the House dismisses the appeal. I do not think it possible to formulate with exactitude all the conditions under which the law will in a specific case imply a voluntary undertaking, any more than it is possible to formulate those in which the law will imply a contract. But in so far as your lordships describe the circumstances in which an implication will ordinarily be drawn, I am prepared to adopt any one of your lordships' statements as showing the general rule; and I pay the same respect to the statement by Denning L.J. in his dissenting judgment in *Candler* v. *Crane, Christmas & Co.* [1951] 2 K.B. 164, at p. 179 about the circumstances in which he says a duty to use care in making a statement exists. . . .

I shall therefore content myself with the proposition that wherever there is a relationship equivalent to contract there is a duty of care. Such a relationship may be either general or particular. Examples of a general relationship are those of solicitor and client and of banker and customer. For the former *Nocton* v. *Lord Ashburton* [1914] A.C. 932 has long stood as the authority and for the latter there is the decision of Salmon J. in *Woods* v. *Martins Bank, Ltd.* [1959] 1 Q.B. 55 which I respectfully approve. There may well be others yet to be established. Where there is a general relationship of this sort it is unnecessary to do more than prove its existence and the duty follows. Where, as in the present case, what is relied on is a particular relationship created ad hoc, it will be necessary to examine the particular facts to see whether there is an express or implied undertaking of responsibility.

I regard this proposition as an application of the general conception of proximity. Cases may arise in the future in which a new and wider proposition, quite independent of any notion of contract, will be needed. There may, for example, be cases in which a statement is not supplied for the use of any particular person, any more than in *McAlister* (or *Donoghue*) v. *Stevenson* [1932] A.C. 562; [1932] All E.R. Rep. 1 the ginger beer was supplied for consumption by any particular person; and it will then be necessary to return to the general conception of proximity and to see whether there can be evolved from it, or was done in *Donoghue* v. *Stevenson* [1932] A.C. 562; [1932] All E.R. Rep. 1, a specific proposition to fit the case. When that has to be done, the speeches of your lordships today as well as the judgment of Denning L.J. to which I have referred – and also, I may add the proposition in the 'Restatement' [See 65 Corpus Juris Secundum title Negligence, pp. 428, 429, §20, which begins 'A false statement negligently made may be the basis of a recovery of damages for injury or loss sustained in consequence of reliance thereon, the American rule, in this respect, being more liberal than the rule in England'] and the cases which exemplify it, will afford good guidance as to what ought to be said. I prefer to see what shape such cases take before committing myself to any formulation, for I bear in mind Lord Atkin's warning, which I have quoted, against placing unnecessary restrictions on the adaptability of English law. I have, I hope, made it clear that I take quite literally the dictum of Lord MacMillan, so often quoted from the same case [1932] A.C. at p. 619, that 'the categories of negligence are never closed'. English law is wide enough to embrace any new category or proposition that exemplifies the principle of proximity.

I have another reason for caution. Since the essence of the matter in the present case and in others of the same type is the acceptance of responsibility, I should like to guard against the imposition of restrictive terms notwithstanding that the essential condition is fulfilled. If a defendant says to a plaintiff:– 'Let me do this for you, do not waste your money in employing a professional, I will do it for nothing and you can rely on me', I do not think that he could escape liability simply because he belonged to no profession or calling, had no qualifications or special skill and did not hold himself out as having any. The relevance of these factors is to show the unlikelihood of a defendant in such circumstances assuming a legal responsibility and as such they may often be decisive. But they are not theoretically conclusive, and so cannot be the subject of definition. It would be unfortunate if they were. For it would mean the plaintiffs would seek to avoid the regidity of the definition by bringing the action in contract as in *De la Bere* v. *Pearson, Ltd.* [1908] 1 K.B. 280 and setting up something that would do for consideration. That to my mind would be an undesirable development in the law and the best way of avoiding it is to settle the law so that the presence or absence of consideration makes no difference. . . .

Lord Pearce stated:

. . . How wide the sphere of the duty of care in negligence is to be laid depends ultimately on the courts' assessment of the demands of society for protection from the carelessness of others. Economic protection has lagged behind protection in physical matters where there is injury to person and property. It may be that the size and the width of the range of possible claims has acted as a deterrent to extension of economic protection. In this sphere the law was developed in the United States in *Glanzer* v. *Shepard* 233 N.Y. 236 (1922), where a public weigher employed by a vendor was held liable to a purchaser for giving him a certificate which negligently overstated the amount of the goods supplied to him. The defendant was thus engaged on a task in which, as he knew, vendor and purchaser alike depended on his skill and care and the fact that it was the vendor who paid him was merely an accident of commerce. This case was followed and developed in later cases. . . .

If an innocent misrepresentation is made between parties in a fiduciary relationship it may, on that ground, give a right to claim damages for negligence. There is also in my opinion a duty of care created by special relationships which, though not fiduciary, gives rise to an assumption that care as well as honesty is demanded.

Was there such a relationship in the present case as to impose on the respondents a duty of care to the appellants as the undisclosed principals for whom National Provincial Bank, Ltd. was making the inquiry? The answer to that question depends on the circumstances of the transaction. If, for instance, they disclosed a casual social approach to the inquiry no such special relationship of duty of care would be assumed (see *Fish* v. *Kelly* 17 C.B.N.S. 194 (1864)). To import such a duty the representation must normally, I think, concern a business or professional transaction whose nature makes clear the gravity of the inquiry and the importance and influence attached to the answer. . . .

Within a year, in the High Court decision of *Securities Trust Ltd.* v. *Hugh Moore & Alexander Ltd.*, *Hedley Byrne* made its way into Irish law.

SECURITIES TRUST LTD. V. HUGH MOORE & ALEXANDER LTD.
[1964] I.R. 417 (High Ct., Davitt P.)

The plaintiff Company, Securities Trust Ltd., brought proceedings in the High Court, claiming damages for negligent misrepresentation in that they were, as alleged, induced to buy preference shares in the defendant Company, Hugh Moore & Alexander Ltd., as the result of an inaccuracy which appeared in a copy of the Articles of Association of the defendant Company supplied by the defendant Company to Kevin Anderson, the chairman and managing director of the plaintiff Company and a registered shareholder of the defendant company. The defendant Company contended that the Memorandum and Articles of Association of the defendant Company supplied to Kevin Anderson were supplied to him in his personal capacity as a member of the defendant Company and not as an agent for the plaintiff Company, that no duty was owed by them to the plaintiff Company to supply an accurate copy, and that they were not negligent.

W. R. C. Parke S.C. (with him *J.E. Lynch*) for the plaintiffs:–

The defendant Company owed a duty to the plaintiff Company to supply them, through their agent, with an accurate copy of their Articles of Association: this duty was owed to them as an intending shareholder. The copy supplied misrepresented the rights of preference shareholders on a winding up. The defendants were negligent in allowing such a copy to be supplied. Such negligent misrepresentation, even though innocent, gives rise to an action for damages: *Hedley Byrne & Co. Ltd.* v. *Heller and Partners Ltd.* [1964] A. C. 465. This case decided that the general proposition that no claim for damages lies in respect of an innocent misrepresentation is wrong: such a proposition is based upon an erroneous view of *Derry* v. *Peek* 14 App. Cas. 337. It has always been the position that where a duty is owed a misstatement made negligently can give rise to an action for damages: *Nocton* v. *Lord Ashburton* [1914] A. C. 932. [He also cited *Candler* v. *Crane, Christmas & Co.* [1951] 2 K. B. 164 and *Woods* v. *Martins Bank Limited* [1959] 1 Q. B. 55).]

R. J. O'Neill S.C. (with him *E. M. Walsh*) for the defendants:–

The plaintiffs have not established that the defendants owed any duty to them nor that the defendants were negligent. *Hedley Byrne & Co. Ltd.* v. *Heller and Partners Ltd.* [1964] A. C. 465 was a case in which both a duty was owed and the person owing the duty was negligent. The duty to make accurate statements must arise by reason of a special relationship between the parties or through special circumstances, and, also, it must be owed to a person. The duty under s. 18 of the Companies Act, 1908, is to supply members with an accurate copy: no duty is owed to non-members.

In the present case, it was Mr. Anderson who was supplied with the copy Articles. In any event, he could have confirmed what he believed from the copy supplied by an inspection in the Companies Office. No liability could arise unless the Articles were supplied to induce a purchase of shares. [He also cited *Peek* v. *Gurney* L. R. 6 H. I., 377 and *Andrews* v. *Mockford* [1896] 1 Q. B. 372)]

Cur. adv. vult.

Davitt P.:

The facts of this case, briefly summarised, appear to be as follows: Mr. Kevin Anderson was at all material times chairman and managing director of the plaintiff Company. in December, 1961, the Company authorised the purchase of shares in the defendant Company. The authority to purchase was a continuing authority, and purchases were made thereunder from time to time. In December, 1961, 200 ordinary shares were bought at twelve shillings per share and 100 preference at 13s. 6d. These shares were purchased by Mr. Kevin Anderson, and were transferred to him respectively on the 6th February, 1962, and the 31st January, 1962. They were registered in his name on the 23rd February, 1962. They were, of course, bought on the Company's behalf.

Early in April, 1962, Mr. Anderson wrote to the secretary of the defendant Company requesting a copy of its Memorandum and Articles of Association, and enclosing the statutory shilling. He did not attach any description to his signature and the letter did not anywhere refer to, or bear the name of, the plaintiff Company. There was nothing in it to indicate that it was written on behalf of the plaintiff Company, or on behalf of anyone other than the writer. On the 9th April he received a reply acknowledging receipt of his shilling and enclosing a copy of the Memorandum and Articles. This was addressed to him personally at the address given in his letter.

Other shares in the defendant Company were purchased as follows: 250 ordinary and 378 preference on the 4th January, 1962 at 15s. 0d. in each case; 100 ordinary at 14s 6d. on the 16th July, 1962; 150 preference on the 25th October, 1962, at 20s. 0d.; 450 preference at 21s. 0d. on the 26th October, 1962; and 250 preference at 21s. 0d. on the 30th October 1962. These shares were registered in the name of the plaintiff Company, the first such registration being made on the 4th May, 1962.

By Article 155 of the defendants' Articles of Association, as it appeared in the copy supplied to Mr. Anderson, it was provided as follows:– 'If the Company shall be wound up, the surplus assets distributable amongst members shall be applied first in repaying to the holders of Preference Shares the amount paid up on the said Preference Shares respectively, with the dividends thereon to date of repayment; and if such assets shall be insufficient to repay same in full, they shall be applied rateably so that the loss shall fall on the holders of Preference Shares in proportion to the amount called up on their Shares respectively; and the balance of such surplus assets (if any) shall be applied in repaying to the holders of Ordinary Shares the amount paid up on their Shares respectively; and if such balance shall be insufficient to repay the said amount in full it shall be applied rateably, so that the loss shall fall on the said holders of Ordinary Shares in proportion to the amount called up on their Shares respectively. If the balance of said surplus assets shall be more than sufficient to repay to the said holders of Shares the whole amount paid up on their Shares, the balance shall be distributed among them in proportion to the amount actually paid up on their Shares respectively.'

There had been rumours of a take-over bid for the shares of the defendant Company as well as of a voluntary winding up; and on the 26th June, 1962, a statement was issued by the chairman which clearly indicated that a voluntary winding up was in contemplation. These circumstances, coupled with the provision contained in the last sentence of Article 155, influenced the plaintiff Company to increase their holdings of Preference Shares; and the last three lots were purchased at par or over, and above their ordinary market value.

On the 30th October, 1962, the secretary of the defendant Company wrote to Mr. Anderson saying that the attention of the directors had been called to the fact that in the reprint of the Articles prepared in 1941 there was a serious printers' error in Article 155. In the original Articles as filed in 1898 the last clause in the Article read: 'If the balance of said surplus assets shall be more than sufficient to repay to the said holders of Ordinary Shares the whole amount paid up on their Shares, the balance shall be distributed among them in proportion to the amount actually paid up on their Shares respectively.' In the reprint, a copy of which had been supplied to Mr. Anderson, the word, 'Ordinary,' had been omitted with the result of making it appear that the holders of Preference Shares were entitled to share in the surplus. On the 4th October, 1962, a resolution to wind up the Company had been passed. The company went into liquidation and Mr. Garnet Walker was appointed liquidator. He refused to allow the claim of the plaintiff Company to participate in the surplus assets in respect of their Preference Shares; and on the 5th February, 1964, they issued their summons in the present proceedings.

In their statement of claim they aver that they applied for a copy of the Memorandum and Articles of Association through their agent, Mr. Anderson, and were supplied with the one containing the printers' error. They claim that by reason of the negligent misrepresentation of the defendant Company they were induced to purchase the 850 Preference Shares at a price exceeding their market value and have thereby suffered damage. The substantial defences raised in the defendants' pleadings are: that the copy of the Memorandum and Articles supplied to Mr. Anderson were not supplied to him as agent for the plaintiff Company; that the defendant Company owed no duty to the plaintiff Company to supply them with an accurate copy of the Memorandum and Articles; that there was no negligence on their part; and that the plaintiff Company did not suffer the alleged or any damage; or, alternatively, that the damages claimed are too remote.

The law to be applied in this case is not in controversy. It would appear that the proposition that innocent (i.e. non-fraudulent) misrepresentation cannot give rise to an action for damages is somewhat too broadly stated, and is based upon a misconception of what was decided by the House of Lords in *Derry* v. *Peek* 14 App. Cas. 337. Such action may be based on negligent misrepresentation which is not fraudulent. This was pointed out in *Nocton* v. *Lord Ashburton* [1914] A. C. 932, particularly in the speech of Haldane L.C. At page 948 he says:– 'Although liability for negligence in word has in material respects been developed in our law differently from liability for negligence in act, it is none the less true that a man may come under a special duty to exercise care in giving information or advice. I should accordingly be sorry to be thought to lend countenance to the idea that recent decisions have been intended to stereotype the cases in which people can be held to have assumed such a special duty. Whether such a duty has been assumed must depend on the relationship of the parties, and it is at least certain that there are a good many cases in which that relationship may be properly treated as giving rise to a special duty of care in statement.' It was apparently considered in some quarters that such a special duty could arise only from a contractual or fiduciary relationship. In *Robinson* v. *National Bank of Scotland* 1916 S. C. (H. L.) 150 Haldane L.C. was at pains to dispel this idea. At page 157 he said:– 'The whole of the doctrine as to fiduciary relationships, as to the duty of care arising from implied as well as express contracts, as to the duty of care arising from other special relationships which the Courts may find to exist in particular cases, still remains, and I should be very sorry if any word fell from me which would suggest that the Courts are in any way hampered in recognising that the duty of care may be established when such cases really occur.'

The proposition that circumstances may create a relationship between two parties in which, if one seeks information from the other and is given it, that other is under a duty to take reasonable care to ensure that the information given is correct, has been accepted and applied in the case of *Hedley Byrne & Co. Ltd.* v. *Heller and Partners Ltd.* [1963] 3 W. L. R. 101, recently decided by the House of Lords. Counsel for the defendant Company did not seek to dispute the proposition. He submitted, however, that the circumstances of this case created no such special relationship.

Sect. 18, sub-s. 1, of the Companies (Consolidation) Act, 1908, provides:– 'Every company shall send to every member, at his request, and on payment of one shilling or such less sum as the company may prescribe, a copy of the memorandum and of the articles (if any).' At the time that Mr. Anderson made his request to the secretary of the defendant Company for a copy of their Memorandum and Articles of Association he was a shareholder. The plaintiff Company had not then been registered as owner of any shares. He was a member of the defendant Company; his Company was not. The position was that he was entitled to receive a copy of the Memorandum and Articles; his Company was not. He was entitled to receive it personally *qua* member; he was not entitled to receive it *qua* agent of the plaintiff Company. In these circumstances I must, I think, conclude that the copy was requested and supplied, in accordance with the provisions of s. 18, sub-s. 1, of the Act, by the defendant Company to Mr. Anderson personally and not as agent for the plaintiff Company. It seems to me that there was no relationship between the parties in this case other than such as would exist between the defendant Company and any person (other than Mr. Anderson) who might chance to read the copy supplied to him; or, indeed, between that Company and any member of the community at large, individual or corporate, who chanced to become aware of the last sentence in Article 155 of the defective reprint of the Memorandum and Articles. It can hardly be seriously contended that the defendant Company owed a duty to the world at large to take care to avoid mistakes and printers' errors in the reprint of their Articles. In my opinion, counsel is correct in his submission that in this case the defendant Company owed no duty to the plaintiff Company to take care to ensure that the copy of the Articles supplied to Mr. Anderson was a correct copy. For these reasons there must, in my opinion, be judgment for the defendant Company.

Notes and Questions

1. Contrast *McSweeney* v. *Bourke*, unreported, High Ct., Miss Justice Carroll, 24 November 1980 (1977–No. 1728P), a decision involving facts almost the converse of the *Securities Trust* case.
2. Does a statement made 'without responsibility' mean: (a) that no duty of care arises in the first place, or (b) that although a duty does arise it may be met with a defence under section 34(1)(*b*) of the *Civil Liability Act 1961*? Is the answer to this question important? Does *Dublin Port & Docks Board* v. *Britannia Dredging Co. Ltd.* [1968] I.R. 136 (Sup. Ct.) throw any light on the problem?
3. To what extent, if any, do those in business undertake responsibility for advice given to clients or customers which extends beyond their area of operation? *Cf. Mutual Life & Citizens' Assurance Co. Ltd.* v. *Evatt* [1971] A.C. 793; *Esso Petroleum Co. Ltd.* v. *Mardon* [1976] Q.B. 801; *Howard Marine & Dredging Co. Ltd.* v. *A. Ogden & Sons (Excavations) Ltd.* [1978] Q.B. 574.
4. May a public authority be sued for negligent misstatement? *Cf.* Buckley, "Hedley Byrne" Marches On: Duty of Public Authority in Providing Information to Enquiries' 76 Incorp. L. Soc. of Ir. Gazette 197 (1982); *Anns* v. *Merton London Borough Council* [1978] A.C. 728, (extracted *supra*, pp. 280–284). See also the cases cited *supra*, p. 284.

BANK OF IRELAND V. SMITH

An advertisement of land for sale in Court in a mortgage suit erroneously stated that portion of the lands was sown with barley and undersown with permanent pasture. This statement was made honestly but mistakenly by the auctioneers who were the agents for the vendors. The purchaser sued for damages for (*inter alia*) innocent and negligent misstatement.

Kenny J.:

. . . The next contention was that the decision of the House of Lords in *Hedley Byrne & Co. Ltd.* v. *Heller* [1964] A.C. 465 had established that a person who relies on an innocent misrepresentation and suffers loss as a result is entitled to damages.

The speeches in that case establish that, in some cases, a negligent misrepresentation made to anyone who, to the knowledge of the speaker or writer will rely on it and will be damaged if it is incorrect, gives a right to damages: they do not establish that every innocent misrepresentation gives such a right. I shall be dealing with this decision in a later part of this judgment in connexion with the claim for negligence against the auctioneers. . . .

. . . I think I should deal with the other ground on which the purchaser based his claim. It was said that an auctioneer acting for a vendor should anticipate that any statements made by him about the property will be relied on by the purchaser and that he, therefore, owes a duty of care to the purchaser and is liable in damages to him if the statement was incorrect and was made carelessly. In my opinion, the decision in *Hedley Byrne & Co.* v. *Heller* [1964] A.C. 465 does not give any support to this startling proposition. It decides that, if a person seeks information from another in circumstances in which a reasonable man would know that his judgement is being relied on, the person giving the information must use reasonable care to ensure that his answer is correct, and if he does not do. so, he is liable in damages: but the relationship between the person seeking the information and the person giving it, if not fiduciary or arising out of a contract for consideration, must be, to use the words of Lord Devlin, 'equivalent to contract,' before any liability can arise. The basis of the decision in *Hedley Byrne & Co. Ltd.* v. *Heller & Partners Ltd.* is, I think, contained in the speech of Lord Devlin when he said (at p. 528):– 'I think, therefore, that there is ample authority to justify your Lordships in saying now that the categories of special relationships which may give rise to a duty to take care in word as well as in deed are not limited to contractual relationships or to relationships of fiduciary duty, but include also relationships which in the words of Lord Shaw in *Nocton* v. *Lord Ashburton* [1914] A.C. 932 are 'equivalent to contract' that is, where there is an assumption of responsibility in circumstances in which, but for the absence of consideration, there would be a contract. Even if an auctioneer's fees are paid by the purchaser (and in this case the vendors are liable for them), a contractual relationship between the vendors' auctioneers and the purchaser does not exist. The decision of Davitt P. in *Securities Trust Limited* v. *Hugh Moore & Alexander Limited* [1964] I.R. 417 supports this conclusion. Moreover, the purchaser has not proved that Mr. Mulcahy was negligent. He was told by an employee of Mr. Smith that the lands had been undersown, he visited them on many occasions and the error which he made is one which could be made by the most careful of auctioneers. The claim in negligence against the vendors fails . . .

Notes and Questions

1. Do you agree with Kenny J.'s approach?
2. A man is in a strange city where he has to be at a particular office by 11 a.m. or else he will miss a big business deal. He stops a pedestrian, explains his plight, and asks for directions to the office. The pedestrian carelessly misdirects him and the man loses the deal. May he sue the pedestrian? *Cf. Howard Marine & Dredging Co. Ltd.* v. *A. Ogden & Sons (Excavations) Ltd.* [1978] Q.B. 574, at 591 (C.A., *per* Lord Denning, M.R.). Would the case be different if the man had instead asked (a) a Garda; (b) the receptionist in a hotel; (c) a postman; (d) an employee in the tourist office?
3. A building society engages a firm of valuers and surveyors to value a house for the purpose of granting a mortgage. The prospective purchasers are given written notice that an advance from the building society does not imply that the purchase price is reasonable. The valuers and surveyors are negligent in their valuation. The plaintiffs, who have not commissioned any independent survey, buy the home and suffer loss. Are the valuers and surveyors in breach of any duty of care to the plaintiffs? *Cf. Yianni* v. *Edwin Evans & Sons* [1982] Q.B. 438.

WALL V. HEGARTY
Unreported, High Court, Barrington, J., 19 June 1980 (1979–No.2552P)

This case raises a neat point of law.

The facts have been admitted on the Pleadings or at the Bar during the course of the hearing. They are as follows:

The plaintiff is the executor named in a purported will of William Wall, deceased, later of Glenturkin, Whitegate, Co. Cork. The plaintiff was also a beneficiary named in the said purported will and was, under its terms, to receive a legacy of £15,000.

The defendants are a firm of solicitors.

In the month of October, 1975, the defendants took instructions from the said William Wall to draw up his last will and testament. They duly prepared a draft will and a solicitor in the defendants' firm attended at the testator's residence to have the will executed. The will was duly executed by the testator and witnessed by the solicitor referred to. The solicitor then apparently returned to his office where, in the absence of the testator, a typist appended her signature to the will, purporting to act as a witness to the execution thereof by the testator.

Later in the same month, the testator wished to alter his will in a manner not material for the purposes of these proceedings. A codicil was drawn up, executed by the testator, and witnessed by the same solicitor. Again, there was no second witness to the execution of the will by the testator but, on the solicitor's return to his office, the typist purported to sign the will as witness to the testator's signature.

Neither the will nor the codicil therefor, was attested as required by Section 78 of the Succession Act 1965.

The testator died without having purported to revoke or alter his said purported will or codicil.

After the testator's death, the defendant firm sent to the plaintiff a copy of the said purported will and codicil in his capacity as the executor named therein. The will and codicil appeared on their face to be in order but, of course, were, unbeknownst to the plaintiff, totally invalid.

However, word of the irregularities in the witnessing of the will and codicil apparently reached the ears of the testator's next-of-kin. They issued proceedings to have the purported will condemned, and it was necessary for the plaintiff to take instructions on the allegations being made by the next-of-kin. The defendants, when these matters were drawn to their attention, properly admitted that the allegations being made by the next-of-kin were true. The plaintiff had accordingly no choice but to concur in the will being condemned.

The testator was apparently a man of some substance. The plaintiff claims to have suffered the loss of the legacy of £15,000 which he would otherwise have received, and also to have suffered loss in the form of legal costs in getting himself involved in litigation which he would not have got involved in, had not the purported will been originally represented to him as being a valid document. At the hearing it was decided that I should defer the question of the quantification of the plaintiff's loss until I had first dealt with the substantial issue of whether a solicitor retained by a testator to draw up his will owes any duty to a legatee named in the will to ensure that the will and the legacy are valid.

There is no doubt that he does owe a duty to a testator to show reasonable care and to exercise professional skills appropriate to a solicitor in ensuring that the testator's wishes are carried out. But if a legacy fails, the testator and his estate may suffer little or no damage. The legatee may suffer substantial damage but may have no right of action against the solicitor. The testator's estate may have a right of action against the solicitor in contract or in tort, but may be entitled only to nominal Damages.

The plaintiff, in his Statement of Claim, pleads that a solicitor retained by a testator to prepare a will owes a duty to an executor and beneficiary named in the will to ensure that the testator's benevolent intentions in respect of the executor and beneficiary are not frustrated through lack of reasonable care on the part of the solicitor. At paragraph 7 of the Statement of Claim, he pleads:–

'The Defendants and each of them as Solicitors for William Wall, deceased, were obliged at all material times to conduct the affairs of the deceased in such manner as would ensure and protect the best interests of the Plaintiff as the person named as his Executor by the deceased and as a beneficiary under his said Will and of all persons entitled to benefit from, or concerned with, the Will of the deceased, which said duty the Defendants failed to discharge.'

Traditionally, English law did not regard a solicitor as owing any such duty to a legatee named in a testator's will and, so far as I am aware, the law of Ireland was no different in this respect.

A passage which appears on page 184 of the 1961 edition of Cordery's 'Law relating to Solicitors', puts the matter as follows:–

'Since the Solicitor's duty to his client is based on the contract of retainer, he owes no duty of care to anyone other than his client, save where he is liable as an Officer of the Court'.

The chief authority relied on, in support of that proposition was *Robertson* v. *Fleming*, 4 (4) Macq. 167. That was a decision of the House of Lords in a Scottish case. It is arguable that the central question in that case was whether an issue which had been settled in the Second Division of the Court of Session properly raised the question of fact in dispute between the parties. But it is also arguable that this question of fact would have been irrelevant if a solicitor owed a duty, not only to his client, but also to the person for whose benefit his services had been retained. In any event, as Sir Robert McGarry has stated in the recent Case of *Ross* v, *Caunters*, ([1979] 3 All E.R., 580 (at page 585)), the dicta, whether they were of the ratio or not, are clearly of high authority.

In that case, Lord Campbell, L.C., rejected in the strongest possible terms, the suggestion that a solicitor retained by a testator might owe any duty to a legatee who was a stranger to him.

In a passage which appears at page 177 of the Report, he says:–

'I never had any doubt of the unsoundness of the doctrine, unnecessarily (and I must say, unwisely) contended for by the Respondent's Counsel, that A. employing B., a professional lawyer, to do any acts for the benefit of C., A. having to pay B.,and there being no intercourse of any sort between B.and C.,– if,through the gross negligence and ignorance of B., in transacting the business, C. loses the benefit intended for him by A., C. may maintain an action against B., and recover Damages for the loss sustained. If this were law, a disappointed legatee might sue the Solicitor employed by a testator to make a Will in favour of a stranger, who the Solicitor never saw or before heard of, if the Will were void for not being properly signed and attested. I am clearly of opinion that this is not the law of Scotland, nor of England, and it can hardly be the law of any country where jurisprudence has been cultivated as a science.'

While Lord Campbell was in a minority in other aspects of the case, it would appears that a majority of his colleagues agreed with him on this point.

However, since *Robertson* v. *Fleming* was decided, there have been two major advances in the law, material to the consideration of the present question. First was the development of negligence as an independent tort and the line of Authority running from *Donoghue* v. *Stevenson* ([1932] App. Cas., page 562, [1932] All E.R., page 1.) to *Hedley Byrne & Co. Ltd.* v. *Heller & Partners Ltd.,* ([1964] App. Cas., page 465; [1963] 2 All E.R., page 575). In particular, was the famous passage in Lord Atkin's speech in *Donoghue* v. *Stevenson*, where he stressed the duty to take reasonable care to avoid injuring one's neighbour, and went on to inquire –

'Who, then in law is my neighbour?
The answer seems to be persons who are so closely and directly affected by my act that I ought reasonably to have them in contemplation as being so affected when I am directing my mind to the acts or omissions which are called into question.'

Lord Atkin went on to stress that the concept of 'neighbour' did not include merely persons in close physical proximity to the alleged tortreasor; but also, all such persons as stood in such direct relationship with him, as to cause him to know that they would be directly affected by his careless act. (See [1932] App. Cas., page 580).

The second important legal development which has taken place since *Robertson* v. *Fleming*, is that it is now finally established, so far, at any rate, as the law of Ireland is concerned, that a solicitor owes two kinds of duties to his client. First, is his duty in contract to carry out the terms of his retainer. Second is a duty in tort to show reasonable professional skill in attending to his client's affairs. It is clear that this duty in tort arises simply because he is purporting to act as a solicitor for his client and is independent of whether he is providing his professional services voluntarily or for reward. (See the judgment of the Supreme Court in *Finlay* v. *Murtagh* [1979] I.R. 249. See also, the judgment of Oliver J., in *Midland Bank* v. *Hett, Stubbs & Kemp*, [1978] 3 All E.R., page 167.)

The Supreme Court in *Finlay* v. *Murtagh* was merely dealing with a new point of law as to whether a Solicitor owed a duty to a client in tort as well as in contract, but it is quite clear that the Court, in holding that he did, derived the duty from the proximity principle outlined by Lord Atkin in *Donoghue* v. *Stevenson*. For instance, the following passages appears in the judgment of Kenny, J. –

'The professional person, however, owes the client a general duty and not one arising from contract but from the "proximity" principle (*Donoghue* v. *Stevenson* [1932] App. Cas., page 562, *Hedley Byrne & Co.* v. *Heller & Partners Ltd.* ([1964] App. Cas., page 465) to exercise reasonable care and skill in the performance of the work entrusted to him. This duty arises from the obligation which springs from the situation that he knew or ought to have known that his failure to exercise care and skill would probably cause loss and damage. This failure to have or to exercise reasonable skill and care is tortious or delictual in origin.'

Indeed, Henchy, J., in a passage in his judgment, appears to anticipate the situation which has arisen in the present case. He says:–

'The solicitor's liability in tort under the general duty of care extends not only to a client for reward, but to any person for whom he undertakes to act professionally without reward, and also to those (such as beneficiaries under a will, persons entitled under an intestacy, or those entitled to benefits in circumstances such as a claim in respect of a fatal injury) with whom he has made no arrangement to act, but who, as he knows or ought to know, will be relying on his professional care and skill. For the same default there should be the same cause of action. If others are entitled to sue in tort for the Solicitor's want of care, so also should the client.'

Since the decision of the Supreme Court in *Finlay* v. *Murtagh*, the specific question which arises in the present case, arose for consideration in the English High Court in the case of *Ross* v. *Caunters*, [1979] 3 All E.R., page 580).

In that case, the testator instructed solicitors to draw up his will to include gifts of chattels and a share of his residuary estate to the plaintiff, who was his sister-in-law. The solicitors drew up the will naming the plaintiff as legatee. The testator requested the solicitors to send the draft will to him at the plaintiff's home where he was staying, to be signed and attested. The solicitors sent the will to the testator with a covering letter giving instructions on executing it, but failed to warn him that under Section 15 of the Wills Act, 1837, attestation of the will by the beneficiary's spouse would invalidate the gift to the beneficiary. The plaintiff's husband attested the will which was then returned to the solicitors who failed to notice that he had attested it. In fact, prior to the execution of the Will, the testator had, in correspondence, raised with his solicitors, the question 'Am I right in thinking that beneficiaries may not be witnesses?' The solicitors unfortunately did not answer this question which clearly provided them with an opportunity to warn the testator that the spouse of a beneficiary should not be a witness either.

The testator died two years after the execution of the will. Some time later, the solicitors wrote to the plaintiff informing her that the gifts to her under the will were void because her husband had attested it. The plaintiff brought an action against the solicitors claiming damages for negligence for the loss of the gifts under the will. Sir Robert Megarry V.C., after an exhaustive analysis of the authorities, held that she was entitled to succeed.

In the present case, Mr. Walsh, on behalf of the plaintiff, has relied strongly on *Ross* v. *Caunters*. Mr. Matthews, on behalf of the Defendants, has drawn the distinction that in *Ross* v. *Caunters* there was a valid will – only the bequest was invalid – whereas in the present case there was no valid will. He has also stated that I should not, by following *Ross* v. *Caunters*, extend the traditional boundaries of the law of negligence in this country. However, it appears to me that the decision of the English High Court in *Ross* v. *Caunters* was already anticipated by the decision of our own Supreme Court in *Finlay* v. *Murtagh* and, for my own part, I find the reasoning of Sir Robert Megarry in *Ross* v. *Caunters* unanswerable.

I do not think that the fact that there was a valid will in *Ross* v. *Caunters*, and that there is not a valid will in the present case is a material distinction. The question is whether the testator's solicitor owes any duty at all to the named legatee. If he owes such a duty and if the legacy fails because of his failure to observe it, it is immaterial whether the gift fails because of a defect in the the words granting the legacy or because of a defect in the will itself.

I fully accept the reasoning of Sir Robert Megarry that in a case such as the present, there is a close degree of proximity between the plaintiff and the defendant. If a solicitor is retained by a testator to draft a will, and one of the purposes of the will is to confer a benefit on a named legatee, the solicitor must know that if he fails in his professional duty properly to draft the will, there is considerable risk the legatee will suffer damage. To use Sir Robert's words, his contemplation of the plaintiff is 'actual, nominate and direct.'

Likewise, I accept Sir Robert's reasoning that there can be no conflict of public policy in holding that a solicitor has a duty to take care in drafting a will, not only to the testator but also to a named legatee in the will. There is no possible inconsistency between the duty to the testator and the duty to the legatee. Recognising a duty to a legatee tends to strengthen the chances that the testator's wishes will in fact be properly expressed in the will. The two duties march together.

The authorities are, as I said, analysed by Sir Robert Megarry with consummate ability in his judgment in *Ross* v. *Caunters*, and it would be otiose for me to repeat here the exercise which he has carried out in his judgment. Suffice it to say that I am satisfied on the basis of the decision in *Finlay* v. *Murtagh* that a solicitor does owe a duty to a legatee named in a draft will, to draft the will with such reasonable care and skill as to ensure that the wishes of the testator are not frustrated and the expectancy of the legatee defeated through lack of reasonable care and skill on the part of the solicitor.

If a solicitor owes any duty to a named legatee, then it is quite clear that the solicitor in the present case has failed to show the appropriate care and skill. It is unnecessary to labour the point. The case has been frankly met. No effort has been made to defend what was done, except to say that the defendants owed no duty to the plaintiff.

To turn now, to the question of the plaintiff's loss. Mr. Matthews has suggested that the plaintiff had no more than a 'spes'. His loss, it is suggested, is too remote to be taken into consideration by the law. I cannot accept this. The testator died without revoking his purported will. Had, therefore, the will been validly drawn, the plaintiff would have received his bequest of £15,000. There might, of course, be circumstances in which the plaintiff would suffer no loss. There might, for instance, be an earlier and valid will under which the plaintiff would receive financial benefits of equal value. The testator's estate might have been insolvent and the plaintiff might have received nothing even if the will had been valid. Or the will might have been invalid on some other collateral ground in respect of which the solicitor had no responsibility. I understand that none of these factors apply to the present case though the defendants have asked for formal proof of the value of the testator's estate, and they are clearly entitled to this before the plaintiff's loss is finally quantified.

Apart from that, the plaintiff has suffered loss in that he got involved in legal proceedings to have the will upheld. It appears to me that a solicitor who draws up a will in which an executor is named and which, on its face appears to be in order, must foresee or anticipate that the executor will or may attempt to have the will admitted to probate. It is clearly the proper thing for the executor to attempt to have the will admitted to probate so that the testator's wishes may be upheld. It therefore appears to me that ordinary costs incurred by the executor, prior to being put on notice of any irregularity, in having the will admitted to probate, flow naturally from the solicitor's lack of care and are recoverable against him. In this respect there may be a distinction between the position in the pesent case and the position in *Ross* v. *Caunters*. There it was held that legal costs incurred by the plaintiff in investigating her own claim against the solicitor, were not recoverable as damages against the defendants. They were recoverable as costs, if at all. The present question is quite distinguishable. We are not dealing here with costs incurred by the plaintiff investigating his own claim. We are dealing with costs incurred by him in upholding the will at a time when he had every reason to believe that the will was a valid one. It appears to me that this item of loss could also be recovered on a different basis. After the testator's death, the defendants sent to the plaintiff a copy of the testator's will without drawing to his attention a fact (which someone in the firm must have known) that while the testator's signature appeared on the face of the will, to have been properly attested it had not in fact been properly attested. Even therefore, if the plaintiff's loss in getting involved in legal proceedings to prove the will did not flow directly from the original carelessness in drafting the will on the principles of *Donoghue* v. *Stevenson*, it appears to me that the loss would still be recoverable because of the fact of the circumstances in which the will was sent to the plaintiff on the principles of the *Hedley Byrne Case* ([1963] 2 All E.R., page 975; [1964] App. Cas., at page 465.)

Apart from the foregoing there appears to me to be another heading under which the plaintiff is entitled to recover damages. Had the will been valid, the plaintiff would, in the normal course, have been entitled to interest on his legacy at the conclusion of the executor's year at the rate which the law allows, there being no express provision for the payment of interest on legacies in the will. Whether the plaintiff would have been entitled to recover interest in the circumstances of the present case, however, where he, himself, was the executor is a matter on which I would like to hear further argument.

Under these circumstances I propose to adjourn the case for the assessment of damages (if any) under these three heads.

Notes and Questions

1. After this decision, has recovery for pure economic loss been placed on the straightforward principle of reasonable foreseeability? If not, what did the decision hold? If so, is there any more a need for retaining the *Hedley Byrne* principle, or has it been rendered obsolete?
2. Statute has recently supplemented the protection available to victims of misrepresentation in a contractual context. Part V of the *Sale of Goods and Supply of Services Act 1980* introduces provisions broadly similar to those of the English *Misrepresentation Act 1967*. An important limitation, however is that only a narrow range of contracts falls within its scope: Section 43 defines 'contract' as meaning a contract of sale of goods, a hire-purchase agreement, an agreement for the letting of goods or a contract for the supply of service. Section 45(1) provides that:
   'Where a person has entered into a contract after a misrepresentation has been made by him by another party thereto and as a result thereof he has suffered loss, then, if the person making the misrepresentation would be liable to damages in respect thereof had the misrepresentation been made fraudulently, that person shall be so liable notwithstanding that the misrepresentation was not made fraudulently, unless he proves that he had reasonable ground to believe and did believe up to the time the contract was made that the facts represented were true.'
   A few points should be noted about this provision. Unlike the situation at common law, it is not necessary for the victim of the misrepresentation to prove the existence of any particular relationship of reliance between him and the party guilty of misrepresentation. Moreover the onus is on the person who makes the misrepresentation to prove not only that it was based on reasonable grounds but also that he believed it to be true up to the time the contract was made. But the statutory provision is more restrictive than the common law in that it imposes liability only on a *party* to a contract: a person whose misrepresentation leads the victim to enter a contract with another does not fall within the scope of the Act.
   There is some uncertainty as to whether the measure of damages (including remoteness of damage) in the statutory action should be regarded as akin to fraud, negligence or breach of contract. See *McMahon & Binchy*, p. 414; Taylor, 'Expectation, Reliance and Misrepresentation' 45 Modern L. Rev. 139 (1982).
3. To what extent does the common law impose liability for negligent misstatement in a contractual setting? Cf. *Stafford* v. *Mahony, Smith and Palmer*, unreported, High Ct., Doyle, J., 21 March 1980 (1976 No.1668P). See also Symmons, 'The Problem of the Applicability of Tort Liability to Negligent Misstatements in Contractual Settings' 21 McGill L. J. 79 (1975).

Chapter 18

INTERFERENCE WITH RELATIONSHIPS

TORTS AFFECTING FAMILY RELATIONSHIPS

Spouses

Tort law through a variety of actions has afforded members of a family some protection against intentional and negligent interference in their relationships with each other. The structure of these actions is antiquated, being based on legal fictions which have been regarded with increasing distaste in the community in recent years. The *Family Law Act 1981* abolished three of these actions. The first was that of criminal conversation, which enabled a man to obtain damages from a person who had sexual intercourse with his wife. (The question whether a woman had a similar right of action in respect of a woman who had sexual intercourse with her husband was never resolved by an Irish court.) The other actions abolished by the 1981 Act were for enticement and harbouring of a spouse.

As regards inter-spousal relationships, the action for loss of *consortium* remains.

SPAIGHT V. DUNDON
[1961] I.R. 201 (Supreme Court, 1960)

Kingsmill Moore J.:

This is an action in which husband and wife, as co-plaintiffs, are suing the defendant for negligence resulting in serious injuries to the wife. The wife has been awarded £7,000 in respect of those injuries and there is no appeal against such award. The husband sues for the expenses of medical, surgical and nursing attention which he has provided and will have to provide for his wife, for the cost of domestic assistance which he has been forced to obtain and may have to obtain in the future by reason of his wife's incapacity to carry out domestic duties, and for the past loss and possible future loss of his wife's society and service. He was awarded £5,210 by the jury and this is an appeal on the ground that such award was excessive.

The injuries to the wife were serious and have undoubtedly involved the husband in heavy expenses. Her leg was amputated at the knee and she was some four months in hospital at Limerick. She then had to go to Roehampton to have an artificial leg fitted and to be trained in its use, and subsequently had to pay a second visit for the fitting of a better leg. In all she was completely separated from her husband for periods totalling nearly a year. The wife's sister came to look after the household and the husband agreed to pay her £4 a week and maintain her. The maintenance he estimates at £2 a week, making a total weekly expense to him of £6, for a period of 72 weeks. The trial Judge accepted that the total expenses to which the husband had been put, including a sum of £468 in respect of wages and maintenance for the wife's sister, amounted at the date of the trial to £1,346.

There will be considerable expenses in the future. Evidence was given that the servicing and replacements of the artificial limb would amount to an average of £40 a year. At present rates of interest this could be obtained by an investment of £666 in a 6 per cent Government security. Income tax would have to be paid but the capital would be intact at the wife's death. I think the maximum which could be allowed under this head could not be more than £600. There is also the possibility of the expense of a future operation to procure a better stump for fitting an artificial leg. Domestic help will be required until the wife has mastered the use of her artificial limb, and perhaps some minor assistance subsequently. I will assume a jury might award £1,500 in respect of future expenses. Finally, there is the total loss of consortium for approximately a year. In so far as the consortium includes servitium, allowance has already been made for this in the sum of £468 awarded in respect of the wages and maintenance of the sister. But the husband is entitled to damages for the total loss of his wife's companionship during the period of approximately a year when she was in hospital or undergoing fitting of the limb and training in London. Juries are always directed to assess this head of damages moderately and I do not think a sum of more than £200 could reasonably be allowed.

The total of all those sums is £3,046. The jury awarded £5,210. This discrepancy is too big to be supported unless some further head of damages can be considered. Mr. Costello says there is such a head. In addressing the jury at the opening of the case he submitted that the husband was entitled to damages for what he suffered in the disruption of his life, his mental torture and the injury to his prospects in his married life. He was also entitled to be compensated because his wife was disfigured and her mental outlook and temperament might be affected. Mr. Liston submitted to the Judge that damages could be awarded for the impairment, as opposed to the total loss, of consortium. The companionship of the wife, he suggested, would in future be less valuable than before. She would not be able to go about with him on social occasions. The trial Judge directed the jury that these considerations must be left out of account, and Mr. Liston took objection to this direction and asked the Judge to recall and re-direct the jury according to his earlier submissions. This the learned Judge refused to do.

At the hearing of the appeal counsel for the defendant contended that the sum awarded to the husband, if it represented damages for matters which properly formed a ground for damages, was so excessive that it must be set aside; and that its amount was evidence that the jury must have taken into account the elements which had been pressed by counsel for the husband, but which had been excluded by the Judge. Mr. Costello in a vigorous argument submitted that the learned Judge was wrong in his ruling and that damages might and should be given for the impairment to the consortium which would occur in the future as a result of the injuries. If such an element could be taken into account the damages, he said, were in no way excessive. Alternatively he submitted that even leaving this element out of account the amount awarded could be justified.

I have already indicated that in my opinion the damages are excessive if the additional elements, which Mr. Costello says are a proper ground for damage, are to be left out of account. I will also assume, though without so deciding, that if these elements are to be taken into account the award can be justified.

The decision of this appeal turns therefore on a single and net question of law: can a husband whose wife has been injured by the negligence of a third party successfully maintain an action for the impairment (as opposed to the total loss) of her consortium arising from the injury?

No Irish authority was cited on this point, but the question has recently been argued with great fullness and research in England and has given rise to weighty opinions in the Court of Appeal and the House of Lords. The case to which I refer is *Best v. Samuel Fox & Co. Ltd.* [1951] 2 K. B. 629; [1952] A. C. 716. The plaintiff, a married woman, sued the defendant company for the loss of her husband's consortium. Her husband had been injured by the negligence of the company, and, as a result, had become incapable of sexual intercourse. The husband sued and recovered against the defendants in respect of his injuries and the wife subsequently brought a second action for loss of consortium.

For the defendants it was argued first, that a married woman could not maintain an action for loss of consortium arising from injuries negligently caused; and secondly, that, even if such an action lay, it lay only where there was a total loss of consortium, (though such loss might only be temporary) and did not lie for mere injury to or impairment of consortium however permanent such injury or impairment might be. In the Court of Appeal Birkett L.J. held that a wife might successfully sue for a total loss of consortium, Asquith L.J. took the contrary view, and Cohen L.J. preferred not to commit himself on this point. All three Lord Justices were, however, of opinion that, even if a wife could maintain an action for *loss* of consortium, she could not maintain an action for mere impairment of consortium in one or more respects; and this is the ground of their decision.

On appeal to the House of Lords the case was decided on a different ground, for the Law Lords held unanimously that a wife could not recover damages even for a total loss of consortium, and, accordingly, it became unnecessary to decide the nature of consortium or whether damages could be recovered for its impairment. Nevertheless four out of the five Law Lords expressed opinions on this question. Lord Porter gave it as his tentative opinion that mere impairment was insufficient. Lord Goddard agreed with him. Lord Reid's view was to the contrary and Lord Oaksey adopted the judgment of Lord Reid. Lord Morton preferred not to express any opinion.

All the judges who considered the question treated it as being open and unconcluded by authority. In Ireland we are equally devoid of authority. I will attempt therefore to state shortly the reasons for their opinions given by the judges in *Best* v. *Samuel Fox & Co. Ltd.*

Lord Justice Birkett says, at p. 664:– 'There would appear to be no case where damages have been recovered save for the loss of, as distinct from any impairment of, the consortium.' He then quotes a passage from the Restatement of the Law of Torts promulgated by the American Law Institute which suggests that damages could be recovered by a husband for 'impairment of his wife's capacity in sexual relations,' and continues:– 'This statement does more than assert the proprietary interest of the husband alone: it assumes that the consortium may be split up and the various strands which are interwoven into the whole may be separated and dealt with singly and apart.

'The view I am inclined to hold is that consortium cannot be dealt with in that way. The history of the action giving the husband his rights shows its somewhat artificial character. But, if consortium is to be capable of separation into many and extremely diverse elements, so that the impairment of any one element, however slight, will give a cause of action, then the prospects are rather overwhelming. Companionship, love, affection, comfort, mutual services, sexual intercourse – all belong to the married state. Taken together, they make up the consortium; but I cannot think that the loss of one element, however grievous it may be, as it undoubtedly is in the present case, can be regarded as the loss of the consortium within the meaning of the decided cases. Still less could any impairment of one of the elements be so regarded. Consortium, I think, is one and indivisible. The law gives a remedy for its loss, but for nothing short of that.'

Lord Justice Cohen, at p. 665, said that he agreed entirely with the conclusion of Birkett L.J. that an action by a wife based on loss of consortium owing to the negligent, but malicious, act of a third party causing injury to her husband cannot succeed unless the wife can prove loss, as distinct from impairment, of that consortium.

Lord Asquith also held that there must be a total, even though temporary, loss of consortium to give a cause of action. 'No case can be found in actions by the husband where, some separable constituent element only of the consortium being destroyed, an action has been held to lie. Consortium is, in my view, one and indiscerptible. The alternative view, the view that you can disengage a particular strand in the consortial bond and say that, because that strand has been severed, that is enough – in other words the view that impairment of the consortium as opposed to destruction of it will suffice – finds no support in the precedents and leads to insoluble problems in practice. Is a wife to be entitled to sue her husband's employer because, through his neglig- ence, her husband has been lamed, and hence that element of their consortium which consisted in long country walks which they used to share has perished? This seems to me wrong. No-one disputes the importance of the particular ingredient in the consortium which has been extinguished in this case, which includes the wife's capacity to bear children in wedlock: but, once you permit the segregation of a particular ingredient and say that when that has gone the consortium has gone, you enter a region of extreme perplexity and complication. For these reasons I am of opinion that the appeal should be dismissed.'

In the House of Lords [1952] A. C. 716, Lord Porter, after referring to the views expressed in the Court of Appeal that consortium was one and indivisible and that it was lost as a whole or not at all, continued, at p. 728:–'I think there is much to be said for this view, and, indeed, I find it difficult to draw the boundary between what is and what is not loss of consortium or to divide it into its component parts.' He did not however find it necessary to come to a final decision on this point having decided the case on other grounds.

Lord Goddard, at p. 733, said that he was in agreement with the views of the Court of Appeal. 'Consortium seems to me to be essentially an abstraction. Where the exercise of a profession or the call of duty involves prolonged absence abroad of one of the spouses there is not an interruption of consortium, nor is there because one of them may become a permanent invalid to be waited on and nursed by the other. Again there may be loss of affection but provided the spouses continue to live together as man and wife it seems to me that it still exists however different life may be from the days of the honeymoon. Sexual relations are doubtless a most important part of the marriage relation, but if age or illness or even disinclination impairs the potency of either of the spouses who continue to live together as husband and wife I do not think the consortium is affected. It would be only if on this account one of them withdrew and decided to live apart. In truth I think the only loss that the law can recognise is the loss of that part of the consortium that is called servitium, the loss of service.'

As Lord Reid was the only judge in either Court to give reasons for the view that impairment of consortium would afford a claim for damages I give his words at some length. He says: 'In the old cases a number of words are used to describe the husband's loss or damage. He has, by the act of the wrongdoer, lost his wife's services, assistance, comfort, society, etc. Sometimes the word consortium is used in conjunction with one or more of these words; sometimes it appears to be intended to include them. I doubt whether there was any fixed practice. But it would seem that there was only one single cause of action in respect of loss in all these matters. There was not one action for loss of consortium and another for loss of servitium, and in the same cause of action loss or damage under any of these heads could properly be taken into account, though often the main emphasis might be on the value of the services or assistance which the husband had lost. The origin of the husband's right of action seems to have been that he was regarded as having a quasi-proprietary right, and I think that it included a right to his wife's society as well as to her services. I can see no sign of any difference in quality between his right to her assistance and his right to her society, and indeed it would be difficult to say where in fact assistance ends and society begins, either to-day or in the Middle Ages. No doubt her services and assistance had an additional value because her comfort and society went with them. I do not think that consortium was an abstraction: it seems to me rather to be a name for what the husband enjoys by virtue of a bundle of rights, some hardly capable of precise definition.

'I do not think that it is open to doubt that an impairment of a wife's capacity to render assistance to her husband was enough to found an action. Certainly an injury which temporarily incapacitated her was sufficient, and I cannot find any ground for the view that an injury which did not produce complete incapacity at any time was insufficient even if it resulted in serious and permanent impairment of her capacity to render services. Any such injury might well deprive the husband to a large extent of his wife's comfort and society but at no time deprive him wholly of it, and I have seen nothing to lead me to think that in such a case that impairment of the consortium must be left out of account, and, if impairment of the consortium is enough, I have seen nothing to lead me to think that the destruction of a wife's capacity for sexual intercourse should not be regarded as such an impairment.'

At least four of the judges who were of opinion that there could be no action even by a husband for impairment of consortium, seem to have been influenced by their views that the action for loss of consortium was an anomalous survival of medieval outlook and should not be extended an inch further than authority prescribed. Their attitude appears most clearly expressed where they were considering whether a wife could sue for loss of consortium, there being no clear authority that she could. But the same consideration would apply to the question whether a husband could sue for impairment as opposed to loss of consortium. If the claim based on total loss of consortium is to be considered anomalous in theory and only sustainable because of binding authority there is no ground for extension of the anomaly to a claim based merely on impairment of consortium for which there is no such authority.

Thus Cohen L.J. says, at p. 666:– 'The husband's right to recover [for total loss] . . . is, no doubt, now so clearly established that, at any rate in this Court, it must be recognised. It seems to me, however, an anomaly. The whole idea of the right of consortium is a vague right. There is nothing concrete about it, with the consequence that a person may trespass on that right without knowing of its existence, for he may not know that the wife is a married woman. It is difficult to see on what principle the right was recognised. It is to be observed, however, that, so far as I have been able to ascertain, in every case where the right was recognised the action was for the loss of consortium et servitium. The *ratio decidendi* may therefore have been that, the husband being entitled to the services of his wife, she was in a certain sense to be regarded as his property.' And at p. 667 he says:– 'So here I think it may be said that the right of the husband to recover damages in cases such as are indicated by the third count in Bullen & Leake's Precedents of Pleadings (3rd ed.), at p. 340' [a case where the husband sues for loss of consortium arising from an assault made by a third party on his wife], 'is an anomaly . . .'

Lord Asquith says, at p. 669, that he agrees that, if the husband's right had first come into question as *res integra* today, it would probably have been negatived, but that as it is 'deeply entrenched in authority' the intervention of the Legislature would be needed to abolish it.

In the House of Lords Lord Porter says, at p. 728:– 'I agree with the Lord Chief Justice that today a husband's right of action for loss of his wife's consortium is an anomaly and see no good reason for extending it.' Lord Goddard, at p. 731, illustrates the illogical and anomalous nature of an action for loss of consortium, and at p. 733 he says:– 'I agree with Cohen L.J. and Lord Asquith that if the matter were now *res integra* the law, they say "probably," while I am tempted to say "certainly," would refuse to give an action to the husband merely for loss of consortium due to negligence. It is too late now for the Courts to deny an action which has existed for hundreds of years. It is an anomaly at the present day that a husband can obtain damages for an injury to his wife, but English law is free neither of some anomalies nor of everything illogical, but this is no reason for extending them. There is this about it that is neither anomalous nor illogical, still less unjust; a husband nowadays constantly claims and recovers for medical and domestic expenses to which he has been put owing to an injury to his wife. As to the first, I think his claim really lies in his legal obligation to provide proper maintenance and comfort, including medical and surgical aid, for his wife, and the fact that a wrong does cause that obligation to be incurred is regarded as giving him a right to recover, while the latter is truly a remnant, and perhaps the last, of his right to sue for the loss of servitium; for, to use Lord Wensleydale's words, it is to the protection of such material interests that the law attends rather than mental pain or anxiety.'

I agree with the eminent judges who considered the action for loss of consortium to be anomalous and founded on a medieval view that the husband had a proprietary – or at least a quasi-proprietary right – in his wife, analogous to his right to the servitium of his servant. Human relationships are so varied that an injury to one person nearly always involves injury of some kind or another to other people but, except where loss of consortium is produced, the common law treats such injury as too remote to found an action for damages. It needed statutory interference to give the dependants of a man, who had been killed by a tortious act, damages for the pecuniary loss caused to them. The anomalous nature of an action for loss of consortium may be brought out by an instance. A married woman owns a small business. She has a growing family, and her widowed and invalid mother lives with her. As a result of a street accident she becomes a permanent invalid and must spend the rest of her life in a nursing home. Her employees have to be dismissed, her children are deprived of her care and influence, her mother no longer has a daughter to look after her. None of these can claim against the person whose negligence has caused the injuries. But the husband, who may have been on the worst of terms with his wife, can claim damages for loss of consortium. His right is supported by authority which cannot be questioned or reversed, unless by the Legislature. For myself, I refuse to extent it. None of the cases cited to us, and none of numerous other cases which I have examined, seem to give him a right of action for mere injury to his consortium, and the judges whose opinion I have quoted have also failed to find any authority for a claim founded on partial injury of consortium as opposed to loss thereof.

To admit such a claim would be to allow damages to be given for injuries extending over a vast field and of the most indefinite nature. Again I resort to an illustration. A woman of great beauty is involved in an accident, caused by negligence, and has her face hideously and permanently scarred by flying glass. Physically she makes a complete recovery but as a result of the loss of her appearance she is sensitive about appearing in public, can no longer bear to go to dances and becomes moody and irritable. All these unfortunate results can be taken into account by a jury in arriving at their decision on the quantum of damages to be awarded to her. But the husband has also been adversely affected. He has no longer the company of his wife at dances, he is deprived of the aesthetic pleasure of contemplating her beauty, the domestic harmony is impaired. These losses may be very real but it would be almost impossible to lay down any principles on which damages could be assessed, even if they could in theory be given. It appears to me that in general policy the law is sound in refusing to extend liability for a tort beyond the injuries to the person against whom the tort is directly committed. Otherwise I can see no limit to the number of the persons who could claim that they had been indirectly affected to their detriment or to the nature of the claims that could be made. It does appear that the law has made one exception for the husband in respect of one type of claim, total loss of consortium. But there does not seem to me any reason to extend the exception in regard to the nature of the claim any more than in regard to the persons who can claim.

There is no doubt that the husband can recover for the medical and surgical expenses which he has been put to by the injury to his wife and for extra domestic expenses in which he has been involved: *Best* v. *Samuel Fox & Co. Ltd.* [1952] A. C. 716, per Lord Porter, at p. 728; per Lord Goddard, at p. 733. These are pecuniary losses easily ascertained where already incurred and capable of fair estimation for the future. In addition he is entitled to damages for the total deprivation of his wife's company, even if such deprivation is for a limited period or periods. Such damages should not be too generous: *Hare* v. *British Transport Commission* [1956] 1 All E.R. 578, at p. 579 per Lord Goddard at p. 579: *Sellars* v. *Best* [1954] 2 All E.R. 389 per Pearson J., at p. 394. No further grounds for awarding damages can be entertained.

It follows that, in my opinion, the award of damages in this case must be set aside and a new trial ordered on the issue of damages.

Maguire J.:

In my opinion there is, in the common law of Ireland, no authority and no precedent for the recovery of damages for partial loss of consortium in an action for damages for negligence against a third party, a complete stranger, who has accidentally caused personal injuries to a plaintiff's wife in a road accident. That is this case. It differs completely from an action for criminal conversation or an action founded on enticement or deceit. The considerations which apply to such actions are so different, the principles of law are so different, that even an analogy cannot be drawn between such actions and an action for damages for negligence as presented in this case.

Counsel for the respondent husband strongly relies upon what he calls the 'bundle of rights' under which the husband enjoys the right of consortium with his wife. The phrase is adapted from the speech of Lord Reid in *Best* v. *Samuel Fox & Co. Ltd.* [1952] A. C. 716, at p. 736:– 'The origin of the husband's right of action seems to have been that he was regarded as having a quasi-proprietary right, and I think that it included a right to his wife's society as well as to her services. I can see no sign of any difference in quality between his right to her assistance and his right to her society, and indeed it would be difficult to say where in fact assistance ends and society begins, either to-day or in the Middle Ages. No doubt her services and assistance had an additional value because her comfort and society went with them. I do not think that consortium was an abstraction: it seems to me rather to be a name for what a husband enjoys by virtue of a bundle of rights, some hardly capable of precise definition.'

It seems to me that if rights are to be presented in bundles, the clarity of vision necessary for their examination and definition may be more than a little obscured, and it may become difficult if not impossible to segregate or define them, or to ascertain or prescribe precisely their extent and limitations. Lord Reid mentions, at

p. 735 of the report, that this part of his speech is not material to a decision of the case he was considering, and that he felt some hesitation in dealing with this aspect of the matter. I find myself quite unable to accept the argument based on the bundle of rights, however strongly it has been urged.

In the case we now have to consider the husband and wife are happily married. They are living happily together in the enjoyment of their married life before and since the accident. There is no evidence whatever to suggest anything to the contrary. There is no evidence of invasion, or attempted invasion, of their marital rights, or of any attack upon them. There is nothing to suggest loss of consortium in the true meaning of the term, as accepted generally, either partially or wholly.

The wife of the respondent has been adequately compensated by the appellant in so far as money can compensate her for the severe injuries she undoubtedly sustained. She has recovered damages, £7,000, in this action. Against that part of the verdict there is no appeal. The plaintiff is entitled to recover damages under two heads:– 1, the medical, surgical and nursing expenses etc. incurred by him, and 2, the extra domestic expenses which he has incurred or will incur, by reason of his wife's injuries. This he is entitled to by law, though it seems to me that since the Married Women's Property Acts the wife could recover the medical, surgical and nursing expenses herself in her own action.

The plaintiff respondent has been awarded £5,210 damages by the jury. The special damage[s] to which he is entitled under the heads I have mentioned are capable of approximate determination. On no basis of reasonable computation can this verdict be sustained unless a substantial sum of approximately £3,000 is included for loss of partial consortium. If this sum has to be eliminated, as I think it must, then the verdict of the jury is grossly excessive and it cannot be sustained.

There is in this case fortunately no question of double payments or overlapping claims which must be guarded against in cases of this kind.

A serious case like this falls heavily on the defendant. It is sought to extend his liability by the addition of a claim for partial loss of consortium for which there is no precedent. The law in Ireland will no doubt seek to protect the rights of husband and wife if and when these rights are challenged or attacked. But it seems to me that to impose a new liability of the kind now sought, if there was power to impose it, which there is not, apart from legislation, would open up an entirely unknown and dangerous vista for claims for damages. It would add another terror to the perils of the roads.

I agree generally with the judgment of Mr. Justice Kingsmill Moore. There must be a new trial of the action on the amount of damages recoverable by the respondent.

Ó Dálaigh and **Lavery JJ.** concurred with **Kingsmill Moore J.**

Maguire C.J. (dissenting):

. . . I see no reason if damages may be recovered for complete loss of consortium why they may not be recovered for a partial loss. It is true of course that drawing a line poses a difficulty. In my opinion, however, a jury should be able from the evidence to form an opinion as to the extent which the bundle of rights which make up the consortium have been interfered with. It is to my mind not proper to take into consideration, as some of the Judges in *Best* v. *Samuel Fox & Co. Ltd.* did, that the right to damages for loss of consortium is based upon a conception of the relationship of husband and wife which in modern times may be regarded as an anomaly. The alteration in the position of a wife *vis-a-vis* her husband by various legislative enactments may be a good reason for changing the law and abolishing the right of the husband to damages for loss of consortium. While the right exists it seems to me illogical to deny a husband a right to damages for its impairment.

The question remains whether the jury have awarded an excessive amount under this head of damage. The figure awarded I take to be somewhere in the region of £3,000. Having regard to the grave physical and psychological change brought about by the injuries to the wife, I am unable to say that the figure is so unduly large that this Court should interfere.

I would dismiss this appeal.

O'HARAN V. DIVINE
100 I.L.T.R. 53 (Supreme Court, 1964)

Kingsmill Moore J.:

This is an appeal by the defendant against an award by a jury to the female plaintiff of £9,000 for personal injuries and an award of £350 to her husband the male plaintiff for loss of consortium. The first award is challenged on the ground that the damages are excessive, the second on the ground that damages are excessive and also on the ground that as the loss of consortium was only partial no damages are recoverable.

The plaintiff Denis William O'Haran and the plaintiff Marie Elizabeth O'Haran are husband and wife. On July 12th 1961, both were involved in a motor accident caused by the negligence of the defendant. The husband's injuries were slight but those of his wife serious and their sequelae even more serious.

[Having considered the award of damages to Mrs. O'Haran and having held that it was not excessive, **Kingsmill Moore J.** continued:]

The award of £350 to Mr. O'Haran for loss of consortium was attacked on novel ground. In *Spaight* v. *Dundon* [1961] I.R. 201 the Supreme Court, while affirming the continued existence of a right of action for loss of consortium caused by negligent action of a third party, laid down that such right lay only where there was a total loss of consortium and not merely an impairment of consortium by loss or reduction of some of the elements which together made up the concept of consortium. Consortium was regarded as the sum total of the benefits which a wife may be expected to confer on her husband by their living together – help, comfort, companionship, services and all the amenities of family and marriage. If by the negligent action of the defendant a husband was deprived of all these, even for a limited period, he was entitled to recover damages; but if the deprivation was merely of one or more elements of consortium while other elements continued to be enjoyed no action lay. I expressed the opinion that the action for – consortium was anomalous, founded on a medieval view that a husband had a proprietary – or at least a quasi-proprietary right – in his wife analogous to his right to the servitium of his servant; and as no case could be found where damages had been given for impairment as distinguished from deprivation of consortium refused to extend a right which seemed already anomalous. In conclusion I said that '. . . he [a husband] is entitled to damages for total deprivation of his wife's company, even if such deprivation is for a limited period or periods. Such damages should not be too generous.' *Hare* v. *British Transport Commission* [1965] 1 All E.R. 578, *per* Lord Goddard at p. 579, *Sellars* v. *Best* [1954] 2 All E.R. 389, *per* Pearson J. at p. 394. Lavery J. and O' Daly J. (as he was then) agreed with my judgment. Maguire J. while 'agreeing generally' with my judgment gave a judgment of his own in which he said– 'In my opinion there is, in the common law of Ireland, no authority and no precedent for the recovery of damages for partial loss of consortium in an action for damages for negligence against a third party, a complete stranger, who has accidentally caused personal injuries to a plaintiff's wife in a road accident.'

In the present case the wife was separated from her husband for twenty-nine weeks during her treatments in hospital and for thirteen weeks of necessary convalescence in Guernsey, a total of forty-two weeks. Mr. FitzGerald points out that her husband was able to visit her while in hospital and could have communicated with her by letter or telephone while in Guernsey. This, he says, prevents the loss of consortium from being total. There remained the opportunity for interchange of thought, a valuable part of the conception of consortium. On the evidence the wife when in hospital was in almost continual pain and was naturally somewhat obsessed by her suffering. The interchange of thought must have been somewhat limited. But I do not rest on this. It seems to me that the question must be looked at somewhat broadly. A healthy companion and helper was reduced to a condition where she had to be separated from her husband for restoration of her health. All the innumerable advantages, pleasures and consolations of married life were brought to an end – save a limited measure of communication. It would be unreal to say that the husband had not been effectively deprived of consortium. I hold that such deprivation may and should be regarded as sufficient to give a claim for damages.

Damages were awarded to the husband under a separate heading for any expenses he had incurred for his wife's treatment and for the hire of domestic help to take the place of her services in the home. The £350 is an estimate of the loss he sustained by being deprived for forty-two weeks of her wifely companionship in the fullest sense of the term. It is impossible to lay down any exact standard of measurement and different juries might vary widely but honestly in their estimates. I have come to the conclusion that the sum of £350 is not so much in excess of what a reasonable jury might give as would warrant a new trial of this item of damages.

Ó Dálaigh C.J., Haugh and **Walsh JJ.** concurred. **Lavery J.** also concurred subject to a slight qualification as to assessment of damages.

Notes and Questions

1. Can *Spaight* v. *Dundon* and *O'Haran* v. *Divine* be reconciled?
2. Has a wife the right to sue for the loss of *consortium* of her husband? *Cf. McMahon & Binchy*, p. 414.
3. Does the action for loss of *consortium* serve a useful purpose? Should it be abolished? Should any other action replace it? *Cf.* the Law Reform Commission's Working Paper No.7 – 1979, *The Law Relating to Loss of Consortium and Loss of Services of a Child*, and its *First Report on Family Law*, pp. 9–11 (1981).

(ii) *Parents and Children*

The relationship between parent and child is protected against outside interference by four actions: for seduction, enticement, harbouring and loss of services of the child. Each will be considered in turn below, but first it is necessary to examine the legal basis on which they proceed. Essentially the law endorses what is in many cases a fiction in order to entitle parents to obtain damages in respect of what is – or, at all event, used to be – regarded as behaviour deserving of legal sanction. This fiction is to the effect that the parent is the 'master' of the child, since the child may perform services (usually of a domestic nature) for the parent when living in the home. Since this fiction is an inherent part of the action, the defendant may escape liability on the somewhat technical basis that the relationship of master and servant at the relevant time or times has not been established in the particular case. This is a particular danger in the action for seduction. See *Hamilton* v. *Long, infra*, pp. 431–433 and *Murray* v. *Fitzgerald* [1906] 2 I.R. 254.

Seduction

Where a woman or girl is seduced this may, of course, result in pregnancy. In such a case some parents have taken action against the man for damages. The essence of the damage is the injury to the 'honour' and respectability of the family, but the action must proceed on the basis that the seduction has resulted in some interference with the services performed for the parent of the seduced woman or girl. It should be noted that it is not essential that pregnancy result from the act of sexual intercourse: illness or disease could also suffice: *Manvell* v. *Thomson* 2 C. & P. 303, 172 E.R. 137 (1826); *Quinlan* v. *Barber* Bat. Rep. 47 (K.B., 1825). Nor is it necessary to show that the defendant applied any undue persuasion: he will be liable whether or not the act of intercourse was forced, improperly induced or entirely consensual.

HAMILTON V. LONG
[1905] 2 I.R. 552 (C.A.), aff'g. [1903] 2 I.R. 407 (K.B. Div., 1902)

Lord O'Brien L.C.J.:

The facts of this case are compressed within a very narrow compass. Sarah Hamilton, the daughter of the plaintiff, lived with her father and mother in the county Longford. The father appears to have been a farmer in a very small way. During the lifetime of the father, and whilst she lived in his household, the daughter Sarah was seduced by the defendant. After the father's death the girl lived with her mother, and assisted her in the household duties, and was confined of a child, the result of the seduction which took place in the lifetime of the father. The question for our determination is, can the mother, who is the plaintiff, maintain an action under these circumstances? It is contended that she can. I can find no shred of authority, not even a suggestion, in any of our law books in support of that proposition – and the absence of all authority, or, as I have said, of even suggestion, is a very strong argument that the proposition is not well-founded. The action of seduction has been for centuries known to our law. It is, as Mr. Justice Willes pointed out in *Evans* v. *Walton* L. R. 2 C. P. 615, at p. 621, referred to in the Year Book of 11 H 4, fo. 2, and from that time to this, often as references to actions for seduction occur in the books, there is nothing whatever to warrant the suggestion that at common law such an action could be maintained, and indeed the Chief Baron, who tried this case, was of this opinion, because he said that if maintainable at all it is by reason of the Married Women's Property Acts. His impression was that, having regard to these Acts, the action might be maintained. I shall consider later on the effect of these statutes.

Now, at common law the action would not, in my opinion, be maintanable for this reason, namely, that to sustain an action of seduction it must be shown that the act of seduction took place whilst the relation of master and servant existed, and that relation in the father's lifetime existed exclusively between the father as head of the family, and the daughter as his child, and one of the family and one of the household which he maintained. The wife may have been alive, and have directed the daughter in the discharge of her domestic duties, but these duties were rendered in respect of the house and family of which the father was the head; and, whilst the father was in that position, in the eye of the law the relation of master and servant was confined to him exclusively; indeed the wife had no separate existence apart from the husband so as to enable her to sue, save in those very exceptional instances where, for example, she was meritoriously entitled, as where she rendered services with her own hands and brain under a contract for good consideration, and even in those cases she could be met by a plea of abatement which necessitated the adding of the husband as a co-plaintiff. No doubt a contractual relation between father and daughter was not essential to the maintenance of the action; the relation of master and servant is enough, and this relation may be inferred from actual service, or the relation of parent and child. Mr. Justice Willes, in giving judgment in *Evans* v. *Walton* L. R. 2 C. P, 615, at p. 622, said:– 'I feel no difficulty in holding that, upon authority, as well as in good sense, the father of a family, in respect of such service as his daughter renders him from her sense of duty and filial gratitude, stands in the same position as an ordinary master. If she is in his service, whether *de bon gre* or *sur* retainer, he is equally entitled to her services, and to maintain an action against anyone who entices her away.' And Mr. Justice Blackburn said in *Terry* v. *Hutchinson* L. R. 3 Q. B. 599 that during the minority of the child the father had the right to the service, that is to say, a right complete in its character, or one of imperfect obligation. Now, according to *Terry* v. *Hutchinson* L. R. 3 Q. B. 599, the right to the service would be, during the minority of the daughter, in the father exclusively; it was never pretended or suggested it could be in father and mother at the same time. This being so, Mr. Cooke pertinently asked, if the right to the service was in the father exclusively during the minority, what occurred to change that relation between her attaining the age of twenty-one, and the time when she was seduced, that is, when she was between twenty-four and twenty-five years of age? The father was still alive. He continued to be head of the family, and the daughter remained in the household which the father continued to maintain.

I think if the matter rested with the common law there would be no doubt that the action was not maintainable; but it is said that a change was effected by the Married Women's Property Acts. In my opinion these Acts do not in any way affect the question; they leave it as it was at common law. As against the application of these Acts it is argued that the power of contracting thereby conferred is dependent upon the possession of separate estate, and that as it could not be pretended that the mother in the present case had any separate estate the position remained unchanged. As regards this, it has been contended that the effect of the Married Women's Property Acts is to change the *status* of a married woman; that they give her a general power to contract independently of the husband and irrespective of the possession of separate estate – that the contractual power is indefinitely enlarged, but that a judgment against a married woman could not be made good unless there be separate estate out of which it might be levied. Whatever the true view of the effect of the Married Women's Property Acts may be, whether they enlarge the contractual powers indefinitely or make the power to contract conditional upon the possession of separate estate, it is plain that these Acts were conversant with real contracts founded upon a sufficient consideration and enforceable at law. They deal with realities and not with fictions. A married woman may maintain an action as a *feme sole* if she sustains a real wrong by which real injury has been inflicted upon her. She may sue in tort or in contract, but then the tort or the contract must be a reality and not a mere fiction. The relation of master and servant, or as it is more properly described the *supposed* relation of master and servant, which flows from the relation of parent and child, is a mere figment of the law. We are clearly of opinion that the action cannot be maintained.

Having regard to the moral merits of the case, I had hoped to be in a position to dispose of the case on the grounds that the point taken was late; it was not taken until after the verdict was found, and I referred to *Foundation* v. *Keatinge* I. R. 9 C. L. 278; but this ground was plainly not relied on before the Lord Chief Baron; on the contrary the matter was argued on the morning after the trial, and the only question then raised was that the Married Women's Property Acts gave the plaintiff a separate existence apart from the husband so as to confer a cause of action upon her. However, Mr. Drummond, counsel for the plaintiff, said he would not argue the point as to lateness in face of what had taken place, and rested his case upon the general legal merits.

Gibson and **Madden JJ.** delivered concurring judgments.

Notes and Questions

1. In the light of *Hamilton* v. *Long* as well as subsequent legal and constitutional developments (as to which see *McMahon & Binchy*, p. 418) try to state the *existing* law as to entitlement to sue in an action for seduction.
2. The action for seduction may well be non-sexist in that, on principle, it is difficult to see why it does not apply to all permutations of sexual relationships irrespective of the sex of the parties: *cf. McMahon & Binchy*, pp. 420–421. Is this a point in favour of the action or against it, in your view?
3. All seem united that the present law cannot be defended, but how should it be reformed? By abolition? By replacement by a family action for the benefit of all members of the family unit? *Cf.* the Law Reform Commission's Working Paper No. 6–1979, *The Law Relating to Seduction and the Enticement and Harbouring of a Child*, ch. 8 and its *First Report on Family Law*, pp. 11–14 (1981).
4. Has the Constitution any relevance to the question of sexual relationships of young people? Article 41, perhaps? Or Article 40? *Cf. McGee* v. *A.G.* [1974] I.R. 284 (Sup. Ct., 1973), *Norris* v. *A.G.*, Supreme Court, 22 April 1983.

Enticement and Harbouring of a Child

Where a person entices a child away from his or her parent, or harbours a child who has left or has been removed from his or her parents' control, the parent has a right to sue that person for damages. The actions, like seduction, are based on the fiction of loss of services. Whether the actions are available in respect of a child of full age is unclear: the fiction of the master-servant relationship would not exclude such a child in all cases, but the (realistic) concentration on parental rights *qua* guardians would suggest the contrary.

The case law is meagre: only two decisions have been reported in England and none in this country. The type of situation where these actions may be contemplated today may well involve a young person joining an unconventional religious sect or socially unorthodox community. It is clear that these actions have not yet been sufficiently developed and refined to deal adequately with the very important issues raised by these new situations of conflict. It is more likely that they will be resolved through other proceedings, including those for *habeas corpus*, wardship and applications under the *Guardianship of Infants Act 1964*. Moreover, the Constitution may well have an important role, since the guarantees of freedom of conscience and of free profession and practice of religion would require appropriate consideration.

For possible avenues of reform of the law, see the Law Reform Commission's Working Paper No. 6 – 1979, *The Law Relating to Seduction and the Enticement and Harbouring of a Child*, ch. 9 and its *First Report on Family Law*, pp. 14–15 (1981).

Action for the Loss of a Child's Services

Seduction, enticement and harbouring of a child are not the only types of conduct to which tortious liability may attach at the suit of the child's parents. The action for loss of a child's services allows a parent to sue for any losses sustained by the parent from injury to a child occasioned by the commission of a tort in relation to the child. This action is also based on a service relationship between parent and child. Only the loss of services of a domestic nature are compensable: *Chapman* v. *McDonald*, [1969] I.R. 188 (High Ct., O'Keeffe, P.). For reform proposals, see the Law Reform

Commission's Working Paper No.7–1979, *The Law Relating to Loss of Consortium and Loss of Services of a Child* and its *First Report on Family Law*, pp. 9–11.

Note

The common law position relating to recovery for pre-natal injury has been supplemented by statute. Section 58 of the *Civil Liability Act 1961* provides that:
    'For the avoidance of doubt it is hereby declared that the law relating to wrongs shall apply to an unborn child for his protection in like manner as if the child were born, provided the child is subsequently born alive.'

TORTS AFFECTING BUSINESS RELATIONS

The action per quod servitium amisit

The action *per quod servitium amisit* traces its origin to mediaeval times, being based on the concept of the servant as falling within the proprietorship of his master. Where a person commits a tort against a servant, whether by taking him away from the master, imprisoning him or (more usually) injuring him and the master is thereby deprived of his services, the action *per quod servitium amisit* is available to the master, but not in respect of 'public' servants such as soldiers: *cf. A.G.* v. *Ryan's Car Hire Ltd.* [1965] I.R. 642 (Sup. Ct., 1964).

INTERFERENCE WITH CONTRACTUAL RELATIONS
The tort of interference with contractual relations has developed greatly from its origins in the Black Death in England in 1348, which produced a scarcity of labour. The *Statute of Labourers* made it an offence for a third party to receive or regain in his service a servant who had left his previous service prematurely. In the famous decision of *Lumley* v. *Gye* 2 El. & Bl. 216, 118 E.R. 749 (1853), it was held that any malicious interference with a contractual relationship was tortious, and that it was not necessary that the party prevailed upon to break his contract should be a 'servant'. Since then the courts have repeatedly recognised that not only contracts of personal service but also those of a purely commercial nature may be the subject of the action.

Persuasion Distinguished from Mere Information or Advice

HYNES V. CONLON
[1939] Ir. Jur. Rep. 49 (High Ct., Hanna, J.)

Appeal by the defendants from a judgment and order of the Circuit Court of Justice sitting at Sligo on July 26, 1938, whereby a decree for £70 damages and costs was given against the defendants.

    The plaintiff claimed £100 damages 'for that the defendants, or some one or more of them, on or before 1st January 1938, and subsequently, unlawfully procured and induced Messrs. Kilcawley, Maloney and Taylor, building contractors, with whom the plaintiff was employed, to break their contract of service with the plaintiff as a result of which the plaintiff was dismissed by his said employers from his employment, and unlawfully interfered with the plaintiff's right to dispose of his labour. In consequence of the said unlawful acts or some one or more of them the plaintiff suffered loss and damage in the above mentioned amount.'

    The defendants in their defence pleaded *inter alia* that they were 'officials and members of the Irish Transport and General Workers' Union, which said union were parties to an agreement in writing made between the Federation of Building Trade Employers, of which the said firm of Kilcawley, Maloney and Taylor were one, whereby it was agreed that Messrs. Kilcawley, Maloney and Taylor would employ workmen from recognised societies. For greater certainty the defendants would refer at the hearing to the said agreement in writing. The defendants and each of them say that if the plaintiff's contract of service with the said firm of Messrs. Kilcawley, Maloney and Taylor was broken (which is not admitted) the said contract was broken or determined by Messrs. Kilcawley, Maloney and Taylor because the plaintiff was not at any material date a member of a recognised society and not by any act of the defendants or either of them.' The defendants also pleaded the Trade Disputes Act, 1906.

Hanna J.:

I am satisfied that this decree cannot stand. It is obvious to me that there were two agreements entered into between the representatives of the union and the contractors. The first of these agreements was that the contractors would not employ non-union labour. That was contained in the agreement which had been signed by Messrs. Kilcawley, Maloney and Taylor as members of the Federation of Building Trade Employers and the union. The second agreement was a verbal agreement which was given by Mr. Taylor to the union deputation after the four workmen – Mattimoe, Moore, Devins and Oates – had been discharged. That second agreement was that the four would get preference for re-employment subject to there being suitable work for them.

It is clear, and is in fact admitted, that at the time of this trouble, 31st December or 1st January, Hynes was forty-eight weeks in arrears with his subscriptions to the union, and, accordingly, on the face of agreement the contractors were not entitled to employ him – in fact it was a breach of their agreement with the union to employ him. The mere fact of the union giving grace from time to time to workmen who at the date of employment were lapsed members and giving them an opportunity of becoming qualified does not affect the legal position of the union, because the contract was made and signed that non-union men were not to be employed. The contractors did employ Hynes, and they did so under the impression that he was a union member. However, as soon as the representatives of the union heard of that they, of course, took the matter up not only on the ground that he was a lapsed member, but also on the ground that he was given preference to some other men who had been relieved of their employment and for whom the union had been working. The facts are that the defendants as representatives of the union went and saw the representatives of the contractors, and on the discussion that took place the question of Hynes being a lapsed member of the union, and, therefore, a non-union member, was discussed or mentioned, and also the fact that three or four men should be given preference in accordance with the agreement made by Mr. Taylor with the union.

It is a matter for congratulation that relations between the contractors and the union were friendly and the relations between the union and its members were the same. Trade unions are now recognised institutions in the law, and they have certain powers that must be exercised for the good of workmen and for the good of the community they represent. As long as they keep within their rules and the law, it is the duty of the Court to recognise their rights when they have to carry out duties which are sometimes unpleasant. I am quite sure it is very unpleasant for any member of the committee who has to go and say that a man has to be dismissed or that there is a breach of any conditions.

I am satisfied that two questions arose – that he was a lapsed member and that they had a complaint against the employer because there was to be preference given to men who had previously been dismissed. I am satisfied on the evidence which has been very frankly given by Mr. Conlon, that when he was talking to Mr. Taylor and Mr. Pilkington he intimated to them that by reason of these matters they would have to get rid of this man in pursuance of the agreement made. But I am satisfied that there was nothing improper in anything these gentlemen did and that they were all well within the law. There was nothing in the nature of a threat to the employer or in the nature of a severe warning that might be construed into a threat, and the view I take of what took place was that it was no more than telling the employer the attitude which the union was taking up. If union officials could not do what was done in this case, they would be of little use. There was conflict between the witnesses as to who was to take the responsibility. The workman was left with whatever remedy he had in law against the union if they acted illegally, but in order to do that they had to do something illegal. So far as I can see in this case there were no threats, no warnings and no violence.

In the view I take of the case the questions can be decided on common law. A person is not entitled to induce another person to break a contract of service by unlawful means. It seems to me that the question which arose in this case about Hynes was brought to the notice of the union, and the chairman, secretary, and Mr. Lynch, a member of the committee, knowing the views of the committee, went on the deputation to the contractors. I have come to the conclusion that they did not exceed their authority and I am also of the opinion that they did not use any threats or warnings of an illegal character nor was there any unlawful interference. For these reasons I think that the decree that the jury gave against the defendants should be reversed and the action should be dismissed.

So far as Hynes is concerned he is now a member of the union, and as they mention in one of their resolutions protesting against victimisation, I hope that they will remember that when they come to deal with him. I have to make an order for costs against Hynes, in this Court and in the Court below, but I hope they will be lenient with him.

Appeal allowed

Notes and Questions

With the utmost good manners and polite language I inform you that, if you do not hand over your wallet, there is a strong likelihood that I will feel obliged, in conscience, to injure you. Have I *threatened* you or merely given you an intimation of what is likely to happen in the future?

What degree of knowledge of the existence of the contract must be proved?

McMAHON V. DUNNE
99 I.L.T.R. 45 (High Court, Budd, J., 1964)

Budd J.:

The plaintiffs in these proceedings are timber merchants and builders' providers carrying on business in Limerick. The first named defendant is the general secretary of the Marine, Port and General Workers' Union (hereinafter generally referred to as the Union). The second named defendant is a member of the union and is the head checker employed by Messrs. George Bell and Company, stevedores.

The plaintiffs issued proceedings on the 20th October last against the defendants claiming an injunction to restrain the defendants or their servants or agents, in combination or otherwise, from interfering with, or preventing, the performance of certain contracts between the plaintiffs and certain firms stated and named in the plenary summons, or procuring, or inducing breaches of such contracts. There was also a claim for damages for conspiracy to procure breaches of contract and for damages for wrongfully procuring the same. The summons contained the usual claim for further or other relief.

The plaintiffs having obtained an interim injunction from Henchy J. on October 20th, 1964, then served the notice of motion now before me seeking an interlocutory injunction restraining the defendants, and each of them, and their respective servants and agents, until after the trial of this action from preventing, or interfering with, or authorising the prevention or interference with, the delivery or removal of goods consigned to the plaintiffs which are now in the port of Dublin. The plaintiffs have sought an amendment to this notice of motion to cover further consignments of goods expected shortly to arrive. The plaintiffs state that they accidentally confined themselves in their application to seeking an injunction that only covered goods at present in the port of Dublin. Since further cargoes are due to arrive it will obviously lack all reality in the circumstances if any injunction to be given was confined to cargoes at present in the port. Such a course would lead to an utterly unnecessary expenditure in costs, because, if an injunction with regard to the goods at present in the port were to be granted, the plaintiffs could obviously come in tomorrow and obtain an injunction with regard to future cargoes. In my view it is therefore right and proper to grant the amendment sought. The application to amend was opposed but it was agreed that if the amendment was to be granted the form of the amendment should be to insert in the notice of motion after the word 'now' the words 'or may arrive in the port of Dublin pending the trial of the action by doing any act tending to further or promote any interference with the removal or movement of the said goods' in lieu of the words originally in the notice of motion after the word 'now'. Accordingly I will grant an amendment in that form. The allegations of conspiracy were not pursued at this stage of the proceedings.

The proceedings arise out of the following circumstances. The plaintiffs had of recent times entered into contracts with the companies or firms specified in the plenary summons, foreign suppliers of timber, for the sale to them of certain quantities of timber to be deivered to the plaintiffs in Dublin. Ten lots of the timber so ordered arrived in the port of Dublin during the months of August, September and October of this year, were discharged over the ship's side and duly paid for. The plaintifs are also expecting the arrival of these further cargoes of timber in the near future. The plaintiffs say that they have been prevented and impeded from removing the aforesaid cargoes from the port of Dublin to their business premises and that the vendors have been prevented from delivering the timber in question to the plaintiffs in breach of their contracts, as a result of an embargo placed on all building materials lying at the port of Dublin by reason a trade dispute between workers employed by builders' providers in the Dublin area and their employers. They say that this embargo has been implemented by the Union directing the 'checkers' in the port, who are members of the Union, to withdraw their labour in connection with the said building materials and other goods consigned to builders' providers, including the above-mentioned cargoes. This the plaintiffs say resulted in the employees of the plaintiff company being unable or unwilling to carry out their employers' instructions with regard to taking delivery of the said timber.

From what the plaintiffs say it would appear that it is necessary in order to complete the delivery of the said timber that it should be examined by a 'checker', who is an employee of the shipping agent or stevedore or other persons in similar positions concerned with the ship in which the goods have arrived and its unloading. They also say that it is the duty of a 'checker' having examined the cargo when unloaded to issue to the consignee a delivery note to enable the timber to be removed by the consignee from the dock in order that the contract between the vendor and the consignee may be completed. The withdrawal of the 'checkers' labour in the above connection they say has resulted in the vendors not delivering the said goods in breach of their contracts. That breach the plaintiffs say was procured *inter alia*, by the first named defendant as regards all the contracts and by the second named defendant with regard to some.

An alleged instance of failure to issue the necessary delivery note on the part of the second named defendant is referred to in the affidavit of Mr. Fennessey, the secretary of the plaintiff company, used in support of the application. It is alleged that, when employees of the plaintiffs attended at the docks on September 7th, 1964 for the purpose of taking delivery of the timber referred to, they were informed by the second named defendant that the plaintiff company had been included on a list, compiled by the Union, of firms whose goods would not be handled at the port owing to such firms being involved in a trade dispute in progress with building workers in the Dublin area. The checkers were thereupon, it is said, directed to withdraw their labour in connection with the above-mentioned cargoes, which they did, resulting in the employees of the plaintiff company being unable or unwilling to carry out their employers' instructions regarding the timber. It is further alleged that the second named defendant gave as the reason for this inclusion of the plaintiff company in the said list (referred to by the plaintiffs as a 'black' list) the fact that the plaintiff company held a controlling interest in a firm of builders' suppliers in Dublin named James McMahon (Dublin) Ltd., a fact disputed.

The second named defendant denies these allegations and says that in fact no embargo existed on the date mentioned at the instigation of the Union and that no withdrawal of labour in relation to the checking out of materials to the plaintiff company took place until after September 11th. There is thus a disputed question of fact which cannot however be resolved at this stage. The allegations are however there even though disputed. It is perhaps of more importance that it appears from Mr. Dunne's affidavit that the embargo was implemented as from September 11th against the plaintiffs. No doubt the facts will be further illuminated at the trial if the injunction is granted.

Apart from the above matter I should point out at this stage that the second named defendant himself states that a lorry driver of the plaintiffs did approach him to obtain delivery of timber on October 13th, 1964, that he was at first authorized by the Union to release it and proceeded to do so, but that the officials of the Union came down to the docks and countermanded the order for its release. He stops short there, but the plaintiffs say that the implication is that the second named defendant must in the circumstances have positively refused to release the timber as distinct from doing nothing. It is common case, however, that an embargo of the kind mentioned was imposed by the Union and implemented as stated. Further, it is conceded that the first named defendant, as secretary of the Union, conveyed directions to the 'checker' members of his Union, to withdraw their labour in connection with the type of goods above-mentioned and the cargoes referred to. There is no question but that the embargo covered goods consigned to the plaintiffs passing through the port from some time in early September.

None of the plaintiffs' employees are members of the Marine, Port and General Workers' Union. The plaintiffs have no trade dispute with their employees and allege that none exists between them and the defendants or the Union.

As soon as the plaintiffs ascertained that the embargo applied to them they commenced these proceedings and obtained the interim injunction mentioned from Henchy J. on the 20th October, 1964, which was in similar terms to that sought in the notice of motion as unamended.

A short reference to the background of the situation may serve to clarify the position. On or about August the 18th of this year, consequent upon a trade dispute which had arisen between the Federation of Builders, representing a number of Dublin building firms, on the one part and a group of trade unions representing workers in the said firms on the other part, a strike commenced which resulted in the withdrawal of labour from the said employers and other industrial action. This strike continued until on or about the 16th October. Neither the plaintiffs nor the defendants were directly concerned with this strike, though affected by it in certain ways. The strike, however, had repercussions and towards the end of August certain members of the Timber, Cement and Fireclay Branch of the Federated Union of Employers, who were builders' providers, issued protective notice to their employees that their employment might be terminated if the building strike continued. On or about the 7th September last the Union served on the member firms of the said Timber, Cement and Fireclay Branch of the Federated Union of Employers a notice on behalf of the members of the Union employed by the said firms claiming a reduction in their hours of labour. On the 10th September the said firms gave notice to their employees that they were closing down from that evening. The Union regarded this as an unjustified lock out. Arising out of this state of affairs and the union's view thereon the labour of the checkers on the docks, who were members of the union, was withdrawn to the extent that such labour was required to obtain the release of the supplies in the docks to firms which had shut down and the Union say that a trade dispute either then or shortly afterwards came into existence between the aforesaid parties. According to the plaintiffs this dispute cut across deliveries to them, and they took up the matter with the union. The building strike was settled, apparently, on the 16th October. On the same date the Union gave notice to the Federated Union of Employers, Timber, Cement and Fireclay Branch, that on and from the 19th October a trade dispute would exist between the Union and the branch, in relation to the claim for the forty hours week. Also on the same date the Executive Committee of the Union resolved that instructions should be given to 'checker' members on the Dublin docks to withdraw their labour insofar as it was required for securing the release of materials for the building industry or in any way concerned with it or required for firms of builders' providers in any part of the country, unless the Union should authorise them to do otherwise. According to the affidavits sworn by the first-named defendant the purpose of this resolution was to place a total embargo on the release of any building materials or anything in the nature of building materials from the docks pending the settlement of the trade dispute. It is relevant to note that the embargo was in fact in existence before this resolution was passed. Mr. Dunne in his first affidavit says that it applied at all material times to the plaintiffs as well as to the firms above referred to but from what he says this must mean after September 10th.

The first named defendant claims that these actions were taken in furtherance of the said trade dispute and for the purpose of bringing pressure to bear on the firms directly concerned and also upon all firms in any way connected with the trade or industry of builders' providers to use their influence to bring about a settlement of the dispute.

On October 19th Mr. Dunne informed the plaintiffs through their solicitor that the embargo extended to their goods.

The plaintiffs allege that the tort of inducement of a breach of contract has been committed against them by the first named defendant. They say that the actions of the first named defendant in communicating the resolution of the Executive Committee of the Union to the 'checker' members of the Union and his giving them directions a to the withdrawal of their labour, *pro tanto* as regards the delivery of the plaintiffs' goods to them, resulted in such withdrawal of labour. That withdrawal of labour they say resulted in the consignors of the goods, parties to the various contracts referred to, being unable fully to perform their contractual obligations to the plaintiff company in that they were unable to deliver the goods to the plaintiffs as the plaintiffs maintain the various contracts required. This then resulted in the procurement of a breach of these commercial contracts and an unlawful interference with the plaintiffs' trade or business. Such breaches of contract, they further say, were brought about by unlawful means, that is to say, by procuring the checkers to commit a breach of their contracts with their respective employers in failing to carry out the normal duties of their employment, which they say are sufficiently indicated in Mr. Fennessey's affidavit to support this allegation.

They also say that the actions of the second named defendant in refusing to release the goods in the manner alleged constituted the procuring of breaches of two or more of the contracts by the commission of unlawful breaches of his contract of employment and therefore by unlawful means.

The tort of intentionally procuring a breach of contract by one party thereto, without legal justification, and resulting in damage to the other party thereto, is now well established. It had its origin in *Lumley* v. *Gye* (1853) 2 E. & B. 215, a decision so familiar to lawyers as to make it unnecessary to expatiate on it. It is also true to say that it is also authoritatively accepted that the tort extends in its ramifications to the case of the procurement of a breach of contract by unlawful means, such as the procuring of a breach of a contract of employment on the part of an employee of the contract breaker. That this ingredient may also extend to the case of procuring a breach of the contract of employment of an employee of a third party appears to have grounds of support will appear later. The difficulty however exists of stating, in the first instance, precisely what the ingredients of the tort are. That is not fully and authoritatively decided here. Furthermore the application of the law to the facts, and deciding whether established facts bring any particular case within the scope of the ingredients of the tort, established or thought likely to be established, is not without difficulty. It has only to be stated that recently the House of Lords reversed the Court of Appeal in England in a case bearing a good deal of analogy to this case, after a lengthy hearing for an interlocutory matter, and after taking time for consideration, for it is to be seen that a formidable task confronts any Judge of first instance charged with the matter of dealing with the various facets of law and fact touched on in this case. I turn to an examination of the relevant law and matters in issue.

Salmond on Torts (1961 Edition) at page 657 describes the tort as follows:– 'Intentionally and without lawful justification to induce or procure anyone to break a contract made by him with another is a tort actionable at the suit of that other, if damage has resulted to him.'

It is pointed out at page 659 of the work above referred to, adopting in this respect the pronouncements of Jenkins, L.J., in *Thomson* v. *Deakin* [1952] Ch. at 693, that, apart from cases of conspiracy to injure, 'Acts of a third party lawful in themselves do not constitute an actionable interference with contractual rights merely because they bring about a breach of contract, even if they were done with the object and intention of bringing about such a breach'. Certain instances of cases where the necessary ingredients of an actionable interference with contractual rights exist are then, however, cited. No. 5 at page 660 is as follows:– 'When a third party, with knowledge of the contract and intent to secure its breach, definitely and unequivocally persuades, induces, or procures the servant of one of the parties to break his contract of employment, provided that the breach of contract forming the alleged subject of interference in fact ensues as a necessary consequence of the breach of the contract of employment.' This is in fact a paraphrase of the views of Lord Justice Jenkins in the same case at page 696, relating to the necessary ingredients, in his view, of the tort of procuring of a breach of contract by unlawful means. The author goes on to say that it must be clearly shown that the effect of the withdrawal of the services of the particular servant concerned was to render it quite impracticable for the contract breaker to perform his contract, and that it must be distinctly shown that unlawful means were advocated with the intent of interfering with the performance of a particular contract. A *prima facie* reasonable and logical argument can be made, in my view, for the extension of the ingredient of procuring by unlawful means to the case of the procuring of the servants of a person, not one of the parties to the contract, to break their contracts of employment. Such a view appears to be implicit in the speeches in the House of Lords in *Stratford* v. *Lindley* [1964] 3 All E.R. 102.

Having made reference to the views of Jenkins L.J., stated in the case of *Thomson* v. *Deakin* it would only be right and proper to state them fully, especially since they were much relied upon by the defendants. He says that he would hold the form of actionable interference, dealt with in Salmond above as strictly confined to cases where it is clearly shown, 'first, that the person charged with actionable interference knew of the existence of the contract and intended to procure its breach; secondly, that the person so charged did definitely and unequivocally persuade, induce or procure the employees concerned to break their contracts of employment with the intent (he had mentioned); thirdly, that the employees so persuaded, induced or procured did in fact break their contracts of employment; and, fourthly, that breach of the contract forming the alleged subject of interference ensued as a necessary consequence of the breaches by the employees concerned of their contracts of employment'.

He also had some observations to make with regard to the expression 'necessary consequence' which I also quote:

'I should add that by the expression "necessary consequence" used here and elsewhere in this judgment I mean that it must be shown that, by reason of the withdrawal of the services of the employees concerned, the contract breaker was unable, as a matter of practical possibility, to perform his contract; in other words, I think the continuance of the services of the particular employees concerned must be so vital to the performance of the contract alleged to have been interfered with as to make the effect of their withdrawal comparable, for practical purposes, to a direct invasion of the contractual rights of the party aggrieved under the contract alleged to have been interfered with, as, for example (in the case of a contract for personal services), the physical restraint of the person by whom such services are to be performed.'

The facts of the case of *J. T. Stratford & Son Limited* v. *Lindley*, to which I have referred as appearing to extend the nature of the ingredient relating to the unlawful means, are briefly as follows. In 1963 a company named Bowker and King Limited, having previously rejected joint invitations of the Transport and General Workers' Union and of the Watermen, Lightermen, Tugmen and Bargemen's Union to negotiate terms and conditions of employment, came to agreement in negotiation with the Transport Union alone, the Watermen's Union not being informed of the negotiations. The agreement covered the terms and conditions of service of all Bowker and King's union employees. These were forty-eight in number, forty-five of whom belonged to the Transport Union and three belonged to the Watermen's Union. The respondents were officers of the Watermen's Union. Having learnt of this agreement and knowing that Mr. Stratford was chairman of J. T. Stratford & Sons Limited (hereinafter sometimes referred to as Stratfords) a company that controlled Bowker and King Limited, as well as chairman of Bowker and King Limited, the union struck at Stratfords by placing an embargo on their union's members handling barges of Stratfords. That latter company did not employ members of either union. Stratfords owned and hired out barges and repaired barges. The hirers of the barges employed lightermen to take charge of the barges, to deliver cargo and return the barges to Stratfords. Master lightermen had dock workers allocated to them pursuant to certain dock regulations made in England. As a result of the embargo Stratfords were caused heavy financial loss, their barges being immobilised, mainly by being tied up by the watermen to the nearest buoy after having been used for the hirer's business and not returned to Stratfords. Barges also were not brought in for repair. If damages were recoverable the respondents would in fact be unable to pay, so that damage would be irreparable. J. T. Stratford & Sons Limited brought an action against the respondents and obtained an interlocutory injunction which was discharged on appeal. An interlocutory injunction was however granted by the House of Lords.

The House of Lords took the view that Stratfords had made out a *prima facie* case that the respondents, with sufficient knowledge of the barge hiring contracts, had either induced breaches by the barge-hirer customers of their contracts with Stratfords by failing to return barges to Stratfords at the conclusion of hirings, and had induced such breaches by unlawful means, that is to say by procuring breaches of their contracts of employment with the master lightermen by the union members' refusal to handle Stratfords' barges or had induced such breaches without lawful justification. On either view loss had thereby been inflicted on Stratfords and they were accordingly, *prima facie*, entitled to recover, on the principle of *Lumley* v. *Gye* (1859) E. & B. 216, damages for the wrong done to them by the respondents.

I should say with regard to the above synopsis of the facts of the case that it was the view of Lord Upjohn that the contracts of employment of the bargemen were with the master lightermen and that my reading of what Lord Reid and Lord Radcliffe said leads to the view that they came to the same conclusion. On this basis the procuring of a breach of a contract of employment existing between a servant and an employer, not a party to the contract, the breach of which is complained of, constitutes the use of unlawful means sufficient so far as that ingredient is concerned to support the tort.

The interlocutory injunction was granted to preserve the *status quo* pending the hearing because the respondents would suffer no loss therefrom whereas Stratfords would suffer heavy financial loss if the embargo continued, which the respondents would be unable to make good.

With reference to the breaches of their contracts of employment by the bargemen there is a passage in the speech of Viscount Radcliffe to which I think it is useful to refer. He says at page 108:– 'The immediate thing that the embargo was intended to achieve was that the union's order to "black" the appellants' barges was to be imposed on a dock worker's normal duty to carry out his employers' lawful directions in his job. To that extent they were to obey the union, not the employer, I regard that as a direct instruction to the dockers not to obey their employers' orders *pro tanto*.' The plaintiffs in these proceedings say that the embargo placed by the Marine, Port and General Workers' Union had the same result with regard to a 'checker's' normal duty to carry out his employer's lawful directions in his job. It resulted in the checkers refusing and failing to carry out the normal duties of their employment with regard to the issue of delivery notes and the release of the goods of the plaintiffs and there is thus a similar position here to that existing in the above case, the plaintiffs contend. They say also that the decision is authority, *prima facie* at any rate, for the proposition that inducing the breach of a contract of employment with a third party, as distinct from procuring a breach of a contract of employment existing between one of the parties to a contract and his employees, would be a use of unlawful means assuming that a breach of contract was procured thereby. Furthermore they claim that the decision shows, *prima facie* again, that it is unnecessary to prove *actual* knowledge on the part of the intervener of the existence of any specific contract of which the procuring of the breach is alleged on the part of the intervener or its precise terms. It is sufficient if the intervener can be fixed with implied or constructive knowledge of the existence of such a contract containing terms of the kind of which it is alleged a breach was procured. The analogy which the plaintiffs draw with regard to the knowledge of the defendants of the contracts of which a breach is alleged to have been procured I deal with later.

While I have touched upon certain matters involved in the above decision relevant to the facts of the present case it should be stated that it was the view of the House of Lords that a trade dispute did not exist between the respondent's union and the appellants so as to enable the respondents to rely on such protection as the Trade Disputes Act, 1906, might afford them in the circumstances. The position in this case is somewhat different in that the defendants say that a genuine trade dispute of the nature outlined above exists between their members employed by the builders' providers above mentioned and the members of the defendant's union employed by them, and they further claim that the existence of such trade dispute entitled them lawfully to take industrial action against persons not actually parties to that dispute for the purpose of bringing pressure on them so that they in their turn might be moved to bring pressure on the employers of the defendants' union members to persuade them to come to terms on the matter of the existing trade dispute and it is claimed that their actions are protected by the provisions of the Trade Disputes Act, 1906.

So far I have referred in a general way to the facts of the case and to some relevant matters of law claimed by one party or the other to be relevant thereto. Certain particular submissions still remain to be dealt with, but, before proceeding to consider them it is appropriate to remark that this is an interlocutory application on which no final determination is made on the facts at issue or as to the correct interpretation of the law to be applied to them, unless in a very clear case. Such observations as I make on both matters are to be read in that light. The correct approach in dealing with an application of this kind is set out in the decision of the Supreme Court in the case of the *Educational Company of Ireland Limited* v. *Fitzpatrick and Others* 96 I.L.T.R. 161; [1961] I.R. 323. It is convenient at this stage to refer briefly to portions of the judgments therein.

Lavery J., in the course of his judgment, quoted with aproval from Kerr on Injunctions. Paraphrasing these quotations as far as relevant in the present proceedings the following principles emerge. An interlocutory injunction does not conclude a right but is merely provisional in its nature, the effective object being to keep matters in *status quo* until the hearing. The Court does not, in general, profess to anticipate the determination of rights but merely gives its opinion that there is a substantial question to be tried and that until trial a case has been made out for the preservation of the property in *status quo*. It is sufficient for a person seeking an interlocutory injunction to show that he has a fair question to be raised as to the existence of the right which he alleges and for the preservation of the property meantime. A fair *prima facie* case must be made in support of the title which he asserts and he must show that there are substantial grounds for doubting the existence of the alleged legal right the exercise of which he seeks to prevent. The Court must, before disturbing any man's legal rights, or stripping him of legal rights, be satisfied that the probability is in favour of his case ultimately failing. The mere existence of a doubt as to the plaintiff's right, interference with which he seeks to restrain, does not of itself constitute a sufficient ground for refusing an injunction, though it is always a circumstance which calls for the attention of the Court.

It is highly relevant to point out that Lavery J. said that the case then before the Court raised questions which had not been decided in any Court whose decision bound the Supreme Court. It had been submitted that the decision of the Court of Appeal in England in the case of *White* v. *Riley* [1921] 1 Ch. 1 had been accepted and that so far as interlocutory relief was concerned it should be accepted. The learned Judge, having pointed out that they plaintiffs had to establish that there was a fair question to be decided at the trial, took the view that the arguments heard indicated that there was such a fair question and in his view a difficult one. He then proceeded to consider what Order should be made on the basis that a fair question for trial had been established. He quoted with approval some passages of the article on Injunctions in the Hailsham edition of Halsbury's Laws of England. In the first part of the quotation is contained the statement: 'in the absence of very special circumstances (the Court) will impose only such restraint as will suffice to stop the mischief and keep things as they are until the hearing'. The quotation continues:–

'Where any doubt exists as to the plaintiff's right, or if his right is not disputed, but its violation is denied, the Court, in determining whether an interlocutory injunction should be granted, takes into consideration the balance of convenience to the parties and the nature of the inquiry which the defendant, on the one hand, would suffer if the injunction was granted and he should ultimately turn out to be right, and that which the plaintiff, on the other hand, might sustain if the injunction was refused and he should ultimately turn out to be right. The burden of proof that the inconvenience which the plaintiff will suffer by the refusal of the injunction is greater than that which the defendant will suffer, if it is granted, lies on the plaintiff.'

Some other passages in the judgment were submitted to be relevant to the facts of the present case and I think that they are. The injunction sought was to restrain picketing and the plaintiffs claimed that the damage might be caused by the continuance of the picketing pending the trial would be serious and in the sense in which the word is used in this connection, 'irreparable'. Lavery J. said: 'Clearly it would be very difficult, if not impossible, for the plaintiffs to show that loss of trade or diminution of their profits, if sustained, should be attributed to the picketing and not to other circumstances or combination of circumstances.' Having pointed out that the defendants were in that case asserting what they considered to be a fundamental principle and agreeing that it was of very great importance, the learned Judge took the view that in that particular case no serious damage could be caused to them if, by order of the Court, the picketing was restrained until the trial of the action. He further stated his view that the case came to be decided under the principle which *Smyth* v. *Beirne and Anr.* was decided by the Supreme Court, the grounds of the decision being twofold. First, that the facts might be in dispute and second, that a serious question of law arose as to whether there was a trade dispute in existence. He was also of opinion that further facts might well be elicited at the trial. Kingsmill Moore J. also stated that he was not convinced that all the relevant facts were established or admitted. He was of opinion that a plaintiff was entitled to have his case fully investigated in the ordinary course of legal procedure and that it would be undesirable in the absence of consent to decide a legal question of the magnitude there involved merely on the affidavits filed for the purpose of the interlocutory motion.

Have the plaintiffs then shown that they have raised a fair question or questions to be decided at the trial?

First of all there arises what may be described as a preliminary point. The plaintiffs in the first instance rely on the procuring of breaches of the contracts referred to. The defendants say that on the true construction of the contracts in question no breach of contract ever occurred. Accordingly the action is unsustainable and interlocutory relief sought should not be granted.

The contracts were produced and appear, with a possible exception, to provide for delivery in Dublin. The plaintiffs say that on their true construction, viewed in the light of the surrounding circumstances this must mean delivery to them in Dublin. They cannot be delivered *in vacuo* so to speak. This construction is not agreed to by the defendants who say that the contracts were completed by delivery over the ship's side and that thus no breach of contract was procured. The plaintiffs' construction would appear however to be reasonably open. The opposite contention does not appear to me to be so clearly correct as would justify a ruling in favour of the defendants' contention at this stage. The true construction would appear to be a matter for determination at the trial if it is otherwise thought proper to grant the injunction sought.

On the matter of the knowledge of the contract (the procurement of the breach of which is alleged) on the part of the intervener, a good deal of debate took place. It was contended on the one side at first that before the intervener could be fixed with liability he must be shown to have known of the existence of the particular contract the breach of which he is charged with procuring. It was said that there was no room for 'ought to know' or 'should be presumed to know'. It was however then conceded, as I understand it, that it need not be shown that the intervener had a knowledge of the particular contract in fact existing between the parties thereto, the breach of which is alleged to have been procured. It would suffice if the intervener had actual knowledge that a contract existed between these parties, without full knowledge of its terms and, I take it, from what was said, that the intervener had sufficient knowledge of it to know that what he was doing or causing to be done, or not done, would result in a breach thereof. There is, I think, involved in this, some departure from the nature of the ingredient of knowledge laid down by Jenkins L.J. in *Thomson* v. *Deakin*, which would appear to require knowledge of the contract.

The plaintiffs contended that it was unnecessary to support their action in respect of this particular tort to show that the defendants had actual knowledge of any of the particular contracts involved. That it was sufficient if the defendants could be fixed with constructive, as distinct from actual, knowledge, that a contract existed either between the actual contracting parties or between the party injured and some other party; the important thing was that the intervener would know that his intervention would procure a breach of contract, which would result in injury to a known party to the contract. They say that as regards the law they have raised a fair question to be tried as to what precise degree of knowledge the law requires in this way. They say that there is no reason, in principle, why a plaintiff should be held in any straight-jacket as regards the requirements as to knowledge. If he is entitled to obtain damages in a case where he can show that the intervener had knowledge of an actual contract between known parties, is there any reason in principle, they ask, for refusing him compensation where the wrongdoer knows full well that a contract exists with the plaintiff of such a nature that his actions will procure a breach of it, to the plaintiffs' damage? They thus rely on constructive or implied knowledge of the contract.

With regard to the law on the matter of knowledge certain observations relative to the matter of the sufficiency of constructive knowledge were made in the case of *Stratford* v. *Lindley*. Lord Reid thought it reasonable to infer, at that stage at any rate, that the respondents were sufficiently aware of the terms of the contracts between the appellants and the barge hirers by reason of the fact that they knew that the barges were always promptly returned at the completion of the job and it must have been obvious to them that this was done under contract between the appellants and barge hirers. The evidence before the House also satisfied Viscount Radcliffe that the defendants should be treated as having sufficient knowledge of the existence and notice of the hiring contracts. Lord Pearse took the view that the hiring contracts were to be implied from an established course of dealing and under them the hirers were under an obligation to return the barges to the appellants when finished with. It was in his view no answer to a claim based on wrongly inducing a breach of contract to assert that the defendants did not know with exactitude all the terms of the contract. The relevant question was whether they had sufficient knowledge of it to know that they were inducing a breach of contract. The evidence, at the trial, he said, would illuminate this point further. Lord Upjohn also did not agree with a limited view on this matter and was satisfied that *prima facie* case had been made of knowledge of a *prima facie* breach of the hiring contracts on the part of the respondents, though the matter might have to be explored more fully at the trial. These observations, made by whom they were and on a matter where the law of England and Ireland is in most respects similar, entitles the plaintiffs in my view to say that so far as the law is concerned they have strong support for the proposition that constructive knowledge is sufficient knowledge in the context. Just what type of constructive knowledge is sufficient is a new point yet to be decided here. If we have moved to the stage where constructive knowledge is sufficient is there any reason for confining the ingredient of knowledge to knowledge of a specific contract between specific parties or actual knowledge of any particular contract? In many instances in modern life it must be obvious to the ordinary onlooker that some transaction is taking place on foot of some contract, particularly where matters of payment and delivery are concerned. This applies *a fortiori* where the intervener has special knowledge of the course of dealing, the customs prevailing and the surrounding circumstances.

Where a contract is obvious there must also be many instances in which the terms or at least some of the terms of the contract are likewise obvious. If some term, such as one requiring delivery to someone, clearly a party to the contract, is itself clearly discernible in the particular circumstances to a person to whom the existence of the contract is obvious, and that person procures a breach of that particular term of the contract, to the detriment of one of the parties is there any valid reason in principle for exempting him from liability for what he has done, merely because he did not know who the other party was or of the existence of any particular form of contract or its exact conditions? I would think that, *prima facie*, a reasonable argument could be made for fixing such a person with liability on the basis of his constructive knowledge.

It may be decided that strict proof will be required of knowledge of some particular contract or it may be that it will be held sufficient if it is proved that in fact a breach of a contract or of some contract was in fact procured and that the intervener had, from the surrounding facts and circumstances, sufficient knowledge of that contract or of some contract to know that his actions would result in a breach of contract injurious to one of the parties to the contract.

These are matters on which I can come to no decision on an interlocutory application. I am satisfied, however, that a fair question has been raised as to these matters which should be decided at the trial of the action.

On the questions of fact with regard to the matter of knowledge of the contract Mr. Finlay made certain submissions. He was prepared to agree that the defendants might know of the existence of a contract between the actual parties from their work, gleaning it from a course of dealing. He pointed out, however, that neither defendant could have known of the contracts produced and, moreover, submitted that it had not been adequately shown that the defendants had sufficient knowledge of any contract between the plaintiffs and the vendors as would show that they had sufficient knowledge to know that their actions would lead to a breach of contract injurious to the plaintiffs. How could the plaintiffs know, he said, that the particular type of contracts here involved existed as distinct from any other type of contract? There were many contracts relative to these goods which could have been entered into between the vendors and the plaintiffs. There might have been contracts whereby the plaintiffs would have been responsible for the carriage of the goods. The plaintiffs might have had contracts with carriers to carry the goods. There might well have been many other sorts of contracts entered into between the plaintiffs and yet other persons for the collection and delivery of the goods. How were the defendants, he said, to know in these circumstances what particular type of contract the plaintiffs had entered into?

The plaintiffs say, in reply, that they have made a sufficient *prima facie* case on the facts with regard to knowledge. They say that the defendants were in a position, from the nature of their work and the everyday knowledge gained therein, to know in a well informed way, as to what goes on with relation to commercial contracts relating to the import of goods. They could scarcely, in Mr. McKenna's words, think that the timber came to the plaintiff company like 'manna from heaven'. They would know that a commercial dealing was involved. The plaintiff company would not be importing timber save under contract, being a commercial firm, and sending their lorries for it would indicate also that they were parties to commercial contracts. All this shows, the plaintiffs say, that they have made a good, *prima facie*, case to fix the defendants with constructive knowledge of a contract. It can, at least, be said that a vendor and purchaser contract was almost certainly involved. Evidence in future to be given at the trial may also very well show that the documents in the hands of checkers or even the markings on the goods would show who the vendors were, thus establishing the other parties to the contracts. It is not going too far to say that there would be constant communications between members of the union on the docks and the general secretary of the union as to which particular lots of goods came under the embargo in the course of which he would hear of the whole nature of the traffic and the parties involved, in such fashion at least, as would fix him with constructive knowledge of the established mode of dealing. That applies, *a fortiori*, to a 'checker'. Then the communications with the plaintiffs and their solicitors, relating to these goods, would appraise him of the fact that they in particular were concerned as parties to the contract particularly having regard to the incident that took place on October 13th. All this, it may be reasonably said, would lead him to the inevitable conclusion that the plaintiffs were involved in a commercial dealing and that it would be naive to suggest that he would not know that a contract was involved with whomever they were buying from. The same remarks apply to any other contract likely to be involved such as for the carriage of the goods. All would have the common factor that delivery of the goods to the plaintiffs would be part of the terms of the contract.

It all depends of course on what species of knowledge is required in law before one can say just what must be proved in order to show that the intervener had the requisite degree of knowledge. The plaintiffs submit that they have placed before the Court sufficient material to show, *prima facie*, that the defendants had sufficient knowledge of the contracts involved to know that their actions would produce a breach of the contracts involved or at least that their actions would procure a breach of a contract to which the plaintiffs were parties, along with another. It cannot, they say, really matter whom the contract is with provided that its existence is evident to the intervener. Again, in so far as the facts are concerned it is impossible, they say, to cover every point fully on an interlocutory application, based on affidavits, and that a much fuller investigation of the facts will take place at the trial which will enable a finding to be made as to whether or not the defendants had such knowledge of the existence of the contract or a contract as the law requires.

In any event I am satisfied that a sufficient *prima facie* case as to the knowledge of the defendants of the contracts or a contract has been made out.

There is also another point with regard to the actual contracts which the plaintiff's had which may be conveniently dealt with at this stage. The form of the contracts with regard to the goods in question is known. They contain clauses exempting the seller from liability in case of *force majeure*. It was suggested that where such a clause exists and delivery in such a case as I am dealing with is prevented by reason of industrial action taken by persons outside the control of the seller resulting in the frustration of the contract, no breach of contract ensues and that it cannot therefore be said that a breach of contract has been procured by the intervener. I do not very well follow this reasoning because it would seem that such a clause predicates a right to delivery and merely exempts the seller from liability in the case of the intervention of *force majeure*. In any event I am quite satisfied that there is a fair question to be tried on this matter.

As regards certain other matters of law argued the plaintiffs say that they have established fair questions. The defendants concede that the tort of inducement of a breach of contract is well established but as I understood them took their stand on the ingredients of the tort as stated by Jenkins L.J. in *Thomson* v. *Deakin* already referred to. Unless there is strict proof of those ingredients they say that the plaintiffs must fail and that *prima facie* proof of the facts necessary to constitute the required ingredients is not forthcoming. But the plaintiffs say that they do not accept the nature of some of these ingredients stated by that learned Judge and they pointed out that while Jenkins L.J. is a Judge to whom the greatest respect is due on any pronouncement of the law, the precise ingredients of the tort have not been authoritatively decided in our Courts, which seems to be the fact.

His views as to some of the necessary ingredients of the tort as laid down by him might not now be followed in England or here, it was pointed out. He appears to confine the ingredient of a procurement of a breach of contract by unlawful means to the instance of a procurement of a breach of the contract of employment existing between one of the parties to the contract, the breach of which is induced, and an employee of that party. The plaintiffs say that the case of *Stratford* v. *Lindley* indicates that a wider view is clearly open and that that case indicates that proof of the procuring of a breach of contract of employment between a third party and his employees is sufficient to sustain the tort. I agree with that to the extent that a most arguable proposition on the point is shown and it follows that a fair question to be tried has been raised on this point.

It was further submitted by the defendants that it is a necessary ingredient of the tort to show that the person charged with procuring the breach of contract alleged intended to procure the breach and did procure it by unlawful means. Granted that this is so but a person is presumed to intend the ordinary and necessary consequences of his acts. If the ordinary and probable consequences of the actions of either defendant would be such as to cause a breach of contract then the intent would ordinarily be presumed.

Since I have found that there is a fair question to be tried on the point that the procuring of the employees of a *third* party to break their contract of employment constitutes the procuring of a breach of contract by unlawful means, the point arises first as to whether or not a *prima facie* case has been made out that a breach of the contracts of employment between the checkers and their employers, be they shipping agents or stevedores or other persons employing the checkers, has been made out. The suggestion is that the stevedores or shipping agents may have acquiesced in the conduct of the checkers. This is not substantiated in any way so far. There does not however seem to be any question but that it is a normal part of the checkers' work to check out deliveries and give a delivery note to the consignee. A *prima facie* case is thus made out that the checkers are in breach of contract with their employers. The second question is: did the first named defendant, *prima facie*, procure the breach of the commercial contracts by unlawful means. Admittedly the procuring of the checkers to withdraw their labour *pro tanto* was procured, *inter alia*, by the first-named defendant and again, *prima facie*, that constitutes an unlawful act. Failure to take the necessary steps to enable consignees to take delivery of goods from the port would, *prima facie*, involve a breach of a contract which involved delivery to the consignee.

It all depends, of course, on the ultimate finding as to what degree of knowledge of the contract or a contract the law requires and whether the facts ultimately found show that the defendants had whatever degree of knowledge is required in law. Admittedly the question of intent is bound up with that of knowledge. If the plaintiffs fail on the knowledge point they will fail on the intent point also. However since I have found that a fair question has been raised as to knowledge of the contract it would seem to me that there is a fair question also to be tried on the question of intent.

There is thus, it would seem to me, also sufficient *prima facie* evidence that a breach of the commercial contracts was procured by unlawful means by the first named defendant. There is also I think, *prima facie*, evidence that the second named defendant by his actions already related procured a breach of the commercial contract by the unlawful means of breaking his own contract of employment.

As to intent, there is before me the terms of the resolutions passed by the general committee of the union relating to the embargo. It is in wide terms. Its object has also been stated. I have already referred to both. It has been communicated to the plaintiff company that the embargo applies to them and their goods. I have also referred to what occurred on October 13th when an order to release the plaintiffs' goods were countermanded. The embargo has been implemented against the plaintiffs by both defendants. If knowledge of a contract is assumed for the moment, there is thus *prima facie* evidence of an intent to procure its breach since the actions of the defendants would, *prima facie*, at any rate necessarily breach since the actions of the defendants have that result. I am not overlooking Mr. Finlay's point that you cannot have the intention of breaking a contract that you do not know of.

It was next submitted by the defendants that it must be shown that the breach of the commercial contracts ensued as a necessary consequence of the breach of contract by the employees concerned. The suggestion is that some way around might have been found to get delivery of the goods. I think that a reasonable interpretation of the second-named defendant's affidavit is that he did not release the goods by reason of the embargo. Mr. Fennessey also swears in his affidavit that by reason of the wthdrawal of their labour by the checkers the plaintiffs' employees were unable or unwilling to collect the goods. All the evidence with regard to what happens when a trade dispute takes place cannot of course be put on affidavit but it may be safely assumed that when the case is fully investigated evidence will be before the Court with regard to the practicability of giving delivery on the part of the vendor and taking it on behalf of the purchaser. At the moment it seems to me that to suggest that it was practicable for the plaintiff company to get these goods when an industrial dispute existed and an embargo had been placed on their goods is somewhat unreal. For the present I think that sufficient has been shown to indicate, *prima facie*, that it is not practicable to give or obtain delivery of these goods. With regard to all these matters I have just dealt with relating to the facts I think that the plaintiffs have established that there are fair questions raised to be decided at the trial. . . .'

Note

The subject of injunctions is considered in more detail in chapter 27, *infra*. See especially pp. 617–622, dealing with interlocutory injunctions in relation to industrial disputes.

The Wrongful Procurement

The wrongful interference with contractual relations may be by (a) direct inducement or threat, (b) direct intervention of another type (such as by kidnapping the contracting party, or by damaging the machinery whereby the contract is to be performed); or (c) indirect procurement, where the defendant induces a third party to do an act in itself wrongful so as to prevent performance of a contract by a fourth party with the plaintiff. See *McMahon & Binchy*, pp. 434–437.

TALBOT (IRELAND) LTD. V. A.T.G.W.U.
Supreme Court, 30 April 1981, as reported in The Irish Times, 1 May 1981.

The Supreme Court yesterday dismissed with costs an appeal by the executive council of the Irish Congress of Trade Unions and Matthew Merrigan, district secretary of the Amalgamated Transport and General Workers Union, against an interlocutory injunction granted by Mr. Justice McWilliam in the High Court on April 10th.

The injunction granted to Talbot (Ireland) Ltd restrained the defendants from inducing or attempting to induce a breach of contract between the company and its dealers, and between the company and its parent company, Talbot (UK) Ltd. or attempting to interfere with their economic relations.

The Supreme Court, dismissing the appeal with costs, varied the order of the High Court to an order restraining the defendants or any person who has notice of the order, until after judgment in the action, or until further order, from inducing or procuring any breach of a commercial contract between the company and any third party and in particular between the company and Talbot (UK) Ltd. and between the company and its dealers.

The judgment was delivered by Mr Justice Henchy (presiding) with whom Mr

Justice Griffin and Mr Justice Kenny agreed. Mr Justice Kenny said that the Trade Disputes Act, 1906, had no application in the case.

Earlier this month Mr Merrigan was committed to prison for contempt of court for failing to obey the High Court order, but that order was not implemented so the appeal could be taken to the Supreme Court.

Mr Justice Henchy (with whom Mr Justice Griffin and Mr Justice Kenny agreed) said it appeared that the executive council of the ICTU at a meeting on March 27th endorsed the embargo a[nd] as a result Mr Merrigan issued two documents.

These two documents, read together, showed that the purpose was that all members of unions affiliated to the Congress would lend their support to a total embargo throughout Ireland, North and South, on the importation and movement of Talbot cars, spare parts and other components and also on services in connection with the company's activities. The court knew from the uncontradicted affidavit before it that those two documents were implemented.

It was clear that the effect of the embargo was that there had been a breach of contract and of more than one contract between the company and those with whom it did business, particularly dealers, not to speak of 2,900 people who bought Talbot vehicles which were within the guarantee period.

The court learned of other effects of the embargo, including the effect on the company's premises relat[ing] to ancillary commercial contractual relationships dealing with the servicing and maintenance of machinery; post not being delivered; petrol and oil firms refusing to supply the company; and refuse not being collected.

Mr Justice Henchy said he instanced those matters to indicate that the effect of the embargo as circulated had been no mere empty request, but had been an implemented direction which in effect had procured the breach of many contracts between the company and third parties.

The case had been made by the defendants that the predominant object of the action taken by them had been to advance the cause of the workers represented by the union, and he had no doubt that that was a correct view. They had relied on the *Harris Tweed* case as supporting the proposition that once the object was lawful, even though the result may be disastrous, if the predominant object was legitimate in the sense of helping the workers, it was sufficient to defeat the plaintiffs' claim. That submission would be correct if the case were laid in conspiracy, but the tort relied on in this case was not the tort of conspiracy.

It was well-established that where a defendant, knowing of a contract between the plaintiff and a third party, intentionally induced a third party to break the contract and thereby cause loss to the plaintiff, a tort was committed unless there was justification for the defendant's action.

In this case Mr Justice McWilliam found in effect that the effect of the embargo was that the defendants, knowing that contracts were in existence, executory or otherwise, between the company and its parent company in England; between the company and its suppliers; between the company and the Post Office etc., nevertheless chose to extend the effect of the industrial action to the stage where they induced breaches of contract with third parties.

Consequently a tort was committed. Subsequent events had shown that the inducement resulted in an actual procurement of breaches of contracts with third parties.

Whether there was a trade dispute or not, a body or bodies must operate within the constitutional framework and the constitutional guarantees in Article 40, and it would have to be borne in mind that innocent persons could not be damnified – and when he spoke of innocent persons he was not referring to the union or the company but to persons such as dealers who had no dispute with anybody, or the owners of vehicles who had no dispute with anybody but who, because of this embargo, could not get their vehicles serviced – a service they were entitled to under their contract.

In this case it was clear that there had been an inducement of the various workers in the various unions affiliated to the Congress to procure breaches of contract between the company and the persons and bodies mentioned, and that was a tort, and that it had not been done with any lawful excuse. For that reason he would support the conclusion that was reached in the High Court that there had been a tort.

It was quite clear that the legitimacy of the trade dispute that existed was not in question. It had been suggested that what had happened was an embargo only in name and that the effect was no more than an all-out strike.

But what had happened had gone far beyond that – far beyond any picket; far beyond any strike, far beyond any legitimate industrial action. He had no doubt that the ICTU, which was a reputable and honorable body, acted inadvertently in placing this total embargo, and no doubt once this matter had been determined by the order, they would abide by the decision given. For those reasons he would dismiss the appeal but he would vary the order made in the High Court in the manner stated.

When the hearing was resumed yesterday, Mr Feargus Flood, SC (for Mr Merrigan) replying to the submissions of Mr Niall Fennelly (for Talbot), asked was it to be said in that court that the ICTU had sat down for the purpose of surgically carving up and closing Talbot (Ireland), or was it that it has as its purpose the consideration of how it could assist its member organisations in the conduct of a dispute with the company?

Mr. Flood submitted that it was beyond all doubt that the whole purpose and object was not the dismembering of Talbot (Ireland), but had the advancement and assistance of a member union as its primary purpose, and that the object was a lawful object.

In this country, or any civilised country, one was entitled to say:– 'This is a legitimate purpose: it should receive the support of all right-thinking people.' If they were not entitled to say that, the freedom of expression of opinion was certainly a very limited freedom in this country.

'I know that throughout this case your Lordships have had an unholy fascination for the fact that if we maintain the embargo Talbot would close, but that fascination is also true of any strike,' said Mr Flood.

If everybody was going to be pig-headed than somebody was going to go to the wall. That was the whole object of striking or picketing – all the forces that brought people to the negotiation table. That was why it was ridiculous to say that the ICTU had sat down to dismember a source of employment.

Notes and Questions

1. For analysis of the decision see *McMahon & Binchy*, pp. 436–437; von Prondzynski, 'Why the Trade Unions Face an Explosive Issue Today' *Irish Independent*, 1 May 1981; von Prondzynski & McCarthy, 'Is the Law Above the Trade Unions?' *Irish Times*, 18 May 1981; von Prondzynski & McCarthy, 'Labour Law – The Freedom to Strike and the Protection of Third Parties' [1981] D.U.L.J. 99; Kerr, 'Trade Disputes, Economic Torts and the Constitution: The Legacy of Talbot' 16 Ir. Jur. (n.s.) 241 (1981). Mr. Kerr suggests that the Irish Constitution may offer the conceptual basis on which a line may be drawn between an embargo of the kind used in *Talbot* and an all-out-strike. For the development of this argument, see *id.*, at 254ff.

2. *Cf.* von Prondzynski, 'Trade Disputes and the Courts: The Problem of the Labour Injunctions' 16 Ir. Jur. (n.s.) 228 at 238 (1981), who states that the decision in *Talbot* –
   'with enormous implications for trade disputes law, was reached at the interlocutory stage.

Highly complex arguments and a number of difficult authorities were submitted to the court, and there clearly was insufficient time to consider these fully or work out the implications of the decision. The balance of convenience was not mentioned at all. The difficulty inherent in deciding complex legal issues on affidavit and under considerable pressure of time, factors which prompted the *Cyanamid* decision [[1975] A.C. 396] in the first place, was apparently ignored here. It is clearly not a good model for decisions of this kind.'

Do you agree? See further *infra*, pp. 617–622.

Intimidation

The tort of intimidation consists of a threat delivered by the defendant to a person whereby the defendant intentionally causes that person to act or refrain from acting in a manner in which he is entitled to act, either to his own detriment or to the detriment of another. It is only relatively recently that the tort has been commonly described as 'intimidation', as the cases extracted below indicate.

COOPER V. MILLEA
[1938] I.R. 749 (High Ct., Gavan Duffy, J.)

Gavan Duffy J.:

The plaintiff, John Cooper, is a widower, aged 54; his home at all material times was and is at Waterford; he joined the railway service in 1916 as a porter and under the Railways Act (No. 29 of 1924), became a servant of the Great Southern Railways; for a few years he was a member of the National Union of Railwaymen (the 'N.U.R.') and then for some years a member of no Union, until 1934, when, upon the formation of a new trade union, the Federation of Road and Rail Workers, registered under trade union law, he became a pioneer for that Union in Waterford, where a branch was established. In March, 1935, that Union declared a strike on the railway and the plaintiff went out on strike; the strike collapsed after a week, and most, but not all, of the men on strike were taken back by the Railway Company, the plaintiff being assigned to duty at the North Wall, Dublin. The Federation continued to function as a trade union, but the Waterford branch ceased to exist; the plaintiff continued to be a member of that Union. At the North Wall he was asked several times to join the N.U.R., but he put off the canvassers until September, 1935, when an organiser for the N.U.R. urged him to join; he replied that he was a member of the Federation and, at the organiser's request, produced his paid up card to the secretary of the local branch of the N.U.R. The local branch thereupon decided that it would not work with plaintiff, refusing to recognise the Federation as a trade union, and a very few men at the North Wall stopped work; the stoppage did not last more than half an hour; the Company's local agent had immediately sent for the plaintiff and suggested that he should apply for a transfer from Dublin; he applied for a transfer to Waterford, his home town, and he was transferred to Waterford next day, the 17th of September, 1935. There Mr. Brewer, the local superintendent, directed him not to resume duty until further orders, telling him that he would receive full pay in the meantime. On the 20th of September he was instructed to report for duty next morning at the Waterford Goods Store; he did so, but had hardly begun work when he was summoned by Mr. Brewer, who told him that, because the Waterford men would not work with him, the Company offered him a transfer to Belturbet (a very long way from Waterford). In vain plaintiff protested; he was told that he must take the transfer or go; he refused Belturbet and was discharged with a week's wages in lieu of notice. He now claims damages from the men whom he regards as mainly responsible for his dismissal; he has failed to obtain any but the most casual employ-ment since. His amended claim charges the defendants with having procured his dismissal by illegal means. Mr. Brewer testifies that plaintiff had always been a satisfactory employee.

The defendant, Peter Millea, was in 1935 and still is secretary of the Waterford No. 1 Branch of the N.U.R.; the defendant, William McBride, was the chairman of the branch in September, 1935, and the defendant, John Drohan, its vice-chairman. On the morning of the 21st of September these three men called upon Mr. Brewer, Millea acting as spokesman, and informed him that they were a deputation from the No. 1 Branch and that, if plaintiff were allowed to take up duty, the men had decided that they would withdraw their labour; they meant, and were understood to mean, an immediate withdrawal – there is no dispute about that. Consequently Mr. Brewer, acting upon instructions from Dublin, where some trouble of this kind had been feared, took the action that he did against the plaintiff. He says that he understood that a general strike, involving the whole line, was threatened, because, if the strike were sanctioned by the N.U.R., it would be general so far as their members, who were very numerous, were concerned; the defendants had stated that they rep-resented the branch, but he took them, he says, to represent the Union; perhaps he was not justified in so understanding them, but that is a side issue. It is material to note that the threatened strike would have involved a breach of their contracts by the men concerned, who had weekly contracts. I use the word 'threat' in this judgment for convenience, but 'pre-intimation' would serve equally well, if anyone prefers it.

The defendants say that Millea and McBride had been in Dublin on Union business on the 17th of September, when they learned of the stoppage at the North Wall, due to plaintiff's refusal to join the N.U.R. and were told that it was thought that he was to be transferred to Waterford; Mr. Watters, the Irish Secretary and Chief Organiser in Ireland of the N.U.R., sent for them; he saw them next day, and in their presence he telephoned to the Company, when he was able to tell them that he had got an assurance that plaintiff would not be transferred to Waterford. They went home, having first wired to one of the Waterford members to convene a special meeting of the branch for 9 o'clock that night for important business. The meeting was called in the usual way for special meetings by posting notice of it in three places where the men at Waterford work, but, whereas two or three days' notice was sometimes given, only a few hours' notice was given on this occasion, so that there is little doubt even some of the men working in Waterford did not hear of the meeting; this course was adopted on the ground of urgency. The No. 1 Branch covers a large area extending to Tipperary and Clonmel, but members in outlying places were not notified; the defendants say that these men were not in the habit of attending meetings and could not afford to do so. It appears that the chairman and secretary told the meeting about the strike at the North Wall, and its success, and about the assurance obtained by Mr. Watters; it was decided to await events, the secretary being instructed to convene another special meeting if he learnt that plaintiff was taking up duty at Waterford. A second special meeting was convened for 9 p.m. on the 20th of September, by notices posted as before on the afternoon of the same day. The meeting was told that plaintiff was to take up duty in Waterford next morning; it was resolved that immediate strike action be taken in the morning if he did take up duty and the defendants were appointed as a deputation to wait on Mr. Brewer. No one had asked the plaintiff to join the N.U.R. since his return to Waterford; perhaps it was assumed that any such request would be quite useless. The policy of refusing to work with a man who was not a member of the N.U.R. was a very grave departure from the existing practice on the line; the policy was quite new, except for the irregular action taken at the North Wall against the plaintiff; the new policy had not received the sanction of the Executive Council of the N.U.R., as required by the rules of the Union, nor had the sanction of that Council, required by the rules, been obtained for the contemplated strike.

In a case of this kind the apparent antinomy between the rights of organised labour and the rights of the private citizen may easily lead to confusion. It is the duty of the Courts firmly to uphold the legal rights of workingmen to combine; the right of combination, recognised by statute in 1824 (when a repressive code, elaborated through three centuries in England, was repealed), has now been securely established, but only after a very severe struggle during the 19th century and through the indomitable courage and perseverance of workingmen against heavy odds; and the right to form unions, subject to control in the public interest, is expressly recognised by the Constitution. At the same time, as a matter of national social policy, every citizen is declared to have the right to adequate means of livelihood and, as a matter of law, every man is entitled to be protected against unlawful interference with his means of living, and that protection he is entitled to seek and obtain from the Courts. In the social conflict there will often be an apparent clash between these rights and, if there be any such clash in the present case, it must be resolved on principle; the rule of law in this country would be gravely impaired if sympathy (for I have been invited to shed tears) or other extraneous considerations were allowed to influence a decision. The interests of the individual and of organised labour must frequently collide; if the union wins, the victim may be crushed; yet his ruin may be as irrelevant in a Court of law as the failure or success of a trade union's policy, for the injured man must prove that the law has been broken before the Courts can give him any redress. It is regrettable that conflicting rights in this sphere of law are not more extensively regulated by statute; the inevitable result under the jurisprudence of this country and of England has often been that important questions as to how far organised labour may go have had to be decided by the conceptions of individual Judges as to what may or may not be lawful in the milky way of the common law, and some such judgments are by no means a certain guide. In the present case, however, I hope that it will be possible to find solid ground in the common law without resorting to juristic speculation and to confine my judgment to principles that are not seriously controverted. The governing principle is that trade unionists may lawfully combine for lawful common purposes, even though their action inflict irreparable harm upon an individual, so long, and so long only, as they confine their activities to lawful methods.

Some of the circumstances attending the defendants' campaign are worth noting. The defendants acted rather recklessly, but with a considerable measure of good faith; apart from a minor question as to whether plaintiff should be allowed to return to Waterford before certain other men, they were forcing the pace in favour of a new policy by reason of an objection, strongly felt by a number of the Waterford men, to the return of plaintiff as an active worker for a rival Union, whose strike had in fact proved very unfortunate for some of the men involved. The defendants, greatly encouraged, no doubt, by the success of the irregular action at the North Wall and by the assurance given to Mr. Watters, were entitled to press their views on this question of policy, but there is a right way and a wrong way of asserting one's convictions and plaintiff's opponents blundered badly; first, since there are no rules as to length of notice for special meetings, any reasonable practice must be supported, but there was no such urgency in the new departure as could justify the precipitate summoning of the vital second meeting without adequate notice; the defendants say that it was intended to call out only the men working at the depot in Waterford, but even these local men were not duly notified and the meeting purported to be a meeting of the branch and to speak for the branch as a whole. Secondly, there is no doubt that the defendants professed to be delegates from the branch, on whose behalf they warned Mr. Brewer of a withdrawal of labour, if plaintiff were allowed to work in Waterford, but, as the branch had not been properly convened, the branch had come to no such decision and the branch had appointed no deputation to Mr. Brewer. Thirdly, no minutes were recorded of the two important meetings until 18 months later, when this action was begun, whereas other meetings generally seem to have been regularly recorded in the minute book. Worse still, at least two of the defendants and probably all three knew that according to their rules the branch had no right to take strike action without the prior sanction of the Executive Committee of the N.U.R., and a strike by the Waterford men alone would have paralysed an important section of the line. Sect. 55 of the Railways Act, 1924 (No. 29 of 1924) may be important in this connection; it requires the conditions of service of railway employees to be regulated in accordance with agreements between the trade unions and the railway companies, thus giving to the unions concerned, of which the N.U.R. is one of the principals, a statutory participation in the government of the railways, and it is admitted that the unions making such agreements do so on behalf of the men in the grades covered by the agreements, whether members of the signatory unions or not. It may be that one effect of sect. 55 is in appropriate cases to give to the companies and the men affected a specific interest in the faithful observance of a union's strike regulations by the members of these unions. Again, agreements as to conditions of service affect status, and it may be that the existing agreements affect the right of the railways to discharge summarily a satisfactory servant, for the object of the section and of the unions must be (among other things) to provide for the men at least such a degree of security of tenure as the railway companies may feel safe in conceding. These important questions have only been touched upon in the course of this case; they have not been argued. Moreover, I am not satisfied that all the agreements governing the plaintiff's conditions of service have been proved, nor has the question of the burden of proof of those conditions been discussed, nor is any reliance placed on any rights derived from sect. 55 in the pleadings; accordingly, while I think that it is necessary to call attention to the section, I must decide this case without regard to it. I have placed it among the surrounding circumstances which it seemed necessary to note in drawing a picture of this case, but in my view of the position a clear and simple *ratio decidendi* for this case is to be found without regard to these incidentals.

The main question to which I shall address myself is the question whether or not the action taken by the defendants was lawful or unlawful at common law; to that question I think the common law gives a clear answer; the answer to that question of law must, of course, depend upon the relevant conclusions of fact to which the evidence leads me, and those findings, together with some others that are necessarily interwoven with them, I shall now summarise as briefly as the circumstances allow.

The defendants' purpose was to drive the plaintiff out of the service at Waterford; that meant securing his removal or dismissal. Their motive was to further their trade union interests, as they saw them; it was not malicious in the popular sense of the word, and their combination adds nothing to the plaintiff's cause of action. Their methods were these:– being officials of a local branch of a powerful Union, they called on the local superintendent as a deputation authorised by that branch to threaten an immediate withdrawal of their labour by the members if plaintiff were allowed to work in Waterford; they had no such authority, but the plaintiff, while complaining in general terms of the use of illegal means, refrains from suing for injurious falsehood; had that been the cause of action, I should probably have found that the defendants believed that they had the authority of the branch, though they knew that the rules of the Union as to strikes were being broken; I should then have had to determine whether in this state of affairs they had a lawful excuse for representing themselves as a deputation from the branch. However, that issue does not arise. The threat was calculated to make a powerful impression on its recipient and, since it was to be expected that plaintiff in the circumstances would refuse to leave Waterford, its direct and proximate result was his discharge. The essential fact is that that result was obtained by the threat of a strike in breach of their contracts with the Company by the men concerned.

This civil bill belongs to the elusive category of actions for intentional interference with a man's employment by illegal means; see Digest of English Civil Law, 3rd ed., par. 984. It is incontestable that the defendants interfered with the plaintiff's employment by illegal means; for a strike in breach of contract is unlawful and a threat or pre-intimation of unlawful action constitutes illegal means; the right of action is thus established; see Lord Dunedin's speech in *Sorrell* v. *Smith* [1925] A. C., at p. 730. The fact that plaintiff could have retained his employment by going to the West is no defence; the Company's instructions to Mr. Brewer, upon which Mr. Brewer acted, in effect gave plaintiff the option and its one concern was to pacify the men by getting him out of the service in Waterford. Nor, in view of the unlawful threat, can sect. 3 of the Trade Disputes Act, 1906, afford a defence, even if there was an actual or contemplated trade dispute; to find any such dispute here would be to ignore the serious irregularities in the creation of the dispute, but the trade dispute question does not arise on my view of that Act and of the facts.

The plaintiff, apart from any improvement which may have been made in his tenure under sect. 55 of the Act of 1924, was at the time of his discharge employed at a weekly wage; when taken back into the service after the strike he had suffered a loss of status: in the event of dismissals for redundancy he would, I am told, have been liable to dismissal before many men who, prior to the strike, would have had to go before him; no written agreement governing this matter of precedence was put in, nor have I seen any seniority lists showing the precise position of precedence of the plaintiff before and after the strike of March, 1935, but I have no doubt that the loss of status in fact occurred and that it was correctly represented to me by Mr. Watters at the trial; before the strike the plaintiff and large numbers of other men had been excepted from the payment of unemployment insurance upon a certificate of the Minister for Industry and Commerce (see the Unemployment Insurance Act, 1920, Schedule I, Part II) to the effect that they were not liable to dismissal except for misconduct or neglect of duty or unfitness; on rejoining the service after the strike the plaintiff lost his immunity and he was not likely to regain it for at least three years; hence, upon dismissals for redundancy, he would be liable to discharge before the excepted men. On the evidence given before me in July last it is reasonably clear that, as matters stood in September of 1935, the plaintiff could legitimately look forward to being retained indefinitely in the Company's service during good behaviour, unless a time should come when the Company had to discharge him for redundancy, and upon the evidence before me that was not likely to happen; it is notorious that extensive reductions of staff for redundancy have been made in earlier years under the Act of 1924 and an amending Act of 1926, and the question before me is not affected by any developments in the railway position which may have occurred since the trial.

I come now to the question of damages. The plaintiff does not allege that the Railway Company committed any breach of its contract with him in paying him off with a week's wages, and I shall assume that he suffered no breach of contract at the hands of the Company, but this assumption does not help the defendants, since the plaintiff is not suing them for breach of contract, but for a tort, claiming compensation for a wilful invasion of his employment through illegal interference between himself and his employers whereby he has been gravely injured. Damage, the temporal loss actually sustained, is the gist of this action, where no contractual right has been disturbed, and I have carefully considered the case law as to the damages which the plaintiff may recover; as, however, this aspect of the matter has not been discussed, I need only say that it is no new law that 'in all cases where a man has a temporal loss or damage by the wrong of another, he may have an action on the case, to be repaired in damages' (Com. Dig., tit. 'Action on the Case' – A). It is quite clear that the fact that the plaintiff might, as between himself and the Company, have been thrown out of the service at any moment on a week's notice will not prevent him from recovering the damage that he has actually suffered by the loss of his livelihood through the wrongful act of the defendants. The law is that every reasonable presumption should be made as to the benefits likely to have accrued to the plaintiff but for his dismissal. The insecurity of the plaintiff's tenure must, of course, be taken into account, but it cannot loom large as an element in reducing damages where there is no evidence whatever before the Court that this satisfactory workman was likely to be discharged; the plaintiff's prospect before the dismissal of retaining his employment for a considerable time was good, but it depended on his continuance in life and health and on various hazards, while his prospect after dismissal, as an unskilled worker, in the fifties, of finding employment was, and remains, remote. As a regular employee of the Company he was earning 45s. a week; in nearly three years since his discharge he says that he has earned less than £10 at casual work; he has thereore suffered serious loss as the direct consequence of the wrongful conduct of the three defendants, and he has given me particulars of that loss, as he sees it. I have carefully considered what sum a jury should and would give him by way of damages for the wrong inflicted upon him, and on a review of all the facts I am of opinion that the sum of £250, which the plaintiff recovered before the learned Circuit Court Judge who first tried the case, represents the just measure of his damages. I shall accordingly enter judgment for him against the defendants in that amount, with costs in the High Court and the costs already awarded to him in the Circuit Court.

Notes and Questions

1. See also *Riordan* v. *Butler* [1940] I.R. 347 (High Ct., O'Byrne, J.)
2. In *Rookes* v. *Barnard* [1964] A.C. 1129 (H.L. (Eng.)), the tort of intimidation was first given full recognition. Of particular interest to Irish readers is the passage from Lord Evershed's opinion, where he stated:

> . . . I therefore agree with the view expressed by the Court of Appeal that there has been established as a wrong and as part of the English law the tort of intimidation. I am willing to concede that the tort is one of relatively modern judicial creation (though Pearson, L.J., in the course of his analysis [1963] 1 Q.B. at pp. 686–696 referred to some authorities of respectable antiquity) and that its full extent and scope have not (at least before the present case) been authoritatively determined and may well, indeed, even by your Lordships' judgments in this case, still not have been finally stated. But that is, after all, in accordance with the well-known principles of our law, one of the characteristics of which is (as has been pointed out by many eminent legal scholars, including Cardozo, C.J.), that its principles are never finally determined, but are and should be capable of expansion and development as changing circumstances require, the material subject matter being 'tested and re-tested' in the law's laboratories, namely, the courts of justice, *Nature of the Judicial*

Process (Yale University Press), p. 33. Moreover, as observed by Professor Holdsworth in his history of the Law of England, vol. 8, pp. 392ff, the tort of conspiracy, as now understood, is also one of relatively modern exposition, differing from the ancient tort of conspiracy (which as Professor Holdsworth points out is in reality now equivalent to malicious prosecution) and has arisen out of the circumstances of modern industrial relations. So also, as I conceive, has the tort of intimidation. Counsel for the respondents forcibly argued on an analysis of the various cases in which the alleged tort has arisen, that it was in truth originally and still is no more than an aspect of the law of tort of nuisance. According to counsel for the respondents, it was in truth invented by Sir John Salmond.

With all respect to counsel for the respondents' argument, it is now, as I have said, in my opinion too late to deny the reception of the tort of intimidation into the company of English wrongs. So far, I have agreed with the Court of Appeal; but I respectfully differ from the Court of Appeal in thinking that the wrong of intimidation must stop short so as to comprehend only threats of criminal or tortious acts, and thus to exclude threats of breaches of contract. I am aware that the only direct authorities for such an extension of the wrong are the two Irish cases of *Cooper* v. *Millea, McBride and Drohan* [1938] I.R. 749 before Gavan Duffy, J. and *Riordan* v, *Butler* [1940] I.R. 347, in which O'Byrne, J. [1940] I.R. at p. 353, followed Gavan Duffy, J. I am aware also that in the former case the learned judge erred in attributing a dictum in support of his view to Lord Dunedin in *Sorrell* v. *Smith* [1925] A.C. 700 and that in fact the noble Lord in that case used the words which I have quoted [1925] A.C. at p. 730 '. . . that action must be either per se a legal action or an illegal, i.e., a tortious action'. I cannot, however, think that by his use of the formula 'id est' Lord Dunedin was intending to lay it down that only threats of tortious actions would constitute the wrong of intimidation. The attention of your lordships was also properly drawn to all the relevant dicta that have fallen from the judges since that of Bowen, L.J., in the *Mogul Steamship* case (1889) 23 Q.B.D. at pp. 611–620 down to the present time, and I would concede that on the face of them these dicta may tend more to support the restriction of the tort than its extension so as to include threats of breach of contract – though they cannot be said in that respect to be uniform: see, for example, the use of the word 'unlawful' by Lord Lindley in *South Wales Miners' Federation* v. *Glamorgan Coal Co. Ltd.* [1905] A.C. 239 at p. 253:

> To break a contract is an unlawful act; or, in the language of Lord Watson in *Allen* v. *Flood* [1898] A.C. at p. 96, "A breach of contract is in itself a legal wrong". . . . a breach of contract would not be actionable if nothing legally was involved in the breach.'

To this last citation Donovan, L.J., referred in his judgment in the present case [1963] 1 Q.B. at p. 679. I venture, like Lord Lindley, to refer to Lord Watson's opinion in *Allen* v. *Flood* [1898] A.C. at p. 94 where the noble lord cited and adopted the language of Bowen, L.J., in the *Mogul Steamship* case (1889), 23 Q.B.D. at p. 612 '. . . the term "wrongful" imports in its term the infringement of some right'. But in none of the reported cases (except the Irish cases *Cooper* v. *Millea* [1938] I.R. 749 and *Riordan* v. *Butler* [1940] I.R. 347) was the question with which your Lordships are now concerned raised as relevant for decision, and the language in the many judgments to which your Lordships have been referred was, as I conceive, intended to be but illustrative and was in any event on the present question *obiter*.

I feel therefore free to approach the question as a matter of principle; and, so approaching it, I cannot for my part see any persuasive basis for drawing the line so as to exclude from the wrong of intimidation threats of breaches of contract. I cannot find in accordance with logic, reason or common sense anything between threats to do tortious or criminal acts, on the one hand, and threats to break contracts on the other, which amounts, in the simile used by Lord Herschell in *Allen* v. *Flood* [1898] A.C. at p. 121 to a chasm. . . .

Conspiracy

Is there a Separate Tort of Conspiracy to Commit a Tort
DILLON V. DUNNE'S STORES (GEORGE'S STREET) LTD.
Unreported, Supreme Court, 20 December 1968 (131–1966)

[The facts of the case and portions of the judgment of **Ó Dálaigh C.J.** are set out, *supra*, pp. 126–130. The passage set out below consists of the Chief Justice's analysis of the plaintiff's claim based on conspiracy by the defendants to falsely imprison her.]

. . . The trial Judge left a second cause of action to the jury for their consideration viz. conspiracy to imprison, and the jury found there was such a conspiracy. What has already been said in analysing the evidence with regard to the jury's finding that the Dunnes *agreed* with the Gárdai to falsely imprison the plaintiff is directly in point. If, as we have held, there is no evidence of an agreement to imprison and the finding of agreement to imprison has been set aside, the finding of conspiracy must fall with it: *agreement* and *conspiracy* are one and the same thing. It follows that the judgment which the Court would enter up in favour of Mr. Ben and Miss Margaret Dunne and the company discharges these three defendants in respect of both causes of action.

It was moreover submitted on behalf of the Dunnes and the company that conspiracy to commit a tort is not an independent tort. The plaintiff's submission that it is a tort is novel and without precedent.

If one considers the difference between conspiracy in criminal law and the tort of conspiracy it will, in our opinion, become clear why there is no room in civil law for the independent tort of conspiracy to commit a tort. What this difference is is well summarised in the words used by Simon L.C. in the opening passages of his speech in *Crofter Handwoven Harris Tweed Co.* v. *Veitch* [1942] A.C. 435, 439–40. He said: 'Conspiracy when regarded as a crime is an agreement of two or more persons to effect any unlawful purpose, whether as its ultimate aim or only as a means to it and the crime is complete if there is such an agreement even though nothing is done in pursuance of it . . . The crime consists in the agreement though in most cases overt acts done in pursuance of the combination are available to prove the fact of agreement. But the tort of conspiracy is constituted only if the agreed combination is carried into effect in a greater or less degree and damage to the plaintiff is thereby produced. It must be so, for, regarded as a civil wrong conspiracy is one of those wrongs like fraud or negligence which sound in damage, and a mere agreement to injure, if it was never acted upon at all and never led to any result affecting the party complaining could not produce damage to him.' The 'conspirators' would, in effect, have committed the tort. It is therefore easy to see why the common law has not found the need to find a place for conspiracy to commit a tort as an independent tort. Instead of having 'conspirators' the common law has been satisfied with joint tort-feasors. Denning L.J. (as he then was) has expressed the same idea in the observations which he made in the course of his judgment in *Ward* v. *Lewis* [1955] 1 W.L.R. 9, 11: 'It is important to remember . . . that when a tort has been committed by two or more persons an allegation of prior agreement to commit the tort adds nothing. The prior agreement merges in the tort. It is sometimes sought, by charging conspiracy, to get an added advantage, for instance in proceedings for discovery, or by getting in evidence which would not be admissible in a straight action in tort or to overcome substantive rules of law, such as here, the rules about republication of slander. When the court sees attempts of that kind being made it will discourage them by striking out the allegation of conspiracy on the simple ground that the conspiracy adds nothing when the tort has in fact been committed.'

On such argument we have heard we favour the view that there it is not a tort of conspiracy to commit a tort; but in the circumstances of this appeal it is not necessary to express a concluded view on the matter. . . .

Question

What do you think of the argument against recognising conspiracy to commit a tort as a separate tort? *Cf. McMahon & Binchy*, pp. 443–444.

McGOWAN V. MURPHY
Unreported, Supreme Court, 10 April 1967 (119–1964)

Walsh J. (for the Court):

This is an appeal brought by the plaintiff against the order of Mr Justic Teevan made the 13th day of November 1964 withdrawing from the jury the plaintiff's claim for damages for conspiracy against the defendants.

The plaintiff's action was brought for various reliefs including a declaration that he had been wrongfully expelled from his trade union, the Electrical Trades Union Ireland, of whom the defendants were members of the resident executive committee. One of the reliefs sought was damages for conspiracy and at the trial of the matter before Mr Justice Teevan and a jury the only issue at trial was the claim for damages for conspiracy. A finding for the plaintiff on this issue would more than likely have ruled all the other issues but it is not necessary to deal with that matter at the moment.

The conspiracy alleged was a conspiracy to prevent the plaintiff earning his living. That is putting the matter rather generally and shortly though the pleadings in the case did not spell out the particular conspiracy. For the purpose of this appeal, however, it may be regarded as a conspiracy to injure the plaintiff.

The origin of the dispute between the plaintiff and his trade union arose from a trade dispute, which was not authorised by the union, occurring in the course of work on Dromoland Castle in Newmarket-on-Fergus, County Clare on July 4th and 5th 1963 and in which, it was alleged, the plaintiff was involved. It was claimed by the union, at the time and subsequently, that the plaintiff took part in unofficial strike action and that in so doing he acted in disobedience to and in defiance of the rules of the union. On the 9th July 1963 the defendants decided unanimously to expel the plaintiff from membership of the union because of the incident but this purported expulsion was not acted upon presumably because, as the evidence discloses, the inquiry which had been held by the defendants was one of which the plaintiff had been given no notice and the rules of the union require that he should be given notice of any such inquiry. On the 15th July 1963 notice was given to the plaintiff that the purported expulsion was withdrawn and that his membership of the union was restored as from the 9th July, 1963. About the 16th July 1963 the defendants invited the plaintiff to attend at the union offices in Dublin to show cause why he should not be dealt with in accordance with the rules because of his alleged part in the unofficial strike action already mentioned. A meeting of the defendants as such executive committee was held on the 19th July 1963 at which the plaintiff attended and the matter was dealt with. In the result the plaintiff received notice of his expulsion from the union as of the 6th August, 1963. The gist of the conspiracy claim is that the hearing on the 19th July 1963 was not a genuine one, that the matter had already been prejudged, that it was only gone through as a matter of form and in effect was part of a conspiracy by the defendants to injure the plaintiff.

For the purpose of dealing with the legal issues it is not necessary to express any views on the merits of the case made against the plaintiff by the defendants alleging that he did take part in unofficial strike action. It is claimed that the effect of expelling the plaintiff from the trade union would, for all practical purposes, make him unemployable as an electrician as no contractor would take a non-union electrician because of the objections of union electricians on the same job and that this would apply particularly to a person who had been expelled from a union. The essence of the action therefore is that the conspiracy to injure the plaintiff was a conspiracy to procure his expulsion from his trade union.

There can be no doubt that in law the defendants would have been quite entitled to advise the trade union to terminate the membership of the plaintiff where the matter did not go beyond advice and did not amount to inducing it or procuring it. When the matter goes beyond mere advice a different situation may arise depending upon the circumstances. If the defendants combined to procure the expulsion of the plaintiff from the trade union and in so doing had as their sole or main purpose or object the injuring of the plaintiff and the plaintiff suffered damage by reason of it the defendants would be guilty of the actionable tort of conspiracy, even if the expulsion was not in breach of the rules of the union. To that extent a combination of persons in such circumstance is in a less favoured position than an individual doing the same act. See *Crofter Harris Tweed Co.* v. *Veitch* [1942] 1 All E.R. 142. If, however, the real purpose of the combination was not to injure the plaintiff but to defend the interests of the trade union by maintaining discipline then no wrong was committed and no action will lie even though damage to the plaintiff resulted provided that the means used were not in themselves unlawful. See the case *Sorrell* v. *Smith* [1925] A.C. 700. The plaintiff submits firstly that the evidence clearly established that the object and purpose of the defendants in combination was to injure him by making it virtually impossible for him to earn his living as an electrician or alternatively, if the object was wholly or mainly to protect the interests of the trade union, that the defendants employed illegal means in that the hearing which they gave to the matter was not a bona fide hearing and was never intended to be such, that the matter had been prejudged and that in reality they constituted what might be called a 'kangaroo court'. If this latter claim could be established then undoubtedly the means employed would be illegal because they would constitute a conspiracy on the part of the defendants to deprive the plaintiff of his contractual right to an inquiry or hearing in accordance with Rules 205 and 206 of the Rules of the union before he could be expelled. In my view the rules constitute a contract between the trade union and the plaintiff to be observed on both sides.

To succeed in this appeal, therefore, the plaintiff must establish that the evidence given before the jury was sufficient to enable a jury reasonably to find that the defendants had combined to expel him from the trade union having as their main object or purpose injury to the plaintiff and that he suffered damage thereby or alternatively that the defendants in combination, even if they had as their main object and purpose the good of the union, employed illegal means, namely setting up a hearing in purported pursuance of rules 205 and 206 of the Rules having previously agreed that it would not be a genuine or bona fide hearing in accordance with the rules, and that the plaintiff suffered damage.

So far as the question of damage is concerned there is sufficient evidence on which the jury could reasonably hold that he has suffered financial loss by reason of the episode.

In examining the evidence given at the trial to see whether it sustains the plaintiff's submissions that there was a case fit to go to the jury on the question of conspiracy this Court is not concerned nor was the trial judge concerned to decide whether the evidence showed that the findings of the defendants that the plaintiff had been guilty of unofficial action was probably supportable on the evidence which was before them. The question is whether the evidence discloses a situation which the jury could reasonably hold to amount to the conspiracy alleged on the part of the defendants.

In their letter of the 9th July 1963 to the plaintiff the defendants disclosed that they had been informed that he had taken part in a meeting of members at Newmarket-on-Fergus and that he had given his consent to take part in unofficial strike action. There is no evidence in the case to indicate that they were not so informed. There is certainly evidence to indicate that if they were so informed a jury could hold that they were misinformed but that is not an issue which bears upon the question now to be decided. The letter of the 9th July 1963 was the one which informed the plaintiff of his expulsion in the first instance. On the 10th July 1963 the plaintiff wrote to the secretary of the union asking to be furnished with particulars of the specific rule or rules which the defendants 'used when they made their decision to expel me'. In reply the plaintiff was informed that the defendants had acted in pursuance of rule 198(b) (which states that in no case shall strike action be taken unless authorised by the National Executive Council) and rule 205(f) and (i). (f) is one which deals with a charge against a member who is charged with conduct which in the opinion of the National Executive Committee or of a branch meeting, has brought injury or discredit on the union or any member thereof, and (i) relates to allegations of refusal to obey the rules or to comply with the orders of any branch meeting or of any branch officer or committee, such orders being by the rules authorised. The letter also, however, acknowledged that the defendants had been advised that their letter of the 9th July giving notice of the expulsion from the union should be withdrawn and the plaintiff was notified that his membership was restored as and from the 9th July. The letter went on to add: 'Your conduct is nevertheless regarded by the Executive Council as being a flagrant breach of the rules of the union. Full liberty to take such further action as is deemed necessary, in respect of this conduct, is therefore reserved.' The letter of the 9th July had indicated that the defendants had been unanimous in their decision to expel him from membership.

On the 16th July the plaintiff received a letter requesting him to attend at the Dublin offices of the union on the afternoon of the 19th July and to show cause why he should not be dealt with in accordance with rules 198(b) and 205(f) and (i) adding: 'arising out of you taking part in unofficial action during the week ending the 6th July 1963.' The plaintiff duly attended the meeting on the 19th July.

It is fairly clear from the evidence given in the High Court that the proceedings following the plaintiff's appearance before the defendants on the 19th July were not the most amiable and that the plaintiff took the occasion to tell the defendants that they had acted in a 'silly fashion'. The plaintiff's evidence before the defendants was to the effect that on the evening of the 4th July when there had been a meeting of the members of the union working on the site at Newmarket-on-Fergus no decision had been made to take unofficial strike action the next day and that on the next morning, Friday, he, the plaintiff, was not in that area at all but was in Portlaoighaise when in fact some form of unofficial strike took place on the site. It was acknowledged at the trial in the High Court that the plaintiff was not on the site but was in fact in Portlaoighaise on the morning in question and therefore could not have taken part in an unofficial strike, at least not in so far as actual presence and participation was required. It was also agreed that the plaintiff, who was a shop steward of the union, had instigated an unofficial strike the previous April. That fact was referred to during the plaintiff's appearance before the defendants. There is also evidence to the effect that the defendants appeared to be unaware that the plaintiff had not been on the site on the morning of the 5th July but had been in Portlaoghaise. The plaintiff, in his evidence in the High Court, alleged that his whole appearance before the defendants took no longer than ten minutes. The plaintiff acknowledged during that appearance that he had attended a meeting on the Thursday evening when there was a discussion on the course which might be adopted by the plaintiff and his friends on Friday the 5th July in the event of a union official not arriving to discuss their grievances with them. A resolution passed at the meeting was to the effect that they would go to work on the Friday morning, show up at the gate next morning and wait for an official. The plaintiff voted in favour of this resolution.

The plaintiff himself, in the course of his evidence in the High Court, described his appearance before the defendants as 'a mock trial' and went on: 'It is the fact of being brought in again to the same man who threw you out before. I would like to say that if I had got a trial first I think I would never have been expelled because we could have put our case before them.' What the plaintiff said contained the essence of the submissions made by his counsel both in the High Court and here. Put more elaborately they were reduced to four propositions. (1) That the defendants were proved to have unanimously decided to expel the plaintiff upon a set of facts which were true in regard to some of the other members of the union but not to the plaintiff. (2) That the defendants invited the plaintiff to attend before them and show cause why he should not be expelled. (3) That at that inquiry the defendants were made aware that the facts were true as regards other members [but] were not true as regards the plaintiff and (4) that the defendants treated the plaintiff in exactly the same manner as the other union members who in fact, it is claimed, were guilty of the matters for which the accused was charged. There was evidence adduced at the trial upon which the jury could find that all of these submissions, so far as they concerned fact, were true. But even assuming that the jury would accept all these submissions as being factually accurate, is it sufficient to enable them to go on to find as a reasonable inference from these facts that the inquiry conducted by the defendants on the 19th July was a mock inquiry because of a prior agreement between the defendants that it should be so? In my view no such inference is reasonably open on the evidence. As I have already said the jury in the High Court was not concerned with the correctness or otherwise of the decision of the defendants upon the facts of the case as such but if the decision was so patently perverse that the only reasonable explanation would indicate a conspiracy, rather than other reason such as a refusal to believe the plaintiff's account, however irrational such refusal might appear to be, or a simple failure to give the plaintiff an adequate opportunity to make his case or to understand the case being made against him, or that the defendants' judgment in the matter had been clouded by feelings of anger towards the plaintiff caused either by their previous experience of the plaintiff or by his attitude on his appearance before them, I think the matter would have had to be left to the jury. The evidence does not however indicate any such degree of perversity on the part of the defendants. The fact that the proceedings might be impugned for any of the other reasons mentioned would not of itself constitute evidence of a conspiracy. In my view the learned trial judge was correct in holding that there was no evidence at the close of the plaintiff's case upon which the jury could reasonably find that the defendants had been guilty of conspiring to have a mock trial as alleged.

With regard to the other leg of the case, while there appears to be evidence that the defendants did consider that the union would be better off without the plaintiff's membership that is a very far cry from the allegation that their main object and purpose was not the benefit and protection of the union but the desire to injure the plaintiff. I do not see any evidence whatever which supports the submission that the defendants were actuated in any degree by a desire to injure the plaintiff rather than protect the union.

In my view the provisions of the Trade Disputes Act of 1906 do not affect these proceedings at all. Sections 1 and 3 of the Trade Disputes Act deal with acts done by persons in contemplation or in the furtherance of a trade dispute. The dispute between the plaintiff and the defendants, which deals only with the procedure adopted for his expulsion or purported expulsion from the union, is not a trade dispute in the meaning of the section. In my view section 4 is of no application either even though the immunity conferred by that section is not limited to acts arising in contemplation or furtherance of a trade dispute. The immunity granted by the section is confined to actions against a trade union or against any members or officials thereof on behalf of themselves and all other members of the trade union in respect of any tortious act alleged to have been committed by or on behalf of the trade union. No such allegation is made by the plaintiff in this case, the action being one only against the defendants as individuals.

For the reasons I have given in my opinion the appeal should be dismissed.

There is one matter I would like to add. In the course of the hearing of this appeal regret was expressed by members of the Court that a matter of this kind, which basically concerns the plaintiff's membership or non-membership of the union, should have had to be litigated. In the hope that perhaps further and unnecessary litigation may be prevented I would like to draw attention again to something I indicated during the course of the appeal. It appears to me that under rule 206 of the rules the plaintiff was entitled to have been present to hear the case to be made against him when it was being made. That procedure was not followed and it is reasonably clear from the evidence that the case against him had already been communicated to the defendants either in the form of written submissions or oral evidence or otherwise at a time when the plaintiff had not been requested to attend. It appears to me therefore extremely doubtful whether the expulsions of July 19th was valid.

Note and Questions

1. For a detailed analysis, see Mathews, 'The Tort of Conspiracy in Irish Labour Law' 8 Ir. Jur. (n.s.) 252 (1973).

2. Are you happy that it is possible in practice – or, indeed, in theory – to identify as a 'main', 'sole' or 'real' purpose the object of injuring the plaintiff|or|of defending the interests of the trade union by maintaining discipline? Was the importance of this distinction in the minds of the defendants? If not, is it fair to make the commission of a serious tort depend on such a distinction?

MESKELL V. CORAS IOMPAIR EIREANN
[1973] I.R. 121 (Supreme Court, 1972)

Walsh J.:

On the 29th October, 1960, the defendants dismissed the plaintiff from his employment as a bus conductor in their service. He had been employed in that capacity for a period of 15 years and this action arose out of his dismissal. At all times during his employment the plaintiff had been a member in good standing of a trade union. For seven or eight years preceding his dismissal he had been a member of the Workers Union of Ireland and prior to that he had been a member of the Irish Transport and General Workers Union. When the plaintiff joined the service of the defendants, trade-union membership was not an obligatory term of his employment and it was not required that he should remain a member of a trade union. Trade-union membership was made a condition of contracts of employment of persons joining the defendants' service as from the year 1958.

During the following years complaints were made by trade unions and by their members that some of their members in the employment of the defendants were falling into arrears with their union dues, and the other members resented working with them. The plaintiff was one of those who expressed this resentment. The trade unions endeavoured to put pressure upon the defendants to do something about it and specifically suggested to the defendants that they should withhold from such defaulting persons the benefits obtained by the unions for their workers in the defendants' employment. On this point the defendants were advised by counsel that it would not be possible to debar trade-union defaulters from the benefits of agreements made by the defendants with the trade unions, or from local practices and arrangements where introduced by the management with or without the concurrence of the trade unions. This legal view was expressed in relation to those employees who were engaged before union membership became a condition of employment. It is unnecessary to decide in this case whether this could or could not have been done but it is of interest to draw attention to the fact that this very question has been the subject of decisions in other jurisdictions in relation to its impact upon the constitutional rights of the individuals involved. The defendants were also advised that they could not dismiss such men or compel them to join a trade union under threat of dismissal. It does not appear that the trade unions ever asked directly for the dismissal of the men concerned but in the course of many negotiations the trade unions indicated that there was an obligation upon the defendants to take such action as would in effect compel the non-union employees or the defaulting ones to join a union or to put themselves into good standing with the unions of which they were nominally members. There was even a threat of a strike on the part of the union members to compel the defendants to take such a step. The legal opinion which the defendants had obtained was made known to the trade unions concerned.

The final result of all the negotiations between the trade unions and the defendants was that an agreement was arrived at between them whereby all the workers, about 3,000 in all, would be dismissed and at the same time would be offered new contracts of employment on all the terms and conditions existing before plus one addition. The additional condition was that each worker would bind himself to be at all times a member of a representative trade union. It is clear beyond all doubt that the object of this agreement between the trade unions and the defendants was not merely to compel all the persons in their employment to become members of a representative trade union but to remain such while they were in the employment. The plaintiff, who was at all material times a member in good standing of a representative trade union, refused to accept this arrangement. His refusal was indicated by his refusal to accept re-employment with the added condition.

The notice of dismissal to the plaintiff, after setting out the address from which it emanated, namely, the Road Passenger Manager's Office, and the name, number, grade and depot of the plaintiff, was as follows:–

'Agreement has been reached with the trade unions representative of the road passenger operative grades that it will be a condition of employment of each person employed in those grades that he shall be at all times a member of a union representative of such grades. It was further agreed with the unions to give effect to this agreement by terminating the employment of the employees concerned and at the same time offering them immediate re-employment on the same terms and conditions as heretofore with the added condition that each employee will agree to be a member of a trade union representative of the said grades. Accordingly your services with the Board will terminate on the 29th October, 1960, and you will be re-employed on that date if you have completed and returned the attached application for re-employment to your Garage Superintendent.'

The attached application referred to was in the following terms:–

'To Manager, Road Passenger Section, Amiens Street. I aply for employment by the Board on the same terms and conditions as hitherto with the added condition of employment which I hereby accept that I shall be at all times a member of a trade union representative of the road passenger operative grades.'

This was then followed by the name, grade, depot, staff number of the applicant, together with his signature and date. Pursuant to the arrangement made between the trade unions and the defendants, approximately 3,000 employees had their employment terminated in this form and all the employees, with two exceptions, appeared to accept this arrangement because they applied for re-employment on the new terms and were accepted. The plaintiff was one of the exceptions. According to the memorandum furnished to the personnel manager of the defendants the plaintiff, when approached by a supervisor, stated that on principle he had no intention of signing such a form under duress. It also appeared that when the matter had been discussed before this at a meeting of the members of the plaintiff's trade union, the Workers Union of Ireland, a majority of those present had voted by a show of hands in favour of adopting the procedure of dismissal and re-employment, but that the plaintiff abstained on the grounds that the proposal was a violation of the individual's freedom of choice. In the result, the plaintiff's notice of dismissal became effective; he ceased to be in the employment of the defendants and forfeited such benefits as might accrue to him from continued employment with the defendants and he was compelled to seek employment elsewhere.

On the 25th January, 1962, the plaintiff instituted proceedings against the defendants seeking a declaration that his dismissal on the 29th October, 1960, was effected for the purpose of wrongfully coercing him to be at all times a member of one of the trade unions designated and was an unlawful interference with his rights under the Constitution. He also claimed a declaration that his dismissal was in pursuance of a conspiracy and a combination between the defendants and the Irish Transport and General Workers Union and the Workers Union of Ireland and other bodies and persons who had agreed together with the defendants that the plaintiff should be dismissed from his employment for the purpose of wrongfully coercing him to undertake at all times to be a member of one of the designated trade unions, and that his dismissal was a denial and violation of and an unlawful interference with his rights under the Constitution. He also claimed damages. The defendants denied that the plaintiff's dismissal was effected for any of the purposes alleged. They also claimed that, by virtue of his membership of the Workers Union of Ireland, the plaintiff had agreed to submit these new conditions of employment to the defendants and that the plaintiff had authorised the said union as his agent to enter into the agreement to which the defendants were parties, and that he is now estopped by his conduct from saying the agreement is unlawful or malicious or amounted to a conspiracy.

The learned trial judge, Teevan J., made no finding and did not base any part of his judgment on the claim of estoppel. In my opinion, on the evidence in this case he could not have done so because, while the plaintiff was a member of the Workers Union of Ireland, there is no evidence whatever to indicate that the plaintiff authorised the union on his behalf to have his employment terminated on the basis of an offer of re-employment on the conditions complained of, nor did he acquiesce in that course; this is borne out by the evidence which points to the fact that the notice of termination was given personally to the plaintiff and that the application for re-employment was to be made personally by him. Nothing in this appeal turns upon that question.

The learned trial judge dismissed the plaintiff's action. First, he said that he knew of no right of action such as that claimed for damages for what was described as the positive duty of the defendants to abstain from interfering with the plaintiff's rights and freedom, by which I presume he meant the constitutional rights claimed by the plaintiff to have been infringed. In my view, the learned judge was incorrect in this. It has been said on a number of occasions in this Court, and most notably in the decision in *Byrne* v. *Ireland* [1972] I.R. 241, that a right guaranteed by the Constitution or granted by the Constitution can be protected by action or enforced by action even though such action may not fit into any of the ordinary forms of action in either common law or equity and that the constitutional right carries within it its own right to a remedy or for the enforcement of it. Therefore, if a person has suffered damage by virtue of a breach of a constitutional right or the infringement of a constitutional right, that person is entitled to seek redress against the person or persons who have infringed that right. As was pointed out by Mr. Justice Budd in *Educational Company of Ireland Ltd.* v. *Fitzpatrick (No. 2)* [1961] I.R. 345, 368, it follows that 'if one citizen has a right under the Constitution there exists a correlative duty on the part of other citizens to respect that right and not to interfere with it.' He went on to say that the Courts would act so as not to permit a person to be deprived of his constitutional rights and would see to it that those rights were protected.

The learned trial judge went on to treat the action as one for damages for conspiracy. In the course of dealing with this aspect he said:—'Even were I to assume that the plaintiff suffered damage as a result of the action of the defendants and the unions (and I am far from concluding that he did) the case must fail, for the object or purpose of the agreement was not to injure the plaintiff. The test is: "what is in truth the object in the minds of the combiners when they acted as they did?" ' That test was stated by Viscount Simon L.C. in *Crofter Hand Woven Harris Tweed Co. Ltd.* v. *Veitch* [1942] A.C. 435, which the trial judge said had been incorporated into the law of this country by the judgment of the Supreme Court in *McGowan* v. *Murphy* (Supreme Court, 10th April, 1967). The learned trial judge was not quite correct in this reference to *McGowan* v. *Murphy*. The only reference in that decision to the *Crofter Case* [1942] A.C. 435 was as an authority for the proposition that a combination of persons was in a less favoured position than an individual when the whole or main purpose of the combination was the injuring of a person and that person suffers damage. In other words that there can be conspiracy when the object of the agreement is unlawful even when the means are not unlawful. The passage the learned trial judge may have been thinking of was one which was based on the decision in *Sorrell v. Smith* [1925] A.C. 700 and which appeared in the judgment delivered in the Supreme Court as follows:– 'If, however, the real purpose of the combination was not to injure the plaintiff but to defend the interests of the trade union by maintaining discipline then no wrong was committed and no action will lie even though damage to the plaintiff resulted provided that the means used were not in themselves unlawful.' The key phrase there are the words 'provided that the means used were not in themselves unlawful.'

In the present case one may assume for the purpose of the decision that the object of the agreement between the defendants and the trade unions was the well-being of the defendants and of the unions, and even of the members of the unions. The complaint made here is that the means adopted to achieve this end were unlawful. If that is so, then there was a conspiracy. To infringe another's constitutional rights or to coerce him into abandoning them or waiving them (in so far as that may be possible) is unlawful as constituting a violation of the fundamental law of the State; in so far as such conduct constitutes the means towards an end which is not in itself unlawful, the means are unlawful and an agreement to employ such means constitutes a conspiracy. If damage results, it is an actionable conspiracy. It is not necessary in this judgment to decide whether or not it amounts to a criminal conspiracy. The decision in the *Crofter Case* [1942] A.C. 435 does not in any way indicate that, because the predominant purpose of an agreement is not unlawful, the agreement cannot amount to a conspiracy even if unlawful means are used. In the present case the learned trial judge concentrated entirely upon the object or purpose of the agreement, and he overlooked the means employed which were the matters complained of in the action.

The plaintiff's case rested upon the provisions in Article 40, s. 6, sub-ss. 1 (iii) and 2, of the Constitution, and upon the decision of the former Supreme Court of Justice in *Educational Company of Ireland Ltd. v. Fitzpatrick (No. 2)* [1961] I.R. 345. That case decided that the right of citizens to form associations and unions conferred also the implicit right to abstain from joining associations or unions, which might be called the right of dissociation.

One of the questions which was argued in detail in the present appeal was the effect of the constitutional right to form an association, or the constitutional right not to belong to an association, on the ordinary common-law rights of an employer to engage or dismiss his workers when, in doing so, he was not in breach of contract. If an employer threatens an employee with dismissal if he should join a trade union, the employer is putting pressure on the employee to abandon the exercise of a constitutional right and is interfering with his constitutional rights. If the employer dismisses the worker because of the latter's insistence upon exercising his constitutional right, the fact that the form or notice of dismissal is good at common law does not in any way lessen the infringement of the right involved or mitigate the damage which the worker may suffer by reason of his insistence upon exercising his constitutional right. If the Oireachtas cannot validly seek to compel a person to forgo a constitutional right, can such a power be effectively exercised by some lesser body or by an individual employer? To exercise what may be loosely called a common-law right of dismissal as a method of compelling a person to abandon a constitutional right, or as a penalty for his not doing so, must necessarily be regarded as an abuse of the common-law right because it is an infringement, and an abuse, of the Constitution which is superior to the common law and which must prevail if there is a conflict between the two. The same considerations apply to cases where a person is dismissed or penalised because of his insistence upon, or his refusal to waive, his right to dissociate. In each of these cases the injured party is entitled, in my view, to recover damages for any damage he may have suffered by reason of the dismissal or penalty resulting from his insistence upon exercising his constitutional right, or his refusal to abandon it or waive it. As there is no claim in the present case for reinstatement, I do not need to consider that matter.

The present case is one relating to dismissal only. The defendants, in their submissions in this Court, claimed that neither the constitutional rights mentioned nor the other Articles of the Constitution guarantee to any citizen the right to any particular employment or class of employment, irrespective of membership or non-membership of a trade union. In my view, that point does not arise for consideration in this case and could arise only if this action arose out of a refusal to engage or hire a person seeking employment on the grounds that he was a member of a trade union or on the grounds that he was not, or on the ground that he had refused to give an undertaking either way. I do not wish to express any view on such a case until there is one brought to this Court.

In my view, upon the facts proved in this case the plaintiff is entitled to a declaration that his dismissal was a denial and a violation of and an unlawful interference with his constitutional rights, and that the agreement between the trade unions concerned and the defendants to procure or cause that dismissal was an actionable conspiracy because the means employed constituted a breach or infringement of the plaintiff's constitutional rights. In my view, the plaintiff is entitled to such damages as may, upon inquiry, be proved to have been sustained by him.

Lastly, the defendants relied upon s. 10 of the Railways Act, 1933, as applied by s. 46 of the Transport Act, 1950. Those sections provide that the rates of pay, the hours of duty and other conditions of service of the road transport employees shall be regulated in accordance with agreements made or to be made from time to time between the trade union representatives of such employees on the one part and the defendants on the other part. The defendants say that the agreement, the subject matter of the present litigation, was such an agreement and was expressly provided for by statute and, as such, could not constitute an actionable conspiracy. In effect, therefore, the defendants say that the statute contemplates that an agreement between the trade unions and the defendants could contain a condition requiring trade-union membership, or membership of a particular trade union, to be a condition of a contract of service between the defendants and their workmen. Article 9 of the Constitution of Saorstát Éireann guaranteed the right to 'form associations or unions.' For the reasons already given by the former Supreme Court of Justice in the *Educational Company of Ireland Ltd.* v. *Fitzpatrick (No. 2)* [1961] I.R. 345, I am of opinion that this guarantee also carried with it the implicit guarantee of the right of dissociation. Bearing in mind the observations of the Chief Justice in *The State (Quinn)* v. *Ryan* [1965] I.R. 70 at p. 119 and my own observations at p. 125 of the report, it follows that s. 10 of the Act of 1933 would be construed on the presumption that it was in accordance with the Constitution of the day and that the Oireachtas of the day did not intend it to be otherwise. If s. 10 of the Act of 1933 had purported to give power to the trade unions concerned and the railway company to do what was done in the present case, it would clearly have been in breach of the guarantee contained in Article 9 of the Constitution of Saorstát Éireann, 1922.

I do not think that s. 10 of the Act of 1933 is capable of any such interpretation. On the ordinary rules of construction the reference to other conditions of service, being preceded by the express reference to rates of pay and hours of duty, could not be held to include matters so different in kind from the ones mentioned as compulsory membership of trade unions or of some particular trade union or trade unions. In my view, what the statute did aim at was uniformity of rates of pay, hours of duty, and similar conditions of service of the road-transport employees irrespective of whether they were members of trade unions or not.

Section 10 of the Act of 1933 applied to road-transport employees of a railway company identical provisions as those applicable to certain railway employees under s. 55, sub-s. 1, of the Railways Act, 1924. The class of railway employees referred to in the Act of 1924 was set out in the eighth schedule to that Act. Both of these statutory provisions were the subject of a decision in this Court in *Transport Salaried Staffs Association* v. *Córas Iompair Éireann* [1965] I.R. 180. In my own judgment in that case at p. 200 of the report I used the following words which are applicable to both s. 55, sub-s. 1, of the Act of 1924 and s. 10 of the Act of 1933: 'That Act, among its other objects, provided for the amalgamation of various railway companies then in existence and one of the objects of the section was quite clearly to achieve a degree of uniformity in the conditions of employment and the rates of pay of the employees of the same or similar classes or grades employed in the various companies. As employees were not necessarily represented by what one might call "house unions" in these particular companies but were catered for by one or more trade unions whose membership covered some or perhaps all of the companies, it was clearly a practical way of achieving uniformity to permit or authorise the companies and the unions to agree on the matters referred to without regard to the size or area of any particular company. Furthermore, it appears to me that the object of the section was to enable this uniformity to be achieved for grades of employees as such rather than the particular members of these grades who happened to be members of a trade union. The object of the section was not to have these agreements negotiated on behalf of employees in the sense that the trade unions might be taken to be the negotiating agents with the power to contract on behalf of each individual member, but rather to set up a uniform standard of rates of wages, conditions of service, hours of duty, etc., which would, by virtue of the statutory provision, be required to be contained in each individual contract of employment between an employee in the grades concerned and his employing railway company.' In my view there is nothing in s. 10 of the Act of 1933 on which the defendants can rely to justify the step they took against the plaintiff in the present case.

It is also of interest to note that *Transport Salaried Staffs Association* v. *Córas Iompair Éireann* [1965] I.R. 180 clearly established that those who have an interest in enforcing a statutory duty have a right of action even where the statute itself provides no penalty for breach of the obligations imposed by it and does not indicate any way in which the duty was to be enforced. *A fortiori*, a person whose constitutional rights have been infringed may sue to enforce them or he may sue for damages suffered by reason of the infringement.

In my opinion the order of the High Court should be set aside and an order made in the terms I have already indicated.

Ó Dálaigh C.J. and **Budd J.** concurred

Note
See generally Cooney & Kerr, 'Constitutional Aspects of Irish Tort Law' [1981] D.U.L.J.1; Heuston, 'Personal Rights under the Irish Constitution' 11 Ir. Jur. (n.s.) 205, at 222 (1976); Whyte, 'Industrial Relations and the Irish Constitution' 16 Ir. Jur. (n.s.) 35 (1981).

TRADE DISPUTES

The principal legislation affecting trade disputes is the *Trade Disputes Act 1906*, as amended by the *Trade Union Act 1941*. The 1906 Act provides as follows:

1. The following paragraph shall be added as a new paragraph after the first paragraph of section three of the Conspiracy and Protection of Property Act, 1875:–

'An act done in pursuance of an agreement or combination by two or more persons shall, if done in contemplation or furtherance of a trade dispute, not be actionable unless the act, if done without any such agreement or combination, would be actionable.

2.–(1) It shall be lawful for one or more persons, acting on their own behalf or on behalf of a trade union or of an individual employer or firm in contemplation or furtherance of a trade dispute, to attend at or near a house or place where a person resides or works or carries on business or happens to be, if they so attend merely for the purpose of peacefully obtaining or communicating information, or of peacefully persuading any person to work or abstain from working.

(2) Section seven of the Conspiracy and Protection of Property Act, 1875, is hereby repealed from 'attending at or near' to the end of the section.

3. An act done by a person in contemplation or furtherance of a trade dispute shall not be actionable on the ground only that it induces some other person to break a contract of employment or that it is an interference with the trade, business, or employment of some other person, or with the right of some other person to dispose of his capital or his labour as he wills.

4.–(1) An action against a trade union, whether of workmen or masters, or against any members or officials thereof on behalf of themselves and all other members of the trade union in respect of any tortious act alleged to have been committed by or on behalf of the trade union, shall not be entertained by any court.

(2) Nothing in this section shall affect the liability of the trustees of a trade union to be sued in the events provided for by the Trade Union Act, 1871, section nine, except in respect of any tortious act committed by or on behalf of the union in contemplation or in furtherance of a trade dispute.

5.–(1) This Act may be cited as the Trade Disputes Act, 1906, and the Trade Union Acts, 1871 and 1876, and this Act may be cited together as the Trade Union Acts, 1871 to 1906.

(2) In this Act the expression 'trade union' has the same meaning as in the Trade Union Acts, 1871 and 1876, and shall include any combination as therein defined, notwithstanding that such combination may be the branch of a trade union.

(3) In this Act and in the Conspiracy and Protection of Property Act, 1875, the expression 'trade dispute' means any dispute between employers and workmen, or between workmen and workmen, which is connected with the employment or non-employment, or the terms of the employment, or with the conditions of labour, of any person, and the expression 'workmen' means all persons employed in trade or industry, whether or not in the employment of the employer with whom a trade dispute arises; and, in section three of the last-mentioned Act, the words 'between employers and workmen' shall be repealed.

Note that sections 11(1) of the *Trade Union Act 1941* limits the scope of these provisions as follows:

Sections 2, 3 and 4 of the Trade Disputes Act, 1906, shall apply only in relation to authorised trade unions which for the time being are holders of negotiation licences and the members and officials of such trade unions, and not otherwise.

See generally Kerr, 'In Contemplation or Furtherance of a Trade Dispute . . .' [1979–80] D.U.L.J. 59.

Picketing
'Peacefully Obtaining or Communicating Information'

E.I. CO. LTD. V. KENNEDY
[1968] I.R. 69 (Supreme Court, revg. High Court, Henchy, J.)

Henchy J.:

This is an application by the plaintiff company (which I shall call 'the company') for an interlocutory injunction to restrain the defendants from picketing the premises of the company at Shannon Airport. The first four defendants are officials of the Irish Transport and General Workers Union (which I shall call the union) and the remaining five defendants are members of the union who are employed by the company. I have already granted an interim injunction and it is now sought to have the injunction continued pending the determination of the company's action for a perpetual injunction. It is agreed that my decision on the matter in this action will govern a similar application in another action (*E. I. Co. Ltd.* v. *Taylor and Others* – 1968, No. 720 P.) in which the company is the plaintiff and 39 members of the union are defendants. The defendants are entitled to picket the company's premises only if they can show, first, that there is a 'trade dispute' as defined by s. 5, sub-s. 3, of the Trade Disputes Act, 1906, and secondly that the picketing was done in contemplation or furtherance of such trade dispute and was for the purpose of peacefully obtaining or communicating information or of peacefully persuading any person to work or abstain from working: sec s. 2, sub-s. 1, of the Act of 1906. The principles on which I should decide whether or not to grant the interlocutory injunction are those laid down by the Supreme Court in *Educational Company of Ireland Ltd.* v. *Fitzpatrick and Others* [1961] I.R. 323.

Counsel for the company contends that the one and only dispute between the company and the union in the present case is that arising from the refusal of the company to recognise the union as the trade union representing all the company's hourly employees, and that such a recognition dispute is not covered by the statutory definition of a 'trade dispute.' I am told that there is no reported decision in this country on the question whether such a recognition dispute is a 'trade dispute,' and the only English decision on the matter to which I have been referred, *Beetham* v.*Trinidad Cement Ltd.* [1960] A. C. 132, is one in which the point was not argued. There is, therefore, a fair question to be decided at the trial and, on the principles set out in the *Educational Company Case* [1961] I. R. 323, particularly per Lavery J. at pp. 336–7 of the report, I should grant the interlocutory injunction sought if this is the 'trade dispute' relied on.

Counsel for the defendants agrees, but he says that non-recognition is not the sole ground of the trade dispute alleged by the defendants to exist. He points to six claims which were put forward by the union on behalf of its members in respect of their conditions of employment, all of which were rejected by the company, and he submits that any one of these disputed claims is sufficient to constitute a 'trade dispute.' I do not propose to recount in detail the history of the dispute now existing between the union and the company, but I think the following is a fair summary of the defendants' version of it.

In the month of June, 1966, the union first sought to negotiate with the company about wages and conditions of service. The company repeatedly refused to negotiate with them. In January, 1967, the union sought to arrange discussions with the company with a view to their recognition as the trade union qualified to negotiate.

The request was repeated unsuccessfully in July, 1967. In August, 1967, a meeting of the union's members, employed by the company, resolved to ask their National Executive Council to sanction the serving of strike notice in support of their claims and because of the failure of the company to recognise the union. On the 29th September, 1967, the union wrote to the company confirming that its members were claiming improvements in their conditions of employment in six respects and seeking an employment agreement covering these conditions. By a letter of the 6th October, 1967, the union threatened strike action unless these demands were met by the 21st October, 1967.

At this stage the Labour Court intervened and a number of discussions took place. In these discussions, disputes as to conditions of service were not pursued, but the question of recognition of the union was pursued. On the 2nd November, 1967, the union informed the members of its National Executive Council that it had won recognition from the company. This proved to be a misinterpretation of the result of the discussions. After further meetings it was agreed that a referendum would be held amongst the company's employees to determine the union's position. The union took exception to certain conduct on the part of the company preparatory to the referendum and, on the 9th March, 1968, served strike notice for the 19th March, 1968, on the ground of the company's failure to grant recognition or to negotiate on five specified complaints relating to conditions of employment. The referendum was held on the 14th March, 1968, and a majority voted against recognition of the union. The strike commenced on the 19th March, 1968.

The union says that the dispute is founded on the specified complaints about conditions of employment as well as the question of recognition. They say that there has been a continuing dispute about conditions of employment since the year 1966, even though it was put in abeyance while the Labour Court intervened and negotiations were taking place about recognition of the union. The company disagrees with that version. They say that the only real dispute at any relevant time was the recognition dispute and that the complaints about conditions of employment were merely a facade. They point to a letter from the union of the 5th April, 1967, which, they say, shows that the union then had no complaints about conditions of employment. They maintain that the documentary evidence does not give a full or true picture; and that, if the matter is investigated at a plenary hearing by the examination and cross-examination of witnesses, it will transpire that the full story of conferences, Labour Court negotiations, and the referendum etc. will show that there was no real dispute about conditions of employment and that the one and only dispute was that concerning recognition of the union.

In dealing with this aspect of the case I respectfully adopt and apply the following passage from the judgment of Kingsmill Moore J. in *Educational Company of Ireland Ltd.* v. *Fitzpatrick and Others* [1961] I. R. 323, 342:– 'Mr. Costello for the plaintiffs does not accept that all relevant facts have been established and says that there are further facts which he hopes to establish if the case goes to a full hearing, and if he can avail himself of discovery, interrogatories, and cross examination to elicit them. I am of opinion that a plaintiff is entitled to have his case fully investigated in the ordinary course of legal procedure and that it would be undesirable in the absence of consent to decide a legal question of this magnitude merely on the affidavits filed for the purpose of the interlocutory motion. In *Smith and Another* v. *Beirne and Another* 89 I.L.T.R. 24 the defendants (who were the picketers) resisted the motion for an interlocutory injunction on the grounds that they did not agree that all facts necessary to decide the issue were established or admitted, and the Court, while granting an interlocutory injunction, did not make any attempt then and there to decide the question of law. I think similar weight must be given to the refusal of the plaintiffs to agree that all necessary facts are established or admitted.'

I think that the company is entitled to a full investigation of the circumstances of the alleged complaints as to conditions of employment at a plenary hearing and that the company should not be subjected to the risk of irreparable damage by picketing until the matter is fully explored by the company and eventually decided by the Court. The interlocutory injunction sought is necessary to ensure that. If I grant the interlocutory injunction, which I propose to do, the worst that will happen to the defendants, if they have a right to picket, is that that right will be postponed until a full hearing has taken place. The balance of possible hardships requires that I grant the interlocutory injunction.

However, the matter does not end there. The defendants have no right to picket unless they comply with the statutory requirement that the picketing be for the purpose of peacefully obtaining or communicating information, or of peacefully persuading any person to work or abstain from working. It is of the very essence of legal picketing that it be peaceful. If the picketing is such as to frighten, intimidate or overawe, it loses its statutory protection and becomes illegal. The affidavit of Matthew J. Dannagher, which was sworn on the 19th March, 1968, states that on the morning the strike commenced he saw some 135 persons at the entrance, to the rear of the company's factory; he saw 24 placards, some carrying the words 'I.T. & G.W.U. on strike here' and some carrying the words 'Yankee, you can't dictate.' A number of those who were assembled there surrounded a bus, bringing employees to work, and shouted at those getting off the bus 'Come out and join us.' Persons holding placards tapped them against the windows and sides of the buses; some persons shouted at the bus-drivers 'You scab' and 'You blackleg' and 'Hold on to your job, you won't get another.'

These matters are not denied in any of the affidavits sworn on behalf of the defendants, but counsel on their behalf submits that the defendants have not been identified with such conduct or language. However, I consider that the company is justified in its submission that, if the matter is fully investigated before and at a plenary hearing the participation of the defendants or some of them, in what is prima facie non-peaceful picketing may be proved. In the affidavit of Earl F. Bradford, an American executive of the company, which was sworn on the 20th March, 1968, it is stated that while picketing on the first morning of the strike the defendant Michael Mullen, who is the senior adviser to the National Executive Council of the union, addressed Mr. Bradford in a hostile way and said 'You are a Yank, we don't want you here.' Mr. Mullen has made an affidavit but has not denied or disavowed such conduct. In an affidavit made by Mr. Bradford on the 26th March, 1968, he says that on the first morning of the strike the defendant Joseph Power, who is the branch secretary of the union for the Shannon area, pushed open the door of one of the buses taking employees to work and, while standing on the steps of the bus, shouted at the driver 'You Goddam scab.' Mr. Power has made an affidavit but has not denied or disavowed such conduct.

It is not for the Court to tell trade union officials how to conduct their affairs, but if, as in the present case, there is prima facie evidence that they have in the course of picketing engaged in conduct or used words which go beyond the purpose of peacefully obtaining or communicating information or of peacefully persuading any person to work or abstain from working, it is the duty of the Court to restrain such picketing. I grant an interlocutory injunction in the same terms as those of the interim injunction.

[The defendants appealed to the Supreme Court]

Ó Dálaigh C.J. [after reviewing the evidence]:

. . . Putting aside the interesting question as to whether a so called recognition dispute (in either the wide or narrow meaning) is in law a trade dispute, it is, in my opinion, manifest from the foregoing analysis of the evidence that there was, and is, in existence between the company and its employees who are members of the union a dispute with regard to their conditions of employment and this is, unmistakably, a trade dispute. The defendants' right to attend at or near the plaintiff company's premises cannot therefore be questioned if they attend merely for the purpose of peacefully obtaining or communicating information or of peacefully persuading any person to work or abstain from working.

That there is evidence that the conduct of some of the defendants on the 19th March, 1968, was otherwise than is authorised for lawful picketing is not to be doubted: indeed the evidence in some instances is that the conduct was such as was likely to lead to a breach of the peace. Mr. Justice Henchy's interim injunction was well warranted. Again, after the granting of the interlocutory injunction there is evidence, in the case of some of the defendants, of acts done in disobedience of the Court Order which, if unexplained, might well have rendered them liable to severe punishment. That matter, however, is not now before this Court. The single question is, has the gross and excessive conduct complained of on the occasion of the opening day of the strike been persisted in? The evidence satisfied me that it has not. The affidavits of Mr. Power, and particularly the affidavit of Mr. Mullen, indicate that the early excesses have been curtailed. These affidavits were sworn on 24th March and were filed on the 25th March, 1968. Mr. Bradford swore a replying affidavit on 26th March; he does not complain of any recrudescence. It will, however, be clear that all reference to racial origins is outside the protection of the Act of 1906, as also is all reference to the recognition dispute until that issue has been decided in the defendants' favour.

I would allow this appeal and discharge the interlocutory injunction. I would also make the same order in *E. I. Co. Ltd.* v. *Taylor and Others.*

Haugh J.:

I agree with the Chief Justice.

Walsh J.:

. . . So far as I am aware there is no decision by the Courts in this country on the question of whether a trade dispute, within the definition contained in s. 5 of the Trade Disputes Act, 1906, embraces either (a) a union's claim to be recognised as the sole representative of all the workers in a particular category of employment with an employer whether such workers are members or not, or (b) a claim by such employees as are members of a trade union to have that trade union accepted as the spokesman and representative of such member employees in any negotiations on questions of terms of employment or conditions of employment whether or not there is currently a dispute between the members and the employer under either of those headings. I am of opinion, therefore, that picketing of an employer's premises upon the claim that such a dispute would be a trade dispute within the meaning of the Act of 1906 ought to be restrained by an injunction, if sought by the employer, until there has been a full trial of the legal issues raised on these points, on the ground that the issues raise fair questions to be decided at the trial and that in the meanwhile the status quo ante should be preserved.

In the present case the plaintiffs have contended that these are the only issues involved. The plaintiffs in fact allege or claim that it is the latter one (namely, the question of whether the employees who are members of the union can be represented by the union) which is the only issue. It would appear from the judgment of the learned judge in the High Court that the issue, as it appeared to him, on this topic was not the one which I have just mentioned but that it was rather the first one, namely, whether the refusal of the company to recognise the union as the sole representative of all the company's hourly employees was a matter which could constitute a trade dispute within the meaning of the Act of 1906. The plaintiffs say that that was never their case and that this reference by the learned High Court judge must have been made in error for the latter of the two types of what I would call 'representation disputes', for want of a better description.

It was submitted by the defendants that, while there was such a 'representation dispute,' there was also a dispute with regard to the terms of employment and the conditions of labour of their members in the employment of the plaintiff company.

[After reviewing the evidence, **Walsh J.** continued:]

It is not disputed in the present proceedings that the employees of the plaintiff company who were members of the union did in fact instruct their union to write the letters already referred to and that the demands sent to the company were made on their behalf. What is suggested by the company is that the demands were specious and were virtually invented to provide a vehicle for what the company regards as the real issue, namely, an attempt to force the company to accept the union officials as the nominated representatives of the employee members. In law an employer is not obliged to meet anybody as the representative of his worker, nor indeed is he obliged to meet the worker himself for the purpose of discussing any demand which the worker may make. The fact that an employer has a right to refuse to do so does not, however, necessarily condition the consequences which may legally follow. There can be no doubt that the employees in question are workmen within the meaning of s. 5 of the Trade Disputes Act, 1906, and in my view the five demands which were set forth in the letter of the 9th March, 1968, are in respect of claims which prima facie fall within the expression 'terms of the employment, or with the conditions of labour' set forth in s. 5, sub s. 3, of that Act. The fact that the employees were previously, and even currently, endeavouring to wring from the plaintiffs an acceptance of the claim of right to be represented at any such negotiations by their union, or the union officials, is relied upon by the plaintiffs as the ground for the claim that the enumerated demands were specious. The plaintiffs' attitude to these demands has been a refusal expressly based upon a consideration of the merits of these claims and, whatever the company's policy towards unions, this matter of representation was not offered as the basis for refusing to negotiate. One must assume therefore as the matter stands that, even if the employees were never represented by a union and made these claims, the claims would have been refused for the reasons already given by the company. The fact that the claims were made through the medium of the union on the instructions of the members is not a factor which can affect the genuineness of the claims, even though it may be a procedure which is also aimed at securing the recognition which is being sought simultaneously.

I do not think that simply to claim on an interlocutory application that at a full hearing the company would hope to be able to demonstrate that the employees' demands were specious is a sufficient ground for granting such an injunction in a case like this. The matter raised upon this point is entirely an issue of fact and is not a hitherto undecided point of law.

Reliance was placed upon the judgments given in the former Supreme Court in the *Educational Company of Ireland Ltd.* v. *Fitzpatrick and Others* [1961] I. R. 323 when considering the part of that case which dealt with the interlocutory injunction. The point primarily at issue in the *Educational Company Case* [1961] I. R. 323 was a point of law and the interlocutory application in that case was granted on the grounds that all the facts necessary to decide the law point were not yet established or admitted. The matter which this Court has to consider at the moment is not the same. If the present dispute is a genuine dispute as to terms of employment and conditions of labour, then it is admitted that it is a trade dispute. The fact that there may be also other matters such as the question of recognition, whether sole recognition or otherwise, is an additional point but it is not the point to be decided upon the present application. Therefore the controversy, as to whether there is or there is not a genuine trade dispute on terms of employment or conditions of labour, resolves itself solely into an issue of fact and not into a question of deciding or ascertaining all the facts which may be necessary to decide a law point hitherto undecided. In my view the plaintiffs have not shown that there is a prima facie case in support of their contention that the dispute raised as to the terms of employment and conditions of labour is a specious one. If it should turn out, upon a full trial of the facts, that the dispute was indeed a specious one, the consequences may be grave for the defendants, or some of them, but that is not a matter which need be considered at this stage. In my view the evidence shows a prima facie case in support of the view that there is a trade dispute upon the matters which I mentioned. If there is a trade dispute, the employees in dispute and such other persons as are included in s. 2 of the Act of 1906 have a legal right to attend at or near the plaintiffs' place of business at Shannon for the purpose of peacefully obtaining or communicating information or peacefully persuading any person to abstain from working there. When I am of opinion there is a prima facie case in favour of the existence of a trade dispute, I could not at the same time support an injunction to restrain the exercise of the rights conferred by s. 2 of the Act of 1906.

The next matter to be raised is the question of whether or not the picketing indulged in was in excess of that permitted by the Act of 1906. In my view there can be little doubt but that the conduct engaged in by the defendants on the 19th March, 1968, that is the first day of the strike, was grossly in excess of that permitted by law and that the interim injunctions were properly granted against such of the defendants as were present. It may well be that some of the defendants were not in fact responsible for what happened, but as the evidence stands there is ground for believing that the matters complained of arose out of a concerted action on the part of all those present. The same inference would not arise in respect of those persons concerned with the strike who were not present on that occasion. The use of words such as 'scab' or 'blackleg' are historically so associated with social ostracism and physical violence as to be far beyond anything which might be described as mere rudeness or impoliteness and go beyond what is permitted by law. In the present context the references made to the race or nationality of the employers could produce the same disorderly response and also go beyond what is permitted by law. Excessive numbers in pickets may also go beyond what is reasonably permissible for the communication of information or for the obtaining of information and may amount to obstruction or nuisance or give rise to a reasonable apprehension of a breach of the peace. It is, however, unnecessary to examine the details of what happened on the 19th March to any greater extent because the points to be considered by this Court at the moment are the grounds which underlie the granting of an interlocutory injunction.

When the interlocutory injunction was sought and obtained there was no evidence that the disorderly scenes of the 19th March had continued, nor was there any expression of apprehension that they would be repeated unless restrained by the Court. There is, I think, some substance in the submission made on behalf of the defendants that in the nature of things matters may not be fully, or properly, organised on the first day of the strike, but the fact that they are not should not necessarily give rise to the inference that they will continue to be disorderly. My own view is that an application for an interlocutory injunction should be based upon the state of affairs continuing since the interim injunction, if any, was granted and the conditions prevailing at the time of the application for the interlocutory injunction. In my view the evidence given in support of the interim injunction did not warrant any inference that that conduct was continuing at the date of the grant of the interlocutory injunction. I would therefore discharge the interlocutory injunctions granted in these two cases and leave the defendants to the exercise of the rights which they have under the Trade Disputes Act, 1906, within the limitations imposed by that Act. For the reasons I have already given picketing can be justified upon the grounds that there is a trade dispute concerning terms of employment and conditions of labour on the five points put forward by the employees, but a claim in such picketing that there is a trade dispute concerning the question of recognition could be restrained by injunction until that issue has been determined by the High Court. It is scarcely necessary to add that the plaintiffs, if they are so advised, can always move in the High Court for an order restraining any activities in excess of those permitted by law.

Budd and **Fitzgerald JJ.** delivered dissenting judgments.

Note
See also *Brendan Dunne Ltd* v. *Fitzpatrick* [1958] I.R. 29 (High Ct., Budd, J., 1957).

Constitutional Limitations

EDUCATIONAL CO. OF IRELAND V. FITZPATRICK (No. 2)
[1961] I.R. 345 (Supreme Court, aff'g. High Court, Budd, J.)

Kingsmill Moore J.:
. . . The two plaintiff Companies, although separate entities in law, are interconnected in the one business. The second-named Company is in fact a subsidiary of the first, which owns all the shares in the second Company. The first-named plaintiffs carry on business at 86/89 Talbot Street and the second-named Company's premises adjoins the first-named Company's premises in Beresford Lane. The plaintiffs are manufacturing stationers, printers, publishers and distributors of school books. There is a retail shop in the premises in Talbot Street.

The staff of the plaintiff Companies numbers one hundred and fifty-seven and of these forty-five are clerical workers. Prior to the happening of the matters giving rise to the present action seven different trade unions catered for the staff, but there were a number of employees who did not belong to any trade union. Most of these non-union workers were members of what may be broadly described as the clerical staff of the business.

The defendants are members of the Irish Union of Distributive Workers and Clerks (hereinafter called 'the Union') and the first named defendant, W. J. Fitzpatrick, is the general secretary of the Union.

In August, 1959, two clerical employees of the plaintiffs, who were dissatisfied with their wages, the method of calculating overtime, and certain minor discomforts in their place of work, got into touch with Mr. Corish, the secretary of the Dublin

North City Branch of the Union. They joined the Union and persuaded eleven others of the clerical staff also to join. Their grievances were taken up by the Union and, as a result of a conference on the 28th October between Mr. Corish for the men and Mr. Lyons and Mr. Fitzsimmons, for the plaintiffs, a new wages scale was agreed.

Difficulties were not at an end. The members of the staff who had joined the Union conceived it to be in their interest to bring further clerical workers into the Union. They persuaded three men to join, but nine others, whom they wished to enrol, refused to do so. Letters were written to the nine by Mr. Corish but without effect.

On the 15th January, 1960, Mr. Corish wrote to Mr. Fitzsimmons a letter, telling him of the failure to induce certain members of the staff to join the Union and stating:– 'The present situation has now been considered by my Branch Committee and by our members in your employment and it has been decided that a ballot vote will be taken as to whether or not our members are prepared to continue working with the non-members.'

Mr. Fitzsimmons replied on the 18th January to the effect that, as previously agreed, the Union was entitled to make every effort to recruit members of the staff, who were free to make up their own minds; that the management had no intention of interfering one way or another; and that it would continue its policy of allowing the staff to choose for themselves. On the 1st February Mr. Corish wrote stating that his Branch Committee had again considered the matter and that he had been directed to call a further meeting of the staff, when a secret ballot vote would be taken as to whether or not they would be prepared to work with non-union labour. On the 10th February Mr. Fitzpatrick, the general secretary of the Union, wrote a further letter in which he said:– 'Having endeavoured by all reasonable means to complete organisation and to avoid friction with the Company, the organised members have now decided – in a secret ballot vote – to refuse to remain at work with the following, who are not members of this Union.' Then follow the names of nine members of the clerical staff. The selection was somewhat arbitrary. No claim was made in regard to women clerical workers or persons in a supervisory capacity, and one or two others seem to have been regarded as having a satisfactory reason for not joining. The letter concluded by a suggestion that a conference might be held. Mr. Fitzsimmons answered on the 11th February that he would be prepared to hear the representatives of the Union, but re-iterated that the management would not compel any member of the staff either to join or stay out of a trade union. Mr. Fitzpatrick replied on the 17th February:– 'In view of the mandate given by our members the Executive Committee must advise that, unless the nine non-members mentioned had joined the Union in the meantime, our members would be instructed not to resume duty after finishing time on Saturday, 27th instant.'

On the 27th February the sixteen members ceased work and on the 29th February pickets were put on the front and back entrances to the plaintiffs' premises, carrying placards announcing a trade dispute.

The plaintiffs moved quickly. On the 1st March they issued the summons in the present action, claiming an injunction to prevent the defendants from picketing, watching and besetting, disturbing the plaintiffs in the conduct of their business, and interfering with the plaintiffs their employees or customers in such a way as to constitute a nuisance. On the same day they obtained from Mr. Justice Haugh an interim injunction and on the 8th March, from Mr. Justice Teevan, an interlocutory injunction restraining picketing until the hearing of the action. The order of Mr. Justice Teevan was affirmed on appeal.

The action came on for hearing before Mr. Justice Budd in May, 1960, and lengthy evidence was tendered on both sides. I do not consider it necessary to refer to it in detail. To my mind the good faith of all the persons concerned was demonstrated. The sixteen considered it to be in their interests to increase the bargaining power of the Union by enrolling further members. They had no personal spite or malevolence against the nine and would have preferred that the management should have persuaded them to join the Union, but if the nine did not yield to persuasion, their attitude was that the nine were to be induced to join by threat of dismissal and, if they still proved obdurate, they were to be dismissed. The sixteen were striking to force the management into persuading the nine to join, or dismissing them if they did not. The nine on the other hand did not wish to join the Union and did not consider their interests would be forwarded by so doing. The plaintiffs, faced with this difference in opinion among their workmen, adopted a course which seems to me not only legal and unexceptionable but, on any ethical standard, entirely commendable. They allowed the Union officials every facility to persuade the nine to join the Union. They refused to interfere in any way, by persuasion or threats, with the free choice and free action of their employees and declined to take sides. The complaint of the Union against them is not that they were partial but that they were impartial. The Union consider that the employers should definitely have allied themselves with the sixteen and have used first their powers of persuasion and, if necessary, their ability to dismiss, in order to force the nine into the Union. In his letter to Mr. Corish of the 18th January, 1960, Mr. Fitzsimmons says that he believes his attitude to be constitutionally correct. It certainly appears to be conceived in the spirit of the Constitution and to be consonant with all fair and liberal principles. But the Court is concerned only with the lawfulness of actions and, if the actions of the defendants are lawful, the unexceptionable conduct of the plaintiffs cannot avail to save them from irreparable damage.

Mr. Justice Budd held that the picketing amounted to watching and besetting and was illegal, unless there was a trade dispute as defined by the Trade Disputes Act, 1906: that there was a trade dispute: and that the picketing would be justified by that Act if not inconsistent with the Constitution: but that if the Act authorised picketing in order to force men into an association against their will the Act was to that extent unconstitutional. Accordingly he granted the injunction sought. Against his judgment and order the defendants now appeal. They contend that the picketing was lawful at common law: that even if they are wrong in this contention it was justified by the Trade Disputes Act: and that the provisions and effect of that Act in no way conflict with the Constitution.

On the first point there has been a difference of opinion in the decided cases. The question seems to have been argued very perfunctorily in the Court of trial if argued at all – there is a difference between counsel in their recollection – and not a great deal of evidence was given as to the nature of the picketing. Apparently there was a picket of six men, subsequently reduced to four, in front of the plaintiffs' premises, and four more at the rear. They carried placards announcing a trade dispute and asserted a trade dispute orally, but there is no evidence that their manner was threatening or aggressive. Mr. Fitzsimmons gave evidence that the effect of such a picket was to prevent customers from coming to the premises and trade unionists from passing the picket to deliver or remove goods. I think we may rely on our common knowledge and our observation to confirm this. That picketing as ordinarily conducted interferes very seriously with the user and enjoyment of the premises picketed and amounts to a common law nuisance can hardly, I think, be contested.

J. Lyons & Sons v. *Wilkins* came twice before the English Court of Appeal, first on an appeal against an interlocutory injunction ([1896] 1 Ch. 811) and secondly on an appeal against a final injunction ([1899] 1 Ch. 255). In the first case the Court,

Lindley L.J., Kay L.J., and A. L. Smith L.J., held the picketing to be unlawful as it was not confined to the mere object of giving or receiving information but was designed to put pressure on persons to do or abstain from doing what they had a right to abstain from doing or to do, and that it amounted to a common law nuisance. The second case came before Lindley M.R., Chitty L.J., and Vaughan Williams L.J. Lindley M.R. adhered to his former decision, Chitty L.J. gave judgment to the same effect, but Vaughan Williams L.J., while holding himself bound by the previous judgment of the Court, indicated his view that communications by a picket properly made, though designed to bring pressure on the employers, were not sufficient to make the picketing illegal; and he also considered that on the facts proved there had been no common law nuisance.

Ward, Lock and Co. Ltd. v. *Operative Printers' Assistants' Society* 22 T. L. R. 327 is not altogether easy to understand. It was an appeal from the findings of a jury on a number of different issues and the Court, Vaughan Williams, Stirling and Fletcher Moulton L.JJ, held that there was no evidence to support such findings. In the course of arriving at this conclusion Vaughan Williams and Fletcher Moulton L.JJ, decided that s. 8 of the Conspiracy and Protection of Property Act, 1875, did no more than make criminal certain acts which were already tortious before its enactment, and made nothing civilly actionable which was not so before. This part of the decision was approved and followed by the Court of Appeal in *Fowler* v. *Kibble* [1922] 1 Ch. 487. Vaughan Williams L.J. held also that the picketing was not unlawful, even if it was done with a view to compelling the plaintiffs to do an act which they had a right to abstain from doing, unless the picketing was carried on in such a way as to amount to a common law nuisance; and thought that there was not evidence of acts amounting to a nuisance. Fletcher Moulton L.J. held that there was no evidence that the picketing was designed to compel the plaintiffs to abstain from doing anything which they had a right to do, and no evidence that a nuisance had been caused. It is clear that the Court took a more limited view of what constituted a common law nuisance than did the Court in *Lyons* v. *Wilkins* [1899] 1 Ch. 255. They were of opinion that if there was no violence or obstruction or direct intimidation no nuisance was caused: and that picketing to induce a person to cease employment or picketing which in fact did interfere with the business of the employers was not necessarily a nuisance.

The Trade Disputes Act, 1906, by ss. 2 and 3 put an end to the question in cases where there was a trade dispute as defined by that Act. Sect. 2 provides that 'it shall be lawful for one or more persons, acting on their own behalf or on behalf of a trade union or of an individual employer or firm in contemplation or furtherance of a trade dispute, to attend at or near a house or place where a person resides or works or carries on business or happens to be, if they so attend merely for the purpose of peacefully obtaining or communicating information, or of peaceably persuading any person to work or abstain from working.' Sect. 3 provides that 'an act done by a person in contemplation or furtherance of a trade dispute shall not be actionable on the ground only that it induces some other person to break a contract of employment or that it is an interference with the trade, business, or employment of some other person, or with the right of some other person to dispose of his capital or his labour as he wills.'

Since the passing of that Act there have been very numerous cases where an injunction was sought to restrain picketing, and the fight always centred round the question as to whether there was or was not a trade dispute. In no case to which we were referred, and in no case of which I am aware, did counsel seek to argue that, if there was no trade dispute, picketing, when carried on without threats, violence or overt intimidation, was lawful at common law. They seem to have realised that picketing is, in the words of counsel in this case, 'a murderous weapon,' and that, even if carried on with scrupulous avoidance of any expressed threats, its inevitable effect is to intimidate customers and to cause such a conditioned reflex in all trade unionists, as inevitably to interfere with the business of the party picketed and with the ordinary user and enjoyment of his property in such a way as to constitute a common law nuisance. In *Esplanade Pharmacy Ltd.* v. *Larkin and Others* [1957] I. R. 285 Mr. Justice Lavery said, at p. 291:– 'The picketing is clearly unlawful and constitutes a "watching and besetting" of the premises unless it is justified by the provisions of the Trade Disputes Act, 1906,' and Mr. Justice O'Daly said, at p. 298:– 'Picketing, otherwise watching and besetting, a premises is lawful only in the conditions defined in the Trade Disputes Act.' The other members of the Court agreed with these judgments. As the argument that the picketing was lawful at common law does not seem to have been advanced in the latter case the Court is not absolutely bound by this decision, nor by *Smith and Another* v. *Beirne and Others* 89 I. L. T. R. 24 in which also it was assumed that picketing was unlawful unless there was a trade dispute as defined by the 1906 Act. Accordingly I approach the question as if it were not concluded by authority. So approaching it I concede that it may perhaps be possible to picket a premises so discreetly and unobtrusively as not to cause any intimidation or interference with the proper and convenient use of an employer's premises: so to convey and receive information as not to bring any pressure other than reasoned argument on anyone to do or abstain from doing anything which he has a right to abstain from doing or to do. But it does not appear to me that picketing as ordinarily conducted, and as conducted in this case, falls within this category and I am of opinion that Mr. Justice Budd was correct in holding it to be illegal unless it was conducted in furtherance of a trade dispute.

This raises the second question. Was there a trade dispute as defined by the 1906 Act, namely, 'any dispute between employers and workmen, or between workmen and workmen, which is connected with the employment or non-employment or the terms of employment, or with the conditions of labour of any person'? Before considering the authorities I ask what were the disputes in this case. First, there was a dispute between workmen and workmen. The sixteen said to the nine:– 'You must join the union.' The nine replied:– 'We will not join.' The sixteen rejoined:– 'If you do not join we will not allow you to work and will take steps to see that you are dismissed.' Second, there was a dispute between workmen and employer. The sixteen said in effect to the plaintiffs:– 'You must persuade the nine to join the union, if necessary by threat of dismissing them, and if they do not join you must dismiss them. Otherwise we will strike.' The plaintiffs declined to persuade and refused to dismiss. Whatever may be said about the first dispute the second seems to be 'connected with the employment or non-employment' of the nine. The authorities are not uniform. In *Valentine* v. *Hyde* [1919] 2 Ch. 129 four unions, working in concert, objected to the plaintiff belonging to a fifth union and demanded that he should join a branch of one of the four unions. The plaintiff refused and thereupon Hyde threatened to get him dismissed, 'downing tools' if the manager of the works did not discharge him. As a result of pressure from the four unions, for whom the defendants acted as spokesmen, notice of dismissal was served on the plaintiff. Thereupon the plaintiff sued the defendants to restrain them from interfering with his employment and the defendants relied on the Trade Disputes Act. Mr. Justice Astbury held that there was no trade dispute between workmen and workmen. The ground of his decision (at p. 151) was that 'a trade dispute within the Act must be a dispute connected directly with employment or non-employment, and not a dispute about some entirely different subject-matter, the non-settlement of which may result in employment of non-employment, the existence, terms or conditons of which are not in contest. . . . The dispute between the plaintiff and the defendants was whether the former would or would not join the Walkden branch. The consequences with which he was threatened, if he refused, formed no part of the subject-matter of the dispute. The fact of his employment, his rate of wages and his conditions of service were not questioned or objected to.'

Hodges v. *Webb* [1920] 2 Ch. 70 was a similar case. The defendant was the District Secretary of a union which objected to workmen being employed unless they belonged to that union. The plaintiff belonged to a different union. Webb asked him to join Webb's union and on his refusal called out the men and told the manager of the company which employed the plaintiff that no further work would be done till the plaintiff was removed. Thereupon the plaintiff was dismissed. He sued the defendant who pleaded the Trade Disputes Act. Mr. Justice Peterson held that there was a dispute between workmen and employers as to whether workmen belonging to the plaintiff's union should be employed side by side with workmen belonging to the defendant's union, and he indicated his view that there was also a dispute betweeen workmen and workmen.

The same question arose in *White* v. *Riley* [1921] 1 Ch. 1. The plaintiff was a member of the Workers' Union, the defendant of the Curriers' Union. The Curriers' Union required all workmen working at the trade of currier to be members of that union. The plaintiff refused to join and thereupon the defendant wrote a letter on behalf of the shop to the plaintiff's employer, giving notice that the men would cease work unless the plaintiff joined the society or left the employment. After some negotiations the employer suspended and then discharged the plaintiff, who sued the defendant, Riley, and another for conspiracy to injure and procurement of a breach of contract. The Court of Appeal, Sterndale M.R., Warrington and Younger L.JJ., held unanimously that on the facts there had been no actionable conspiracy to injure and no procurement of a breach of contract, and that this was sufficient to decide the case. But, as the Trade Disputes Act had been pleaded, Sterndale M.R. and Warring- ton L.J. went on to consider if a trade dispute had arisen. Both held that the existence or non-existence of a trade dispute was a question of fact. Sterndale M.R. (at p. 19) said:– 'The only fair conclusion of fact is that there was a dispute between workmen and workmen in connection with the employment of a person – namely, the plaintiff.' He considered that there might also be a trade dispute between workmen and employers. He preferred the reasoning of Peterson J. in *Hodges* v. *Webb* [1920] 2 Ch. 70 to that of Astbury J. in *Valentine* v. *Hyde* [1919] 2 Ch. 129. Warrington L.J. also preferred the reasoning of Peterson J. and criticised the reasoning of Astbury J., saying (at p. 27):– 'He treats the matter as if the dispute was whether or not the workman in question should join the particular union. In my judgment that is only an incident in the dispute. The dispute is whether while he is not a member of the union to which the other men belong he should be employed by the employers. It is really a dispute as to the terms upon which he should continue in the employment.' Younger L.J. agreed with the views expressed by his brethren.

White v. *Riley* [1921] 1 Ch. 1 has stood for forty years and counsel were not able to point to any case in which the views there expressed had been criticised. Whether there is or is not a trade dispute, is a matter of fact. I have set out what I consider to have been the essence of the dispute in this case and it seems to me that there was a dispute between the sixteen and the plaintiffs, and probably also a dispute between the sixteen and the nine, as to whether the nine should continue to be employed while they refused to join the Union, in other words, a trade dispute within the meaning of the 1906 Act.

It remains then to consider whether the operation of the Trade Disputes Act has been affected by the provisions of the Constitution. Article 50 provides that, *subject to the Constitution and to the extent that they are not inconsistent therewith*, the laws in force in Saorstát Éireann immediately prior to the date of the coming into operation of the Constitution shall continue to be of full force and effect until the same or any of them shall have been repealed or amended by enactment of the Oireachtas.

Article 73 of the Free State Constitution provided that *subject to that Constitution and to the extent to which they are not inconsistent therewith,* the laws in force in the Irish Free State at the date of the coming into force of that Constitution should continue to be of full force and effect till repealed or amended.

The Trade Disputes Act of 1906 thus first became part of the law of the Irish Free State and subsequently part of the law of our present Republic, subject always to the provisions of the two constitutions and to the extent to which it was not inconsistent therewith.

Article 9 of the Free State Constitution provided that 'the right . . . to form associations or unions is guaranteed for purposes not opposed to public morality. Laws regulating the manner in which the right of forming associations . . . may be exercised shall contain no political, religious or class distinction.

Article 40, 3,1°, of our Constitution provides:– 'The State guarantees in its laws to respect, and, as far as practicable, by its laws to defend and vindicate the personal rights of the citizen.'

Article 40, 3, 2°, provides that 'The State shall, in particular, by its laws protect as best it may from unjust attack and, in the case of injustice done, vindicate the . . . property rights of every citizen.'

Article 40, 6, 1°, provides that 'The State guarantees liberty for the exercise of the following rights, subject to public order and morality. . . .

'i. The right of the citizens to express freely their convictions and opinions. . . .

'iii. The right of the citizens to form associations and unions.'

Laws however may be enacted for the regulation and control in the public interest of the exercise of the foregoing rights.

Article 40, 6, 2°, provides that 'Laws regulating the manner in which the right of forming associations and unions . . . may be exercised shall contain no political, religious or class discrimination.'

Finally I would call attention to Article 15, 4, 2°, which provides that every law enacted by the Oireachtas which is in any respect repugnant to the Constitution or to any provision thereof shall, but to the extent only of such repugnancy, be invalid. As I cannot conceive that the Constitution laid down a more stringent test for the validity of laws passed by the Oireachtas than it did for the continued validity of statutes or law carried forward into our *corpus juris* by Article 50, I must interpret the words in Article 50, 'Subject to this Constitution and to the extent to which they are not inconsistent therewith,' as negativing the carrying forward of any statute or law which is 'in any respect repugnant to the Constitution or to any provision thereof' to the extent of such repugnancy.

The first step in the constitutional argument of the plaintiffs was an attempt to show that the Constitution guaranteed the right of citizens not to join associations or unions if they did not so desire, and the right not to be coerced into so joining. The Constitution does not give such a guarantee in express terms, but I think it does so by necessary implication. The right to express freely convictions and opinions, guaranteed by Article 40, 6, 1°, i, must include the right to hold such convictions and opinions and the right not to be forced to join a union or association professing, forwarding, and requiring its members to subscribe to contrary opinions. The undertaking in Article 40, 3, 2°, to protect the property rights of every citizen may perhaps include an undertaking to protect his right to dispose of his labour as he wills, and would include impliedly a right not to be forced against his will into a union or association which exacts from him a regular payment. Moreover I think a guarantee of a right to form associations and unions is only intelligible where there is an implicit right to abstain from joining such associations or unions or, to put it another way, to associate and unite with those who do not join such unions. In *National Union of Railwaymen and Others* v. *Sullivan and Others* [1947] I. R. 77 Murnaghan J., giving the judgment of the Court, emphasised at p. 102 the constitutional right of the citizen to a free choice of the persons with whom he would associate and the decision seems to me to establish that a person shall not be coerced, at any rate by legislative action, into joining an association which he is not willing to join. Accordingly I hold that there is an implicit guarantee in the Constitution that citizens shall not be coerced to join associations or unions against their will.

I have used the word 'coerced' (which does not appear in the Constitution) and it is necessary to explain the sense in which I use that word, and also to indicate the nature of the coercion which the law may restrain as violating the exercise of the rights granted by the Constitution. I am unable to accept the view of Lord Watson that a person cannot properly be said to be coerced if, having two courses open to him, he follows the course which he considers conducive to his own interests. Coercion to my mind consists in forcing a person by action or threat of action to do or abstain from doing something which he is unwilling to do or abstain from doing, and which, but for such action or threats of action, he would not do or abstain from doing. Attempted coercion is the attempt (which may not be successful) by action or threat of action to produce a similar result. If a highwayman presents a pistol to my head and says, 'Your money or your life,' he attempts to coerce me, though he gives me a choice of two courses. I may, indeed, adopt a heroic attitude and say, 'Shoot away,' but, if discretion or pusillanimity prevail and I disgorge my money, it seems to me idle to say that I have not been coerced into so doing. Similarly if I give money to a blackmailer, under threat of exposure, I may properly be said to have been coerced.

It seems to me that any form of pressure which compels me to act in a way in which I would not have acted but for such pressure is a form of coercion and any such pressure designed to deprive me of a right given me by the Constitution is against the spirit of the Constitution; but certain forms of pressure do not come within the province of the law to restrain. Unpopularity or social ostracism may be coercive to prevent me from exercising a right guaranteed to me, but the law has no concern with them, nor will it, in general, interfere with economic pressure exercised by another person in pursuance of his own legitimate interests. The Constitution guarantees my right to join an association, no matter how extreme its tenets may be, provided it is not illegal. Nevertheless my membership may involve me in unpopularity, loss of friendship, social ostracism, all designed to make me forgo my right. An employer may hesitate to engage me, anticipating that my membership will cause trouble. These forms of pressure may coerce me to resign my membership against my desires, but they are not restrainable by the law.

It is a very different matter when the Legislature intervenes to authorise or facilitate coercion by attempting to legalise acts, directed to that end, which previously were illegal and restrainable. I agree with Murnaghan J. when he said, giving the judgment of the Supreme Court in *National Union of Railwaymen and Others* v. *Sullivan and Others* [1947] I. R. 77, at p. 100:– '. . . in a Constitution like our own Constitution, the object of stating a principle in the Constitution is to limit the exercise by the Legislature of its otherwise unlimited power of legislation.' A statute of the Oireachtas prohibiting me from joining an association (which was not illegal) or forcing me to join an association against my will, would be unconstitutional and invalid. Equally unconstitutional to my mind would be a statute which purported to legalise acts of a nature previously illegal and restrainable by law, in so far as such acts were legalised when used for a purpose of interfering with rights guaranteed by the Constitution. If the Trade Disputes Act had not been passed, but an identical Act were to be put on the statute book tomorrow, I conceive that it would be unconstitutional to the extent that it purported to legalise the use of picketing (an act previously illegal) for the purpose of interfering with the exercise of my guaranteed constitutional right of association or dissociation. The same tests must in my opinion be applied to a statute of the Imperial Parliament passed before 1922 when considering whether and to what extent it is incorporated into our law by the continuation articles of the two Constitutions. It is only incorporated to the extent that it is not inconsistent with the Constitution.

It was suggested in the course of the hearing that, if picketing in aid of a strike to force men into a union could be restrained by injunction, so equally could the strike itself be restrained. This contention may be put forward in a future case and so I will say only that, as at present advised, the claim to picket and the claim to strike seem to me to involve very different considerations. The right to dispose of one's labour and to withdraw it seems to me a fundamental personal right which, though not specifically mentioned in the Constitution as being guaranteed, is a right of a nature which I cannot conceive to have been adversely affected by anything within the intendment of the Constitution. But the matter does not arise for decision in this case. Mr. Costello for the plaintiffs expressly disclaimed any intention of attacking the right of the sixteen to withdraw their work, and the order of the trial Judge does not interfere with the right. I wish to make it clear that my opinion deals with picketing and not with strikes; and with picketing only where it is carried on for the purpose of coercing into an association persons who are unwilling to join. My reasons can be re-stated shortly. Picketing in the sense of watching and besetting, was an illegal activity until legalised by the Trade Disputes Act when pursued in contemplation or furtherance of a trade dispute. A trade dispute may be a dispute as to whether persons shall be coerced into joining a union against their wishes. The Constitution implicitly guarantees the right of a person not to be so coerced. A statute which authorises or facilitates such coercion, if now passed by the Oireachtas would be to that extent unconstitutional. A statute passed before 1922 authorising or facilitating such coercion is not incorporated in our law by the continuation clauses of the Free State Constitution or our present Constitution in so far as it is inconsistent therewith. The Trade Disputes Act, 1906, can no longer be relied upon to justify picketing in aid of a trade dispute, where that dispute is concerned with an attempt to deprive persons of the right of free association or free dissociation guaranteed by the Constitution. The definition of trade dispute must be read as if there were attached thereto the words, 'Provided that a dispute between employers and workmen or between workmen and workmen as to whether a person shall or shall not become or remain a member of a trade union or having as its object a frustration of the right of any person to choose with whom he will or will not be associated in any form of union or association shall not be deemed to be a trade dispute for the purposes of this Act.'

I would dismiss the appeal.

Haugh J. delivered a concurring judgment.

Ó Dálaigh J. concurred with **Kingsmill Moore J.'s** judgment.

Maguire C.J. (dissenting):

. . . If the facts in this case are on all fours with the facts in *National Union of Railwaymen and Others* v. *Sullivan and Others* [1947] I. R. 77 there is nothing more to be said. That decision is binding upon this Court. In my opinion, however, this case is distinguishable. The Court in that case was considering provisions of Part III of the Trade Union Act, 1941, which permitted a trade union to apply to a tribunal set up under the Act for a determination that it alone should have the right to organise in a trade union workmen of a particular class. It was held that these provisions, by purporting to deprive citizens of the choice of the persons with whom they would associate, were at variance with the emphatic assertion in Article 40 of the Constitution of the citizens' right to form associations and unions and are therefore invalid. To my mind there is a clear distinction between such a provision in a statute of the Oireachtas and the action of the trade union in this case. There is no question here of forbidding or preventing the workmen who refuse to join a particular union to form associations or unions. They are quite free to form a union of their own or to join other unions. It is to be observed that *White* v. *Riley* [1921] 1 Ch. 1 was not mentioned in the course of the argument in *National Union of Railwaymen and Others* v. *O'Sullivan and Others* [1947] I.R. 77. This suggests to my mind a tacit assumption that the decision was not in conflict with the Constitution. The plaintiffs in that case could hardly have anticipated that the argument upon which they relied would later be advanced in support of the contention that the provisions of Article 40 had reversed the decision in *White* v. *Riley* [1921] 1 Ch. 1.

Moreover, it is a strange feature of this case that the plaintiffs hesitate to press their argument to its logical conclusion. If the contention is right that action which aims at persuading non-union men to join a union is a denial of the rights given by Article 40, 6, iii, it would seem to me that each step taken with this end in view is an infringement of the Article. The demand upon the employers that men shall be dismissed if they do not join the union, the threat of a strike to support this demand and, above all, the strike itself would seem to me just as much a derogation of the right of the non-union workmen as the placing of a picket on the premises. Yet it is conceded that none of these steps does violence to the constitutional rights of the non-union workmen or of their employers.

I am unable to understand this inconsistency of the plaintiffs and their refusal to face the logical results of their argument.

To my mind the position is simple and clear.

The defendants are exercising the right which they have of refusing to associate with workmen who are not members of their Union. The reasonableness of this objection may be questioned but it seems to me that union members act lawfully in trying to strengthen their union by bringing in all those upon whose behalf they will be acting in negotiating with employers. Whatever was said as regards the negation of choice in *National Union of Railwaymen and Others* v. *Sullivan and Others* [1947] I. R. 77 I am of opinion that there is no such negation here, not is there coercion in the legal sense. The Union is acting *bona fide* in its own interests just as was the union in the *Crofter's Case* [1942] A. C. 435.

As was said by Peterson J. in *Hodges* v. *Webb* [1920] 2 Ch. 70, at p. 86, ' "Coercion" implies some negation of choice,' and I respectfully adopt the view of Lord Watson in *Allen* v. *Flood* [1898] A.C. 1 that 'an employer cannot properly be said to be coerced if having two alternative courses presented to him he follows the course which he considers conducive to his own interests.' In that sense the plaintiffs here are not being 'coerced' and there is no negation of choice. The situation is not any different to the position which frequently arises in the rivalries in many spheres, particularly in that of business rivalry. The defendants' aim is to strengthen their Union by bringing into it all workmen of a certain category on whose behalf their Union may seek to negotiate with the employers. They say in effect to the non-unionists:– 'We do not wish to work with you unless you become members of our Union.' They next inform the employers of this attitude and intimate that they will withdraw their labour unless the non-unionist workmen become members. Implicit is the intimation that the weapon of picketing will be used to further the dispute. As I see it the unionist workmen are entitled to invoke Article 40, 6, iii, in protection of their rights to choose their associates and so bring members into their Union.

The basis of the decision in *White* v. *Riley* [1947] I. R. 77 was that workmen may assert the right to choose with whom they will work and may inform an employer of their objection to continue to work with non-unionists. Although the action of the defendants may make it difficult and disadvantageous for the non-unionists to remain outside the union, their choice of a course of action is not denied them. As I have said, they may join or refuse to join and form another union. It seems to me that the most that can be said to arise is a clash between the positive right of the unionist workmen and what may be called the negative right of those who are unwilling to join. Even if such clash can be said to exist I am unable to interpret Article 40, 6, iii, as denying the rights of the unionist workmen to take the steps they have taken.

In my view the judgment and order of the High Court should be reversed and this action dismissed.

Lavery J. also delivered a dissenting judgment.

Note

For critical analysis of the decision see Casey, 'Some Implications of Freedom of Association in Labour Law: A Comparative Survey with Special Reference to Ireland' 21 I.C.L.Q. 899 (1972); Whyte, 'Industrial Relations and the Irish Constitution' 16 Ir. Jur. (n.s.) 35, at 50ff. (1981).

'Employment or Non-Employment'

GOULDING CHEMICALS LTD. V. BOLGER
[1977] I.R. 211 (Supreme Court 1977, aff'g High Court, Hamilton, J., 1976)

O'Higgins C.J.:

This is an appeal by the plaintiff company from the judgment and order of Mr. Justice Hamilton dismissing its claim for an injunction against picketing and for associated relief. The defendants are all members of the Irish Transport and General Workers Union (ITGWU) and were all former employees of the plaintiff company, being part of the workforce at the plaintiffs' plant at East Wall, Dublin. The issues which have arisen on this appeal require, in my view, to be considered in the light of facts which were established in evidence before the learned trial judge. A short reference to these facts would appear appropriate.

The plaintiff company had two plants for the manufacture of fertilizers – one at East Wall in Dublin and the other in Cork. By reason of consistent and substantial falling off in the plaintiffs' sales on the home market, it was decided to close down the East Wall plant and to concentrate future effort on the Cork plant. The date for the closure of the East Wall plant was to be the 30th July, 1976. Having been reached by the management of the plaintiff company, this decision was communicated to a specially-convened meeting of the staff and payroll unions representing all of those employed at the East Wall plant. This meeting was held on the 14th June, 1976, and it was the first of a series of meetings between the management of the plaintiff company and the different unions having as their objective the acceptance by the unions of the inevitability of the closing of the East Wall plant and the working out of satisfactory compensation terms for all of those who would become redundant as a result. These meetings resulted in the acceptance, at a joint general meeting of all the unions representing those employed at the East Wall (some eleven in number), of a six-point statement issued on behalf of the plaintiffs on the 23rd July, 1976. Having reiterated that the East Wall plant would close 'permanently' on the 30th July and that wages and salaries for employees would cease on that date, this statement set out terms for compensatory payments to employees, based on service, which were significantly higher than would have been payable under the Redundancy Payments Acts. The acceptance of these terms by the joint general meeting of all the unions took place on the 27th July.

If this agreement had been honoured and observed by all those to whom it was intended to apply, no further problem would have arisen and the plaintiffs could have devoted their efforts towards making their continuing operations viable. Unfortunately this was not to be so. Upon the closing of the East Wall plant on the 30th July, 1976, the defendants refused to leave the factory premises and staged a 'sit-in' on these premises; all the defendants were former employees of the plaintiffs and members of ITGWU, which was one of the unions which had accepted the settlement. This led to High Court proceedings on the part of the plaintiffs and the granting of an injunction against the defendants in respect of this trespassing. This injunction was obeyed and the sit-in ceased. However, on the 23rd August, 1976, the defendants commenced to picket the East Wall premises and this led to a further application by the plaintiffs for an injunction to restrain such picketing.

The plaintiffs contended that this picketing was unjustified and illegal and that the effect of it was to prevent them removing from the East Wall premises a considerable tonnage of valuable fertilizer material which could be sold or used in Cork. They also complained that it interfered with the 'mothballing' and preservation of the valuable machinery in the plant and with the provision of necessary security arrangements. The defendants contended that their action was lawfully taken in pursuance of a trade dispute relating to the closing of the plant and the non-employment of the defendants in the work still requiring to be done at the plant, whether in relation to mothballing the machinery, removing the assets or providing security.

It is apparent from the transcript that while some of the defendants took part in the meetings between management and staff which led to the plaintiffs' six-point statement of the 23rd July, 1976, all the defendants (including those who attended such meetings) were at all times opposed to the closing of the plant and to the conclusion of any agreement with the plaintiffs. The defendants maintained this attitude throughout the negotiations and prior to and after the final meeting at which the plaintiffs' proposals were accepted by a majority. Their action in picketing the plaintiffs' premises was in accordance with their declared attitude of hostility to the conclusion of any agreement which would facilitate the closing of the plant and the cesser of their employment.

The learned trial judge refused the plaintiffs' claim for an injunction and held that the picketing complained of was in pursuance of a bona fide trade dispute; this appeal has been brought by the plaintiffs. At the hearing of the plaintiffs' claim for an injunction in the High Court and because of the urgency of the matter, pleadings were dispensed with and the issue was decided by the learned trial judge on the affidavits filed on behalf of each of the parties and on the oral evidence which he heard. On the lodging of the appeal this Court thought it desirable, in view of the absence of pleadings, to require written submissions to be filed by the parties.

In addition, the Court permitted one matter to be argued on the appeal which had not been argued before the learned trial judge; this related to the application, meaning, and effect of s. 11, sub-s. 1, of the Trade Union Act, 1941. As a question of the section's constitutionality had been raised by the defendants, the Court directed that notice be served on the Attorney General and that he be heard on the appeal. The latitude which was given to the parties in this respect to enable all possible issues between them to be ventilated on the appeal, even though some of the issues were not raised in the High Court, is unusual and, in my view, ought not to be regarded as a precedent. It was permitted here only with considerable misgivings and because there was no procedure under which the appropriate arguments could then be initiated in the High Court.

I now turn to the issues which have arisen on this appeal and I propose to consider first the meaning and effect of s. 11 of the Act of 1941. [*The Chief Justice referred to the provisions of s. 11 of the Act of 1941, and continued*] It was submitted on behalf of the plaintiffs that the effect of this section is to confine the protection given by ss. 2, 3 and 4 of the Trade Disputes Act, 1906, to such authorised trade unions holding negotiation licences issued under the Act of 1941 and to the members and officials of such unions acting with the authority, or pursuant to a decision, of their union. If this be the true meaning and effect of s. 11 of the Act of 1941 then, on the facts of this case, the protection of the Act of 1906 could not be available to the defendants. The defendants have acted in this case on their own and in defiance of a settlement reached through the proper channels with the organised labour force employed by the plaintiffs. In addition they have acted in opposition to the views and, therefore, without the approval of their own union. If s. 11 of the Act of 1941 confined the right to picket to those unions which hold a negotiation licence and to their members and officials acting as such, then it brought about a major change and reform in trade-union law which has gone almost unnoticed through nearly four decades. Can this be the effect of the section? If it is, then it is the duty of this Court so to declare whatever may be the consequences.

In construing a statute certain rules have been laid down which, when observed, lead to some certainty of construction. In the first place, one seeks the intention in the words used which must, if they are plain and unambiguous, be applied as they stand. The words used in s. 11, sub-s. 1, of the Act of 1941 state, and state plainly, that the three named sections of the Act of 1906 shall 'apply only' to the described trade unions and 'the members and officials of such trade unions.' The section goes on to add finally in relation to the application of the three sections the words 'and not otherwise.' Here the words used appear to be used without ambiguity and appear clearly to confine the protection of the Act of 1906 to the unions and the persons indicated. Therefore, it seems to me that one starts off in construing the sub-section by accepting the clear effect of the words used as being to abolish the protection previously provided generally by ss. 2, 3 and 4 of the Act of 1906 except in the case of the unions and persons mentioned. But the problem of construction does not end at this. Section 11, sub-s. 1, of the Act of 1941 must now be read in conjunction with the three sections of the Act of 1906 which are now declared to operate only in the confined area permitted by s. 11, sub-s. 1, of the Act of 1941. As one looks at the language of these three sections now applied to the confined area by s. 11, sub-s. 1, some further rules of construction require to be mentioned. It seems to me that one must regard s. 11, sub-s. 1, of the Act of 1941 as having the effect of re-enacting ss. 2, 3 and 4 of the Act of 1906 as applying to the unions and persons mentioned by that sub-section.

It is well established that, if there is nothing to modify, nothing to alter, nothing to qualify the language which a statute contains, the words and sentences must be construed in their ordinary and natural meaning. It is to be presumed that words are not used in a statute without a meaning and, accordingly, effect must be given, if possible, to all the words used, for, as has been said, 'the legislature is deemed not to waste its words or to say anything in vain' – *per* Lord Sumner in *Quebec Railway, Light, Heat and Power Co.* v. *Vandry* [1920] A.C. 662, 676.

Here one notes that in s. 2 of the Act of 1906 which is now to operate as provided by s. 11, sub-s. 1, of the Act of 1941, the protection given is accorded to 'one or more persons, acting on their own behalf or on behalf of a trade union.' How are these words to be construed in the new application of the section? They cannot be ignored. It must be assumed that they were contemplated by the Oireachtas as being words in a section which would operate as indicated by s. 11, sub-s. 1, of the Act of 1941. It seems to me that one is driven to the conclusion that the protection given by s.2 of the Act of 1906 is by s. 11, sub-s. 1 of the Act of 1941 to apply to authorised trade unions holding a negotiation licence and to the officers and members of these unions whether such officers and members act on behalf of the union or on their own behalf. In relation to s. 3 of the Act of 1906, it has been pointed out in argument to this Court that the words 'trade union' nowhere appear. This, of course, is true but one must seek a meaning and a sense in the application of that section by s. 11, sub-s. 1, of the Act of 1941. In so doing, I find it not unreasonable to conclude that s. 3 of the Act of 1906 appears to apply under s. 11, sub-s. 1, of the Act of 1941 to persons who are officers or members of a trade union holding a negotiation licence, whether such persons are acting on behalf of the union or on their own behalf. No problem arises with regard to the application of s. 4 of the Act of 1906 in the limited field provided by s. 11, sub-s. 1, of the Act of 1941.

In my view, therefore, the effect of s. 11, sub-s. 1, of the Act of 1941 is to confine the protection and immunities given by ss. 2, 3 and 4 of the Act of 1906 to authorised trade unions holding negotiation licences and to the officials and members of such unions whether acting on behalf of their unions or on their own behalf. If this be the effect of s. 11, sub-s. 1, of the Act of 1941 then the submission made by the plaintiffs on this aspect of the case fails. All the defendants are members of an authorised trade union holding a negotiation licence. On the view I have taken, the provisions of s. 11, sub-s. 1, of the Act of 1941 do not delimit in any way their rights under the Act of 1906.

The defendants have raised the question of the constitutionality of s. 11, sub-s. 1, of the Act of 1941 if its true meaning and effect were as contended for by the plaintiffs. This Court indicated a tentative or provisional opinion as to the meaning and effect of s. 11, sub-s. 1, which was along the lines just expressed by me in this judgment and, accordingly, did not feel it necessary or proper at that stage to enter into the question of its constitutionality. By reason of the view I have formed as to the meaning and effect of s. 11, sub-s. 1, of the Act of 1941, I do not think that this Court should now entertain an argument or pronounce a judgment on the constitutionality of the section.

I turn now to consider the other submissions made on behalf of the plaintiffs on the hearing of this appeal. These related to the other four grounds of appeal as set out in the written submissions lodged by the plaintiffs pursuant to the direction of this Court. I will take these in the order in which they were dealt with on the appeal.

First, it was submitted that on the facts of this case no true dispute existed and that on that account the picketing complained of was illegal. This submission was put forward on two distinct grounds. In the first place it was said that a trade dispute must relate to the employment or non-employment or the terms of employment or the conditions of labour of any person. It was said that the plaintiffs had ceased to carry on their operations, and that they had lawfully terminated the contracts of service of their employees and were in the process of locking up and preserving their empty plant. It was submitted that in such circumstances there could not be any question of employment or non-employment because such could only arise when the plaintiffs had a choice to employ or to refuse employment, and that such a choice did not exist on the facts of this case. Put in another way, it was suggested that the reality was that the picketing was in pursuance of a claim by the defendants to be employed or to have the plant remain open or to have employment guaranteed to them at some future date, and that this would not be sufficient to constitute a trade dispute. In support of these submissions reliance was placed on *Conway* v. *Wade* [1909] A.C. 506; *Barton* v. *Harten* [1925] 2 I.R. 37; and *British and Irish Steampacket Co. Ltd.* v. *Branigan* [1958] I.R. 128. The second ground of this submission was that, as the plaintiffs' dismissals of the defendants were lawful in that their contracts of service were lawfully terminated, there could in such circumstances be no trade dispute. Reliance in support of this contention was placed on the decision and reasoning of Overend J. in *Doran* v. *Lennon* [1945] I.R. 315.

I have considered this ground of appeal and the submissions made in support of it very carefully. I have considerable sympathy with the contention that for a trade dispute to exist there must be some reality in the question of possible employment in the sense that there must be an employer having employment available. However, I fear that this contention is irrelevant on the facts of this case. As I read the transcript and the facts, as found by the learned High Court Judge, it was precisely because they claimed that the plaintiffs had employment to give that they were picketing the premises. It is clear that after the closing of the plant employment became available on the premises in relation to the removing of certain raw materials which were intended to be sold or used in Cork, in maintaining and mothballing machinery, and generally in relation to the security of the plant and such machinery and other assets as remain there. As was made clear in evidence, the defendants felt that they should have been employed on some of this work. While their original opposition inside their union and at general staff meetings to the conclusion of any agreement with the plaintiffs may have had as its object the impossible aim of preventing the plaintiffs closing down their operations and, to that extent, may not have constituted a trade dispute, it seems clear that their subsequent conduct was actuated by the failure or refusal of the plaintiffs to employ them or other East Wall employees on the work which required to be done at the East Wall plant as a consequence of the closure of the plant itself. For this reason it seems that, irrespective of its merits, this has been a dispute between the defendants as workmen and the plaintiffs as employers connected with the non-employment of the defendants or of other former employees of the plaintiffs at the East Wall premises in the work continuing to be done on such premises. Therefore, on the evidence and facts of this case I am of the opinion that a trade dispute existed.

The second of the plaintiffs' submissions in support of this ground of appeal was to the effect that where a dismissal of a workman was lawful no trade dispute could be raised in relation to it. It was not disputed that the contracts of service of all the defendants had been lawfully terminated, and so it was contended that none of them could raise a bona fide trade dispute in relation to what was lawfully done by their employers, the plaintiffs. As a corollary, it was also urged that the defendants, having been properly and lawfully dismissed, were no longer workmen since they were not in employment and, therefore, could not raise a trade dispute. Reliance was placed on *Doran* v. *Lennon* [1945] I.R. 315 where Overend J. held that workers who had walked off the job and who were, on that account, dismissed could not raise a trade dispute. At p. 326 of the report he said:–

'If it were otherwise, then every employee of a commercial firm, who broke his contract and was dismissed for cause, would be entitled to picket his late master's premises and yet claim the protection of the statute.'

While the facts of *Doran* v. *Lennon* [1945] I.R. 315 are somewhat peculiar and special, it does appear from these facts and from the passage of his judgment which I have quoted that Overend J. was of the opinion that a lawful dismissal precluded the raising of a trade dispute. I cannot agree with this view and I think it is erroneous. The definition of 'trade dispute' in the Trade Disputes Act, 1906, permits of no such limitation and, indeed, is sufficiently wide and general to include any dispute between employers and workmen provided only it is connected with the employment or non-employment, or the terms of employment or the conditions of labour of any person. Such a definition can comprehend a dispute as to whether an employer ought to have exercised his contractual right to terminate a particular employment or employments. Such dispute would clearly be 'connected with' the employment of the persons in question or with their non-employment. The fact that the termination of the employment or employments in question was lawful and for good and substantial reasons appears to me to be completely irrelevant once such termination led to a dispute as to whether the employer should have acted as he did. It is true that the definition of 'workmen' who may engage in a trade dispute is 'all persons employed in trade or industry.' In my view 'employed' here does not mean in actual present employment but rather refers to the occupation or way of life of those who are to be regarded as 'workmen.' Any other meaning could have the effect of withdrawing the protection of the Act from workmen by the simple device of dismissing them and this would have its maximum effect at a time of general unemployment. In *Ferguson* v. *O'Gorman* [1937] I.R. 620 Meredith J., in relation to the issue as to whether the defendants were competent to raise a trade dispute (an issue which was not involved in the hearing of the appeal in that case), said at p. 634 of the report:– 'A workman does not cease to be a workman because he has been dismissed and is out of employment or has been forced to take up other work.' I concur with this view. I have also had regard to the decisions in *R.* v. *National Arbitration Tribunal* [1947] 2 All E.R. 693 and *Wilkinson* v. *Barking Corporation* [1948] 1 K.B. 721. For these reasons I feel that the second submission put forward in support of this ground of appeal also fails.

The second ground of appeal put forward by the plaintiffs was based on the acceptance by all the unions concerned (including ITGWU of which the defendants are members) of the plaintiffs' proposals for the closing of their plant. These proposals were designed to ensure that the closing would be accepted by the unions as being in the circumstances unavoidable and that satisfactory monetary compensation would be paid to all employees. It was of course implicit in the proposals and in their acceptance by the unions that there would be no trade dispute and, of course, no picketing. The six-point proposal or statement from the plaintiffs which was accepted by the unions was a business-like document and had all the appearances of being intended to create legal relations between the unions which accepted and the plaintiffs who proposed. I would regard the agreement resulting from the acceptance of these proposals as being similar in effect to that dealt with in *Edwards* v. *Skyways Ltd.* [1964] 1 W.L.R. 349 and, there being nothing to suggest the contrary, in my view a valid contract was thereby created between these unions and the plaintiffs. However, this is not the point of this ground of appeal.

The plaintiffs' contention is that this valid enforceable agreement has the effect of binding the defendants who are all members of one of the unions involved. This submission must be considered in the light of the evidence, which was uncontradicted, that the defendants at all times opposed the conclusion of any agreement with regard to the closing of the plant and made it abundantly clear, both inside the union and to the plaintiffs, that they would not accept any agreement to this effect. I find it hard to accept that in such circumstances the defendants can be bound by an agreement which they have expressly repudiated and opposed. It seems to me that to hold them bound would be contrary to all principle. The only basis put forward for suggesting that they should be bound was that they did not resign and continued to be members of their union. The rules of the union were not put in evidence but I would find it very difficult to accept that membership of an association like a union could bind all members individually in respect of union contracts merely because such had been made by the union. I cannot accept for these reasons that this ground of appeal is well founded.

The next ground of appeal was to the effect that the Redundancy Payments Acts, 1967–1973, have the effect of amending the Trade Disputes Act, 1906, by necessary intendment so as to withdraw the protection of that Act from employees who became entitled to redundancy payment. This ground of appeal, having been opened in argument, was later abandoned and therefore it is not necessary for me to deal with it further.

The final ground of appeal was to the effect that the picketing of the plaintiffs' premises did not qualify for protection under s. 2 of the Act of 1906 because it was not done for any of the purposes set out in the section. In the course of the argument particular emphasis was laid on the use of the word 'merely' in the section, and it was suggested that in this case the motive behind the picketing was to prevent the winding up of the plaintiffs' operations and the consequent mothballing of the machinery. Reference was made to the judgment of Mr. Justice Henchy in *Becton Dickinson* v. *Lee* [1973] I.R. 1, 44 as indicating the importance to be attached to the word 'merely.' It seems to me that in this argument there is some confusion between the motive or reason for an action and the purpose or object to be obtained from the action if taken. First of all, the action which is protected by s. 2 of the Act of 1906 must be in contemplation or furtherance of a trade dispute. What motives inspire this trade dispute do not arise. If in furtherance of the dispute it is decided to picket, again the motive for such decision is irrelevant. What is relevant and, indeed, crucial is that those who attend to picket do so only for one or more of the purposes permitted by the section. If, for example, they picket in order to frighten or to intimidate, as may be established by the manner of picketing or the numbers involved, then such would not be lawful under the section. In this case it seems clear that the defendants were opposed at all times to the closing of the plant and to the conclusion of any orderly arrangement or settlement with the plaintiffs. Originally this was their dominant aim and this, of course, they failed to achieve.

However, the evidence suggests that the defendants' attitude eventually hardened into a bid to secure employment in the post-closure operations being carried on in the plant in the removal of raw materials, the moth-balling of machinery and the general security arrangements. The evidence shows that it was for this purpose that they conducted a sit-in on the premises and later a picket which is now under consideration. I am satisfied on the evidence that this picket is acting in furtherance of their disputed claim to employment. I am equally satisfied on the evidence that it merely has as its purpose the matters set out in s. 2 of the Act of 1906. For these reasons this ground of appeal also fails.

The result, in my view, is that this appeal by the plaintiffs fails and that the plaintiffs' action should be dismissed.

This case highlights the extent to which immunity for picketing is given by statute to small minorities of workmen regardless of the wishes of their fellow workmen, including their fellow trade unionists, and irrespective of how the picketing is calculated to damage the particular trade or industry or to conflict with the common good. Whether the degree of immunity for picketing granted by the law should be put on a more rational and just basis is something that might well merit consideration by those charged with the framing and enactment of our laws.

Henchy J.

I agree.

Griffin J.

I also agree with the judgment delivered by the Chief Justice.

Kenny J.

. . . The plaintiffs argued that there is not a 'trade dispute,' as defined in s. 5, sub-s. 3, of the Act of 1906, between the defendants and them because a trade dispute must relate to the employment or non-employment or the terms of employment of the defendants. They say that there cannot be a trade dispute as the trial judge found that the defendants had been validly dismissed. The definition of 'trade dispute' in s. 5, sub-s. 2, of the Act of 1906 is 'any dispute between employers and workmen, or between workmen and workmen, which is connected with the employment or non-employment, or the terms of the employment, or with the conditions of labour, of any person' and the word 'workmen' is defined as 'all persons employed in trade or industry, whether or not in the employment of the employer with whom a trade dispute arises.' The Act of 1906 was introduced to redeem an election pledge of the Liberal Party to overrule the decision of the House of Lords in *Taff Vale Railway* v. *Amalgamated Society of Railway Servants* [1901] A.C. 426, and there are many indications in it that it was hurriedly drafted and that its wording did not receive adequate consideration. Section 2 of the Act of 1906 authorises peaceful picketing and those who do this are not usually employed by anyone: in many cases the picket takes place because those picketing have been dismissed. I think that the word 'employed' in the definition of 'workmen' means 'engaged' and that the fact that those picketing have been validly dismissed does not have the consequence that there is not a trade dispute between the employers and them.

All the reported authorities except one support the view that an employee who has been validly dismissed is a workman for the purposes of the Act of 1906. In *Ferguson* v. *O'Gorman* [1937] I.R. 620 Meredith J., who was then a judge of the High Court, said at p. 634 of the report:– 'A workman does not cease to be a workman because he has been dismissed and is out of employment or has been forced to take up other work.' When giving the advice of the Privy Council in *Bird* v. *O'Neal* [1960] A.C. 907 Lord Tucker said at p. 925 of the report:– 'Their Lordships also agree with the trial judge's rejection of the submission that the lawful dismissal of a workman cannot be the subject of a trade dispute.' In *Quigley* v. *Beirne* [1955] I.R. 62 Dixon J. decided in the High Court that there was not a trade dispute because the employees had been lawfully dismissed but this Court reversed his judgment and held that there was although the men whose dismissal was the cause of the dispute were not employed by the employer. The only authority which supports the plaintiffs' argument is the passage in the judgment of Overend J. in *Doran* v. *Lennon* [1945] I.R. 315 which is quoted in the judgment of the Chief Justice. In my opinion the passage and, indeed, the decision itself were wrong and should not now be followed. Accordingly, I reject the argument that there was not a trade dispute because the defendants had been lawfully dismissed from their employment.

The defendants contended that the six-point statement and its acceptance by the unions did not constitute an enforceable agreement. An agreement between parties is enforceable by the law unless the agreement itself or the surrounding circumstances show that the parties did not intend to enter into legal relations (*Rose and Frank Co.* v. *J. R. Crompton and Bros. Ltd.* [1923] 2 K.B. 261) and reliance was placed on the decision of Lane J. in *Ford Motor Co. Ltd.* v. *A.E.F.* [1969] 2 Q.B. 303 where it was held that two collective agreements did not, having regard to their background, constitute a legally enforceable agreement. In *Edwards* v. *Skyways Ltd.* [1964] 1 W.L.R. 349 Megaw J. held that an agreement by the defendants to make *ex gratia* payments to their employees whom they were dismissing created an enforceable agreement. I have considerable doubts about the correctness of the decision in the *Ford Motor Company Case* [1969] 2 Q.B. 303 particularly as Lane J. did not say anything about the decision in *Edwards* v. *Skyways Ltd.* [1964] 1 W.L.R. 349 although it was cited to him. It seems to me that the six-point agreement was intended to create legal relations and was intended to be a contract between the plaintiffs and the unions engaged in the negotiations. I think that Megaw J. was right when he said that when an apparent agreement in relation to business relations is entered into, the onus on the party who asserts that it was not intended to have legal effect is a heavy one. In my opinion the six-point statement and its acceptance created a valid enforceable contract between the plaintiffs and the unions who took part in the negotiations.

The plaintiffs then argued that if the six-point statement and its acceptance by the unions created a contract the defendants, as members of the union, were bound by it because the majority of their co-members had accepted it. No authority to support this argument was cited and the rules of the union, which would show the authority of the majority, were not referred to or proved. I think that the contention is wrong in principle and that all the reported cases on this matter are against it. Membership of a corporate body or of an association does not have the consequence that every agreement made by that corporate body or association binds every member of it. None of the defendants are parties to the agreement and as they consistently opposed it, no question of their being bound by acquiescence can arise. In addition, there is the negative evidence against the contention provided by a section in the Industrial Relations Act, 1946. The two decisions that I have been able to find on this matter are against the plaintiffs' contention.

In *Holland* v. *London Society of Compositors* (1924) 40 T.L.R. 440 the plaintiff was a member of a provincial trade union which made an agreement with a London trade union that a member of the former union should, if he came to London, be admitted to membership of the latter union. The plaintiff was offered a position in London but was refused membership of the London union and, therefore, could not accept the position. He brought an action against the London union for a declaration that he was entitled to membership of it and for an injunction. The court decided that the agreement was made not between the plaintiff and the London union but between the two trade unions only and that, as the plaintiff was neither directly nor indirectly a party to it, the action failed. In *Young* v. *Canadian Northern Railway Co.* [1931] A.C. 83 the defendants had entered into an employment agreement with a trade union and the plaintiff sought to rely on the terms of it when he was dismissed by the defendants. The Privy Council held that, having regard to the terms and nature of the agreement, it did not constitute a contract between any individual employee and his employer. There is in addition the negative argument that the Oireachtas assumed in 1946 that an employment agreement to which a trade union was a party did not bind the individual members of it. Section 30, sub-s. 1, of the Industrial Relations Act, 1946, reads:–

'A registered employment agreement shall, so long as it continues to be registered, apply, for the purposes of this section, to every worker of the class, type or group to which it is expressed to apply, and his employer, notwithstanding that such worker or employer is not a party to the agreement or would not, apart from this subsection, be bound thereby.'

Therefore, I reject the plaintiffs' argument that the defendants are bound by the six-point agreement or that there is any contractual relationship between the plaintiffs and them.

The plaintiffs argued that the Redundancy Payments Acts, 1967–1973, recognised that employers might be compelled to dismiss employees as a result of economic or financial pressures and that, in providing for the payment of redundancy moneys, the Trade Disputes Act, 1906, was by necessary implication amended so as to withdraw the protection of that Act from employees who were entitled to redundancy payments under these Acts. When I was a judge of the High Court I rejected this contention in *Cunningham Brothers Ltd.* v. *Kelly and Others* (18th November, 1974) and I have not heard anything which has induced me to change my mind. It seems to me that the redundancy payments provided for by the Oireachtas are a minimum which the employer must pay, and that trade unions representing the redundant employees or the employees themselves are entitled to demand a sum greater than that provided for by the legislation. If this demand is refused, there is a trade dispute.

The plaintiffs' next contention was that the picketing was not protected by s. 2 of the Act of 1906 because the predominant motive of those picketing was not to obtain or communicate information or to persuade any person to work or abstain from working but was to compel the plaintiffs to re-open the factory. [*The judge referred to the provisions of s. 2, sub-s. 1, of the Act of 1906 and continued*] This section has presented judges with many difficulties of interpretation; for example, what is the force of the word 'merely'? If an employer dismisses all his staff without notice and they picket the premises with the predominant motive of being reinstated, I think everyone with or without a legal training would regard such a dispute as a trade dispute and would think that the employees were entitled to picket. Yet, if the predominant motive must be to peacefully obtain or communicate information or to peacefully persuade any person to work or abstain from working, the picket would not be protected by s. 2 of the Act of 1906 for the predominant motive would be the reinstatement of the employees. The power of a picket comes from the refusal of workmen employed by other employers, or the fellow employees of those picketing, to pass it unless they are directed to do so by their unions. It is thus an immensely powerful weapon which closes the business of those against whom it is used.

I think that s. 2 of the Act of 1906 is not dealing with the predominant motive of those picketing but with the aim to be achieved by the picketing. If the section had the meaning contended for by the plaintiffs it would have read:– 'It shall be lawful for one or more persons acting on their own behalf or on behalf of a trade union or of an individual employer or firm in contemplation or furtherance of a trade dispute to attend at or near a house or place where a person resides or works or carries on business or happens to be, for the purpose of peacefully obtaining or communicating information or of peacefully persuading any person to work or abstain from working.' The repetition of the word 'attend' in the words 'if they so attend' shows that the industrial weapon of picketing must be used for the purpose of peacefully obtaining or communicating information or peacefully persuading any person to work or abstain from working. It is not the predominant motive of those picketing which is relevant but the aim of the attending at or near a premises. In this case the purpose of attending as a picket at East Wall was and is to persuade peacefully persons not to work. While this may seem a very fine distinction, it is the only interpretation which gives meaning to the repetition of the word 'attend' in the section. The purpose of those picketing is not relevant to any question under s. 2 of the Act of 1906: what is to be looked at is the aim of attending at or near the premises.

We were referred to the decision of the House of Lords in *Hunt* v. *Broome* [1974] A.C. 587 but that case is of no assistance. In it the question was whether a person, who was a member of a picket, committed a criminal offence under the Highways Act, 1959, when in the course of picketing he stood in front of a lorry in order to persuade its driver not to go into a factory which was being picketed. The argument on behalf of the accused was that his right to persuade a person to work or abstain from working would be negatived if he could not speak to the lorry driver. That question has no relevance to this case.

It is singularly unfortunate that no questions whatever were directed to those members of the picket who gave evidence as to their motives and this Court must act on its conclusions drawn from the evidence given. It is admitted that the picket is peaceful and, in my opinion, those attending as a picket are doing so for the purpose of informing others that they are in dispute with the plaintiffs and persuading persons not to work with or for the plaintiffs.

Another argument advanced related to the effect of the provisions of s. 11, sub-s. 1, of the Trade Union Act, 1941. This Act was passed to provide for the licensing of bodies carrying on negotiations for fixing wages or other conditions of employment and to provide for the establishment of a tribunal which was to have power to restrict the rights of organising trade unions. This latter purpose, which was sought to be achieved by Part III of the Act, has been held by this Court to be unconstitutional: see *National Union of Railwaymen* v. *Sullivan* [1947] I.R. 77. The plaintiffs in this case argued that the meaning of the section was that persons could picket only if they represented authorised trade unions or were members or officials of one of them and were authorised by them to picket. This would mean that the section would have to be read:– 'and the members and officials of such trade unions as such.' They also argued that the section was an implied repeal of the words 'acting on their own behalf' in s. 2 of the Act of 1906. I do not accept either of these contentions. I think that the effect of s. 11 of the Act of 1941 is to confine the immunities given by ss. 2, 3 and 4 of the Act of 1906 to authorised trade unions and their officials and members. Membership of an authorised trade union is essential if the picket is to be lawful. Those who are not members of an authorised trade union cannot picket. As all the defendants are members of the union, s. 11 of the Act of 1941 does not make it unlawful for them to picket. Therefore, it is unnecessary to consider whether s. 11 is repugnant to the Constitution and I expressly reserve this point for future consideration.

A faint-hearted attempt was made to invoke the principle decided in the *Educational Company of Ireland Ltd.* v. *Fitzpatrick (No. 2)* [1961] I.R. 345. The argument was that the majority of the members of the unions have a right to have the agreement implemented and that the defendants who are a minority are interfering with this right and, therefore, interfering with the right of association of the majority. The short answer is that the right of the majority of the union employed by the plaintiffs was to receive the sums provided for in the six-point agreement. The evidence shows that they have received these payments and, therefore, their rights are not interfered with in any way.

It follows, in my opinion, that this appeal fails and should be dismissed. I reach this conclusion with considerable reluctance. During the two years before the 30th July, 1976, the plaintiffs were suffering huge losses in their trading at East Wall and they decided to close the factory in Dublin after much anxious consideration and in order to end the losses. The terms under which the factory was closed were generous and were approved by the very responsible trade-union officials who saw that the closure of the factory in Dublin was inevitable. They were approved by a majority of the union members affected after a long and bitter debate. The picketing of the factory is without economic sense. If industrial chaos is to be avoided, the authority of trade-union officials and of majority resolutions of unions must be upheld. Section 30 of the Industrial Relations Act, 1946, makes a registered employment agreement binding on all the members of the union which negotiated it. If a similar provision had been passed making all agreements made by trade unions with employers and approved by a majority of their members binding on all the members, the picketing in this case would be contrary to law. I think that the Minister for Labour should give urgent attention to the introduction of legislation which will provide that any registered agreement made between employers and a union which is approved by a majority of the members of that union or, where the agreement relates to a worker employed by one employer, is approved by a majority of all the workers employed by that employer who are members of the union, should be binding on all the members of that union despite the fact that they are not parties to the agreement.

Parke J.

I agree that this appeal should be dismissed for the reasons expressed in the judgments already delivered. I derive no gratification in finding myself obliged to come to this conclusion because I believe that the result of this case may well cause concern to both employers and trade-union leaders who desire a well-ordered industrial society.

The Trade Disputes Act, 1906, was a child of political expediency, hastily conceived and prematurely delivered. It has now survived more than the allotted span of life with all its inbred imperfections still uncorrected. Indeed, I suspect that apart from such of those imperfections as have already become apparent others may yet be discovered by those of agile and ingenious mind. Those who caused it to be enacted believed that it would enable trade unions to make effective use of collective bargaining for the benefit of their members by putting into their hands the powerful weapon of peaceful picketing which could be used against employers with whom it was impossible to reach agreement by other means. It could hardly have been contemplated that this very weapon would be used by trade union members against an employer with whom their own union had entered into an agreement with the full support of the overwhelming majority of their fellow workers.

The defendants are a small minority of the large work force formerly employed by the plaintiffs in their factory at East Wall, Dublin. Upon the closure of that plant the leaders of all the trade unions involved engaged in lengthy negotiations with the plaintiffs in order to obtain the best possible redundancy payments for the benefit of their members. These negotiations appear to have been conducted on both sides in a highly responsible manner and the agreement which was ultimately reached can, I think, be described as very advantageous to the former employees. The plaintiffs had done the best they possibly could for their workers, and the trade-union negotiators could have felt considerable satisfaction in believing that their efforts had been rewarded by obtaining terms which were much to the benefit of their members, some of whom received almost £8,000 free of tax. That such a feeling was justified is demonstrated by the fact that the proposals were agreed to by the majority of the workers and honoured by all of the workers with the exception of the defendants. The defendants, however, have wholly disregarded the views of the majority of their fellow workers and have declined to accept the advice and instructions of those union officials who were elected under the rules of the union to which the defendants themselves subscribe.

Whatever may be the practical result of the defendants' actions, what they have done appears to be a defiance of the normal democratic procedures and to strike at the whole principle of orderly collective bargaining under the authority of properly elected union representatives. It is a step towards industrial chaos which must be deplored by all responsible leaders in industry whether they be representative of employers or employees. As the law now stands it is a step which this Court is powerless to restrain. It is the duty of this Court to interpret the law. The power of making new law or to amend those laws which already exist belongs to other constitutional organs of State.

Note

See generally Kerr, 'Trade Disputes Act 1906 – "Employment or Non-Employment" ' 74 Incorp. L. Soc. of Ireland Gazette 191 (1980).

Secondary Action

ELLIS V. WRIGHT
[1976] I.R. 8 (High Court, Butler, J., 1975)

Butler J.

The defendants are employees of William Ellis and Sons Limited and are members of the Irish Transport and General Workers' Union. They are in dispute with the company and are on strike; the strike is an official one. The business of the company is sand and gravel quarrying, the manufacture of general concrete products, general contracting, and the delivery of ground limestone; it acts as an agent for the supply and delivery of fertilizers. The company does not and never has engaged in farming and is not empowered to do so save as a convenient or necessary ancillary to its main business. The plaintiff is a director of the company and he works with it on a full-time basis and in a managerial capacity. The plaintiff's father is the managing director of the company and effectively controls it. Father and son hold or control the bulk of the shares in the company and they run what, in effect, is a family business. The offices and the principal depot of the company are at Ballyvolane where it also has a quarry. It has at least two other quarries – one at Carrigtwohill and another at Rafeen.

In the course of the dispute the union has placed pickets on all the company's premises. No question arises as to the legality of these pickets. The defendants, however, have picketed a farm at Castleview, Little Island, which is owned by the plaintiff. Placards and notices carried by them on that picket indicate that it is mounted as part of the industrial action against the company. The farm at Castleview comprises some 180 acres and is run mainly as a dairy-farm; there are 160 milch cows with an average daily output of 700 gallons of milk, and the milk is collected in a bulk tanker from Ballinahina Dairies. While there was a picket at the plaintiff's farm, the men driving the milk tanker would not pass the picket. As a result, the plaintiff was unable to dispose of his milk.

In these circumstances on the 16th April, 1975, the plaintiff issued proceedings and obtained from this court an interim injunction to restrain the defendants from picketing his farm on the grounds that no dispute exists between him and any of his employees on the farm; that no employee of the company works on or has any connection with the farm; and that the company does not own and has no connection with the farm or the business carried on there. That injunction still continues. The present application for the interlocutory injunction was heard on oral evidence and, by consent of the parties, it is to be treated as the trial of the action.

This is the background of the present proceedings. The additional facts which were established in evidence, and about which there is little (if any) dispute, are as follows. The farm at Castleview has never been owned by the company. It was originally the property of the plaintiff's father who transferred it to the plaintiff in the year 1970. The plaintiff also owns land at Carrigtwohill and at Ovens where he lives. In addition, by arrangement with the company, he has the use for agricultural purposes of a small area of land at Rafeen. This land is part of the holding which also comprises the company's quarry there. The work on all these lands is carried out by a farm steward, Mr. Rothwell, and by four other farm workers. This work force is based at and works from Castleview where Mr. Rothwell lives in the farmhouse. None of the farm workers are or ever have been employees of the company. While the farm business is entirely the plaintiff's both as to ownership of the lands, stock and effects and the profits, it is largely carried on by Mr. Rothwell under the general management of the plaintiff's father who regards it as his hobby. The plaintiff's father resides at Little Island in a house which is adjacent to but does not form part of the Castleview holding. The farming operations are highly mechanised and, except for seasonal and casual assistance which I next refer to in detail, the work is carried out by Mr. Rothwell and the other four employees.

The company provides services for the farm in the following ways.

(1) The plaintiff avails of the services of the company's P.A.Y.E. clerk to make up the farm employees' wages. The wages are calculated and the amounts put into pay envelopes in the company's office at Ballyvolane; they are then collected usually by the plaintiff's father and brought out to Castleview and paid. No charge is made by the company for this service which places only a very small additional burden on the wages clerk. The company is fully re-imbursed for the amount paid in wages in this way.

(2) When the farm requires additional or urgent haulage facilities (for example, at harvest or sowing time), lorries and drivers are provided by the company. Several of the defendants have done this work. This happens only very occasionally and the help is usually provided at week-ends or in the evening. The lorry drivers enter particulars of the work done on their time sheets or job sheets and it is charged by the company to the farm. This form of service is also provided by the company to other farmers though not as frequently or as regularly as to the plaintiff. When provided it is similarly priced and charged.

(3) Company lorries carry farm produce, such as beet and grain, when it is sold and they collect the beet pulp drawback from the sugar company factory. This work is similarly priced and charged.

(4) The company, as part of its business of agents for fertilizers, sells and delivers fertilizers to the farm. These are charged to the farm as to an ordinary customer.

(5) When it is necessary to employ outside assistance, maintenance and construction work on the farm is done by company employees. Such work is entered by the

men on their sheets and is charged to the farm.

(6) As part of its daily round, the company's pick-up truck, driven by a company employee, collects milk from Castleview and delivers it to the plaintiff's house at Ovens. The company is paid a fixed charge of £1 a day for this service.

(7) For some months in the year cattle are kept on the lands at Rafeen; during these periods they are looked after on a part-time basis by a quarry worker who is employed by the company at that quarry. Three hours a day of his wages is charged to the farm for this work.

On the other hand the farm occasionally lends tractors to the company and the company is debited with their hire.

Apart from the services of the company's P.A.Y.E. clerk in relation to wages, the company is paid for all these services when accounts are furnished; the payments are made by the plaintiff's father sometimes in cash and sometimes by cheques. These cheques were originally drawn on the private account of one or other of the plaintiff's family but, before the present dispute arose, a separate bank account was opened to deal with the farm business; this account is in the plaintiff's name, and cheques drawn on it can be signed either by the plaintiff or by his father.

The plaintiff's father lends money informally to the company from time to time so as to maintain its liquid cash position. This cash is represented in the company's books as a credit balance in favour of the plaintiff's father; part of it comes from his private monies and part from the farm account. The money due to the company by the farm in respect of wages paid to the farm workers is set off from time to time against this credit.

In these circumstances, the defendants were under the impression, not unnaturally, that the farm business was an ancillary to the company's business, since they knew nothing of the ownership of the farm or of the private financial arrangements between the plaintiff's father and the plaintiff. As is clear from their affidavits, part of the defendants' justification for picketing the farm was that belief. However, I think it clear that, although the farm was able to call on the services of the company with less formality than an ordinary customer could, the services provided by the company were asked for and given on a hireage or contract basis and they were dealt with and paid for as such. I am satisfied that the businesses are distinct and separate in ownership and operation. Consequently, the question of the right of the defendants to picket the farm cannot be considered from the point of view that the company carries on business at Castleview or, as has been submitted, that the businesses are interlocked.

However, this finding is not sufficient to render the picketing unlawful. The provisions of s. 2 of the Trade Disputes Act, 1906, render lawful the peaceful picketing of any place where 'a person' resides or works or carries on business or happens to be, if the picketing is in contemplation or furtherance of a trade dispute and if the picket is merely for the purpose of obtaining or communicating information or of peacefully persuading any person to work or abstain from working. Furthermore, s. 3 of the Act of 1906 provides inter alia that an action done in contemplation or furtherance of a trade dispute shall not be actionable on the ground only that it interferes with the trade or business of some other person; while s. 5, in defining 'trade dispute,' provides that 'workmen' means all persons employed in trade or industry whether or not in the employment of the employer with whom a trade dispute arises. It has repeatedly been noted that these provisions are designedly and necessarily wide. They justify sympathetic and possibly even general strikes and associated actions, and they justify consequential picketing. Their effect is summarised conveniently for my purpose by Dixon J. in *The Roundabout Ltd.* v. *Beirne*

[1959] I.R. 423 where he says at pp. 428–9 of the report:–

'The practical effect of that definition is that, if a trade dispute arises between workmen and employers in one premises, it might, and in most cases would, be permissible for the workmen . . . to picket entirely different premises owned or occupied by a totally different employer. It is an everyday feature of trade disputes that the dispute does not exist with the particular employer who is being picketed; the object of that provision of the Trades Disputes Act is to legalise sympathetic or consequential picketing.'

I am not unmindful of the implications of this interpretation of the statutory right to picket, though I do not accept Mr. Costello's submission that it necessarily legalises the most disruptive and indiscriminate picketing. The fundamental requirement to render a picket lawful is that it must be in contemplation or further-ance of a trade dispute. That necessitates a clearly discernible connection between the premises picketed and the dispute in the sense that the employer (or the workman) affected by the picket is directly concerned with the dispute. Without seeking to define the limits of such connection, I may say that I find it here in the controlling interest that the plaintiff and his father have in the company.

The plaintiff is the owner of the farm business and it is managed to a considerable extent by his father. Between them they effectively control the company and are in a position to concede or negotiate on the defendants' claim in their dispute with the company. Any influence or persuasion that can be brought to bear on the plaintiff and his father is conducive to a satisfactory resolution of the dispute. The picket on Castleview is thus clearly action in furtherance of a trade dispute; the plaintiff is an employer and carries on business at Castleview and, accordingly, in my view the picket is lawful.

If I am incorrect in this reasoning and conclusion I am of opinion that there is a more tenuous though nonetheless valid basis on which the present picket can be justified. A picket is lawful if one of its objects is to persuade any person to work or abstain from working. This provision has been interpreted as allowing a picket to be placed in the course of a strike on any place where employees of the employer with whom the dispute exists attend in the course of their employment, whether such employees are on strike or not. The driver of the company's pick-up truck attends daily as part of his duties to collect the milk from the plaintiff's farm at Castleview. It is clearly necessary for the effectiveness of the strike that he abstains from working. In so far as the picket on Castleview is apt to that end it is, in my opinion, justified by the provisions of s. 2 of the Act of 1906.

For these reasons I must refuse the present application and discharge the interim injunction.

CLEARY V. COFFEY
Unreported, High Court, McWilliam, J., 30 October 1979 (1979–6480P)

McWilliam J.:

The plaintiff is one of the executors of the last will of Alice Connolly, deceased, who died on 3rd April 1979. Alice Connolly was the owner of licensed premises known as The Refuge, Malahide Road, Dublin of off-licence premises at No. 1, Millmount Terrace, Drumcondra. By her will she gave the off-licence premises to her manager, Patrick Sheehy, and gave the remainder of her estate, including the licensed premises at Malahide Road, amongst a number of her relations to whom the plaintiff was one and thereby became entitled to a one twelfth share of the property comprising the residuary estate.

It was necessary to sell the licensed premises at Malahide Road for the purposes of the administration of the estate and the nine employees at these premises were given notice of the termination of their employment there on 24th August 1979. These employees were paid the full redundancy payments to which they were entitled but they also claimed and continue to claim to be entitled to further payments under the heading of 'Disturbance Claims Payments'. It is alleged that such payments are always made in the licensed trade over and above the statutory redundancy payments.

The plaintiff is the owner of licensed premises at 53, Sarsfield Road, Inchicore. It is not suggested that there is now or ever has been any business association between these premises and the premises owned by Alice Connolly. These proceedings have been brought to restrain the defendants from picketing her premises at 53, Sarsfield Road, Inchicore.

Although the claim in the plenary summons and this application for an interlocutory injunction relate only to the premises at 53, Sarsfield Road, the case has been presented on behalf of the plaintiff that there is no trade dispute with regard to any of the premises or between the employees and the owners of any of the premises. I cannot accept this contention. It appears to me to be clear that there is a trade dispute between the employees of the late Alice Connolly and her successors in title whether the claim by the employees is sustainable under their contracts of employment or is reasonable on other grounds or not. A dispute does not cease to be a trade dispute within the meaning of the Trade Disputes Act, 1906 merely because the claim by the employees appears to be unreasonable. A 'trade dispute' within the meaning of the Act is 'any dispute between employers and workmen, . . . which is connected with the employment or non-employment or the terms of the employment, or with the conditions of labour, of any person.' This dispute is between employers and workmen and is connected with the terms of the employment of the employees of the late Alice Connolly. The employees are claiming that, in the licensed trade, on the termination of employment employees are entitled to substantially more than the statutory redundancy payments. This claim may or may not be correct, but it appears to me that it constitutes a trade dispute within the meaning of the Act.

This, however, does not conclude the matter. As it appears to me I have two questions to decide. The first is whether the personal representative of a deceased person is so identified with a dispute relating to the business of his deceased that the employees of the deceased are entitled to picket the premises of such personal representative. The second is whether one of numerous residuary legatees of a deceased is sufficiently identified with such a dispute as to be legally subject to such picketing.

These are very difficult questions and I have not been referred to any authorities relating to either of them. To take an extreme instance, which must regularly arise on the first question, a solicitor or a bank may be appointed to be the executor or the owner of a business who disposed of his estate in such a manner that it was necessary for the proper administration of the estate that the business should be sold. Are the employees who allege a breach of the conditions of their employment as a result of that sale entitled to picket the offices of the solicitor who is executor or all or any of the branches of the bank so appointed, in addition to the premises in which the deceased carried on business? Similarly, with regard to one of several residuary legatees who is given no interest in the business of the deceased and, because of his small share in the residue, has no control over the disposal of the business.

I have been referred to the case of *Ellis* v. *Wright* [1976] I.R. 8. In that case Butler, J., said, at p. 13, 'The fundamental requirement to render a picket lawful is that it must be in contemplation or furtherance of a trade dispute. That necessitates a clearly discernible connection between the premises picketed and the dispute in the sense that the employer (or the workman) affected by the picket is directly concerned with the dispute.' I referred to this passage in my judgment in the case of *Bradbury* v. *Duffy & Whelan* earlier this year. It appeared to me then, on the authority of *Barton* v. *Harten* [1925] I.R. 37, that a 'clearly discernible connection' is not always sufficient to justify industrial action in the context of non-employment and that there must be something more than a mere 'clearly discernible connection' to justify it although I was not then and have not now been referred to any principle as to how this 'something more' should be ascertained. I would, however, emphasise the expression 'directly concerned' in the judgment of Butler, J. In the *Bradbury* case I came to the conclusion that, in the absence of any guidance, it is left to the Court to decide, on the facts of each case, whether the connection is sufficiently close. Although that case was one in which I had to decide whether there was a trade dispute or not and I did there decide that there was a trade dispute within the meaning of the Act, the principle appears to me to apply to the resolution of the two questions I have mentioned, notwithstanding that I have already decided that there is a trade dispute.

In the present case, the fact that the Plaintiff is engaged in the same kind of business appears to me to be irrelevant. It has not been alleged that there is or at any time was any business connection between the premises of the deceased and those of the Plaintiff. Nor has it been alleged that the Plaintiff at any time carried on business in the premises of the deceased or took over any of the stock-in-trade of the deceased. All that she has done is to realise the assets of the deceased in order to administer the estate according to law. She has not been given any beneficial interest in the business as such. She has merely been given a small interest in the residue of the estate; which is quite a different thing. Although there is a clearly discernible connection between the Plaintiff and the dispute, it seems to me that the connection is not sufficiently close to justify picketing of her premises as there is no feature which associates the Plaintiff with the dispute in any way other than as personal representative of the deceased and as being entitled to a small share in the residue of the estate of the deceased.

Accordingly, I will accede to the application of the Plaintiff for an interlocutory injunction restraining picketing of her premises at 53, Sarsfield Road, Inchicore, pending the hearing of the action, upon the usual terms as to damages.

Note

See generally Kerr, 'In Contemplation or Furtherance of a Trade Dispute . . .' [1979–80] D.U.L.J. 59, at 82–87.

Chapter 19

TRESPASS TO LAND

The tort of trespass to land consists of intentionally or negligently entering on, or directly causing anything to come into contact with, land in the possession of another, without lawful justification. The most frequent justification will, of course, be that the entrant has been permitted by the occupier to come onto the property, whether for consideration or gratuitously. On occasion, of course, it may be difficult to determine the precise scope of his permission: see, e.g., *Rudd* v. *Rea* [1921] 1 I.R. 223 (Powell, J.). Where an entrant abuses the terms of the permission to be on the property, does he become a trespasser? Clearly he does where the person who has invited him onto the property becomes aware of this abuse and requests him to leave. But what is the position where the abuse remains a secret? And does the status of an entrant change where, having entered the property in good faith, he subsequently forms a secret intention to abuse the terms of the invitation? These questions were raised by Walsh J. in *Purtill* v. *Athlone U.D.C.* [1968] I.R. 205, at 210 (Sup. Ct.). In several English cases these have been discussed: see J. Smith, *The Law of Theft*, 172–174 (4th ed., 1979); E. Griew, *The Theft Acts 1968 and 1978*, 63–64 (3rd ed., 1978).

The right to entry onto property may be conferred by statute. Thus, for example, factory and health inspectors may enter premises ensuring the humane slaughter of animals or seeking the prevention of oil pollution. Whereas using the highway for the purposes of picketing might be a trespass, section 2(1) or the *Trade Disputes Act 1906* renders lawful attendance 'at or near' a house or place where a person resides or carries on business, if those attending there are acting in contemplation or furtherance of a trade dispute or are there merely for the purpose of peacefully obtaining or communicating information, or of peacefully persuading any person to work or abstain from working. This provision has been interpreted as rendering lawful picketing on the highway, as opposed to on the premises of another: *Larkin* v. *Belfast Harbour Commissioners* [1908] 2 I.R. 214; *McCusker* v. *Smith* [1918] 2 I.R. 432; *Ferguson* v. *O'Gorman* [1937] I.R. 620 (Sup. Ct.); *Ryan* v. *Cooke* [1938] I.R. 512 (High Ct., Johnston, J.).

Acts Amounting to an Intention to Assume Possession

HEGAN V. CAROLAN
[1916] 2 I.R. 27 (K.B.Div., Pim, J., 1915)

The plaintiff's predecessor in title let a field in conacre to the defendant for the season ending on 1 November 1914. The plaintiff bought the field in April 1915. The defendant continued to keep his cattle on the field, in spite of the plaintiff's protests. On 22 July 1915 two of the plaintiff's workmen, on his instructions, entered the field and cut down a tree. Two days later the plaintiff broke a lock which the defendant had put on the gate of the field, and put his own cattle on the field, but almost immediately the defendant drove them away. The defendant remained in occupation of the field. The plaintiff sued him for trespass to land.

Pim J.:

. . . What (if anything) took place between April and July is not very clear; but no evidence sufficient to establish a deliberate attempt to assume possession was given. On the 22nd July, however, the plaintiff did an act which cannot be passed over as of no importance. On that day he and his servant, or servants, entered on the field of Anny, and cut down some trees. This fact is admitted by the son of the defendant himself. That was an act which was consistent only with a determination to assert a claim to possession. Again, on the 24th July the plaintiff broke the lock on the gate of the field, and entered and put his own cattle there. The cattle were almost immediately afterwards driven off by the defendant; but for a short period of time they were there. Since then the plaintiff has done nothing which could be construed into an assumption of possession, and the defendant has remained on in occupation. What I have to decide is, were the acts of the 22nd and 24th July sufficient to give the plaintiff such possession as the law requires in order to enable him to maintain an action for trespass? The law, as propounded by [counsel for the defendant], is incontrovertible, viz., there must be actual possession before an action of trespass can be brought. Now, how can actual possession be acquired? It cannot be necessary for one who is asserting his rights to walk over every inch of a field. That would be absurd. All that is necessary is that he should do some act from which it may reasonably be inferred that he claimed the whole, and intended to assert his right to the whole. I need only refer to three authorities – *Butcher* v. *Butcher* 7 B. & C. 399, *Jones* v. *Chapman* 2 Ex. 803, and *Lows* v. *Telford* 1 A.C. 414. In *Butcher* v. *Butcher* 7 B. & C. 399, Lord Tenterden C.J. says (at p. 402): 'if he who has the right to land enters and takes possession, he may maintain trespass. It is not necessary that the party who makes the entry should declare that he enters to take possession; it is sufficient if he does any act to show his intention. Here his servants ploughed the land. It is manifest, therefore, that he intended to take possession.' In the case I am trying the plaintiff on one occasion entered and cut down some trees, and on another broke the lock of the gate, entered into the field, and put his cattle thereon. Is it not manifest from these acts that he intended to take possession, and entered and did the acts in assertion of his right? In *Jones* v. *Chapman* 2 Ex. 803, Maule J. lays down the law with great clearness. 'I agree,' he says, at p. 820, 'with the exception of the plaintiff in error, that the question raised by the issue of "Not Possessed" is, whether the plaintiff was in *actual possession* or not; but it seems to me that, as soon as a person is entitled to possession, and enters in the assertion of that possession, or, which is exactly the same thing, any other person enters by command of that lawful owner, so entitled to possession, the law immediately vests the actual possession in the person who has so entered. If there are two persons in a field, each asserting that the field is his, and each doing some act in the assertion of the right of possession, I answer, the person who has the title is in actual possession, and the other person is a trespasser.' If that is so, how can the presence of cattle belonging to the person disputing the right (assuming they were there) affect the matter, if the presence of the person himself who asserts the right does not? The law as laid down by Maule J. was quoted with approval by Lord Selborne in the case of *Lows* v. *Telford* 1 A.C. 414, at p. 426, and he adds: 'And in *Harvey* v. *Brydges* 14 M. & W. 442, it is pointed out that so far as relates to the fact of possession and its legal consequences, it makes no difference whether it has been taken by the legal owner forcibly or not.' I am constrained, by the evidence, to hold that the plaintiff intended to assume possession on the 22nd and 24th of July, and that he did the acts proved in the assertion of his rights; and, by the cases, to hold that the plaintiff thereby obtained actual possession of the field, and that consequently trespass will lie; and I give judgment for him with £2 damages.

Notes and Questions

1. Is the requirement of possession fair or sensible?
2. It will not normally be a defence for a person sued for trespass to land to show that the plaintiff has no right to possession of the land in question, because the right (*jus*) rests in a third party (*tertii*). But where the defendant has entered the land with the authority of the person with the true right to possession he will have a good defence. What policy lies behind this rule? Is it defensible?
3. In *Clarke* v. *Midland Great Western Railway Co.*, [1895] 2 I.R. 294, at 304–305 (Q. B. Div., 1893), Holmes J., stated:

   'Concurrently . . . with the rule that only one action is permitted for one wrong, there is the principle that if a trespass or the interference with a right is continuous in its character, it is regarded as a succession of wrongs, for which action after action may be brought as long as the trespass or interference continues. Continuous torts are simple enough in theory, but it is not always easy to distinguish them for practical purposes. A man builds a wall on another's land. This is a continuing trespass, and a judgment against the wrongdoer will not be a bar to a second action, if the wall is permitted to remain. On the other hand, a man digs a hole or cuts down a tree on another's land, and only one action can be brought. So, too, a house is built or altered in such a way as to interfere with the access of light through the ancient windows of a neighbouring house; this is a continuing wrong, and there may be a succession of actions until the obstruction is taken away. On the other hand, where the removal of a house deprives an adjoining house of the support to which it is entitled, damages must be sued for once for all. What is the principle that underlies these distinctions? It cannot depend upon the nature of the injury sustained, or upon the fact that such injury is of a continuing character. The right to enjoy one's land free from the incumbrance of a wall does not differ in kind from the right to enjoy it free from the inconvenience of a hole. The element of continuity must, I think, be looked for not in the right interrupted by in the acts that cause the interruption. Where a man commits a trespass by placing something upon another's land, it is reasonable to regard him as responsible for its continuance until he takes away what is in its nature removable, or until the owner of the lands by refusing him permission to remove it adopts what has been done. But a tree cut down is gone forever. Compensation can be made for it, but it cannot be brought back. So, too, in the case of an excavation; it may no doubt be filled up, but not so as to make the excavated place what it was before. An equivalent can be given, but restoration, strictly speaking, is impossible. The distinction I have suggested will be found to accord with ordinary thought and language. We naturally think and speak of the man who has built a wall as keeping the wall where he had placed it. He has taken possession of certain land by building on it, and he retains possession of it as long as the building is allowed to stand. No such idea attaches to the person who makes an excavation or cuts down a tree. He may retain for his own use, or otherwise dispose of, the matter excavated, or the timber, but his trespass on the lands ceases when the act is done. So, too, in the case of interference with the easements to which I have referred. We speak of the wrongdoer as obstructing the access of light and air as long as the obstruction continues, but once the support to which an adjoining house is entitled has been removed, the injury is described in the past tense.

   For these reasons, I think the true test of whether the tort is continuing or not is whether the act of trespass or interference is in its nature continuing, and not whether the consequences of such an act continue to be felt. I admit that it is often difficult to apply the test to individual cases . . .'

   The difficulty in applying the test to individual cases, mentioned by Holmes J. was evident in *Clarke's* case itself, where there was a two-two split in the Queen's Bench Division, the Court of Appeal holding unanimously in favour of the plaintiff.
4. There has been no recent Irish decision on the limits of the scope of the action for trespass to airspace. In England, in *Bernstein of Leigh (Baron)* v. *Skyviews & General Ltd.* [1977] Q.B. 479, at 488 (Q.B.D.) Griffiths, J. stated that such infringement may constitute an actionable trespass, at all events, up to 'such height as is necessary for the ordinary use and enjoyment of [one's] land and the structures upon it.' Is this the best approach? The flight of aircraft is subject to statutory provision: *cf. Air Navigation and Transport Act 1936*, section 55 (No. 40).
5. Where parties share grazing rights in common, an action for overstint rather than trespass may lie: cf. *O'Connor* v. *O'Connor* 114 I.L.T.R. 63 (Judge Wellwood, 1976).

Chapter 20

NUISANCE

Nuisance in tort law consists essentially of the unreasonable interference with another person in the exercise of his or her rights generally arising from or connected with the occupation or use of land. The action traces its origin to mediaeval times, yet it displays continuing vitality, being capable of adjustment to contemporary notions of ecological balance and the control of pollution.

A nuisance may be either a *public* nuisance or a *private* nuisance. Each will be considered in turn.

PUBLIC NUISANCE

A public nuisance is a crime, the essence of which is injury to the reasonable convenience of the public or a section of the public. Obstructing the highway or placing dangers upon it are examples of public nuisance, but other disparate activities, such as keeping a common gaming-house or holding a pop festival that generates an excessive degree of noise, may also be held to be public nuisances.

Where the public or some section of it is injured by a public nuisance, the general rule is that only the Attorney-General may take civil proceedings. But where a person has suffered 'particular' or 'special' damage over and above that suffered by other members of the public, he may take civil proceedings.

BOYD V. THE GREAT NORTHERN RAILWAY CO.
[1895] 2 I.R. 556 (Ex. Div.)

Andrews J.:

We have not had the advantage of hearing counsel for the Railway Company, who have not appeared on the argument of this case; but having regard to the findings of fact by Mr. Justice Gibson, I feel no difficulty in deciding the question he reserved for the opinion of the Court, viz. whether on the facts proved the defendants are liable to the plaintiff in this action. The Railway Company are not entitled either under the 47th sect. of the Railways Clauses Consolidation Act, 1845, or any other enactment to obstruct the public highway, which they obtained power to cross on a level, for a longer period than is reasonably necessary for their own authorised purposes, and the protection of the public using the highway; and even without any such expression of judicial opinion as is to be found in the case of *Wyatt* v. *The Great Western Railway Company* 6 B. & S. 709; 34 L. J., Q. B. 204, I should have been quite prepared to hold the defendants liable in the present case. By the findings the only two material questions of fact are affirmatively determined, viz. whether the defendants on the occasion in question unreasonably and unnecessarily obstructed the highway, and if so, whether the plaintiff suffered thereby some appreciable damage peculiar to himself beyond that suffered by other members of the public ordinarily using the highway. The learned Judge has found that an actual delay of twenty minutes was occasioned by the defendants, not by any necessity arising from their traffic or otherwise, and that the delay was unreasonable, and the result of negligence on the part of the defendants. He has also found that the plaintiff is a medical man, in very large practice, whose time was of pecuniary value, and that he had sustained personal pecuniary damage from the delay of twenty minutes, which the learned Judge estimated at ten shillings. Everything, therefore, which is necessary in point of law to entitle the plaintiff to recover damages in this action, has been established in point of fact, and our answer to the question reserved for our opinion must be that on the facts proved the defendants are liable to the plaintiff.

The learned Judge will, upon our decision being communicated to him, reverse the dismiss, and give the plaintiff a decree for ten shillings, with such costs as he shall think it proper to award, and we shall order the defendants to pay to the plaintiff £10 for the costs of the argument before us.

Murphy J. concurred.

Notes and Questions

1. See also *Smith* v. *Wilson* [1903] 2 I.R. 45 (K.B.Div., 1902), in which the requirement of proof by the plaintiff of particular damage is exhaustively analysed.
2. If I pollute a bay and commercial fishermen lose their livelihood as a result, have they suffered 'particular' damage such as will enable them to sue me for public nuisance? *Cf. Hickey* v. *Electric Reduction of Canada* 21 D.L.R. (3d) 368 (1970); *Union Oil* v. *Oppen* 501 F. 2d 558 (9 C.A., 1974). See also *Hanna* v. *McKibben* [1940] N.I. (K.B. Div., Murphy L.J.).
3. Do you think that the requirement of proof of particular damage is a sensible one?
4. Another decision on public nuisance included in the casebook is *Cunningham* v. *MacGrath Bros., supra*, pp. 6–9.

PRIVATE NUISANCE

Private nuisance 'is really a field of tortious liability rather than a single type of tortious conduct: the feature which gives it unity is the interest invaded – that of the use and enjoyment of land' (*Salmond*, p. 48). The dimensions of the tort have changed over the years, the trend being to expand the scope of liability in terms of who may sue and who may be sued, but contracting its scope so far as the standard of liability is concerned – here the trend is towards aligning nuisance with negligence.

A private nuisance is not generally actionable *per se*, and actual damage must be proved. The damage may consist of either (a) physical injury to land, (b) a substantial interference with the enjoyment of land, or (c) an interference with servitudes. The last of these categories overlaps with the mainstream of property law and will not be discussed in this chapter.

(a) *Physical injury to land*

Physical injury to land constituting a nuisance may result from blasting, vibrations, noise, dust, fumes or sewage, or from the encroachment of tree branches or roots, for example.

Whether personal injuries come within the scope of private nuisance is not clear. This is because the tort of nuisance (like negligence) is in a state of development and what was formerly outside its scope is not necessarily so today. Historically, since nuisance is a tort based on injury to the use of property, it was not invoked where personal injuries were sustained except in cases where the injuries were the incidental consequence of some clear interference with the use of the property – as with illness caused by noxious gases from an adjoining factory, for example. On principle, compensation should be due for personal injuries to the same extent as for other injuries.

PATTERSON V. MURPHY
Unreported High Ct., Costello J., 4 May 1978 (1977 – No.6215P)

Costello J.:

The plaintiffs herein instituted proceedings for damages and injunction arising out of alleged acts of nuisance for which they claimed the defendants were responsible. They sought interlocutory relief and on the hearing of their motion a date was fixed for the trial of the action . . .

The plaintiffs married in 1967. Both are, by profession, musicians, Mr. Patterson being a singer and Mrs. Patterson a pianist and harpist. They lived in Paris between 1967 and 1971. In 1971 they returned to Ireland, renting a cottage in Brittas, County Dublin. They liked the area and sought somewhere in it where they could settle permanently. Late in 1972 Mr. Patterson found Shillelagh Lodge. It was a small two-storeyed house, very old and in a dilapidated and run-down condition, but it ideally suited his requirements and the plaintiffs decided to purchase it and renovate it. It was situated in a very beautiful part of the countryside, and some distance from the main road. Access to it was by means of a narrow laneway. It was purchased in April 1973, along with 5 acres of land and a right-of-way up the laneway. The Pattersons did a lot of renovation work to the house, and built on a music room and moved into their new home in the month of September 1973.

The laneway ends beside the entrance to Shillelagh Lodge at an old gateway which leads into a field (which, for ease of reference I will refer to as the 'quarry field'). This field is a little over 4 acres in area. Mr. Patterson took a walk in it before buying his new home, and he noticed that some of the top soil had been scraped away leaving areas of broken rock and shale. He said (and I accept his evidence) that the total area involved was approximately 25 yards square and the rest of the field appeared to consist of rough grazing and heather. He took the precaution of inspecting the Planning Register in the County Council offices and found that no permission to use the field as a quarry had been given but that permission to erect a dwelling on the other side of the lane existed. In fact the plot of ground opposite Shillelagh Lodge had been purchased by Mr. O'Sullivan who, not long after the Pattersons' purchase built a bungalow for himself (which is now known as Aughfarrel) which he moved into after his marriage in September 1974.

The owner of Shillelagh Lodge, and Aughfarrel, had been Mrs. Murphy. She also owns the quarry field, the land over which the laneway runs and other land in the vicinity amounting in all to over 100 acres. Her home is lower down the lane closer to the main road. She is now a remarkable old lady of 91 who, as a child, was brought up in Shillelagh Lodge. Her husband, for many years, farmed the land and also carried on a sand and gravel business until he got into ill-health in the year 1964. Thereafter her son, Michael Murphy, has managed the family business and the farm and, in fact, all the negotiations in relation to the sale of the property and the dealings relating to the quarry field were conducted by Mrs. Murphy's son on her behalf. Not surprisingly, Mrs Murphy's recollection of events is infirm, and the principal evidence in the case was given by her son. Some time in the month of August or September 1973 Mr. and Mrs. Patterson called on Mrs. Murphy. As they were shortly to be neighbours they wanted to introduce themselves to Mrs. Murphy and also raise with her the question of the gates on the lane. At that time there were two gates on the laneway and Mr. Patterson hoped that an arrangement to keep them open could be made. In the course of the conversation Mr. Patterson was told that a 'big quarry' was to be operated in the quarry field. This was the first he learnt of this possibility. I should make it clear that I do not accept the suggestion that he had been told about this possible development by Mr. Michael Murphy at or about the time he had effected the purchase some months previously. I think, however, that it is probable that Mr. Michael Murphy was not in his mother's home when the Pattersons called to see her.

The possibility that a quarry might be opened up in the adjoining field came closer to reality in the month of July 1974. An explosion then took place in the field and a considerable quantity of rock was displaced. Mr. Patterson went to his solicitor and to the County Council offices and, no doubt as a result of his representations, a Notice to Cease Development dated the 25th September 1974 was served on Mr. Murphy. The Notice stated that the 'use of lands as a quarry' was being carried out without a grant of permission under the relevant Act and was unauthorised development. For approximately four weeks after the blast rock was removed by means of lorries but thereafter the situation reverted to the normally peaceful conditions which had existed prior to July. What those conditions were I will examine in greater detail later. But a new development and a most startling one from the Pattersons' point of view occurred in the early summer of 1977. Large items of equipment and vehicles were brought up the laneway by the second-named defendants. Blasting rock on an extensive and regular basis commenced. Crushing equipment was used to reduce the size of the rocks, to produce 4 inch stones and a very considerable volume of traffic of heavy lorries commenced. In fact, quarrying operations on a considerable commercial scale had begun.

The plaintiffs claim that they have been subjected to a nuisance as a result of the quarrying operations carried on in the adjoining quarry field and by virtue of the traffic on the laneway and they seek damages and relief by way of Injunction.

Acts of Nuisance

I should begin my examination of the nuisance claim by considering a submission of the second-named defendant. It is this. In ascertaining whether the noise, vibration and dust complained of in these proceedings amounts in law to a nuisance it is submitted that the standard of comfort to be applied is that of the ordinary and reasonable man in the locality in which the plaintiffs reside (see *Salmond on Torts* 17th edition, p. 56); that as the plaintiffs came to reside in what was termed a 'mining area' the standard of comfort to which they are entitled is less than would apply in an ordinary rural area; that by applying the proper standards no nuisance has been established. In connection with this submission evidence was adduced both as to the nature of the locality in which Shillelagh Lodge was situated and, also, the user of the quarry field adjoining the plaintiffs' home. From the evidence I find the following facts:–

1. Shillelagh Lodge is in fact situated on a hillside. It is surrounded by fields which are used for coarse grazing. The quarry field itself was covered to a considerable extent by heather. To the west of the field a large state forest commences. On the lane way close to Murphy's house there was a gravel pit and further away beside the main road there was a larger gravel pit formerly operated by Messrs. Roadstone. At the time of the plaintiffs' purchase, this gravel pit had been worked out. About three quarters of a mile from Shillelagh Lodge there was a quarry known as Tracey's Quarry from which stone was extracted. The environs of Shillelagh Lodge are well illustrated in the fine panoramic photographs taken by Dr. O'Rahilly.

2. Later I will examine the use of the quarry field prior to October 1964. For the purposes of this part of the case I find that from 1964 to 1969 the quarry field was used very intermittently by Mr. Murphy to obtain shale. For this purpose a mechanical shovel was used to scrape the top of the soil and to put the shale into lorries.

3. The quarry field was more intensively worked by a Mr. Mansfield in the year 1969 (not the year 1970 as he thought). Mr. Mansfield entered into an agreement with Mr. Murphy and as a result of this he was given permission to take shale. He did this by using a Caterpillar bulldozer. He worked the field only for some weeks. During this time the bulldozer scraped to a depth of between seven to ten feet in portions of the field. When Mr. Mansfield left the field the area exploited was that as subsequently seen by the plaintiff and described by him in evidence.

4. After Mr. Mansfield vacated the field it was, again, only used very intermittently for the purpose of obtaining shale. It was, in fact, let from time to time by Mr. Murphy for sheep grazing. Mrs. Nocter (who moved into a house on the lane way in the year 1972) was in a good position to describe how the lane way and the quarry field were used. I accept her evidence (and that of Mr. Leavy junior who grazed sheep on an adjoining field) to the effect that the lane way and the quarry field were very little used in the years from 1972. It is true that Mr. Murphy produced in evidence tenders for the years subsequent to 1969 which he said had been accepted by the Dublin County Council for the supply of shale. But these documents did not establish the amount of shale he actually supplied or from where it was obtained.

I conclude, therefore, that the existence of the gravel pits and the quarry some distance away from Shillelagh Lodge and the use actually made by the defendant of the quarry field do not reduce the standard of comfort to which the plaintiff was entitled when he purchased his new home. The standard to which he was entitled and which I should apply in considering the nuisance claim is that which an ordinary reasonable person would expect whose home was on a country lane in an area used for normal and common agricultural purposes.

The new developments which occurred from about the middle of 1977 were these. In the month of May of that year Mr. Murphy and Mr. Daragh, the Managing Director of 'Trading Services' (the second-named defendant) entered into an oral agreement about the use of the quarry field. Mr. Daragh wrote out a Memorandum of the agreement, part of which reads – 'permission to install crusher screeners and conveyors and necessary equipment for the purpose of manufacturing stone'. Not long after their agreement Trading Services brought into the quarry field a large crushing plant, a Parker Screening plant, an excavator, two dumpers, a loading shovel, a compressor and a drill. Basically, the operations which Trading Services began were these. From time to time large quantities of rock were blasted by means of explosives. The blasted rock was loaded by the excavator into a dumper. The dumper transferred the rock into a hopper at the rear of the crusher. The material travelled by conveyor belt (having been crushed in the crushing machine) to the screening plant. The crushed stones fell from the screening plant into a hopper and the four inch stones were loaded into lorries and taken away. As stated in the written memorandum the object of the operations was the manufacture of these stones. It appears that between twelve and twenty men were employed in the operations, and that they began at 8 o'clock in the morning and finished at 5.30 p.m. Large 30 ton lorries were used to take away the stone, and these, naturally, were driven up and down the laneway close to the plaintiffs' house. The intensity of the traffic varied. Sometimes lorries came in convoys of four and five and on some days more than eighty lorries would pass by the plaintiffs' entrance. The evidence establishes to my satisfaction that from the middle of 1977 until after the institution of the present proceedings the operations carried on in the quarry field were extensive and intense. To obtain the raw material for the manufacture of stone blasting occurred on the 26th July, the 8th August, the 15th September, the 28th September, the 11th October, the 20th

October, the 8th December. By arrangement made in the course of these proceedings a further blast occurred on the 30th March of the present year. The total amount of explosives used in each blast varied. On the 30th March last a total charge was 1130 pounds; whilst on the 8th August 1977 well over 2000 pounds were used. Blasting took place at distances from 500 feet from the plaintiffs' house to about 675 feet or thereabouts. The rock face of the quarry is now 10 to 12 metres high at its highest point. The crusher is about 175 yards from the house.

I have heard evidence from Mr. and Mrs. Patterson and Mr. and Mrs. O'Sullivan as to the effect of the operations which I have described. I have no hesitation in accepting their evidence. Each gave their testimony without exaggeration, with care for accuracy, and conscientiously. None could be regarded as being in any way abnormally sensitive. Turning, firstly to the allegation relating to noise and dust, I accept that the noise from the operations in the quarry field was continuous and loud and calculated to fray the nerves of any normal person. The noise came from the plant, including the crushing plant which was used continuously; it came from the movement of the rocks and stones as they were shifted in the different parts of the operation which I have described. I accept that the noise became so intolerable that Mrs. Patterson was forced to leave her home and live elsewhere and that, similarly, Mrs. O'Sullivan was driven from her home by it. Equally, I accept that serious nuisance from dust was created by the operations in the quarry field. The level of dust, naturally, varied according to the climatic conditions but I accept the evidence that on some occasions the dust could actually be felt on the face; that it created a film over the house and gardens; that it was such as to require windows to be kept closed, and prohibited Mr. and Mrs. Pattison from sitting in their garden.

Apart from the noise and dust emanating from the quarry field the evidence establishes to my satisfaction that further acts of nuisance were occasioned by the lorries travelling to and from the quarry field. The laneway was unmetalled and in fine weather very considerable dust came into the plaintiffs' house and garden both from the loads being carried on the lorries but principally from the surface of the laneway. In addition the size of the lorries and the frequency of the journeys created an excessive amount of noise. In wet conditions the laneway became a morass and almost impassable on occasions, and the laying of stones from the quarry on the laneway proved an ineffective remedy.

I find, accordingly, that the plaintiffs have established acts of nuisance to a serious degree arising from the emanation of noise and dust from the quarry field and from the emanation of noise and dust from the laneway. I will now turn to deal with the allegations relating to the blasting operations.

The evidence satisfies me that if delayed detonators had been used in the blasting operations no physical damage to the plaintiffs' house would have occurred. Unfortunately, on the 29th September when Mr. Daragh personally supervised the blasting operation delayed detonators were not used. A very considerable amount of explosives were used on that occasion and physical damage was, I am quite satisfied, caused to the plaintiffs' house by the blast set off on that day. I will now examine the claim arising out of this damage.

The blast of the 29th of September was a very severe one. The window of the living-room was shattered, and part of an old boundary wall was knocked down. Mr. Patterson gave evidence of cracking appearing on the interior walls of the house which was not there before the blast and Mr. Purcell, the well known architect, described these cracks as he saw them on his visit on the 3rd of October. I am quite satisfied that the cracks described by Mr. Purcell were caused by the explosion on the 29th September. A further explosion took place on the 11th of October and Mr.

Purcell visited the premises on the 14th of October and described three additional cracks which he then saw. Although it does appear that in all probability delayed detonators were used for the 11th of October explosion, I am satisfied that, on the balance of probabilities, the extra cracks seen on that day were produced by the combined effect [of] explosions carried out in the quarry field. Mr. Purcell again examined the house after the 30th March explosions. Some of the cracks had increased in width and length and for the first time he noticed external cracks. These external cracks (which he described in detail) were not present when he examined the premises in October. Controversy exists as to whether or not they were old cracks unassociated with the explosions. I am satisfied that the plaintiffs have discharged the onus which is on them of establishing that, on the balance of probabilities, all the cracks described by Mr. Purcell were attributable to vibration from explosion and not otherwise. I am, however, not satisfied that the explosions caused any damage to the plaintiffs' chimney as has been alleged. It had been imperfectly constructed and had, in fact, given trouble long before the plaintiffs purchased the premises. Cracks in walls can of course, be serious or insignificant. In this case, none of the cracks are in any way serious; and they are, indeed, difficult to see. The blasting has not affected the structure of the premises. In sum, the physical damage to the house was, fortunately, small.

I will now consider the other aspects of the claim arising from the blasting operations. The blast on the 29th of September occurred in the afternoon. Mrs. Patterson was lying down (she was then expecting a baby) and had actually gone to sleep. She was awoken by a very loud explosion which actually threw her up into the air and causing her to hit her head at the head-rest of the bed. She thought a bomb had gone off. She found the living-room in chaos and the couch (on which normally she would have been resting) was covered in glass from the blown-in window. Her first reaction was anger at what had been done and she immediately went down to the quarry to see someone in charge. Later she got a severe pain in her chest and she then started to worry that she might have a miscarriage. The experience was, I am quite satisfied, a very frightening one. She was present on subsequent occasions when blasting took place. She found them very frightening and she is now of the view that she could not stay in the house if she thought any future explosions would take place.

The evidence establishes to my satisfaction that if delayed detonators had been used no physical damage would have been caused to the premises. But the blasting constituted an actionable interference with the enjoyment by the Plaintiffs of their home. The evidence further satisfies me that if blasting operations were continued with the volume of charges employed by Trading Services as heretofore their effect would be in the future to cause material discomfort to the plaintiffs' enjoyment of their premises both by the noise involved and the nervous strain associated with the explosives.

As to consequential loss, the plaintiffs left Shillelagh Lodge on the 12th of December 1977 and rented a house at 6 Firhouse Grove, Tallaght. This is a semi-detached house and because of its proximity to other dwelling-houses Mr. Patterson was unable to practise his singing and prepare for concerts in the way he had been able to do at Shillelagh Lodge. The rent has been £90 per month. I appreciate that Mrs. Patterson was expecting her baby at the end of December but I am quite satisfied that the plaintiffs would not have left Shillelagh Lodge but for the nuisance of which they complain. They were, in effect, driven out of their home. In this connection it is relevant to observe that Mr. and Mrs. O'Sullivan were likewise driven from their home and I am satisfied that they, too, were not displaying any exaggerated degree of sensitivity in acting as they did. A case for consequential damage has been, without doubt, established.

I should add that even if a lower standard of comfort, as urged on behalf of the defendants, were to be applied, the conditions produced by the operations I have described fell far short of the standards which an ordinary reasonable person would expect to enjoy in the sort of 'mining area' invisaged by the defendant's counsel.

Defendants' Liability

I now turn to consider the liability of the defendants for the wrongful acts which I have found occurred. I have already referred to the fact that an agreement was entered into between Mr. Murphy and Mr. Daragh in the month of May 1977. It was an oral agreement and the written memorandum made at the time by Mr. Daragh faithfully records its terms. The parties agreed that Trading Services would take a 'lease' of the field which I have termed the 'quarry field' for three years with an option to renew. It was expressly agreed that permission was given to them 'to install crusher screeners and conveyors and necessary equipment for the purpose of manufacturing stone'. This provision clearly shows what was in the contemplation of the parties. Shale had been won from the field at irregular intervals over many years but Mr. Murphy, I am quite satisfied, had in mind throughout these years that sometime commercial quarrying and the manufacture of stone would take place in the field. For this purpose the machinery mentioned in the memorandum was required. In addition, of course, substantial blasting operations would have to be undertaken so that the rock would be produced from which the stone could be manufactured. In relation to the rock which had been blasted in 1974 the parties agreed at a price at which it would be sold. In relation to other rock a royalty was fixed which Mr. Murphy was to receive. It was also agreed that Mr. Murphy could himself collect material which had been produced by Trading Services and he would pay Trading Services for this 'half the price he can buy anywhere else'.

The first matter which arises from my consideration on this part of the case is the relationship created by the oral agreement to which I have referred. I am satisfied that the parties used the phrase 'lease' in their agreement and that they intended that the occupation by Trading Services of the field would be an exclusive one. I conclude that it was intended that the relationship of landlord and tenant would be created between the parties. No legal problem arises in relation to the liability of Trading Services once I have found that the operations carried on by them in the quarry field caused a nuisance; as occupiers of the field and creators of the nuisance they are liable. But is Mrs. Murphy concurrently liable with them? To answer this question I should refer, briefly, to three decisions relating to the liability of a landlord for nuisance caused by the act of his tenant.

The leading case on the subject is *Harris* v. *James* (1876) 45 L.J. Q.B. 545. In that case the landlord let a field for the purpose of it being worked as a lime quarry. The ordinary way of getting limestone was by means of blasting and the landlord authorised the quarrying of the stone and the erection of the lime kilns in the field. A nuisance was caused to the adjoining occupier by the blasting and by the smoke from the kilns and he took proceedings against the tenant and the landlord. It was held that the landlord was liable. In the course of his judgment Blackburn J. said;

'There can be no doubt that where a person authorises and requires another to commit a nuisance he is liable for that nuisance; and if the authority be given in the shape of a lease he is none the less liable. I do not think when a person demises property he is to be taken to authorise all that the occupier may do . . . In the present case, as I understand the averments, the field was let for the very purpose and object of being worked as a lime quarry and for erecting lime kilns and burning lime. When, then, it is stated as a fact that the injury complained of arose from the natural and necessary consequence of carrying out this object and as a result of lime getting and lime burning, then I think we must say that the landlord authorised the lime burning and the nuisance arising from it as being the necessary consequence of letting the field in the manner and with the objects described.'

In this country *Harris v. James* was followed by Mr. Justice Overend in *Goldfarb and Anor.* v. *Williams and Company Limited and Ors.* ([1945] I.R. 433). This was a case in which Messrs. Williams made a letting of the second floor of premises in Henry Street to the Trustees of a Social and Athletic Club. The landlords were aware that the club would use the premises inter alia for holding dances. The dances were conducted in a reasonable and normal manner but none the less noise was transmitted to the plaintiffs' overhead premises. It was held that the landlords were liable in nuisance as they had authorised the nuisance which was inevitable if the premises were used as intended. In the course of his judgment Mr. Justice Overend stated;

> 'As between the club and the lessors I am of opinion that, inasmuch as dancing was one of the purposes specifically mentioned during the negotiations, the club was entitled to use the premises for that purpose in a reasonable manner, notwithstanding the restrictive provision against causing nuisance or annoyance. I therefore think the lessors are responsible as having authorised such nuisance, which was inevitable if the premises were used as intended: *Harris* v. *James*'.

More recently, *Harris v. James* was considered in England in the case of *Smith* v. *Scott and Ors.* ([1973] 1 Ch. 314). One of the defendants was a local authority which had placed as tenants in the house adjoining that of the plaintiff a family known by the Corporation to be likely to cause a nuisance. The action against the Local Authority was dismissed, the Vice Chancellor holding that the Corporation were not liable for a nuisance committed by their tenants for they had neither expressly nor impliedly authorised the nuisance. In the course of the judgment it was pointed out that the person to be sued in nuisance is the occupier of the property from which the nuisance emanates; that in general a landlord is not liable for nuisance committed by his tenant; but to this rule there is a recognised exception, namely, that the landlord is laible if he authorised his tenant to commit the nuisance. It was stated that:

> 'This exception has, in the reported cases, been rigidly confined to circumstances in which the nuisance has either been expressly authorised or is certain to result from the purposes for which the property is let . . . I have used the word 'certain' but 'certainty' is obviously a very difficult matter to establish. It may be that, as one of the textbook suggests, the proper test in this connection is 'virtual certainty' which is another way of saying a very high degree of probability, but the authorities are not, I venture to think, altogether satisfactory in this respect.' (p. 321).

I think that I should follow the formulation of the principle as stated in *Harris* v. *James*. Accordingly for the plaintiff to succeed in these present proceedings against Mrs. Murphy I must firstly ascertain what was the purpose and object of the letting agreement with Trading Services (the creators of the nuisance) and secondly determine whether the injury complained of arose from the natural and necessary consequence of carrying out that object.

Dealing firstly with the nuisance emanating from the quarry field (otherwise than from blasting) I am satisfied that the object and purposes of the agreement between Mr. Murphy and Mr. Daragh was that stone would be manufactured. For this purpose rock would be blasted and then crushed on the site into stones of a predetermined size. I am satisfied that it was contemplated that this operation would be carried out on a considerable scale and by the aid of heavy machinery and plant. The natural consequences of these contemplated operations were that nuisance resulting from the noise and nuisance arising from dust would be caused and I conclude that Mrs. Murphy authorised these acts of nuisance by virtue of the agreement entered into on her behalf by Mr. Michael Murphy.

As to the allegation of nuisance created by blasting, it seems to me that the natural consequence of carrying out the object of the agreement was that blasting would occur at regular intervals and on a substantial scale. I do not think that it was a natural consequence of what was contemplated that damage to property would result as the evidence satisfies me that blasting could be performed (by the use of delayed detonators) without causing physical damage to property. It follows that Mrs. Murphy is not liable for the physical damage resulting from the explosion of the 29th of September and thereafter, nor is she liable for the frightening experience suffered by Mrs. Patterson on that day. But in my judgment it was a natural consequence of blasting on the scale contemplated that a substantial nuisance to the plaintiffs' enjoyment of their house would result by virtue of the noise, nervous strain and inconvenience thereby arising. For this aspect of the damage sustained by the plaintiffs from the nuisance from blasting Mrs. Murphy is liable.

Nuisance arising from the use of the lane way is in a somewhat different position. No letting was made by Mrs. Murphy of the lane way to Trading Services and the relationship of landlord and tenant did not exist between them in relation to it. But by implication, a right of way was granted to Trading Services over the lane way in respect of their own and their customers' lorries. It follows, therefore, that the acts of nuisance in relation to the lorries were authorised by Trading Services when they permitted the lorries to come to the quarry and take away loads of material. They were also authorised by Mrs. Murphy in granting Trading Services a right of way for this purpose. Both defendants, therefore, are liable in so far as the nuisance arises from the user of the lane way.

The Plaintiffs' remedies
(a) *Damages*
I will now deal with the damages recoverable by the plaintiffs.
(i) *Physical damage to property*
The plaintiffs' premises were damaged in the way I have described. Evidence has been given as to the cost of repairing the damage by Mr. Stapleton. The total figure, including repairing the internal and external cracks and redecoration, is £850. I approach the measure of damages by applying the principles set out by Mr. Justice Finlay in *Munnelly* v. *Calcon Ltd.* [1978] I.R. 387. In *Munnelly's Case* the Court was concerned with a claim arising from damage done to a house by the negligent removal of its support. One of the issues which had to be considered was whether damages should be based on the market value of the premises or on the cost of reinstatement. In the course of his judgment the learned President laid down certain general principles of law relating to the measure of damage when damage to property occurs. The following two are relevant to the present case;

> '(1) The owner of a building as distinct from the owner of a chattel is, when the building is damaged or destroyed by the tort of another, entitled by way of damages to the cost of repairing or restoring the building unless (a) the Court is satisfied that he has not got a bona fide intention of restoring or rebuilding the premises, in

which case he is entitled to the amount of the reduction in its value or, if destroyed, its original value, less any salvage, or (b) the Court is satisfied that for the Plaintiff to, repair or restore the building even though he might wish to do so is a failure on his part to take reasonable steps to mitigate his loss in that there is available to him an alternative method of reasonably restoring him to the position in which he was before the damage or destruction which imposes a less onerous burden on the defendant;

(2) Whilst the difference between the burden imposed upon the wrongdoer by a cost of repair or restoration and the alternative assessment on the basis of diminution in value or pre-accident market price is a factor and an important factor to be taken into consideration in arriving at a conclusion as to whether it is reasonable for the plaintiff to repair or rebuild it is not a determining factor. If the Court is satisfied that the only reasonable method of restoring the plaintiff's position is the repair or restoration required it should not deny him that by reason even of a substantial difference between that cost and the cost of the alternative method of assessing his compensation.'

Applying these principles to this case, I have come to the conclusion that it is not necessary for the plaintiffs to repair the cracks described by Mr. Purcell and that payment of damages based on the diminution in value of the house would adequately compensate them in respect of this injury. The diminution in value is obviously slight. No cause of action arises from the defect in the chimney. The plaintiffs are entitled to the cost of repairing the window and the cost of rebuilding the boundary wall. Whilst I have no direct figures as to the actual costs of these items I think I am entitled to measure a figure for them. Doing this and calculating the diminution in the value of the house I award the sum of £450 in respect of damage to property. This is payable by Trading Services alone to the plaintiffs as joint owners of the property.

(ii) *Cost of alternative accommodation*

The plaintiffs acted reasonably in seeking somewhere to live away from the nuisance of which they rightly complained. The rent of £90 per month which they had to pay is not an excessive one and this sum is recoverable from both defendants from the 12th of December last to the present time. I award £450 under this heading. I do not think that the costs of heating to which reference was made in the course of evidence have been established as a proper head of loss. The sum of £450 is payable by both defendants to the plaintiffs.

(iii) *Further consequential loss*

I accept Mr. Patterson's evidence that he had intended to carry out extensive additions to his home in the autumn of last year and I accept Mr. Stapleton's evidence that the cost now of doing the same work has increased by £1,567. A question arises, however, as to whether this loss is recoverable from the defendants. I do not think that it was necessary for the plaintiffs to have lived in the house when the additions were being made. Nor do I think that the nuisance was such as to prohibit Mr. Stapleton's workmen from doing the work. Mr. Patterson postponed the work, I am satisfied, because of the uncertainty arising about the plaintiffs' future use of the house arising from the nuisance and these proceedings. As a matter of law, is the loss which he thereby suffered recoverable from the defendants? It seems to me that it is not. The expenditure proposed could have been undertaken nothwithstanding the infringement of the plaintiffs' rights. The decision to postpone it was taken by the plaintiffs having regard to their own particular interest. But the plaintiffs must take reasonable steps to mitigate the loss to them resulting from the defendants' wrong, and I do not think that a plaintiff can say to a defendant, in effect: 'I am entitled to damages and an injunction, but in case I am not, I am postponing the additions to my house; you, of course, must pay the extra costs arising from the postponement if I win my case'. The loss which has resulted from the postponement of the expenditure in this case should in my view not fall on the defendants.

(iv) *Mrs. Patterson's Damages*

Mrs. Patterson suffered a very frightening and an extremely upsetting experience as a result of the blast of the 29th of September. I measure the damages which she suffered as a result at £100. This is payable by Trading Services to her alone.

(v) *General damages*

General damages are payable to each of the plaintiffs separately for annoyance, discomfort, inconvenience and mental distress. In measuring the sums payable I have taken into account not just the conditions at Shillelagh Lodge from the summer of last year until the 12th of December but also of the fact that the plaintiffs had to move to rented accommodation with all the inconvenience thereby resulting. Whilst it may be that Mrs. Patterson suffered more acutely than Mr. Patterson from the nuisance it must be borne in mind that Mr. Patterson had an additional strain associated with his professional career as he was most particularly affected by the lack of proper facilities for practice in the rented accommodation. I conclude that a sum of £500 should be paid to each under this general heading and that both defendants are jointly liable for these payments. I do not think that the plaintiffs' condition described in the medical evidence is attributable to the tort complained of.

The amount of damages for which the defendants are jointly liable under paragraphs (ii) and (v) is £1,450. Cross notices have been served by each defendant on the other claiming a contribution or indemnity under the provisions of the *Civil Liability Act 1961*. I will consider these issues at a later part of this judgment. Before doing so I will consider the plaintiffs' claim for relief by way of injunction.

(b) *Injunction*

The defendants have submitted that even if an infringement of the plaintiffs' rights has been established the Court has the discretion to award damages in lieu of an injunction and that it should do so in this case. I agree that relief by way of injunction is a discretionary remedy. There are, however, well established principles on which the Court exercises this discretion. The relevant ones for the purposes of this case can be summarised as follows:

1. When an infringement of the plaintiff's right and a threatened further infringement to a material extent has been established the plaintiff is prima facie entitled to an Injunction. There may be circumstances however, depriving the plaintiff of this prima facie right but generally speaking the plaintiff will only be deprived of an Injunction in very exceptional circumstances.
2. If the injury to the plaintiff's rights is small, and is one capable of being estimated in money, and is one which can be adequately compensated by a small money payment, and if the case is one in which it would be oppressive to the defendant to grant an Injunction, then these are circumstances in which damages in lieu of an Injunction may be granted.
3. The conduct of the plaintiff may be such as to disentitle him to an Injunction. The conduct of the defendant may be such as to disentitle him from seeking the substitution of damages for an Injunction.

4. The mere fact that a wrong-doer is able and willing to pay for the injury he has inflicted is not a ground for substituting damages. (See: *Shelfer* v. *City of London Electric Company* [1895] 1 Ch. 322; and *Kerr on Injunctions*, 6th Edition, 656, 657).

I was referred to the judgment of Mr. Justice Gannon in *Halpin* v. *Tara Mines Ltd* (unreported: 16 February 1976).It is, however, clear that was a case in which an injunction was refused because of the improved working standards employed subsequent to the plaintiffs'original complaint, and was not one of the substitution of damages for an injunction.

In the present case there are no circumstances which can deprive the plaintiffs of the relief to which they are prima facie entitled. The infringement of their rights is a most serious one; the injury which they have suffered and will suffer if the nuisance is permitted to continue has been and will be a considerable one; damages would not adequately compensate them. I should add that whilst I am conscious of the financial consequences for the defendants of the granting of an injunction I do not think, bearing in mind that the sale to the plaintiffs took place at a time when Mr. Murphy was aware of the possibility that quarrying operations in the adjoining field might take place, and bearing in mind that both defendants must have fully appreciated the great inconvenience to the plaintiffs which the quarrying operations would cause, that relief by way of an injunction could be termed oppressive.

In the course of Counsel's submissions I was referred to *Miller* v. *Jackson* ([1977] 1 Q.B. 966), a case in which the Plaintiff claimed an injunction to stop the playing of cricket. I do not think this is an authority which helps the defendants in the present case. The three Judges of the Court of Appeal took different views of the matter before them. Cummings-Bruce, L.J. took the view that the defendants were liable in negligence and nuisance to the plaintiffs but considered an injunction should not be granted, quoting with approval the following passage from Spry on 'Equitable Remedies' (1971 Ed. p. 365):

'. . . Where the plaintiff has prima facie a right to specific relief the Court of Equity will if occasion should arise weigh the disadvantage or hardship which he will suffer if relief were refused against any hardship or disadvantage which should be caused to third persons or to the public generally if relief were granted'.

He held (as did the Master of the Rolls) that it was in the public interest on the facts which he was considering that damages rather than an injunction should be granted. In the present case no question of any hardship or disadvantage to the public arises if an injunction is granted.

I will now turn to the defendants' second line of defence on this part of the case: to their submission that an injunction should not issue because the nuisance can be and will be remedied. It was clear from the evidence that serious consideration to remedial action was only given during the course of the hearing. It was unsupported by any professional opinion. As to the nuisance from noise from the quarry field, Mr. Daragh proposed moving the crusher and screening plant about seventy yards further away from the plaintiffs' house, lowering the hopper so that the distance which the material had to fall was reduced, putting rubber lining on the chute, and putting another silencer on the machine to reduce engine noise. I regret to say that I have no doubt that these measures would have at best only a marginal affect on the noise levels at the plaintiffs' house and I accept Mr. Tennyson's opinion in this regard that they would not abate the nuisance. I also accept his evidence on the proposals made to suppress the dust from the quarry field. Mr. Magee a director of a Northern

Ireland firm specialising in this work, gave evidence about a dust control system marketed by his firm. The system was based on the use of water to which a chemical wetting agent is added. The water is sprayed on to the material by means of nozzles attached to the machines. Spraying on waste material can be also undertaken. Whilst the system he proposed might be of assistance in reducing the level of dust to which the operatives at the site are exposed, I do not think that it would adequately deal with the nuisance in this case; In Mr. Tennyson's opinion (which I accept) the spraying techniques are not, in practice, satisfactory and in the present case would not be adequate to deal with the many sources from which dust escapes from the quarry field. As to the nuisance from the lane way, Mr. Daragh said that access to the quarry could be obtained by another route. No evidence was given by the Murphys in this connection and I am not satisfied that such an alternative route is feasible or readily available. Even if it was, however, in the absence of any undertaking to discontinue the present use of the lane way a proposal of an alternative route does not disentitle the plaintiffs to an injunction in relation to the present user of the lane way. It follows that the plaintiffs are entitled to injunctions to stop the nuisance complained of. I will make no order at present for a mandatory injunction as sought in paragraph (d) of the last paragraph of the Statement of Claim [requiring the lane way to be put in good and proper condition – *eds*.], but give liberty to apply in relation to it.

Contribution between the defendants
Each defendant has claimed against the other a contribution or indemnity under the *Civil Liability Act 1961*. By virtue of Section 21 the amount of the contribution recoverable from a contributor is such as is just and equitable having regard to the degree of the contributor's fault, and the contribution to be recovered may amount to a complete indemnity of the other wrong-doer. The Supreme Court in *Carroll* v. *Clare County Council* ([1975] I.R. 221) considered the meaning of Section 34 of the *Civil Liability Act 1961* by which, in the case of contributory negligence, the damages recoverable by the Plaintiff are to be reduced by such amount as 'the Court thinks just and equitable having regard to the degrees of fault of the plaintiff and the defendant'. It seems to me that I should interpret Section 21 of the Act in the same way as the Supreme Court interpreted Section 34. In the course of his judgment in *Carroll's Case* Mr. Justice Kenny pointed out that Section 34 did not require a reduction of damages by reference to degrees of *negligence* but by reference to degrees of *fault*, and, having referred to the Supreme Court's decision in *O'Sullivan* v. *Dwyer* [1971] I.R. 275) be said:–

'I think fault in Section 34 of the Act of 1961 means a departure from a norm by a person who, as a result of such departure, has been found to have been negligent and that 'degrees of fault' expresses the extent of his departure from the standard of behaviour to be expected from a reasonable man or woman in the circumstances. The extent of that departure is not to be measured by moral considerations, for to do so would introduce a subjective element while the true view is that the test is objective only. It is the blameworthiness, by reference to what a reasonable man or woman would have done in the circumstances, of the contribution of the plaintiff and defendant to the happening of the accident which is to be the basis of the apportionment.

Following this test I should consider the blameworthiness of the contribution which each defendant made to the damages which the plaintiffs suffered by reason of the acts complained of – the test of blameworthiness being an objective one and applied by reference to what a reasonable man or woman would have done in the circumstances of the present case. Approaching the problem this way I conclude as follows. Trading Services actually committed the nuisance which emanated from the quarry field; they were in control of the operations and determined their intensity. Theirs is the major share of fault. But Mrs. Murphy authorised the nuisance (other than the nuisance resulting from the blast of the 29th of September) and must bear some blame. Both defendants authorised the nuisance which emanated from the lane way but the major blame must again attach to Trading Services who were responsible for the actual level of the activities from which the various nuisances resulted. I think the justice of this case would be met if I apportion damages which are jointly payable by the defendants on the basis that Trading Services bear 75% of them and Mrs. Murphy 25%.

Judgment will be entered accordingly on the findings I have made. . . .

Note

See also *Sampson* v. *Hodson – Pressinger* [1981] 3 All E.R. 710 (C.A.), noted by Owen, [1982] Camb. L.J. 38.

Notes and Questions

1. Do you agree with the Court's balancing of the respective interests of the parties in this case?
2. *Cf. New Imperial & Windsor Hotel Co. Ltd.* v. *Johnson*, [1912] 1 I.R. 327 (Barton, J.). Does this case imply that urban industrial and recreational proprietors have a virtual *carte blanche* to make noise, provided the purpose of their business is socially beneficial? *Cf. Polsue & Alferi Ltd.* v. *Rushmer* [1907] A.C. 121 (H.L. (Eng.)); *Crump* v. *Lambert*, L.R. 3 Eq. 409 (Lord Romilly, M.R., 1867); *Dublin Corporation* v. *Sandyford Printers Ltd. & Healy Holdings Ltd.*, unreported, High Ct., Gannon, J. 26 July 1982, *Irish Times*, 27 July 1982, *Walsh* v. *Tedcastle McCormack & Co. Ltd.*, unreported, High Ct., Kenny, J., 23 June 1967 (1963–No. 1891P). For an excellent analysis of the policy issues, see Tromans, 'Nuisance – Prevention or Payment?' [1982] Camb. L. J. 87.
3. May residents of a middle-class suburb avail themselves of an action for nuisance if a smallpox hospital is built in their area? *Cf. A.G. (Boswell)* v. *Rathmines & Pembroke Joint Hospital Board* [1904] 1 I.R. 161 (C.A., 1904 rev'g Chatterton, V.C., 1903); *Earl of Pembroke & Montgomery* v. *Warren* [1896] 1 I.R. 76. May they obtain damages for the reduction in the value of their property. What about a gaol? Or a hostel or home for drug addicts or displaced persons? Is a Court action the proper forum for resolving these important social questions? Does our Constitution prevent segregation?
4. In *Earl of Pembroke & Montgomery* v. *Warren* [1896] I.R. 76, at 140, Walker L.J. said that 'what would be a nuisance . . . in Merrion-Square involves very different considerations from what would be a nuisance – say at the North Wall.' Is this a defensible proposition?
5. Where noise or other disturbance results from malice rather than necessity, the courts have shown scant sympathy for attempted rationalisations by defendants: *cf. Christie* v. *Davey* [1893] 1 Ch. 316 (North J., 1892); *Hollywood Silver Fox Farm Ltd.* v. *Emmett*, [1936] 1 All E.R. 825 (K.B.D., MacNoughton, J.):

MULLIN V. HYNES
Unreported, Supreme Court, 13 November 1972 (46–1969)

Henchy J.:

The plaintiffs, Mr. and Mrs. Mullin, live with their son in a three-bedroom bungalow at the edge of the town of Templemore, Co. Tipperary. Up to 1961 the road in question could be described as entirely residential. Behind the house were green fields and across the road were the grounds of the Garda Síochána Training Centre. The plaintiffs, therefore, enjoyed the degree of tranquility that can be expected in a dormitory area on the fringe of a town the size of Templemore.

About the year 1961 the defendant built and opened up next door to the plaintiffs' bungalow the 'Las Vegas' ballroom. This is a dance hall with floor space for 1,000 dancers and having a concrete forecourt with space for some 50 parked cars. The defendant, as licensee of the hall, became entitled to hold a dance every Sunday and Church Holidays from 9 p.m. until 1 a.m. The effect of the introduction of these dances into this quiet road was what one might expect: the peace of the night was shattered by the sounds emanating from the hall – the amplified drums, wind instruments, electronic guitars, announcers and singers – and the revving of engines, slamming of doors, loud talk and the other noises that were made on the nights of dances until about 2.30 a.m. by departing dancers.

The principal sufferers were the plaintiffs. Unfortunately, the hall was designed and sited with little regard for the fact that the plaintiffs' bungalow was next door, and the south side of the hall, from which a considerable amount of noise escaped, was only a short distance from the north bedroom of the bungalow, in which Mrs. Mullin slept. To make matters worse, Mrs. Mullin is a semi-invalid, having been operated on for a colostomy about ten years ago and therefore having to suffer the permanent physical disability that such a drastic surgical process entails. She was particularly badly affected by the noise, since her bedroom was nearest to the hall, but sleep was also disrupted in the other two bedrooms, in which her husband and son slept.

It was not until May, 1964, that the plaintiffs complained that the degree of noise to which they were being subjected amounted to a nuisance which the defendant should abate. It is clear that not alone was the defendant unwilling to reduce the intrusive and disturbing noise but the plaintiffs' well-founded complaint was summarily brushed aside and the noise continued to invade the plaintiffs' house at a level of intensity that is now agreed to have been grossly excessive on the part of the defendant and intolerable to the plaintiffs. One particular unfortunate result of the defendant's tortious misconduct was that Mrs. Mullin, who as a semi-invalid and the occupier of the bedroom next to the hall was the principal sufferer, has had her nerves so shattered by the noise that she has been rendered hypersensitive to the point of being unable to tolerate even the reduced degree of noise that later emanated from the hall.

II

The plaintiffs commenced proceedings against the defendant on the 26th January, 1967, by a plenary summons claiming an injunction and damages for nuisance. The action came on for hearing in April, 1968, when Teevan J. granted a perpetual injunction restraining the defendant from running the dance hall 'in such a manner as to cause nuisance by noise emanating from the said dance hall to the plaintiffs or either of them or their successors or assigns as owners or occupiers' of the bungalow.' Execution on foot of that injunction was stayed for three months so as to give the defendant an opportunity of abating the nuisance.

Some work was done on the hall by the defendant with a view to reducing the noise to a tolerable level. The windows on the side of the hall facing the bungalow were blocked up, sound-absorbing material was introduced into the hall, a screen was placed at eave level along the wall of the hall facing the bungalow, and a second ceiling, made of softboard, was placed under the existing ceiling of the hall. The result was that the high-pitched sounds were largely eliminated, but the low-pitched sounds, particularly the throbbing rhythmical beat of amplified drums, bass instruments and electronic guitars, in the opinion of the plaintiffs, still penetrated the bungalow and were a continuing nuisance. The plaintiffs put down a notice of motion to have the defendant attached for contempt of the order granting the injunction. This application came on for hearing before Teevan J. on the 25th November, 1968, and after a six-day hearing he reserved judgment. On the 24th February, 1969, he gave judgment in which he held that, despite the ameliorative measures taken since the earlier hearing, the defendant had only partly abated the nuisance and was therefore in contempt of the injunction, but since the contempt was held not to have been deliberate, no penalty was imposed.

The matter now comes before this Court as an appeal by the defendant against so much of the order of Teevan J. as held the defendant to be continuing to cause a nuisance by noise emanating from the hall and to be therefore in contempt of the injunction restraining such noise. Counsel for the defendant reads the judgment of Teevan J. as holding that the type and degree of noise now emanating from inside the hall are only such as to affect a hypersensitive person, as Mrs. Mullin is admitted to be, so that the finding of a continuing nuisance was wrong in law. It is contended that on the authorities a nuisance could not be found unless the noise complained of were shown to affect someone other than Mrs. Mullin, who, it is agreed, is abnormally sensitive to noise coming from the hall. That is the essence of the case as argued by counsel for the appellant.

III

The private nuisance in respect of which the injunction was granted arose from the use by the defendant of his property so that noise was created to such a degree as to be a tortious interference with the plaintiffs' user of their property. In a claim for a private nuisance of this kind the judge has to act as an arbiter between the competing interests of the respective property users. He has to decide which is to prevail, the defendant's claim to use his property in the impugned manner or the plaintiff's claim to use his property free from the damage caused by the defendant. In the present case it is admitted that the trial judge was correct in holding at the time he granted the injunction that the noise caused by the defendant was such as to constitute a private nuisance and to warrant the granting of a perpetual injunction restraining it. But, say counsel for the defendant, the noise has now been so reduced that it affects only Mrs. Mullin in her present hypersensitive condition, and since on the authorities the present degree of noise can be held to be a nuisance only if it causes damage to an average person, the judge was wrong in law in holding the defendant to be in breach of the injunction, for the reason that Mrs. Mullin's inability to tolerate the reduced noise coming from the dance hall is not that of an average person.

The authorities cited in support of this proposition seem to be examples of the application of the maxim *de minimis non curat lex*. For example, in *Gaunt* v. *Fynney* (1982) L.R. 8 Ch. App. 8, at p. 13, Lord Selborne L.C. said: 'A nervous, or anxious, or propossessed listner hears sounds which would otherwise have passed unnoticed, and magnifies and exaggerates into some new significance, originating within himself, sounds which at other times would have been passively heard and not regarded.' And in *Walter* v. *Selfe* (1851) 4 De G. & Sm. 315, at p. 322 Knight Bruce V.–C. disposed of a claim for nuisance by posing the rhetorical question: 'Ought this inconvenience to be considered in fact as more than fanciful, more than one of mere delicacy or fastidiousness, as an inconvenience materially interfering with the ordinary comfort physically of human existence, not merely according to elegant or dainty modes and habits of living, but according to plain and sober and simple notions among the English people?' Such observations are but examples of the unwillingness of the courts to grant relief where the damage claimed is in respect of trivial, fanciful or exaggerated inconvenience. They do not enshrine any wider principle and, in particular, they are no warrant for the proposition that the dominant test is the tolerance of an average or reasonable or ordinary person of the inconvenience complained of.

Both counsel for the plaintiffs and counsel for the defendant accept that the broad test is that laid down by Lord Cooper in *Watt* v. *Jamieson* 1954 S.C. 56 at p. 57–8 where he says that 'the proper angle of approach to a case of alleged nuisance is rather from the standpoint of the victim of the loss or inconvenience than from the standpoint of the alleged offender. . . . The critical question is whether what he was exposed to was *plus quam tolerabile* when due weight has been given to all the surrounding circumstances of the offensive conduct and its effects.' For my part I consider that test to be a fair and sufficiently flexible basis for deciding in the present case whether the defendant's use of his property should be allowed to prevail over the inconvenience suffered by the plaintiffs. I must therefore look at the matter from the standpoint of these particular plaintiffs, not that of an ordinary or average user of a house.

IV

It is necessary first to see what was the basis of the decision of Teevan J. that the defendant was in breach of the injunction. Counsel for the defendant say that the sole reason for the finding against the defendant was that the judge held that the modified noise emanating from inside the hall is a substantial and continuing inconvenience to Mrs. Mullin in her present condition of abnormal sensitivity to noise from that quarter. Assuming that to be the sole foundation of the judgment, I must then test the correctness of the judgment by asking whether after due weight is given to all the circumstances, including the origin, nature, extent and effect of the noise complained of and the past and present conduct of the parties, the inconvenience now suffered by Mrs. Mullin is more than she should reasonably be expected to put up with.

The following facts seem to be established beyond question: this dance hall was designed and built in a residential area with scant regard for the fact that it would emit a considerable amount of noise; when the plaintiffs, as the chief sufferers from the noise, complained to the defendant, their well-founded complaint was spurned and they were subjected for a considerable period to a bombardment of noise that was a gross invasion of their rights as occupiers of their home; the result has been that Mrs. Mullin, who was not physically robust, has been so traumatically affected by the defendant's admittedly illegal conduct that she is unable to tolerate the reduced degree of noise that now comes from the hall, so that every Sunday night she suffers physically and psychologically from the noise and cannot sleep until the dance is over. Ought she therefore to be expected to put up with that discomfort on the ground that the noise she complains of is so reduced that it would be quite tolerable by a person of more normal sensitivity? It seems to me that an answer favourable to the defendant could be given only by not paying due regard to one of the crucial circumstances of the case: that Mrs. Mullin's present acute inability to cope with the reduced noise is the direct consequence of the defendant's earlier tortious misconduct in bombarding her with excessive noise over a long period. Because of this, she is not to be equated with the over-fastidious or over-sensitive plaintiff for whose idiosyncracy the defendant is in no way to blame. Since this defendant has unlawfully caused Mrs. Mullin to be unable to tolerate the reduced noise, it does not lie with him to say, as in effect he does say, that she must either put up with that noise, to the probable further detriment of her health, or else go to live elsewhere. If the judgment of Teevan J. rested solely on Mrs. Mullin's subjective complaints, I would be prepared to uphold his finding of a breach of the injunction.

However, since this was not the sole ground on which the judge decided the matter, the plaintiffs' case in this appeal is not thus limited. It is true that the greater part of the judgment is devoted to Mrs. Mullin's complaint of inability to sleep in her bedroom on the nights of dances, but reference is also made to the evidence of Mr. Mullin and the noise experts who gave evidence. Having quoted extensively from the evidence of Mr. Ward, the defendant's expert, the Judge said:

> 'This evidence supports Mr. McAteer [the plaintiffs' expert] in that the noise penetrating the house, although very much reduced from its former volume and intensity, is such as would prevent the plaintiff Mrs. Mullin from sleeping. (Mr. McAteer is also of opinion that while it would not awaken a person already asleep it would prevent the ordinary person from falling asleep).'

The evidence of Mr. Mullin, who recorded in his diary the degree of noise he found on different nights, is summed up in the answer he gave to Q. 424:

> 'The vocalists and the announcers are muffled and are (*sic*) the only effect of the recent measures they have taken. Before that, in my room, in any room, I was subject to this droning noise from the hall. I could say that I can now sleep in my room with the door closed but when the cars start they waken me. I have to put up with them, but I could not sleep in my wife's bedroom or the bedroom in the back – in the back room bedroom – nobody could sleep in either of those rooms.'

If that evidence was accepted by the judge, then it was not a question of an abnormally sensitive person being unable to sleep in one of the bedrooms; sleep was impossible for anybody in two of the three bedrooms. The judge concluded his judgment by dealing with Mr. Mullin's evidence as follows:

> 'In conclusion I must comment on the keeping of diary entries by the plaintiff Michael Mullin. No doubt these record the facts correctly but this whole idea is open to objection. If one is waiting with pen in hand, so to speak, for noises the latter will be heard in an exaggerated quality. What might have passed unnoticed will be noticed. The court may be concerned with two questions, the fact of the existence of the noise complained of and then if it is found to exist, its likely effect on the normal reasonable person. The evidence I refer to would be material to the first question but open to mislead on the second question: rather, perhaps, it tends to weaken the evidence of the complaining party on the latter question. On the other hand I suppose it might be said that witnesses for the defence might in like manner be affected the other way, subconsciously in search of the innocuous. In any case I think it natural that a person will be kept awake and disturbed by the sounds he has been waiting for and anticipating, which without such predisposition might have escaped him.'

I read that passage as holding, if not expressly then by necessary implication, that Mr. Mullin was correct in his evidence that the noise from the hall would prevent a normal person from sleeping in two of the three bedrooms. That being so, there was clearly a breach of the injunction and the judge was correct in finding the defendant to be in contempt.

I would accordingly dismiss the appeal.

ÓDálaigh C.J. and **Fitzgerald J.** concurred.

Note and Questions

1. Do you agree with this decision? Are there practical difficulties in accepting that a person rendered over-sensitive by the conduct of another should thereafter be able to require that that other conduct his business so as not to offend this over-sensitive condition? Should not such a principle have limitations?
2. See also *Connell* v. *Porter,* unreported, High Ct., Teevan, J., 21 December 1967 (1966–No. 1939P.)

Chapter 21

THE RULE IN RYLANDS V. FLETCHER

The rule in *Rylands* v. *Fletcher*, L.R. 3 H.L. 330 (1868), aff'g L.R. 1 Ex. 265 (1866), is a source of much controversy. As Prosser has stated: 'There are few cases upon which such magnificat edifices of theory have been erected, and few which in the process have been so sadly misunderstood', *The Principle of Rylands* v. *Fletcher*, Ch. 3 of W. Prosser, *Selected Topics in the Law of Torts*, at 135 (1954). The rule has given rise to very little reported litigation in Ireland. It is difficult to see why this should be: the volume of reported cases in regard to the related tort of nuisance, for example, is high. Moreover, the clash of rural and industrial values which the rule seeks to superintend is surely one that has been of continuing importance in this country.

The facts in *Rylands* v. *Fletcher,* briefly, were that the plaintiff was mining coal with the permission of the land-owner. The defendants obtained the same land-owner's permission to build a reservoir to supply water to their mill on his land. This work was done by independent contractors. The contractors negligently failed to discover that there was a disused shaft of a mine under the reservoir which communicated with the plaintiff's mine. In due course water from the reservoir broke into the shaft and flooded the plaintiff's mine.

The plaintiff in launching his action faced some formidable difficulties. The defendants had not been negligent (the arbitrator found). No trespass had been committed since the damage by flooding had not been a direct consequence of the defendants' activity. The defendants were not guilty of nuisance, since there had been a single escape; nor (at that time) would they be considered liable for the negligence of an independent contractor.

Liability was nonetheless imposed on the defendants. Blackburn J., in the Court of Exchequer Chamber stated:

> 'We think that the true rule of law is that the person who for his own purposes brings on his lands and collects and keeps there anything likely to do mischief if it escapes, must keep it in at his peril, and, if he does not do so, is *prima facie* answerable for all the damage which is the natural consequence of its escape.'

The House of Lords affirmed. Lord Cairns included in his judgment a passage that has caused some confusion in subsequent decisions:

> '[I] the defendants, not stopping at the natural use of their close, had desired to use it for any purpose which I may term a non-natural use for the purpose of introducing into the close that which in its natural condition was not in or upon it, for the purpose of introducing water either above or below ground in quantities and in a manner not the result or any work or operation on or under the land; and if in consequence of their doing so, or in consequence of any imperfection in the mode of their doing so, the water came to escape and pass off into the close of the plaintiff, then it appears to me that that which the defendants were doing they were doing at their own peril; and if in the course of their doing it the evil arose to which I have referred – the evil, namely, of the escape of the water and its passing away to the close of the plaintiff and injuring the plaintiff, then for the consequence of that, in my opinion, the defendants would be liable. . . .'

CONOLLY V. THE CONGESTED DISTRICT BOARDS FOR IRELAND
52 I.L.T.&Sol. J. 52 (County Court, Judge Wakely, 1917)

Wakely J.:

The facts of this case proved before me are as follows (there was very little dispute as to the facts):– About the spring of 1915 the defendants acquired a property at a place called Cloonerco, in this county; on this property there is a considerable amount of bog. And in particular there is a tract of bog, which is coloured blue and marked 'A' on the map which has been put in and proved and admitted by both parties to this case to be correct. This tract of bog has between it and the county road, to the south-east, a tract of low-lying land, consisting of cut-away bog and marsh. Then, on the other side of the county road, to the south-east, is land belonging to the plaintiff, and in respect of the flooding of which he brings this action. This latter land is coloured yellow on the map, and it forms part of the holding of the plaintiff, and the only part which has to do with this action. The watershed on this property acquired by the defendants changes at the pink line marked on map 'boundary of catchment.' From that pink line – going in a southerly and south-easterly direction – all the water goes south-east, and north of that pink line the water goes north, and with the latter water this case is not concerned. The water from the bog area coloured blue and marked 'A' on the map goes in a southerly and south-easterly direction towards the county road, and is carried under the county road by a rather small culvert at letter 'D' on the map, and thence by a drain across the plaintiff's lands in a south-easterly direction, and thence in the same direction into the Ballin-trillick River at 'E' on the map, passing through other lands on the way, between the plaintiff's lands and the river. The water is carried from the defendant's bog to the culvert under the county road at 'D' by a drain along the black line on the east of the defendant's bog and marsh land, and which I have marked 'P R' and continuing towards the culvert at 'D' it is more a depression in the marshy land than a defined made drain: drain 'P R' is old water course. The water is also carried to the culvert at 'D' from defendant's bog by a drain along the north side of the county road, and which drain I have marked 'S S' and it is an old water course also. In 1915 the defendants, in order to provide fuel for the tenants on this property and other properties 'belonging' to them in this district, commenced to make drains in the bog area 'A' (blue) on the map and to make and lay out turf banks. The plaintiff and his witnesses deposed that there was not much making of drains for these purposes in 1915, and that his land was not much flooded in that year. In 1916 the defendants, in order to provide more fuel for their tenants on this and other property of theirs in this neighbourhood, drained more of the bog 'A' marked blue on the map, and laid out more turf banks thereon, and their tenants cut turf on a large number of turf banks on this bog. In 1916 from 70 to 80 of such tenants cut turf on this bog. Mr. Chute, the engineer, examined for the plaintiffs, deposed that the defendants, between new drains made to drain the bog and so make the turf fit to be cut and used as fuel and new drains made by the actual cutting of the turf banks or bog holes, as they are called, made certainly three miles of new drains in this bog marked 'A' on the map and coloured blue, and this was not denied or disputed by the defendants. Mr. Chute also deposed that the defendants cleaned and improved and deepened several existing drains on the same bog, and this also was not disputed by the defendants. Mr. Chute and all the witnesses for the plaintiff admitted and deposed that the only water which got into and is carried by these new and improved and cleaned and deepened drains is water off this bog of the defendants and off the cutaway and marsh land of the defendants to the south and south-east of the bog, and that no water was or is brought into or on the plaintiff's land, but the water on this bog and land of the defendants, and which is produced by the rain which falls on the bog and land of the defendants. It was also proved before me that all these new drains made by the defendants were well and properly made, and that the drains improved, cleaned and deepened were well and properly done, and that these new drains and the cleaning, improving, and deepening of the existing drains were necessary in order (1) to make the turf fit to cut for fuel; and (2) in order to cut and save the turf as fuel, and this was not disputed by the plaintiff. It was proved on behalf of the plaintiff that all this drainage work on this bog by the defendants greatly increased the flow of water from this bog ('A') of the defendants to the culvert 'D' on map and into the drain across the plaintiff's land, and so that this drain, which is a small one and not deep, was quite incapable of carrying away all this water, especially at the time of turf cutting in the late spring and early summer of 1916, and that the consequence of this was that this extra water flowed over the banks of the drain and flooded the plaintiff's lands so that he could not cut or save any of the meadow on it. The defendants somewhat disputed this, and they also proved that 1916 was in this, as in many other districts, a very wet year, and that the plaintiff did not clean his drains, and that the land of the plaintiff and the land between it and the Ballintrillick River is marshy and very flat. But I find, as a juror, that, taking into consideration the heavy rainfall, the somewhat bad state of the plaintiff's drain, the marshy and flat nature of the plaintiff's land, and the land between it and the Ballintrillick River, the thing that caused the chief flooding to the plaintiff's land was this extra water coming from the defendants' bog 'A'. It was admitted that the Ballintrillick River is a mountain river which clears quickly after heavy rains, so that there would not be much backing up of water from flood in the river in the plaintiff's drain. The level of plaintiff's land at the culvert at 'D' on the map is about 14 inches below the flood level of the river at 'F' on the map, and it is about 18 inches above the normal level of the river at the same place. The plaintiff admitted that in 1907 this same land of his was flooded so that he could not cut or save the meadow on it, but he deposed that in that year there was a very heavy rainfall, and that the banks of the Ballintrillick River burst so that the water flooded all the lands and could not be carried away, and I believed him as to this. I also find as a juror that all the said drainage works done by the defendants were well and properly done and were done without negligence, and that there was no negligence on their part. I also find as a juror that all the said drainage works done by the defendants were necessary for, and were only done for, the purpose of providing turf as fuel for their said tenants. After allowing for the abnormally wet year, the somewhat bad and uncleaned state of the plaintiff's drain, and the marshy nature of his land I am of opinion that the damage measured in money done to the plaintiff by the extra water so brought to his land by the defendants' said drainage work is £12 in 1916. I also find as a juror that the water which so came to the plaintiff's land came only from the defendants' said bog, and that they did not bring on their said bog, or to the plaintiff's land, water from anywhere else, and I find that this water was caused by the rain which from time to time fell on the defendants' said bog 'A', and that it flowed naturally, by gravitation, to plaintiff's land. Mr. Carson, for the plaintiff, argued that the maxim *sic utere tuo ut alienum non laedas* applied, and that the defendants were liable because they flooded the plaintiff's land, and that negligence on their part was not necessary for his case.

Mr. Fetherstonhaugh argued that the defendants only used their bog for a purpose for which it might in the ordinary course of the enjoyment of land be used, that the bog was only used for the natural purpose of cutting and saving turf, that for that purpose these drainage works were necessary, that the defendants had not brought any water to their lands but only drained their land of water which from rain was on it, and that this water, by natural gravitation, had passed on to the plaintiff's land. Both counsel referred me to several authorities. As the case seemed of importance to both parties and to farmers all over the country and as it was intimated to me that there would be an appeal in any event, I reserved my decision from Sligo Easter Sessions to this Trinity Sessions at Sligo. First, I must note that in this case the defendants are in the position of an ordinary individual, and that there is no statute which protects them from liability or assists them in this case. I do note this, as there are several statutes relating to the Congested Districts Board and giving that Board various powers. Next, I think that to make the defendants liable it is not necessary to prove negligence on their part, nor even knowledge that their acts would cause damage. Lord Cranworth, in *Rylands* v. *Fletcher*, L. R. 3 H. L. 330, says, at p. 341:–

'In considering whether a defendant is liable to a plaintiff for damage which the plaintiff may have sustained, the question in general is not whether the defendant has acted with due care and caution, but whether his acts have occasioned the damage. This is all well explained in the old case of *Lambert* v. *Bessey*,' reported by 'Sir Thomas Raymond' (Sir T. Raymond 421). 'And the doctrine is founded on good sense. For when one person in managing his own affairs causes, however innocently, damage to another it is obviously only just that he should be the party to suffer. He is bound *sic ut tuo ut non laedat alienum*.'

In the case of *Rylands* v. *Fletcher* A. was a mine owner and had worked his mine up to a spot where there were vertical shafts and passages of old mines which communicated with the land above and had been out of use for years. B. was a mill owner of a mill standing on land adjoining that under which the mines were worked. B. constructed a reservoir on his land and over where these vertical shafts were, and his engineers did not block up these shafts. When water was brought into the reservoir it broke through these shafts and flooded A.'s mine, and A. was held entitled to recover damages from B. The headnote says:– 'Where the owner of land, without wilfulness or negligence, uses his land in the ordinary manner of its use, though mischief should thereby be occasioned to his neighbour, he will not be liable in damages. But if he brings upon his land anything which would not naturally come upon it and which is in itself dangerous and may become mischievous if not kept under proper control, though in so doing he may act without personal wilfulness or negligence, he will be liable in damages for any mischief thereby occasioned.' Lord Cairns says in that case, at p. 338:– 'My Lords, the principles on which this case must be determined appear to me to be extremely simple. The defendants, treating them as the owners or occupiers of the close on which the reservoir was constructed, might lawfully have used that close for any purpose for which it might, in the ordinary course of the enjoyment of land, be used, and if in what I may term the natural use of that land there had been any accumulation of water, either on the surface or underground, and if by the operation of the laws of nature that accumulation of water had passed off into the close occupied by the plaintiff, the plaintiff could not have complained that that result had taken place. If he had desired to guard himself against it, it would have lain upon him to have done so by leaving or by interposing some barrier between his close and the close of the defendants in order to have prevented that operation of the laws of nature. As an illustration of that principle I may refer to a case which was cited in the argument before your Lordships in the case of *Smith* v. *Kenrick* in the Court of Common Pleas' (7 C. B. 515). 'On the other hand, if the defendants, not stopping at the natural use of their close, had desired to use it for any purpose, which I may term a non-natural use, for the purpose of introducing into the close that which in its natural condition was not in or upon it for the purpose of introducing water either above or below ground in quantities, and in a manner not the result of any work or operation on or under the land, and if in consequence of their doing so, or in consequence of any imperfection in the mode of their doing so, the water came to escape and to pass off into the close of the plaintiff, then it appears to me that that which the defendants were doing they were doing at their own peril, and if in the course of their doing it, the evil arose to which I have referred, the evil – namely, of the escape of the water and it passing away to the close of the plaintiff and injuring the plaintiff – then, for the consequences of that, in my opinion, the defendants would be liable. As the case of *Smith* v. *Kenrick* is an illustration of the first principle to which I have referred, so also the second principle is well illustrated by another case in the same Court, the case of *Baird* v. *Williamson*. 15 C. B. (N.S.) 367, which was also cited in the argument at the Bar.'

The case of *Smith* v. *Kendrick* was:– A., owner of a mine on a higher level, worked out all his coal, leaving no barrier between his mine and the mine on the lower level, so that the water, percolating through the upper mine, flowed into the lower mine and obstructed the owner of it in getting his coal. It was held that the owner of the lower mine had no ground of complaint. The defendant, the owner of the upper mine, had a right to remove all his coal. In *Baird* v. *Williamson* the defendant, the owner of the upper mine, did not merely suffer the water to flow through his mine without leaving a barrier between it and the mine below, but, in order to work his own mine beneficially, he pumped up quantities of water, which passed into the plaintiff's mine in addition to that which would have naturally reached it, and so occasioned him damage. Though this was done without negligence and in the due working of his own mine, yet he was held to be responsible for the damage so occasioned. There are many references in the text-books and many cases on this point. Coulson and Forbes, Law of Waters, 2nd ed. (1902), p. 136, *et seq*., contains most of the law on the subject. In Halsbury's The Laws of England, Vol. XXI., pp. 401, 402, it is stated: 'The question of the natural or non-natural user of the land is material in considering the origin of the injuries, but it is not conclusive of liability.'

Thus an owner of mining rights is entitled to exercise them to the full, and is not liable for injury resulting to his neighbour's mine through the percolation of water, even if the percolation is guided by artificial means not in the ordinary course of mining, but such right does not extend to throwing a greater burden upon his neighbour by operations in the course of mining which discharge into his neighbour's mine a greater quantity of water than would naturally gravitate there, and the cases of *Wilson* v. *Waddell* (1876), 2 App. Cas. 95; *Baird* v. *Williamson (supra)* and other cases are cited. In Vol. XXVIII, of the same work, p. 453, it is stated: 'When water escapes or overflows from land the owner of that land is not liable for the consequences, if this happens in the ordinary use of the land without any wilful act or negligence on his part,' and *Wilson* v. *Waddell (supra)*, *Fletcher* v. *Smith*, 2 App. Cas. 781, and *Walley* v. *Lancashire and Yorkshire Railway Co*. (1884) 13 Q.B.D. 131 (C.A.), are cited. Again, at p. 455: 'Injuries caused by the escape of water due to the effect of gravitation or percolation in the proper and ordinary use and working of the land give no cause for damages, though the pumping of water to another's land, even when done without negligence and in the due working of a mine, renders the owner liable unless he can show that his operations do not throw any burden on the land which it had not been subjected to before.' The law is also discussed in Beven on Negligence, 3rd ed., Vol. I., pp. 476, 477, 478, 479. In the Scotch case of *Armistead* v. *Bowerman*, 15 Rettie 814, a claim was made by the proprietor of a 'fish hatchery' against the purchaser of timber higher up the stream for dragging his timber across the stream which fed the 'fish hatchery,' and thereby fouled and damaged it. The

Court held that, apart from a right given in the grant to the pursuer restricting the removal of timber in the ordinary way of business, the pursuer had no right to recover, since the defendant was only performing an ordinary and legitimate operation in the ordinary and usual way. And the Scotch Law is the same as our law on this point (see *Blair* v. *Hunter, Finlay & Co.*, 9 Macph. 204). I think that the cases of *Rawstron* v. *Taylor*, 11 Ex. 369 (1856), and *Broadbent* v. *Ramsbottom*, 11 Ex. 602, referred to by Mr. Fetherstonhaugh, do not apply in this case. They were cases of defendants using surface waters which were on their lands in no definite channels, though they had for years gone on to the plaintiffs' lands and were used by the plaintiffs for their mills, and by defendants' user were stopped from reaching the plaintiffs' lands, and I think that the words used by the judges in those cases are confined to such cases.

I have referred to these various authorities, as it seems to me that this is a case of great importance to all farmers in Ireland, especially now when farming is improving, and therefore the drainage of lands increasing, and also when tillage is increasing, as well-drained land is essential to good tillage, also because it is so important to all persons whou burn turf as fuel in Ireland, as well-drained bogs are essential to good turf and bad turf is nearly always caused by badly drained bogs. I have come to the conclusion that the defendants in this case have only worked their bog according to the natural user of the land, and that their drainage works were necessary to obtaining turf for their tenants, and that the water from their drains went in its natural course to the plaintiff's lands, and that within what Lord Cairns said in *Rylands* v. *Fletcher (supra),* they are not liable, and that this action should be dismissed on the merits.

McDONNELL V. TURF DEVELOPMENT BOARD
78 I.L.T.R. 94 (High Court, Murnaghan, J., 1944)

Murnaghan J.:

The plaintiff, being in possession of a County Council cottage and plot attached, planted some potatoes in a small area of the plot. I have now to investigate an injury to those potatoes caused by flooding. It is suggested by the plaintiff that the flooding was caused by the Turf Development Board, who had acquired about 70 acres of adjoining bog, on which they opened a number of drains for the development of the bog, and that heavy rain fell in the month of August, 1942, and was discharged out of those drains into a main drain or stream, which runs at the foot of plaintiff's plot, and that this main drain or stream overflowed its banks and the overflow went over the intervening road and on to plaintiff's potatoes. The defendants, on the other hand, say that it was not water from their bog that flooded the plaintiff's garden; that the real cause of the flooding was the heavy rainfall which fell on the plaintiff's gargen or plot and accumulated in the part of the plot in which the potatoes were planted. To support this theory of the accumulation of the rainfall in the potato part of the plot, the defendants say that the place where the potatoes were is at a lower level than the rest of the garden, and further, that the general slope of the plot is towards where the potatoes were. Secondly, they contend that even if the flooding was caused by water which came from their bogland, it came as a result of ordinary and natural user of the bogland and that they are not liable in law for this. . . .

The plaintiff's evidence was vague as compared with the expert evidence given by the Board's engineer. The plaintiff's case is that he saw his plot flooded. He believes that the water came across the road and bank into his garden. Just at this plot there is a culvert in the road, which is described as good by the Board's engineer. It would carry off ordinary water flowing from the road. There is no suggestion that at the time this culvert was constructed by the County Council it was intended that it should carry a great volume of water from the bog. This culvert was simply capable of taking an ordinary flow of water.

There was evidence given that the month of August, 1942, was extremely wet; figures for rainfall at this period went to show that the rainfall was 2 inches in four days. Such a heavy fall accumulating in one place would be a great volume of water indeed. The plaintiff's plot was extremely small when compared with the large area of 70 acres. I have to decide whether this water which caused the flooding came from the defendants' bog or whether it was the accumulation of all the water that fell on the plaintiff's plot. I think the balance of probability is in favour of the plaintiff and I find as a fact that the water came from defendants' land.

Next I have to decide whether the defendants as owners of the bogland, did anything that makes them liable to the plaintiff in making the drains for the discharge of the water off the bogland. The legal position is that if the owner of land makes natural use of his land he is entitled to do whatever he pleases with it. The defendants admit that they intend to use heavy machinery in bog development; for this the surface of the bog must be firm, and in order that the desired firmness may be secured a five-year drainage scheme must be applied to the bog. I do not think this comes under the heading of ordinary and natural user of land. If a farmer opened the drains on his bog I think the position might be different. I think, therefore, on this point the plaintiff is entitled to succeed. . . .

I must affirm the decision of the Court below and dismiss the appeal with costs.

Notes and Questions

1. Can *McDonnell* v. *Turf Development Board* and *Connolly* v. *Congested Districts Board for Ireland* be reconciled? *Cf.* Carroll, 'The Rule in Rylands v. Fletcher: A Re-Assessment,' 8 Ir. Jur. (n.s.) 208, at 219 (1973).
2. In *Rylands* v. *Fletcher*, Blackburn, J. spoke of a person bringing and collecting on his lands 'anything likely to do mischief if it escapes . . .' In *A.G.* v. *Corke*, [1933] Ch. 89, liability was imposed in respect of caravan-dwellers who were licensees of the defendant on his land. This approach has not found general favour: *cf. Smith* v. *Scott*, [1973] Ch. 314; *Matheson* v. *Northcote College Board of Governors* [1975] 2 N.Z.L.R. 106. The action for nuisance would appear to be more appropriate in such circumstances: *cf. Ellis* v. *Dun Laoghaire Corporation*, unreported, Circuit Ct., Judge Ryan, 29 January 1982, *Irish Times*, 30 January 1982.
3. Does the rule in *Rylands* v. *Fletcher* extend to those who bring wild animals onto their property? *Cf.*, *Brady* v. *Warren*, [1900] 2 I.R. 632, at 651 (Q.B. Div., *per* Johnson, J.); *Gibb* v. *Comerford* [1942] I.R. 295, at 304 (High Ct., Maguire, P., 1939). What about domestic animals? *Cf.*, *id.*; see also *Noonan* v. *Hartnett* 84 I.L.T.R. 41 (Circuit Ct., Judge O'Brian, 1950).

HEALY V. BRAY URBAN DISTRICT COUNCIL
[1963–1964] Ir. Jur. Rep. 9 (Supreme Court, 1961)

Kingsmill Moore J.:

The plaintiff, a woman of middle age, while walking on the public footpath which runs round Bray Head at about 100 feet above sea level, was struck and somewhat seriously injured by a loose rock which had rolled down the hill, in all probability from a spot 210 yards distant and about 350 feet higher than the path. The upper slopes are owned in perpetuity by the defendant council under an indenture of the 27th October, 1923, which contains a covenant by the Council to use the lands solely for the purpose of a public park for the inhabitants of and visitors to the town of Bray. The strip of land over which the public right of way runs at the scene of the accident is also owned by the Council, under a different title, an agreement of the 31st March, 1932, whereby the Great Southern Railway Company let to the Council on a yearly tenancy, subject to determination by six months' notice in writing and to a variable rent, three parcels of land: first, a small park situate at the end of Bray esplanade bordered by the sea on one side and the railway line on the other, coloured red on the map attached to the conveyance, and referred to in the conveyance as 'the said Park'; second, a strip of ground, coloured brown on the map, over which runs the path in question; third, a strip of ground coloured blue on the map, which could be utilised to provide a further way to the Park. Those three portions of ground are referred to in the conveyance as 'the said premises.' The 'said Park' is granted on the express conditions that the same 'shall be used solely as a public park for recreation purposes for the people or general public' but I am of opinion that on the construction of the document this condition does not extend to the strip coloured brown, over which the public path runs.

The Council maintained the plot marked red on the map as a park for the public. They inspected and supervised the path and maintained its surface, but the path was not subject to the bye-laws. No evidence was given as to the user of the lands conveyed by the earlier indenture of 1923 but it was admitted that the public was given free access to these lands. From a map put in evidence by the plaintiff it would appear that the more level portions of these lands, situate on or near the top of the head, had been planted and provided with paths but the steep seaward slopes were left in their natural untouched condition. If any member of the public chose to walk over these slopes and enjoy the view he was at liberty to do so.

The plaintiff put her case on four grounds. First she relied on the principle of absolute liability laid down in *Rylands* v. *Fletcher* and said that the rock which hit her was something of a dangerous nature brought and kept by the Council on their land, for the escape of which they were responsible. . . .

To understand the arguments based on these submissions it is necessary to describe somewhat fully the general physical features of the scene of the accident and the circumstances, so far as they are known, of the descent of the stone.

Bray Head is a solid bluff of Cambrian rock rising to about 700 feet above sea level, sloping seawards at varying angles. At its base, some 50 feet above the sea, runs the railway line, in steep sided cuttings and tunnels cut through the live rock and on rocky ledges and shelves. About fifty feet higher on the landward side and closely parallel with the railway line runs the path. It is separated from the steep slope of the railway cutting by a carefully built masonry wall 2′ 6″ high and on the other side of the path a mass concrete wall 2′ high supports the earth and prevents it from shingling down on to the path. The surface of the path appears to be compacted stones and gravel and from the photographs it is clear that the path, at all events where the accident occurred, was at some time cut out of the hillside and, with its side walls, artificially constructed at a considerable expenditure of time and labour. Above the path the side of the head stretches up to a height of over 600 feet. The gradient is at an angle of 30° to 38° and the surface is covered with a natural growth of bracken, furze, brambles and coarse grass. In this vegetation, buried or partially buried, lie some stones and boulders, the result of past erosion, and in places the rock outcrops in small knolls of bare stone, the lower sides of which lie at a somewhat steeper angle than the main slope. Except for the walls to which I am about to refer the slope appears never to have been interfered with by the hand of man and to have reached its present state as the result of natural agencies – water, wind, ice, sun and frost – operating throughout the many millions of years since the formation was laid down.

There are on the hillside two stone walls substantially built and apparently of considerable age, which are admittedly boundary walls of the property conveyed by the deed of 1923, though in age antedating that conveyance. One stretches straight up the slope and forms the boundary between that property and the Meath estate. The other runs parallel with the path and about 25 feet above it and constituted the boundary between that property and the land formerly owned by the railway. It was claimed by the plaintiff that this wall was built as a protection for persons using the path against any stones that might roll down the slope, and undoubtedly, so long as it was intact, it would have served to intercept anything but a large boulder: but the trial judge, on a comparison of this wall with the other wall and on the admitted fact that it ran along the boundary of the two properties, told the jury, rightly in my opinion, that it should be regarded as a boundary wall and that there was nothing to warrant the conclusion that it was built to protect the path. This wall, though clearly very old, is generally in good repair but over one stretch of about 30 yards someone has removed the coping stones and immediately above the spot where the accident happened there is a gap about 15 feet wide at the top and 9 feet wide at ground level. It is not a new gap, for the grass has grown over it and there is no sign of the stones which must have come from it; and no evidence was given to fix even its approximate age.

The circumstances which led to the fall of the stone are established in broad outline. Six boys were descending the Head in a straggling group and the stone was dislodged from where it was lying by one of them, either accidentally or wantonly. It rolled down the hill, found its way through the gap in the wall and came to rest in the middle of the path, striking the plaintiff just as it came to rest. In weight it was between two and three hundred-weight and its dimensions are stated to have been about $2' \times 1\frac{1}{2}' \times 1'$. Its shape is described as being 'wedge shaped' and three sided. Photographs of the stone were put into evidence but they only show two faces, which are rectangular with rounded corners. As far as I can judge from the description and the photographs, if stood on end, it would have a rectangular base and top and the sides would be rectangular with the corners rounded. The base and two of its sides appeared to have been in contact with the earth; the third side was weathered.

One of the boys who had been on the hill pointed out to an Inspector of the Garda the spot from which he thought the stone had come. There was a hole 17' deep on the upper side and 16' across, but owing to the declivity there was little or no supporting earth on the sea side. The Inspector said that if the stone has been in place it would have been 'like an egg in an egg cup with one third of the side of the egg cup broken away on the lower side'. This depression was on a small outcrop and, immediately below, the ground fell very sharply for about 100 feet so that if the stone was once dislodged from its bed it would rapidly gain impetus which might be sufficient to carry it on down the somewhat gentler, but still steep, gradient to the path. This was what had happened for the Inspector was able to trace the marks of its descent in an irregular course to where it came to rest on the path.

Mr. Purcell, an engineer called for the plaintiff, said that on examination he has found on the inside of the wall a few stones which had apparently, at some time or another, come down the hill; but he did not specify their size, nor whereabouts in the length of wall he had found them.

I have summarised the evidence given by the witnesses and contained in the maps, plans and photographs. In addition, certain interrogatories administered by the plaintiff and answered by the Town Clerk to the Council were put into evidence by the plaintiff. From the answers it appeared that the Council had no knowledge of any previous falls of rock on Bray Head or on to the path; that no reports of any such falls had ever been made to them; that no claims had been made on them nor, as far as the records went, on any previous occupier, in respect of such falls. It was admitted that the Council supervised and inspected Bray Head and the footpath, and maintained the surface of the footpath, but they did not in any way inspect, supervise or maintain the wall, which was alleged to be merely a boundary wall marking the extent of the property. No representations had at any time been made to the Council as to the danger from falling rock or stones nor had the existence of any such danger come to the knowledge of the Council or its members or staff. It was admitted that the footpath was a public highway, having been dedicated by user from time immemorial. No invitation to use the path had ever been issued, nor permission given, nor had any warning been given to persons using the footpath, that there was a danger from falling stones or that they used the footpath at their own risk. Although there were bye-laws governing the use of the park, these did not extend to cover the footpath.

At the conclusion of the case for the plaintiff, Mr. Peart, for the defendants, applied to have the case withdrawn from the jury on the ground that the evidence did not establish any duty on the Council to prevent the fall of the stone. The trial judge refused to accede to this application and, on the defendants electing not to call evidence, the judge left to the jury the following questions:

(1) Was the boulder which struck the plaintiff dislodged by human agency?
(2) Was the said boulder insecure if not interfered with by human agency?
(3) If so, did the defendants know that the said boulder was insecure as aforesaid?
(4) If not, should the defendants reasonably have known the said boulder was insecure?
(5) Were the defendants negligent?
(6) Damages.

We are told that the four grounds of liability which I have mentioned were advanced by counsel for the plaintiff in the course of his argument resisting a direction, and in his speech to the jury, but the learned judge in his charge did not direct the jury on the law of nuisance, nor on the liability to invitees and licensees, nor on the principle of *Rylands* v. *Fletcher*. He left the case to the jury as a straight case of negligence or no negligence, and further directed the jury that it was within their province not to answer the specific questions but to bring in a general verdict in the form of 'We find for the defendants' or 'We find for the plaintiff.' In the result the jury gave no answer to questions 1 to 4, answered question 5 'Yes' and assessed damages at £1,457.

From this verdict and the judgment given thereon the defendant Council appeals, assigning numerous grounds of appeal, of which it is only necessary to note two – first that the learned judge was wrong in refusing the direction sought by the defendants at the conclusion of the plaintiff's case, and second 'in holding that there were any facts in evidence from which it could be concluded that any duty lay upon the defendants towards the plaintiff, a breach of which might give rise to any claim based on negligence in this action.'

As Mr. Ó Síocháin did not object to the charge of the learned judge, except in one respect to which the judge acceded, I doubt if any question other than common law negligence is open for argument; but the Court allowed Mr. Ó Síocháin to rely on the other grounds which I have mentioned and therefore I will deal with them briefly.

The rule in *Fletcher* v. *Rylands* has no application. In that case the rule was stated by Blackburn J. in the Exchequer Chamber as follows– 'The true rule of the law is that the person who for his own purposes brings on his lands and collects and keeps there anything likely to do mischief if it escapes, must keep it at his peril.' The defendants did not bring the rocks or outcrop on to [their] land for their own purpose (or at all). They are there as a result of natural forces operating in geological time, as indeed is the land. They are, in short, the land itself and not things brought on to it. See also *Pondardawe R.D.C.* v. *Moore-Gwyn* [1929] 1 Ch. 656, a decision of Eve J. which appears to me to be clearly correct.

Notes and Questions

1. If the rock had not escaped from the defendant's land, no claim could have been brought under the rule in *Rylands* v. *Fletcher*. As Viscount Simon, L.C. explained in *Read* v. *Lyons* [1947] A.C. 156, at 168, there has to be an 'escape from a place where the defendant has occupation of or control over land to a place which is outside his occupation or control.' Is this a sensible limitation?
2. Do you support exemption from liability where the thing that does damage is on the defendant's land 'as the result of natural forces operating in geological time'? What about a tree? Should it be vitally important whether a ninety-year-old tree had been planted by the landowner or naturally sown? *Cf.* Moore, J.'s dissenting judgment in *Mullan* v. *Forrester* [1921] 2 I.R. 412.
3. For a discussion of the defences to the action, see *McMahon & Binchy*, pp. 507–510.

Chapter 22

LIABILITY FOR FIRE

Fire is a basic necessity but it is a dangerous servant: it respects no boundaries, it can be started intentionally or by accident, by adult or child, by the sane or the insane, by occupier or trespasser, or indeed on occasion by forces of nature without any human intervention. So varied are these permutations and so disproportionate the injury that may flow from a venial act of carelessness, that tort law has had some difficulty in establishing a coherent set of principles of liability for damage caused by fire.

Historically, liability for fire concentrated on injury in the context of the spread of fire from one person's property to the property of another. The law has tended to be discussed even today primarily in terms of liability arising from occupation or ownership of land. But this emphasis should not blind us to the possibilities of actions against others, who have started fires (whether intentionally or negligently) or who, by their action or inaction, have culpably brought about injury in respect of fires not of their making. See *McMahon & Binchy*, pp. 511, 515–517.

RICHARDSON V. ATHLONE WOOLLEN MILLS CO. LTD.
[1942] I.R. 581 (Sup. Ct.)

A fire originated accidentally in woollen mills, the property of the defendants, and spread to, and destroyed, adjoining premises occupied by the plaintiffs. In an action based on the defendants' liability at common law for damage caused by the fire, the defendants claimed that they were exonerated from their common law liability by a statute enacted in 1715 (*An Act for preventing Mischief by fire*, 2 Geo. 1, c.5), section 1 of which provided that 'Whereas by the common law of this Kingdom every person or persons, in whose house, chamber, or out-house, any fire should accidentally happen, was compellable to make recompense and satisfaction for all damages suffered or occasioned thereby, to the impoverishment and utter ruin frequently of such persons: for remedy whereof, be it enacted . . . no action, suit, or process whatsoever shall be had, maintained, or presented against any person or persons in whose house or chamber any fire shall . . . accidentally begin.' The jury found that the defendants were not guilty of any negligence in allowing the fire to spread. The tial judge held that, in such circumstances, the defendants were exempt from liability by virtue of section 1. The defendants appealed to the Supreme Court.

O'Byrne J.:
. . . In the present case a fire originated accidentally in a factory, the property of the defendant Company, and caused damage to the plaintiffs' property, and the question for decision is whether the defendants are protected by the foregoing section. This involves and depends upon the question whether the factory, in which the fire originated, is a 'house' within the meaning of the section. It is admitted that it is not a 'chamber' within the meaning of that section.

I accept as good law the proposition laid down by the Earl of Halsbury L.C. in *Grant* v. *Langston* [1900] A.C. 383 that the word 'house' has no common or ordinary meaning so fixed and definite that by the mere use of the word you can determine in what sense the Legislature has used it. Accordingly, regard must be had, in each case, to the subject-matter and the context, for the purpose of determining the meaning of the term.

If s. 1 stood alone I do not think there would be much difficulty in affixing a definite meaning to the term; but regard must be had to the remaining provisions of the Act, and particularly, to s.4 which provides that if any menial or other servant or servants, through negligence or carelessness, shall fire, or occasion the burning of, any dwelling-house, or out-house, or houses, such servant or servants, being thereof lawfully convicted, shall be liable to the penalties prescribed by the section. This section, occurring in the same statute, strongly suggests that the word 'house' has a different, and probably wider, signification than the word 'dwelling-house'; though, even in this section, I think its meaning is considerably restricted by two considerations arising on the section. First, the object of the section is to impose penalties on menial or other servants. If the term 'other servants' is, as I think it should be, construed ejusdem generis with 'menial servants' it will be seen that the section is confined to the class of servants that would ordinarily be employed in, or in connection with, a dwelling-house. Secondly, the term is used in conjunction with the term 'dwelling-house' and 'out-house' and seems to me to be coloured and restricted by this collocation. The ordinary meaning of 'out-house' (as appears from the Oxford Dictionary) is 'a house or building, belonging to and adjoining a dwelling-house, and used for some subsidiary purpose; e.g., a stable, barn, wash-house, tool-house or the like.' Accordingly, it seems to me that, even in s.4, the word 'house' must be restricted to a building used in some way in connection with a dwelling-house.

I come now to the material section, viz., s.1. In reciting the mischief aimed at and sought to be remedied, it refers to accidental fires happening in any *house, chamber or out-house*; but the remedy is confined to fires which originate in *a house or chamber*. In this section the word 'house' is used in conjunction with the word 'out-house' and in a sense which obviously does not include the latter. It, therefore, to my mind, cannot have been used in the extended sense (contended for by the respondents) as denoting a building; and I am of opinion that some more restricted meaning must be given to the term.

The primary meaning of the word 'house' (I again refer to the Oxford Dictionary) is 'a building for human habitation; especially a building that is the ordinary dwelling-place of a family.' That it was, in fact, used in this sense in the Act is strongly borne out by its use in conjunction with the term 'chamber' and 'out-house.' I have already referred to the meaning of the term 'out-house'. The same idea of connection with a dwelling-house is conveyed by the term 'chamber', which normally means a room or apartment in a house, usually appropriated to the use of one person, especially a sleeping apartment or bedroom. It is used in this sense by Swift in the year 1711 (four years before the Act in question was passed), and I take this to be a well recognised meaning of the term at the time when the Act was passed.

I am, therefore, of opinion that, having regard to the context and the subject-matter, the word 'house', as used in s. 1 of the Act, merely denotes a dwelling-house, or, at any rate, some building closely associated with, or used in connection with, a dwelling-house. Construing the term in this way, it clearly does not include, or refer to, the building in which the fire originated in this case. That building was a factory – constructed and used as such, which was never used, or intended to be used, as a residence – which was not suitable for such use, and which was not, in any way, used in connection with a dwelling-house.

It was strongly urged upon us, by counsel for the respondents, that this was a remedial statute, passed for the purpose of removing an anomaly theretofore existing in the common law, and that it should be so construed as to remedy, as far as possible, the mischief at which it was aimed. The principle of construction so contended for, is well recognised, and, in cases of doubt or ambiguity, is a useful canon of construction.

In the present case, however, it is clear that the statute was only intended to remove partly the anomaly. According to the common law, the doctrine for responsibility for damage caused by accidental fires was not confined to fires originating in buildings. If a fire originated accidentally in defendant's close and spread to and damaged the plaintiff's property, the defendant was responsible: *Tuberville* v. *Stamp* 1 Ld. Raym. 264. Accordingly, as pointed out by the Lord Chancellor, Lord Lyndhurst, in *Canterbury* v. *Attorney-General* 1 Ph. 306, with reference to the corresponding English statute (6 Anne, c.31), if the statute was intended to put an end to the anomaly, it was obviously defective, inasmuch as it is clearly confined to fires originating in buildings. It seems to me impossible to contend that the statute was intended to effect a complete remedy.

It is difficult, at this stage, to say with any certainty upon what principle the common law doctrine was based. One theory is that it was based upon presumed negligence; but the mere statement of the doctrine would appear to negative the idea of negligence. A more reasonable theory would appear to be that it had its origin in some such principle as that recognised in the well-known case of *Fletcher* v. *Rylands*, viz., that if a person keeps upon his land anything which is likely to do mischief if it escape, he is answerable for all the damage which is the natural consequence of its escape. No doubt, these cases are sometimes treated as being founded upon negligence; but negligence, either in the keeping, or in connection with the escape, of the commodity, does not form any part of the gist of the action. If, as I am inclined to think, the doctrine was founded upon that principle, it may well have been considered unduly harsh and improper to continue it in connection with the keeping of domestic fires in dwelling-houses, where they were absolutely essential for the ordinary purposes of life.

I have arrived at the foregoing conclusion without any reference to the several statutes passed, in pari materia, by the English Parliament. A reference to these statutes, however, strengthens the conclusion at which I have arrived. The earlier statutes were, substantially, to the same effect as the Irish statute; but, in the year 1774, Parliament considered it necessary or desirable to enact that no action, suit, or process whatever, should be maintained or prosecuted against any person in whose house, chamber, stable, barn or other building or on whose estate any fire should, after the date therein mentioned, accidentally begin (14 Geo. 3, c.78, s. 86). It may well be that the time has arrived when similar provision should be made in this country; but, in the meantime, the Courts must administer the law as they find it.

For these reasons, I am of opinion that the statute relied upon affords no protection to the defendants, and that this appeal should be allowed, and the action remitted to the High Court with a view to having the damages assessed.

Murnaghan and **Meredith JJ.** delivered concurring judgments; **Sullian C.J.** and **Geoghegan J.** dissented.

Notes and Questions

1. The following year the legislature responded. Section 1(1) of the *Accidental Fires Act 1943* (No. 8) provides that:
   'Where any person (in this section referred to as the injured person) has suffered damage by reason of fire accidentally occurring . . . in or on the building or land of another person, then, notwithstanding any rule of law . . . no legal proceedings shall be instituted in any court by the injured person or any person claiming through or under him or as his insurer against such other person an account of such damage.'
   'Building' is defined (by section 1(3)) as including 'any structure of whatsoever material or for whatever purpose used'.

2. What does 'accidentally' mean in this context? Unintentionally? Without negligence? See Osborough, 'Liability in Tort for Unintended Fire Damage' 6 Ir. Jur. (n.s.) 205, at 206–207 (1971).
3. Must the defendant have been negligent in relation to the creation of the fire or will failure to control it adequately also be a basis of liability?

WOODS V. O'CONNOR
[1958] Ir. Jur. Rep. 71 (Circuit Ct., Judge Deale, 1957)

The plaintiff was a guest in the defendant's hotel. During his stay there a fire broke out, and whilst attempting to escape from the flames the plaintiff suffered personal injuries. He sued the defendant for damages, claiming that there had been a breach of an implied warranty in that the premises were not as safe as reasonable care and skill could make them, or, alternatively that there was negligence and/or breach of statutory duty by the defendant in that there was a failure to provide a premises that was safe and proper for the business being carried on there.

Judge Deale:

I am of opinion that this action fails. [Counsel for the plaintiff] that the injuries to the plaintiff arose because of a defect in the hotel premises, in consequence of which, when he was put in peril as a result of the fire, he sustained personal injury. He further submits that the Accidental Fires Act, 1943, does not apply because the injury was caused by defective premises.

It is of course true that the means of exit used by the plaintiff was not safe, and that there was no other means open to him when the fire cut him off from the stairs. But, he was only using this exit because of the fire; if there had been no fire, and he had wished to leave his room, he would have used the door, landing and stairs. It is clear therefore that the fire was the cause of the injuries, and there is no evidence to show what started the fire. This means that the plaintiff has failed to show that the fire was not accidental, and so has failed to take the case out of the protection afforded to the defendant by the Accidental Fires Act, 1943.

[Counsel for the plaintiff] also submitted that, even if the fire was accidental, the 1943 Act did not protect the defendant because the Act only barred the actions where the injured person had suffered 'damage' by reason of the fire, and did not apply where the injured person had suffered personal injury. The distinction [counsel] sought to make was between 'damage' in the sense of loss or injury to property, and 'injury' in the sense of 'personal injury' i.e. to the person.

In my opinion this submission also fails. The word 'damage' used in the Act is, in my opinion, inclusive both of damage to property and injury to the person. When a party suffers 'personal injury' – this is, injury to his body – he suffers 'damage' in legal parlance.

Accordingly, it appears to me that [counsel for the defendant]'s application for a non-suit succeeds, and I therefore dismiss the action with costs.

Notes and Questions

1. Do you agree with the holding of this case? *Cf.* Osborough, 'Liability in Tort for Unintended Fire Damage' 6 Ir. Jur. (n.s.) 205, at 210 (1971).
2. It seems clear that section 1(1) of the *Accidental Fires Act 1943 (No. 8)* does not foreclose an action for negligence: *cf.* Osborough, *supra*, at 215–216. An action for breach of statutory duty might also possibly be available: *cf. id.*, at 216; and *Gaynor* v. *McGinn* [1933] L.J. Ir. 70. See also *Hallet* v. *Nicholson*, 1979 S.C. 1.

3. The plaintiffs' action may, of course, be met by the defence of contributory negligence. *Cf. Kelly* v. *McElligott*, 85 I.L.T.R.4 (Sup. Ct., 1949). (Note that this case was decided before apportionment was introduced by the *Civil Liability Act 1961*).
4. The *Fire Services Act 1981*, enacted in the wake of the Stardust tragedy, includes a number of provisions that should be noted particularly.

   Section 18 of the Act provides as follows:

   '(1) This section applies to premises or any part thereof put to any of the following uses –
   (*a*) use as, or for any purpose involving the provision of, sleeping accommodation, excluding premises consisting of a dwelling house occupied as a single dwelling;
   (*b*) use as, or as part of, an institution providing treatment or care;
   (*c*) use for purposes of entertainment, recreation or instruction or for the purpose of any club, society or association;
   (*d*) use for purposes of teaching, training or research;
   (*e*) use for any purpose involving access to the premises by members of the public, whether on payment or otherwise; and
   (*f*) use for any other prescribed purpose, but excluding –
      (i) premises used as a factory within the meaning of the Safety in Industry Acts, 1955 and 1980;
      (ii) premises used as a store and subject to licensing under regulations made under the Dangerous Substances Act, 1972;
      (iii) a magazine, store or registered premises within the meaning of the Explosives Act, 1875; and
      (iv) an oil jetty within the meaning of regulations under the Dangerous Substances Act, 1972.

   (2) It shall be the duty of every person having control over premises to which this section applies to take all reasonable measures to guard against the outbreak of fire on such premises, and to ensure as far as is reasonably practicable the safety of persons on the premises in the event of an outbreak of fire.

   (3) It shall be the duty of every person, being on premises to which this section applies, to conduct himself in such a way as to ensure that as far as is reasonably practicable any person on the premises is not exposed to danger from fire as a consequence of any act or omission of his.

   (4) A fire authority may give advice in relation to fire safety to the owner or occupier of any premises or to any person having control over any premises.'

   The 'duty' laid down by this section appears to be of a criminal nature: *cf.* section 5, especially subsection (2). Would civil liability also attach? See also sections 25 to 29, but note that section 36 provides immunity from civil liability for the Minister for the Environment, fire authorities and sanitary authorities in respect of injury to persons or property alleged to have been caused or contributed to by the failure to comply with any functions conferred by the Act. Does subsection (4) of section 18 impose a duty to rescue where this is 'reasonably practicable'?

   See also the *Report of the Tribunal of Inquiry on the Fire at the Stardust, Artane, Dublin on the 14th February 1981* (Pl. 853, 1982), pp. 31 ff., for reference to the relevant legislation.

Chapter 23

ANIMALS

Introduction

The owner of an animal may become liable for damage caused by the animal either under special rules relating to animals or under the general rules of tort such as negligence, nuisance etc. The special rules of liability, which render the owner strictly liable for damage caused by his animals, include liable for injury caused (1) by wild animals, or (2) by domestic animals with a known mischievous propensity, or (3) by cattle trespassing, or (4) by dogs worrying cattle (the *Dogs Act 1906*). The cases selected provide examples of liability under both the general and the special rules. The curious immunity afforded to persons whose animals stray on the highway and cause damage is also noted.

DOGS ACT 1906

1.–(1) The owner of a dog shall be liable in damages for injury done to any cattle by that dog; and it shall not be necessary for the person seeking such damages to show a previous mischievous propensity in the dog, or the owner's knowledge of such previous propensity, or to show that the injury was attributable to neglect on the part of the owner.

(2) Where any such injury has been done by a dog, the occupier of any house or premises where the dog was kept or permitted to live or remain at the time of the injury shall be presumed to be the owner of the dog, and shall be liable for the injury unless he proves that he was not the owner of the dog at that time:

Provided that where there are more occupiers than one in any house or premises let in separate apartments, or lodgings, or otherwise, the occupier of that particular part of the house or premises in which the dog has been kept or permitted to live or remain at the time of the injury shall be presumed to be the owner of the dog.

(3) If the damages claimed under this section do not exceed five pounds they may be recovered under the Summary Jurisdiction Acts as a civil debt.

(4) Where a dog is proved to have injured cattle or chased sheep, it may be dealt with under section two of the Dogs Act, 1871, as a dangerous dog.

2.–(1) The Diseases of Animals Act, 1894, shall have effect as if, amongst the purposes for which the Board of Agriculture and Fisheries may make orders under section twenty-two of that Act, there were included the following purposes:–

    (*a*) for prescribing and regulating the wearing by dogs, while in a highway or in a place of public resort, of a collar with the name and address of the owner inscribed on the collar or on a plate or badge attached thereto:

    (*b*) with a view to the prevention of worrying of cattle, for preventing dogs or any class of dogs from straying during all or any of the hours between sunset and sunrise.

(2) Orders under this section may provide that any dog in respect of which an offence is being committed against the orders, may be seized and treated as a stray dog.

[Sections 3 and 4 make provision for seizure of stray dogs. Section 5 exempts sheep dogs, etc. from excise licence.]

6. Any person who shall knowingly and without reasonable excuse permit the

carcase of any head of cattle belonging to him to remain unburied in a field or other place to which dogs can gain access shall be liable on conviction under the Summary Jurisdiction Acts to a fine not exceeding forty shillings.

7. In this Act the expression 'cattle' includes horses, mules, asses, sheep, goats, and swine.

[Sections 8 and 9 extend the Act, with modifications, to Scotland and Ireland.]

DOGS (PROTECTION OF LIVESTOCK) ACT, 1960

AN ACT FOR THE PROTECTION OF LIVESTOCK FROM WORRYING BY DOGS. [*16th June, 1960.*]

BE IT ENACTED BY THE OIREACHTAS AS FOLLOWS:–

1.–In this Act –

'agricultural land' means land used as arable, meadow or grazing land,

'livestock' means cattle, sheep, pigs, poultry or horses,

'occupier' includes a person who owns and occupies as well as a person who occupies only.

2.–(1) Where a dog worries livestock on agricultural land, the owner of the dog, and, if the dog is in the charge of a person other than the owner, that person also, shall be guilty of an offence unless the dog is owned by or in the charge of –

(*a*) the occupier of the land, a member of his family or a person employed by him, or

(*b*) the owner of the livestock, a member of his family or a person employed by him.

(2) It shall be a good defence in a prosecution for an offence under this section if the defendant proves that reasonable care was taken to prevent the worrying of the livestock.

(3) A person who is guilty of an offence under this section shall be liable on summary conviction –

(*a*) except in a case falling within paragraph (*b*) of this subsection, to a fine not exceeding twenty pounds, and

(*b*) in a case where the person has been convicted previously of an offence under this section in respect of the same dog, to a fine not exceeding fifty pounds.

3.–(1) Where in the case of a dog found on agricultural land –

(*a*) the dog has been worrying livestock on the land, and

(*b*) no person is present who admits to being the owner of the dog or in charge of it,

a member of the Garda Síochána may seize the dog, and thereupon the provisions of sections 3 and 9 of the Dogs Act, 1906, in relation to seized stray dogs shall apply.

(2) Where in the case of a dog found on agricultural land when worrying livestock lawfully on the land no person is present who admits to being the owner of the dog or in charge of it, the finder may seize the dog and deliver it to a member of the Garda Síochána at the nearest Garda Síochána station, and thereupon the provisions of sections 3 and 9 of the Dogs Act, 1906, in relation to seized stray dogs shall apply.

4.–In an action for damages for the shooting of a dog, it shall be a good defence if the defendant proves –

(*a*) that the dog was shot when worrying livestock on agricultural land,

(*b*) that the livestock were lawfully on the land,

(*c*) that the defendant was –

   (i)   the occupier of the land, a member of his family or a person employed
          by him, or
   (ii)   the owner of the livestock, a member of his family or a person employed
          by him, and
(*d*)   that the defendant notified the shooting within forty-eight hours to a member
          of the Garda Síochána at the nearest Garda Síochána station.
5.–This Act may be cited as the Dogs (Protection of Livestock) Act, 1960.

Questions

What justification is there for having separate rules of liability for damage caused by dogs? Why
should not the special liability be extended to *all* damage caused by dogs?

   *Liability may be imposed on the owner of animals under the general principles of
tort law. Negligence.*

HOWARD B. BERGIN, O'CONNOR & CO.
[1925] 2 I.R. 110

O'Connor J.:
   This action was brought to recover damages for injuries occasioned to the plaintiff
when walking on the footpath in Lord Edward Street, Dublin, by being knocked
down by a bullock which belonged to the defendants, and which at the time of the
occurrence was at large and unattended. Two defences were raised:– That there was
no negligence; that even if there were negligence, it gave no cause of action under the
circumstances.
   The case is an important one for the public and of interest for lawyers.
   The material facts are these:– The defendants are cattle salesmen who carry on
business in Prussia Street, Dublin, where they keep cattle-yards. They bought in
Roscrea, in County Tipperary, seventeen head of cattle, and caused them to be
entrained there for delivery at Kingsbridge, Dublin. At Kingsbridge there is a special
place for unloading cattle with special arrangements for the purpose. One of these is
the provision of strong wooden fences constructed so as to prevent the escape of
cattle when being unloaded. The purpose is obvious, and indeed was admitted. Cattle
on being unloaded after being pent up in trucks during a railway journey are inclined
to break loose and get scattered, and it is all important to keep the entire consignment bunched together as they are being driven from the unloading place. If they are
let loose immediately on detrainment the leaders may be well ahead of those in the
rear, and it would be impossible for the drovers usually employed to guide and
control the lot. Further, if cattle are kept well together they go more quietly and are
more easily driven and managed.
   According to the evidence given at the trial all cattle trains, that is, trains which
contain cattle only are brought to the landing place I have mentioned, and there
unloaded. But cattle are sometimes carried in trucks which are attached to passenger
trains, and these trains are brought to the ordinary passenger platforms. Such trains
are, as I understand, so composed that the cattle trucks are at the end of the train.
When the train is brought to a stop, while the passenger carriages and usual luggage
vans are actually brought into the covered terminus, the cattle trucks behind are left
outside, just at the end of the platform, where there is an extended place where livestock may land.
   The cattle in question were transported to Kingsbridge in trucks attached to a
passenger train. These trucks when the train stopped were opposite to the enlrged

space I have mentioned. This space is enclosed by a wall with a gate capable of being closed. The evidence is that this place is frequently used for unloading cattle which come by passenger trains. There are there no fences such as are provided at the usual place for unloading cattle, but the enclosing wall and gateway, if closed, serves the purpose, because the cattle could be 'bunched' before being driven out.

The defendants' cattle were in two trucks, and on arrival were taken in charge by John Nugent, the defendants' foreman drover. His evidence is all-important, and I think that the whole case turns upon it. He said: 'There is a cattle bank for the unloading of cattle at Kingsbridge (he is here speaking of the place for unloading cattle trains). There are strong wooden fences to prevent the escape of cattle when they are being unloaded. *We have to take precautions when unloading*. They are liable to take fright when they are being unloaded.' In this part of his evidence he shows the necessity for the pens. He then goes on to say: 'I was entirely in charge of the unloading of the cattle – not the Railway Company. If the waggons were not in a suitable place for unloading it would be my duty to request the Railway Company to put them at a suitable place.' Then, as I understand his evidence, he gave an explanation why he did not require the waggons to be drawn to the proper landing place. He said: 'This was on a Wednesday. The cattle market is on Thursday. These were intended for the market on the following day. I was anxious to get them up as soon as I could and give them a good rest before the market. At this place there were no pens at all.' In other words, he made no objection to the place where there were no pens, the advantage of which he recognised, because he could get his cattle home sooner. Now, let us see whether, having dispensed with the pens, he took precautions, which he said were necessary, because cattle take fright during unloading. There were no pens, but there was at the actual unloading place what served the purposes of a pen. There was a wall enclosing the place with a gate in it capable of being closed, and which, he said, 'can be closed very easily.' If that gate were closed no cattle could have escaped. What happened? The two trucks were unloaded. Two of the cattle were excited, and dashed wildly about. The foreman drover stood at the gate to guard it, but the two cattle dashed through and escaped. Now, by standing at the gate he showed that he thought it required to be guarded. The observation is open that the obviously effective way of guarding it was to close it, and that it would not be an unreasonable opinion to form that the foreman drover did not take proper precautions having regard to his own evidence about the likelihood of cattle taking fright on being unloaded and the necessity for pens.

The two cattle escaped into the City. The foreman drover and an assistant named Hannon remained with the remaining fifteen, as, indeed, I think they were obliged to do, because they could not abandon fifteen on the chance of reclaiming two. These two men drove the fifteen cattle down the quays, and no doubt they hoped to overtake the two which had escaped. They did not do so, and, meeting a drover named Hefferman who was known to Nugent, the latter asked him to search for them, and when he had found them to come back to him in order that he might go to them with more cattle and bring them back quietly. Hefferman went off and found the missing cattle in a yard in Bull Lane. Having located them there, he left them and returned to give the information to Nugent. Meantime the owner of the yard found the cattle on his premises doing damage to his property, and turned them out on the public street. Left there, they again proceeded to wander, one of them found its way to Lord Edward Street, and there knocked down the plaintiff on the footpath, inflicting on her serious injuries. It is very unlikely that there was any vicious attack by the animal. It is much more probable that it was running in a state of fright – the state which one would expect any animal to be in, which was taken from green fields and found itself in the unaccustomed surroundings of a city thoroughfare.

Putting aside for a moment the question of negligence, I will address myself to one of the points made by the defendants' counsel, viz.:– That the damage done to the plaintiff was not the natural and probable consequence of the escape.

It is, no doubt, true that the defendants or their agent could not possibly have foreseen the special accident which is complained of; but it is equally true that anyone allowing a bullock absolutely fresh from the country to wander at large in a crowded city thoroughfare ought to know that anything might happen – the knocking down of an old man, the overturning of a perambulator, a dash into a china shop, or any other mishap impossible to specify. In the present case the mishap was the collision of the beast with the plaintiff. That belonged to the class of things anyone would have apprehended from the escape. But then it was urged that the mishap to the plaintiff was not caused by the escape from the railway premises – that that originating cause had spent itself when the offending animal found an asylum in Kelly's yard – that, there, the chain of causation had stopped – and that he, a *novus interveniens*, by driving out the two cattle started them on an entirely new career of dangerous activity. It appears to me, however, that his action was in law identical with that of the intervening squib-thrower in *Scott* v. *Shepherd* 2 Wm. Bl. 892. As the result of the original escape the cattle found their way to Kelly's private yard where they were playing havoc with his goods, and he drove them out – just as the intervening squib-thrower got rid of the squib. Indeed, in the adventures of a wandering beast there is always the likelihood of an *interveniens*. A bullock is seen rushing down a street and a man with a stick may stop him. It may then divert to another course, from which he may be driven by the shouts of boys, and so on. These interferences are only the natural incidents proceeding from the original escape. They may mark twists and turns, but they do not mark breaks in the chain of causation.

I hold, then, that the final event in the bullock's career, that is, the knocking down of the plaintiff, was the natural consequence of the escape – that that consequence was not too remote, and gave a cause of action if the escape was the result of the defendants' negligence, and if negligence threw legal responsibility on the defendant. I have already indicated that there was evidence of negligence on which the jury might find a verdict for the plaintiff. The learned Judge put the question: 'Did Nugent and Hannon take proper precautions at the unloading of the cattle at Kingsbridge to prevent them escaping on to the public street?' The answer was: 'No, inasmuch as the cattle should have been unloaded at the proper unloading bank.' I read that answer as meaning that there was negligence in allowing the cattle to be unloaded at an unsafe place, or in unloading them at an improper place without taking proper precautions against the attendant risks. The learned Judge interpreted the answer as meaning that the defendants did take proper precautions at the actual unloading, coupled with an expression of opinion that the unloading ought to have taken place at another place. With the utmost respect, I beg to say that this is an impossible interpretation, directly opposed to the language used. I am clearly of opinion that the jury intended to find, and did find, negligence, and that the language of the answer is explained by the evidence of Nugent that he was in entire charge, that, in effect, he accepted the landing place for the special reason that he alleged, and that pens were a most desirable precaution against escape, and in the absence of pens he did not provide against an escape by closing a gate which he admitted he might easily have closed.

But the defence did not stop there. Mr. Fitzgerald, counsel for the defendants, with his usual ability, took up two other lines of defence. Firstly, he maintained that the owner of an animal *manseutae naturae*, unless it be trespassing on private property or unless there be the scienter of vice, is not liable for damage done by such an animal.

No doubt this, as a general proposition, is true, but it must be subject to qualifications; if it is not, it is impossible to understand well-recognised cases of authority. A horse is *manseutae naturae*, and yet if a horse, no matter how well trained and docile, is left unattended in a public street, and if, owing to some special circumstances, her runs away and does damage the owner is liable. If a well-trained and docile horse, accustomed to the traffic of a public street, may occasion actionable damage if unattended and left without control, why should not a bullock, left without any control in a public street and subjected to disturbing surroundings to which it is wholly unaccustomed and which are most likely to produce fright, entail similar consequences? True, the bullock may have no vice, but because he is a bullock he is subject to fright under what are, to it, abnormal circumstances. The rustic coming to town for the first time is more likely to be run over than the townsman. The bullock taken from the serene quietude of his native fields and subjected to the din and noise of a city is more likely to run down the townsman. I do not think that the general proposition on which Mr. Fitzgerald relied covers a case like the present. But, if necessary, I would hold that there was a *scienter* in this case. Nugent said that cattle unloaded from a train are liable to take fright. Fright may not be a vice, properly so called, but it produces a condition which, in a public thoroughfare, is very dangerous, and the owner of the frightened animal is found to take the necessary precautions. I have searched for authority against this proposition and I could find none. I think that it is consistent with all the authorities which were cited during the argument.

The leading case of *Cox* v. *Burbidge* 13 C.B.N.S. 430 was strongly relied upon by the defendants, but the judgment turned entirely upon the improbability of the horse in that case kicking the plaintiff, an event altogether contrary to the habits of the horse. Erle C.J. said 13 C.B.N.S. 430, at p. 436: 'It appears that the horse was on the highway, and that, without anything to account for it, he struck out and injured the plaintiff. I take the well-known distinction to apply here, that the owner of an animal is answerable for any damage done by it, provided it be of such a nature as is likely to arise from such an animal, and the owner knows it . . . The owner of a horse must be taken to know that the animal will stray if not properly secured, and may find its way into his neighbour's corn or pasture. For a trespass of that kind the owner is, of course, responsible. But, if a horse does something which is quite contrary to his ordinary nature, something which his owner has no reason to expect he will do, he has the same sort of protection that the owner of a dog has.' The same law applies to a bullock; but does it mean any more than this: that in usual circumstances a horse and a bullock may be expected to remain harmless when straying on a highway? It does not mean that a bullock normally harmless ought to be expected to continue so, if put out on the highway in a state of excitement caused by fright. Nugent, the drover, said that precautions had to be taken. Why? Because beasts were liable to take fright during unloading. Here is the evidence of the *scienter* – not, perhaps, of a vicious disposition, but of a disturbed condition equally fruitful of harm, which requires precaution. In *Cox* v. *Burbidge* 13 C.B.N.S. 430 the surroundings were rural, apparently those which the horse was accustomed to. How different were they from the circumstances of the present case!

In *Heath's Garage, Ltd.,* v. *Hodges* [1916] 2 K.B. 370 the liability of an owner of animals allowed by him to stray on a public highway was fully considered. It was held that he was not liable because the animals were harmless domestic animals not known to have any dangerous propensity. The offending animal in that case was the most harmless of all domestic animals, a sheep, and the least likely to injure anyone. The idea underlying all the judgments is expressed by Lord Cozens-Hardy, who said (p. 376):– 'I am prepared to hold that in ordinary circumstances, in an ordinary highway' – which was a rural highway – 'it is no breach of duty not to prevent harmless animals like sheep from straying on to the highways, and that it makes no difference whether the action is sought to be based on negligence or on a nuisance to the highway.' The present case is not one of an escape in ordinary circumstances in an ordinary highway. We have the special elements of apprehension on the part of the drover which dictated precaution against the very event which happened. I should also observe that the negligence referred to by Lord Cozens-Hardy was only negligence in not having proper fencing, not negligence in not taking precautions against the escape of an animal in an excitable, and therefore dangerous, condition.

Now I come to Mr. Fitzgerald's last line of defence, maintained with equal ability and courage. His argument was, as I understand it, that by the common law of England – which is also the common law of Ireland – the occupier of a close adjoining a public highway is not under a legal obligation to maintain fences to prevent his animals *mansuetae naturae* from straying on the public highway, and that he is not liable for any accident which is occasioned by such straying under any circumstances. I interjected, during the course of the argument, that if that proposition were to be accepted the possibilities were appalling. It involves this – that a cattle salesman, having stock yards abutting upon a public street, is under no obligation to confine his stock, and may with impunity, so far as damage to individuals is concerned, allow twenty, fifty, or even a hundred head of cattle to stray on the public streets. Or, to take the very case with which we are dealing, if Nugent and his assistant in sheer negligence allowed the whole consignment of seventeen cattle to escape into the public street and if they did damage all round, the defendants would incur no liability to the injured parties. Such consequences must put us on enquiry, because our respect for the common law must make us unwilling to admit that it involves extravagant conclusions.

In my opinion the broad proposition cannot be maintained. In the first place, the cases I have already cited establish that animals *mansuetae naturae* known to have a dangerous propensity may not be allowed by the owner to stray with impunity. In the second place, I am inclined to the opinion (although, as I will show later on, it is unnecessary to decide the question in the present case), that the common law, which relieves the owners and occupiers of land adjoining highways from fencing their lands, does not apply to cities. I have not been able to find any authority to this effect, but I was urged to the conclusion I am inclined to adopt when seeking for an explanation of the common law. Its origin is involved in obscurity, but I think it arose in this way:– When roads were first made they ran through unenclosed country. The imposition of an obligation on the owners of the lands on either side to raise fences would have been intolerable. Indeed, I think it never occurred to anyone to impose such a liability, because there was no necessity for fences. The traffic was so meagre and so slow that the obstruction of cattle was not of any importance whatever. These are the days of motor cars, but in the time of Charles the Second the stage-coach took two days to do the journey from London to Oxford. That, and pack horses, were almost the only traffic on the road. There may have been another reason against the obligation of fencing. The adjoining owners were accredited with the ownership of the soil of the road *ad medium filum viae*, and should not, therefore, be shut out from it; and it also occurs to me that the common law right of diversion for a traveller into the adjoining land, when a portion of the roadway became impassable, was inconsistent with the existence of fences. In modern times the country became enclosed. Owners of lands put up road fences, not for the convenience of travellers, but for their own, and the erection of such fences could impose no liability upon them. But these explanations of the common law have no application to cities. For instance, the ownership *ad medium filum viae* is unknown in cities. For these reasons I am inclined to think that the common law proposition has no application to the conduct of business in cities, and I feel almost driven to this view by a consideration of the consequences which would ensue from non-liability for escape of animals from enclosures abutting upon public streets. It is, further, very remarkable that all the cases which have been cited were concerned with escapes from enclosures in rural districts. But, as I said, it is not necessary to decide that the common law, which was relied upon, does not apply to cities. We are dealing here with premises of an exceptional character – the terminus of a large railway which is an emporium for the consignment of cattle of all kinds, most of which may be quite docile, but others very excitable and unmanageable after the severe strain of a railway journey. To say that such animals may be let loose indiscriminately on crowded highways would, I think, be against the reason and spirit of the common law, which represents what was the common custom of the realm in days gone by.

For these reasons I am of opinion that the plaintiff is entitled to judgment on the finding by the jury, as I read it, that the defendants were guilty of negligence.

Kennedy C.J.:

. . .[W]e must, in my opinion, take it to be admitted and assume (as counsel on both sides have assumed in argument) as if the jury had formally so found, that the bullock which injured the plaintiff, as soon as it was released from the railway waggon, got wild on the platform, and in that wild state rushed out of the railway premises on to the public streets, and that the defendants' servants, Nugent and Hannon, were fully aware of its condition of wildness from the moment it came out of the waggon.

We have the further admission of Nugent, speaking from his experience, that it is necessary 'to take precautions when unloading. They are liable to take fright when they are being unloaded.'

It could not be, and was not suggested that the bullock was at any time after its escape from the railway station in the character of an animal being lawfully driven along a public highway or street, and, in my opinion, decisions relating to the state of facts have no direct application to the admitted facts of the present case.

The main line of argument presented with great force by Mr. Fitzgerald for the defendants was that by the common law there is no duty on an owner of cattle, being of the class of animals *mansuetae naturae*, to fence or otherwise keep them off the highway, and that if they stray and do damage he is not liable unless he had knowledge of a mischievous propensity in the animals, against which alone he should take precautions. Mr. Fitzgerald relied very strongly on *Heath's Garage, Ltd., v. Hodges* [1916] 2 K.B. 370. The argument assumes the absence of a mischievous propensity from the black bullock, or, alternatively, that such propensity (if any) was not proved to be known to the defendants. This argument of course proceeds on the assumption that the wild state of the bullock before its escape was not a 'mischievous propensity,' an assumption which also underlies the judgment of Johnston J.

It appears to me that the argument and the judgment proceed upon the further assumption that the 'mischievous propensity' mentioned in the reported cases means something of a chronic character, though it may be only intermittently active, in the nature of a particular animal. In my opinion, however, what is called a 'mischievous propensity' may be as well a passing or temporary phase of the character or temper of the particular animal as a chronic or permanent element of its nature. If this opinion needs any authority to support it, reference may be made to, *inter alia, Turner* v. *Coates* [1917] 1 K.B., per Lush J., at p. 674; *Manton* v. *Brocklebank* [1923] 2 K.B., per Warrington L.J., at p. 227.

Moreover, the expression 'a mischievous propensity' is not, in my opinion, to be limited to mean only what may be termed a 'specialised propensity,' as for instance in the case of a particular horse, generally mild, but with a special propensity in certain circumstances to kick, or, in the case of bull which has acquired what in view of the famous *dictum* of Blackburn J. must be described as an idiosyncrasy which impels him to gore. I understand by the expression 'a mischievous propensity,' a propensity to do mischief, a tendency to do harm or cause injury, whether, in one case, by some single characteristic action such as kicking or goring or biting, or, in another case, generally, when mischief may be done in any of a variety of ways. As an example of the latter, or general propensity to mischief, take the case of an ox, ordinarily mild, brought to slaughter. It is said that the animals show an instinctive revulsion from the smell of the slaughter house and often become wild. In my opinion if a beast, having become maddened in such circumstances, were allowed by the butcher to escape and run amuck in a crowded street, the butcher must be held to know that the beast was abroad with a mischievous propensity, that is to say, with a general propensity to mischief, though acquired only in the very surroundings from which it had escaped. I think that this view is an element of the *ratio decidendi* in such cases as *Turner* v. *Coates* [1917] 1 K.B. 670. The judgment of Atkin L.J. in *Manton* v. *Brocklebank* [1923] 2 K.B. 212 is to be considered in this connection. Mr. Fitzgerald's argument must logically result in a denial of any responsibility in law on the part of the butcher in the case I have put. I am satisfied that no such immunity is given by the law.

Now, in the case under appeal, the black bullock on emerging from the railway waggon displayed its wild condition to the defendants' servants in such a way as, in my opinion, to deprive them of the benefit of the doctrine of 'the *prima facie* harmlessness of domestic animals as frequenters of the highway' (so put by Neville J. in *Heath's Garage, Ltd.,* v. *Hodges* [1916] 2 K.B. 370, at p. 382). The animal had to the knowledge of Nugent and Hannon become 'an exception to its class' (the phrase is that of Willes J. in *Cox* v. *Burbidge* 13 C.B. (N.S.) 430, at p. 440), and the duty of controlling it as though it belonged to the class of animals *ferae naturae* had fallen on the defendants and their servants: *Cox* v. *Burbidge* 13 C.B. (N.S.) 430, per Willes J.; *Manton* v. *Brocklebank* [1923] 2 K.B. 212, per Atkin L.J., at p. 231; *Turner* v. *Coates* [1917] 1 K.B. 670, per Lush J., at p. 674. The bullock had acquired a propensity to mischief, and it 'did exactly the damage which the owner must have anticipated it would do if the circumstances arose, which in fact arose in this case' (see per Bailhache J. in *Turner* v. *Coates* [1917] 1 K.B., at p. 675), that is to say, it dashed blindly along colliding with or overturning human impediments to its wild progress.

Apart from the defendants' knowledge of the mischievous propensity actually acquired by the animal before the escape, which, in my opinion, takes them out of the defined immunity given to owners of domestic animals, it is to be added that they had prior knowledge on their own admission of the tendency of cattle when being unloaded from the railway to get frightened and to become wild and restless.

I will now consider the case in the view that the claim has been based on negligence only. The third question put to the jury and the answer to that question have been interpreted by Johnston J. as a finding that the defendants did take proper precautions at the actual unloading at the Military Siding coupled with an expression of opinion that the unloading ought to have taken place at another place, namely, the cattle bank. I regret to say that I am at a complete loss to understand how the learned Judge arrives at this interpretation of the finding. It appears to me that the jury have found in the plainest terms that, inasmuch as the cattle were unloaded at the passenger platform and not at the cattle unloading bank, the precautions taken or arrangements made for the unloading (which might have been sufficient and proper at the cattle bank) were not sufficient or proper precautions at the actual place of unloading, and, accordingly, the answer to this question is, in my opinion, a finding of negligence against the defendants.

Such a finding of negligence is amply supported by the evidence. At the cattle bank there are pens for 'bunching' the cattle as they come out of the waggons, which enables control to be established over the animals before they are driven out on the public road. There are no such pens at the Military Siding where the defendants knew the animals would be discharged, and, in fact, caused them to be discharged by sending them by passenger train. The defendants' witnesses said that cattle are liable to take fright when being unloaded. Only two men were sent to take the cattle from the train. The defendants' witness, O'Connor, said in his direct examination that he 'would like to have three men at the unloading of them.' Hannon said in his direct examination that 'no two men could have stopped them.' Further, we have it proved by the defendants, that, opposite to the waggons as they were unloaded, there is a gate leading on to the public road, and that this gate was open; that Nugent stood by it; that it is a gate which moved on wheels, and can be closed very easily, but that Nugent did not close it, and the bullock escaped through it. There is, therefore, evidence to support a finding of negligence both at the earlier stage, namely, at and prior to the actual unloading, and at the later stage, namely, when the bullocks had become wild.

With regard to the fourth question, in answer to which the jury found that Heffernan was guilty of negligence, but negligence which cannot be brought home to the defendants for want of a finding that Heffernan was a servant of the defendants, I must respectfully disagree with the learned Judge who did not put that question to the jury on the ground that 'there was no evidence that Heffernan was in the service of the defendants.' Nugent was, on his own evidence, in complete charge of the business of transferring the cattle from the railway to the defendants' premises, and he was their regular foreman drover. In my opinion it was open to the jury to find on the evidence that Nugent had authority to obtain further assistance in such circumstances as arose here, and that he did within such authority enlist the services of Heffernan for the recapture of the bullocks. In my view of the third finding, however, the plaintiff will not suffer by the gap which defeats the fourth finding.

The suggestion that the action of Kelly, who, when he found the two bullocks smashing up his goods, drove them out of his yard, was a *novus actus interveniens* which broke the chain of causation and cut the plaintiff off from remedy against the defendants could not be seriously pressed. It is too clearly ruled by the principle of *Scott* v. *Shepherd* 2 Wm. Bl. 892. Actually, in that famous case, the analogy is made in one of the judgments with the case of a mad ox turned loose in a crowd, and in another of the judgments with the case of the diverting of the course of an enraged ox.

I am of opinion, therefore, that this appeal must be allowed with costs, and the judgment entered by Johnston J. for the defendants must be set aside, and that in lieu thereof judgment should be given for the plaintiff for £250 damages on the findings of the jury, with costs of action.

[**Fitzgibbon J.** also felt that the verdict in favour of the defendants should not stand. He felt, however, that a new trial should be ordered, for to give a verdict for the plaintiff would be to usurp the functions of the jury.]

KAVANAGH V. STOKES
[1942] I.R. 596

Gavan Duffy J.:

The plaintiff was an invitee and paying guest staying in the defendant's house, and in my opinion it was the duty of the defendant in this case to provide reasonably safe access from the road to the hall-door of her house for people staying in the house, and in my opinion she failed to do so.

I think that negligence has been proved and that, in the special circumstances, there is no need to examine the doctrine of *scienter*, though there was evidence of a previous bite by the dog in question.

The dog was a largish sheep dog, kept as a watch-dog, and its principal duty as such would be to guard the house during the night. The dog hardly knew the girls, of whom the plaintiff was one. They were guests in the house, and had only arrived there the day before. They went to the neighbouring town of Gorey for a dance and told the defendant that they would be back about 11 or 11.30 p.m., and arranged that she should leave the hall-door on the latch for them. They came in about 11.30 p.m. It was the watch-dog's duty and nature to give warning of intruders at night, and of course it might go further than give warning when a number of strange people came to the house late at night.

It is not unusual for young people returning from a dance to be somewhat noisy, though these girls seem to have come in quietly enough, and I think that the defendant, in leaving the dog at large when she knew that the girls, new visitors, would be returning home at a late hour, was careless for the safety of her guests on a dark night, and failed to act reasonably in leaving the dog at large, where he might well be a danger to the girls.

There was evidence that the dog was a dog that rather distrusted strangers. The girls all came in together; four of them ran in, because the dog barked excitedly, but the plaintiff stayed behind to close the gate and the dog bit the plaintiff. There was no evidence before me that the plaintiff had irritated the dog: the suggestion was that she patted him; and I think that the evidence of the plaintiff generally was correct.

Mr. Crivon [counsel for the plaintiff] referred to the observations of Greer L.J. in *Sycamore* v. *Ley* 147 L.T.R. 342, at p. 345, which are in point.

I hold that, in leaving this watch-dog out under the circumstances that I have outlined, the defendant failed in her duty to take reasonable precautions to ensure the safety of, or prevent danger to, the plaintiff and those accompanying her, and that there was no negligence on the part of the plaintiff.

There must be judgment for the plaintiff for the following special damages:–£8 8s. 0d. fees due to Dr. Freedman, £3 3s. 0d. Mr. Pringle's fee, £3 18s 0d. loss of earnings, and 19s 6d. for medicine. Over and above these items I shall allow £30 general damages making a total of £46 8s. 6d.

GIBB V. COMERFORD
[1942] I.R. 295

Maguire P.:

In this action the plaintiff seeks to recover damages for injuries and loss suffered by reason of the negligence of the defendant. There is an alternative claim based on a nuisance. The Circuit Court Judge dismissed the action and it now comes before me on appeal.

The facts, as they appear from the evidence of the plaintiff and of the witnesses called on his behalf, are as follows:– On the 1st September of last year the plaintiff was cycling along a public road in the vicinity of Clonskeagh. A companion was with him, cycling ahead of him. Both of them were keeping properly to their left side of the roadway. According to this companion, a wire-haired fox terrier ran out from the defendant's premises 'Annanaar' and rushed across the road. A motor car was coming towards the plaintiff. It nearly ran over the dog, which then 'dashed back like the shot of a gun' towards the plaintiff and hit the front wheel of his bicycle. The plaintiff applied his brakes but was thrown to the ground. His bicycle was slightly damaged and he suffered certain bodily injuries, principally to one of his fingers. I have no doubt that he did suffer these injuries and no doubt that, as a result of these injuries, he has been prevented from doing his normal work as a painter and decorator since the date of the accident. This was a very unfortunate result from what he may well have regarded as a trivial accident. His losses, although perhaps exaggerated, are serious.

I shall not deal with the question of the identity of the dog involved as I have not heard evidence for the defendant. Ownership is not admitted. I am told, moreover, that, having heard all the evidence, the Circuit Court Judge was not satisfied on this point. As the case stands at the close of the evidence for the plaintiff there is sufficient evidence to satisfy me, if that evidence stood alone and uncontradicted, that the dog which caused the accident belonged to the defendant. The defendant, if I hold there is a case to answer, may be able to satisfy me that it was not his dog which was involved.

I am, however, asked to non-suit the plaintiff on the ground that he has not shown any legal cause of action. The law applicable has been elaborately discussed by Mr. Fahy, and in order fully to review the numerous cases to which he has referred me it would be necessary to reserve judgment. I feel so clear in my own mind, however, as to the legal principles applicable to the facts here, that I do not think that any good purpose would be served by doing so.

The plaintiff grounds his claim firstly on negligence. The law as to domestic animals straying on the highway seems to me to be well settled. A long line of authorities has laid it down that, in the absence of proof of knowledge that a particular domestic animal has a mischievous propensity, the owner is ordinarily under no liability for the acts of such an animal.

The evidence here is that the dog came out of the open gate of the defendant's property, dashed across the road and, as a result of being frightened by an oncoming car, turned back and struck the plaintiff's bicycle, knocking the plaintiff down. There is a complete absence of evidence as to any mischievous propensity in this dog. There is, in fact, positive evidence before me of its harmless disposition.

The law applicable in such circumstances has been clearly and well stated in the judgment of Neville J. in *Heath's Garage Ltd.* v. *Hodges* [1916] 2 K. B. 370. In that case, Neville J. observes (at p. 382):– 'In my opinion the experience of centuries has shown that the presence of domestic animals upon the highway is not inconsistent with the reasonable safety of the public using the road. I am unable to draw any distinction in this regard between domestic animals. I think horses, cattle, sheep, pigs, fowl and dogs all fall into the same category for this purpose. There is no doubt that the advent of motor cars has greatly increased the danger resulting from the presence of loose animals on the road, owing to the speed at which the cars travel and the difficulty shared by man and beast of avoiding them. It was only yesterday, however, that, as mechanically propelled carriages, the right of motor cars to use the roads was subject to conditions which rendered great speed unattainable, and I think that to-day those who use them must take the roads as they find them and put up themselves with such risks as the speed of their cars occasions not only to themselves but to others. The *prima facie* harmlessness of domestic animals as frequenters of the highway is, I think, established as a legal doctrine.'

The learned Judge then goes on, in an interesting passage, to discuss modern conditions of traffic and their possible effect on this doctrine. 'If,' he continues, 'the character of domestic animals with regard to highways had come to be considered for the first time when roads were tarred and motor traffic abounded, it is possible that a different view might have prevailed with regard to their harmlessness on the highway, for, however strongly the instinct of self-preservation may appeal to them, their perceptions may prove inadequate to such a judgment of the speed of the prevailing traffic as will always ensure their safety and consequently the safety of the traffic; but in my opinion it is not competent to the Courts to re-consider the classification of former times and to include domestic animals of blameless antecedents in the class of dangerous animals even when wandering on the roadsides.'

This is the law not alone in England but in this country also. In the Irish case of *Howard* v. *Bergin, O'Connor & Co.* [1925] 2 I.R. 110, the above passage from *Heath's Garage Ltd.* v. *Hodges* [1916] 2 K. B. 370 is referred to with approval by the late Chief Justice Kennedy. In that case a bullock, one of a number which were being unloaded from a train in Dublin, escaped and injured the plaintiff. The Chief Justice in his judgment says (at p. 125): 'Now, in the case under appeal, the black bullock on emerging from the railway waggon displayed its wild condition to the defendants' servants in such a way as, in my opinion, to deprive them of the benefit of the doctrine of "the *prima facie* harmlessness of domestic animals as frequenters of the highway" ' – these last words being quoted from the judgment of Neville J. to which I have referred.

It appears to me difficult to take this case out of the line of authorities of which *Cox* v. *Burbidge* 13 C. B. (N. S.) 430 is an example. Mr. Fahy, however, seeks to persuade me to treat this case as falling within another line of authorities, not dealing with *scienter*. He argues that there was a duty on the defendant to keep his dog under control, a breach of which duty led to this accident. If I do not hold with him that the law as it stands gives the plaintiff a cause of action he asks that the law be extended so as to give a remedy. The Court, he says, should avail itself of the flexibility of the common law and extend it where modern conditions so require. I cannot lose sight of the fact that the changed circumstances arising from modern conditions of traffic were present to the mind of Neville J. in *Heath's Garage, Ltd.* v. *Hodges* [1916] 2 K. B. 370. Road traffic was perhaps not so great in 1916 as it is now, although the traffic at that time in England must have been much the same as it is here to-day. Moreover, as recently at 1925, the principle laid down by Neville J. was accepted by the Supreme Court in this country in *Howard* v. *Bergin, O'Connor & Co.* [1925] 2 I.R. 110 to which I have already referred.

Even if I were convinced of the reasonableness of extending the principles of negligence, I see no justification for doing so in this case and there are many reasons against my doing so. Mr. Fahy, on the other hand, argues that there is no need to extend the common law if I follow a line of authorities, of which recent English cases cited by him are examples, and which, if I apply to the facts here, establish the liability of the defendant. These recent cases, he contends, establish the principle that the owner of a dog who allows it to have uncontrolled access to the highway is in the same position as one who brings his dog upon the highway. The main authority he cites in support of this proposition is *Deen* v. *Davies* [1935] 2 K. B. 282. Although I am not bound by an English decision of that year, I am not disposed to quarrel with the decision of such a Court without very good reason. If I were shown that the facts were substantially the same as in this case I should hesitate before refusing to follow such a decision.

In *Deen* v. *Davies* [1935] 2 K. B. 282 the facts were as follows: A farmer brought his pony into town and tied it up in a stable adjoining a public street; he tied it so loosely, however, that it escaped into the street and caused injury to the plaintiff. The farmer was held negligent and the plaintiff recovered damages for her injuries. As has been emphasised over and over again, each of these cases depends on its own facts, and the facts in that were not on all fours with the facts in the present case. The Court in *Deen* v. *Davies* [1935] 2 K. B. 282 accepted the general principles to which I have already referred. Mr. Fahy relied in particular on the judgment of Romer L.J.

As I read that judgment, the learned Judge seems to have accepted the principles laid down in *Heath's Garage Ltd.* v. *Hodges* [1916] 2 K. B. 370 and followed here by our Supreme Court. Romer L.J. says (at p. 292):– 'Counsel for the appellant, in the course of his interesting argument, properly called our attention to a series of cases in which the Court had to deal with the position of the owner of an animal that escapes from land adjoining a highway on to the highway and there injures somebody who is lawfully using the highway.' He goes on to say:– 'In reading the judgments in these cases it is essential to distinguish between those parts where the Court is dealing with the question of what duty is owned to the public by the owner of an animal which is in a field, say, adjoining the highway and those where it is dealing with the question whether, if he does owe a duty not to let the animal escape on to the highway, the damage sustained by the plaintiff is the natural consequence of his breach of that duty. An interesting illustration of that is to be found in *Cox* v. *Burbidge* 13 C. B. (N. S.) 430.' He then considers *Cox* v. *Burbidge*:– 'In that case . . . a horse that had no vicious propensities escaped from a field adjoining a highway on to the highway by reason of the fact that there were gaps in the hedge separating the field from the road. Having got on to the road, it damaged the plaintiff in the action by kicking him. The decision, which was in fact in favour of the defendant, could have been supported on either of two grounds: either because, the horse having no vicious propensity, there was no duty on the part of the defendant to prevent him getting on to the highway, or because, if there was a duty to prevent the horse from getting on to the highway, the damage done to the plaintiff was not the necessary or probable cause [Query: For 'cause' read 'consequence'? –*eds*.] of that breach of duty, because it was not the habit of that horse to kick. The result would have been a little strange if the Court had arrived at the conclusion that the owner of an animal that is in a field adjoining a highway owes a duty to the public to prevent it getting on to the highway, because if the plaintiff had then been damaged merely by the horse trotting along the highway in the natural manner the defendant would have been liable, but if the plaintiff had been damaged by reason of the horse kicking him, which was an unnatural act on the part of the animal, the defendant would not have been liable. However, the Court decided in favour of the defendant on both grounds.' In his judgment (at p. 294) Romer L.J. says:– 'But there is another series of cases to which our attention was called. . . . Those were cases in which the Court had to deal with the position of the owner of an animal which he himself has brought upon the highway and which, having been so brought, damages somebody else who is lawfully using the highway. Again, on examining those cases, it is very necessary to draw a distinction between two different matters. There is, first of all, the question whether the owner of such an animal owes any duty at all to the public; and secondly, there is the question of whether, if he does owe such a duty, he has committed a breach of it; because, if he does owe a duty to take all reasonable care that the animal he has brought on to the highway does not damage other parties, reasonable care in one case may not be reasonable care in another. Therefore, in some cases where a man has so brought an animal on to the highway he has been held liable for damage caused to another party, and in other cases he has not been held liable. As I read those cases, bearing that distinction again in mind, it has been clearly established that the owner of an animal who brings it on to the highway does owe a duty to those who are using the highway to use all reasonable care to prevent the animal damaging other parties. Reasonable care in the country may not be reasonable care in the town: reasonable care in the case of one animal may not be reasonable care in the case of another. In one of the cases to which Slesser L.J. has referred, the owner of a colt, which he had tethered behind a cart or which was following a cart which colt was of an excitable disposition (as most untamed colts are), was held liable for the damage done to a person using the highway by the colt suddenly swerving to one side: and it was held that, having regard to the nature of the animal, he had not taken all reasonable care to prevent the animal from damaging somebody else. In these cases the general principle is established, that the owner of an animal which he brings on to the highway must use all reasonable care to prevent the animal doing damage.'

In that case it will be seen that Romer L.J. draws a clear distinction between the obligation of owners of animals straying on the highway and animals brought on to the highway by their owner. The Court of Appeal held that the case fell within the second of these categories. In the present case, however, the plaintiff's case is that the defendant had his dog on his own premises whence it strayed on to the highway. It seems to me that to apply that case here would have the effect of abolishing the distinction drawn in the judgment of Romer L.J. in that case.

Another case cited by the plaintiff is *Pitcher* v. *Martin* [1937] 3 All E. R. 918. The facts in that case were that an owner brought her dog on the road on a long lead which she held so loosely that the dog escaped and the lead became entangled with the plaintiff's legs, causing the plaintiff to fall. In giving judgment in favour of the plaintiff, Atkinson J. remarks:– '*Prima facie*, there would here be a case of liability. I have no difficulty in holding that a dog with a loose lead in the streets of London is a cause of danger to users of the highway, and a dog with a loose lead, being free in the streets, is something which calls for explanation by the person in control, to rebut the allegation of negligence.' Surely that case falls within the second class of cases to which Romer L.J. refers, and is entirely distinct from the class of cases concerned with animals straying unattended on the highway.

I might go on to discuss the other cases referred to by counsel for the plaintiff, such as *Sycamore* v. *Ley* 147 L.T.R. 342, and *Milligan* v. *Henderson* 1915 S.C. 1030, but to my mind the distinction between the two lines of authority is quite clear, and I see no ground for refusing to apply the accepted principle of the *prima facie* harmlessness of domestic animals straying on the highway.

In the alternative, Mr. Fahy asks me to hold that the defendant is liable in nuisance. I can understand that the rule in *Rylands* v. *Fletcher* may apply in the case of wild animals, but it appears to me to have no application to a domestic animal.

I have great sympathy with the plaintiff, but I must dismiss this action. If the law needs modification there is no difficulty in our Legislature making such a modification, should modern conditions be thought to require it; but it is not for me to change the law.

Questions

1. Is the distinction between animals that stray on to the highway on the one hand, and animals that are brought onto the highway on the other, a sound one?
2. If *Gibb* v. *Comerford* were to have been decided in 1983, what do you think would have been the result? Why?

Liability for mischievous propensity of domestic animal. Scienter.

BENNETT & ANOR. V. WALSH
70 I.L.T.R. 252

(Circuit Ct., Judge Davitt, 1936)

The infant plaintiff, Yvonne Bennett, claimed £300 for damages for personal injuries occasioned to her on August 28, 1935, in a garden at 43 Strand Road, Sandymount, Dublin (the defendant's residence) by a dog (an Irish terrier) owned and kept by the defendant, which attacked and bit the plaintiff. It was alleged that the dog was of a fierce and mischievous nature and accustomed to attack and bite mankind and that the defendant wrongfully kept the dog, well knowing that it was of such fierce and mischievous nature and so accustomed.

The infant's father, Albert Bennett, on the same Civil Bill, claimed £36 15s. 0d. for special damages in respect of loss and expense occasioned to him in the circumstances, *i.e.*, doctors' fees, medicines, nursing, etc.

The defendant pleaded in his defence, *inter alia*, denials that he owned or kept the dog: that it was of a fierce or mischievous nature or accustomed to attack or bite mankind; that he knew it was of such nature or so accustomed.

Evidence was given on behalf of the infant plaintiff, a girl, aged 6 years, who appeared in Court, of her being attacked by the dog on August 28, 1935, when it was in charge of the defendant's daughter, Ann Walsh, aged about 9 years, in the defendant's garden, and being severely bitten in the face, resulting in serious injury, bleeding and shock, which necessitated surgical operations resulting in permanent scars in the absence of treatment by plastic surgery.

Evidence was given also as follows:– By Yvonne Bennett's mother that she was present with Ann Walsh and others when the dog snapped at a little boy, Barton Brown, in May or June, 1935. Ann Walsh was rebuked by one of those present (Barton Brown's mother) who ordered Ann Walsh to take the dog and bring it home, which she did.

By Mita O'Rourke as to the above incident and as to an incident in July, 1935, when the dog turned on and snapped at her child. She ordered Ann Walsh to take and keep the dog away. Mita O'Rourke, in August, 1935, saw the dog, then unaccompanied, 'charge up to' two little children and catch one of them by the hair.

By Barton Brown's mother that when the dog snapped at her son she hunted the dog away and ordered Ann Walsh to take the dog away, which she did.

By Bernard Burns that one evening the dog charged out and ran after him. The dog did not actually bite him.

None of the witnesses as to the dog's disposition and activities complained to the defendant or his wife, whose daughter lived with them.

At the close of evidence for the plaintiff *McGilligan* asked for a direction to the jury that there was no case to answer on the grounds, *inter alia*, that there was no evidence of notice to the defendant of the dog's mischievous propensities.

The learned Judge, having referred to *Baldwin* v. *Casella*, (1872) L. R. 7 Exch. 325, establishing that knowledge by a servant, who has charge of a dog, of its mischievous propensities is equivalent to knowledge of the master –

Brereton Barry cited *Elliott* v. *Longden* (1901) 17 T. L .R. 618, where its owner was held liable in respect of a dog which was mischievous to the knowledge of the owner's son, a boy aged 11 years.

Judge Davitt ruled that it was sufficient in the circumstances to prove that Ann

Walsh had knowledge of the vicious propensities of the defendant's dog.

The defendant giving evidence denied knowledge of the alleged previous attacks. His daughter, for whom the defendant had got the dog as a present, also denied knowledge of them. It was admitted by the defendant's wife that Ann Walsh had told her of the dog's attacking and devouring a litter of kittens.

At the close of the defendant's case a further submission was made on the defendant's behalf by *McGillian* that there was no case to go to the jury on the grounds:– That there was not sufficient evidence of viciousness in the dog; that whatever knowledge Ann Walsh had in respect of his dog was not in the circumstances distinct knowledge of viciousness and that on the evidence the defendant, through his daughter, could not be said to have knowledge of the dog's viciousness.

Reference was made to *Gladman* v. *Johnson*, (1867) 36 L. J. C. P. 153; *Line* v. *Taylor*, 3 F. & F. 731; *Knott* v. *London County Council*, [1931] 1 K. B. 126.

The jury returned a verdict that the dog was vicious on August 28, 1935, and that the defendant's daughter knew. The foreman indicated that the jury were under the impression that both the defendant and his daughter knew that the dog was vicious. On being asked to answer categorically the questions: 'Did the defendant's daughter know?' 'Did the defendant know?' the jury found that the father knew through the daughter.

Damages for the plaintiff Yvonne Bennett, £100. Special damages for the adult plaintiff, £31.

Question

Will the owner of an animal be liable in *scienter* for knowledge of the mischievous propensity where

    (a) he has no personal knowledge of the propensity but his wife has?

    (b) he has no personal knowledge of the propensity but his servant has?

    (c) he has no personal knowledge of the propensity but a teenage member of his household has?

    (d) he has no personal knowledge of the propensity but his nine year old daughter has?

QUIN V. QUIN
39 I.L.T.R. 163 (Lord O'Brien, L.C.J., 1905)

Appeal from a decision of the Country Court Judge of Limerick, heard at Limerick Spring Assizes, 1905. The Civil Bill was for £17, loss and damage sustained by the plaintiff, for that the defendant in April, 1904, allowed two of his pigs to wander into the plaintiff's cow-stall and tear and eat off two of a cow's paps, by reason of which the cow died. The plaintiff and defendant occupied the same land, and had the joint use of a stall, with a timber partition dividing the plaintiff's portion from the defendant's. The Plaintiff requested the defendant to put up a substantial partition, but the defendant did not do so, and one of his sows, having got into the portion of the stall occupied by the plaintiff's cow, attacked it and tore its paps, by reason of which injuries the cow died. Evidence was given by the plaintiff that on a previous occasion the same sow, in the presence of the defendant, had attacked and killed some cocks and hens.

Lord O'Brien L.C.J.:

This case, as presented before me, has a perfectly different aspect from that which it presented before the County Court Judge, for a new volume of evidence has been added here. I believe that the sow eat (sic) the cocks and hens in the presence of the defendant as deposed to by the plaintiff. The question then is whether this particular sow was a sow of mischievous propensities with a taste for blood. A cock or hen is an animal, and a cow is an animal and they both have blood. Therefore the sow had a mischievous disposition to take blood, and as I am certain the defendant saw the birds being attacked, the mischievous disposition was evidenced before the defendant. It pre-eminently stands out in the case that the sow bit the cow, blood poisoning ensued, the plaintiff lost her cow. It was killed by a sow with mischievous propensities known to the defendant, and consequently I give a decree for £10.

Questions

1. If the sow in *Quin*, after attacking the cocks, had attacked a child, would the owner of the sow have been liable?
2. X's greyhound has shown a tendency to 'fight' while racing at track meetings. This tendency takes the form of snapping at other greyhounds who try to pass him. Is X liable if the greyhound in X's backyard bites Y's child?
3. Is a 'Beware of the Dog' sign on a gate a licence to bite? *Cf. Forster* v. *Donovan, Ireland and Attorney-General* 114 I.L.T.R. (High Ct., Costello J., 1980).

Liability for damage caused to adjoining property by 'tamed' dear and wild rabbits.

BRADY V. WARREN
[1900] 2 I.R. 632

Palles, C.B.:

One of the questions argued in this case is interesting. It is, whether Lord Justice Fitzgibbon should, at the trial, have directed a verdict for the defendant on the claim for trespass of deer, upon the ground that there was no evidence that the deer were tame or 'reclaimed.'

The action was brought to recover damages for injuries to the plaintiff's crops, caused by deer and rabbits which were alleged to be 'kept' by the defendant. The jury found that those animals were the defendant's; and what, to my mind, is the same thing in another form, that they were 'kept' by him. They further found that reasonable care to prevent them injuring the plaintiff's farm had not been taken; and they assessed, for the damage caused by the deer, £102 8s, and for that by the rabbits, £10. Judgment was entered for the sum of these two amounts; and the present application is to change the verdict, on the ground that there was no evidence of any liability on the defendant, or for a new trial, on the ground that the verdict was against the weight of evidence.

The plaintiff is a tenant in occupation of certain farms, which adjoin Warrenscourt demesne, in the county Cork. The defendant has been, since January, 1898, in occupation of that demesne, which contains between 600 and 700 acres. Within the demesne is a walled enclosure of about 40 acres, called the 'Deer Park,' but which is not a park in the feudal sense of that term. Fallow deer were kept in this park during the entire time which is covered by the evidence; but up to a date, which is fixed by the defendant at 1893, none of them lived in the demesne outside the park. In that year there appears to have been a breach in the park wall, and in consequence some of the deer escaped into the demesne. Some repairs were effected to the wall of the park, but the deer that had escaped were not brought back into the park. The plaintiff gave evidence that so long as the former owner, Sir Augustus Warren, was in possession of the demesne, that is, till the beginning of the year 1898, its boundary wall was kept in repair by him, by which I suppose is meant that it was so kept as to enclose the deer; but still he says that the trespass of deer upon his farms began about eight years ago. But however this may have been during the possession of Sir Augustus Warren, there is evidence that 'in recent years,' by which I suppose is meant, during the defendant's occupation of the demesne, the deer crossed the wall whenever they liked. The plaintiff says: 'There is no more to prevent trespass of deer from the demesne on my farm than if it was an open street.' It is the case of the defendant also that there was not such an enclosure of the deer in the demesne as would have prevented them leaving it had they so desired, and this must be deemed a common fact in the case. But, notwithstanding this, there is a body of evidence, as well in the defendant's as in the plaintiff's case, from which a reasonable inference is that the deer which escaped from the park, instead of straying about the country, and becoming wild, remained in the demesne as their home, in the same way as they would have remained in it, had it been sufficiently enclosed; that they bred there and increased in numbers; and that when they occasionally left the demesne and went on the plaintiff's lands, they returned to the demesne. The defendant says that about thirty escaped out of the park into the demesne; and he fixes at about sixty (and the plaintiff at from eighty to 100) the number now in the demesne. In addition, many were shot by the defendant and his friends. The defendant was cross-examined as to the absence of straying habits in the deer. He says: 'I have heard of deer being seen in the neighbourhood. I cannot say when or where. I heard about a year ago of a deer being seen outside the demesne. I did not look on it as extraordinary. I forget really whose it was. It was not a deer of mine. I do not say who it belonged to: it might be one of my own deer. I really don't know if there are any other deer than mine in the whole district.' Murphy, the defendant's woodranger, who was examined for him, says:– 'They (the deer) go out of the demesne, and miles away. I have known them to go three miles across the townland to Doonisky. I do not know if they came back.'

These two passages are the only ones I can find as to straying habits in the deer; and contrasting them, general and unsatisfactory as they are, with the body of testimony, appearing as well in the evidence of the defendant's as of the plaintiff's witnesses, that the deer remained in the demesne, bred there, came from there into the plaintiff's farm, returned there from the plaintiff's farm, and there increased in numbers, I entertain no doubt that the jury might reasonably have arrived at the conclusion that there was, on the part of the deer, by reason of their or their ancestors having been bred in the park, some attraction, or relation in the nature of an attraction, to the demesne, different from that which they had to any other place; that they remained there, usually and almost constantly, as in their home; that their absence from it was occasional, and arising from external causes, such as the existence at times upon the plaintiff's farm of food of a kind which they preferred to that which was then available in the demesne; and that as a rule they returned to the demesne, as soon as they had satisfied the immediate desire which induced them to leave it. The distinction, then, between these deer, as they were in the demesne, and deer, as they would have been in the demesne had it been so enclosed as to prevent them leaving it, is that in the latter case they would have been coerced to remain within it, whatever might be their habit or desire, whereas in the actual case we have to determine they remained there in consequence of habit or desire.

The defendant, of course, admits that he would be answerable for any damage caused by the trespass of the deer which were in the walled park; but he insists that the deer in the demesne outside the park are *ferae naturae*, for whose acts he is not responsible; and further, that either there was no evidence at the trial that any of the damage sued for was caused by the park deer, or, if there was, that no distinction was drawn by the learned Lord Justice, in his summing up, as to the defendant's liability in respect of these two classes of animals. No objection, however, to this effect was taken at the trial; and it cannot, I think, be denied that there was evidence for the jury that some of the damage was caused by the park deer. Mr. McMullen, a surveyor, examined for the plaintiff, proved that upon the Monday before the trial there was, in the park wall, the appearance of four gaps having been recently filled up; that in one of these, 15 feet wide, the wall had been reduced to 3 feet in height; and that in the three others, of widths of 13 feet, 12 feet, and 9 feet, the wall, as reduced, did not exceed 2 feet, or 2 feet 9 inches. This witness was not cross-examined. The evidence of the plaintiff himself was to the same effect, although not so particular. 'The deer park wall,' he says, 'is broken down: the deer can go in and out in several places.' The defendant said that he had seen other breaches since 1893; that they were mended up immediately that he knew nothing of recent gaps, but that his men had orders to make them up, that a storm would make them. He adds, however, that no deer got out of the park, to his knowledge, since 1893.

It was also proved – which, to my mind, is a matter of great importance – that Sir Augustus Warren fed the deer during the winter with hay, laurels, and oats. This evidence is not very specific as to time, but taking it in the context in which it occurs, it would appear to me that Sir Augustus was, during his time, in the habit of feeding them through the winter. The statement occurs in the portion of the plaintiff's evidence which deals with the damage sustained. He says that 'the deer did £20 damage in 1895; that they trespassed in like manner in 1896, getting heavier every year; that they broke out when they were tired of their own place.' Then he says: 'In 1897 they were worse again. Sir Augustus fed them through the winter with hay, laurels and oats. The present man, his son, did not feed them, so far as I know.' This would appear to contrast the state of things in Sir Augustus' time, to the end of 1897, with that during the defendant's occupation, since that year.

Lastly, it was proved that the defendant's agent, Mr. Carroll, promised the plaintiff that the deer would be kept off his farm. Carroll was not called to contradict this.

Some statements made by Murphy, the wood-ranger, were relied upon during the argument; but as I have not thought it necessary to take them into consideration in arriving at my conclusion, I do not occupy time by referring to them.

Now, as to the defendant's application to direct a verdict for him, it might be sufficient without entering the main subject of controversy, to say that there was abundant evidence from which the jury might assume that a substantial part of the damage was caused by deer which were within the enclosure, and passed out through the breaches in the wall; but as the case has been mainly argued by the plaintiff upon the ground that the defendant was responsible in law for the trespass of the deer in the demesne, as well as of those in the park, and as the jury appear to have assessed as damages the full amount proved by the plaintiff, we could not sustain the verdict if the plaintiff is not correct in his contention as to the defendant's liability. The question then is, was there evidence from which the jury might reasonably arrive at the conclusion that these deer in the demesne were tame for it is admitted that, if they were, there is abundant evidence that they were kept by the defendant.

Is there, then, evidence that they were tame? The reason of the distinction between the right of property in animals which are of a tame and domestic nature, as distinct from *ferae naturae*, is elementary. Blackstone states it to be (vol. ii., book ii., chap. I) because the former 'continue perpetually in his occupation, and will not stray from his house or person, unless by accident or fraudulent enticement, in either of which cases the owner does not lose his property.' This distinction is kept in view in determining whether animals *ferae naturae* have been tamed. Bracton's view on this subject is thus translated by Sir Travers Twiss (edit. 1878, vol. i., p. 67): 'If wild animals have been tamed, and they by habit go out and return, fly away and fly back, such as deer, swans, and sea-fowl, doves, and such like; another rule has been approved, that they are so long considered as ours, as long as they have a disposition to return,' *quamdiu habuerint animum revertendi*. 'For if they have no disposition to return, they cease to be ours; but they seem to cease to have the disposition to return when they have abandoned the habit of returning': *revertendi autem animum videntur desinere habere cum consuetudinem revertendi desinuerint*. This view, which is taken from the civil law (Gaius, ii. 68; Inst. 2, i. 15), is to be found in all our law books which treat of this subject. It is to be observed of the civil law, that in the passage from Gaius, from which Bracton probably took the words I have read, deer are, as they are in Bracton, specially mentioned as being among the class of animals which may have this habit of going and returning, and by reason of this habit may be subjects of property. The habit there mentioned, however, is of going into and coming back from 'the woods': *item cervisque in sylvas ire et redire solent*. The woods referred to were, doubtless, not land in the actual occupation of mankind, as is the plaintiff's farm here, but the wild forests, beyond the resort of man, which would be the natural habitation of such deer if they returned to their original wildness. The habit of going into such woods, although accompanied by a habit of returning, involves more of a desire to become wild again than merely breaking into an adjoining farm and returning from it, as if they permanently remained in the wild forests they would be deemed to have become wild again. No such result would follow from their permanently remaining on the plaintiff's farm.

Further, the fact that deer are more usually domesticated now than they were in feudal times has, for more than a century and a half, been recognised as matter of law. In *Davies* v. *Powell* (Willes' Rep. 16, 48) the question was whether deer in an enclosed place were distrainable. Willes, C.J., in contrasting the view which the law took of deer, in the time of Lord Coke, with that then held, says. 'Besides, the nature of things is now very much altered, and the reason which is given for the rule fails. Deer were formerly kept only in forests or chases, or such parks as were parks either by grant or prescription, and were considered rather as things of pleasure than of profit; but now they are frequently kept in enclosed grounds which are not properly parks, and are kept principally for the sake of profit, and, therefore, must be considered as other cattle.' Again, he adds (ibid. p. 51): 'When the nature of things changes, the rules of law must change too. When it was holden that deer were not distrainable, it was because they were kept principally for pleasure, and not for profit, and were not sold and turned into money as they are now. But now they are become as much a sort of husbandry as horses, cows, sheep, or any other cattle. Whenever they are so, and it is universally known, it would be ridiculous to say that, when they are kept merely for profit, they are not distrainable as other cattle, though it has been holden that they were not so when they were kept only for pleasure.' The principle is recognised and approved of in *Morgan* v. *The Earl of Avergavenny* (8 C. B. 768, 798), the judgment in which, prepared by Wilde, C.J., and 'in substance assented to' by the entire Court, contains this sentence: 'In considering whether the evidence warranted the verdict upon the issue whether the deer were tamed and reclaimed, the observations made by Lord Chief Justice Willes in the case of *Davies* v. *Powell* (Willes' Rep., 46, 48) are deserving of attention. The difference in regard to the mode and object of keeping deer in modern times from that which anciently prevailed, as pointed out by Lord Chief Justice Willes, cannot be overlooked. It is truly stated that ornament and profit are the sole objects for which deer are now ordinarily kept, whether in ancient legal parks, or in the modern enclosures so called, the instances being very rare in which deer in such places are kept and used for sport: indeed, their whole management differing very little, if at all, from that of sheep, or of any other animals kept for profit.' To the same effect is the judgment of Lord Hatherley, when Vice-Chancellor, in *Forde* v. *Tynte* (2 J. & H. 150; 31 L. J. Ch. 177). In reference to this last mentioned case, as well as to *Morgan* v. *Abergavenny*

(8 C.B. 768), it is to be observed that the question in each was not whether the deer in question were or were not property, but was whether they were parcel of the inheritance, or personal property. In determining this question the mode in which the parks were enclosed was immaterial. In the present case, however, the circumstance that the demesne is, to a certain extent, fenced, although not in such a way as to prevent the deer leaving it if they desire, is one that cannot be left out of consideration, as it is evidence on the question whether the deer were under the control of the defendant.

I do not think it necessary to contrast the evidence of the 'management' of the deer with that in either of the cases I have last mentioned, as each case of this description must depend upon its individual facts. Here, as in each of the two cases I have referred to, there was evidence of 'management' of the deer, and of management of them as the property of the defendant. Therefore, the present case can be well determined on one or other, or both of two separate considerations, viz.:–

(1.) That it is a reasonable inference from the evidence that these deer had the habit of remaining in the demesne, a place of quasi captivity, although they had the opportunity of escaping from it, and the habit of returning to it when they occasionally left it for the plaintiff's farm.

(2.) That it is also a reasonable inference from the evidence that they were managed in the same way as other domestic cattle, oxen, sheep, &c., making allowance for the difference of their nature.

Having regard to these considerations, taken in connection with the nature of the animals in question, fallow deer, always easily tameable, and in the present day usually tamed and kept for profit, I entertain no doubt that there was evidence to go to the jury that the deer in the demesne were tame, were under the defendant's control, in his possession, were his, and were kept by him, and that the findings in the affirmative of these questions were in accordance with the weight of the evidence.

The verdict, therefore, on this head of the plaintiff's claim must stand.

The second claim was for trespass by rabbits. As to this there is more difficulty. It is laid down in *Boulston's Case* (Rep., Part V., 101 b; more fully Cro. Eliz. 517 (21)), that 'if a man makes cony burrows in his own land, which increase in so great numbers that they destroy his neighbour's land next adjoining, his neighbour cannot have an action on the case against him who makes the said cony burrows'; and the reason is given, 'for as soon as the conies go on his neighbour's land he may kill them, for they are *ferae naturae*, and he who makes the cony burrows has no property in them.' To the same effect is *Hinsley* v. *Wilkinson* (Cro. Car. 387), and *Boulston's Case* (Rep., Part V., 104 b; more fully Cro. Eliz. 547 (21)) is cited with approval by Bayley, J., in delivering the judgment of the full Court of King's Bench, in *Hannam* v. *Mockett* (2) B. & C. 934, 939); and is admitted by both parties to be now law. Accordingly, the Lord Justice directed the jury that the defendant was not answerable for any amount of damage caused by the natural and reasonably to be expected trespass of rabbits, having regard to the existence of rabbits in the locality. To this direction no objection was taken. The Lord Justice, however, proceeded to leave to the jury the question whether the defendant *kept* rabbits upon his land in such *extra* numbers, or under such circumstances, as to cause *further or additional* damage; but only so far as he could have prevented it by reasonable fencing, or by killing a large number, or by other reasonable means; and he further told the jury that, before they could find for the plaintiff, they should be satisfied that there was a use of the rabbits by the defendant as his property, which would impose upon him the duty of reasonable care not to injure his neighbour in the mode of using his own property. This direction I regard as having been given, not as expressing the Lord Justice's own final or deliberate opinion of the law, but to render unnecessary a second trial, in the event of the Court holding that the action lay.

The question is, was there evidence to go to the jury that the defendant was liable for any part of the trespass of the rabbits? The principal evidence upon which this question was left, and the only evidence relied upon during the argument in support of it, is compendiously summed up by the Lord Justice as that 'of stocking, or trapping for profit, and of the offer of compensation by Mr. Carroll.' No other portion of the evidence has been relied on for the plaintiff.

The following is the substance of the evidence thus referred to: Sir Augustus Warren, who was in the habit of selling the rabbits, brought two Belgian rabbits there and subsequently some years since, brought some bucks to the demesne, let them into the burrows, and reared a great quantity from them. Shortly afterwards the plaintiff commenced to complain of their trespass, and he continued to do so till this action was brought. When the defendant succeeded Sir Augustus in the possession, he continued to kill, trap, and sell rabbits for profit. As to the number sold by him, he stated in answer to questions of the Lord Justice, that the most he sold in any year was 4,000, that he sold that number five years ago, when he was managing for his father, that in 1899 he sold about 3,000, and in 1898 less. Mr. Carroll, the defendant's agent, offered to allow the plaintiff half a year's rent, £8 15s., for the damage caused by the rabbits.

In determining whether the facts I have stated amount to evidence of liability in the defendant, I desire to confine myself to the exact question in issue. I purposely refrain from considering whether an action would lie against a person who by his own act, such as *bringing* rabbits on his land, caused them to increase to such an unreasonable extent that his neighbour's lands are thereby injured to a greater extent than they would have been, had the natural growth of the wild rabbits already on the lands not been effected. No actual decision on that question has been cited. In *Hitton* v. *Greene* (2 F. & F. 821), *Birkbeck* v. *Paget* (31 Beav. 403), *Paget* v. *Birkbeck* (3 F. & F. 683), and *Farrer* v. *Nelson* (15 Q. B. D. 258), the question was the liability to the occupier of the land of a person entitled to a right of shooting over that occupier's land, not his liability to an adjoining occupier. In all such cases the question must be whether the act of bringing the animals on the land is authorised by the right granted to the defendant, and necessarily is wholly different from that between adjoining occupiers which does not depend on grant. Undoubtedly, however, in *Farrer* v. *Nelson* (15 Q. B. D. 258), Pollock, B., expressed the opinion, apparently with the assent of Day, J., that such an action as I have mentioned will lie. 'I will first deal,' he says, 'with the question whether an action can be brought by a neighbour against any person who collects animals upon his land so as to injure the crops of his neighbour; and I should say that, beyond doubt, such an action would lie, and that the rule upon which it would be founded would be not so much negligence as upon an infraction of the rule *sic utere tuo ut alienum non laedas.*' I cannot say that I think we can gain much assistance from this maxim, as to bring any case within it you must first show that the act complained of does 'injury' (in a legal sense) to the neighbour: *damnum sine injuria* would not be sufficient, and to ascertain whether the act is an 'injuria,' it must be shown that it was a breach of an obligation due by the defendant to the neighbour, and thus we come back to the question which it was proposed to solve (El. Bl. & El. 643). Further, I am of opinion that the proposition can hardly have been intended to be taken in its broad generality or otherwise than subject to some restriction in respect of the occupier's reasonable use of his own lands. For the purpose of this judgment, however, I assume it to be law, and I further assume that which I think may well be subject to some doubt, that notwithstanding *Boulston's Case* (Rep., Part V., 104 b; more fully, Cr. Eliz. 547 (21)), rabbits are 'animals' within the rule, and that the proved acts of Sir Augustus Warren amounted to a bringing of the rabbits upon the land. Further, I assume that which I also gravely doubt, that there was evidence of the rabbits being in such extra numbers (over and above that which would have existed but for the introduction of the bucks), as to cause damage additional to that which would have been caused by the 'natural and reasonably to be expected trespass' of rabbits whose breeding had not been interfered with by Sir Augustus. Making all these assumptions, I come to the one single proposition on which I decide this portion of the case. It is this: that although these assumed circumstances *might be* sufficient to maintain the action, had it been brought against Sir Augustus Warren in his lifetime, he is not the defendant here. The action is against a person who, subsequently to the rabbits being turned on, became entitled to the possession of the land. When the defendant so became entitled, the rabbits which had been turned on by Sir Augustus, and their progeny, were wild. It is not proved that the defendant himself brought rabbits to the land, or personally interfered in relation to their being brought by Sir Augustus. If, therefore, the bringing of them is to render him liable, he can be so liable only, as a *subsequent occupier* of land which continued to be affected by a wrongful act of Sir Augustus. I cannot, however, see that that act of Sir Augustus can, in law, impose upon the land a quasi servitude, rendering its occupier liable in respect of wild rabbits, under circumstances in which no liability is imposed upon him by the common law. The case does not appear to me to be analogous to that of a continuing nuisance as it might have been had the rabbits been tame when the defendant came into possession. Had they then been tame, there would have been evidence that he 'kept' them, and the case would have been different.

The two matters left to the consideration of the jury by the learned Lord Justice, in addition to the stocking or turning on of the rabbits by Sir Augustus, were the defendant's user of them for profit by selling them, and the agent's offer to allow half a year's rent for the damage. But if the rabbits were on the defendant's land under such circumstances that the defendant was not liable for their trespass, then whilst he as occupier of the land was entitled to trap or shoot on that land as many as he thought proper, he was not under any obligation to the plaintiff, the adjoining occupier, to do so. The number that he trapped was a matter entirely for himself. The trapping of rabbits on the plaintiff's land is out of the case, as this was done by his licence. As to the agent's offer to allow money for the damage, had there been *any* evidence of the liability of the defendant, sufficient to be left to the jury, this offer might legitimately be considered as adding to the *weight* of it; but it cannot, in my opinion, per se amount to evidence of a liability which is negatived by all the other facts in evidence.

I am therefore of opinion that the plaintiff's only remedy for the trespass was to kill the trespassing rabbits, and that the verdict, so far as it relates to this cause of action, should be entered for the defendant.

[**Johnson J.** in a separate judgment agreed with **Palles C.B.'s** judgment while **Boyd J.** agreed as to the rabbits but felt that there be no liability in respect of the deer.]

Note

See also *Cream* v. *Nolan*, *supra* p. 26.

Liability for 'mass of animals forming an obstruction of the highway.'

CUNNINGHAM V. WHELAN
52 I.L.T.R. 67 (1917)

Molony, L.J.:

This civil bill was brought by the plaintiff to recover damages for personal injury, and raises an interesting question as to the liability of owners for cattle straying on the highway. There has been no great conflict of evidence in the case, as no person representing the defendant was present, or had any knowledge of the occurrence at the time. According to the evidence of the plaintiff, he was proceeding in an empty cart from Ballynahanagh to Kilmacthomas, and when he was going along the public road he saw 24 bullocks and heifers, the property of the defendant, some distance in front of him. There was nobody in charge of them, and when he came near he slowed down his horse and came to a standstill, but notwithstanding this the bullocks and heifers pressed in on the cart, upset it, and threw him out, and thereby damaged the cart and injured the plaintiff. John Walsh was examined on the part of the defendant, and said the defendant had land adjoining the roadway, and that it was most likely the cattle had got on to the highway through the gate, which was open. It is not necessary to discuss how the cattle were on the roadway, as it is admitted they were there when the plaintiff came up, and that nobody was in charge. Now, in these circumstances, what is the liability of the owner of the cattle, apart from the Petty Sessions Act or from the Highway Acts, as they are in England, in respect of cattle straying on the highway? There is abundant authority for saying that, apart from an animal of a vicious propensity, there is no liability on the owner of cattle for the mere trespass of an animal on the highway. He is liable for proceedings summarily for trespass of cattle on the highway: but the mere fact of the animal being on the highway and not known to be of a vicious propensity does not create liability in respect of the animals for the mere act of trespass. The ordinary rule is well illustrated in the case of *Jones* v. *Lee* 106 L. T. R. 126. In that case a young horse escaped owing to a defective hedge on to the highway, and caused injury to a motorist. The County Court Judge held that the horse was not vicious, and the defendant was not liable, and this decision was affirmed on appeal. Bankes, J., stated that 'by common law the owner or occupier of land adjoining a highway is under no duty to fence, so as to keep his animals off the highway.' *Jones* v. *Lee* was, in the same year, considered by the Court of Appeal in the case of *Ellis* v. *Banyard* (106 L. T., p. 51, C. A.). In that case the plaintiff was cycling along the highway and was injured by a cow the property of the defendant, which had strayed on to the highway from the adjoining lands of the defendant through a gate, which had been left open by the defendant. The County Court Judge held that the opening of the gate was evidence of negligence. That, of course, would be a decision on the main facts in favour of the plaintiff here; but when it went to a Divisional Court the judges differed, because Mr. Justice Horridge adopted the view of the County Court Judge, and Mr. Justice Phillimore said it should be shown that the opening of the gate should be proved to be an act of his servant. In the Court of Appeal all the three judges entered judgment for the defendant, and adopted the judgment of Bankes, J., in *Jones* v.*Lee*. We have here to deal with the negligence of not a single cow, but of 24 cows, being on the highway at the same time, and the accident being the result of these 24 – not one or two, but the 24 being there together. There is no doubt that if in the ordinary course the plaintiff was going along the roadway if there were two or three cows he would have escaped injury – the cows would have gone to one side or the other, and nothing would have happened. But in consequence of the cows being there in one mass when he came up to them, and they dispersed, their combined force was sufficient to upset the cart. But when you are dealing with the combined mass, sufficient in themselves by their impact to overturn the cart, then we must see the difference between such a case and *Ellis* v. *Banyard*. Well, that very point was dealt with in that case. Lord Justice Vaughan Williams (p. 52) said: 'At the same time I am far from saying that it is impossible that a man should be sued for putting his cattle in such a place or position that the natural result is that they go out of that place or position and, if in large numbers, obstruct the highway, and cause damage to those who use it.' Kennedy, L.J., in the same case said: 'I should be also slow to infer that because a harmless cow or sheep is allowed to get into the highway without giving rise to a cause of action, that rule applies to crowds of cattle, whose mass might constitute an obstruction to travellers along the highway.' There may be a case of duty arising in the case of a mass or number, even of the most 'harmless animals, which would not apply where it was only the case of a single animal.' Both *Jones* v. *Lee*, and *Ellis* v. *Banyard* were considered by the Court of Appeal in *Heath's Garage, Limited,* v. *Hodges,* [1916] 2 K. B. 370, where it was again laid down in express terms that an owner or occupier of land adjoining an ordinary highway is not bound to fence it, so as to prevent harmless animals like sheep from straying on the highway. Pickford, L. J., refers to the observations above quoted of Vaughan Williams and Kennedy, L.JJ., and suggests that the distinction may be that although a single animal may probably so act as to cause an obstruction, it will not necessarily do so, and whether it so acts or not depends upon its own will and that, therefore, the owner cannot expect an obstruction to be the natural consequence of its straying; whereas, in the case of large numbers, the obstruction is inevitable merely by reason of the numbers. It is, I think clear that while, in ordinary circumstances an owner is not bound to prevent his cattle or other domestic animals from straying on the highway, he is bound to use such care or caution that they will not stray in such numbers so as to render the highway positively unsafe or dangerous to those who use it. If he omits to do so, and allows his cattle to wander or be there, it is a breach of duty on his part, and if that breach is the approximate cause, he is liable. I am satisfied that no damage would have occurred if it were only a single cow, or two or three, but here it was caused by 'a mass' of cattle, to use the words of Lord Justice Kennedy, forming an obstruction and danger to travellers on the highway. Now, the only possible suggestion to negative the liability of the defendant was that this man might have got off and led his horse, or might have driven the cattle away; and I daresay it is true that if he had done so, and walked his horse along and waited for the cattle to disperse at one side and the other, nothing would have happened; but still, it was not unreasonable for him to act as he did. While it is clear that an owner is not liable for the consequence of a harmless animal straying on the highway, I hold in the present case that the defendant is liable by reason of the mass of animals forming an obstruction of the highway, and thereby causing the damage, and I affirm the decree.

Questions

Would the defendant have been liable in *Cunningham* if the obstruction had been caused by six (twelve, eighteen) cattle? Would the width of the road be a relevant factor in deciding this question? Would the rule in *Cunningham* apply in the case of twenty-four hens? Or eight pigs?

Cattle Trespass

KENNEDY V. McCABE
103 I.L.T.R. 110 (Circuit Ct., Judge Ryan, 1969)

The plaintiff claimed damages for trespass by the defendant's cattle on his land. There was a public road between the lands of the plaintiff and the defendant. The plaintiff found nine cows and a goat in his field which was some distance up an open laneway. When challenged by the plaintiff the defendant admitted that the cattle were hers and drove them from the plaintiff's field back to her own lands. No evidence was called for the defendant in either Court. In the District Court the solicitor for the defendant referred to *Moloney* v. *Stephens* [1945] Ir. Jur. Rep. 37, and also argued that there could be no liability for trespass from the public road without proof of negligence. The District Justice dismissed the plaintiff's action.

Judge Ryan:
The plaintiff must succeed in this case. I reserved my judgment to enable me to refer to Glanville Williams on 'Liability for Animals'. The following passage from that work at page 373 appears to cover this case: 'The animals that escaped must have been lawfully on the highway – i.e., they must have been there in pursuance of the right of passage, and not merely straying upon it. This was laid down in *Dovaston* v. *Payne* (1795); the rule is analogous to that which exists in the case of prescriptive and statutory duties to fence. Its justification at the present day is that damage done by straying cattle is not one of the risks that those who have property adjacent to a highway may be expected to assume. Where cattle stray in this way the landowner may lawfully replace them on the highway or distrain them damage feasant; in the former case he may also bring an action of cattle-trespass.'
Decree for the plaintiff.

Cattle Trespass. Remoteness.

McCABE V. DELANEY
[1951] Ir. Jur. Rep. 10

The plaintiff, Owen McCabe, claimed damages for trespass against the defendant, Annie Delany, for the loss of a horse, his property, which had been gored and killed by a cow, the property of the defendant. It appeared that at the time of the occurrence the horse was lawfully grazing in a field which was let by the defendant to the plaintiff for grazing, and was attacked by the cow which, with calf at foot, had broken into and entered the field. There was no evidence of *scienter* nor as to whether the conduct of the cow in the circumstances or the cow itself had been abnormal. The Circuit Court (Judge Sheehy) allowed the plaintiff's claim and from the decision the defendant appealed.

Black J.:
The plaintiff in this case had at the material time such rights in respect of a certain fied as entitled him to sue for trespass upon it. I find as a fact that the defendant's cow, while trespassing upon the field, gored and killed the plaintiff's horse which was lawfully there. The plaintiff claims the value of the horse as damages. Having regard to my findings, the only defence I have to consider is the contention that the damage is too remote.
A cow belongs to the class *mansuetae naturae*. When such an animal is in a place

where it is not trespassing, and there attacks and injures another animal, then, in the words of Lord Sterndale M.R. in *Manton* v. *Brocklebank* [1923] 2 K. B. at p. 223, the owner is entitled to assume that being *mansuetae naturae* it is '*prima facie* an innocent animal'. Unless this *prima facie* presumption is rebutted, and it is also proved that the owner of the offending animal knew that it was likely to be dangerous in the circumstances of the case, he cannot be held guilty of negligence in causing or permitting the animal to be in the place in question.

But if at the material time, the animal is trespassing, or if by reason of some contractual obligation the owner is guilty of lack of due care in causing or permitting the animal to be where it is when it does the damage, then in my opinion this presumption of harmlessness cannot be relied upon. If it could *Ellis* v. *Loftus* L.R. 10 C.P. 10 must have been a wrong decision; for half the Court, not being satisfied as to negligence, based the decision upon trespass. It would therefore, have been wrong if th defendants could have relied on a presumption that their horse, being *mansuetae naturae*, was harmless. They failed, and the decision has never been said to have been wrong. Where the presumption exists it carries with it the onus of proving *scienter*. In *Theyer* v. *Purnell* [1918] 2 K.B. 333, Abory J. clearly thought that the doctrine of *scienter* had no application to a care where the animal was trespassing. Thus, in *Cooke* v. *Waring* 2 H. & C. 332 the action, which was founded on negligence, failed for lack of proof of *scienter*. But Serjeant Pigot, for the defendant, admitted, as apparently clear law, that if an action were brought upon trespass, alleging injury by the kick of an animal, it would not be necessary to prove either *scienter* or negligence.

I am, therefore, of opinion that this being a claim in trespass, the defendant cannot object that *scienter* has not been proved or rely upon any *prima facie* presumption that the cow, being *mansuetae naturae*, was harmless. Similarly the doctrine of *scienter* and the accompanying presumption of harmlessness do not apply where the owner of the offending animal is under a contract to take due care, as in the case of an agistment. This was the decision in *Smith* v. *Cook* 1 Q.B.D. 79. In my view, the strength of the defence here lies, not in any attempt to invoke a presumption that the cow was harmless, but in the contention that for a cow to attack and gore a horse is not in accordance with the ordinary nature of a cow, and that the owner of an animal *mansuetae naturae*, even when it is trespassing on the land of another person, is liable only for such damage done by it as it is in accordance with the ordinary nature of such an animal to do.

This doctrine will be found in the text-books. It is commonly traced back to *Cox* v. *Burbidge* 13 C.B.N.S. 430 which is regarded as a leading case on the subject. There half the Court clearly affirmed this doctrine, and both Erle C.J. and Williams J. went so far as to assert that where the damage is not of such a nature as is likely to arise from such an animal *scienter* must be proved, even though the owner was guilty of negligence or trespass – a view which does not accord with that of Avory J. in *Theyer* v. *Purnell*. However, in *Fletcher* v. *Rylands* 1 Ex. 265 Blackburn J., in what has been called his 'classic judgment', quotes with apparent approval what Williams J. said in *Cox* v. *Burbidge* 13 C.B.N.S. at p. 438, namely, that in the case of a trespassing animal the owner is 'liable for any trespass it may commit, and for the ordinary consequences of that trespass'. The inference is plainly that the owner is not liable for any extra-ordinary consequence of that trespass.

Although, as I shall show presently, there is a great weight of authority for grounding this doctrine upon the decision in *Cox* v. *Burbidge*, I should myself presume to think that so far as that case is concerned it must rest on the opinions of only half the Court, namely Erle C. J. and Williams J.; for a third Judge said nothing about it, and Willes J., whose judgments carry such great weight, expressed himself as follows (at p. 441):– 'Does, then, the fact of the horse being on the highway make any difference? No doubt, if the horse was trespassing there, the owner of the highway might have an action against the owner of the horse'. Now, if Willes J. meant – and I think it is a natural meaning of his words – that if the person kicked by the horse had been himself the owner of the highway, he might, in an action of trespass – assuming there was a trespass – have recovered damages for the personal injury, it must follow that the damage would not have been too remote merely because the act of the horse was something which the owner had no reason to expect that it would do. Actually the plaintiff was a child who happened to be on the highway. I cannot resist a feeling that the view of Willes J. in *Cox* v. *Burbidge* was very like that of Kennedy L.J. in *Bradley* v. *Wallaces, Ltd.* [1913] 3 K.B. 629 where he thus expressed himself: 'Let it be assumed, however, that in bringing the horse into the yard the appellants became, in point of law, trespassers upon the land of the respondents. What is the legal result? That, if the horse did damage to the respondents, the owners of the land, the appellants would have to pay for it: not that injury done by the horse, not known by his owners to be vicious, kicking a third party on the premises, is, because the horse is a trespassing horse, an actionable wrong for which that third party can sue' [1913] 3 K.B. at pp. 636–7. Thus Kennedy L.J., like Willes J. in *Cox* v. *Burbidge*, drew a distinction between the owner of the land suing for trespass and a person who was not the owner of the land trying by framing his action in trespass to get damages for personal injuries caused by a trespassing animal, without proving either negligence or *scienter*.

However all this may be, the doctrine attributed to the Court in *Cox* v. *Burbidge* has been repeatedly reaffirmed by individual judges. Thus, in *Bradley* v. *Wallaces, Ltd.* Swinfen Eady L.J. said:– 'The guiding principle is that a person is liable only for the natural and probable consequences occasioned by or resulting from trespass or negligence' Ibid at p. 641. Again, in *Manton* v. *Brocklebank* [1923]2 K.B. at p. 230 Atkin L.J. expressly affirmed the view expressed by Erle C.J. in *Cox* v. *Burbidge* which I have quoted already, and in *Buckle* v. *Holmes* [1926] 2 K.B. 125 Atkin L.J. was still more explicit, saying, 'Where the owner is liable for the animal's trespasses it may be material to consider whether the damage it does is the result of a normal propensity. For this damage the owner is liable; but for damage resulting from an abnormal propensity not known to him he is not in my opinion liable, though he would of course be liable for the ordinary consequences of the trespass' [1926] 2 K.B. at p. 130. Finally, in *Deen* v. *Davies* [1935] 2 K.B. 282 Romer L.J. said of *Cox* v. *Burbidge* that the second ground of that decision was that, even supposing the defendant was guilty of a breach of a duty to the plaintiff in allowing the horse to be upon the highway, 'yet, inasmuch as the plaintiff had been damaged by the horse behaving not in a natural manner, but in a way which the defendant could not reasonably have expected it to do, the damage was too remote.' From all this it follows that if the doctrine just enunciated upon such formidable authority is good law, then the liability of the defendant depends upon whether the act of her cow was due to an abnormal propensity or whether it could be said to be in accordance with the ordinary instincts of cows under the circumstances which existed at the time.

As against all this it has been contended that the doctrine in question is no longer good law, if it ever was, being consistent with the principle laid down by the English Court of Appeal in *In re Polemis and Furness, Withy & Co.* That principle was that given a breach of duty constituting negligence – and logically it must surely be the same if one substitutes trespass for negligence – and given the damage as a direct result of that negligence or trespass, then, in the words of Bankes L.J. 'the anticipations of the person whose negligent act has produced the damage appear . . . irrelevant . . . The damages claimed are not too remote' [1921] 3 K.B. at p. 572. Scrutton L.J. said in the same case, *ibid.* at p. 576:– 'I cannot think it useful to say the damage must be the natural and probable result.' The same principle had already been laid down in *Smith* v. *London & South-Western Railway Co*. 6 C.P. 14, in *H.M.S. London* [1914] p. 72, and by Lord Sumner in *Weld-Blundell* v. *Stephens* [1920] A.C. 956. *In re Polemis* was treated as good law by a later Court of Appeal in *Hambrook* v. *Stokes* [1925] 1 K.B. 141. There, Atkin L.J. referring to *In re Polemis* and the line of authorities I have last quoted said: 'If the plaintiff can prove that her injury was the direct result of a wrongful act or omission by the defendant, she can recover, whether the wrong is a malicious and wilful act, is a negligent act, or is merely a failure to keep a dangerous thing in control, as for instance to keep a wild beast in control' [1925] 1 K.B. at p. 156. I cannot say whether he would have excepted a tame beast that did damage to a person while trespassing upon his land; but logically I see no justification for such an exception. Atkin L.J. proceeded to say 'Once a breach of duty to the plaintiff is established, one has no longer to consider whether the consequences could reasonably be anticipated by the wrongdoer. The question is whether the consequences causing the damage are the direct result of the wrongful act or omission.'

Thus, we have two conflicting lines of authority, each of very great weight, the one initiated by the pronouncements I have quoted in *Cox* v. *Burbidge* and followed by many weighty judicial utterances in the same sense, and the other illustrated by *In re Polemis, Smith* v. *London & S.W. Railway, Weld-Blundell* v. *Stephens, H.M.S. London*, and *Hambrook* v. *Stokes*. The problem thus raised has been learnedly discussed in such publications as *The Cambridge Law Journal, The Harvard Law Review*, and the *Law Quarterly Review*, but I fear without any convincing solution. In the last named publication, vol. 38, at p. 166, Sir Frederick Pollock wrote: 'If the authority of *Cox* v. *Burbidge*, and of Willes J's learned judgment therein, is to be saved, it must be by a distinction between trespass to land and other wrongs and defaults, for which no better reason can be assigned than a desire to make a distinction somehow.' I have already said that I myself doubt whether the judgment of Willes J. in *Cox* v. *Burbidge* supports the view taken by his colleagues Erle C.J. and Williams J. and undoubtedly upheld by Blackburn J. in *Fletcher* v. *Rylands*, and by the various other judges whose words I have quoted in later cases. But, I do agree with Sir Frederick Pollock that this latter view, whether it be that of Willes J. or not, can only be reconciled with the principle of *In re Polemis* and its supporting cases by making a distinction between trespass to land and other wrongs 'for which no better reason can be assigned than a desire to make a distinction somehow'.

A satisfactory solution of such a problem can be found only by a court of final appeal. If I could decide this case without attempting to propound such a solution, it would be fortunate. But, can I? If, without deciding whether or not the defendant can only be held liable if the act of the cow in killing the horse was due to an ordinary, and not an abnormal, propensity of the cow, I assume that such is the legal position, can I hold the defendant liable? I have rejected the idea that in an action framed in trespass, where the only question is one of remoteness of damage, the defendant can rely on any *prima facie* presumption that the cow was harmless.

If it is material to consider whether the killing was in the circumstances due to an abnormal propensity, making the cow 'an exception to her class', I must decide that question as best I can upon the evidence, and without making any *prima facie* presumption of abnormality. Unfortunately, there was no evidence given as to whether such an act by a cow with calf at foot was abnormal or not. All I know is that the cow broke into the plaintiff's field, that she had a calf at foot, that the plaintiff's horse was grazing there, and that the cow in fact gored it. In such circumstances the question of onus of proof seems to me very important.

In *Turner* v. *Coates* which was a case of injury done by an unbroken colt being led along the highway, Bailhache J. remarked to the defendant's counsel, 'In order to succeed you have to satisfy us that the damage that occurred was not likely to be done by the colt in the circumstances' [1917] 1 K.B. at p. 672. As the colt was not trespassing on the highway, it might have been argued that, being an animal *mansuetae naturae*, the onus was upon the plaintiff to prove *scienter*, or if not, at least to prove that in the special circumstances it ought reasonably to have been anticipated that the colt was likely to cause damage, though, as Lush J. said, 'not by doing something mischievous', but merely by taking fright and colliding with people. It is unnecessary for me to express any opinion about this; but at least if the colt had been trespassing, I should have been inclined to think that what Bailhache J. said as to onus was right. My reason is this. Abnormality is generally *prima facie* improbable in any given case, precisely because it is abnormality. What any given animal, not proved to have been abnormal, does in given circumstances is more likely to be what others of its species and variety would be apt to do in the like circumstances than to be due to some freakish propensity. In other words, I think that generally it is rational and justified by experience, when considering any act which an animal has been proved to have done, to start with at least a slight presumption that the animal and the act were not abnormal. If I am right in this, then in the absence of any specific evidence on the point either way, the onus of shewing abnormality should rest on the person who relies upon it. Here, it is the defendant who relies upon the supposed abnormality of the cow. She has given no evidence of it. In stating the view just mentioned, I have used the word 'generally', because there are cases in which, without any evidence either way, I should not consider a presumption of normality admissible. For instance, there are certain types of behaviour on the part of well-known domestic animals which everybody who knows anything about them would at once pronounce to be notoriously abnormal. An extreme example would be the facts of performing animals which people pay to see, precisely because the things they have been taught to do are known by everybody to be highly abnormal and unnatural.

If it were to my knowledge notorious, or even if I myself reliably knew, that it was alien to the nature of a cow, though she might have a calf at foot, to butt such an animal as a horse that might be grazing close to her, I might take judicial notice of that as a fact, and naturally any contrary presumption would be out of the question. But, I have no such knowledge. There are, moreover, certain facts which are notorious and which tend to encourage the inference that the act of the cow in question, in the special circumstances, was more probably due to a normal than to an abnormal propensity. One of these facts is that cows will often butt at dogs – even large dogs – which come close to them. I require no evidence of this, nor would I accept any evidence that denied it; for even a judge is not bound to accept testimony which would discredit what he has seen happen on countless occasions. The dog is rarely hurt; but that is because he is too nimble for the cow. She butts at him because her instinct is that he is going to interfere with her. It is her self-defence, and that is what her horns are for. Naturally, some cows are more given to butt in this way than others. But, it cannot be said to be alien to cow nature to do so, and if a cow, given to butt at dogs, is not deterred even by a large dog it seems to me not improbable that such cows, without being freaks, might not be deterred by the size of a horse. Another fact is that most, if not all, animals tend to become daring when they have young. Many of them which are ordinarily very docile display quite surprising courage and offensiveness when they have young to protect. It seems likely that cows are no exception to the rule. I suppose that most people with experience of the country have heard of cross cows. I should not call a cross cow a freak or an abnormality though she might represent a minority of her species.

Bearing all this in mind, I was not surprised on reading the report of the case of *Pinn* v. *Rew* 32 T.L.R. 451 to find that evidence was given there which satisfied the

Court that a cow with a calf at foot might become dangerous if it met a dog, or that the cow in question rushed at the plaintiff and tossed her more than six feet in the air. Atkin and Sankey J.J. held that the owner was liable, although the cow was not trespassing, but was being driven along the highway.

I have thought it right to take all the foregoing matters into consideration in endeavouring to weigh the probabilities. In the result, my conclusion is that the act of the defendant's cow, not being either proved, or known to me, to be inherently improbable on the part of a normal cow with a calf at foot, not only cannot be presumed to have been due to abnormality, but justifies a contrary presumption, even if it be slight which has not been rebutted.

I must accordingly hold that the plaintiff is entitled to recover damages, which upon the evidence I have no difficulty in assessing at the figure of £50.

Question

Cattle Trespass is a strict tort. In determining what damage may be too remote would you favour 'the reasonable foreseeability rule' or 'the direct consequence' rule?

Cattle Trespass. Defence. Wrongful Act of Third Party.

MOLONEY V. STEPHENS
[1945] Ir. Jur. Rep. 37

A third party left the defendant's gate open so that his cattle strayed onto the plaintiff's property.

Judge O'Briain:

This case involves an interesting question of law, and one which, as appears from the reports, has not received much consideration. My personal reaction to the case apart from authority was that the defendant should not be held liable.

As I read *M'Gibbon* v. *M'Curry* 43 I.L.T.R. 132 it is an authority binding on me and in favour of the defendant. The report is not free from ambiguity, but the several references in it to trespass, and the fact that Salmond on Torts, in repeated editions, has taken it as an authority on cattle trespass determine my attitude. I am faced with a decision of the Courts prior to 1922 but incorporated into the law of this State by the Constitutions. I hold that the defendant has established a good defence in law to this action by showing that the trespass complained of was caused by the wrongful acts of a third party. Accordingly, I affirm the order of the learned District Justice, and dismiss the appeal.

Question

If the defendant knew that some person had wrongfully left the defendant's gate open, would it make any difference in determining his liability?

CARROLL V. PARKS
47 I.L.T.R. 88 (1913)

The plaintiff sought damages from the defendant for the wrongful distress of sheep. The plaintiff had, with others, a right of grazing on Annaloughan Mountain. Immediately adjoining the Annaloughan Mountain is the Rockmarshall Mountain, leased for grazing purposes to the defendant Robert Parks. The only division between the two mountains was the usual loosely built stone wall, which was not in good repair. The defendant found sheep (some of which he subsequently learned belonged to the plaintiff) trespassing upon Rockmarshall Mountain, where he had sheep of his own. He drove all the sheep to his yard at Killen, where he separated his own sheep from the trespassing sheep, and then drove the latter to the pound at Carlingford, a distance of about seven miles. A pound at Annaverna was the nearest pound to the place where the sheep were found trespassing, but the Carlingford pound was the nearest to the place where the defendant segregated his own sheep from the plaintiff's. The sheep sustained injury in being driven to the more distant pound. A summons was brought by Carroll against Parks charging him that on May 8, 1912, he 'did unlawfully impound three sheep belonging to complainant by impounding them when he knew the owner thereof, and further did on same date unlawfully impound said sheep at Carlingford, in the County of Louth, said pound at Carlingford not being the nearest pound of the county, contrary to the provisions respectively of s. 20 (1) and s. 19 (6) of 14 & 15 Vict., c. 92, in each case. The case was heard before the Justices at Ravensdale Petty Sessions on July 6, 1912, when the Justices made the following order: Defendant convicted, 'That he did on May 8, 1912, unlawfully impound said sheep in Carlingford pound, Co. Louth, said pound not being the nearest pound of the county, and is ordered to pay as penalty the sum of one shilling, and for costs the sum of seven shillings and sixpence forthwith, and in default of payment to be imprisoned in Dundalk gaol for the period of forty-eight hours without hard labour unless said sums be sooner paid, and remaining charge in summons is dismissed without prejudice.' There was a cross civil bill by Parks against Carroll for damages for the trespass by Carroll's sheep during the previous twelve months. There were other civil bills by other plaintiffs against Parks for wrongful distress and trespass to sheep and cross civil bills by Parks against them for trespass by sheep, but the facts of each case were similar to those in *Carroll* v. *Parks*. The County Court Judge dismissed all the civil bills and cross civil bills.

*   *   *

Cherry L.J. was of the opinion that the conviction at petty sessions was no bar to the bringing of a civil action in respect of the same wrongful impounding. He would have a decree for £1 for the injury it had been proved the sheep sustained in being driven to a pound which was not the nearest pound; and in the cross civil bill he would give a decree for £1 for the trespass of Carroll's sheep.

Plaintiff whose animal strays on to highway may be guilty of contributory *negligence.*

CODY V. PLAYER & WILLS (IR.) LTD.
109 I.L.T.R. 32

The plaintiff's field was fenced and was next to the public highway. In it were two horses and some cattle. On the evening in question a heifer broke out of this field. Two of the plaintiff's horses followed it. Stock had never broken out of the field before. The plaintiff admitted in evidence that it was a known thing that horses would follow cattle out of a field in which both were kept. He also said that the horse probably got out through a small gap beside the gate. The defendant was driving along the public highway beside the plaintiff's field. A motorist coming towards him flashed his lights at the defendant three or four times to warn him of the presence of the horse on the road. The defendant's car collided with the horse and the horse was killed. The plaintiff claimed damages in the Circuit Court for the negligence of the defendant.

Judge Sheridan stated that the defendant was negligent in not avoiding a collision with the plaintiff's horse, having been warned of its presence on the highway by the oncoming car. The question then before the Court was whether or not the plaintiff could be found guilty of contributory negligence in allowing his animal to stray onto the highway.

Judge Sheridan:

Although the defendant in this case would be unable to maintain an action in negligence against the plaintiff, I am, however, of the opinion that it is possible to find the plaintiff guilty of contributory negligence, namely fault in relation to the protection of his own property, in allowing his own animal to stray onto the highway in the manner described. I find him so guilty and attribute 20% of the fault to him and 80% to the defendant, damages to be assessed accordingly.

Questions and Note

How should the law relating to animals be reformed? Is strict liability the answer? Or should a general principle of liability in negligence be imposed? See the Law Reform Commission's *Report on Civil Liability for Animals* (L.R.C. No. 2–1982).

1. Where animals stray as a result of the failure of a third party to keep them secure, their owner may have a right of action in negligence if they are injured: see *Clune* v. *Clare Co. Co.* 114 I.L.T.R. 58 (Circuit Ct., Judge O'Briain, 1972).

Chapter 24

INTERFERENCE WITH CHATTELS

1. *TRESPASS TO CHATTELS*

The tort of trespass to chattels consists of wrongfully and directly interfering with the possession of chattels. This may be done by taking the chattel out of the possession of another (*e.g. Sligo Corporation v. Gilbride* [1929] I.R. 351 (Sup. Ct.), moving it from one place to another, or doing damage to it. The commentators are generally of the view that the tort is actionable *per se*, but the judicial authorities are less than compelling: *cf. McMahon & Binchy*, pp. 536–537. The fact that the defendant does not appreciate that his interference is wrongful will not exempt him from responsibility: thus, the deliberate use of a chattel in the mistaken belief that it is one's own will constitute a trespass. But where a person uses a chattel without having obtained the permission of the owner he may be excused where the situation was one of some urgency (albeit created by the defendant himself) if the intervention is in protection of the owner's interests and it is not possible to obtain the consent of the owner beforehand: *cf. Ross v. Dunphy*, unreported, High Ct., Finlay, P., 13 February 1978 (1976–2375P). For a general, penetrating analysis of the entire subject of tortious interference with chattels (including detinue and conversion), see Samuel, 'Wrongful Interference with Goods' 31 Int. & Comp. L.Q. 357 (1982).

ELECTRICITY SUPPLY BOARD V. HASTINGS & CO. LTD.
[1965] Ir. Jur. Rep. 51 (High Ct., O'Keeffe, J., 1966)

The defendants, civil engineering contractors, were engaged by Dublin Corporation to re-surface a road. In the course of their work, they directed the driver of their mechanical shovel to open a trench of a particular depth for the purpose of laying a drain. While opening the trench, the shovel came into contact with, and damaged, an underground high tension cable which had been laid by the plaintiffs pursuant to statutory powers. The precise position of the cable was unknown to the defendants beforehand. The plaintiffs sued the defendants in trespass.

O'Keeffe, J.:

. . . The defendants submit that an action for trespass does not lie in this case, and put forward three propositions which they submit the plaintiffs must establish in order to succeed. These are briefly as follows. First, the plaintiffs must prove that the act complained of is the act of the defendants. They say that an employer is not responsible for the trespass of his servant in the same way as he is liable for his servant's negligent act, and they say that it must be shown that the employer either commanded the servant to commit the act of trespass complained of or commanded him to do something which, in the circumstances and to the knowledge of the employer, would necessarily result in an invasion of the plaintiffs' rights.

Secondly, they submit that in order to be actionable a trespass must be either wilful or negligent, and thirdly, they submit that the plaintiffs must have possession or a right to possession of the chattel in respect of which the trespass is committed.

It is convenient to approach these three submissions in inverse order. Taking the third submission first, I am of opinion that the plaintiffs have established such a right of possession as entitles them to maintain this action. The cable was laid by them under their statutory powers. Their ownership of it is pleaded in the Statement of

Claim and is not put in issue. The cable was at the time of the trespass being used as part of their system for the transmission of electric current, and although it lay buried some four feet below the public highway I think that they at all times retained possession of it and dominion over it. They are, in my opinion, entitled to sue in respect of a trespass to it.

In support of the second proposition of law the defendants cite *National Coal Board v. Evans & Co. (Cardiff) Ltd.* [1951] 2 K.B. 861 and *Fowler v. Lanning* [1959] 1 Q.B. 426. These cases appear to support the proposition sufficiently for me to accept it as being correct. I have, however, come to the conclusion that the defendants were negligent in what they did.

Although the high tension cable was not shown on any map sent to the Corporation the plaintiffs did take steps to warn the defendants of the possibility of damaging their cables. One of their employees, Mr. John Walsh, was detailed to keep an eye on the work from time to time, and did so. I do not accept that he warned the defendants' driver and foreman as many times as he said, viz. about ten times, but the evidence of Mr. Gilheany, the defendants' foreman, establishes that a short time before the accident to the cable Mr. Walsh spoke to him and to the driver of the mechanical shovel and told him that there were cables crossing the Green. Mr. Gilheany did not trouble to ascertain the exact position of the cables as the work which was being done was merely skimming off the surface of the Green, and he did not know of the intention to dig a deep trench through the Green. Unfortunately on the day of the accident he was ill and not supervising the work. If he were, I believe that the accident would not have happened, as he would have taken steps to ascertain the precise position of the cable before proceeding with the trenching. The foreman who acted in his absence did not know of the conversation between Mr. Walsh and Mr. Gilheany, and accordingly he made no such inquiry.

On the day when Mr. Gilheany was warned of the existence of a cable under the Green, the driver of the machine which was being used to skim the surface was also warned, but as it happened he was not the driver who was working the machine which did the damage. Had he been instructed to dig a trench through the Green, he would probably have remembered the warning and asked for some information about the cable, but the driver who was actually doing the work was, like the acting foreman, unaware of the existence of the cable.

In my view this case can be distinguished from the case of *National Coal Board v. Evans & Co. Ltd* [1951] 2 K.B. 861. In that case the cable which was damaged was laid wrongfully under the land the property of the Glamorgan County Council, and the Council and their contractors were wholly unaware of its existence. In the present case the cable was lawfully laid by the plaintiffs in the exercise of their statutory powers, and although it was not shown on the map returned to the Corporation in December, 1962, the contractors were, through their foreman, and one of their drivers, given a specific warning of the existence of an underground cable near where their machine was working. I think that they were put on notice sufficiently to render them liable for the trespass, and that it is not sufficient for them to say that Mr. Walsh may not have conveyed to Mr. Gilheany the precise location of the cable in question.

Coming finally to the first proposition put forward by the defendants, I am of opinion that it affords no defence to this case. An employer may not be liable for the trespass committed by his servant if the servant is doing an act which does not involve a trespass and in the course of doing that act he, of his own volition, commits an act of trespass. In this case the contractors were directed by the Corporation to dig a trench in the precise place where the cable lay. Their driver could not have excavated the trench to the required depth without coming into contact with the cable. He was doing the very act which his employer required him to do, and that act necessarily involved a trespass on the cable, even though is employers were not aware of this. In my view they cannot escape liability for that trespass by saying that the hand which directed the machine was the hand of a servant.

In my view the plaintiffs were entitled to judgment . . .

Notes and Questions

1. This decision does not discuss the question of onus of proof. Do the English decisions cited in the decision answer the question satisfactorily? *Cf.* Diplock, J., in *Fowler* v. *Lanning* [1959] 1 Q.B. 426, at 439–441.
2. The cutting of electricity cables has given rise to much litigation in recent years, since significant economic loss may result, frequently to businesses having no direct proprietary interest in the cable itself (as in the *E.S.B.* case). Liability has been imposed in negligence but the courts have shown some uncertainty as to where and how to draw the line beyond wich recovery of damages will not be permitted. *Cf. supra*, pp. 196–198. Should the extent of recovery hinge on whether the plaintiff owned the damaged cable? If so, why?

2. *DETINUE*

The essence of the action for detinue is the wrongful refusal by the defendant to deliver up to the plaintiff a chattel, after demand has been made by the plaintiff to do so. Of course, where a person wrongfully detains the property of another, detinue may not be the only available legal response: the tort of conversion (*infra*, pp. 589–595) may be more suitable, or, indeed, a straightforward action for breach of contract. Nevertheless there are times where detinue constitutes the best avenue on which to proceed, as for example, where for some reason a contractual claim does not arise (e.g. where the delivery was gratuitous rather than for consideration) or where the plaintiff wants recovery of the chattel rather than merely monetary compensation for its loss.

Adverse possession is normally proved by establishing a demand by the plaintiff for the return of the chattel and a refusal by the defendant to do so.

POOLE V. BURNS
[1944] Ir. Jur. Rep. 20 (Circuit Ct., Judge Davitt, 1943)

The plaintiff sent a horse to the defendant, an auctioneer, to have it sold by public auction. At the auction, on 9 December 1942, the reserve price was not reached and the animal was withdrawn. Later that day the defendant was informed by another person that the horse was her property, that it had been stolen from her and that it should not be sold. The following day the plaintiff asked the defendant for the return of the horse but was refused, and on the next day a Garda officer, who was investigating the alleged larceny, told the defendant to retain the horse while the investigation was going on. It was 'eventually ascertained' that the animal was the property of the plaintiff. [The report is not clear as to when this fact was ascertained by either the Gardaí or the defendant. – *eds.*]

There was correspondence between the parties. On 14 January, 1943, the defendant telephoned the Gardaí and, as a result, on 16 January, the defendant's solicitor wrote to the plaintiff's solicitor, asking that the animal be removed on the 18th of the month, without prejudice to the defendant's claim for livery. In the meantime, on 15 January, a civil bill had been served by the plaintiff on the defendant, containing a claim for return of the horse.

The defence alleged (*inter alia*) that any delay in the matter on the part of the defendant was due to a *bona fide* doubt as to the ownership of the animal and was not unreasonable in the circumstances.

Judge Davitt:

If this had been a claim for conversion I should have had no hesitation in dismissing it, as I am satisfied that the defendant made no claim to this property, and never attempted to convert it to his own use. But the claim is for wrongful detention, and I am satisfied that a detention of some kind, against the will of the plaintiff has taken place. [Counsel for the defence] seeks to justify that detention by evidence that the defendant was in *bona fide* doubt as to the true ownership of the property, owing to the conflicting claims made by the plaintiff and by a Miss Sheil who alleged the mare had been stolen from her. The cases he has cited establish the proposition that a bailee of property, who is in *bona fide* doubt as to the ownership thereof, is legally entitled to detain that property for a reasonable time in order to make enquiries or to have enquiries made as to who is the proper owner.

I have great sympathy with auctioneers and pawnbrokers and other people of that sort who are frequently placed in such a difficult position. But I have come to the conclusion that in this case the defendant detained the animal for more than a reasonable time. If she had made an effort she would probably have speeded up the police investigations, and it was the duty of her and not the plaintiff to do everything possible to secure the release of the animal. Instead of that she did nothing until her solicitor rang up the police on the 14th January and secured the release of the plaintiff's property on the 16th.

I have no intention of giving heavy damages, because I am satisfied that the loss suffered on resale of the animal had nothing to do with the unlawful detention. That being so, the plaintiff has suffered no financial loss, but in my opinion a technical wrong has been committed by the defendant and I give a decree for 1/- with costs.

Questions

Do you agree with Judge Davitt's judgment? Does it strike a fair balance?

THE MAYOR, ALDERMEN AND BURGESSES OF WATERFORD V. O'TOOLE
Unreported, High Court, Finlay, J., 9 November 1973 (1969–271 Sp.)

This is an action brought on Plenary Summons by the plaintiffs who are the Corporation of the City of Waterford against the defendant claiming firstly an order for the return of two stone plaques which have been erected by the defendant on his premises known as the Maryland Guest House which are situate in the Mall in the City of Waterford. Secondly for a Mandatory Injunction directing the defendant to take down and remove the plaques from the premises and to yield up and deliver the same to the plaintiffs and in the alternative there is a claim for damages for detention.

The facts out of which this claim arises I find to be as follows.

Probably in or about the year 1912 a number of persons by voluntary subscription created a fund with which it was intended to commemorate by a statue placed in the City of Waterford the well known composer William Vincent Wallace. The plaques, the subject matter of the claim, where I am satisfied brought into existence with the intention that they should form part of a decorative pedestal for the statue.

It was not possible for anyone to prove nor is it of any relevance to the issue before me what happened in regard to the statue and in regard to certain other plaques that were intended to be placed on it. With regard to these two plaques however, there is clear evidence that they came into the possession of a carrier named Mr. Valette whose daughter gave evidence before me and who was a general carrier carrying on business in Waterford under the name of Hackett & Company. By 1950 these two plaques had, I am satisfied, been for a considerable time in a store yard, the property of Mr. Valette, and were almost certainly being held by him by virtue of the lien which he was entitled to exercise over them for the unpaid amounts of charges due for carriage. Mr. Valette died in 1950 and left the entire of his business to his wife who died on the evidence before me in the same year. She in turn left the entire of the business to their daughter Miss Valette. I am satisfied that the legal position then was that Miss Valette as the successor to the carrier's business of Hackett & Company had a right to retain possession of these plaques by way of lien by virtue of the charges due to the firm for their carriage. She decided to sell the business and the premises in which it was carried on in the year 1951 and amongst other premises which she was then selling was a store at Mary Street where the plaques were then situated. I am satisfied on the evidence that she then decided that it was of more importance to clear the plaques out of the store than to seek to continue her lien and try and recover the cost of the carriage of them – something which had manifestly become impractical. In those circumstances on her own evidence she gave the plaques to a Mr. O'Keeffe who was then associated with the Waterford Choral Society as she put it, 'to take care of.' The right of lien which existed in Miss Valette as the successor to the business of Hackett & Company, did not, I am satisfied, include a right of sale and was not a transferable right and it seems to me as a matter of strict law that she had not got the authority to deliver up possession of these plaques to Mr. O'Keeffe unless she was delivering them to him as a bailee to retain on her behalf in exercise of her lein, his possession in those circumstances being in her possession. On the evidence, I am satisfied that this was not the intention nor the form of the transfer of actual possession of the plaques by Miss Valette to Mr. O'Keeffe and that she chose him to take care of the plaques because she felt that his association with the Waterford Choral Society made him the most suitable person to have control and actual possession of plaques commemorating Waterford's best known musician and composer.

Mr. O'Keeffe is now dead and I have no evidence as to what he intended to do or sought to do with the plaques, but I am satisfied on the evidence of Mr. Edward James that by the year 1955 the plaques had become situated in a yard in Mary Street which was then owned by Strangman's Brewery of which Mr O'Keeffe was an employee. Strangman's Brewery was in that year taken over and the yard was purchased by Messrs. Arthur Guinness Son & Company Limited and it is clear from the evidence of Mr. James that Guinnesses who were carrying out an extensive demolition of the yard in which the plaques were lying were anxious to clear them from their premises and at the same time took the view that they were of historical interest and should not be destroyed or thrown out.

In those circumstances they wrote to the then Mayor of the Waterford Corporation offering to present the plaques to the Corporation and this offer was gratefully accepted by the Mayor on behalf of the Corporation and actual possession then transferred from Messrs. Guinnesses' yard at Mary Street to the Corporation premises. Subsequently and for a great number of years the Waterford Corporation had the plaques in the basement portion of a building known as Reginald's Tower which is maintained as a civic museum. In the year 1969 alterations being carried out to Reginald's Tower necessitated the removal of the plaques and they were brought to the ordinary Corporation store at Bolton Street.

It was in or around this time that Mr. Vincent O'Toole, the defendant, became interested in the situation with regard to these plaques. I am satisfied on the genuine interest in the life and works of William Vincent Wallace and as a result of his researches had discovered firstly the project for the erection of the statue which had become frustrated and secondly the existence of these plaques in the possession of the Waterford Corporation. He therefore conceived, in the year 1969 in association with the Festival of Light Opera annually held in Waterford, a plan for the unveiling of these plaques on some prominent public place associated with choral singing by children and associated with a considerable amount of publicity which he was satisfied would enhance the reputation and general organisation of the festival.

Mr. O'Toole is the owner of a Guest House known as the Maryland Guest House situated at the Mall in the City of Waterford which is close to and in actual sight of the house in which the composer Wallace lived. The house in which the composer Wallace lived was in 1969, I am satisfied, in a dilapidated condition and for that reason Mr. O'Toole decided that the most suitable place in which to place the plaques was on the wall of his own guest house.

I am fully satisfied that in choosing this he had not got a personal profit or ulterior motive and was simply anxious to secure the erection of the plaques in a prominent and suitable public place.

With this end in view he asked Mr. William Carroll, who was then chairman of the festival to approach the City Manager for the purpose of obtaining permission to have the plaques erected on the Maryland Guest House at the expense of Mr. O'Toole. Mr. William Carroll in turn sought the assistance of Alderman Thomas Brennan who is now the Mayor of Waterford and who was in 1969 an Alderman on the Waterford Corporation. An interview then took place between the City Manager, Mr. Cassidy and Mr. Carroll and Alderman Brennan, as he then was. After that interview Mr. Carroll and Alderman Brennan returned to Mr. O'Toole and a conversation then took place about which there has been considerable controversy in the evidence.

Mr. Carroll's version of what was then said by him and Mr. Brennan to Mr. O'Toole was that they told Mr. O'Toole that the City Manager had said that he saw no objection to his taking the plaques, that there were no plans about them in the Corporation to do anything otherwise with them, but that he would have to wait for the formal permission of the Corporation at its next meeting. The version given by Mr. Brennan was that they told Mr. O'Toole that he couldn't have possession of the plaques until the Council met on the following Monday and took a Council decision. Mr. O'Toole's version of this conversation is again different and was that he was told 'the plaques are yours but you must put them up by a builder and not by a handyman and the City Manager's decision will be ratified at the next meeting of the Waterford Corporation 'and furthermore that the Corporation should not be involved in any expense in putting up the plaques. I am satisfied that whatever this conversation consisted of it almost certainly took place on the 1st of September 1969. I think the difference in the accounts of the conversation given by the various persons who were at it is to be explained by the lapse of time since then and also to an extent by the fact that this has become a controversial question in which obviously Mr. O'Toole feels very strongly and in which Alderman Brennan may well have strong views as well. I am satisfied and find as a fact that the substance of the message then conveyed to Mr. O'Toole was that the City Manager was agreeable to his taking the plaques and having them erected on his premises but, that that would have to be ratified at a meeting of the Corporation but I am also satisfied that the meaning was then conveyed to Mr. O'Toole that this ratification was not considered anything more than a formality.

On the same day, that is to say the 1st of September 1969, I find that Mr. O'Toole went to the Bolton Street premises of the Corporation and I accept his evidence that his arrival was expected and that he was shown the plaques by employees of the Corporation and he then arranged that they would be removed on the following day by Messrs. Hearne & Company who are substantial builders and contractors carrying on business in the City of Waterford. The reason why permission was then given, as I am satisfied it was, by the officials of the Corporation for the removal of the plaques by Messrs. Hearn & Company was that Mr. O'Toole's telephone conversation with Mr. Cassidy, the City Manager, which he Mr. Thomas Carroll, interpreted as being a direction that he should hand over the plaques to Mr. O'Toole or to any person coming on his behalf. Mr. Cassidy gave evidence before me that he did not intend to give any such order to Mr. Carroll and that on his recollection he did not give those instructions. Mr. Carroll struck me as being a meticulous and careful public official and he wrote a report on the 3rd of September confirming the instructions which he understood he had received and the action which he had taken in pursuance of them.

I take the view that the Waterford Corporation in law held out Mr. Carroll, the City Engineer, as a person having authority to deal with a matter such as this and that therefore they must be taken for the purposes of the issues arising in this case, to have handed over at that time possession of these plaques to Mr. O'Toole. I will deal later with the terms and conditions on which, as a matter of law, I find that they were handed over.

The next events that occurred were that Mr. O'Toole, having collected the plaques through Messrs. Hearn & Company the contractors on the 2nd of September, had extensive renovation and cleaning work done to them and by the 5th of September, I am satisfied, had got as far as erecting one of the two plaques in the wall of the Maryland Guest House set in a massive area of concrete with iron bars holding it into the concrete and was in the process of erecting the other plaque. He was then visited by Mr. Ryan who is a Staff Officer with the Waterford Corporation and who was on terms of personal acquaintanceship and friendship with him. A conversation then took place between Mr. Ryan and Mr. O'Toole in respect of which again there is substantial conflict on the evidence before me. I am satisfied that the substance of that conversation consisted of a warning by Mr. Ryan that the motion to confirm or ratify the City Manager's decision which was coming before the Waterford Corporation might be prejudiced to the disadvantage of Mr. O'Toole if he were observed to have taken it as a foregone conclusion and proceeded to erect the plaques. There was not, I am satisfied, a formal demand for the return of the plaques nor is there any evidence of any direct communication between the City Manager and Mr. O'Toole on that occasion protesting about the removal of the plaques from the Corporation yard or about the erection of them which was then in process.

The erection of the two plaques on the wall of the Maryland Guest House was, I am satisfied, completed on the following day, that is to say the 6th of September 1969.

The next meeting of the Waterford Corporation took place on Monday the 8th of September 1969 and at that meeting a proposal to ratify the handing over of the plaques to Mr. O'Toole for the purpose of their erection on the Maryland Guest House was defeated and a resolution was taken to demand the return of the plaques and to make provision for their erection elsewhere in the City of Waterford. It is of some importance that Mr. O'Toole knew that the question of the final authority of the Corporation for the removal and erection of the plaques remained to be decided at that meeting for he wrote a long letter on the 8th September 1969 to the then Mayor of the Corporation setting out the reasons why he believed that the erection of the plaques in the manner and for the purpose which I have indicated was in the interest of the people of Waterford. On the 9th of September 1969 both the City Engineer, Mr. Carroll, and the City Manager, Mr. Cassidy, wrote to Mr. O'Toole demanding the return of the plaques. Mr. O'Toole, I am satisfied, refused to return the plaques and eventually after correspondence from the Law Agent to the Corporation wrote on the 8th of October 1969 indicating that it was not now possible in the view of builders to remove the plaques without breaking them. These proceedings were then instituted and Mr. O'Toole in his defence denies the ownership of the plaques by the Waterford Corporation, denies his wrongful removal of them, denies that he detained them or that he continues to detain them and asserts that he is the lawful owner of the two plaques or that in the alternative that he is the lawful custodian of them.

Mr. O'Toole in his evidence here expressly disclaimed ownership of the plaques. There are only two other portions of the evidence which it is necessary to refer to. (1) The evidence of Mr. William Maguire Architect, which I accept, that removal of these plaques from the premises of Mr. O'Toole would now only be possible by what might be described as a massive operation removing a very considerable section of the corner of the house, having supported the balance, and taking a large part of the structure of the house away with the plaques. And (2) the evidence of Miss Valette that the defendant had paid to her a sum of £40 in discharge of the amounts due to her late father's firm for carriage of these plaques and she had executed a purported assignment of her interest in the plaques to the defendant. This transaction which took place in September 1969 had not got the legal effect of transferring any title or right of possession to Mr. O'Toole. Miss Valette having parted with possession of the plaques had then no right over them which she could transfer.

On these facts as I find them, the following legal consequences ensue. I am satisfied that Miss Valette had lawful possession of these plaques up to the year 1951 by virtue only of a lien against them in respect of charge due for their carriage. I am satisfied as a matter of law that she could not transfer or assign that lien and that in the circumstances in which it occurred her purported handing over of possession of these plaques to Mr. O'Keeffe was not any lawful transfer of title nor of possession.

I am further satisfied that Messrs. Guinness Son & Company by 1955 were entitled to a lawful possession of these plaques upon the basis that they were the owners and occupiers of the land and premises on which they were to be found and that against everyone except the true owner of them they were entitled to possession.

This conclusion leads me also to decide that the origin of the possession of the Waterford Corporation of these plaques was lawful and that Messrs. Guinness Son & Company Limited had got authority to hand over possession of them and to transfer to the Waterford Corporation a right to possession good against anyone except the rightful owners.

It has been urged on behalf of the plaintiffs that they held the plaques as trustees for the citizens of the City of Waterford. This was as I understood it put in two alternative ways, one that they held all such objects by virtue of the fact that they were the Corporation of the City of Waterford as trustees for the citizens and secondly that the circumstances under which they received them from Messrs. Guinness & Company made them trustees.

I am satisfied that this is not so and that whereas no doubt the intention of presenting them to the Corporation of Waterford on the part of Messrs. Guinness was that they should be made available in Waterford and as an amenity to Waterford that there is no form of trust which was created in respect of them.

As I have already indicated in my findings of the facts in this case, I am satisfied that there was a transfer of the possession of these plaques to the defendant on the 2nd of September 1969 and I take the view that he received them as a bailee, the terms of the bailment being that if and when the Council of the Corporation had ratified the decision made by the City Manager that he, Mr. O'Toole, should erect and maintain these plaques on his own premises, the Maryland Guest House, at his own expense.

I am satisfied as a matter of law that the disposal or more properly the erection and display of these plaques on any particular premises was not a reserved function under the City of Waterford Management Act and that it was within the power of the City Manager to have made any arrangement he liked with Mr. O'Toole in regard to the plaques without obtaining the ratification or approval of the City Council. I am equally satisfied however, as a matter of fact that it was not the intent of Mr. Cassidy to make such a decision without the ratification of the Council and I am satisfied that Mr. O'Toole was at all material times aware that a ratification on the part of the Council was necessary. In these circumstances I am satisfied that what could be described as the condition of Mr. O'Toole's bailment failed and that he had an obligation after the rejection of the proposal by the Council on the 8th of September to return the plaques to the Waterford Corporation. Although the evidence goes very close indeed to establishing that it was no longer within his power to do that, I do not consider that that was fully established, although it was clear that the expense and physical difficulty of doing it was out of all proportion to either the value of the plaques or the circumstances surrounding their delivery to Mr. O'Toole.

The power of a Court to order the specific return of a chattel in an action for detinue is a discretionary power and has in my view been correctly stated as one which should not be exercised where damages are an adequate remedy. Whereas Mr. O'Toole must have known that a ratification on the part of the Council was still necessary before the decision to erect the plaques on his house was a final and complete decision, he was undoubtedly left under the impression that that was a mere formality and I think whatever words were spoken to him by Mr. Brennan and Mr. William Carroll which led him to this belief must have been heavily reinforced when the plaques were handed out to him with the full authority of the City Engineer. This was therefore his state of mind and I am satisfied his honest belief at the time he took steps of inserting these plaques into the wall of his own building. By the time they were inserted, which occurred I am satisfied before the meeting on the 8th of September when the Council decided not to ratify the City Manager's decision though not literally impossible of restoration to the plaintiffs they were practically impossible of being restored in the condition in which they originally were and furthermore were practically impossible of being restored without an altogether unwarranted expense and damage to the defendant's property. In these circumstances I do not grant any order for the return of the goods nor do I therefore in my discretion grant the alternative Mandatory Injunction for their removal from the building.

As already indicated I am however satisfied that there was sufficient knowledge in Mr. O'Toole of the lack of finality in the decision of the City Manager to make him at the time he inserted these plaques in the wall of his building a bailee of them with a condition attached technically to that bailment that he should return them if the Council failed to ratify the City Manager's decision. I have considered carefully as to whether at the time of the first demand for the return of these plaques which I am satisfied took place on the evening of the 8th of September it was within the power of the defendant to return them. If it was not then he was not guilty in law of detinue. Whilst as I have indicated I consider that as a practical matter it was almost impossible then to return them and certainly was out of all proportion to the value of the subject matter concerned, I am not satisfied that as a matter of law it could be said to be physically impossible to return them. In those circumstances he has committed a detinue of these goods and the plaintiffs are entitled to damages for that.

The plaintiffs failed to prove and their Counsel indicated the impossibility of estimating any particular value for these goods. I am satisfied that the proper interest of the plaintiffs in these two plaques was to ensure that they would be preserved for the benefit of the citizens and visitors to the City of Waterford and placed suitably in a prominent place. They have in my view been preserved for the benefit of the citizens and visitors to Waterford and are suitably placed in a prominent place and it is in this regard that some importance may attach to the attendance of the then Mayor and several members of the Council to the unveiling of the plaques in 1969. In these circumstances the damages suffered by the plaintiffs by reason of the technical detinue of the plaques is in my view nominal only and I award to them £1 damages for detinue.

Question

Do you think that Finlay, J. was compelled to his conclusion by the application of legal principles, or do you feel that somewhat broader, commonsense, considerations of justice also had their effect?

3. *CONVERSION*

The tort of conversion consists of any act relating to the goods of another that amounts to an unjustifiable denial of his title to them. Conversion may be committed by wrongfully taking possession of the goods, abusing possession already acquired or otherwise denying the title of the other person to them, whether or not possession has been acquired. The tort in detinue may provide an alternative basis of laibility in some cases. Thus we find that in many of the reported cases, both detinue and conversion are pleaded, and the court's analysis may not clearly distinguish between the two actions.

Taking possession of another's property will not always constitute conversion: it will do so only where the defendant deals with the goods in a manner inconsistent with the right of the true owner. *Cf. Fouldes* v. *Willoughby* 8 M. & W. 540, 151 E.R. 1153 (1841).

Difficulties may arise where a person is the *involuntary* recipient of another's goods. *Cf.* Burnett, 'Conversion by an Involuntary Bailee' 76 L. Q. Rev. 364 (1960); *McMahon & Binchy*, pp. 542–543. Section 47 of the *Sale of Goods and Supply of Services Act 1980* deals with the problem of unsolicited goods. It provides as follows:

'(1) Where –

(*a*) unsolicited goods are sent to a person with a view to his acquiring them and are received by him, and

(*b*) the recipient has neither agreed to acquire nor agreed to return them,

and either –

(i) during the period of six months following the date of receipt of the goods the sender did not take possession of them and the recipient did not unreasonably refuse to permit the sender to do so, or

(ii) not less than 30 days before the expiration of that period the recipient gave notice to the sender and during the following 30 days the sender did not take possession of the goods and the recipient did not unreasonably refuse to permit the sender to do so,

then the recipient may treat the goods as if they were an unconditional gift to him and any right of the sender to the goods shall be extinguished.

(2) The notice referred to in subsection (1) shall be in writing and shall state –

(*a*) the recipient's name and address and the address at which the sender may take possession of the goods (if not the same) and

(*b*) that the goods are unsolicited.

(3) A person who, not having reasonable cause to believe there is a right to payment, in the course of any business, makes a demand for payment, or asserts a

present or prospective right to payment for what he knows are unsolicited goods sent to another person with a view to his acquiring them, shall be guilty of an offence.

(4) A person who, not having reasonable cause to believe there is a right to payment in the course of any business and with a view to obtaining any payment for what he knows or ought to know are unsolicited goods –

    (*a*) threatens to bring any legal proceedings,

    (*b*) places or causes to be placed the name of any person on a list of defaulters or debtors or threatens to do so, or

    (*c*) invokes or causes to be invoked any other collection procedure or threatens to do so,

shall be guilty of an offence.

(5) In this section –

"acquire" includes hire,

"send" includes deliver,

"sender" includes any person on whose behalf or with whose consent the goods are sent and any other person claiming through or under the sender or any such person,

"unsolicited" means, in relation to goods sent to any person, that they are sent without any prior request by him or on his behalf.'

Note and Questions

Do you consider that this section adequately protects the recipient of unsolicited goods? Were you previously aware of its existence and its scope? Note that the section does not alter the law as regards the obligation of care of recipient of the goods in respect of their safety during the period before either the six months, or the thirty days, has elapsed.

An honest but mistaken belief that one has the right to deal with another's goods will not afford a good defence in an action for conversion.

DELANEY V. WALLIS & SON
14 L.R. Ir. 31 (C.A., 1884 affirming Exchequer Division, 1883)

Sir Edward Sullivan C.:

This is a case of considerable importance, not merely in relation to the position of salemasters in Dublin and elsewhere, but to the public. It arises on a Special Case stated in an action brought by Denis Delaney against John Wallis & Sons, for the sum of £71 8s., claimed as damages for the conversion by the Defendants of twenty-one sheep of the Plaintiff; and there is a count also for money had and received by the Defendants for the Plaintiff's use. The Defendants' defence was a denial of the acts of conversion, and a denial that any money was received by them for the use of the Plaintiff. It is necessary to be very clear as to the particular facts stated by the parties in the Special Case, and what we think are the fair inferences to a drawn therefrom. The Special Case states that the Plaintiff is a farmer, residing at Roskeen, in the Queen's County, and that the sheep the subject-matter of the action were, on or about the 17th January, 1883, stolen off his land by a man named Michael Crossan. That the Defendants are public salemasters, and transact their business in that capacity in the new cattle-market established by the Corporation of Dublin, under the provisions of the Dublin Improvement Act (12 & 13 Vic. c. 79, s. 80). That on every Thursday a public market for the sale of cattle and sheep is held in this market, the legal hour for commencing sales being eight o'clock in the morning. That on Thursday, the 18th January, 1883, Michael Crossan, accompanied by two other men, brought the twenty-one sheep, which had been so stolen by him from the Plaintiff, to the stand of the Defendants in the new cattle-market, between eight and nine o'clock, and asked the Defendants to have the sheep sold for him. The Defendants did not know Michael Crossan, or either of the men with him, and were entirely ignorant that the sheep had been stolen. The name given by Michael Crossan was 'John Cullen;' and the name Dunne was also mentioned. The sheep were, within a few minutes, purchased by Mr. P. Graves, butcher, Rathgar, at 63s. each; and this price, less £1 13s. for commission, and 2s. handed to Michael Crossan in cash, was paid to Michael Crossan by Defendants. The entry in Defendants' books as to the transaction, made at the time, is in the words and figures following:–

'JOHN CULLEN (OR DUNNE)

'Twenty-one sheep – Graves – 63s.		£66 3 0
Commission,	£1 13 0	
Cash,	2 0	
	————	
		1 15 0
		————
	Cash,	£64 8 0'

And the invoice given to said Michael Crossan at the time he received the £64 8s., which was paid him by cheque, was in the following words and figures:–

'JOHN WALLIS & SONS,
Cattle and Sheep Salesmen, Corn and Wool Brokers,

'Dublin, Liverpool and Manchester.

Office – 33, Bachelor's-walk.

Cattle-market, Dublin, 18th January, 1883.
Sold for MR. JOHN CULLEN:

Cattle	Sheep	Buyer		Rate per Head	£	s.	d.
. . .	21	Graves, . . .		63s.	66	3	0
		Comm, ... £1 13 0					
		Keep, ...					
		Tolls, ...					
		Drivings, ...					
		Cash, ... 2 0			1	15	0
		Cash, ...		. . .	£64	8	0

The Special Case then states that the twenty-one sheep were taken away by Mr. Graves immediately after his purchase; and that the whole transaction was closed by payment to Michael Crossan by nine o'clock in the morning. That on the day following the sale, the Plaintiff informed the Defendants, at their office in Dublin, that the sheep had been stolen off his lands; and that this was the first information the Defendants had on the subject. That the Defendants informed the Plaintiff of the facts hereinbefore stated, including the name and address of the purchaser of the sheep.

Now, on the statement of the facts that I have read, we think that we must assume that the possession of those sheep which were brought to the stand of the Defendants in the public market, and which Crossan asked the Defendants to have sold for him, was given to the Defendants for the purpose of the sale. The facts of the case are inconsistent with any other supposition. We also think that we must assume that the twenty-one sheep, when taken away by Graves, were taken away from the stand of the Defendants, the sellers, and that the Defendants were the persons who gave the sheep over to the purchaser to take away.

It has been suggested that the position of the Defendants was not different from that of a bystander listening to and promoting a bargain between a person selling in a public market and a purchaser, and not having possession of the articles sold. The case, in our opinion, is entirely inconsistent with such a state of facts. The statements that the Defendants are salemasters, that they have a stand in the Cattle-market, and that Crossan employed them to have the sheep sold for him, are pregnant with this, that the Defendants got possession of the sheep to sell, and having that possession sold them, and delivered them to the buyer. A very important question then arises, whether, this being a market overt, and the Defendants giving a good title to the purchaser of the sheep by their sale, the Defendants are liable to the real owner for the value of them. We are all of opinion that the Court of Exchequer was right in giving judgment for the Plaintiff, and holding that the Defendants were guilty of conversion of the sheep. When the facts are stated as we find them, there is no doubt as to the law. The principle applicable to such a case received a good deal of attention in a case bearing some resemblance to the present, that of *Ganly* v. *Ledwidge* Ir. R. 10 C. L. 33, where Lord Fitzgerald and Lord Justice Barry held that salemasters who had sold a cow that had been stolen from the plaintiff, and had delivered the beast to the purchaser, were liable in trover. The Lord Chief Justice Whiteside was of a different opinion. I beg respectfully to express my dissent from his judgment. He would appear to have been led astray by some observations in the case of *Greenway* v. *Fisher* 1 C. & P. 190, as to persons acting in a public employment being protected. Certainly, the judgments of Lord Fitzgerald and Lord Justice Barry commend themselves to my mind as being entirely right, there being no warrant for the proposition that a seller in market overt is protected as well as a buyer. It is said that this is a case of great hardship on the Defendants. I do not see that it is so. If one of two innocent parties must suffer, the responsibility must rest where the law casts it; but I really think that salesmasters may very well be required to make some inquiry as to the persons who bring them cattle for sale before they effect a sale for them.

The law bearing on this subject has been most exhaustively treated in a case of *Hollins* v. *Fowler* L. R. 7 H. L. 757. The facts of that case are very different from the present, but the principles of law applicable are, I think, very clearly stated in the judgments in the House of Lords; and I think it will be found that those principles are clearly applicable to the present case. That was not so strong a case as the present for holding the defendants liable, for there the defendants had not done any act which changed the property in the goods sold by them, while here the salesmasters put the property in the animals sold into the purchaser by their sale of them in market overt. There, Lord Chelmsford says (p. 795): 'To my mind the principle which fits this case is, that any person who, however innocently, obtains possession of the goods of a person who has been fraudulently deprived of them, and disposes of them, whether for his own benefit or that of any other person, is guilty of a conversion.' Apply that p[rop]osition to this case. These Defendants innocently got possession of the sheep, they disposed of them, and they deprived the Plaintiff of his right of property by making this sale to Mr. Graves. They are therefor, if the proposition of laws is rightly stated in the judgment I have quoted, guilty of a conversion. In his judgment Lord

Chelmsford refers to the case of *Stephens* v. *Elwall* 4 M. & S. 259, mentioned by Mr. Justice Blackburn in his opinion delivered to the House of Lords, and repeats Lord Ellenborough's observations:– 'The clerk acted under an unavoidable ignorance, and for his master's benefit, when he sent the goods to his master, but nevertheless his acts may amount to a conversion; for a person is guilty of conversion who intermeddles with my property and disposes of it; and it is no answer that he acted under the authority of another, who had himself no authority to dispose of it.' And adds: 'This case was decided sixty years ago, and I do not find that the authority of it has ever been disputed.' Lord Cairns opens his judgment with this observation: 'My Lords, in this case, having had the advantage of reading beforehand the opinion of my noble and learned friend who has moved the judgment of your Lordships, and agreeing entirely with that opinion, I do not delay your Lordships by any reference to the facts of the case.' The other Lords concurred.

Now, the familiar case of an auctioneer, which was put at an early stage of the case by the Lord Chief Justice of the Common Pleas, illustrates very well the true state of the law. The auctioneer who gets possession of the articles sent to be sold by him, for the purpose of sale, and sells them, is liable to the true owner, on all the authorities. The fact of his exercising a public employment is no protection to him. The case cited in argument, *Cochrane* v. *Rymill* 40 L. T. (N.S.) 741, is a very remarkable confirmation of that doctrine. There, Lord Justice Bramwell says:– 'It no doubt is a very hard case for the defendant, who has acted throughout innocently in the matter; but, setting aside the hardship of the case, the law applicable to it is perfectly clear. Here is Peggs, a man who is not the true owner of these goods, but appearing to act as such, and who has no power whatever to sell, takes them to the defendant, and gets a loan from him upon them. The defendant keeps them, and finally sells them in such a way as to pass the property in them to the buyers; and if that is not a conversion, then I think there can be no such thing.' He unquestionably puts the case, which has here been suggested at the Bar, of a man bringing a horse by the bridle to an auctioneer, and saying, 'I want to sell my horse,' and the auctioneer thereupon finding him a purchaser, and the horse being sold while the owner is still holding him by the bridle, and he himself giving the horse to the purchaser: it is suggested, rightly enough, that in such a case the auctioneer may not be liable to the right owner, as having never got possession of the horse he might not be regarded as guilty of conversion. That state of things, as I have already shown, does not exist here. We find that the Defendants got possession of the Plaintiff's sheep, that they sold the sheep when in their possession, and gave possession of them to the purchaser.

We affirm the judgment of the Exchequer Division, and give judgment for the Plaintiff for the sum of £71 8s., and costs.

Morris C.J. concurred

FitzGibbon L.J.:
The only doubt I entertain is upon the sufficiency of the statements in the Special Case to elucidate the facts. I am not quite certain that we should not act more prudently by declining to give our decision unless the parties can agree to amend the case by stating that before the sale the custody of the sheep was, for the purpose of sale, given to the Defendants, who accepted it by placing the sheep upon their stand; and also that the Defendants made the sale, paid the seller, looked to the purchaser for the price, and in pursuance of the sale delivered the sheep to the purchaser. It, however, I think, sufficiently appeared that all these matters of fact are in accordance with the truth; they are consistent with, if not implied by, the statements of the Special Case; and, assuming them to be established, I have no hesitation in

concurring with the Lord Chancellor and Chief Justice. The Defendants had such a special possession of the sheep as would have entitled them to maintain an action of trover against a wrongdoer; having such a possession they parted with the sheep to a purchaser, with the intention of passing the property, and they are on first principles liable for sending the Plaintiff's property in a wrong direction, by a sale and transfer to which they were parties. As to the argument *ab inconveniente*, I think there is no hardship or injustice in holding salesmasters liable if they wrongfully sell property for people of whose title they are ignorant, and of whom they know nothing. Here it appears that the Defendants did not ascertain even the name of the person for whom they acted.

Barry L.J.:

Assuming the facts to be specified by the Lord Chancellor and Lord Chief Justice Morris (and I think we are justified in so inferring from the Case Stated), I do not think that the question so elaborately discussed in *Hollins* v. *Fowler* L. R. 7 H. L. 757 arises at all. The position of the Defendant here does not, in my opinion, resemble that of the broker who acts as a mere intermediary between an intending vendor and an intending purchaser. The Defendant here had the physical possession of the animals, he effected the sale, delivered them to the buyer, and by the sale, being in market overt, he divested the owner's property until conviction of the thief. I think his action in the transaction constituted a conversion, and that the decision of the Exchequer must be affirmed.

Where the true owner of a chattel cannot be discovered, the finder of the chattel generally has a title against all others.

QUIN V. COLEMAN
33 I.L.T.R. 79 (Circuit Case, Gibson, J., 1898)

The plaintiff found a lost purse in Thurles. Subsequently a person obtained the purse from her by the false pretence that he was its owner. This person was later tried and convicted, but no order was made for the return of the purse to the plaintiff. The purse remained with the defendant, a police officer. Advertisements were inserted for the owner, but without success. Some time later the plaintiff unsuccessfully sought the return of the purse from the defendant. She sued him in an action for trover and detinue. Her action was dismissed and she appealed.

Gibson J.:

. . . [A] reasonable time for enquiry has elapsed, and there is no prospect of the true owner being found. The plaintiff, as finder of the purse, asks to have it returned to her. The action was defended by the Constabulary authorities. Counsel for the defendant did not allege that there was any statute governing the case, but relied on *Buckley* v. *Gross* 3 B. & S. 566 as establishing that the plaintiff could not recover. There the plaintiff was a wrongdoer; the true owners were known, and the plaintiff's possession was divested by an order of the Justices under a statute. The case has no application to the facts before me. The plaintiff was an innocent finder; the true owner cannot be discovered, and the defendant cannot protect his possession by any statute. The dismiss therefore must be reversed . . .'

Notes and Questions

1. Compare this decision with *Crinion* v. *Minister for Justice* [1959] Ir. Jur. Rep. 15 (Circuit

Ct., Judge Conroy). The plaintiff, who was a serving member of the Garda Síochána, found a sum of money on the public footpath while he was on duty. He handed the money over to the local station sergeant; extensive enquiries were made but the money was never claimed. After the expiration of a year and a day, the plaintiff wrote to the Garda Síochána seeking the return of the money but his request was refused. His action for conversion was dismissed by Judge Conroy who stated (at 17) that:

'The general principle of law is that a servant or agent acts for his principal. The plaintiff in this case was a member of the Garda Síochána on duty and was in the service of the State at the time when he found the money. The plaintiff never took full possession of the money so as to establish his claim to it. The plaintiff is not entitled to succeed . . .'

2. In England, In *Parker* v. *British Airways Board* [1982] All E.R. 834, the Court of Appeal held that an occupier of a building has rights superior to those of a finder of chattels on or in, but not attached to the building, 'if, but only if, before the chattel is found, he has manifested an intention to exercise control over the building and the things which may be on or in it'. Such an occupier, the Court held, is under an obligation to take reasonable measures to ensure that lost chattels are found, and, on their being found, whether by him or a third party, to acquaint the true owner of the finding and to care for the chattels meanwhile.

Conversion and Contributory Negligence

Prior to 1961, the effect of the plaintiff's contributory negligence on an action for conversion was a matter of some doubt. Section 34(2)(*d*) of the *Civil Liability Act 1961* now provides that:

'the plaintiff's failure to exercise reasonable care in the protection of his own property shall, except to the extent that the defendant has been unjustly enriched, be deemed to be contributory negligence in an action for conversion of the property.'

Since, as we have seen, the defendant in an action for conversion may be entirely morally blameless, there is much to be said for his provision, which ensures that an owner who has been careless about minding his property cannot insist without qualification that others be more careful than he himself was. Do you think that Section 43 of the *Civil Liability Act 1961* could have relevance in some cases? *Cf. Williams*, para. 79.

Chapter 25

PASSING OFF

Much of the law relating to unfair competition is now the subject of statutory control. The law relating to trade marks and copyright, for example, has been regulated by statute in relatively recent times. There remains, however, an area of common law protection falling within the scope of the tort of passing off.

The tort appears to have its origin in the concept of deceit, but the requirement of fraudulent intent has long since been abandoned. The essence of the tort is that one trader represents his goods or services as those of another, so as to be likely to mislead the public and involve an appreciable risk of detriment to the plaintiff.

The tort is essentially designed to protect the plaintiff's proprietary interest in his goodwill rather than to protect the interests of the consumer: thus it is no defence to show that the defendant's goods or services are better or cheaper than those of the plaintiff or that the resultant competition is good for the consuming public.

ADIDAS SPORTSCHUHFABRIKEN ADI DASSLER K.A. V. O'NEILL & CO. LTD.
[1983] I.L.R.M. 112 (Sup. Ct., 1982)

O'Higgins C.J. (with whom **Hederman J.** concurred):

The Appellants (hereinafter referred to as Adidas) appeal to this Court against the dismissal by Mr. Justice McWilliam of their claim for passing off brought against the Respondents (hereinafter referred to as O'Neill).

Adidas originate in Germany but has now an international basis and standing. It manufactures and sells sports equipment of all kinds including boots, shoes, clothing, bags, footballs and various accessories. It has at present factories in nineteen countries situate in western and central Europe and the Far East. In addition it has a large international sales organisation. It was formed in 1947 and its growth over the years has been rapid and sustained. The process has been supported by an extensive advertising campaign, not only in newspapers, magazines and other periodicals, but also on radio and television in different countries. As a part of its promotional and advertising campaign, Adidas has concentrated on having its products worn and used by competitors in the big international athletic and sporting events which would be the cynosure of world television. When Adidas commenced operations in 1947 it confined its activities to the manufacture and sale of sports footwear of all kinds – football and other boots; track, tennis and other types of sports shoes. This footwear was manufactured and marketed with a distinctive design or fashion of three diagonal coloured stripes on the instep and outer side of each boot or shoe. As a result of the use of Adidas footwear by competitors at athletic and other events and the television coverage, this particular design or fashion became well known. In 1967 Adidas decided to launch into textiles and sportswear generally. To this end it proceeded to manufacture and sell, through its organisation football shorts, shirts, singlets, track suits, anoraks, bathing costumes and a variety of sporting and leisure gear. Most of these garments, in addition to bearing the word 'Adidas' or a particular trefoil, which are Adidas trade marks, also carried the design of three coloured stripes, not diagonal, but straight down the side of the arms or legs, where that was possible. Again, to the extent that competitors at Olympic or other sporting events used Adidas sports gear, the three-stripe design necessarily received extensive television coverage. So far as Ireland is concerned it appears that Adidas footwear came on the market in limited quantities in the late 1960's. Footwear was then subject to quota restrictions and such small quantities of Adidas products as were imported were brought in by commission agents. One of these was a Mr. Michael O'Connell. In 1970 when quota restrictions on footwear came to an end Mr. O'Connell succeeded in securing the sole agency for Adidas in Ireland. In 1971 he formed a company called Three Stripes International Limited, through which this agency operated. Initially, Mr. O'Connell's importation of Adidas products consisted of footwear although he did sell a small quantity of track suits and other sports gear. In 1976 Mr. O'Connell persuaded Adidas to commence manufacturing in Ireland and since then has been, on behalf of Adidas, in competition with O'Neill in the sport market for textiles.

O'Neill is an Irish company which was formed in 1918. It commenced with the manufacture and sale of footballs for the three codes of football in this country. Its products were identified by the name 'O'Neill's' written across them. In the middle 1920's it produced a white football known as 'The O'Neill All-Ireland' which has since become the standard ball for big GAA games. In 1927 in association with an English company called Umbro, O'Neill started importing sports gear – mostly shorts and jerseys – and supplied these on order to teams playing the different codes of football. As a result of difficulties of supply and import restrictions both during and subsequent to the last War, O'Neill decided in 1960 to manufacture its own textile products. Initially these consisted of football shorts and jerseys which were supplied on order, mostly to GAA teams. Apparently, the business expanded quickly. In 1965 O'Neill started putting stripes on its products. The number of stripes varied, according to what was ordered, from one to three. In 1967 track suits first appeared on the Irish market, having been imported from Poland. Their appearance apparently started a fashion in Ireland and O'Neill responded by manufacturing its own track suits. Again in response to orders O'Neill commenced putting stripes on these articles. Initially the number of stripes varied in accordance with the order from one to three. O'Neill faced particular technical difficulties in affixing stripes to their products. However, because stripes were popular and were demanded, it persisted in efforts to overcome this difficulty and eventually secured a machine which enabled stripes to be added to the garment in a satisfactory and economical manner. By 1976 O'Neill had four striping machines in production and were manufacturing in two centres – one in Dublin and one in Strabane. At this stage, and for some years before, it had concentrated on three stripes down the side of the legs and arms of jerseys and shorts and also on track suits. At this stage, also, O'Neill's products were extensively used by supporters of the three football codes in Ireland. It had a virtual monopoly in the supply to the GAA of footballs and hurling balls and they supplied to clubs in the three codes the majority of the sporting gear used. In addition, their products were stocked by sports shops and were freely purchased by the public.

This was the situation which confronted Adidas when it decided in 1976 to open a factory in this country and thereby seriously to compete for the Irish sports gear market. It had the year before secured the registration in Ireland of a trade mark consisting of a trefoil with three horizontal stripes. This trade mark was in no way associated with a design of stripes on garments. However, faced with the fact that O'Neill's garments were then commonly on sale with the three stripe design, Adidas in May 1976 instructed their trade mark agent to write to O'Neill claiming that this was an infringement of Adidas' registered design. This letter only referred to track suits. In fact Adidas had no such design registered in Ireland. O'Neill's reply indicated that if such design were registered it was invalid as 'a three-stripe pattern in ornament has been applied to sportswear since at least the late 1950s . . . Furthermore

decorations of three stripes are widely used throughout the clothing trade.'
Subsequent to this letter, on the 22nd December 1976, through their trade mark
agents Adidas applied for a registration of a trade mark consisting of 'three equally
spaced stripes, each of the same colour and width' on the arms and legs of sports
clothing. This application has not yet been dealt with. This is probably due to the fact
that these proceedings were commenced by Adidas against O'Neill's and involve
incidentally the whole question as to whether any particular exclusive property or
reputation can be claimed by Adidas in respect of the three-stripe design on clothing.

Adidas's claim in these proceedings is that O'Neill by putting three coloured
stripes down the arms and legs of the shorts, jerseys and track suits which it manufactures and sells, has been passing off these products as the products of Adidas. The
claim is confined to the use of this three-stripe design in the manner indicated. No
suggestion has been made that Adidas's name or trade marks have been used or that
any other form of representation has been made. It is, therefore, a claim for passing
off based exclusively on the alleged imitation of the general appearance or 'get up' of
Adidas products so as to confuse and mislead the public. A claim for passing off so
based is rare. In Kerly's *Law of Trade Marks* 10th Edition, at 419, this fact is noted in
the following passage:

> 'It is usually true in some degree that a trader's goods are recognised as his by their
> general appearance, or "get up". Accordingly, resemblance of "get up" is not
> uncommonly an ingredient in passing off, and it is possible for imitation of "get
> up" alone to amount to passing off. Such cases are rare, since few traders rely on
> "get up" alone to distinguish their goods, so that trade names and word trade
> marks are ordinarily present too; and in these days, in this country, a difference in
> names is enough to warn the public that they are getting one trader's goods and not
> the other's. Accordingly, there can hardly be passing off by "get up" alone unless
> the resemblance between the goods is extremely close, so close that it can hardly
> occur except by deliberate imitation; and even that may not be enough.'

Even if its claim be rare or exceptional, Adidas is entitled to succeed if it can establish
that the three-stripe design used in the manner indicated is clearly associated in the
public mind with its products, and with those of no other trader, so that it has a clear
reputation in the use thereof; and further, that what has been done by O'Neill is
calculated to cause such confusion in the minds of probable customers of Adidas as
would be likely to lead to O'Neill's goods being bought and sold as the goods of
Adidas. I think it proper to add that the public mind which is to be considered in
relation to the establishment of a reputation for Adidas in the three-stripe design is
the public mind in this country and, further, that the confusion which is relevant is the
confusion of probable customers here. In this respect this case differs from *C & A
Modes and C & A (Ireland)* v. *C. & A. (Waterford) and Others* [1976] I.R. 198 where
the passing off which was injuncted was the use of an established and well known
trade name, although the Plaintiffs carried on no trade within the State. The Court
held that the good will attached to the established name and that, as such was well
known within the State, the owners of that name were intitled to protection. The
distinction between such a case and a claim in respect of a given mark or 'get up' was
noted by Mr. Justice Kenny in his judgment in that case. He quoted from the
judgment of Lord Justice Jenkins in *Alain Bernadin* v. *Pavilion Properties Limited*
[1976] R.P.C. 581 as follows:

> 'It is of course essential to the success of any claim in respect of passing off based on
> the use of a given mark or get up that the plaintiff should be able to show that the
> disputed mark or get up has become by user in this country distinctive of the

plaintiff's goods so that the use, in relation to any goods of the kind dealt in by the plaintiff, of that mark or get up will be understood by the trade and the public in this country as meaning that the goods are the plaintiff's goods.'

Mr. Justice Kenny added in his own judgment as follows:

'This passage relates to passing off by the use of a trade mark or "get up" of goods (as the judge emphasises) and has no application to passing off by the use of a well known name.'

In this case if the complaint had been that the name 'Adidas' or a name similar thereto or an imitation thereof had been used in association with O'Neill's goods, although no Adidas products were on sale in this country, I have no doubt that a good will and a potential in relation to customers would have been established and protection given. We are dealing, however, not with a well known name but with a particular design and its exclusive association with the goods of Adidas in Ireland must be established if the claim made is to succeed. One other matter should be mentioned. The fact is that Adidas have, over the years, projected their products with the three-stripe design in every advertising medium available. This fact, however, does not give title to Adidas to complain if a trader attracted by the design or susceptible to the fashion which its prominence creates, decides to copy or imitate. The mere copying of a design or the anticipation of a fashion or the taking advantage of a market or demand created by another's advertising is not of itself sufficient to support an action for passing off if the trader against whom the complaint is made has sufficiently distinguished his goods so that confusion is not created. (See *Cadbury-Schweppes* v. *Pub Squash Company* [1981] W.L.R. 193).

I think it proper now to refer again to some of the evidence in the case and then to consider the findings of fact made by the learned trial Judge. As already indicated, O'Neill is a well established and well known Irish firm which both manufactures and wholesales its products. Its products in footballs and in sporting gear of all kinds have been bought and sold over many years in athletic and sporting circles in this country. As already mentioned, it commenced experimenting with stripes on its textile products in the late sixties and by 1971 freely advertised in its price list two and three-stripe jerseys. Shortly after this, having perfected a process for attaching stripes to other garments, it proceeded to market shorts and track suits with a three-stripe design. In doing so, O'Neill may have been aware of the growing attraction of stripes on sporting gear due to the television coverage of international sporting events. If so, in this respect, it was not alone, as other firms, about this time, also commenced to use a striped effect on their products. Indeed one French firm, which had a branch in Canada, used a three-stripe design. The evidence establishes that O'Neill's products were always delivered to retail outlets in clearly marked O'Neill boxes or packages and that each garment bore the O'Neill name written across a white circle intended to indicate the O'Neill All-Ireland football. While there was evidence that in some shops garments such as track suits were displayed in rows, on hangers, so that the sides of the garments with the stripes on the shoulders and legs would normally be observed by customers, it was not suggested that this was done by O'Neill or that it was done in order to deceive. In any event it must be assumed in relation to the possibility of confusion that customers will look fairly at the goods on display and that such goods will be shown fairly without the distinguishing features being concealed (*Schweppes Limited* v. *Gibbens* (1905) 22 R.P.C. 601; *Lever Brothers Limited* v. *Bedingfield* (1898) 16 R.P.C. 3). As already indicated, Adidas commenced manufacturing textiles in 1967 and very quickly put on international markets all forms of sporting gear including track suits with a three-stripe design. However, by reason of import restrictions, very few of Adidas' products reached this country at that time. Some footwear and a limited amount of textiles were imported but it was not until 1976, when they opened a factory here, that Adidas posed a real challenge to O'Neill for the Irish market in sporting gear. At this stage O'Neill's products with a three-stripe design were well established and well known. These were on the market clearly marked as O'Neill's products with the O'Neill sign. At the trial Mr. Justice McWilliam had to consider all this evidence and also the evidence of a number of witnesses who, as he put it, 'were almost equally divided in numbers as to whether they did or did not assume that any garment with three stripes was an Adidas garment'. He came to the conclusion, in effect, that Adidas had failed to establish that essential reputation in this country in relation to the three-stripe design which was vital to the success of their claim and, further, that no confusion had been caused by the use by O'Neill of that particular design.

I have considered very carefully all the evidence which was before the learned trial Judge and also the conclusions which he reached. As he pointed out in his Judgment, this is not a claim for an infringement of a registered mark or design. Had Adidas succeeded in registering a three-stripe design in this country, different considerations might apply. This, however, is a claim for passing off which involves not only the use of another's 'get-up' but also, and, essentially, a resulting confusion in the marketplace. As indicated, he was not satisfied that Adidas had established in this country an exclusive association of the three-stripe design with their garments. On the contrary, he was impressed by evidence which showed the opposite to be the position. More important than this, however, was his finding of fact that no confusion had been caused. In this respect he noted the evidence that Adidas had two registered trade marks, the word 'Adidas' and the design with three elliptical leaves crossed by three horizontal stripes, and that one or other or both these marks appear on all their products, except where sports organisations preclude such during public events. Similarly, in relation to O'Neill's products he noted the evidence that all such were sold clearly marked with the O'Neill emblem or trade mark in boxes or packets indicating clearly the firm by which they were made. In this respect he said:

> 'Certainly, in so far as O'Neill's garments were sold in or with the packages in which they are made up and delivered to retailers, there could not, to my mind, be any possibility of confusion. Nor has the likelihood of confusion been demonstrated with regard to other garments unless it is assumed that customers do not observe the name O'Neill's written on them and believe that all garments with three stripes are made by Adidas.'

He formed the view, on the evidence, that the use of stripes of varying colours and numbers on sports gear was a fashion in the trade and that O'Neill had done no more than to adopt this fashion and to use on their products the same number of stripes as Adidas did on their products, and that in doing so O'Neill had not attempted to deceive or pass off and had in fact not done so. In my view, the learned trial Judge's finding of the fact the conclusions which he reached were fully justified and his findings cannot be disturbed. I would accordingly dismiss this appeal.

Henchy J. (dissenting):
    . . . The trial judge, in the course of his judgment, said of the claim made by Adidas:

> 'The case for the Plaintiff seems to me to involve a most dangerous extension of the principle of passing off and [I think] that there must be something more than mere adoption of a fashionable trend in clothing, no matter how ingenious the person who started the fashion'.

That comment would be apt if Adidas were asserting an exclusive right to man-ufacture and sell sportswear with stripes, or even with three stripes, for that would be no more than an impermissible attempt to corner the market in what appears to be a fashionable trend in sportswear. But that is not their claim. Their claim is that they have made their own the design of a particular kind of three-striped sportswear. And where I respectfully differ from the trial judge is in my holding that the evidence shows, not only the genuineness and correctness of that claim, but that the market (by which I mean the generality of those who buy and sell sports garments) regard garments with that particular mark or get-up as emanating from Adidas. In other words, the design or get-up has become part of the goodwill of Adidas. That may be an unwelcome conclusion to those who resent the power over personal taste and preference exercised by lavish advertising, free handouts and suchlike influences on purchasing habits that are a feature of the media-dominated society in which we live. But, whether we like it or not, the accrual to Adidas of a goodwill in this particular mark or get-up is shown by the evidence to be an accomplished and proven fact. It is therefore sufficient to found an action for passing off.

Finally, there is the question whether the passing off operated to the actual or likely detriment of Adidas. The evidence on this aspect of the case was quite clear. . . .

There was . . . ample and uncontroverted evidence that custom intended for Adidas was being deceptively diverted to the defendants and that the cause was the passing off as Adidas's garments of garments with the Adidas get-up, manufactured for the defendants and sold to shopkeepers by the defendants with that get-up. Because it was calculated to damage the goodwill of Adidas, it was a wrongful filching from Adidas of trade intended by the customer for Adidas. The misrepresen-tation is emphasised by the fact that the defendants could have manufactured with impunity garments with any other arrangement of three stripes. One is drawn to the conclusion that in choosing to use this particular arrangement of three stripes they intended to capture part of the Adidas goodwill.

In case I have not made it clear, I would like to stress that a person who has initiated or exploited a trend or fashion in clothes or other goods does not thereby acquire a right, by means of a passing-off action, to warn off competitors who might wish to trade in such articles or goods. In such circumstances, competitive trading remains open to all until, by the use of a name, a mark, a get-up, or other novel or distinctive feature, a particular trader acquires a goodwill as a result of such use. Even then, that trader does not get a right of action against a rival trader for passing off until a rival puts forth goods for sale bearing that distinctive indication or a tolerable imitation thereof, thereby misrepresenting his goods as those of the person who has acquired the goodwill or proprietary repute created by the distinctive feature and, by such unfair trading, causing a degree of financial loss, actually incurred or likely to be incurred by the person who has acquired the goodwill or 'the intangible property right' created by the idiosyncratic mark, design or get-up. . . .

Note
For commentary favouring the approach of the majority, see Phillips, 5 Dublin U.L.J. 105 (1983).

Chapter 26

DAMAGES

Although in some cases, in preference to monetary compensation, the plaintiff may seek an injunction to stop the defendant committing a tort, in most cases the plaintiff will seek damages as compensation for the wrong committed.

Appellate Functions Regarding Jury Awards

FOLEY V. THERMOCEMENT PRODUCTS LTD.
90 I.L.T.R. 92 (Supreme Court, 1954)

Maguire C.J.:

This appeal raises the question whether the amount of damages awarded by the jury was excessive . . .

No complaint was made of the directions given by the learned trial judge in regard to the heads which the jury should consider when measuring damages. They awarded the sum of £5,765, of which £210 was for special damages. The appellants ask this Court to say that this sum is too much.

The principles to be applied by this Court when considering whether it will set aside a verdict on the grounds that the damages are excessive, are well established. They are stated by Palles C.B. in terms accepted by this Court in *M'Grath* v. *Bourne* I.R. 10 C.L. 160 at p. 164. He laid it down that a verdict should not be set aside only because the damages are more than the appellate Court would be disposed to give if it were fixing the figure, but that there is some amount of damages which will be sufficient to induce the Court to interfere. In other words, a line must be drawn somewhere. The problem in each case is to decide where it is to be drawn. The Chief Baron approved of a test suggested by his brother Fitzgerald in the course of argument that to justify interference by the Court '. . . the amount should be such that no reasonable proportion existed between it and the circumstances of the case'. The court must, however, adopt the view of the evidence most favourable to the plaintiff. Having regard to the view I take I do not think that it is proper to deal with the various heads under which damages are claimed in an attempt to estimate a figure which would in my view be reasonable in the circumstances of the case. I have, however, come to the conclusion, taking a view of the facts most favourable to the plaintiff that no reasonable proportion exists between the figure I would be inclined to give and that awarded by the jury.

Accordingly I would set aside this verdict and order a new trial.

Lavery J.:

. . . The jurisdiction of this Court to set aside a verdict on the grounds that the damages are either excessive or inadequate and the principle upon which it should be exercised is well established and is not in controversy.

The jury is the constitutional tribunal to determine the amount of damages and their decision is not to be interfered with merely because the court reviewing it would itself be disposed to give a greater or a lesser sum – even a substantially greater or lesser sum.

There is, however, a degree of disproportion between the damages awarded and the damages which, in the opinion of the Court of review, should be awarded which will require that the verdict should be set aside and the action be remitted for a new assessment. What this degree is has been variously expressed by judges. Adopting the words of Palles C.B. in *M'Grath* v. *Bourne* I.R. 10 C.L. 160 the test to be applied is:–

If, of the various views of the facts which are capable of being taken by reasonable men, we adopt that which is most favourable to the plaintiff and if, adopting this view, we arrive at the conclusion that no reasonable proportion exists between the damages which we should be inclined to give and the amount awarded by the jury, then the verdict ought not to stand.

English Courts have expressed the same idea in somewhat different words. Thus, Greer L.J., in *Flint* v. *Lovell* [1935] 1 K.B. 354 at p. 360 said 'the Court should be convinced either that the judge acted on some wrong principle of law, or that the amount awarded was so extremely high or so very small as to make it, in the judgment of this Court, an entirely erroneous estimate of the damages to which the plaintiff is entitled.' MacKinnon L.J., in *Greenfield* v. *London and North Eastern Railway Co.* [1944] 2 All E.R. 438 at p. 440 – also reported in [1945] 1 K.B. 89 – stated the problem thus:– 'We do not interfere merely because we might ourselves have given rather more or rather less, but only (a) if it appears that the judge below has omitted some relevant consideration, or admitted some irrelevant consideration, or (b) if we think the amount fixed is so excessive, or insufficient, as to be plainly unreasonable.'

It is to be noted that in these English decisions the damages were fixed by a judge and not by a jury and the Court of Appeal, may, therefore, have had a somewhat wider discretion to interfere.

On the other hand there has to be borne in mind the circumstance adverted to in *M'Greene* v. *Hibernian Taxi Co.* [1931] I.R. 319, that unanimity of a jury is no longer required and that the verdict of a majority of nine members of the jury has been made sufficient to determine the verdict. Kennedy C.J. and Fitzgibbon J. both observed that this circumstance should be borne in mind in maintaining the authority to set aside a verdict of a jury as against the weight of evidence – which was the question there involved. The same consideration should apply to the question of the amount of damages. There is not, however, any material difference between the statements of the principle – if it is precise enough to be called a principle – of the several judges.

It seems that what the judge in the Court of Appeal has to do is to make his own estimate of the damages he would award and then compare this estimate with the verdict and say whether there is a reasonable proportion between the sums or whether the verdict is an entirely erroneous estimate of the damage or is plainly unreasonable. In making this estimate the judge must adopt the view at all points most favourable to the plaintiff and must keep in mind that the jury had the advantage, which he has not had, of hearing the evidence and of seeing the witnesses and in particular hearing and seeing the plaintiff.

No one will deny that this is a most difficult task. It is especially difficult in a case where personal injuries are the subject of the claim. There is no standard by which pain and suffering, facial disfigurement or indeed, any containing disability can be measured in terms of money. All that can be said is that the estimate must be reasonable and different minds will inevitably arrive at widely differing conclusions as to what is reasonable. The task must, however, be undertaken. . . .

I consider that I am entitled to have regard to my experience of the amounts awarded by juries and judges and sustained in this Court in other cases of personal injuries. No precise standard can be established but within wide limits something like uniformity should be aimed at. . . .

My conclusion is that the jury have awarded a wholly unreasonable sum for damages, either on the head of facial disfigurement or, on some of the other heads or have admitted into their computation of damages some irrelevant consideration and that their verdict should be set aside and a new trial on the issue of the damages ordered.

Kingsmill Moore J.: – I agree with the judgments delivered by Maguire C.J., and Lavery J.

Ó Dálaigh J. dissented.

Computation Under Separate Headings

SEXTON V. O'KEEFFE
[1966] I.R. 204 (Supreme Court, 1964)

Lavery J. (dissenting):

The plaintiff is an unmarried lady now aged 65. On the 28th December, 1961, she suffered serious personal injuries when travelling as a passenger in a car which was the property of the defendant and was being driven by the defendant's wife, who was the sister of the plaintiff.

At the trial of her action against the defendant, in which she claimed damages for negligence, she obtained a verdict for £10,499.

The defendant has appealed to this Court on the grounds that the driver of the car was not negligent and that the amount awarded for damages is wholly excessive.

This Court, having heard the appeal, has dismissed it in so far as the issue of negligence is concerned and has given judgment on that issue, but reserved the question of damages for consideration.

This issue has now to be disposed of.

I have come to the conclusion that the damages are excessive to a degree wholly out of proportion to the loss suffered and I would therefore set aside the verdict on this issue and direct that the action should be sent back to the High Court for a re-assessment of damages.

The other members of the Court have come to the contrary conclusion. They are of the opinion that the sum of £10,499 is within the limits of compensation which a jury could reasonably award and that, on the well-established principles upon which this Court acts in reviewing a verdict on damages, the judgment should stand and the appeal be dismissed.

This being the case, I am not called on to explain in detail my own conclusion, but as I have, of course, considered the matter fully, I think I should set out as shortly as possible my reasons and why I differ from my colleagues.

The injuries suffered by the plaintiff were indeed serious and permanently disabling. They are described in the judgment which Mr. Justice Kingsmill Moore will deliver and which I have had an opportunity of reading and studying.

The major injuries were to her nose and fractures to both thighs and to the left knee joint.

She suffered great pain over a long period and underwent a number of serious operations.

Her present condition, which may be regarded as permanent, is that she requires crutches to walk and even with their aid can only drag herself for short distances. Her nose is deformed and her breathing is impeded at times.

It is obvious that these injuries, the pain and suffering involved, and the permanent disability would justify and require a very large sum in compensation.

The plaintiff was in the employment of Hospitals Trust Limited and was earning

£10 10s. od. per week. Since her accident the wages paid by the Trust have been increased and she might have expected to be now earning £11 per week, with something additional for overtime work.

Given good health and capacity, she might have expected to continue in her employment till she reached the age of 70 and could on these conditions have continued to the age of 72.

It is claimed, and reasonably claimed, that she will require domestic help having regard to her physical condition and it is suggested this would require £5 per week.

Her loss of earnings up to the date of trial were calculated at £1,150 and her medical expenses were £945, and these together amount to £2,095.

Since the accident she has been living with her sister and, though she has not paid for her support, she says a sum of £5 per week has been discussed as an appropriate payment. Certainly some provision of this kind would fairly be due and should be provided for.

Putting aside for the moment the item of compensation for loss of future earnings, if I were acting as a juror I would consider that full compensation for the other items of damage I have enumerated would be about £5,000 or at most £6,000.

I am fully conscious of the criticism which may be made of this apparently cold-blooded approach to a matter of human suffering but I have to face, as a jury has to face, the really impossible task of translating such suffering and distress into terms of money.

The jury of course did not explain how they arrived at their verdict.

Assuming – and it may be a large assumption – that they approached the problem by assessing the damages for the heads of damage other than loss of future earnings and allowed £5,000 or £6,000, they have awarded something between £5,499 and £4,499 for loss under this head.

In my opinion this is grossly excessive in the circumstances.

It is at this point that I unfortunately find myself differing from the view of Mr. Justice Kingsmill Moore.

His approach has been the opposite to mine. He first estimates the future loss of earnings and reaches a figure of £4,267 as the present value which not only does he consider not excessive but is the figure he has calculated and considers might be reasonably awarded.

Deducting this from the verdict gives £6,232 in respect of the other items of damage, which sum he does not consider excessive – at least, not excessive to the degree which would justify this Court in interfering.

Although this figure is substantially in excess of my highest figure of £6,000, I should not seriously disagree on this point.

The difference between our views is therefore on a net point, but I think on a point of importance, which indeed is the only justification for this judgment.

Mr. Justice Kingsmill Moore reaches the figure of £4,267 by making the following assumptions:–

1. That the plaintiff's expectation of life was 13.07 years, because that is the figure given as the expectation of life of a female aged 65 years in the Registrar General's Decennial Supplement, England and Wales, 1931, Life Tables;

2. That the plaintiff's working life might reasonably be taken to continue to the age of 72 years;

3. That her future earnings, but for the accident, might reasonably be capitalised by the application of the 5 per cent Innwood's Tables.

No such case was presented to the jury. These tables were not proved or explained by expert or other evidence.

The Court does not know how the case was presented at the trial or what directions the trial Judge gave the jury on damages. There was no objection to the charge but it is, I should think, certain that he did not direct them on the basis of these tables. There was no evidence upon which he could have done so.

Nevertheless, Mr. Justice Kingsmill Moore considers that this Court may test the verdict in this way.

I do not doubt that a judge is entitled to use and apply any material at his command or any knowledge or experience he may have in estimating general damages.

In my opinion, however, this calculation is not realistic. I do not know if these life tables can be usefully applied to the plaintiff's case or to any particular case. Before applying them I should certainly require expert assistance.

Life tables are generally used by insurance companies, Government Departments and other organisations in the framing of pension schemes and similar projects. There are, I believe, different tables for various countries, areas and for different categories of persons.

To establish that 100,000 – or perhaps a larger number – of persons of a particular age have an average expectation of life of so many years tells little or nothing about the expectation of life of any one of them. A life table tells nothing whatever about any person's continued ability to continue in employment.

The age factor is not the most important one in estimating an individual's expectation of life, and still less the expectation of an individual's continued ability to earn. The nature of the employment and the security of tenure (in this case undoubtedly good), the health, strength, habits and character of the person and even the family history are more important. All the vicissitudes of life have to be regarded.

Whether life tables and other actuarial material are admissible evidence – and, if so, the value of such evidence – may be doubtful. This cannot be usefully discussed and cannot be decided in this case as no evidence of the kind was given.

Much has been said on this topic. I content myself with referring to the words of Cotton L. J. in *Phillips* v. *London and South Western Railway Co.* 5 C. P. D. 280, at p. 293 of the report:– 'In my view a fair compensation for the pecuniary loss is not to be arrived at by any arithmetical process; it cannot be said that the amount of the income being known, the loss is reduced to a mere matter of calculation.'

I look at this case as the jury on the evidence before it could, I think, only look at it.

What would be fair compensation for money loss if an elderly woman of 65 years of age, in secure employment and earning £11 per week, is disabled from continuing in such employment?

I cannot but think that £4,500 – and there may be a larger sum involved in the verdict – is wholly out of proportion to the real loss.

Kingsmill Moore J.:

The plaintiff, a woman then over 63 years old, was thrown out of a motor-car on the 28th December, 1961. Her injuries were very serious. I leave out of account numerous bruises, abrasions and cuts over face, limbs and body which, though painful at the time, would have healed rapidly. Her major injuries were to her nose, which was split down the centre right through to the skull leaving the flesh turned back on each side over her eyes with the bones of the nose shattered and displaced; to her right femur which was badly fractured at the neck and displaced; to her left femur which had an extensive and complicated fracture in the lower third extending into the knee joint; and to her left tibia which was shattered just below the knee, involving the entire lower portion of the knee joint.

The repair and treatment of these injuries was complicated and prolonged. In all she had to be anaesthetised nine times and underwent four major operations, all of which involved very considerable subsequent pain.

On the 9th November, 1962, she was discharged. Her bones had united and her condition had become static. Her left knee is now almost completely stiff, her right hip badly deformed, her nose somewhat deformed. She cannot walk without crutches, though with their aid she can drag herself for a distance of up to half a mile by a process of advancing the left leg and pulling the right leg up to it. She requires a prop when standing. She cannot go up steps. The passage of air through her nose is impeded and when she gets a cold in the nose it produces headaches. No improvement in any of these disabilities can be expected.

At the time of the accident she was earning ten guineas a week as an employee of Hospitals Trust Limited, and the payment for the work she was doing has, since the 28th October, 1963, been increased to £11 per week. In addition she earned about £34 in the year for overtime. The trial took place on the 18th November, 1963. Counsel agreed that her loss of earnings up to the date of the trial might be reckoned at £1,200, a figure some £50 over what might be reached by strict calculation, but which takes into account the fact that payment is made in arrears.

The jury awarded a sum of £10,499 damages and the defendant appeals against this sum as being excessive. The jury were not asked to segregate their award between special damages for expenses and monetary loss, on the one hand, and general damages for pain and suffering, disability and deprivation of enjoyment on the other. Such a separation and the award of damages under those two separate heads, in many cases of which this is one, would greatly facilitate the Court in arriving at satisfactory conclusions in the event of an appeal, and would help to concentrate the attention of the jury on the matters to be taken into consideration. I am of opinion that it is a practice which could with advantage be adopted in all cases where special damages are likely to form a considerable proportion of the award.

It is, however, possible by analysis to arrive at a close approximation to the sum which could have been awarded as special damages. Medical and hospital expenses were agreed at £945 and, as I have mentioned, £1,200 was accepted as a sum to cover loss of earnings to the date of the trial. Probable future earnings depend on several factors.

At the date of the trial the plaintiff was aged just over 65, and on the figures of expectation of life compiled by the British Registrar General and reproduced at page 39 of Kemp's Quantum of Damages (2nd ed., 1961), she could have looked forward to living for another 13 years.

The evidence of Mr. Kinsella, staff manager of Hospitals Trust Limited, was that she could have retired at 70 on a pension of £4 per week or £208 per year, but that retirement at that age was not compulsory. Having regard to the work she was doing it seems reasonable to suppose that she could have continued at work till the age of 72. This is admittedly an arbitrary figure and a jury might have taken a couple of years more or less as representing her full working life, but in my opinion the age of 72 for retirement cannot be very far wrong.

Her earnings at the date of the trial would have been £11 per week and £34 per year in overtime, making a total of £606 per year.

Thus, for the estimated remainder of her life she would have received £4 per week (£208 per year), and for 7 years, that is until she retired, she would have received an additional £398 a year, being the excess of her working salary of £606 over her 'retiring' salary of £208.

Applying the 5 per cent tables to be found at page 74 of Innwood's Tables, the present value of £208 per year payable for 13 years (her expectation of life) would be £1,954, which figure is arrived at by multiplying the annual sum of £208 by 9.39357; and the present value of £398 per year payable for the remaining 7 years of her estimated working life would be £2,313, which figure is arrived at by multiplying the annual sum of £398 by the appropriate figure of 5.78637. The total of £4,267 represents the present value at the date of the trial of her estimated loss of earnings for the rest of her life.

In making these calculations the earnings of the plaintiff have been taken in gross, without any deduction in respect of the income tax exigible in respect of these earnings. It has not been customary in our Courts to make a deduction for income tax and no argument was addressed to us that such deductions should be made. If the sum awarded in this case in respect of loss of earnings is invested, income tax will have to be paid on the dividends but, if the income tax which would have been paid on the dividends be set against the income tax which would have been paid on the earnings, the difference would not be a substantial sum – one indeed which could be more than offset if the jury had been minded to add to the award, as they would have been entitled to do, something extra for the cost of domestic help rendered necessary by reason of the plaintiff's crippled condition and had also taken into account the high probability of an increase in the rate of wages during the period of the future service. I desire, however, to make it clear that while I have made no notional deduction in respect of income tax I am not deciding that such deduction is never permissible. Such a decision could only be given after full argument.

To the figure of £4,267 for estimated loss of future earnings must be added the £945 for medical and hospital expenses and the £1,200 for loss of earnings to the date of the trial, making a grand total of £6,412 for special damages. I have arrived at this conclusion with the aid of the Registrar General's figures for expectation of life and on the accepted actuarial basis for calculating the present value of a sum payable annually over a period of years. This assistance was not available to the jury but could have been afforded by any actuary and I consider such assistance would have been not only permissible but desirable.

The actuary can, of course, only speak with authority as to the method of calculation on given assumptions. I refer to the words of Mr. Justice Walsh giving the judgment of the Court in *Swords* v. *St. Patrick's Copper Mines* [1965] Ir. Jur. Rep. 63: 'It must be emphasised that the actuary is not the judge of the case and that his real value is to act as a guide on the mathematical calculations which must be made to arrive at a figure. It is, therefore, quite open to a jury to give a figure differing from his, whether it be higher or lower, if the evidence or the inferences to be drawn from the evidence warrant that course: that is to say, the jury may postulate a different set of assumptions and calculate accordingly, guided of course by the method of system which has been explained and elaborated by the actuary.'

In arriving at the figure of £4,267 for loss of earnings I have set forth the facts which have been proved and the assumptions which I think a jury could reasonably and properly have made, and have made the calculation of present value on such facts and assumptions, applying a basis which an actuary could have applied. The figure which emerges is not necessarily one which a jury took; it is one which a jury could reasonably have taken. In testing whether the figure they awarded was so excessive as to warrant this Court in setting it aside, one of the steps must be to see what the jury might reasonably have awarded under the various heads of damages. This I have tried to do.

It was suggested that a jury might also have been entitled to add a sum for domestic assistance rendered necessary by the plaintiff's crippled condition and a further sum to allow for an anticipated rise in wages over the period when the plaintiff might have been expected to be employed if she had not been injured. I have already indicated that I think some addition under these heads would have been permissible. I do not, however, find it necessary to add any sum to the special damages in respect of these items, as on the figure already calculated, it would appear that the sum awarded for general damages may not be in excess of £4,087. Having regard to the extent of her injuries, the permanent nature of her disablement and the suffering she undoubtedly underwent over a long period, I do not consider this sum to be so out of proportion to her injuries as to warrant setting the verdict aside and ordering a new trial.

Walsh J.:

I agree with the judgment which has been delivered by Mr. Justice Kingsmill Moore. In particular I wish to emphasise the desirability of giving a jury the benefit of the evidence of an actuary in any case in which loss of future earnings forms a substantial portion of a plaintiff's claim. It is very undesirable in such cases that a jury should be left at large to form their own impressions as to expectation of life and the computing of loss dependent upon it without the expert assistance of an actuary who can inform the jury of the precise mathematical calculations involved and to be applied according to the jury's findings on the relevant facts.

Collateral Benefits

McELROY V. ALDRITT
Unreported, Supreme Court, 11 June 1953 (5–1953)

Lavery J. (for the Court):

. . . [One] ground of appeal is that the learned Judge misdirected the jury on the question of damages generally and particularly in relation to the plaintiff's alleged loss of earnings.

The particular matter argued is that the plaintiff having given evidence that his employers had continued to pay his wages after the accident on an arrangement that if he succeeded in the proceedings against the defendant he would repay the amount paid, the plaintiff had suffered no loss of earnings and that the judge should have so directed the jury.

In fact the Judge told the jury that the employers having paid the wages – or an amount equivalent to the wages – voluntarily (as is admitted to be the case) the jury were entitled to award as part of the damages such sum for loss of earnings as in their opinion represented [the] period during which the plaintiff was disabled by the injuries from working and unable to earn wages. This summarises the very full direction given by the learned Judge.

In my opinion this direction was correct. The plaintiff so far as the evidence goes was employed by the week. He was disabled for the very considerable period of 89 weeks and did not work for his employers during this time – though in the latter part of this period he was able to do some work for his father, a fact to which the Judge drew the attention of the Jury.

It is impossible for the defendant as the wrongdoer to mitigate the damges for which he is responsible by relying on voluntary payments made by a third person to provide for the support of the plaintiff on an arrangement that he should be recouped if and when the plaintiff was in a position to do so and it can make no difference that that person was the employer of the plaintiff.

Note

On collateral benefits generally, see *McMahon & Binchy*, pp. 576–578.

Non-Pecuniary Loss

As a matter of practice, non-pecuniary loss is broken down into a number of elements. These may, for convenience, be listed as follows:

1. Pain and sufffering;
2. Loss of amenities;
3. Loss of expectation of life.

1. *Pain and Suffering*

Since pain is subjective, it raises particular difficulties of proof and of computation of damage, where obviously 'there can be no exact measurement' (*Ebbs* v. *Forkin*, unreported, Supreme Court, 6 May 1963 (107–1961), *per* Lavery, J.). Some of these difficulties are apparent in the decisions extracted below.

BOURKE V. BOURKE
Unreported, Supreme Court, 27 July 1971 (53–1970)

Fitzgerald J.:

The plaintiff in this case, Mary Bourke, is a farmer's wife and is aged some forty-four years. On the 24th December, 1967 she was a passenger in a car owned and driven by her husband, James Bourke, when the car collided with a vehicle the property of Messrs. Batchelors Limited. The plaintiff sustained serious injuries and instituted these proceedings claiming damages for negligence from both her husband and Messrs. Batchelors. The defendants joined in their defence which was confined to a denial of the alleged injuries, loss and damage.

The action came to trial before Mr. Justice Murnaghan and a jury on the 30th April, 1970, and the 1st May, 1970, the only issue being the amount of damages. The jury awarded the plaintiff £6,000 of which £25 was for damage to property and £5,975 for general damages. The defendants have appealed to this Court against the figure for general damages, contending that the figure is excessive.

The plaintiff's injuries consisted of:–
(1) a comminuted fracture of the left femur,
(2) a comminuted fracture of the first metatarsal bone of the right foot,
(3) lacerations of the forehead on the left eyebrow,
(4) a laceration near the left ankle,
(5) concussion causing loss of consciousness,
(6) bruising of the chest and arms, and
(7) shock.

Her injuries necessitated her detention in hospital for three months, during which she had to undergo an operation of the left femur and the insertion of a surgical pin. This fracture united but left her with a half inch to three-quarter inch shortening of the leg which caused her to limp. The fracture of the metatarsal bone united without requiring re-setting but left her with an irregularity of the instep. The laceration of the forehead healed satisfactorily but has left a depression on her forehead on the left hand side. This has not caused any disability and it was not alleged that it was a serious cosmetic blemish. The laceration of the left ankle appears to have healed fully with no resulting disability. The head injury has, according to the plaintiff, caused insomnia, dizziness, some deafness and nervousness in travelling by car. Prior to the accident she was learning to drive and now lacks the courage to resume her course of training. She appears to have made a full recovery from the bruising of the chest and arms. She still complains of insominia, dizziness and nervousness attributable to the concussion and shock.

The plaintiff in evidence complained of great difficulty in carrying on her work as a farmer's wife. She said that the left leg affected her in walking on rough ground and prevented her from working around the farmyard and in negotiating stairs. She said the left knee was stiff and that the leg and her right foot were painful and that, as a result, she could not work outside the house, was not able to use the milking machine, and was seriously restricted in working indoors. When discharged from hospital, while the plaster had been removed from her left leg, she had to use crutches which were ultimately discarded in 1968, from which time she has used a stick. She still complained of the above mentioned consequences of the concussion and shock.

Her complaints of her continuing disabilities were only partially supported by her doctor, Surgeon Baker. He said that the limp would cause her some difficulty on rough ground but would not restrict her household duties too much. On cross-examination he agreed that a half inch lift inside her left shoe would compensate for the shortening and help to steady her. He was further of the opinion that the irregularity of the right instep did not call for operative treatment but would restrict her in wearing stylish shoes. He expected that her symptoms from the concussion would have cleared up within two years but their continued presence, as she alleged, depended upon when [sic] you accepted her evidence and that she might be, to some degree, subject to litigation neurosis.

Ignoring the evidence called for the defendants it is clear that the evidence of the plaintiff and that of her surgeon as to her present incapacity and future condition cannot be reconciled. Dr. Baker agrees that the limp in the left leg can be corrected or certainly greatly reduced by a half inch lift in the shoe and that the irregularity of the right instep does not call for removal or cause any loss of function other than ensuring that she must avoid selecting shoes which might press or rub on it. He further agreed that her subjective symptoms are possibly protracted by the pending litigation. This is a very different picture from that presented by the plaintiff's own evidence.

Making all due allowances for the fact that an injured person may feel a pain, for which his or her doctor cannot account, and that a jury are entitled to accept a plaintiff's complaint as to the existence of a pain notwithstanding the doctor's inability to account for it, it appears to me that, where a plaintiff has a series of complaints indicating a serious permanent incapacity and calls in support of her claim her own doctor who fails to support the incapacity alleged, the jury is not entitled to proceed on the basis that the plaintiff is right and that her doctor is wrong. They must, in my view, have some regard to the medical evidence called for the plaintiff to support her case. They are certainly not entitled to ignore it.

I am of the opinion that the verdict of almost £6,000 for general damages in this case does not bear any reasonable relationship to the injuries proved to have been sustained and that the appeal should be allowed.

Budd J. concurred with **Fitzgerald J. Ó Dálaigh C.J.** dissented.

Questions

1. As a juryman, would you find the direction suggested by Fitzgerald J., on the question of conflict between doctor and patient a meaningful one? Could you still decide in favour of the patient? Is it simply a matter of credibility or is something more at issue? If the latter, what is this 'something more'?

2. *Loss of Amenities*

Where a person loses an amenity or faculty, such as an eye or leg, he is, of course, entitled to compensation. But how is that loss to be measured? On one view, which adopts an objective approach, the plaintiff is entitled to substantial compensation for the loss, irrespective of any consideration of whether he was ever aware of it: thus a person rendered totally unconscious by the injury and who lost a leg would not have his damages significantly reduced on account of his unconscious state even if he never regained consciousness. On another, subjective and more utilitarian, view, the true purpose of compensation is to fill the void experienced by the victim of the injury; where, therefore, the victim experiences little or no loss (on account of unconscious-ness or otherwise), his damages under this heading should be reduced to virtually nothing. Which approach would you favour? Why?

3. *Loss of Expectation of Life*

McMORROW V. KNOTT
Unreported, Supreme Court, 21 December 1959 (29–1959)

Maguire C.J. [This is described as an 'unrevised' judgment; no copy of the revised judgment has been preserved – *eds*.]:

This is an appeal against the amount of damages awarded by a jury in an action of negligence on the ground that it is excessive.

The plaintiff was a solicitor practising in the town of Carrick-on-Shannon, Co. Leitrim. He was so badly injured that it is extremely doubtful if he will ever again be able to resume the practice of his profession and even if he does so his activities will be restricted to office work. It is clear that he will be an invalid and will require skilled nursing and medical attention for the rest of his life.

Damages are claimed under the following heads:–

(a) Special damages.
(b) Pain and suffering.
(c) Loss of future income.
(d) Future nursing and medical attention.
(e) Shortening of the plaintiff's life.
(f) The cost of providing a dwelling and office adapted to his needs having regard to his disability and the necessity of providing constant nursing.

The jury awarded the sum of £87,402.

The grounds of appeal relied upon are misdirection by the trial Judge on the method to be adopted in assessing damages under heads (c), (d), (e) and (f) and that the damages are excessive.

In support of the claim for loss of future income there was evidence from an actuary based upon the usual statistical tables as regards the plaintiff's expectation of life and on the basis that he should be given a sum which would purchase an annuity based upon his earnings in the last year before the accident. When considering this evidence the jury should have been instructed that while it was open to them to consider these figures they should realise that the figure of expectation of life was an artificial one based on statistics and that they were not bound to accept the figure as unalterable in an individual case. They were of course entitled to consider the plaintiff's physical condition at the time of the accident but must take into account the ordinary recognised hazards of life to which he would be subject. Moreover they were bound to consider the obvious risks in connection with his practice as a solicitor. It might expand as was suggested but as with any calling depending upon individual effort it might diminish. This was not made as clear to the jury as it should have been.

The learned Judge also in my opinion erred in the way he dealt with the claim for future nursing and medical expenses. The jury were directed as to this on the basis that the same actuarial tables might be applied as in connection with loss of income. This was clearly wrong. It is obvious that the compensation to be awarded under this head depended in the first place not upon the expectation of life of the plaintiff at the time of the accident but as at the time of the trial. When he recalled the jury the learned Judge did something to set this right. In one important sentence, however, he put the matter on a different but equally wrong basis. He said: 'It is only right to say, and I have been asked to say, that of course I didn't tell you that if you were to come to the conclusion that the plaintiff's life may be shortened by the injury he sustained that he might pass away in one of these "flare-ups". If you thought that was likely you would pay due regard to the evidence of Dr. Guttmann that the longest known life is 18 years . . . If you think the plaintiff's life will be shortened as a result of his injury he is entitled to general damages in regard to that and the one may balance the other.'

The head of damage for the shortening of life should not in my opinion be considered on an actuarial basis. It is a difficult matter to lay down a precise method for estimating a figure. The learned Judge's failure to deal with this head of damage may have been due to the view which he expressed in the absence of the jury 'that there was nothing in the evidence of Dr. Guttmann to suggest that the plaintiff was not to have a normal expectation of life'. This does not seem to be a correct view on the evidence. It has been suggested with a good deal of reason that this head of damages might properly be considered as an element of pain and suffering. In considering it and the other heads of damages I have mentioned the jury should have been told that it is quite impossible in a case such as this to give perfect compensation. In one sense nothing would compensate the plaintiff for the dreadful consequences of an accident for which admittedly he had no blame. A jury must, however, be just and towards this end must be reasonable in arriving at a figure.

I cite with approval a well-known passage from the judgment of Parke J. in *Armsworth* v. *South Eastern Rly.*, 11 Jur. p.758:

'Here you must estimate the damage by the same principle as if only a wound had been inflicted. Scarcely any sum could compensate a labouring man for the loss of a limb, yet you don't in such a case give him enough to maintain him for life; and in the present case you are not to consider the value of his existence as if you were bargaining with an annuity office; for in that view you would have to calculate all the accidents which might have occurred to him in the course of it, which would be a very difficult matter. I therefore advise you to take a reasonable view of the case and give what you consider a fair compensation.'

As I take the view that the jury were not correctly directed in regard to certain important matters affecting the proper consideration of the case it is unnecessary to deal with the other heads of damages although I may say that it seems to me that the claim in respect of the provision of a proper house was put on an incorrect basis.

In view of the misdirection this verdict cannon stand.

It should, however, be made clear even if misdirection was not established that this Court is entitled to set aside a verdict of a jury if in its opinion the amount of damages is excessive. Apart altogether from the grounds mentioned I would hold that the amount measured by the jury in this case is excessive because to use the oft quoted words of Baron Fitzgerald as adopted by Palles C.B. in *McGrath* v. *Bourne* 10 I.R.C.L. 'no reasonable proportion exists between it and the circumstances of the case.'

There should in my opinion be a new trial limited of course as the notice of appeal limits it to the question of damages.

Ó Dálaigh, J.:

The issue of the amount of damages to which the plaintiff is entitled should in my opinion – and I have reached this conclusion not without regret – be the subject of a new trial.

Of the matters to have been considered at the trial one of first importance was the effect of the plaintiff's catastrophic injuries on his expectation of life. Was it open to the jury, on the evidence placed before them, to find that his expectation of life had been unaffected or virtually unaffected? I am satisfied it was not. I have re-examined Dr.

Guttmann's evidence – see his answers to questions 8–14, 34–38, 44, 51, 62, 68, 77–78 and 138 – and I have borne in mind the doctor's tribute to Mr. McMorrow's outstanding courage and determination (q.43) and to his profound will to live (q.132). The effect of Dr. Guttmann's evidence – I speak of probabilities – is plain; it is that the plaintiff's expectation of life has been seriously affected. The doctor's answers, though given with delicacy, are of sufficient degree of plainness as not to admit of misunderstanding.

Nevertheless, while this was the state of the medical evidence it appears that the case went to the jury upon the basis that it was open to them to find that there was no loss of expectation of life or no appreciable loss, subject however to this addition; that, if they did find there was loss of expectation of life, the amount of damages might not be different from the damages that would be awarded on the basis of no loss of expectation of life, because the damages in respect of such loss might be equated with the saving in the cost of nursing, the one (as it was said) balancing the other.

As will be seen, three main reasons now emerge why the issue of damages should be retried. I shall state them very briefly. Firstly: the loss of future earnings and the cost of future nursing were two of the plaintiff's principal heads of damages. The one was proper to be examined by reference to the plaintiff's expectation of life before injury and the other by reference to his expectation of life after injury. At the trial, however, these two distinct and important heads of damage were not segregated but were treated as being subject to a common time element; thus, as it seems to me, importing a wrong principle into the jury's calculations.

Secondly: in the circumstances of this case – and this was only to be stated to become clear – damages in respect of loss of expectation of life could not be equated with the consequent saving in nursing expenses. Compensation for shortening of life is a difficult question; but it will now suffice to observe that the Courts have been consistent in declining to allow in respect of his head of damages other than moderate sums of compensation, in no way comparable with the amount which a saving of nursing expenses in this case would be likely to represent. Here then, also, a wrong principle has been imported into the jury's calculations.

Thirdly: I have already indicated what limitations the medical evidence in my opinion imposed on the jury in their consideration of the issue of damages. Bearing those limitations in mind I have, as this Court in *Foley* v. *Thermocement Products Ltd.* (90 I.L.T.R. 92) indicated should be done, formed my own estimate of the amount of damages I would be inclined to award; and as I find that no reasonable proportion exists between my figure and the jury's assessment I am constrained to say the jury's assessment is excessive and the verdict therefore ought not to stand.

Finally, it will, I think, not be out of place to refer to two other matters, one specific and the other general. The first matter concerns the provision of an invalid bay attached to the plaintiff's house for the plaintiff's special nursing needs. It was not controverted that the defendant could be properly called upon to answer for this, save, perhaps, for some allowance for capital value. But the costs of making this provision was not, I think, sufficiently isolated from the cost of erecting a house for the ordinary household needs of the plaintiff and his family and, on that account, I incline to the view that the jury may have considered this head of damage on a basis entirely too broad.

The other matter concerns the use of actuarial evidence. Actuarial evidence can furnish guidance to a jury in its deliberations, but it must as a basis for ascertaining loss be acted upon with caution.

Such evidence has to be re-orientated by reference to the special problems raised by the evidence in the case and other countervailing circumstances, such as the ups and downs of life in health and business, have to be allowed for. Damages in a case of personal injuries are not to be assessed by pricing each element of damage separately and taking the total. A figure thus arrived at does not present a true picture. The several elements of damage instead of being just totalled have to be fused, because the final assessment should be informed by a view of the case not as seen in segregation but as a whole.

Lavery J. [Draft judgment: in a communication with the Registrar of the Supreme Court, dated 21 December 1965 enclosing this draft judgment, which he 'believe[d] to have been prepared' by him, Lavery, J. stated that '[f]or some reason which I do not recall this judgment was not delivered. It may still be of some help.' – *Eds.*]

I am of opinion that the sum awarded by the jury in this case is excessive and that accordingly there should be a new trial.

Ordinarily it would be unnecessary and perhaps undesirable to say more. I consider, however, that it might be helpful to the judge who will re-try the case to say something on the principles which should be followed in measuring damages in a case such as this.

The plaintiff was a practicising solicitor aged 38 years. In the last full year before the accident he had earned £1,350 – allowing for deduction of income tax his earnings were £1,110. He is totally incapacitated and can only look forward to the life of an invalid in future. The nature of his injuries are such that to keep him alive will require skilled nursing and medical attention for the rest of his life. It is estimated that the expense of nursing and caring for him will be the sum of £1,835 per year. He is entitled to compensation for the loss he has [sustained] and will sustain through inability to attend to his profession. How far this may be lessened by the chance of his resuming practice in a restricted manner suggested in evidence is a matter for the jury. At the trial evidence was given by an actuary of the expectation of life appropriate to a man of his age. On the basis of standard tables it was stated in evidence that his expectation of life would have been 34 years. On this assumption an actuary gave evidence that it would require £1,573 to purchase an annuity of £100. In my opinion it is proper for a jury to consider this evidence. They should, however, be told while he was entitled to full and fair compensation that perfect compensation is impossible and might be unjust. It should be explained to them that this figure of 34 years is an artificial figure worked out by Insurance Companies on basis of averages. They should realise that as regards the individual case there are the ordinary hazards and although the fact that he was a healthy man and the son of long-lived parents might be relied upon there is always the risk that he might not live this number of years. They should also remember that his income was not a fixed annual figure but was subject to all the hazards of a professional life and might fluctuate. It might conceivably disappear altogether.

The second head of damages viz. the prospective nursing and medical expenses must be approached on quite a different basis. In calculating compensation under this head the expectation of life of the plaintiff must be estimated in a different way. The actuarial tables as to his probable length of life put forward in connection with the first head of damage have no application. The only witness who dealt with this aspect was Dr. Guttmann. His evidence amounted to no more than saying that in view of the improved technique which he has applied with such remarkable success the figure of two or three years formerly accepted as the probable duration of life of a person who suffers injury of the type which the plaintiff suffered no longer applies. He did not give a figure for the probable duration of the plaintiff's life. He did say that one patient in a similar condition had survived for 18 years. It is, to my mind, quite obvious that the hazards which the plaintiff will encounter are great. His evidence did not provide any firm ground upon which an estimate might be made. They would, in my opinion, be justified in holding that the chances are that the plaintiff will not live more than a few years. The case went to the jury in a very loose way. They were first of all instructed on the basis that the actuarial tables should be applied in the same way in arriving at figures under both heads of damage. When the learned judge recalled the jury he altered his direction by saying: 'If you think that the plaintiff's life would be shortened as a result of his injury he is entitled to general damages in regard to that and the one may balance the other.' This surely was wrong as in effect it maintained the position that the jury might estimate both heads of damage in the same way.

The next head of damage discussed was that of loss of expectation of life. To lay down any rule with reference to this head of damage is undoubtedly a matter of considerable difficulty. Whether the plaintiff could reasonably look forward to a happy life or a miserable one, the loss to him is, in one sense, inestimable. Lord Wright at p. 848 said: 'In one sense it is true that no money would be compensation for life or the enjoyment of life and in that sense it is impossible to fix compensation for the shortening of life. But it is the best the law can do. It would be paradoxical if the law refused to give any compensation at all because none would be adequate.' This decision is said to have caused chaos 'not much relieved', according the Mr. Heuston, in a number of judgments in the Court of Appeal. [See *Salmond on the Law of Torts*, p. 316 (12th ed., by R.F.V. Heuston, 1957) – *eds.*] The present tendency is to give very moderate amounts. It seems to me that a jury should understand that perfect compensation could not be given – they must be reasonable and add what they think appropriate to the damages for pain and suffering.

Of the other heads of damage there is no need to say anything. The figure for special damage is large but there is little dispute about it. Neither is there any difficulty as to damages for pain and suffering. The plaintiff has suffered terrible injuries for which in a sense, no money can compensate him. He is entitled to a substantial sum under this head of damage but again the jury must keep a sense of proportion.

I have dealt with various aspects of the case and have endeavoured to give some guidance as to how a jury should be instructed to deal with a claim of the kind with which we are concerned. It is to be remembered, however, that it is not necessary to establish misdirection or misconduct of the jury to entitle this Court to interfere where damages are excessive as in my opinion they are in this case. The verdict should be set aside and there should be a new trial.

Note

See also *Murray* v. *John Sisk & Son (Dublin) Ltd.* [1965] Ir. Jur. Rep. 41, at 42 (Sup. Ct., *per* Lavery, J., 1964); *O'Sullivan* v. *Dwyer,* [1971] I.R. 275 (Sup. Ct.). Generally, *cf. McMahon & Binchy*, pp. 581–583.

Property Damage

Problems may arise in attempting to apply the principle of *restitutio in integrum* in cases where property has been severely damaged or destroyed. The plaintiff may claim that he is entitled to the cost of reinstatement of the property; the defendant may reply that compensation should be limited to the diminution of its value. Our courts have adopted a pragmatic approach to the question, investigating a wide range of factors before determining which solution should be adopted. See *Munnelly* v. *Calcon Ltd.* [1978] I.R. 387 (Sup. Ct.); *Quinn* v. *Quality Homes Ltd.*, unreported, High Ct., Finlay, P., 21 November 1977 (1975–2242P).

Chapter 27

INJUNCTIONS

In many cases the victim or apprehended victim of a tort will not regard an award of damages as an appropriate remedy. His real concern may be that a wrongful act may be committed or continued in the future or that it will recur; he may much prefer that the defendant be ordered to cease doing the wrongful act than that he obtain damages in the form of monetary compensation. Such an order by the Court is called an injunction. The injunction may be (a) *prohibitory*, that is, one restraining the defendant from continuing or repeating a wrongful act, (b) *mandatory*, that is, one ordering the defendant to do some positive act to end a wrongful state of affairs that has been created by him; or (c) *quia timet*, that is, one restraining wrongful conduct that has not yet been committed but is merely apprehended.

Some other modes of categorising injunctions should also be noted. A *perpetual* injunction is issued at the end of the trial of the action on its merits. *Interlocutory* and *interim* injunctions are merely provisional, being designed to preserve matters *in statu quo* until the complete hearing of the case. An interim injunction is an injunction of an interlocutory nature granted by the Court on application to it *ex parte* by the plaintiff. It is very much an emergency 'holding operation' until proceedings with both parties appearing can take place, usually within a few days.

THE EDUCATIONAL COMPANY OF IRELAND LTD. V. FITZPATRICK
[1961] I.R. 323 (Supreme Court, aff'g. High Court, Teevan, J., 1960)

The plaintiffs, the Educational Company of Ireland Ltd. and Edward Hely and Co. Ltd., carried on the business, *inter alia*, of manufacturing stationery and the production of school textbooks. They employed forty-five clerical workers of whom sixteen were members of the Irish Union of Distributive Workers and Clerks. A discussion took place between Mr. Corish, branch secretary of the Union and Mr. Fitzsimmons, a director of the first-named plaintiff Company. Mr. Fitzsimmons, on behalf of the management of both Companies, agreed that the Union was entitled to make every effort to recruit members of the staff. He also agreed that the Companies would make no effort to prevent any or all of the staff from joining the Union; that it was a matter for each individual to decide for himself and that the Companies would not interfere in any way.

At a meeting held subsequently on the 6th February, 1960, which was attended by fourteen out of the sixteen Union members, these members passed a resolution refusing to remain at work with nine other members (who were named) of the clerical staff who were not members of the Union. On the 9th February a letter was written by Mr. Corish to Mr. Fitzsimmons acquainting him of the result of the meeting, and on the 10th February a letter was written by Mr. Fitzpatrick, general secretary of the Union, referring to the meeting and to the vote and suggesting a conference between the representative of the executive committee of the Union and the management of the Companies. To this Mr. Fitzsimmons replied, on the 11th February, stating that he was prepared to hear anything put forward but that the Companies would once again repeat that they could not, nor were they prepared to, compel any member of their staff either to join or to stay out of the Union. The Union took this to mean – and so communicated by letter dated the 17th February to Mr. Fitzsimmons – that the Companies felt that a conference would not achieve any change of attitude on the part of the management in the matter. The Union further stated that unless the nine members mentioned had joined the Union in the meantime, the Union members would be instructed not to resume duty after finishing time on Saturday, the 27th February. On the 29th February, the sixteen members of the Union did not turn up for work and a picket was placed on the plaintiffs' premises in the customary way.

On the 1st March the plaintiffs issued a summons, in the High Court, naming Mr. Fitzpatrick and the sixteen Union members as defendants, claiming an injunction restraining the defendants and each of them from attending at or near the plaintiffs' premises at 86/89 Talbot Street in the City of Dublin and at Beresford Lane off Lower Gardiner Street in the City of Dublin for the purpose of watching or besetting or picketing the said premises and from disturbing the plaintiffs in the conduct of the business carried on by them in the said premises and from interfering with or attempting to interfere with the plaintiffs, their employees or customers or any of them, in any way which would, or would tend to be, a nuisance or annoyance to the plaintiffs, their employees or customers or any of them. Damages and ancilliary relief were also claimed.

On the same day as the summons was issued it came before Mr. Justice Haugh, who granted an interim injunction in the terms of the claim as set out above and gave the plaintiffs liberty to serve the defendants with short notice of motion, returnable for the 7th March, 1960, for an interlocutory injunction. Mr. Justice Haugh also gave liberty to the plaintiffs prior to the service of the order upon the defendants to give notice thereof by telephone or telegram or both directed to the said defendants respectively. On the 8th March an order was made by Mr. Justice Teevan, sitting for Mr. Justice Budd, granting an interlocutory injunction in the above terms.

Teevan J.:

I am satisfied that the main consideration which I should bear in mind in approaching the present application is the balance of the convenience and inconvenience which is likely to result to the parties from the granting or refusing of the order sought. In this respect, and indeed in regard to the question of the damage which is likely to result to the respective parties as a result of my decision on this application, Mr. McKenna's statement as to the intentions of his clients in regard to the members of their staff who have gone on strike simplifies my task very considerably.

Mr. FitzGerald, appearing for the defendants, submits that the legal position is crystal clear; that the facts before the Court bring the case within the judicial pronouncement in the decisions in this branch of law, and that there is nothing left which can be said to be in doubt or in issue in the case. He contends that it is clearly established that there is a trade dispute in existence, and that such being the case I should not continue the injunction.

In my opinion there are certain matters which can be made the basis of contentious issues in the case. The question of fact as to whether an agreement was made between the plaintiffs and the Union as outlined in the correspondence commencing with the letter of the 16th November, 1959, is in issue between the parties. There is also the question as to why only nine non-union members are singled out by the Union. There may be some explanation for this matter; however, the plaintiffs say that the matter warrants investigation at a full hearing of the action. Furthermore, legal issues of some importance, and which the plaintiffs seek an opportunity to debate at a full hearing of this case, may well arise for decision. Cogent arguments have been advanced for distinguishing the present case from that of *Ryan* v. *Cooke and Quinn* [1938] I.R. 512. However, *Ryan* v. *Cooke and Quinn* [1938] I. R. 512 is the law in this country, and it is not criticised in the subsequent cases. Some distinguishing features are mentioned in the judgment of O'Byrne J. in *Riordan* v. *Butler and Others* [1940] I. R. 347, but he does not disagree with the earlier decision. In addition, whether a trade dispute exists is always a question of fact, as is made clear by the decision of the House of Lords in *White* v. *Riley* [1921] 1 Ch. 1. There are clearly some matters in issue between the parties.

On the other hand, the position as regards damages and the balance of convenience is made very simple. I have a clear undertaking from the plaintiffs that the members of their staff who are on strike will be taken back to their pre-strike jobs at their usual wages pending the hearing of this action, and that return to work will not be used in any way to prejudice the defendants' position in this action. It appears to me to be clear that a continuation of picketing pending the hearing of this action will cause grave and irreparable damage to the plaintiffs. The defendants if they avail of the offer will suffer no loss other than the loss of wages which they have already voluntarily suffered. Accordingly, the defendants are not prejudiced and are in a position to avoid all damage and inconvenience, if the injunction is continued. The plaintiffs, on the other hand, will suffer irreparable damage and considerable inconvenience if the present application is refused. I cannot see that these employees – the most junior of whom, in regard to length of time in employment with the plaintiffs, has waited seven years before feeling that he could not work with non-union workers – will suffer inconvenience or disturbance if I continue the injunction as requested, and whilst I do not base my decision on the attitude of the Union, I do not see that they will suffer serious inconvenience by the making of such an order. In my opinion justice demands that the parties should have an opportunity of having the issues argued in the fullest manner, and that the *status quo* be preserved pending the hearing of the action. I should add that the plaintiffs have undertaken to proceed with the action with all possible speed. Accordingly I shall make an order continuing the injunction until the hearing of the action, it being agreed by the plaintiffs that they will have the statement of claim filed and delivered within ten days from today.

[From the above judgment the defendants appealed to the Supreme Court.]

Lavery J.:
. . . The defendants submit that the facts . . . are not in controversy and that established law shows that on these facts there is in existence a trade dispute which justifies their conduct and that accordingly an interlocutory injunction should not be granted.

The defendants offered to have the motion for the interlocutory injunction treated as the trial of the action; this is a course which is not unusual where the facts are admitted. The plaintiffs declined to agree to this and it is conceded that in doing so they were within their rights. This appeal must therefore be dealt with as one from an interlocutory order.

The principles upon which the High Court and this Court on appeal from the High Court (with some modification where an appeal is being considered) deal with the granting of an interlocutory injunction are well settled.

I quote from the authoritative text-book, Kerr on Injunctions (6th ed., 1927, at p. 2):– 'The interlocutory injunction is merely provisional in its nature, and does not conclude a right. The effect and object of the interlocutory injunction is merely to keep matters *in statu quo* until the hearing or further order. In interfering by interlocutory injunction, the Court does not in general profess to anticipate the determination of the right, but merely gives it as its opinion that there is a substantial question to be tried, and that till the question is ripe for trial, a case has been made out for the preservation of the property in the meantime *in statu quo*. A man who comes to the Court for an interlocutory injunction, is not required to make out a case which will entitle him at all events to relief at the hearing. It is enough if he can show that he has a fair question to raise as to the existence of the right which he alleges, and can satisfy the Court that the property should be preserved in its present actual condition, until such question can be disposed of.'

I also quote from pp. 15 and 16 of the same book:– 'The office of the Court to interfere being founded on the existence of the legal right, a man who seeks the aid of the Court must be able to show a fair *prima facie* case in support of the title which he asserts. He is not required to make out a clear legal title, but he must satisfy the Court tat he has a fair question to raise as to the existence of the legal right which he sets up, and that there are substantial grounds for doubting the existence of the alleged legal right, the exercise of which he seeks to prevent. The Court must, before disturbing any man's legal right, or stripping him of any of the rights with which the law has clothed him, be satisfied that the probability is in favour of his case ultimately failing in the final issue of the suit. The mere existence of a doubt as to the plaintiff's right to the property, interference with which he seeks to restrain, does not of itself constitute a sufficient ground for refusing an injunction, though it is always a circumstance which calls for the attention of the Court.'

The case now before the Court raises questions which have not been decided in any Court whose decision binds this Court. But it is submitted that the decision of the Court of Appeal in England in the case of *White* v. *Riley* [1921] 1 Ch. 1 has been accepted and that so far as interlocutory relief is concerned it should be accepted.

The plaintiffs have to establish that there is a fair question raised to be decided at the trial. The arguments, lasting three days in this Court, show I think that there is such a question to be determined.

I have read and studied the cases cited to the Court: *Gaskell* v. *Lancashire and Cheshire Miners' Federation* 28 T. L. R. 518; *White* v. *Riley* [1921] 1 Ch. 1; *Valentine* v. *Hyde* [1919] 2 Ch. 129; *Larkin* v. *Long* [1915] A. C. 814; *Riordan* v. *Butler and Others* [1940] I.R. 347; *Sherriff* v. *McMullen* [1952] I. R. 237; *Smith and Another* v. *Beirne and Another* (decided on 29th January, 1953, but unreported on the application for an interlocutory injunction); *National Union of Railwaymen and Others* v. *Sullivan and Others* [1947] I. R. 77.

It would be inappropriate to discuss them on this appeal. The Chief Justice has stated the issues and other members of the Court will state them. Sufficient to say that in my opinion they raise a question and a difficult one.

So, if the fair question for trial is established, what should be the order on the plaintiffs' application for an interlocutory injunction? As to the considerations which should guide the Court, I refer to the article on 'Injunctions' in Halsbury's Laws of England (Hailsham ed., vol. 18, p. 33, paras, 48 and 49). The author of the article is Mr. Justice Eve. I abbreviate the quotation:– '. . . in the absence of very special circumstances [the Court] will impose only such restraint as will suffice to stop the mischief and keep things as they are until the hearing.

'Where any doubt exists as to the plaintiff's right, or if his right is not disputed, but its violation is denied, the Court, in determining whether an interlocutory injunction should be granted, takes into consideration the balance of convenience to the parties and the nature of the injury which the defendant, on the one hand, would suffer if the injunction was granted and he should ultimately turn out to be right, and that which the plaintiff, on the other hand, might sustain if the injunction was refused and he should ultimately turn out to be right. The burden of proof that the inconvenience which the plaintiff will suffer by the refusal of the injunction is greater than that which the defendant will suffer, if it is granted, lies on the plaintiff.'

The plaintiffs have stated that the damage which may be caused by the continuance of picketing pending the trial of the action will be serious and, in the sense in which the word is used in this connection, 'irreparable.' Clearly, it would be very difficult, if not indeed impossible, for the plaintiffs to show that loss of trade or diminution of their profits, if sustained, should be attributed to the picketing and not to other circumstances or combination of circumstances.

The defendants are asserting what they consider to be a fundamental principle, which indeed is so, and one of very great importance. In the particular case no serious damage will be caused to them if by order of the Court the picketing is restrained till the trial of the action. It is true that the defendants, other than Mr. Fitzpatrick, are out of employment and at the loss of their wages, but this loss, serious though it is, is not related to the issue as to picketing save in the sense, as Mr. FitzGerald submitted, that if picketing is continued the plaintiffs may be compelled to surrender. But this is not a legal consideration which should affect the Court in favour of the defendants. In my opinion this case comes within the principles upon which *Smith and Another* v. *Beirne and Another (supra)* was decided in this Court. Unfortunately this case is unreported, but the Chief Justice has obtained from the Registrar a note of the judgment of the Court delivered by him. The grounds of the decision were twofold. First, that the facts might be in dispute, and second, that a serious question of law arose as to whether there was a trade dispute in existence.

In this case there may well be further facts elicited at the trial, but there can be no doubt that a serious question of law arises.

The manner in which a Court of Appeal should approach the decision of a Court of first instance in interlocutory matters is well settled and understood.

In the case of *Baker* v. *White* 1 T. L. R. 64 it was held by Bowen and Fry L.JJ. that the Court of Appeal will not interfere with the exercise of the discretion of a judge who has granted an injunction until the trial of an action. Of course, this is not an absolute rule, but it is one to be applied unless a case is made out showing that the judge either acted on a wrong principle or completely misunderstood the facts.

In our Courts it is of the first importance that this principle should be enforced and perhaps extended. The structure of the Court system has been simplified. Dealing only with the High Court and the Supreme Court, there is a hearing in the High Court and an appeal from the decision therein to the Supreme Court. This appeal is the first and also the final appeal. Gone is the motion for judgment in the Divisional Court, the appeal to the Court of Appeal and the ultimate appeal, where allowed, to the House of Lords. This simplification is suitable to the needs of the country. The multiplication of appeals and the costs thereby involved are to be avoided. There are, however, certain dangers in the system which should be noted and which increase the responsibility of this Court.

This Court has to pronounce the law finally and there is no opportunity for a review of its decision in the particular case. The Oireachtas may, of course, change the law generally within the limits imposed by the Constitution.

It is my opinion that the cases in which this Court, charged with the responsibility which I have explained, should declare the law on an interlocutory appeal reversing the decision of the judge of the High Court are few and that this is not such a case.

In my opinion the judgment of Mr. Justice Teevan was correct and he, more briefly than I have done, but adequately, stated the principles upon which he had to act.

I would dismiss the appeal.

Ó Dálaigh J.:

. . . Although the question under the Act of 1906 is *res integra* in this jurisdiction, I accept it that there is persuasive authority in favour of the view put forward by the defendants; but, as at present advised, I incline to the view that the constitutional issue raised by the plaintiffs is *prima facie* sufficient to turn the scales once more in their favour. Accordingly, the only remaining matter is balance of convenience.

I have little doubt where that lies. Not to grant this injunction might well effectively deprive the plaintiffs of having this action tried out in the proper forum;
pending trial, they might well find themselves with no choice except either to close
down their business or to act (as I incline to think) unconstitutionally by bringing
pressure on their employees to join a union not of their own choice. On the other
hand, for the defendants the only inconvenience which they would suffer is a
limitation of temporary duration on their permission to picket.

I am therefore of opinion that the injunction should be maintained and this appeal
dismissed.

Kingsmill Moore J. delivered a concurring judgment. **Maguire J.** also concurred.
Maguire C.J. dissented.

Notes and Questions

1. Interlocutory injunctions are frequently availed of by employers in industrial disputes. See
   Casey, 'The Injunction in Labour Disputes in Eire' 18 Int. & Comp. L. Q. 347 (1969);
   Stewart, 'Injunctions and the Right to Strike', 109 I.L.T.&Sol. J. 289 (1975). They are a
   source of much controversy. *Cf.* von Prondzynski, 'Trade Disputes and the Courts: The
   Problem of the Labour Injunction' 16 Ir. Jur. (n.s.) 228, at 230–231 (1981):
   > 'The interlocutory injunction is . . . a means of maintaining or restoring the *status quo ante*
   > until the actual trial and of preventing the infliction of irreparable damage . . .
   > The problem here is that the realities of industrial conflict are not easily reconcilable with
   > this kind of reasoning. The main flaw is that a full trial, on which the above theory really
   > depends, rarely if ever follows an interlocutory injunction granted against strikes. Where
   > an injunction has stopped a union in its tracks, the prospect of taking the strike up again
   > should the case go in its favour later is virtually irrelevant; the momentum is lost, and the
   > issues which underlie the dispute are unlikely to survive the considerable delay before the
   > hearing commences.' (Footnote reference omitted.)

   In England, the House of Lords in *American Cyanamid Co.* v. *Ethicon Ltd.,* [1975] A.C.
   396, held that the proper approach for a court to adopt in determining whether to grant an
   interlocutory injunction was to decide whether there was a serious question to be tried and,
   if there was, to determine where the balance of convenience lay.

   In Ireland, the judicial response to *American Cyanamid* has been divided: *cf.* McMahon &
   Binchy, p. 589, fn. 24. In the context of industrial disputes, it has been argued by von
   Prondzynski, *supra*, at 233–235, that greater stress should be placed in Ireland on one of the
   practical realities stressed by Lord Diplock in his speech in the *American Cyanamid* case and
   in *N.W.L.* v. *Woods* [1979] 3 All E.R. 614.
2. To what extent should the *public interest*, irrespective of considerations of the balance of
   convenience, require the granting of an interlocutory injunction? *Cf.* von Prondzynski,
   'Trade Disputes and the Courts: The Problem of the Labour Injunction' 16 Ir. Jur. (n.s.)
   228, at 236–237 (1981).

BELLEW V. CEMENT LTD.
[1948] I.R. 61 (Supreme Court, 1946, affirming Gavan Duffy, P.)

James Bellew brought a plenary summons against the defendant company claiming an injunction to restrain them from continuing to carry on blasting operations at
their quarry at Mell, North Road, Drogheda, in such proximity to the plaintiff's
dwellinghouse, glass-houses, out-offices and premises at Moneymore, North Road,
aforesaid, or with such heavy charges as to cause damage or injury to the said
premises by the shock of the explosions or by hurling rocks or stones into or upon the
premises and for damages.

It appeared from the statement of claim that the plaintiff alleged that ever since
the month of December, 1944, the defendants had carried on blasting operations, at

first at a distance of between two hundred and three hundred yards from Mr. Bellew's dwellinghouse, but gradually at lesser distances until, at a date before action brought, they were blasting at a distance between one hundred and one hundred and fifty yards from the house.

On the 29th July, 1946, the plaintiff applied, on notice, to Gavin Duffy P. for an interlocutory injunction to restrain the defendants from blasting in their quarry during the period which must elapse before the hearing of the action. The application was supported by affidavits made by the plaintiff and by architects on his behalf. These affidavits supported the allegations in the pleadings and described damage, alleged to have been done to the plaintiff's premises by vibration, caused by blasting, and claimed that irreparable damage would be done by the continuance of blasting operations during the long vacation.

On behalf of the defendants, affidavits were made by the managing director of the company, Mr. Harold Osterberg, and by a number of architects, engineers and employees of the company. The defendants said that no damage had been caused to the plaintiff by blasting and they further showed that, as a result of plaintiff's representations, the maximum amount of explosives used in any one blast had been reduced from 1,115 lbs. in 1945 to 150 lbs. between the 23rd of May, 1946, and the 22nd of July, 1946, which latter amount, they said, could not harm plaintiff's premises. They also alleged that they had bought the lands on which the quarry now was, from the plaintiff in 1935, and that he had been well aware that it was intended to blast in the said quarry. Notwithstanding his knowledge of the defendants' operations, the plaintiff built his present house and premises where they now stood in the years 1943 and 1944.

Gavan Duffy P. granted the plaintiff an interlocutory injunction, in the terms of his endorsement of claim, upon the plaintiff's undertaking as to damages.

From this order the defendants appealed to the Supreme Court.

C. Lavery K.C. (with him, *E.C. Micks*), for the appellants:–

If there is any injury being done to the plaintiff, it is clear that damages would be an adequate remedy. The Court should not grant an injunction where a plaintiff can be compensated in damages.

In order to succeed, the plaintiff must show that the defendants are making an unusual use of their land. The plaintiff, himself, sold the land to the defendants for use as a quarry. It cannot be said that blasting is an unusual user of a quarry. The fact that the plaintiff chose to build a house where he did, cannot make the defendants' user of their own quarry an unusual one. In any case the introduction of the lighter charges has reduced vibration to a negligible level at the plaintiff's premises.

If the Court is of opinion that the affidavits are too contradictory to admit of a firm conclusion on the evidence, the injunction should be refused: *Mitchell* v. *Henry* 15 Ch. D. 181.

If this injunction be granted, it will be impossible to manufacture the cement which is urgently needed for building and inconvenience to the public will result. The Court is entitled, in the exercise of its discretion, to consider matters of public convenience. Especially is this so, when the Court is considering which of several remedies should be granted.

J. A. Costello K.C. (with him, *A. C. Newett*), for the respondents:–

The affidavits made on behalf of the plaintiff, clearly show that he is being gravely prejudiced in his occupancy. If blasting is allowed to continue, a state of affairs may arise, in which it is no longer safe to reside in the place where the plaintiff has built his house. Damages cannot be regarded as a remedy for this progressive deterioration.

The Court should move to preserve the *status quo* until the action can be determined.

Questions of public convenience cannot be permitted to influence the judgment of the Court when the rights of private parties have to be determined.

Cur. adv. vult.

Maguire C.J.:

In my opinion this appeal should be dismissed and the interlocutory injunction, granted in the Court below, should stand.

It is unnecessary, and perhaps undesirable, to discuss in detail, the evidence contained in the affidavits. It appears, however, clear that, for a time at least, there was a nuisance to Mr. Bellew through the company's blasting operations. It is true that, in order to meet Mr. Bellew's complaints, an alteration was made in the company's methods. I am not satisfied, however, that the change made is sufficient to justify a refusal of Mr. Bellew's application for an interlocutory injunction. In my opinion, the affidavits show that there is a substantial question of fact to be tried. I take the view that, as there is a substantial question raised, the Court should interfere to preserve the *status quo* as far as possible. It was mainly with a view to preserving the *status quo* that the injunction was granted, and I am of opinion that, in all the circumstances, the proper course is to see that the *status quo* is preserved.

A large part of the argument in this Court was devoted to the question of public convenience. I am afraid that I cannot attach very much importance to the effect of this injunction upon the public convenience. It is suggested that, to restrain the company in the way in which the injunction would restrain them, would have a serious effect on building operations throughout the entire country. I am not altogether clear how far it was intended to press that argument, but I am of the opinion that the Court is not entitled to take the public convenience into consideration when dealing with the rights of private parties. This matter is a dispute between private parties, and I think that the Court should be concerned, only, to see that the rights of the parties are safeguarded. It is my view, on the affidavits, that blasting, with charges on the scale recently adopted, should not be carried on, pending the trial of this action. There is no doubt that it constitutes a grave inconvenience to Mr. Bellew, and I am not satisfied that it has been established that any greater inconvenience would be caused by granting this injunction, than by refusing it.

For these reasons I am of the opinion that this appeal must be dismissed and the injunction granted by the High Court allowed to stand.

Murnaghan J.:

I also am of opinion that this appeal must be dismissed.

The method of blasting used by the defendant company is a highly scientific method and should be quite unobjectionable if the company owned lands of considerable area. But when the method of blasting in use is carried on quite near to the house of a different owner, the defendants must be regarded as making an unusual user of the lands owned by them. The plaintiff was aware of the existence of the quarry when he built his house, having, in fact, sold the land to the company and the evidence on behalf of the company is that one of their employees – Mr. Dolan – advised the plaintiff not to build a house where it was built. No argument was, however, advanced that the plaintiff was not entitled to build on that particular spot if he chose to do so – and the impression left upon my mind, from this evidence, is that Mr. Dolan contemplated that the defendant's activities would seriously interfere with the plaintiff's use of his house.

It is admitted on both sides that there is a certain amount of vibration in this house when the blastings take place. It seems to me that Mr. Bellew has made a strong case that, up to May of this year, he was substantially interfered with in the enjoyment of his house. The real question is, of course, whether he has made a *prima facie* case that what went on in June and July substantially interfered with his right of property and right of comfort. Having regard to what happened previously, I think that the onus is on the company to show that Mr. Bellew is not being interfered with in the enjoyment of his property.

In my view, the learned President had sufficient material before him to enable him to arrive at the conclusion that Mr. Bellew was being interfered with. Mr. Bellew satisfied the learned President, *prima facie*, that there was considerable interference with his private rights and with the enjoyment of his house. In those circumstances, I do not think that we are entitled to deprive Mr. Bellew of his legal rights on some idea of public convenience. In my opinion, the learned President was entitled to grant an injunction, and I do not think that this Court should interfere with his discretion in the matter.

Geoghegan J.:
I agree.

O'Byrne J. (dissenting):
I have arrived at a different conclusion, not on any question of law, but in my view of the facts of this case.

The question which the trial Judge had to determine was, whether Mr. Bellew had made such a case as would justify the Court in interfering, by way of interlocutory injunction, with the operations of the Company. For this purpose it was necessary to show that substantial damage was being done to the plaintiff and his family, that there was reasonable apprehension that such damage would continue and that the damage was of such a nature that it could not properly be compensated by means of damages.

The question which this Court has to consider is whether the trial Judge, on the evidence, ought reasonably to have been satisfied on the foregoing matters.

The evidence before the Court was extremely conflicting on almost every point. I am satisfied that, during the earlier operations, there was considerable interference with the peace and comfort of the plaintiff and his family: but, following representations which the plaintiff made to the company, the company made extensive alterations in its method of blasting and there was no suggestion that it did not intend to adhere to the method as so altered. The charges were drastically reduced until in May of this year, they were only 150 lbs. I am not satisfied on the evidence, and, in my opinion, the trial Judge ought not to have been satisfied, that this altered method of blasting caused any substantial interference with the plaintiff's enjoyment of his property. If any interference did result, it was, in my view, of such an unsubstantial character that the Court would not be entitled to intervene, by injunction, pending the trial of the action.

I do not accept the proposition that the onus lay on the company to show that Mr. Bellew is not being, and will not be, damnified. In my opinion the onus lay on Mr. Bellew to show that there was reasonable apprehension that he would be damnified in such a way that the Court ought to interfere by way of interlocutory injunction. The damage, if any, which is likely to arise might well, in my view, be compensated by way of damages.

If Mr. Bellew had made out a clear case for an interlocutory injunction, I do not think that the Court would be entitled to have regard to questions of public convenience; but where, as in this case, public convenience is involved, the Court should be careful to see that a clear case has been established before an injunction is granted.

It may well be that when the case comes on for trial, Mr. Bellew will establish his claim; but, on the evidence before the trial Judge and before this Court, it seems to me that the whole question has been left too much in doubt.

For these reasons, I am of opinion that the application for an interlocutory injunction should not have been granted but should have been allowed to stand over until the trial of the action.

Black J. (dissenting):

I am of opinion that this appeal should be allowed, and for two reasons which I shall explain separately.

The first reason is that, taking the affidavits on both sides together, it seems to me probable that when this case comes to a definitive hearing, it will be found that damages would be an adequate and proper remedy for any grievance that the plaintiff may establish to the satisfaction of the Court.

In *Kine* v. *Jolly* [1905] 1 Ch. 480, Kekewich J. granted a mandatory injunction in respect of a nuisance caused by obstruction of light. The expert evidence was that the value of the plaintiff's house had been diminished, by the nuisance, to the extent of £20 to £25 a year and Kekewich J. estimated the capitalised injury, in terms of money, at £300 to £400. The Court of Appeal, without questioning the learned Judge's findings in these respects, held that damages was the proper remedy. Cozens-Hardy L.J. said (at p. 504):– 'It is not a case of irremediable damage, or of the house being rendered uninhabitable, nor is it a case in which damages cannot be regarded as reasonable and adequate compensation. I think it is impossible to doubt that the tendency of the speeches in the House of Lords in *Colls* v. *Home and Colonial Stores, Ltd.* [1904] A. C. 179, is to go a little further than was done in *Shelfer* v. *City of London Electric Lighting Co.* [1895] 1 Ch. 287, and to indicate that as a general rule the Court ought to be less free in granting mandatory injunctions than it was in years gone by.'

The present case, likewise, is not one 'of irremediable damage or of the house being rendered uninhabitable.'

When Cozens-Hardy L.J. spoke of the tendency of the House of Lords to go a little further than was done in *Shelfer's Case* [1895] 1 Ch. 287, he can only have been alluding to the suggestion of Smith L.J., in his well-known 'working rule,' that damages should only be substituted for an injunction when the injury is small. Accordingly, turning to *Colls* v. *Home and Colonial Stores, Ltd.* [1904] A. C. 179, I find that Lord Macnaghten said (at p. 192):– 'It has been said that an injunction ought to be granted when substantial damages would be given at law. I have some difficulty in following out this rule. . . . I rather doubt whether the amount of the damages which may be supposed to be recoverable at law affords a satisfactory test. In some cases, of course, an injunction is necessary – if, for instance, the injury cannot fairly be compensated by money – if the defendant has acted in a high-handed manner – if he has endeavoured to steal a march upon the plaintiff or to evade the jurisdiction of the Court. In all these cases an injunction is necessary, in order to do justice to the plaintiff and as a warning to others. But if there is really a question as to whether the obstruction is legal or not, and if the defendant has acted fairly and not in an unneighbourly spirit, I am disposed to think that the Court ought to incline to damages rather than to an injunction.'

I think that in the present case, judging by the affidavits which are all we have before us at this stage, the defendants have not done anything which satisfies me that a Court, applying Lord Macnaghten's tests, ought not, as he said, 'to incline to damages rather than to an injunction.' Those tests were quoted and expressly approved of by Vaughan Williams L.J., and were applied by the Court of Appeal in *Kine* v. *Jolly*. Kekewich J. in that case, on the evidence, which he accepted, put the damages which he would have given, if he had not erroneously thought that he must grant an injunction, at £300 to £400.

Even if, contrary to Lord Macnaghten's view that the amount of the damages is not a satisfactory test, the choice of remedy were to depend on the probable amount of damages fairly recoverable, I do not think that that amount, in this case, would be likely to exceed the amount estimated by Kekewich J. in *Kine* v. *Jolly* [1905] 1 Ch. 480, especially as the affidavits indicate that appliances to end the whole trouble complained of could be procured within six months or a year, and an undertaking could be required that this would be done. In these circumstances, being far from satisfied by the affidavits that the case is not one in which, upon the above authorities, the Court ought to incline to damages, rather than to an injunction, I think that the irreparable course of granting an injunction ought not to be taken on an interlocutory application, whatever view may prove to be justified after a full trial of the action.

The second, but by no means the lesser, reason for which, in my opinion, this appeal should be allowed is the reason which was regarded by the English Court of Appeal in *Mitchell* v. *Henry* 15 Ch. D. 181, as decisive against granting an interlocutory injunction. That reason was that the conflict of testimony in the affidavits created a doubt which it would not be safe to resolve upon mere affidavits or without applying fully the test of cross-examination at a full trial. The action was for an alleged infringement of trade-marks. The judgments in that case are, of course, not binding upon me; but emanating from the English Court of Appeal, they command my high respect, and the more so since I entirely agree with them. The following citations are very germane to our present problem.

James L.J. said (at p. 191):– 'As regards the evidence, I will not give any opinion on which side the balance of evidence appears to me to lie. There is a great amount of evidence in support of the plaintiffs' case, and there is on the other hand a great amount of evidence on the part of the defendants . . . but there is such a conflict of evidence that in my opinion the matter cannot be safely dealt with upon an interlocutory application when the witnesses have not been cross-examined. In order to come to a satisfactory conclusion, it is necessary to know what the witnesses would say when they are using their own words in answer to questions not leading, whereas we have before us only affidavits which are answers in the solicitor's words to questions the most leading possible.'

Cotton L.J. said (at p. 195):– 'Now I do not say that, on the materials before us I should arrive at a conclusion adverse to the plaintiffs. My impression at the present moment is in their favour. But there is a conflict of testimony between the expert witnesses, and there is, so far as I am concerned, a difficulty in arriving at a satisfactory conclusion, and I think the better course is to let the motion stand to the hearing, and then, after cross-examination of the witnesses, and after hearing the evidence in Court, the Court can decide . . . On that ground I think that we ought not to grant any interlocutory injunction . . .'

Thesiger L.J. said (at p. 197):– 'There is clearly a conflict of evidence, and such a conflict of evidence as makes it undesirable that this Court should decide the matter on motion.'

I have no doubt that in that case the plaintiffs and their experts made a strong *prima facie* case – strong enough, indeed, to make Cotton L.J. form an impression in their favour – but their *prima facie* case was not deemed sufficient by the Court of Appeal to justify the grant of an interlocutory injunction when once it was seriously challenged on affidavit. The same, in my opinion, applies to the plaintiff's *prima facie* case here. There is before us a serious conflict of testimony, and everything that was said by the Appeal Judges in *Mitchell* v. *Henry* 15 Ch. D. 181 is decisive in favour of this appeal, unless we reject the grounds of those judgments. For myself, I heartily accept them.

There is a further consideration in the case. In Kerr on Injunctions, 6th edn. p. 24, there is the following passage:– 'In doubtful cases where the question as to the legal right is one on which the Court is not prepared to pass an opinion, or the legal right being admitted, the fact of its violation is denied, the course of the Court is either to grant the injunction pending the trial . . . or to order the motion to stand over. . . . In determining which of these two alternatives it shall adopt, the Court is governed by the consideration as to the comparative mischief or inconvenience to the parties which may arise from granting or withholding the injunction. . . . In doubtful cases, if it appears, upon the balance of convenience . . . that greater damage would arise to the defendant by granting the injunction in the event of its turning out afterwards to have been wrongly granted, than to the plaintiff from withholding it in the event of the legal right proving to be in his favour, the injunction will not be granted, but the motion will be ordered to stand over until the hearing.'

Here the violation of the legal right is denied. The case is rendered as doubtful by the conflict of the affidavits as was *Kine* v. *Jolly* [1905] 1 Ch. 480. What then of the balance of inconvenience? There is grave risk that the granting of an injunction may cause the defendant company to close down for six months or three months, or may bring about a serious reduction of its output. On the other hand, the annoyance caused to the plaintiff is due to intermittent vibration vastly different from the constant unceasing noise of the electrical machinery in *Colwell* v. *St. Pancras Borough Council* [1904] 1 Ch. 707; yet even in that case, Joyce J., while obliged to grant an injunction, granted a suspension of its operation for six months. It seems to me probable from the affidavits that a six months' suspension of an injunction in the present case would mean that by then, the nuisance, if such it be, would have ceased to exist.

In my opinion, it must be plain that the inconvenience to the company entailed by an injunction would transcend, perhaps a hundred-fold, the inconvenience that would result to the plaintiff from its refusal pending the trial. Nor is it the defendants alone that would suffer. To stop their work must have grave consequences for the public at a time when, as stated, more than four-fifths of the entire cement used in this country is produced by the defendants, and at a time when houses are badly wanted, and when the building trade is expected to be about to awake from its long torpor. No doubt, as has often been laid down, public convenience cannot justify refusal of a remedy for a nuisance. It is another matter to say that it cannot, or ought not to, affect the way in which a nuisance should be dealt with. In *Price's Patent Candle Co., Ltd.* v. *London County Council* [1908] 2 Ch. 526, Cozens-Hardy M.R. said (at p. 544):– 'Considerations of public welfare may justify the suspension of an injunction upon terms, but they do not justify the denial of relief to the private person whose rights have been affected.' In both *Prince's Cast* [1908] 2 Ch. 526 and in *Colwell's Case* [1904] 1 Ch. 707 which I previously quoted, the injunction was only granted at the trial of the action and not on an interlocutory motion. It is not suggested in the present case that the plaintiff should be denied relief, if he establishes that his rights have been affected. What I have suggested is, not that relief, but that the particular form of relief by injunction should be denied him, if it turns out, after investigation at a full trial, that an alternative form of relief by way of damages would be an adequate, and, in all the circumstances, a less objectionable remedy.

I have also suggested, for the reasons stated, and not, I think, without the support of high authority, that neither the question of whether an actionable nuisance exists nor the question of whether, in case it does, the remedy should be by injunction or by damages, should be determined in so doubtful a case upon an interlocutory application. I think it highly undesirable and dangerous to grant an injunction pending the proper trial and that the application therefore should have been refused, and that the order of the High Court should be discharged.

Notes and Questions

1. Which approach do you prefer? Why?
2. In England the judges have recently evinced some disagreement as to this question. See *Miller* v. *Jackson* [1977] Q.B. 966; *Kennaway* v. *Thompson* [1980] 3 All E.R. 329. See also *Patterson* v. *Murphy supra*, pp. 512–524.

SINCLAIR V. GOGARTY
[1937] I.R. 377 (Supreme Court, affirming Hanna J.)

Hanna J.:

On May 11th, 1937, a plenary originating summons was issued by the plaintiff, H. M. Sinclair, against the defendants, Dr. Oliver St. John Gogarty, who resides in Dublin, and Messrs. Rich and Cowan, Ltd., who carry on business as publishers in London, for damages for libel on the plaintiff, contained in a book entitled 'As I Was Going Down Sackville Street,' of which the defendant, Dr. Gogarty, is the author, and for an injunction restraining the publication of the said book.

Service of this writ was accepted on behalf of Dr. Gogarty on the 19th May, and on the 22nd May the notice of motion which is before me was served asking for an interlocutory injunction restraining the publication of the book complained of pending the trial of the action.

On the 13th May an order was made giving liberty to serve a concurrent writ out of the jurisdiction upon the defendants, Rich and Cowan, Ltd., and liberty was also given to serve a notice of this motion upon them. These defendants, Rich and Cowan, have not been served in accordance with the order of the Court and have not entered an appearance in the action and did not appear upon this motion. Accordingly, as they are resident out of the jurisdiction no order can be sought against them.

The book complained of is the work of the defendant, Dr. Gogarty, and the defendants, Rich and Cowan, are his publishers. From the description of the book it seems to be mainly a survey of Irish and Dublin life, past and present, and I gather that it is described by the publishers as 'an extraordinary book,' while in the affidavit of the plaintiff it is sworn that it has a wide circulation in Saorstát Éireann and that it is 'a reservoir of filth and the grosser forms of vulgarity,' which has attracted widespread notoriety not only here but in Great Britain and in America.

This alarming statement as to the character of the book has not been contradicted by the defendant, but it does not affect the present application, which is only concerned with the question of the extent of the publication.

The plaintiff and his brother, the late William Sinclair, were twins and of the Jewish faith. They carried on a well-known business in Dublin as antique and art dealers and jewellers, their business premises, until a recent date, being in Nassau Street, but are now in Grafton Street, Dublin. The business was carried on by the two brothers in succession to their grandfather, Morris Harris, who died in 1909. William Sinclair died recently, on the 4th May, 1937. In connection with his business the plaintiff claims that his clientele extends not only to Saorstát Éireann but to Great Britain and the United States of America.

The libel complained of is contained in two passages in the book, one at page 65 and the other at page 70, these two passages being, on the plaintiff's allegation, linked up by the references therein contained. These passages are set out in full in the affidavit of the plaintiff, but it is unnecessary to set them out in my judgment. The first paragraph at page 65, if it refers to the plaintiff, holds him and his brother up to ridicule, but the passage at page 70, if it refers to the plaintiff, his brother and his grandfather, goes far beyond mere ridicule and contempt and contains a very grave charge against them – a charge which would completely destroy any personal character for respectability, decency or morality that the plaintiff would have either in his relations towards the public in his own community or amongst his customers.

The questions for the Court are:– 1. Do these passages clearly refer to the plaintiff? 2. Are they clearly libellous? 3. Are the circumstances such that in the interests of justice an immediate stop to their publication should be made by injunction, or, whether, in the alternative, should the plaintiff be left to a trial to be recompensed by damages?

As to the first question, whether these passages refer to the plaintiff and his brother and grandfather, I have before me the uncontradicted evidence of the plaintiff and of Mr. Beckett that they do refer to them. The evidence of Mr. Beckett is more important as being that of an outsider and he states in the most unequivocal manner that on reading the book he understood these passages to refer to the plaintiff, his brother William, and their grandfather. He knew to some extent the circumstances and relationship of the Sinclair and Harris family, and it is clear that there are sufficient *indicia* in the passages to give to any one who knew the family the necessary clue to their identity. The author, by giving their business place as Sackville Street instead of Grafton Street or Nassau Street, and referring to the Jewish grandfather as a usurer instead of an antique dealer, has only resorted to the usual devices of those who lampoon others and seek to escape liability. No affidavit has been put in by Dr. Gogarty stating that he did not in fact, or in intent, refer to the Sinclairs or their grandfather – a statement which would have been some palliation, so I must act solely upon the evidence before me, and I am satisfied beyond doubt that the Sinclairs were referred to.

On the second point, whether the statements are libellous, I have no doubt. In particular, the passage at page 70 clearly constitutes a wicked and grossly scurrilous libel of a very serious nature.

The last and most important question on this application is whether, under these circumstances, an interlocutory injunction pending the trial should be granted. The Courts have always regarded this procedure as falling under a delicate jurisdiction in libel actions, to be exercised only in special circumstances and only in clear cases. Would it be just or fair on the evidence before me that the publication of these injurious passages in the book should continue for months until this action can be tried? On the authorities, the highest test against the plaintiff's application is whether, if a jury found that these passages were not libellous, such a verdict could stand. I am satisfied, as there is no special defence suggested, such as appear in some of the cases on the subject, that, if the matter came before a jury on the evidence as it stands before me, they could not, as reasonable men, come to any other conclusion than in favour of the plaintiff, and if any other verdict were given, I am of the opinion that it would be set aside as unreasonable. This may not be the only test applicable in the case of the special nature of the one under consideration, where personal character is attacked so as to cause serious, immediate and continuing loss of reputation. I am of opinion that the loss of reputation to the plaintiff by the continued publication of the libellous passages in this book could not be properly compensated by damages alone.

I shall, accordingly, grant the application. As Rich and Cowan, as I have indicated, are outside the jurisdiction and have not submitted to the Court, or entered an appearance, I shall not give any relief against them, but as they are the agents of Dr.

Gogarty for the publication of the book a further order is not necessary.

I accordingly grant an order for the interim injunction against Dr. Gogarty, his agents and servants, from further publication of the book with the passages complained of, pending judgment in this action; but, as this restraint upon publication would cause damage to the defendants in the event of the defendants succeeding in the action, this order is made on condition of the usual undertaking by the plaintiff through his counsel to abide any order the Court may make as to such damages as the Court hereafter may be of opinion that the defendants may have suffered by reason of this order, in the event of judgment being given for the defendants.

The costs of each side of this application shall abide the result of the trial.

[The defendant, Dr. Gogarty, appealed to the Supreme Court before Sullivan C.J., FitzGibbon, Murnaghan, Meredith and Geoghegan JJ.]

J. M. Fitzgerald K.C. and *R. B. Barry K.C.* (with them *O. Gogarty*) for the appellant:–

The Court must be satisfied that the alleged libel refers to the plaintiff before granting an injunction. The alleged libel cannot, it is submitted, refer to the plaintiff unless one ignores the actual language used in the book. As to whether the matter complained of is libellous or not, Lord Halsbury L.C. in his judgment in *Neville* v. *Fine Art and General Insurance Co.* [1897] A. C. at p. 73 states that 'because some person may choose, not by reason of the language itself, but by reason of some fact to which it refers, to draw an unfavourable inference, it does not follow that therefore such matter is libellous.'

An injunction in a case of this kind must prejudice the jury when the case comes on for trial as the jury would have in effect to overrule the Judge who granted the injunction if they wished to find a verdict for the defendant. The question of 'libel or no libel' is for the jury: *Monson* v. *Tussauds, Ltd.* [1894] 1 Q.B. 671. In that case the injunction given in the Queen's Bench Division was dissolved by the Court of Appeal. We submit that the rule in *Bonnard* v. *Perryman* [1891] 2 Ch. 269 has not been observed, and that the trial Judge arrogated to himself the functions of the jury. On the evidence before him it would have been reasonable for a jury to find a verdict for the defendant.

The test laid down by Hanna J. is not the true test. The evidence to be considered is not only the evidence which comes before the Judge on the hearing of the motion but also the evidence which will come before the jury on the trial of the action: *Bonnard* v. *Perryman* [1891] 2 Ch. 269. The same principle was laid down in *Coulson* v. *Coulson* 3 T. L. R. 846. In that case Lindley L.J. points out the danger of granting injunctions upon evidence by affidavit before the trial.

The question of 'libel or no libel' is not the only question to be considered. Even assuming that the publication were libellous, the effect of it upon the respondent can only be finally disposed of by a jury, and, on this ground, the Court in *Bonnard* v. *Perryman* [1891] 2 Ch. 269 refused to grant an interlocutory injunction. [They also cited *Gallagher* v. *Touhy* 58 I. L. T. R. 134; *Cullen* v. *Stanley* [1926] I. R. 73.]

There is no evidence that the defendant, Dr. Gogarty, is publishing the book, and the order should not be allowed to stand as it has no legal effect if he is not the publisher.

A. E. Wood K.C. and *J. A. McCarthy K.C.* (with them *E. Wood*) for the respondent:–

The book is clearly defamatory of someone. The question is, does it refer to the plaintiff?

There is evidence before the Court that Mr. Beckett understood the passages to refer to the plaintiff, in addition to the affidavit of the plaintiff himself, and it is immaterial whether the defendant intended to refer to the plaintiff or not: *Hulton & Co., Ltd.* v. *Jones* [1910] A. C. 20.

The test to be applied in deciding whether an interlocutory injunction should be granted or not is: 'Do the affidavits disclose a case on which the jury at the trial of the action could properly find only a verdict for the plaintiff?' *per* Lord Davey in *Monson* v. *Tussauds, Ltd.* [1894] 1 Q. B. at p. 697.

The trial Judge certainly came to the conclusion that there was a very serious and very grave libel. The evidence that the libel refers to the plaintiff is unchallenged and there is no suggestion of justification. Consequently this case is not covered by the decision in *Bonnard* v. *Perryman* [1891] 2 Ch. 269. No affidavit has been filed on behalf of the defendant, and no assurance has been given as to the attitude the defendant intends to adopt. On the evidence no jury could find otherwise than in favour of the plaintiff, and if they did not so find, the Court would set aside the verdict as unreasonable.

J.M. Fitzgerald K.C. in reply:–

The defendant is not bound to offer any evidence so long as he claims that there is a question to be tried by a jury.

Sullivan C.J.:

I am of opinion that this appeal should be dismissed. . . .

On the hearing of an interlocutory application such as this, it is undesirable that I should say any more than is necessary for the purpose of giving my decision. I realise that in granting an interlocutory injunction to restrain the publication of a libel the Court is exercising a jurisdiction which has been described as a jurisdiction of a delicate nature.

The principle upon which the Court should act in considering such applications was stated by Lord Esher M.R. in *Coulson* v. *Coulson* 3 T.L.R. 846, and his statement of the principle was approved of and adopted by the Court of Appeal in *Bonnard* v. *Perryman* [1891] 2 Ch. 269. The principle is this, that an interlocutory injunction should only be granted in the clearest cases where any jury would say that the matter complained of was libellous, and where if the jury did not so find the Court would set aside the verdict as unreasonable. It is unnecessary for me to decide whether that principle is applicable in all cases. I accept it as applicable in the present case.

There are two questions to be considered in this case:–

(1). Is the matter complained of clearly defamatory?
(2). Does it clearly refer to the plaintiff?

The matter complained of consists of two passages in the book, one at page 65 and the other at page 70. Whatever doubt I might have as to the defamatory nature of the former passage, I am clearly of opinion that the latter passage is a libel, and that no reasonable jury could hold that it was not.

As regards the second question, I am of opinion that a Judge must deal with an application on the evidence that is before him, and the only evidence before Hanna J., and before us, is that the passages in question refer to the plaintiff. Mr. Beckett states in his affidavit that he understood the passages as referring to the plaintiff, and no affidavit has been made on behalf of the defendant to suggest that they do not.

I think that Hanna J. was right in granting an interlocutory injunction, and that his order should be affirmed and this appeal dismissed.

FitzGibbon, Murnaghan, Meredith and **Geoghegan JJ.** concurred.

Notes and Questions

1. Does this case hold that the right to free speech takes priority over the right to a reputation?
2. Do you regard defamation cases as raising any distinctive problem in relation to injunctions? Is the risk that I will take away your name to be treated in the same way as the risk that I will take away your property?
3. Are damages an adequate remedy for loss of a reputation, which could have been prevented had the court granted an injunction? Should a defamed plaintiff be satisfied with punitive damages? *Cf. Cassell & Co. Ltd.* v. *Broome* [1972] A.C. 1027 (H.L.)
4. Do you see dangers of rich and powerful organisations 'muzzling' free speech if an interlocutory injunction against defamation were granted on conditions easier than those adopted in *Sinclair* v. *Gogarty*? *Cf.* Martin, 'Interlocutory Injunctions in Libel Actions', 20 U. Western Ontario L. Rev. 129 (1982).
5. Of what relevance, if any, is the Constitutional protection of freedom of speech under Article 40.6.1.i? In the United States, judicial interpretation of the First Amendment protection of free speech has led to a situation where restraint of publication is a nearly unheard-of remedy. The courts take the view that they should not restrain the commission of a libel or slander, 'for that is prior censorship – a basic evil' denounced by the Constitution: *Northwestern Pacific Railway Co.* v. *Lumber & Sawmill Workers' Union*, 189 P.2d 277, at 282 (Cal., 1948).

Damages in Lieu of an Injunction

Since *Lord Cairns' Act 1858*, the Court has been empowered to award damages either in addition to or in lieu of an injunction. The discretion conferred on the Court is untramelled, but attempts have been made in some of the decisions to articulate general guidelines. In *Patterson* v. *Murphy* [extracted *supra*, pp. 512–514], Costello, J. summarised these guidelines as follows:

'1. When an infringement of the plaintiff's right and a threatened further infringement to a material extent has been established the plaintiff is prima facie entitled to an Injunction. There may be circumstances, however, depriving the plaintiff of this prima facie right but generally speaking the plaintiff will only be deprived of an Injunction in very exceptional circumstances.

2. If the injury to the plaintiff's right is small, and is one capable of being estimated in money, and is one which can be adequately compensated by a small money payment, and if the case is one in which it would be oppressive to the defendant to grant an Injunction, then these are circumstances in which damages in lieu of an injunction may be granted.

3. The conduct of the plaintiff may be such as to disentitle him to an Injunction. The conduct of the defendant may be such as to disentitle him from seeking the substitution of damages for an Injunction.

4. The mere fact that a wrongdoer is able and willing to pay for the injury he has inflicted is not a ground for substituting damages.'

Other attempts have been made to express the general guiding principles, as is clear from the following decision.

McGRATH V. MUNSTER & LEINSTER BANK LTD.
[1959] I.R. 313 (High Ct., Dixon, J.)

[The plaintiff, a solicitor, occupied as tenant a first floor office adjoining the defendants' property. The defendants demolished a building and constructed on the site a much larger building, which interfered substantially with the plaintiff's right to light. Dixon, J. held that this interference constituted a nuisance and continued:]

... The question remains as to the nature and extent of the relief to which she is entitled.

In *Colls* v. *Home and Colonial Stores Ltd.* [1904] A.C. 179 Lord Macnaghten pointed out (at pp. 192 and 193) that the award of damages in lieu of an injunction was a matter of judicial discretion and that the probable amount of damages was not a satisfactory test. He went on (at p. 193):– 'In some cases, of course, an injunction is necessary – if, for instance, the injury cannot fairly be compensated by money – if the defendant has acted in a high-handed manner – if he has endeavoured to steal a march upon the plaintiff or to evade the jurisdiction of the Court. In all these cases an injunction is necessary, in order to do justice to the plaintiff and as a warning to others. But if there is really a question as to whether the obstruction is legal or not, and if the defendant has acted fairly and not in an unneighbourly spirit, I am disposed to think that the Court ought to incline to damages rather than to an injunction.' I respectfully adopt this passage and, applying it to the present case, the appropriate remedy is damages rather than an injunction. There are the additional circumstances that the plaintiff has only a limited interest in the office premises and that her original claim for an injunction was not pressed.

It is not easy to assess damages in a matter of this kind, as the greatest injury to the plaintiff is in the rather intangible realm of loss of convenience and amenity in the use of her office. There is no real likelihood of any loss of business or of profits, except in so far as the greater use of artificial light entails additional expense. She has incurred, and will incur, additional expense on this account, in addition to some expense in providing a different and better type of artificial lighting for her typist. The cost of the contemplated re-decoration and of moving the position of the waiting room was estimated at £120 with an upkeep cost of about £30 every four years. The re-decoration will, of course, to some extent offset the additional cost of artificial lighting.

As stated, the interest of the plaintiff in the premises is a limited one. She took the office first on a quarterly tenancy in June, 1944. She subsequently obtained a lease for 21 years from the 5th June, 1949, at the yearly rent of £75 in addition to the payment of rates and responsibility for internal repairs. There was not suggested to be anything in the lease or in the circumstances of its grant that would disentitle her to whatever statutory right of renewal there may be at the end of that period. The lease prohibits assigning, sub-letting, or parting with possession without the previous consent of the lessors in writing. This does not, of course, render the plaintiff's interest wholly incapable of assignment. The house agent, who gave evidence on her behalf, estimated that the fair and true rent of the office in the present circumstances would be £55 per annum with rates, a depreciation of £20 per annum.

I assess the damages at £500 and I will give judgment for that amount as damages in lieu of an injunction.

Chapter 28

LIMITATIONS

Tort actions are subject to periods of limitation within which proceedings must be commenced. The reasons are fairly clear: it would be unfair for a person to be subjected to litigation many years after he is alleged to have committed a tort, where the plaintiff has slept on his rights; moreover, fresh evidence is more likely than stale to yield a just and accurate determination of the case. As against this, it can be appreciated that there are sometimes good reasons for delay in taking proceedings. Our law steers a middle course between, on the one hand, allowing the Court a broad discretion to extend the periods of limitation in cases that appear desirable, and, on the other, having no regard to reasons that might justify delay.

The law on the subject is principally contained in the *Statute of Limitations 1957*, which consolidated and amended the previous law.

The general period of limitation for an action founded on tort is six years from the date on which the cause of action accrued. Three years is the appropriate period, however, for an action claiming damages for negligence, nuisance or breach of duty, where the damages claimed by the plaintiff comprise or include damages for personal injuries to any person.

Persons Under a Disability

Special provisions as to limitation apply to persons under a disability, the law taking a broad view that such persons are as a class in need of special protection. Who, then, is a person 'under a disability'? The law allows for three categories:

(a) an infant; that is, a person under the age of twenty-one years;
(b) a person of unsound mind;
(c) a convict subject to the operation of the *Forfeiture Act 1870*, in whose case no administrator or curator has been appointed under that Act.

A number of somewhat complex provisions apply to persons under a disability. The general rule is that if, on the date when a right of action accrued, the person to whom it accrued was under a disability, the action may be brought at any time before the expiration of six years from the date when the person ceases to be under a disability or dies, whichever event first occurs, nothwithstanding that the period of limitation has expired. Thus, for example, where a person of unsound mind has a right of action, the appropriate period will not begin to run until he regains his sanity or until he dies, whichever is the sooner.

To this rule there are exceptions.

First, where the right of action originally accrued to some person *not* under a disability through whom the person under a disability claims, *no* extension will be permitted.

Secondly, where a right of action which has accrued to a person under a disability accrues, on his death while still under a disability, to *another person under a disability*, no further extension of time is allowed by reason of the disability of the second person.

A provision that has given rise to some controversy and constitutional litigation in section 49(2) of the *Statute of Limitations 1957*, which is to the following effect:

'(a) In the case of actions for damages for negligence, nuisance or breach of duty (whether the duty exists by virtue of a contract or of a provision made by or under a statute or independently of any contract or of any such provision) where the damages claimed by the plaintiff for the neglegence, nuisance or breach of duty consist of or include damages in respect of personal injuries to any person –

(i)   subsection (1) of this section shall have effect as if for the words "six years" there were substituted the words "three years", and

(ii) this section shall not apply unless the plaintiff proves that the person under the disability was not, at the time when the right of action accrued to him, in the custody of a parent.

(b)   For the purposes of paragraph (a) of this subsection, "parent" in relation to a person under a disability means his father, mother, grandfather, grandmother, stepfather or stepmother, notwithstanding that the relationship is illegitimate or in consequence of adoption under the Adoption Act, 1952.'

The twofold purpose of this provision is relatively clear: it was to reduce the general limitation period to three years in the case of personal injury litigation, and to make the special extensions in respect of persons under a disability not apply to cases where the person under the disability was in the custody of a parent when the right of action accrued to him.

The legislature was apparently of the view that:

'where the disability was that of infancy, it was not reasonable to extend the period of limitation beyond that afforded to a person of full age in those particular cases in which the infant was in such a position that, by virtue of the natural relationship that existed between it and a parent, the parent would normally and reasonably be expected to look after the child's legal interests and see that such action was taken as would protect those interests.' [*Currie* v. *Fairy Hill Ltd.* [1968] I.R. 232, at 237–238]

The first purpose was achieved without difficulty; the second has given rise to some difficulty, as the following decisions show.

O'BRIEN V. KEOGH
[1972] I.R. 144 (Supreme Court, reversing O'Keeffe, P.)

Trial of point of law.

The plaintiff was born on the 1st September, 1952; he was injured on the 8th September, 1963, when a motor car driven by his father, the second defendant, was in collision with a motor car belonging to the first defendant. At the time of the collision the plaintiff was a passenger in his father's car and was in the custody of his parents. On the 16th January, 1968, the plaintiff by his next friend issued a plenary summons in which he claimed damages for the negligence of the defendants in causing his injuries. The plaintiff delivered a separate statement of his claim against each defendant, and each defendant delivered a separate defence in which he pleaded that the plaintiff's claim was statute-barred by the provisions of s. 49, sub-s. 2(a)(ii), of the Statute of Limitations, 1957. The plaintiff challenged the constitutional validity of these provisions in the High Court. O'Keeffe, P. held against the challenge and the plaintiff appealed to the Supreme Court.

As the Statute of Limitations, 1957, was passed after the Constitution of Ireland came into operation, the decision of the Supreme Court (consisting of Ó Dálaigh C.J., Walsh, Budd, FitzGerald and McLoughlin JJ.) was pronounced by one of the judges of that Court in accordance with the provisions of Article 34, s. 4, sub-s. 5, of the Constitution. [Cf. [1970] I.R., at 325].

Limitations 637

Ó Dálaigh C.J. (delivering the judgment of the Court):

The Act of 1957 is expressed to be an act to consolidate, with amendments, certain enactments relating to the limitation of actions and arbitrations. The Act is divided into four parts. Part I (ss. 1–9) is preliminary and generally Part II (ss. 10–46) fixes the periods of limitations for different classes of action. Part II (ss. 47–72) provides for extension of limitation periods in a case of disability (ss. 48, 49), acknowledgements (ss. 50–60), part-payment (ss. 61–70), and fraud and mistake (ss. 71, 72). Finally, Part IV deals with the application of the Act and other limitation enactments to arbitrations. Part II opens by providing in s. 10 that the provisions of Part II shall have effect subject to the provisions in Part III for extension of the peroids of limitation in the case of disability, acknowledgment, part-payment, fraud and mistake. Section 11 then sets out the periods of limitation in actions for contract and tort and certain other actions. Sub-section 2 of s. 11 deals with actions founded on tort and the general provision, contained in paragraph (*a*), is that an action founded on tort shall not be brought after the expiration of six years from the date on which the cause of action accrued; this period is reduced to a period of three years by paragraph (*b*) in actions claiming damages for negligence, nuisance or breach of duty where the damages claimed consist of or include damages in respect of personal injuries to any person; and by paragraph (*c*) a similar reduction is made in the case of actions for damages for slander.

The extension of these, and other, limitation periods in case of disability is to be found in ss. 48 and 49. Section 48 defines a person under disability as (*a*) an infant, (*b*) a person of unsound mind, and (*c*) a person who is a convict subject to the operation of the Forfeiture Act, 1870, for whom no curator or administrator has been appointed under that Act. The general extension effected for cases of disability is that contained in sub-s. 1(a) of section 49: a person under disability at the date of the accrual of his right of action is given six years from the cesser of his disability within which to bring his action. There follow a number of limitations of this general extension. For instance, the extension is not to apply at all where the right of action accrued to some person (not under a disability) through whom the person under a disability claims; nor, where a right of action which has accrued to a person under a disability accrues on the death of that person to another person under disability, is any further extension allowed by reason of the disability of the second person; nor, in an action for the recovery of land or for money charged on land, can any action be brought by any person after the expiration of thirty years from the date of the accrual of the right of action to that person or to some person from whom he claims.

Sub-section 2 of s. 49 contains the modifications which have given rise to the question in this case. Sub-section 2, in full, is as follows:–

'(2)   (a)   In the case of actions for damages for neglegence, nuisance or breach of duty (whether the duty exists by virtue of a contract or of a provision made by or under a statute or independently of any contract or any such provision) where the damages claimed by the plaintiff for the negligence, nuisance or breach of duty consist of or include damages in respect of personal injuries to any person –

        (i)   subsection (1) of this section shall have effect as if for the words "six years" there were substituted the words "three years", and

        (ii)   this section shall not apply unless the plaintiff proves that the person under the disability was not, at the time when the right of action accrued to him, in the custody of a parent.

  (b)   For the purposes of paragraph (a) of this subsection, "parent" in relation to a person under a disability means his father, mother, grandfather, grandmother, stepfather or stepmother, notwithstanding that the relationship is illegitimate or in consequence of adoption under the Adoption Act, 1952 (No. 25 of 1952).'

The complaint is that sub-paragraph (ii) of sub-s. 2(a) of s. 49 is repugnant to Article 40 of the Constitution and specifically to the provisions of ss. 1 and 3 of that Article. It will be convenient to set out these sections in juxtaposition to the impugned provision of the statute. Sections 1 and 3 of Article 40 of the Constitution are as follows:

'1. All citizens shall, as human persons, be held equal before the law.
    This shall not be held to mean that the State shall not in its enactments have due regard to differences of capacity, physical and moral, and of social function.
3. 1° The State guarantees in its laws to respect and, as far as practicable, by its laws to defend and vindicate the personal rights of the citizen.
    2° The State shall, in particular, by its laws protect as best it may from unjust attack and, in the case of injustice done, vindicate the life, person, good name, and property rights of every citizen.'

The President in his judgment was of the view that it was not contrary to the Constitution to differentiate in favour of infants as against adults, nor was it unequal to differentiate as between particular classes of infants – i.e. those under the control of a parent and those not under such control – and that the defence of the statute must therefore succeed.

The argument against the Act of 1957 has been that the Act differentiates unfairly between infants under disability who are in the custody of a parent and those infants under disability who are not in the custody of a parent. The former are only allowed the limitation period appropriate to an adult who is not under a disability, while the latter have until their infancy ceases and the appropriate adult limitation period thereafter. It has been submitted that this is a differentiation based on where the infant is (*i.e.*, as his physical location) and it is said that the differentiation offends against the guarantee of equality before the law contained in s. 1 of Article 40 of the Constitution. The answer that has been made to this submission is that it is too narrow a view of the provision of the statute to say that it is based on the physical location of the infant; it is said that the distinction between infants in the custody of a parent and those who are not in such custody is a distinction related to moral capacity and social function, and that therefore the distinction is valid under s. 1 of Article 40.

The second limb of the plaintiff's argument is that the right to sue for personal injuries is a chose in action and a property right, and that it is one of the personal rights of a citizen which the State (under s. 3 of Article 40) has the duty to respect, defend, protect and vindicate; the plaintiff submits that sub-paragraph (ii) of sub-s. 2(a) of s. 49 of the Act of 1957 has patently failed to do this in the case of infants who are in the custody of a parent. The answer on behalf of the Attorney General has been that the statute assumes that infants in the custody of their parents should be looked after, and that this was a reasonable basis from which to legislate and that it was within the competence of the Oireachtas to choose to legislate as it did.

The principles to be applied by the Courts in deciding whether or not any part of an Act of the Oireachtas is repugnant to the Constitution have been stated on many occasions. Acts of the Oireachtas enjoy the presumption of not being repugnant to the Constitution unless such repugnancy is clearly shown: *The State (Quinn)* v. *Ryan* [1965] I.R. 70, 125; *The State (Sheerin)* v. *Kennedy* [1966] I.R. 379, 386; *McDonald* v. *Bord nag Con* [1965[I.R. 217, 239 and *East Donegal Co-Operative* v. *The Attorney General* [1970] I.R. 317, 340. The meaning of the provision which is here impugned is clear, and therefore there is no room for a choice between two constructions, of which one would be constitutional and the other unconstitutional, or of doubtful constitutionality as occurred in *East Donegal Co-Operative* v. *The Attorney General* [1970] I.R. 317, 340. Nor can there be any question that nothing is to be found in the statute which debars a parent from invoking the statute against his infant child, as has been done in this case; however, it should be said that the second defendant pleaded the statute not for lack of parental affection but probably because of certain pre-accident contractual obligations.

Counsel for the Attorney General was right to concede that the right to litigate claims was a personal right of the citizen within Article 40 of the Constitution. [See [1966] I.R. 345.] Mr. Justice Kenny pointed out in *Ryan* v. *The Attorney General* [1965] I.R. 294, 313 that there are many personal rights of the citizen which follow from the Christian and democratic nature of the State and which are not mentioned in Article 40 at all, and that the general guarantee in Article 40 extends to rights not specified therein. This Court, in affirming his judgment in that case, agreed that the personal rights mentioned in s. 3, sub-s. 1, of Article 40 are not exhausted by the enumeration of 'life, person, good name, and property rights' in sub-s. 2 of that section.

In the opinion of the Court the first submission, *viz.*, that the principle of equality before the law enunciated in s. 1 of Article 40 is infringed by the provisions of the impugned sub-paragraph, is not sound and should be rejected. The distinction made between those in the custody of a parent, as defined in the section, and those not in such custody is not a distinction based on physical location. Difference of physical location is an accidental difference; the essential difference is between being in the custody of a person who is either a parent or is, in effect, *in loco parentis* on the one hand and not being in such custody on the other hand. Far from effecting inequality, the purpose of the provision would appear to attempt to establish equality between the two groups. As was said in the judgment of this Court in *The State (Hartley)* v. *Governor of Mountjoy Prison* (21st December, 1967) 'a diversity of arrangements does not effect discrimination between citizens in their legal rights. Their legal rights are the same in the same circumstances. This in fact is equality before the law and not inequality . . .' Article 40 does not require identical treatment of all persons without recognition of differences in relevant circumstances. See [1966] I.R. at p. 639. It only forbids invidious discrimination.

The plaintiff's second submission raises a more serious problem. Has the State in the provision which it has made with regard to infant citizens protected, as best it may, from unjust attack and, in the case of injustice done, vindicated the property rights of such citizens? Prior to the passing of the Act of 1957 all persons under the disability of infancy enjoyed the same rights whether or not in the custody of a parent: see s. 22 of the Common Law Procedure Amendment Act (Ireland), 1853. That provision was repealed by s. 9 of the Act of 1957 and the impugned provision has been substituted. It would appear that the impugned provision is a transcription of the British Act of three years earlier: see s. 2, sub-s. 2, of the Law Reform (Limitation of Actions, &c.) Act. 1954. It does not bear any evidence of having been considered in the light of the requirements of Article 40, s. 3, of the Constitution. It may first be noted that the parental custody which is being discussed is custody at the time when the right of action accrues. During the course of the argument a member of the Court put the case of a family party in an omnibus or car which is involved in a collision and the infant children and parents alike being injured, and the parents (father and mother) die later as the result of their injuries. In such case the statute, with its three-year limitation, begins immediately to run against the orphan children who, in the circumstances supposed, may now be inmates of a public-welfare institution. This is not a far-fetched case but one which could readily occcur if, indeed, it has not occurred. It is not a sufficient answer for counsel for the Attorney General to say that the State has made exceptions, that these are reasonable and that the Oireachtas is entitled to choose. The indications are that the broad division into infants (or others suffering from a disability) in parental custody and infants not in such custody is not calculated to bring up for consideration the matters that should be borne in mind if infants' rights are to be given reasonable protection. The case was also put in argument of an infant being injured when a passenger in his father's car due to the parent's negligent driving. Here again we are dealing with events which, far from being improbable, are of too frequent occurrence. In such case what adequate safeguards are made for the infant's rights? The parent, as has happened here, may raise the statute against proceedings not taken within three years of the accrual of the right of action.

It is not possible to save by deletion some part of the impugned paragraph. The provision has no purpose without the words that establish the date of the running of the statute. It must therefore for its constitutional frailty fall in its entirety.

The infant plaintiff, it has been noted, was at all relevant times in the custody of one or other of his two parents; but it is clear that he has a sufficient *locus standi* to challenge the constitutional propriety of sub-paragraph (ii) of s. 49, sub-s. 2 (a), of the Act of 1957. First and foremost because the parent to whom he might reasonably have looked to protect his rights is permitted to raise the statute against him. Secondly, because, where a question of the constitutionality of a statutory provision is raised before the Court, the Court's duty in testing the provision is to examine it in as wide a manner as if the provision had been the subject of a reference under Article 26 of the Constitution; that is to say, the Court must advert as best it can to the full scope of the provision away and beyond the problem presented by the circumstances of the particular case then before the Court.

Sub-paragraph (ii) of s. 49, sub. s. 2 (a), of the Act of 1957, it has been demonstrated, fails to match up to the guarantee contained in Article 40, s. 3, of the Constitution; therefore the Court will declare that the sub-paragraph is repugnant to the Constitution and invalid.

MOYNIHAN V. GREENSMYTH
[1977] I.R. 55 (Supreme Court, affirming Murnaghan, J.)

Trial of point of law.

The plaintiff (née Cecelia O'Shea on the 16th April, 1950) was injured on the 6th August, 1966, when a motor car in which she was a passenger collided with a bridge near Glenflesk in the county of Kerry. William Greensmyth was the driver of the car and he was killed in the accident, which was caused by his negligence. On the 5th August, 1969, the plaintiff (suing by her next friend, Christopher O'Brien) issued a plenary summons in the High Court and claimed damages in respect of her injuries from the defendant in his capacity as personal representative of William Greensmyth deceased. The plaintiff attained her majority on the 16th April, 1971, and on the 12th February, 1972, she married Denis Joseph Moynihan.

Section 8 of the *Civil Liability Act, 1961*, provides:–

'(1) On the death of a person on or after the date of the passing of this Act all causes of action (other than excepted causes of action) subsisting against him shall survive against his estate.

(2) Where damage has been suffered by reason of any act in respect of which a cause of action would have subsisted against any person if he had not died before or

at the same time as the damage was suffered, there shall be deemed, for the purposes of subsection (1) of this section, to have been subsisting against him before his death such cause of action in respect of that act as would have subsisted if he had died after the damage was suffered.'

Section 9 of the said Act of 1961 provides:–

'(1) In this section "the relevant period" means the period of limitation prescribed by the Statute of Limitations or any other limitation enactment.

(2) No proceedings shall be maintainable in respect of any cause of action whatsoever which has survived against the estate of a deceased person unless either –

(a) proceedings against him in respect of that cause of action were commenced within the relevant period and were pending at the date of his death, or

(b) proceedings are commenced in respect of that cause of action within the relevant period or within the period of two years after his death, whichever period first expires.'

Section 11, sub-s. 2(b), of the *Statute of Limitations, 1957*, provides that (subject to s. 49) an action claiming damages for negligence in which the damages claimed include damages in respect of personal injuries shall not be brought after the expiration of three years from the date on which the cause of action accrued. Section 49 of the Statute of 1957 provides that where the right of action in such circumstances has accrued to a person under disability (including infancy), he may bring his action before the expiration of three years from the date when he ceased to be under the disability; it was this period of limitation which was replaced, so far as the plaintiff was concerned, by the provisions of s. 9 of the Act of 1961.

The plaintiff challenged the constitutional validity of section 9 of the *Civil Liability Act 1961*. Murnaghan, J. rejected the challenge and the plaintiff appealed to the Supreme Court.

O'Higgins C.J., delivering the judgment of the Court:

. . . Before considering the constitutional aspects of this appeal, it is well to set out the historical background in relation to actions for tort against the estate of a deceased person and also the statutory provisions which, from time to time, applied in relation to the limitation of such actions.

At common law the maxim which applied in relation to personal actions was *actio personalis moritur cum persona*. This maxim expressed the rule that a personal representative of a deceased could not sue or be sued in his lifetime for any tort committed against or by the deceased. The only case in which, apart from breach of contract express or implied, a remedy for a wrongful act could be pursued against the estate of a deceased person was where the property, or the proceeds or value of property, belonging to another had been appropriated by the deceased and added to his own estate. Certain modifications to this rule were made by statute but, generally speaking, the liability in respect of a tort terminated on the death of the wrongdoer.

The first major change took place in 1933 when compulsory motor insurance was introduced. By s. 171 of the Road Traffic Act, 1933, it was provided that the liability of any person for injury caused by him or his servant's negligent driving of a mechanically propelled vehicle should not terminate with his death, but that it should continue to be a liability of his estate and be enforceable against his personal representative. By s. 6 of the Fatal Injuries Act, 1956, it was provided that, in the event of a fatal injury, the liability of a wrongdoer should not be limited to himself or be terminated by his death, but should be a liability of his estate. The Road Traffic Act, 1961, repealed the Act of 1933 but s. 117 of the Road Traffic Act, 1961, contains provisions similar to s. 171 of the repealed Act of 1933.

The Civil Liability Act, 1961, which was passed a few weeks after the Road

Traffic Act, 1961, repealed both s. 117 of the Road Traffic Act, 1961, and the Fatal Injuries Act, 1956. In their place was enacted the provision contained in s. 8 of the Civil Liability Act, 1961, with regard to causes of action subsisting against deceased persons, and in Part IV of the same Act with regard to fatal injuries. As to the limitation of actions, the former rules were those laid down in the Common Law Procedure Amendment Act (Ireland), 1853. Section 20 of that Act laid down different periods of limitation for different causes of action. Six years would have been the appropriate period in relation to the plaintiff's claim. Section 22 of that Act provided that where, at the time of the accrual of such a right of action to any person, such person was under 21 years of age, he or she could bring the action within six years after attaining that age. These provisions continued to apply until the Statute of Limitations, 1957, by which they were repealed.

By s. 11, sub-s. 2 (b), of the Statute of 1957 a period of three years was provided as the period of limitation in an action, such as the plaintiff's, where the claim is for damages for personal injuries based on negligence. Section 49 of the Statute of 1957 provides for an extension of time in case of disability, which includes infancy. In a claim such as the plaintiff's, where the incapacity of infancy exists, this section has the effect that an action may be brought at any time before the expiration of three years after the plaintiff reaches the age of 21 years: see s. 49, sub-s. 2(a)(i), of the Statute of 1957. Therefore, the position was that, had the plaintiff's accident occurred after the passing of the Statute of 1957 and before the enactment of the Civil Liability Act, 1961, it could not have become statute barred until the expiration of three years after the plaintiff reached the age of 21 years. The accident occurred on the 6th August, 1966, at which date the Civil Liability Act, 1961, was already law. Section 5 of that Act repealed s. 117 of the Road Traffic Act, 1961, and in its place there had been substituted the general provisions of s. 8 of the Civil Liability Act, 1961, by which it was provided that thenceforth all causes of action (other than excepted causes) subsisting against a person should on his death survive against his estate.

On the date of the plaintiff's accident it was these provisions of s. 8 of the Civil Liability Act, 1961, and not the former provisions of s. 117 of the Road Traffic Act, 1961, which gave the plaintiff a right of action against the estate of the late William Greensmyth. However, the provisions of s. 8 of the Civil Liability Act, 1961, were followed and qualified by the provisions of s. 9 of the same Act. By s. 9 it is provided that no proceedings shall be maintainable in respect of any cause of action which has survived against the estate of a deceased person unless either '(a) proceedings against him in respect of that cause of action were commenced within the relevant period and were pending at the date of his death, or (b) proceedings are commenced in respect of that cause of action within the relevant period or within the period of two years after his death, whichever period first expires.' Sub-paragraph (a) applies only where proceedings had been commenced within the appropriate period laid down in s. 11 of the Statute of 1957 and were pending at the death; obviously this has no relevance in the plaintiff's case. In her case, sub-paragraph (b) applies and the period of limitation laid down is two years from the death. As the death of the late William Greensmyth occurred in the accident in which the plaintiff was injured, the plaintiff's proceedings (which were issued on the 5th August, 1969) were 12 months later than the period laid down in s. 9 of the Civil Liability Act, 1961.

In these circumstances it has been contended on behalf of the plaintiff that s. 9 of the Civil Liability Act, 1961, is repugnant to the Constitution because, in its enactment, the State failed to observe the duty (prescribed by Article 40, s. 3, sub-s. 2, of the Constitution) to protect from unjust attack the property rights of the plaintiff. Reliance was placed by counsel on behalf of the plaintiff on two decisions of this

Court, namely, *O'Brien* v. *Keogh* [1972] I.R. 144 and *O'Brien* v. *Manufacturing Engineering Co. Ltd.* [1973] I.R. 334.

In *O'Brien* v. *Keogh* [1972] I.R. 144 the Court considered the validity of sub-paragraph 2 of sub-s. (2)(a) of s. 49 of the Statute of 1957. That sub-paragraph provided that the extension of time given in relation to incapacity would not apply unless it was proved that the person under incapacity was not in the custody of a parent when the right of action accrued. The Court held this sub-paragraph to be invalid because it offended against Article 40, s. 3, sub-s. 1, of the Constitution. The basis of this decision was that the common-law right of action of the infant plaintiff in that case was a property right which, the Court held, by reason of the enactment of the sub-paragraph of the Statute of 1957 had not been protected and vindicated by the State as it ought to have been under the provisions of Article 40, s. 3, sub-s. 1, of the Constitution.

In *O'Brien* v. *Manufacturing Engineering Co. Ltd.* [1973] I.R. 334 the Court was asked to consider the validity of s. 6, sub-s. 1, of the Workmen's Compensation (Amendment) Act, 1953, having regard to the provisions of the Constitution. This section of the former Workmen's Compensation code provided that an injured workman who had accepted compensation under the Workmen's Compensation Acts could maintain a common-law action in respect of his injury – but only if he brought it within two years of the accident. As this provision made a distinction between injured workmen who had accepted compensation and other injured plaintiffs who had three years to sue under the Statute of 1957, it was contended that the sub-section offended both s. 1 and s. 3 of Article 40 of the Constitution. The Court held against these contentions, but accepted that a cause of action at common law for damages for personal injuries caused by negligence is a property right which is protected by the provisions of sub-s. 2 of s. 3 of Article 40 of the Constitution: see the portion of the judgment of the Court at p. 367 of the report.

In both *O'Brien* v. *Keogh* [1972] I.R. 144 and *O'Brien* v. *Manufacturing Engineering Co. Ltd.* [1973] I.R. 334 the Court acted on the assumption that a right to litigate a particular claim was a property right and that, as such, its protection was guaranteed by Article 40, s. 3, sub-s. 2, of the Constitution. In neither of those cases does it seem that the Court's attention was directed to its earlier decisions in *Foley* v. *Irish Land Commission* [1952] I.R. 118 and in *Attorney General* v. *Southern Industrial Trust Ltd.* (1957) 94 I.L.T.R. 161. In these cases it was held, in effect, that the property rights guaranteed by Article 40, s. 3, sub-s. 2, of the Constitution are not rights over particular items of property but are the property rights guaranteed by Article 43, namely, *the natural right to the private ownership of external goods* and *the general right to transfer, bequeath and inherit property*. To divest a citizen of the ownership of a particular item of property in certain circumstances was held to be permissible under Article 43, s. 2, of the Constitution. If this opinion were to be adhered to, the reasoning underlying the decisions in the two *O'Brien* cases would seem to be incompatible with the Court's ruling in *Foley* v. *Irish Land Commission* [1952] I.R. 118 and *Attorney General* v. *Southern Industrial Trust Ltd.* (1957) 94 I.L.T.R. 161. Accordingly, in order to give a comprehensive answer to the question posed by the present case, it would be necessary for the Court to give a considered ruling as to whether the right claimed by the plaintiff is a property right and, if so, whether it is one of the property rights guaranteed by Article 40, s. 3, sub-s. 2 of the Constitution. For that purpose it would be necessary to review the Court's decisions in *O'Brien* v. *Keogh* [1972] I.R. 144; *O'Brien* v. *Manufacturing Engineering Co. Ltd.* [1973] I.R. 334; *Attorney General* v. *Southern Industrial Trust Ltd.* (1957) 94 I.L.T.R. 161; and in earlier cases such as *Foley* v. *Irish Land Commission* [1952] I.R. 118 and *Buckley and Others (Sinn Féin)* v. *The Attorney General* [1950] I.R. 67 – not all of which decisions are reconcilable with each other.

However, counsel for the defendant and counsel for the Attorney General have conceded that the right claimed by the plaintiff is a property right and it has not been contended that such property right does not come within the category fo property rights guaranteed by Article 40, s. 3, sub-s. 2, of the Constitution.

Therefore, the Court is constrained to decide this appeal on the basis of those two concessions or assumptions but it wishes to make it clear that, in doing so, it does not necessarily accept that those concessions or assumptions are well founded. The points have not been argued in this case, so the Court is unable to express any opinion on them. In particular, the Court reserves for a case in which the point has been duly raised and argued the question whether it was correctly decided in *O'Brien* v. *Keogh* [1972] I.R. 144 that s. 49, sub-s. 2(a)(ii), of the Statute of Limitations, 1957, is repugnant to the Constitution.

Proceeding, therefore, on the assumption that the right to sue claimed by the plaintiff is a property right which is guaranteed by Article 40, s. 3, sub-s. 2, of the Constitution, the question is whether that right has been subjected to unjust attack or whether there has been an injustice which required vindication by the State. It is noted that the guarantee of protection given by Article 40, s. 3, sub-s. 2, of the Constitution is qualified by the words 'as best it may.' This implies circumstances in which the State may have to balance its protection of the right as against other obligations arising from regard for the common good.

As the law stood, prior to the passing of s. 9 of the Civil Liability Act, 1961, an infant could wait up to three years after attaining majority before suing the personal representative of a deceased motorist in respect of his negligent driving. This could mean that the administration of an estate might be greatly delayed or, alternatively, that after many years those entitled on a death might be subjected to a claim for damages of which there had been no prior notice. Obviously in such circumstances severe hardship might be caused and injustice done to innocent people. As the law then stood, this could only happen to those who represented, or shared in, the estate of a person who had been guilty of negligent driving. In relation to others the common-law rule continued to apply and liability terminated at the death of the wrongdoer.

When it was decided to provide generally for the survival of causes of action, a general limitation period of two years was provided in the impugned provisions of s. 9, sub-s. 2(b), of the Civil Liability Act, 1961. It was conceded in argument that this could not be regarded as an unjust attack on those not suffering from incapacity and that, in such circumstances, the period was reasonable and fair. In relation to those (such as the plaintiff) who at the time of the accrual of the cause of action are under 21 years of age, is a two-year period from the death of the wrongdoer so unreasonably short as to constitute an unjust attack on their rights? Bearing in mind the State's duty to others – in particular those who represent the estate of the deceased, and beneficiaries – some reasonable limitation on actions against the estate was obviously required. If the period of infancy were to form part of the period of limitation, as was formerly the case, then the danger of stale claims being brought would be very real and could constitute a serious threat to the rights of beneficiaries of the estate of a deceased. The alternative was to apply a period of limitation which would have general application. It had to be either one or the other; and it does not appear that any compromise was possible.

In these circumstances, in the view of the Court, having regard to the conflicting claims on the State's protection, this sub-section cannot be regarded as constituting an unjust attack nor can its enactment be a failure to vindicate the alleged property right of infants. In the view of the Court it has not been shown that the State has not fulfilled its obligations under Article 40, s. 3, sub-s. 2, to protect from unjust attack and, in the case of injustice done, to vindicate the property rights of the plaintiff. Accordingly, this appeal is dismissed.

The specific answer the Court will give to the question set out in the issue is that, on a consideration of even the restricted arguments put foward in this case, it has not been shown that s. 9 of the Civil Liability Act, 1961, is repugnant to Article 40, s. 3, sub-s. 2, of the Constitution; and that the plaintiff's claim is, therefore, not statute barred.

CAMPBELL V. WARD
[1981] I.L.R.M. 60 (High Court, Carroll, J.)

The plaintiff was born in May 1955. She was involved in an accident in June 1972 and she reached her majority in May 1976. A plenary summons was issued in July 1978. The question before the court was whether her claim was statute barred.

Carroll J. delivered her judgment on 28 April 1981 saying: . . . By virtue of the decision of the Supreme Court in the case of *O'Brien* v. *Keogh* [1972] IR 44, s.49(2)(a)(ii) of the Statute of Limitations 1957 was held to be unconstitutional.

In the case of *Moynihan* v. *Greensmyth* [1977] IR 55 the Supreme Court, in its judgment delivered by the learned Chief Justice, indicated that the decisions in *O'Brien* v. *Keogh* and in a later case of *O'Brien* v. *Manufacturing Engineering Co Ltd* [1973] IR 344 seemed to be incompatible with the court's rulings in *Foley* v. *The Irith Land Commission* [1952] IR 118 and the *Attorney General* v. *Southern Industrial Trust Limited* (1957 94 ILTR 161) and it is stated as follows at page 71: 'In particular the court reserves for a case in which the point has been duly raised and argued the question whether it was correctly decided in *O'Brien* v. *Keogh* that section 49 sub-section 2(a)(ii) of the Statute of Limitations 1957, is repugnant to the Constitution.'

I do not consider that these words give me liberty to hear any arguments as to whether the case of *O'Brien* v. *Keogh* was correctly decided. I consider that I am bound by the existing decision of the Supreme Court in that case until such time as the Supreme Court reviews its decision.

Accordingly, following the existing decision in *O'Brien* v. *Keogh* which holds that section 49 (2)(*a*)(ii) of the Statute of Limitations 1957 is unconstitutional, I hold that the plaintiff's claim is *not* statute barred having been commenced by the issue of proceedings within three years of her ceasing to be under the disability of infancy, in accordance with section 49(1)(*a*) and section 49(2)(*a*).

[This case is on appeal to the Supreme Court.]

Fraud

Fraud may affect the limitation periods, Where either:

'(*a*) an action is based on the fraud of the defendant or his agent or of any person through whom he claims or his agent, or
(*b*) the right of action is concealed by the fraud of any such person,'

then the period of limitation does not begin to run until the plaintiff has discovered the fraud or could with reasonable diligence have discovered it. (Sect. 70(1) of the *Statute of Limitations, 1957*.)

The word 'fraud' as used in paragraphs (*a*) and (*b*) has two different meanings. In paragraph (*a*) it means such fraud as will itself give rise to a right of action – in other words the tort of deceit; in paragraph (b), on the other hand, it has 'the same meaning as "fraud" in the *Real Property Limitation Act 1833* and in the general equitable principles on which this section of the Act is based and which it extends': *Breaman* v. *A.R.T.S. Ltd.* [1949] 1 K.B. 550, at 567 (C.A., *per* Somervell, L.J.). Thus, no degree of moral turpitude is required, and the term here includes conduct 'which, having regard to some special relationship between the two parties concerned, is an unconscionable thing for the one to do towards the other': *Kitchen* v. *R.A.F. Association* [1958] 1 W.L.R. 563, at 573 (C.A., *per* Lord Evershed, M.R.).

The extension of the limitation period in the case of fraud will not permit the recovery of property that has been purchased for valuable consideration by a person not party to the fraud.

Extinction of Title in Conversion and Detinue

Prior to 1957, the expiration of the limitation period merely barred a right of action for conversion and detinue, and did not divest the owner of the chattel of his title to it. Thus, if he could recover it otherwise than by action, he was entitled to do so. Furthermore, any further conversion or wrongful detention of the chattel by a third person entitled the owner to sue in respect of it, his action running from the time of the subsequent wrongful act.

Section 12 of the *Statute of Limitations 1957* has changed the position on both these points. Now, the owner's title to the chattel is extinguished after the expiry of the relevant limitation period, unless he has in the meantime recovered possession of it. Moreover, where a chattel has been converted or wrongfully detained, and before the owner recovers possession of it a further conversion or wrongful detention takes place, no action may be brought in respect of this subsequent tort after the expiration of six years from the accrual of the cause of action in respect of the original conversion or detention.

Special Periods of Limitation

Some special periods of limitation may be noted.

(a) Actions for Contribution under the Civil Liability Act 1961

An action for contribution under Chapter II of the *Civil Liability Act 1961* may be brought within the same period as the injured person is allowed in law for bringing an action against the contributor, or within two years after the liability of the claimant is ascertained, or the injured person's damages are paid, whichever is the greater. It was held by Finlay, P., in *Buckley* v. *Lynch* [1978] I.R. 6, at 11 (High Ct., 1977), that:

'the entire right to recover contribution, and any legal procedure created for the enforcement of that right by the Act of 1961, must be deemed to be an action for contribution . . .'

within the meaning of the limitation provision.

(b) Maritime Conventions Act 1911

Section 8 of this Act provides for a general period of limitation of two years for any claim 'in respect of any damage or loss to [a] vessel, her cargo or freight, or any property on board her, or damages for loss of life or personal injuries suffered by any person on board her' caused by the fault of another vessel. The period *may* be extended by the Court in any action 'to such extent and on such conditions as it thinks fit', and *must* be extended if the Court is satisfied that there has not, during the period, been any reasonable opportunity of arresting the defendant vessel within the jurisdiction of the Court or within the territorial waters of the country to which the plaintiff's ship belongs or in which the plaintiff resides or has his principal place of business: in such latter case, the period must be extended 'to an extent sufficient to give such reasonable opportunity'.

INDEX